THE
POCKET OXFORD
GERMAN
DICTIONARY

THE
POCKET OXFORD
GERMAN
DICTIONARY

THE
POCKET OXFORD
GERMAN
DICTIONARY

GERMAN-ENGLISH

COMPILED BY

M. L. BARKER

AND

H. HOMEYER

ENGLISH-GERMAN

COMPILED BY

C. T. CARR

OXFORD
AT THE CLARENDON PRESS

Oxford University Press, Walton Street, Oxford OX2 6DP

Oxford New York Toronto
Delhi Bombay Calcutta Madras Karachi
Petaling Jaya Singapore Hong Kong Tokyo
Nairobi Dar es Salaam Cape Town
Melbourne Auckland
and associated companies in
Beirut Berlin Ibadan Nicosia

Oxford is a trade mark of Oxford University Press.

Published in the United States by
Oxford University Press, New York

First published 1975
First published in Paperback 1980
Reprinted 1982, 1983, 1986

British Library Cataloguing in Publication Data

The pocket Oxford German dictionary.
1. German language – Dictionaries – English
2. English language – Dictionaries – German
I. Barker, Marie Louise   II. Homeyer, Helene
III. Carr, Charles Telford
433'.2'1   PF3640   76 – 35 1958
ISBN 0 – 19 – 864138 – 9

Printed in Hong Kong

PREFACE TO THE
THIRD EDITION

THE dictionary has again been completely revised so as to include new material particularly from recent political, scientific, and literary sources. Technical terms borrowed from English or American vocabulary have been omitted.

The compiler wishes to express sincere gratitude to Dr. Fritz Homeyer who has given valuable advice and made many useful suggestions.

H. H.

PREFACE TO THE
SECOND EDITION

THIS edition has been completely revised and brought up to date. It not only incorporates the addenda and corrections of the two earlier reprints, but also contains important additions to the current vocabulary of spoken and written German. Special care has been devoted to this fresh material, which includes political, economic, literary, scientific, and technical terms now used in books and newspapers, in educational and trade journals, and by television and radio broadcasters.

The original introduction follows; the Grammar Section has been slightly extended.

It is with sincere regret that I record the death of Dr. M. L. Barker on 3 January 1961. Her enthusiasm for the work and her wide teaching experience were a most valuable help in compiling the Dictionary, particularly in its first stages.

H. H.

INTRODUCTION

This *Oxford German–English Dictionary* has been planned on the modern and generally useful lines of the *Concise Oxford French–English Dictionary*.

It aims at presenting, in a small but scholarly volume, the German language in such a way as to reflect the *current* vocabulary of daily life and its manifold activities. It is also intended to provide the language student with word-material which will train him in translation and sense of style and will stimulate him in his search for the 'right' word.

The compilers have therefore given great attention to the various uses and meanings of the German words and the selection of their English equivalents. Comparison with other German–English dictionaries will show that 'traditional' translations have been carefully sifted and that frequently a German word or phrase has been given an improved rendering or a more 'exact' translation.

As in the *Concise Oxford French–English Dictionary* a special typographical sign ⌂ warns the reader against words liable to mistranslation because of similarity to English spelling, e.g. *Harm, Justiz, Lektüre*.

VOCABULARY

To illustrate the present-day language as fully as possible and yet keep within the limit of approximately 40,000 words, a rigorous selection had to be made. While more consideration than is usual in a small dictionary has been given to the vocabularies of *literature, music, theology, modern science, political science*, and *typography*, the following groups of words have been omitted: OBSOLETE AND RARE WORDS, e.g. *dero, Seiger, Maut*; DIALECT WORDS OR WORDS OF LOCAL USAGE, unless they have become part of the general vocabulary or occur in modern literature, e.g. *Dirndl, Stulle, Metzger*; HIGHLY SPECIALIZED TECHNICAL TERMS; DIMINUTIVE NOUNS ending in *-chen* or *-lein*, unless their meaning differs from the parent noun's meaning, e.g. *Kränzchen, Hörnchen*; FEMININE NOUNS ending in *-in*, unless the English feminine differs from the masculine, e.g. 'tiger', 'tigress'; 'fox', 'vixen'; DERIVATIVE NOUNS ending in *-heit, -keit*, or *-ung*, since their meaning can often be guessed from the adjective or verb from which they are derived, e.g. *Brüderlichkeit* from *brüderlich*, *Erkämpfung* from *erkämpfen*.

ARRANGEMENT

Words etymologically related and having a common root are generally grouped under one main article. This grouping will help the student to remember words of the same word-family more easily. The verb, however, has usually been given a special article.

Within each article a strict alphabetical order has been kept practically throughout, i.e. no distinction has been made between derivatives and compounds, e.g. **Herz** ~grube, ~haft, ~ig, ~innig.

Where an article would have become unduly long or an important word deserved special treatment, it has been broken up, e.g. **Arbeit, Arbeiter~, Arbeits~.**

An idiom or phrase containing a noun will usually be found under that noun, e.g. *im Auge behalten* will be found under **Auge.** Where an idiom contains two nouns the reader will find it under the first noun, e.g. *außer Rand und Band* under **Rand.** Idioms containing no nouns are placed under the word on which the main emphasis is laid, e.g. *sich zu eigen machen* under **eigen** but *sich gut anlassen* under **anlassen.** As it is often doubtful on which word the main emphasis is laid the reader should look up each possible word before abandoning the search.

GRAMMAR

The main grammatical facts of the German language are set out below. Within the vocabulary itself only the following grammatical hints could be given:

The genitive singular and nominative plural of all the important simple nouns are indicated within brackets immediately after the gender, e.g.:

Abend *m.* (-s, -e), where (-s, -e) stands for **Abends, Abende.**

Hand *f.* (-, ̈e), where (-, ̈e) stands for **Hand, Hände.**

If the genitive singular alone or the nominative plural alone is given the case omitted either does not exist or is not used. Omission of both cases means that the noun is hardly ever used except in the nominative singular.

But to help the reader as much as possible all irregular verbs* are indicated as such within the vocabulary (*st.* stands

---

* See List of Strong and Irregular Verbs, p. 449.

for strong conjugation). In addition, to save 'hunting', irregular verb-forms are quoted with reference to the main verb, e.g. **kann** *1st & 3rd pers. sing. pres. of* **können.**

Intransitive verbs conjugated with *sein* are marked thus: *vws.i.*

Adjectives formed from past participles are indicated only as adjectives, e.g. **gelassen** *a.* (*fig.*) calm.

ETYMOLOGY

It has been considered helpful to include a few etymological hints in square brackets at the end of an article. They either refer to the immediate source of a borrowing or are cognate equivalent words, e.g. **Kuvert** [F]. **Dach** [THATCH]. As etymology is a very complex study the selection in a small dictionary is necessarily casual.

SPELLING AND PUNCTUATION

The spelling of German words is that used in the latest revised edition of *Der Große Duden* (15th, revised edn., Mannheim, 1961).

In the English translation all equivalents with the same meaning are separated by commas. Different meanings are introduced by semicolons, but the line between the groups could not always be sharply drawn.

Brackets within the German text mean that both forms—the long and the short—can be used equally well.

Brackets in the English text contain explanations referring to either the meaning or the grammatical use of a word.

SIGNS

Words spelt alike but unrelated either in etymology or meaning have been given separate entries and are marked with figures, e.g. **arm¹** *a.* poor; **Arm²** *m.* arm.

The danger sign ⚠ signalizes German words which are spelt as in English but which differ from the English word in meaning.

The sign | in the German headword in heavy type indicates a glottal stop as in **Ab|art** or a break between a voiceless and voiced consonant, e.g. **Ab|bild.**

For the stress sign ′ see PRONUNCIATION, p. ix.

University of Saarbrücken   H. H.
University of Edinburgh   M. L. B.

THE GERMAN ALPHABET
IN GOTHIC TYPE

𝔄	𝔞	A	a
𝔅	𝔟	B	b
ℭ	𝔠	C	c
𝔇	𝔡	D	d
𝔈	𝔢	E	e
𝔉	𝔣	F	f
𝔊	𝔤	G	g
ℌ	𝔥	H	h
ℑ	𝔦	I	i
𝔍	𝔧	J	j
𝔎	𝔨	K	k
𝔏	𝔩	L	l
𝔐	𝔪	M	m
𝔑	𝔫	N	n
𝔒	𝔬	O	o
𝔓	𝔭	P	p
𝔔	𝔮	Q	q
ℜ	𝔯	R	r
𝔖	𝔰 𝔣	S	s
𝔗	𝔱	T	t
𝔘	𝔲	U	u
𝔙	𝔳	V	v
𝔚	𝔴	W	w
𝔛	𝔵	X	x
𝔜	𝔶	Y	y
ℨ	𝔷	Z	z

PRONUNCIATION

ACCENT. In German the stress or force with which a syllable is pronounced is considerably stronger than in English. As with English, the first syllable of a German word usually has a strong stress, and words that conform to this rule are not marked. When a strong stress falls on a later syllable, it is indicated, where possible, by the stress mark ′ BEFORE it, e.g. *Abgötte′rei*.

SOUNDS. The symbols used, with a few exceptions, are those of the *Association Phonétique Internationale*. As it was impossible in such a small dictionary to give the pronunciation of every German word only the pronunciation of common German words often mispronounced by students is given in round brackets immediately after the German headword, e.g. **Sache** (zaxə). The pronunciation of some other important words or difficult parts of words is also given, e.g. **Arz′nei** (artsnai), **Peter′silie** (-zi:liə). The sign : indicates that the preceding vowel is long.

GERMAN VOWEL SOUNDS

Phonetic Symbol	German examples	Nearest English equivalent
i	bin, ich	bin, bit
i:	*Biene*, mir, *ihr*, *Vieh*	bean
e:	*Meer*, mehr	may, gate (Sc.*)
ɛ, ɛ:	Bett, Ähre	getting, air
a	Kamm	come, lum (Sc.)
a:	kam	calm
ɔ	kommen	common
o	Astronom	French eau
o:	Sohn	zone (Sc.)
u	Mutter	foot, could
u:	Mut	moot
y	füllen	None. Pronounce with lips protruded.
y:	fühlen	None. Pronounce with lips protruded.
œ	Hölle	None. Pronounce as ɛ with lips slightly rounded.
ø:	Höhle	None. Pronounce as e with lips protruded.
ə	gehoben	Unstressed like a in again.

Nasalized Vowels. ɛ̃ in Bass*in*, ã in Chance, ɔ̃ in Ball*on*, œ̃ in Parf*um*, are pronounced as in French.

DIPHTHONGS. ai in m*ein* is pronounced as in mine (Sc.*); au in Haus (a:+u); ɔi in *euch* as in boy, boil.

* Sc. indicates that the Scottish pronunciation is closer to German than the English.

GERMAN CONSONANT SOUNDS. The phonetic symbols p, b, t, d, k, g, m, n, f, s, z, h, as in German *Paar*, *bei*, *Tor*, *du*, *kam*, *Gott*, *Mann*, *nein*, *fein*, *es* (as in yes), *sah* (as in *Zoo*), *Hand*, have approximately their English values in *pit*, *bit*, &c.

The following special symbols are used:

Phonetic Symbol	German examples	Nearest English equivalent
ŋ	e*ng*	si*ng*
ʃ	*Sch*uh	*sh*oe
v	*Schw*ester	*v*ain
ʒ	Lo*g*is	a*z*ure
ç	Köni*g*	*b*ig
j	*j*a	*y*es
x	a*ch*	lo*ch* (Sc.)

Notes on the Consonants. German *w* as in *wo* is pronounced approximately as *v* in *vote*.

German final *b, d*, as in *ab*, *Bild*, are pronounced *p, t* (*ap, bilt*).

German *r*, as in *Rose*, resembles the *Scottish* rolled *r*. The *French* *r*, as in *heureux*, may be used instead.

The final consonant *s* as in *es* is pronounced *s* as in *yes*.

The initial consonant *s* as in *sah* is pronounced *z* as in *Zoo*.

    „   „   *v* „ *Vater*   „   *f* „ *fat*.

    „   „   *z* „ *Zeit*   „   *ts* „ *gets*.

SYNOPSIS OF GERMAN GRAMMAR
THE DEFINITE ARTICLE

The definite article is declined as follows:

	singular			plural
	m.	f.	n.	
Nom.	der	die	das	die
Gen.	des	der	des	der
Dat.	dem	der	dem	den
Acc.	den	die	das	die

THE INDEFINITE ARTICLE

The indefinite article is declined as follows:

	singular			
	m.	f.	n.	
Nom.	ein	eine	ein	No plural
Gen.	eines	einer	eines	
Dat.	einem	einer	einem	
Acc.	einen	eine	ein	

NOTES ON DECLENSIONS OF NOUNS

In the Models of Declensions below note (1) that the ending of the genitive singular of most masculine nouns and all neuter nouns is *-s*, or *-es* after a monosyllable, e.g. *Gottes*; (2) that the dative plural always ends in *-n*.

MASCULINE PLURAL: To form the masculine plural add *-e* or *-er* to the singular, e.g.:

der Anfang, die Anfänge
der Gott, die Götter

The root vowel is usually modified (*ä, ö, ü*).

Masculine and neuter nouns ending in *-el, -en, -er*, are invariable except in the genitive singular and dative plural, e.g. *der Himmel*, gen. sing. *des Himmels*; dat. pl. *den Himmeln*.

NEUTER PLURAL: Same endings as masculine, but most neuter monosyllables form the plural by adding *-er*, e.g. *das Licht, die Lichter*.

All FEMININE NOUNS are invariable in the singular. The PLURAL is formed by adding *-n* or *-en* to the singular, e.g. *die Wiese, die Wiesen*. About 30 monosyllables add *-e* and modify, e.g. *die Nacht, die Nächte*; *die Wand, die Wände*.

Models of Strong Declension. Plural in -er

	m. sing.	plural	n. sing.	plural
Nom.	der Gott	die Götter	das Licht	die Lichter
Gen.	des Gottes	der Götter	des Lichtes	der Lichter
Dat.	dem Gott(e)	den Göttern	dem Licht(e)	den Lichtern
Acc.	den Gott	die Götter	das Licht	die Lichter

No feminines form the plural by adding *-er*.

Strong Declension. Plural in -e

	m. sing.	plural	f. sing.	plural
Nom.	der Anfang	die Anfänge	die Frucht	die Früchte
Gen.	des Anfangs	der Anfänge	der Frucht	der Früchte
Dat.	dem Anfang	den Anfängen	der Frucht	den Früchten
Acc.	den Anfang	die Anfänge	die Frucht	die Früchte

	n. sing.	plural
Nom.	das Meer	die Meere
Gen.	des Meeres	der Meere
Dat.	dem Meer(e)	den Meeren
Acc.	das Meer	die Meere

Strong Declension. Plural without Suffix

	m. sing.	plural	n. sing.	plural
Nom.	der Himmel	die Himmel	das Zeichen	die Zeichen
Gen.	des Himmels	der Himmel	des Zeichens	der Zeichen
Dat.	dem Himmel	den Himmeln	dem Zeichen	den Zeichen
Acc.	den Himmel	die Himmel	das Zeichen	die Zeichen

Only two feminine nouns, *Mutter* and *Tochter*, have no suffix in the plural. They both modify in the plural.

Models of Weak Declension

	m. sing.	plural	f. sing.	plural
Nom.	der Mensch	die Menschen	die Wiese	die Wiesen
Gen.	des Menschen	der Menschen	der Wiese	der Wiesen
Dat.	dem Menschen	den Menschen	der Wiese	den Wiesen
Acc.	den Menschen	die Menschen	die Wiese	die Wiesen

The Mixed Declension

1. A few masculine nouns belong to the strong declension in the singular and to the weak declension in the plural, e.g. *Strahl, Staat, Stachel.*

2. Also a few neuter nouns: *Auge, Ende, Ohr, Hemd, Bett, Insekt.*

3. Also a few borrowed nouns: *Doktor, Professor.*

The genitive singular of all these nouns ends in -s or -es, the plural in -n or -en.

Diminutives

The terminations -chen and -lein form diminutives, e.g. *der Mann, das Männchen, die Magd, das Mägdlein.* These diminutives are always neuter. They add an s in the genitive singular. The other cases are invariable.

PRONOUNS

The German PERSONAL PRONOUNS are declined as follows:

	singular	plural	singular	plural
Nom.	ich, I	wir, we	du, thou	ihr, ye Sie, you
Gen.	meiner	unser	deiner	euer Ihrer
Dat.	mir	uns	dir	euch Ihnen
Acc.	mich	uns	dich	euch Sie

	singular			*plural*
Nom.	er, *he*	sie, *she*	es, *it*	sie, *they*
Gen.	seiner	ihrer	seiner	ihrer
Dat.	ihm	ihr	ihm	ihnen
Acc.	ihn	sie	es	sie

The REFLEXIVE PRONOUNS are identical with the personal pronouns except in the third person. *Sich* is used as the dative and accusative of the reflexive pronoun of the third person in all genders and in both numbers.

The DEMONSTRATIVE PRONOUN *der* differs from the definite article in the genitive singular (m. *dessen*, f. *deren*, n. *dessen*) and in the genitive and dative plural (gen. *derer* or *deren*, dat. *denen*).

The RELATIVE PRONOUN *der* differs from the demonstrative pronoun in the genitive plural, only *deren* being used.

The words *dieser* and *jener*, 'this' and 'that', are declined like the definite article. They are used both as pronouns and as adjectives. As *dieser* are declined *jeder, solcher, mancher, welcher, keiner*.

POSSESSIVE PRONOUNS

The POSSESSIVE PRONOUNS used as adjectives are:

m.	f.	n.		corresponding to ich, *I*
mein	meine	mein	,,	du, *thou*
dein	deine	dein	,,	er, *he*
sein	seine	sein	,,	sie, *she*
ihr	ihre	ihr	,,	es, *it*
sein	seine	sein	,,	wir, *we*
unser	unsere	unser	,,	ihr, *ye*
euer	eure	euer	,,	Sie, *you*
Ihr	Ihre	Ihr	,,	sie, *they*
ihr	ihre	ihr		

Note. The possessive pronouns are declined exactly like the indefinite article. Also *kein*, 'not any', 'not one', 'no'.

DECLENSION OF ADJECTIVES

ADJECTIVES used predicatively are not declined, e.g. *der Anfang war gut*; *die Wiese war grün*; *das Wasser war tief*. But adjectives immediately preceding the nouns to which they belong are declined to agree with those nouns in gender, number, and case. Adjectives may be declined in three ways:

1. Without article or pronoun.
2. After the indefinite article or a pronominal adjective declined like it.
3. After the definite article or a pronominal adjective declined like it,

e.g. *singular masculine* noun preceded by adjective:

	(1)	(2)	(3)
Nom.	guter Anfang	ein guter Anfang	der gute Anfang
Gen.	guten Anfangs	eines guten Anfangs	des guten Anfangs
Dat.	gutem Anfang	einem guten Anfang	dem guten Anfang
Acc.	guten Anfang	einen guten Anfang	den guten Anfang

plural (1 and 2) gute Anfänge   *plural* (3) die guten Anfänge
        guter Anfänge   der guten Anfänge
        guten Anfängen   den guten Anfängen
        gute Anfänge   die guten Anfänge

singular feminine noun preceded by adjective:

	(1)	(2)	(3)
Nom.	grüne Wiese	eine grüne Wiese	die grüne Wiese
Gen.	grüner Wiese	einer grünen Wiese	der grünen Wiese
Dat.	grüner Wiese	einer grünen Wiese	der grünen Wiese
Acc.	grüne Wiese	eine grüne Wiese	die grüne Wiese

plural (1 and 2) grüne Wiesen   *plural* (3) die grünen Wiesen
        grüner Wiesen   der grünen Wiesen
        grünen Wiesen   den grünen Wiesen
        grüne Wiesen   die grünen Wiesen

singular neuter noun preceded by adjective:

	(1)	(2)	(3)
Nom.	tiefes Wasser	ein tiefes Wasser	das tiefe Wasser
Gen.	tiefen Wassers	eines tiefen Wassers	des tiefen Wassers
Dat.	tiefem Wasser	einem tiefen Wasser	dem tiefen Wasser
Acc.	tiefes Wasser	ein tiefes Wasser	das tiefe Wasser

plural (1 and 2) tiefe Wasser   *plural* (3) die tiefen Wasser
        tiefer Wasser   der tiefen Wasser
        tiefen Wassern   den tiefen Wassern
        tiefe Wasser   die tiefen Wasser

VERBS

Tenses. German verbs have only two tenses formed by inflection—the Present and the Past (Imperfect). The other tenses are formed, as in English, by the use of Auxiliaries. These are: **haben**, 'to have'; **sein**, 'to be'; and **werden**, 'to become'.

haben, to have

INDICATIVE MOOD

Present ich habe, du hast, er hat, wir haben, ihr habt, sie haben.
Imperfect ich hatte, du hattest, er hatte, wir hatten, ihr hattet, sie hatten.

COMPOUND TENSES

Perfect	ich habe gehabt	I have had
Pluperfect	ich hatte gehabt	I had had
Future	ich werde haben	I shall have
Future perfect	ich werde gehabt haben	I shall have had

CONDITIONAL MOOD

Present	ich würde haben (*or* ich hätte)	I should have
Imperfect	ich würde gehabt haben (*or* ich hätte gehabt)	I should have had

Present subjunctive ich habe, du habest, er habe, wir haben, ihr habet, sie haben.

Imperfect subjunctive ich hätte, du hättest, er hätte, wir hätten, ihr hättet, sie hätten.

Imperative habe, *have thou*; habt (*or* haben Sie), *have (ye) or (you).*

Participles habend, *having*; gehabt, *had.*

sein, to be

INDICATIVE MOOD

Present ich bin, du bist, er ist, wir sind, ihr seid, sie sind.

Imperfect ich war, du warst, er war, wir waren, ihr war(e)t, sie waren.

The compound tenses of **sein** are formed with *sein* as auxiliary.

Perfect	ich bin gewesen	*I have been*
Pluperfect	ich war gewesen	*I had been*
Future	ich werde sein	*I shall be*
Future perfect	ich werde gewesen sein	*I shall have been*

CONDITIONAL MOOD

Present	ich würde sein (*or* ich wäre)	*I should be*
Imperfect	ich würde gewesen sein (*or* ich wäre gewesen)	*I should have been*

Present subjunctive ich sei, du seiest, er sei, wir seien, ihr seiet, sie seien.

Imperfect subjunctive ich wäre, du wärest, er wäre, wir wären, ihr wäret, sie wären.

Imperative sei, *be thou*; seid (*or* seien Sie), *be (ye) or (you).*

Participles seiend, *being*; gewesen, *been.*

werden, to become

Present indicative ich werde, du wirst, er wird, wir werden, ihr werdet, sie werden.

Imperfect indicative ich wurde, du wurdest, er wurde, wir wurden, ihr wurdet, sie wurden.

Present subjunctive ich werde, du werdest, er werde, wir werden, ihr werdet, sie werden.

Imperfect subjunctive ich würde, du würdest, er würde, wir würden, ihr würdet, sie würden.

The compound tenses of **werden** are formed with *sein* as auxiliary.

Perfect ich bin geworden.

Pluperfect ich war geworden.

Future ich werde werden; *Conditional* ich würde werden.

Future perfect ich werde geworden sein; *Conditional imperfect* ich würde geworden sein.

Imperative werde, werdet.

Participles werdend, *becoming*; geworden, *become* (but as auxiliary, worden, *been*).

CONJUGATION OF A WEAK VERB

machen, to make (*machen, machte, gemacht*)

The weak conjugation forms the past tense by adding the suffix *-te* to the root, and the past participle by adding the suffix *-t* and the prefix *ge-*.

INDICATIVE MOOD

Present ich mache, du machst, er macht, wir machen, ihr macht, sie machen.
Imperfect ich machte, du machtest, er machte, wir machten, ihr machtet, sie machten.
Perfect   ich habe gemacht
Pluperfect   ich hatte gemacht
Future   ich werde machen
Future perfect ich werde gemacht haben

SUBJUNCTIVE MOOD

Endings of present tense: *-e, -est, -e, -en, -et, -en.* Endings of past tense: Same as indicative.

CONDITIONAL MOOD

Present ich würde machen   *I should make*
Past   ich würde gemacht haben *I should have made*

CONJUGATION OF A STRONG VERB

sprechen, to speak (*sprechen, sprach, gesprochen*)

In German the strong conjugation forms the past tense from the root or stem by altering the root vowel; and the past participle by adding the prefix *ge-* and the suffix *-en,* and generally with a further change of vowel.

INDICATIVE MOOD

Present ich spreche, du sprichst, er spricht, wir sprechen, ihr sprecht, sie sprechen.
Imperfect ich sprach, du sprachst, er sprach, wir sprachen, ihr spracht, sie sprachen.

SUBJUNCTIVE MOOD

Present ich spreche, -est, -e, -en, -et, -en.
Imperfect ich spräche, -est, -e, -en, -et, -en.
The Compound tenses are formed exactly like those of **machen.**

Verbs of motion, as *gehen,* 'to go', are conjugated with *sein,* similarly verbs denoting a change of state, as *wachsen,* 'to grow'.
Reflexive verbs are always conjugated with *haben.*

PASSIVE VOICE

werden forms the whole of the passive voice, e.g.:

Present	es wird gemacht		*it is made*
Past	„ wurde „		„ *was made*
Perfect	„ ist „	worden	„ *has been made*
Pluperfect	„ war „	„	„ *had been made*
1 Future	„ wird „	werden	„ *will be made*
2 Future	„ „ „	worden sein	„ *will have been made*

MODAL AUXILIARIES

There are six auxiliaries of mood:

dürfen (*may*), *to be allowed*	mögen (*may*), *to like*
können (*can*), *to be able*	müssen (*must*), *to be obliged*
sollen (*shall*), *to be bound, ought*	wollen (*will*), *to want*

Past participle

gedurft	gekonnt	gesollt	gemocht	gemußt	gewollt

After an infinitive a past participle identical with the infinitive is used: Ich habe nicht kommen **können** (I have not been able to come).

Present indicative, 1st person sing. and plural

darf	kann	soll	mag	muß	will
dürfen	können	sollen	mögen	müssen	wollen

Present subjunctive

dürfe	könne	solle	möge	müsse	wolle

Imperfect indicative

durfte	konnte	sollte	mochte	mußte	wollte

Imperfect subjunctive

dürfte	könnte	sollte	möchte	müßte	wollte

The auxiliary of these verbs is *haben*.

INSEPARABLE AND SEPARABLE PREFIXES

There are sixteen inseparable prefixes:

be-, ge-, ent-, emp-, er-, ver-, zer-, miß-; über, unter, wider, um, durch, hinter; wieder, voll.

Verbs compounded with these have no accent on the prefix, and do not add the prefix *ge-* for the past participle, e.g. *behalten*, 'to keep', *behielt*, 'kept', *behalten*, 'kept'; *ich habe es behalten*, 'I have kept it'; *vollenden*, 'to finish', *vollendet*, 'finished'.

Verbs compounded with separable prefixes insert the prefix *ge-* for the past participle, e.g. *abschließen*, 'to lock up', *abgeschlossen*, 'locked up'.

Verbs with a preposition or adverb as prefix are usually separable. This prefix is STRESSED, e.g. *'zumachen*, 'to shut'.

CONJUGATION OF A SEPARABLE VERB

INDICATIVE MOOD

Present	*Imperfect*
ich mache . . . 'zu.	ich machte . . . 'zu.

Perfect	*Future*
ich habe . . . 'zugemacht.	ich werde . . . 'zumachen.

PREPOSITIONS

The following prepositions always take an ACCUSATIVE: *durch, für, gegen, ohne, um, wider, bis, sonder, gen.*

The following always govern the DATIVE: *aus, außer, bei, mit, nach, seit, von, zu, gegenüber, nächst, zunächst, nebst, samt, zuwider, entgegen, gemäß, binnen.*

The following take the ACCUSATIVE if they denote 'motion towards a place', the DATIVE if they denote 'rest at a place': *an, auf, hinter, in, neben, vor, über, unter, zwischen.*

The following generally govern the GENITIVE: *während, anstatt, statt, kraft, wegen, trotz, unweit, unfern, mittels, laut, vermöge, ungeachtet, unbeschadet, oberhalb, unterhalb, innerhalb, außerhalb, diesseits, jenseits, halber, um ... willen, inmitten, zeit, betreffs, infolge, anfangs, angesichts, namens.*

COMPARISON OF ADJECTIVES

The comparative and superlative are formed, as in English, by adding *-er* and *-est* or *-st*; as *mild, milder, mildest (der mildeste).*

Most monosyllabic adjectives modify the root vowel, *a, o, u*: *alt, älter, ältest (der älteste).* Similarly: *kalt, warm, hart, lang, rot, jung, kurz,* and the adverb *oft.* But the great bulk of adjectives do not modify the root vowel.

Irregular comparisons are: *gut, besser, best; viel, mehr, meist; groß, größer, der größte; hoch, höher, der höchste; nahe, näher, der nächste.* Adverbs: *bald, eher, am ehesten; gern, lieber, am liebsten.*

NUMERALS

Cardinals

1 eins	6 sechs	11 elf	16 sechzehn	21 einundzwanzig
2 zwei	7 sieben	12 zwölf	17 siebzehn	22 zweiundzwanzig
3 drei	8 acht	13 dreizehn	18 achtzehn	30 dreißig
4 vier	9 neun	14 vierzehn	19 neunzehn	40 vierzig
5 fünf	10 zehn	15 fünfzehn	20 zwanzig	50 fünfzig

60 sechzig   70 siebzig   80 achtzig   90 neunzig
100 hundert   101 hundert und eins   1000 (ein) tausend
1000000 eine Million   0 Null

Ordinals

To form the ORDINALS add *-te* up to and including 19; from 20 onwards add *-ste*, e.g. *der, die, das zweite,* 'the second'; *der zwanzigste,* 'the 20th'. 1st and 3rd are irregular: *der erste, der dritte.*

ABBREVIATIONS

♤ pitfall! beware of apparent analogy
&c., etcetera
a., aa., adjective(s)
abbr., abbreviation
acad., pertaining to academical customs, &c.
acc., accusative
adv., advv., adverb(s)
agric., agriculture
anat., anatomy
app., appendix
Arab., Arabic
archaeol., archaeology
archit., architecture
art., article
astron., astronomy
av., aviation

bibl., biblical
biol., biology
bot., botany

carp., carpentry
chem., chemistry
colloq., colloquial
commerc., commercial
comp., comparative
compd., compound
compp., compounds
conj., conjunction
contempt., contemptuously
cook., cookery
Cz., Czech

dat., dative
def., definite
dem., demonstrative
derog., derogatory
dial., dialect
dressm., dressmaking
Du., Dutch

E., English
eccl., ecclesiastical
educ., education
electr., electricity
excl., exclamation

F., French
f., feminine
fig., figuratively
fut., future

gen., genitive
geogr., geographical
geol., geology
geom., geometry
Gk., Greek
gram., grammatical
gym., gymnastics

h., haben
Hebr., Hebrew
herald., heraldry
hort., horticulture

i., intransitive
imper., imperative
imperf., imperfect
impers., impersonal
indecl., indeclinable
indic., indicative
insep., inseparable
int., interjection
interrog., interrogative
iron., ironically
irreg., irregular
It., Italian

joc., jocose

L., Latin
leg., legal
lit., literature, literary

m., masculine
mach., machinery
math., mathematics
med., medicine
meteor., meteorology
mil., military
min., mineralogy
ML., Middle Latin
motor., motoring
mount., mountaineering
mus., music

n., neuter

naut., nautical
nom., nominative
N.T., New Testament
num., numeral

obs., obsolete
opt., optics
o.s., oneself

p., participle, participial
paint., painting
parl., parliament
part., particle
pass., passive voice
path., pathology
perf., perfect
phil., philosophy
phot., photography
phys., physics
pl., plural
poet., poetical
pol., political
pp., participle past
pred. a., predicative adjective
pref., prefix
prep., preposition
pres., present tense
pron., pronoun
pros., prosody
psych., psychoanalysis

r., reflexive
rail., railways
R.C., Roman Catholic
relig., religion
Russ., Russian

s., sein
Sc., Scotch
Scand., Scandinavian
sci., science
sculp., sculpture
sep., separable
sing., singular
sl., slang
Slav., Slavonic
sport., sporting
st., strong (conjugation)
sth., something

subj., subjunctive mood	univ., university	v.t., verb transitive
subst., substantive	usu., usually	vulg., vulgar
sup., superlative		vwh., verb conjugated with *haben*
	v., vv., verb(s)	vws., verb conjugated with *sein*
t., transitive	v. aux., verb auxiliary	
tech., technical	vet., veterinary	
tel., telephony	v.i., verb intransitive	
theatr., theatrical	v. impers., verb impersonal	
theol., theology		w., weak (conjugation)
Turk., Turkish	v. st., verb following strong conjugation	
typ., typography		zool., zoology

German abbreviations see p. 443.

A

A, a (a:) *n.* the letter A, a; (*mus.*) a; *das große A* capital A.

a. *See* App. II.

Aal *m.* (-es, -e) eel. **~en** *v.r.* (*colloq.*) to be lazy, relax. **~glatt** *a.* slippery, elusive.

Aar *m.* (-es, -e) eagle.

Aas *n.* (-es, Äser) carcass, carrion; (*vulg. sl.*) swine. **~en** (*mit*) *v.i.* (*colloq.*) to waste.

ab (ap) *adv. & sep. pref.* off; down; away; from; *~Lager* (*commerc.*) ex store; *~ Ostern* from Easter (on); *~ 1. März* on and after March 1st; *~ und an, ~ und zu* from time to time, now and then; *von nun ~* henceforth; *~ sein* (*colloq.*) to be exhausted.

ab|änder-n *v.t.* to change, alter; to modify. **~ung** *f.* change, alteration. **~ungsantrag** *m.* (*parl.*) amendment.

ab|ängstigen *v.r.* to be worried or alarmed.

ab|arbeiten *v.t.* to work off. *v.r.* to work hard, overwork oneself.

ab|ärgern *v.r.* to be annoyed, feel vexed.

Ab|art *f.* variety; variation. **~en** *vws.i.* to degenerate; to deviate; to vary.

ab|ästen *v.t.* to poll (trees), lop, trim.

ab|balgen *v.t.* to skin, flay.

Ab|bau *m.* working (of mine); reduction, cutting down (of prices, &c.); (*chem.*) disintegration, decomposition. **~en** *v.t.* to break up; to work (mine); to reduce, cut down (prices); to dismiss, axe; (*chem.*) to decompose.

ab|beißen *v.t.* to bite off.

ab|bekommen *v.t.* to get, get a share of; *etwas ~* to get hurt.

ab|berufen *v.t.* to call away, recall.

ab|bestellen *v.t.* to countermand, discontinue, cancel.

ab|betteln *v.t.* to wheedle out of (one).

ab|biegen *v.t.* to bend off, bend aside. *vws.i.* to turn, bend, branch off.

Ab|bild, *n.* copy; image; likeness. **~en** *v.t.* to copy, portray; to model. **~ung** *f.* illustration, picture; representation.

ab|binden *v.t.* to untie, undo; (*med.*) to tie off.

Ab|bitte *f.* apology; *~ leisten* to apologize (for). **~n** *v.t.* to beg one's pardon; to apologize.

ab|blasen *v.t.* to blow off or away; (*mil.*) to sound the retreat; to release (gas); (*fig.*) to call off, cancel.

ab|blättern *v.t.* to strip of leaves. *vws.i. & r.* to shed its leaves; to exfoliate; to scale off.

ab|blenden *v.t.* to screen, shade, dim (lights); (*phot.*) to dim; to fade down (sound or picture).

ab|blitzen *vws.i.* to be rebuffed; *~ lassen* to snub.

ab|blühen *v.i.* to cease blooming; to fade, wither.

ab|brausen *v.t.* to douche.

ab|brechen *v.t.* to pluck, pick; to break off, break up; to pull down, demolish (house); to raise (siege); to strike (tents). *v.i.* to cease, interrupt, stop short; to drop (subject).

ab|bremsen *v.t.* to brake.

ab|brennen *v.t. & vws.i.* to burn down; to fire off; to let off (fireworks).

ab|bringen *v.t.* to lead away; to remove (stain); (*fig.*) to dissuade, divert.

ab|bröckeln *vws.i.* to crumble away.

Ab|bruch *m.* breaking off; pulling down, demolition (of house); damage, loss; *auf ~ verkaufen* to sell as scrap; *~ tun* to damage, injure. **~reif** *a.* dilapidated.

ab|brühen *v.t.* to scald; to parboil.

ab|buchen *v.t.* to write off; to balance (accounts).

ab|bürsten v.t. to brush, brush off.

ab|büßen v.t. to expiate, atone for; to serve (sentence).

AB'C n. alphabet; (fig.) rudiments. ~buch n. primer. ~schüler, ~schütze m. beginner.

abdach-en v.t. to slope; to cope (wall). ~ung f. slope, declivity.

abdämmen v.t. to dam, dam up.

Abdampf m. exhaust steam. ~en vi. to evaporate; (colloq.) to clear off.

abdämpfen v.t. to soften, tone down.

abdank-en v.t. to dismiss, discharge. v.i. to retire, resign; to abdicate. ~ung f. dismissal; resignation; abdication.

abdarben v.r. to stint oneself of.

abdeck-en v.t. to uncover, unroof; to skin, flay (cattle); to clear (table); to turn down (bed); to pay off (debts). ~er m. knacker. ~e'rei f. knacker's yard.

abdestillieren v.t. to distil off.

abdichten v.t. to stop up, seal.

abdienen v.t. (mil.) to serve (one's time).

abdingen v.t. to beat down (price); to obtain by negotiating.

abdrängen v.t. to push aside.

abdrehen v.t. to wring (neck); to turn off (gas, tap); to switch off (light). v.i. (naut.) to veer.

abdrosseln v.t. (tech.) to throttle; (motor.) to stall; to stop, switch off engine.

Abdruck m. impression; copy, proof, print; (plaster) cast; stamp, mark. ~en v.t. to print off, reprint; to publish. ~srecht n. copyright.

abdrücken v.t. & i. to press the trigger, fire.

abdunkeln v.t. to darken; to black out; to deepen (colour).

ab|ebben v.i. to ebb away; (fig.) to quieten, die down.

Abend m. (-s, -e) evening, night; (poet.) eve; Heiliger ~ Christmas Eve; am ~ in the evening, at night; gestern ~ last night; heute ~ tonight; neulich ~ the other night; es wird ~ it is getting dark; zu ~ essen to have supper;

~andacht f. even-song. ~blatt n. evening paper. ~brot, ~essen n. supper. ~gesellschaft f. evening party. ~kasse f. box-office for ev. performance. ~land n. west, occident. ~ländisch a. western, occidental. ~lich a. (of) evening. ~mahl n. Holy Communion. ~rot n., ~röte f. sunset glow. ~s adv. in the evening, at night. ~toilette f. evening dress. [EVE]

Abenteu-er n. (-ers, -er) adventure. ~erlich a. adventurous; strange, romantic; venturesome. ~ern v.i. to seek adventures. ~rer m. adventurer. ~rerin f. adventuress. [F]

aber conj. but; yet; however. adv. again; tausend und ~tausend thousands and thousands. ~malig a. repeated. ~mals adv. again, once more.

Aber-glaube m. superstition. ~gläubisch a. superstitious. ~witz m. craziness. ~witzig a. foolish; crazy.

ab|erkenn-en v.t. to deprive of; to disallow; to give verdict against. ~ung f. (leg.) dispossession; ~ung bürgerlicher Rechte deprivation of civil rights.

ab|ernten v.t. to reap, to harvest.

abfädeln v.t. to string (beans).

abfahr-en vos.i. to depart, leave; to start; (naut.) to sail; (skiing) to glissade. v.t. to carry or cart away; to wear out (tyre); ~en lassen (fig.) to snub. ~t f. departure, start; descent, glissade. ~tssignal n. starting-signal. ~tszeit f. time of departure.

Abfall m. falling-off; slope, declivity; waste, refuse, offal; defection, revolt; apostasy. ~eimer m. garbage pail, dustbin. ~en vos.i. to fall off; to slope; to be wasted; to desert, revolt; to slope (away); (fig.) to decrease, deteriorate; ~ für to be profitable for; to be left.

abfällig a. unfavourable; derogatory.

abfangen v.t. to catch, intercept; (hunt.) to stab; (av.) to pull out of a dive, flatten out.

abfärben v.i. to stain; to lose colour; ~ *auf* to influence.

abfass-en v.t. to compose, write, draw up; to catch (thief). ~**ung** f. composition, writing.

abfaulen v.i. to decay; to putrefy.

abfegen v.t. to sweep off.

abfeilen v.t. to clip; to file off.

abfertig-en v.t. to dispatch, send off; to serve, deal with; (*customs*) to clear; *kurz* ~*en* to snub. ~**ung** f. dispatch, expedition; attention, service; clearance; dismissal.

abfeuern v.t. to fire off, discharge.

abfiltrieren v.t. to filter off.

abfind-en v.t. to satisfy, compensate. ~**v.r.** to settle (with); to resign oneself (to), put up (with). ~**ung** f. compensation, (*leg.*) composition.

abflachen v.t. to flatten; to level.

abflauen v.i. to abate, drop; to decrease, ease off; to slacken.

abfliegen vws.i. to fly off; (*av.*) to take off.

abfließen vws.i. to flow off.

Abflug m. (*av.*) take-off, start.

Abfluß m. flowing off; discharge; outlet. ~**graben** m. culvert, drain. ~**rohr** n. drain, pipe.

Abfolge f. succession, sequence.

abfordern v.t. to demand.

abformen v.t. to model, mould.

abforsten v.t. to clear of trees, deforest.

abfragen v.t. to interrogate; to hear (lesson).

abfrieren vws.i. to be nipped by frost; to be frostbitten.

Abfuhr f. (-, -en) removal; (*fig.*) rebuff.

abführ-en v.t. to lead off, carry away; to take into custody; to pay off, pay over; to discharge (debts). v.i. (*med.*) to purge. ~**mittel** n. aperient, laxative, purgative.

abfüllen v.t. to draw off, decant.

abfüttern v.t. to feed; to line (dress).

Abgabe f. delivery; tax, duty; ~ *von Stimmen* voting. ~**nfrei** a. duty-free; tax-exempt. ~**npflichtig** a. taxable.

Abgang m. departure; leaving (school); (*theatr.*) exit; (*commerc.*) sale; tare, loss, waste. ~**szeit** f. time of departure; time of dispatch. ~**szeugnis** n. (school) leaving certificate.

Abgas n. exhaust gas, waste gas.

abgearbeitet a. worn out.

abgeben v.t. to give, deliver up; to part with; to share with; *einen guten Lehrer* ~ to be a good teacher. v.r. to have to do (with); to occupy oneself (with); to associate (with).

abgebrannt a. (*fig.*) stony-broke.

abgebrüht a. (*fig.*) hard boiled.

abgedroschen a. (*fig.*) trite, hackneyed.

abgefeimt a. cunning; insidious.

abgegrast a. (*fig.*) well-covered (ground).

abgegriffen a. well-thumbed; (*of coins*) worn.

abgehen vws.i. to start, go off, depart; to branch off; to leave (school); to resign (office); to come off, be loose; (*commerc.*) to sell; (*math.*) ~ *von* to be deducted from; *gut* ~ to end well; *von s. Meinung* ~ to change one's view; *geht ab* (*theatr.*) exit; *sich nichts* ~ *lassen* to deny oneself nothing.

abgekämpft a. worn out; (*colloq.*) fagged.

abgeklärt a. (*fig.*) wise, mellow.

abgelebt a. decrepit, worn.

abgelegen a. remote.

abgelten v.t. to pay (off); to meet (demand).

abgemessen a. calculated; formal.

abgeneigt a. disinclined; averse.

Abgeordnete(r) m. (-n, -n) deputy; Member of Parliament. ~**nhaus** n. House of Commons.

abgerissen a. ragged; (*fig.*) abrupt, disconnected.

abgesagt a. (*fig.*) declared, sworn.

Abgesandte(r) m. (-n, -n) delegate, envoy, deputy.

abgeschabt a. (*fig.*) threadbare, worn.

abgeschieden a. secluded, retired; deceased. ~**heit** f. solitude, seclusion.

abgeschliffen a. polished.

abgeschlossen *a.* secluded; self-contained (flat); settled; complete.

abgeschmackt *a.* silly, in bad taste.

abgesehen *pp.* ~ *von* apart from, not to mention; *es auf etwas* ~ *h.* to aim at.

abgespannt *a.* (*fig.*) tired out, run down.

abgestanden *a.* stale, flat.

abgestumpft *a.* blunt; (*fig.*) dull; indifferent to.

abgewinnen *v.t.* to obtain, secure from; *Geschmack* ~ to get to like.

abgewöhnen *v.t.* to wean from, to break (person of habit). *v.r.* to give up (habit).

abgezehrt *a.* emaciated.

abgießen *v.t.* to pour off, decant; (*sculp.*) to cast.

Abglanz *m.* reflection; (*fig.*) image.

abgleiten *vws.i.* to slide, slip off; *alles an sich* ~ *lassen* to be proof against everything.

Abgott *m.* idol.

Abgött-e'rei *f.* idolatry. ~**isch** *a.* idolatrous; ~**isch lieben** to idolize.

abgraben *v.t.* to drain off, draw off; *einem das Wasser* ~ to take the bread out of one's mouth.

abgrämen *v.r.* to pine away.

abgrasen *v.t.* to graze; (*fig.*) to search thoroughly.

abgrenzen *v.t.* to mark off, demarcate; to define.

Abgrund *m.* abyss; precipice.

abgründig *a.* precipitous; (*fig.*) inscrutable, impenetrable.

abgucken *v.t.* to learn by watching.

Abguß *m.* pouring off; cast, copy.

abhaben *v.t. etwas* ~ *wollen* to want one's share.

abhacken *v.t.* to chop off.

abhaken *v.t.* to unhook; to tick off (items).

abhalftern *v.t.* to unharness.

abhalt-en *v.t.* to hold off, keep off; to hinder, prevent; to hold (meeting); to give (lesson); to hold out (child). ~**ung** *f.* hindrance; holding (of meeting).

abhand-eln *v.t.* to beat down (price); to get by bargaining;

to discuss, treat of. ~**lung** *f.* treatise, paper, dissertation.

ab'handen *adv.* ~ *kommen* to get lost.

Abhang *m.* slope.

abhäng-en *v.t.* to take down; (*tel.*) to hang up; (*tech.*) to disconnect. *v.i.* ~*en von* to depend on. ~**ig** *a.* dependent; ~**ige Rede** indirect speech. ~**igkeit** *f.* dependence; (*gram.*) subordination.

abhärmen *v.r.* to pine away, grieve.

abhärt-en *v.t.* to harden. ~**ung** *f.* toughening.

abhaspeln *v.t.* to reel off; (*fig.*) to rattle off.

abhauen *v.t.* to cut off; (*sl.*) to scram.

abhäuten *v.t.* to skin.

abheben *v.t.* to lift (off); to withdraw (money); to cut (cards); *sich* ~*von* to stand out (against).

abheilen *vws.i.* to heal up.

abhelfen *v.i.* to help, remedy, redress.

abherzen *v.t.* to hug and kiss.

abhetzen *v.t.* to hunt down, to harass. *v.r.* to rush about, tire oneself out.

Abhilfe *f.* remedy, help, relief, redress.

abhobeln *v.t.* to plane, plane off.

abhold *a.* ~ *sein* to be averse (to).

abholen *v.t.* to fetch, call for, collect; to meet.

abholzen *v.t.* to deforest, cut down trees.

abhorchen *v.t.* to listen, sound; (*med.*) to auscultate.

abhör-en *v.t.* to listen, listen in, overhear, intercept; to hear (lesson). ~**apparat** *m.* stethoscope.

abirr-en *vws.i.* to lose one's way, go astray. ~**ung** *f.* deviation; (*opt.*) aberration.

Abi'tur *n.* (-s, -e) school leaving examination. ~**i'ent** *m.* candidate for sch. l. examination.

abjagen *v.t.* to overdrive; to retrieve, snatch away.

abkanten *v.t.* to bevel, trim.

abkanzeln *v.t.* to reprimand.

abkarten *v.t.* to prearrange; to

plot; *abgekartetes Spiel* plot, put-up job.

abkauen *v.t.* to bite off, gnaw off.

abkaufen *v.t.* to buy from.

Abkehr *f.* (-) withdrawal, alienation. **~en** *v.r.* to turn away.

abklappern *v.t.* to scour, rove; *abgeklapperte Redensarten* hackneyed expressions.

abklären *v.t.* to clarify, clear.

Abklatsch *m.* impression, copy; stereotype-plate; (*fig.*) poor imitation.

abklingeln *v.i.* (*tel.*) to ring off; to give starting-signal.

abklingen *v.i.* to die away.

abklopfen *v.t.* to knock off; (*med.*) to auscultate. *v.i.* to rap with baton to stop music.

abknabbern *v.t.* to nibble off.

abknallen *v.t.* to fire off; to shoot down.

abknappen, abknapsen *v.t.* to stint, curtail.

abknicken *v.t.* to break off, snap off.

abknöpfen *v.t.* to unbutton; (*fig.*) *einem etwas ~* to do a person out of.

abkochen *v.t.* to decoct, boil; to scald (milk). *v.i.* to cook (in camp).

abkommandieren *v.t.* to detach, detail.

Abkomme *m.* (-n. -n) descendant.

abkommen *vws.i.* to deviate; to lose (one's way); to give up (plan); to get off or away; to become obsolete, fall into disuse. *subst. n.* agreement; treaty.

abkömm-lich *a.* free; (to be) available. **~ling** *m.* descendant; (*chem.*) derivative.

abkonterfeien *v.t.* to portray.

abkoppeln *v.t.* to uncouple.

abkratzen *v.t.* to scrape off, scratch off; (*sl.*) to push off.

abkriegen *v.t.* to get (a share of); to get hurt; (*sl.*) to be punished.

abkühl-en *v.t. & i.* to cool; to chill. *v.r.* to cool down. **~ung** *f.* cooling.

Abkunft *f.* (-) descent, origin, birth; breed.

abkürz-en *v.t.* to shorten, abbre-

viate; to reduce; to curtail. **~ung** *f.* abbreviation; short-cut.

ablade-n *v.t.* to unload, discharge, dump. **~platz** *m.*, **~stelle** *f.* goods-yard; dumping-ground.

Ablage *f.* depot; dump.

ablagern *v.t.* to deposit; to store; *abgelagert* matured (wine). *v.r.* to deposit, settle.

Ablaß *m.* (Ablasses, Ablässe) indulgence. **~brief** *m.* letter of indulgence. **~ventil** *n.* blow-off valve.

ablassen *v.t.* to drain off (water); to let off (steam); to reduce (in price); to sell, give up. *v.i.* to leave off, desist, cease.

Ablativ *m.* (-s, -e) ablative.

Ablauf *m.* running off; outlet; lapse, expiration (of time). **~en** *vws.i.* to run off, flow down; to expire; (*of clock*) to run down; (*sport.*) to start; *gut ~en* to end well. *v.t.* to scour, rove; to wear out (shoes); *sich die Beine ~en* to run oneself off one's feet.

Ablaut *m.* vowel-permutation.

abläuten *v.i.* to give starting-signal; (*tel.*) to ring off.

Ableben *n.* death, decease.

ablecken *v.t.* to lick off.

ablegen *v.t.* to put away, lay aside, lay down; to take off; to give up (habit); to file (letters); to distribute (types); to pass (examination); *bitte, legen Sie ab!* please, take off your things; *abgelegte Kleider* cast-off clothing.

Ableger *m.* (-s, -) layer, slip, shoot; (*bot.*) branch.

ablehn-en *v.t.* to decline, refuse; (*leg.*) to challenge. **~end** *a.* negative; critical. **~ung** *f.* refusal, rejection.

ableisten *v.t.* to perform duly; (*mil.*) to serve (one's time).

ableit-en *v.t.* to turn aside, divert; to shunt (current); (*gram.*) to derive. **~ung** *f.* diversion; derivation.

ablenk-en *v.t.* to divert, distract; to deflect; (*opt.*) to diffract. **~ung** *f.* diversion; deflection; diffraction; (*fig.*) distraction;

recreation; **~ungsmanöver** *n.* (*fig.*) red herring.

ablesen *v.t.* to pick off, pluck off; to read off.

ableugnen *v.t.* to deny, disown.

abliefer-n *v.t.* to deliver, hand over. **~ung** *f.* delivery.

abliegen *v.i.* to lie remote; to mature.

ablisten *v.t.* to trick (a person) out of.

ablocken *v.t.* to get by coaxing.

ablohnen *v.t.* to pay off.

ablöschen *v.t.* to blot out.

ablös-en *v.t.* to remove, detach, loosen; to change or relieve (guard); (*commerc.*) to redeem. *v.r.* to come off, scale off; to relieve one another, alternate. **~ung** *f.* loosening; relief; redemption. **~ungsmannschaft** *f.* relief (party).

abmach-en *v.t.* to remove, loosen, detach; to settle, arrange; *abgemacht!* agreed! **~ung** *f.* arrangement, settlement, agreement.

abmagern *vws.i.* to get thin, lose flesh.

abmähen *v.t.* to mow, cut down.

abmahnen *v.t.* to dissuade, warn.

abmalen *v.t.* to paint, portray, copy.

Abmarsch *m.* marching off; start. **~bereit** *a.* ready to start.

abmatten *v.t.* to fatigue, exhaust.

abmeld-en *v.t.* to give notice of removal or departure. **~ung** *f.* notice of departure.

abmess-en *v.t.* to measure off, gauge, survey; to weigh (one's words). **~ung** *f.* measurement.

abmieten *v.t.* to rent; to hire.

abmontieren *v.t.* (*tech.*) to dismount; to dismantle.

abmühen *v.r.* to exert oneself.

abmustern *v.t.* to pay off (crew).

abnagen *v.t.* to gnaw off.

Abnahme *f.* (-, -n) taking off, removal; sale, purchase (of goods); decrease, decline, diminution; loss (in weight); (*med.*) amputation; (*mach.*) test.

abnehm-en *v.t.* to take off, remove; to gather, pick; to take over; to buy (goods); to cut

(cards); to take in (in knitting); (*med.*) to amputate. *v.i.* to decrease, diminish; (*of person*) to lose weight; (*of moon*) to wane; (*of days*) to grow shorter. **~er** *m.* buyer, customer.

Abneigung *f.* aversion, dislike; antipathy.

ab'norm *a.* abnormal.

abnötigen *v.t.* to extort (from).

abnutz-en, abnütz-en *v.t.* to wear out, use up. **~ung** *f.* wear and tear; attrition.

Abonne'ment (-mã:) *n.* (-s, -s) subscription; (*rail.*) season-ticket.

Abo'nn-ent *m.* (-enten, -enten) subscriber. **~ieren** *v.t.* to subscribe.

ab|ordn-en *v.t.* to delegate, depute. **~ung** *f.* delegation, deputation.

Ab|ort¹ *m.* (-s, -e) lavatory, W.C.; latrine; cloak-room.

A'bort² *m.* (*med.*) abortion.

abpassen *v.t.* to measure, fit; to time; to watch for (opportunity).

abpflücken *v.t.* to pluck off, pick.

abplacken, abplagen *v.r.* to drudge, work hard, toil.

abplatten *v.t.* to flatten.

abprägen *v.r.* to leave an impress.

Abprall *m.* rebound, recoil. **~en** *vws.i.* to rebound, recoil; (*mil.*) to ricochet; (*fig.*) to glance off.

abprotzen *v.t.* to unlimber.

abputzen *v.t.* to clean, polish; to rough-cast.

abquälen *v.r.* to worry oneself; to toil, work hard.

abquetschen *v.t.* to squeeze off.

abrackern *v.r.* to slave, toil.

abrahmen *v.t.* to skim (milk).

abrasieren *v.t.* to shave off.

abraspeln *v.t.* to rasp off.

abraten *v.t.* to dissuade (from), warn (against).

Abraum *m.* rubbish. **~halde** *f.* slag heap.

abräumen *v.t.* to take away, clear away, remove.

abrechn-en *v.t.* to deduct. *v.i.* to settle (accounts). **~ung** *f.* deduction; balancing (of accounts), settlement. **~ungsstelle** *f.* clearing house.

Abrede *f.* agreement; *in ~ stellen*

to deny. ~n *v.t.* to dissuade (from).

abreib-en *v.t.* to rub off, rub down. ~ung *f.* rubbing, rub down; (*med.*) friction.

Abreise *f.* departure. ~n *vws.i.* to leave (for).

abreiß-en *v.t.* to tear off; to pull down (house). *vws.i.* to break off, snap. ~kalender *m.* tear-off calendar.

abrennen *v.r.* sich die Beine ~ to run oneself off one's feet.

abrichten *v.t.* to train (animal); to break in (horse).

abriegeln *v.t.* to bolt; to close or barricade (street).

Abriegelungsfeuer *n.* box barrage; back barrage; defensive barrage.

abrinden *v.t.* to bark (tree).

abringen *v.t.* to wrest (from).

abrinnen *vws.i.* to flow down.

Abriß *m.* draft, sketch; summary; compendium; abstract.

abrollen *v.t.* to roll off; to forward (goods); to unwind (film). *v.r.* (*fig.*) to unroll, unfold.

abrücken *v.t.* to move off. *vws.i.* to march off; to depart; (*fig.*) to draw back.

Abruf *m. auf ~* at call. ~en *v.t.* to call away or off; to call out (train).

abrunden *v.t.* to round off; to make round (sum).

abrupfen *v.t.* to pluck off.

abrüst-en *v.t. & i.* to disarm. ~ung *f.* disarmament.

abrutschen *vws.i.* to slide down or off.

absäbeln *v.t.* (*colloq.*) to hack off.

absacken *vws.i.* to sink; (*av.*) to pancake.

Absage *f.* refusal; cancellation. ~n *v.t. & i.* to cancel; to call off; to refuse, decline; to revoke, renounce.

absägen *v.t.* to saw off; (*colloq.*) to sack.

absatteln *v.t.* to unsaddle. *v.i.* to dismount.

Absatz *m.* section, paragraph; pause, stop; landing (on staircase); heel (of shoe); sale (of goods); circulation (of newspaper, &c.). ~gebiet *n.* market.

abschaben *v.t.* to scrape off.

abschaff-en *v.t.* to do away with, abolish; to give up. ~ung *f.* abolition; dismissal.

abschälen *v.t.* to peel, pare, shell.

abschalten *v.t.* to switch off.

abschätz-en *v.t.* to value, estimate; to assess. ~ig *a.* derogatory, contemptuous, disparaging. ~ung *f.* valuation, estimate; assessment.

Abschaum *m.* scum; (*fig.*) dregs.

abschäumen *v.t.* to skim off.

abscheiden *v.t.* to separate; to refine. *vws.i.* to die. *v.r.* (*chem.*) to be precipitated.

abscheren *v.t.* to cut (hair); to shear (sheep).

Abscheu *m.* aversion, horror, loathing. ~lich *a.* horrible, abominable, detestable, atrocious. ~lichkeit *f.* ugliness; atrocity.

abscheuern *v.t.* to scrub, scour. *v.r.* to wear off.

abschicken *v.t.* to send off, dispatch.

abschieben *v.t.* to push off; to turn out; to deport; *etwas von sich ~* to get out of something. *vws.i.* (*colloq.*) to buzz off.

Abschied *m.* (*-s, -e*) departure, parting, leave; dismissal; ~ *nehmen von* to take leave of; to say good-bye to; *seinen ~ nehmen* to resign; *den ~ bekommen* to be dismissed; to be placed on the retired list. ~sbesuch *m.* farewell visit. ~sgesuch *n.* resignation.

abschießen *v.t.* to shoot, fire; to shoot off, shoot down; to launch (rocket); to down (plane); *den Vogel ~* (*fig.*) to take the cake.

abschinden *v.r.* to slave, drudge.

abschirmen *v.t.* to screen, shield.

abschirren *v.t.* to unharness.

abschlachten *v.t.* to slaughter, butcher.

Abschlag *m.* fall in price; *auf ~* by instalments. ~en *v.t.* to beat off, knock off; to cut down; to repel (attack); to refuse (request).

abschlägig *a.* negative.

abschleifen *v.t.* to grind, polish.

abschlepp-en *v.t.* to drag off, tow away. *v.r.* to tire oneself out (carrying things). **~dienst** m. breakdown service. **~wagen** m. breakdown lorry.

abschließen v.t. & i. to lock up, shut off; to finish (work); to strike (bargain); to balance (account); to come to terms. **~d** a. conclusive, final.

Abschluß m. close, conclusion, settlement; balance; sale. **~prüfung** f. final(s). **~rechnung** f. final account.

abschmecken v.t. to taste.

abschmeicheln v.t. to coax out of.

abschmelzen v.t. & vws.i. to melt off; to separate by melting.

abschmieren v.t. (motor.) to grease.

abschminken v.r. (theatr.) to take off one's make up.

abschnallen v.t. to unbuckle.

abschneiden v.t. to cut off; Ehre ~ to slander; das Wort ~ to interrupt. v.i. gut ~ to come off well.

abschnellen v.t. & vws.i. to jerk off; to fly off with a jerk.

Abschnitt m. cut; division; epoch, period; (math.) segment; (mil.) sector, section; part, paragraph, passage (of book); (commerc.) coupon.

abschnüren v.t. (med.) to tie off.

abschöpfen v.t. to skim off.

abschrägen v.t. to slope; to bevel.

abschrauben v.t. to unscrew, screw off.

abschrecken v.t. to frighten, dishearten, deter; to chill, cool (metals); **~d aussehen** to look forbidding; **~des Beispiel** lesson, warning.

Abschreckungsmittel n. deterrent.

abschreib-en v.t. to copy; (lit.) to plagiarize; to crib (in school); (commerc.) to write off, deduct. v.i. to send written refusal. **~er** m. copyist; plagiarist.

abschreiten v.t. to pace off.

Abschrift f. copy, duplicate, transcript. **~lich** a. in duplicate.

abschuften v.r. to slave, drudge.

abschuppen v.t. to scale off; to scrape (fish).

abschürf-en v.t. to scratch off, scrape off; sich die Haut **~en** to tear one's skin. **~ung** f.

abrasion.

Abschuß m. firing-off, discharge; (mil.) knocking out; (av.) downing, shooting-down; launching.

abschüssig a. steep, precipitous.

abschütteln v.t. to shake off.

abschwächen v.t. to weaken, diminish; to soften.

abschwatzen v.t. to talk (person) out of (something).

abschweif-en vws.i. to stray; to deviate, digress. **~ung** f. digression, deviation.

abschwellen vws.i. to grow less; to die down; (med.) to go down.

abschwenken vws.i. to turn off; (mil.) to wheel.

abschwindeln v.t. to swindle out of.

abschwören v.t. to deny upon oath; to abjure, renounce (faith).

absegeln vws.i. to sail away, set sail.

absehbar a. within sight; in **~er** Zeit before long.

absehen v.t. to foresee (the end of sth.); to copy; es ~ auf to aim at; ~ von to desist from, disregard; not to take into account.

abseifen v.t. to soap.

abseihen v.t. to strain, filter off.

abseilen v.t. to rope down, lower by rope. v.i. to descend on rope.

absein v.i. (colloq.) to be tired out; weit ~ to be far off.

abseits adv. & prep. aside, apart, away from.

absend-en v.t. to send off, send away, forward, dispatch. **~er** m. sender; consignor. **~ung** f. sending, dispatch.

absengen v.t. to singe off.

absenk-en v.t. to layer. **~er** m. offshoot, layer.

absetz-en v.t. to put down, deposit; to depose (king); to take off (hat); to dismiss, remove (official); to put down; to deduct (sum); to sell (goods); to withdraw (play); (typ.) to set up. v.i. to break off, stop, pause. v.r. (mil.) to disengage o.s. (from); (chem.) to be precipitated. **~ung** f. deposition; dismissal.

Absicht f. (-, -en) intention, purpose, view; aim; in der ~ with the intention; mit ~ on purpose; in böser ~ with malice afore-

thought. **~lich** a. intentional.
adv. on purpose.

absingen v.t. to sing at sight.

absitzen v.i. vom Pferde ~ to dismount. v.t. to do time (in prison).

abso'lut a. absolute. **~ismus** m. absolutism.

absol'vieren v.t. to finish (one's studies); to absolve.

ab'sonderlich a. peculiar, strange, unusual. **~keit** f. peculiarity.

absonder-n v.t. to separate, isolate, detach; (med.) to secrete. v.r. to withdraw, retire. **~ung** f. separation, isolation; secretion.

abspalten v.t. to split off; to separate.

abspann-en v.t. to unharness (horse); to unbend (bow). **~ung** f. fatigue, exhaustion.

absparen v.t. sich etwas ~ to stint oneself of something.

abspeisen v.t. (fig.) to put off (with).

abspenstig a. ~ machen to estrange; ~ werden to desert.

absperr-en v.t. to shut off, lock; to bar, block, stop; to turn off (gas); to isolate, separate. **~hahn** m. stop cock. **~ung** m. shutting off; blocking; stoppage; barrier; cordon; barrage; isolation.

abspiegeln v.t. to reflect, mirror.

abspielen v.r. (fig.) to take place. v.t. to wear out (mus. instr.).

absplittern v.t. & vws.i. to splinter off.

Absprache f. agreement.

absprechen v.t. to deny, deprive of. **~d** a. slighting, deprecatory.

abspringen vws.i. to leap off, jump off; (av.) to bale out; to rebound; to crack off; (fig.) to digress; to desert (party).

Absprung m. jump; (av.) baling out, descent (by parachute).

abspulen v.t. to wind off, unwind.

abspül-en v.t. to wash up, wash off, rinse. **~wasser** n. dish-water.

abstamm-en vws.i. to descend; to be derived. **~ung** f. descent, lineage; derivation.

Abstand m. distance; interval; (fig.) difference. ~ nehmen von to desist from, give up. **~geld** n. indemnification, compensation.

abstatten v.t. to give, render, pay; to return (thanks).

abstauben, abstäuben v.t. to dust.

abstech-en v.t. to cut; to stick (pig). v.i. **~en von** to contrast with, stand out against. **~er** m. excursion; détour; (fig.) digression.

absteck-en v.t. to unpin; to mark out, stake out. **~pfahl** m. stake, post, picket.

abstehen v.i. to stand off; to desist (from); to get stale; to stick out.

absteifen v.t. to prop up, support.

absteig-en vws.i. to come down, descend; to dismount; to alight; to put up (at an inn). **~equartier** n. accommodation, night's lodging.

abstellen v.t. to put down; to stop (machine); to turn off (gas); to park (vehicle); (fig.) to abolish, do away with; to redress, remedy (an evil).

abstempeln v.t. to stamp.

absteppen v.t. to quilt.

absterben vws.i. to die away; to fade, wither; to grow numb; (med.) to mortify.

Abstieg m. (-s, -e) descent.

abstimm-en v.t. to tune; to shade off (colours); to adjust, coordinate. v.i. to vote; **~en lassen** to put to the vote. **~knopf** m. tuner. **~skala** f. tuning-dial. **~ung** f. tuning-in; voting; (parl.) division; plebiscite; geheime **~ung** ballot.

Absti'nenz f. (-) total abstinence. **~ler** m. teetotaller.

abstoß-en v.t. to knock off, push off, rub off; to sell off (goods); (fig.) to repel; to repulse. **~d** a. repellent, repulsive.

abstottern v.t. to pay by instalments.

abstra'hieren v.t. to abstract.

ab'strakt a. abstract.

abstrapazieren v.t. to wear out; to tire out.

abstreichen v.t. to strike off; to deduct (sum); to wipe (shoes).

abstreifen v.t. to strip off, pull off; to skin; to wipe (shoes on mat).

abstreiten v.t. to dispute; to deny.

Abstrich m. deduction, cut; down-stroke (in writing); (med.) ~ machen to take a swab; (fig.) to withdraw, revoke.

abstuf-en v.t. to gradate, graduate; to grade. ~ung f. grad(ua)tion; grade.

abstumpfen v.t. to blunt, dull. vws.i. (fig.) ~ gegen to become insensible to.

Absturz m. fall, crash; zum ~ bringen to bring down, shoot down.

abstürzen vws.i. to fall, fall down; to descend steeply; (av.) to crash.

abstützen v.t. to prop, support.

absuchen v.t. to search; to scour (the country); to sweep (sky); to pick (off).

Absud m. (-s, -e) decoction; extract.

Ab'szeß m. (-sses, -sse) abscess.

Abt m. (-s, "-e) abbot. ~'ei f. abbey.

abtasten v.t. to palpate; (fig.) to probe.

abtakeln v.t. to unrig.

Abteil n. compartment. ~en v.t. to divide off; to separate. ~ung f. division, section; department; compartment; ward (in hospital); (mil.) unit.

abtelegraphieren v.t. to cancel by telegram.

Äb'tissin f. (-, -nen) abbess.

abtönen v.t. to shade off; to tone down.

abtöten v.t. to destroy; to mortify (the flesh).

Abtrag m. einem ~ tun to injure someone. ~en v.t. to carry away, clear away; to pull down (house); to level (hill); to pay (debt); to wear out (clothes). **abträglich** a. injurious; detrimental.

Abtransport m. transportation; removal; evacuation.

abträufeln vws.i. to trickle down.

abtreib-en v.t. to drive away; (med.) to procure abortion. vws.i. to drift off. ~ung f. abortion.

abtrennen v.t. to separate, detach; (dressm.) to rip off, undo.

abtret-en v.t. to leave, retire;

tritt ab (theatr.) exit. v.t. to tread down; (fig.) to cede, yield; to transfer. ~ung f. cession, surrender; transfer.

Abtritt m. (theatr.) exit; lavatory, W.C.

abtrocknen v.t. to dry, dry off, wipe.

abtröpfeln, abtropfen vws.i. to drip down, trickle down.

abtrotzen v.t. to wrest, wrench away.

abtrudeln vws.i. (av.) to go into or come down in a spin.

abtrünnig a. unfaithful, disloyal; apostate. ~keit f. desertion; apostasy.

abtun v.t. to take off, put away; to dispose of, finish.

ab|urteilen v.t. to pass sentence upon. v.i. to criticize severely.

abvermieten v.t. to sublet.

abwägen v.t. to weigh, consider.

Abwahl f. revocation (at election).

abwälzen v.t. to roll off; (fig.) to shirk; to shift (blame) on.

abwand-eln v.t. to vary; (gram.) to inflect; to decline; to conjugate. ~lung f. inflexion; declension; conjugation.

abwander-n vws.i. to wander off; to migrate. ~ung f. exodus (of capital).

abwarten v.t. & i. to wait for, await, wait and see.

abwärts prep. & adv. down, downwards.

abwasch-en v.t. to wash off; to wash up. ~magd f. scullerymaid. ~ung f. ablution. ~wasser n. dish-water.

Abwasser n. waste water.

abwechs-eln v.t. to vary, change. v.i. to alternate, take turns. ~elnd a. alternate. adv. alternately, by turns. ~lung f. change, variety; zur ~lung for a change.

Abweg m. wrong way; detour; auf ~e geraten to go astray. ~ig a. devious; misleading.

Abwehr f. defence. ~en v.t. to ward off; to keep off; to defend; to avert. ~ung f. defensive.

abweich-en vws.i. to deviate, depart from; to differ; to diverge; (phys.) to decline. ~end a.

different. ~ung f. deviation; difference; divergence; declination; exception.

abweiden v.t. to graze.

abweis-en v.t. to refuse, reject, send away; (leg.) to dismiss; to repel (attack). ~ung f. refusal, rejection.

abwend-en v.t. to avert, prevent; to ward off; to turn aside, turn away. ~ig a. ~ig machen to estrange.

abwerfen v.t. to throw off, cast off; to shed (leaves); to drop (bombs); to yield (profit).

abwerten v.t. to depreciate; to devalue (money).

abwesen-d a. absent; (fig.) absentminded. ~heit f. absence.

abwickeln v.t. to unwind; (fig.) to wind up, finish.

abwiegen v.t. to weigh out; to weigh (one's words).

abwimmeln v.t. (colloq.) to keep off, ward off.

Abwind m. down-current.

abwinken v.i. to warn off.

abwirtschaften v.t. to ruin, mismanage; abgewirtschaftet h. to be ruined; abgewirtschaftet s. to be done for.

abwischen v.t. to wipe, wipe off.

abwracken v.t. to break up (ship).

Abwurf m. throwing down; dropping.

abwürgen v.t. to throttle, strangle.

abzahl-en v.t. to pay off, pay by instalments. ~ung f. payment on account; auf ~ung by instalments.

abzähl-en v.t. to count, count off.

abzapfen v.t. to draw off; (fig.) to bleed; to fleece.

abzäumen v.t. to unbridle.

abzäunen v.t. to fence off or in.

abzehr-en vws.i. to waste away. ~ung f. emaciation; consumption.

Abzeichen n. badge; stripe; sign, mark.

abzeichnen v.t. to copy, draw; to mark off. v.r. to stand out (against).

Abziehbild n. transfer-picture.

abziehen v.t. to take off, take out; to strip (bed); to string (beans);

to skin; to strop; to draw off (beer); to distil; (typ.) to pull (phot.) to print; to subtract, deduct (sum); to divert (attention). vws.i. to march off, move off; (of smoke) to escape, disperse.

abzielen (auf) v.i. to aim (at).

abzirkeln v.t. to measure with compasses.

Abzug m. departure; outlet; trigger; (typ.) proof; (phot.) print; (commerc.) rebate, discount; deduction, allowance; in ~ bringen to deduct. ~sgas n. burnt gas. ~skanal m. drain; sewer.

abzüglich adv. ~ der Unkosten less charges, expenses.

abzupfen v.t. to pull off, pick off.

abzwacken v.t. to extort (from).

abzweigen vws.i. & r. to branch off.

ach (ax) int. ah! oh! alas! ~ so! oh, I see; ~ was!, ~ wo! nonsense, not a bit of it. subst. n. lamentation; mit ~ und Krach by the skin of one's teeth, only just.

A'chat m. (-s, -e) agate.

Achse (aksə) f. (-, -n) axle; (math.) axis. ~nblech n. axle-guard. ~nschnitt m. axial section.

Achsel (aksəl) f. (-, -n) shoulder; auf die leichte ~ nehmen to make light of; über die ~ ansehen to look down on. ~band n. shoulder-strap. ~bein n. shoulder-blade. ~drüse f. axillary gland. ~höhle f. armpit. ~klappe f. shoulder-piece. ~träger m. time-server, doubledealer. ~zucken n. shrug(ging) of the shoulders.

acht¹ (axt) a. & subst. f. eight; heute in ~ Tagen today week; a week today. ~e a. eighth. ~eck n. octagon. ~eckig a. octagonal. ~el n. eighth (part). ~elnote f. quaver. ~ens adv. eighthly. ~er m. figure eight; eight (-oared boat). ~hundert a. eight hundred. ~mal adv. eight times. ~stundentag m. eighthour day. ~zehn a. eighteen. ~zig a. eighty.

Acht² (axt) f. (-) care, attention; ~ geben, ~ haben to pay attention to, take notice of; *sich in ~ nehmen* to take care, beware; *außer ~ lassen* to disregard, take no notice (of). ~**bar** *a.* respected, respectable. ~**barkeit** *f.* respectability. ~**enswert** *a.* worthy of esteem. ~**los** *a.* careless, negligent. ~**losigkeit** *f.* carelessness, negligence. ~**sam** *a.* careful, attentive. ~**samkeit** *f.* carefulness, attention.

Acht³ (axt) *f.* ban, outlawry; *in die ~ erklären* to outlaw.

acht-en *v.t.* to esteem, regard, respect. *v.i.* to pay attention (to), see (to). ~**ung** *f.* esteem, regard; (*excl.*) attention! beware! look out! ~**unggebietend** *a.* commanding respect. ~**ungsvoll** *a.* respectful.

ächt-en *v.t.* to outlaw, proscribe. ~**ung** *f.* outlawing, proscription.

achter *prep. & a.* aft. ~**deck** *n.* quarter-deck. ~**luke** *f.* after-hatch.

ächzen *v.i.* to groan.

Acker *m.* (-s, *ä*) field, arable land, soil. ~**bau** *m.* agriculture, farming. ~**bauend**, ~**bautreibend** *aa.* agricultural. ~**bestellung** *f.* tillage. ~**boden** *m.*, ~**land** *n.* arable land. ~**gaul** *n.* farmhorse. ~**gerät** *n.* agricultural implement. ~**knecht** *m.* farm labourer. ~**krume** *f.* mould, surface soil. ~**smann** *m.* ploughman. [ACRE]

ackern *v.t. & i.* to till, plough.

a'ddieren *v.t.* to add up.

a'de *int.* good-bye; farewell.

Adel *m.* (-s) nobility, aristocracy. ~**ig, adlig** *aa.* noble. ~**sbrief** *m.*, ~**sdiplom** *n.* patent of nobility. ~**sstand** *m.* peerage. ~**sstolz** *m.* pride of birth.

adeln *v.t.* to raise to the peerage; to ennoble.

Ader *f.* (-, -n) vein; grain, streak (in wood); *zur ~ lassen* to bleed. ~**ig, äderig** *aa.* veined. ~**laß** *m.* bleeding.

adi'eu (adjø:) *int. & subst. n.* good-bye, farewell. [F]

Adjektiv *n.* (-s, -e) adjective.

Adler (a:-) *m.* (-s, -) eagle. ~**nase**

f. aquiline nose.

Admi'ral (-a:l) *m.* (-s, -e) admiral. ~**i'tät** *f.* admiralty. ~**sschiff** *n.* flag-ship. ~**sstab** *m.* naval staff.

adop't-ieren *v.t.* to adopt. ~**ivkind** *n.* adopted child.

Adre'ssat *m.* (-en, -en) addressee.

A'dreßbuch *n.* directory.

A'dress-e *f.* (-e, -en) ✦ address (of letter); speech. ~**ennachweis** *m.* registry office, agency. ~**ieren** *v.t.* to address.

a'drett *a.* smart.

Ad'vent *m.* (-s, -e) advent.

Ad'verb (-vɛrp) *n.* (-s, -ien) adverb.

Advo'kat (-a:t) *m.* (-en, -en) advocate, solicitor, barrister.

Aero-dynamik *f.* aerodynamics. ~**nautik** *f.* aeronautics. ~**plan** *m.* (-s, -e) aeroplane. ~**statik** *f.* aerostatics.

A'ffäre *f.* (-, -n) affair.

Affe *m.* (-n; -n) ape, monkey. ~**npinscher** *m.* griffon.

A'ffekt *m.* (-es, -e) ✦ excitement, passion. [L]

affek'tiert *a.* ✦ affected = full of affectation. ~**heit** *f.* affectation.

äff-en *v.t.* to mock. ~**in** *f.* she-ape.

After *m.* (-s, -) anus. ~**beredsamkeit** *f.* empty eloquence. ~**gelehrsamkeit** *f.* sham erudition. ~**mieter** *m.* sub-tenant. ~**rede** *f.* slander, calumny.

A'gende *f.* (*eccl.*) liturgy, ritual.

A'gent *m.* (-en, -en) agent. ~**ur** *f.* agency.

A'gide *f.* aegis.

a'gieren *v.i.* to act.

agita-to'risch *a.* inflammatory, inciting. ~**ieren** *v.i.* to agitate.

Ago'nie *f.* ✦ death-struggle, death-agony.

A'graffe *f.* (-, -n) brooch, clasp. [F]

A'grarier *m.* (-s, -) agrarian.

Ahle *f.* (-, -n) awl.

Ahn *m.* (-en, -en) ancestor, forefather. ~**e**, ~**frau**, ~**in** *f.* ancestress. ~**ennachweis** *m.* proof of ancestry. ~**enpass** *m.* certificate of ancestry. ~**entafel** *f.* genealogical tree. ~**herr** *m.* ancestor.

ahnd-en *v.t.* to punish; to revenge.

~ung f. punishment; revenge.
ähneln v.i. to resemble.
ahn-en v.t. & i. to have a presentiment of; to guess; to suspect. ~ung f. presentiment; keine (blasse) ~ung not the slightest idea. ~unglos a. unsuspecting. ~ungsvoll a. full of forebodings.

ähnlich a. similar, like; ~ sehen to resemble; to be like. ~keit f. similarity, likeness, resemblance.
Ahorn m. (-s, -e) maple.
Ähre f. (·, -n) ear (of corn). ~nlese f. gleaning. ~nleser m. gleaner.
Ais n. (mus.) A sharp.
Aka-de'mie f. academy; university; school. ~'demiker m. academician; graduate. ~'demisch a. academic.

A'kazie f. (·, -n) acacia.
akklimati'sieren v.t. to acclimatize.
A'kkord m. (-s, -e) accord; contract, agreement; (mus.) chord. ~arbeit f. piece-work. ~arbeiter m. piece-worker. ~'ieren v.t. & i. to agree, come to terms with. ~lohn m. wages for piece-work.
akkredi'tieren v.t. to accredit. ~iv n. letter of credit.
Akku-mu'lator m. accumulator. ~ladestelle f. battery-charging plant.
akku'rat a. accurate, exact.
Akkusativ m. (-s, -e) accusative.
A'kontozahlung f. payment on account; instalment.
Akro'bat m. (-en, -en) acrobat. ~ik f. acrobatics. ~isch a. acrobatic.
Akt m. (-es, -e) action, deed; (theatr.) act; nude. ~modell n. life model, nude. ~
Akten f. pl. deeds, documents, records, files; zu den ~ nehmen to file; to register; zu den ~ legen to pigeon-hole. ~klammer f. paper clip. ~mappe f. document case, portfolio. ~mäßig a. authentic, documentary. ~schrank m. filing cabinet. ~ständer m. pigeon-holes. ~stück n. (official) document. ~zeichen n. reference (-number).
Aktie (aktsia) f. (-, -n) share, stock. ~ngesellschaft f. joint-stock company. ~ninhaber, Ak-

tionär m. shareholder. ~nkapital n. share-capital.

ak'tiv (-if) a. active; (mil.) serving with the colours, regular. ~a n.pl. assets. ~i'tät f. activity.
Aktu-ali'tät f. actuality. ~'ell a. ♢ actual = of present interest; topical.
A'kust-ik f. acoustics. ~isch a. acoustic.
a'kut a. ♢ (med.) acute; burning (question).
Ak'zent (-tsɛnt) m. (-s, -e) accent, stress. ~u'ieren v.t. to stress.
Ak'zept n. (-s, -e) acceptance (of bill). ~'ant m. acceptor. ~'ieren v.t. to accept; to honour (bill).
Akzi'denz-arbeit f. job-work. ~ien n.pl. occasional emoluments.
Ala'baster m., ~n a. alabaster.
A'larm m. (-s, -e) alarm, warning, alert; blinder ~ false alarm; ~ schlagen to sound an alarm. ~bereit a. on the alert; in constant readiness. ~bereitschaft f. stand-by. ~glocke f. alarm bell. ~ieren v.t. to alarm.
A'laun m. alum. ~erde f. alumina.
Albe f. (·, -n) alb.
albern a. silly, foolish. v.i. to behave foolishly. ~heit f. silliness, foolishness.
Alchi'mie f. alchemy.
Alfanze'rei f. tomfoolery.
Alge f. (·, -n) alga, seaweed.
Algebra f. (·) algebra. ~isch a. algebraical.
Ali'mente n.pl. alimony.
alkalisch a. alkaline.
Alkohol m. (-s, -e) alcohol. ~frei a. non-alcoholic; (colloq.) soft. ~iker m. alcoholic. ~schmuggel m. bootlegging.
Al'koven m. (-s, -) alcove, recess.
All 1. n. (-s) universe. 2. a. all, entire, whole; every, each, any; ~ und jeder each and every; ~e Tage every day; ~e Welt everybody; auf ~e Fälle in any case, whatever happens; trotz ~em in spite of everything; vor ~em above all; zu ~em Unglück to crown it all; ohne ~en Grund for no reason at all; in ~er Eile in a great hurry; ~es in ~em (genommen) all things consi-

dered; *wer* ~*es?* who; *Mädchen für* ~*es* maid-of-all-work. **3.** *adv.* ~*e sein* (*colloq.*) to be gone or done; (*fig.*) to be all in.

all-'abendlich *a.* every evening. ~be'kannt *a.* notorious.

A'llee *f.* (-, -n) ⚏ avenue.

Alle-go'rie *f.* allegory. ~'orisch *a.* allegorical.

a'llein **1.** *pred. a.* alone; single; solitary, apart; *von* ~ without assistance; of one's own accord. **2.** *a.* only, merely. **3.** *conj.* only, but. ~betrieb, ~handel *m.* monopoly. ~herrschaft *f.* absolute power; sovereignty. ~hersteller *m.* sole manufacturer. ~ig *a.* sole, exclusive. ~mädchen *n.* maid-of-all-work. ~sein *n.* solitude, loneliness. ~seligmachend *a.* (*eccl.*) claiming the monopoly of all means of grace. ~stehend *a.* detached, isolated; single, unmarried. ~vertrieb *m.* monopoly.

alle-mal *adv.* always, every time; *ein für* ~*mal* once and for all. ~nfalls *adv.* if need be; perhaps. ~nthalben *adv.* everywhere.

aller-art *indecl. a.* diverse, sundry. ~best *a.* very best. ~dings *adv.* certainly, to be sure; of course. *conj.* though. ~enden *adv.* everywhere. ~erst *a.* very first, first and foremost. ~gnädigst *a.* most gracious. ~hand *indecl. a.* all sorts, all kinds of. ~heiligen *n.* All Saints' Day. ~heiligste *n.* (*eccl.*) Holy of Holies. ~höchst *a.* highest of all. ~lei *indecl. a.* diverse, all kinds of. ~subst. ~ medley. ~letzt *a.* very last, latest; *zu* ~*letzt* last of all. ~liebst *a.* most charming; *am* ~*liebsten* best of all. ~meist *a.* most. *adv.* most of all, chiefly. ~mindest *a.* least; least of all. ~nächst *a.* nearest of all. ~neu(e)st *a.* very latest. ~orten, ~orts *adv.* everywhere. ~seelen *pl.* All Souls' Day. ~seits *adv.* on all sides; to all (of you). ~wärts, ~wege *adv.* everywhere. ~weltskerl *m.* smart fellow. ~wenigst *a.* least of all.

Allerg-ie *f.* allergy. ~isch *a.* allergic.

alle-samt *adv.* all together, one and all. ~zeit *adv.* always, at all times.

allgegenwärtig *a.* omnipresent.

allgemach *adv.* gradually.

allgemein *a.* universal; general; *im* ~*en* in general. ~befinden *n.* general health. ~heit *f.* universality, generality; general public. ~verständlich *a.* popular.

All'heilmittel *n.* universal remedy.

Alli-'anz *f.* alliance. ~'ierte(r) *m.* ally.

all-jährlich *a.* yearly, annual; every year. ~macht *f.* omnipotence. ~mächtig *a.* omnipotent. ~mählich *a.* gradual. *adv.* gradually, by degrees. ~monatlich *a.* every month. ~morgendlich *a.* every morning. ~nächtlich *a.* every night.

Allo'path *m.* (-en, -en) allopathist.

A'llotria *n. pl.* tomfoolery.

all-seitig *a.* universal; all round; versatile. ~tag *m.* every day, week-day, working-day. ~täglich *a.* daily, every day; commonplace. ~überall *adv.* everywhere. ~umfassend *a.* all-embracing. ~vater *m.* Father of all. ~waltend *a.* supreme. ~wissend *a.* omniscient. ~wissenheit *f.* omniscience. ~wöchentlich *a.* weekly, every week. ~zu *adv.* too, much too. ~zubald *adv* much too soon. ~zumal *adv.* at once, altogether. ~zuviel *adv* too much, overmuch.

Alm *f.* (-, -en) Alpine pasture.

Almanach *m.* (-s, -e) almanac.

Almosen *n.* (-s, -) alms, charity. ~büchse *f.* poor-box. ~empfänger *m.* pauper.

Alp *m.*, ~drücken *n.* ~traum *m* nightmare. [ELF]

Alp-(e) *f.* Alpine pasture; *pl.* (-en Alps. ~englühen *n.* Alpine glow ~enveilchen *n.* cyclamen. ~enverein *m.* Alpine Club.

Alpha'bet *n.* (-[e]t) *n.* (-s, -e) alpha bet. ~isch *a.* alphabetical.

Älpler *m.* (-s, -) native of the Alps.

Al'raune *f.* (-, -n) mandrake.

als *conj.* as, like; when; (*in comparisons*) than; ~ *ob* as if, as though; *sobald* ~ as soon as; *sowohl* ~ *auch* as well as; *kein andrer* ~ none other than, nobody but; *nichts (weiter)* ~ nothing but; *er ist zu jung, als daß er verstehen könnte* he is too young to understand. ~**bald** *adv.* at once, forthwith; soon. ~**dann** *adv.* then, thereupon.

also (-z-) *adv.* thus, so, in this way. *conj.* therefore, consequently, hence, so.

alt[1] *a.* old, aged; ancient; antique; stale; worn; *alles beim* ~ *lassen* to leave things as they were; *mein* ~*er* (*Herr*) (*colloq.*) the governor, the old man; ~*e Geschichte* ancient history; ~*e Sprachen* ancient languages, classics; *die* ~*en* the ancients. ~**angesessen** *a.* long established. ~**backen** *a.* stale. ~**bewährt** *a.* of long standing. ~**ehrwürdig** *a.* venerable. ~**eisen** *n.* scrap-iron. ~**englisch** *a.* Old English. ~**enteil** *n.* part of estate set aside for parents' use. ~**fränkisch** *a.* old-fashioned, quaint, antiquated. ~**gläubig** *a.* orthodox. ~**hergebracht** *a.* customary, traditional. ~**hochdeutsch** *a.* Old High German. ~**jüngferlich** *a.* old-maidish. ~**klug** *a.* precocious. ~**material** *n.* salvage, scrap, junk. ~**meister** *m.* past-master, highest authority. ~**modisch** *a.* old-fashioned. ~**papier** *n.* waste paper. ~**philologie** *f.* the classics. ~**silber** *n.* oxidized silver. ~**väterisch** *a.* old-fashioned, antiquated. ~**vordern** *pl.* ancestors. ~**warenhändler** *m.* second-hand dealer. ~**weibersommer** *m.* Indian summer.

Alt[2] *m.* (*mus.*) alto. ~**ist** *m.*, ~**istin** *f.* alto singer.

Al'tan *m.* (-s, -e) gallery, balcony.

Al'tar *m.* (-s, Altäre) altar. ~**bild** *n.* altar-piece.

Alter *n.* (-s, -) age; old age; seniority; antiquity; *blühendes* ~ prime of life; *biblisches* ~ a great age; *mittleren* ~*s* of middle age; *von*

~*s her*, of old, of yore; *vor* ~*s* in ancient days. ~**serscheinung** *f.* symptom of old age. ~**sgenosse** *m.* person of the same age, coeval; contemporary. ~**sgrau** *a.* hoary, grey. ~**sgrenze** *f.* age limit. ~**sheim** *n.* home for the aged. ~**sklasse** *f.* age group. ~**srente** *f.* old-age pension. ~**sschwach** *a.* decrepit. ~**sschwäche** *f.* senility, decrepitude. ~**sstufe** *f.* stage of life. ~**sversorgung** *f.* old age pension. ~**tum** *n.* antiquity. ~**tümelei** *f.* antiquarianism. ~**tümlich** *a.* antique; archaic. ~**tumsforscher** *m.* antiquary, archaeologist. ~**tumsforschung** *f.* archaeology. ~**tumshändler** *m.* dealer in antiques. ~**tumskunde** *f.* archaeology.

ält-er *a.* older; elder, senior. ~**est** *a.* oldest; eldest, senior. ~**lich** *a.* oldish, elderly.

altern *vi.* & *vws.i.* to grow old, to age.

am = **an dem**; ~ *1. März* on March 1st; *Bonn* ~ *Rhein* Bonn on the Rhine; ~ *besten* best.

amalga'mieren *v.t.* & *i.* to amalgamate.

Amboß *m.* (-sses, -sse) anvil.

Ambu'lanz *f.* (-, -n) ambulance.

Ameise *f.* (-, -n) ant. ~**nhaufen** *m.* ant-heap. ~**nsäure** *f.* formic acid. [EMMET]

Amen *n.* & *int.* amen; *ja und* ~ *sagen* to agree.

Amme *f.* (-, -n) nurse, wet-nurse. ~**nmärchen** *n.* (*fig.*) cock-and-bull story.

Ammer *f.* (-, -n) yellow-hammer, bunting.

Ammoni'ak *n.* ammonia.

Amnes'tie *f.* (-, -n) amnesty. ~**ren** *v.t.* to pardon.

A'möbe *f.* (-, -n) amoeba.

Amok *m.* ~ *laufen* to run amuck.

amorph *a.* amorphous.

Amortis-ati'on *f.* amortization. ~**ieren** *v.t.* to pay off, redeem (loan).

Ampel *f.* (-, -n) hanging lamp.

Am'phibie *f.* (-, -n) amphibium.

Am'pulle *f.* (-, -n) ampulla; (*med.*) ampoule.

ampu'tieren *v.t.* to amputate.

Amsel *f.* (-, -n) blackbird. **~schlag** *m.* blackbird's song.

Amt *n.* (-es, ⁻er) office, charge, post, employment, appointment; duty; board; magistracy; (*tel.*) exchange; (*eccl.*) Mass; *stilles* ~ Low Mass; *Auswärtiges* ~ Foreign Office; ~ *antreten* to enter upon one's official duties; *seines* ~*es walten* to officiate, perform one's official duties; *kraft seines* ~*es* by virtue of one's office; *von* ~*s wegen* ex officio, officially; *in* ~ *und Würden stehen* to be in office, be a person of position.

amt-'ieren *v.i.* to officiate. **~lich** *a.* official. **~mann** *m.* bailiff.

Amts-alter *n.* seniority. **~antritt** *m.* entry on the duties of an office. **~befugnis** *f.* competence, authority. **~bereich** *m.* jurisdiction. **~blatt** *n.* official gazette. **~bruder** *m.* colleague. **~dauer** *f.* term, tenure of office. **~diener** *m.* usher, beadle. **~eid** *m.* oath of office. **~entsetzung** *f.* dismissal from office. **~führung** *f.* administration. **~geheimnis** *n.* official secret. **~gericht** *n.* county court; police court. **~inhaber** *m.* functionary. **~miene** *f.* (*fig.*) solemn air. **~richter** *m.* district judge. **~schimmel** *m.* red-tape. **~stunden** *f. pl.* office hours. **~tracht** *f.* robes of office. **~überschreitung** *f.* official excess. **~vertreter** *m.* deputy, locum tenens. **~weg** *m.* official channel. **~wohnung** *f.* official residence.

Amu'lett *n.* (-s, -e) amulet.

amü's-ant *a.* amusing. **~ieren** *v.t.* to amuse. *v.r.* to enjoy oneself, have a good time.

an 1. *prep.* on, by, in, at, near, close to; along; to; up to; about; about; ~ *der Donau* on the Danube; ~ *der Wand* on the wall; ~ *der Türe* at the door; ~ *einer Schule* in a school; ~ *der Arbeit sein* to be at work; ~ *die Arbeit gehen* to go to work; *es ist* ~ *mir* it is my turn; *jung* ~ *Jahren* young in years; ~ *die tausend Menschen* about a

thousand people; *bis* ~ *den Rand* up to the edge; ~ (*und für*) *sich* in itself, in themselves, per se. 2. *adv.* on, onward, up; *von nun* ~ from now on, henceforth. 3. *sep. pref.*

ana'log *a.* analogous. **~ie** *f.* analogy.

Analpha'bet *m.* (-en, -en) illiterate. **~entum** *n.* illiteracy.

Ana'ly-se (-y:za) *f.* (-se, -sen) analysis. **~'sieren** *v.t.* to analyse. **~tiker** *m.* analyst. **~tisch** *a.* analytical.

Anä'mi-e *f.* an(a)emia. **~sch** *a.* an(a)emic.

Ananas *f.* (-, -se) pineapple.

Anar'chie *f.* anarchy.

Ana'tom *m.* (-en, -en) anatomist. **~ie** *f.* anatomy; dissecting department. **~isch** *a.* anatomical.

anbahnen *v.t.* to pave the way for, open up, prepare.

anbändeln *v.i.* to make up (to); to flirt (with).

Anbau *m.* cultivation (of a field); addition (to a building), wing, annex. **~en** *v.t.* to cultivate, grow, till; to add to, build on. *v.r.* to settle. **~fläche** *f.* arable acreage.

Anbeginn *m.* beginning, commencement, outset.

anbehalten *v.t.* to keep on (coat, &c.).

an'bei *adv.* herewith, enclosed.

anbeißen *v.t. & i.* to bite, bite at; (*fig.*) to take the bait.

anbelangen *v.t.* to concern. See anlangen.

anbellen *v.t.* to bark at.

anbequemen *v.r.* to adapt oneself to.

anberaumen *v.t.* to fix (a time).

anbet-en *v.t.* to worship, adore. **~er** *m.*, **~erin** *f.* worshipper; admirer. **~ung** *f.* worship; adoration.

Anbetracht *in* ~ *der Lage* considering the situation.

anbetreffen *v.t.* to concern; *was mich anbetrifft* as for me, for my part.

anbetteln *v.t.* to solicit alms from.

anbiedern *v.r.* to make friends (with); (*colloq.*) to chum up.

anbieten v.t. to offer. v.r. to offer to, volunteer.

anbinden v.t. to tie to; (fig.) kurz angebunden sein to be short, to be curt.

Anblick m. sight, view, spectacle. **~en** v.t. to look at.

anblinzeln v.t. to blink at, wink at.

anbohren v.t. to bore, pierce; to tap (cask).

anbraten v.t. to roast gently.

anbrechen v.t. to start on. vws.i. to begin; (of day) to break, dawn.

anbrennen v.t. to light, light up, kindle. vws.i. to catch fire; (of soup, &c.) to burn.

anbringen v.t. to bring; to lodge (complaint); to fix, put up; to sell, dispose of (goods); gut angebracht appropriate, suitable, fitting; schlecht angebracht out of place, unsuitable.

Anbruch m. beginning, opening; bei **~** des Tages at daybreak; vor **~** der Nacht before nightfall.

anbrüllen v.t. to roar at, shout at.

Andacht f. (-, -en) devotion; (eccl.) prayers. **~svoll** a. devout.

andächtig (c-) a. devout, pious; (fig.) attentive.

andauern v.i. to continue, last. **~d** a. continuous, incessant; lasting.

Andenken n. (-s, -) memory, remembrance; souvenir; keepsake; zum **~** (an) in memory (of); as a souvenir.

ander a. & pron. other, another; different; second; next; etwas **~es** another thing, something different; nichts **~es** als nothing but; ein **~es** Mal, ein **~** Mal another time; ein ums **~e** Mal alternately; einen Tag um den **~n** every other day; **~er** Meinung sein to be of a different opinion, differ; unter **~em** among other things; am **~n** Morgen next morning. **~(e)nfalls** adv. (or) else, otherwise. **~(e)nteils** adv. on the one hand. **~(er)seits** adv. on the other hand or side. **~wärts** adv. elsewhere. **~weitig** a. other,

further; adv. elsewhere, at another time; in a different way.

ändern v.t. to alter, change. **~ung** f. alteration, change.

anders adv. otherwise, differently; niemand **~** nobody but; wer **~** who else; **~** sein als to be different from; **~** werden to change; ich kann nicht **~** als lachen I cannot help laughing. **~denkend** a. of a different opinion, dissenting. **~gesinnt** a. differently minded. **~gläubig** a. heterodox. **~wo** adv. elsewhere. **~woher** adv. from elsewhere. **~wohin** adv. to some other place.

anderthalb indecl. a. one and a half.

andeut-en v.t. to indicate; intimate, hint. **~ung** f. indication, intimation, hint.

andichten v.t. to write poems (to); (fig.) to impute to.

Andrang m. run, rush; (med.) congestion.

andrängen, andringen vws.i. to press on, push on.

andrehen v.t. to turn on; (motor.) to start up; (fig.) to palm off (goods) upon.

androh-en v.t. to threaten, menace with. **~ung** f. threat, menace.

Andruck m. (typ.) proof.

anecken v.i. (colloq.) to give offence.

an|eifern v.t. to stimulate, rouse.

an|eign-en v.r. to acquire, appropriate, adopt, take possession of. **~ung** f. acquisition, appropriation.

anei'nander adv. together; to or against one another; **~geraten** vws.i. to fly at each other; to come to grips.

Anek'dote f. (-, -n) anecdote.

an|ekeln v.t. to disgust.

An|erbe m. heir (to a farm).

An|erbieten n. (-s, -) offer, proposal.

an|erkanntermaßen adv. admittedly.

an|erkenn-en v.t. to recognize, acknowledge, admit; to appreciate; to honour (bill). **~end** a. appreciative. **~enswert** a. praiseworthy. **~ung** f. recognition, acknowledgement; appreciation.

anfachen *v.t.* to blow, fan; to stimulate.

anfahren *v.t.* to convey, carry (goods); to collide with, run into; (*naut.*) to call at (port); (*fig.*) to fly at, give a blowing-up. *vws.i.* to drive up.

Anfahrt *f.* arrival; (carriage-) drive; (*naut.*) landing-place; (*mining*) descent.

Anfall *m.* attack, assault; (*med.*) attack, fit; (*leg.*) succession to, reversion of. **~en** *v.t.* to attack, assail, assault; (*leg.*) to fall to.

anfällig *a.* susceptible (to).

Anfang *m.* (-s, Anfänge) beginning, commencement, start; origin. **~s** *adv.* in or at the beginning. **~sbuchstabe** *m.* initial letter. **~sgeschwindigkeit** *f.* initial velocity. **~sgründe** *m.pl.* fundamental principles, elements, rudiments.

anfangen *v.t. & i.* to begin, set about; (*colloq.*) to do.

Anfäng-er *m.* (-ers, -er) beginner. **~lich** *a.* initial, incipient. *adv.* in the beginning, at first.

anfassen *v.t.* to handle, touch; take hold of, seize; (*fig.*) to set to work; *mit~* to lend a hand. *v.r.* to feel.

anfauchen *v.t.* to spit at.

anfecht-bar *a.* contestable. **~en** *v.t.* to dispute, contest; (*leg.*) to challenge; to attack; to trouble; (*relig.*) to tempt. **~ung** *f.* attack; impeachment; temptation.

anfeind-en *v.t.* to bear ill will; to attack, oppose. **~ung** *f.* hostility, persecution.

anfertig-en *v.t.* to make, manufacture. **~ung** *f.* making, manufacture, production.

anfeuchten *v.t.* to moisten, damp, wet.

anfeuern *v.t.* to fire, inflame, stimulate.

anflehen *v.t.* to implore.

anfliegen *v.i.* (*av.*) to touch, call, land at.

Anflug *m.* (*av.*) approach flight; (*fig.*) touch, trace, tinge.

anforder-n *v.t.* to exact, demand. **~ung** *f.* demand, claim; hohe **~ungen stellen an** to make great

demands (on); to expect great things from.

Anfrage *f.* inquiry; *auf ~ on* application. **~n** *v.i.* to ask, inquire.

anfreunden *v.r.* to become friends; to make friends (with).

anfrieren *vws.i.* to freeze on (to).

anfügen *v.t.* to join, attach, affix (to).

anfühlen *v.t. & r.* to feel.

Anfuhr *f.* carriage (of goods); supply.

anführ-en *v.t.* to lead, conduct; to quote, cite; to allege; to dupe, cheat, trick. **~er** *m.* leader, commander, chief; ring-leader. **~ung** *f.* leadership, lead; quotation. **~ungsstrich** *m.*, **~ungszeichen** *n. pl.* quotation marks, inverted commas.

anfüllen *v.t.* to fill, fill up.

Angabe *f.* declaration, assertion, statement; data; instruction; *nähere ~n* particulars.

angaffen *v.t.* to gape at, stare at.

angängig *adv.* possible; admissible.

angeb-en *v.t.* to state, declare; to give (one's name); to indicate, explain; to pretend; to denounce; *Ton ~en* to set the fashion, take the lead. *v.i.* to deal first (at cards); (*colloq.*) to swagger. **~er** *m.* informer. **~erei** *f.* denunciation. **~lich** *a.* alleged; pretended, ostensible.

Angebinde *n.* (-s, -) present, gift.

angeboren *a.* inborn, innate; hereditary, congenital.

Angebot *n.* (-s, -e) offer; bid; tender; *~ und Nachfrage* supply and demand.

angedeihen *v.i. ~ lassen* to grant, bestow upon.

Angedenken *n.* remembrance, recollection.

angedonnert *a.* thunderstruck.

angegossen *a.* (*fig.*) *wie ~ sitzen* to be a perfect fit, to fit like a glove.

angegriffen *a.* (*fig.*) tired, exhausted.

angeheiratet *a.* by marriage.

angeheitert *a.* slightly tipsy, merry.

angehen *v.t.* to apply to, ask for; (*vws.*) to concern. *vws.i.* to begin; to catch fire; to be passable, to be tolerable; ~ *gegen* to repress; to fight against; *das geht dich nichts an* that's none of your business; *was mich angeht* as for me; *angegangenes Fleisch* slightly tainted meat. **~d** a. beginning, incipient; future.

angehör-en v.i. to belong to. **~ig** a. belonging to. **~ige(r)** m. relation, relative; (*pl.*) family, people; next of kin.

Angeklagte(r) m. (-n, -n) accused, defendant.

Angel[1] (-n-) f. (-, -n) hinge; *aus den ~n heben* to revolutionize; *zwischen Tür und ~* at the last moment, just before leaving. **~punkt** m. cardinal point. **~weit** a. wide (open).

Angel[2] f. fishing-hook. **~gerät** n. fishing-tackle. **~schnur** f. fishing-line. [ANGLE]

angelegen a. *sich etwas ~ sein lassen* to make it one's business. **~heit** f. affair, concern, business. **~tlich** a. pressing, urgent, earnest.

angeln (-n-) v.t. & i. to angle, fish.

angeloben v.t. to vow.

angemessen a. suitable, adequate.

angenehm a. agreeable, pleasant.

angenommen pp. ~ *daß* supposing that.

Anger (-n-) m. (-s, -) green, common.

angesäuselt a. slightly tipsy.

angesehen a. distinguished, respected, esteemed.

angesessen a. resident, settled.

Angesicht n. face, countenance; *von ~ zu ~* face to face. **~s** prep. in view of, considering.

angespannt a. (*fig.*) tense; adv. with intensity.

angestammt a. hereditary.

Angestellte(r) m. (-n, -n) employee.

angetan a. clad (in); *danach ~ sein* to be likely to; to be suitable for; ~ *sein von* to be captivated by.

angetrunken a. tipsy.

angewandt a. applied.

angewöhnen v.t. to accustom (to). v.r. to contract (habit).

Angewohnheit f. habit; custom.

angewurzelt a. (*fig.*) rooted to the spot.

angleichen v.t. to assimilate; to approximate.

Angler (-n-) m. (-s, -) angler.

anglieder-n v.t. to attach; to annex. **~ung** f. annexation; affiliation.

Ang'list (-n-) m. (-en, -en) student of English language and literature. **~ik** f. study of English philology.

anglotzen v.t. to stare at, gape at.

angreifbar a. vulnerable.

angreif-en v.t. to handle, seize hold of; to undertake; to encroach upon (one's capital); to break into (supplies); to attack; to affect; to exhaust. **~end** a. aggressive; trying, exhausting. **~er** m. aggressor, assailant.

angrenzen v.i. to border on, adjoin. **~d** a. adjoining, adjacent.

Angriff m. (-s, -e) attack; *in ~ nehmen* to set about. **~sfläche** f. (*fig.*) spot open to attack. **~skrieg** m. offensive war. **~slustig** a. aggressive. **~sziel** n. objective, goal.

angrinsen v.t. to grin at.

Angst (-n-) f. (-, -e) anxiety, anguish, fear; *ich habe ~, mir ist* ~ I am afraid; *es mit der ~ bekommen* to get frightened; *einem ~ machen* to alarm someone. **~beklommen** a. oppressed with fear. **~meier** m. coward. **~schweiß** m. cold sweat. **~voll** a. full of fear.

ängst-igen (-n-) v.t. to frighten. v.r. to be frightened; *sich ~igen vor* to be afraid of; *sich ~igen um* to feel anxious about, worry about. **~lich** a. anxious; nervous, timid; scrupulous. **~lichkeit** f. timidity, uneasiness; scrupulousness.

anhaben v.t. to wear, have on; (*einem*) *nichts ~ können* not to be able to find any fault or weak spot (in).

anhaften v.i. to adhere to, stick to.

anhaken v.t. to hook on to; tick off (items).

Anhalt m. support; fact, evidence;

~ *gewähren* to afford a clue. **~spunkt** *m.* essential fact, clue; instruction.

anhalten *v.t.* to stop, pull up; to spur on (to). *v.i.* to stop, halt; to continue, go on; to last; ~ *um* to propose to. *v.r.* to hold on. **~d** *a.* continuous, incessant; lasting; persistent.

Anhang *m.* appendage; appendix, supplement; adherents, followers, hangers-on. **~en** *v.t.* to adhere to, stick to.

anhäng-en *v.t.* to hang on; to append, add; (*tel.*) to hang up, ring off; to palm off (goods) upon; (*fig.*) *einem etwas* ~ to make insinuations against. *v.i.* to cling to, adhere to. **~er** *m.* **1.** adherent, supporter. **2.** trailer. **3.** locket. **~erschaft** *f.* partisanship. **~eschloß** *n.* padlock. **~ig** *a. Prozeß ~ig machen* to take legal proceedings. **~lich** *a.* attached; faithful. **~lichkeit** *f.* attachment. **~sel** *n.* appendage.

Anhauch *m.* breath; trace, tinge. **~en** *v.t.* to breathe upon; (*colloq.*) to blow up.

anhäuf-en *v.t. & r.* to heap up, accumulate. **~ung** *f.* accumulation; agglomeration.

anheben *v.t.* to lift, raise. *v.i.* to begin.

anheften *v.t.* to attach (to), fasten (to).

anheilen *vws.i.* to heal up.

anheimeln *v.t.* to make one feel at home. **~d** *a.* cosy, snug.

an'heim-fallen *vws.i.* (*of property*) to fall to; to devolve upon. **~geben, ~stellen** *v.t.* to leave to, submit to.

anheischig *v.r. sich* ~ *machen* to pledge oneself.

anheizen *v.t.* to kindle a fire.

anheuern *v.t.* to hire; *sich* ~ *lassen* to sign on.

Anhieb *m. auf* ~ at the first go, right away.

anhimmeln *v.t.* (*colloq.*) to gush.

Anhöhe *f.* hill, elevation, rising ground.

anhören *v.t.* to listen to. *v.r.* (*impers.*) to sound.

ani'malisch *a.* animal; natural.

ani'mier-en *v.t.* to animate; to encourage, urge on. **~kneipe** *f.* low saloon-bar.

ankämpfen *v.t.* to fight (against).

Ankauf *m.* purchase. **~en** *v.t.* to buy. *v.r.* to buy property, settle (at a place).

Anker (-ŋ-) *m.* (-s, -) anchor; (*electr.*) armature; ~ *werfen, vor* ~ *gehen* to anchor; *vor* ~ *liegen* to ride at anchor. **~boje** *f.* anchor-buoy. **~fest** *a.* well-moored. **~grund** *m.* anchorage. **~mast** *m.* mooring mast. **~winde** *f.* windlass, capstan.

ankern *v.t. & i.* to anchor, to moor.

anketten *v.t.* to chain (to).

ankläffen *v.t.* to bark at.

Anklage *f.* accusation, charge. **~bank** *f.* dock. **~rede** *f.* speech for the prosecution. **~schrift** *f.* indictment. **~vertretung** *f.* prosecution.

anklagen *v.t.* to accuse, impeach, charge.

Ankläger *m.* (-s, -) accuser; plaintiff, pursuer.

anklammern *v.t.* to clip on. *v.r.* to cling to.

Anklang *m.* reminiscence; ~ *finden* to meet with approval, become popular.

ankleben *v.t.* to stick (on). *vws.i.* to stick (to).

ankleiden *v.t. & r.* to dress.

anklingeln *v.t. & i.* (*tel.*) to ring up.

anklingen *v.i.* (*fig.*) to remind (of).

anklopfen *v.i.* to knock (at).

anknipsen *v.t.* to switch on (light).

anknüpf-en *v.t.* to fasten (to), tie (to); (*fig.*) to begin; to establish (relations). *v.i.* to resume, refer (to); take up. **~ungspunkt** *m.* point of contact; starting-point.

ankommen *vws.i.* to arrive; to approach; to reach; (*colloq.*) to get a job; *gut* (*schlecht*) ~ to be well (ill) received; *schön* (*iron.*) to get left; *darauf* ~ to depend on; *es kommt darauf an, ob* it all depends on whether; *darauf kommt es an* that's the main thing; *es kommt nicht darauf an* it doesn't matter; *es darauf* ~ *lassen* to chance it.

v.t. to befall; *es kam ihn die Lust an* he was overcome with a desire (to); *es kommt mich schwer an* I find it hard.

Ankömmling *m.* (-s, -e) newcomer, arrival.

ankreiden *v.t.* to chalk up.

ankünden, ankündig-en *v.t.* to announce; to publish, notify; to advertise. **~ung** *f.* announcement; notification; advertisement.

Ankunft *f.* (-) arrival. **~sbahnsteig** *m.* arrival platform.

ankurbeln *v.t.* (*motor.*) to start, crank up; (*fig.*) to stimulate; to step up; (*colloq.*) to ginger up.

anlächeln *v.t.* to smile at.

anlachen *v.t.* to smile at; to laugh in one's face.

Anlage *f.* plan, draft, sketch, structure; (*typ.*) layout; park, grounds; works, plant, installation; investment (of capital); enclosure (in letter); (*fig.*) talent, ability; tendency, predisposition. **~kapital** *n.* stock (capital); funds.

anlangen *vws.i.* to arrive, reach. *v.t.* to concern; *was das anlangt* as regards this matter, as for this.

Anlaß *m.* (Anlasses, Anlässe) occasion, cause; *ohne allen ~* for no reason at all.

anlassen *v.t.* to keep on; to leave on; (*motor.*) to start, turn on; to temper (metal); *sich gut ~* to promise well.

Anlasser *m.* self-starter.

anläßlich *prep.* on the occasion of.

anlasten *v.t.* to charge (with).

Anlauf *m.* start, run; onset, attack; (*av.*) take-off run; *einen ~ nehmen* to take a starting-run, (*fig.*) to make an effort. **~en** *vws.i.* to begin to run; to run (against); (*motor.*) to start; to swell; (*med.*) to mount up; (*of glass, &c.*) to dull, tarnish; *rot ~en* to blush. *v.t.* to touch at, call at (a port).

Anlaut *m.* initial sound.

anläuten *v.t. & i.* to ring up.

anleg-en *v.t.* to put against; to

apply to; to put on (dress); to set up; to found; to lay out (garden); to set (fire to); (*mil.*) to take aim (at); to invest (money). *v.i.* (*naut.*) to land, touch (at); *es ~en auf (fig.)* to aim at. **~estelle** *f.* landing-place. **~ung** *f.* application; laying out, planning; construction.

anlehn-en *v.t.* to lean (against); to leave (door) ajar. *v.r.* (*fig.*) to rely on; to follow (the example of); to be modelled (after). **~ung** *f.* support; *in ~ung an* in imitation of.

Anleihe *f.* (-, -n) loan.

anleimen *v.t.* to glue on.

anleit-en *v.t.* to guide (to), instruct (in). **~ung** *f.* guidance, instruction.

anlernen *v.t.* to teach, train.

anliegen *v.i.* to lie near, be adjacent (to), border on; (*of dress*) to fit well; *einem ~* to entreat someone. *subst. n.* request; concern, matter; aim.

Anliegerverkehr *m.* road reserved for residents (only).

anlocken *v.t.* to allure, entice.

anlügen *v.t.* to lie to.

anmachen *v.t.* to attach, fix; to mix, to dress (salad); to light (fire).

anmalen *v.t.* to paint.

Anmarsch *m.* approach, advance. **~'ieren** *vws.i.* to march on, advance.

anmaß-en *v.r.* to presume; to pretend to, assume. **~end** *a.* arrogant. **~ung** *f.* arrogance.

anmeld-en *v.t.* to announce; to notify, report, register; to give notice of arrival. **~epflichtig** *a.* notifiable. **~eschein** *m.* registration form. **~ung** *f.* announcement; notification, report.

anmerk-en *v.t.* to remark, note; to notice. **~ung** *f.* remark; note, comment, annotation.

anmessen *v.t.* to measure for (suit).

anmustern *v.t.* (*naut.*) to sign on.

Anmut *f.* (-) grace; charm, sweetness. **~ig** *a.* graceful; charming.

anmuten *v. impers.* to seem to (one).

annageln *v.t.* to nail on (to).

annähen v.t. to sew on.

annäher-n v.t. to approximate (to). v.r. to approach. ~nd a. approximate. ~ung f. approach, advance; rapprochement.

Annahme f. (-, -n) acceptance; (fig.) assumption, hypothesis. ~verweigerung f. non-acceptance (of letter, &c.).

A'nnalen f. pl. annals, records.

annehm-bar a. acceptable. ~en v.t. to take, accept, receive; to assume, suppose; to adopt (child); to contract (habit). v.r. to take care of, take an interest in. ~lichkeit f. amenity; comforts.

annek'tieren v.t. to annex.

Annexi'on f. annexation.

A'nnonc-e (anõ:sə) f. (-, -n) advertisement. -'ieren v.t. & i. to advertise.

annullieren v.t. to annul, cancel.

an|öden v.t. (colloq.) to bore.

ano'nym (-ny:m) a. anonymous. -i'tät f. anonymity.

an|ordn-en v.t. to order; to arrange, dispose. ~ung f. order, regulation; arrangement, disposition.

anpacken v.t. to seize, grasp.

anpass-en v.t. to fit, suit, adapt. v.r. to adapt oneself (to). ~ung f. adaptation. ~ungsfähig a. adaptable. ~ungsvermögen n. adaptability.

anpflanz-en v.t. to plant, cultivate. ~ung f. cultivation; plantation.

anpflöcken v.t. to tether (to).

anpöbeln v.t. to abuse, vilify.

anpochen v.i. to knock (at a door).

Anprall m. (-es) collision, impact; shock; brunt. ~en vws.i. to strike, bound (against).

anprangern v.t. to denounce, pillory.

anpreisen v.t. to extol, praise, commend; to cry (wares).

Anprob-e f. fitting-on. ~en, ~ieren v.t. to try on (dress).

anpumpen v.t. (colloq.) to touch (for), borrow money.

anraten v.t. to advise, recommend. subst. n. auf sein ~ on his advice.

anrauchen v.t. to start to smoke (cigar), to season (pipe).

anrechn-en v.t. to charge; to ascribe to; zu viel ~ to overcharge; hoch ~ to value greatly. ~ung f. in ~ung bringen to charge (to account).

Anrecht n. claim, title; ~ haben auf to be entitled to.

Anrede f. address. ~n v.t. to address; speak to; to accost.

anreg-en v.t. & i. to incite, stimulate, excite; to suggest. ~end a. stimulating; interesting. ~ung f. stimulation, stimulus; diversion; suggestion.

anreichern v.t. to enrich; (commerc.) to accumulate.

anreihen v.t. to string (beads); to add. v.r. to rank (with); to queue up.

anreiß-en v.t. to tear off; to break in upon. ~er m. (sl.) tout.

Anreiz m. incitement, stimulus. ~en v.t. to incite; to induce.

anrempeln v.t. to jostle against.

anrennen v.t. to run against.

Anrichte f. dresser, sideboard. ~n v.t. to cause, do; to serve up (meal); es ist angerichtet dinner is ready.

anrüchig a. disreputable.

anrücken vws.i. to approach, draw near.

Anruf m. call; appeal. ~en v.t. to call to, hail; to ring up; to appeal to; to invoke. ~ung f. invocation.

anrühren v.t. to touch; (cook.) to stir, mix together.

ans = an das.

Ansage f. (-, -n) announcement; notification. ~n v.t. & r. to announce; to notify; to intimate; to call (a card). ~r m. announcer; compère.

ansamen v.r. to grow from wind-borne seeds.

ansamm-eln v.t. to collect, accumulate, gather; to amass; to assemble. ~lung f. collection, accumulation; concentration; heap; crowd.

ansässig a. domiciled, settled; resident.

Ansatz m. start; beginning; mouthpiece (of mus. instr.); in ~ bringen to take into account. **~punkt** m. starting-point.

anschaff-en v.t. to procure, provide, buy. **~ung** f. purchase; (pl.) provisions, supplies. **~ungskosten** pl. prime cost.

anschalten v.t. to switch on.

anschau-en v.t. to look at; to contemplate. **~lich** a. evident, clear; vivid, graphic. **~lichkeit** f. clearness, vividness. **~ung** f. contemplation; perception, intuition; view, idea. **~ungsmaterial** n. illustrations. **~unterricht** m. visual education.

Anschein m. appearance, look; allem ~ nach to all appearances; den ~ erwecken, sich den ~ geben to pretend, to look (as if). **~end** a. apparent, seeming, to all appearance.

anschicken v.r. to prepare, set about.

anschießen v.t. to shoot first; to test (gun); to wound.

anschirren v.t. to harness.

Anschlag m. stroke, striking; (mus.) touch; poster, bill, placard, notice; plot, design; attempt (on one's life); (commerc.) estimate; in ~ bringen to take into account, allow for; (mil.) im ~ halten to point (a gun) at. **~brett** n. notice-board. **~säule** f. advertisement-pillar.

anschlagen v.t. to strike (against); to ring (bell); (mus.) to touch; to affix; to stick up, post up; (commerc. & fig.) to estimate, value; (mil.) to take aim (at). v.i. to strike; (of birds) to sing; (of dogs) to bark, give tongue; (of waves) to break; (of food) to agree with; (of medicine) to take effect.

anschließen v.t. to chain up; to fasten; to add, annex; (electr.) to connect. v.r. to join; to close the ranks; to follow; (of dress) to fit close. **~d** a. following. adv. after (that); afterwards.

Anschluß m. annexation; joining; (rail.) connexion; supply (of gas, water); communication; ~ erhalten (tel.) to get through; ~ suchen to seek company; im ~

an referring to. **~dose** f. (electr.) junction-box.

anschmieden v.t. to forge on (to); to put in irons.

anschmieg-en v.r. to nestle (against), snuggle up (to); to fit; to fit in (with). **~sam** a. pliant, supple; (fig.) compliant.

anschmieren v.t. to smear, daub; (collog.) to cheat.

anschnallen v.t. to buckle on.

anschnauz-en v.t. (collog.) to bully, snarl at. **~er** m. blowing-up.

anschneiden v.t. to cut; to broach (subject).

Anschnitt m. first cut, first slice.

anschrauben v.t. to screw on.

anschreib-en v.t. to write down; to charge, enter (debt); to score; bei einem gut (schlecht) angeschrieben sein to be in someone's good (bad) books.

anschreien v.t. to shout at.

Anschrift f. address.

anschuldig-en v.t. to charge (with), accuse (of). **~ung** f. accusation.

anschwärmen v.t. to adore.

anschwärzen v.t. to blacken; (fig.) to slander.

anschwell-en vws.i. to swell (to); to rise, increase. **~ung** f. swelling.

anschwemm-en v.t. to wash up, wash ashore. **~ung** f. wash of sea against shore; alluvium.

anschwindeln v.t. to swindle; to lie to.

ansegeln v.t. to make for (a port); (of ship) to fall foul of.

ansehen v.t. to look at; to consider, regard; take (for); to examine; to see, perceive; einem etwas ~ to tell by a person's face. subst. n. appearance, esteem, respect, authority; dem ~ nach to all appearance; in ~ stehen to be esteemed; ohne ~ der Person without respect of persons; von ~ kennen to know by sight; sich ein ~ geben to give oneself airs.

ansehnlich a. imposing; considerable.

anseilen v.t. (mount.) to rope.

ansetzen v.t. to put (to); to affix; to apply; to add (to); to take up (the bow); to fix (price), charge, estimate; to put forth (leaves); to put on (flesh) (chem.) to prepare, mix. *v.i.* to take a short run (before jumping); to try. *v.r.* to be deposited.

Ansicht *f.* (-, -en) view, sight; inspection; (*fig.*) opinion; *nach meiner* ~ in my opinion; *zur* ~ on approval. **~ig** *a.* ~*ig werden* to catch sight of. **~skarte** *f.* picture postcard. **~ssache** *f.* matter of opinion.

ansied-eln *v.t.* to settle, colonize. **~ler** *m.* settler, colonist. **~lung** *f.* colonization; settlement, colony.

Ansinnen *n.* demand.

anspann-en *v.t.* to stretch, bend; to harness (to); (*fig.*) to strain, exert. **~ung** *f.* tension, strain.

anspeien *v.t.* to spit at, spit upon.

anspiel-en *v.i.* to begin to play; ~*en auf* to hint at, allude to. **~ung** *f.* allusion, hint, insinuation.

anspinnen *v.t.* to plot. *v.r.* to begin; to develop.

anspitzen *v.t.* to sharpen (pencil).

Ansporn *m.* spur, stimulus. **~en** *v.t.* to spur on, stimulate.

Ansprache *f.* speech, address.

ansprechen *v.t.* to speak to; to accost; (*fig.*) to please, appeal to. **~d** *a.* attractive.

ansprengen *vws.i.* to gallop up.

anspringen *v.t.* to jump up at; *angesprungen kommen* to come skipping along. *vws.i.*(*motor.*) to start.

anspritzen *v.t.* to splash, spray.

Anspruch *m.* claim, pretension, title, demand; ~ *haben auf* to be entitled to; ~ *machen auf* to lay claim to; *in* ~ *nehmen* to take up (time); to engross, absorb (attention). **~slos** *a.* unassuming, modest, unpretentious. **~slosigkeit** *f.* modesty, unpretentiousness. **~svoll** *a.* pretentious, fastidious; exacting.

anspucken *v.t.* to spit at.

anspülen *v.t.* to wash ashore; to deposit.

anstacheln *v.t.* to goad on; to spur on, stimulate, incite.

Anstalt *f.* (-, -en) arrangement, preparation; establishment, institution; (*med.*) asylum; ~*en treffen* to prepare, set about, make arrangements.

Anstand *m.* 1. propriety, decorum, seemliness, etiquette, manners, decency; *ohne* ~ without hesitation; ~ *nehmen* to hesitate, doubt. 2. (*hunt.*) stand. **~sbesuch** *m.* formal call. **~sgefühl** *n.* tact. **~shalber** *adv.* for propriety's sake. **~slos** *adv.* without hesitation, readily. **~swidrig** *a.* improper, indecent.

anständig *a.* becoming, decorous, proper; decent, respectable. **~keit** *f.* propriety; decency, respectability.

anstarren *v.t.* to stare at.

an'statt *prep. & conj.* instead of.

anstaunen *v.t.* to gaze at.

anstechen *v.t.* to prick; to broach (cask).

ansteck-en *v.t.* to fasten, pin on; to put on (ring); to light (cigar), to set fire to; (*med.*) to infect, contaminate. *v.i.* to be infectious. *v.r.* to catch (infection), become infected. **~end** *a.* infectious, contagious, catching. **~ung** *f.* infection, contagion.

anstehen *v.i.* to fit, suit; ~ *nach* to queue up for; ~ *lassen* to defer (payment); ~ *zu tun* to hesitate to do.

ansteigen *vws.i.* to ascend, mount; to rise; to increase.

anstell-en *v.t.* to appoint, employ, engage, take on; to turn on (radio, &c.); to start (engine), to make, cause. *v.r.* to queue up; (*fig.*) to behave; to feign, pretend; to make a fuss. **~ig** *a.* skilful, handy; able. **~ung** *f.* appointment, post, employment.

Anstich *m.* broaching (of a cask).

Anstieg *m.* (-s) ascent.

anstieren *v.t.* to stare at.

anstift-en *v.t.* to cause; to plot; to incite (to). **~er** *m.* instigator, author. **~ung** *f.* instigation.

anstimmen *v.t.* to sing, strike up.

Anstoß *m.* (*fig.*) impulse, initiative; (*footb.*) kick-off; *ohne* ~ fluently, without hesitation; *Stein des* ~*es* stumbling-block;

~ erregen to give offence; **~ nehmen** to take offence. **~en** v.t. to push, strike, knock against. v.i. to bump against; to stammer; to clink glasses; to adjoin, border (on); **~en bei** to hurt (someone), give offence to; *mit der Zunge* **~** to lisp; *angestoßenes Obst* bruised fruit.

anstößig a. offensive, obnoxious, improper.

anstrahlen v.t. to shine on, cast rays on; to flood-light; (*fig.*) to beam upon.

anstreben v.t. to strive for, aspire to.

anstreich-en v.t. to paint; to mark, tick off; *weiß* **~en** to whitewash. **~er** m. housepainter.

anstreng-en v.t. to strain, exert; *Prozeß* **~en** to bring an action (against). v.r. to make an effort. **~end** a. tiring, trying, exacting. **~ung** f. exertion, effort; strain.

Anstrich m. paint, painting; coat; colour; (*fig.*) tinge; appearance, air.

anstricken v.t. to knit on (to); to foot (stockings).

anstücke(l)n v.t. to piece, patch.

Ansturm m. assault; run, rush.

anstürmen vws.i. to assault, storm, charge.

ansuchen v.t. **~ um** to ask for, petition for. *subst. n.* request.

Ant'arktis f. the Antarctic.

antasten v.t. to touch; (*fig.*) to violate, infringe.

Anteil m. share, part, portion; (*fig.*) interest; **~ nehmen** to take an interest (in); to sympathize (with). **~nahme** f. sympathy. **~schein** m. share certificate.

antelephonieren v.t. & i. to ring up.

An'tenne f. (-, -n) antenna; aerial.

Anthrazit m. anthracite.

Antialkoholiker m. teetotaller.

an'tik (-ik) a. antique. **~e** f. antique; antiquity.

Antilope f. antelope.

Antipa'thie f. (-, n) antipathy.

antippen v.t. to touch lightly, tap.

An'tiqua (-ti:kva:) f. (-) Roman type.

Anti'quar (-kva:r) m. (-s, -e) ⚹

second-hand bookseller; dealer in antiques. **~i'at** n. second-hand bookshop. **~isch** a. secondhand.

Antiquitätenhändler m. antique dealer.

Antise'mit m. (-en, -en) anti-Semite. **~isch** a. anti-Semitic. **~ismus** m. anti-Semitism.

Anti'these f. (-, -n) antithesis.

Antlitz n. (-es, -e) face, countenance.

Antrag m. (-s, Anträge) proposition, proposal; application, request, appeal; (*leg.*) **~ machen** to propose; (*parl.*) motion; **~ stellen** to move. **~en** v.t. to offer, propose. **~steller** m. proposer; mover; applicant; petitioner.

antrauen v.t. to marry to.

antreffen v.t. to meet; to find.

antreiben v.t. to drive, push on, propel. vws.i. to drift ashore.

antreten v.t. to start; to set out on (a journey); to take up (office); to take possession of (inheritance). vws.i. to take one's place; (*mil.*) to fall in.

Antrieb m. impulse, motive, incentive; (*electr.*) drive, power.

Antritt m. entrance (upon); beginning. **~sbesuch** m. first visit. **~srede** f. inaugural address.

antun v.t. to put on (dress); to do, inflict; to injure, insult; *sich etwas* **~** to commit suicide; *es einem* **~** to bewitch someone.

Antwort f. (-, en) answer, reply. **~en** v.t. & i. to answer. **~schein** m. (International) reply coupon.

anvertrauen v.t. to entrust; to confide. v.r. to confide in, unbosom oneself to.

anver.vandt a. related.

anwachsen vws.i. to grow on (to); to take root; (*of river*) to swell, rise; (*fig.*) to increase.

Anwalt (-v-) m. (-s, Anwälte) lawyer, counsel, solicitor, attorney, advocate; (*fig.*) defender, champion.

anwand-eln v.t. *Lust wandelte mich an* I was seized with a desire (to). **~lung** f. attack, fit; impulse.

anwärmen v.t. to warm slightly.

Anwärter *m.* (*leg.*) reversioner; candidate.

Anwartschaft *f.* reversion.

anwehen *v.t.* to blow upon.

anweis-en *v.t.* to direct, instruct, show, guide; to assign (money); *angewiesen sein auf* to depend on. **~ung** *f.* instruction, direction, order; cheque, draft, (money-) order.

anwend-bar *a.* applicable; practicable. **~en** *v.t.* to employ, use, apply. **~ung** *f.* use, application; practice.

anwerben *v.t.* to levy, raise.

anwerfen *v.t.* to start (motor).

Anwesen *n.* (-s, -) estate, property.

anwesen-d *a.* present. **~heit** *f.* presence.

anwidern *v.t.* to disgust.

Anwohner *m.* (-s, -) neighbour.

Anwuchs *m.* growth, increase.

Anwurf *m.* roughcast; (*fig.*) reproach, abuse, slander.

anwurzeln *vws.i.* to take root.

Anzahl *f.* number; quantity. **~en** *v.t.* to pay on account. **~ung** *f.* payment on account.

anzapfen *v.t.* to tap.

Anzeichen *n.* sign, indication, symptom; omen.

Anzeige *f.* (-, -n) notice, intimation; advertisement; announcement; (*leg.*) denunciation. **~n** *v.t.* to intimate, notify, report; to announce; to advertise; to lodge a complaint, inform (against); *ohne angezeigt halten* to consider it advisable. **~nannahme** *f.* advertising agency.

anzetteln *v.t.* to plot, scheme.

anzieh-en *v.t.* to draw, pull; to tighten, stretch; to draw in (reins); to drive home (screw); to put on (dress), to dress; (*fig.*) to interest, attract. *v.i.* to draw; to draw near; to absorb; (*of prices*) to rise; to move first (in chess). **~end** *a.* attractive. **~ung** *f.* attraction **~ungskraft** *f.* (power of) attraction; gravitation. F; gravitation.

Anzug *m.* (-s, Anzüge) suit; dress; opening move (in chess); *im ~ sein* to approach; to be imminent.

anzüglich *a.* suggestive; personal. **~keit** *f.* suggestive remark; personalities.

anzünd-en *v.t.* to light, set fire to. **~er** *m.* lighter.

anzweifeln *v.t.* to doubt.

a'part *a.* ♣ uncommon, interesting. [F]

Apa'thie *f.* apathy. **a'pathisch** *a.* apathetic.

Apfel *m.* (-s, ⸚) apple; *in die sauren ~ beißen* to swallow a bitter pill. **~auflauf** *m.* apple soufflé. **~most**, **~wein** *m.* cider. **~mus** *n.* purée of apples. **~schimmel** *m.* dapple-grey horse. **~sine** *f.* orange.

A'postel *m.* (-s, -) apostle. **~geschichte** *f.* Acts of the Apostles.

Aposto'lat *n.* (-s, -e) apostleship.

Apo'stroph *m.* (-o:f) *m.* (-s, -e) apostrophe.

Apo'theke (-e:ke) *f.* (-, -n) chemist's shop. **~r** *m.* chemist, druggist. **~rwaren** *f.pl.* drugs; druggist's articles.

Appa'rat (-a:t) *m.* (-s, -e) apparatus, appliance, instrument; camera; telephone; *am ~ bleiben* to hold the line. **~ur** *f.* apparatus, equipment.

A'ppell *m.* (-s, -e) roll-call; (*fig.*) appeal. **~ieren** *v.t.* to appeal (to).

Appe'tit (-ti:t) *m.* (-s) appetite. **~lich** *a.* appetizing, dainty.

applau'dieren *v.t. & i.* to applaud.

A'pplaus *m.* (-es) applause.

appor'tieren *v.t.* (*of dog*) to fetch, retrieve.

appre'tieren *v.t.* to dress, finish.

appro'biert *a.* certified, approved.

Apri'kose *f.* (-, -n) apricot.

A'pril *m.* (-s) April.

Apsis *f.* (-, Apsen) apse.

Aqua'rell *n.* (-s, -e) water-colour. **~ieren** *v.i.* to paint in water-colour.

Ä'quator (ɛkva:-) *m.* (-s) equator.

Äqui'va'lent *n.* equivalent.

Ar *m. or n.* (-s, -e) are.

Ära *f.* (-) era.

Ara'beske *f.* (-, -n) arabesque.

Arbeit *f.* (-, -en) work, task; labour, toil; job, employment; workmanship, piece of work;

(*lit.*, &c.) essay, paper; *in ~ geben* to commission; *keine ~ h.* to be out of work; *körperliche ~* manual work.

arbeiten *v.t. & i.* to work, labour; to make, manufacture.

Arbeiter *m.* (-s, -) worker; workman, labourer; *~ der Stirn* brain-worker; *gelernter ~* skilled worker. **~frage** *f.* labour question. **~mangel** *m.* labour shortage. **~partei** *f.* labour party. **~schaft** *f.* workmen; working class. **~siedlung** *f.* workers' housing estate. **~stand** *m.* working class.

Arbeiterin *f.* (-, -nen) workingwoman, workwoman; factorygirl or -woman.

Arbeit-geber *m.* employer. **~nehmer** *m.* employee. **~sam** *a.* industrious, diligent. **~samt** *n.* Labour Exchange. **~sanzug** *m.* working clothes; (*mil.*) fatigue dress. **~sausfall** *m.* loss of work; absenteeism. **~sbeutel** *m.* work-bag. **~sdienst** *m.* labour service. **~seinstellung** *f.* strike. **~sfähig** *a.* able-bodied. **~sfeld** *n.* sphere of action, field of activity. **~sgang** *m.* stage, phase. **~sgemeinschaft** *f.* study group. **~shaus** *n.* penitentiary. **~skorb** *m.* work-basket. **~skraft** *f.* capacity for work; worker, labourer; (*pl.*) hands. **~slager** *n.* labour camp. **~slohn** *m.* wages. **~slos** *a.* out of work, unemployed. **~slosenunterstützung** *f.* dole, unemployment relief. **~slosigkeit** *f.* unemployment. **~smarkt** *m.* labour market. **~snachweis** *m.* Labour Exchange. **~sscheu** *a.* work-shy. **~ssperre** *f.* lock-out. **~stier** *m.* (*fig.*) glutton for work. **~sunfähig** *a.* unfit for work, disabled. **~svermittlung** *f.* Labour Exchange; employment agency. **~sverwendungsfähig** *a.* fit for labour duties (only). **~szeit** *f.* working hours. **~szeug** *n.* tools. **~szimmer** *n.* study.

Arche *f.* (-, -n) ark.

Archi'pel *m.* (-s, -e) archipelago.

Archi'tek-t *m.* (-ten, -ten) architect. **~tonisch** *a.* architectonic. **~tur** *f.* architecture.

Ar'chiv *n.* (-s, -e) archives, record-office. **~ar** *m.* keeper of the archives; archivist.

Areal *n.* area.

arg (-k) *a.* bad, evil; mischievous; severe; (*colloq.*) awful, very. *subst. n. ohne ~* without malice; *nichts ~es denken* to mean no harm; *im ~en liegen* to be in a bad way. **~list** *f.* craftiness, cunning. **~listig** *a.* crafty, cunning. **~los** *a.* harmless, unsuspecting, innocent. **~wohn** *m.* suspicion. **~wöhnen** *v.t.* to suspect. **~wöhnisch** *a.* suspicious.

ärger[1], **ärgst** *comp. & sup. of* arg.

Ärger[2] (ergər) *m.* (-s) annoyance, vexation, anger, worry, irritation. **~lich** *a.* annoying, provoking, vexatious; angry; *~lich sein auf* to be cross with. **~n** *v.t.* to annoy, vex, irritate. *v.r.* to be annoyed (at). **~nis** *n.* scandal; offence; annoyance, vexation.

argumentieren *v.i.* to argue.

Arie (a:riə) *f.* (-, -n) aria.

Arier *m.*, **arisch** *a.* aryan.

Aristo'krat (-a:t) *m.* (-en, -en) aristocrat. **~ie** *f.* aristocracy. **~isch** *a.* aristocratic.

Arith'meti-k (-ik) *f.* arithmetic. **~sch** *a.* arithmetical.

Arktis *f.*, **arktisch** *a.* arctic.

arm[1] *a.* poor, indigent; penniless, impecunious, hard-up; barren, destitute, devoid (of); deficient. **~enhaus** *n.* workhouse, almshouse. **~enkasse** *f.* poor-box; relief fund. **~enpflege** *f.* charity organization, poor-relief. **~enrecht** *n.* poor-law. **~esünder** *m.* criminal. **~esündergesicht** *n.* hang-dog look. **~selig** *a.* poor, miserable, wretched; paltry, mean. **~seligkeit** *f.* misery, wretchedness.

Arm[2] *m.* (-es, -e) arm; tributary (of river); branch. **~band** *n.* bracelet. **~banduhr** *f.* wrist-watch. **~binde** *f.* armlet, sling; badge. **~blätter** *n.pl.* dress-shields. **~brust** *f.* cross-bow.

~höhle *f.* armpit. ~lehne *f.* arm of chair, elbow-rest. ~leuchter *m.* chandelier. ~schiene *f.* vambrace; (*med.*) splint. ~sessel *m.* arm-chair, easy chair.

Arma'turen *f. pl.* fittings. ~brett *n.* instrument board.

Ar'mee *f.* (-, -n) army. ~befehl *m.* operation order. ~lieferant *m.* army contractor. ~~Oberkommando *n.* Army H.Q.

Ärmel *m.* (-s, -) sleeve; *aus dem ~ schütteln* to do easily. ~aufschlag *m.* cuff. ~kanal *m.* the Channel. ~schoner *m.* sleeve-protector.

ärmer, ärmst *comp. & sup. of* arm.

ar'mier-en *v.t.* to equip, arm. ~ung *f.* equipment, armament. ~ungstruppen *f. pl.* labour units.

ärmlich *a.* poor, miserable; mean. ~keit *f.* poverty, misery, shabbiness, meanness.

Armut *f.* (-) poverty, penury. ~szeugnis *n.* *sich ein ~szeugnis geben* to prove one's incapacity.

arran'gieren *v.t.* to arrange.

A'rrest *m.* (-es, -e) seizure, arrest, detention. ~ant *m.* prisoner, person in custody. ~lokal *n.* lock-up; guard-room. ~strafe *f.* detention, confinement.

arre'tieren *v.t.* to arrest, take into custody.

Arsch *m.* (-es, "e) (*vulg.*) behind, backside.

Arsen *n.* arsenic.

Art *f.* (a:rt) *f.* (-, -en) kind, sort; manner, mode, way; behaviour; method; type; description; nature; (*sci.*) species; breed, stock, race; *aus der ~ schlagen* to degenerate; (*colloq.*) to be a black sheep. ~en *on rws.i.* to take (after); *gut geartet* good-natured. ~fremd *a.* racially different, alien. ~ung *f.* mode; nature.

Ar'terie *f.* (-, -n) artery. ~nverkalkung *f.* arteriosclerosis.

ar'tesisch *a.* Artesian.

artig (-ç) *a.* good, well-behaved; polite, courteous, civil, gallant; pretty. ~keit *f.* good behaviour; politeness; (*pl.*) compliments.

Ar'tikel *m.* (-s, -) article; (com-

merc.) commodity.

artiku'lieren *v.t.* to articulate.

Artille'r-ie *f.* (-ie, -ien) artillery. ~iefeuer *n.* cannonade. ~ist *m.* gunner, artilleryman.

Ar'tist *m.* (-en, -en) ♃ artiste.

Arz'nei (artsnai) *f.* (-, -en) medicine. ~glas *n.* phial. ~kasten *m.* medicine-chest. ~kunde *f.* pharmacy, pharmacology. ~mittel *n.* remedy, medicine. ~pflanze *f.* medicinal herb. ~trank *m.* potion.

Arzt *m* (a:rtst) *m.* (-es, "e) doctor, medical practitioner, physician. [ML]

Ärzt-in *f.* (-, -innen) woman doctor. ~lich *a.* medical.

As¹ *n.* (*mus.*) A flat. ~ *Dur n.* A flat major.

As² *n.* (-ses, -se) ace.

Asch-e *f.* (-e, -en) ashes, ash; *in ~e legen* to burn down. ~e-bahn *f.* cinder-track. ~(en)-becher *m.* ash-tray. ~enbrödel *n.* Cinderella. ~ensalz *n.* potash. ~ermittwoch *m.* Ash Wednesday. ~fahl, ~grau *au* ashen, ash-grey.

äsen *v.i.* to graze, feed, browse.

As'ke-se (-ke:-) *f.* (-se) asceticism. ~t *m.* (-ten, -ten) ascetic. ~tisch *a.* ascetic.

asozial *a.* antisocial.

asphal'tieren *v.t.* to asphalt.

aß *imperf. of* essen.

Assel *f.* wood-louse.

assimi'lieren *v.t.* to assimilate.

Assi'stent *m.* (-en, -en) assistant.

Ast *m.* (-es, "e) branch, bough. ~loch *n.* knot-hole. ~werk *n.* branches.

Aster *f.* (-, -n) aster.

Äs'thet *m.* (-en, -en) aesthete. ~ik *f.* aesthetics. ~isch *a.* aesthetic.

Asth'mati-ker *m.*, ~sch *a.* asthmatic.

Astro'log *m.* (-en, -en) astrologer. ~ie *f.* astrology. ~isch *a.* astrological.

Astro'nom *m.* (-en, -en) astronomer. ~ie *f.* astronomy. ~isch *a.* astronomical.

A'syl n. (-s, -e) asylum, refuge; (fig.) sanctuary. **~recht** n. right of sanctuary.

Atelie'r (-e:) n. (-s, -s) studio. [F]

Atem m. (-s) breath; in ~ halten to keep on the move; to keep in suspense. **~holen** v. breathing, respiration. **~los** a. breathless. **~not** f. asthma; heavy breathing. **~pause** f. breathing-space, respite. **~raubend** a. breath-taking; (fig.) exciting. **~zug** m. breath.

Athe'ismus m. (-) atheism.

Äther (ɛːtər) m. (-s) ether. **~isch** a. ethereal.

Ath'let (atleːt) m. (-en, -en) athlete. **~isch** a. athletic.

Atlas¹ m. (-ses, Atlanten) atlas.

Atlas² m. (-ses) satin.

atm-en (aː-) v.i. to breathe. **~ung** f. breathing, respiration. **~ungsorgan** n. respiratory organ.

Atmos'phär-e (-sfɛːrə) f. (-e) atmosphere. **~isch** a. atmospheric.

A'tom (-oːm) n. (-s, -e) atom. **~ar** a. atomic. **~forschung** f. atomic research. **~ion** f. atomic ion. **~kern** m. atomic nucleus. **~kontrolle** f. atomic energy control. **~lehre** f. atomic theory. **~meiler** m. atomic pile. **~müll** m. fall-out. **~physik** f. atomic physics. **~waffe** f. nuclear weapon. **~zerfall** m. nuclear fission. **~zertrümmerung** f. splitting of the atom.

ätsch int. it serves (you, &c.) right!

Atten-'tat n. (-tats, -tate) assault; attempted murder. **~'täter** m. assailant, assassin.

A'ttest n. (-es, -e) certificate, attestation.

A'ttrappe f. (-, -n) dummy; trap.

Attri'but n. (-s, -e) attribute.

atzen v.t. (rare) to feed.

ätz-en v.t. to corrode; to etch; to bite; (med.) to cauterize. **~kalk** m. caustic lime. **~kunst** f. etching. **~mittel** n. corrosive, caustic.

au! int. expressing pain.

auch (-x) conj. & adv. also, too, likewise; even; sowohl . . . als ~ both . . . and; ~ nicht neither, nor; wer ~ whoever; was ~ whatever; wo ~ wherever; wenn ~ even if, even though, although.

Audi'enz (-rnts) f. (-, -en) ♃ audience = interview.

Audionröhre f. detector valve.

Audi'torium n. (-s) lecture room; audience = hearers.

Aue f. (-, -n) meadow, field(s). [ISLAND]

Auerhahn m. capercailye.

auf 1. prep. with dat. on, upon, in, at; ~ der Straße in the street; ~ Erden on earth. 2. prep. on, in, at, to, towards, for; ~ einen Augenblick for a moment; ~ meine Bitte at my request; ~ Englisch in English; ~ einmal suddenly; ~s beste in the best way possible; alle bis ~ einen all except one; es hat nichts ~ sich it doesn't matter much; ein Viertel ~ drei a quarter past two. 3. adv. up, upwards; ~ und ab up and down; ~ und davon gehen to run away, make off; von klein ~ from childhood. 4. conj. ~ daß in order that; ~ daß nicht lest, for fear that. 5. int. on! frisch ~ go to it! 6. sep. pref. [UP]

auf|arbeiten v.t. to work up; to clear up (arrears); to finish; to renovate; to upholster (chair, &c.).

auf|atmen v.i. to breathe again; to utter a sigh (of relief).

aufbahr-en v.t. to lay out. **~ung** f. lying in state.

Aufbau m. building up, structure, construction; composition. **~en** v.t. to build up, erect, construct. **~schule** f. intermediate school.

aufbäumen v.r. to rear, prance; (fig.) to rebel.

aufbauschen v.t. to swell out; (fig.) to exaggerate.

aufbegehren v.i. to remonstrate.

aufbehalten v.t. to keep on (hat); to keep (one's eyes) open.

aufbeißen v.t. to bite open.

aufbekommen v.t. to get open; to have (a lesson) set.

aufbereiten v.t. to dress (ore); to prepare (coal); to arrange.

aufbessern *v.t.* to raise, increase.

aufbewahr-en *v.t.* to keep, preserve; to store. **~ung** *f.* keeping, preservation; storage.

aufbieten *v.t.* to proclaim, summon; to publish (banns); to raise (army); *alles* **~** to strain every nerve, do one's utmost.

aufbinden *v.t.* to untie, loosen, undo; to tie up; *(fig.)* to impose on.

aufblähen *v.t.* to swell out, puff up. *v.r.* to boast, be puffed up.

aufblasen *v.t.* to blow up; to inflate.

aufblättern *v.t.* to open (a book).

aufbleiben *vws.i.* to sit up, stay up; *(of door)* to remain open.

aufblicken *v.i.* to look up.

aufblitzen *v.i.* to flash.

aufblühen *vws.i.* to open; *(fig.)* to flourish.

aufbrauchen *v.t.* to use up.

aufbrausen *v.i.* to roar; (*chem.*) to effervesce; *(fig.)* to flare up.

aufbrechen *v.t.* to break open, force open. *vws.i.* to burst (open); to depart, set out.

aufbreiten *v.t.* to prepare, set up.

aufbringen *v.t.* to get (door) open; to raise (money); to summon up (courage); to provoke, irritate (person); to capture (ship); to bring up (child).

Aufbruch *m.* break-up, departure; rising (of nation).

aufbrummen *v.t.* to load (with); to sentence (to).

aufbügeln *v.t.* to iron.

aufbürden *v.t.* to burden with, lay upon, impose on.

aufdecken *v.t.* to uncover; to lay (cloth); *(fig.)* to expose; to disclose.

aufdonnern *v.r.* to dress up; to doll up.

aufdrängen *v.t.* to force on to. *v.r.* to obtrude (up)on.

aufdrehen *v.t.* to wind (up); to untwist; to unscrew; to turn on (gas, &c.); to switch on (light).

aufdringlich *a.* importunate; strong (odour). **~keit** *f.* importunity.

Aufdruck *m.* imprint; impress;

stamp. **~en** *v.t.* to imprint, stamp.

aufdrücken *v.t.* to imprint, press on to; to open (ulcer).

auf|ei'nander *adv.* one after the other; successively; one on top of the other; one against the other. **~folge** *f.* succession; series. **~folgen** *vws.i.* to succeed. **~folgend** *a.* successive. **~stoßen** *vws.i.* to clash, conflict.

Aufenthalt *m.* (-s, -e) stay; residence; delay; stop, halt. **~sdauer** *f.* duration of stay.

auf|erlegen *v.t.* to inflict, impose; to enjoin.

auf|ersteh-en *vws.i.* to rise from the dead. **~ung** *f.* resurrection.

auf|erweck-en *v.t.* to raise from the dead, restore to life. **~ung** *f.* raising from the dead.

auf|essen *v.t.* to eat up.

auffädeln *v.t.* to string.

auffahr-en *vws.i.* to ascend, rise; to jump up; to start (up); to drive up; *(naut.)* to run aground; *(fig.)* to flare up. *v.t.* to bring up (guns). **~end** *a.* irascible. **~t** *f.* driving up; drive; ascent; *(rail.)* ramp.

auffallen *vws.i.* to fall upon; *(fig.)* to strike. **~d, auffällig** *aa.* striking, conspicuous.

auffangen *v.t.* to catch (up); to snap up; to intercept (letters); to parry (blow).

auffärben *v.t.* to redye; to touch up.

auffass-en *v.t.* *(fig.)* to conceive, comprehend, understand; to interpret. **~ung** *f.* conception, comprehension, view; interpretation. **~ungsgabe** *f.* perceptive faculty; intellectual grasp.

auffinden *v.t.* to find out, trace; to discover.

aufflackern *vws.i.* to flare up, flicker up.

aufflammen *vws.i.* to flame up, blaze up.

auffliegen *vws.i.* to fly up, soar up; to rise; to fly open; to explode.

aufforder-n *v.t.* to call upon; to ask, request, demand; to invite; to summon; to challenge. **~ung** *f.* request, demand; invitation; summons; challenge.

aufforsten *v.t.* to afforest.

auffressen *v.t.* to eat up, devour.

auffrischen *v.t.* to freshen up; to touch up; (*fig.*) to revive; (*colloq.*) to brush up.

aufführ-en *v.t.* to build, erect; to present, produce; to perform, act (play); to quote; to enter, specify (items). *v.r.* to behave. **~ung** *f.* building, erection; performance; specification; behaviour, conduct. **~ungsrecht** *n.* acting rights.

Aufgabe *f.* task, duty; aim, end, object; problem, proposition; lesson, exercise; asking (a riddle); posting (of letters); booking, registration (of luggage); resignation; giving up, shutting down (of business). **~nbereich** *m.* sphere of action. **~nheft** *n.* exercise-book. **~ort** *m.* issuing station. **~schein** *m.* bill of delivery; post-office receipt. **~stempel** *m.* postmark.

aufgabeln *v.t.* (*colloq.*) to pick up.

Aufgang *m.* rising, rise; ascent; staircase, stairs.

aufgeben *v.t.* to commission, order, set (task); to ask (riddle); to post (letter); to hand in (telegram); to book, register (luggage); to give up, abandon, relinquish; to resign.

aufgeblasen *a.* puffed up, inflated.

Aufgebot *n.* notice; banns (of marriage); body of men; calling out of troops; levy; *mit ~ aller Kräfte* with might and main.

aufgebracht *a.* angry, furious.

aufgedonnert *a.* dressed up (to kill).

aufgedunsen *a.* bloated.

aufgehen *vws.i.* to rise; to come up; to open; break up; to come undone; (*math.*) to leave no remainder; to be consumed, end (in smoke); (*fig.*) to dawn (on one); *~ in* to be absorbed in.

aufgeknöpft *a.* (*fig.*) communicative.

aufgekratzt *a.* (*fig.*) in high spirits, jolly.

Aufgeld *n.* agio; extra charge; premium.

aufgelegt *a. gut ~ sein* to be in a good mood.

aufgeräumt *a.* (*fig.*) merry, in good humour.

aufgeschlossen *a.* open-minded.

aufgeschmissen *a.* helpless, stranded.

aufgeweckt *a.* (*fig.*) bright, quick-witted, clever.

aufgeworfen *a.* turned up, pursed up.

aufgießen *v.t.* to pour upon; to infuse (tea).

aufgliedern *v.t.* to break up, divide into, classify.

aufgraben *v.t.* to dig up.

aufgreifen *v.t.* to take up; to seize.

Aufguß *m.* infusion.

aufhaben *v.t.* to have on, wear; to have open; to have to do (lesson).

aufhacken *v.t.* to hack open, hew open; to hoe up.

aufhaken *v.t.* to unhook, undo.

aufhalsen *v.t.* to saddle with.

aufhalten *v.t.* to hold open, keep open; to delay; to stop; to stem (tide, &c.). *v.r.* to stay, stop; to dwell on; *sich ~ über* to find fault with.

aufhäng-en *v.t.* to hang up. **~er** *m.* loop, hanger.

aufhäufen *v.t.* to heap up, amass. *v.r.* to accumulate.

aufheb-en *v.t.* to lift up, raise; to hold up; to pick up; to keep, preserve, put by; to abolish, annul; to cancel (agreement); to raise (siege); to reduce (a fraction) to its lowest terms; *Tafel ~en* to rise from table. *v.r.* (of colours) to compensate. *subst. n. kein ~ens machen* to make no fuss; *viel ~ens* much ado, much fuss; *gut aufgehoben sein* to be well looked after. **~ung** *f.* lifting (up); raising; suspension; abolition; repeal; annulment; dissolution, ending.

aufheitern *v.t.* to cheer up. *v.r.* (*of weather*) to clear up.

aufhelfen *v.t.* to help up.

aufhellen *v.t.* to brighten. *v.r.* to clear up.

aufhetzen *v.t.* to rouse, stir up; to incite.

aufholen *v.t.* to make up (for loss); (*naut.*) to hoist up, haul up.

aufhorchen *v.i.* to listen.

aufhören *v.i.* to stop, cease, leave off; *da hört doch alles auf* that's the limit.

aufjauchzen *v.i.* to shout with joy.

aufkaufen *v.t.* to buy up.

Aufkäufer *m.* buying-agent, speculator.

aufklappen *v.t.* to open.

aufklär-en *v.t. & i.* to clear, clear up; to enlighten; to explain, elucidate, solve; to set right, correct; (*mil.*) to reconnoitre. **~ung** *f.* explanation; enlightenment; (*age of*) rationalism; reconnaissance. **~ungsabteilung** *f.* recce unit. **~ungsdienst** *m.* reconnoitring. **~ungsflug** *m.* reconnaissance flight.

aufklauben *v.t.* to pick up; to glean.

aufkleb-en *v.t.* to stick on, paste on; to affix. **~eadresse** *f.* gummed label.

aufklinken *v.t.* to unlatch.

aufknacken *v.t.* to crack open.

aufknöpfen *v.t.* to unbutton; to open.

aufkochen *v.t.* to boil, boil up.

aufkommen *vws.i.* to get up; to recover; to grow up, prosper; to arise; to come into use; **~** *für* to be responsible for, to make good; *nicht ~ gegen* to be no match for.

aufkratzen *v.t.* to scratch up or open.

aufkrempe(l)n *v.t.* to turn up (sleeves).

aufkriegen *v.t.* (*colloq.*) to get open; to have (a lesson) set.

aufkündigen *v.t.* to give notice; to renounce; to recall; to call in (mortgage).

auflachen *v.i.* to burst out laughing.

aufladen *v.t.* to load; to saddle with.

Auflage *f.* tax, duty; edition (of book); circulation (of newspaper; (*tech.*) support, rest.

auflassen *v.t.* to leave open; (*leg.*) to convey; (*av.*) to make climb.

auflauern *v.i.* to lie in wait for.

Auflauf *m.* crowd; mob; riot;

(*cook.*) soufflé. **~en** *vws.i.* to accumulate; to increase; (*naut.*) to run aground. *v.r.* to get footsore.

aufleben *vws.i.* to revive.

auflecken *v.t.* to lick up.

auflegen *v.t.* to lay (on); to put on; to publish (book).

auflehn-en *v.t.* to lean (against); to rest (on). *v.r.* (*fig.*) to rebel (against). **~ung** *f.* rebellion.

auflesen *v.t.* to pick up, gather; to glean.

aufleuchten *v.i.* to flash, light up.

aufliegen *v.i.* to be exposed (for sale); to be on show. *v.r.* to develop bedsores.

auflockern *v.t.* to loosen.

auflodern *vws.i.* to blaze up.

auflös-bar *a.* soluble; resolvable. **~en** *v.t. & r.* to loosen; to unravel; to undo; to disband (troops); to solve; (*mus.*) to resolve; (*chem.*) to analyse, dissolve; to decompose; to melt **~ung** *f.* loosening; solution; dissolving, dissolution; disbandment; (*mus.*) resolution, analysis; decomposition. **~ungszeichen** *n.* (*mus.*) natural.

aufmach-en *v.t.* to open, unlock; to undo; to make up. *v.r.* to set out. **~ung** *f.* get-up (of book, &c.); make-up.

Aufmarsch *m.* marching-up, drawing-up (of troops). **~gelände** *n.* assembly area; operational basis. **~'ieren** *vws.i.* to march up, draw up (in line); to deploy.

aufmerk-en *v.i.* to attend (to). **~sam** *a.* attentive; polite. **~samkeit** *f.* attention; attentiveness; politeness; small gift.

aufmunter-n *v.t.* to rouse; to cheer, encourage. **~ung** *f.* encouragement.

aufnäh-en *v.t.* to sew on. **~er** *m.* tuck, false hem (on dress).

Aufnahme *f.* (-, -n) taking up; reception; admission; enrolment; borrowing, loan (of money); drawing of map; taking of survey, of photo; making of record; map; survey; photograph, snapshot; record; (*chem.*) absorption. **~bedingungen** *f. pl.*

entrance requirements. ~fähig *a.* receptive; capable of absorbing. ~gebühr *f.* admission fee. ~gerät *n.* recording apparatus. ~prüfung *f.* entrance examination. ~raum *m.* (B.B.C.) studio.

aufnehmen *v.t.* to lift up, pick up; to take up; to take in, receive; to admit; to raise (loan); to survey (land); to take a photograph of; to shoot (film); to record (voice); to make (inventory); to draw up (minutes); to take down (telegram); to find (scent); to contain, hold; (*chem.*) to absorb; *es* ~ *mit* to cope with.

aufnorden *v.t.* to improve the Northern race (eugenically).

aufnötigen *v.t.* to force upon.

aufopfer-n *v.t.* to sacrifice. *v.r.* to sacrifice oneself; to devote oneself (to). ~ung *f.* (self-) sacrifice, sacrificing; devotion.

aufpäppeln *v.t.* to coddle, pamper.

aufpass-en *v.i.* to pay attention; to observe; to watch; *einem* ~*en* to waylay someone; *aufgepaßt!* attention! look out! ~er *m.* supervisor; spy.

aufpeitschen *v.t.* to stir up.

aufpflanzen *v.t.* to set up; to fix. *v.r.* to plant oneself.

aufpfropfen *v.t.* to graft (upon).

aufplatzen *vws.i.* to burst open.

aufplustern *v.r.* (*of birds*) to ruffle feathers; (*fig.*) to give oneself airs.

aufpolstern *v.t.* to stuff, upholster.

aufprägen *v.t.* to imprint, stamp (on).

aufprallen *vws.i.* to bounce (against); to strike (the ground).

aufprobieren *v.t.* to try on.

aufprotzen *v.t.* (*mil.*) to limber up.

aufpumpen *v.t.* to pump up.

Aufputz *m.* dress; finery. ~en *v.t.* to smarten up; to dress up.

aufquellen *v.t.* to soak. *vws.i.* to well up; to swell up.

aufraffen *v.t.* to snatch up. *v.r.* to pull oneself together.

aufragen *v.i.* to rise (on high); to tower up.

aufrauhen *v.t.* to tease (cloth).

aufräum-en *v.t.* to tidy up; to clear up, mop up; (*fig.*) to make

a clean sweep (of). ~ungsarbeiten *f.pl.* salvage work; clearing of debris; mopping-up.

aufrechnen *v.t.* to reckon up; *gegeneinander* ~ to settle accounts.

aufrecht *a.* erect; upright. ~erhalten *v.t.* to maintain; to keep up, preserve. ~erhaltung *f.* maintenance.

aufreden *v.t.* to talk (someone) into.

aufreg-en *v.t.* to stir up, to rouse; to excite; to incite. *v.r.* to be excited, to work oneself up. ~ung *f.* excitement; agitation.

aufreiben *v.t.* to rub open; (*mil.*) to destroy. *v.r.* to worry oneself to death; to wear oneself out.

aufreihen *v.t.* to string (beads).

aufreißen *v.t.* to tear open; to break up; to open (eyes, &c.) wide.

aufreizen *v.t.* to rouse, stir up, excite; to egg on.

aufricht-en *v.t.* to lift up, raise; to erect, set up; (*fig.*) to console, comfort. *v.r.* to sit up; to rise. ~ig *a.* sincere; frank; straightforward. ~igkeit *f.* sincerity; straightforwardness.

aufriegeln *v.t.* to unbolt.

aufringeln *v.r.* to coil up.

Aufriß *m.* sketch; elevation.

aufritzen *v.t.* to slit or scratch open.

aufrollen *v.t.* to roll up; to coil; to unroll; to broach (question).

aufrücken *vws.i.* to be promoted; to move up; (*mil.*) to close the ranks.

Aufruf *m.* call; summons; appeal; manifesto. ~en *v.t.* to call up; to call in (bank-notes); *namentlich* ~*en* (*mil.*) to call the roll.

Aufruhr *m.* (-s, -e) uproar; revolt, insurrection, mutiny, riot.

aufrühr-en *v.t.* to stir up; to incite to rebellion; to rake up, bring up, revive (memory of). ~er *m.* agitator; rioter; rebel; mutineer. ~erisch *a.* seditious; inflammatory; mutinous; rebellious.

aufrunden *v.t.* to round off.

aufrüst-en *v.t. & i.* to arm, rearm. ~ung *f.* rearmament.

aufrütteln *v.t.* to shake up; to rouse.

aufs = auf das.

aufsagen *v.t.* to recite; *Dienst* ~ to give notice.

aufsässig *a.* rebellious, refractory.

Aufsatz *m.* head-piece, top; essay, paper, treatise.

aufsaugen *v.t.* to suck up; to absorb.

aufschauen *v.i.* to look up (to); to glance up (from).

aufscheuchen *v.t.* to scare.

aufscheuern *v.t.* to scrub; to scour; to chafe (skin).

aufschichten *v.t.* to pile up; to stack; to stratify.

aufschieben *v.t.* to push open; (*fig.*) to put off, defer; to delay; to postpone, adjourn.

aufschießen *vws.i.* to shoot up; to leap up.

Aufschlag *m.* striking; impact; lapel, revers, facings (of coat, &c.); rise (in price); service (in tennis). ~**en** *v.t.* to break open; to open (eyes, book, &c.); to cut (one's knee); to turn up (trousers); to put up (bed, scaffolding); to pitch (camp); to take up (one's abode); to raise (price). *vws.i.* to strike, hit.

aufschließen *v.t.* to unlock; to open (up). *v.i.* (*mil.*) to close the ranks. *v.r.* to pour out (one's heart).

aufschlitzen *v.t.* to slit open, rip.

Aufschluß *m.* explanation; information. ~**reich** *a.* informative, instructive.

aufschlüsseln *v.t.* to distribute in a fixed ratio.

aufschnallen *v.t.* to unbuckle; to buckle on.

aufschnappen *v.t.* to snap up; (*fig.*) to pick up. *vws.i.* to spring or fly open.

aufschneid-en *v.t.* to cut open; to cut (pages); to carve (meat); (*med.*) to dissect; (*fig.*) to brag, exaggerate. ~**er** *m.* braggart, boaster. ~**e'rei** *f.* boasting, bragging.

Aufschnitt *m.* (*kalter*) ~ cold meats.

aufschnüren *v.t.* to unlace, untie.

aufschrauben *v.t.* to unscrew; to screw on.

aufschrecken *v.t.* to startle. *vws.i.* to start, jump.

Aufschrei *m.* scream, shriek; (*fig.*) outcry. ~**en** *v.i.* to cry out, scream, shriek.

aufschreiben *v.t.* to write or note down; to charge (to account).

Aufschrift *f.* inscription; address; label, ticket; legend (on coin).

Aufschub *m.* postponement; delay; adjournment; respite; reprieve.

aufschürfen *v.t.* to graze, abrade (skin).

aufschütteln *v.t.* to shake up.

aufschütten *v.t.* to heap up.

aufschwatzen *v.t.* to talk (someone) into.

aufschwingen *v.r.* to soar, rise.

Aufschwung *m.* rise; progress; prosperity; stimulus; flight (of fancy).

aufseh-en *v.i.* to look up. *subst. m.* stir, sensation. ~**er** *m.* keeper; custodian; attendant; overseer; superintendent.

aufsein *v.i.* to be up; to be open.

aufsetzen *v.t.* to put on; to set (up); to put in; to add, build on; to draw up (letter, &c.). *v.r.* to sit up (straight).

Aufsicht *f.* inspection; supervision; surveillance; guardianship; care; charge. ~**sbeamte(r)** *m.* superintendent, supervisor; keeper. ~**srat** *m.* board of directors.

aufsitzen *v.i.* to sit upon; to sit up; to mount (horse); (*naut.*) to run aground; (*fig.*) ~ *lassen* to leave in the lurch.

aufspalten *v.t.* to split.

aufspannen *v.t.* to stretch; to mount (canvas); to spread or set (sails); to put up (umbrella); *Saiten* ~ to string (an instrument).

aufsparen *v.t.* to save, save up, lay by; to reserve.

aufspeichern *v.t.* to store up.

aufsperren *v.t.* to unlock; to open (wide); to gape.

aufspielen *v.t. & i.* to strike up. *v.r.* to put on airs, to pose.

aufspießen *v.t.* to lift (with fork); to impale; to gore.

aufspringen *vws.i.* to jump up; to open, spring open; (*of skin*) to chap; to crack; to burst.

aufspüren *v.t.* to trace or smell out; to find out.

aufstacheln *v.t.* to goad; to incite.

aufstampfen *v.i.* to stamp one's foot.

Aufstand *m.* (-s, Aufstände) rebellion, insurrection.

aufständisch *a.* rebellious, seditious, revolutionary.

aufstapeln *v.t.* to pile up, stack up.

aufstechen *v.t.* to prick open; (*surg.*) to lance.

aufstecken *v.t.* to stick on; to pin up (dress); (*fig.*) to give up; *Licht* ~ to enlighten.

aufstehen *vws.i.* to get up, to rise; (*of door*) to stand open; ~ *gegen* to revolt, rebel.

aufsteigen *vws.i.* to ascend; to rise; to mount; to climb up, go up; to well up; (*av.*) to take off, climb.

aufstell-en *v.t.* to put up, set up, erect; to post (guards); to draw up (troops); to set (trap); to prepare (balance); to lay down (principle); to make (assertion); to nominate (candidate). *v.r.* to place oneself (in position); (*mil.*) to draw up, form up. ~**ung** *f.* putting-up; drawing-up, formation; assertion; list; inventory; statement; nomination.

aufstemmen *v.t.* to prize open; to lean upon.

Aufstieg *m.* (-s) ascent; (*fig.*) rise.

aufstöbern *v.t.* to stir up; to ferret out.

aufstocken *v.t.* to add a storey.

aufstören *v.t.* to disturb, rouse.

aufstoßen *v.t.* to push open; to bump against. *v.i.* to belch; (*naut.*) to run aground; (*fig.*) to strike. *subst. n.* eructation.

aufstreben *v.i.* to rise; to aspire (to).

aufstreichen *v.t.* to spread (on).

aufstreifen *v.t.* to tuck up (sleeves).

aufstreuen *v.t.* to sprinkle (on); to strew (upon).

Aufstrich *m.* spread, paste; upstroke (of pen).

aufstülpen *v.t.* to turn up (sleeves); to put on (hat).

aufstützen *v.t.* to prop up. *v.r.* to lean or rest (on).

aufsuchen *v.t.* to search for; to seek (out); to look up, visit.

auftakeln *v.t.* to rig up; (*fig.*) *aufgetakelt sein* to be togged up.

Auftakt *m.* anacrusis; (*mus.*) unaccented beat; (*fig.*) prelude; initial phase (of operation).

auftauchen *vws.i.* to emerge; to appear; to arise.

auftauen *v.t. & vws.i.* to thaw; to unfreeze (capital).

auftischen *v.t.* to serve up.

Auftrag (-k) *m.* (-s, Aufträge) commission; order; mission; charge; instruction; *im* ~ *von* by order of, on behalf of. ~**geber** *m.* employer; consignor.

auftragen *v.t.* to serve (food); to lay on (colour); to wear out; to send (greetings); to ask (to do sth.); *dick* ~ (*fig.*) to lay it on thick.

auftreffen *v.i.* to impact.

auftreiben *v.t.* to raise; to start; to hunt up, get hold of, obtain; (*med.*) to swell up, distend.

auftrennen *v.t.* to undo.

auftreten *v.t.* to kick open. *vws.i.* to tread (upon); to appear; to come forward; to behave; to arise; to break out. *subst. n.* behaviour, bearing, demeanour; appearance; occurrence; outbreak.

Auftrieb *m.* buoyancy; driving of cattle into Alpine pasture; (*fig.*) stimulus, impetus; rise.

Auftritt *m.* (*theatr. & fig.*) scene; appearance.

auftrumpfen *v.i.* to boast; to exult; to go one better.

auftun *v.t.* to open; to start.

auftürmen *v.t.* to heap up, pile up. *v.r.* to tower up; to accumulate.

aufwachen *vws.i.* to wake up, awake(n).

aufwachsen *vws.i.* to grow up.

aufwall-en *vws.i.* to boil up. ~**ung** *f.* emotion; transport; fit.

Aufwand *m.* (-es) expenditure; luxury; flow (of language).

aufwärmen *v.t.* to warm up; (*fig.*) to repeat (old stories).

Aufwart-efrau *f.* charwoman. **~en** *v.i.* to wait on; to serve (a person). **~ung** *f.* visit; (*colloq.*) charwoman, help.

Aufwärter *m.* attendant.

aufwärts *adv.* upward(s). **~haken** *m.* upper-cut.

aufwaschen *v.t.* wash up.

aufwecken *v.t.* to waken, wake up.

aufweichen *v.t.* to soften; to soak.

aufweinen *v.i.* to weep loudly.

aufweisen *v.t.* to show, exhibit.

aufwend-en *v.t.* to spend (upon); to take (pains) to bestow (upon). **~ig** *a.* expensive.

Aufwendungen *pl.* expenditure; expenses.

aufwerfen *v.t.* to throw open; to throw up; to dig; to raise (question). *v.r.* to set oneself up (for).

aufwert-en *v.t.* to revalorize. **~ung** *f.* revalorization.

aufwickeln *v.t.* to roll up; to wind up; to put (hair) in curlers; to unroll; to unwind; to unwrap.

aufwieg-eln *v.t.* to incite, stir up. **~ler** *m.* agitator. **~lerisch** *a.* inflammatory, seditious **~(e)-lung** *f.* incitement, instigation.

aufwiegen *v.t.* to counterbalance; to compensate (for).

Aufwind *m.* up-current.

aufwinden *v.t.* to hoist; to haul up; to weigh (anchor).

aufwirbeln *v.t.* to whirl up; to raise (dust).

aufwischen *v.t.* to wipe up, to clean.

aufwühlen *v.t.* to turn up (ground); to dig up, grub up; (*fig.*) to agitate, stir up.

aufzählen *v.t.* to count up; to enumerate; to pay down.

aufzäumen *v.t.* to bridle.

aufzehren *v.t.* to use up, consume; to waste.

aufzeichn-en *v.t.* to draw; to sketch; to note down; to record. **~ung** *f.* note, record.

aufzeigen *v.t.* to show; to exhibit.

aufziehen *v.t.* to draw up; to put

up; to hoist; to raise; to haul up; to weigh (anchor); to draw (curtain); to open (sluice-gate); to wind up (watch); to mount, stretch on (canvas); to put on (strings); to bring up, rear (child); to rear, cultivate, grow; (*fig.*) to tease, make a fool of; *groß* **~** to bring up. **aufziehen** *vws.i.* to march up; *auf Wache* **~** to mount guard; to approach; (*of storm*) to gather; to appear.

Aufzucht *f.* breeding; rearing.

Aufzug *m.* procession; train; parade, cavalcade; pageant; getup, dress, attire; (*theatr.*) act; (*tech.*) lift, elevator; crane.

aufzwängen, aufzwingen *v.t.* to press or force upon.

Aug|apfel *m.* eye-ball; (*fig.*) apple of one's eye.

Auge (-s) *n.* (-s, -n) eye; point, pip (on card); (*bot.*) bud; *gute* (*schlechte*) **~n haben** to have good (bad) eyesight; *kein* **~ zutun** not to sleep a wink; *im* **~ behalten** to keep in mind; *aus den* **~n verlieren** to lose sight of; *unter vier* **~n** between ourselves; privately; *ein* **~ zudrücken** to wink or connive at; *ins* **~ sehen** (*fig.*) to face. [EYE]

Augen-arzt *m.* oculist. **~blick** *m.* moment, minute. **~blicklich** *a.* instantaneous; present; momentary. *adv.* immediately, just now. **~blicks** *adv.* immediately; instantly; just now. **~bogen** *m.* orbital ridge. **~braue** *f.* eyebrow. **~fällig** *a.* obvious, evident. **~flimmern** *n.* vibration of iris. **~heilkunde** *f.* ophthalmology. **~höhle** *f.* eye-socket. **~licht** *n.* eyesight. **~lid** *n.* eyelid. **~maß** *n. gutes* **~maß** accurate eye. **~merk** *n.* attention. **~schein** *m.* appearance, view; inspection. **~scheinlich** *a. & adv.* apparent(ly), obvious(ly), evident(ly). **~spiegel** *m.* ophthalmoscope. **~stern** *m.* pupil. **~täuschung** *f.* optical illusion. **~trost** *m.* (*bot.*) eyebright. **~weide** *f.* feast for the eyes. **~wimper** *f.* eyelash. **~zeuge** *m.* eyewitness.

äugeln v.i. to ogle.

äugen v.i. to look about carefully.

Au'gust m. (-s) August.

Aukti'on (-tsio:n) f. (-, -en) sale, auction. ~'ator m. auctioneer.

Aula f. (-, Aulen) (large) hall.

aus 1. prep. out of; from; of; for; by; on, upon, on account of, in; ~ Berlin from B.; ~ Holz of wood; ~ Liebe for love; ~ Mangel an Geld for want of money; ~ unserer Mitte from among us; ~ dem Deutschen übersetzen to translate from the German. 2. adv. out; over; up; finished; von hier ~ from here; von mir ~ for my part; (colloq.) I don't care; von Haus ~ originally; mit ihm ist es ~ he is done for; weder ein noch ~ wissen to be at one's wit's end; ~ ! finis. 3. sep. pref.

aus|arbeit-en v.t. to work out; to compose; to elaborate. v.r. to take exercise. ~ung f. elaboration, perfecting; composition.

aus|arten vws.i. to degenerate; (fig.) to get out of hand.

aus|atm-en v.t. to exhale, breathe out. ~ung f. exhalation.

ausbaden v.t. (fig.) to suffer for.

ausbaggern v.t. to dredge.

Ausbau m. extension; completion; consolidation. ~en v.t. to enlarge; to extend; to complete.

ausbauchen v.t. to belly, puff out.

ausbedingen v.t. to stipulate (for).

ausbesser-n v.t. to mend; to repair; to restore; to refit (ship); to correct (essay). ~ung f. mending, repair.

Ausbeut-e f. gain; profit; yield. ~en v.t. to exploit. ~er m. exploiter. ~ertum n. sweating-system; slave-driving. ~ung f. exploitation.

ausbiegen vws.i. to make way for.

ausbieten v.t. to cry (wares), cry up.

ausbild-en v.t. to form; to develop; to cultivate; to educate; (mil.) to drill; to train. ~ung f. formation; development; cultivation; education; instruction; drilling; training.

ausbitten v.t. sich ~ to ask for;

to insist on; das bitte ich mir aus I (must) insist on that.

ausblasen v.t. to blow out.

ausbleiben vws.i. to fail to appear, not to come; to stay away. subst. n. absence; failure.

Ausblick m. view, prospect, outlook.

ausbohren v.t. to bore, drill.

ausbooten v.t. to disembark; (fig.) to oust.

ausbrechen v.t. to break out; to vomit. vws.i. to break out, escape; to burst out (laughing).

ausbreit-en v.t. to spread out; to stretch; to display. v.r. to extend, spread. ~ung f. spreading; circulation.

ausbrennen v.t. to cauterize; to scorch. vws.i. to burn out; to cease burning.

ausbringen v.t. jemandes Gesundheit ~ to propose a person's health.

Ausbruch m. outbreak; eruption; escape; (fig.) outburst.

ausbrüten v.t. to hatch; to plot.

Ausbuchtung f. indentation; salient.

ausbuddeln v.t. (coll.) to dig out.

Ausbund m. paragon; prodigy; quintessence; embodiment.

ausbürgern v.t. to deprive of citizenship.

ausbürsten v.t. to brush, brush out.

Ausdauer f. perseverance; assiduity; endurance. ~n v.i. to hold out. ~nd a. persistent, persevering.

ausdehn-bar a. expansible, extensible. ~barkeit f. expansibility. ~en v.t. & r. to extend, stretch; to extend; to prolong. ~ung f. expansion, extension; extent; dimension. ~ungsvermögen n. expansive force.

ausdenken v.t. to think out; to conceive. v.r. to think of; to imagine; to invent.

ausdeuten v.t. to interpret; to explain.

ausdienen v.i. to serve one's time.

ausdorren vws.i. to dry up.

ausdörren v.t. to parch, dry up.

ausdrehen v.t. to turn out; to switch off (light); to turn off (tap).

Ausdruck m. (-s, Ausdrücke) expression; term; word, wording. **~slos** a. expressionless; blank; vacant. **~svoll** a. expressive; significant; suggestive.

ausdrucken v.t. (typ.) to work off; to finish printing.

ausdrück-en v.t. to press out; to put out (cigar); (fig.) to express; *sich klar ~en* to speak plainly; *sich kurz ~en* to be brief. **~lich** a. explicit; intentional; express. *adv.* expressly.

ausdünst-en v.t. & i. to exhale; to sweat out; to perspire; (bot.) to transpire; (chem.) to evaporate. **~ung** f. exhalation; perspiration; evaporation.

aus|ei'nander adv. apart, asunder; separately. **~brechen** v.t. to break. *vws.i.* to break (in two). **~bringen** *vws.i.* to separate. **~fahren** *vws.i.* to separate suddenly; (of crowd) to scatter. **~fallen** *vws.i.* to go to pieces. **~gehen** *vws.i.* to separate; to disperse; to break (up); to come or get loose. **~halten** (fig.) v.t. to distinguish between. **~setzen** v.t. to explain. *v.r.* to come to terms; to settle. **~setzung** f. explanation; statement; discussion; argument; dispute; (leg.) settlement; *feindliche ~setzung* fight.

aus|erkoren a. chosen; elect.

aus|erlesen a. choice; select; picked; exquisite.

aus|ersehen v.t. to single out; to choose; to destine.

aus|erwählen v.t. to choose, select.

aus|essen v.t. to eat up; to finish; (fig.) to pay or suffer for.

ausfahr-en v.t. to take out for a drive. *vws.i.* to go for a drive or ride; (naut.) to put to sea; (min.) to ascend; *ausgefahrene* (road) full of ruts. **~t** f. drive; departure; sailing; exit.

Ausfall m. (-s, Ausfälle) loss; deficiency; deficit; falling-out (of hair); attack, invective; (mil.) sortie, sally; (fenc.) lunge; result, issue. **~en** *vws.i.* to fall out; to be omitted; to be deducted; (fig.) not to take place; (mil.) to

attack; to make a sortie, sally forth; to lunge; *gut ~en* to turn out well. **~end** a. aggressive. **~stor** n. sally-port. **~straße** f. arterial road.

ausfasern v.t. & i. to unravel; to ravel out.

ausfechten v.t. to fight out.

ausfegen v.t. to sweep out.

ausfeilen v.t. to file out; (fig.) to elaborate.

ausfertig-en v.t. to draw up; to execute; to issue; to dispatch; to make out (bill). **~ung** f. drawing up; execution; dispatch; *in zweifacher ~ung* in duplicate.

ausfinden, ausfindig machen v.t. to find out, discover.

ausflicken v.t. to patch.

ausfliegen *vws.i.* to fly out; to leave home; to make an excursion.

ausfließen *vws.i.* to flow out; to emanate (from).

Ausflucht f. (-, Ausflüchte) evasion, excuse.

Ausflug m. trip; excursion.

Ausflügler m. (-s, -) excursionist; tourist; tripper, hiker.

Ausfluß m. flowing out; mouth, outlet (of river); (med.) discharge; (phys.) emanation; (fig.) result; expression.

ausfolgen v.t. to deliver, hand over.

ausforschen v.t. to find out, search out; to explore; to investigate.

ausfragen v.t. to question, interrogate; to examine; to pump.

ausfransen v.t. & i. to fray out.

ausfressen v.t. to eat up; (chem.) to corrode; (colloq.) to make mischief.

Ausfuhr f. (-, -en) exportation, export. **~artikel** m. exports.

ausführbar a. practicable, feasible; exportable. **~keit** f. practicability, feasibility.

ausführ-en v.t. to take out; to export (goods); to carry out, execute, work out; to make; to perform; to explain. **~lich** a. detailed, ample, full. *adv.* in detail, fully. **~lichkeit** f. fullness, copiousness. **~ung** f. exportation; execution, completion, performance; realization; statement, explanation; (commerc.) description; quality.

ausfüll-en v.t. to fill out; to fill up; to pad; to fill (post); to occupy; to engross. **~ung** f. filling up.

Ausgabe f. expense; expenditure; outlay; delivery (of letters); issue (of ticket, &c.); edition (of book). **~buch** n. cash-book.

Ausgang m. going out; exit, way out; end, close; issue, unshot; (servant's) day out, time off. **~spunkt** m. starting-point.

ausgeben v.t. to give out; to deliver; to issue (order); to spend (money); to deal (cards). v.i. (colloq.) to suffice. last. v.r. to spend all one has; *sich ~ für* to pass oneself off for.

Ausgeburt f. product; creature; *der Hölle* fiend.

ausgedehnt a. ample, vast, extensive.

ausgefallen a. (fig.) unusual, out-of-the-way.

ausgeglichen a. well-balanced.

ausgehen vws.i. to go out; to fall out, come out; (of colour) to fade; to run out of, be short of (supplies); to be spent; to come to an end; to proceed, start (from); to emanate (from); *auf* to aim at, be bent on; *leer ~* to get nothing, be left out in the cold.

ausgekocht a. (colloq.) cunning, wily.

ausgelassen a. (fig.) wild, exuberant; in high spirits. **~heit** f. exuberance.

ausgeleiert a. worn out.

ausgenommen part. & conj. save, except, with the exception of.

ausgerechnet adv. just, precisely.

ausgeschlossen a. impossible; out of the question.

ausgeschnitten a. low-necked (dress).

ausgesprochen a. (fig.) marked, decided.

ausgestalt-en v.t. to shape; to elaborate. **~ung** f. shaping; arrangement, decoration.

ausgesucht a. selected, choice, exquisite; picked.

ausgezeichnet a. excellent; distinguished.

ausgiebig a. abundant, rich.

ausgieß-en v.t. to pour out. **~ung** f. pouring-out; descent (of the Holy Ghost).

Ausgleich m. (-es, -e) settlement, arrangement, agreement; adjustment; compensation; (sport.) handicap. **~en** v.t. to make even; to equalize; to settle, arrange; to compensate; to balance (account); to make up (quarrel). **~getriebe** n. (motor.) differential. **~ung** f. settlement; compensation; balance.

ausgleiten, ausglitschen vws.i. to slip.

ausglühen v.t. (tech.) to anneal; (chem.) to calcine.

ausgrab-en v.t. to dig out or up; to exhume (corpse). **~ung** f. digging-out; exhumation; (archaeol.) excavation.

ausgreifen v.i. to step out. **~d** a. (fig.) far-reaching.

Ausguck m. (-s, -e) look-out.

Ausguß m. sink; gutter; spout (of jug).

aushacken v.t. to hack out; to pick out (eyes).

aushaken v.t. to unhook.

aushalten v.t. to bear, endure, stand; to support, keep. v.i. to hold out; to persevere; to last.

aushändigen v.t. to hand over.

Aushang m. notice.

Aushänge-bogen m. (print.) clean sheet. **~n** v.t. & i. to hang out; to unhinge (door). **~schild** n. signboard.

ausharren v.t. to hold out; to persevere.

aushauchen v.t. to breathe out; to exhale; *Seele* ~ to expire.

aushauen v.t. to hew out; to cut out; to thin (wood).

ausheb-en v.t. to lift out; to pull out; to dig up; to raid; to unhinge (door); *sich den Arm* ~en to dislocate one's arm; (mil.) to enlist (recruits). **~ung** f. conscription; levy, draft of soldiers.

aushecken v.t. to concoct, devise.

ausheilen vws.i. to heal up; to be healed.

aushelfen v.i. to help out; to aid, assist.

Aushilf-e f. (temporary) help; assistance, aid; stop-gap. **~stellung** f. temporary post.

aushöhlen v.t. to hollow out; to excavate.

ausholen v.t. to sound, pump (person). v.i. to lunge; zum Schlag ~ to raise one's arm to strike (blow); zum Sprung ~ to take a run (before jumping); (fig.) weit ~ to go far back.

aushorchen v.t. to sound, pump.

aushülsen v.t. to shell (peas, &c.).

aushungern v.t. to starve out.

ausjäten v.t. to weed out.

auskämmen v.t. to comb out.

auskaufen v.t. to buy out, buy up.

auskehlen v.t. to flute, channel.

auskehren v.t. to sweep out.

auskennen v.r. to know, know about; to know what's what.

auskernen v.t. to stone (fruit); to shell.

ausklagen v.t. to sue for.

Ausklang m. end.

auskleiden v.t. & v.r. to undress; to line, coat; to decorate (with).

ausklingen v.i. (of sound) to die away; to end (in).

ausklopf-en v.t. to beat, beat out. **~er** m. carpet-beater.

ausklügeln v.t. to puzzle out; to calculate.

auskneifen vws.i. to run away, slip away; (sl.) to hook it.

ausknipsen v.t. to switch off (light).

ausknobeln v.t. to gamble for (with dice); to toss for; (fig.) to puzzle out.

auskochen v.t. to boil thoroughly; to extract by boiling.

auskommen vws.i. to get away; to escape; to manage (with), make do; to get on (with a person). subst. n. livelihood; income; competency; es ist kein ~ mit ihm there is no getting on with him.

auskömmlich a. sufficient.

auskosten v.t. to enjoy to the full.

auskramen v.t. to display; to turn out (drawer).

auskratzen v.t. to scratch out. vws.i. (sl.) to hook it.

auskriechen vws.i. to creep out,

come out.

auskundschaften v.t. to explore; to reconnoitre.

Auskunft f. (-, Auskünfte) information; intelligence; particulars. **~ei**, **~sstelle** f. information bureau, inquiries.

auslachen v.t. to laugh at.

ausladen v.t. to unload; to disembark; to cancel invitation. v.i. (archit.) to project; **~de Geste** sweeping gesture.

Auslage f. outlay; expenses; display (of goods); shop-window.

Ausland n. foreign country; im ~ leben to live abroad; ins ~ gehen to go abroad.

Ausländ-er m. (-ers, -er) foreigner, alien. **~isch** a. foreign, alien; (bot.) exotic.

auslass-en v.t. to let out; to leave out, to omit; (cook.) to melt; (dressm.) to let out, let down; to give vent to (anger). v.r. to speak one's mind. **~ung** f. leaving out; omission; utterance.

auslasten v.t. to make full use (of).

Auslauf m. hen-run; outlet; (sport.) the finish; (av.) landing run. **~en** vws.i. to run out; to leak; (naut.) to put to sea; (fig.) to end (in).

Ausläufer m. errand-boy; spur (of mountains); (bot.) runner.

auslaugen v.t. to steep in lye; to leach out; (fig.) to exhaust.

Auslaut m. final sound (at end of word). **~en** v.i. to end (in).

ausläuten v.t. to ring out.

ausleben v.r. to live fully.

ausleer-en v.t. to empty, clear; to drain; **~ung** f. emptying, clearing; draining; (med.) evacuation, motion.

ausleg-en v.t. to lay out (money) for; to display; to inlay; to tile; (fig.) to explain, interpret, expound. **~er** m. outrigger. **~ung** f. explanation, interpretation, exposition.

ausleiden v.i. to cease suffering.

Ausleihe f. issuing counter in lending library.

ausleihen v.t. to lend, lend out; sich etwas ~ to borrow something (from).

auslernen *v.t. & i.* to finish learning; to finish one's apprenticeship.

Auslese *f.* choice, selection; (wine from) selected grapes; the pick. **~n** *v.t.* to select, choose; to read through, finish (book).

ausliefer-n *v.t.* to deliver; to give up; to hand over; to extradite (criminal). **~ung** *f.* delivery; extradition.

ausliegen *v.i.* to be on show.

auslöffeln *v.t.* to spoon out.

auslöschen *v.t.* to extinguish, put out, quench; to wipe out, blot out; to efface.

auslos-en *v.t.* to draw lots for; to draw. **~ung** *f.* drawing of bonds.

auslös-en *v.t.* to loosen; to redeem (pledge); to ransom (prisoner); (*tech.*) to release; to uncouple; (*fig.*) to cause; to awaken, kindle, (*phot.*) trigger, release. **~er** *m.* (*phot.*) trigger, release. **~ung** *f.* ransom; redemption.

Auslug *m.* look-out.

ausmachen *v.t.* to put out (fire); to constitute, come to, make; to settle, arrange; to decide; to agree upon; *das macht nichts aus* it does not matter.

ausmalen *v.t.* to paint; to decorate; (*fig.*) to depict, describe; to amplify; *sich etwas ~* to imagine something.

Ausmarsch *m.* marching-out, departure. **~ieren** *vws.i.* to march out, set out on march.

Ausmaß *n.* measure, degree, extent; scale, proportion.

ausmauern *v.t.* to wall (up); to line with bricks or masonry.

ausmeißeln *v.t.* to chisel; to carve; to chase.

ausmergeln *v.t.* to emaciate; to impoverish; to exhaust.

ausmerzen *v.t.* to reject; to expurgate, eliminate.

ausmess-en *v.t.* to measure; to survey. **~ung** *f.* measurement; survey(ing).

ausmisten *v.t.* to clear of dung.

ausmitteln *v.t.* to find out; to ascertain.

ausmünden *v.i.* to flow (into); to open (into).

ausmustern *v.t.* to sort out, pick out; (*mil.*) to reject.

Ausnahm-e *f.* (-e, -en) exception. **~efall** *m.* exceptional case. **~ezustand** *m.* state of emergency. **~slos** *a.* without exception. **~sweise** *adv.* exceptionally; by way of exception.

ausnehmen *v.t.* to take out; to draw (poultry); to except, exclude; to exempt. *v.r.* to show, look. **~d** *a.* exceptional. *adv.* exceedingly.

ausnutzen, ausnützen *v.t.* to make good use of, turn to account; to exploit.

auspacken *v.t.* to unpack.

auspeitschen *v.t.* to whip, flog.

auspfeifen *v.t.* to hiss; (*sport.*) to boo.

auspflanzen *v.t.* to bed out; to pot out.

ausplaudern *v.t.* to blab out; to let out, divulge (secret).

ausplündern *v.t.* to plunder, pillage.

auspolstern *v.t.* to stuff, pad; to upholster.

ausposaunen *v.t.* to blazon forth.

ausprägen *v.t.* to coin, stamp. *v.r.* to show itself. *ausgeprägt* pronounced, well marked.

auspressen *v.t.* to press out, squeeze out; (*fig.*) to extort from.

ausprob-en, ~ieren *v.t.* to try, test; to taste.

Auspuff *m.* exhaust. **~klappe** *f.* exhaust valve. **~rohr** *n.* exhaust pipe. **~topf** *m.* silencer.

auspumpen *v.t.* to pump out; to exhaust.

auspusten *v.t.* to blow out (light, &c.).

Ausputz *m.* ornamentation. **~en** *v.t.* to clean; to decorate. *v.r.* to deck oneself out, dress up.

ausquartieren *v.t.* to billet out; to remove.

ausquetschen *v.t.* to squeeze out.

ausradieren *v.t.* to erase.

ausrangieren *v.t.* to cast off; to discard; to shunt out (train).

ausrauben *v.t.* to rob, pillage.

ausräuchern *v.t.* to smoke out; to fumigate.

ausraufen *v.t.* to tear out, pluck out, pull out.

ausräumen v.t. to clear away; to empty.

ausrechn-en v.t. to reckon out; to calculate. ~**ung** f. calculation; computation.

Ausrede f. excuse; evasion; pretence. ~**n** v.i. to finish speaking. v.t. einem etwas ~**n** to dissuade someone from something. v.r. to wriggle out of.

ausreiben v.t. to rub out.

ausreichen v.i. to suffice, be sufficient.

Ausreise f. departure, going abroad; sailing.

ausreiß-en v.t. to pull out, draw, extract. ~ v.i. to tear, split; (fig.) to run away; to desert. ~**er** m. runaway; deserter.

ausreiten vws.i. to ride out, go for a ride.

ausrenken v.t. to dislocate.

ausrichten v.t. (mil.) to dress (ranks); to deliver (message); to execute, do; to see to; to obtain, get, subst. n. alignment.

ausringen v.t. to wring out; (fig.) ausgerungen haben to cease suffering; to have died.

Ausritt m. ride on horseback.

ausroden v.t. to root up; to clear (forest).

ausrotten v.t. to root out; to exterminate, stamp out, extirpate.

ausrücken vws.i. to march out; (colloq.) to decamp.

Ausruf m. cry; exclamation. ~**en** v.t. to cry out, call out; to proclaim. ~**er** m. crier. ~**ewort** n. interjection. ~**ungs** f.exclamation; proclamation. ~**ungszeichen** n. exclamation-mark.

ausruhen v.t., i., & r. to rest.

ausrüst-en v.t. to furnish; (mil. & naut.) to equip, arm, fit out; (fig.) to endow. ~**ung** f. equipment, armament; outfit.

ausrutschen vws.i. to slip, skid.

Aussaat f. sowing; seed corn.

aussäen v.t. to sow; (fig.) to disseminate, scatter.

Aussage f. statement, assertion; account; declaration; (leg.) deposition, evidence; (gram.) predicate. ~**n** v.t. to affirm, assert,

declare; to depose, give evidence.

Aussatz m. (-es) leprosy; scab.

aussätzig a. leprous. ~**e(r)** m. leper.

aussaug-en v.t. to suck out; (fig.) to exhaust, drain, bleed. ~**er** m. sponger; extortioner.

ausschachten v.t. (mining) to sink; to excavate.

ausschalten v.t. to cut out; to switch out or off; (fig.) to eliminate, remove.

Ausschank m. (-es) retailing of liquor; retail licence; public bar.

Ausschau f. ~ **halten** to watch for; to be on the look-out for. ~**en** v.t. to look out (for). v.i. to look.

ausscheid-en v.t. to separate; (med.) to secrete. vws.i. to withdraw; to retire. ~**ung** f. (med.) secretion; (sport.) withdrawal. ~**ungsspiel** n. final (game).

ausschelten v.t. to scold.

ausschenken v.t. to pour out; to retail (liquor).

ausscheuern v.t. to scour out, scrub out.

ausschicken v.t. to send out, dispatch.

ausschießen v.t. to shoot out; to shoot for (prize); (fig.) to reject, cast out; (typ.) to impose.

ausschiff-en v.t. to disembark, land. vws.i. to put to sea. ~**ung** f. disembarkation, landing.

ausschimpfen v.t. to abuse, revile.

ausschirren v.t. to unharness.

ausschlachten v.t. to cut up; (fig.) to exploit.

ausschlafen v.i. to have one's sleep out. v.t. to sleep off (effects of drink).

Ausschlag m. (med.) rash; deflexion (of magnet); turn (of scale); (motor.) lock; den ~ geben to decide the issue. ~**en** v.t. to knock out, beat out; to line; to decline, refuse. v.i. to strike out; to kick; to sprout, bud; to show damp; to turn; to deflect; (fig.) to turn out. ~**gebend** a. decisive. ~**gebende Stimme** casting vote.

ausschließ-en v.t. to shut out,

lock out; (*sport.*) to disqualify; (*fig.*) to exclude. **~lich** *a.* exclusive.

ausschlüpfen *vws.i.* to slip out.

Ausschluß *m.* exclusion; disqualification; exception; *unter ~ der Öffentlichkeit* behind closed doors, in camera.

ausschmück-en *v.t.* to adorn, decorate; to embellish. **~ung** *f.* decoration; embellishment.

ausschrauben, ausschneuzen *v.r.* to blow one's nose.

ausschneiden *v.t.* to cut out.

Ausschnitt *m.* cutting; cut; section; low neck (of dress); (*geom.*) sector.

ausschöpfen *v.t.* to scoop out; to drain (off); (*fig.*) to exhaust.

ausschreiben *v.t.* to write out, write out in full; to finish writing; to copy; to plagiarize; to publish, announce, proclaim; to summon; to advertise (vacancy); to issue writs (for elections); to invite (competition).

ausschreien *v.t.* to cry, cry out.

ausschreit-en *vws.i.* to step out, to pace. **~ung** *f.* excess; (*pl.*) riots.

Ausschuß *m.* 1. refuse. 2. committee, board. **~sitzung** *f.* committee meeting. **~waren** *f.pl.* damaged goods.

ausschütteln *v.t.* to shake out.

ausschütten *v.t.* to pour out; to empty; to pay (dividends); to unburden (one's heart); *sich vor Lachen ~* to be convulsed with laughter.

ausschwärmen *vws.i.* to swarm out; (*mil.*) to extend.

ausschwefeln *v.t.* to fumigate with sulphur.

ausschweif-en *v.i.* to lead a dissolute life. **~end** *a.* bulging; (*fig.*) dissolute, dissipated. **~ung** *f.* excess, debauch.

ausschwenken *v.t.* to rinse.

ausschwitzen *v.t.* to exude.

Aus|segnung *f.* (*R.C.*) The absolution for the dead.

aus|sehen *v.i.* to look out (for); to look, appear; *es sieht nach Regen aus* it looks like rain; *nach et-*

was ~ to look important. *subst. n.* appearance; look, air.

aus|sein *v.i.* to be out; to be over; *~ auf* to be after.

außen (-s-) *adv.* out; without; outside; outwardly; *nach ~* outwards; *von ~* from the outside, from without. **~aufnahme** *f.* (*filming*) exterior shooting. **~bordmotor** *m.* outboard motor. **~dienst** *m.* outdoor service; (*mil.*) duties outside barracks. **~handel** *m.* foreign trade, export trade. **~minister** *m.* Foreign Minister. **~politik** *f.* foreign policy. **~seite** *f.* outside. **~seiter** *m.* outsider. **~stände** *pl.* outstanding debts; liabilities. **~welt** *f.* external or visible world. **~winkel** *m.* exterior angle.

aus|senden *v.t.* to send out.

außer (-s-) 1. *prep.* outside, out of; beyond; besides; except; *~ sich* beside oneself; *~ Hause* out of doors; *~ Kraft setzen* to annul; *~ Kurs setzen* to withdraw from circulation; *~ Landes gehen* to go abroad. 2. *conj.* except; unless; save; but; *~ wenn* unless. **~amtlich, ~dienstlich** *aa.* unofficial, private. **~dem** *adv.* besides, moreover. **~ehelich** *a.* illegitimate. **~gewöhnlich** *a.* extraordinary, unusual. **~halb** *prep.* outside. *adv.* on the outside. **~ordentlich** *a.* extraordinary. **~planmäßig** *a.* supernumerary. **~stand(e) sein** to be unable.

äußer-e (-s-) *a.* outward; outer; exterior; external. *subst. n.* outside; exterior; external appearance; *Minister des ~en* Foreign Minister. **~lich** *a.* external, outward, (*fig.*) superficial. **~lichkeit** *f.* formality; superficiality; *pl.* externals. **~st** *a.* outermost; extreme, utmost. *adv.* extremely, exceedingly; *sein ~stes tun* to do one's best; *es zum ~sten treiben* to drive to extremities; *aufs ~ste gefaßt sein* to be prepared for the worst. **~ung** *f.* expression, utterance, saying, remark.

äußer-n *v.t.* to utter, express; to manifest, show. *v.r.* to say, remark; to express oneself. **~ung** *f.* remark; manifestation.

aus|setzen *v.t.* to set out; to put out; to expose; to lower (boat); to land (crew); to maroon; to offer (reward); to bequeath (legacy). *v.i. & i.* to interrupt; to stop; to put off; (*mech.*) to break down, (*colloq.*) to conk out; *etwas ~ an* to find fault with. *v.r.* to expose oneself to.

Aus|sicht *f.* (-, -en) view, prospect; *~ haben auf* to have a chance. **~slos** *a.* without prospects; hopeless.

Aussiedlung *f.* (compulsory) transfer (of population).

aus|söhn-en *v.t. & r.* to reconcile. **~ung** *f.* reconciliation.

aus|sondern, **aus|sortieren** *v.t.* to separate; to sort out; to select.

ausspann-en *v.t.* to spread out, stretch; to unharness (horse). *v.i.* (*fig.*) to relax. **~ung** *f.* relaxation, rest.

aussparen *v.t.* (*paint.*) to leave space; (*mil.*) to by-pass; to leave unshelled.

ausspeien *v.t. & i.* to spit out.

aussperren *v.t.* to shut out; to lock out.

ausspielen *v.t. & i.* to finish playing; to lead (card); (*fig.*) to play off (one against another).

ausspinnen *v.t.* to spread out, enlarge upon; to devise.

auspionieren *v.t.* to spy out.

Aussprache *f.* pronunciation, accent; discussion, (heart to heart) talk.

aussprechen *v.t.* to pronounce; to express; to declare, utter. *v.i.* to finish speaking. *v.r.* to speak one's mind.

aussprengen *v.t.* to spread (rumour).

ausspritzen *v.t.* to squirt out; (*med.*) to syringe.

Ausspruch *m.* utterance, remark, saying; verdict.

ausspucken *v.t. & i.* to spit out.

ausspülen *v.t.* to wash out, rinse.

ausspüren *v.t.* to track, trace.

ausstaffieren *v.t.* to furnish, fit out, equip; to smarten up.

Ausstand *m.* strike; (*pl.*) outstanding debts.

ausständig *a.* on strike.

ausstanzen *v.t.* to punch out.

ausstatt-en *v.t.* to equip, fit out; to give a dowry to; (*fig.*) to endow, bestow upon. **~ung** *f.* equipment, outfit; fittings; marriage dowry; get-up; scenery; endowment. **~ungsstück** *n.* transformation-scene; spectacular show.

ausstechen *v.t.* to dig out; to put out; (*fig.*) to cut out; to supplant; to outshine.

ausstehen *v.i.* to be still expected; to be outstanding. *v.t.* to endure, bear; *nicht ~ können* (*colloq.*) to hate, loathe.

aussteigen *vvs.i.* to get out, alight; to disembark.

aussteinen *v.t.* to stone.

ausstell-en *v.t.* to exhibit; to display; to make out (bill, &c.); to issue (draft); *~en an* to find fault with. **~er** *m.* exhibitor; drawer (of bill). **~ung** *f.* exhibition, show; drawing (of bill); (*fig.*) *~ungen machen* to find fault, criticize. **~sstück** *n.* exhibit.

Aussterbeetat *m.* *auf dem ~ stehen* (*fig.*) to die out.

aussterben *vvs.i.* to die out; to become extinct; *ausgestorben* deserted (street, &c.).

Aussteuer *f.* marriage dowry; trousseau. **~n** *v.t.* to portion, endow.

Ausstieg *m.* exit.

ausstopfen *v.t.* to stuff.

ausstoßen *v.t.* to push out; (*fig.*) to expel; to utter (cry).

ausstrahl-en *v.t. & i.* to radiate; to emit. **~ung** *f.* radiation.

ausstrecken *v.t.* to stretch out; to extend.

ausstreichen *v.t.* to strike out, cross out; to smooth out (crease).

ausstreuen *v.t.* to scatter; to spread.

ausströmen *vvs.i.* to stream out,

flow out; to emanate; to escape; (*fig.*) to radiate.

aussuchen *v.t.* to pick out; to select, choose.

austapezieren *v.t.* to paper.

Austausch *m.* exchange, barter. **~en** *v.t.* to exchange; to barter.

austeilen *v.t.* to distribute; to administer.

Auster *f.* (-, -n) oyster. **~nfischer** *m.* (*zool.*) oyster-catcher. **~n-fischerei** *f.* oyster-dredging.

austilgen *v.t.* to wipe out, efface; to extirpate.

austoben *v.i.* to cease raging. *v.r.* to romp; (*fig.*) to sow one's wild oats.

Austrag *m.* (-s) decision; issue. **~en** *v.t.* to deliver; to distribute; to decide (fight); *Kind* **~en** to carry child for full term.

austreib-en *v.t.* to drive out; to expel; to cast out, exorcize. **~ung** *f.* expulsion; exorcism.

austreten *v.t.* to tread under foot, trample; to tread out; to wear out. *vws.i.* to retire, leave; to overflow.

austrinken *v.t.* to drink up, drain.

Austritt *m.* stepping out; overflow; retirement, leaving.

austrocknen *v.t. & vws.i.* to dry up; to desiccate; to drain.

austrompeten *v.t.* to trumpet forth.

austüfteln *v.t.* to puzzle out.

aus|üb-en *v.t.* to practise, exercise; to execute; to exert (influence); to carry on (trade); to commit or perpetrate (crime). **~ung** *f.* practice; exercise; execution; perpetration.

Ausverkauf *m.* (clearance) sale. **~en** *v.t.* to sell off or out.

auswachsen *vws.i.* to sprout, germinate; to grow up. *v.r.* to develop.

Auswahl *f.* choice, selection; assortment.

auswählen *v.t.* to choose, select.

Auswander-er *m.* emigrant. **~n** *vws.i.* to emigrate; to migrate. **~ung** *f.* emigration; migration.

auswärt-ig *a.* foreign; abroad; **~iges Amt** Foreign Office. **~s** *adv.* outward(s); out of doors;

abroad.

auswaschen *v.t.* to wash out, wash away.

auswechsel-bar *a.* interchangeable. **~n** *v.t.* to exchange; to change for; to replace.

Ausweg *m.* way out.

ausweich-en *vws.i.* to make way (for); to side-step; to avoid, evade; to dodge; (*fig.*) to shirk. **~end** *a.* evasive. **~stelle** *f.* siding. **~straße** *f.* by-pass.

ausweiden *v.t.* to eviscerate, draw.

ausweinen *v.r. sich die Augen* **~** to cry one's eyes out.

Ausweis *m.* (-es, -e) proof; identity card; passport; permit; ticket. **~en** *v.t.* to expel, banish; to show. *v.r.* to prove one's identity. **~papiere** *n.pl.* identity papers. **~ung** *f.* expulsion; banishment. **~ungsbefehl** *m.* extradition order.

ausweiten *v.t.* to widen, stretch.

auswendig *a.* outward, exterior; (*fig.*) by heart; from memory.

auswerfen *v.t.* to knock out; to throw out; to eject; to cast (anchor); to fix (salary); (*med.*) to expectorate.

auswerten *v.t.* to make full use of.

auswetzen *v.t.* (*fig.*) to make amends for, make up for; to avenge.

auswickeln *v.t.* to unwrap, unroll.

auswiegen *v.t.* to weigh out, balance.

auswirken *v.t.* to procure, get. *v.r.* to operate, take effect.

auswischen *v.t.* to wipe out or away; (*fig.*) *einem eins* **~** to deal a person a blow.

Auswuchs *m.* (-es, Auswüchse) excrescence; (*fig.*) abuse.

Auswurf *m.* refuse, dregs, scum; (*med.*) discharge; expectoration.

auszacken *v.t.* to notch, indent; to scallop.

auszahl-en *v.t.* to pay out or down. **~ung** *f.* payment.

auszählen *v.t.* to count out.

auszehr-en *v.t. & i.* to consume; to waste away. **~ung** *f.* consumption.

auszeichn-en *v.t.* to mark out; to distinguish, excel; (*commerc.*) to mark price. **~ung** f. mark; distinction; decoration.

ausziehen v.t. to pull out, extract; to take off (dress); to make out (bill); to ink in (sketch). v.r. to undress. vws.i. to set out; to march off; to move, remove.

auszischen v.t. to hiss off (stage).

Auszug m. departure; marching out; exodus; removal; extract; summary; statement (of account); abstract (of account).

auszupfen v.t. to pluck out; to unravel.

Auto n. (-s, -s) motor-car. **~bahn** f. motor-road. **~bahnzubringer** m. feeder road, approach road. **~brille** f. goggles. **~droschke** f. taxi-cab. **~falle** f. police trap. **~heber** m. jack. **~hupe** f. hooter, horn. **~mobilist** m. motorist. **~schlosser** m. mechanic.

Auto-biographie f. autobiography. **~didakt** m. self-taught person. **~gen** a. **~gene Schweißung** oxyacetylene welding. **~gramm** n. autograph. **~'krat** m. autocrat. **~'mat** m. automaton; slot-machine. **~'matisch** a. automatic. **~'nom** a. autonomous. **~no'mie** f. autonomy.

Autor m. (-s, -en) author, writer. **~i'sieren** v.t. to authorize. **~i'tär** a. authoritarian. **~i'tät** f. authority. **~schaft** f. authorship.

Avi'atik f. (-) aviation.

avi'sieren v.t. to advise.

Axt (akst) f. (-, ¨e) axe, hatchet.

A'zur (atsu:r) m. (-s) azure. **~n** a. azure.

B

B, b (be:) n. the letter B, b; (mus.) B flat.

babbeln v.i. to babble, prattle.

Babyausstattung f. baby-linen; layette.

ba'cchantisch a. bacchanal, bacchic.

Bach (bax) m. (-es, ¨e) brook,

rivulet, stream. **~stelze** f. wagtail. **~weide** f. water-willow.

Bache f. (-, -n) wild sow.

Back f. (-, -en) forecastle; mess; bowl. **~bord** n. port.

Back-e f. (-e, -en) cheek. **~enbart** m. whiskers. **~enzahn** m. molar. **~pfeife** f. box on the ear.

back-en v.t. & i. to bake; to fry. **~fisch** m. fried fish; (fig.) flapper, teenager. **~obst** n. dried fruit. **~ofen** m. oven. **~pflaume** f. prune. **~pulver** n. baking-powder. **~stein** m. brick. **~trog** m. kneading-trough. **~werk** n. pastry, fancy cakes.

Bäcker m. (-s, -) baker. **~ei** f. bakery.

Bad (ba:t) n. (-es, ¨er) bath; watering-place; spa.

Bade-anstalt f. baths; swimming-pool. **~anzug** m. bathing-costume. **~arzt** m. doctor at a spa. **~gast** m. visitor taking the cure. **~hose** f. bathing-shorts. **~kappe** f. bathing-cap. **~kur** f. treatment; course of baths. **~laken**, **~tuch** n. bath-towel. **~mantel** m. bathing-wrap, bath-robe. **~meister** m. bath attendant; swimming-instructor. **~ofen** m. geyser. **~ort** m. watering-place; spa. **~strand** m. bathing-beach. **~wanne** f. bath(-tub). **~zeug** n. bathing-things. **~zimmer** n. bathroom.

baden v.t. to bath. v.t. & i. to have a bath; to bathe (in sea).

Bader m. (-s, -) barber.

baff int. **~ sein** to be flabbergasted.

Ba'gage (ga:ʒə) f. (-) luggage, baggage; (fig.) rabble.

Bagger m. (-s, -) dredger. **~n** v.t. to dredge.

bähen v.t. (med.) to foment.

Bahn (ba:n) f. (-, -en) track, road, way, course; orbit (of planets); trajectory (of missile); width (of cloth); railway; tram; **~ frei!** carry on! go (ahead)! line clear! **~anlagen** f.pl. railway sites, installations. **~arbeiter** m. railway man. **~beamte(r)** m. railway official. **~brechend** a. pioneering; epoch-making. **~brecher**

m. pioneer. **~damm** *m.* railway embankment. **~gleis** *n.* track. **~hof** *m.* station. **~hofsvorsteher** *m.* station-master. **~körper** *m.* permanent way. **~lagernd** *a.* to be kept at station. **~linie** *f.* line. **~netz** *n.* railway system. **~sperre** *f.* platform-gate. **~steig** *m.* platform. **~steigkarte** *f.* platform-ticket. **~strecke** *f.* line. **~übergang** *m.* bridge, railway crossing. **~wärter** *m.* signalman. **~häuschen** *n.* signal-box.

bahnen *v.t.* to open a way; *(fig.)* to pave the way for; *sich einen Weg ~* to force one's way (through).

Bahr- (*f.* (-e, -en) stretcher; bier. **~tuch** *n.* pall.

Bai *f.* (-, -en) bay.

Baisse (bɛːsə) *f.* (-, -en) slump.

Bajo'nett *n.* (-s, -e) bayonet.

Bake *f.* (-, -n) beacon.

Bakelit *n.* bakelite.

Bak'terie *f.* (-, -n) bacterium. **~nhaltig** *a.* containing bacteria.

Ba'lanc-e (-lã:sə) *f.* (-e, -en) balance; equilibrium. **~ieren** *v.t. & i.* to balance.

bald (-t) *adv.* **1.** soon; shortly; **~ . . . ~** sometimes . . . sometimes, now . . . now. **2.** almost, nearly. **~ig** *a.* quick, speedy, early. **~möglichst** *adv.* as soon as possible.

Baldachin *m.* (-s, -e) canopy. [IT.]

Bälde *f. in ~* soon.

Baldrian *m.* (-s, -e) valerian.

Balg *m.* (-es, ̈-e) skin; *(pl.)* bellows (of organ). *m. & n. (colloq.)* imp. **~(en)treter** *m.* organ-blower. [BELLY]

Balge *f.* (-, -n) wash-tub.

balg-en *v.r.* to romp, fight. **~e'rei** *f.* romp; scuffle.

Balken *m.* (-s, -) beam; rafter; baulk; girder. [BALK]

Bal'kon *m.* (-s, -e) balcony.

Ball¹ *m.* (-es, ̈-e) ball; globe; sphere. **~spiel** *n.* game of ball.

Ball² *m.* (-es, ̈-e) ball, dance. **~kleid** *n.* evening dress. **~saal** *m.* dancing-hall, ball-room.

Ba'llade *f.* (-, -n) ballad.

Ballast *m.* (-es, -e) ballast.

Ballen¹ *m.* (-s, -) bale, pack; ball (of foot, &c.).

ballen² *v.t.* to clench. *v.r.* to gather.

Ba'llett *n.* (-(e)t) *n.* (-s, -e) ballet.

Ba'llon (-lõ:) *m.* (-s, -e) balloon.

Balsam (balz-) *m.* (-s, -e) balsam, balm. **~ieren** *v.t.* to embalm. **~isch** *a.* balmy, fragrant.

Balz (-ts) *f.* (-, -en) pairing-time (of birds). **~en** *v.i.* to call.

Bambus *m.* (-ses, -se) bamboo.

bammeln *v.i.* to dangle.

Banali'tät *f.* (-, -en) banality.

Ba'nane *f.* (-, -n) banana. **~nstecker** *m.* banana plug.

Ba'nause *m.* (-n, -n) low fellow, philistine.

band¹ *imperf. of* binden.

Band² (-t) **1.** *n.* (-es, ̈-er) ribbon; band; tape; hoop (of cask); *(anat.)* ligament; *(pl. -e) (fig.)* tie, bond; *(only pl.)* fetters; *in ~en* in chains; *laufendes ~* conveyor belt; *am laufenden ~* on the assembly line; *(fig.)* uninterruptedly. **2.** *m.* (-es, ̈-e) volume; tome. **~'age** (-a:ʒə) *f.* bandage. **~a'gieren** *v.t.* to bandage. **~eisen** *n.* hoop-iron. **~maß** *n.* tape-measure. **~nudeln** *f.pl.* ribbon vermicelli. **~säge** *f.* band-saw. **~scheibenvorfall** *m.* prolapsed intervertebral disk. **~schleife** *f.* favour, knot of ribbons. **~waren** *f.pl.* haberdashery. **~wurm** *m.* tape-worm.

Bande *f.* (-, -n) band, gang; (billiard) cushion. **~nkrieg** *m.* guerrilla warfare.

bändereich *a.* voluminous.

bändig-en *v.t.* to tame; to break in; *(fig.)* to subdue; to restrain. **~ung** *f.* taming; breaking-in.

Ban'dit *m.* (-en, -en) bandit.

Ban'donion *n.* (-s, -s) concertina.

bang-e (-ŋə) *a.* afraid, alarmed; uneasy, anxious; *~e machen* to frighten. *subst. f. keine ~e!* don't worry! **~en** *v.i.* to be afraid; *mir bangt davor* I am afraid of it; *sich ~en um* to be worried about; *sich ~en nach* to long or yearn for. **~igkeit** *f.* fear, anxiety. **~igkeit** *f.* fear, anxiety.

bänglich *a.* rather anxious, timid.

Bank¹ *f.* (-, ̈-e) bench, seat; form

(in school); pew (in church); *durch die* ~ all, without exception; *auf die lange* ~ *schieben* to put off, delay.

Bank² f. (-, -en) bank; *die* ~ *sprengen* to break the bank. ~**abschluß** m. balance-sheet. ~**aktie** f. share. ~**anweisung** f. cheque. ~**beamte(r)** m. bank clerk. ~**fach** n. banking-business. ~**halter** m. banker. ~**note** f. bank-note. ~**wesen** n. banking.

Bänkelsänger m. ballad-singer.

bank(e)rott *subst.* m. bankruptcy; (*fig.*) ruin; ~ *anmelden* to declare (o.s.) bankrupt; ~ *machen* to go bankrupt.

Bankert m. (-s, -e) bastard.

Bankett n. (-s, -e) banquet.

Banki'er (-e:) m. (-s, -s) banker.

Bann m. (-es) ban; proscription; (*eccl.*) excommunication; (*fig.*) spell. ~**fluch** m. anathema. ~**kreis** m. (*fig.*) spell, sphere of influence. ~**meile** f. boundary. ~**ware** f. contraband.

Banner n. (-s, -) banner, flag, standard. ~**träger** m. standard-bearer. [F]

bar¹ (ba:r) a. bare, naked; destitute of; devoid of; ~*er Unsinn* sheer nonsense; ~*es Geld* ready money, cash; ~ *zahlen* to pay cash; ~*e Münze* (*fig.*) face value. ~**auslage** f. outlay incurred. ~**ertrag** m. net proceeds. ~**fuß**, ~**füßig** aa. barefoot(ed). ~**geld** n. ready money, cash. ~**geldlos** a. cashless. ~**häuptig** a. bare-headed. ~**preis** m. cash-price. ~**schaft** f. cash, ready money. ~**scheck** m. open or uncrossed cheque. ~**sortiment** n. wholesale bookstore. ~**zahlung** f. cash-payment.

Bar² f. (-, -s) bar. ~**dame** f. barmaid.

Bär (bɛ:r) m. (-en, -en) bear; *der Große (Kleine)* ~ the Great (Lesser) Bear. ~**beißig** a. grim, grumpy. ~**enhaut** f. *auf der* ~*enhaut liegen* to be idle. ~**in** f. she-bear.

Ba'racke f. (-, -n) hut, barrack.

~**nlager** n. hutment.

Bar'bar (-ba:r) m. (-en, -en) barbarian. ~**ei** f. barbarism; barbarity. ~**isch** a. barbarous.

Bar'bier (-bi:r) m. (-s, -e) barber. ~**en** v.t. to shave.

Barchent m. (-s, -e) fustian. [ARAB.]

bar'dauz int. bump! bang!

Barde f. (-n, -n) bard, minstrel.

Ba'rett n. (-s, -e) biretta.

barg imperf. of **bergen**.

Bar'kasse f. (-, -n) launch.

Barke f. (-, -n) barque.

Bärme f. (-) leaven, yeast.

barm'herzig a. merciful, compassionate; ~*e Schwester* Sister of mercy; *der* ~*e Samariter* the good Samaritan. ~**keit** f. mercy, compassion.

Ba'rock n. (-s) baroque.

Baro'meterstand m. height of barometer.

Ba'ron m. (-s, -e) baron. ~**in** f. baroness.

Barre f. (-, -n) bar; ingot.

Barren m. (-s, -) parallel bars.

Barri'ere (-ɛ:rə) f. (-, -n) barrier; (*rail.*, &c.) gate.

Barri'kade f. (-, -n) barricade.

Barsch¹ m. (-es, -e) perch.

barsch² a. harsh, gruff, rough, rude. ~**heit** f. rudeness, roughness.

barst imperf. of **bersten**.

Bart m. (-es, "e) beard; whiskers (of cat); wattle (of cock); bit (of key).

bärtig a. bearded.

Ba'saltbruch m. basalt quarry.

Ba'sar (-za:r) m. (-s, -e) bazaar.

Base¹ (-za) f. (-, -n) cousin.

Base² f. (-e, -en) (*chem.*) base. ~**ieren** v.t. to base, found (upon). v.i. to be based, rest (upon). ~**is** f. basis, foundation.

Baskenmütze f. beret.

Baß m. (Bass-es, "e) bass.

Baß'sänger m. (Bass-es, "e) bass singer.

Ba'ssin (-sɛ̃:) n. (-s, -s) basin, dock, reservoir.

Bast m. (-es) bast. ~**en** a. made of bast. ~**seide** f. tussore silk.

basta int. *damit* ~! that's enough!

Bastard m. (-s, -e) bastard.

Ba'stei, Basti'on f. (-, -en) bastion.

bast-eln *v.t.* to build up, rig up; to potter; to work at a hobby. **~ler** *m.* amateur; dabbler.

bat *imperf. of* **bitten**.

Bataill'on (-jo:n) *n.* (-s, -e) battalion.

Ba'tist *m.* (-es, -e) cambric.

Batte'rie *f.* (-, -n) battery; troop.

Batzen *m.* (-s, -) heap, lump.

Bau *m.* (-es, -ten) building, erection, construction; edifice, building; pile; structure, organism, build, frame; cultivation; cultivation, den (of animals). **~amt** *n.* Board of Works. **~art** *f.* style; type, design. **~fach** *n.* architecture; building trade. **~fällig** *a.* tumble-down, dilapidated. **~führer** *m.* overseer, manager. **~gelände** *n.* building site. **~genossenschaft** *f.* building society. **~gerüst** *n.* scaffolding. **~gewerbe** *n.* builder's trade. **~herr** *m.* builder, owner. **~hütte** *f.* (*archit.*) shed, barracks. **~kasten** *m.* box of bricks. **~kommission** *f.* Board of Works. **~kunst** *f.* architecture. **~leute** *pl.* workmen. **~lich** *a.* architectural; structural. **~meister** *m.* masterbuilder. **~plan** *m.* ground-plan. **~platz** *m.* building-lot. **~polizei** *f.* official surveyors. **~riß** *m.* plan of building. **~sparkasse** *f.* building society. **~stein** *m.* brick. **~stelle** *f.* building-lot; b.-site; (road) repairs. **~stoff** *m.* building materials. **~unternehmer** *m.* building builder, contractor. **~werk** *n.* building. **~zaun** *m.* hoarding.

Bauch (-x) *m.* (-es, ⁓e) belly, stomach; (*fig.*) body; bottom (of ship). **~binde** *f.* body-belt. **~fell** *n.* peritoneum. **~fellentzündung** *f.* peritonitis. **~grimmen**, **~kneifen**, **~weh** *n.* stomach-ache, colic. **~höhle** *f.* abdominal cavity. **~laden** *m.* box of small wares. **~redner** *m.* ventriloquist. **~speicheldrüse** *f.* pancreatic gland.

bauchen (-x-) *v.r.* to bulge out.

bauchig *a.* bellied, bulging.

bäuchlings *adv.* lying prone.

bauen (-an) *v.t. & i.* to build, construct; to cultivate, till; to work

(a mine); (*fig.*) to rely (on).

Bauer¹ = **Erbauer**.

Bauer² *m. & n.* (-s, -) bird-cage.

Bauer³ *m.* (-n, -n) peasant, farmer; (*fig.*) boor; (*card*) knave; (*chess*) pawn. **~naufstand** *m.* peasant rising. **~nbursche** *m.* country lad. **~ndirne** *f.* country lass. **~nfänger** *m.* crook. **~ngut** *n.* **~nhof** *m.* farm. **~nregel** *f.* peasant lore. **~nschaft** *f.* **~nschenke** *f.* village inn, country pub. **~nschlau** *a.* canny, shrewd. **~nstand** *m.* peasantry. **~ntracht** *f.* peasant dress. **~nvolk** *n.* peasants, countryfolk. **~nfrau** *f.* farmer's wife. **~nsleute** *pl.* peasants. **~nsmann** *m.* peasant, farmer. [BOOR]

Bäuer-in *f.* (-, -innen) peasant woman, farmer's wife. **~lich** *a.* rural, rustic, country. **~isch**, **bäurisch** *aa.* rustic; boorish.

Baum *m.* (-es, ⁓e) tree; pole; beam; (*naut.*) boom. **~kuchen** *m.* pyramid cake. **~lang** *a.* tall as a lamp-post. **~rinde** *f.* bark. **~säge** *f.* garden-saw. **~schere** *f.* pruning-shears. **~schlag** *m.* foliage trees. **~schule** *f.* nursery. **~stamm** *m.* trunk. **~strunk** *m.* stump. **~stumpf** *m.* stump. **~wolle** *f.* cotton. **~wollen** *a.* cotton. **~wollgarn** *n.* cotton thread, twist. **~wollspinnerei** *f.* cotton-mill. **~zucht** *f.* nursery.

baumeln *v.i.* to dangle.

bäumen *v.r.* to rear, prance.

Bausch *m.* (-es, ⁓e) pad; bolster; compress; *in ~ und Bogen* in the lump. **~en** *v.t. & r.* to swell, puff out. **~ig** *a.* baggy, puffy, puffed out.

Ba'zill-us (-tsil-) *m.* (-us, -en) bacillus. **~enträger** *m.* carrier.

be'absichtigen *v.t.* to intend, mean to.

be'acht-en *v.t.* to take notice of; to observe; to notice. **~enswert**, **~lich** *aa.* worth consideration; noteworthy. **~ung** *f.* consideration; attention.

Be'amte(r) *m.* (-n, -n) official, civil servant. **~nschaft** *f.* civil service. **~ntum** *n.* officialdom.

be'ängstig-en *v.t.* to alarm. ~ung *f.* alarm, anxiety.

be'anlagt *a.* gifted.

be'anspruch-en *v.t.* to claim, demand; to engross (attention); to take up (time); **stark** ~t *s.* to be fully occupied.

be'anstand-en *v.t.* to object to; to reject; to contest (election).

be'antrag-en *v.t.* to move, propose.

be'antwort-en *v.t.* to answer, reply to. ~ung *f.* answering; answer, reply.

be'arbeit-en *v.t.* to work; to work on, influence; to fashion; to cultivate, till; to treat; to deal (with); to revise, adapt (book, &c.). ~ung *f.* cultivation; revision, adaptation; arrangement.

be'argwöhnen *v.t.* to suspect, be suspicious of.

be 'aufsichtig-en *v.t.* to supervise, superintend; to look after. ~ung *f.* supervision, inspection.

be'auftrag-en *v.t.* to commission, instruct. ~te(r) *m.* deputy, agent.

be'bändert *a.* beribboned.

be'bauen *v.t.* to build on; to cultivate.

beben (be:-) *v.i.* to tremble, shake; **vor Angst** ~ to quake with fear. *subst. n.* shaking, trembling.

be'bildert *a.* illustrated.

be'brillt *a.* bespectacled.

Becher (-çər) *m.* (-s, -) cup, goblet, mug; (dice-)box. ~n *v.i.* to tipple, booze. [BEAKER]

Becken *n.* (-s, -) basin; (*mus.*) cymbal; (*anat.*) pelvis.

be'dachen *v.t.* to roof.

be'dacht *a.* thoughtful (of); mindful (of); intent (on). *subst. m.* consideration; forethought; deliberation. ~sam *a.* considerate; circumspect. ~samkeit *f.* thoughtfulness; circumspection.

bedachte *imperf. of* bedenken.

be'dächtig *a.* prudent, circumspect; slow, deliberate. ~keit *f.* circumspection; slowness.

be'danken *v.r.* to thank.

Be'darf *m.* (-s) need, requirement; requisites, supply. ~artikel *m.*

commodities; requisites; utensils. ~sfall *m. im* ~sfall in case of need; if necessary. ~s-haltestelle *f.* request stop.

be'dauer-lich *a.* regrettable, deplorable. ~n *v.t.* to regret (something); to pity (someone); to be sorry for. *subst. n.* regret, sympathy; pity. ~nswert *a.* regrettable, deplorable; pitiable.

be'deck-en *v.t.* to cover. ~t *a.* overcast (sky). ~ung *f.* covering, protection; (*mil.*) escort.

be'denk-en *v.t.* to think, think over, reflect, consider; to provide (with); to bequeath; *sich eines andern* ~en to change one's mind. *subst. n.* consideration; hesitation; scruple; doubt; ~en tragen to hesitate; to have misgivings. ~lich *a.* doubtful, serious, risky; scrupulous. ~zeit *f.* time for reflection.

be'deut-en *v.t.* to mean, signify; to be of importance; to portend; to inform, advise (a person). ~end *a.* considerable, important, great. ~sam *a.* significant. ~ung *f.* meaning; significance; importance. ~sgleich *a.* synonymous. ~slehre *f.* semantics. ~slos. *a.* insignificant, of no account; meaningless. ~s-wandel *m.* semantic change. ~svoll *a.* momentous; portentous, meaningful.

be'dien-en *v.t.* to serve, attend; to work (machine); to follow suit (in cards). *v.r.* to use; to help oneself (at table). ~stete(r) *m.* employee. ~te(r) *m.* servant. ~ung *f.* service, attendance, attention; servants.

be'ding-en *v.t.* to stipulate; to involve, imply. ~t *a.* limited; conditional; conditioned. ~ung *f.* condition; stipulation; terms. ~ungslos *a.* unconditional. ~ungssatz *m.* conditional clause. ~ungsweise *adv.* conditionally.

be'dräng-en *v.t.* to press hard; to oppress; to afflict. ~nis *f.* oppression; trouble; distress.

be'droh-en *v.t.* to threaten, menace. ~lich *a.* threatening. ~ung *f.* threat, menace.

be'drucken *v.t.* to imprint.

be'drück-en *v.t.* to oppress; to harass. ~er *m.* oppressor. ~t *a.* depressed. ~ung *f.* oppression.

be'dünken *v. impers. mich bedünkt* I think; it seems to me.

be'dürf-en *v.i.* to need, require, want, have need of. ~nis *n.* need, want; necessity. ~nisanstalt *f.* lavatory. ~nislos *a.* frugal; unassuming, unpretentious. ~nislosigkeit *f.* frugality; modesty. ~tig *a.* needy, poor. ~tigkeit *f.* need, necessity; indigence. ~tigkeitsnachweis *m.* means test.

be'duselt *a.* fuddled; tipsy.

be'ehren *v.t.* to honour. *v.r.* to have the honour (to).

be'eidigen *v.t.* to confirm by oath; *einen* ~ to put someone on his oath.

be'eilen *v.t. & r.* to hasten, hurry.

be'eindrucken *v.t.* to impress.

be'einfluss-en *v.t.* to influence. ~ung *f.* influence; interference.

be'einträchtig-en *v.t.* to injure, impair; to prejudice. ~ung *f.* injury; prejudice.

be'endig-en *v.t.* to finish, end, terminate. ~ung *f.* finish, conclusion, end.

be'engen *v.t.* to narrow, cramp; to hamper; *sich beengt fühlen* to feel oppressed or ill at ease.

be'erben *v.t.* to be heir to.

be'erdig-en *v.t.* to bury. ~ung *f.* funeral. ~~sinstitut *n.* funeral services.

Beere (-e:-) *f.* (-, -n) berry.

Beet (-e:t) *n.* (-es, -e) bed, border.

Beete *f.* (-, -n) *rote* ~ beetroot.

be'fähig-en *v.t.* to enable; to qualify. ~t *a.* fit (for); talented, gifted. ~ung *f.* capacity; ability; fitness; qualification; competence.

befahl *imperf. of* befehlen.

be'fahr-bar *a.* practicable; (*naut.*) navigable. ~en *v.t.* to drive over or on; to navigate.

be'fallen *v.t.* to befall; to attack.

be'fangen *a.* shy, self-conscious, biased, prejudiced; *in einem Irrtum* ~ *sein* to labour under a misapprehension. ~heit *f.* constraint; timidity; bias, prejudice.

be'fassen *v.r.* to occupy oneself (with); to deal (with).

be'fehden *v.t.* to make war upon; to attack.

Be'fehl *m.* (-s, -e) order, command. ~en *v.t. st.* to order, command, bid, dictate, *v.r.* (*bibl.*) to commend or commit oneself (to). ~igen *v.t.* to command, lead. ~serteilung *f.* issuing of orders. ~storm *f.* (*gram.*) imperative mood. ~sgewalt *f.* authority of command. ~shaber *m.* commander. ~shaberisch *a.* imperious, dictatorial.

be'festig-en *v.t.* to fasten; (*mil.*) to fortify; (*fig.*) to strengthen. ~ung *f.* fastening; fortification. ~ungsanlagen, ~ungswerke *pl.* defences.

be'feuchten *v.t.* to wet, moisten.

Beffchen *n.* (-s, -) (*obs.*) bands.

be'fiedert *a.* feathered.

befiehl *imperat. of* befehlen.

befiel *imperf. of* befallen.

be'find-en *v.t.* to find, deem. *v.r.* to be; to feel. *subst. n.* health; condition; opinion. ~lich *a.* being, existing.

be'flaggen *v.t.* to flag, deck with flags.

be'fleck-en *v.t.* to stain, spot; (*fig.*) to pollute. ~ung *f.* defilement, pollution.

be'fleißigen *v.r.* to take great pains to; to apply oneself to.

be'flissen *a.* studious (to do something); intent upon. ~heit *f.* assiduity.

be'flügeln *v.t.* to wing; to lend speed to; (*fig.*) to accelerate; to inspire.

be'fohlen *pp. of* befehlen. *Gott* ~ good-bye.

be'folg-en *v.t.* to follow; to obey; to observe. ~enswert *a.* worth following. ~ung *f.* following; adherence (to); observance (of).

beförder-n *v.t.* to forward, dispatch; to carry, transport; (*fig.*) to promote. ~ung *f.* forwarding, dispatch; conveyance; (*fig.*) promotion. ~ungsmittel *n.* means of transport; vehicle.

be'frachten *v.t.* to load; to freight.

be'frackt *a.* in tail-coat, in tails.

be'fragen *v.t.* to question, interrogate.

be'frei-en *v.t.* to free, set free, deliver; to liberate, release; to relieve; to exempt (from). ~er *m.* liberator, deliverer. ~ung *f.* liberation, deliverance; exemption. ~ungskrieg *m.* war of liberation or independence.

be'fremd-en *v.t.* to appear strange to, surprise; to impress unfavourably. *subst. n.* surprise; consternation; dislike. ~lich *a.* odd, strange, surprising.

be'freund-en *v.t.* to befriend; *sich* ~ *mit* to make friends, become friends (with); to reconcile oneself to; ~*et s.* to be on intimate terms (with).

be'fürcht-en *v.t.* to apprehend, fear. ~ung *f.* apprehension, fear.

befrieden *v.t.* to pacify.

be'friedig-en *v.t.* to satisfy, content. ~end *a.* satisfactory. ~ung *f.* satisfaction; gratification.

be'friste-n *v.t.* to fix a time (limit); ~*ter Vertrag* temporary contract.

be'frucht-en *v.t.* to fertilize; to impregnate; (*fig.*) to stimulate. ~ung *f.* fertilization; impregnation.

Be'fug-nis *f.* (-nis, -nisse) authority; right; warrant; powers. ~t *a.* authorized; competent.

be'fühlen *v.t.* to feel, touch.

Be'fund *m.* state, condition; finding, report; diagnosis.

be'fürwort-en *v.t.* to recommend. ~ung *f.* recommendation.

be'gab-en *v.t.* to bestow upon; to endow (with). ~t *a.* gifted, talented. ~ung *f.* gift, talent, ability, endowment.

Be'gängnis *n.* (-ses, -se) funeral.

begann *imperf.* of beginnen.

be'gatt-en *v.r.* to copulate. ~ung *f.* copulation.

be'gaunern *v.t.* to cheat.

be'geben *v.r.* to go, proceed (to); to set out (for); (impers.) to happen, occur; (*bibl.*) to come to pass; (*with gen.*) to give up, forgo. *v.t.* to negotiate, sell (bill). ~heit *f.* event, occurrence, happening.

be'gegn-en *vws.i.* to meet with, encounter; to happen to; to treat; to prevent, take measures against. ~ung *f.* meeting, encounter; reception, treatment.

be'geh-en *v.t.* to walk (on); to traverse; to commit (error); to celebrate. ~ung *f.* traversing; commission, perpetration; celebration.

Be'gehr *m. & n.* (-s) desire, wish. ~en *v.t.* to want, desire; to demand; to covet; ~*t sein* to be sought after; to be in demand. *subst. n.* desire. ~enswert *a.* desirable. ~lich *a.* desirous; covetous. ~lichkeit *f.* greediness, covetousness. [YEARN]

be'geister-n *v.t.* to inspire; to fill with enthusiasm. *v.r.* to be enthusiastic (about). ~t *a.* inspired; enthusiastic. ~ung *f.* inspiration; enthusiasm.

Be'gier, ~de *f.* (-de, -den) desire, longing; appetite. ~ig *a.* desirous, eager; covetous (of).

be'gießen *v.t.* to water; (*cook.*) to baste.

Be'ginn *m.* (-es) beginning. ~en *v.t. & i. st.* to begin, start. *subst. n.* undertaking, enterprise.

be'glaubig-en *v.t.* to attest, certify; to accredit (to). ~ung *f.* attestation. ~ungsschreiben *n.* credentials.

be'gleich-en *v.t.* to settle, pay. ~ung *f.* settlement, payment.

Be'gleitadresse *f.* declaration form.

be'gleit-en *v.t.* to accompany; to attend; (*mil.*) to escort; *nach Hause* ~*en* to see home. ~er *m.* companion; attendant; (*mus.*) accompanist. ~erscheinung *f.* attendant phenomenon; concomitant symptom. ~schiff *n.* escort vessel. ~schreiben *n.* letter of advice; covering letter. ~umstand *m.* concomitant circumstance. ~ung *f.* company; escort; retinue; accompaniment.

be'glück-en *v.t.* to make happy. ~wünschen *v.t.* to congratulate.

be'gnaden *v.t.* to bless, favour (with).

be′gnadig-en v.t. to pardon. ~ung
f. pardon, reprieve, amnesty.

be′gnügen v.r. to be satisfied
(with); to content oneself (with).

begonnen p.p. of beginnen.

be′gönnern v.t. to patronize.

be′graben v.t. to bury.

Be′gräbnis n. (-ses, -se) funeral,
burial. ~platz m. burial ground.

be′greif-en v.t. to comprehend,
understand, grasp; in sich ~en
to include, contain, imply;
begriffen sein to be; to be
about (to do). ~lich a. comprehensible, conceivable. ~licher-
weise adv. naturally, of course.

be′grenz-en v.t. to bound, border;
(fig.) to limit, confine. ~theit f.
limitation; narrowness. ~ung f.
limitation, boundary; restriction.

Be′griff m. idea, conception,
notion; schwer von ~ dull,
stupid; im ~ sein zu to be on the
point of, be about to. ~lich a.
notional. ~sbestimmung f. definition. ~sstutzig a. dull-witted,
slow, stupid.

be′gründ-en v.t. to found, establish; to confirm; to prove; to
give as reason (for). ~er m.
founder. ~ung f. foundation,
establishment; proof; reason.

be′grüß-en v.t. to greet; to
welcome. ~ung f. greeting,
welcome; reception.

be′günstig-en v.t. to favour; to
promote; to patronize; (leg.) to
aid and abet. ~ung f. encouragement; patronage; favouritism; aiding and abetting.

be′gutachten v.t. to give an opinion, give an expert judgement
on; to evaluate.

be′gütert a. rich, well-off.

be′gütigen v.t. to appease, placate,
soothe.

be′haart a. hairy; (bot.) pilose.

be′häbig a. portly, corpulent,
stout; comfortable.

be′haftet a. burdened (with); infected or afflicted (with); subject (to).

be′hag-en v.i. to suit, please.
subst. n. comfort, ease, enjoyment. ~lich a. comfortable,
cosy, snug. ~lichkeit f. com-

fort, ease, cosiness.

be′halten v.t. to keep, retain; to
remember.

Be′hält-er m. (-ers, -er) ~nis n.
container, case, box; receptacle;
bin; tank; reservoir; vessel.

be′hand-eln v.t. to handle; to
treat, deal with; to manage;
(med.) to attend; to dress
(wound). ~lung f. treatment;
management.

Be′hang m. hanging; fringe;
drapery.

be′hängen v.t. to hang (with),
drape (with).

be′harr-en v.i. to persist, persevere; to remain firm; ~en auf
to insist on; to stick to. ~lich
a. persistent, persevering, constant; tenacious. ~lichkeit f.
persistence; determination;
constancy; tenacity. ~ungsver-
mögen n. (phys.) inertia. ~ungs-
zustand m. permanence; persistence; resistance (of machine).

be′hauen v.t. to hew; to trim; to
lop.

be′haupt-en v.t. to maintain, uphold; to assert, affirm. v.r. to
hold one's own; to hold out;
(of prices) to keep up, be firm.
~ung f. assertion, statement;
proposition; argument.

Be′hausung f. (-, -en) dwelling,
lodging, home.

be′heben v.t. to remove; to repair,
remedy.

be′heimatet a. domiciled.

Be′helf m. (-es, -e) help, expedient,
makeshift; device. ~en v.r. to
manage (with); to make do; to
resort (to); to do (without).
~smäßig a. provisional; makeshift; temporary.

be′hellig-en v.t. to importune,
molest, bother. ~ung f. molestation, bother.

be′hend(e) a. agile, nimble, quick,
smart. ~igkeit f. agility,
nimbleness, quickness, smart-
ness.

be′herbergen v.t. to lodge, shelter,
put up; to harbour.

be′herrsch-en v.t. to rule over; to
govern; to have command of; to
master. v.r. to control oneself.

~er *m.* ruler; governor. **~ung** *f.* rule; command; mastery; self-control.

be'herz-igen *v.t.* to take to heart; to consider. **~igenswert** *a.* worthy of consideration. **~igung** *f.* consideration, reflection. **~t** *a.* courageous, plucky, brave. **~theit** *f.* courage, pluck, daring.

be'hexen *v.t.* to bewitch.

be'hilflich *a.* **~ sein** to help, assist.

be'hinder-n *v.t.* to hinder; to handicap. **~ung** *f.* obstacle; impediment; handicap.

Be'hörd-e *f.* (-e, -en) authority, authorities, governing body. **~lich** *a.* official.

Be'huf (-u:-) *m. zu diesem ~* for this purpose. **~s** *prep.* for the purpose of; concerning.

be'hüten *v.t.* to guard, preserve; *(Gott) behüte!* God forbid! certainly not.

be'hutsam *a.* cautious, wary, careful. **~keit** *f.* caution; care.

bei *prep. & sep. pref.* at, by, near, in, among, with, on; *~ der Hand* at hand; *~ m Bäcker* at the baker's; *~ Tage* by day; *~ weitem* by far; *~ weitem nicht* far from being, by no means; *~ alledem* for all that; *~ sich haben* to have about one.

beibehalten *v.t.* to keep, retain.

Beiblatt *n.* supplement.

Beiboot *n.* dinghy; pinnace.

beibringen *v.t.* to bring forward; to adduce; to produce (witness); to inflict, deal, administer; to teach; to impart (to).

Beicht-e *f.* (-e, -en) confession. **~en** *v.t. & i.* to confess; to go to confession. **~iger** *m.* Father confessor. **~kind** *n.* penitent. **~stuhl** *m.* confessional.

beide *a. & pron.* both; either; *wir ~* both of us, we two; *alle ~* both (of them); *einer von ~n* one of the two; *keiner von ~n* neither of them. **~mal** *adv.* both times. **~rlei** *indecl. a.* both kinds, of either sort. **~rseitig** *a.* on both sides, mutual, reciprocal. **~rseits** *adv.* on both sides, mutually.

beidrehen *v.t. & i.* (*naut.*) to

heave to.

beiei'nander *adv.* together.

Beifahrer *m.* assistant driver, relief driver.

Beifall *m.* (-s) approval, approbation; applause. **~sruf** *m.* cheer.

beifällig *a.* assenting, approving.

Beifilm *m.* supporting or supplementary film.

beifolgend *a.* herewith, enclosed, annexed.

beifügen *v.t.* to add, append, enclose.

Beigabe *f.* addition; extra; supplement; free gift.

beigeben *v.t.* to add to; *klein ~* to draw in one's horns.

Beigeschmack *m.* smack, flavour, tinge.

beigesellen *v.t. & r.* to associate with.

Beiheft *n.* supplement.

Beihilfe *f.* aid, help, assistance; subsidy; allowance; (*leg.*) aiding and abetting.

beikommen *vws.i.* to get at.

Beil *n.* (-es, -e) hatchet, axe.

Beilage *f.* addition; enclosure; supplement; (*cook.*) vegetables.

Beilager *n.* nuptials.

beiläufig *a.* incidental, casual. *adv.* by the way, incidentally.

beileg-en *v.t.* to add; to enclose; to attribute to, confer (title on); attach to; to settle (dispute); *sich ~en* to assume (name). *v.i.* (*naut.*) to heave to. **~ung** *f.* addition; settlement.

bei'leibe *adv.* **~ nicht** on no account.

Beileid *n.* sympathy; *~ bezeigen* to condole with. **~sbrief** *m.* letter of condolence.

beiliegen *v.i.* to lie with; to be enclosed; (*naut.*) to lie to.

beim = bei dem.

beimengen *v.t.* to add; to mix with.

beimessen *v.t.* to attribute, impute, ascribe to; *Glauben ~* to believe.

beimischen *v.t.* to mix with.

Bein *n.* (-es, -e) leg; bone; *einem ein ~ stellen* to trip a person up; *sich kein ~ ausreißen* not to hurry, take one's time; *sich auf* die ~e machen to be off, (sl.) to get a move on; einem ~e machen to hurry one on. ~bruch m. fracture of the leg. ~ern a. bony, made of bone. ~haus n. charnel-house. ~kleid n. trousers; knickers. ~schiene f. splint. [BONE]

beinah(e) adv. nearly, almost.

Beiname m. surname; nickname.

bei|ordnen v.t. to adjoin; to co-ordinate.

Beipferd n. led horse, extra horse.

beipflichten v.i. to agree with; to assent to.

Beirat m. adviser.

be'irren v.t. to confuse; to divert from; sich nicht ~lassen to stick to.

bei'sammen (-z-) adv. together.

Beischlaf m. cohabitation.

Beischläfer m. bedfellow. ~in f. concubine.

beischließen v.t. to enclose.

Beisein (-z-) n. presence.

bei'seite (-z-) adv. aside, apart.

beisetz-en v.t. to put to, put beside; to bury; to spread or unfurl (sail). ~ung f. burial.

Beisitzer m. (-s, -) assessor.

Beispiel n. (-s, -e) example; zum ~ for example; abschreckendes ~ awful warning, deterrent example. ~haft a.exemplary. ~los a. unprecedented, unparalleled, unheard of. ~shalber, ~sweise advv. for instance. [SPELL]

beispringen vws.i. to help, succour.

beiß-en v.t. & i. st. to bite; to smart; to burn; to prick; to sting; ins Gras ~en to die; in den sauren Apfel ~en to swallow a bitter pill. ~end a. mordant, biting, sarcastic. ~korb m. muzzle. ~zange f. pliers.

Beistand m. help, assistance; counsel.

beistehen v.i. to help, stand by.

Beisteuer f. contribution. ~n v.t. to contribute (to).

beistimmen v.i. to agree with; to assent to.

Beistrich m. comma.

Beitrag m. (-s, ⁻e) contribution; subscription; share. ~en v.t.

& i. to contribute (to); to help.

beitreiben v.t. to collect; to requisition.

beitreten vws.i. to join; (fig.) to accede, assent to.

Beitritt m. joining; enrolment.

Beifwagen m. side-car.

Beiwerk n. accessories.

beiwohnen v.i. to be present at, attend; to cohabit with.

Beiwort n. adjective; epithet.

beizählen v.t. to reckon among.

Beize (-tsa) f. (-e, -en) 1. corrosion; corrosive; stain; mordant. 2. hawking. ~en v.t. to corrode; to mordant; to stain (wood); to tan (hides); (med.) to cauterize.

bei'zeiten (-ts-) adv.betimes, early.

be'jahen v.t. & i. to answer in the affirmative; to assent, to accept. ~denfalls adv. if the answer is positive.

be'jahrt a. aged.

be'jammern v.t. to bewail, lament. ~swert a. deplorable, lamentable.

be'kämpf-en v.t. to combat, fight; to oppose. ~ung f. combat, fight; struggle; control.

be'kannt pp. of bekennen. a. well-known, known; acquainted; ~ machen mit to introduce to. ~e(r) m. acquaintance, friend. ~ermaßen, ~lich advv. as is known. ~machung f. publication; announcement; notice; advertisement. ~schaft f. acquaintance.

be'kehr-en v.t. to convert. ~ung f. conversion.

be'kenn-en v.t. to confess, admit, own up; to profess (a religion); to follow (method); Farbe ~en to follow suit; (fig.) to be frank. v.r. to acknowledge; sich schuldig ~en to plead guilty. ~er m. confessor. ~tnis n. confession, avowal; creed. ~tnisschule f. denominational school.

be'klag-en v.t. to lament, deplore, pity. v.r. to complain (about or of). ~enswert a. lamentable, deplorable, regrettable. ~te(r) m. accused, defendant.

be'klatschen v.t. to applaud.

be'kleben v.t. to paste on; to stick on; to line (with paper).

be'kleckern, be'klecksen v.t. to spot, blot, bespatter.

be'kleid-en v.t. to dress, clothe; to hang; to wainscot; (fig.) to invest; to hold (office). ~**ung** f. clothing, clothes, dress; lining; investiture; tenure. ~**ungs-gegenstände** m.pl. clothing, clothes.

be'klemmen v.t. to oppress. ~**ung** f. oppression, anguish.

be'klommen a. anxious, uneasy, oppressed. ~**heit** f. uneasiness; anxiety.

be'klopfen v.t. to percuss, tap.

be'kommen v.t. to get, receive, obtain; to have; to catch (illness; train, &c.); es fertig ~ (fig.) to bring about; to dare. vus.i. (of food) to agree with.

be'kömmlich a. digestible; beneficial, wholesome.

be'köstig-en v.t. to feed, board. ~**ung** f. board, food.

be'kräftig-en v.t. to confirm, corroborate. ~**ung** f. confirmation.

be'kränzen v.t. to crown, decorate with garland.

be'kreuzigen v.t. to make the sign of the cross upon. v.r. to cross oneself.

be'kriegen v.t. to make war upon.

be'kritteln v.t. to carp at.

be'kritzeln v.t. to scrawl upon.

be'krönen v.t. to crown with.

be'kümmern v.t. to grieve, distress, trouble. v.r. to be anxious; to trouble (about), care (for). ~**is** f. affliction, grief.

be'kunden v.t. to state, depose; to manifest, show.

be'lächeln v.t. to smile at.

be'lachen v.t. to laugh at.

be'laden v.t. to load; to burden.

Be'lag m. (-es, -e) meat, relish, spread, fillings; coating; fur (on tongue); foil (on mirror); film (on teeth); covering (of floor).

be'lager-n v.t. to besiege. ~**ung** f. siege.

Be'lang m. (-es, -e) importance; interest(s); nicht von ~ of no account; inconsiderable. ~**en** v.t. to concern; gerichtlich ~**en** to sue. ~**los** a. unimportant, insignificant. ~**reich** a. considerable, important.

be'lassen v.t. es dabei ~ to leave things as they are.

be'last-en v.t. to load, burden; to accuse; to charge; erblich belastet sein to have an hereditary disposition (to). ~**end** a. incriminating. ~**ung** f. load, burden; debit; (hereditary) taint. ~**ungsprobe** f. (loading) capacity-test; (fig.) crucial test. ~**ungszeuge** m. witness for the prosecution.

be'lästig-en v.t. to molest, trouble, bother, pester. ~**ung** f. molestation, annoyance.

be'laubt a. covered with foliage, leafy.

be'lauern v.t. to lie in wait for.

be'laufen v.r. to amount (to).

be'lauschen v.t. to listen to; to overhear.

be'leb-en v.t. to animate, enliven; to revive. ~**t** a. animated, lively; bustling; crowded. ~**ung** f. animation, revival, stimulus.

be'lecken v.t. to lick.

Be'leg (-e:k) (-s, -e) proof, evidence; example, illustration; record, document, deed; voucher. ~**en** v.t. to cover; to reserve (seat); to take (course of lectures); to prove, verify; to cover (mare); mit Bomben ~**en** to bomb. ~**exemplar** n. author's copy. ~**schaft** f. personnel, staff; shift (of miners). ~**stelle** f. quotation, authority. ~**stück** n. copy; record. ~**t** a. reserved, taken; coated (tongue); strained (voice); ~**te** Brötchen sandwiches.

be'lehn-en v.t. to invest; to enfeoff. ~**ung** f. investiture, enfeoffment.

be'lehr-en v.t. to enlighten; to instruct; to inform; eines Besseren ~**en** to set right, correct. ~**end** a. instructive; didactic. ~**ung** f. instruction; information; correction.

be'leibt a. stout, corpulent.

be'leidig-en v.t. to offend, insult. ~**end** a. offensive, insulting. ~**ung** f. offence, insult.

be'lesen *a.* well-read.

be'leucht-en *v.t.* to light up, illuminate, illumine; (*fig.*) to throw light on, elucidate. ~ung *f.* lighting, illumination; lights. ~ungskörper *m.* lighting-fixture.

be'leumdet, be'leumundet *aa. gut* (*schlecht*) ~ in good (bad) repute.

be'licht-en *v.t.* to expose to light. ~ung *f.* exposure. ~ungs-messer *m.* exposure meter.

be'lieb-en *v.t.* to like. *v.i.* to please; *wie* ~t? I beg your pardon? *subst. n.* will; pleasure; discretion. ~ig *a.* any (you like). ~t *a.* favourite; popular; *sich* ~t *machen* to ingratiate oneself (with). ~theit *f.* favour, popularity, vogue.

be'liefern *v.t.* to supply; to cater (for).

bellen *v.i.* to bark.

Belle'tristik *f.* (-) belles-lettres; fiction.

be'lobig-en *v.t.* to praise, commend. ~ung *f.* praise, commendation.

be'lohn-en *v.t.* to reward, recompense. ~ung *f.* reward, recompense.

be'lügen *v.t.* to lie to.

be'lustig-en *v.t.* to amuse, entertain. ~ung *f.* amusement, entertainment.

be'mächtig-en *v.r.* to seize; take possession of. ~ung *f.* seizure.

be'mäkeln *v.t.* to find fault with.

be'malen *v.t.* to paint, paint over.

be'mängeln *v.t.* to find fault with.

be'mann-en *v.t.* to man. ~ung *f.* manning; (*naut. & av.*) crew.

be'mäntel-n *v.t.* (*fig.*) to cloak; to palliate. ~ung *f.* cloaking; palliation.

be'meistern *v.t.* to master.

be'merk-bar *a.* perceptible, noticeable. ~en *v.t.* to notice, note; to observe, remark. ~enswert *a.* noteworthy, remarkable. ~ung *f.* remark, observation; note, annotation.

be'messen *v.t.* to measure out; to apportion (to); (*of time*) *Knapp* ~ *sein* to be short of.

be'mitleiden *v.t.* to pity, be sorry

for. ~swert *a.* pitiable, deplorable.

be'mittelt *a.* well-off, wealthy.

be'mogeln *v.t.* to cheat.

be'moost *a.* mossy; (*fig.*) old.

be'müh-en *v.t.* to trouble. *v.r.* to take pains; to endeavour, strive, try; to apply (for), seek (post); *~en Sie sich nicht* don't trouble, don't bother. ~ung *f.* effort, trouble, endeavour.

be'müßigt *pp. sich* ~ *fühlen* to feel bound (to); to feel obliged (to do something).

be'muttern *v.t.* to mother.

be'nachbart *a.* neighbouring.

be'nachrichtig-en *v.t.* to inform, advise, send word (to). ~ung *f.* information; advice.

be'nachteilig-en *v.t.* to prejudice. ~ung *f.* prejudice, detriment, injury.

be'nebelt *a.* (*fig.*) tipsy.

bene'deien *v.t.* to bless.

Bene'fizvorstellung *f.* benefit performance.

be'nehmen *v.t.* to take away. *v.r.* to behave. *subst. n.* behaviour, conduct; manners; *sich ins* ~ *setzen* to get in touch (with), come to terms (with).

be'neiden *v.t.* to envy. ~swert *a.* enviable.

be'nenn-en *v.t. st.* to name, call; denominate. ~ung *f.* name, appellation; designation; term; denomination.

be'netzen *v.t.* to moisten, wet.

Bengel (-n-) *m.* (-s, -) heavy stick, club; clapper (of bell); boy, urchin; rude fellow, hooligan. [BANG]

be'nommen *a.* benumbed; confused.

be'nötigen *v.t.* to be in want of, require.

be'nutz-en *v.t.* to use, employ, utilize. ~ung *f.* use; utilization.

Ben'zin (-tsi:n) *n.* (-s, -e) benzine; (*motor.*) petrol; gas(oline).

Ben'zol (-tso:l) *n.* (-s, -e) benzene, benzole.

be'obacht-en *v.t.* to observe, watch; (*fig.*) to keep, perform; *heimlich* ~en to shadow. ~er *m.* observer. ~ung *f.* observa-

tion; observance. ~ungsstand
m. look-out; observation post.

be'ordern v.t. to order, command.

be'packen v.t. to load, charge.

be'pflanzen v.t. to plant.

be'pflastern v.t. to pave; (med.) to
plaster.

be'quem (-kve:m) a. suitable,
convenient; easy-going, lazy, indolent. ~en v.r. to condescend
(to); to comply (with), submit
(to). ~lichkeit f. convenience;
comfort, ease; indolence, laziness. [BECOME]

be'rappen v.t. (colloq.) to pay up.

be'rat-en v.t. to advise. ~ to
deliberate. ~end a. advisory;
consultative. ~er m. adviser;
consultant. ~schlagen v.t. & r.
to deliberate; to consult; to confer with. ~ung f. deliberation;
consultation; conference; guidance, advice.

be'raub-en v.t. to deprive (of);
to rob; to bereave. ~ung f. deprivation; robbing.

be'rauschen v.t. to intoxicate;
(fig.) to enchant. v.r. (fig.) to
become enraptured (with).

Berberitze f. barberry.

be'rechn-en v.t. to calculate; to
estimate; to charge. ~end a.
calculating. ~et a. (fig.) pre-
meditated, intended. ~ung f.
calculation, computation.

be'rechtig-en v.t. to justify, entitle; to authorize. ~ung f.
authorization; right(s); qualification.

be'red-en v.t. to talk over; to
persuade. v.r. to confer (with).
~samkeit f. eloquence. ~t a.
eloquent.

Be'reich m. & n. reach, range;
sphere; area, zone.

be'reichern v.t. to enrich; to
enlarge.

be'reifen v.t. to hoop (cask);
(motor.) to fit with tyres.

be'reift a. covered with hoar-frost.

be'reinigen v.t. to settle, clear up.

be'reisen v.t. to travel through,
visit.

be'reit a. ready, prepared; ~
halten to keep ready; to tender
(money); ~stellen to provide,

prepare. ~s adv. already.
~schaft f. readiness; (mil.)
stand-to, alert. ~ung f. preparation. ~willig a. ready,
willing. ~willigkeit f. willingness; alacrity.

be'reiten¹ v.t. to prepare, get
ready; to cause, give.

be'reiten² v.t. to ride across; to
break in (horse).

be'rennen v.t. to assault.

be'reuen v.t. to repent, regret; to
rue.

Berg (-k) m. (-es, -e) mountain,
hill; über den ~ sein (fig.) to be
out of the wood or over the
worst; hinterm ~e halten to hold
back, keep in the dark; die
Haare standen ihm zu ~e his
hair stood on end; goldene ~e
extravagant promises. ~ab
adv. downhill. ~an, ~auf adv.
uphill. ~arbeiter m. miner.
~bau m. mining. ~bewohner
m. mountaineer. ~geist m.
mountain sprite. ~gipfel m.
top or summit of mountain.
~halde, ~lehne f. mountain
slope or side. ~ig a. mountainous, hilly. ~kamm m.
crest. ~knappe m. miner.
~kristall m. rock-crystal.
~mann m. (pl. -leute) miner.
~partie f. climbing-excursion.
~predigt f. Sermon on the
Mount. ~rücken m. moun-
tain-ridge. ~rutsch m. landslip.
~schäden m.pl. (damage due to)
mining subsidence. ~steiger m.
mountain-climber. ~wand f.
mountain side. ~werk n. mine.
[BARROW]

berg-en v.t. st. to save, secure; to
salvage; to conceal; to contain;
to take in (sail). ~ung f.
salvage. ~ungsarbeit f. salvage
operations; rescue work.

Be'richt (-çt) m. (-es, -e) report,
account; commentary; narrative. ~en v.t. to report; to inform (person of sth.): to relate.
~erstatter m. reporter; com-
mentator; correspondent.

be'richtig-en v.t. to correct, rectify, amend; to settle (bill). ~
ung f. correction, amendment.

be'riechen *v.t.* to smell, sniff at.

be'rieseln *v.t.* to irrigate.

be'ringt *a.* covered with rings.

Bernstein *m.* amber.

be'ritten *a.* mounted.

bersten *vws.i. st.* to burst, crack, split.

be'richtigt *a.* notorious.

be'rücken *v.t.* to inveigle; to fascinate, enchant.

be'rücksichtig-en *v.t.* to consider, bear in mind, allow for, take into account. **~ung** *f.* consideration, regard.

Be'ruf *m.* (-s, -e) profession; occupation; trade, business; vocation, calling. **~lich** *a.* professional. **~smäßig** *a.* professional. **~spädagogik** *f.* (teacher's) educational training. **~schule** *f.* college of education; technical college. **~ssprache** *f.* jargon. **~stätig** *a.* having a job; working (as employee). **~ung** *f.* call; appointment; (*leg.*) appeal; **~ung einlegen** to appeal; **unter ~ung auf** with reference to.

be'rufen[1] *v.t.* to call; to appoint; to convoke; (*colloq.*) to tempt providence. *v.r.* to refer (to); to appeal (to); *sich ~ fühlen* to feel called upon (to).

be'rufen[2] *a.* competent, well-qualified.

be'ruhen *v.i.* to rest (on), be based (on), be due (to), depend (on); *auf sich ~ lassen* to let alone.

be'ruhig-en *v.t.* to quiet, soothe, calm. *v.r.* to calm down; to compose oneself; to acquiesce (in). **~ung** *f.* calming down; comfort; reassurance. **~ungsmittel** *n.* sedative.

be'rühmt *a.* famous, renowned, celebrated. **~heit** *f.* fame, renown; celebrity.

be'rühr-en *v.t.* to touch; (*fig.*) to touch on, mention, allude to; to border on. **~ung** *f.* contact, touch. **~ungslinie** *f.* tangent.

be'sagen *v.t.* to say; to purport, mean, signify.

be'saiten *v.t.* to string; *zart besaitet* sensitive, touchy.

Be'samung *f.* propagation (of seed, insemination.

Be'san *m.* (-s, -e) mizzen.

be'sänftig-en *v.t.* to soften; to appease, calm, assuage, soothe. *v.r.* to calm down. **~ung** *f.* softening, appeasement; mitigation.

be'sät *a.* covered, studded; be-spangled (with stars).

Be'satz *m.* trimming, border, edge; facings; piping. **~ung** *f.* garrison; (*naut. & av.*) crew. **~ungsheer** *n.* army of occupation.

be'saufen *v.r.* (*vulg.*) to get drunk.

be'schädig-en *v.t.* to damage, injure, harm. **~t** *a.* damaged; injured, disabled. **~ung** *f.* damage, injury.

be'schaff-en *v.t.* to procure, supply. *a.* **~en sein** to be, be constituted or conditioned. **~enheit** *f.* state, condition; quality; disposition. **~ung** *f.* providing, procuring; supply.

be'schäftig-en *v.t.* to occupy, engage; to employ. **~t** *a.* busy, occupied. **~ung** *f.* occupation; work; something to do. **~ungslos** *a.* unemployed, out of work. **~ungstherapie** *f.* occupational therapy.

be'schälen *v.t.* to cover (mare).

be'schäm-en *v.t.* to make ashamed, shame; to confound, confuse. **~end** *a.* shameful. **~t** *a.* ashamed. **~ung** *f.* (feeling of) shame; confusion.

be'schatten *v.t.* to shade, overshadow; (*fig.*) to shadow.

be'schau-en *v.t.* to look at; to view, behold; to inspect; to contemplate. **~er** *m.* looker-on, spectator; inspector. **~lich** *a.* contemplative; comfortable, tranquil. **~lichkeit** *f.* contemplation; tranquillity.

Be'scheid *m.* (-es, -e) answer; information; decision; **~ geben** to inform; **gehörig ~ sagen** to give (a person) a piece of one's mind; **~ wissen** to know; to know what's what; **~ tun** to drink to the health of. **~en 1.** *v.t.* to allot; to instruct, inform; *zu sich ~en* to send for, summon; *sich ~en* to acquiesce in. **2.** *a.*

moderate; modest, unassuming; plain. **~enheit** *f.* modesty.

be'scheinen *v.t.* to shine upon.

be'scheinig-en *v.t.* to certify, attest; to acknowledge (receipt). **~ung** *f.* certificate; voucher; receipt.

be'schenken *v.t.* to present (with).

be'scher-en *v.t.* to present with; to mete out to; to give. **~ung** *f.* giving of presents; *eine schöne ~ung* a nice mess.

be'schicken *v.t.* to send to; to put in order; to exhibit (at exhibition); to charge (furnace).

be'schieden *a.* given, allotted, granted.

be'schieß-en *v.t.* to fire upon; to bombard, shell. **~ung** *f.* bombardment.

be'schiff-en *v.t.* to navigate. **~ung** *f.* navigation.

be'schimpf-en *v.t.* to insult; to abuse. **~ung** *f.* affront, insult.

be'schirm-en *v.t.* to protect, defend. **~er** *m.* protector, defender.

be'schlafen *v.t.* to lie with; (*fig.*) *etwas ~* to sleep on it.

Be'schlag *m.* (metal) mounting or cap or clasp; fittings; shoe (of horse); moisture (on glass); *in ~ nehmen, mit ~ belegen* to seize; to sequestrate, confiscate; to engross (attention); to take up (time). **~en** *v.t.* to mount; to cover; to stud; to fit (with metal, &c.); to shoe (horse). *vws.i.* to become coated (with moisture); *~en sein in* (*fig.*) to be conversant with, be well versed in, know well. **~nahme** *f.* seizure; sequestration; requisition; (*naut.*) embargo. **~nahmen** *v.t.* to seize; to commandeer; to confiscate.

be'schleichen *v.t.* to steal up to; to stalk; (*fig.*) to overcome, seize.

be'schleunig-en *v.t.* to hasten, expedite; to accelerate. **~ung** *f.* haste; acceleration.

be'schließen *v.t.* to end, close, finish, conclude, terminate; to decide, resolve on; to vote; to carry (motion).

Be'schluß *m.* end, close, con-

clusion; decision, resolution, decree; carrying (of motion). **~fähig** *a.* competent to pass resolutions; **~fähige Anzahl** quorum. **~fassung** *f.* passing of a resolution.

be'schmieren *v.t.* to smear, dirty; to spread (jam, &c.) on; *mit Butter ~* to butter; to scrawl or scribble on (paper, &c.).

be'schmutzen *v.t.* to dirty, foul, soil.

be'schneid-en *v.t.* to cut; to clip; to trim; to prune; to circumcise; (*fig.*) to curtail, reduce. **~ung** *f.* curtailment; (*relig.*) circumcision.

be'schneit *a.* snowy, snow-covered.

be'schnüffeln, beschnuppern *v.t.* to sniff at.

be'schönig-en *v.t.* to extenuate, gloss over, explain away. **~ung** *f.* excuse, extenuation.

be'schottern *v.t.* to metal (a road).

be'schränk-en *v.t.* to limit, confine; to restrict. **~t** *a.* limited; restricted; (*fig.*) narrow-minded. **~theit** *f.* narrowness; scantiness; narrow-mindedness. **~ung** *f.* limitation, restriction.

be'schreib-en *v.t.* to write upon; to describe; *Bahn ~en* (*astron.*) to revolve. **~ung** *f.* description.

be'schreiten *v.t.* to walk on; to take (road, &c.).

be'schrift-en *v.t.* to letter; to inscribe. **~ung** *f.* lettering; inscription; caption.

be'schuhen *v.t.* to shoe (horse).

be'schuldig-en *v.t.* to accuse, charge with. **~ung** *f.* accusation, charge.

be'schummeln *v.t.* (*colloq.*) to cheat.

Be'schuß *m.* bombardment.

be'schützen *v.t.* to protect, defend. **~er** *m.* protector, defender.

be'schwatzen *v.t.* to persuade, talk (a person) into.

Be'schwer, Be'schwerde *f.* (-, -den) burden; hardship, trouble; infirmity; complaint, grievance; *~de führen* to lodge a complaint.

be'schwer-en *v.t.* to weight; to burden; to lie heavy on; (*fig.*) to trouble. *v.r.* to complain (about).

be'schwichtigen *v.t.* to calm, pacify, appease; to compose (quarrel).

be'schwindeln *v.t.* to swindle, cheat.

be'schwingt *a.* winged, on wings; speedy; lofty.

be'schwipst *a.* (*colloq.*) tipsy.

be'schwör-en *v.t.* to affirm on oath; to implore; to raise (spirits); to exorcize. **~er** *m.* conjurer; exorcist. **~ung** *f.* confirmation by oath; conjuration; exorcism.

be'seel-en *v.t.* to animate; to inspire. **~ung** *f.* animation.

be'sehen *v.t.* to look at; to inspect.

be'seitig-en *v.t.* to set aside; to abolish; to remove; to do away with. **~ung** *f.* removal; elimination.

be'seligen *v.t.* to make happy, fill with bliss.

Besen (be:z-) *m.* (-s, -) broom. **~stiel** *m.* broomstick. [BESOM]

be'sessen *pp.* of **besitzen**. *a.* possessed.

be'setz-en *v.t.* to trim; to set; to fill; to occupy; to man. **~t** *a.* occupied, crowded; full up (*tel., &c.*) engaged. **~tzeichen** *n.* engaged signal. **~ung** *f.* occupation; filling (of post); cast or casting (of play); (*mus.*) complement.

be'sichtig-en *v.t.* to view; to inspect; to visit (the sights). **~ung** *f.* view; inspection; sight-seeing.

be'sied-eln *v.t.* to settle; to settle in; to colonize; *dicht~elt* densely populated. **~(e)lung** *f.* colonization; settlement.

be'siegeln *v.t.* to seal.

be'sieg-en *v.t.* to conquer, overcome; to beat, defeat. **~er** *m.* conqueror, victor.

be'singen *v.t.* to praise, laud, celebrate.

be'sinn-en *v.r.* to consider, reflect, think of; to remember, recollect; *sich eines Besseren ~en* to think

better of. **~lich** *a.* contemplative; thoughtful. **~ung** *f.* consciousness; recollection; reflection. **~ungslos** *a.* unconscious, insensible; (*fig.*) mad.

Be'sitz *m.* possession; property; estate. **~anzeigend** *a.* (*gram.*) possessive. **~en** *v.t.* to possess, own; to have, be endowed with. **~er** *m.* proprietor, owner. **~nahme** *f.* taking possession of; occupation. **~tum** *n.* property. **~ung** *f.* possession; property; estate. **~urkunde** *f.* title-deed.

be'soffen *pp.* of **besaufen**. *a.* drunk.

be'sohlen *v.t.* to sole.

be'sold-en *v.t.* to pay a salary. **~ung** *f.* pay, salary.

be'sonder *a.* particular, special; peculiar, exceptional; separate. **~heit** *f.* particularity; peculiarity; speciality. **~s** *adv.* especially, particularly; exceptionally; chiefly; separately.

be'sonnen *pp.* of **besinnen**. *a.* sensible; cautious; discreet. **~heit** *f.* prudence, discretion, circumspection.

be'sonnt *a.* sunlit, sunny.

be'sorg-en *v.t.* to take care (of); to fetch, procure, provide; to see to, manage; to do, execute. *v.i.* to fear, apprehend. **~nis** *f.* fear, alarm. **~t** *a.* solicitous, anxious, apprehensive. **~theit** *f.* anxiety, uneasiness; concern. **~ung** *f.* care; management; purchase, commission; **~ungen machen** to go shopping.

be'spannen *v.t.* to harness to; to stretch; to span; to string (instrument); *mit Pferden bespannt* horse-drawn.

be'spiegeln *v.r.* to look at oneself in the glass; (*fig.*) to admire oneself.

be'spitzeln *v.t.* to spy on.

be'spotten, **be'spötteln** *v.t.* to ridicule.

be'sprech-en *v.t.* to discuss, talk over; to criticize, review (book); to conjure (spirits). **~er** *v.t.* confer (with). **~ung** *f.* discussion; conference; consultation; criticism; review; conjuration.

be'sprengen *v.t.* to besprinkle, water.

be'spritzen *v.t.* to splash; to spray.

be'spülen *v.t.* to wash (against).

besser *a. comp.* better; *umso ~* so much the better.

besser-n *v.t.* to make better; to mend. *v.r.* to improve, get better; to reform. ~ung *f.* improvement; recovery; *gute ~ung* speedy recovery. ~ungs-anstalt *f.* reformatory, remand home.

best *a. sup.* best; *der erste ~e* the first comer; *aufs ~e* as well as possible; *zum ~en geben* to treat; to entertain; *zum ~en der Armen* for the benefit of the poor; *zum ~en haben* to tease, rag. ~enfalls *adv.* at best. ~ens *adv.* as well as possible.

be'stall-en *v.t.* to appoint (to); to invest (with). ~ung *f.* appointment; investiture.

bestand¹ *imperf. of* bestehen.

Be'stand² *m.* duration, continuance; stability; stock, store; amount; cash (in hand); balance; *von ~ sein* to last. ~(s)auf-nahme *f.* stock-taking. ~teil *m.* ingredient; constituent; component.

be'ständig *a.* constant, continual, permanent; steady; stable, settled, steadfast. ~keit *f.* constancy; stability; steadiness.

be'stärken *v.t.* to support; to confirm.

be'stätig-en *v.t.* to corroborate, confirm; to ratify (treaty); to acknowledge (letter). *v.r.* to be confirmed, prove true. ~ung *f.* confirmation; ratification; acknowledgement.

be'statt-en *v.t.* to bury, inter. ~ung *f.* burial, interment, funeral.

be'stauben *v.t. & i.* to cover with dust; to get dusty.

be'stäuben *v.t.* to dust; to powder; (*bot.*) to pollinate.

be'stech-en *v.t.* to bribe, corrupt. ~end *a.* fascinating, brilliant. ~lich *a.* corrupt. ~ung *f.* bribery, corruption.

Be'steck *n.* (-s, -e) knife, fork, and spoon; (*med.*) set of instruments, instrument case. ~en *v.t.* to stick (with pins); to plant (seedlings, &c.).

be'stehen *v.t.* to go through, undergo, stand; to overcome; to pass (exam.); *nicht ~* to fail (exam.). *v.i.* to exist; to continue, last; *~ auf* to insist on; *~ aus* to consist of; *bestanden mit* planted or covered with. ~d *a.* existing.

be'stehlen *v.t.* to rob, steal from.

be'steig-en *v.t.* to climb; to mount; to board (ship, &c.); to ascend (throne). ~ung *f.* ascent; mounting; accession (to throne).

be'stell-en *v.t.* to arrange, set in order; to till, cultivate (land); to do (errands); to deliver (letter); to send (greetings); to order (goods); to book (seats); to appoint; *zu sich ~en* to send for; *es ist schlecht um ihn ~t* he is in a bad way. ~er *m.* customer. ~ung *f.* management; tillage; delivery; message, order, commission; appointment. ~zettel *m.* order-form.

be'sternt *a.* decorated with orders.

be'steuer-n *v.t.* to tax. ~ung *f.* taxation.

besti'alisch *a.* bestial; beastly.

Bestie *f.* (-, -n) beast, brute.

be'stimm-en *v.t.* to decide; to determine; to fix; to define; to appoint; to induce (person to do something); *~en über* to dispose of. ~t *a.* decided, determined; fixed; firm, peremptory; destined (by fate); certain; (*gram.*) definite; (*naut.*) bound (for). *adv.* definitely, surely, certainly. ~theit *f.* determination; certainty; precision. ~ung *f.* determination; definition; destiny; *gesetzliche ~ung* regulation. ~ungsort *m.* destination.

be'stirnt *a.* starry.

be'stoßen *v.t.* to knock against; to damage.

be'straf-en *v.t.* to punish; to sentence. ~ung *f.* punishment; penalty.

be'strahl-en *v.t.* to shine upon; (*med.*) to expose to X-rays.

~ung f. irradiation; radiation; X-ray treatment.

be'streb-en v.r. to endeavour. ~en n., ~ung f. endeavour, attempt; aspiration.

be'streichen v.t. to spread over, smear; (mil.) to rake, sweep.

be'streiten v.t. to dispute; to deny; to defray the expenses, pay for; Gespräch ~ to do all the talking.

be'streuen v.t. to strew, sprinkle over.

be'stricken v.t. (fig.) to ensnare; to captivate.

be'stücken v.t. to arm with guns.

be'stürmen v.t. to storm; (also fig.) to assail; mit Bitten ~ to implore.

be'stürz-en v.t. to disconcert, perplex. ~t a. disconcerted, dismayed. ~ung f. alarm, consternation.

Be'such m. (-es, -e) visit; visitor(s), company; attendance. ~en v.t. to visit, call on; to attend (lecture). ~er m. visitor, caller, guest; frequenter; (pl.) audience.

be'sudeln v.t. to dirty, soil.

be'tagt a. aged.

be'tasten v.t. to touch; to handle, finger.

be'tätig-en v.t. to set in motion; to practise. v.r. to work, take an active part in. ~ung f. operation; activity; participation.

be'täub-en v.t. to deafen; to stun; to narcotize; (med.) to anaesthetize; (fig.) to deaden; to stupefy. ~ung f. deafening; numbness; torpor; stupor; anaesthesia. ~ungsmittel n. anaesthetic; narcotic; dope.

be'taut a. dewy.

be'teilig-en v.t. to give a share (in). v.r. to take part (in), join; to take an interest (in); ~t sein to participate; to have a share (in); die ~ten the parties concerned. ~ung f. share; participation; support; interest; attendance (at lecture).

bet-en v.i. & t. to pray; to say one's prayers. ~er m. worshipper.

be'teuer-n r.t. to aver, assert; to protest. ~ung f. assertion; protestation.

be'titeln v.t. to call; to entitle.

Be'ton m. (-s) concrete. ~'ieren v.t. to build with concrete.

be'ton-en v.t. to stress, accent; to emphasize. ~ung f. stress, accentuation; emphasis.

be'tören v.t. to delude; to infatuate.

Be'tracht m. in ~ kommen to come into question; in ~ ziehen to take into consideration; nicht in ~ kommen to be out of the question. ~en v.t. to look at; to examine; to consider. ~er m. onlooker, spectator. ~ung f. view; contemplation; consideration; meditation.

be'trächtlich a. considerable.

Be'trag m. (-s, ⁀e) amount, sum, total. ~en v.i. to amount to. v.r. to behave oneself. subst. n. behaviour, conduct.

be'trauen v.t. to entrust (with).

be'trauern v.t. to mourn for; to deplore.

Be'treff m. in ~ with regard to. ~s prep. concerning, as to.

be'treffen v.t. to befall; to concern; to surprise (a person); was mich betrifft so far as I am concerned, as for me. ~d a. concerning; concerned, in question; respective.

be'treiben v.t. to pursue (calling); to carry on (business); to prosecute (studies); to hasten, urge on, push forward. subst. n. auf ~ at the instigation (of).

be'treten v.t. to walk on, tread on; to enter. a. embarrassed, disconcerted.

be'treuen v.t. to take care of.

Be'trieb m. management; working; firm; service; trade; works, plant; (fig.) bustle, activity; in ~ sein to be working; außer ~ not working; closed down; in ~ setzen to start, set in motion. ~sam a. industrious; officious. ~samkeit f. industry, activity. ~skapital n., ~smittel n. pl. working capital. ~sklima n. atmosphere amongst firm's employees. ~skosten pl. working expenses; operating costs. ~sleiter *m*. manager. ~smaterial *n*. rolling-stock. ~sordnung *f*. regulations. ~srat *m*. works council. ~ssicher *a*. safe to operate, foolproof. ~sstoff *m*. petrol; fuel. ~störung *f*. breakdown. ~swirtschaft *f*. industrial economics; business management. ~szelle *f*. (*pol*.) factory-cell.

be'trinken *v.r*. to get drunk.

be'troffen *pp*. of betreffen. *a*. amazed, perplexed, taken aback.

be'trüb-en *v.t*. to grieve, distress. ~lich *a*. sad. ~nis *f*. grief, distress. ~t *a*. distressed, dejected, sad; sorry (for).

Be'trug *m*. (-s) deception; fraud; swindle.

be'trüg-en *v.t*. to deceive; to defraud; to trick (out of). ~er *m*. deceiver, cheat, impostor. ~e'rei *f*. fraud; swindle. ~erisch *a*. deceitful, fraudulent.

be'trunken *a*. drunk, intoxicated.

Bett *n*. (-es, -en) bed; *das* ~ *hüten* to be confined to bed. ~bezug *m*. bed-linen. ~decke *f*. counterpane; bedspread; quilt; blanket. ~lägrig *a*. bedridden, confined to bed. ~laken, ~tuch *n*. sheet. ~statt, ~stelle *f*. bedstead. ~wäsche *f*., ~zeug *n*. bed-clothes, bed-linen.

Bettel *m*. (-s) trash; rubbish. ~arm *a*. desperately poor. ~brief *m*. begging-letter. ~bruder *m*. beggar. ~ei *f*. begging. ~mönch *m*. mendicant friar. ~pack, ~volk *n*. beggars, paupers. ~stab *m*. *an den* ~*stab bringen* to reduce to beggary.

betteln *v.i*. to beg (for).

betten *v.t*. to make up a bed; to put to bed.

Bettler *m*. (-s, -) beggar.

be'tulich *a*. busy; attentive.

be'tupfen *v.t*. to dab; to spot; to dot.

beug-en *v.t*. to bend, bow; (*gram*.) to inflect. *v.r*. to humble oneself; to submit to. ~sam *a*. pliant, flexible. ~ung *f*. flexion; inflexion. [BOW]

Beule *f*. (-, -n) bump, lump, swelling; dent; boss. ~npest *f*. bubonic plague.

be'unruhig-en *v.t*. to disturb; to alarm, upset; to harass. ~ung *f*. disturbance; uneasiness, alarm.

be'urkunden *v.t*. to authenticate.

be'urlaub-en *v.t*. to grant leave of absence. *v.r*. to take leave. ~t *a*. absent on leave.

be'urteil-en *v.t*. to judge; to criticize. ~er *m*. judge; critic. ~ung *f*. judgement; criticism; review.

Beute *f*. (-, -n) booty, spoil; prey. ~zug *m*. raid.

Beutel *m*. (-s, -) bag; pouch; purse; (*med*.) cyst; sac. ~n *v.t*. to shake. *v.r*. to pucker, bag. ~schneider *m*. pickpocket. ~tier *n*. marsupial.

be'völker-n *v.t*. to people, populate; *spärlich* ~*t* sparsely populated. ~ung *f*. population; inhabitants. ~ ~sdichte *f*. density of population.

be'vollmächtig-en *v.t*. to empower, authorize. ~te(r) *m*. deputy; plenipotentiary; (*leg*.) attorney. ~ung *f*. authorization; power of attorney.

be'vor *conj*. & *sep. pref*. before.

be'vor-munden *v.t*. to act as guardian; (*fig*.) to patronize; to domineer over. ~mundung *f*. guardianship; tutelage. ~rechten *v.t*. to privilege. ~stehen *v.i*. to be imminent, impend; to be in store. ~zugen *v.t*. to prefer, favour. ~zugung *f*. preference; favouritism.

be'wachen *v.t*. to watch over; to guard.

be'wachsen *a*. overgrown (with).

be'waffn-en *v.t*. to arm. ~ung *f*. arming; armament; equipment.

be'wahr-en *v.t*. to preserve, keep; to guard, protect (from); *i* not a bit of it! ~heiten *v.t*. to verify. *v.r*. to prove true.

be'währ-en *v.t*. to confirm. *v.r*. to prove true; to stand the test. ~t *a*. tried; approved; trustworthy. ~ungsfrist *f*. period of probation.

be'waldet *a*. wooded.

be'wältig-en *v.t.* to master; to overcome; to finish.

be'wandert *a.* versed, experienced, proficient (in).

Be'wandtnis *f.* case, state (of affairs), condition.

be'wässern *v.t.* to water; to irrigate.

be'weg-en *v.t.* to move; to stir. *v.t. st.* to induce (person to do something). *v.r.* to move, move about; to take exercise; to range. **~grund** *m.* motive. **~lich** *a.* movable; mobile; nimble, quick; lively; touching. **~lichkeit** *f.* mobility; agility; nimbleness; versatility, sprightliness. **~t** *a.* agitated, troubled, *(fig.)* touched; **~te** See rough sea. **~ung** *f.* movement, stir; commotion, motion; exercise; emotion, agitation. **~ungskrieg** *m.* mobile warfare. **~ungslehre** *f.* mechanics; kinetics. **~unglos** *a.* motionless, immobile. **~ungsspiele** *n.pl.* outdoor games.

be'wehrt *a.* armed.

be'weibt *a.* married.

be'weihräuchern *v.t.* to cense; *(fig.)* to flatter, butter up.

be'weinen *v.t.* to lament, bewail, weep for.

Be'weis *m.(-es,-e)* proof; evidence. **~ erbringen** to furnish proof. **~aufnahme** *f.* argumentation; hearing of evidence. **~bar** *a.* demonstrable, provable. **~führung** *f.* demonstration; argumentation; reasoning. **~grund** *m.* argument. **~kräftig** *a.* conclusive; convincing.

be'weisen *v.t. st.* to prove; to demonstrate.

be'wenden *v.i. es ~ lassen bei* to acquiesce in. *subst. n. dabei muß es sein ~ haben* there the matter must rest.

be'werb-en *v.r.* to apply (for); to compete (for); to court, woo. **~er** *m.* applicant, candidate; competitor; suitor. **~ung** *f.* application; *(sport.)* entry; courtship, wooing.

be'werfen *v.t.* to throw at; to plaster.

be'werkstelligen *v.t.* to effect,

accomplish, manage.

be'werten *v.t.* to assess; to value. **~ung** *f.* valuation; assessment; rating.

bewies *imperf.* of **beweisen.**

be'willig-en *v.t.* to consent to, grant, concede. **~ung** *f.* concession; permit; grant; licence.

be'willkommnen *v.t.* to welcome.

be'wirken *v.t.* to effect, cause, bring about.

be'wirt-en *v.t.* to entertain. **~schaften** *v.t.* to manage, conduct; to work upon. **~schaftung** *f.* management; control; regulation. **~ung** *f.* entertainment; reception; treat; food.

be'witzeln *v.t.* to chaff, ridicule.

bewog *imperf.* of **bewegen.**

be'wohn-bar *a.* inhabitable. **~en** *v.t.* to inhabit, live in. **~er** *m.* inhabitant, resident; inmate.

be'wölk-en *v.t.* to cloud over. *v.r.* to become overcast or cloudy. **~ung** *f.* cloud; cloudiness.

Be'wunder-er *m.* (-ers, -er) admirer. **~n** *v.t.* to admire. **~nswürdig** *a.* admirable. **~ung** *f.* admiration.

Be'wurf *m.* plastering; plaster.

be'wußt *a.* conscious (of); known, in question; deliberate; *sich einer Sache ~ sein* to be conscious or aware of something. **~los** *a.* unconscious; senseless. **~losigkeit** *f.* unconsciousness; insensibility. **~sein** *n.* consciousness; knowledge.

be'zahl-en *v.t.* to pay; *sich ~t machen* to pay, be lucrative. **~ung** *f.* payment.

be'zähmen *v.t.* to tame; *(fig.)* to restrain, check, control.

be'zaubern *v.t.* to bewitch, enchant; to charm. **~d** *a.* charming; enchanting.

be'zechen *v.r.* to get drunk.

be'zeichn-en *v.t.* to mark, denote, label; to call, term. **~end** *a.* characteristic. **~ung** *f.* marking, mark, sign; notation; name.

be'zeig-en *v.t.* to show, manifest, express. **~ung** *f.* manifestation.

be'zeug-en *v.t.* to attest; to testify (to), certify. **~ung** *f.* attestation; testimony.

be'zichtigen *v.t.* to charge with; to accuse of.

be'zieh-bar *a.* habitable; obtainable. ~en *v.t.* to cover; to change (the bed-linen); to string (instrument); to move into (house); to enter (university); (*mil.*) to mount (guard); to receive, draw (salary); to obtain, buy (goods); to take in (newspaper); to apply (to); to refer (to), relate (to); to become overcast or cloudy. ~er *m.* subscriber; customer. ~ung *f.* connexion, relation; reference; respect; *in jeder ~ ~* in every respect. ~ungsweise *adv.* respectively; relatively; or, or else.

be'ziffern *v.t.* to number. *v.r.* to amount (to).

Be'zirk *m.* (-s, -e) district; borough; circuit; (policeman's) beat.

Be'zug *m.* covering, cover, case; supply (of goods); (*pl.*) income; salary; fees; subscription; *in ~ auf* with regard to, as to; *~ nehmen auf* to refer to. ~nahme *f. unter ~nahme auf* with reference to. ~sbedingungen *f.pl.* terms of purchase; terms of delivery. ~spreis *m.* buying price; rate of subscription. ~squelle *f.* source of supply. ~sschein *m.* coupon; indent form.

be'züglich *a.* relative to. *prep.* respecting, referring to.

be'zwecken *v.t.* to aim at, intend.

be'zweifeln *v.t.* to doubt.

be'zwing-en *v.t.* to conquer, vanquish, overcome. *v.r.* to control oneself. ~ung *f.* conquest.

Bibel *f.* (-, -n) Bible, Scripture. ~auslegung *f.* exegesis. ~fest *a.* well up in the Bible. ~kunde *f.* biblical research. ~spruch *m.* text. ~stelle *f.* biblical passage.

Biber *m.* (-s, -) beaver.

Biblio'graph *m.* (-en, -en) bibliographer. ~ie *f.* bibliography.

Biblio'thek *f.* (-, -en) library. ~ar *m.* (-ars, -are) librarian.

biblisch *a.* biblical, scriptural.

Bickbeere *f.* bilberry.

bieder *a.* honest, honourable, upright; commonplace. ~keit *f.*

probity, honesty, respectability. ~mann *m.* honest man.

bieg-en *v.t. & r. st.* to bend, bow; to curve. *vws.i.* to turn (the corner). *subst. n. auf ~en und Brechen* by hook or by crook. ~sam *a.* flexible, pliant; supple; (*fig.*) yielding. ~ung *f.* bend, turn, turning, curve; winding. [BOW]

Biene *f.* (-, -n) bee. ~nkorb, ~nstock *m.* beehive. ~nzüchter *m.* bee-keeper.

Bier *n.* (-es, -e) beer; *helles ~* pale beer; *~ vom Faß* draught. ~brauer *m.* brewer. ~brauerei *f.* brewery. ~eifer *m.* excessive zeal. ~filz *m.* mat. ~krug *m.*, ~seidel *n.* beer-mug.

Biese *f.* (-, -n) piping (on uniform).

Biest *n.* (-es, -er) beast; brute.

bieten *v.t. st.* to offer; to bid; *sich alles ~ lassen* to put up with everything.

Biga'mie *f.* (-, -n) bigamy.

bi'gott *a.* bigoted.

Bi'lanz *f.* (-, -en) balance; *aktive ~* credit balance. ~prüfer *m.* auditor.

Bild *n.* (-t) (-es, -er) image, figure, picture; illustration; portrait, likeness; representation; description; metaphor, simile; idea; sight; *lebendes ~* tableau; *im ~e sein* to see, understand. ~band *n.* film strip. ~gerät *n.* video tape recorder. ~bericht *m.* documentary report. ~feld *n.* (*phot.*) field of vision. ~fläche *f.* surface screen; perspective plane; *auf der ~fläche erscheinen* to appear upon the scene. ~funk *m.* television. ~haft *a.* plastic. ~hauer *m.* sculptor. ~hauerei *f.* sculpture. ~karte *f.* relief map. ~kraft *f.* creative power. ~lich *a.* pictorial; (*fig.*) figurative, metaphorical. ~ner *m.* artist; pedagogue. ~nis *n.* image, portrait, likeness, picture. ~sam *a.* receptive, capable of development; flexible; adaptable. ~säule *f.* statue. ~schirm *m.* (tele)screen. ~schnitzer *m.* wood-carver. ~schön *a.* very beautiful. ~seite *f.* face; head (of coin). ~stock *m.*, ~stöckel *n.* wayside shrine. ~streifen *m.* film strip. ~sucher *m.* view finder. ~telegraphie *f.* phototelegraphy. ~wand *f.* projection screen. ~werfer *m.* (slide) projector. ~werk *n.* sculpture.

bilden *v.t.* to form, shape, fashion; to mould, model; (*educ.*) to educate, cultivate, train, improve; to constitute, to be. *v.r.* to form; to arise; to improve one's mind. ~d *a.* formative; instructive; ~de Kunst Fine Arts.

Bilder-bogen *m.* sheet of pictures. ~buch *n.* picture-book. ~dienst *m.* idolatry; photo service. ~rätsel *n.* picture puzzle. ~schrift *f.* pictorial writing. ~sprache *f.* metaphorical language. ~stürmer *m.* iconoclast.

Bildung *f.* (-, -en) formation; forming; constitution; shape; structure; organization; education, culture; creation; coinage (of word). ~sanstalt *f.* educational establishment; school.

Billard (-jart) *n.* (-s, -e) billiards. ~kugel *f.* ball. ~stock *m.* cue.

Bi'llett (-jet) *n.* (-s, -e) ticket; note. ~ausgabe *f.* booking-office.

billig *a.* just, reasonable, fair; cheap, moderate. ~en *v.t.* to approve of; to sanction. ~erweise *adv.* in fairness; justly. ~keit *f.* justice, reasonableness, fairness; cheapness. ~ung *f.* approval, consent; sanction.

Bilsenkraut *n.* henbane.

bimmeln *v.i.* to tinkle, ring.

Bimsstein *m.* pumice-stone. [L]

bin 1 *pers. sing. pres. of* sein.

Binde-f. (-e, -en) band; badge; tie, fillet; (*med.*) ligature; sling; sanitary towel. ~egewebe *n.* connective tissue. ~eglied *n.* connecting link. ~ehaut *f.* conjunctiva. ~ehautentzündung *f.* conjunctivitis, pink-eye. ~emittel *n.* binding agent; cement. ~estrich *m.* hyphen. ~ewort *n.* conjunction. ~faden *m.* string. ~ung *f.* binding; (*mus.*) ligature, slur; (*fig.*) obligation; bonds.

binden *v.t. st.* to bind; to tie, fasten; to hoop (cask); to

thicken (soup, &c.); (*fig.*) to tie down. *v.r.* to feel bound, compelled (to). ~d *a.* binding, obligatory.

binnen *prep.* within. ~fischerei *f.* freshwater fishing. ~gewässer *n.* inland water(s). ~hafen *m.* inland harbour, basin. ~handel *m.* inland trade. ~land *n.* inland, interior. ~meer *n.* landlocked sea. ~reim *m.* internal rhyme. ~schiffahrt *f.* inland navigation. ~verkehr *m.* inland traffic.

Bi'nom *n.,* ~isch *a.* binomial.

Binse *f.* (-, -n) rush. ~nwahrheit *f.* platitude. [BENT]

Bio'graph (-a:-) *m.* (-en, -en) biographer. ~ie *f.* biography. ~isch *a.* biographical.

Bio'log-e *m.* (-en, -en) biologist. ~ie *f.* biology. ~isch *a.* biological.

birgst, birgt 2 *& 3 pers. sing. pres. of* bergen.

Birk-e *f.* (-e, -en) birch tree. ~en *a.* birchen. ~enreis *n.* birchrod. ~hahn *m.* cock, heath-cock. ~huhn *n.* moor-hen.

Birn-baum *m.* pear-tree. ~e *f.* pear; (*elcctr.*) bulb.

birst 2 *& 3 pers. sing. pres. of* bersten.

bis *prep.* to; up to; down to; till, until; as far as; between; or; except; ~ auf Weiteres for the present; ~ zwei ~ drei Pfund two to three pounds; alle ~ auf einen all except one. *conj.* till, until; ~ 'her *adv.* hitherto, till now. wie ~~ as before. ~herig *a.* up to now, until now, hitherto existing. ~'lang *adv.* so far, as yet. ~'weilen *adv.* sometimes, occasionally.

Bisam *m.* (-s, -e) musk.

Bischof *m.* (-s, *̂e*) bishop. ~smütze *f.* mitre. ~ssitz *m.* see. ~sstab *m.* crosier.

bischöflich *a.* episcopal.

Bis'kuit (-kvi:t) *m.* (-s, -e) biscuit; rusk; sponge-cake.

biß¹ *imperf. of* beißen.

Biß² *m.* (Biss-es, -e) bite; sting.

bißchen *indecl. a. & subst. n.* a little bit.

Biss-en *m.* (-ens, -en) morsel, bite, mouthful, tit-bit. **~enweise** *adv.* bit by bit, in bits. **~ig** *a.* biting, snappish; (*fig.*) cutting, sarcastic. **~igkeit** *f.* snappishness; sarcasm.

bist 2 *pers. sing. pres. of* sein.

Bistum *n.* (-s, ⸚er) bishopric; diocese.

Bitt-e *f.* (-e, -en) request; entreaty; prayer. **~gang** *m.* procession of pilgrims. **~gesuch** *n.*, **~schrift** *f.* petition. **~steller** *m.* petitioner. [BEAD]

bitten *v.t. & i. st.* to ask (for); to beg; to implore; to intercede (for); *zu Gast ~* to invite; *bitte* please; don't mention it; *wie, bitte?* I beg your pardon? [BID]

bitter *a.* bitter; biting; severe. **~böse** *a.* very angry; very wicked. **~feind** *a.* very hostile. **~keit** *f.* bitterness; sarcasm. **~lich** *a.* bitterish. *adv.* bitterly. **~nis** *f.* bitterness. **~salz** *n.* Epsom salt.

Biwak (-vak) *n.* (-s, -s) bivouac. **~ieren** *v.i.* to bivouac.

bi'zarr (-tsar) *a.* bizarre.

Blachfeld *n.* open field.

blaffen *v.i.* to bark.

bläh-en *v.t. & r.* to inflate; to swell, swell out. *v.i.* to cause flatulence. **~ung** *f.* flatulence, wind. [BLOW]

blaken (-a:-) *v.i.* to smoke.

Bla'mage (-ma:ʒə) *f.* (-, -n) disgrace, shame. [F]

bla'mieren *v.t.* to expose to ridicule; to compromise. *v.r.* to disgrace oneself; to make a fool of oneself.

blank *a.* bright, shining, polished, clean; bare; *~ ziehen* to draw one's sword. [BLANK]

blanko *a.* blank. **~vollmacht** *f.* unlimited power.

Bläschen (blɛːsçən) *n.* (-s, -) bubble; (*med.*) pustule; pimple; blister.

Blase (-zə) *f.* (-, -n) bubble; blister; bleb (in glass); (Harn)**~** bladder. **~nziehend** *a.* blistering.

blas-en *v.t. & i. st.* to blow; (*mus.*) to play, sound. **~ebalg** *m.* bellows. **~instrument** *n.*

wind-instrument. **~musik** *f.* brass band. **~rohr** *n.* blowpipe; pea-shooter.

Bläser *m.* (-s, -) player on wind-instrument.

bla'siert (-zi:rt) *a.* blasé.

Blasphem-'ie *f.* (-ie, -ien) blasphemy. **~isch** *a.* blasphemous.

blaß *a.* pale; *keine blasse Ahnung* not the foggiest idea.

Blässe *f.* (-) paleness; pallor.

Blatt *n.* (-es, ⸚er) leaf; petal; blade (of sword, oar); sheet (of paper); (news)paper; *ein unbeschriebenes ~* (*fig.*) an unknown quantity; innocent; *kein ~ vor den Mund nehmen* to speak plainly, not to mince matters; *vom ~ singen* to sing at sight; *das ~ hat sich gewendet* the tide has turned. **~gold** *n.* gold-leaf. **~grün** *n.* chlorophyll. **~laus** *f.* plant-louse; green-fly. **~metall** *n.* sheet metal. **~pflanze** *f.* foliage plant. **~salat** *m.* young lettuce. **~stiel** *m.* stalk. stem. **~werk** *n.* foliage. [BLADE]

Blatter *f.* (-, -n) blister; (*pl.*) small-pox. **~narbe** *f.* pock-mark. **~narbig** *a.* pock-marked. **~nimpfung** *f.* vaccination. [BLADDER]

blätter-n *v.i.* to turn over the leaves. **~teig** *m.* puff-pastry.

blau *a.* blue; **~ machen** to take a day off; **~ sein** (*fig.*) to be drunk; *mit einem ~en Auge davonkommen* to get off lightly; *ins ~e hinein reden* to talk at random; *Fahrt ins ~e* mystery tour, journey into the unknown. **~äugig** *a.* blue-eyed. **~beere** *f.* bilberry. **~blütig** *a.* aristocratic. **~felchen** *n.* blue char. **~fuchs** *m.* arctic fox. **~kraut** *n.* red cabbage. **~meise** *f.* tomtit. **~papier** *n.* carbon paper. **~pause** *f.* blueprint. **~säure** *f.* prussic acid. **~stift** *m.* blue-pencil. **~strumpf** *m.* blue-stocking.

Bläu-e *f.* (-e) blueness. **~en** *v.t.* to blue (linen). **~lich** *a.* bluish.

blauen *v.i.* to be blue.

Blech (-ɛç) *n.* (-es, -e) tin; sheet metal; *gewalztes ~* rolled metal;

(*fig.*) nonsense. **~büchse** *f.* tin box. **~ern** *a.* tin. **~gefäß**, **~geschirr** *n.* (*mil.*) mess-tin. **~musik** *f.* brass band. **~schmied** *m.* tinsmith.

blechen *v.t.* (*colloq.*) to pay, fork out.

blecken *v.t.* *Zähne* ~ to show one's teeth.

Blei *n.* (*-es, -e*) lead; (*naut.*) plummet. *m.* pencil. **~bergwerk** *n.* lead-mine. **~ern** *a.* leaden. **~gewicht** *n.* dead weight. **~kugel** *f.* bullet. **~säure** *f.* plumbic acid. **~soldat** *m.* tin-soldier. **~stift** *m.* pencil. **~stifthalter** *m.* p.-holder. **~stiftspitzer** *m.* p.-sharpener. **~wage** *f.* plumb-line. **~weiß** *n.* white lead.

Bleibe *f.* abode, dwelling, home. (*colloq.*) shelter, hostel; (*sl.*) digs.

bleiben *vws.i. st.* to remain, stay; to continue, keep, last; *es bleibt dabei* agreed; *sich gleich ~* to be always the same; *stehen ~* to stop; to stand still; *fern ~* to stay away; *etwas ~ lassen* to let alone; *dabei ~* to stick to this; *bei der Sache ~* to keep to the point. **~d** *a.* permanent; abiding; lasting. [LEAVE]

bleich *a.* pale, wan, pallid; faint; faded. **~e** *f.* bleaching-ground. **~mittel** *n.* bleaching agent; bl. powder. **~sucht** *f.* anaemia. **~süchtig** *a.* anaemic. [BLEAK]

bleichen *v.t.* to whiten; to bleach.

Blend-e *f.* (*-e, -en*) sham window; sham door; blind; (*phot., &c.*) diaphragm, shutter; stop; (*min.*) blende; (*naut.*) dead-lights. **~er** *m.* (*fig.*) bluffer. **~laterne** *f.* dark-lantern, bull's-eye. **~leder** *n.* blinker. **~scheibe** *f.* diaphragm. **~werk** *n.* delusion, illusion; mirage; deception.

blenden *v.t.* to blind; to dazzle; (*fig.*) to deceive, hoodwink. *v.i.* to glare, dazzle. **~d** *a.* dazzling; brilliant; (*colloq.*) marvellous.

Blesse *f.* (*-, -n*) blaze; horse with white spot.

bleuen *v.t.* to beat.

blich *imperf.* of bleichen.

Blick *m.* (*-es, -e*) look, glance,

gaze; view; *flüchtiger* ~ glimpse; *feindlicher* ~ glare; *böser* ~ evil eye; *auf den ersten* ~ at first sight. **~fang** *m.* (advertising) stunt. **~feld** *n.* field of vision. **~feuer** *n.* signal-fire; flash-light. **~punkt** *m.* point of sight, visual point.

blicken *v.i.* to look; *sich ~ lassen* to appear; *tief ~ lassen* to be an eye-opener.

blieb *imperf.* of bleiben.

blies *imperf.* of blasen.

blind *a.* blind; (*of glass*) dim, dull; **~er Gehorsam** implicit obedience; **~er Lärm** false alarm; **~er Passagier** deadhead; *to fire away (on ship)*; ~ *schießen* to fire blank cartridges; ~ *schreiben* to type by touch. **~darm** *m.* appendix. **~darmentzündung** *f.* appendicitis. **~ekuh** *f.* blind-man's-buff. **~enanstalt** *f.* blind-asylum. **~endruck** *m.*, **~enschrift** *f.* braille. **~gänger** *m.* dud; misfire. **~heit** *f.* blindness. **~lings** *adv.* blindly, blindfold. **~schleiche** *f.* slow-worm.

blink-en *v.i.* to glitter, gleam, twinkle; to signal (with lamps). **~feuer**, **~zeichen** *n.* intermittent light; revolving light; lamp signal. [BLINK]

blinzeln (*-ts-*) *v.i.* to blink, wink.

Blitz *m.* (*-es, -e*) lightning; flash. **~ableiter** *m.* lightning-conductor. **~blank** *a.* very bright, shining. **~licht** *n.* flash-light. **~sauber** *a.* spruce; shining. **~schlag**, **~strahl** *m.* flash of lightning. **~schnell** *a.* like a flash, quick as lightning.

blitzen *v.i.* to lighten, emit lightning; to flash, sparkle.

Block *m.* (*-es, "-e*) block; log; (paper) pad; stocks; bar (of soap). **~adebrecher** *m.* blockade-runner. **~haus** *n.* log-hut; blockhouse. **~schrift** *f.* block-letters. **~stelle** *f.* signal-box. **~wagen** *m.* truck.

blo'ckieren *v.t.* to block up; to obstruct; to blockade; to lock.

blöd-e *a.* imbecile; shy, timid. **~igkeit** *f.* coyness, bashfulness. **~sinn** *m.* imbecility; nonsense, rubbish. ~sinnig *a*. silly, idiotic.

blöken *v.i.* to bleat; to low.

blond *a*. fair, blonde. ~ine *f*. blonde.

bloß (-o:s) *a*. bare, naked; uncovered; unprotected; (*fig*.) mere, pure. *adv*. merely, only. ~stellen *v.t.* to expose. [BLOT]

Blöße (-ø:-) *f*. (-, -n) bareness, nakedness; weakness; (*fig*.) *sich eine ~ geben* to lay oneself open to attack; *sich keine ~ geben* to save one's face.

blühen (bly:an) *v.i.* to bloom, blossom, flower; (*fig*.) to flourish. [BLOW]

Blume (-u:ma) *f*. (-, -n) flower, blossom; bouquet, flavour (of wine); tail (of hare); *durch die ~ sprechen* to speak figuratively. ~nflor *m*. show of flowers. ~nkohl *m*. cauliflower. ~nladen *m*. flower-shop. ~nlese *f*. (*fig*.) selection. ~nmuster *n*. floral pattern. ~nstock *m*. potted plant. ~ntopf *m*. pot-plant; flower-pot. ~nzucht *f*. floriculture. ~nzwiebel *f*. bulb. [BLOOM]

blumig *a*. flowery.

Bluse (-u:za) *f*. (-, -n) blouse.

Blut (-u:t) *n*. (-es) 'blood; *geronnenes ~* gore; race; parentage, birth; *böses ~ machen* to arouse ill feeling; *im ~ liegen* (*fig*.) to run in the blood. ~andrang *m*. congestion. ~apfelsine *f*. blood orange. ~arm *a*. anaemic; (*fig*.) very poor. ~bad *n*. slaughter. ~buche *f*. copper-beech. ~druck *m*. blood pressure. ~dürstig *a*. bloodthirsty. ~egel *m*. leech. ~er *m*. bleeder. ~erguß *m*. extravasation (of blood). ~fluß *m*. haemorrhage. ~gefäß *n*. blood-vessel. ~gerinnsel *n*. clot of blood. ~gerüst *n*. scaffold. ~gier *f*. bloodthirstiness. ~hund *m*. blood-hound. ~ig *a*. bloody, gory; sanguinary. ~jung *a*. very young. ~körperchen *n*. blood-corpuscle. ~leer, ~los *aa*. bloodless, anaemic. ~probe *f*. blood test. ~rache *f*. vendetta, blood-feud. ~rünstig *a*. bloody; blood-shot. ~sauger *m*. blood-sucker, ex-

tortioner. ~schande *f*. incest. ~spender *m*. blood-donor. ~stillend *a*. blood-stanching, styptic. ~sturz *m*. haemorrhage. ~sverwandt *a*. related by blood. ~tat *f*. bloody deed, murder. ~übertragung *f*. blood transfusion. ~ung *f*. bleeding, haemorrhage. ~unterlaufen *a*. blood-shot. ~urteil *n*. sentence of death. ~vergießen *n*. bloodshed, slaughter. ~vergiftung *f*. blood-poisoning. ~wasser *n*. blood serum. ~wenig *adv*. very little. ~wurst *f*. black pudding. ~zeuge *m*. martyr.

Blüte (-y:ta) *f*. (-, -n) blossom, flower; (*fig*.) prime, heyday. ~nblatt *n*. petal. ~nkelch *m*. calyx. ~nlese *f*. anthology. ~nstaub *m*. pollen. ~nstengel *m*. stalk, peduncle. ~nweiß *a*. snow-white. ~nzeit *f*. flowering time; prime; golden age.

bluten *v.i.* to bleed.

Bö *f*. (-, -en) gust, squall. ~ig *a*. squally.

Bobbahn *f*. bob-sleigh run.

Bock *m*. (-es, ¨e) 1. (*zool*.) ram; he-goat; buck. 2. trestle; coach box; (*gym*.) horse; (*fig*.) obstinacy; *einen ~ schießen* (*fig*.) to make a blunder. ~beinig *a*. pigheaded. ~ig *a*. obstinate. ~shorn *n*. *ins ~shorn jagen* to intimidate, bully. ~sprung *m*. caper.

bocken *v.i.* to prance; (*fig*.) to be obstinate.

Boden (-o:-) *m*. (-s, ¨en) ground; soil; base; floor; bottom (of sea); loft; attic. ~bearbeitung *f*. cultivation of the soil. ~belag *m*. flooring. ~erhebung *f*. undulation, rising ground. ~fenster *n*. attic-window. ~ fläche *f*. acreage, acres. ~kammer *f*. attic, garret. ~kredit *m*. loan on landed property. ~los *a*. bottomless; (*fig*.) unheard of. ~luke *f*. skylight; dormer-window. ~mannschaft *f*. (*av*.) ground staff. ~raum *m*. attic. ~reform *f*. agrarian reform. ~satz *m*. dregs, grounds; deposit; sediment. ~schätze *m.pl*.

mineral wealth. ~senkung f. declivity. ~ständig a. indigenous; permanently located. ~treppe f. attic-stair. ~tür f. trap-door, door of loft. [BOTTOM]

Bodme'rei f. (-) bottomry.

Bofist m. (-es, -e) (bot.) puff-ball.

bog imperf. of biegen.

Bogen¹ (bo:g) m. (-s, ") bow, bend; curve; arc; arch. ~fenster n. bay-window; oriel. ~förmig a. curved, arched. ~führung f. bowing. ~gang m. colonnade, arcade. ~lampe f. arc-lamp. ~schluß m. keystone.

Bogen² (bo:g) m. (-s, ") bow. ~schießen n. archery. ~schütze m. archer.

Bogen³ (bo:g) m. (-s, "") (mus.) bow. ~führung f., ~strich m. bowing technique.

Bogen⁴ (bo:g) m. (-s, "") sheet (of paper); in rohen ~ in sheets. ~größe f. folio size. ~weise adv. by the sheet, in sheets. ~zahl f. (typ.) number of sheets.

Bohle f. (-, -n) board, plank.

Bohne f. (-, -n) bean; grüne ~n French beans; weiße ~n haricot beans; dicke ~n broad beans; (fig.) blaue ~n bullets. ~nkaffee m. pure coffee. ~nstange f. bean-pole.

bohner-n v.t. to wax, polish. ~lappen m. polishing-cloth. ~wachs n. floor polish.

bohr-en v.t. to bore, drill; to pierce; in den Grund ~en to sink, scuttle (ship). v.i. (fig.) to pester, harass. ~er m. borer; bore; gimlet; drill. ~loch n. bore-hole; gimlet-hole. ~maschine f. boring- or drilling-machine. ~turm m. drilling-derrick. ~wurm m. ship-worm.

Boje (bo:jə) f. (-, -n) buoy.

Böller m. (-s, -) small cannon.

Bollwerk n. bulwark; bastion; rampart.

Bolsche'wismus m. Bolshevism.

Bolsche'wi-st m. (-sten, -sten) Bolshevik, Bolshevist, (sl.) Bolshy. ~stisch a. bolshevist.

Bolzen m. (-s, -) bolt; arrow; peg.

Bombarde'ment (-mã:) n. bombardment. ~ieren v.t. to bomb, bombard, shell, strafe.

Bombe f. (-, -n) bomb, shell. ~nabwurf m. dropping of bombs. ~nattentat n. bomb outrage. ~neinschlag m. bomb hit. ~nerfolg m. huge success. ~nsicher a. bomb-proof; (fig.) quite certain. ~r m. bomber.

Bon'bon (bõbõ:) m. & n. (-s, -s) sweet.

Bonze m. (-n, -n) bonze, (colloq.) bigwig.

Boot (bo:t) n. (-es, -e) boat. ~sfahrt f. boating. ~shaken m. boat-hook. ~shaus n. boat-house.

Bor n. (-s) boron. ~salbe f. boric ointment. ~säure f. boric acid, boracic acid.

Bord¹ m. (-es, -e) edge, border, rim; an ~ on board, aboard. ~buch n. log-book. ~flugzeug n. ship-borne aeroplane. ~funker m. (av.) wireless operator. ~linie f. water-line. ~schwelle f. kerb(-stone). ~wand f. ship's side.

Bord² Bord n. (-es, -e) board; shelf.

Bor'dell n. (-s, -e) brothel, disorderly house.

Bor'düre (-dy:rə) f. (-, -n) edging; edge; border.

Borg m. (-es) borrowing; auf ~ on credit. ~en v.t. to lend. v.t. & r. to borrow.

Borke f. (-, -n) bark, rind.

Born m. (-es, -e) spring, well.

bor'niert a. narrow-minded.

Börse (bœrzə) f. (-, -n) purse; (commerc.) stock exchange. ~nbericht m. money-market report. ~nfähig a. negotiable. ~ngeschäft n. stock-exchange transaction. ~nmakler m. stockbroker. ~nschwindler, ~nspieler m. speculator. ~nzettel m. stocklist, market report.

Borst-e f. (-e, -en) bristle. ~ig a. bristly; (fig.) surly, irritable.

Borte f. (-, -n) trimming, edging, border; braiding.

bös(-e) (bø:zə) a. bad, ill, evil,

wicked; angry; sore; ~ *sein* to be angry (with); ~*e Zeiten* hard times; *der* ~*e* the devil. ~artig *a.* ill-natured; wicked; malicious, malignant; (*med.*) virulent. ~ewicht *m.* villain, scoundrel, rogue. ~lich, ~willig *aa.* malevolent, malicious; wilful.

Böschung *f.* (-, -en) slope; embankment.

bos-haft (bo:s-) *a.* malicious; mischievous; wicked, spiteful. ~heit *f.* malice; spite. ~

boss-eln, ~ieren *v.t. & i.* to emboss; to model (in wax).

bot *imperf. of* bieten.

Bo'tan-ik *f.* botany. ~iker *m.* botanist. ~isch *a.* botanical. ~i'sieren *v.i.* to botanize. ~i'siertrommel *f.* vasculum.

Bot-e (-o:-) *m.* (-en, -en) messenger. ~engang *m.* errand. ~enjunge *m.* errand-boy, officeboy. ~schaft *f.* news; message; embassy, legation. ~schafter *m.* ambassador.

botmäßig *a.* subject. ~keit *f.* dominion; rule, power; jurisdiction.

Böttcher *m.* (-s, -) cooper. ~'ei *f.* cooperage.

Bottich *m.* (-s, -e) tub; vat; barrel. [ML]

Boui'llon (buljɔ̃) *f.* (-, -s) clear soup. ~würfel *m.* soup cube.

Bowle (bo:lə) *f.* (-, -en) (claret-) cup, iced fruit-cup; (silver or glass) tureen.

box-en *v.t.* to box. ~er *m.* boxer. ~kampf *m.* boxing-match.

boyko'ttieren *v.t.* to boycott.

brach¹ *imperf. of* brechen.

brach² (-a:x) *a.* fallow, unploughed, untilled. ~acker *m.*, ~feld *n.* fallow land. ~monat *m.* June.

brachte *imperf.* bringen.

Brachvogel *m.* curlew.

Bracke *m.* (-n, -n) *& f.* hound; pointer; setter.

Brack-gut *n.* refuse, trash, lumber. ~wasser *n.* brackish water.

bramarbasieren *v.t.* to brag, swagger.

Bramsegel *n.* topgallant sail.

Brand (-t) *m.* (-es, ⸚e) burning; fire, conflagration; fire-brand; (*med.*) gangrene; (*bot.*) blight, mildew; *in* ~ *geraten* to catch fire; *in* ~ *legen or stecken* to set on fire. ~blase *f.* blister. ~bombe *f.* incendiary bomb. ~brief *m.* threatening letter. ~er *m.* fire-ship. ~fackel *f.* incendiary torch, fire-brand. ~geschoß *n.* incendiary shell. ~ig *a.* blasted, blighted; (*med.*) gangrenous; (*of smell*) burnt. ~mal *n.* scar, brand. ~marken *v.t.* to brand. ~mauer *f.* fire-proof wall. ~opfer *n.* burnt-offering. ~rede *f.* inflammatory address. ~rot *a.* fiery red. ~salbe *f.* ointment for burns. ~schaden *m.* damage by fire. ~schatzen *v.t.* to levy a contribution on; to plunder. ~sohle *f.* welt. ~stifter *m.* incendiary. ~stiftung *f.* arson, incendiarism. ~wunde *f.* burn, scald.

brand-en *v.i.* to break, surge. ~ung *f.* breakers, surf, surge.

brannte *imperf. of* brennen.

Branntwein *m.* spirits; brandy. ~brennerei *f.* distillery.

Brasse *f.* bream.

brassen *v.t.* (*naut.*) to brace.

Brat-apfel *m.* baked or roasted apple. ~fisch *m.* fried fish. ~huhn *n.* roast chicken. ~kartoffeln *f. pl.* fried potatoes. ~pfanne *f.* frying-pan; roasting-tin. ~rost *m.* gridiron, grill. ~spieß *m.* spit. ~wurst *f.* fried sausage.

braten (bra:t-) 1. *v.t. & i. st.* to roast; to bake; to grill; to fry. 2. *subst. m.* roast; *den* ~ *riechen* (*fig.*) to smell a rat. ~fett *n.* dripping. ~rock *m.* dress-coat.

Bratsch-e (bra:t-) *f.* (-e, -en) viola, bass-viol. ~ist *m.* viola player.

Bräu(haus) *n.* brewery; tavern, public house.

Brauch *m.* (-es, ⸚e) usage, use; custom. ~bar *a.* useful, serviceable; practicable. ~barkeit *f.* usefulness; fitness. ~en *v.t.* to

use, employ; to need, want, require. ~tum *n.* customs.

Braue *f.* (-, -n) eyebrow.

brau-en *v.t.* to brew. **~er** *m.* brewer. **~e'rei** *f.* brewery.

braun *a.* brown; bay (horse); sun-burnt, sun-tanned. **~äugig** *a.* brown-eyed. **~kohle** *f.* brown coal, lignite.

Bräun-e *f.* (-e) brown colour, brownness; (*med.*) Vincent's angina. **~en** *v.t.* to brown; to tan. **~lich** *a.* brownish.

Braus *m.* bustle, tumult.

Brause (-zə) *f.* (-, -n) shower; douche; spray; rose (of watering-pot); (*chem.*) fermentation. **~kopf** *m.* hot-headed fellow. **~limonade** *f.* fizzy lemonade. **pulver** *n.* effervescent powder.

brausen (-z-) *v.i.* to storm, rage, bluster; to roar, rush; to hum, buzz; (*of organ*) to peal; (*chem.*) to effervesce.

Braut *f.* (-, ⁓e) fiancée, intended; bride. **~ausstattung** *f.* trousseau. **~führer** *m.* best man. **~jungfer** *f.* bridesmaid. **~kleid** *n.* wedding-dress. **~leute** *pl.*, **~paar** *n.* engaged couple. **~schleier** *m.* wedding-veil. **~staat** *m.* bridal attire.

Bräutigam *m.* (-s, -e) fiancé, intended; bridegroom.

bräutlich *a.* bridal.

brav (-f) *a.* honest; excellent; brave; good, well-behaved. **~heit** *f.* honesty, uprightness; good behaviour. **~oruf** *m.* shout of bravo; acclamation; (*pl.*) cheers.

Brech-bohnen *f.pl.* French beans. **~durchfall** *m.* cholera nostras. **~eisen** *n.* crow-bar. **~er** *m.* breakers, heavy seas; stone-crusher. **~mittel** *n.* emetic. **~reiz** *m.* retching; nausea. **~stange** *f.* crow-bar. **~ung** *f.* breaking; (*phys.*) refraction.

brechen *v.t. st.* to break; to quarry (stone); to pick (flower); to fracture (bone); (*phys.*) to refract. *v.r.* to be refracted; (*med.*) to vomit, be sick. *vws.i.* to break; (*of eyes*) to grow dim.

Bregen *m.* (-s, -) (*cook.*) brains.

Brei *m.* (-es, -e) pap, mash; pulp. **~ig** *a.* pulpy.

breit *a.* broad, wide; flat; **einen ~schlagen** to persuade; **sich ~ machen** to take up much room; (*fig.*) to swagger. **~treten** to dilate upon, thrash out. **~beinig** *a.* straddling, straddle-legged.

Breit-e *f.* (-e, -en) breadth, width; (*geogr.*) latitude; (*fig.*) verbosity, prolixity. **~engrad** *m.* degree of latitude. **~randig** *a.* broad-brimmed; (*of book*) with wide margins. **~schult'er**ig *a.* broad-shouldered. **~seite** *f.* broadside. **~spurig** *a.* wide-gauge; (*fig.*) swaggering.

breiten *v.t.* to spread; to extend.

Brems-e¹ *f.* (-e, -en) brake. **~hebel** *m.* brake lever. **~klotz** *m.* brake-shoe, brake-block. **~vorrichtung** *f.* brake mechanism.

Bremse² *f.* (-, -n) gad-fly.

bremsen *v.t. & i.* to brake, put the brake on; (*colloq.*) to stop.

brenn-bar *a.* combustible; inflammable. **~er** *m.* distiller; burner. **~e'rei** *f.* distillery. **~glas** *n.* burning-glass. **~holz** *n.* firewood. **~material** *n.* fuel. **~(n)essel** *f.* stinging nettle. **~punkt** *m.* focal point, focus. **~schere** *f.* curling-tongs. **~spiegel** *m.* concave or burning-mirror. **~spiritus** *m.* methylated spirits. **~stahl** *m.* blister-steel. **~stoff** *m.* fuel. **~weite** *f.* focal distance.

brennen *v.t. st.* to burn; to brand; to bake (bricks); to roast (coffee); to wave (hair); to distil (spirits); (*med.*) to cauterize. *v.i.* to burn, be on fire; (*of wounds*) to smart, sting; **es brennt!** fire! **vor Neugier ~** to be consumed with curiosity; **darauf ~** (*zu*) to be dying to know, &c.).

brenzlich *a.* burnt (taste or smell); (*fig.*) risky, doubtful.

Bresche *f.* (-, -n) breach, gap; **eine ~ schlagen** to thrust forward, clear the way.

bresthaft *a.* decrepit.

Brett n. (-es, -er) board, plank; shelf; (pl.) stage, boards. ~**erbude** f. booth, shed. ~**ern** a. boarded, planked. ~**erwand** f. wooden partition. ~**erzaun** m. wooden fence. ~**spiel** n. draughts, chess, &c.

Bre'vier (-vi:r) n. (-s, -e) breviary.

Brezel f. (-, -n) B-shaped roll or cracknel. [L]

brichst 2 pers. sing. pres. of brech-en.

Brief m. (-es, -e) letter. ~**ablage** f. letter-files; letter-sorter. ~**adel** m. patent nobility. ~**beschwerer** m. paper-weight. ~**bestellung** f. delivery of letters. ~**bogen** m. sheet of note-paper. ~**bote**, ~**träger** m. postman. ~**einwurf** m. slit; letter-box. ~**fach** n. pigeon-hole. ~**geheimnis** n. secrecy of correspondence. ~**kasten** m. letter-box. ~**lich** a. by letter. ~**mappe** f. document-case; writing-case. ~**marke** f. stamp. ~**ordner** m. letter-file. ~**papier** n. writing-paper, note-paper. ~**porto** n. postage. ~**schaften** pl. letters, papers, documents. ~**steller** m. letter-writer; guide for letter-writing. ~**tasche** f. wallet, pocket-book. ~**taube** f. carrier-pigeon. ~**träger** m. postman. ~**umschlag** m. envelope. ~**verkehr** m. correspondence; postal service. ~**waage** f. letter balance. ~**wechsel** m. correspondence. [BRIEF]

Bries n. (-es) sweetbread.

briet imperf. of braten.

Bri'gade (-ga:də) f. (-, -n) brigade.

Bri'gant m. (-en, -en) brigand.

Brigg (-k) f. (-, -s) brig.

Bri'kett n. (-s, -s) briquette.

bril'lant (-jant) a. brilliant. subst. m. (-en, -en) brilliant.

Brille f. (-, -n) spectacles, glasses. ~**nfutteral** n. spectacle-case. ~**nglas** n. lens. ~**nschlange** f. cobra. [Gk.-L]

Brim'borium n. (-s) fuss, to-do.

bringen (-ŋən) v.t. st. to bring, fetch; to convey; to carry, take;

to make; to accompany; an sich ~ to acquire; nachhause ~ to see home; dazu ~ to induce (to); um etwas ~ to deprive (of); unter sich ~ to get into one's power; es zu etwas ~ to achieve something; fertig ~, zustande ~, zuwege ~ to bring about, accomplish; es mit sich ~ (fig.) to involve.

Brisan-z f. detonating violence. ~**t** a. (fig.) highly effective.

Brise (-i:zə) f. (-, -n) breeze.

bröckel-n v.t. & vrs.i. to crumble. ~**ig** a. crumbly, friable.

Brocken m. (-s, -) morsel, crumb; fragment; scrap. v.t. to break (bread). ~**sammlung** f. collection of junk (for sale). ~**weise** adv. bit by bit, piecemeal.

brodeln (-o:-) v.i. to bubble.

Brodem m. (-s) steam; exhalation. [BREATH]

Bro'kat (-a:-) m. (-s, -e) brocade.

Brom (-o:m) n. (-s) bromine. ~**kalium** n. potassium bromide. ~**säure** f. bromic acid. ~**silber** n. silver bromide.

Brombeere f. (-, -n) blackberry, bramble.

Bronchi'alkatarrh m. bronchial catarrh.

Bronnen m. (-s, -) (poet.) spring, well, fountain.

Bronz-e (brõ:sə) f. (-e, -en) bronze. ~**efarben** a. bronze-coloured. ~**en** a. bronze. ~**ezeit** f. Bronze Age. ~**ieren** v.t. to bronze.

Brosame (-za:mə) f. (-, -n) crumb.

Brosche (-ʃə) f. (-, -n) brooch.

bro'sch-ieren v.t. to stitch, sew. ~**iert** a. in paper covers. ~**üre** f. pamphlet; booklet. [F]

Brösel (-ø:z-) m. (-s, -) crumb, morsel. ~**n** v.i. to crumble.

Brot (-o:t) n. (-es, -e) bread; loaf; sein ~ verdienen to earn one's living. ~**beutel** m. haversack. ~**erwerb** m. livelihood. ~**herr** m. master, employer. ~**korb** m. bread-basket; den ~korb höher hängen to keep on short commons. ~**krume** f. bread-crumb. ~**los** a. unemployed; ~lose Kunst unprofitable art. ~**neid** m.

professional jealousy. **~rinde** f. crust. **~röster** m. toasting-fork; toaster. **~scheibe**, **~schnitte** f. slice of bread. **~schneidemaschine** f. bread-slicing machine. **~studium** n. vocational study.

Brötchen (-ø:tç-) n. (-s, -) roll.

Bruch[1] (-u:x) m. & n. (-es, =e) marsh, bog, fen. [BROOK]

Bruch[2] (-ux) m. (-es, =e) breach, break, breaking, breakage; fracture; crease, fold; debris, rubble, scrap; (med.) rupture, hernia; (math.) fraction; (leg.) infringement, violation; **~ machen** (av.) to crash; in die Brüche gehen to break, fall to pieces; (fig.) to come to grief. **~band** n. truss. **~landung** f. (av.) crash-landing. **~rechnung** f. fractions. **~spalte** f. fault cleft. **~strich** m. division sign. **~stück** n. fragment. **~teil** n. fraction. **~zahl** f. fractional number.

brüchig a. fragile; brittle; full of cracks.

Brücke f. (-, -n) bridge; rug; dental arch; **~ schlagen** to bridge (a river); alle **~n** hinter sich abbrechen to burn one's boats. **~nkopf** m. bridge-head. **~npfeiler** m. pier, pile. **~nwaage** f. weigh-bridge.

Bruder (-u:-) m. (-s, =) brother; friar; (sl.) warmer **~** homosexual. **~krieg** m. fratricidal war. **~mord** m. fratricide. **~schaft** f. fraternity; religious brotherhood. **~volk** n. sister nation.

Brüder-lein n. little brother. **~lich** a. brotherly, fraternal. **~schaft** f. brotherhood; close friendship.

Brüh-e (-y:ə) f. (-e, -en) broth; gravy, sauce. **~en** v.t. to scald. **~warm** a. boiling-hot; (fig.) fresh, (colloq.) hot.

brüllen v.i. to roar; to bellow; to low; to bawl, shout; to howl.

Brumm-bär m. bear; (fig.) grumbler. **~baß** m. bourdon; bass voice; double bass. **~eisen** n. Jew's harp. **~er** m. bluebottle. **~ig** a. grumbling.

peevish, grumpy. **~kreisel** m. humming-top. **~schädel** m. headache, hang-over.

brummen v.t. & i. to growl, grumble; to hum, buzz; to mutter, mumble; (colloq.) to do time.

brünett a. brunette.

Brunft f. (-) rut, heat. **~zeit** f. rutting-time.

Brünne f. (-, -n) breast-plate.

Brunnen m. (-s, -) spring, well, fountain; mineral spring; spa. **~kresse** f. water-cress. **~kur** f. spa-treatment.

Brunst f. (-) passion, lust; rut.

brünstig a. lustful; in heat; (fig.) ardent.

brüsk a. curt; gruff; offhand.

Brust f. (-, =e) breast; chest; bosom; sich in die **~ werfen** to boast, give oneself airs. **~bein** n. breastbone. **~bild** n. half-length portrait. **~drüse** f. mammary gland. **~fellentzündung** f. pleurisy. **~kasten**, **~korb** m. chest, thorax. **~latz** m. bib. **~schwimmen** n. breast stroke. **~ton** m. chest-note. **~warze** f. nipple. **~wehr** f. parapet.

brüst-en v.r. to give oneself airs, brag, boast. **~ung** f. parapet.

Brut f. (-u:t) f. (-, -en) brood; hatch; fry, spawn; (fig.) pack, rabble. **~apparat** m. incubator. **~henne** f. sitting-hen. **~kasten** m. spawn-hatcher. **~stätte** f. breeding-place; (fig.) hotbed.

bru'tal (-a:l) a. brutal. **~i'tät** f. brutality.

brüten (-y:t-) v.i. & t. to sit (on eggs), hatch; (also fig.) to brood. [BREED]

brutto adv. gross. **~gewicht** n. gross weight. **~registertonnen** f. pl. gross register(ed) tons.

brutzeln v.i. to splutter.

Bub-e (bu:bə) m. (-en, -en) boy, lad; rogue, scamp; (card) knave. **~enstreich** m., **~enstück** n. boy's trick; piece of villainy. **~ikopf** m. bobbed hair.

Büb-e'rei f. piece of villainy. **~isch** a. mischievous; villainous, vile.

Buch (bu:x) *n.* (-es, ̈er) book. **~binder** *m.* bookbinder. **~binderei** *f.* bookbinding; bookbinder's workshop. **~deckel** *m.* cover, binding. **~druck** *m.* printing, typography. **~drucker** *m.* printer. **~druckerei** *f.* printing-works or -office. **~führung,** book-keeping. **~gemeinschaft** *f.* book club. **~gewerbe** *n.* graphic trade. **~halter** *m.* book-keeper. **~handel** *m.* book-trade. **~händler** *m.* bookseller. **~handlung** *f.,* **~laden** *m.* book-shop. **~macher** *m.* book-maker. **~prüfer** *m.* accountant. **~umschlag** *m.* jacket. **~ung** *f.* entry. **~verleih** *m.* lending library. **~zeichen** *n.* book-mark. See also **Buchstabe.**

Buch-e (bu:xə) *f.* (-e, -en) beech-tree. **~ecker** *f.* beech-nut. **~fink** *m.* chaffinch. **~weizen** *m.* buckwheat. **~weizengrütze** *f.* buckwheat porridge.

buchen (bu:x-) *v.t.* to enter, book.

Bücher-abschluß *m.* closing or balancing of books. **~bord,** **~brett** *n.* book-shelf. **~ei** *f.* library. **~gestell** *n.* bookcase, book-shelves. **~kunde** *f.* bibliography. **~mappe** *f.* satchel. **~narr** *m.* bibliomaniac. **~revisor** *m.* accountant, auditor. **~schau** *f.* review of books. **~schrank** *m.* bookcase. **~stütze** *f.* book-stand, book-rest. **~verzeichnis** *n.* list, catalogue. **~wurm** *m.* maggot; *(fig.)* book-worm. **~(bestell)zettel** *m.* (book) order-form.

Buchsbaum *m.* box-tree.

Buchse *f.* (*tech.*) bush.

Büchse (byksə) *f.* (-, -n) tin, case, box, canister; rifle, gun. **~nfleisch** *n.* tinned meat. **~n-macher** *m.* gunmaker. **~nmilch** *f.* tinned milk. **~nöffner** *m.* tin-opener.

Buchstab-e *m.* (-en, -en) letter; *(typ.)* character; type; *großer (kleiner)* capital (small) letter. **~enmensch** *m.* pedant. **~enrätsel** *n.* anagram. **~ieren** *v.t.* to spell.

buchstäblich *a.* literal. *adv.* literally.

Bucht *f.* (-, -en) bay, creek, inlet.

Buckel *m.* (-s,) humpback, hump; *(colloq.)* back; boss, umbo. **~ig** *a.* hunchbacked. [L]

bück-en *v.r.* to stoop, bend; to bow. **~ling¹** *m.* bow.

Bückling² *m.* (-s, -e) smoked herring.

buddeln *v.t. & i.* to dig.

Bude (bu:də) *f.* (-, -n) booth, stall; *(sl.)* digs.

Büdner *m.* (s, -) cottager.

Bü'ffett (byf't) *n.* (-s, -e) dresser, sideboard; buffet, refreshment bar.

Büffel *m.* (-s, -) buffalo. **~n** *v.i.* *(colloq.)* to swot, grind.

Bug (bu:k) *m.* (-es, -e) *(naut.)* bow; shoulder-bone. **~spriet** *n.* bowsprit.

Bügel (by:g-) *m.* (-s, -) handle; frame; coat-hanger; stirrup. **~brett** *n.* ironing-board. **~eisen** *n.* flat-iron. **~falte** *f.* crease (in trousers).

bügeln (by:g-) *v.t.* to iron; to press.

bug'sieren *v.t.* to tow; *(fig.)* to take in tow.

Büh(e)l *m.* (-s, -) hill, hillock.

Buhl-e *m. & f.* (-en, -en) *(obs.)* sweetheart, beloved; *(now)* paramour, mistress. **~erin** *f.* paramour; prostitute. **~erisch** *a.* wanton, lewd; amorous. **~schaft** *f.* love-affair, amour.

buhlen *v.i.* to make love to; to have illicit intercourse (with); *(fig.)* to strive (for).

Buhne *f.* (-, -n) groyne; dike.

Bühne *f.* (-, -n) stage; scaffold; platform. **~nanweisung** *f.* stage direction. **~nausstattung** *f.* scenery; scenes, décor. **~nbild** *n.* stage-picture; background; *(pl.)* scenes. **~ndichter** *m.* playwright, dramatist. **~nleiter** *m.* stage-manager. **~nsprache** *f.* standard speech. **~nwirksam** *a.* 'good theatre'.

buk *imperf. of* **backen.**

Bu'kett *n.* (-s, -s) bouquet, bunch of flowers.

Bu'lette *f.* (-, -n) meat-ball, rissole.

Bull|auge n. port-hole; bull's-eye.

Bull-e¹ m. (-en, -en) bull. **~dogge** f., **~enbeißer** m. bulldog. **~enhitze** f. (colloq.) oppressive heat.

Bulle² f. (-, -n) papal bull.

bullern v.i. (colloq. of fire) to roar.

Bummel m. (-s, -) stroll. **~ei** f. dawdling; carelessness, negligence. **~ig** a. slow; careless. **~leben** n. dissipated life. **~zug** m. slow train.

bumm-eln v.i. to saunter, stroll; to dawdle; to loiter about, slack. **~ler** m. idler, loafer, dawdler, gadabout.

bums int. bang! crash! bump! **~en** v.i. to bump; to fall with a bump.

Buna m. (-) synthetic rubber.

Bund (bunt) **1.** m. (-es, ˙˙e) waistband; tie; league; alliance; confederacy, confederation, (bibl.) covenant. **2.** n. (-es, -e) bundle; bunch (of keys). **~esbruder** m. fellow member of students' association. **~esgenosse** m. confederate, ally. **~eslade** f. Ark of the Covenant. **~esrepublik** f. Federal Government. **~esstaat** m. federal state. **~estag** m. Federal Diet.

Bündel n. (-s, -) bundle; bunch; packet; (opt.) pencil (of rays). **~n** v.t. to bundle, bundle up.

bünd-ig a. convincing; concise; curt. **~nis** n. alliance, league.

Bunker m. (-s, -) dug-out, pill-box; (naut.) bunker.

bunt a. coloured; variegated, mottled, motley; spotted; stained (glass); (fig.) lively, gay; wild; das ist zu ~ that's going too far; ~er Abend social evening; ~ durcheinander topsy-turvy; ~e Reihe machen to mix the sexes. **~druck** m. colour-printing. **~gefiedert** a. of gay plumage. **~gefleckt**, **~scheckig** aa. speckled, spotted, piebald. **~schillernd** a. iridescent, opalescent. **~specht** m. spotted woodpecker. **~stift** m. crayon, coloured pencil.

Bürde (-yr-) f. (-, -n) burden, load.

Bureau see **Büro**.

Burg (-k) f. (-, -en) castle; citadel, stronghold, fort. **~frieden** m. precincts (of castle); party-truce. **~graben** m. moat. **~graf** m. burggrave. **~verlies** n. dungeon, keep. **~vogt** m. castellan, steward. [BOROUGH]

Bürg-e m. (-en, -en) bail; guarantee; surety. **~en** v.i. to go bail (for); to become security (for); to vouch (for); to guarantee. **~schaft** f. bail, surety; security; **~schaft leisten** to give bail; **gegen ~schaft freilassen** to release on bail.

Bürger m. (-s, -) citizen, townsman; middle-class man; commoner. **~krieg** m. civil war. **~kunde** f. sociology; civics. **~lich** a. civic; civil; middle-class; plain; **~liches Gesetzbuch** code of Civil Law. **~mädchen** n. girl of the middle classes. **~meister** m. mayor, (Sc.) Lord Provost. **~pflicht** f. duty as a citizen. **~recht** n. civic rights; citizenship; freedom of a city. **~schaft** f. townspeople, citizens. **~stand** m. citizens; middle classes. **~steig** m. pavement, sidewalk. **~tum** n. citizens; middle classes. **~wehr** f. Home Guard; militia.

bur'lesk a. burlesque.

Bü'ro n. (-s, -s) office. **~bedarf** m. stationery, office equipment. **~bote** m. office-boy. **~klammer** f. paper-clip or -fastener. **~'krat** m. (-en, -en) bureaucrat. **~'kra'tie** f. bureaucracy; red tape. **~kratisch** a. bureaucratic. **~vorsteher** m. chief or head clerk.

Bursch-e m. (-en, -en) youth, fellow, lad; boy; man-servant; batman; member of students' association. **~enherrlichkeit** f. Old College days. **~enschaft** f. students' association. **~i'kos** a. boisterous, rough; free and easy.

Bürste f. (-, -n) brush. **~n** v.t. to brush. **~nabzug** m. brush proof. **~nbinder** m. brush-maker.

Bürzel m. (-s, -) rump, croup; tail (of boar, &c.).

Busch *m.* (-es, ̈-e) bush, shrub; copse, thicket; woodland; bunch, tuft; shock (of hair). **~ig** *a.* bushy; shaggy. **~klepper** *m.* bush-ranger. **~werk** *n.* brushwood.

Büschel (by-) *n.* (-s, -) tuft, bunch; sheaf; plume.

Busen (bu:z-) *m.* (-s, -) bosom; breast; heart; bay, gulf. **~nadel** *f.* tie-pin.

Bussard *m.* (-s, -e) buzzard.

Buß-e (bu:sə) *f.* (-e, -en) penitence, repentance; atonement; compensation; fine, penalty; **~e tun** to do penance. **~fertig** *a.* penitent, repentant; contrite. **~fertigkeit** *f.* penitence, repentance; contrition. **~psalm** *m.* penitential psalm. **~tag** *m.* day of prayer and repentance. **~übung** *f.* penance.

büß-en (by:s-) *v.t. & i.* to atone for, suffer for; to expiate; *seine Lust ~en* to indulge one's passion, satisfy one's desire. **~er** *m.* penitent.

Bu'ssole *f.* (-, -n) compass. [F]

Büste *f.* (-, -n) bust. **~nhalter** *m.* brassière, bust-bodice.

Butt *m.* (-es, -e) brill; turbot; flounder.

Bütt-e *f.* (-e, -en) tub, vat. **~enpapier** *n.* hand-made paper. **~ner** *m.* cooper.

Büttel *m.* (-s, -) beadle; bailiff; jailer; executioner.

Butter *f.* (-) butter. **~blume** *f.* buttercup. **~brot** *n.* slice of bread and butter. **~brotpapier** *n.* grease-proof paper. **~dose** *f.* butter-dish. **~faß** *n.* churn. **~teig** *m.* short pastry.

buttern *v.t. & i.* to churn.

Butzen (buts-) *m.* (-s, -) core. **~scheibe** *f.* bull's-eye pane.

C

(See also under **K**, **Sch**, and **Z**)

C, c (tse:) *n.* the letter C, c; (*mus.*) c.

Ce'llist (tʃ-) *m.* (-en, -en) violoncellist.

Cello (tʃ-) *n.* (-s, -s) violoncello.

Cembalo (tʃ-) *n.* (-s, -s) harpsichord.

Ces (tsɛs) *n.* (*mus.*) C flat.

Cha'grin (ʃagrɛ̃) *m.* (-s) shagreen.

Chaise'longue (ʃɛzlõ:(ŋ)) *f.* (-, -) couch, divan.

Cha'mäleon (k-) *n.* (-s, -s) chameleon.

Cham'pagner (ʃampanjər) *m.* (-s) champagne.

Champignon (ʃampinjõ) *m.* (-s, -s) (edible) mushroom.

Chaos (ka:ɔs) *n.* (-) chaos.

cha'otisch *a.* chaotic.

Cha'rakter (k-) *m.* (-s, -e) character; disposition; nature; type, print, letter; title, dignity; energy, willpower. **~fest** *a.* of moral strength. **~istik** *f.* characterization. **~istikum** *n.*, **~zug** *m.* characteristic. **~istisch** *a.* characteristic. **~los** *a.* unprincipled; weak.

charakteri'sieren *v.t.* to characterize.

Charg-e (ʃarʒə) *f.* (-e, -en) rank. **~ierte(r)** *m.* leader of a students' corps.

Chau'ffeur (ʃofø:r) *m.* (-s, -e) chauffeur.

chauf'fieren *v.t. & i.* to drive (car).

Chau'ssee (ʃose:) *f.* (-, -n) main road, road, highway, thoroughfare. **~graben** *m.* roadside ditch. **~wärter** *m.* roadman. [F]

Chef (ʃɛf) *m.* (-s, -s) ♠ chief, head, principal; manager; boss. **~redakteur** *m.* chief editor.

Chem-ie (çemi:) *f.* chemistry. **~i'kalien** *pl.* chemicals. **~iker** ('çe:-) *m.* ♠ analytical chemist; student or teacher of chemistry. **~isch** *a.* chemical.

Chiffre (ʃifər) *f.* (-, -n) cipher. **~schlüssel** *m.* cipher-code.

chi'ffrieren *v.t.* to encipher, to code.

China see App. I. **~rinde** *f.* Peruvian bark.

Chi'nin (çini:n) *n.* (-s) quinine.

Chiroman'tie (c-) *f.* palmistry.

Chi'rurg (çirurk) *m.* (-en, -en) surgeon. **~ie** *f.* surgery. **~isch** *a.* surgical.

Chlor (klo:r) *n.* (-s) chlorine. **~haltig** *a.* containing chlorine. **~id** *n.* chloride. **~kalium** *n.* potassium chloride. **~kalk** *m.* chloride of lime; bleaching powder. **~kalzium** *n.* calcium chloride. **~säure** *f.* chloric acid. **~wasserstoff** *m.* hydrogen chloride; hydrochloric acid.

chlorofor'mieren *v.t.* to chloroform.

cho'lerisch (-le:-) *a.* choleric.

Chor (ko:r) *m.* (-es, ¨-e) chorus; choir; (*archit.*) choir, chancel. **~'al** *m.* (-als, -äle) chorale, hymn. **~gang** *m.* aisle. **~gesang** *m.* chorus, anthem. **~hemd** *n.*, **~rock** *m.* surplice. **~herr** *m.* canon, prebendary. **~'istin** *f.* chorusgirl. **~knabe** *m.* choir-boy. **~nische** *f.* apse. **~sänger** *m.* chorister. **~schranke** *f.* chancelscreen. **~stuhl** *m.* choir-stall.

Christ (krist) *m.* (-en, -en) Christian; *der Heilige ~* Christmas. **~enheit** *f.* Christendom. **~entum** *n.* Christianity, Christian religion. **~kind** *n.* Christ-child. **~lich** *a.* Christian. See also under **Weihnachts~**.

Chrom (kro:m) *n.* chromium, chrome. **~'atisch** *a.* chromatic. **~gelb** *n.* chrome yellow; Cologne yellow.

Chron-ik (kro:-) *f.* (-ik, -iken) chronicle. **~isch** *a.* chronic. **~ist** *m.* chronicler. **~olo'gie** *f.* chronology. **~o'logisch** *a.* chronological.

Cis (tsis) *n.* (*mus.*) C sharp.

Clique (klikə) *f.* (-, -n) clique, set, coterie.

Cou'pé *n.* (-s, -s) compartment (in train). [F]

Couplet *n.* music-hall song.

Cour (ku:r) *f.* (-) *die ~ machen to* court (girl). **~macher**, **~schneider** *m.* admirer; ladies' man, suitor.

Creme *f.* (-) cream.

D

D, d (de:) *n.* the letter D, d; (*mus.*) d.

da (da:) *adv. & sep. pref.* (*place*) there, here; (*time*) then, at that time. *conj.* when; because, as, since.

da'bei *adv.* near, near by, close to, besides, moreover, yet, but, withal, as well, at the same time; *was ist ~* what does that matter; *~ kommt nichts heraus* nothing is to be gained by it. **~bleiben** *vws.i.* to persist in; to insist on; *~ bleibt es* there the matter ends, that is agreed. **~sein** *v.i.* to be present, take part (in); to be on the point of. **~stehen** *vws.i.* to stand near, stand by.

dableiben *vws.i.* to stay, remain.

Dach (-x) *n.* (-es, ¨-er) roof; (*fig.*) house, shelter; *unter ~ und Fach* safe; under cover. **~antenne** *f.* roof aerial. **~balken** *m.* rafter, beam. **~boden** *m.* loft. **~decker** *m.* slater, tiler. **~fenster** *n.* attic or dormer-window; skylight. **~first** *m.* ridge of a roof. **~gesellschaft** *f.* holding company. **~kammer** *f.* attic, garret. **~luke** *f.* dormer-window; (*av.*) turret roof door. **~pappe** *f.* tarred roofing-paper. **~reiter** *m.* ridge turret. **~rinne** *f.* gutter. **~sparren** *m.* rafter. **~stuhl** *m.* framework of roof, roof-truss. **~ziegel** *m.* tile. [THATCH]

Dachs (daks) *m.* (-es, ¨-e) badger. **~bau** *m.* burrow.

dachte *imperf. of* **denken.**

Dackel *m.* (-s, -) dachshund.

dadurch (-c) *adv.* through it; thereby; by this means; *~ daß* through the fact that.

dafür *adv.* for that, for it; instead of it; *~ sein* to be in favour of, vote for; *ich kann nichts ~* it is not my fault; *nach meinem ~halten* in my opinion.

da'gegen *adv.* against it, against that; in comparison with; in return (for), in exchange (for); *nichts ~ haben* to have no objection (to). *conj.* on the other hand; whereas.

da'heim *adv.* at home.

daher *adv.* thence, from that place, from there. *conj.* therefore, hence. *sep. pref.* along.

daherum *adv.* thereabouts.

dahin *adv. & sep. pref.* thither, to that place; to that time; so far (that); along; away, gone, lost. **~bringen** *v.t.* to manage to; to induce, persuade. **~geben** *v.t.* to give up, sacrifice. **~gehen** *vus.i.* to walk along; (*of time*) to pass. **~stehen** *v.i. es steht ~* it is undecided. **~stellen** *v.t. es ~gestellt sein lassen* to leave undecided.

da'hinten *adv.* behind.

da'hinter *adv.* behind that. **~kommen** *vus.i.* to find out.

damal-ig *a.* then, of that time. **~s** *adv.* then, at that time.

Da'mast *m.* (-es) damask. **~en** *a.* damask.

damas'zieren *v.t.* to damascene.

Dam-bock, **~hirsch** *m.* fallow-buck, fallow-deer. **~wild** *n.* fallow-deer.

Dambrett *n.* draught-board.

Dame (da:me) *f.* (-, -n) lady; (dance) partner; queen (at cards); king (at draughts). **~nbinde** *f.* sanitary towel. **~nsattel** *m.* side-saddle. **~nwelt** *f.* ladies, fair sex. **~nspiel** *n.* draughts. [F]

Däm-(e)lak *m.* fat-head. **~lich** *a.* stupid.

damit *adv.* with it; with that. *conj.* so that, in order that; *~ nicht* lest, in order that ... not, for fear that.

Damm *m.* (-es, ̈-e) dam, dike; mole; pier; embankment, bank; causeway, roadway; *auf dem ~ sein* to be O.K., be in the pink. **~bruch** *m.* bursting of a dike.

dämmen *v.t.* to dam; (*fig.*) to stop, check, restrain.

Dämmer *m.* (-s) dusk, twilight. **~ig** *a.* dusky; dim. **~licht** *n.*, **~schein** *m.* dusk, twilight. **~schoppen** *m.* evening pint. **~ung** *f.* dawn; twilight. **~zustand** *m.* semi-conscious state.

dämmern *v.i.* to grow light, dawn; to get dark, grow dusky; (*fig.*) to dawn on; *vor sich hin ~* to be semi-conscious.

Dämon *m.* (-s, -en) demon. **~isch**

a. demoniac; demoniacal; demonic.

Dampf *m.* (-es, ̈-e) vapour, steam. **~bad** *n.* vapour-bath. **~boot** *n.*, **~er** *m.* steamboat, steamer. **~ig** *a.* steamy, vaporous. **~kessel** *m.* boiler. **~kraft** *f.* steam-power. **~maschine** *f.* steam-engine. **~roß** *n.* locomotive. **~schiffahrt** *f.* steam-navigation. **~walze** *f.* steam-roller. [DAMP]

dampfen *v.i.* to give off vapour, to steam; to smoke.

dämpf-en *v.t.* to damp; to tone down (colour); to deaden (sound); to mute (violin), muffle (drum); to extinguish (fire); to subdue (light); (*cook.*) to steam; (*fig.*) to suppress, restrain. **~er** *m.* silencer, damper; mute (on violin); shock-absorber.

danach (-x) *adv.* after that, thereupon; accordingly, according to that; *ich frage nichts ~* I don't care (about it); *es sieht ~ aus* it looks like it.

da'neben *adv.* near it, next to it, close by. *conj.* besides, moreover, at the same time, also. **~gehen** *vus.i.* (*colloq.*) to miss, fail.

dang *imperf. of* **dingen.**

da'nieder *adv.* down, on the ground. **~liegen** *v.i.* to be laid up; (*fig.*) to degenerate, perish.

Dank 1. *m.* (-es) thanks; gratitude; reward, recompense; *herzlichen* or *schönen ~* many thanks; *Gott sei ~* thank God; *zum ~* as a reward; *~ wissen* to be grateful; *zu ~ verpflichten* to oblige. 2. *prep.* thanks to. **~adresse** *f.* vote of thanks. **~bar** *a.* grateful; thankful; profitable. **~barkeit** *f.* gratitude. **~enswert** *a.* deserving of thanks, meritorious. **~fest** *n.* thanksgiving (festival). **~opfer** *n.* thank-offering. **~sagung** *f.* (returning) thanks, acknowledgement; (*eccl.*) thanksgiving.

danke! thank you, thanks; no, thank you; *~ schön* thank you very much.

danken *v.i.* to thank, return thanks. *v.t.* to owe (something) to, be indebted (to someone) for.

dann adv. then; thereupon; ~ und wann now and then.

dannen adv. von ~ thence, away.

daran, dran adv. at it, on it (or that); to it, near it; in regard to it; by it; of it; was liegt ~ what does it matter; ich bin ~ it is my turn; gut ~ sein to be well off; nahe ~ sein to be on the point of, be near. ~gehen vws.i. to set to work. ~setzen v.t. to risk, stake.

darauf, drauf adv. on it, upon it; after that; ein Jahr ~ a year later; ~ aus sein to be out to, to aim at; gerade ~ zu straight towards; drauf und dran sein to be on the point of. ~hin adv. thereupon, on the strength of that. ~kommen to hit upon; to recall, remember.

daraus, draus adv. from there, from thence; hence; of it; ich mache mir nichts ~ I don't care for it much.

darben v.i. to suffer want, starve.

darbiet-en v.t. to offer; to present. ~ung f. entertainment; performance.

darbringen v.t. to bring, present, offer.

darein, drein adv. into it, therein. ~finden v.r. to submit to. ~reden v.i. to interrupt. ~schlagen v.i. to strike hard. ~willigen v.i. to consent (to).

darf 1 & 3 pers. sing. pres. of **dürfen**.

darin, drin adv. in it, therein. ~nen adv. within, inside.

darleg-en v.t. to explain, expound. ~ung f. explanation, exposition.

Darlehen n. (-s, -) loan.

Darm m. (-es, "e) gut, intestine. ~blutung f. intestinal haemorrhage. ~saite f. catgut. ~verschlingung f. stoppage of the bowels.

darob, drob adv. on that account.

Darr-e f. (-e, -en) kiln-drying; kiln; (vet.) phthisis. ~ofen m. drying-kiln.

darreichen v.t. to present, offer; to administer (sacrament).

darstell-en v.t. to describe, repre-

sent; to exhibit; to produce, prepare; (theatr.) to perform, act. ~er m. actor. ~erin f. actress. ~ung f. description, representation; presentation; preparation, production; performance.

dartun v.t. to demonstrate; to prove.

darüber, 'drüber adv. over it, above it; about it; in the meantime, meanwhile; before that; (and) more; ~ hinaus beyond that; further; in addition.

darum, drum adv. round it; for it; about it; therefore, for that reason; alles Drum und Dran everything connected with it. ~kommen vws.i. to lose.

darunter, 'drunter adv. under it, below it; underneath; among them, between them, in the midst of them; by that; drunter und drüber topsy-turvy.

das (neuter of **der**) the; that, which. Compp. of **das** see **der-**.

dasein (-z-) v.i. to exist; to be present; ist der Postbote dagewesen? has the postman called? subst. n. existence, life, presence. ~sberechtigung f. right to exist.

da'selbst adv. there, in that very place.

daß (-s) conj. that; ~ doch if only, would it were, I wish (it were); ~ nicht lest, for fear that; es sei denn, ~ unless.

Dat-enverarbeitung f. programming of data. ~ieren v.t. to date. ~o adv. bis ~o till now. ~um n. (-ums, -en) date; pl. particulars.

Dativ m. (-s, -e) dative (case).

Dattel f. (-, -n) date (fruit).

Daube f. (-, -n) stave.

Dauer f. (-) length, duration; continuance; auf die ~ for long, in the long run. ~auftrag m. standing order. ~brandofen m. anthracite stove. ~brenner m. oven with slow-burning fire. ~flug m. non-stop flight. ~haft a. durable, lasting. ~karte f. season-ticket. ~lauf m. long-distance race. ~marsch m. forced march. ~stellung f. permanent job. ~welle f. permanent wave. ~wurst f. hard sausage.

dauern[1] *v.i.* to last, continue; *lange* ~ to take a long time. ~d *a.* continuous, constant.

dauern[2] *v.t.* to be sorry for, regret; *er dauert mich* I am sorry for him.

Daumen *m.* (-s, -) thumb. ~**abdruck** *m.* thumb-print. ~**lutscher** *m.* thumb-sucker. ~**schraube** *f.* thumb-screw.

Däumling *m.* (-s, -e) thumb-stall; (*lit.*) Tom Thumb.

Daune *f.* (-, -n) down. ~**ndecke** *f.* eider-down, quilt.

Daus *n.* (-es, -e) deuce, ace.

da'von (-fon) *adv.* of it, from it; about it; away, off; *das kommt* ~ that's the result. ~**kommen** *vws.i.* to escape. ~**machen** *v.r.* to run away, make off. ~**tragen** *v.t.* to carry off; to win.

da'vor (-fo:r) *adv.* in front of; before; of it; from it; against it.

da'wider *adv.* against it.

da'zu (-tsu:) *adv.* to it; for it, for that purpose; in addition to that. ~**gehören** *v.i.* to belong to it. ~**mal** *adv.* at that time, in those days. ~**tun** *v.t.* to add to.

da'zwischen (-tsvi∫) *adv.* among (them), amongst, in the midst of; between times. ~**fahren** *vws.i.* to interfere (brusquely). ~**kommen** *vws.i.* to come between; to intervene. ~**kunft** *f.* intervention. ~**stehen** *v.i.* to stand between. ~**stellen** *v.t.* to interpose.

De'batt-e *f.* (-e, -en) debate. ~**enschrift** *f.* parliamentary shorthand. ~**ieren** *v.t. & i.* to debate.

Debet *n.* (-s, -s) debit.

De'bit *n.* (-s) ♀ sale.

debü'tieren *v.i.'* to make one's début.

De'chant (-çant) *m.* (-en, -en) dean.

dechiff'rieren *v.t.* to decipher, decode.

Deck *n.* (-s, -e) deck. ~**adresse** *f.* accommodation address. ~**bett** *n.* feather-bed. ~**blatt** *n.* outside leaf of cigar. ~**farbe** *f.* body-colour. ~**mantel** *m.* (*fig.*) cloak, pretence. ~**name** *m.* pseudonym; code word. ~**offi-**

zier *m.* warrant-officer. ~**wort** *n.* code word.

Decke *f.* (-, -n) cover, blanket, coverlet, rug; ceiling (of room); sheet (of ice); *unter einer* ~ *stecken* to conspire together, be accomplices; *sich nach der* ~ *strecken* to adapt expenditure to resources. ~**nbeleuchtung** *f.* ceiling lamp(s). ~**ngemälde** *n.* painting on ceiling.

Deckel *m.* (-s, -) cover, lid.

deck-en *v.t.* to cover; to protect, guard, secure; to roof; to lay (table); to reimburse; to meet (bill). *v.r.* to coincide; to be identical (with). ~**ung** *f.* cover, shelter, protection, guard; covering; reimbursement; funds; security; *in* ~**ung** *gehen* to take cover. ~**weiß** *n.* zinc white.

dedi'zieren *v.t.* to dedicate.

dedu'zieren *v.t.* to deduce; to infer.

De'fekt *m.* (-s, -e) defect, deficiency. *a.* defective, damaged.

defi'lieren *vws.i.* to defile, march past.

defi'n-ieren *v.t.* to define. ~**i'tiv** *a.* definite; final.

Defizit *n.* (-s, -e) deficit.

Defrau'dant *n.* (-en, -en) defrauder.

defrau'dieren *v.t. & i.* to defraud.

Degen[1] *m.* (-s, -) warrior. [THANE]

Degen[2] *m.* (-s, -) sword. ~**koppel** *f.* sword-belt. ~**scheide** *f.* scabbard, sheath. [DAGGER]

degene'rieren *vws.i.* to degenerate.

degra'dieren *v.t.* to degrade.

dehn-bar *a.* extensible; malleable, ductile; elastic; (*fig.*) vague, wide. ~**en** *v.t.* to extend; lengthen, stretch; to expand; to drawl (speech). ~**ung** *f.* extension; lengthening.

Deich *m.* (-[c]) *m.* (-es, -e) dike, dam. ~**graf**, ~**hauptmann** *m.* dike-reeve.

Deichsel (daik-) *f.* (-, -n) shaft, pole. ~**n** *v.t.* to wangle, manage.

dein (dain) *pron. & a.* your; yours; (*bibl. & poet.*) thy, thine. ~**erseits** *adv.* on your part. ~**esgleichen** *pron.* such as you, the like of you. ~**ethalben**,

~etwegen, ~etwillen *advv.* for your sake. ~ige *pron.* yours; thine.

Deka'denz *f.* (-) decadence.

De'kan (-a:-) *m.* (-s, -e) dean. ~at *n.* office of Dean.

Deklam-ati'on *f.* declamation. ~ieren *v.t. & i.* to recite; to declaim.

dekla'rieren *v.t.* to declare (goods).

Deklinati'on *f.* (-, -en) declension; (*astron.*) declination.

dekli'nieren *v.t.* to decline.

De'kokt *n.* (-es, -e) decoction.

dekolle'tiert *a.* low-necked.

Dekor-a'teur (-ateurs, -ateure) decorator, painter; upholsterer. ~ati'on *f.* (*theatr.*) scenery. ~ationsmaler *m.* decorator, painter; (*theatr.*) scenic painter. ~ieren *v.t.* to decorate.

De'kret (-kre:t) *n.* (-s, -e) decree.

dele'gier-en *v.t.* to delegate. ~te(r) *m.* delegate.

deli'kat (-ka:t) *a.* delicate; delicious; ticklish, difficult (question). ~esse *f.* delicacy, tact; dainty (morsel). ~essenhandlung *f.* delicatessen shop.

deli'rieren *v.i.* to rave, be delirious.

Delle *f.* (-, -n) dent.

Del'phin (-fi:n) *m.* (-s, -e) dolphin.

Delta *n.* (-s, -s) delta.

dem (de:m) *dat. sing.* of *der* and *das*; wenn ~ so ist if that is so; wie ~ auch sei be that as it may, however that may be it. ~entsprechend, ~gemäß, ~nach, ~zufolge *advv.* accordingly. ~nächst *adv.* soon, shortly. ~unerachtet, ~ungeachtet *advv.* nevertheless, for all that.

Dema'gog-e *m.* (-en, -en) demagogue. ~ie *f.* demagogy. ~isch *a.* demagogic.

De'mant see Diamant.

demas'kieren *v.t.* to unmask.

De'ment-i *n.* (-is, -is) denial. ~ieren *v.t.* to deny (truth of statement). [F]

demobili'si-eren *v.t. & i.* to demobilize. ~ati'on *f.* demobilization.

Demo'krat (-kra:t) *m.* (-en, -en) democrat. ~ie *f.* democracy.

~isch *a.* democratic.

demo'lieren *v.t.* to demolish.

Demon'strant *m.* (-en, -en) ⚔ (*pol.*) demonstrator.

demon'strieren *v.t. & i.* to demonstrate.

Demontage *f.* dismantling.

demorali'sieren *v.t.* to demoralize.

Demut (de:mu:t) *f.* (-) humility, meekness.

demütig *a.* humble, meek, submissive. ~en *v.t.* to humble; to humiliate. ~ung *f.* humiliation.

den (de:n) *acc. sing. & dat. pl.* of *def. art.* ~en *dat. pl.* of *dem. pron.*

denatu'rieren *v.t.* (*chem.*) to denature.

dengeln *v.t.* to sharpen (scythe).

Denk-art *f.* manner of thinking. ~bar *a.* conceivable; imaginable. ~er *m.* thinker. ~faul *a.* slow (to think). ~kraft *f.* brainpower. ~mal *n.* monument, memorial. ~münze *f.* (commemorative) medal. ~schrift *f.* memorial; memoir. ~spruch *m.* maxim. ~stein *m.* memorial stone, monument. ~würdig *a.* memorable, notable. ~zeichen *n.* token, keepsake. ~zettel *m.* reminder, punishment.

denken (dɛŋkən) *v.i. & t. st.* to think, reflect; to intend, purpose; ~ an to remember, think of. ~ v.r. to imagine; *denk (dir) nur!* imagine! fancy!

denn *conj. & adv.* for, because; then; *es sei* ~ except, unless; *mehr* ~ *je* more than ever.

dennoch *conj.* yet, still, however, nevertheless, though.

Denunzi'ant (-tsi-) *m.* (-en, -en) informer, denouncer.

denun'zieren *v.t.* to denounce.

De'pesch-e *f.* (-e, -en) telegram, wire. ~ieren *v.t. & i.* to telegraph, wire. [F]

depo'nieren *v.t.* to deposit.

depor'tieren *v.t.* to deport.

Depo'siten-(gelder) *pl.* deposits. ~kasse *f.* branch office (of bank).

De'pot (-po:) *n.* (-s, -s) depot, dump; storehouse; deposit.

depri'mieren *v.t.* to depress.

Depu'tierte(r) *m.* (-n, -n) deputy.

der, die, das *def. art.* the. *dem. & rel. pron.* that, who, which.

der-art *adv.* in such a way; to such an extent; so much. **~artig** *a.* such, of that kind. **~einst** *adv.* some day, in days (years) to come. **~einstig** *a.* future. **~enthalben**, **~entwegen**, **~entwillen** *adv.* for her (their, whose) sake. **~gestalt** *adv.* in such a manner, so. **~gleichen**, **~lei** *indecl. aa.* such, of that kind. **~jenige, diejenige, dasjenige** *pron. & a.* that one, the one, he, she, it. **~maleinst** *adv.* hereafter, in days to come. **~maßen** *adv.* so much, to such an extent. **~selbe, dieselbe, dasselbe** *pron.* the same. **~weil** *conj.* whilst. **~zeitig** *a.* at the time, for the time being.

derb *a.* firm, strong, solid; sturdy, robust; rough, rude, coarse, blunt. **~heit** *f.* solidity; sturdiness; roughness, rudeness.

Deri'vat *n.* (-es, -e) derivative.

Derwisch *m.* (-es, -e) dervish.

des *gen. sing.* of **der** and **das**. **~gleichen** *adv.* likewise, ditto. **~halb**, **~wegen** *adv. & conj.* therefore, for that reason.

Des *n.* (inv.) D flat.

Deser'teur *m.* (-s, -e) deserter.

desertieren *vws.i.* to desert.

Desinfektion *f.* (-, -en) disinfection. **~smittel** *n.* disinfectant.

desinfi'zieren *v.t.* to disinfect.

Des'pot (-po:t) *m.* (-en, -en) despot. **~ie** *f.* despotism. **~isch** *a.* despotic.

dessen *gen. sing.* of **der, das, welcher, welches**. **~thalben**, **~twegen**, **~twillen** *advv.* on that account; on account of which. **~ungeachtet** *adv.* nevertheless, for all that.

Desti'llat (-a:t) *n.* (-es, -e) distillate. **~'eur** *m.* distiller; publican.

De'still-e *f.* (-e, -en) (*sl.*) pub. **~ierapparat** *m.* distilling apparatus, still. **~ieren** *v.t.* to distil. **~ierkolben** *m.* distilling flask.

desto *adv.* the (more so); **~ besser** so much the better.

De'tail-handel *m.* retail trade. **~lieren** *v.t.* to detail; to retail.

Detek'tiv (-ti:f) *m.* (-s, -e) detective.

De'tektor *m.* (-s, -en) detector.

deucht *obs. sing. pres. of* **dünken**.

Deut *m.* doit, farthing; **keinen ~ wert** not worth a fig.

Deute'lei *f.* (-, -en) strained interpretation.

deuteln *v.t. & i.* to subtilize; to twist (the meaning of).

deut-en *v.i.* to point (to or at). *v.t.* to explain, interpret. **~lich** *a.* distinct, clear. **~lichkeit** *f.* distinctness, clearness. **~ung** *f.* interpretation, explanation.

deutsch, Deutschland *see* **App. I.**

De'vise (-vi:zə) *f.* (-, -n) motto; foreign bill (of exchange), foreign currency. **~nbewirtschaftung** *f.* foreign currency control. **~nschieber** *m.* foreign currency smuggler.

de'vot (-vo:t) *a.* humble, submissive.

De'zember (de:tsεm-) *m.* (-s, -) December.

dezent *a.* ♧ modest, unobtrusive.

Dezernat *n.* department.

Dezernent *m.* head of department.

Dezi'm-albruch *m.* decimal fraction. **~alwaage** *f.* weigh-bridge. **~ieren** *v.t.* to decimate.

dia'bolisch *a.* diabolic, diabolical.

Dia'dem (-de:m) *n.* (-s, -e) diadem.

Dia'gnose (-gno:zə) *f.* (-, -n) diagnosis.

diagnosti'zieren *v.t.* to diagnose.

diago'nal *a.*, **Diago'nale** *f.* (-, -n) diagonal.

Dia'kon (-ko:n) *m.* (-s, -e) deacon. **~issin** *f.* deaconess.

Dia'lekt *m.* (-s, -e) dialect. **~isch** *a.* dialectic.

Dia'log (-lo:k) *m.* (-s, -e) dialogue.

Dia'mant *m.* (-en, -en) diamond. **~en** *a.* diamond. **~schleifer** *m.* diamond-cutter.

Diaposi'tiv, Dias *n.* (-s, -e) (*phot.*) colour-slide, transparency; (lantern) slide.

Di'ari-um *n.* (-ums, -en) diary.

Diar'rhöe (-rø:) *f.* (-, -n) diarrhoea.

Di'ät (-ε:t) *f.* (-, -en) diet; *pl.* daily allowance; **~ leben** to diet.

dich *acc. of* du.

dicht (diçt) *a.* dense, thick, compact; tight; close; impervious (to water). *adv.* ~ **an**, ~ **bei** near by, close to. ~**e, ~igkeit** *f.* density, tightness, closeness. ~**halten** *v.i.* (*fig.*) not to breathe a word, not let it go further. [TIGHT]

dicht-en[1] *v.t.* to make tight, tighten; to caulk, stop up. ~**ungsring** *m.* washer.

dicht-en[2] *v.t. & i.* to compose, to write poetry; to invent. ~**er** *m.* poet. ~**ergabe** *f.* poetic gift. ~**erin** *f.* poetess. ~**erisch** *a.* poetical. ~**erling** *m.* poetaster. ~**kunst** *f.* (art of) poetry, poetic art. ~**ung** *f.* poetical work, poem; poetry; fiction.

dick *a.* thick; fat, stout, corpulent; big, large, bulky; voluminous; rich; (*colloq.*) ~**e Luft** trouble; (*sl.*) hot water; ~**e Milch** curdled milk; *sich* ~*tun* (a brag, boast. ~**bäckig** *a.* chubby. ~**bäuchig** *a.* paunchy. ~**darm** *m.* large intestine. ~**e** *f.* thickness; corpulency; bigness; size, bulkiness. ~**fellig** *a.* thick-skinned. ~**flüssig** *a.* viscous, viscid, thick. ~**häuter** *m.* pachyderm. ~**icht** *n.* thicket. ~**kopf** *m.* blockhead. ~**köpfig** *a.* stubborn. ~**leibig** *a.* corpulent; (*fig.*) bulky. ~**wanst** *m.* paunch.

die *fem. of* der. ~**weil** *adv. & conj.* while, whilst; because; whereas.

Dieb *m.* (-es, -e) thief, burglar. ~**e'rei** *f.* thieving, pilfering. ~**(e)sgeselle** *m.* accomplice. ~**(e)sgut** *n.* stolen goods. ~**essicher** *a.* burglar-proof. ~**isch** *a.* thievish. *adv.* (*colloq.*) awfully. ~**stahl** *m.* theft, robbery; burglary.

Diele *f.* (-, -n) board, plank; floor; hall, vestibule.

dien-en *v.t.* to serve; *womit kann ich* ~? can I help you? ~**er** *m.* (man-)servant; bow. ~**erin** *f.* maid. ~**erschaft** *f.* servants, household staff. ~**lich** *a.* serviceable, useful.

dienern *v.i.* to bow (and scrape).

Dienst *m.* (-es, -e) service; duty; situation, post, employment; *außer* ~ off duty, (*mil.*) retired; ~ **leisten** to help, oblige; *zu* ~ *stehen* to be at (a person's) disposal. ~**abzeichen** *n.* badge. ~**alter** *n.* seniority (in office, armed services). ~**bar** *a.* subservient; subject. ~**beflissen** *a.* ~**eifrig, ~fertig** *aa.* zealous, officious. ~**bote** *m.* servant, domestic. ~**eid** *m.* official oath. ~**enthebung** *f.* suspension (from duty). ~**grad** *m.* rank. ~**habend** *a.* on duty. ~**leistung** *f.* service. ~**leute** *pl.* servants, domestics. ~**lich** *a.* official. ~**mädchen** *n.* servant-girl, maid. ~**mann** *m.* porter, messenger; (*obs.*) vassal. ~**pflicht** *f.* compulsory (military) service, conscription. ~**sache** *f.* official communication. ~**stelle** *f.* headquarters; depot; centre; office, administrative department. ~**stunden** *pl.* office hours. ~**tauglich** *a.* fit for service. ~**untauglich** *a.* unfit for active service. ~**weg** *m.* official channels. ~**willig** *a.* ready to serve, obliging. ~**wohnung** *f.* official residence.

Dienstag *m.* (-s, -e) Tuesday. ~**s** *adv.* on Tuesdays; every Tuesday.

dies-bezüglich *a.* referring thereto or to this. ~**jährig** *a.* this year's, of this year. ~**mal** *adv.* this time; for once. ~**malig** *a.* this, present. ~**seitig** *a.* on this side. ~**seits** *adv. & prep.* on this side. *subst. n.* this world, this life.

dieser, diese, dies(es) *a. & pron.* this; the latter.

diesig *a.* hazy, misty.

Dietrich *m.* (-s, -e) skeleton key, picklock.

diffamieren *v.t.* to defame.

Differenti'alrechnung *f.* differential calculus.

Diffe'renz *f.* (-, -en) difference. ~**iert** *a.* (*fig.*) discriminating, refined.

diffe'rieren *v.i.* to diverge, differ.

Dik'tat (-a:t) *n.* (-s, -e) dictation; dictated. ~**o'risch** *a.* dictatorial. ~**ur** *f.* dictatorship. ~**zeichen** *n.* reference (number).

dik'tieren v.t. & i. to dictate.

Dile'ttant m. (-en, -en) amateur. ~isch a. amateurish.

dile'ttieren v.i. to toy (with subject), dabble (in).

Ding (-p) n. (-es, -e) thing; object; matter; *guter ~e sein* to be in high spirits; *vor allen ~en* first of all. ~*fest machen* to arrest. ~lich a. material; concrete; objective. ~sda m., f., n. thingamy, thingumbob; what's-its-name.

dingen v.t. st. to hire.

di'nieren v.i. to dine.

Diö'zese (diötse:zə) f. (-, -n) diocese.

Diphthe'r-ie, -itis f. diphtheria.

Diph'thong m. (-es, -e) diphthong.

Di'plom (-plo:m) n. (-s, -e) diploma; certificate. ~*at* m. diplomat. ~a'tie f. diplomacy. ~atisch a. diplomatic. ~'iert a. certificated. ~ingenieur m. certified civil engineer.

dir (di:r) dat. sing. of **du**.

di'rekt a. & adv. direct; straight; ~er Wagen through-carriage. ~i'on f. direction; management. ~or m. managing director, head, principal, governor; headmaster. ~'orium n. board. ~rice f. manageress.

Diri'gent m. (-en, -en) (mus.) conductor.

diri'gieren v.t. & i. to direct; (mus.) to conduct.

Dirndl n. (-s, -n) (dial.) maid, lass. ~kleid n. Bavarian girl's dress.

Dirne f. (-, -n) girl; prostitute.

Dis n. (mus.) D sharp.

Disharmo'nie f. (-, -en) disharmony; discord.

dishar'monisch a. disharmonious.

Dis'kant m. (-s, -e) treble, soprano. ~schlüssel m. treble clef.

Dis'kont m. (-s, -e) discount. ~'ieren v.t. to discount (bill).

diskredi'tieren v.t. to bring disrepute upon.

Diskrepanz f. discrepancy.

dis'kret a. ⚭ discreet = tactful, cautious; reserved. ~i'on f. ⚭ discretion.

Diskussi'on f. (-, -en) discussion, debate.

disku'tieren v.t. & i. to discuss, debate.

Dis'pens m. (-es, -e) ⚭ dispensation = exemption. ~'ieren v.t. to exempt.

dispo'nibel a. available, at one's disposal. ~'nieren v.i. to dispose (of); to arrange. ~siti'on f. disposition; arrangement.

Dis'put (-pu:t) m. (-s, -e) dispute. ~'ieren v.t. to dispute, debate.

disqualifi'zieren v.t. to disqualify.

Dissertation f. dissertation, thesis.

Dissident m. dissenter, nonconformist.

Disso'nanz f. (-, -en) dissonance.

Dis'tanz f. (-, -en) distance.

Distel f. (-, -n) thistle. ~fink m. goldfinch.

Dis'trikt m. (-es, -e) district.

Diszi'plin (distsipli:n) f. (-, -en) discipline. ~arisch a. disciplinary. ~arverfahren n. disciplinary action. ~arvergehen n. disciplinary offence.

di'vers a. sundry.

Divi'dend m. (-en, -en), ~e f. dividend.

divi'dieren v.t. to divide (by).

Diwan (-v-) m. (-s, -e) divan, sofa, settee.

doch (dox) adv. & conj. however, nevertheless; after all; though, yet, but; (after negatives) yes, oh, yes; *ja ~*! but of course; *nicht ~*! certainly not; don't!

Docht (doxt) m. (es, -e) wick.

Dock n. (-s, -s) dock, dockyard. ~en v.t. to dock (ship).

Docke f. (-, -n) skein; baluster; (obs.) doll.

Dogge (dogə) f. (-, -n) German breed of Great Dane. [DOG]

Dogm-a n. (-as, -en) dogma. ~'atiker m. dogmatist. ~'atisch a. dogmatic.

Dohle f. (-, -n) jackdaw.

Doktor m. (-s, -en) doctor; physician; *den ~ machen* to take the degree of doctor. ~arbeit f. thesis for doctorate. ~vater m. supervisor for doctoral thesis.

Doku'ment n. (-s, -e) document. ~'arisch a. documentary. ~'ieren v.t. to prove (by documents).

Dolch *m.* (-es, -e) dagger. **~stoß** *m.* stab with a dagger.

Dolde *f.* (-, -n) umbel. **~ntragend** *a.* umbelliferous.

Dole *f.* drain; sewer.

dolmetsch-en *v.t.* to interpret. **~er** *m.* interpreter. [TURK.]

Dom (do:m) *m.* (-es, -e) cathedral; dome; (*fig.*) vault. **~freiheit** *f.* cathedral close. **~herr** *m.* canon, prebendary. **~pfaffe** *m.* bullfinch.

Do'mäne *f.* (-, -n) domain; crownland.

Domi'nante *f.* (-, -n) dominant.

domi'nieren *v.i.* to domineer.

Dominikaner *m.* Dominican friar.

Dominospiel *n.* dominoes.

Domi'zil (-tsi:l) *n.* (-s, -e) domicile.

Domp'teur (domto:r) *m.* (-s, -e) trainer, tamer.

Donner *m.* (-s, -) thunder; *vom ~ gerührt* thunderstruck. **~schlag** *m.* thunder-clap, thunderbolt. **~wetter** *n.* thunderstorm; (*fig.*) blowing-up; *zum ~wetter!* dash it all! damn it!

donnern *v.i.* to thunder, roar. **~d** *a.* thunderous.

Donnerstag *m.* (-s, -e) Thursday.

Doppel *n.* (-s, -) duplicate. **~adler** *m.* two-headed eagle. **~bereifung** *f.* twin-tyres. **~boden** *m.* false bottom. **~decker** *m.* biplane. **~deutig** *a.* ambiguous. **~ehe** *f.* bigamy. **~gänger** *m.* double. **~gleisig** *a.* doubletrack. **~griff** *m.* (*mus.*) double stop. **~kohlensauer** *a.* bicarbonate of. **~kreuz** *n.* (*mus.*) double sharp. **~läufig** *a.* doublebarrelled. **~punkt** *m.* colon. **~reihig** *a.* double-breasted. **~schalter** *m.* duplex switch. **~schlag** *m.* (*mus.*) turn. **~seitig** *a.* on both sides. **~sinn** *m.* double meaning. **~sinnig** *a.* ambiguous. **~spat** *m.* Iceland spar. **~spiel** *n.* double game. **~steuerung** *f.* (*av.*) dual control. **~stück** *n.* duplicate. **~zentner** *m.* quintal. **~zimmer** *n.* twinbedded room. **~züngig** *a.* double faced.

doppelt *a.* double, twofold; **~e** *Buchführung* double entry. *adv.*

doubly, twice.

Dorf *n.* (-es, "er) village, hamlet. **~bewohner** *m.* villager. **~geistliche(r)** *m.* country parson. **~krug** *m.*, **~schenke** *f.* village inn. **~schulze** *m.* village magistrate. [THORP]

Dörf-ler *m.* (-lers, -ler) villager. **~lich** *a.* rustic.

Dorn *m.* (-es, -en) thorn, prickle, spike; spine. **~busch**, **~strauch** *m.* thorn- or brier-bush. **~hecke** *f.* hedge of thorns. **~enkrone** *f.* crown of thorns. **~envoll**, **~ig** *aa.* thorny. **~röschen** *n.* The Sleeping Beauty.

dörr-en *v.t.* to dry, desiccate, parch. **~obst** *n.* dried fruit.

Dorsch *m.* (-es, -e) torsk, codling.

dort *adv.* there; yonder. **~her** *adv.* from there, thence. **~hin** *adv.* thither; that way; there. **~ig** *a.* of that place; there. **~zulande** *adv.* in that country, over there.

Dose (do:za) *f.* (-, -n) box; can; tin. **~nöffner** *m.* tin-opener. [DU.]

dös-en *v.i.* to doze. **~ig** *a.* sleepy, dull; stupid.

dos-'ieren *v.t.* to measure out. **~is** *f.* dose.

Dotter *m.* & *n.* (-s, -) yolk (of egg). **~blume** *f.* marsh-marigold. [DOT]

Do'zent *m.* (-en, -en) university lecturer. [L]

do'zieren *v.t.* & *i.* to lecture, teach.

Drache(n) *m.* (-n, -n) dragon; kite; (*fig.*) termagant.

Drachme *f.* (-, -n) drachm; dram.

Dra'goner (-go:-) *m.* (-s, -e) dragoon.

Draht (dra:t) *m.* (-es, "e) wire, cable, line. **~anschrift** *f.* telegraphic address. **~antwort** *f.* telegraphic reply. **~bericht** *m.* telegram, wire. **~haarig** *a.* wirehaired. **~los** *a.* wireless. **~netz** *n.* wire gauze, wire netting. **~schere** *f.* wire-cutters. **~seilbahn** *f.* funicular railway. **~verhau** *m.* wire entanglement. **~zange** *f.* pliers. **~zieher** *m.* wire-drawer; (*fig.*) wire-puller. [THREAD]

drahten *v.t.* & *i.* to telegraph, wire.

dra'konisch *a.* Draconian.

drall[1] *a.* buxom; firm; sturdy.

Drall[2] *m.* (-es, -e) twist of rifling.

Dra'mat-iker *m.* (-ikers, -iker) dramatist, playwright. ~isch *a.* dramatic. ~i'sieren *v.t.* to dramatize. ~'urg *m.* ◊ (*theatr.*) producer. ~ur'gie *f.* dramaturgy; theory or technique of dramatic art.

dran see daran.

drang[1] *imperf. of* dringen.

Drang[2] (-ŋ) *m.* (-es) pressure; oppression; stress; distress; impulse. ~sal *f, n.* affliction, distress, hardship. ~sa'lieren *v.t.* to afflict, oppress; to worry, torment. [THRONG]

drängeln *v.t. & i.* to push, shove, press.

drängen (-ŋən) *v.t. & i.* to push, press, crowd; to hurry, to urge. *gedrängt voll* crammed full, closely packed.

drä'nieren *v.t.* to drain.

dra'pieren *v.t.* to drape.

drastisch *a.* drastic.

dräuen (*obs.*) see drohen.

drauf see darauf. ~gänger *m.* daredevil.

draus see daraus.

draußen *adv.* outside; out of doors; abroad.

Drechs-elbank *f.* turning-lathe. ~eln *v.t.* to turn on a lathe. ~ler *m.* turner. ~lerware *f.* turnery.

Dreck *m.* (-s) dirt, filth, muck, mud. ~ig *a.* dirty, filthy, muddy.

Dreh-bank *f.* turning-lathe. ~bleistift *m.* propelling pencil. ~bolzen *m.* axis pin, pivot-belt. ~buch *n.* scenario. ~bühne *f.* revolving stage. ~er *m.* turner. ~krankheit *f.* staggers; giddiness. ~kreuz *n.* turnstile. ~orgel *f.* barrel-organ. ~punkt *m.* pivot, fulcrum. ~scheibe *f.* turn-table; potter's wheel, revolving disk; dial. ~strom *m.* three-phase current. ~stuhl *m.* revolving chair. ~tür *f.* revolving door. ~ung *f.* turn; rotation; revolution. ~zahl *f.* revolutions per minute.

drehen *v.t. & r.* to turn, rotate,

revolve; to roll, wind, twist; to veer; to shoot (film); (*av.*) to spin; *sich ~ um* (*fig.*) to be a question (whether), to hinge on.

drei *a. & subst. f.* three. ~achteltakt *m.* three-eight time. ~blatt *n.* trefoil. ~blättrig *a.* three-leaved. ~bund *m.* Triple Alliance. ~eck *n.* triangle. ~eckig *a.* triangular. ~einig *a.* triune. ~einigkeit *f.* (the) Trinity. ~erlei *indecl. a.* of three kinds. ~fach *a.* threefold, treble. ~faltigkeit *f.* (the) Trinity. ~farbendruck *m.* three-colour print. ~fuß *m.* tripod; trivet. ~gestrichen *a.* thrice accented. ~jährig *a.* three-year-old; triennial. ~kantig *a.* three-cornered. ~käsehoch *m.* tiny fellow. ~klang *m.* triad. ~königstag *m.* Epiphany, Twelfth-day. ~mal *adv.* three times, thrice. ~malig *a.* thrice repeated. ~master *m.* three-master; threecornered hat. ~monatig *a.* threemonths-old; lasting three m. ~monatlich *a.* quarterly. ~rad *n.* tricycle. ~schenkelig *a.* threelegged. ~seitig *a.* trilateral. ~silbig *a.* trisyllabic. ~ßig *a.* thirty. ~stellig *a.* of three digits. ~stimmig *a.* for three voices. ~stöckig *a.* three-storied. ~teilig *a.* in three parts, tripartite. ~vierteltakt *m.* triple time. ~zack *m.* trident. ~zehn *a.* thirteen.

drein see darein.

dreist *a.* bold, daring, audacious; cheeky, impudent. ~igkeit *f.* boldness; impudence.

Drell *m.* (-s) ticking.

Dresch-e *f.* (-e) (*colloq.*) thrashing. ~en *v.t. st.* to thrash, thresh. ~er *m.* thrasher. ~flegel *m.* flail.

Dre'ss-eur *m.* trainer. ~ieren *v.t.* to train; to break in. ~ur *f.* training, breaking-in. [F]

Drill *m.* (-es) drill. ~bohrer *m.* drill. ~en *v.t.* to drill.

Drillich (-c) *m.* (-s) ticking.

Drilling[1] *m.* (-s, -e) 1. triplet. 2. three-barrelled gun.

Drilling[2] *m.* (-s, -e) lantern-wheel.

drin, drinnen see **darin**.

dring-en v.i. st. to penetrate; to get in; to enter; *in einen* ~en *auf* to insist on; *in einen* ~en to urge a person; *sich gedrungen fühlen* to feel compelled. ~**end** a. urgent. ~**lich** a. pressing, urgent. ~**lichkeit** f. urgency. ~~**sliste** f. priority list. ~~**sstufe** f. high priority.

drischt 3 *sing. pres. ind. of* **dreschen**.

dritt-e a. third. ~**el** n. a third (part). ~**eln** v.t. to divide into three. ~**ens** adv. thirdly. ~**letzt** a. last but two.

droben adv. up there; above; on high.

Drog-e (dro:gə) f. (-e, -en) drug. ~**e′rie** f. chemist's shop. ~′**ist** m. druggist.

Droh-brief m. threatening letter. ~**en** v.i. to threaten. ~**ung** f. threat.

Drohne f. (-, -n) drone.

dröhnen (-ø:-) v.i. to roar; to rumble; to boom.

drollig a. droll, funny, comical.

Drome′dar n. (-s, -e) dromedary.

drosch imperf. of **dreschen**.

Droschke f. (-, -n) cab. ~**nkutscher** m. cabby, cabman. [RUSS.]

Drossel[1] f. (-, -n) thrush.

Drossel[2] f. (-, -n) throat. ~**klappe** f., ~**ventil** n. throttle-valve. ~**n** v.t. to throttle.

drüben (-y:b-) adv. over there, yonder.

drüber see **darüber**.

Druck m. (-es, -e) **1.** pressure; compression; squeeze; (*fig.*) weight, strain, burden. **2.** print, printing; impression; *kleiner* ~ small type. ~**bogen** m. proof, proof-sheet. ~**buchstabe** m. type; block letter. ~**erlaubnis** f. imprimatur; licence. ~**farbe** f. printer's ink. ~**fehler** m. misprint, printer's error. ~**fertig**, ~**reif** aa. ready for the press. ~**knopf** m. press-stud; patent-fastener; push-button. ~**legung** f. printing. ~**luft** f. compressed air. ~**luftbremse** f. pneumatic brake. ~**messer** m. pressure gauge. ~**ort** m. place of printing. ~**probe** f. specimen,

sample. ~**pumpe** f. pressure pump. ~**reif** a. ready for the press. ~**sache** f. printed matter. ~**schrift** f. type; publication. ~**stock** m. (*typ.*) wood-block; plate.

Drückeberger m. (-s, -) shirker, skulker; malingerer.

drucken v.t. to print; *wie gedruckt lügen* to tell whopping lies.

drück-en v.t. to press, clasp, squeeze; to pinch; to bring down; to lower (record); to undercut (wages); (*fig.*) to depress. v.r. to sneak off, steal away; to shirk. ~**end** a. heavy; oppressive; (*of air*) sultry. ~**er** m. latch; trigger.

Drucker m. (-s, -) printer. ~′**ei** f. printing-works. ~**schwärze** f. printer's ink.

drucksen v.i. to waver, hesitate.

Drude f. (-, -n) witch. ~**nfuß** m. pentagram; (*bot.*) club-moss.

drum see **darum**.

drunten adv. down there, below.

Druse f. (-, -n) druse; (*vet.*) glanders.

Drüse f. (-, -n) gland.

Dschungel m., f., & n. jungle.

du pron. thou; you; *auf* ~ *und* ~ *stehen* to be on intimate terms.

Dualismus m. dualism.

Dübel m. (-s, -) dowel, peg, plug.

Du′blette f. (-, -n) duplicate.

duck-en v.t. to stoop, duck; to humble. v.r. to bow one's head; to stoop; to knuckle under; to sing small. ~**mäuser** m. coward.

dudel-n v.i. to play on the bagpipes. ~**sack** m. bagpipes.

Du′ell n. (-es, -e) duel. ~′**ieren** v.r. to fight a duel.

Du′ett n. (-es, -e) duet.

Duft m. (-es, -ͤe) scent, smell, fragrance. ~**en** v.i. to smell sweet, be fragrant. ~**ig** a. sweet-smelling, fragrant; airy, light; hazy.

Du′katen m. (-s, -) ducat.

duld-en v.t. & i. to endure, bear, suffer; to tolerate, allow. ~**er** m. sufferer; martyr. ~**sam** a. enduring, long-suffering; tolerant.

Dult f. (-, -en) fair.

dumm a. stupid, dull, slow, silly,

ignorant. ~dreist a. impertinent. ~heit f. stupidity; blunder. ~kopf m. stupid fellow, noodle, dunce. [DUMB]

dumpf a. muggy, damp, musty, stuffy; hollow, deep-sounding; (fig.) dull, gloomy. ~ig a. damp, musty. [DUMPS]

Düne f. (dy:na) f. (-e, -en) dune. ~enhafer m. bent(s). ~ung f. swell, surf. [DOWN]

Dung m. (-es) dung. ~gabel f. dung-fork. ~grube f. manure-pit. düngen v.t. to manure, fertilize. ~er m. manure, fertilizer. ~erhaufen m. dung-heap, dung-hill. ~mittel n. fertilizer.

dunkel a. dark, dusky, dim; gloomy; (fig.) obscure; vague. subst. n., ~häutig a. dark-skinned. ~heit f. darkness; obscurity. ~kammer f. darkroom. ~mann m. obscurantist.

Dünkel m. (-s) conceit; presumption; pride. ~haft a. conceited; haughty, arrogant.

dunkeln v.i. to grow dark.

dünken v.i. es dünkt mich (or mir) it seems to me, I think. v.r. to fancy oneself.

dünn a. thin; dilute; weak; rare. ~bier n. small beer. ~darm m. small intestine. ~druckausgabe f. India paper edition. ~e, ~heit f. thinness; weakness. ~flüssig a. watery, fluid. ~gesät a. sparsely sown; thinly scattered; (fig.) scarce.

Dunst m. (-es, ~e) vapour; haze; fume; blauen ~ vormachen to humbug (one); keinen blassen ~ h. not to have the foggiest notion. ~gebilde n. phantom. ~ig a. vaporous; hazy; damp, moist. ~kreis m. atmosphere. [DUST]

dunsten v.i. to evaporate; to steam.

dünsten v.t. to stew.

Dupli'kat n. (-s, -e) duplicate.

Dur a. (mus.) major. [L]

durch (durç) prep., adv., & pref. through; across; by, by means of, out of; owing to, because of; during, throughout; die ganze Zeit durch the whole time, all the time.

durch|arbeiten v.t. to work

through, study thoroughly; to train (body). v.r. to get through, force one's way through.

durchaus adv. thoroughly, quite; absolutely, by all means; ~ nicht not at all, by no means.

durchbeißen v.t. to bite through. v.r. to fight one's way through.

durchbilden v.t. to develop thoroughly; to educate (highly).

durchblättern v.t. to turn over (pages), skim (book).

Durchblick m. view, vista. ~en v.t. to look through; ~en lassen to hint, suggest.

durchbohren v.t. to bore or pierce through; to pierce, perforate.

durchbrechen v.t. & i. to break through; to pierce, penetrate.

durchbrennen v.i. to burn through; (electr.) to fuse; (fig.) to abscond.

durchbringen v.t. to carry through; to squander (money). v.r. to support oneself.

durch'brochen a. filigree, openwork.

Durchbruch m. break-through; breach; rupture. ~arbeit f. filigree work, net work, pinking.

durchdenken v.t. to think over.

durchdringen v.t. to penetrate, get through; to succeed. durch'dringen v.t. to penetrate, permeate; to fill. ~d a. penetrating, piercing, shrill.

durchdrücken v.t. to press or squeeze through; (fig.) to enforce.

durchdrungen a. ~s. to be convinced (of), inspired (by).

durcheinander adv. confusedly, in disorder. subst. n. confusion, disorder, muddle, medley.

durchfahr·en v.t. & vvs.i. to drive through; to traverse; (fig.) to flash across. ~t f. thoroughfare, passage.

Durchfall m. failure; (med.) diarrhoea. ~en vvs.i. to fall through; (fig.) to fail.

durchfechten v.t. to fight out. v.r. to fight one's way through.

durchfinden v.r. to find one's way through.

durchfliegen v.t. & vvs.i. to fly through; (fig.) to skim over, glance through; (colloq.) to fail (in exam).

durchfließen v.t. & vws.i. to flow through.

Durchfluß m. flowing through.

durch'forschen v.t. to search through; to investigate.

durchfressen v.t. & i. to eat through; to corrode. v.r. (fig.) to struggle through.

durchfrieren vws.i. to be chilled right through.

Durchfuhr f. transit.

durchführ-bar a. practicable, feasible. **~en** v.t. to convey through; (fig.) to execute, accomplish. **~ung** f. accomplishment, performance, execution.

durch'furcht a. wrinkled, furrowed.

Durchgabe f. (radio) announcement.

Durchgang m. passage; transit; kein ~ no thoroughfare. **~sverkehr** m. through-traffic; transit-trade. **~swagen** m. through-carriage.

Durchgäng-er m. (-ers, -er) runaway horse. **~ig** adv. throughout, without exception.

durchgehen vws.i. to go through; (of horse & fig.) to bolt, run away; (of law) to pass, be adopted. v.t. to examine, peruse, work through; ~ lassen to let pass. **~d** a. fast, through (train); continuous. **~ds** adv. generally, without exception, universally.

durch'geistigt a. spiritual; of superior intelligence.

durch'glühen v.t. to heat red-hot; (fig.) to inflame, inspire.

durchgreifen v.i. to put one's hand through; (fig.) to take vigorous action. **~d** a. decisive.

durchhalten v.i. to hold out, carry through.

durchhauen v.t. to cut through; to thrash, flog. v.r. to hack one's way through.

durchhecheln v.t. to hackle (flax); (fig.) to pull to pieces.

durchkommen vws.i. to get through; to pass (exam); (fig.) to manage.

durch'kreuzen v.t. to cross; (fig.) to thwart.

Durchlaß m. (Durchlass-es, ⸗sse) passage, opening, outlet.

durchlassen v.t. to let through; to let pass.

durchlässig a. permeable, pervious, penetrable.

Durchlaucht f. (-, -en) Serene Highness.

durchlaufen vws.i. to run through; to filter through. v.t. to wear out (shoes).

durch'leben v.t. to live through, go through.

durchlesen v.t. to read through, peruse.

durchleuchten v.i. to shine through. **durch'leuchten** v.t. to illuminate; (med.) to X-ray.

durchliegen v.r. to get bed-sores.

durch'loch-en v.t. to punch. **~t** a. perforated.

durch'löcher-n v.t. to perforate; to pierce; to make holes. **~t** a. ragged; holey (shoe); riddled (with bullets).

durchmachen v.t. to go through, suffer.

Durchmarsch m. march through. **~ieren** vws.i. to march through.

durch'messen v.t. to traverse.

Durchmesser m. (-s, -) diameter.

durch'nässen v.t. to wet through, soak, drench.

durchnehmen v.t. to work through, go over; to deal with.

durchpausen v.t. to trace; to copy.

durchpeitschen v.t. to whip soundly.

durchprügeln v.t. to thrash soundly.

durch'pulst a. full (of), vibrating (with).

durch'queren v.t. to cross, traverse.

durchrechnen v.t. to reckon up, count over.

Durchreise f. journey through, passing through, transit. **~n** vws. i. & t. to travel through; to traverse, cross. **~nde(r)** m. through-passenger. **~visum** n. transit-visa.

durchreißen v.t. to tear in two, break. vws.i. to get torn.

durchrennen vws.i. & v.t. to run through.

durchrieseln *vws.i. & v.t.* to flow through; to run through.

Durchsage *f.* announcement. **~n** *v.t.* to announce.

durchschauen *v.i.* to look through.

durch'schauen *v.t.* to see through.

durch'schauern *v.t.* to shudder; *es durchschauert ihn* he quivers (with fear, etc.).

durchscheinen *v.i.* to shine through. **~d** *a.* transparent, translucent.

durchschießen *v.t.* to shoot through; to interleave (book); (*typ.*) to space out, lead.

Durchschlag *m.* colander, strainer, filter; carbon copy. **~en** *v.t.* to beat through; to strain. *v.i.* to penetrate; to blot; (*fig.*) to be effective; to be successful. *v.r.* to fight one's way through; to rough it. **~end** *a.* powerful, decisive. **~papier** *n.* copying-paper, carbon paper. **~skraft** *f.* penetrating power; force of percussion.

durchschlängeln *v.r.* to wind (one's way) through.

durchschleusen *v.t.* to pass through the locks.

durchschlüpfen *vws.i.* to slip through.

durchschneiden *v.t.* to cut through; to intersect (line).

Durchschnitt *m.* cut; intersection; cross-section; (*fig.*) average. **~lich** *a.* average, on an average.

durch-schreiben *v.t.* to copy, make a copy. **~schrift** *f.* carbon copy.

Durchschuß *m.* woof, weft; (*typ.*) leads, space-line; interleaf.

durchsehen *v.i.* to see or look through. *v.t.* to examine, look over.

durchseihen *v.t.* to strain, filter.

durchsetzen *v.t.* to achieve; to enforce. *v.r.* to succeed, make one's way. **durch'setzen** *mit* to mix, intersperse with.

Durchsicht *f.* view, vista; (*fig.*) inspection, perusal; revision. **~ig** *a.* transparent, clear.

durchsickern *vws.i.* to ooze, trickle through; (*fig.*) to leak out.

durchsieben *v.t.* to sift.

durchsprechen *v.t.* to talk over.

durchspülen *v.t.* to rinse, to flush.

durchstech-en *v.t.* to pierce through; to transfix; to cut through. **~e'rei** *f.* plotting, intriguing.

durchstehen *v.i.* to sit out; to see through.

Durchstich *m.* cutting; cut.

durchstöbern *v.t.* to rummage through, ransack.

durchstoßen *v.t. & i.* to pierce, transfix, stab; to break through.

durchstreichen *v.t.* to strike out, cancel.

durch'streifen *v.t.* to roam through.

durchströmen *v.t. & vws.i.* to flow through; to run through.

durchsuch-en *v.t.* to search through, search all over. **~ung** *f.* search; (police) raid.

durch'tränkt *a.* saturated, impregnated.

durchtreiben *v.t.* to drive through.

durch'trieben *a.* cunning, sly, artful.

durch'wachsen *a.* streaky.

durchwärmen *v.t.* to warm through.

Durchweg *m.* passage. *adv.* throughout, all.

durchweichen *v.t. & vws.i.* to soak; to become wet or soft.

durch'wirken *v.t.* to interweave.

durchwühlen *v.t.* to root up; to ransack, rummage.

durchzeichnen *v.t.* to trace.

durchziehen *v.t.* to draw through; to thread (needle); to interlace; (*of rivers, &c.*) to run through; to pass or march through. *vws.i.* to pass or march through.

durch'zucken *v.t.* to flash through.

Durchzug *m.* march through, passage; through-draught.

dürfen *v.i. st.* to be allowed, be permitted, may; to venture, dare; *er darf nicht* he must not; *darf ich bitten?* will you, please…?

dürftig *a.* needy, indigent, scanty, poor; insufficient. **~keit** *f.* indigence, need, want; scantiness, meagreness.

dürr *a.* dry, parched, arid; dried,

withered; lean, skinny; barren, sterile, poor; ~e *Worte* plain or blunt language. ~e f. dryness; drought.

Durst m. (-es) thirst. ~en, **dürsten** vv.i. to be thirsty; (*fig.*) to long (for), crave (for). ~ig a. thirsty.

Dusche f. (-, -n) douche; shower-bath. ~n v.t. to douche.

Düse f. (-, -n) nozzle, jet. ~nantrieb m. jet propulsion; *mit* ~nantrieb jet propelled. ~nflugzeug n. jet-plane. ~njäger m. jet-fighter. ~nrohr n. blast pipe.

Dusel m. (-s) stupor, dizziness; (*colloq.*) luck. ~ig a. sleepy, dizzy. ~n v.i. to be half asleep, doze.

düster a. dark, gloomy; sad, melancholy. ~heit, ~keit f. darkness, dusk, gloom.

Dutzend n. (-s, -e) dozen. ~mal adv. dozens of times. ~weise adv. by the dozen.

Duz-bruder m. intimate friend. ~en v.t., *auf* ~fuß *stehen* to say 'du' to.

Dy'namik (-na:-) f. (-) dynamics. **Dyna'mit** n. (-s) dynamite. **Dy'namo** m. (-s, -s) dynamo. **Dynas'tie** f. (-, -en) dynasty. **D-Zug** m. (de:-) express train.

E

E, e (e:) n. the letter E, e; (*mus.*) e.

Ebbe f. (-, -n) ebb or low tide. ~n v.i. to ebb.

eben (e:-) a. even, level, flat, smooth; (*math.*) plane; *zu* ~er *Erde* on the ground-floor. adv. just, even; evenly; exactly; ~ *erst* just now. ~bild n. likeness, image. ~bürtig a. equal in birth; equal. ~da, ~dort adv. in that place, there, ibidem. ~derselbe pron. the very same. ~deshalb adv. for that very reason. ~falls adv. likewise, too, also. ~maß n. symmetry, harmony, due proportion. ~mäßig a. symmetri-

cal, proportionate. ~so adv. just as, just so, quite as.

Ebene (e:-) f. (-, -n) plain; (*math.*) plane; (*fig.*) level.

Ebenholz n. ebony.

Eber (e:-) m. (-s, -) boar.

Eber|esche f. mountain ash.

ebnen (e:-) v.t. to level, smooth.

Echo (εço:) n. (-s, -s) echo. ~n v.i. to echo.

echt (εçt) a. genuine, true, real; unadulterated (wine); pure (metal); fast (colour); real, own (hair); legitimate; authentic (text). ~heit f. genuineness; fastness; authenticity; legitimacy.

Eck-e f. (-e, -en) corner; angle; edge; turning; *an allen* ~en *und Enden* everywhere; *um die* ~e *bringen* to murder. ~ig a. angular; cornered; (*fig.*) awkward. ~stein m. corner-stone. ~zahn m. eye-tooth.

Ecker f. (-, -n) acorn; beech-nut.

edel (e:-) a. noble, well-born; generous; precious (stone); *edle Teile* vital parts. ~frau f. titled lady. ~hirsch m. stag, red deer. ~knabe m. page. ~mann m., ~leute pl. nobleman, nobles. ~metall n. precious metal. ~mut m., ~sinn m. magnanimity, generosity. ~mütig a. magnanimous, generous. ~obst n. choice fruit. ~stein m. precious stone, jewel. ~tanne f. silver fir.

E'dikt n. (-es, -e) edict.

Efeu (e:foi) m. (-s) ivy.

E'ffekt m. (-s, -e) effect; (pl. -en) stocks. ~enhandel m. stock(-exchange) business. ~enhändler m. stockbroker. ~hascherei f. showing-off, claptrap. ~iv a. ♃ actual, real. ~voll a. effective.

e'gal (e:ga:l) a. alike, the same; all one.

Egel (e:-) m. (-s, -) leech.

Egge f. (-, -n) harrow; ~n v.t. to harrow.

Ego-'ismus m. (-) egoism. ~'ist m. egoist. ~'istisch a. egoistic. ~zentrisch a. egocentric.

ehe[1] (e:ə) conj. before; until. ~dem, ~mals advv. before this

time, formerly, of old. **~malig**
a. former; late. **~r** adv. sooner;
rather; umso **~r** all the sooner;
nicht **~r** not until. **~stens** adv.
as soon as possible, very soon,
at the earliest. [ERE]

Ehe² (e:ǝ) f. (-, -n) matrimony;
marriage; wilde **~** concubinage;
~brechen to commit adultery.
~brecher m. adulterer. **~bre-
cherin** f. adulteress. **~bruch** m.
adultery. **~bund** m. marriage-
tie; matrimony. **~frau** f. wife,
spouse. **~gatte** m. husband.
~hälfte f. better half. **~leute**
pl., **~paar** n. married couple.

ehelich a. matrimonial, conjugal;
legitimate. **~en** v.t. to marry.

Ehe-losigkeit f. celibacy.
~mann m. husband. **~recht** n.
marriage law. **~scheidung** f.
divorce. **~scheidungsklage** f. divorce suit. **~schließung** f. marriage. **~stand** m. married state,
wedlock. **~stifter** m. match-
maker. **~versprechen** n. promise
of marriage. **~weib** n. wife,
spouse.

ehern a. brazen; brass; bronze;
mit **~er** Stirn brazen-faced.

Ehr-abschneider m. slanderer.
~bar a. respectable, honourable,
honest. **~begier(de)** f. ambition.

Ehre f. (-, -n) honour; reputation;
respect; privilege.

ehren v.t. to honour; sehr geehrter
Herr! Dear Sir.

Ehren-amt n. honorary post.
~amtlich a. honorary. **~be-
zeigung** f. mark of respect,
salute. **~bürger** m. honorary
citizen. **~doktor** n. honorary
doctor. **~gabe** f. donation,
presentation. **~gast** m. guest
of honour. **~geleit** n. retinue,
suite. **~gericht** n. court of
honour. **~haft** a. honourable,
high-principled. **~halber** adv.
for honour's sake. **~handel** m.
affair of honour. **~kleid** n.
ceremonial dress. **~kränkung**
f. affront, insult, libel. **~mal** n.
monument; cenotaph. **~mann**
m. man of honour. **~mitglied** n.
honorary member. **~preis** m.
prize. n. (bot.) speedwell. **~recht**

n. bürgerliche **~rechte** civic rights.
~rettung f. vindication, apology.
~rührig a. defamatory, libellous.
~voll a. creditable, honourable.
~wert a. respectable. **~wort** n.
word of honour. **~wörtlich** a. on
one's word of honour. **~zeichen**
n. decoration, medal.

ehr-erbietig a. respectful, reverential. **~erbietung** f. deference,
respect, veneration. **~furcht** f.
respect, awe, reverence. **~fürch-
tig** a. reverential. **~gefühl** n.
sense of honour; self-respect.
~geiz m. ambition. **~geizig** a.
ambitious. **~lich** a. honest, fair.
~lichkeit f. honesty. **~los** a.
dishonourable. **~losigkeit** f.
dishonesty, infamy. **~sam** a.
respectable, decent. **~sucht** f.
ambition. **~vergessen** a. unprincipled, infamous. **~verlust**
m. loss of civic rights. **~widrig**
a. disgraceful, discreditable.
~würden m. (The) Reverend.
~würdig a. venerable, reverend.

ei¹ interj. ah! why! indeed!

Ei² n. (-es, -er) egg; wie aus
dem **~** gepellt spick and span.
~dotter, **~gelb** n. yolk. **~er-
becher** m. egg-cup. **~erkuchen**
m. omelet. **~erschale** f. egg-
shell. **~erschnee** m. whisked
white of eggs. **~erstock** m.
ovary. **~förmig** a. oval, oblong.
~weiß n. white of egg, albumen; protein. **~weißhaltig** a.
containing protein. **~weißstoff**
m. protein. [EGG]

Eibe f. (-, -n) yew.

Eich-amt n. gauging office. **~maß**
n. standard.

Eich-e f., **~baum** m. oak(-tree).
~el f. acorn; (anat.) glans;
(card) club. **~elhäher** m. jay.
~enlaub n. oak leaves. **~hörn-
chen**, **~kätzchen** n. squirrel.
[OAK]

eichen¹ v.t. to gauge.

eichen² a. of oak, oaken.

Eid m. (-es, -e) oath; **~ablegen**,
~leisten to take an oath, attest.
~brecher m. perjurer. **~bruch**
m. perjury. **~esformel** f. form
of oath. **~esstattlich** a. in lieu
of oath. **~genossenschaft** f. con-

federacy; Confederation. ~lich *a.* on oath, by oath, sworn; ~liche Erklärung *affidavit.* ~schwur *m.* oath.

Eidam *m.* (-s, -e) *(obs.)* son-in-law.

Eidechse (-dɛksə) *f.* (-, -n) lizard.

Eiderdaunen *f.pl.* eider-down.

Eifer *m.* (-s) zeal, ardour, fervour. ~er *m.* zealot. ~sucht *f.* jealousy. ~süchtelei *f.* petty jealousy. ~süchtig *a.* jealous.

eifern *v.i.* to take great pains, endeavour; ~ *über* to get angry about; ~ *gegen* to inveigh against; ~ *um* to vie with (someone) in (doing a thing).

eifrig *a.* eager, keen, zealous.

eigen *a.* own, proper; particular, special, separate; exact; peculiar, strange, odd; *sich zu ~ machen* to adopt, utilize. ~art *f.* peculiarity, individuality. ~artig *a.* special, peculiar. ~brödler *m.* crank, eccentric. ~dünkel *m.* self-conceit. ~geschwindigkeit *f.* *(phys.)* initial velocity; *(av.)* air speed; characteristic speed. ~gewicht *n.* dead weight; net weight. ~händig *a.* with one's own hand; autograph (letter). ~heit *f.* peculiarity; idiosyncrasy; idiom. ~liebe *f.* egotism, self-complacency. ~lob *n.* self-praise. ~mächtig *a.* arbitrary, autocratic; unauthorized. ~name *m.* proper name; noun. ~nutz *m.* selfishness, egotism. ~nützig *a.* self-seeking, selfish. ~schaft *f.* quality; property; feature; attribute; capacity. ~schaftswort *n.* adjective.

eigen-s *adv.* on purpose, particularly, expressly. ~sinn *m.* wilfulness, obstinacy. ~sinnig *a.* stubborn, self-willed. ~ständig *a.* independent. ~ständigkeit *f.* autonomy. ~tlich *a.* true, real; essential; proper; intrinsic. *adv.* really, exactly. ~tum *n.* property. ~swohnung *f.* owner-occupier flat. ~tümer *m.* proprietor, owner. ~tümlich *a.* proper; specific; peculiar, strange, odd. ~tümlichkeit *f.* peculiarity, characteristic. ~wärme *f.*

specific heat; body heat. ~willig *a.* self-willed; wilful.

eign-en *v.r.* to be suited, be adapted, be qualified (for). ~er *m.* owner. ~ung *f.* aptitude, qualification; suitability.

Eiland *n.* (-s, -e) island.

Eil-bestellung *f.* express delivery. ~bote *m.* courier; *(on letters)* per ~boten express. ~brief *m.* express letter.

Eil-e *f.* (-e) hurry, haste, speed. ~fertig *a.* hasty, rash. ~fertigkeit *f.* hastiness. ~fracht *f.*, ~gut *n.* express goods. ~ig *a.* quick, hurried; urgent; *es ~ig haben* to be in a hurry. ~marsch *m.* forced march. ~post *f.* express delivery. ~zug *m.* fast train.

eilen *v.i.* & *r.* to hurry, hasten. ~ds *adv.* speedily, quickly, hastily.

Eimer *m.* (-s, -) pail, bucket. [L]

ein 1. *art.* a, an; ~ *jeder* each one. 2. *pron.* one; ~ *und derselbe* the very same; *manch ~er* many a one; ~s *ums andre Mal* alternately. 3. *num.* a, one; ~er *von beiden eins* either; ~ *für alle Mal* once and for all; *in ~em fort* continuously, incessantly; *mit ~s* suddenly; *um ~s* at one o'clock. See also einer and eins.

ein² *adv. nicht ~ und aus wissen* to be at one's wit's end; ~ *und aus gehen* to frequent. *sep. pref.* For words not given under ein- see the simple nouns and verbs.

einachsig *a.* two-wheeled.

Einakter *m.* (-s, -) one-act play.

ein'ander *indecl. pron.* each other, one another.

einarbeiten *v.r.* to get used to, familiarize oneself with.

einarmig *a.* one-armed.

ein'äscher-n *v.t.* to burn to ashes; to cremate. ~ung *f.* cremation; incineration. ~ungshalle *f.* crematorium.

einatm-en *v.t.* to inhale. ~ung *f.* inhalation.

einäugig *a.* one-eyed.

Einbahnstraße *f.* one-way street.

einbalsamieren *v.t.* to embalm.

Einband *m.* binding. **~decke** *f.* cover.

einbändig *a.* in one volume.

einbauen *v.t.* to install, fit; to build in.

Einbaum *m.* log-canoe.

einbegreifen *v.t.* to include, comprise.

einbehalten *v.t.* to keep back, detain.

einbeinig *a.* one-legged.

einberuf-en *v.t.* to convene, summon; (*mil.*) to call out, call up. **~ung** *f.* summoning; calling up.

einbett-en *v.t.* (*fig.*) to embed, surround with). **~ig** *a.* single (-bedded).

einbeziehen *v.t.* to include, implicate.

einbiegen *v.t.* to bend inwards. *vws.i.* to turn (into).

einbild-en *v.r.* to imagine, fancy, think, believe; to pride oneself (on). **~ung** *f.* imagination, fancy; conceit, presumption.

einbinden *v.t.* to bind (book).

einblasen *v.t.* to blow into; (*fig.*) to whisper, prompt.

Einbläser *m.* prompter, insinuator.

Einblattdruck *m.* broadsheet, offprint, leaflet.

einbläuen, einbleuen *v.t.* to drum in.

Einblick *m.* insight.

einbrech-en *v.t.* to break open, smash in. *vws.i.* to break through; to break in, (*colloq.*) burgle; to set in; *Nacht bricht ein* night is falling. **~er** *m.* burglar.

einbrennen *v.t.* to brand; to burn.

einbring-en *v.t.* to bring in; to yield; to make up for, retrieve. **~lich** *a.* profitable.

einbrocken *v.t.* to crumble; *sich etwas ~* to put one's foot in it.

Einbruch *m.* housebreaking, burglary; break through; **~** *der Nacht* nightfall. **~diebstahl** *m.* burglary. **~ssicher** *a.* burglarproof.

Einbuchtung *f.* (-, -en) dent; bay.

einbürger-n *v.t.* to naturalize; to adopt (foreign word, &c.). *v.r.* to become naturalized; to be adopted. **~ung** *f.* naturalization.

Einbuße *f.* loss; damage.

einbüßen *v.t.* to lose; to forfeit.

eindämmen *v.t.* to dam up; (*fig.*) to check.

eindeck-en *v.r.* to lay in a store (of). **~er** *m.* monoplane.

eindeutig *a.* clear, plain.

eindeutschen *v.t.* to translate into German, to Germanize.

eindicken *v.t.* to thicken; to inspissate.

eindring-en *vws.i.* to penetrate; to invade. **~lich** *a.* impressive; urgent. **~ling** *m.* intruder; gate-crasher.

Eindruck *m.* (-s, "e) impression. **~svoll** *a.* impressive.

eindrück-en *v.t.* to break; to crush, squash; to impress. **~lich** *a.* impressive; emphatic.

ein|ebnen *v.t.* to level.

Ein|ehe *f.* monogamy.

einen *v.t.* to unite.

ein|engen *v.t.* to narrow; to compress; to cramp.

Einer *m.* (-s, -) unit; digit; single-sculler. **~lei** *indecl. a.* of one kind; the same; all the same; **~lei** *ob* regardless whether. *subst. n.* sameness; monotony. **~seits, einesteils** *adv.* on the one hand.

ein|exerzieren *v.t.* to drill, train.

einfach *a.* single; simple; plain; modest; primary; elementary. *adv.* simply. **~heit** *f.* simplicity.

einfädeln *v.t.* to thread (needle); (*fig.*) to contrive.

einfahr-en *v.t.* to bring in; to break in (horse). *vws.i.* to enter, drive in; (*mining*) to descend. **~t** *f.* drive, entrance, gateway; harbour entrance; descent.

Einfall *m.* falling down, collapse; (*mil.*) invasion; incidence (of ray); (*fig.*) idea, brain-wave; whim. **~en** *vws.i.* to fall down, collapse; to interrupt; (*mus.*) to join in, chime in; (*mil.*) to invade, overrun; (*opt.*) to be incident; *mir fällt ein* it occurs to me; *es fällt mir nicht ein* I cannot think of it or remember it; *es fällt mir nicht ein, das zu tun* catch me doing that; *was fällt dir ein?* what do you mean by it? **~slot**

n. perpendicular. **~swinkel** *m.* angle of incidence.

Einfalt *f.* (-) simplicity; innocence; naïveté. **~spinsel** *m.* simpleton; noodle.

einfältig *a.* simple; innocent; foolish.

Einfamilienhaus *n.* self-contained house; villa, bungalow.

einfangen *v.t.* to catch, capture.

einfarbig *a.* of one colour; plain.

einfass-en *v.t.* to border, to trim, edge, bind; to set (jewel); to mount (in gold); to enclose. **~ung** *f.* border; edging, trimming, binding; setting; mounting; enclosure; railing.

einfetten *v.t.* to grease, lubricate.

einfinden *v.r.* to appear, arrive, turn up.

einflechten *v.t.* to plait; to adorn with; to interlard with; to put in (a word).

einfliegen *v.t.* to test a plane. *v.i.* to enter by air.

einfließen *vws.i.* to flow in; (*fig.*) **~ lassen** to remark casually.

einflößen *v.t.* to administer, give; (*fig.*) to inspire (with), call forth.

Einflug *m.* (reconnaissance) flight; raid.

Einfluß *m.* flowing in; influx; (*fig.*) influence. **~reich** *a.* influential. **~rohr** *n.* inlet-pipe.

einflüstern *v.t.* to whisper to; to insinuate.

einfordern *v.t.* to call in (debts); to collect (tax).

einförmig *a.* uniform; monotonous. **~keit** *f.* uniformity; monotony.

einfried(ig)en *v.t.* to enclose, fence.

einfrieren *vws.i.* to freeze.

einfügen *v.t.* to insert. *v.r.* to fit in, adapt oneself (to).

einfühl-en *v.r.* to understand (sympathetically). **~ung** *f.* sympathetic understanding; (*phil.*) empathy.

Einfuhr *f.* (-) importation; import. **~kontingent** *n.* import quota. **~sperre** *f.* embargo on imports. **~zoll** *m.* import duty.

einführ-en *v.t.* to introduce; to install; to inaugurate; to import

(goods); (*tech.*) to lead in. **~ung** *f.* introduction; installation; importation.

einfüllen *v.t.* to fill in, pour in.

Eingabe *f.* petition; memorial.

Eingang *m.* entrance(-gate); entry; arrival, coming in; introduction; beginning; *pl.* (*commerc.*) goods received; **kein ~** no entry; **nach ~** on receipt. **~s** *adv.* at the beginning. **~szoll** *m.* import duty.

eingeb-en *v.t.* to give, administer; to send in, present; to inspire with; prompt. **~ung** *f.* inspiration.

eingebildet *a.* imaginary; conceited.

eingeboren *a.* innate; native; (*bibl.*) only-begotten. **~e(r)** *m.* native.

eingedenk *a.* mindful of, remembering.

eingefallen *a.* emaciated, hollowcheeked.

eingefleischt *a.* inveterate.

eingehen *vws.i.* to arrive, come in; to cease, stop, come to an end; (*of animals*) to die; (*of plants*) to wither, decay; (*of wool*) to shrink; **~ auf** to agree to; to enter into. *v.t.* to contract (marriage); to make (bet). **~d** *a.* exact; thorough; searching.

Eingemachte(s) *n.* preserves; jam.

eingemeinden *v.t.* to incorporate.

eingenommen *a.* prepossessed (in favour of); prejudiced (against); **von sich ~** conceited.

eingeschrieben *a.* registered (letter).

eingesessen *a.* resident, established.

Eingeständnis *n.* avowal, confession.

eingestehen *v.t.* to admit, confess, own up.

eingestrichen *a.* (*mus.*) onceaccented.

eingetragen *a.* registered.

Eingeweide *n.* (-s, -) intestines, bowels, entrails.

eingewöhnen *v.r.* to accustom oneself (to).

eingewurzelt *a.* deep-rooted, inveterate.

eingezogen *a.* retired, secluded; (*mil.*) called up.

eingießen *v.t.* to pour in; to pour out (tea, &c.).

eingittern *v.t.* to rail off; to fence in.

Einglas *n.* monocle.

eingleisig *a.* single-track.

eingliedern *v.t.* to incorporate.

eingraben *v.t. & r.* to dig in, entrench; to bury; (*fig.*) to engrave.

eingravieren *v.t.* to engrave.

eingreifen *v.i.* to catch; (*mach.*) to interlock; (*motor.*) to gear; (*mil.*) to come into operation; (*fig.*) to intervene; to interfere, interrupt; to join.

Eingriff *m.* intervention; interference; infringement, encroachment; (*med.*) operation.

einhaken *v.t.* to hook into; to fasten; to catch, pin down. *v.r.* to link arms.

Einhalt *m.* ~ gebieten to put a stop to; to check. ~en *v.t.* to observe, follow, keep to. *v.i.* to stop, pause. ~ung *f.* observance.

einhämmern *v.t.* to hammer into; (*fig.*) to drive home.

einhändigen *v.t.* to hand over, deliver.

einhängen *v.t.* to hang, put in, put on hinges.

einhauchen *v.t.* to instil, inspire with.

einhauen *v.t. & i.* to hew in, cut into; (*mil.*) to fall upon, attack; (*colloq.*) to tuck in.

einheften *v.t.* to file (papers).

einheimisch *a.* native; indigenous (plant); home (product).

einheimsen *v.t.* (*fig.*) to reap; to rake in.

einheiraten *v.i.* to marry into.

Einheit *f.* (-, -en) unity, union; (*math.*) unit. ~lich *a.* uniform, homogeneous; centralized. ~lichkeit *f.* uniformity. ~spreis *m.* uniform *or* standard price.

einheizen *v.t. & i.* to light a fire; to heat.

einhellig *a.* unanimous.

ein'her (-he:r) *adv. & sep. pref.* along, forth. ~gehen *vws.i.* to walk along.

einholen *v.t.* to bring in; to collect, gather; to seek (counsel); to make up for; to catch up with;

(*naut.*) to haul in or down. *v.t. & i.* to shop; ~ gehen to go shopping.

Einhorn *n.* unicorn.

einhüllen *v.t.* to wrap up, envelop.

einig[1] *a.* in agreement; united; unanimous, at one. ~en *v.t.* to unite, unify. *v.r.* to come to terms, to agree. ~keit *f.* harmony, concord, union; agreement. ~ung *f.* agreement, settlement.

einig[2]-emal *adv.* several times. ~ermaßen *adv.* to some extent, somewhat. ~es *a.* some, any (of it); (*pl.*) several, some, a few.

ein|impfen *v.t.* to inoculate, vaccinate.

einjagen *v.t. Angst* ~ to alarm, frighten.

einjährig *a.* one-year-old; annual.

einkapseln *v.t.* to capsule; (*med.*) to encyst.

einkassieren *v.t.* to cash, collect.

Einkauf *m.* purchase; buying. ~en *v.t.* to buy, purchase; to shop. ~spreis *m.* cost price.

Einkäufer *m.* buyer.

Einkehr *f.* (-) stop at an inn; (*fig.*) contemplation. ~en *vws.i.* to stop at an inn; to call at.

einkeilen *v.t.* to wedge in, hem in.

einkellern *v.t.* to cellar.

einkerben *v.t.* to notch, score.

einkerkern *v.t.* to imprison.

einkesseln *v.t.* to encircle.

einklagen *v.t.* to sue for.

einklammern *v.t.* to bracket, put in parentheses; (*mech.*) to cramp.

Einklang *m.* unison; harmony.

einkleiden *v.t.* to fit out; to invest with; (*eccl.*) to robe.

einklemmen *v.t.* to jam, squeeze; (*med.*) *eingeklemmt* strangulated (hernia).

einklinken *v.t.* to latch.

einknicken *v.t. & vws.i.* to turn down; to bend in; to give way.

einkochen *v.t.* to boil down; to make jam, preserve.

einkommen *vws.i.* to come in; ~ um to apply for. *subst. n.* income, emoluments, revenue. ~steuer *f.* income-tax.

einkreisen *v.t.* to encircle, surround.

Einkünfte *f. pl.* income, revenue.

einladen[1] *v.t.* to load, ship.

einlad-en[2] *v.t.* to invite. **~end** *a.* inviting, tempting. **~ung** *f.* invitation.

Einlage *f.* enclosure; (bank) deposit; stake (wager); (med.) instep raiser, support.

einlagern *v.t.* to store.

Einlaß *m.* (-(ss)es) entrance; admission; inlet. **~karte** *f.* ticket. **~ventil** *n.* inlet-valve.

einlassen *v.t.* to admit, let in. *v.r.* to have dealings (with); *sich ~ auf* to engage in, meddle with, have (anything) to do with.

Einlauf *m.* arrival; (med.) enema. **~en** *vws.i.* to arrive, come in; to enter (harbour); (of cloth) to shrink; *sich ~en* (motor.) to run in; *in einem das Haus ~en* to pester someone.

einleben *v.r.* to settle down (in); to familiarize oneself (with).

einleg-en *v.t.* to put in, enclose; to inlay; to insert; (cook.) to preserve; to pickle. **~esohle** *f.* insole; sock.

einleit-en *v.t.* to begin, initiate; to introduce; (leg.) to institute, open. **~ung** *f.* introduction; prelude; preamble.

einlenken *v.i.* to turn (in); (fig.) to give in; to become more reasonable.

einlernen *v.t.* to hammer in, teach.

einleuchten *v.i.* to be clear, be intelligible. **~d** *a.* evident.

einliefern *v.t.* to deliver up; to take to.

einliegend *a.* enclosed.

einlösen *v.t.* to redeem; to honour (bill).

einlullen *v.t.* to lull to sleep; to lull into.

einmach-en *v.t.* to preserve; to bottle; to pickle. **~glas** *n.* preserving bottle or jar.

einmal *adv.* once; once, formerly; one day, some time; *~ dies, ~ das* now this, now that; *auf ~* all at once, suddenly; *noch ~* once again; *nicht ~* not even. **~eins** *n.* multiplication table. **~ig** *a.* single, solitary; unique, happening only once.

Einmarsch *m.* entry, marching in. **~ieren** *vws.i.* to march in.

einmauern *v.t.* to wall in; to immure.

einmeng-en, einmisch-en *v.r.* to meddle with, interfere. **~ung** *f.* interference, intervention.

einmotorig *a.* single-engined.

einmotten *v.t.* to protect (clothes) against moths.

einmünden *v.i.* to run into, join, flow into.

einmütig *a.* unanimous. **~keit** *f.* unanimity.

Einnahme *f.* (-, -n) capture; occupation, conquest; receipt; income, revenue. **~quelle** *f.* source of income.

einnebeln *v.t.* to lay a smoke screen.

einnehmen *v.t.* to engage; to occupy; to take; to receive, collect (tax); (fig.) to charm, captivate. **~d** *a.* taking, engaging, captivating.

einnicken *vws.i.* to fall asleep, nod.

einnisten *v.r.* to build one's nest; to settle down; (colloq.) to squat.

Ein|**öde** *f.* (-, -n) desert, solitude.

ein|**ölen** *v.t.* to oil, grease.

ein|**ordnen** *v.t.* to arrange, classify; to file (letters).

einpacken *v.t.* to pack; to wrap up.

einpauken *v.t.* (colloq.) to cram.

einpferchen *v.t.* to pen in; to coop up.

einpflanzen *v.t.* to plant; (fig.) to implant, inculcate.

einpfropfen *v.t.* to cork up; to engraft.

einpökeln *v.t.* to pickle.

einpräg-en *v.t.* to impress, imprint; (fig.) to impress upon. *v.r.* to note, remember. **~sam** *a.* easily remembered; impressive.

einpuppen *v.r.* to change into a chrysalis.

einquartier-en *v.t.* to billet; to quarter troops. **~ung** *f.* billeting, quartering; billeted soldiers.

einrahmen *v.t.* to frame.

einrammen *v.t.* to ram in.

einräumen *v.t.* to put in order; to furnish (room); to give up; to admit, grant; to concede.

einrechnen *v.t.* to include; to allow for.

Einrede f. objection; contradiction, protest. **~n** v.t. & i. to persuade, make (one) believe; **~n auf** to urge (a person) to; to keep on talking to interrupt.

einregnen vws.i. to be caught in a deluge (of rain).

einreiben v.t. to rub, rub into.

einreichen v.t. to hand in, deliver; to present, submit.

einreih-en v.t. to insert, include; to arrange; to enroll. **~ig** a. single-breasted.

Einreise f. entry into a country. **~erlaubnis** f. permit to enter.

einreißen v.t. to pull down; to tear. vws.i. (fig.) to spread, gain ground.

einrenken v.t. to set; (fig.) to set right.

einrennen v.t. to run against, dash against, force open; einem das Haus ~ to pester someone.

einricht-en v.t. to arrange, prepare; to manage; to furnish (house); to set (bone). **~ung** f. arrangement; institution; furnishings; fittings.

einrollen v.t. to roll up.

einrosten vws.i. to rust; (fig.) to get rusty.

einrücken vws.i. to enter, march into; (mil.) to join up; (typ.) to indent. v.t. to insert (advertisement).

eins a. & subst. f. one. adv. the same; **~ sein** to be at one; **~ werden** to agree, come to terms; es kommt auf **~ hinaus** it comes to the same thing.

einsalzen v.t. to salt; to pickle.

einsam (-z-) a. lonely, solitary. **~keit** f. loneliness, solitude.

einsammeln v.t. to gather; to collect.

einsargen v.t. to coffin.

Einsatz m. inset; insertion; container; nest (of tables); stake; (cards) pool; (mus.) entry, striking up; (mil., &c.) employment, use; effort; (av.) sortie; unter ~ des Lebens at the risk of one's life; zum ~ bringen to put into action. **~bereitschaft** f. ready devotion; readiness for action.

einsaugen v.t. to suck in; to absorb.

einsäumen v.t. to hem in; to surround.

einschachteln v.t. to put one box into another.

einschalt-en v.t. to insert; to put in; to interpolate; to intercalate; to connect; to switch on (light); to engage (gear). **~ung** f. insertion; interpolation; intercalation.

einschärfen v.t. to impress upon; to inculcate.

einscharren v.t. to bury.

einschätzen v.t. to assess, value; to form an estimate of.

einschenken v.t. to pour in; to pour out; reinen Wein ~ (fig.) to tell the unvarnished truth.

einschicken v.t. to send in.

einschieb-en v.t. to put in; to insert; to intercalate. **~sel** n. intercalation; interpolation.

einschießen v.t. to shoot down; to test (gun); to pay in. v.r. to practise shooting.

einschiff-en v.t. & r. to embark. **~ung** f. embarkation.

einschlafen vws.i. to fall asleep; (of limbs) to become numb; (fig.) to die.

einschläf-ern v.t. to lull to sleep; (med.) to narcotize. **~ernd** a. somnolent, lulling. **~rig** a. single-bedded.

Einschlag m. impact; burst (of bomb); woof, weft; tuck, fold; (fig.) touch. **~papier** n. wrapping-paper.

einschlagen v.t. to drive in (nail); to break (glass); to knock out; to wrap up; to put a tuck in, to shorten (dress); to take (road). v.i. to shake hands; to agree; (of lightning) to strike; (fig.) to catch on.

einschlägig a. respective, pertinent; relative to, on the subject.

einschleichen v.r. to steal in, creep in.

einschleppen v.t. to bring in; to drag in.

einschließ-en v.t. to lock up; to enclose; (mil.) to encircle; (fig.) to include. **~lich** a. inclusive.

einschlummern *v.i.* to fall asleep; (*fig.*) to die.

Einschluß *m.* inclusion; *mit ~* including, inclusive.

einschmeicheln *v.r.* to insinuate oneself (into), ingratiate oneself (with).

einschmelzen *v.t.* to melt down.

einschmieren *v.t.* to grease, oil; to smear.

einschmuggeln *v.t.* to smuggle in.

einschnappen *vws.i.* to click, catch; (*fig.*) to take offence.

einschneiden *v.t.* to cut into; to notch. **~d** *a.* decisive, strict.

einschneien *vws.i.* to snow up.

Einschnitt *m.* incision, cut; cutting; (*fig.*) turning-point.

einschränk-en *v.t.* to curtail; to limit, restrict. *v.r.* to retrench. **~ung** *f.* curtailment; limitation, restriction; retrenchment.

Einschreibe-brief *m.* registered letter. **~gebühr** *f.* registration fee. **~n** *v.t.* to enter, note down; to register (letter). *v.r.* to enrol; to matriculate; to enter one's name.

einschreiten *vws.i.* to intervene; to interfere; to take steps; to proceed (against).

einschrumpfen *vws.i.* to shrink, shrivel up.

Einschub *m.* interpolation; insertion.

einschüchtern *v.t.* to intimidate.

einschulen *v.t.* to send to school; to train.

einschwenken *v.i.* to wheel (round).

einsegn-en *v.t.* to consecrate; to confirm. **~ung** *f.* consecration; confirmation.

einsehen *v.t.* to look into; to examine; (*fig.*) to comprehend, realize, understand. *subst. n. ein ~ haben* to be reasonable.

einseifen *v.t.* to soap; to lather; (*fig.*) to take in.

einseitig *a.* one-sided; on one side; partial. **~keit** *f.* one-sidedness; partiality.

einsenden *v.t.* to send in; to contribute.

einsenken *v.t.* to sink; to plant.

einsetz-en *v.t.* to put in; to insert; to employ, use; to appoint,

make, install (in office); to plant; (*fig.*) to stake, risk. *v.r.* to stand up (for), side (with); *sich voll ~en* to pull one's weight. *v.i.* to set in, begin; (*mus.*) to strike up. **~ung** *f.* institution; appointment; installation. **~ungsworte** *pl.* (*theol.*) Words of the Institution of the Lord's Supper.

Einsicht *f.* insight; inspection, examination; (*fig.*) understanding, judgement, reason. **~ig** *a.* sensible, prudent, judicious. **~nahme** *f. zur ~nahme* on approval; for inspection.

einsickern *vws.i.* to trickle in, soak into.

Einsied-e'lei *f.* hermitage. **~ler** *m.* hermit. **~lerisch** *a.* secluded, solitary.

einsilbig *a.* monosyllabic; (*fig.*) taciturn. **~keit** *f.* taciturnity.

einsinken *vws.i.* to sink in; to give way.

einsitzig *a.* single-seated.

einspannen *v.t.* to harness; to stretch.

Einspänner *m.* one-horse vehicle.

einsparen *v.t.* to economize.

einsperren *v.t.* to lock in; to imprison.

einspielen *v.r.* to train (as a team); to become practised in playing (music) together.

einspinnen *v.r.* (*zool.*) to cocoon; (*fig.*) to be absorbed (in); to seclude oneself (from).

Einsprache *f.* objection, protest.

einsprechen *v.t.* to talk to; *einem Mut ~* to encourage s.o.

einsprengen *v.t.* to damp; (*geol.*) to intersperse.

einspringen *vws.i.* to jump in; (*of lock*) to snap, catch; (*of angle*) to re-enter; (*fig.*) to help; to step into the breach.

einspritz-en *v.t.* to inject. **~ung** *f.* injection.

Einspruch *m.* protest, objection; *~ erheben* to object (to), protest (against).

einspurig *a.* single-track.

einst *adv.* once; one day; in days to come. **~ig** *a.* former; future. **~mals** *adv.* once, formerly.

~weilen adv. meanwhile, for the present. **~weilig** a. temporary, provisional.

einstampfen v.t. to pulp.

Einstand m. (tennis) deuce.

einstauben vws.i. to get dusty.

einstecken v.t. to put in; to pocket; (colloq.) to jail, run in; (fig.) to swallow (insult).

einstehen vws.i. to be responsible (for); to guarantee, answer (for).

einsteigen vws.i. to get in.

einstell-en v.t. 1. to put in; to garage (car); (opt.) to focus; to turn on (radio), tune in; (motor.) to adjust, set; to engage (worker); (mil.) to enlist. 2. to stop, cease, leave off; (leg.) to stay, withdraw; Arbeit **~en** to strike; Betrieb **~en** to close down. v.r. to appear, come; sich **~en** auf to be prepared for. **~ig** a. of one figure. **~skala** f. front scale (of typewriter). **~ung** f. 1. adjustment; engagement; enlistment; (fig.) attitude. 2. cessation, stoppage; suspension; (leg.) stay, withdrawal (of charge).

einstimm-en v.i. to join in; (fig.) to agree (with), consent (to). **~ig** a. for one voice; (fig.) unanimous.

einstöckig a. one-storied.

einstoßen v.t. to push in; to smash, break.

einstreichen v.t. to pocket (money).

einstreuen v.t. to strew in, scatter; (fig.) to intersperse, interlard.

einstudieren v.t. to study; to rehearse (play).

einstuf-en v.t. to classify; to range; to rate. **~ung** f. classification; rating.

einstündig a. one hour's.

einstürmen vws.i. to assail; to rush upon.

Einsturz m. collapse; caving-in, subsidence.

einstürzen vws.i. to collapse.

eintägig a. lasting one day; ephemeral.

Eintagsfliege f. May-fly.

Eintänzer m. gigolo.

eintauchen v.t. & vws.i. to dip, plunge.

eintauschen v.t. to exchange.

einteil-en v.t. to divide, distribute; to arrange; to graduate (a scale). **~ung** f. division; distribution; arrangement; classification.

eintönig a. monotonous.

Eintopf m. hot-pot; one-course (meal).

Eintracht f. (-) harmony, union, concord.

einträchtig a. united; harmonious.

Eintrag m. (-s, ⁻e) damage, harm; entry. **~en** v.t. to carry in; to enter (in book); to register; to yield, bring profit. **~ung** f. entry; registration.

einträglich a. lucrative, profitable.

eintränken v.t. einem etwas **~** to make a person pay for it.

einträufeln v.t. to instil drop by drop.

eintreffen vws.i. to arrive; (fig.) to happen; to be fulfilled, come true.

eintreiben v.t. to drive home (cattle); to collect (tax).

eintreten vws.i. to go in, enter, step in; (mil.) to join up; (fig.) to stand up (for), intercede (for); to set in; to take place. v.t. to kick open. v.r. to run (thorn) into one's foot.

eintrichtern v.t. (fig.) to drum into one's head.

Eintritt m. entrance, entry; admission; commencement, setting in. **~sgeld** n. admission fee. **~skarte** f. ticket.

eintrocknen vws.i. to dry up.

eintröpfeln v.t. to drop in, instil.

Eintrübung f. (meteor.) cloudiness; becoming overcast.

eintunken v.t. to dip in.

ein|üben v.t. to practise; to drill; to train.

einverleiben v.t. to imbibe; (fig.) to incorporate; to annex.

Einvernehmen n. consent; understanding.

einverstanden pp. agreed; **~** sein to agree.

Einverständnis n. agreement; consent.

Einwand m. (-s, ⁻e) objection;

protest. ~frei a. faultless; irreproachable; perfect.

Einwander-er m. (-ers, -er) immigrant. ~n vws.i. to immigrate.
~ung f. immigration.

einwärts (-verts) adv. inwards, inward, turned-in.

einwechseln v.t. to change
(money).

einwecken v.t. to bottle, preserve.

einweichen v.t. to steep, soak.

einweih-en v.t. to consecrate; to
inaugurate; to open; to initiate.
~ung f. consecration; inauguration; opening; initiation.

einweisen v.t. to direct into; to
introduce.

einwend-en v.t. to object. ~ung f.
objection.

einwerfen v.t. to break, smash; to
throw in; (fig.) to interject; to
object.

einwickel-n v.t. to wrap up,
envelop. ~papier n. wrapping-
paper.

einwillig-en v.i. to consent; to
agree. ~ung f. consent.

einwirken v.i. ~ auf to influence;
impress; to act on.

einwohn-en v.r. to begin to feel at
home. ~er m. inhabitant. ~er-
schaft f. inhabitants.

Einwurf m. slit; aperture; slot;
(fig.) objection.

einwurzeln vws.i. to take root.

Einzahl f. singular (number).

einzahl-en v.t. to pay in. ~ung
f. payment.

einzäun-en v.t. to fence in. ~ung
f. fence, enclosure.

einzeichnen v.t. to mark; to draw
in. v.r. to enter one's name.

Einzel-arrest m. solitary confinement. ~fall m. particular or
individual case. ~gänger m.
outsider, lone wolf. ~handel m.
retail business. ~heit f. detail,
particular. ~kampf m. hand-to-
hand fight; (sport.) single match.
~spiel n. a single.

einzellig a. unicellular.

einzeln a. individual, particular;
single; odd; isolated; ~es some.

einziehen v.t. to pull in, draw in;
to thread (needle); to lower (flag,
sail); (mil.) to call up, draft; to

withdraw; (leg.) to confiscate;
to collect (tax); to call in (coins);
to make (inquiries); to absorb
(liquid). vws.i. to march in; to
move in(to house); (chem.) to
soak in, infiltrate.

einzig a. only; sole; single;
unique; ~ und allein only.
~artig a. unique.

einzuckern v.t. to sugar.

Einzug m. entry, entrance; moving in (to house).

einzwängen v.t. to squeeze in.

Eis¹ ('e:is) n. (mus.) E sharp.

Eis² (ais) n. (-es) ice; ice-cream.
~bahn f. rink. ~bär m. polar
bear. ~bein n. pickled pork
trotters. ~beutel m. ice-bag.
~bombe f. ice-bomb. ~decke
f. sheet of ice. ~frei a. clear of
ice. ~gang m. drifting of the
ice. ~treiben m. drifting of the
ice. ~grau a. hoary. ~heiligen
(die drei) pl. the 11th, 12th, and
13th of May. ~ig a. icy. ~kalt
a. icy-cold. ~kegeln n. curling.
~kübler m. ice-pail. ~laufbahn
f. skating-rink. ~läufer m.
skater. ~maschine f. freezer.
~meer n. polar sea. ~pickel
m. ice-axe. ~scholle f. floe.
~schrank m. refrigerator. ~vogel
m. kingfisher. ~zapfen m. icicle.
~zeit f. Ice Age, glacial period.

Eisen (aizən) n. (-s, -) iron;
horseshoe; iron implement, iron
tool; in ~ legen to put in irons;
zum alten ~ werfen to scrap.
~abfall m. scrap iron. ~bahn
f. railway, railroad; train.
~bahner m. railway man. ~bahnfahrt
f. railway journey. ~bahnknotenpunkt
m. railway junction. ~bahnkreuzung
f. railway crossing. ~bahnnetz
n. network of railway lines.
~bahnschwelle f. sleeper. ~bahnübergang
m. level crossing.
~bahnwagen m. railway carriage. ~beton m. reinforced
concrete. ~blech n. sheet iron.
~erz n. iron-ore. ~fresser m.
bully, fire-eater. ~gießerei f.
iron-foundry. ~guß m. cast
iron. ~haltig a. containing iron,
ferruginous. ~hammer m. ironworks. ~hut m. aconite, monks-

hood. ~hütte f. ironworks, forge. ~hüttenkunde f. ferrous metallurgy. ~oxyd n. ferric oxide. oxydul n. ferrous oxide. ~waren f.pl. ironmongery, hardware. ~zeit f. Iron Age.

eisern (aizərn) a. iron; (fig.) inflexible; ~er Bestand reserve stock; permanent fund; iron rations; ~es Kreuz Iron Cross; ~er Vorhang safety-curtain.

eitel a. vain, conceited; empty; idle; (indecl.) only, nothing but. ~keit f. vanity; conceit. [IDLE]

Eiter m. (-s) pus, matter. ~beule f. abscess. ~ig a. purulent, festering. ~n v.i. to suppurate, fester. ~ung f. suppuration.

Ekel (e:-) m. (-s) nausea; aversion, disgust, loathing. n. (colloq.) nasty fellow. ~haft a. disgusting, loathsome. ~ig a. disgusting; unpleasant, nasty. ~n v.i. mir ~t vor or es ~t mich I loathe it, it disgusts me. v.r. to loathe, feel disgusted.

Eks'tase (-ta:zə) f. (-, -n) ecstasy.

Ek'zem (-tse:m) n. (-s, -e) eczema.

e'lasti-sch a. elastic. ~zi'tät f. elasticity.

Elch (-ç) m. (-es, -e) elk.

Ele'fant m. (-en, -en) elephant. ~enzahn m. tusk.

ele'gan-t a. elegant. ~z f. elegance.

Ele'gie f. (-, -n) elegy.

e'legisch a. elegiac; mournful, melancholy.

elektrifi'zieren v.t. to electrify.

E'lektri-ker m. (-kers, -ker) electrician. ~sch a. electric; die ~sche the tram. ~sieren v.t. to electrify; to give electric treatment. ~zi'tät f. electricity. ~zitätsmesser m. electrometer. ~zitätswerk n. power-plant.

Elektro-'lyse f. electrolysis. ~techniker m. electrical engineer; electrician.

Elektron n. (-s, -en) electron. ~enlehre f. electronics.

Ele'ment n. (-s, -e) element; rudiment; (electr.) cell. ~'ar a. elementary, first; elemental, violent. ~'arbuch n. primer. ~'argewalt f. elemental power.

Elen (e:-) (-s, -), ~tier n. elk.

Elend (e:lənt) n. (-s) misery; misfortune; distress, need, want. a. miserable, wretched; ill. adv. miserably, wretchedly. ~sviertel n. slums.

elf⁴ a. & subst. f. eleven. ~te a. eleventh.

Elf² m. (-en, -en), ~e f. (-, -en) elf, fairy. ~enhaft a. like a fairy.

Elfenbein n. ivory. ~e(r)n a. (of) ivory.

elimi'nieren v.t. to eliminate.

E'litetruppen pl. picked troops.

Eli'xier (-ksi:r) n. (-s, -e) elixir.

Ell-e f. (-e, -en) ell; (anat.) ulna. ~(en)bogen m. elbow. ~bogenfreiheit f. elbow-room. ~enlang a. (colloq.) very long.

E'llips-e f. (-se, -sen) ellipse; (gram.) ellipsis. ~tisch a. elliptical.

Elster f. (-, -n) magpie.

elter-lich a. parental. ~n pl. parents. ~nlos a. orphaned. [ALDERMAN]

E'mail (-maij) n. (-s) enamel. ~'lieren (-ji:r-) to enamel.

emanzi'pieren v.t. to emancipate.

Embo'lie (-li:) f. (-, -n) embolism.

Emi'grant m. (-en, -en) emigrant.

empfahl imperf. of empfehlen.

empfand imperf. of empfinden.

Em'pfang -(n) m. (-s, ~e) receipt; reception; nach ~ on receipt. ~nahme f. receipt. ~sanlage f. receiving-set. ~sdame f. receptionist. ~sschein m. receipt. ~sstörung f. (radio) interference; atmospherics; jamming.

em'pfangen v.t.st. to receive, take; to welcome. v.i. to conceive.

Em'pfäng-er m. (-ers, -er) receiver; recipient; addressee; consignee. ~lich a. susceptible, responsive; impressionable. ~lichkeit f. susceptibility; impressionability. ~nis f. conception. ~nisverhütung f. contraception.

em'pfehl-en v.t.st. to recommend; ~en Sie mich give my regards (to) ... v.r. to take one's leave; (impers.) to be advisable. ~enswert a. commendable. ~ung f.

recommendation; compliments;
(pl.) regards. **~ungsschreiben** *n.*
letter of introduction.

Empfinde'lei *f.* (-, -en) sentimentality.

em'pfind-en *v.t.* *st.* to experience,
feel; to perceive. **~lich** *a.* sensitive; touchy; delicate; painful. **~lichkeit** *f.* sensitiveness;
touchiness. **~sam** *a.* sentimental; sensitive. **~samkeit** *f.* sentimentality; sensitiveness. **~ung**
f. sensation, feeling; perception; sentiment. **~ungslos** *a.*
insensitive; unfeeling. **~ungsvermögen** *n.* perceptive faculty.

empfing *imperf.* of **empfangen**.

empfohlen *pp.* of **empfehlen**.

empfunden *pp.* of **empfinden**.

Em'pha·se (-fa:zə) *f.* emphasis.
~tisch *a.* emphatic.

em'pirisch (-pi:r) *a.* empirical.

em'por (-po:r) *adv.* up, upwards;
(poet.) on high. **~blicken** *v.i.* to
look up. **~kömmling** *m.* upstart. **~ragen** *v.i.* to tower up.

Em'pore *f.* (-, -n) gallery; choirloft.

em'pör-en *v.t.* to rouse to indignation,
excite, shock. *v.r.* to rebel;
to be furious (about). **~end** *a.*
shocking, disgraceful. **~er** *m.*
insurgent, rebel. **~t** *a.* indignant. **~ung** *f.* rebellion; indignation.

emsig (-z-) *a.* busy; active; industrious, assiduous. **~keit** *f.*
industry, assiduity; diligence.

Endbahnhof *m.* railhead, terminus.

End·e *n.* (-es, -en) end; result;
close, conclusion; aim, purpose,
point, extremity; *am* **~e** *in the
end; after all, eventually; letzten*
~es when all is said and done,
finally; *zu* **~e** *führen* to finish;
zu **~e** *gehen* to come to an end;
to run short. **~ergebnis** *n.* final
result. **~esunterzeichnete(r)** *m.*
undersigned. **~geschwindigkeit**
f. terminal velocity. **~gültig** *a.*
final, definite. **~lich** *a.* finite;
final, ultimate. *adv.* at last,
finally. **~lichkeit** *f.* finiteness;
limitation. **~los** *a.* endless.
~punkt *m.* end-point; farthest
point. **~silbe** *f.* final syllable.

~station *f.* terminus; railhead.
~ung *f.* ending, termination. **~zweck** *m.* goal, aim, purpose.

enden, endigen *vv.t.* to finish, end.
v.i. to cease, stop; to terminate
(in); to die

Endivie *f.* endive.

Ener'gie (-gi:) *f.* (-, -n) energy;
(electr.) power. **~los** *a.* lacking in
energy. **~zufuhr** *f.* supply of
power.

e'nergisch *a.* energetic, vigorous.

eng (ɛŋ) *a.* narrow; tight; close;
(fig.) intimate; **~er machen** to
tighten; *~ere Wahl* short list;
im ~eren Sinne strictly speaking. **~brüstig** *a.* asthmatic.
~e *f.* narrowness; tightness;
closeness; defile; *(fig.)* straits;
in die ~e treiben to corner.
~herzig *a.* narrow-minded;
strait-laced. **~maschig** *a.* closemeshed. **~paß** *m.* defile; pass.

enga'gieren (-ʒi:r-) *v.t.* to engage.

Engel (ɛŋəl) *m.* (-s, -) angel. **~haft**
a. angelic. **~schar** *f.* angelic
host. **~sgeduld** *f.* patience of
Job.

Engerling *m.* (-s, -e) larva of cockchafer.

Engländer *m.* (-s, -) adjustable
spanner, monkey-wrench. See
also App. I.

englisch *a.* English; *(poet.)* angelic;
~er Gruß Ave Maria; **~e**
Krankheit rickets; **~es Pflaster**
court-plaster.

en'gros (ãgro:) *adv.* wholesale.
[F]

Enkel[1] *m.* (-s, -) ankle.

Enkel[2] *m.* (-s, -) grandson. **~in**,
~tochter *f.* grand-daughter. **~kind** *n.* grandchild.

e'norm *a.* enormous, huge.

ent'art-en *vvs.i.* to degenerate.
~ung *f.* degeneration.

ent'äußern *v.r.* to give up; to
part with.

ent'behr-en *v.t.* to be without,
lack; to miss; to do without.
~lich *a.* superfluous; spare.
~ung *f.* privation; want.

ent'bieten *v.t.* to send; to send for.

ent'bind-en *v.t.* to set free; to release; to disengage; *(med.)* to deliver; *entbunden werden* to give

birth (to). **~ung** f. confinement.
~ungsanstalt f. maternity hospital.

ent'**blättern** v.t. to strip of leaves.
v.r. to shed leaves.

ent'**blöden** v.r. sich nicht ~ to
have the impudence (to).

ent'**blöß-en** v.t. to bare, expose; to
uncover. **~ung** f. baring, exposing; deprivation.

ent'**brennen** vws.i. to break out;
to be inflamed, seized (with).

ent'**deck-en** v.t. to discover, detect,
find out; to confide (in). **~er** m.
discoverer. **~ung** f. discovery;
disclosure.

ent**dunkeln** v.t. to remove the
blackout.

Ente f. (-, -n) duck; (med.) urine
bottle; (fig.) canard, hoax. **~n-
braten** m. roast duck. **~njagd**
f. duck-shooting. **~rich** m.
drake.

ent'**ehren** v.t. to dishonour; to
disgrace; to degrade.

ent'**eign-en** v.t. to expropriate; to
dispossess. **~ung** f. expropriation.

ent'**eilen** vws.i. to hurry away.

ent'**eisen** v.t. to defrost; to de-ice.

ent'**erben** v.t. to disinherit.

Enter-haken m. boat-hook; grappling-iron. **~n** v.t. to board; to
grapple.

ent'**fachen** v.t. to kindle; to fan.

ent'**fahren** vws.i. to escape.

ent'**fallen** vws.i. to fall from; to
slip from (one's) memory; ~ auf
to fall to one's share.

ent'**falten** v.t. to unfold; to unfurl; to develop; to display. v.r.
to open; to expand.

ent'**färben** v.r. to lose colour; to
grow pale.

ent'**fern-en** v.t. to remove; to
take away. v.r. to go away,
depart. **~t** a. & adv. distant;
far off; far from; (fig.) slight,
faint; nicht im ~testen not in the
least; not in the slightest degree.
~ung f. distance; range; removal. **~ungsmesser** m. rangefinder.

ent'**fesseln** v.t. to unchain; to let
loose.

Ent'fettungskur f. treatment for

obesity, slimming cure.

ent'**flammen** v.t. to inflame; to
kindle.

ent'**fliehen** vws.i. to run away,
escape; (of time) to pass quickly.

ent'**fremd-en** v.t. to estrange; to
alienate. **~ung** f. estrangement; alienation.

ent'**führ-en** v.t. to carry off; to
elope with; to abduct; to kidnap. **~ung** f. abduction; elopement; kidnapping.

ent'**gegen** 1. adv. & prep. towards;
opposed to; against; in face of;
contrary to. 2. sep. pref. **~-
arbeiten** v.i. to work against;
to counteract. **~gehen** vws.i. to
go to meet; to face. **~gesetzt**
a. opposite; contrary. **~halten**
v.t. to object; to contrast. **~kommen** 1. vws.i. to come to
meet; to meet half-way. 2.
subst. n. willingness to oblige,
kindness. **~kommend** a. obliging; kind, helpful. **~laufen** vws.i.
to run to meet. **~nehmen** v.t.
to accept, receive. **~sehen** v.i.
to look forward to; to expect.
~setzen, ~stellen v.t. to oppose;
to contrast. **~strecken** v.t. to
stretch out towards. **~treten** vws.i. to advance towards; to
oppose. **~wirken** v.t. to counteract; to thwart.

ent'**gegn-en** v.t. to reply, answer;
to retort. **~ung** f. reply, answer; retort.

ent'**gehen** vws.i. to escape (from);
to elude.

ent'**geistert** a. thunderstruck, flabbergasted.

Ent'gelt m. & n. (-s) remuneration; reward. **~en** v.t. to pay
for, atone for.

ent'**giften** v.t. to decontaminate.

ent'**gleis-en** vws.i. to run off the
rails; (fig.) to make a faux pas.
~ung f. derailment.

ent'**gleiten** vws.i. to slip from.

ent'**göttert** a. without gods; profaned.

ent'**gräten** v.t. to bone (fish)

ent'**haar-en** v.t. to remove hair.
~ungsmittel n. depilatory.

ent'**halt-en** v.t. to contain, hold;

to include. *v.r.* to refrain from, abstain from. ~**sam** *a.* abstemious; abstinent; temperate. ~**samkeit** *f.* abstemiousness; abstinence; temperance; continence.

ent'**haupt-en** *v.t.* to behead, decapitate; to execute. ~**ung** *f.* beheading, decapitation; execution.

ent'**heb-en** *v.t.* to relieve of; to free, exempt from; to suspend from (office). ~**ung** *f.* exemption; dismissal.

ent'**heiligen** *v.t.* to profane, desecrate.

ent'**hüll-en** *v.t.* to unveil; to expose; (*fig.*) to reveal. ~**ung** *f.* unveiling; exposure, revelation.

ent'**hülsen** *v.t.* to shell, husk.

Enthusi'**as-mus** (-tuzi-) *m.* (-mus) enthusiasm. ~**tisch** *a.* enthusiastic.

ent'**jungfern** *v.t.* to deflower, ravish.

ent'**kernen** *v.t.* to stone (fruit).

ent'**kleiden** *v.t.* to undress; to divest.

ent'**kommen** *vws.i.* to escape.

ent'**korken** *v.t.* to uncork, open.

ent'**körpert** *a.* disembodied.

ent'**kräft-en** *v.t.* to weaken, exhaust; (*fig.*) to invalidate; to refute. ~**ung** *f.* enervation, exhaustion.

ent'**kuppeln** *v.t.* (*motor.*) to declutch.

ent'**lad-en** *v.t.* to unload; to discharge. *v.r.* to go off; to burst. ~**ung** *f.* discharge.

ent'**lang** (-n) *adv. & prep.* along.

ent'**larven** *v.t.* to unmask.

ent'**lass-en** *v.t.* to dismiss; to discharge; to release. ~**ung** *f.* dismissal, discharge. ~**ungsgesuch** *n.* resignation.

ent'**last-en** *v.t.* to unburden; to relieve; (*commerc.*) to credit with; to clear (a person's) account; to exonerate. ~**ung** *f.* exoneration, relief; help. ~**ungsangriff** *m.* diversionary attack. ~**ungszeuge** *m.* witness for the defence.

ent'**laubt** *a.* leafless.

ent'**laufen** *vws.i.* to run away.

ent'**lausen** *v.t.* to delouse.

ent'**ledigen** *v.r.* to get rid of; to perform, execute.

ent'**leer-en** *v.t.* to empty. ~**ung** *f.* (*med.*) evacuation.

ent'**legen** *a.* remote, distant.

ent'**lehnen** *v.t.* to borrow.

ent'**leiben** *v.r.* to commit suicide.

ent'**leihen** *v.t.* to borrow.

Ent'**lobung** *f.* breaking of engagement.

ent'**locken** *v.t.* to elicit; to draw from.

ent'**lohnen** *v.t.* to pay off.

ent'**machten** *v.t.* to deprive of power.

ent'**mannen** *v.t.* to castrate; (*fig.*) to emasculate.

ent'**menscht** *a.* inhuman; brutal.

entmilitari'**sieren** *v.t.* to demilitarize.

ent'**mündigen** *v.t.* to put under tutelage.

ent'**mutigen** *v.t.* to discourage, dishearten.

Ent'**nahme** *f.* (-, -n) taking; drawing; withdrawal.

ent'**nazifieren** *v.t.* to denazify.

ent'**nehmen** *v.t.* to take from; to gather, understand; (*commerc.*) to draw upon.

ent'**nerven** *v.t.* to weaken, enervate.

Entomo'**log-e** *m.* (-en, -en) entomologist. ~**'ie** *f.* entomology.

ent'**puppen** *v.r.* to burst the cocoon; (*fig.*) to reveal oneself (as).

ent'**raten** *v.i.* to do without.

ent'**rätseln** *v.t.* to decipher; to solve.

ent'**rechten** *v.t.* to deprive of rights.

ent'**reißen** *v.t.* to tear or snatch from; to save from.

ent'**richten** *v.t.* to pay.

ent'**ringen** *v.t.* to wrest from. *v.r.* (*of words or sighs*) to escape.

ent'**rinnen** *vws.i.* to run away, escape.

ent'**rollen** *v.t.* to unroll; to unfurl (flag). *v.r.* to unfold.

ent'**rück-en** *v.t.* to remove, move out of sight. ~**t** *a.* entranced, carried away.

ent'**rümpeln** *v.t.* to clear out (for salvage).

ent'rüst-en *v.t.* to provoke, irritate, make angry. *v.r.* to become angry. ~**ung** *f.* anger, indignation.

ent'sag-en *v.i.* to renounce; to waive, abandon; *dem Thron* ~*en* to abdicate. ~**ung** *f.* renunciation; resignation.

Ent'satz *m.* relief.

ent'schädig-en *v.t.* to compensate, indemnify. ~**ung** *f.* compensation, indemnity. ~**ungsklage** *f.* action for damages.

ent'schärfen *v.t.* to render safe; (*fig.*) to mitigate, disarm.

Ent'scheid *m.* (-s, -e) answer, decision. ~**en** *v.t.* to decide; to pass sentence, to rule. *v.r.* to be decided. ~**end** *a.* decisive; critical. ~**ung** *f.* decision; judgement, sentence.

ent'schieden *a.* decided; firm, resolute; peremptory. *adv.* certainly. ~**heit** *f.* determination; certainty.

ent'schlafen *vws.i.* to fall asleep; (*fig.*) to die.

ent'schlagen *v.r.* to give up, dismiss.

ent'schleiern *v.t.* to unveil.

ent'schließ-en *v.r.* to decide, make up one's mind. ~**ung** *f.* resolution.

ent'schlossen *a.* determined; resolute. ~**heit** *f.* determination.

ent'schlummern *vws.i.* to fall asleep; (*fig.*) to pass away.

ent'schlüpfen *vws.i.* to escape.

Ent'schluß *m.* resolution, decision.

ent'schlüsseln *v.t.* to decode.

ent'schuld-bar *a.* excusable. ~**igen** *v.t.* to excuse. *v.r.* to apologize; ~*igen Sie, bitte!* excuse me, please! I beg your pardon. ~**igung** *f.* excuse; apology; *um* ~*igung bitten* to beg pardon, apologize. ~**ung** *f.* sinking *or* wiping out of debts.

ent'schwinden *vws.i.* to vanish, disappear.

ent'seelt *a.* dead, lifeless.

ent'setz-en 1. *v.t.* to dismiss from; (*mil.*) to relieve; to frighten. *v.r.* to be horrified, to be shocked. 2. *subst. n.* horror, terror. ~**lich** *a.* terrible, dreadful.

ent'sichern *v.t.* to release safety-catch.

ent'sinnen *v.r.* to remember, recollect, recall.

ent'spann-en *v.r.* to relax. *v.t.* (*mil.*) to uncock; to relieve (tense situation). ~**ung** *f.* relaxation, rest, recreation.

ent'spinnen *v.r.* to begin, ensue.

ent'sprechen *v.i.* to be in accordance with, conform to; to comply with (request). ~**d** *a.* adequate, suitable, appropriate; corresponding, matching; *dem* ~*d* accordingly.

ent'springen *vws.i.* to escape from; to rise, spring from; (*fig.*) to arise.

ent'stammen *vws.i.* to descend from, come from.

ent'steh-en *vws.i.* to arise; to originate; to break out. ~**ung** *f.* rise, origin; formation.

ent'stell-en *v.t.* to disfigure; (*fig.*) to distort, misrepresent. ~**ung** *f.* disfigurement; distortion; misrepresentation.

ent'stören *v.t.* to eliminate jamming.

ent'sühnen *v.t.* to absolve.

ent'täusch-en *v.t.* to disappoint. ~**ung** *f.* disappointment.

ent'thronen *v.t.* to dethrone.

ent'völkern *v.t.* to depopulate.

ent'wachsen *vws.i.* to outgrow.

ent'waffnen *v.t.* to disarm.

ent'walden *v.t.* to deforest.

ent'warn-en *v.t.* to give the 'all-clear' signal. ~**ungssignal** *n.* 'all-clear' signal.

ent'wässern *v.t.* to drain; to dehydrate.

entweder *conj.* either.

ent'weichen *vws.i.* to escape; to abscond; to disappear.

ent'weih-en *v.t.* to desecrate, profane. ~**ung** *f.* desecration, profanation.

ent'wenden *v.t.* to pilfer; to embezzle.

ent'werfen *v.t.* to sketch; to draft; to outline.

ent'werten *v.t.* to depreciate; to cancel (stamps).

ent'wick-eln *v.t.* to develop; to explain; (*mil.*) to deploy. *v.r.*

to develop. ~ler *m.* developer.
~lung *f.* development; evolution; (*phot.*) developing; (*tech.*) processing. ~lungsjahre *n.pl.* (period of) adolescence, puberty. ~lungsländer *pl.* developing countries.

ent'winden *v.t.* to wrest from.

ent'wirren *v.t.* to disentangle; to unravel.

ent'wischen *vws.i.* to escape.

ent'wöhnen *v.t.* to wean (child, &c.); to break of.

ent'würdigen *v.t.* to degrade; to disgrace.

Ent'wurf *m.* (-es, ⸚e) sketch; draft; plan, project; rough copy.

ent'wurzeln *v.t.* to uproot.

ent'zieh-en *v.t.* to deprive of; to take away from. *v.r.* to withdraw from; to shun. ~ungskur *f.* treatment (for drug-addicts).

ent'ziffer-n *v.t.* to decipher; to decode. ~ung *f.* deciphering; decoding.

ent'zück-en 1. *v.t.* to delight, charm, enchant; ~t sein to be delighted (with). 2. *subst. n.* delight, rapture; transport. ~end *a.* charming, delightful.

Entzug *m.* withdrawal; deprivation.

ent'zünd-en *v.t.* to kindle, set fire to; (*med.*) to inflame. *v.r.* to catch fire. ~lich *a.* inflammatory. ~ung *f.* inflammation.

ent'zwei (-tsvai) *adv. & sep. pref.* in two; asunder; torn; broken. ~en *v.t.* to estrange, alienate. *v.r.* to fall out, quarrel. ~gehen *vws.i.* to break. ~schlagen *v.t.* to smash. ~t *a.* hostile; at daggers drawn. ~ung *f.* estrangement, quarrel; dissension.

Enzian (-tsia:n) *m.* (-s, -e) gentian.

En'zyklik-a *f.* (-a, -en) encyclic.

Epide'mie *f.* (-, -n) epidemic.

epi'demisch *a.* epidemic.

Epi'gone (-go:nə) *m.* (-n, -n) descendant (of great men).

Epi'gramm *n.* (-s, -e) epigram.

Ep-ik (e:-) *f.* epic poetry. ~iker *m.* epic poet. ~isch *a.* epic. ~os *n.* (-os, -en) epic poem.

Epiku'reer *m.* Epicurean.

Epi-lep'sie *f.* epilepsy. ~'leptiker

m., ~'leptisch *a.* epileptic.

Epi'log *m.* (-s, -e) epilogue.

E'pistel *f.* (-, -n) epistle.

E'poche (-pɔxa) *f.* (-, -n) epoch, era.

Eppich (-ç) *m.* celeriac; ivy.

Equi'page (tkipa:ʒə) *f.* (-, -n) carriage.

er[1] (e:r) *pron.* he; ~ selbst he himself.

er-[2] (ɛr) *insep. pref.*

er'achten *v.t.* to think, consider; meines ~s in my opinion.

er'arbeiten *v.t.* to get by working, earn.

Erb-adel *m.* hereditary nobility. ~anspruch *m.* claim to an inheritance. ~begräbnis *n.* family vault. ~berechtigt *a.* having an hereditary title to.

er'barm-en *v.r.* to feel pity; to have mercy. *subst. n.* pity, compassion; mercy. ~er *m.* God of Mercy. ~ungslos *a.* merciless, pitiless, remorseless.

er'bärmlich *a.* pitiful; miserable.

er'bau-en *v.t.* to erect, build; (*fig.*) edify. ~er *m.* builder; founder. ~lich *a.* edifying. ~ung *f.* erection, building; (*fig.*) edification.

Erb-e (ɛrbə) *m.* (-en, -en) heir. *n.* (-es) heritage; inheritance. ~fehler *m.* inherited defect. ~feind *m.* hereditary enemy. ~folge *f.* succession. ~hofbauer *m.* owner of family estate. ~in *f.* heiress. ~krank *a.* suffering from hereditary disease. ~lasser *m.* testator. ~lich *a.* hereditary. ~masse *f.* all the hereditary factors. ~onkel *m.* uncle. ~prinz *m.* prince's heir. ~recht *n.* right of succession. ~sasse *m.* lord of the manor. ~schaft *f.* inheritance; legacy. ~schaftsgericht *n.* probate court. ~schaftsmasse *f.* (*leg.*) estate. ~schaftssteuer *f.* death-duty, legacy duty. ~schleicher *m.* legacy-hunter. ~stück *n.* heirloom. ~sünde *f.* original sin. ~teil *n.* portion of inheritance. [ORPHAN]

er'beben (-be:b-) *vws.i.* to tremble, shake, quiver.

erben *v.t.* to inherit; to succeed to.

er'beuten *v.t.* to capture.

er'bieten *v.r.* to offer, volunteer.

er'bitten *v.t.* to ask, beg.

er'bitter-n *v.t.* to embitter; to exasperate. ~**t** *a.* exasperated. ~**ung** *f.* animosity, exasperation.

er'blassen, er'bleichen *vws.i.* to turn pale.

erblich¹ *a.* hereditary.

er'blich² *imperf. of* erbleichen.

er'blicken *v.t.* to catch sight of; to see, perceive.

er'blind-en *vws.i.* to grow blind. ~**ung** *f.* loss of sight.

er'bosen (-bo:z-) *v.t.* to make angry. *v.r.* to get vexed *or* angry.

er'bötig (-bø:t-) *a.* ready, willing.

er'brechen *v.t.* to break open; (*also v.r.*) to vomit. *subst. n.* vomiting.

Erbse (crp-) *f.* (-, -n) pea.

Erd-achse *f.* axis of the earth. ~**antenne** *f.* ground aerial. ~**apfel** *m.* potato. ~**arbeiter** *m.* navvy. ~**ball** *m.* terrestrial globe. ~**beben** *n.* earthquake. ~**beere** *f.* strawberry. ~**boden** *m.* ground; soil; earth.

Erd-e (e:rdə) *f.* (-e, -en) earth, ground; soil; *auf ~en* on earth; *zu ebener ~e* on the ground-floor; *zu ~e werden* to return to dust; *der ~e gleich machen* to level to the ground. ~**geboren** *a.* earth-born, mortal. ~**geschoß** *n.* ground-floor. ~**ig** *a.* earthy. ~**innere** *n.* interior of the earth. ~**kreis** *m.* globe. ~**kunde** *f.* geography. ~**leitung** *f.* ground wire, earth connexion. ~**messer** *m.* geodesist. ~**mine** *f.* land mine. ~**nähe** *f.* perigee. ~**öl** *n.* petroleum. ~**reich** *n.* earth, ground; soil; (*bibl.*) Earthly Kingdom. ~**rinde** *f.* earth's crust. ~**rund** *n.* earth, globe. ~**rutsch** *m.* land-slide. ~**schluß** *m.* earth connexion, ground. ~**scholle** *f.* clod. ~**streitkräfte** *f.pl.* ground forces. ~**strich** *m.* region, zone. ~**teil** *m.* continent. ~**umfang** *m.* circumference of the earth. ~**vermessung** *f.* geodesy.

erden *v.t.* to earth, ground. ~**bahn** *f.* earthly course. ~**bürger** *m.* human being, mortal. ~**wallen** *n.* (*poet.*) earthly pilgrimage.

er'denk-en *v.t.* to think out; to conceive; to invent. ~**lich** *a.* imaginable.

er'dichten *v.t.* to invent; to fabricate.

er'dolchen *v.t.* to stab.

er'dreisten *v.r.* to venture; to have the cheek (to do).

er'drosseln *v.t.* to strangle, throttle.

er'drücken *v.t.* to stifle; to crush; to squeeze to death; *~de Übermacht* overwhelming superiority.

er'dulden *v.t.* to suffer, endure.

er'eifern *v.r.* to get excited.

er'eign-en *v.r.* to happen, occur, come to pass. ~**is** *n.* event; occurrence, incident.

er'eilen *v.t.* to overtake, catch up.

Ere'mit (-mi:t) *m.* (-en, -en) hermit.

er'fahr-en *v.t.* to hear, learn; to experience. *a.* experienced, expert, skilled. ~**ung** *f.* experience; *aus ~ung* by experience; *in ~ung bringen* to learn; to ascertain. ~**ungsgemäß** *adv.* from experience; empirically.

er'fassen *v.t.* to catch hold of; to seize; to include; to register; (*fig.*) to grasp, understand.

er'find-en *v.t.* to find out, discover; to invent. ~**er** *m.* inventor. ~**ergeist** *m.* ingenuity. ~**erisch** *a.* inventive. ~**ung** *f.* invention, device; fiction.

er'flehen *v.t.* to implore or beg for.

Er'folg (-k) *m.* (-es, -e) success; result, outcome. ~**en** *vws.i.* to ensue, result, follow. ~**los** *a.* unsuccessful, fruitless. ~**reich** *a.* successful.

er'forder-lich *a.* necessary, requisite. ~**n** *v.t.* to need, require, call for. ~**nis** *n.* exigency, requisite.

er'forsch-en *v.t.* to explore; to investigate. ~**ung** *f.* exploration; investigation.

er'fragen *v.t.* to inquire, ascertain.

er'frechen *v.r.* to dare; to have the cheek (to do).

er'freu-en *v.t.* to give pleasure to; to gladden. *v.r.* to be pleased or glad; to enjoy, rejoice in. ~**lich** *a.* delightful; gratifying; satisfactory. **~licherweise** *adv.* fortunately. **~t** *a.* glad, pleased, delighted.

er'frieren *vws.i.* to die of cold; to freeze to death.

er'frisch-en *v.t.* to refresh. **~ung** *f.* refreshment.

er'füll-en *v.t.* to fill; to fulfil; to comply with (request); to do (one's duty); to keep (promise); to carry out (agreement). *v.r.* to come true; to be realized. **~ung** *f.* fulfilment. **~ungsort** *m.* destination.

er'gänz-en *v.t.* to complete; to restore; to supplement; to replenish. **~ung** *f.* completion; restoration; supplement; replenishment. **~ungsband** *m.* supplementary volume. **~ungswinkel** *m.* complementary angle.

er'gattern *v.t.* to get hold of; to pick up.

er'geb-en 1. *v.t.* to produce; yield; to result in; to make, amount to. *v.r.* to surrender; to devote oneself to; to take to (drink) to; to acquiesce in, resign oneself to; to follow, result (from). 2. *a.* devoted; *Ihr ~ener* yours faithfully. **~enheit** *f.* devotion. **~enst** *a.* obedient, respectful. **~nis** *n.* result; yield; output; sum. **~nislos** *a.* without result. **~ung** *f.* submission, resignation.

er'gehen 1. *v.r.* to walk, stroll; (*fig.*) to dwell upon; to indulge in. *vws.i.* to be published, be issued; to be promulgated; (*leg.*) to be passed; *über sich ~ lassen* to endure, bear. *v. impers.* to go, fare with; *wie ist es Ihnen ergangen?* how did you get on? 2. *subst. n.* condition, state of health; way of living.

er'giebig *a.* productive; lucrative; fertile. **~keit** *f.* productiveness; fertility.

er'gießen *v.r.* to discharge, flow (into).

er'glühen *vws.i.* to glow.

er'götz-en (-gœts-) *v.t.* to amuse, delight. *v.r.* to enjoy oneself. *subst. n.* delight, joy. **~lich** *a.* diverting, amusing, funny.

er'grauen *vws.i.* to get grey.

er'greif-en *v.t.* to seize; to take hold of; to take; to take up; to move, touch. **~end** *a.* moving, touching. **~ung** *f.* seizure; capture.

er'griffen *a.* moved, touched, affected. **~heit** *f.* emotion.

er'grimmen *vws.i.* to get angry.

er'gründen *v.t.* to fathom; to probe, look into.

er'guß *m.* effusion.

er'haben *a.* projecting; raised, elevated; prominent; lofty, noble, sublime; *~e Arbeit* relief; *~ sein über* to be above. **~heit** *f.* eminence; sublimity.

Er'halt *m.* (-es) receipt.

er'halt-en *v.t.* to receive, get, obtain; to preserve, keep; to save; to support, maintain. **~er** *m.* supporter. **~ungszustand** *m.* state of preservation, condition.

er'hältlich *a.* obtainable.

er'hängen *v.t. & r.* to hang.

er'härten *v.t.* to harden; (*fig.*) to confirm.

er'haschen *v.t.* to catch, snatch, seize.

er'heb-en *v.t.* to raise; to lift up; to praise; to extol; to bring (action) against; to collect (taxes); *ins Quadrat ~en* to square. *v.r.* to rise; to arise; to rebel (against); to assume a superiority. **~end** *a.* elevating, impressive. **~lich** *a.* considerable. **~ung** *f.* raising; elevation; collection; rebellion, revolt; Gallup poll; *~ungen anstellen* to make inquiries.

er'heischen *v.t.* to require, demand.

er'heiter-n *v.t.* to cheer, amuse. **~ung** *f.* amusement, diversion.

er'hellen *v.t.* to light up, illuminate. *v.i.* to become clear, be evident.

er'hitzen *v.t.* to heat, warm. *v.r.* to grow hot, become heated; (*fig.*) to fly into a passion.

er'höh-en *v.t.* to raise; to exalt; to increase, heighten. **~ung** *f.* elevation, eminence; increase, advance, rise.

er'hol-en *v.r.* to recover, get better; to rest, relax; to improve.

~ung f. recovery; rest, recreation.

er'hör-en v.t. to hear; to grant. ~ung f. hearing, granting.

Erika f. bell-heather.

er'|inner-lich a. present to one's mind. ~n v.t. to remind; dagegen ~n to object. v.r. to remember, recollect. ~ung f. remembrance, memory; recollection; reminiscence; reminder; zur ~ung an in memory of.

er'kalten vws.i. to cool down; to grow cold.

er'kält-en v.r. to catch (a) cold. ~ung f. cold, chill.

er'kämpfen v.t. to get by fighting.

er'kaufen v.t. to buy; teuer ~ (fig.) to pay dearly for.

er'kecken v.r. to dare, be so bold as to.

er'kenn-bar a. recognizable, perceptible. ~en v.t. to recognize; to perceive; to know; to understand, realize, see; (commerc.) to credit; schuldig ~en to return a verdict of guilty; zu ~en geben to show, indicate; sich zu ~en geben to make oneself known. ~tlich a. recognizable; grateful. ~tlichkeit f. gratitude. ~tnis f. knowledge; cognition; perception; understanding. ~tnistheorie f. theory of cognition. ~ung f. recognition. ~ungsmarke f. identification disk. ~ungsmelodie f. signature tune. ~ungswort n. password. ~ungszeichen n. distinguishing sign.

Erker m. (-s, -) alcove. ~fenster n. oriel, bay-window.

er'kiesen v.t. (poet.) to choose.

er'klär-en v.t. to explain; to account for; to declare; ~lich a. explicable; understandable. ~t a. professed, declared. ~ung f. explanation; interpretation; commentary; declaration.

er'klecklich a. considerable.

er'klettern, er'klimmen vt.s. to climb.

er'klingen v.i. to sound; to resound; to ring.

er'koren a. chosen.

er'krank-en vws.i. to fall ill, be taken ill. ~ung f. illness.

er'kühnen v.r. to venture (to), dare.

er'kund-en v.t. to ascertain; (mil.) to reconnoitre. ~ung f. reconnaissance.

er'kundig-en v.r. to inquire (for person and about a thing); to make inquiries. ~ung f. inquiry.

er'künstelt a. affected.

er'lahmen vws.i. to become lame; (fig.) to get tired, flag.

er'langen v.t. to reach, attain; to get, obtain; to acquire.

Er'laß m. (-(ss)es, -(ss)e) decree; remission; pardon.

er'lass-en v.t. to issue; to remit, release from; to dispense with. ~ung f. remission.

er'laub-en v.t. to allow, permit. v.r. to presume, dare. ~nis f. permission, leave; licence.

er'laucht a. illustrious, noble.

er'läuter-n v.t. to explain; to illustrate; to comment on. ~ung f. explanation; comment, illustration, note.

Erle f. (-, -n) alder-tree.

er'leb-en v.t. to experience; to live to see. ~nis n. event, occurrence; experience; adventure.

er'ledig-en v.t. to carry through; to wind up; to do; to dispatch; to settle, finish; ~tes Amt vacant post; ~t sein to be dead tired. ~ung f. execution; carrying out, completion; dispatch.

er'legen v.t. to kill; to pay down.

er'leichter-n v.t. to facilitate; to ease, lighten; to relieve. ~ung f. facilitation; relief; alleviation; (pl.) facilities.

er'leiden v.t. to suffer, bear, endure.

er'lernen v.t. to learn, acquire.

er'lesen v.t. to select, choose. a. select, choice.

er'leucht-en v.t. to light up, illuminate; (fig.) to enlighten. ~ung f. illumination; enlightenment.

er'liegen vws.i. to be defeated; to succumb to; to die of (an illness).

Erlkönig m. king of the elves.

er'logen a. false, untrue; fabricated.

Er'lös m. (-es, -e) net proceeds.

er'löschen vws.i. st. to be extinguished, go out; (fig.) to cease to exist; to expire; to die.

er'lös-en v.t. to save; to redeem, deliver; to get (proceeds). ~**er** m. deliverer; Redeemer, Saviour. ~**ung** f. redemption; release, deliverance.

er'mächtig-en v.t. to empower, authorize. ~**ung** f. authorization, authority.

er'mahn-en v.t. to exhort, admonish. ~**ung** f. exhortation, admonition.

er'mangel-n v.i. to lack; ~n zu tun to fail to do; in ~ung von for want of, in default of, failing.

er'mannen v.r. to take heart.

er'mäßig-en v.t. to abate; to reduce, lower. ~**ung** f. abatement; reduction.

er'matt-en v.t. to tire, weary, exhaust, vws.i. to grow weary or tired, feel exhausted. ~**ung** f. weariness, fatigue, exhaustion.

er'messen v.t. to judge; to consider. subst. n. judgement; opinion; discretion.

er'mitt-eln v.t. to find out; to ascertain. ~**lung** f. inquiry; ascertainment. ~**lungsverfahren** n. preliminary investigations.

er'möglichen v.t. to make possible or feasible; to enable (person to).

er'mord-en v.t. to murder, assassinate. ~**ung** f. murder, assassination.

er'müd-en v.t. to tire out, weary. vws.i. to become tired, grow weary. ~**ung** f. fatigue, weariness.

er'munter-n v.t. to wake up; (fig.) to rouse; to incite.

er'mutigen v.t. to encourage.

er'nähr-en v.t. to nourish; to feed; to support, maintain. ~**er** m. breadwinner. ~**ung** f. nourishment; food; feeding; nutrition; support, maintenance.

er'nenn-en v.t. to nominate; to appoint. ~**ung** f. nomination; appointment.

er'neu-en, -ern vv.t. to renew, renovate; to replace; to repeat. ~**erung** f. renewal, renovation;

replacement; repetition.

er'niedrig-en v.t. to lower; to humble, humiliate; to degrade; (mus.) to depress. ~**ung** f. lowering; humiliation; degradation. ~**ungszeichen** n. (mus.) flat.

Ernst 1. m. (-es) seriousness; earnest(ness); gravity; severity; im ~, allen ~es in all seriousness; seriously; ~ machen mit to put into practice. 2. a. (also ~**haft**) serious; earnest; grave; severe. ~**fall** m. emergency. ~**haftigkeit** f. seriousness. ~**lich** a. serious, earnest.

Ernte f. (-, -n) harvest, crop. ~**arbeit** f. harvesting. ~**dankfest** n. harvest thanksgiving. ~**monat** m. August. ~**segen** m. rich harvest.

ernten v.t. & i. to harvest; to reap, gather in.

er'nüchter-n v.t. to sober, sober down; to disillusion. ~**ung** f. sobering down; disillusionment.

er'ober-n (-o:b-) v.t. to conquer, to capture. ~**er** m. conqueror. ~**ung** f. conquest.

er'öffn-en v.t. to open; to start; to disclose, inform; to probate (will). ~**ung** f. opening; inauguration; communication; disclosure.

er'örter-n v.t. to discuss. ~**ung** f. discussion.

e'rotisch a. erotic.

Erpel m. drake.

er'picht a. ~ sein auf to be keen on.

er'press-en v.t. to extort; to blackmail. ~**er** m. blackmailer. ~**ung** f. extortion; blackmail.

er'proben v.t. to try, test.

er'quick-en v.t. to refresh. ~**ung** f. refreshment.

er'raten v.t. st. to guess.

er'ratisch a. erratic.

er'rechnen v.t. to reckon out.

er'reg-bar a. excitable; irritable. ~**en** v.t. to excite, stir up. ~**er** m. (sci.) agent. ~**ung** f. excitement; agitation; excitation.

er'reich-bar a. attainable; within reach, get-at-able. ~**en** v.t. to reach, attain, achieve; to arrive at. ~ung f. reaching; attainment.

er'rett-en v.t. to save, rescue, deliver. ~ung f. saving, rescue, deliverance; salvation.

er'richt-en v.t. to erect, put up; to found, establish. ~ung f. erection; foundation, establishment.

er'ringen v.t. to gain, win; to achieve.

er'röten vws.i. to blush. subst. n. blushing, blush.

Er'rungenschaft f. (-, -en) acquisition; achievement.

Er'satz (-zats) m. (-es) substitute; surrogate; amends, compensation, equivalent; (mil.) reserve, drafts. ~anspruch m. claim (for compensation). ~blei m. refill lead. ~mann m. substitute. ~mannschaft f. fresh draft. ~mittel n. substitute, surrogate. ~pflichtig a. liable for damages. ~rad n. spare wheel. ~reifen m. spare tyre. ~teil m. spare part. ~wahl f. by-election.

er'saufen vws.i. to be drowned.

er'säufen v.t. to drown.

er'schaff-en v.t. to create, produce. ~er m. creator. ~ung f. creation.

er'schallen vws.i. to ring, resound.

er'schauern vws.i. to shiver, tremble, shudder.

er'schein-en vws.i. to appear; (of book) to come out, be published; to seem. ~ung f. appearance; figure; apparition, vision; publication; (sci.) phenomenon; (med.) symptom; (eccl.) ~ung Christi Epiphany.

er'schieß-en v.t. to shoot (dead). ~ung f. shooting, execution.

er'schlaffen vws.i. to grow slack, slacken, relax. v.t. to enervate, slacken.

er'schlagen v.t. to kill, slay.

er'schleichen v.t. to obtain surreptitiously.

er'schließen v.t. to open; to make accessible; to infer, conclude.

er'schöpf-en v.t. to exhaust. ~end a. exhaustive. ~ung f. exhaustion.

er'schrecken v.t. to frighten,

startle. vws.i. st. to be frightened, be alarmed.

er'schrocken a. frightened, terrified.

er'schütter-n v.t. to shake; to upset; (fig.) to shock, affect deeply. ~ung f. shaking, concussion; shock; agitation, violent emotion.

er'schweren v.t. to make more difficult; to aggravate.

er'schwingen v.t. to afford. ~lich a. within one's means.

er'sehen v.t. to see, perceive; to learn.

er'sehnen v.t. to long for.

er'setzbar a. reparable; replaceable.

er'setzen v.t. to replace; to take the place of; to restore; to repair; to compensate; to recover (expenses); to make up (for).

er'sichtlich a. obvious, evident.

er'sinnen v.t. to think out; to devise.

er'spähen v.t. to espy, spot.

er'spar-en v.t. to save, economize. ~nis f. saving; savings.

er'sprießlich a. useful, profitable; beneficial.

erst a. first; (fig.) foremost, leading, prime, best; der ~e beste the first that comes; fürs ~e for the present; der ~ere the former; zum ~en, zweiten, dritten! going, going, gone! adv. first; at first, at the beginning, first of all; only, just; eben ~ just now; ~ als not till, only when; ~ recht all the more. ~aufführung f. first performance. ~druck m. first edition. ~enmal adv. zum ~enmal for the first time. ~ens adv. firstly. ~geboren a. first-born. ~geburt f. primogeniture. ~klassig, ~rangig aa. first-class, first-rate. ~lich adv. first, firstly. ~ling m. first-born; first-fruit(s); first production. ~malig a. & adv. first; for the first time.

er'starken vws.i. to grow strong, gain strength.

er'starr-en vws.i. to grow stiff, to congeal, solidify; to be paralysed (with fear). ~t a. benumbed. ~ung f. stiffness, numbness; freezing; coagulation, solidification.

er'statt-en *v.t.* to replace; to refund; *Bericht* ~*en* to report. ~*ung f.* compensation; restitution; return.

er'staun-en *v.t.* to astonish. *vws.i.* to be astonished. *subst. n.* astonishment, amazement, surprise. ~*lich a.* astonishing, amazing, surprising.

er'stechen *v.t.* to stab.

er'stehen *v.t.* to buy, purchase. *vws.i.* to arise; to rise.

er'steig-en *v.t.* to climb, ascend; to scale. ~*ung f.* ascent.

er'sterben *vws.i.* to die away.

er'stick-en *v.t.* to suffocate, choke, stifle; *im Keime* ~*en* to nip in the bud. *vws.i.* to be suffocated. ~*ung f.* suffocation.

er'strahlen *v.i.* to radiate.

er'streben *v.t.* to strive for, aspire to. ~*swert a.* desirable, worthwhile.

er'strecken *v.r.* to extend; to stretch to, reach to.

er'stürm-en *v.t.* to storm, take by storm. ~*ung f.* storming.

er'suchen *v.t.* to request, beg. *subst. n.* request.

er'tappen *v.t.* to catch; to surprise.

er'teil-en *v.t.* to give, impart; to place (an order); to bestow on; to grant. ~*ung f.* giving, imparting; granting.

er'tönen *vws.i.* to sound, resound.

er'töten *v.t.* to deaden, smother, stifle; to mortify.

Er'trag *m.* (-es, ⁼e) produce, yield, profit; proceeds; returns. ~*en v.t.* to bear, endure; to suffer, tolerate. ~*fähigkeit f.* productivity.

er'träg-lich *a.* bearable, endurable; tolerable; passable. ~*nis n.* = Ertrag.

er'tränken *v.t.* to drown.

er'träumen *v.t.* to dream of.

er'trinken *vws.i.* to be drowned.

er'trotzen *v.t.* to extort (from).

er'tüchtig-en *v.t.* to make fit, train, harden. ~*ung f.* training, hardening.

er'übrigen *v.t.* to save, put by; to spare. *v.r.* to be unnecessary, be superfluous.

er'wachen *vws.i.* to awake.

er'wachsen *vws.i.* to grow up; (*fig.*) to arise, spring from, accrue from. *a.* grown-up. ~*e(r) m.* adult, grown-up.

er'wäg-en *v.t.* to consider, weigh. ~*ung f.* consideration; reflection.

er'wählen *v.t.* to choose, elect.

er'wähn-en *v.t.* to mention. ~*ung f.* mention.

er'wärm-en *v.t.* to warm; to heat.

er'wart-en *v.t.* to expect; to wait for, await. ~*ung f.* expectation. ~*ungsvoll a.* expectant, full of hope.

er'weck-en *v.t.* to awaken, rouse; to restore to life, resuscitate; (*fig.*) to arouse; to raise. ~*ung f.* awakening; resuscitation; reviving, revival.

er'wehren *v.r.* to defend oneself against; to keep off; to refrain from.

er'weichen *v.t.* to soften; to move.

Er'weis *m.* (-es, -e) proof; evidence. ~*en v.t.* to prove, show; to render, do, pay. *v.r.* to prove oneself to be; to turn out to be. ~*lich a.* demonstrable.

er'weiter-n *v.t.* to widen; to expand, extend; to enlarge; to amplify. ~*ung f.* widening; expansion; extension; enlargement; amplification.

Er'werb (-verp) *m.* (-es, -e) acquisition; gain, profit; living. ~*sfähig a.* capable of earning one's living. ~*slos a.* unemployed, out of work. ~*slosenunterstützung f.* dole, unemployment relief. ~*squelle f.* means of living. ~*stätig a.* working. ~*sunfähig a.* unfit for work; incapable of earning a living. ~*szweig m.* branch of industry, line of business.

er'werben *v.t.* to acquire; to gain; to earn.

er'wider-n (-vi:d-) *v.t.* to return; to reply, retort, rejoin. ~*ung f.* return; reply, retort, rejoinder.

er'wiesenermaßen *adv.* as has been proved.

er'wirken *v.t.* to procure, secure.

er'wischen *v.t.* (*colloq.*) to catch.

er'wünscht a. desired; desirable.

er'würgen v.t. to strangle, throttle.

Erz¹ (-ts) n. (-es, -e) ore; metal; brass; bronze. ~ader f. vein of ore. ~en a. metal, brazen, bronze. ~förderung f. output of ore. ~gießerei f. brass-foundry. ~haltig a. containing ore. ~reich a. rich in ore.

erz-² pref. arch-. ~betrüger. ~gauner. ~schelm m. thorough scoundrel. ~bischof m. arch-bishop. ~dumm a. extremely stupid. ~engel m. archangel. ~feind m. arch-enemy. ~herzog m. archduke. ~lügner m. arch-liar. ~vater m. patriarch.

er'zähl-en v.t. to tell, relate, narrate. ~er m. narrator, story-teller; novelist, writer. ~ung f. story, tale, narrative; report.

er'zeugen v.t. to show; to render.

er'zeug-en v.t. to beget, procreate; to breed; to produce; to manufacture; to cause, create; (chem.) to generate. ~er m. father; producer, manufacturer. ~nis n. produce; product; production. ~ung f. begetting, procreation; production; generation.

er'zieh-en v.t. to bring up; to educate; to train. ~er m. teacher, tutor. ~erin f. teacher, governess. ~erisch a. educational, pedagogic. ~ung f. education, upbringing, bringing up. ~ungswesen n. educational system.

er'ziel-en v.t. to obtain, attain, achieve; to produce; to realize (profit). ~ung f. attainment, achievement.

er'zürnen v.t. to anger, enrage. v.r. to get angry; to fall out (with).

er'zwingen v.t. to force, enforce; to extort.

es¹ pron. it.

Es² n. (mus.) E flat.

Esche f. (-, -n) ash-tree.

Esel (ezal) m. (-s, -) ass, donkey. ~ei f. stupidity, folly. ~in f. she-ass. ~sbrücke f. crib. ~sohr n. (fig.) dog's-ear.

eskor'tieren v.t. to escort.

Espe f. (-, -n) asp, aspen; zittern

wie ~nlaub to tremble like an aspen-leaf.

eß-bar a. eatable, edible. ~ge-schirr n. mess-tin. ~löffel m. table-spoon. ~lust f. appetite. ~tisch m. dining-table. ~waren f.pl. provisions, victuals. ~zimmer n. dining-room.

Esse f. (-, -n) chimney, chimney-stalk; forge, smithy.

ess-en v.t. & i. st. to eat; to dine; (mil.) to mess. subst. n. food; meal. ~enszeit f. meal-time, dinner-time. ~er m. eater.

E'ssenz (-ts) f. (-, -en) essence.

Essig (-ç) m. (-s) vinegar. ~gurke f. pickled cucumber. ~sauer a. acetic, acetate of. ~säure f. acetic acid. [ACID]

Estrich m. (-s, -e) plaster floor. [L]

etab'lieren v.t. to establish, set up. v.r. to start a business.

E'tag-e (-ta:ʒə) f. (-e, -en) floor, story, flat. ~enwohnung f. flat. ~ere f. stand. [F]

E'tappe f. (-, -n) stage; (mil.) base. [F]

E'tat (e:ta:) m. (-s) estimate, budget. ~sjahr n. financial year. ~smäßig a. (of official, &c.) on the establishment; permanent. [F]

etepe'tete (e:təpə'te:tə) pred. a. (colloq.) finicky, particular.

Ethi-k (e:tik) f. (-k) ethics. ~sch a. ethical.

Ethno'graph m. (-en, -en) ethnographer. ~isch a. ethnographic.

Ethno'log-e m. (-en, -en) ethnologist. ~ie f. ethnology.

Eti'kett-e f. (-e, -en) etiquette; ticket, label. ~ieren v.t. to ticket, label.

etliche a. & pron. pl. some; a few.

E'tui (-tvi:) n. (-s, -s) case. [F]

etwa (etva) adv. nearly, about; perhaps, by chance. ~ig a. eventual.

etwas (-vas) pron. something; anything. indecl. a. some, any. adv. somewhat; a little.

Etymo'log-e m. (-en, -en) etymologist. ~ie f. etymology. ~isch a. etymological.

euch (oiç) acc. & dat. of pron. you; to you.

Eucha´ristie f. (-) eucharist.

euer (ɔiər) pron. & a. your; yours.

Eule (ɔilə) f. (-, -n) owl. ~nspiegelei f. tomfoolery.

eur-erseits adv. on your part; in your turn. ~esgleichen indecl. pron. like you, of your kind. ~ethalben, ~etwegen, ~etwillen adv. for your sake; because of you; on your account. ~ig a. yours.

Euter (ɔi-) n. (-s, -) udder.

evaku´ieren v.t. to evacuate.

evan´geli-sch a. evangelical; Protestant. ~um n. (-ums, -ien) gospel.

Eventu-ali´tät (-t:r) f. eventuality. ~ell a. ⚕ possible. adv. if occasion arises; perhaps; possibly.

Ew. (obs.) = Euer.

Ewer m. (-s, -) smack, fishing-smack.

ewig (e:viç) a. eternal, everlasting; endless, continual; perpetual (snow); der ~e Jude the wandering Jew; auf ~ for ever (more). ~keit f. eternity; age, ages. ~lich adv. for ever; eternally.

e´xakt a. exact. ~heit f. exactness, exactitude.

exal´tiert a. ⚕ over-excited; highly strung.

E´xam-en (-ksa-) n. (-ens, -ina) examination. ~ensarbeit f. thesis, paper. ~i´nator m. examiner. ~i´nieren v.t. to examine.

E´xemp-el n. (-els, -el) example; (math.) problem, sum. ~lar n. sample; specimen; copy. ~larisch a. exemplary. ~lifi´zieren v.t. to exemplify.

E´xequien (ɛksɛ:kviən) n.pl. obsequies.

exer´zier-en (-tsi:r-) v.t. & i. to drill. ~meister m. drill-sergeant, instructor. ~platz m. drill-ground. [L]

Exer´ziti-um n. (-ums, -en) exercise; meditation.

E´xil (ɛksi:l) n. (-s, -e) exile.

Existentia´lismus m. existentialism.

Exis´tenz (-stɛnts) f. (-, -en) existence; (means of) livelihood; position.

exis´tieren v.i. to exist; to live.

exkommuni´zieren v.t. to excommunicate.

exmatriku´lieren v.r. to leave the university, to go down.

exorzi´(s)ieren v.t. to exorcise.

e´xotisch a. exotic.

Exped-i´ent m. forwarding clerk. ~ieren v.t. to dispatch, forward. ~iti´on f. forwarding; forwarding department; expedition.

Experi´ment n. (-s, -e) experiment. ~ell a. experimental. ~ieren v.i. to experiment.

Ex´pert-e m. (-en, -en) expert. ~ise f. expert's report.

explo-´dieren vws.i. to explode. ~si´on f. explosion. ~sivstoff m. explosive.

expo´nieren v.t. to expound, explain; to expose.

Ex´port m. (-s, -e) export, exportation. ~eur m. exporter. ~ieren v.t. to export.

ex´preß a. by express. ~(ss)io-´nistisch a. expressionist.

Exsu´dat n. (-s, -e) exudate, exudation.

Ex´tase f. ecstasy.

Extempo´r-ale n. exercise in class. ~ieren v.t. & i. to extemporize.

Extrablatt n. special edition.

extra´hieren v.t. to extract.

Ex´trakt m. & n. (-es, -e) extract.

ex´trem (-trɛ:m) a. extreme; exaggerated. subst. n. extreme. ~i´täten f.pl. extremities.

Exze´llenz (-lɛnts) f. (-, -en) Excellency.

ex´zentrisch a. eccentric.

exzer´pieren v.t. to make excerpts from.

Ex´zeß m. (-(ss)es, -(ss)e) excess, riot.

F

F, f (ɛf) n. the letter F, f; (mus.) f.

Fabel f. (-, -n) fable; story; plot

FABELN column:

(of play). **~ei** f. tale, fiction. **~haft** a. fabulous; amazing; (colloq.) marvellous. **~schmied** m. story-teller. **~wesen** n. fabulous being.

fabeln (fa:-) v.i. & t. to tell stories; to spin yarns.

Fa'brik (-bri:k) f. (-, -en) factory; mill; plant. **~anlage** f. plant. **~ant** m. manufacturer; factory owner. **~arbeiter** m. factory worker. **~at** n. manufacture; article. **~at'ion** f. making, manufacture. **~ationsfehler** m. flaw. **~marke** f., **~zeichen** n. trade mark. **~mäßig** a. machine-made. **~ware** f. manufactured goods.

fabri'zieren v.t. to manufacture, make.

fabu'lieren v.i. to invent stories.

Fa'cett-e f. (-e, -en) facet. **~iert** a. faceted.

Fach (fax) n. (-es, "er) compartment; shelf; drawer; pigeon-hole; (fig.) subject, speciality; branch; line; department; vom **~** by profession; specialist in; ins **~** schlagen to be (in) one's line. **~arbeiter** m. specialist; skilled worker. **~ausbildung** f. professional education or training. **~ausdruck** m. technical term. **~gelehrte(r)** m. specialist. **~genosse** m. colleague. **~geschäft** n. (special) supply store. **~gruppe** f. professional section; trade section. **~kenntnis** f. specialist or technical knowledge. **~lich** a. professional, special. **~literatur** f. special literature. **~mann** m. (pl. **~leute**) expert, specialist. **~männisch** a. professional; expert. **~schule** f. technical school. **~simpeln** v.i. to talk shop. **~werk** n. framework. **~werkbau** m. half-timbered building. **~wissenschaft** f. special branch of science. **~zeitschrift** f. technical or scientific periodical.

fäch-eln (fɛç-) v.t. to fan. **~er** m. fan. **~erförmig** a. fan-shaped.

Fackel f. (-, -n) torch. **~n** v.i. (fig.) to hesitate. **~zug** m. torch-light procession. [L]

FAHRBAHN column:

Fädchen n. small thread.

fade (fa:də) a. insipid; stale; flat; dull. [FADE]

Faden (fa:-) m. (-s, ") thread; twine, string; filament; fibre; fathom; an einem **~** hängen to hang by a thread; keinen guten **~** an einem lassen not to have a good word to say for; keinen trocknen **~** am Leibe haben to get wet through; den **~** verlieren (fig.) to lose the thread. **~heftung** f. thread-stitching (of books). **~nudeln** f.pl. vermicelli. **~rolle** f. reel of thread, cotton reel. **~scheinig** a. threadbare. **~ziehend** a. stringy. [FATHOM]

Fa'gott n. (-es, -e) bassoon. [IT.]

fähig (fɛ:ɡ) a. capable of; clever, able. **~keit** f. capability, ability; faculty; talent.

fahl a. fallow; faded; pale; livid.

fahnden v.i. to search (for).

Fahne (fa:-) f. (-, -n) flag; standard; banner; (mil.) colours; (typ.) proof. **~nabzug** m. galley-proof. **~neid** m. (mil.) oath of loyalty. **~nflucht** f. desertion. **~nflüchtige(r)** m. deserter. **~njunker** m. colour-sergeant. **~nstange** f. flagstaff. **~nträger** m. standard-bearer. **~nweihe** f. consecration of the colours.

Fähn-lein n. pennon; (obs.) squad, troop. **~rich** m. cadet; ensign; (naut.) midshipman.

Fahr-bahn f. road, roadway; track. **~bar** a. passable; navigable; mobile (equipment). **~damm** m. road, roadway. **~dienstleiter** m. station-master. **~er** m. driver. **~gast** m. passenger. **~geld** n. fare. **~gelegenheit** f. conveyance. **~gestell** n. under-carriage; (motor.) chassis. **~karte** f. ticket. **~kartenausgabe** f., **~kartenschalter** m. booking-office. **~lässig** a. negligent, careless. **~lässigkeit** f. negligence, carelessness. **~plan** m. time-table. **~planmäßig** a. regular; to time, to schedule. **~preis** m. fare. **~prüfung** f. driving test. **~rad** n. bicycle. **~rinne** f. water-way; fairway. **~schein** m. ticket.

~straße f. highway. ~stuhl m. lift, elevator. ~stuhlführer m. lift-boy or attendant. ~verbot n. 'prohibited to traffic'. ~wasser n. channel, fairway; (fig.) element. ~zeug n. vehicle; vessel, craft.

Fähr-e f. (-e, -en) ferry-boat; ferry. ~mann m. ferryman.

fahren v.t. st. to drive; to convey; to take; ~ lassen to give up, let go, abandon; ~de Habe movable property; ~des Volk tramps, vagrants. vws.i. to drive; to ride; to travel; to go; to sail; mit dem Rad ~ to cycle; mit dem Schiff ~ to sail; spazieren ~ to go for a drive; in die Höhe ~ to start up; in die Kleider ~ to throw on one's clothes; aus der Haut ~ to burst; gut (schlecht) ~ (fig.) to come off well (badly); einem durch den Kopf ~ to occur to one; was ist in ihn gefahren? what has come over him? fahre wohl! farewell! ~d a. driving, &c.; vagrant.

Fahrer m. (-, -) driver.

fahrig a. fidgety; careless.

Fahrt f. (-, -en) ride, drive; run; journey; trip; (sea) voyage; course (of ship); in voller ~ at full speed. ~ausweis m. (railway) ticket. ~enbuch n. logbook; record book. ~unterbrechung f. break of the journey. ~verbot n. traffic prohibited.

Fährte f. (-, -en) track; scent; auf falscher ~ on the wrong track.

faksimi'lieren v.t. to make facsimile of.

fakt-isch a. real, actual. ~or m. fact; factor; circumstance; foreman.

Fak'tur (-tu:r) f. (-, -en) invoice. ~ieren v.t. to invoice. [IT.]

Fakul't-ät f. (-ät, -äten) faculty. ~a'tiv a. optional.

falb a. fallow, dun.

Falke m. (-n, -n) falcon. ~nbeize f. falconry, hawking.

Fall m. (-es, ⸚e) fall; drop; downfall; accident; waterfall; (gram., leg., med.) case; instance; zu ~ bringen to ruin; zu ~ kommen to be ruined; auf jeden ~, auf alle

Fälle in any case, at all events; auf keinen ~ on no account; by no means; gesetzt den ~ supposing that; im ~ daß in case; von ~ zu ~ according to its merits; as the case may be. ~beil n. guillotine. ~brücke f. drawbridge. ~grube f. pitfall, trap. ~obst n. fallen fruit, windfall. ~reep n. accommodation ladder, gangway steps. ~schirm m. parachute. ~schirmabsprung m. parachute descent. ~schirmjäger, ~schirmtruppen f.pl. paratroops. ~schirmspringer m. parachutist. ~strick m. snare, noose. ~sucht f. epilepsy. ~tür f. trap-door. ~winkel m. angle of inclination or descent.

Falle f. (-, -n) trap; snare. ~nsteller m. trapper.

fallen vws.i. st. to fall; to sink; to die, be killed; ~ lassen to let fall, drop; leicht (schwer) ~ to find it easy (hard); aus allen Wolken ~ to be thunderstruck; in die Augen ~ to strike (one); in Ohnmacht ~ to faint; in die Rede ~ to interrupt; in den Rücken ~ to attack from behind, stab in the back; mit der Tür ins Haus ~ to blurt out.

fäll-en (fel-) v.t. to fell; to pass (sentence); to lower (bayonet); (geom.) to let fall; (chem.) to precipitate. ~ig a. due, payable. ~igkeit f. expiration, maturity (of bill). ~ung f. precipitation. ~ungsmittel n. precipitant.

fa'llieren v.i. to fail, become bankrupt.

falls conj. in case, if, in the event.

falsch a. wrong, incorrect; false; artificial; forged; counterfeit; bad (money); deceitful; ~ aussprechen to mispronounce; ~ singen to sing out of tune; ~ schwören to perjure; ohne ~ without guile, guileless. ~heit f. falseness; falsehood; duplicity. ~münzer m. forger. ~spieler m. cheat, card-sharper.

fälsch-en v.t. to falsify; to adulterate (food); to forge; to counterfeit (coin); to cook (ac-

counts). ~er *m.* forger. ~lich *a.*
false. ~licherweise *adv.* wrongly;
by mistake. ~ung *f.* falsification;
adulteration; forgery.

Faltboot *n.* collapsible boat.

Falt-e *f.* (-e, -en) fold; pleat;
crease; wrinkle; ~en werfen to
pucker; ~en ziehen to wrinkle,
knit (brow). ~enlos *a.* smooth,
without crease. ~enrock *m.*
pleated skirt. ~enwurf *m.*
drapery. ~ig *a.* folded; pleated;
wrinkled.

fälteln *v.t.* to fold in small pleats.

falten *v.t.* to fold; to plait; to
ruffle.

Falter *m.* (-s, -) butterfly.

Falz (-ts) *m.* (-es, -e) fold; groove;
notch; rabbet. ~bein *n.* folder,
paper-knife. ~en *v.t.* to fold; to
groove; to rabbet.

famili'är *a.* familiar; intimate.

Fa'milie (-mi:liə) *f.* (-, -n) family.
~nabzüge *m.pl.* personal allow-
ances. ~nanschluß *m.* mit
~nanschluß 'as one of the
family'. ~nbeihilfe *f.* family
allowance. ~nname *m.* surname.
~nstand *m.* status (married or
single, &c.).

fa'mos (-mo:s) *a.* capital, fine;
grand, great. [FAMOUS]

Fa'nat-iker *m.* (-ikers, -iker)
fanatic. ~isch *a.* fanatical.
~ismus *m.* fanaticism.

fand *imperf. of* **finden**.

Fan'fare *f.* (-, -n) flourish of
trumpets. [F]

Fang (-ŋ) *m.* (-es, ⁓e) catch;
capture; prey; haul; (*pl.*) tusks,
fangs; claws, talons (of birds).
~eisen *n.* iron trap. ~garn *n.*
snaring-net. ~leine *f.* rope,
painter; harpoon-line.

fangen (faŋən) *v.t. st.* to catch; to
trap; to capture.

Fant *m.* (-es, -e) fop, coxcomb.

Farbband *n.* typewriter ribbon.

Farb-e *f.* (-, -en) colour; hue,
tint; dye, stain, paint; (*of cards*)
suit; ~e bekennen to follow suit;
(*fig.*) to show one's colours. ~
echt *a.* of fast colour. ~en-
blind *a.* colour-blind. ~(en)-
druck *m.* colour-printing; colour-
print. ~enfreudig *a.* multi-

coloured, gay. ~enlehre *f.* theory
of colours, chromatics. ~en-
schmelz *m.* blending of colours.
~enspiel *n.* opalescence. ~holz
n. dye-wood. ~ig *a.* coloured;
stained; *die* ~igen the coloured
races. ~los *a.* colourless; pale.
~stift *m.* coloured pencil or
crayon. ~stoff *m.* dye-stuff, dye;
pigment; stain. ~ton *m.* colour-
tone, shade, tint.

färb-en *v.t.* to colour; to dye
(hair, &c.); to stain. ~emittel
n. colouring agent; dye. ~e'rei
f. dye-works; dry-cleaning shop.
~ung *f.* hue, tinge; (*fig.*) touch.

Farce (-sə) *f.* (-, -n) farce; (*cook.*)
stuffing, force-meat.

Farm *f.* (-, -en) ⚑ colonial settlement; (chicken, &c.) farm. ~er
m. colonial settler; colonial
farmer.

Farn *m.* (-es, -e), ~kraut *n.* fern.

Farre *m.* (-n, -n) bull, bullock.

Färse *f.* (-, -n) heifer.

Fa'san (-za:n) *m.* (-s, -en) pheasant.
~e'rie *f.* pheasant preserve.

Fa'schine (-ʃi:nə) *f.* (-, -n) fascine;
bundle of faggots. ~nmesser *n.*
bill-hook; short sword.

Fasching *m.* (-s, -e) carnival.

Fa'schismus *m.* fascism. ~st *m.*
fascist. ~stisch *a.* fascist.

Fasel'ei (-z-) *f.* (-ei, -eien) twaddle,
drivel. ~ig *a.* silly, drivelling.
~n *v.t. & i.* to twaddle, drivel.

Faser (fa:z-) *f.* (-, -n) fibre; filament; thread. ~gewebe *n.*
fibrous tissue. ~ig *a.* fibrous,
stringy. ~n *v.i.* to fray out;
to ravel out. ~stoff *m.* fibrin;
fibrous material.

Faß (-s) *n.* (Fasses, Fässer) cask,
barrel; keg; butt; churn, tun;
tub, vat; *frisch vom* ~ (beer) on
draught. ~bier *n.* draught beer.
~binder *m.* cooper. ~weise *a.* in
or by barrels. [VAT]

Fa'ssade (-sa:də) *f.* (-, -n) façade.
~nkletterer *m.* cat-burglar.

fass-en *v.t.* to seize, take, hold; to
comprise; to contain, accommo-
date; to mount, set; (*fig.*) to
comprehend, grasp, take in. *v.r.* to
pull oneself together; *sich kurz*
~ to be brief; *ins Auge* ~ to en-

visage; to consider. **~lich** *a.* comprehensible, conceivable. **~ung** *f.* setting, mounting; draft, drafting, wording; version; composure, self-control; *aus der* **~ung bringen** to upset, disconcert. **~ungsgabe** *f.* power of comprehension; mental capacity. **~ungslos** *a.* disconcerted, put out. **~ungsvermögen** *n.* holding, seating, *or* loading capacity; *(fig.)* mental capacity.

Fa'sson (-sɔ̃:) *f.* (-, -s) shape; way; design; style. [F]

fast *adv.* almost, nearly.

fast-en *v.i.* to fast. *subst. n.pl.* **~enzeit** *f.* Lent. **~nacht** *f.* Shrove-tide; carnival.

Fas'zikel *m.* (-s, -) file.

fas zi'nieren (fastsi-) *v.t.* to fascinate.

fa'tal (-ta:l) *a.* ♠ awkward, unfortunate; disagreeable. **~ismus** *m.* fatalism.

Fatzke *m.* (-n, -n) *(dial.)* fool, coxcomb.

fauchen (-x-) *v.i.* to spit; to hiss.

faul *a.* rotten, putrid; bad; *(fig.)* lazy, idle; **~er Zauber** humbug. **~heit** *f.* laziness, idleness, sloth. **~ig** *a.* rotten, putrid, decayed. **~pelz** *m.* lazy-bones, idler, sluggard. **~tier** *n.* *(zool.)* sloth. [FOUL]

Fäul-e, Fäul-nis *f.* (-) rottenness; putrefaction. **~niserreger** *m.* germ of decomposition.

faulen *v.i.* to rot, putrefy. **~zen** *v.i.* to idle, be lazy, lounge. **~zer** *m.* idler, lazy-bones; deck-chair. **~ze'rei** *f.* idling; laziness.

Faust *f.* (-, -̈e) fist; *auf eigene* **~** on one's own responsibility. **~ball** *m.* punch-ball. **~dick** *a.* as big as one's fist; *es* **~dick hinter den Ohren haben** to be sly; **~dicke Lüge** a thumping lie. **~handschuh** *m.* mitten, mitt; boxing-glove. **~kampf** *m.* boxing; boxing-match. **~kämpfer** *m.* boxer. **~pfand** *n.* deadpledge. **~recht** *n.* club-law. **~schlag** *m.* cuff, punch.

Fäust-chen *n.* small fist; *sich ins* **~chen lachen** to laugh in one's

sleeve. **~ling** *m.* mitten.

faustisch *a.* like (Goethe's) Faust.

Favo'rit *m.* (-en, -en) favourite.

Faxen *f.pl.* tomfoolery, tricks. **~macher** *m.* buffoon.

Fazit *n.* (-s) result, sum total. [L]

Februar (fe:-) *m.* (-s, -e) February.

Fecht-boden (fɛçt-) *m.* fencing-room. **~bruder** *m.* beggar, tramp. **~en** *v.i.* *st.* to fight; to fence; to gesticulate; *(sl.)* to go begging. **~er** *m.* fencer. **~meister** *m.* fencing-master.

Feder (fe:-) *f.* (-, -n) feather; plume; pen; nib; *(mach.)* spring. **~ball** *m.* shuttlecock. **~bett** *n.* feather-bed. **~fuchser** *m.* scribbler, quill-driver. **~halter** *m.* penholder. **~kasten** *m.* pencil-case. **~kiel** *m.* quill. **~kleid** *n.* plumage. **~leicht** *a.* light as a feather. **~lesen** *n.* *nicht viel* **~lesens machen** to make short work of. **~strich** *m.* stroke of the pen. **~vieh** *n.* poultry. **~wisch** *m.* feather-duster. **~wischer** *m.* penwiper. **~wolke** *f.* cirrus. **~zeichnung** *f.* pen-and-ink sketch.

feder-n (fe:-) *v.i.* to moult; *(mach.)* to be elastic. **~nd** *a.* light, springy, elastic. **~ung** *f.* springiness, elasticity; *(motor.)* spring suspension.

Fee (fe:) *f.* (-, -n) fairy. **~nhaft** *a.* fairylike. [F]

feg-en (fe:-) *v.t.* to sweep, clean. **~efeuer** *n.* purgatory. [FAIR]

Fehde (fe:-) *f.* (-, -n) feud; quarrel; challenge. **~handschuh** *m.* gauntlet.

Fehl *m.* (-es, -e) blame, blemish. *adv.* amiss, wrong; **~** *am Platz sein* to be out of place. **~anzeige** *f.* negative report. **~bestand** *m.* shortage, deficiency. **~betrag** *m.* deficit. **~bitte** *f.* vain request; *eine* **~bitte** *tun* to meet with a refusal. **~geburt** *f.* miscarriage, abortion. **~gehen** *vws.i.* to go a wrong road; to make a mistake. **~greifen** *v.i.* to miss one's hold; to make a mistake. **~griff** *m.* mistake, blunder. **~guß** *m.* faulty cast. **~leistung** *f.* mistake, slip. ~schlag m. failure, washout. ~schlagen vws.i. to fail, come to nothing. ~schluß m. wrong inference; false conclusion. ~schuß m. miss. ~tritt m. false step, slip; moral lapse. ~urteil n. miscarriage of justice. ~zug m. wrong move. ~zündung f. misfire; (fig.) back-fire.

fehlen (fe:-) v.t. to miss. v.i. to err, make a mistake, blunder; to sin; to be missing, be absent; to be wanting; to lack; was fehlt dir? what's the matter with you? es an nichts ~ lassen to spare no pains. [FAIL]

Fehler m. (-s, -) defect; blemish; flaw; fault, blunder, mistake, error. ~frei, ~los aa. faultless; flawless; correct. ~haft a. faulty, defective, deficient; incorrect.

Fehpelz m. squirrel coat.

Feier f. (-, -n) festival, celebration; ceremony; rest. ~abend m. evening leisure; off-time; ~abend machen to knock off work. ~lich a. solemn; festive; ceremonious. ~lichkeit f. solemnity; ceremony. ~schicht f. idle shift; shift lost by absenteeism. ~stunde f. leisure hour; festive hour. ~tag m. festival; feast; holiday. [L]

feiern v.t. to celebrate. v.i. to rest, take a holiday; to stop work; to be idle.

feig(-e) a. cowardly. ~heit f. cowardice. ~herzig a. cowardly. ~ling m. coward. [FEY]

Feige f. (-, -n) fig. ~nblatt n. figleaf.

feil a. for sale; (fig.) mercenary. ~bieten v.t. to offer for sale. ~halten v.t. to have for sale.

Feil-e f. (-e, -en) file. ~en v.t. to file; (fig.) to polish, elaborate. ~späne m.pl. filings.

feilschen v.i. to bargain; to haggle.

fein a. fine, thin, delicate; distinguished, refined, elegant; subtle; sly, adv. (colloq.) fine! grand! ~bäckerei f. baker and confectioner's (shop). ~fühlig a. of delicate feeling, sensitive,

~gefühl n. tact. ~gehalt m. fineness, standard (of gold, &c.). ~gold n. fine gold. ~heit f. fineness; grace; elegance, refinement; subtlety. ~kosthandlung f. delicatessen (shop). ~mechaniker m. precision tool maker. ~schmecker m. gourmet. ~sinnig a. sensitive, delicate, tasteful. ~sliebchen n. sweetheart. ~zucker m. refined sugar.

Feind (-t) m. (-es, -e) enemy, foe; der böse ~ the Devil. pred. a. hostile. ~lich a. hostile, enemy; inimical. ~schaft f. hostility, enmity. ~selig a. hostile. ~seligkeit f. hostility; animosity. [FIEND]

feist a. fat, plump.

feixen v.i. to grin.

Feld (-t) n. (-es, -er) field; open country; plain; ground; (archit.) panel; (chess) square; (fig.) sphere; scope; ins ~ rücken to take the field; ins ~ führen (fig.) to bring up; im weiten ~ liegen to be still very uncertain. ~apotheke f. field dispensary. ~arbeit f. agricultural labour. ~artillerie f. (field) artillery. ~bett n. camp-bed. ~blume f. wild flower. ~dienstfähig a. fit for active service. ~dienstordnung f. Field Service Regulations. ~dienstübung f. field-day. ~ein, ~aus advv. across country. ~flasche f. water-bottle, flask. ~flüchtige(r) m. deserter. ~geschrei n. war-cry. ~grau a. field-grey (uniform). ~herr m. commander-in-chief. ~herrnstab m. baton. ~küche f. field-kitchen. ~lazarett n. ambulance, fieldhospital. ~marschall m. fieldmarshal. ~marschmäßig a. in full marching order. ~messer m. surveyor. ~prediger m. army chaplain. ~scher m. army surgeon. ~schlacht f. pitched battle. ~spat m. feldspar. ~stecher m. binoculars, fieldglasses. ~webel m. sergeant. ~zeichen n. ensign, standard. ~zeugmeister m. quartermaster. ~zug m. campaign.

Felge f. (-, -n) felloe; wheel-rim.

Fell n. (-es, -e) skin, hide, coat, fur; *ein dickes ~ haben* to be thick-skinned; *einem das ~ über die Ohren ziehen* to fleece a person. **~eisen** n. knapsack.

Fels, Fels-en m. (-ens, -en) rock; cliff; crag. **~block** m. piece of rock; block; boulder. **~enfest** a. firm as a rock; unshaken. **~enriff** n. reef. **~glimmer** m. mica. **~ig** a. rocky, craggy. **~klippe** f. cliff, rocky ridge. **~sturz** m. fall of rock. **~wand** f. wall of rock. [FELL]

Feme f., **Femgericht** n. vehmgericht; vehmic court.

Femi'nin-um n. (-ums, -a) feminine noun.

Fenchel (-çal) m. (-s, -) fennel.

Fenn n. (-s, -e) fen, bog, marsh.

Fenster n. (-s, -) window. **~bank** f., **~brett** n., **~sims** f. windowsill or -ledge. **~flügel** m. casement, (hinged) window-sash. **~kreuz** n. cross-bars. **~laden** m. shutter. **~nische** f. embrasure. **~rahmen** m. frame. **~riegel** m. sash-bolt, windowcatch. **~rose** f. rose-window. **~scheibe** f. pane. **~sturz** m. lintel. [L]

Ferge m. (-n, -n) ferryman.

Ferien (fe:-) pl. holidays, vacation. **~kolonie** f. holiday camp. [L]

Ferkel n. (-s, -) young pig. [FARROW]

Fer'mate (-ma:-) f. (-, -n) pause. [IT.]

fern a. & adv. far, distant, remote; *von ~* from afar, at a distance; *das sei ~ von mir* far be it from me.

Fern-amt n. trunk exchange. **~anruf** m. trunk-call.

Fern-e f. (-e, -en) distance. **~empfang** m. long-distance reception. **~er** a. farther, further. *adv.* moreover, besides. **~erhin** *adv.* henceforth. **~gelenkt** a. guided (missile). **~gespräch** n. trunk-call. **~glas** n. telescope; binoculars. **~heizanlage** f. long-distant heating plant. **~leitung** f. trunk-line. **~leitungsnetz** n.

trunk-line system. **~meldewesen** n. telecommunications. **~meldung** f. phone message. **~mündlich** a. by telephone. **~rohr** n. telescope. **~ruf** m. telephone; (telephone) call. **~schreiber** m. teleprinter. **~sehapparat** m. television set, T.V. set. **~sehbildschirm** m. viewing screen. **~sehen** n. television. **~sicht** f. perspective; vista, prospect; distant visibility. **~sprechamt** n. (telephone-)exchange. **~sprecher** m. telephone. **~sprechstelle** f. (public) telephone; telephone box. **~spruch** m. telephone message, wireless message. **~steuerung** f. remote control. **~verkehr** m. long-distance traffic. **~wirkung** f. telekinesis; long-range effect. **~zug** m. main-line train.

Ferner m. (-s,-) glacier.

Ferse f. (-, -n) heel; *~ngeld geben* to take to one's heels.

fertig a. ready; ready-made; finished; (*fig.*) skilled, accomplished, quick; *~ bringen* to bring about, accomplish; *~ werden mit* to manage; *~ sein mit* to have done with; *sich ~ machen* to get ready. **~en** v.t. to make, manufacture. **~fabrikat** n., **~ware** f. ready-made or manufactured goods. **~keit** f. dexterity, skill; knack; fluency. **~stellen** v.t. to finish, get ready.

Fes n. (mus.) E flat.

fesch a. smart. [FASHIONABLE]

Fessel[1] f. (-, -n) chain, fetter, shackle; (*fig.*) tie. **~ballon** m. captive balloon. **~n** v.t. to chain, fetter, shackle; to tether; (*fig.*) to absorb, to fascinate, captivate; *ans Bett gefesselt* confined to bed. **~tau** n. balloon cable; mooring-rope. **~ung** f. chaining up.

Fessel[2] f. (-, -n) ankle; pastern-joint, fetlock (of horse).

fest[1] a. firm; hard; rigid; solid; compact; tight; fast, fixed; permanent; constant; strong; *~e Nahrung* solid food; *~e Preise* fixed prices; *~e Stellung* permanent post; *~er Schlaf* sound sleep; *~en Fuß fassen* to

gain a firm footing. **~binden**
v.t. to tie, bind (fast). **~fahren**
vws.i. & r. to stick fast; to run
aground; (*fig.*) to be stuck; to
come to a deadlock. **~halten** *v.t.*
to hold (fast); to seize, arrest; to
write down; to picture, portray.
v.r. to hold on. **~land** *n.* mainland; continent. **~legen** *v.t.* to
fix, lay down; to invest (money).
v.r. to tie oneself down to. **~**
machen *v.t.* to fasten; to tighten;
to fix, settle. **~nahme** *f.* seizure, arrest. **~setzen** *v.t.* to fix;
to imprison. *v.r.* to settle, gain a
footing. **~sitzen** *v.i.* to be stuck;
to fit tightly. **~stehen** *v.i.* to
stand firmly; to be certain,
be a matter of fact. **~~d** *a.* constant; established. **~stellen** *v.t.*
to ascertain; to state; to determine; to identify; to establish.
~stellung *f.* statement; determination; identification. **~**
verzinslich *a.* (stock) at a fixed
rate of interest.

Fest² *n.* (-es, -e) feast, festival.
~essen *n.* banquet, public
dinner. **~feier** *f.* festival.
~gabe *f.* gift. **~halle** *f.* ban-
queting-hall. **~lich** *a.* festive;
solemn. **~lichkeit** *f.* festivity;
solemnity. **~ordner** *m.* organizer of a fête. **~schrift** *f.* publication in honour of someone.
~spiel *n.* festival performance.
~tag *m.* holiday, feast. **~zug**
m. festive procession.

Feste *f.* (-, -n) stronghold; (*bibl.*)
firmament.

festig-en *v.t.* to make firm,
strengthen; to consolidate. **~keit**
f. solidity; firmness; (*mach.*)
strength, resistance.

Festung *f.* (-, -en) fortress, stronghold. **~sgraben** *m.* moat of a
fortress. **~shaft** *f.* confinement
in a fortress. **~swall** *m.* rampart.

Fetisch (fe:-) *m.* (-s, -e) fetish.
fett (fɛt) *a.* fat; plump; fertile;
rich; lucrative. *subst. n.* fat;
lard, dripping; grease; **~** *ansetzen* to grow fat, put on flesh.
~auge *n.* drop of grease. **~darm**
m. rectum. **~druck** *m.* heavy

type, bold-faced type. **~drüse**
f. sebaceous gland. **~fleck** *m.*
grease spot. **~haltig** *a.* containing fat, fatty. **~ig** *a.* fatty; fat;
greasy. **~leibig** *a.* corpulent.
~näpfchen *n. ins ~näpfchen*
treten to put one's foot into it.
~sucht *f.* obesity. **~wanst** *m.*
big paunch.

Fetzen *m.* (-s, -) rag; scrap; shred.
feucht (fɔiçt) *a.* damp; muggy;
moist; humid. **~igkeit** *f.* dampness; moisture; humidity. **~ig-
keitsmesser** *m.* hygrometer.

feudal *a.* feudal; (*colloq.*) magnificent.

Feuer (foiər) *n.* (-s, -) fire; firing,
bombardment; brilliance, lustre;
(*fig.*) ardour; **~** *fangen* to catch
fire; **~** *geben* to give one a light;
(*mil.*) to fire, shoot; **~** *und
Flamme sein* to be very enthusiastic.

Feuer-bestattung *f.* cremation.
~eifer *m.* ardent zeal. **~fest**
a. fire-proof. **~gefährlich** *a.*
(highly) inflammable. **~haken**
m. fire-hook; poker. **~lärm** *m.*
fire-alarm. **~leiter** *f.* fire-ladder.
~lilie *f.* orange lily. **~linie** *f.*
front line. **~löschapparat** *m.*
fire-extinguisher. **~löschmann-
schaft** *f.* fire-brigade; fire-fighters.
~melder *m.* fire-alarm. **~probe**
f. ordeal by fire. **~sbrunst** *f.* fire,
conflagration. **~schiff** *n.* light-
ship. **~sgefahr** *f.* danger of
fire. **~sicher** *a.* fire-proof. **~snot**
f. suffering caused through fire.
~speiend *a.* **~er** *Berg* volcano.
~spritze *f.* fire-engine. **~stein** *m.*
flint. **~stelle** *f.* fire-place, hearth.
~taufe *f.* baptism of fire. **~über-
fall** *m.* strafe. **~ung** *f.* fuel; firing,
heating. **~versicherung** *f.* fire-
insurance. **~wache** *f.* fire-
station. **~waffe** *f.* fire-arm.
~wehr *f.* fire-brigade. **~werk**
n. firework. **~werker** *m.* gunner.
~zange *f.* tongs. **~zeug** *m.*
match-box; lighter.

feuern *v.i.* to fire.

feurig *a.* fiery; heady; ardent.

Fi'aker *m.* (-s, -) (*dial.*) cab. [F]

Fibel¹ (fi:-) *f.* (-, -n) primer. [Gk.]

Fibel² *f.* (-, -n) brooch, clasp. [L]

Fiber f. (-, -n) fibre.

ficht 3rd sing. pres. ind. of **fechten**.

Fichte (ficta) f. (-, -n) pine; spruce.

Fideikom'miß n. entail. [L]

fi'del (-de:l) a. merry, jolly. [L]

Fidibus m. spill. [L]

Fieber (fi:-) n. (-s, -) fever; *kaltes ~* ague; *~ messen* to take the temperature. *~haft* a. feverish. *~ig* a. febrile, feverish. *~phantasie* f., *~wahn* m. delirium. *~tabelle* f. temperature-chart. *~thermometer* n. clinical thermometer.

fiebern v.i. to be feverish, have a temperature.

Fied-el f. (-el, -eln) fiddle. *~elbogen* m. bow, fiddlestick. *~eln* v.t. & i. to fiddle. *~ler* m. fiddler.

fiel imperf. of **fallen**.

Fi'gur (-gu:r) f. (-, -en) form, shape, image; diagram; (*sculp., &c.*) figure; chess-man.

fi'gürlich (-gy:r-) a. figurative.

Fikti'on f. (-, -en) ♀ invention; pretence.

fik'tiv a. fictitious.

Fi'let (-le:) n. (-s, -s) network; (meat) fillet. [F]

Fili'ale (-a:lə) f. (-, -n) branch (office).

Fili'gran (-gra:n) n. (-s, -e) filigree.

Film m. (-s, -e) film, coat; film, (*colloq.*) movie, picture; *plastischer ~* stereoscopic film. *~atelier* n. studio. *~aufnahme* f. shooting (of film scenes). *~band* n. film strip. *~bearbeitung* f. film adaptation. *~kassette* f. film magazine. *~prüfstelle* f. film censorship office. *~streifen* m. film-strip. *~text* m. caption. *~verleih* m., *~vertrieb* m. film distributors.

Filt-er m. (-ers, -er) filter. *~ern*, *~rieren* v.t. to filter, strain. *~riertrichter* m. funnel.

Filz (-ts) m. (-es, -e) felt; (*fig.*) skinflint, miser. *~ig* a. felt-like; (*fig.*) mean, stingy. *~schuh* m. felt-slipper.

Fi'nanz (-ts) f. (usu. pl. -en) finances. *~amt* n. revenue office. *~beamte(r)* m. revenue officer. *~iell* a. financial. —

'ieren v.t. to finance; to support. *~minister* m. Chancellor of the Exchequer. *~technisch* a. fiscal, on the financial side.

Findelkind n. foundling.

find-en v.t. st. to find; to discover; to meet with; to think, consider. *v.r.* to find oneself, be found; to come right; *sich ~ein* to put up with, resign oneself to. *~er* m. finder. *~erlohn* m. finder's reward. *~ig* a. clever; ingenious. *~igkeit* f. cleverness; ingenuity. *~ling* m. foundling; erratic block.

fing imperf. of **fangen**.

Finger (fiŋ-) m. (-s, -) finger. *~abdruck* m. finger-print. *~fertig* a. quick- or nimble-fingered. *~fertigkeit* f. dexterity, skill. *~hut* m. thimble; (*bot.*) foxglove. *~ling* m. finger-stall. *~satz* m. (*mus.*) fingering. *~spitze* f. tip of the finger. *~spitzengefühl* n. flair. *~sprache* f. deaf-and-dumb alphabet. *~zeig* m. hint, tip.

fingern v.t. & i. to finger.

fin'gier-en v.t. to feign; *~t* a. feigned; fictitious.

Fink m. (-en, -en) finch.

Finne f. (-, -n) pimple, acne; fin.

finster a. dark, gloomy, obscure. *~nis* f. darkness, gloom, obscurity; eclipse.

Finte f. (-, -n) feint, (*fig.*) trick.

Firlefanz m. (-es, -e) foolery, nonsense. [F]

Firm-a f. (-a, -en) firm, business. *~en(adreß)buch* n. trade directory. *~eninhaber* m. owner of the firm. *~enschild* n. sign-board. *~enzeichen* n. trade-mark.

Firma'ment n. (-s, -e) firmament, sky.

firm-en v.t. to confirm. *~ling* m. candidate for confirmation. *~ung* f. confirmation.

Firn m. (-es, -en) névé, glacier-snow.

Firnis m. (-ses, -se) varnish. *~sen* v.t. to varnish.

First m. (-es, -e) ridge of roof; mountain ridge.

Fis (fis) n. (*mus.*) F sharp.

Fisch m. (-es, -e) fish. *~adler* m.

osprey. **~bein** *n.* whalebone. **~dampfer** *m.* steam-trawler. **~er** *m.* fisherman. **~e'rei** *f.* fishing; fishery. **~geruch** *m.* fishy smell. **~gräte** *f.* fish-bone. **~händler** *m.* fishmonger. **~leim** *m.* fish-glue, isinglass. **~tran** *m.* fish-oil, train-oil. **~zucht** *f.* pisciculture. **~zug** *m.* catch, haul, draught of fish.

fischen *v.t. & i.* to fish; *im Trüben ~* to fish in troubled waters.

fisk·alisch *a.* fiscal. **~us** *m.* exchequer, treasury.

Fistel *f.* (-, -n) fistula. **~stimme** *f.* falsetto.

Fittich (-ç) *m.* (-s, -e) wing, pinion.

fix *a.* fixed; quick; *~ und fertig* quite ready. **~ierbad** *n.* fixing-bath. **~ieren** *v.t.* to fix; to stare at. **~iermittel** *n.* fixing agent, fixative. **~igkeit** *f.* speed. **~stern** *m.* fixed star. **~um** *n.* fixed salary.

Fjord *m.* (-s, -e) fiord.

flach (flax) *a.* flat, plain, level; (*also fig.*) shallow. **~bahn** *f.* flat trajectory. **~land** *n.* flat country, plain. **~relief** *n.* bas-relief. **~rennen** *n.* flat race. **~zange** *f.* pliers.

Fläche (flɛçə) *f.* (-, -n) plain; surface; plane; area. **~ausdehnung** *f.* square dimension. **~inhalt** *m.* area. **~nmaß** *n.* square measure. **~nraum** *m.* area. **~nwinkel** *m.* plane angle. **~nzahl** *f.* square number.

Flachs (-aks) *m.* (-es) flax. **~blond** *a.* flaxen-haired. **~kopf** *m.* flaxen-haired person. **~samen** *m.* linseed. **~spinnerei** *f.* flax-mill.

flächsern (flɛks-) *a.* flaxen, of flax.

flackern *v.i.* to flicker, flare.

Fladen *m.* (-s, -) flat cake.

Flageo'lett (-ʒo-) *n.* (-s, -e) flageolet. **~(t)on** *m.* harmonic; overtone.

Flagg·e *f.* (-e, -en) flag. **~en** *v.t. & i.* to deck with flags; to fly a flag. **~leine** *f.* flag-line. **~schiff** *n.* flagship. [E]

Flak *f.* (*abbr. = Fliegerabwehrkanone*) A.A. gun. **~posten** *m.* A.A. spotter. **~schiff** *n.* flak-ship. **~truppe** *f.* A.A. artillery.

Fla'kon *n.* (-s, -s) phial; scent-bottle. [F]

Flamme *f.* (-, -n) flame; blaze; light; (*colloq.* sweetheart; *in ~n schlagen* to blaze up. **~n** *v.i.* to flame, blaze. **~nbogen** *m.* flaming arc, electric arc. **~nwerfer** *m.* flame-thrower. [ML]

Flammeri *m.* (-s, -s) blancmange. [E]

Fla'nell (-nɛl) *m.* (-s, -e) flannel.

Flank·e *f.* (-e, -en) flank; (*gym.*) side-vault. **~ieren** *v.t.* to flank; to enfilade.

flapsig (-ic) *a.* boorish, uncouth.

Flasche *f.* (-, -n) bottle; flask; phial; *auf ~n ziehen* to bottle. **~nbier** *n.* bottled beer. **~nhals** *m.* neck of bottle. **~nzug** *m.* set of pulleys, block and tackle.

flatter-haft, -ig *aa.* fickle, inconstant. **~haftigkeit** *f.* fickleness, flightiness. **~mine** *f.* contact-mine. **~n** *v.i.* to flutter; to wave, stream.

flau *a.* feeble, weak; faint; flat; dull.

Flaum *m.* (-s) down, fluff. **~feder** *f.* down feather. **~ig** *a.* downy, fluffy.

Flaus, Flausch *m.* (-es, -e) fleecy woollen cloth.

Flause (-zə) *f.* (-, -n) humbug. **~nmacher** *m.* phrase-monger; humbug.

Flaute *f.* (-, -n) calm; dullness.

Flechse *f.* (-, -n) tendon, sinew.

Flecht·e (-ɛçtə) *f.* (-e, -en) plait; (*bot.*) lichen; (*med.*) herpes. **~en** *v.t. st.* to plait, braid; to bind. **~werk** *n.* wickerwork.

Fleck *m.* (-es, -e) place; spot; stain, mark; patch; *vom ~ kommen* to get on, make headway. **~enlos** *a.* spotless. **~fieber** *n.* spotted fever. **~ig** *a.* stained, spotted, speckled. **~typhus** *m.* (spotted) typhus. **~wasser** *n.* stain-remover.

Flecken[1] *m.* (-s, -) spot, stain; blemish, fault; market town, country town.

flecken[2] *v.i.* to spot, stain, mark.

fleddern *v.t.* (*sl.*) to rob.

Fleder-maus *f.* bat. **~wisch** *m.* feather-duster.

Flegel (fle:-) *m.* (-s, -) flail; (*fig.*)

lout, boor. ~ei f. rudeness,
insolence. ~haft a. rude, impertinent. ~jahre n.pl. teens,
hobbledehoy stage. ~n v.r. to
behave rudely.

flehen v.i. to implore, beseech,
entreat. *subst. n.* entreaty, sup-
plication. ~tlich a. beseeching,
fervent.

Fleisch n. (-es) flesh; meat; pulp
(of fruit). ~beschauer m. inspector of butcher's meat. ~
brühe f. broth; beef-tea; clear
soup. ~er, ~hauer m. butcher.
~eslust f. lust, carnal desire.
~faser f. muscular fibre. ~fliege
f. blow-fly. ~fressend a. carnivorous. ~geworden a. incarnate.
~ig a. like flesh; fleshy; plump;
pulpy. ~kloß m. meat-ball.
~konserve f. tinned meat.
~lich a. carnal, sensual. ~los a.
meatless. ~waren f.pl. meat.
~werdung f. incarnation. ~wolf
m. mincer.

Fleiß (-s) m. (-es) diligence, industry; *mit* ~ on purpose, intentionally. ~ig a. diligent,
industrious.

flek'tieren v.t. to inflect.

flennen v.i. to whine, snivel, cry.

fletschen v.t. *die Zähne* ~ to show
one's teeth.

Flexi'on f. (-, -en) inflexion.

flick-en v.t. to patch, mend, repair.
subst. n. patch. ~e'rei f., ~werk
n. patchwork; mending. ~
schneider m. jobbing tailor. ~
schuster m. cobbler. ~wort
n. expletive. ~zeug n. darning-
needle, thread, &c.; puncture-
repair outfit (for bicycles).

Flieder m. (-s, -) elder; *spanischer*
~ lilac. ~tee m. elder-blossom
tea.

Fliege (fli:-) f. (-, -n) fly; (*beard*)
imperial. ~nfänger m. fly-
paper. ~ngewicht n. fly-weight.
~nklappe, ~nklatsche f. fly-
swatter. ~npilz m. toadstool.
~nschrank m. meat safe.

flieg-en (fli:-) vws.i. & vwh.t. st.
to fly; to rush; (*colloq.*) to get the
sack; ~endes Blatt fly-sheet,
pamphlet. ~er m. airman,
aviator, pilot. ~erabwehr f.

anti-aircraft defence. ~erab-
wehrkanone f. anti-aircraft gun.
~eralarm m. air-raid alarm,
alert. See also **Flug-** and
Luft-.

fliehen (fli:-) vws.i. st. to flee, run
away, retreat. v.t. to shun,
avoid.

Fliese f. (-, -n) flagstone; tile.

Fließ-arbeit f. assembly-line work.
~band n. conveyor belt.

fließ-en (fli:sən) vws.i. st. to flow,
rush, stream, run; ~endes
Wasser running water; ~end
sprechen to speak fluently.
~papier n. blotting-paper.

Flimmer m. (-s) glimmer, glitter.
~n v.i. to flicker, glitter.

flink a. quick, brisk, nimble.

Flinte f. (-, -n) gun, rifle; *die*
~ *ins Korn werfen* to throw up
the sponge. ~nlauf m. gun-
barrel.

flirren v.i. to whirr, flit about; to
flicker; (*of air*) to vibrate.

Flirt m. (-es, -e) ⚠ flirtation. ~en
v.i. to make love, flirt.

Flitter m. (-s, -) tinsel, spangles.
~glanz m. false lustre; hollow
pomp. ~kram m., ~werk n.
cheap finery. ~wochen f.pl.
honeymoon.

flitzen vws.i. to dash along.

flocht *imperf.* of **flechten**.

Flock-e f. (-e, -en) flake; flock (of
wool). ~ig a. flaky; fluffy.

flog *imperf.* of **fliegen**.

floh[1] *imperf.* of **fliehen**.

Floh[2] (flo:) m. (-es, ̈e) flea.
~stich m. flea-bite.

flöhen v.t. to rid of fleas.

Flor m. (-o:-) m. (-es, -e) blossom,
bloom; blossoming time; gauze;
crape. ~ieren v.i. to flourish,
prosper.

Flo'rett n. (-s, -e) (*fenc.*) foil. [F]

Floskel f. (-, -n) fine phrase,
flowery language.

floß[1] *imperf.* of **fließen**.

Floß[2] (flo:s) n. (-es, ̈e) raft, float.

Flosse f. (-, -n) fin.

flöß-en (flø:s-) v.t. to float, raft
(wood). ~er m. raftsman, rafter.

Flöt-e (-ø:-) f. (-e, -en) flute, pipe.
~en v.i. to play the flute; to
whistle; ~en *gehen* (*colloq.*) to be

lost. ~enbläser, ~'ist *m.* flute-player, flautist.

flott *a.* afloat, floating; fast; smart; gay; ~ machen to get afloat; to get (vehicle) going again; ~ leben to lead a fast life.

Flotte *f.* (·. -n) fleet, navy. ~nschau *f.* naval review. ~nstützpunkt *m.* naval base. ~nvorlage *f.* navy bill.

Flottille *f.* (-, -n) flotilla.

Flöz (flø:ts) *n.* (-es, -e) layer, stratum, seam.

Fluch (-u:x) *m.* (-es, -e) curse, imprecation; oath. ~beladen *a.* accursed; under a curse. ~en *v.i.* to curse, swear. ~würdig *a.* accursed, execrable.

Flucht (fluxt) *f.* (-, -en) flight, escape; (*archit.*) straight line, row; suite; flight (of stairs). ~artig *a.* hurried, headlong. ~linie *f.* vanishing line.

flücht-en (flyçt-) *vvs.i.* to flee, escape. ~ig *a.* fugitive; transient, fleeting; hasty, hurried; careless, superficial; (*chem.*) volatile. ~igkeit *f.* transitoriness, hastiness; carelessness; volatility. ~ling *m.* fugitive, refugee.

Flug (flu:k) *m.* (-es, -e) flight; flock, covey; im ~e on the wing; (*fig.*) in haste. ~abwehr *f.* anti-aircraft defence. ~bahn *f.* trajectory. ~blatt *n.* leaflet; pamphlet. ~boot *n.* flying-boat, seaplane. ~gast *m.* air-passenger. ~hafen *m.* air-port, landing-ground. ~höhe *f.* altitude. ~klar *a.* ready for flight. ~körper *m.* missile. ~linie *f.* air-line. ~post *f.* airmail. ~sand *m.* quicksand. ~schrift *f.* pamphlet. ~strecke *f.* distance, distance covered. ~wesen *n.* aviation, aeronautics, flying. See also Flugzeug.

Flügel (fly:-) *m.* (-s, -) wing, leaf; (hinged) window-sash, casement; blade (of propeller); arm, sail (of windmill); (*motor.*) mud-guard, wing; (*mus.*) grand piano; (*mil.*) flank. ~decke *f.* (*zool.*) elytron. ~haube *f.* (*motor.*)

helmet. ~lahm *a.* with crippled wings. ~mann *m.* end man of line; flank man. ~mutter *f.* thumb-nut. ~roß *n.* winged horse, Pegasus. ~schlag *m.* beat of a wing. ~spannung *f.* wing-spread. ~tür(e) *f.* folding-door.

flügge (flygə) *a.* fledged.

flugs *adv.* quickly; instantly.

Flugzeug *n.* (-s, -e) aeroplane, aircraft, plane. ~aufnahme *f.* aerial photograph. ~führer *m.* pilot. ~halle *f.*, ~schuppen *m.* hangar, shed. ~mutterschiff *n.* aircraft-carrier. ~staffel *f.* air-squadron. ~träger *m.* aircraft-carrier.

Fluidum *n.* (-s) fluid; (*fig.*) atmosphere; tone; influence.

Flunder *f.* (-, -n) flounder.

flunkern *v.i. & t.* to tell fibs.

Fluor *n.* fluorine. ~es'zieren *v.i.* to fluoresce.

Flur (flu:r) **1.** *f.* (-, -en) field, meadow. **2.** *m.* (-es, -e) hall, corridor. ~hüter *m.* ranger, keeper. ~schaden *m.* damage to crops. [FLOOR]

Fluß (-us) *m.* (Flusses, Flüsse) river; flow, flux; (*tech.*) fusion, state of melting; (*med.*) catarrh; (*fig.*) fluency; im ~ sein (*fig.*) to be in the melting pot. ~abwärts *adv.* down-stream. ~arm *m.* tributary, a. lacking rivers. ~aufwärts *adv.* up-stream. ~lauf *m.* course of a river. ~netz *n.* network of rivers. ~pferd *n.* hippopotamus. ~schiffahrt *f.* river traffic. ~spat *m.* fluorspar, fluorite. ~übergang *m.* passage, ford; river crossing.

flüssig (flysiç) *a.* liquid, fluid; ready (money); (*fig.*) flowing, fluent; Geld ~ machen to realize money. ~keit *f.* liquid; fluid; fluidity.

flüster-n *v.t. & i.* to whisper. ~propaganda *f.* whispering campaign.

Flut (flu:t) *f.* (-, -en) flood, deluge; inundation; water, waves; high-tide, high water. ~en *vvs.i.* to stream, flow.

focht *imperf.* of fechten.

Fock-mast m. foremast. **~segel** n. foresail.

födera'tiv a. federative, confederate.

Fohlen n. (-s, -) foal, colt. v.i. to foal.

Föhn m. (-es, -e) Föhn (wind).

Föhre f. (-, -n) pine, Scotch fir.

Folge f. (-, -n) sequence, succession, order, series; suite, set; continuation; sequel; serial part; consequence; result; conclusion, inference; in der ~ in future, subsequently; ~ leisten to comply with; to obey; to accept; to answer. **~erscheinung** f. consequence, effect. **~ndermaßen** adv. as follows. **~nschwer** a. momentous, weighty. **~recht**, **~richtig** aa. consistent, logical. **~satz** m. conclusion, deduction; corollary. **~widrig** a. inconsistent, illogical. **~zeit** f. future, time to come.

folg-en v.i. to obey, listen to. vws.i. to follow, follow after, succeed; daraus folgt hence it follows. **~lich** adv. consequently, hence, thus, so. **~sam** a. obedient, docile. **~samkeit** f. obedience, docility.

folger-n v.t. to infer, conclude, deduce. **~ung** f. inference, conclusion, deduction.

Foli'ant m. (-en, -en) folio volume.

Folie (fo:lia) f. (-, -n) 1. foil. 2. background.

Folio-bogen m., **~papier** n. foolscap.

Folter f. (-, -n) torture; auf die ~ spannen to put to the rack; (fig.) to torment. **~kammer** f. torture-chamber. **~knecht** m. torturer. **~n** v.t. to torture; to torment. **~ung** f. torture.

Fönapparat m. hair-dryer.

Fond (fã:) m. foundation; (motor.) back seat. **~s** m. funds, capital; stock.

Fon'täne (fɔntɛ:na) f. (-, -n) fountain.

foppen v.t. to hoax; to tease; to chaff.

Förde f. (-, -n) inlet, creek, gulf.

Förder-anlage f. hauling plant. **~band** n. conveyor belt. **~erz** n. crude ore. **~lich** a. useful.

~schacht m. winding shaft. **~ung** f. help, advantage; promotion; (mining) hauling; output.

forder-n v.t. to demand, ask; to claim; to require, exact; (leg.) to summon; (duel) to challenge. **~ung** f. demand; claim; challenge.

förder-n (fœr-) v.t. to further, advance, promote; (mining) to haul. **~er** m. promoter; patron.

Fo'relle f. (-, -n) trout.

Forke f. (-, -n) pitchfork, manure fork.

Form f. (-, -en) form, shape; figure; fashion, cut; model, pattern; (tech.) mould; in aller ~ formally; die ~ wahren to keep up appearances. **~ali'tät** f. formality. **~at** n. size; (fig.) weight, importance. **~el** f. formula. **~ell** a. formal. **~enlehre** f. accidence. **~enmensch** m. formalist, pedant. **~e'rei** f. moulding. **~fehler** m. informality; flaw; social blunder, offence against etiquette. **~gebung** f. fashioning, moulding. **~los** a. shapeless, formless; informal. **~losigkeit** f. shapelessness, formlessness; rudeness. **~sache** f. formality. **~vollendet** a. perfect in form. **~widrig** a. contrary to usage; against good form.

formen v.t. to form, shape, mould, fashion.

for'mieren v.t. to form.

förmlich (fœrm-) a. formal, ceremonious; regular, veritable, real. adv. absolutely, really.

Formu'lar n. (-ars, -are) form. **~ieren** v.t. to formulate, define.

forsch a. smart, dashing, plucky.

forsch-en v.i. to investigate; to seek or search (after); to do research work. **~er** m. investigator; scientist; research worker. **~ung** f. inquiry, investigation; research. **~ungsreisende(r)** m. explorer.

Forst m. (-es, -e) forest, wood. **~haus** n. forester's house. **~meister** m. (head) forester. **~wesen** n., **~wirtschaft** f. forestry.

Förster m. (-s, -) forester; game-keeper. ~**ei** f. forester's house.

Fort[1] (fo:r) n. (-s, -s) fort. [F]

fort[2] (fort) adv. & sep. pref. away, off, gone; forth, forward, on, onward; in einem ~ continually, ceaselessly, without interruption; und so ~ and so on, and so forth.

fort- adv. henceforth, from this time; hereafter. ~**arbeiten** v.i. to go on working, continue working. ~**bestand** m. continuance, continuation; duration. ~**bewegung** f. locomotion, progression. ~**bildung** f. advanced training; further development. ~**bildungsschule** f. continuation school; educational college. ~**dauer** f. continuance, permanence, duration. ~**erben** v.r. to be inherited; be transmitted, go down (to posterity). ~**fahren** v.t. to drive away, remove. vws.i. to drive off. vwh.i. to continue. ~**fall** m. discontinuing, cessation. ~**fallen** vws.i. to be omitted. ~**führen** v.t. to lead away; to go on with, continue; to carry on. ~**gang** m. departure, leaving; continuation; progress. ~**gehen** vws.i. to go away; to go on, continue. ~**gesetzt** a. continuous, incessant. ~**kommen** vws.i. to get away (fig.) to get on. subst. n. living; progress. ~**lassen** v.t. to allow to go; to leave out, omit. ~**laufen** vws.i. to run away, escape; to go on. ~**laufend** a. running; continuous. ~**leben** v.i. to live on. subst. n. survival, after-life. ~**pflanzen** v.t. & r. to propagate; to reproduce; to transmit. ~**pflanzung** f. propagation; reproduction; transmission. ~**schaffen** v.t. to remove; to get rid of. ~**scheren** v.r. to be gone. ~**schleichen** v.i. & r. to sneak off. ~**schreiten** vws.i. to advance; to proceed; to make progress. ~**schritt** m. progress. ~**schrittlich** a. progressive. ~**schwemmen** v.t. to wash away. ~**setzen** v.t. to continue; to pursue. ~**setzung** f. continuation; sequel;

pursuit. ~**stehlen** v.r. to steal away. ~**während** a. continuous, perpetual, incessant. adv. continually, incessantly. ~**ziehen** v.t. to drag along or away. vws.i. to move on; to march off; to leave (a house).

Fracht (-ax-) f. (-, -en) freight; cargo; load. ~**brief** m. bill of lading. ~**dampfer**, ~**er** m. freighter. ~**frei** a. carriage-paid. ~**gut**, ~**stück** n. package, goods. [FRAUGHT]

Frack m. (-es, ⁼e) dress-coat. [FROCK]

Frag-e (-a:-) f. (-e, -en) question; inquiry; query; ohne ~e undoubtedly; in ~e stellen to question, doubt; nicht in ~e kommen to be out of the question. ~**ebogen** m. questionnaire. ~**esatz** m. interrogative sentence. ~**esteller** m. interrogator. ~**estellung** f. formulation of a question. ~**ezeichen** n. question-mark. ~**lich** a. in question; questionable, doubtful. ~**los** adv. unquestionably, undoubtedly. ~**würdig** a. questionable, doubtful.

fragen (-a:-) v.t. & i. to ask, inquire; nichts danach ~ not to care about; es fragt sich the question is whether.

Fragment n. (-s, -e) fragment. ~**arisch** a. fragmentary.

Frakti'on f. (-, -en) parliamentary faction. ~**sbeschluß** m. party resolution.

Frak'tur (-u:r) f. (-, -en) Gothic type.

frank a. frank, open.

fran'kieren v.t. to stamp, pay postage.

Franse (-zə) f. (-, -n) fringe. [L]

Franz-band m. calf-binding. ~**branntwein** m. brandy. ~**mann** m. Frenchman.

fra'pp-ant a. striking. ~**ieren** v.t. to strike. [F]

fräs-en (-z-) v.t. to fraise, mill. ~**maschine** f. fraising machine.

fraß[1] imperf. of fressen.

Fraß[2] (-a:s) m. (-es) food, (for animals) feed; (sl.) grub; (med.) caries.

Fratz m. (-en, -en) naughty child; (*collog.*) little devil. **~e** f. grimace; caricature; *en schneiden* to make faces. **~enhaft** a. grotesque. [IT.]

Frau f. (-, -en) woman; lady of the house; (*on letters*) Mrs.; *meine ~* my wife; *gnädige ~* Madam; *Ihre ~ Gemahlin* your wife; (*eccl.*) *Unsere liebe ~* Our Lady. **~enarzt** m. gynaecologist. **~enfrage** f. question of women's rights. **~engestalt** f. (*lit.*) female character. **~enhaar** n. maidenhair. **~enhemd** n. vest, chemise. **~enkloster** n. nunnery. **~enrechtlerin** f. suffragette. **~ensleute** pl. women-folk. **~enstimmrecht** n. women's suffrage. **~enzimmer** n. woman, female; creature, slut. **~lich** a. womanly.

Fräulein n. (-s, -) young lady; unmarried lady; Miss.

frech (-c) a. impudent, insolent, cheeky. **~dachs** m. cheeky young rascal. **~heit** f. impudence, insolence; cheek. [FREAK]

Fregatte f. (-, -n) frigate.

frei a. free, independent, at liberty; frank, candid, open; liberal; voluntary, spontaneous; vacant, disengaged; gratis, for nothing; prepaid; off (duty); *ich bin so ~* allow me; *aus ~er Hand* freehand (drawing); off-hand; *unter ~em Himmel, im Freien* outside, in the open air. **~beruflich** a. free-lance. **~beuter** m. freebooter. **~billet** n. complimentary ticket; pass. **~bleibend** a. (*commerc.*) if not sold previously; if unsold. **~brief** m. licence, permit; charter. **~denker**, **~geist** m. free-thinker.

frei-en v.t. to court, woo. **~er** m. suitor, wooer; *auf ~ersfüßen gehen* to woo, go courting.

Frei-exemplar n. free specimen, presentation copy. **~frau** f. baroness. **~gabe** f. release. **~geben** v.t. to set free, release. **~gebig** a. liberal, generous. **~gebigkeit** f. liberality, generosity. **~gelassene(r)** m. freedman. **~halten** v.t. to stand

treat. **~händig** a. without support, free-hand; direct (sale). **~heit** f. freedom, liberty; franchise; *poetische ~heit* poetic licence. **~heitlich** a. liberal. **~heitsdrang** m. desire for independence. **~heitskrieg** m. war of independence. **~heitsstrafe** f. imprisonment. **~herr** m. baron. **~herrin** f. baroness. **~herrlich** a. baronial. **~lassen** v.t. to release, set free. **~lassung** f. release. **~lauf** m. free wheel(-ing).

freilich (-c) adv. yes, of course, certainly, to be sure; I admit, indeed.

Frei-lichtbühne f. open-air theatre. **~lichtmalerei** f. plein-air painting. **~machen** v.t. to stamp, to prepay. **~marke** f. stamp. **~maurer** m. freemason. **~mut** m. frankness, candour. **~mütig** a. frank, candid. **~schar** f. volunteer corps, irregulars. **~schärler** m. volunteer, insurgent, guerrilla. **~sinnig** a. liberal; free-thinking. **~sprechen** v.t. to acquit, absolve. **~spruch** m. acquittal. **~staat** m. free state. **~statt, ~stätte** f. asylum, refuge, sanctuary. **~stehen** v.i. to be at liberty, be free. **~d** a. exposed; detached. **~stelle** f. scholarship, bursary, free place. **~stellen** v.t. to give a choice. **~stilringen** n. all-in wrestling, catch-as-catch-can. **~tisch** m. free board. **~tod** m. suicide. **~treppe** f. outside staircase; front steps. **~übung** f. calisthenics; (*sl.*) physical jerks. **~umschlag** m. stamped envelope. **~wild** n. fair game. **~willig** a. voluntary, spontaneous. **~willige(r)** m. volunteer. **~zeitgestaltung** f. organization of leisure-time. **~zeitlager** n. holiday camp. **~zügig** a. free to move about or to choose one's domicile.

Freitag m. Friday.

fremd (-t) a. strange, foreign; unknown; extraneous; exotic; *~es Gut* other people's property; *unter ~em Namen* under an assumed name. **~artig** a. strange, odd. ~e f. foreign country; in der ~e abroad. ~e(r) m. stranger, foreigner; alien; guest. ~enbuch n. visitors' book; hotel register. ~enführer m. guide. ~enlegion f. Foreign Legion. ~enverkehr m. tourist traffic. ~enzimmer n. spare room. ~herrschaft f. foreign rule. ~körper m. foreign body; (pl.) impurities. ~ländisch a. foreign. ~ling m. stranger; foreigner. ~rassig, ~stämmig aa. alien, of different race. ~sprache f. foreign language. ~wort n. foreign word.

frequen~'tieren v.t. to frequent. ~z f. frequency, wave-length.

fress-en v.t. & i. st. to eat; to feed; to devour; (chem.) to corrode. subst. n. food (for animals); ein gefundenes ~en a godsend, the very thing. ~gier f. voracity. ~napf m. dish, trough. ~sack m. glutton. [FRET]

Frettchen n. (-s, -) ferret.

Freud-e f. (-e, -en) joy, gladness, delight, pleasure; ~e haben an to enjoy, delight in. ~enfeuer n. bonfire. ~enhaus n. brothel. ~enmädchen n. prostitute. ~estrahlend a. beaming with joy, radiant. ~ig a. joyful, cheerful. ~los a. joyless, cheerless.

freuen v.t. to gladden, please, delight. v.r. to be glad, be pleased, rejoice; sich ~ auf to look forward to.

Freund (-t) m. (-es, -e) friend. ~lich a. friendly, kind; obliging; amiable; pleasant. ~lichkeit f. friendliness, kindness; pleasantness. ~schaft f. friendship. ~schaftlich a. friendly, amicable. ~schaftsdienst m. kind service, good offices.

Frev-el (-e:f-) m. (-els, -el) sacrilege; crime; wantonness, mischief. ~elhaft, ~entlich aa. sacrilegious; criminal; wanton, wicked, malicious. ~eln v.i. to commit a crime; to blaspheme. ~ler m. criminal; evil-doer, offender; blasphemer.

Fried-e, -en (fri:-) m. (-ens) peace; harmony; im ~en in

peace-time. ~ensbruch m. breach of the peace. ~ensschluß m. conclusion of peace. ~ensstifter m. peacemaker, mediator. ~ensvertrag m. peace treaty. ~fertig, ~liebend aa. peaceloving. ~hof m. churchyard, cemetery. ~lich a. peaceful, peaceable.

frieren (fri:-) v.i. st. to freeze, be freezing; to feel cold; mich friert I am cold.

Fries¹ m. baize.

Fries² m. (-es, -e) (archit.) frieze.

Frieseln pl. (med.) purples.

Frikadelle f. meat ball.

frika'ssieren v.t. to cut up.

frisch a. fresh, cool, refreshing; vigorous, brisk, lively; new, recent; ~ auf! look alive! come on! go it! ~ gestrichen! wet paint! ~e Eier new-laid eggs; ~e Wäsche clean linen; auf ~er Tat in the (very) act of. ~e f. freshness, coolness; briskness, liveliness; brightness. ~esse f. refining furnace. ~ling m. young boar. ~stahl m. natural steel, German steel.

Fri's-eur m. (-eurs, -eure), ~euse f. hairdresser. ~ieren v.t. to dress the hair; sich ~ieren lassen to have one's hair done. ~iermantel m. dressing-jacket; overall, gown. ~iertisch m. dressing-table. ~ur f. hairdressing; hair-do; coiffure. [F]

frißt 3rd pers. sing. pres. of fressen.

Frist f. (-, -en) time; term; respite, delay. ~en v.t. sein Leben ~en to just manage to exist. ~los a. ~lose Entlassung summary dismissal. ~verlängerung f. extension of time-limit.

fri'vol (-v-) a. frivolous.

froh a. glad, joyous, joyful, gay, happy. ~gemut a. cheerful. ~locken v.i. to rejoice, exult (at) triumph (over). ~sinn m. cheerfulness.

fröhlich a. cheerful, happy, merry. ~keit f. cheerfulness, mirth. [FROLIC]

fromm a. pious, religious, godly,

devout; good, patient. **~en**
v.i. to benefit, be of use.
[FRAME]

Frömme'lei *f.* (-) bigotry; hypocrisy.

frömm-eln *v.i.* to affect piety. **~igkeit** *f.* piety, godliness. **~ler** *m.* devotee; hypocrite.

Fron (-o:n) *f.* (-, -en) compulsory or statute labour. **~en** *v.i.* to do compulsory labour. **~herr** *m.* feudal lord exacting statute labour. **~leichnam** *m.* Corpus Christi. **~vogt** *m.* taskmaster.

frönen *v.i.* to labour, slave; to be addicted to, indulge in.

Front *f.* (-, -en) front; face; **~ machen gegen** to oppose; to make a stand against. **~kämpfer** *m.* front(-line) soldier. **~urlaub** *m.* leave from the front.

fror *imperf.* of **frieren**.

Frosch *m.* (-es, ⸚e) frog; (*fireworks*) cracker.

Frost *m.* (-es, ⸚e) frost; cold; chill. **~beule** *f.* chilblain. **~ig** *a.* frosty; cold. **~schaden** *m.* damage done by frost. **~schutzmittel** *n.* anti-freezing agent.

frösteln *v.i.* to shiver, feel chilly.

fro'ttier-en *v.t.* to rub. **~handtuch** *n.* bath-towel. [F]

Frucht (-uxt) *f.* (-, ⸚e) fruit; crop; corn; produce; (*fig.*) result; (*med.*) foetus. **~bar** *a.* fruitful, fertile. **~barkeit** *f.* fruitfulness, fertility, fecundity. **~boden** *m.* (*bot.*) receptacle. **~bonbon** *n.* boiled sweet, acid drop, fruit pastille, jujube. **~bringend** *a.* fruit-bearing; productive; fertile. **~folge** *f.*, **~wechsel** *m.* rotation of crops. **~gelée** *n.* fruit-jelly. **~knoten** *m.* (*bot.*) ovary. **~lese** *f.* gathering of fruit. **~saft** *m.* fruit-juice.

fruchten *v.i.* to bear fruit; to have effect; to avail.

früh (fry:) *a.* early; in the morning; *heute* **~** this morning. **~beet** *n.* hotbed.

Frühe (-y:ə) *f.* (-e) (early) morning; dawn; *in aller* **~e** very early; *heute* **~** this morning. **~er** *a.* earlier, sooner; former. **~estens** *adv.* at the earliest.

~geburt *f.* premature birth. **~jahr** *n.*, **~ling** *m.* spring. **~messe** *f.* early mass; matins. **~reif** *a.* precocious. **~rot** *n.* dawn, red morning sky. **~schoppen** *m.* morning pint. **~stück** *n.* breakfast. **~stücken** *v.i.* to breakfast. **~zeitig** *a.* early; premature.

Fuchs (fuks) *m.* (-es, ⸚e) fox; chestnut horse; (*acad.*) freshman, fresher. **~bau** *m.* earth, hole, kennel. **~eisen** *n.* fox-trap. **~schwanz** *m.* brush; (*tech.*) padsaw; (*bot.*) love-lies-bleeding. **~teufelswild** *a.* in a fearful rage, furious.

fuchsen *v.r.* (*colloq.*) to be frightfully annoyed.

Füchsin (fyksin) *f.* (-, -nen) vixen.

Fuchtel (fux-) *f.* (-, -n) rod, ferule; blow; *unter der* **~** *stehen* to be under (a person's) thumb. **~n** *v.i.* to gesticulate violently.

Fuder (fu:-) *n.* (-s, -) cart-load.

Fug (fu:k) *m.* *mit* **~** *und Recht* with full authority; justly.

Fuge[1] (fu:-) *f.* (-, -n) joint; *aus den* **~n** *sein* to be out of joint; *aus den* **~n** *gehen* to fall to pieces. **~los** *a.* jointless; seamless.

Fuge[2] *f.* (-, -n) fugue.

füg-en (fy:g-) *v.t.* to join, put or fit together; to add; to will, ordain. *v.r.* to submit to, acquiesce in, accommodate oneself to; (*impers.*) to happen, chance. **~lich** *adv.* appropriately, conveniently, rightly. **~sam** *a.* yielding; submissive; docile, obedient. **~ung** *f.* dispensation; coincidence.

fühl-bar *a.* tangible; perceptible; felt; marked. **~en** *v.t. & i.* to feel; to sense; to be sensitive to; *sich gut* **~en** to feel well. **~er** *m.*, **~horn** *n.* feeler, antenna. **~ung** *f.* contact; *in* **~ung** *sein* to be in touch (with).

fuhr *imperf.* of **fahren**.

Fuhr-e (fu:-) *f.* (-e, -en) cart, conveyance; cart-load, load.

~mann *m.* (*pl.* ~leute) carter, wagoner, driver. ~werk *n.* vehicle, carriage, cart.

führ-en (fy:r-) *v.t.* to convey, conduct; to lead; to direct, guide; to carry; to handle, control, manage; to stock (goods); to keep (books); to bear (name, title); to show (proof); to wield (the pen); to wage (war); *zum Munde* ~en to raise to one's lips; *das Wort* ~en to be spokesman. ~er *m.* leader; driver; (*av.*) pilot; guide-book. ~erschaft *f.* leadership; direction; the leaders. ~erschein *m.* driving-licence; pilot's certificate. ~ersitz *m.* driver's seat; cockpit; cab. ~ung *f.* leadership, command; direction, management; behaviour, conduct; keeping (of books). ~ungszeugnis *n.* certificate of good conduct; reference, character.

Füll-e (fyla) *f.* (-e) abundance, plenty; profusion; fullness; stoutness, plumpness; fullness. ~bleistift *m.* propelling pencil. ~feder *f.* ~halter *m.* fountain pen. ~horn *n.* cornucopia. ~ig *a.* corpulent; well rounded. ~sel *n.* stop-gap; (*cook.*) stuffing. ~ung *f.* filling, stopping; packing; (*av.*) inflation; panelling (of door); (*cook.*) stuffing. ~wort *n.* expletive.

füllen¹ (fyl-) *v.t.* to fill; to stop, fill up; to inflate; (*cook.*) to stuff; *auf Flaschen* ~ to bottle.

Füllen² *n.* (-s, -) foal; colt (*m.*); filly (*f.*).

fummeln *v.i.* to fumble; to grope about.

Fund (funt) *m.* (-es, -e) finding; discovery; find, thing found. ~büro *n.* lost-property office. ~grube *f.* mine; (*fig.*) storehouse, rich source. ~ort *m.* place where thing is found; (*biol.*) habitat.

Funda'ment *n.* (-es, -e) foundation.

fun'dieren *v.t.* to lay a foundation, consolidate.

fünf (fynf) *a. & subst. f.* five. ~eckig *a.* pentagonal. ~erlei *a.*

of five kinds. ~fach *a.* fivefold, quintuple. ~seitig *a.* pentahedral. ~stellig *a.* of five digits. ~stöckig *a.* five-storied. ~te *a.* fifth. ~tel *n.* fifth (part). ~tens *adv.* fifthly. ~zehn *a.* fifteen. ~zig *a.* fifty; *ein* ~ziger a man of fifty, a man in his fifties.

fun'gieren *v.i.* to function; to act; to officiate.

Funk *m.* (-s) wireless, radio. ~anlage *f.* wireless station; radio plant. ~apparat *m.* ~gerät *n.* wireless set. ~e (*also* Funken) *m.* spark; sparkle; flash; (*fig.*) particle, bit. ~empfang *m.* wireless reception. ~engeber *m.* sparking device, spark coil. ~ensprühend *a.* sparkling, scintillating. ~entelegraphie *f.* wireless telegraphy. ~er *m.* wireless operator; (*colloq.*) sparks; telegraphist. ~peilstation *f.* radio-location station. ~spruch *m.* wireless message, radiogram. ~station, ~stelle *f.* wireless station; broadcasting station. ~streife *f.* radio patrol squad. ~turm *m.* radio tower, wireless mast. ~zeitung *f.* radio magazine. See also Radio-.

funkel-n *v.i.* to sparkle, glitter, twinkle. ~nagelneu *a.* brand-new.

funken *v.t.* to wireless, broadcast.

Funktionär *m.* functionary; official.

funktio'nieren *v.i.* to function, to work (well).

Funzel *f.* (-, -n) weak (oil) lamp.

für (fy:r) *prep.* for; for the sake of; for the benefit of, on behalf of, in favour of; in return for; instead of; *an und* ~ *sich* of itself, in itself; ~ *und wider* pro and con; *ich* ~ *meine Person* as for me, I for one; *Tag* ~ *Tag* day by day; *was* ~ (*ein*) what kind of. ~baß *adv.* further, forward, on. ~bitte, ~sprache *f.* intercession. ~liebnehmen *v.t.* to put up with. ~sorge *f.* care; relief (of poor). ~sorgeerziehung *f.* child welfare work; training in a remand-home. ~sorgerin *f.* welfare-worker, social worker.

~sorglich a. careful, thoughtful. ~sprecher m. intercessor; advocate. ~wahr adv. truly, indeed, verily, in truth. ~witz m. inquisitiveness; pertness. ~wort n. pronoun.

Fu'rage (-ra:ʒǝ) f. (-) forage, fodder.

Furch-e (-ç) f. (-e, -en) furrow, wrinkle. ~en v.t. to furrow; to wrinkle.

Furcht (furçt) f. (-) fear, fright, dread; anxiety. ~bar a. terrible, dreadful, awful, fearful. ~los a. fearless, intrepid. ~losigkeit f. fearlessness, intrepidity. ~sam a. timid, timorous, nervous. ~samkeit f. timidity.

fürcht-en (fyrçt-) v.t. to fear; to be afraid (of). ~erlich a. terrible, horrible, frightful.

fürder adv. further; henceforward.

Furie (fu:riǝ) f. (-, -n) Fury; termagant.

fur'nier-en v.t. to veneer, inlay. ~holz n. wood for inlaying.

Fürst (fyrst) m. (-en, -en) prince. ~engruft f. royal burial-vault. ~entum n. principality. ~in f. princess. ~lich a. princely; (fig.) sumptuous. [FIRST]

Furt f. (-, -en) ford.

Fu'runkel m. (-s, -) furuncle, boil.

Furz m. (vulg.) fart.

Fusel (fu:z-) m. (-s, -) bad brandy or gin.

füsi'lieren v.t. to shoot (as punishment).

Fuß (fu:s) m. (-es, "e) foot; footing; base; pedestal; bottom; stem (of glass); zu ~ on foot; ~ fassen to gain a footing; stehenden ~es immediately; auf dem ~e folgen to follow hard on; auf freien ~ setzen to set at liberty; auf gutem ~ stehen to be on good terms (with); auf großem ~ leben to live in grand style; auf eigenen Füßen stehen to be independent. ~abstreifer m. doormat, scraper. ~angel f. man-trap. ~ball m. football. ~bank f. footstool. ~boden m. floor. ~breit m. (fig.) foot ~breit every inch. ~bremse f. footbrake. ~ende n. foot, bottom-end. ~fall m. prostra-

tion. ~fällig a. on one's knees. ~gänger m. pedestrian. ~gelenk n. ankle joint. ~knöchel m. ankle. ~lappen m. footbandage. ~note f. footnote. ~pflege f. chiropody. ~punkt m. nadir. ~sack m. foot-muff. ~spitze f. point of the toe, tiptoe. ~spur m. footprint; footstep; track, trace. ~tritt m. kick. ~volk n. infantry. ~vorleger m. rug, mat. ~wanderung f. walking tour, hike. ~weg m. footpath.

fußen v.i. to set foot (upon). ~ to rely (on); to base, found (on).

futsch pred. a. (colloq.) gone, lost.

Futter¹ n. (-s, -) food, fodder, forage. ~napf m. food-dish. ~neid m. (fig.) professional jealousy. ~trog m. trough, manger.

Futter² n. (-s, -) lining; casing. ~al n. case; box, sheath. ~seide f. silk for lining. ~stoff m. lining.

futtern (fut-) v.i. (colloq.) to eat heartily; (sl.) to tuck in.

füttern¹ (fyt-) v.t. to feed. ~ung f. feeding.

füttern² (fyt-) v.t. to line, pad; (tech.) to case. ~ung f. lining; casing.

Fu'tur (-u:r) n. (-s, -e) future tense.

G

G, g (ge:) n. the letter G, g; (mus.) g.

gab imperf. of geben.

Gabe (ga:bǝ) f. (-, -n) present, gift; talent; milde ~n alms, charity.

Gabel (ga:-) f. (-, -n) fork; shafts (of cart); (bot.) tendril; (tel.) rest, cradle. ~frühstück n. lunch. ~n v.r. to fork, branch off, bifurcate. ~ung f. forking, bifurcation.

gackern v.i. to cackle. [GAGGLE]

Gaffel f. (-, -n) (naut.) gaff.

gaff-en v.i. to gape, stare. ~er m. gaper; idle onlooker.

Gage (ga:ʒǝ) f. (-, -n) honorarium, fee. [F]

gähn-en *v.i.* to yawn; to gape. **~krampf** *m.* fit of yawning.

Gala *f.* (-) gala; *in* ~ in full dress.

Ga'lan *m.* (-s, -e) lover. **~t** *a.* ♢ **gallant** = courteous. **~te'rie** *f.* courtesy. **~teriewaren** *f.pl.* fancy goods, trinkets.

Ga'leere (-le:ra) *f.* (-, -n) galley.

Gale'rie (-) *f.* gallery. **Galerist** *m.* gallery owner.

Galgen *m.* (-s, -) gallows, gibbet. **~frist** *f.* respite. **~humor** *m.* grim humour. **~strick**, **~vogel** *m.* rogue.

Gali'onsfigur *f.* figure-head (of ship).

Gallapfel *m.* gall-nut.

Gall-e *f.* (-e) gall, bile; (*fig.*) rancour. **~enanfall** *m.* bilious attack. **~enblase** *f.* gall-bladder. **~enstein** *m.* gall-stone. **~ig** *a.* bilious; bitter; choleric.

Gallert *n.* (-s, -e), **~e** *f.* gelatine, jelly.

galo'niert *a.* lace-trimmed.

Ga'lopp *m.* (-s, -s) gallop. **~ieren** *v.i.* to gallop.

Ga'losche *f.* (-, -n) galosh.

galt *imperf.* of **gelten**.

galvan-i'sieren *v.t.* to galvanize. **~o** *n.* electrotype. **~otechnik** *f.* galvanoplastics.

Ga'masche *f.* (-, -n) gaiter; legging; spat. [F]

Gammastrahlung *f.* γ-radiation, gamma radiation.

Gammler *m.* hippie; drop-out.

Gamsbart *m.* goatee beard.

Gang[1] (gaŋ) *m.* (-es, =e) walk, gait, carriage; progress, march; stroll, walk; way; message, errand; course (of meal); (*boxing*) round; (*archit.*) passage, corridor; (*tech.*) working, action, movement; (*motor.*) gear; (*mining*) vein, lode; worm (of screw); (*anat.*) duct; *in vollem* ~ in full swing; *in* ~ *setzen* to set going, start. **~art** *f.* walk, gait; action, pace (of horse). **~bar** *a.* passable, practicable; (*commerc.*) current; marketable, saleable. **~spill** *n.* capstan.

gang[2] *a.* ~ *und gäbe* customary, usual.

Gängel-band *n.* leading-strings. **~n** *v.t.* to lead (child) by the hand.

gängig *a.* saleable.

Gans (-s) *f.* (-, =e) goose.

Gänse-blümchen *n.* daisy. **~füßchen** *n.pl.* inverted commas, quotation marks. **~haut** *f.* (*fig.*) goose-flesh. **~klein** *n.* giblets. **~leberpastete** *f.* pâté de foie gras. **~marsch** *m.* single file. **~rich** *m.* gander. **~schmalz** *n.* goose-dripping. **~wein** *m.* (*joc.*) water.

ganz (-ts) *a.* whole, entire, undivided, all; complete, total, full; intact; **~e** *Note* semibreve; **~e** *Zahl* integer; *~ London* the whole of L.; *im* **~en** on the whole, in the lump; *von* **~em** *Herzen* with all my heart. *adv.* wholly, entirely, thoroughly, altogether; fairly, quite; ~ *anders* quite different; ~ *besonders* especially; ~ *und gar* wholly; ~ *und gar nicht* not at all. **~e(s)** *n.* whole, totality, bulk; *aufs* **~e** *gehen* to be or go all out (for). **~leder** *n.* leather-binding; calf. **~leinen** *n.* cloth. **~tagsarbeit** *f.* full-time job. **~ton** *m.* major second.

gänzlich *a.* whole, total, entire. *adv.* wholly, totally, entirely.

gar (ga:r) *a.* ready; cooked, done; dressed (leather); refined (metal). *adv.* quite, very, quite; even; ~ *nicht* not at all, by no means; ~ *mancher* many a man. **~aus** *m. den ~aus machen* to kill, do away with. **~küche** *f.* eating-house, cook-shop. [YARE]

Ga'rant *m.* (-en, -en) guarantor. **~ie** *f.* guarantee. **~ieren** *v.t.* to guarantee.

Garbe *f.* (-, -n) sheaf.

Gard-e *f.* (-e, -en) guard, guards. **~ist** *m.* guardsman.

Garde'robe *f.* (-, -n) clothes; wardrobe; cloak-room. **~nfrau**, **Garderobière** *f.* cloak-room attendant. **~nmarke** *f.* cloak-room ticket. **~nständer** *m.* hat-stand. [F]

Gar'dine (-di:nə) *f.* (-, -n) curtain. **~npredigt** *f.* curtain-lecture. **~nstange** *f.* curtain-rail.

gär-en v.i. to ferment; (fig.) to seethe. **~mittel** n. ferment. **~ung** f. fermentation.

Garn n. (-es, -e) yarn; thread; (fig.) net, snare. **~rolle** f. reel of thread.

Gar'nele (-ne:lə) f. (-, -n) shrimp.

garn-'ieren v.t. to trim; to garnish (dish). **~i'tur** f. trimming; outfit, equipment; set; fittings; accessories.

Garni'son f. (-, -en) garrison. **~verwendungsfähig** a. fit for garrison duty.

garstig (-c)a. nasty,loathsome;ugly.

Garten m. (-s, ÷) garden. **~bau** m. gardening, horticulture. **~erde** f. garden-mould. **~haus** n. summer-house. **~land** n. garden-plot. **~laube** f. arbour, summer-house. **~schau** f. flower show. **~schere** f. garden or pruning shears.

Gärtner m. (-s, -) gardener. **~ei** f. gardening; nursery. **~isch** a. horticultural. **~n** v.i. to do gardening.

Gas (ga:s) n. (-es, -e) gas; **~ geben** (mot.) to step on the gas. **~abwehr** f. anti-gas defence. **~anlage** f. gas-fittings. **~anstalt** f., **~werk** n. gas-works. **~brenner** m. gas-burner. **~förmig** a. gaseous. **~(fuß)hebel** m. accelerator. **~glühlicht** n. incandescent light. **~hahn** m. gas-tap. **~kammer** f. gaschamber. **~krieg** m. gas warfare. **~leitung** f. gas-pipes, gas supply. **~maske** f. gas mask. **~messer**, **~ometer** m., **~uhr** f. gas-meter. **~schutz** m. gas defence. **~vergiftung** f. gas poisoning.

Gasse f. (-, -n) narrow street, lane, alley; street. **~nbube** m. streetarab, urchin. **~nhauer** m. popular song. [GATE]

Gast m. (-es, ÷e) visitor, guest; customer, client; stranger; (theatr.) star. **~arbeiter** m. worker of foreign nationality. **~bett** n. spare bed. **~e'rei** f. feast, banquet. **~frei**, **~freundlich**, **~lich** aa. hospitable. **~freundschaft** f. hospitality. **~geber** m. host. **~haus** n., **~hof**

m., **~wirtschaft** f. inn, hotel. **~mahl** n. dinner-party, banquet. **~rolle** f. starring part. **~spiel** n. starring (performance). **~stätte** f. inn, restaurant. **~stättengewerbe** n. catering trade. **~wirt** m. landlord, innkeeper.

Gästebuch n. visitors' book.

gas'tieren v.i. to star.

gastrisch a. gastric.

Gatt-e m. (-en, -en) husband, consort. **~en** v.t. & r. to couple, pair; to copulate. **~in** f. wife. **~ung** f. kind, sort; genus; species, family. **~ungsbegriff** m. generic character. **~ungsname** m. generic name. [GATHER]

Gatter n. (-s, -) railing, fence; enclosure.

Gau m. (-es, -e) district.

Gauk-elbild n. illusion, phantasm, mirage. **~elei** f., **~elspiel** n. **~elwerk** n. juggling, conjuring; trickery, fraud. **~eln** v.i. & t. to juggle; to trick; to flutter about. **~ler** m. juggler, conjurer.

Gaul m. (-es, ÷e) horse.

Gaumen m. (-s, -) palate, roof of mouth. **~laut** m. palatal sound. [GUM]

Gauner m. (-s, -) rogue, swindler, cheat. **~ei** f., **~stück** n. swindle, swindling, cheating, cheat. **~n** v.i. to swindle, cheat. **~sprache** f. thieves' cant.

Gaze (-za) f. (-, -n) gauze.

Ge'ächtete(r) m. (-n, -n) outlaw.

Ge'äder n. (-s) veins. **~t** a. veined; marbled, grained.

Ge'äst n. (-es) branches.

Ge'bäck n. (-es, -e) pastry, cakes.

Ge'bälk n. (-es, -e) beams, timberwork.

gebar imperf. of **gebären**.

Ge'bärde f. (-, -n) gesture, movement. **~n** v.r. to behave; to conduct oneself. **~nspiel** n. gesticulation; dumb show. **~nsprache** f. mimicry.

ge'baren v.r. to behave, conduct oneself. subst. n. behaviour, deportment.

ge'bär-en v.t. st. to bear, bring forth, give birth to. **~erin** f. mother. **~mutter** f. womb, uterus.

Ge′bäude n. (-s, -) building, structure, edifice. **~steuer** f. property tax, burgh rates.

Ge′bein n. body; bones; limbs.

Ge′belfer n. (-s) yelping, barking.

Ge′bell n. (-es) barking.

geben v.t. st. to give, present, bestow; to yield, produce; to play, act; to deal (cards). v.r. to behave; to abate; to get better; to stop; *es gibt* there is, there are; *von sich ~* to utter, express; *etwas ~ auf* to attach value to, set great store by.

Geber m. (-s, -) giver, donor.

Ge′bet (-be:t) n. (-s, -e) prayer.

gebeten pp. of **bitten**.

gebeut (obs.) = **gebietet**.

gebiert 3rd pers. sing. pres. of **gebären**.

Ge′biet (-bi:t) n. (-s, -e) district, territory, area; (fig.) sphere, province. **~en** v.t. to order, command. v.i. to rule (over), govern; to have at one's disposal. **~er** m. master, lord; commander, governor, ruler. **~erin** f. mistress. **~erisch** a. imperious, peremptory.

Ge′bilde n. (-s, -) form; figure, image; creation; creature; structure; formation.

gebildet a. educated, cultured.

Ge′bimmel n. (-s) ringing or tinkling of bells.

Ge′binde n. (-s) bundle; sheaf (of corn); skein, hank; barrel.

Ge′birg-e n. (-es, -e) mountain range; mountains; highlands. **~ig** a. mountainous. **~skamm** m. mountain ridge. **~szug** m. range of mountains. See also **Berg-**.

Ge′biß n. (Gebiss-es, -e) set of teeth; denture; bit.

ge′bissen pp. of **beißen**.

Ge′bläse n. (-s, -) blast apparatus; bellows; blower; supercharger.

geblichen pp. of **bleichen**.

geblieben pp. of **bleiben**.

Ge′blöke n. (-s) bleating; lowing.

ge′blümt a. flowery; figured, sprigged.

Ge′blüt n. (-s) blood; descent; lineage; race.

gebogen pp. of **biegen**.

geboren pp. of **gebären**. a. born; née; *ein ~er Münchner* a native of Munich.

geborgen pp. of **bergen**. a. safe, out of danger.

geborsten pp. of **bersten**.

Ge′bot (-bo:t) n. (-s, -e) order, command; law; (bibl.) commandment; (commerc.) offer; *zu ~ stehen* to be at one's disposal. **~en** pp. of **gebieten**. a. necessary, imperative.

gebracht pp. of **bringen**.

gebrannt pp. of **brennen**.

Ge′bräu n. brewing; brew; mixture.

Ge′brauch (-x) m. use; custom; (pl.) rites. **~en** v.t. to use, make use of. **~sanweisung** f. directions for use. **~sgegenstand** m. commodity. **~sgraphik** f. graphic arts; commercial art. **~smusterschutz** m. registered trade mark. **~twaren** f.pl. second-hand articles.

ge′bräuchlich a. usual, in use, customary; current.

ge′brech-en v.i. to lack; to be wanting; *es gebricht mir an* I am in need of, I am short of. subst. n. infirmity; weakness; defect. **~lich** a. feeble, weak; fragile, frail; decrepit. **~lichkeit** f. feebleness, weakness; infirmity; frailty; decrepitude.

gebrochen pp. of **brechen**.

Ge′brüder pl. brothers.

Ge′brüll n. (-es) roar; lowing (of cow).

Ge′brumm n. (-es) growling, growls; grumbling; humming.

Ge′bühr (-by:r) f. (-, -en) duty; propriety; charge; fee; tax; rate; *über ~* unduly, immoderately. **~en** v.i. to be due; to be proper or fitting. **~end** a. due, proper. adv. duly, deservedly. **~enfrei** a. tax-free; post-free. **~enordnung** f. tariff. **~enpflichtig** a. subject to tax; postage to be paid. **~lich** a. suitable, proper, fitting, becoming.

gebunden pp. of **binden**. a. **~e** Rede verse, poetry.

Ge′burt (-bu:rt) f. (-, -en) birth;

origin, extraction. **~enrege-**
lung f. birth-control. **~enrück-**
gang m. fall in the birth-rate.
~enziffer f. birth-rate. **~sfeh-**
ler m. congenital infirmity.
~shelfer m. obstetrician. **~s-**
helferin f. midwife. **~sjahr**
n. year of birth. **~sort** f.
place of birth. **~sschein** m.
birth certificate. **~stag** m.
birthday. **~swehen** f.pl. labour-
pains. **~szange** f. forceps.

ge'**bürtig** (-iç) a. native (of),
born (in).

Ge'**büsch** n. (-es, -e) bushes;
thicket, copse, underwood.

Geck m. (-en, -en) coxcomb, fop.
~enhaft a. dandified.

ge**dacht** pp. of **denken**.

Ge'**dächtnis** n. (-deçt-) n. (-ses, -se)
memory; remembrance; aus
dem ~ from memory, by heart.
~feier f. commemoration. See
also **Gedenk-**.

Ge'**danke** m. (-ns, -ns) thought, conception, idea; plan; in ~ sein
to be engrossed, be preoccupied;
sich ~n machen to worry;
kein ~! not a bit, not at all.
~ngang m. train of thought.
~nlos a. thoughtless. **~nlosig-**
keit f. thoughtlessness; thoughtlessness. **~nlyrik** f. philosophical poetry. **~nsplitter** m.
flash (of thought), aphorism.
~nsprung m. (sudden) turn of
thought. **~nstrich** m. dash.
~nübertragung f. telepathy.
~nvoll a. thoughtful, pensive;
full of ideas.

ge'**danklich** a. intellectual, mental.

Ge'**därm** n. (-es, -e) intestines,
bowels.

Ge'**deck** n. (-s, -e) cover (at table);
trockenes ~ restaurant meal
(without drinks).

Gedeih m. auf ~ und Verderb for
better or for worse.

ge'**deih-en** vws.i. st. to grow,
thrive, develop; to succeed,
prosper. subst. n. growth; development; success, prosperity.
~lich a. thriving, prosperous.

ge'**denk-en** v.i. & t. st. to think
of, remember; to mention; to
intend (to). subst. n. memory.

~feier f. commemoration. **~-**
stein m. monument, memorial. **~-**
tag m. remembrance day;
anniversary.

Ge'**dicht** n. (-es, -e) poem.

ge'**diegen** (-di:g-) a. pure; solid;
reliable; thorough. **~heit** f.
purity; solidity; reliability;
thoroughness.

gedieh imperf. of **gedeihen**.

Ge'**dinge** n. piece work.

ge'**dräng-e** n. (-es) crowd, throng;
(fig.) difficulty. **~t** a. crowded,
concise, terse.

gedroschen pp. of **dreschen**.

ge'**druckt** pp. printed.

ge'**drückt** a. depressed, oppressed.

ge'**drungen** pp. of **dringen**. a. thick-
set.

Ge'**duld** (-t) f. (-) patience; forbearance; endurance. **~en** v.r.
to have patience, wait patiently.
~ig a. patient; forbearing.
~sfaden m. (colloq.) patience.
~sprobe f. trial of patience.

gedungen pp. of **dingen**.

ge'**dunsen** a. bloated, puffy.

ge'**durft** pp. of **dürfen**.

ge**eicht** a. **~s.** auf to be an expert on.

ge'**eignet** a. suitable, fit, appropriate.

Geest f. (-, -en) high sandy ground.

Ge'**fahr** f. (-, -en) danger, peril;
~ laufen to run the risk. **~los**
a. safe, secure, without danger.
~voll a. dangerous, perilous.
[FEAR]

ge'**fähr-den** v.t. to endanger, imperil, expose to danger. **~lich** a.
dangerous, perilous. **~lichkeit**
f. danger.

Ge'**fährt** n. (-es, -e) vehicle.

Ge'**fährt-e** m. (-en, -en), **~in** f.
companion, comrade.

Ge'**fälle** n. (-s, -) fall, incline, slope,
gradient.

ge'**fall-en¹** v.i. to please; es
gefällt mir I like it; sich ~en
lassen to submit to, put up with.
subst. m. pleasure; kindness,
favour. **~sucht** f. coquetry.
~süchtig a. coquettish.

ge'**fallen²** pp. of **fallen**. **~e** f.
fallen woman. **~e(n)** m.pl. (the)
dead, (the) killed, fallen.

ge'**fällig** (-iç) a. pleasing, pleasant,

Ge'fangen-e(r) *m.* (-en, -en) prisoner, captive. **~nahme**, **~setzung** *f.* capture; arrest; imprisonment. **~schaft** *f.* captivity, confinement.

Ge'fängnis *n.* (-ses, -se) prison, gaol, jail. **~wärter** *m.* gaoler, jailer.

Ge'fäß *n.* (-es, -e) vessel, receptacle; container.

ge'faßt *a.* composed, collected, calm; *sich ~ machen auf* to be prepared for.

Ge'fecht *n.* (-s, -e) fight, combat, action, engagement; *außer ~ setzen* to put out of action, knock out. **~sbefehl** *m.* operation order. **~sklar** *a.* cleared for action. **~sstreifen** *m.* battle zone.

ge'feit *a.* immune (from), proof (against).

Ge'fieder *n.* (-s, -) plumage, feathers. **~t** *a.* feathered; (*bot.*) pinnate.

Ge'filde *n.* (-s, -) fields, open country; domain; *~ der Seligen* Elysium.

Ge'flecht *n.* (-s, -e) wickerwork; network; texture; (*anat.*) plexus.

ge'fleckt *a.* spotted, speckled.

ge'flissentlich *a.* intentional, wilful.

geflochten *pp.* of **flechten**.

geflogen *pp.* of **fliegen**.

geflohen *pp.* of **fliehen**.

geflossen *pp.* of **fließen**.

Ge'flügel *n.* (-s) birds; poultry, fowls. **~händler** *m.* poulterer. **~zucht** *f.* poultry-farming.

ge'flügelt *a.* winged; *~e Worte* familiar quotations, household words.

Ge'flüster *n.* (-s) whispering.

gefochten *pp.* of **fechten**.

Ge'folg-e *n.* (-es, -e) suite, entourage; train; *im ~ e haben* to lead to, result in. **~schaft** *f.* followers; staff (of firm). **~smann** *m.* adherent; vassal.

ge'fräßig *a.* greedy. **~keit** *f.* greediness.

Ge'freite(r) *m.* (-n, -n) lance-corporal; able seaman; aircraftman first class.

ge'frier-en *vws.i.* to freeze; to congeal. **~fleisch** *n.* frozen meat. **~punkt** *m.* freezing-point. **~schrank** *m.* deep-freeze, refrigerator. **~schutzmittel** *n.* antifreeze.

ge'froren *pp.* of **frieren**. **~e(s)** *n.* ice(-cream).

Ge'füg-e *n.* (-es, -e) structure, construction, frame; texture. **~ig** *a.* pliant; docile, tractable; adaptable. **~igkeit** *f.* pliancy; adaptability; tractableness.

Ge'fühl *n.* (-s, -e) feeling, sentiment; emotion; touch; sense; sensation. **~los** *a.* numb; unfeeling, heartless. **~losigkeit** *f.* numbness; heartlessness. **~voll** *a.* feeling; tender; sentimental.

gefunden *pp.* of **finden**.

gegangen *pp.* of **gehen**.

ge'gebenenfalls *adv.* in case.

gegen (ge:-) *prep.* against; contrary to; to, towards; compared with; about; for, in return for. **~angriff** *m.* counter-attack. **~besuch** *m.* return visit. **~beweis** *m.* counter-evidence. **~dienst** *m.* return service. **~einander** *adv.* against each other; towards e.o. **~einanderhalten** to compare with e.o. **~füßler** *m.* antipode. **~gewicht** *n.* counterpoise, counterweight. **~gift** *n.* antidote, antitoxin. **~leistung** *f.* return service. **~liebe** *f.* mutual love. **~maßregel** *f.* countermeasure. **~partei** *f.* (the) opposition. **~rede** *f.* contradiction; reply. **~satz** *m.* contrast; opposition. **~sätzlich** *a.* contrary, adverse; opposite. **~schlag** *m.* counter-blow. **~schrift** *f.* refutation; rejoinder. **~seite** *f.* opposite side; opponent; (the) other party. **~seitig** *a.* mutual, reciprocal. **~seitigkeit** *f.* reciprocity. **~spieler** *m.* opponent, antagonist. **~spionage** *f.* counter-intelligence. **~stand** *m.* object; subject (of talk). **~ständlich** *a.* objective; graphic; perspicuous. **~standslos** *a.* unnecessary, superfluous.

~stoß *m.* counter-thrust. ~stück *n.* companion-picture; counterpart. ~teil *n.* opposite, contrary, reverse; im ~teil on the contrary. ~teilig *a.* opposite; to the contrary. ~über *adv. & prep.* opposite, facing; in the face of. *subst. n.* vis-à-vis. ~überliegen *v.i.* to face. ~überstellen *v.t.* to oppose; to confront; to contrast. ~verkehr *m.* oncoming traffic. ~wart *f.* presence; the present; (*gram.*) present tense. ~wärtig *a.* present; actual, current. *adv.* at present, now, nowadays. ~wehr *f.* defence, resistance. ~wert *m.* equivalent. ~wind *m.* headwind. ~winkel *m.* corresponding angle. ~zeichnen *v.t.* to countersign. ~zug *m.* counter-move.

Gegend (ge:-) *f.* (-, -en) country; region; district; neighbourhood.

geglichen *pp.* of gleichen.

geglitten *pp.* of gleiten.

geglommen *pp.* of glimmen.

Gegner *m.* (-s, -) opponent, adversary; enemy. ~isch *a.* hostile, opposing; of the enemy. ~schaft *f.* opposition, opponents.

gegolten *pp.* of gelten.

gegoren *pp.* of gären.

gegossen *pp.* of gießen.

gegriffen *pp.* of greifen.

Gehabe *n.* (affected) behaviour. ~n *v.r.* to behave, conduct oneself; gehab dich wohl farewell.

Ge'halt *m.* (-s, -e) contents, content; capacity; proportion (of); standard (of coins); (*fig.*) value. *n.* (-s, ̈er) salary, pay. ~en *a.* (self-)controlled; ~en sein zu to be obliged to. ~los *a.* worthless. ~saufbesserung *f.* rise, increase in salary. ~sstufe *f.* salary scale. ~voll *a.* valuable, substantial.

ge'harnischt *a.* clad in armour; (*fig.*) sharp.

ge'hässig *a.* spiteful, malicious. ~keit *f.* spitefulness, malice.

Ge'häuse *n.* (-s, -) box; case, capsule; core; (snail's) shell.

Ge'hege (-he:-) *n.* (-s, -) preserve, deer-forest; enclosure; pen; einem ins ~ kommen to spoil a

person's game.

ge'heim *a.* concealed, hidden; clandestine, secret; ~ halten to keep secret. ~fach *n.* private safe; secret drawer. ~lehre *f.* esoteric doctrine. ~nis *n.* secret; mystery. ~niskrämer *m.* mystery-monger. ~nisvoll *a.* mysterious. ~polizei *f.* secret police. ~rat *m.* privy councillor. ~schrift *f.* code; secret document. ~tuerei *f.* secretiveness. ~wissenschaft *f.* occultism.

Ge'heiß *n.* (-es, -e) order, command.

geh-en *vrs.i. st.* to walk, go, pass, move; to go away; to leave; to extend (to), reach; (*tech.*) to work, run; (of ice) to break up; (of wind) to blow; (of dough) to rise; wie. geht es dir? how are you? es geht ihm gut he is well; das geht nicht that won't do; es geht um it is a matter of; ~en lassen to let go, give up; sich ~en lassen to let oneself go; an die Arbeit ~en to begin work; in sich ~en to repent; vor sich ~en to take place, proceed. ~rock *m.* frock-coat. ~werk *n.* works.

Ge'henk *n.* (-s, -e) sword-belt.

Gehenkte(r) *m.* hanged man.

ge'heuer *a.* nicht ~ unsafe; haunted; uncanny, weird.

Ge'heul *n.* (-s) howling, yelling.

Ge'hilfe *m.* (-n, -n) assistant, help.

Ge'hirn *n.* (-s, -e) brain; brains (*pl.*). ~erweichung *f.* softening of the brain.

gehoben *pp.* of heben. *a.* elevated, high; in ~er Stimmung in high spirits.

Ge'höft *n.* (-s, -e) farm; farm premises.

geholfen *pp.* of helfen.

Ge'hölz (-ts) *n.* (-es, -e) wood, copse.

Ge'hör (-ö:-) *n.* (-s) hearing, ear; nach dem ~ by ear; ~ schenken to listen to; to grant. ~gang *m.* acoustic duct. ~nerv *m.* auditory nerve. ~sinn *m.* sense of hearing.

ge'horchen (-ç-) *v.i.* to obey.

ge'hör-en (-ö:-) *v.i.* to belong to, be owned by; to appertain to. *v.r.* to be fitting, be proper, be right. **~ig** *a.* belonging to; due, necessary; good, sound, proper.

Ge'hörn (-œ-) *n.* (-s, -e) horns; antlers. **~t** *a.* horned; antlered; horny.

ge'horsam *a.* obedient. *subst. m.* obedience.

Geier *m.* (-s, -) vulture.

Geifer *m.* (-s) drivel, slaver, spittle; (*fig.*) venom. **~n** *v.i.* to slaver, drivel; (*fig.*) to foam with rage.

Geige *f.* (-, -n) violin. **~n** *v.i. & t.* to play the violin, play on the violin. **~nkasten** *m.* violin-case. **~r** *m.* violinist.

geil *a.* luxuriant; voluptuous, lascivious. **~heit** *f.* luxuriance; lasciviousness.

Geisel (-z-) *m.* (-s, -n) hostage.

Geiser *m.* (-s, -) geyser.

Geiß *f.* (-, -en) goat. **~blatt** *n.* woodbine, honeysuckle. **~bock** *m.* he-goat, billy-goat.

Geißel (-s-) *f.* (-, -n) whip, lash; (*fig.*) scourge. **~n** *v.t.* to lash, whip, flagellate; (*fig.*) to reprimand, censure. **~ung** *f.* lashing, flagellation; condemnation.

Geist *m.* (-es, -er) spirit; genius; mind, intellect; wit; ghost, spectre; *den ~ aufgeben* to die. **~erbanner**, **~erbeschwörer** *m.* exorcist, necromancer. **~erhaft** *a.* ghostly, ghostlike. **~erseher** *m.* visionary, seer of ghosts. **~esabwesend** *a.* absent-minded. **~esarbeiter** *m.* brain worker. **~esblitz** *m.* brain-wave, stroke of genius. **~esgabe** *f.* talent. **~esgegenwart** *f.* presence of mind. **~eshaltung** *f* mentality. **~eskrank** *a.* of unsound mind, insane. **~eskrankheit** *f.* insanity. **~esschwach** *a.* feeble-minded; imbecile. **~esverfassung** *f.* frame or state of mind. **~esverwandt** *a.* congenial. **~eswissenschaften** *f.pl.* the Arts; humanities. **~ig** *a.* spiritual; intellectual, mental; spirituous (drinks); **~ige** *Arbeit* brain work. **~igkeit** *f.* spirituality; intellectuality. **~lich** *a.* religious, spiritual; ecclesiastical, clerical; sacred. **~liche(r)** *m.* clergyman,

vicar, minister. **~lichkeit** *f.* clergy, ministers. **~los** *a.* spiritless, lifeless; dull. **~reich**, **~voll** *aa.* ingenious; spirited; witty.

geistern *v.i.* to haunt.

Geiz (-ts) *m.* (-es) avarice, covetousness. **~en** *v.i.* to covet; to stint; to economize. **~hals**, **~kragen** *m.* miser, skinflint. **~ig** *a.* avaricious, stingy, miserly.

Ge'jammer *n.* (-s) wailing, lamentation.

Ge'jauchze, **Ge'jubel** *n.* (-s) jubilation, shouting.

Ge'johle *n.* (-s) yelling, hooting; cat-calls.

ge'kachelt *a.* tiled.

ge'kannt *pp. of* kennen.

Ge'keife *n.* (-s) squabbling.

Ge'kicher *n.* (-s) tittering.

Geklimper *n.* strumming, tinkling.

Ge'klingel *n.* (-s) tinkling, jingling.

ge'klommen *pp. of* klimmen.

ge'klungen *pp. of* klingen.

Ge'knatter *n.* (-s) cracking; crackling, roaring.

geknickt *a.* depressed.

ge'kniffen *pp. of* kneifen.

Ge'knister *n.* (-s) rustle, rustling; crackling.

gekonnt *pp. of* können.

Ge'kritzel *n.* (-s) scribbling, scrawl.

gekrochen *pp. of* kriechen.

Ge'kröse *n.* (-s, -) giblets, pluck; (*anat.*) mesentery.

ge'künstelt *a.* artificial; affected.

Ge'lächter *n.* (-s, -) laughter; laughing-stock.

geladen *a.* **~** *s. auf* to be furious at.

Ge'lage *n.* (-s, -) feast, banquet; carouse.

Ge'lände *n.* (-s, -) (tract) of country, country-side; terrain, area, ground; territory, lands. **~abschnitt** *m.* area, sector. **~aufnahme** *f.* land survey; air photograph. **~hindernis** *n.* natural obstacle. **~lauf** *m.* cross-country race *or* run. **~sport** *m.* field-sports; scouting exercises.

Ge'länder *n.* (-s, -) railing; balustrade; banister; parapet.

gelang *imperf.* of gelingen.

ge'langen *vws.i.* to reach, arrive (at); to attain, get (to).

Ge'laß *n.* (Gelass-es, -e) small room.

ge'lassen *a.* calm, collected, composed. ~heit *f.* calmness, composure.

Gela'tine (ʒɛ-) *f.* (-) gelatine.

Ge'laufe *n.* (-s) running to and fro, bustle.

ge'läufig *a.* fluent; familiar; current.

ge'launt *a.* disposed; *gut* ~ in good humour; *schlecht* ~ cross, bad-tempered.

Ge'läut(e) *n.* (-s) ringing of bells; peal of bells, chime.

gelb (-p) *a.* yellow. ~filter *m.* ~scheibe *f.* light-filter. ~gießer *m.* brass-founder. ~lich *a.* yellowish. ~sucht *f.* jaundice.

Geld (-t) *n.* (-es, -er) money; *(pl.)* funds; *bares* ~ cash; *kleines* ~ change; *zu* ~ *machen* to turn into ready money; ~ *anlegen* to put out (at interest). ~abfindung *f.* cash settlement, allowance; service gratuity. ~anweisung *f.* money-order, postal order. ~beutel *m.* purse, money-bag. ~einwurf *m.* slot for coins. ~entwertung *f.* inflation. ~erwerb *m.* money-making. ~gier *f.* avarice. ~quelle *f.* source of income. ~sachen *f.pl.* money matters. ~schein *m.* paper money, banknote. ~schrank *m.* safe. ~sorten *f.pl.* coins. ~strafe *f.* fine. ~stück *n.* coin. ~verlegenheit *f.* financial difficulty.

Ge'lee (ʒəle:) *n.* (-s) jelly. [F]

ge'legen *pp.* of liegen. *a.* situated; convenient, opportune. ~heit *f.* occasion; opportunity; facilities. ~heitsarbeiter *m.* casual labourer. ~heitskauf *m.* bargain. ~heitsmacher *m.* go-between. ~tlich *a.* occasional, incidental; as occasion offers; at some time or other.

ge'lehr-ig (-lc) *a.* docile; teachable. ~igkeit *f.* docility. ~samkeit *f.* learning, scholarship, erudition. ~t *a.* learned, scholarly, erudite.

~te(r) *m.* scholar, savant.

Ge'leise (-zə) *n.* (-es, -e) rut, track; rails, line; *(fig.)* beaten track.

Ge'leit *n.* (-s, -e) accompanying, conducting; *(mil.)* escort; *(naut.)* convoy; *freies* ~ safe conduct. ~en *v.t.* to accompany; to escort, convoy. ~wort *n.* motto; preface. ~zug *m.* convoy.

Ge'lenk *n.* (-s, -e) joint, articulation; link (of chain). ~ig *a.* pliable, supple. ~igkeit *f.* pliability, flexibility; suppleness.

ge'lernt *a.* skilled.

Ge'lichter *n.* (-s) gang, set, rabble.

Ge'liebte *m.* (-n, -n) & *f.* lover; beloved, sweetheart, mistress.

geliehen *pp.* of leihen.

ge'lind(e) *a.* soft, gentle; mild; light, lenient, slight.

ge'lingen *vws.i. st.* to succeed (in doing something); to manage (to do). *subst. n.* success.

Ge'lispel *n.* (-s) lisping, whispering.

gelitten *pp.* of leiden.

gellen *v.i.* & *t.* to yell; to shrill. ~d *a.* shrill, piercing.

ge'loben *v.t.* to promise, vow.

Ge'löbnis *n.* (-ses, -se) solemn promise, vow.

gelogen *pp.* of lügen.

gelt *interrog.* isn't it?; don't you think so?

gelt-en *v.i. st.* to matter, mean; to have influence; to be worth; to be valid, hold good, be current; to be a question of; to be intended for, be aimed at; ~en als to be considered as, be taken for; ~en lassen to let pass; ~end machen to plead, maintain; *sich* ~end machen to make oneself felt; *es gilt!* agreed! ~ung *f.* value; currency; recognition; respect; validity. ~ungsbereich *m.* (leg.) purview. ~ungstrieb *m.* desire to dominate.

Ge'lübde *n.* (-s, -) vow.

gelungen *pp.* of gelingen. *a.* funny.

Ge'lüst *n.* (-es, -e) desire. ~en *v.i.* to long for, hanker after; *sich* ~en lassen to covet, lust after.

Ge'mach (-x) *n.* (-s, "er) room. *adv.* slowly, quietly.

ge'mächlich *a.* slow; comfortable.

adv. slowly, easily. **~keit** *f.* ease, comfort.

Ge'mahl *m.* (-s, -e) husband, consort. **~in** *f.* wife.

ge'mahnen *v.t.* to remind.

Ge'mälde *n.* (-s, -) painting, picture.

ge'mäß *a.* suitable. *prep.* according to. **~igt** *a.* moderate; temperate.

Ge'mäuer *n.* (-s, -) masonry; *altes ~* ruins.

ge'mein *a.* ordinary; general; low, vulgar, common; *der ~e Soldat* the private soldier; **~ haben** *mit* to have in common with; *sich ~ machen mit* to chum up with, be hail fellow well met. **~faßlich**, **~verständlich** *aa.* easy to understand; popular. **~gefährlich** *a.* dangerous to the public. **~gut** *n.* common property. **~heit** *f.* vulgarity; baseness; mean trick. **~hin**, **~iglich** *adv.* generally. **~nutz** *m.* common good. **~nützig** *a.* non-profit making. **~platz** *m.* commonplace, platitude. **~sam** *a.* joint, common; mutual; together. **~schaft** *f.* community; intercourse; communion; association; *in ~schaft mit* together with. **~schaftlich** *a.* common, joint; in common. **~schaftserziehung** *f.* co-education. **~sinn** *m.* public spirit. **~wesen** *n.* public affairs; community; commonwealth. **~wohl** *n.* common weal, public welfare.

Ge'meinde *f.* (-, -n) community; municipality; parish; congregation. **~anger** *m.* common, village green. **~bezirk** *m.* parish, district, borough. **~schule** *f.* council school, elementary school. **~vorstand** *m.* town-council, board. **~vorsteher** *m.* mayor.

Ge'menge *n.* (-s) mixture; mêlée. **~sel** *n.* medley, hotchpotch.

ge'messen *a.* measured; precise; formal.

Ge'metzel *n.* (-s, -) slaughter; massacre, carnage.

ge'mieden *pp.* of meiden.

Ge'misch *n.* (-es) mixture, mixing.

Gemme *f.* (-, -n) gem.

gemocht *pp.* of mögen.

gemolken *pp.* of melken.

Gemse *f.* (-, -n) chamois.

Ge'munkel *n.* (-s) whispers, rumours.

Ge'murmel *n.* (-s) murmur(ing).

Ge'müse *n.* (-s, -) vegetables, greens. **~händler** *m.* greengrocer.

gemußt *pp.* of müssen.

Ge'müt *n.* (-my:t) *n.* (-s) soul; mind; heart; feeling; disposition. **~lich** *a.* good-natured; pleasant, jolly; comfortable, cosy. **~lichkeit** *f.* comfort; cosiness. **~sart** *f.* disposition, temper. **~sbewegung** *f.* emotion. **~skrank** *a.* (*med.*) melancholic. **~sruhe** *f.* peace of mind. **~sverfassung** *f.* frame of mind, humour. **~voll** *a.* kindly, affectionate.

gen = gegen *prep.* towards, to.

genannt *pp.* of nennen.

ge'narbt *a.* granulated, shagreened.

genas *imperf.* of genesen.

ge'näschig *a.* fond of delicacies.

ge'nau *a.* close, tight; exact, accurate; particular, scrupulous, sparing. *adv.* exactly. **~so-wie** exactly-like. **~igkeit** *f.* exactness, accuracy, precision; economy.

Gen'darm (ʒān-) *m.* (-en, -en) policeman, gendarme. **~e'rie** *f.* police station.

Genealo'gie *f.* (-, -n) genealogy.

ge'nehm *a.* agreeable. **~igen** *v.t.* to grant; to agree to, approve. **~igung** *f.* granting; approval, assent; permit; licence.

ge'neigt *a.* inclined (to); friendly; gentle (reader). **~heit** *f.* favour, benevolence.

Gene'ral *m.* (-s, -e) general. **~baß** *m.* thorough-bass. **~feldmarschall** *m.* field-marshal. **~i'tät** *f.* generality; body of generals. **~nenner** *m.* lowest common denominator. **~probe** *f.* dress rehearsal; (*mus.*) full rehearsal. **~stab** *m.* General Staff. **~stabskarte** *f.* ordnance map. **~streik** *m.* general strike. **~versammlung** *f.* general meeting. **~vollmacht** *f.* full authority, power (of attorney).

Generati'on f. (-, -en) generation.

gene'rell a. general.

ge'nes-en *vrs.i. st.* to recover, get better; to be delivered (of a child). **~ung** f. recovery; convalescence.

gen-i'al (-a:l) a. ⚕ full of genius, highly gifted; ingenious. **~iali'tät** f. originality. **~'ie** n. genius.

Ge'nick n. (-s, -e) nape, (back of the) neck. **~starre** f. meningitis, spotted fever.

ge'nieren (ʒə-) *v.t.* to trouble, inconvenience, bother. *v.r.* to feel embarrassed, be shy. [F]

ge'nieß-bar a. eatable: drinkable. **~en** *v.t. st.* to eat; to enjoy; to have the benefit of. **~er** m. epicure, sensualist.

Geni'talien *pl.* genitals.

Genitiv (-i:f) m. (-s, -e) genitive.

genommen *pp.* of **nehmen.**

genoß, genossen *imperf. & pp.* of **genießen.**

Ge'noß, Ge'noss-e m. (-en, -en) companion, comrade, colleague. **~enschaft** f. association, company; co-operative society.

Genrebild n. genre-painting.

ge'nug (-k) a. enough, sufficient. **~sam** a. plentiful; plenty. **~tun** *v.i.* to satisfy (person), give satisfaction. **~tuung** f. satisfaction; compensation, reparation. [ENOUGH]

Ge'nüg-e f. *zur* **~e** sufficiently, enough; *~e tun* to content, satisfy. **~en** *v.i.* to suffice; to satisfy. **~sam** a. easily satisfied, modest, unassuming. **~samkeit** f. contentedness, modesty.

Ge'nuß m. (Genuss-es, =e) enjoyment, pleasure, delight; taking (of food); use, profit. **~mensch** m. epicure; epicurean. **~mittel** n.pl. foodstuffs; luxuries. **~reich** a. enjoyable, delightful. **~sucht** f. craving for pleasure. **~süchtig** a. pleasure-seeking.

Geo-dä'sie f. geodesy. **~graph** m. geographer. **~gra'phie** f. geography. **~graphisch** a. geographical. **~lo'gie** f. geology. **~meter** m. surveyor. **~me'trie** f. geometry. **~metrisch** a.

geometrical.

Geor'gine f. (-, -n) dahlia.

Ge'päck n. (-s, -e) luggage; baggage. **~abfertigung** f. luggage office, cloak-room. **~annahme** f. luggage-office. **~aufbewahrung** f. left-luggage office, cloak-room. **~ausgabe** f. luggage office. **~marsch** m. march with full pack. **~netz** n. luggage rack. **~schein** m. registered-luggage receipt; cloak-room ticket. **~stück** n. bag, parcel. **~träger** m. porter. **~wagen** m. luggage-van.

gepfiffen *pp.* of **pfeifen.**

gepflegt a. well groomed (appearance); well kept; cultivated.

ge'pflogen *pp.* of **pflegen. ~heit** f. habit, custom.

Ge'plänkel n. (-s, -) skirmishing.

Ge'plapper n. (-s) babbling, chatter.

Ge'plätscher n. (-s) splashing, (*poet.*) plashing.

Ge'plauder n. (-s) chat, chatting.

Ge'polter n. (-s) rumble, din.

Ge'präge n. (-s) coinage, impression; (*also fig.*) stamp.

Ge'pränge n. (-s) pomp, splendour.

Ge'prassel n. (-s) crackling, clatter.

gepriesen *pp.* of **preisen.**

ge'punktet a. dotted.

gequollen *pp.* of **quellen.**

Ger m. (-es, -e) spear, javelin.

ge'rad-e (-a:-) a. direct; upright, erect; honest, straight; even (number). *adv.* just, exactly, directly; *nun ~e* now more than ever; *~e das Gegenteil* the very opposite. *subst. f.* straight line. **~eaus** *adv.* straight on. **~ehalter** m. back-board. **~eheraus** *adv.* frankly, bluntly. **~e(s)wegs** *adv.* straightway, at once. **~ezu** *adv.* straight on; plainly, candidly, flatly; directly. **~heit** f. straightness; uprightness. **~linig** a. rectilinear. **~sinnig** a. straightforward.

Ge'ranie (-iə) f. (-, -n) geranium, pelargonium.

gerannt *pp.* of **rennen.**

Ge'rassel n. (-s) clanking; rattle, clatter.

Ge'rät n. (-s, -e) tool, implement, utensil; fittings; apparatus, equipment; set. ~**schaften** f.pl. utensils, implements. ~**eturnen** n. gymnastics with apparatus.

ge'raten 1. vvs.i. to succeed; to turn out well; to come, come upon, hit upon, get into; *aneinander* ~ to come to blows; *außer sich* ~ to get worked up; *in Brand* ~ to catch fire; *ins Stocken* ~ to come to a standstill. **2.** pp. of **raten**. a. advisable.

Gerate'wohl n. aufs ~ at random, haphazard.

ge'raum a. ample; long.

ge'räumig a. roomy, spacious. ~**keit** f. spaciousness.

Ge'räusch n. (-es, -e) noise. ~**los** a. noiseless. ~**voll** a. noisy.

gerb-en v.t. to tan; *weiß* ~**en** to taw; to refine (steel). ~**er** m. tanner. ~**e'rei** f. tannery. ~**säure** f. tannic acid. ~**stoff** m. tannin.

ge'recht a. just, righteous; fair, equitable; ~ *werden* to do justice to; to master. ~**fertigt** a. justified, justifiable. ~**igkeit** f. justice, righteousness; fairness. ~**same** f. privilege, prerogative.

Ge'rede n. (-s) talk; rumour.

ge'reichen v.i. to cause; to turn out to be; to redound to.

Ge'reiztheit f. (-) irritation.

ge'reuen v.t. impers. *es gereut mich* I am sorry for, repent; *sich keine Mühe* ~ *lassen* to spare no trouble.

Geria'trie f. geriatrics.

Ge'richt n. (-s, -e) dish, course; judgement; court of justice, tribunal; *Jüngstes* ~ Last Judgement; *vor* ~ in court; *zu* ~ *gehen mit* (fig.) to take to task. ~**lich** a. judicial, legal; forensic. ~**sbarkeit** f. jurisdiction. ~**sbefehl** m. writ. ~**sbezirk** m. jurisdiction; circuit. ~**sdiener** m. usher. ~**shof** m. court of law. ~**sverfahren** n. legal procedure; trial. ~**sverhandlung** f. hearing; legal proceedings. ~**svollzieher** m. sheriff, bailiff. ~**sweg** m. legal procedure.

ge'rieben pp. of **reiben**. a. cunning.

geriet imperf. of **geraten**.

ge'rillt a. grooved, fluted.

ge'ring a. small, little; unimportant, trifling, slight; modest, humble; inferior, low; *nicht im* ~*sten* not in the least. ~**achten**, ~**schätzen** v.t. to think little of, despise. ~**fügig** a. unimportant, trivial. ~**schätzig** a. disdainful, derogatory. ~**schätzung** f. disdain, contempt.

Ge'rinn-e n. running, flowing; gutter. ~**en** vvs.i. st. to coagulate, curdle. ~**sel** n. rivulet; coagulated mass; clot.

Ge'rippe n. (-es, -e) skeleton; framework. ~**t** a. ribbed; corded; fluted.

ge'rissen pp. of **reißen**. a. sly, cunning, wily.

geritten pp. of **reiten**.

Ger'man-e m. See App. I. ~**ist** m. teacher or student of German philology. ~**istik** f. German philology.

gern adv. with pleasure, gladly, readily; ~ *haben* to like; ~ *geschehen !* don't mention it. ~**egroß** m. upstart.

gerochen pp. of **riechen**.

Ge'röll n. (-s, -e) rubble, boulders.

ge'ronnen pp. of **rinnen**. a. ~*es Blut* coagulated blood.

Gerste f. (-) barley. ~**nkorn** n. barley-corn; sty (on eye). ~**nsaft** m. (poet.) beer. [GORSE]

Gerte f. (-, -n) rod, switch, twig.

Ge'ruch m. (-s, -̈e) smell; scent, odour; (fig.) reputation. ~**los** a. odourless. ~**snerv** m. olfactory nerve. ~**ssinn** m. sense of smell.

Ge'rücht n. (-s, -e) rumour, report.

ge'ruh-en v.i. to deign, condescend. ~**sam** a. leisurely.

Ge'rümpel n. (-s) lumber, rubbish.

Ge'rund-ium n. (-iums, -ien) gerund. ~**iv** n. gerundive.

gerungen pp. of **ringen**.

Ge'rüst n. (-es, -e) scaffolding; stage; stand.

Ges n. (mus.) G flat.

ge'samt a. whole, entire; all; together; total. ~**ausgabe** f. complete edition. ~**ertrag** m.

entire proceeds; total output. ~heit f. the whole; totality. ~schule f. comprehensive school. ~summe f. total amount. ~wohl n. common weal.

ge'sandt pp. of senden. ~(e)r m. envoy; ambassador. ~schaft f. embassy, legation.

Ge'sang m. (-s, ˵e) singing; song; canto. ~buch n. hymn-book; song-book. ~lehrer m. singing-teacher. ~lich a. choral; vocal. ~stimme f. vocal part. ~verein m. choral society.

Ge'säß n. (-es, -e) bottom, buttocks.

Ge'säusel n. (-s) murmuring, rustling.

Ge'schäft n. (-s, -e) business; transaction; commerce, affair; deal; occupation, trade; commercial firm; shop, office. ~ig a. busy, active. ~igkeit f. activity, industry. ~lich a. business, commercial. ~saufgabe f. giving-up of business. ~saufsicht f. legal control. ~sbereich m. sphere of activity. ~sführer m. manager. ~sgang m. course, way, routine. ~sgegend f. business quarter. ~skapital n. working capital. ~slage f. state of business, state of market. ~smann m. (pl. ~sleute) business man, tradesman. ~smäßig a. businesslike; perfunctory. ~sordnung f. standing orders. ~sreisende(r) m. commercial traveller. ~sschluß m. closing-time. ~sstelle f. office, bureau. ~sträger m. representative; chargé d'affaires. ~sviertel n. shopping district. ~szeit f. office hours.

ge'schehen vws.i. st. to take place, happen, occur; to be done; es geschieht ihm recht it serves him right; es ist um mich ~en I'm done for; ~en lassen to permit, allow, tolerate. ~nis n. event, happening.

ge'scheit a. clever, intelligent.

Ge'schenk n. (-s, -e) present, gift.

Ge'schicht-e f. (-e, -en) history; story; (colloq.) affair, thing. ~enbuch n. story-book. ~lich a. historical. ~sbuch n. history book. ~sforscher m. historian. ~sklitterung f. biased account of historical events.

Ge'schick n. (-s, -e) fate, destiny. ~lichkeit f. fitness, aptitude; skill, dexterity. ~t a. apt, fit, capable; clever.

ge'schieben pp. of scheiden.

geschienen pp. of scheinen.

Ge'schirr n. (-s, -e) crockery, dishes; china; harness. ~spüler m. dish washer.

Ge'schlecht n. (-s, -er) sex; genus, kind, species, race; family, stock; generation; (gram.) gender. ~lich a. sexual. ~sakt m. coition. ~skrankheit f. venereal disease. ~sname m. family name, surname. ~sregister n. pedigree. ~sreife f. puberty. ~steile m.pl. genitals. ~strieb m. sexual instinct. ~sverkehr m. sexual intercourse. ~swort n. article.

geschlichen pp. of schleichen.

geschliffen pp. of schleifen.

Ge'schlinge n. (-s) pluck, giblets.

ge'schlossen pp. of schließen. a. closed; complete, whole; united, unanimous; ~e Reihen (mil.) serried ranks; ~e Veranstaltung private show or meeting.

geschlungen pp. of schlingen.

Ge'schmack m. (-s, ˵e) taste; flavour; ~ finden an to like. ~los a. insipid; in bad taste. ~losigkeit f. bad taste. ~sache f. matter of taste. ~voll a. tasteful, elegant.

Ge'schmeide n. (-s, -) jewels, jewellery.

ge'schmeidig a. soft; supple, flexible, pliant. ~keit f. softness; flexibility, suppleness.

Ge'schmeiß n. (-es) droppings; vermin; (fig.) dregs, scum.

Ge'schmier n. (-s) daub, scrawl.

geschmissen pp. of schmeißen.

geschmolzen pp. of schmelzen.

Ge'schnatter n. (-s) cackling; chatter.

ge'schniegelt a. spruce, smart, dressed-up.

geschnitten *pp. of* schneiden.

geschoben *pp. of* schieben.

Ge'schöpf *n.* (-s, -e) creature.

geschoren *pp. of* scheren.

Ge'schoß *n.* (Geschoss-es, -e) projectile, missile; shell; story, floor. **~bahn** *f.* trajectory.

geschossen *pp. of* schießen.

ge'schraubt *a.* affected, stilted.

Ge'schrei *n.* (-s) shouting, screaming; shrieking, screeching; clamour; ado, fuss.

geschrieben *pp. of* schreiben.

geschrieen *pp. of* schreien.

geschritten *pp. of* schreiten.

geschunden *pp. of* schinden.

Ge'schütz *n.* (-es, -e) gun, cannon. **~bedienung** *f.* gun-crew, g.nners. **~feuer** *n.* cannonade, barrage. **~rohr** *n.* barrel of gun. **~stand** *m.* emplacement.

Ge'schwader (-va:-) *n.* (-s, -) squadron. **~flug** *m.* flight in formation.

Ge'schwätz (-vets) *n.* (-es) idle talk, tittle-tattle. **~ig** *a.* talkative, loquacious. **~igkeit** *f.* talkativeness, loquacity.

ge'schweift *a.* arched, curved; with a tail.

ge'schweige *adv.* not to mention, let alone; much less.

geschwiegen *pp. of* schweigen.

ge'schwind *a.* quick, fast, swift, prompt, speedy. **~igkeit** *f.* quickness, rapidity; velocity; speed; rate. **~igkeitsmesser** *m.* speedometer. **~schritt** *m.* double-quick step.

Ge'schwister *pl.* brother(s) and sister(s). **~kind** *n.* first cousin. **~lich** *a.* brotherly, sisterly.

geschwollen *pp. of* schwellen.

geschwommen *pp. of* schwimmen.

ge'schworen *pp. of* schwören. **~e(r)** *m.* juryman; (*pl.*) jury. **~enliste** *f.* panel, jury-list.

Ge'schwulst *f.* (-, -ͤe) swelling, tumour.

geschwunden *pp. of* schwinden.

geschwungen *pp. of* schwingen.

Ge'schwür *n.* (-s, -e) ulcer, abscess.

ge'segnet *a.* *in* ~ *en Umständen* with child, pregnant.

Ge'selchte *n.* (-n) (*dial.*) smoked meat.

Ge'sell-e *m.* (-en, -en) journeyman; fellow; companion. **~enjahr** *n.*, **~enzeit** *f.* journeyman's time of service. **~ig** *a.* sociable; social; *iger Verein* club, society. **~igkeit** *f.* sociability; social life. **~schaft** *f.* society; association, company; social gathering, party; *schaft leisten* to keep (someone) company. **~schafter** *m.* partner. **~schafterin** *f.* lady companion. **~schaftlich** *a.* social. **~schaftsanzug** *m.* evening dress, party dress. **~schaftsreise** *f.* conducted tour. **~schaftsspiel** *n.* round game, party game. **~schaftsvertrag** *m.* deed of partnership. **~schaftswissenschaft** *f.* social sciences, sociology.

ge'sellen *v.r.* to join, associate (with).

gesessen *pp. of* sitzen.

Ge'setz *n.* (-es, -e) law, statute; commandment. **~buch** *n.* statute-book, code. **~entwurf** *m.* draft of a bill. **~gebend** *a.* legislative. **~gebung** *f.* legislation. **~lich** *a.* legal, lawful, statutory; *lich geschützt* patented. **~mäßig** *a.* conforming to law; lawful, legitimate. **~tafeln** *f.pl.* decalogue. **~übertretung** *f.* transgression of the law. **~widrig** *a.* unlawful, illegal.

ge'setzt *pp. & a.* sedate, calm; mature; *den Fall, daß* supposing that.

Ge'sicht *n.* (-s, -e) sight, vision; hallucination; (*pl.* -er) face, countenance; (*fig.*) aspect, appearance; *zweite* ~ second sight; *zu* ~ *bekommen* to catch sight of; *zu* ~ *stehen* to suit; *er schneiden* to make faces. **~sfarbe** *f.* complexion. **~sfeld** *n.* field of vision, range. **~skreis** *m.* (mental) horizon. **~spunkt** *m.* point of view; (*sci.*) point of sight, visual point. **~srose** *f.* erysipelas. **~ssinn** (-tsz-) *m.* sense of sight. **~stäuschung** *f.* optical illusion. **~swinkel** *m.* optic angle; facial angle. **~szug** (-tsts-) *m.* feature.

Ge'sims *n.* (-es, -e) cornice, ledge.

Ge'sinde n. (-s) servants. **~l** n. rabble, mob.

ge'sinnt a. minded, disposed.

Ge'sinnung f. (-, -en) mind, way of thinking; disposition; conviction; *treue ~* loyalty. **~sgenosse** m. partisan, follower. **~slos** a. unprincipled. **~streu** a. loyal. **~swechsel** m. change of opinion, change of front, reversal of one's policy.

ge'sitt-et a. well-mannered; civilized. **~ung** f. good manners; civilization.

gesoffen pp. of **saufen**.

gesogen pp. of **saugen**.

ge'sonnen pp. of **sinnen**. a. disposed, resolved (to do).

gesotten pp. of **sieden**.

Ge'spann n. (-s, -e) team (of horses, &c.).

ge'spannt a. stretched, taut; strained; intent, eager, anxious; *auf ~em Fuß stehen* to be on bad terms (with).

Ge'spenst n. (-es, -er) ghost, phantom, spectre. **~ig**, **~isch** aa. ghostly; ghostlike.

gespieen pp. of **speien**.

Ge'spiele m. (-n, -n) playmate.

Ge'spinst n. (-es, -e) spun yarn; web; tissue.

gesponnen pp. of **spinnen**.

Ge'spött n. (-s) mockery, derision; laughing-stock.

Ge'spräch n. (-s, -e) talk, conversation, discourse; (phone) call. **~ig** a. talkative. **~sstoff** m. topic of conversation, subject. **~sweise** adv. in the course of conversation.

ge'spreizt a. wide apart; (*fig.*) stilted, pompous.

ge'sprenkelt a. speckled.

gesprochen pp. of **sprechen**.

gesprossen pp. of **sprießen**.

gesprungen pp. of **springen**.

Ge'stade n. (-s, -) shore, bank.

ge'staffelt a. staggered (holidays); graded (wage scale).

Ge'stalt f. (-, -en) form; figure, shape; build; stature; frame; aspect, manner, fashion, kind; character. **~en** v.t. to form, shape, mould, fashion; to create. v.r. to turn out. **~los** a.

shapeless. **~ung** f. fashioning, shaping; organization; creation.

Ge'stammel n. (-s) stammering, stuttering.

gestand imperf. of **gestehen**.

gestanden pp. of **stehen** and **gestehen**.

ge'ständ-ig a. confessing; *~ig sein* to plead guilty, confess. **~nis** n. confession, admission.

Ge'stänge n. rod, gear.

Ge'stank m. (-s) stench, stink.

ge'statten v.t. to allow, permit.

Geste f. (-, -n) gesture.

ge'steh-en v.t. to confess, admit. **~ungskosten** pl. prime cost.

Ge'stein n. (-s, -e) rock, stone. **~sgang** m. streak, lode.

Ge'stell n. (-s, -e) stand; rack; frame; trestle. **~ungsbefehl** m. enlistment order.

gest'ern adv. yesterday. **~rig** a. of yesterday.

ge'stiefelt a. booted; in boots.

gestiegen pp. of **steigen**.

gestiku'lieren v.i. to gesticulate.

Ge'stirn n. (-s, -e) star. **~stand** m. constellation. **~t** a. starry, starred.

gestoben pp. of **stieben**.

Ge'stöber n. (-s, -) snow-drift; storm; (snow) flurry.

gestochen pp. of **stechen**.

gestohlen pp. of **stehlen**.

gestorben pp. of **sterben**.

Ge'stotter n. (-s) stammering, stuttering.

Ge'sträuch n. (-s, -e) shrubs, bushes; shrubbery.

ge'streift a. striped, streaky.

ge'streng a. severe, rigorous.

gestrichen pp. of **streichen**.

gestritten pp. of **streiten**.

Ge'strüpp n. (-s, -e) bushes, brushwood, underwood.

Ge'stühl n. (-s) pew(s).

gestunken pp. of **stinken**.

Ge'stüt n. (-s, -e) stud.

Ge'such n. (-s, -e) application; petition, request. **~t** a. in demand, sought after; affected.

ge'sund a. healthy, well; wholesome, beneficial; sound, natural; *~er Menschenverstand* common sense. **~beterei** f. faith-healing. **~brunnen** m. mineral well.

~heit f. health; wholesomeness; *geistige* ~*heit* sanity. ~**heitlich** *a.* as regards health; hygienic, sanitary. ~**heitshalber** *adv.* for the sake of health. ~**heitspflege** *f. öffentliche* ~*heitspflege* public health service. ~**heitszustand** *m.* state of health.

ge'**sunden** *vws.i.* to recover, regain health.

gesungen *pp.* of **singen.**

gesunken *pp.* of **sinken.**

Ge'**täfel** *n.* (-s) wainscoting, panelling.

getan *pp.* of **tun.**

Ge'**tändel** *n.* (-s) trifling, dallying.

Ge'**tier** *n.* (-s) animals, beasts.

Ge'**töse** *n.* (-s) noise, din, uproar.

ge'**tragen** *a.* (*fig.*) grave, solemn, ceremonious.

Ge'**trampel** *n.* (-s) trampling.

Ge'**tränk** *n.* (-s, -e) drink, beverage.

ge'**trauen** *v.r.* to dare, venture.

Ge'**treide** *n.* (-s, -) corn, grain. ~**art** *f.* cereal. ~**bau** *m.* corn-growing. ~**halm** *m.* corn-stalk. ~**speicher** *m.* granary.

ge'**treu** *a.* faithful, true, trusty. ~**lich** *adv.* faithfully.

Ge'**triebe** *n.* (-s, -) bustle; (*tech.*) gear; drive; machinery.

getrieben *pp.* of **treiben.**

ge'**troffen** *pp.* of **treffen** *and* **triefen.**

ge'**trogen** *pp.* of **trügen.**

ge'**trost** *a.* confident.

ge'**trösten** *v.r.* to wait patiently.

getrunken *pp.* of **trinken.**

Ge'**tue** *n.* (*collog.*) fuss, to-do.

Ge'**tümmel** *n.* (-s) bustle, tumult.

Ge'**vatter** (-fat-) *m.* (-s, -n) godfather; relative, neighbour. ~**in** *f.* godmother.

Ge'**viert** (-fi:-) *n.* (-s, -e) square.

Ge'**wächs** (-vɛks-) *n.* (-es, -e) plant, vegetable; vintage; (*med.*) growth, tumour. ~**haus** *n.* conservatory, greenhouse.

ge'**wachsen** *pp. & a. einem* ~ *sein* to be equal to, be a match for.

ge'**wagt** *a.* risky.

ge'**wählt** *a.* choice, selected.

Ge'**wahr** *a.* aware (of). ~**en** *v.t.* to perceive, become aware of. ~**sam** *n.* charge, custody.

Ge'**währ** *f.* (-) security; surety; *ohne* ~ no responsibility taken.

~**en** *v.t.* to grant; ~*en lassen* to let a person do as he pleases. ~**leisten** *v.t.* to vouch for, guarantee. ~**smann** *m.* informant, authority; guarantee. ~**ung** *f.* granting, concession.

Ge'**walt** (-v-) *f.* (-, -en) power; authority; force, violence; *höhere* ~ act of God; force majeure; *mit aller* ~ with all one's might; *einem* ~ *antun* to do violence to; *in der* ~ *haben* to have command of, master; *sich in der* ~ *haben* to have self-control. ~**haber** *m.* person in authority. ~**herrschaft** *f.* despotism. ~**herrscher** *m.* despot. ~**ig** *a.* powerful; violent; huge. ~**marsch** *m.* forced march. ~**probe** *f. eine* ~*probe machen* to use violence. ~**sam** *a.* forcible, violent. ~**streich** *m.* violent measure, arbitrary act; coup de main. ~**tätig** *a.* brutal, violent.

Ge'**wand** (-v-) *n.* (-s, ⸚er) garment, dress; vestment.

ge'**wandt** *a.* agile, skilful; adroit, clever; easy. ~**heit** *f.* agility, skill; cleverness; fluency.

gewann *imperf.* of **gewinnen.**

ge'**wärtig** *a.* expecting, expectant (of). ~**en** *v.t.* to expect, be resigned to.

Ge'**wäsch** *n.* (-es) idle talk, twaddle.

Ge'**wässer** *n.* (-s, -) waters.

Ge'**webe** (-v-) *n.* (-s, -) weaving, web; fabric, tissue; texture. ~**lehre** *f.* histology.

ge'**weckt** *a.* alert, bright, clever.

Ge'**wehr** *n.* (-s, -e) gun, rifle, weapon. ~**feuer** *n.* rifle fire. ~**lauf** *m.* gun barrel.

Ge'**weih** *n.* (-es, -e) antlers, horns. ~**zacken** *m.* prong of antler.

Ge'**werb-e** (-v-) *n.* (-es, -e) trade, business; calling, profession; craft, industry. ~**efleiß** *m.* industry. ~**ekammer** *f.* Board of Trade, chamber of commerce. ~**eschein** *m.* trade licence. ~**eschule** *f.* technical school. ~**etreibend** *a.* industrial, manufacturing. ~**lich** *a.* industrial. ~**smäßig** *a.* professional.

Ge'werkschaft f. trade-union. **~ler** m. trade-unionist.

gewesen pp. of **sein**.

gewichen pp. of **weichen**.

Ge'wicht n. (-s, -e) weight; ins ~ fallen to weigh with. **~ig** a. weighty, important. **~sverlust** m. loss of weight.

ge'wiegt a. experienced.

Ge'wieher n. (-s) neighing.

gewiesen pp. of **weisen**.

ge'willt a. willing.

Ge'wimmel n. (-s) swarming; swarm, crowd, throng.

Ge'wimmer n. (-s) wailing, whimpering.

Ge'winde n. (-s, -) garland, festoon; thread, worm (of screw). **~bohrer** m. screw-tap.

Ge'winn (-v-) m. (-s, -e) winning, profit, gain; prize; winnings; advantage. **~anteil** m. dividend. **~beteiligung** f. profit-sharing. **~bringend** a. profitable, lucrative. **~er** m. winner. **~liste** f. prize-list. **~sucht** f. greed. **~süchtig** a. greedy. **~ung** f. obtaining; production; extraction.

ge'winnen (-v-) v.t. st. to gain, earn; to win; to enlist; to produce, extract; to prepare (chemicals). v.i. to improve; es über sich ~ to bring oneself (to). **~d** a. taking, winning.

Ge'winsel n. (-s) whining, whimpering.

Ge'winst m. (-es, -e) winnings; gain, profit.

Ge'wirr n. (-s) confusion, mass; maze, jumble; tangle.

ge'wiß (-v-) a. certain, sure; fixed. adv. certainly, indeed. **~heit** f. certainty.

Ge'wissen (-v-) n. (-s, -) conscience. **~haft** a. conscientious, scrupulous. **~los** a. unscrupulous. **~sbiß** m. twinge of conscience; remorse. **~szwang** m. coercion of conscience.

ge'wissermaßen adv. to some extent; so to speak, as it were.

Ge'witt-er n. (-ers, -er) thunder-storm. **~ern** v.i. to thunder. **~erregen** m. thunder plump, deluge. **~erschwül** a.

sultry. **~rig** a. thundery.

ge'witzigt a. taught by experience; shrewd.

gewoben pp. of **weben**.

gewogen pp. of **wägen** and **wiegen**. a. well-disposed (towards).

ge'wöhn-en (-vo-) v.t. to accustom. v.r. to get into the habit of, get accustomed to. **~lich** a. usual, customary; average, ordinary; vulgar, common. **~ung** f. accustoming, habit. [WEAN]

Ge'wohnheit (-vo-) f. (-, -en) habit; custom; usage. **~smäßig** a. habitual.

ge'wohnt a. used to, accustomed to; inured to; usual.

Ge'wölbe (-s, -) vault; arch.

Ge'wölk (-vœlk) n. (-s) clouds.

gewonnen pp. of **gewinnen**.

geworben pp. of **werben**.

geworden pp. of **werden**.

geworfen pp. of **werfen**.

Ge'wühl (-v-) n. (-s) turmoil; crowd, throng.

gewunden pp.of **winden**. a.winding, spiral, sinuous; (fig.) tortuous.

ge'würfelt a. chequered.

Ge'würm n. (-s, -e) worms, reptiles.

Ge'würz (-vyrts) n. (-es, -e) spice, seasoning, condiment. **~händler** m. grocer. **~ig** a. spiced, spicy, aromatic. **~nelke** f. clove.

gewußt pp. of **wissen**.

ge'zahnt a. notched; toothed; (bot.) dentate.

Ge'zänk n. (-s) quarrelling, wrangling.

Ge'zeiten (-tsai-) f.pl. tides.

Ge'zeter (-tse:-) n. (-s) screaming, clamour.

ge'ziemen v.r. to be fit, become. **~d** a. proper, becoming, seemly; due.

ge'ziert a. affected, minced.

Ge'zirpe n. (-s) chirping.

Ge'zisch n. (-es) hissing.

Ge'zischel n. (-s) whispering.

gezogen pp. of **ziehen**.

Ge'zücht n. (-s) brood, breed.

Ge'zwitscher n. (-s) twittering; chirping.

gezwungen pp. of **zwingen**.

gibst 2nd pers. sing. pres. of **geben**.

Gicht (-çt) f. (-) gout; (tech.) furnace-mouth. **~brüchig** a.

gouty; palsied; paralytic. **~isch**
a. gouty. **~knoten** *m.* chalk-
stone.

Giebel *m.* (-s, -) gable, gable-end.
~feld *n.* pediment, tympanum.
~fenster *n.* attic-window.

Gier *f.* (-) greed; eagerness,
avidity. **~en** *v.i.* to long eagerly
(for). **~ig** *a.* greedy.

Gieß-bach *m.* torrent. **~en** *v.t.*
st. to pour; to water; to cast.
v.i. impers. to pour (with rain).
~er *m.* caster, founder. **~e'rei**
f. foundry. **~kanne** *f.* watering-
can.

Gift *n.* (-es, -e) poison; venom;
toxin; virus; (*fig.*) malice.
~hauch *m.* blight. **~ig** *a.*
poisonous, venomous. **~mischer**
m. poisoner. **~pilz** *m.* toadstool.
~zahn *m.* poison-fang. [GIFT]

Gi'gant *m.* (-en, -en) giant. **~isch**
a. gigantic.

Gigerl *m.* & *n.* (-s, -) fop, dandy.

Gilde *f.* (-, -n) guild, corporation.

gilt *3rd pers. sing. pres. of* **gelten.**

Gimpel *m.* (-s, -) bullfinch; (*fig.*)
noodle.

ging *imperf. of* **gehen.**

Ginster *m.* (-s, -) broom, gorse.

Gipfel *m.* (-s, -) summit, top, peak;
(*fig.*) climax; zenith, height. **~**
höhe *f.* (*av.*) ceiling. **~leistung** *f.*
record. **~n** *v.i.* to culminate. **~**
punkt *m.* limit; climax. **~**
treffen *n.* summit meeting.

Gips *m.* (-es) gypsum; calcium
sulphate; plaster of Paris. **~en**
v.t. to plaster. **~verband** *m.*
plaster dressing.

Gi'raffe *f.* (-, -n) giraffe.

gi'rieren (ɡɪr-) *v.t.* to endorse (bill);
to circulate.

Gir'lande *f.* (-, -n) garland.

Giro (ɡiːro:) *n.* (-s, -s) endorse-
ment. **~verkehr** *m.* clearing-
house business.

girren *v.i.* to coo.

Gis *n.* (*mus.*) G sharp.

Gischt *m.* (-es) spray, foam. [YEAST]

Gi'tarre *f.* (-, -n) guitar.

Gitter *n.* (-s, -) grating; lattice;
railing; fence; trellis; grid. **~**
bett *n.* cot. **~fenster** *n.* latticed-
window; barred window. **~tor**
n. iron gate.

Gla'cèhandschuh *m.* kid glove.

Glanz (-ts) *m.* (-es) shining, brightness, lustre, glamour; glitter;
gloss, polish; splendour; distinction. **~bürste** *f.* polishing-brush.
~leder *n.* patent leather. **~leis-**
tung *f.* record. **~papier** *n.* glazed
paper. **~punkt** *m.* climax. **~**
voll *a.* brilliant, splendid, glorious.

glänzen *v.i.* to shine, glitter,
gleam. **~d** *a.* shining, lustrous,
glittering; splendid, brilliant.

Glas (ɡlɑːs) *n.* (-es, ̈er) glass;
tumbler. **~auge** *n.* glass eye;
wall-eye. **~bläser** *m.* glass-
blower. **~er** *m.* glazier. **~e'rei**
f. glazier's shop. **~erkitt** *m.*
putty. **~faser** *f.* spun glass.
~glocke *f.* glass-bell. **~sturz** *m.* bell-glass.
~hütte *f.* glass-factory. **~ig**
a. glassy, vitreous. **~kolben** *m.*
glass flask. **~schleiferei** *f.* glass-
grinding *or* -cutting.

gläsern *a.* of glass; glassy, vitreous.

gla's-ieren (-z-) *v.t.* to glaze; to
varnish; (*cook.*) to ice, frost. **~ur**
f. glazing; varnish; icing.

Glast *m.* (-es) glare, radiance.

glatt *a.* even, smooth; slippery;
plain; polished; (*fig.*) flattering,
oily; bland; **~ sitzen** to fit close.
~eis *n.* glazed frost; **aufs ~eis**
führen to lead up the garden-
path. **~rasiert** *a.* clean-shaven.
~weg *adv.* plainly, flatly.

Glätte *f.* (-) smoothness; polish;
slipperiness. **~n** *v.t.* to smooth;
to plane; to polish.

Glatz-e *f.* (-, -en) bald head.
~köpfig *a.* bald-headed.

Glaub-e(n) *m.* (-ens) faith; confidence, trust; belief; credit.
~ensbekenntnis *n.* creed, confession of faith. **~ensgenosse** *m.*
fellow believer. **~haft**, **~lich**
aa. credible, likely, probable.
~würdig *a.* credible, reliable,
authentic. **~würdigkeit** *f.* credi-
bility, reliability, authenticity.

glauben *v.t. & i.* to believe, trust;
to think, suppose.

gläubig *a.* believing, faithful. **~e(r)**
m. believer. **~er** *m.* creditor.
~keit *f.* faith, confidence.

gleich (-ç) *a.* same, similar, alike;

even, level; direct; equal, like, equivalent. *adv.* equally, just, alike; at once, immediately, directly; *es ist mir* ~ it's all the same to me; *es einem* ~*tun* to rival a person; *es einem* ~*tun wollen* to vie with; ~ *darauf* immediately afterwards.

gleich-altrig *a.* of the same age. ~**artig** *a.* of the same kind, homogeneous. ~**berechtigt** *a.* entitled to the same rights. ~**ermaßen** *adv.* in like manner, likewise. ~**falls** *adv.* likewise, also. ~**förmig** *a.* uniform; monotonous. ~**geschlechtlich** *a.* homosexual. ~**gesinnt** *a.* like-minded, congenial. ~**gewicht** *n.* equilibrium, balance, equipoise. ~**gewichtslehre** *f.* statics. ~**gewichtsstörung** *f.* imbalance. ~**gültig** *a.* indifferent; unconcerned. ~**gültigkeit** *f.* indifference. ~**heit** *f.* equality; parity; identity; similarity. ~**klang** *m.* unison, consonance. ~**laufend** *a.* parallel. ~**lautend** *a.* consonant; identical; (*commerc.*) duplicate. ~**machen** *v.t.* to make like; to equalize; *dem Erdboden* ~~ to raze to the ground. ~**maß** *n.* symmetry, proportion. ~**mäßig** *a.* proportionate; symmetrical, equal, even, uniform, regular. ~**mut** *m.* equanimity. ~**mütig** *a.* even-tempered, calm. ~**namig** *a.* having the same name; corresponding; homonymous. ~**nis** *n.* image; simile. ~**richter** *m.* rectifier. ~**sam** *adv.* as it were, almost. ~**schaltung** *f.* (*pol.*) co-ordination; bringing into line. ~**schenk(e)lig** *a.* isosceles. ~**seitig** *a.* equilateral. ~**strom** *m.* direct current. ~**ung** *f.* equation. ~**viel** *adv.* no matter; all the same. ~**wertig** *a.* equivalent, of equal value. ~**wie** *conj.* & *adv.* just as, even as. ~**wohl** *conj.* & *adv.* yet, however. ~**zeitig** *a.* simultaneous; contemporary. *adv.* at the same time.

gleichen *v.i. st.* to be equal; to be like, resemble.

Gleis see **Geleise**. ~**anschluß** *m.*

siding.

Gleisner *m.* (-s, -) hypocrite. ~**isch** *a.* hypocritical.

gleißen *v.i.* to glisten, glitter.

Gleit-bahn *f.* slide; slips. ~**en** *vws.i. st.* to glide, slide, slip. ~**flug** *m.* gliding flight. ~**flugzeug** *n.* glider. ~**schutzreifen** *m.* non-skid tyre.

Gletscher *m.* (-s, -) glacier. ~**spalte** *f.* crevasse. ~**zeit** *f.* glacial period.

glich *imperf. of* **gleichen**.

Glied (-t) *n.* (-es, -er) limb; member; link; (*mil.*) rank, file; (*math.*) term; *männliches* ~ penis. ~**erbau** *m.* structure of body. ~**erfüßler** *m.* arthropod. ~**erlahm** *a.* paralysed. ~**erpuppe** *f.* puppet, marionette. ~**erreißen** *n.* shooting pains, rheumatism. ~**erung** *f.* articulation; arrangement; formation, organization. ~**ermaßen** *pl.* limbs.

gliedern *v.t.* to articulate; to arrange, classify; to organize; to form into ranks, form up. *v.r.* to form, be composed (of), be divided (into).

glimm-en *v.i. st.* to burn faintly, glimmer, glow. ~**er** *m.* glimmer; (*min.*) mica. ~**ern** *v.i.* to glimmer, glow. ~**erschiefer** *m.* slate mica.

glimpflich *a.* mild; light, easy.

glitsch-en *vws.i.* to slide; to slip. ~**ig** *a.* slippery.

glitt *imperf. of* **gleiten**.

glitzern *v.i.* to glitter, glisten; to twinkle.

Globus *m.* (-, Globen) globe.

Glocke *f.* (-, -n) bell; shade; clock. ~**nblume** *f.* harebell. ~**ngießer** *m.* bell-founder. ~**nhell** *a.* clear as a bell. ~**nschlag** *m.* stroke of the clock. ~**nspeise** *f.* bell-metal. ~**nspiel** *n.* chime. ~**nstube** *f.*, ~**nstuhl** *m.* belfry. ~**nturm** *m.* steeple.

Glöckner *m.* (-s, -) bell-ringer, sexton.

glomm *imperf. of* **glimmen**.

Glor-ie (-ia) *f.* (-ie) glory. ~**ienschein** *m.* halo; aureola. ~**reich** *a.* glorious, illustrious.

Glo'ssar *n.* (-s, -ien) glossary.

Glosse f. (-e, -en) gloss. **~ieren** v.t. to gloss.

Glotz-auge f. goggle-eye. **~en** v.i. to goggle, gape, stare.

Glück n. (-es) fortune, good luck; prosperity; happiness; chance; **~ auf!** good luck!; **~ haben** to be lucky; **~ wünschen** to congratulate; **auf gut ~** at a venture; **zum ~** fortunately; **viel ~ !** many happy returns; good luck. **~lich** a. fortunate, lucky; happy. **~licherweise** adv. fortunately, luckily. **~selig** a. blissful, happy, radiant. **~seligkeit** f. happiness, bliss. **~stall** stroke of luck, lucky chance. **~güter** n.pl. earthly goods. **~skind** n. fortune's favourite. **~spilz** m. lucky fellow. **~sritter** m. adventurer. **~sspiel** n. game of hazard. **~ssträhne** f. stroke of luck. **~verheißend** a. auspicious, propitious. **~wunsch** m. congratulation; good wishes; compliments of the season.

Glucke f. (-, -n) clucking hen. **~n** v.i. to cluck; to chuck.

glücken vvs.i. to succeed, be lucky.

glucksen v.i. to gurgle.

Glüh-birne f. electric bulb. **~faden** m. (drawn-wire) filament. **~licht** n. incandescent light. **~strumpf** m. mantle. **~wein** m. negus. **~wurm** m. glowworm.

glühen (-y:-) v.i. to glow. **~d** a. glowing, fervent.

Glut (-u:t) f. (-, -en) glow, heat; glowing embers; (fig.) ardour, fire.

Glykose f. glucose.

Glyze'rin n. (-s) glycerine.

Gly'zinie f. wistaria.

Gnade (-a:-) f. (-, -n) favour; grace; mercy, clemency, pardon; **auf ~ und Ungnade** at discretion, unconditionally. **~nbild** n. miraculous image. **~nbrot** n. bread of charity. **~nfrist** f. respite. **~ngesuch** n. petition for clemency. **~nmittel** f.pl. means of grace. **~nsold** m. gratuity. **~nstoß** m. death-blow, knockout. **~ntod** n. mercy killing.

~nwahl f. predestination. **~nweg** m. act of grace; **auf dem ~nweg** (theol.) by the grace of God.

gnädig a. merciful; gracious, benevolent; condescending; **~e Frau** Madam.

Gneis m. (-es) gneiss.

Gnom m. (-en, -en) gnome.

Gockel m. (-s, -) cock, rooster.

Gold (golt) n. (-es) gold. **~ammer** f. yellow-hammer. **~arbeiter** m. goldsmith. **~braun** a. chestnut. **~en** a. gold; of gold, golden. **~feder** f. fountain pen, gold nib. **~finger** m. ring-finger. **~gewicht** n. troy weight. **~grube** f. goldmine. **~grund** m. gold background. **~haltig** a. containing gold; auriferous. **~ig** a. shining like gold; (fig.) sweet. **~käfer** m. rose-beetle. **~klumpen** m. nugget. **~lack** m. wallflower. **~leiste** f. gilt cornice. **~regen** m. laburnum. **~schaum** m. gold leaf; tinsel. **~schmied** m. goldsmith. **~schnitt** m. gilt edge. **~stück** n. gold coin. **~waage** f. auf die **~waage legen** (fig.) to weigh every word; to be over-particular. **~währung** f. gold standard.

Golf[1] m. (-es, -e) gulf.

Golf[2] n. (-es) golf. **~platz** m. golflinks.

Gondel f. (-, -n) gondola.

gönn-en v.t. not to grudge; to grant, allow; to wish. **~er** m. patron. **~erhaft** a. patronizing.

Göpel m. (-s, -) horse-gin; winch; capstan.

gor imperf. of **gären**.

Gör n. (-s, -en), **~e** f. (dial.) child, brat.

Gösch f. (-, -en) (naut.) jack.

goß imperf. of **gießen**.

Gosse f. (-, -n) gutter; drain.

Gotik f. (archit.) Gothic. See App. I.

Gott m. (-es, "er) God; god; **grüß ~** good day; **~ befohlen** good-bye, farewell; **~ sei Dank** thank God; thank goodness; **leider ~es** alas, sad to say; **um ~es willen** for goodness' sake; **von ~es Gnaden** by the grace of

God. **~esacker** m. churchyard. **~esdienst** m. public worship, (divine) service. **~esfürchtig** a. pious, god-fearing. **~esgelehrte(r)** m. theologian. **~esgericht** n. ordeal. **~eshaus** n. church, chapel, place of worship. **~eslästerer** m. blasphemer. **~eslästerlich** a. blasphemous. **~esleugner** m. atheist. **~gefällig** a. pleasing to God. **~heit** f. deity; divinity; godhead. **~lob** int. thank God, thank goodness. **~los** a. godless, ungodly. **~losigkeit** f. ungodliness. **~seibeiuns** m. the Devil. **~selig** a. godly, pious. **~verlassen** a. godforsaken.

Gött-erdämmerung f. twilight of the Gods. **~erspeise** f. ambrosia; (cook.) cream trifle. **~in** f. goddess. **~lich** a. divine; godlike. **~lichkeit** f. divinity; godliness.

Götze m. (-n, -n) idol. **~ndiener** m. idolater. **~ndienst** m. idolatry.

Gouver'nante (-u-) f. (-, -n) governess.

Gouver'neur (-u-) m. (-s, -e) governor.

Grab (-p) n. (-es, ̈er) grave; tomb; sepulchre. **~esstimme** f. sepulchral voice. **~geläute** n. tolling of bells, knell. **~geleite** n. procession of mourners. **~gesang** m. dirge. **~hügel** m. mound, tumulus. **~legung** f. burial, interment. **~mal** n. tomb, monument. **~platte** f. tombstone. **~rede** f. funeral sermon or oration. **~schrift** f. epitaph. **~stätte** f. burial-place, tomb. **~stein** m. tombstone.

Graben[1] (-a:-) m. (-s, ̈) ditch; (mil.) trench.

grab-en[2] (-a:-) v.t. st. to dig. **~scheit** n. spade, shovel. **~stichel** m. chisel.

Gräberfund m. sepulchral relics.

Grad (-a:t) (-es, -e) degree; rank; grade; stage; rate; in hohem ~ highly, extraordinarily. **~bogen** m. protractor. **~ieren** v.t. to graduate; to refine. **~ierwerk** n. graduation-works. **~messer** m. graduator. **~u'ell**, **~weise** adv.

gradually, by degrees.

grade = **gerade**.

Graf (-a:f) m. (-en, -en) earl; count. **~enkrone** f. earl's coronet. **~schaft** f. earldom; shire; county.

Gräf-in f. (-in, -innen) countess. **~lich** a. belonging to an earl.

Gral (-a:l) m. (-es) grail.

Gram (-a:m) m. (-es) grief, sorrow, a. einem ~ sein to be cross with a person. **~gefurcht** a. careworn. **~voll** a. sorrowful, gloomy.

gräm-en v.r.r. to grieve; to worry, fret. **~lich** a. peevish, morose.

Gramm n. (-es, -e) gram, gramme.

Gra'mmati-k f. (-, -ken) grammar. **~(kali')sch** a. grammatical. **~ker** m. grammarian.

Grammo'phon (-o:n) n. (-s, -e) gramophone. **~platte** f. record.

Gran n. (-s, -e) grain.

Gra'nat-apfel m. pomegranate. **~stein** m. garnet.

Gra'nat-e f. (-e, -en) grenade, shell. **~splitter** m. shell splinter. **~trichter** m. shell crater.

Gra'nit (-i:t) m. (-s, -e) granite. **~en** a. granitic.

Granne f.(-,-n) awn, beard (of corn).

granu'lieren v.t. to granulate.

Graphi-k f. (-, -ken) graphic arts. **~ker** m. illustrator, commercial artist. **~sch** a. graphic; ~sche Darstellung graph, chart, diagram.

Gra'phit m. (-s, -e) graphite.

Grapho'loge m. (-n, -n) graphologist.

graps(ch)en v.t. to snatch, grab.

Gras (-a:s) n. (-es, ̈er) grass; ins ~ beißen to die. **~fressend** a. graminivorous. **~halm** m. blade of grass. **~hüpfer** m. grasshopper. **~ig** a. grassy. **~mücke** f. hedge-sparrow. **~platz** m. green, grass-plot, lawn.

grasen v.i. to graze.

gra'ssieren v.i. to rage.

gräßlich a. terrible, horrible, ghastly; nasty.

Grat m. (-es, -e) edge, ridge; groin. **~linie** f. edge of regression.

Grät-e f. (-e, -en) fish-bone. **~ig** a. full of fish-bones.

Grätsche f. (-, -n) straddling, splits. ~n v.i. to straddle, to do the splits.

Gratu'l-ant m. (-anten, -anten) congratulator, well-wisher. ~ati'on f. congratulation. ~'ieren v.i. to congratulate.

grau a. grey; (fig.) remote, ancient. ~brot n. brown bread. ~tier n. ass, donkey.

grauen[1] v.i. to dawn.

grau-en[2] v. impers. to be afraid, shudder, dread. subst. n. horror, fear, dread. ~enhaft, ~envoll aa. horrible, dreadful, ghastly. ~len v.r. to be afraid.

Graupe f. (-, -n) hulled barley, groats.

Graupeln f.pl. hailstones, sleet. v. impers. to sleet.

Graus m. (-es) horror. ~en v. impers. to shudder, feel horror. subst. n. horror, terror. ~ig a. horrible, dreadful, horrid. ~lich a. hideous, dreadful.

grausam a. cruel. ~keit f. cruelty. [GRUESOME]

Gra'v-eur m. engraver. ~ieren v.t. to engrave. ~üre f. engraving.

Gravi'tät f. (-) gravity. ~isch a. grave, ceremonious.

Gravitationskraft f. force of gravity.

Grazi-e f. (-, -en) grace, charm. ~ös a. graceful.

Greif m. (-es, -e) griffin.

greif-bar a. tangible; palpable; (commerc.) on hand. ~en v.t. & i. st. to seize; to grasp; to catch, catch hold of; (mus.) to touch, strike; ineinander ~en to interlock; um sich ~en to spread, gain ground; unter die Arme ~en to help, support. ~er m. grab. ~zange f. pliers, pincers.

greinen v.i. to whimper, weep. [GRIN]

Greis m. (-es, -e) old man. a. old. ~enalter n. old age. ~enhaft a. senile. ~in f. old woman.

grell a. glaring, dazzling; crude; loud; shrill.

Gremium n. (corporate) body.

Grenz-e f. (-e, -en) frontier; boundary; limit. ~enlos a.

boundless; infinite. ~enlosigkeit f. boundlessness; infinitude. ~fall m. limiting case, extreme case. ~kontrolle f. customs examination. ~linie f. boundary-line. ~mark f. borderland. ~scheide f. boundary. ~verkehr m. frontier trading, frontier traffic. ~wert m. limit, limiting value.

grenzen v.i. to border (on), adjoin.

Greu-el m. (-els, -el) horror, abomination; outrage. ~eltat f. atrocity, horrible deed. ~lich a. horrible, atrocious, frightful.

Grieben[1] f.pl. greaves.

Grieben[2] m. (-s, -) core (of apple).

Gries-gram m. grumbler, grouser. ~grämig a. grumbling, grousing.

Grieß m. (-es, -e) semolina.

griff[1] imperf. of greifen.

Griff[2] m. (-es, -e) grip; grasp; hold; catch; (mus.) touch; handle; knob; handhold; hilt (of sword); ~e klopfen to practise rifle drill. ~brett n. fret-board; keyboard (of piano).

Griffel m. (-s, -) slate-pencil; (bot.) style, pistil.

griffig a. easy to handle; handy.

Grille f. (-, -n) cricket; (fig.) whim, fad; ~n fangen to be in low spirits. ~nfänger m. capricious person; pessimist. ~nhaft a. whimsical, capricious.

Gri'masse f. (-, -n) grimace.

Grimm m. (-es) anger, rage. ~darm m. colon. ~en v.i. colic; gripes. ~ig a. furious, grim.

Grind m. (-es) scab, scurf. ~ig a. scabby.

grinsen v.i. to grin, smirk.

Grippe f. (-, -n) influenza, flu. [F]

grob (-p) a. clumsy; thick; big; coarse; rough; heavy (gun); uncouth, rude; bad. ~heit f. coarseness, roughness, rudeness. ~ian m. boor, rude fellow. ~körnig a. coarse-grained. ~schlächtig a. uncouth. ~schmied m. blacksmith.

gröblich adv. greatly, grossly.

grö(h)len v.i. & v.t. to bawl, squall.

Groll m. (-es) resentment, anger. ~en v.i. to be resentful, be angry; (of thunder) to peal, boom.

Gros[1] *n.* (-, -) gross, twelve dozen.

Gros[2] *n.* main body. [F]

Groschen *m.* (-s, -) *(colloq.)* penny. See App. III.

groß (gro:s) *a.* big, tall, large, high, great, vast, huge; important, eminent, grand; **~tun** to boast; **~ziehen** to bring up; **~er Buchstabe** capital letter; **~e Kinder** grown-up children; **der ~e Ozean** the Pacific; **im ~en und ganzen** on the whole. **~artig** *a.* grand, sublime. **~aufnahme** *f.* close-up. **~eltern** *pl.* grandparents. **~enteils** *adv.* mostly. **~fürst** *m.* grand duke. **~grundbesitz** *m.* landed property (on large scale). **~grundbesitzer** *m.* landed proprietor. **~handel** *m.* wholesale trade. **~herzog** *m.* grand duke. **~hirn** *n.* cerebrum. **~industrie** *f.* heavy industry. **~industrielle(r)** *m.* wholesale manufacturer; captain of industry. **~jährig** *a.* of age. **~macht** *f.* great power. **~mächtig** *a.* high and mighty. **~mannssucht** *f.* megalomania. **~mäulig** *a.* bragging, swaggering. **~mut** *f.* magnanimity, generosity. **~mütig** *a.* magnanimous, generous. **~mutter** *f.* grandmother. **~oktav** *n.* large octavo. **~raum** *m.* im **~raum von London** in Greater L. **~reinemachen** *n.* spring cleaning. **~sprecherei** *f.* boasting, bragging. **~spurig** *a.* arrogant, boasting. **~stadt** *f.* large town. **~städter** *m.* inhabitant of a large town. **~tat** *f.* achievement, exploit, feat. **~vater** *m.* grandfather. **~ziehen** *v.t.* to bring up. **~zügig** *a.* generous, on a large scale.

Größ-e (-ø:sə) *f.* (-e, -en) size; bulk; dimension; largeness, bigness; tallness, height; quantity, value; *(astron.)* magnitude; *(fig.)* greatness; enormity; celebrity, star. **~enwahn** *m.* megalomania. **~enteils** *adv.* for the most part, mostly. **~tmöglich** *a.* greatest possible, as large as possible.

Gro'ssist *m.* (-en, -en) wholesale dealer.

gro'tesk *a.* grotesque.

Grotte *f.* (-, -n) grotto.

grub *imperf.* of **graben**.

Grübchen *n.* (-s, -) dimple.

Grube (-u:-) *f.* (-, -n) pit, mine; hole, cavity; *(fig.)* grave. **~narbeiter** *m.* miner. **~nbrand** *m.* fire in pit. **~ngas** *n.* fire-damp. **~nlampe** *f.* miner's lamp. **~nwetter** *n.* fire-damp.

Grüb-e'lei *f.* brooding, musing. **~eln** *v.i.* to brood, to muse.

Gruft *f.* (-s, "e) grave, vault, tomb.

Grummet *n.* (-s) aftermath.

grün (-y:n) *a.* green; *(fig.)* immature; *auf einen ~en Zweig kommen* to get on well; *vom ~en Tisch aus* only in theory. *subst. n.* green; verdure. **~donnerstag** *m.* Maundy Thursday. **~en** *v.i.* to grow green, sprout. **~futter** *n.* green fodder. **~kern** *m.* green rye. **~kohl** *m.* kale. **~kramladen** *m.* greengrocer's shop. **~land** *n.* meadows. **~lich** *a.* greenish. **~schnabel** *m.* greenhorn. **~span** *m.* verdigris. **~zeug** *n.* herbs.

Grund (-t) *m.* (-es, "e) ground, soil; land, estate; bottom; valley; depth; basis, foundation; dregs; reason, cause, motive; argument; *auf ~ geraten* to run aground; *aus welchem ~e?* for what reason, why; *im ~e* after all, at bottom; *von ~ aus* thoroughly; *auf ~ von* on account of, based on, according to; *auf den ~ gehen* to investigate thoroughly, get to the root (of); *in ~ und Boden* thoroughly. See also **zugrunde-**.

Grund-akkord *m.* fundamental chord. **~begriff** *m.* fundamental idea, basic principle. **~besitz** *m.* landed property, real estate. **~buch** *n.* register of landed property. **~eis** *n.* ground-ice. **~falsch** *a.* radically wrong. **~farbe** *f.* primary colour. **~feste** *f.* foundation, basis. **~fläche** *f.* base, area, basal surface. **~gebühr** *f.* basic or fixed charge. **~gedanke** *m.* fundamental idea. **~gesetz** *n.* constitution; natural law. **~herr** *m.*

lord of the manor. **~kapital** *n.* original stock. **~lage** *f.* foundation, base; groundwork, basis. **~legend** *a.* fundamental. **~linie** *f.* ground-line, base-line. **~los** *a.* bottomless; (*fig.*) groundless. **~riß** *m.* ground-plan, sketch, outline; compendium. **~satz** *m.* principle. **~sätzlich** *a.* fundamental. *adv.* on principle. **~schule** *f.* elementary school. **~stein** *m.* foundation-stone, corner-stone. **~steuer** *f.* land-tax. **~stock** *m.* basis, foundation, stock. **~stück** *n.* piece of land, site, estate. **~stücksmakler** *m.* real estate agent. **~ton** *m.* key-note. **~verschieden** *a.* entirely different. **~wasser** *n.* ground water. **~zahl** *f.* unit, cardinal number. **~zug** *m.* characteristic, main feature.

gründ-en *v.t.* to found, establish; (*commerc.*) to float, promote. *v.r.* to rest (on). **~er** *m.* founder; promoter. **~~zeit** *f.* time of capitalistic expansion. **~lich** *a.* thorough; solid, profound; radical. **~lichkeit** *f.* thoroughness, solidity. **~ling** *m.* groundling; gudgeon. **~ung** *f.* foundation, establishment.

grun'dieren *v.t.* to prime; to size.

grunzen *v.i.* to grunt.

Grupp-e *f.* (-, -en) group, section. **~enweise** *adv.* in sections. **~'ieren** *v.t.* to group.

Grus *m.* (-es) coal-slack.

grusel-ig *a.* uncanny, creepy. **~n** *v. impers.* mir or mich *gruselt* my flesh creeps.

Gruß (-us) *m.* (-es, ⸚e) greeting; (*mil.*) salute.

grüßen *v.t. & i.* to greet; to salute; ~ *lassen* to send one's love or regards.

Grütze *f.* (-, -n) groats; *rote* ~ fruit-flavoured blancmange.

guck-en *v.i.* to look, peep. **~loch** *n.* peep-hole, spy-hole.

guilloti'nieren *v.t.* to guillotine.

Gulasch *n.* (-s) stewed steak. **~kanone** *f.* (*mil. sl.*) field-kitchen.

Gulden *m.* (-s, -) florin; guilder.

---

gültig *a.* valid; binding; available; good, current. **~keit** *f.* validity, currency; legality.

Gummi *m.* (-s) rubber, India-rubber; gum. **~absatz** *m.* rubber heel. **~band** *n.* elastic. **~gutt** *n.* gamboge. **~knüppel** *m.* rubber truncheon. **~mantel** *m.* waterproof, mackintosh. **~schuhe** *m.pl.* galoshes. **~stempel** *m.* rubber stamp. **~unterlage** *f.* rubber sheet. **~zelle** *f.* padded cell. **~zug** *m.* elastic (on boots).

gum'mieren *v.t.* to gum.

Gunst *f.* (-) kindness; favour; partiality; advantage, credit; *zu* ~*en von* in favour of; (*commerc.*) to a person's credit.

günst-ig *a.* kind, favourable, propitious; advantageous, good. **~ling** *m.* favourite. **~~swirtschaft** *f.* favouritism.

Gurgel *f.* (-, -n) throat, gullet. **~n** *v.i.* to gargle. **~wasser** *n.* gargle.

Gurke *f.* (-, -n) cucumber. [GHERKIN]

gurren *v.i.* to coo.

Gurt *m.* (-es, -e) girth, strap; belt, girdle.

Gürt-el *m.* (-els, -el) belt, girdle. **~elrose** *f.* shingles. **~eltier** *n.* armadillo. **~en** *v.t.* to gird. **~ler** *m.* brass-founder.

Guß *m.* (Guss-es, ⸚e) pouring out; downpour, torrent; casting, founding; (*typ.*) fount; *aus einem* ~ (*fig.*) a perfect whole. **~eisen** *n.*, **~eisern** *a.* cast iron. **~stahl** *m.* cast steel.

gut (gu:t) *a.* good, pleasant, beneficial; kind, good-natured, friendly. *adv.* well; ~ *und gern* easily; *schon* ~! all right! that'll do! *kurz und* ~ in short; *im* ~*en* amicably, friendly; *es* ~ *haben* to be well off; ~ *stehen für* to be security for. *subst. n.* (-es, ⸚er) good; property; estate, farm; (*commerc.*) commodity, goods. *See also* GÜTER.

Gut-achten *n.* expert opinion, estimate. **~achter** *m.* valuer, assessor. **~artig** *a.* good-natured; (*med.*) benign. **~dünken** *n.* opinion, discretion. **~gelaunt** *a.*

in a good temper, in good spirits.
~gesinnt *a.* friendly, loyal.
~gläubig *a.* credulous. **~haben**
n. credit, balance. **~heißen** *v.t.*
to approve, sanction. **~herzig**
a. kind-hearted. **~machen** *v.t.*
to make amends for. **~mütig** *a.*
good-natured. **~mütigkeit** *f.*
good nature. **~sagen** *v.t.* to
be security (for). **~sbesitzer** *m.*
landowner; gentleman farmer.
~schein *m.* voucher; token. **~**
schreiben *v.t.* to credit. **~schrift**
f. credit. **~strau** *f.* lady of the
manor, squire's wife. **~herr**
m. lord of the manor, squire.
~shof *m.* farm; estate. **~sver-**
walter *m.* steward, manager of
an estate. **~tat** *f.* kindness;
benefaction. **~willig** *a.* willing;
voluntary.

Güt-e (gy:tə) *f.* (-e) kindness,
goodness, excellence, quality.
~ig *a.* kind, good. **~lich** *a.*
amicable, friendly; *sich ~lich*
tun to enjoy.

Güter-abfertigung *f.* goods office.
~bahnhof *m.* goods station.
~gemeinschaft *f.* joint property.
~trennung *f.* division of property. **~wagen** *m.* van, truck.
~zug *m.* goods train.

Gutta'percha *f.* (-s) gutta-percha.

Gymnasi-'albildung *f.* classical
education. **~'ast** *m.* secondary
schoolboy. **~'um** *n.* secondary
school, grammar-school.

Gym'nasti-k *f.* (-k) gymnastics.
~sch *a.* gymnastic.

Gynäko'log-e *m.* (-en, -en) gynaecologist. **~'ie** *f.* gynaecology.

H

H, h (ha:) *n.* the letter h; (*mus.*)
B natural.

Haar (ha:r) *n.* (-es, -e) hair; nap,
pile (of cloth); *sich die ~e*
machen to do one's hair; *~e*
lassen to get fleeced; *~e auf den*
Zähnen haben to stand up to
(opponent); *aufs ~* exactly, pre-

cisely; *um ein ~* nearly, narrowly; *kein gutes ~ an einem lassen*
to pull to pieces; *sich in die ~e*
geraten to come to blows; *sich in*
den ~en liegen to be at daggers
drawn. **~ausfall** *m.* loss of hair.
~bürste *f.* hairbrush. **~büschel**
n. tuft of hair. **~esbreite** *f. um*
~esbreite by a hair's breadth.
~genau *a.* meticulous, very
exact. **~ig** *a.* hairy. **~klein**
adv. minutely, in full detail.
~künstler *m.* hairdresser. **~**
nadel *f.* hairpin. **~scharf** *a.*
very sharp; very exact. **~spal-**
terei *f.* hair-splitting. **~sträu-**
bend *a.* hair-raising. **~trockner**
m. hair-dryer. **~wasser** *n.* hair
tonic.

haaren *v.i.* to lose hair.

Hab-e (ha:-) *f.* (-e) property,
belongings; *bewegliche ~e* movables; *unbewegliche ~e* immovables; *Hab und Gut* goods and
chattels. **~enichts** *m.* pauper.
~gier *f.* greed, avarice, covetousness. **~gierig** *a.* greedy, avaricious, covetous. **~haft** *a.* **~**
haft werden to obtain possession
of, seize. **~schaft** *f.,* **~selig-**
keiten *f.pl.* belongings, property. **~sucht** *f.* avarice. **~**
süchtig *a.* avaricious.

haben (ha:-) *v.t. irreg.* to have; to
own, possess; to get; *zu ~ sein*
to be obtainable; be had; *sich ~*
to be fussy; *unter sich ~* to be in
charge of; *nichts auf sich ~* to
be of no consequence; *was hast*
du? what's the matter with you?
da hast du's! there you are! *hat*
sich was! nonsense! *subst. n.*
credit.

Habicht *m.* (-s, -e) hawk.

habili'tieren *v.r.* to become qualified as univ. teacher.

Ha'bit *m.* (-s, -e) ♢ dress of
religious order.

Hack-beil *n.* chopper. **~brett** *n.*
chopping-board. **~fleisch** *n.*
minced meat. **~frucht** *f.* root-
crop.

Hacke¹ *f.* (-, -n) hoe, mattock.

Hacke² *m.* (-n, -n) & *f.* (-, -n) heel.

hacken *v.t.* to chop; to mince; to
pick, peck.

Häck-erling, **~sel** *m.* chopped straw, chaff.

Hader (ha:-) *m.* (-s) quarrel, dispute. **~n** *v.i.* to quarrel, dispute, argue.

Haderlumpen *m.* (*dial.*) rag.

Haf-en¹ (ha:-) *m.* (-ens, ⁼en) vessel, pot. **~ner** *m.* potter.

Hafen² (ha:-) *m.* (-s, ⁼) port; harbour, haven. **~anlagen** *f.pl.* port-installations. **~arbeiter** *m.* dockyard labourer, docker. **~damm** *m.* jetty, mole. **~sperre** *f.* embargo; blockade. **~stadt** *f.* seaport. [HAVEN]

Hafer (ha:-) *m.* (-s) oats. **~brei** *m.* porridge. **~flocken** *f.pl.* rolled oats. **~grütze** *f.* groats. **~schleim** *m.* gruel.

Haff *n.* (-es, -e) bay, haff.

Haft *f.* (-) custody, arrest, detention. **~bar** *a.* liable, responsible. **~befehl** *m.* warrant (of arrest). **~geld** *n.* earnest, retaining fee. **~pflicht** *f.* liability, responsibility. **~pflichtig** *a.* liable, responsible. **~ung** *f.* *mit beschränkter ~ung* with limited liability. **~vollzug** *m.* imprisonment.

haften *v.i.* to stick to; to cling to; to adhere to; *~ für* to be security for, answer for.

Häftling *m.* (-s, -e) prisoner.

Hag (ha:k) *m.* (-es, -e) hedge; grove; meadow. **~ebutte** *f.* hip, haw. **~edorn** *m.* hawthorn. **~estolz** *m.* old bachelor.

Hagel (ha:-) *m.* (-s) hail; (*fig.*) shower. **~korn** *n.*, **~schloße** *f.* hailstone. **~schlag** *m.*, **~wetter** *n.* hailstorm.

hageln *v.i.* to hail.

hager (ha:-) *a.* lean, thin; haggard, worn. **~keit** *f.* leanness, thinness.

Häher *m.* (-s, -) jay.

Hahn *m.* (-es, ⁼e) cock; stopcock; tap. **~enfuß** *m.* (*bot.*) crowfoot. **~enkamm** *m.* cockscomb. **~enschrei** *m.* crowing of cock. **~rei** *m.* cuckold.

Hai, Haifisch *m.* (-es, -e) shark. [DU.]

Hain *m.* (-es, -e) grove, wood.

Häkel-arbeit, **~ei** *f.* crochet

work. **~n** *v.t. & i.* to crochet.

Haken (ha:-) *m.* (-s, -) hook, peg; tick, mark; (*fig.*) snag, drawback. **~kreuz** *n.* swastika.

halb (-p) *a.* half. *adv.* by halves; *~ zwei* half past one; *ein ~es Pfund* half a pound; *auf ~em Wege* midway, halfway; *~ so viel* half as much. **~amtlich** *a.* semi-official. **~bildung** *f.* superficial education; smattering (of knowledge). **~blut** *n.* half-caste; half-blood. **~dunkel** *n.* dusk, twilight. **~edelstein** *m.* semi-precious stone. **~fertig** *a.* semi-manufactured. **~gott** *m.* demigod. **~heit** *f.* incompleteness; half-measure. **~insel** *f.* peninsula. **~jährlich** *a.* half-yearly. **~kreis** *m.* semicircle. **~kugel** *f.* hemisphere. **~laut** *a. & adv.* in an undertone. **~leder** *n.* halfcalf. **~messer** *m.* radius. **~mond** *m.* crescent moon, half-moon. **~part** *adv.* **~part machen** to go halves. **~rund** *a.* semicircular. **~schlaf** *m.* doze, drowsy sleep. **~schuh** *m.* shoe, slipper. **~strumpf** *m.* sock. **~tagsarbeit** *f.* part-time job. **~ton** *m.* semitone. **~wegs** *adv.* midway, halfway; tolerably. **~welt** *f.* demimonde. **~wüchsig** *a.* half-grown; teenage. **~zeit** *f.* half-time.

halber *prep.* for the sake of, on account of; by reason of.

hal'bieren *v.t.* to halve; to bisect.

Halbstarke(r) *m.* teddy boy.

Halde *f.* (-, -n) slope, hill-side.

half *imperf. of* **helfen.**

Hälfte *f.* (-, -n) half; *zur ~* half of.

Halfter *m. & n.* (-s, -) halter. [HELVE]

Hall *m.* (-es, -e) sound, peal, clang. **~en** *v.i.* to sound, resound.

Halle *f.* (-, -n) hall; porch; (*av.*) hangar. **~nschwimmbad** *n.* indoor swimming-bath.

Halm *m.* (-es, -e) stalk, blade; straw. **~früchte** *f.pl.* cereals.

Hals *m.* (-es, ⁼e) neck; throat; *~ über Kopf* headlong, helter-skelter; *aus vollem ~e* loudly, immoderately; *um den ~ fallen* to embrace; *auf dem ~ haben* to be saddled with; *sich vom ~e*

schaffen to get rid of; *einem zum*
~e herauswachsen to be bored
to tears with. **~abschneider** *m.*
cut-throat. **~ader** *f.* jugular
vein. **~band** *n.* necklace; collar.
~binde *f.* tie. **~brecherisch**
a. dangerous, risky, perilous.
~krause *f.* ruffle, frill. **~**
länge *f. um eine ~länge* by a
neck. **~schmerzen** *m.pl.;* **~weh**
n. sore throat. **~starrig** *a.*
obstinate, stubborn. **~tuch** *n.*
neckerchief; scarf. [COLLAR]

Halt *m.* (**-es, -e**) stop, halt; support, hold, footing. *int.* stop!
~bar *a.* lasting, durable; tenable. **~barkeit** *f.* durability;
(fig.) defensibility. **~egurt** *m.*
parachute harness. **~estelle** *f.*
stop, station. **~etau** *n.* mooring
cable; guy-rope. **~los** *a.* without
support; unsteady, unprincipled;
untenable. **~losigkeit** *f.* instability; absurdity. **~machen** *v.i.*
to stop, halt. **~ung** *f.* bearing,
carriage; behaviour, attitude;
self-control.

halten *v.t. st.* to hold; to support;
to celebrate; to keep, observe;
to follow; to deliver (speech);
to take in (newspaper); to contain; to think, take (for). *v.i.* to
stop; to last; *(of ice)* to bear.
v.r. to stop, keep oneself; to
hold out, endure; to continue;
an sich ~ to restrain oneself;
sich ~ an (fig.) to keep to, comply
with; *es mit einem ~* to be on a
person's side; *viel ~ auf* to think
highly of; *schwer ~* to be
difficult; *für schwer ~* to think
(it) difficult.

Ha'lunke *m.* (**-n, -n**) rogue,
scoundrel, rascal. [CZ.]

Hamen *m.* (**-s, -**) fishing-hook;
net.

hämisch *a.* malicious, spiteful.

Hammel *m.* (**-s, -**) wether. **~**
braten *m.* roast mutton. **~**
rippchen *n.* mutton chop.

Hammer *m.* (**-s,** **ᵘᵉ**r) hammer;
forge; mallet. **~schmied** *m.*
blacksmith.

hämmern *v.t. & i.* to hammer.

Hämorrho'iden *f.pl.* hæmorrhoids.

Hampelmann *m.* puppet, jumping-

jack.

Hamster *m.* (**-s, -**) hamster. **~er**
m. hoarder. **~n** *v.t.* to hoard.

Hand (**-t**) *f.* (**-,** **ᵘᵉ**) hand; *tote ~*
mortmain; *~ legen an* to set to
work upon; *an sich legen* to
commit suicide; *letzte ~ anlegen*
to put the finishing touch to;
~ und Fuß haben to be to the
purpose; *die ~ im Spiel haben* to
have a finger in the pie; *an die
~ geben (commerc.)* to deliver
(goods) for sale or return;
einem die ~ geben to shake hands
with; *an die ~ gehen* to help,
assist; *auf der ~ liegen* to be
clear; *bei der ~ sein* to be ready,
be handy; *unter der ~* secretly,
underhand; *von der ~ gehen* to
work well; *von langer ~ vorbereiten* to prepare beforehand;
von der ~ weisen to decline,
reject; *zur ~ gehen* to help,
assist; *auf Händen tragen* to
spoil; *mit Händen und Füßen* to
strike with might and main.

Hand-arbeit *f.* manual labour;
needlework. **~bibliothek** *f.* reference library. **~breit** *a.* of a
hand's breadth. **~bremse** *f.*
handbrake. **~feger** *m.* broom,
brush. **~fertigkeit** *f.* manual
skill. **~fesseln,** **~schellen** *f.pl.*
handcuffs. **~fest** *a.* robust,
sturdy. **~feuerwaffen** *f.pl.* small
arms. **~fläche** *f.,* **~teller** *m.*
palm of the hand. **~geld** *n.*
earnest; advance. **~gelenk** *n.*
wrist. **~gemein** *a.* **~gemein**
werden to come to blows.
~gemenge *n.* hand-to-hand
fighting. **~gepäck** *n.* hand luggage. **~gerecht** *a.* handy. **~**
geschöpft *a.* hand-made (paper).
~gewirkt *a.* handwoven. **~**
granate *f.* hand grenade. **~greif-**
lich *a.* manifest, obvious;
~greiflich werden to use one's
fists. **~greiflichkeit** *f.* act of
violence, assault. **~griff** *m.*
handle; manipulation. **~habe**
f. handle; *(fig.)* opportunity,
chance. **~haben** *v.t.* to handle,
manage. **~koffer** *m.* small
trunk; suit-case. **~langer** *m.*
handy-man. **~lesekunst** *f.*

palmistry. **~lich** *a.* handy.
~pferd *n.* led horse. **~reichung** *f.* (manual) help; assistance.
~rücken *m.* back of the hand.
~schelle *f.* handcuff. **~schlag** *m.* shake of the hand. **~schrift** *f.* handwriting; manuscript.
~schriftendeutung *f.* graphology. **~schriftlich** *a.* written, in writing, in manuscript. **~schuh** *m.* glove. **~streich** *m.* surprise attack, coup de main. **~tasche** *f.* handbag. **~tuch** *n.* towel.
~tuchhalter *m.* towel-rack.
~umdrehen *n.* im *~umdrehen* in a trice, in a jiffy. **~werk** *n.* handicraft, trade; *einem das ~werk legen* to stop a person's activities. **~werker** *m.* craftsman, artisan, workman. **~werksbursche** *m.* (travelling) journeyman. **~werksmäßig** *a.* workmanlike; mechanical. **~werkszeug** *n.* tools, implements.
~wurzel *f.* wrist. **~zeichnung** *f.* (free-hand) drawing.
Händedruck *m.* clasp of the hand, pressure of the hand.

Handel *m.* (-s) trade, commerce, traffic; business; bargain; affair; *~ treiben* to trade; *einen ~ abschließen* to conclude a bargain.
~sdampfer *m.* merchantman, cargo steamer. **~seinig** (or **~seins**) *a.* *~seinig werden* to come to terms. **~sflotte** *f.* merchant fleet. **~sgärtnerei** *f.* market-garden. **~sgerichtlich** *a.* **~sgerichtlich eingetragen** legally registered. **~sgewicht** *n.* avoirdupois weight. **~sherr** *m.* wholesale merchant. **~skammer** *f.* chamber of commerce.
~smarine *f.* mercantile marine, merchant service. **~smarke** *f.* trade mark. **~sministerium** *n.* Board of Trade. **~sschiff** *n.* merchantman. **~sschule** *f.* commercial college. **~ssperre** *f.* embargo. **~süblich** *a.* customary in trade. **~svertrag** *m.* commercial treaty, trade agreement.
~sweg *m.* trade route. **~streibend** *a.* trading.
Händel *m.pl.* quarrel(s). **~süchtig** *a.* quarrelsome.

handeln *v.i.* to act, do; *~ mit* to trade, do business with; to deal in (goods); *~ um* to bargain for, haggle for; *~ von* to treat of, deal with, be about; *sich ~ um* to be a matter of, be a question of.
Händler *m.* (-s, -) trader, dealer, merchant.
Handlung *f.* (-, -en) act, action; deed; (*lit.*) plot; (*commerc.*) business, trade; shop. **~sbevollmächtigte(r)** *m.* attorney; representative. **~sreisende(r)** *m.* commercial traveller. **~sunkosten** *pl.* business expenses. **~svollmacht** *f.* power of attorney. **~sweise** *f.* way of acting, method of dealing.
hanebüchen *a.* unheard of, preposterous.
Hanf *m.* (-es) hemp. **~en** *a.* hempen.
Hänfling *m.* (-s, -e) linnet.
Hang *m.* (-es, ⁼e) slope; (*fig.*) inclination, propensity, bent.
Hänge-bauch *m.* paunch, potbelly. **~boden** *m.* loft. **~brücke** *f.* suspension bridge. **~lampe** *f.* hanging lamp. **~matte** *f.* hammock.
hangeln *v.i.* to move in suspended position.
hangen, hängen *v.i. st.* to hang, be suspended; to adhere (to), stick (to); to be attached (to); to depend (on), turn (upon).
~bleiben *vws.i.* to be caught (by or on).
hängen *v.t.* to hang, suspend, attach, fix.
hänseln *v.t.* to tease.
Hans-'narr *m.* tomfool. **~'wurst** *m.* clown, buffoon.
Hantel *f.* (-, -n) dumb-bell.
han'tier-en *v.t.* to handle, manipulate, operate; to manage, carry on a business. **~ung** *f.* handling, manipulation; business, trade.
hapern *v. impers.* to be amiss, be wrong.
Happ-en *m.* (-ens, -en) piece, morsel, mouthful. **~ig** *a.* greedy.
hären *a.* hairy.
Häre'sie *f.* (-, -n) heresy.
Hä'reti-ker *m.* (-kers, -ker) heretic. **~sch** *a.* heretical.

Harfe *f.* (-, n) harp. ~**nist**,
Hartner *m.* harpist.

Harke *f.* (-, -n) rake. ~**n** *v.t.* & *i.*
to rake.

Harm *m.* (-es) ♣ grief, sorrow;
insult, injury. ~**los** *a.* harmless.
~**losigkeit** *f.* harmlessness; innocence. [HARM]

härmen *v.r.* to grieve (about),
fret (over), worry (about).

Harmo'nie *f.* (-, -n) harmony,
concord. ~**lehre** *f.* theory of
harmony. ~**ren** *v.i.* to harmonize; to agree (with).

Har'moni-ka *f.* (-ka, -ken) concertina. ~**sch** *a.* harmonious.
~**um** *n.* harmonium.

harmonisieren *v.t.* (mus. & fig.) to
attune, bring into harmony.

Harn *m.* (-es) urine. ~**blase** *f.*
bladder. ~**fluß** *m.* incontinence
of urine. ~**glas** *n.* urinal. ~
röhre *f.* ureter. ~**säure** *f.* uric
acid. ~**stoff** *m.* urea. ~**treibend**
a. diuretic. ~**zwang** *m.* stran-
gury.

harnen *v.i.* to urinate.

Harnisch *m.* (-es, e) armour; *in*
~ *geraten* to fly into a rage. [F]

Har'pun-e *f.* (-e, -en) harpoon.
~**ieren** *v.t.* to harpoon. [DU.]

Har'pyie *f.* (-, -n) harpy.

harren *v.i.* to wait (for), await.

harsch *a.* harsh, hard, rough.

hart *a.* hard, firm, solid; ~ *an* hard
by. ~**futter** *n.* oats and grain.
~**geld** *n.* coins. ~**gesotten** *a.*
hard-boiled. ~**gummi** *m.* hard
rubber, ebonite. ~**guß** *m.* chill
casting; chilled casting. ~**herzig**
a. hard-hearted. ~**herzigkeit** *f.*
hardheartedness. ~**hörig** *a.*
hard of hearing. ~**köpfig** *a.*
headstrong. ~**leibigkeit** *f.* constipation. ~**näckig** *a.* obstinate,
stubborn; chronic (illness). ~
näckigkeit *f.* pertinacity. ~**spiritus** *m.* solid alcohol.

Härte *f.* (-, -n) hardness; roughness; severity; cruelty. ~**n** *v.t.*
to harden; to temper (steel).

Harz (-ts) *n.* (-es, -e) resin, rosin.
~**ig** *a.* resinous.

Ha'sardspiel *n.* game of chance,
gambling. [F]

Ha'sch-ee (-ʃeː) *n.* (-ees, -ees)
hash. ~**ieren** *v.t.* to hash.

haschen *v.t.* to catch, seize; to
snatch (at), strive (for).

Häscher *m.* (-s, -) bailiff; catch-
pole; guard.

Hase (haːzə) *m.* (-n, -n) hare;
falscher ~ meat roll. ~**nbraten**
m. roast hare. ~**nfuß** *m.* coward.
~**nklein** *n.* jugged hare. ~**npanier** *n. das* ~*npanier ergreifen* to
take to one's heels. ~**nscharte**
f. hare-lip.

Hasel-huhn *n.* hazel-hen. ~**maus**
f. dormouse. ~**nuß** *f.* hazel-
nut.

Häsin *f.* (-, -nen) female hare.

Haspe *f.* (-, -n) hasp, hinge; staple.

Haspel *m.* (-s, -) reel; windlass;
winch. ~**n** *v.t.* to reel.

Haß (-s) *m.* (Hasses) hate, hatred.

hassen *v.t.* to hate. ~**swert** *a.*
hateful, odious.

häßlich *a.* ugly; nasty. ~**keit** *f.*
ugliness.

hast[1] *2 pers. sing. pres. of* **haben**.

Hast[2] *f.* (-) hurry, haste. ~**en**
vws.i. to hurry, hasten. ~**ig** *a.*
hurried, hasty. ~**igkeit** *f.* hastiness.

hätscheln *v.t.* to caress; to coddle,
pamper.

hatte *imperf. of* **haben**.

Haube *f.* (-, -n) hood, cap;
(*motor.*) bonnet; *unter die* ~
bringen to marry off. ~**nlerche**
f. crested lark.

Hau'bitze *f.* (-, -n) howitzer. [cz.]

Hauch (-x) *m.* (-es, -e) breath;
slight breeze, whiff; tinge; (*fig.*)
trace, touch. ~**en** *v.i.* to breathe
v.t. to exhale; to whisper softly.
~**laut** *m.* aspirate. ~**zart** *a.*
delicate, flimsy, filmy.

Hau-degen *m.* broadsword; (*fig.*)
warrior, bully. ~**e** *f.* hoe; pick;
(*colloq.*) thrashing. ~**en** *v.t. st.*
to beat; to hew (trees); to break
(stones). *v.r.* to fight; *um sich*
~*en* to lay about one. ~**er** *m.*
woodcutter, hewer; (*zool.*) fang,
tusk.

Haufe-(n) *m.* (-ns, -n) heap, pile;
quantity; crowd; rabble; *über
den* ~*n werfen* to throw aside,
overthrow. ~**nweise** *adv.* in
heaps; in crowds.

häufeln v.t. to heap; to earth (potatoes).

häuf-en v.t. to heap; to accumulate. v.r. to multiply, increase. **~ig** a. frequent; abundant. **~igkeit** f. frequency. **~ung** f. accumulation. **~ungslinie** f. upper limit.

Haupt n. (-es, ¨er) head; chief, leader; (as prefix) chief, main, principal; aufs ~ schlagen to defeat totally; zu Häupten at the head of. **~aufgabe** f. main task. **~bahnhof** m. main station, central station. **~bestandteil** m. chief constituent. **~buch** n. ledger. **~hahn** m. main tap, main cock. **~mann** m. captain; flight lieutenant. **~merkmal** n. chief characteristic. **~nenner** m. common denominator. **~person** f. principal person; (theatr.) leading character. **~postamt** n. General Post Office. **~probe** f. dress rehearsal; full rehearsal. **~quartier** n. headquarters. **~sache** f. main thing. **~sächlich** a. principal, chief. adv. mainly, especially. **~stadt** f. capital. **~treffer** m. first prize (in lottery). **~verkehrszeit** f. rush hours. **~wort** n. noun, substantive.

Häuptling m. (-s, -e) chieftain, captain. **~s** adv. head foremost.

Haus n. (-es, ¨er) building, house, dwelling; cottage; home, family; (commerce) firm; nach ~e home; zu ~e at home; von ~ aus originally; das ~ hüten to be confined to the house; das ~ bestellen to put one's affairs in order. **~angestellte(r)** m. servant. **~arbeit** f. housework. **~arzt** m. family doctor. **~aufgabe** f. homework. **~backen** a. home-made; (fig.) prosaic. **~dame** f. lady housekeeper. **~flur** m. hall; corridor. **~frau** f. housewife. **~gebrauch** m. domestic use. **~gehilfin** f. housemaid, help. **~halt** m. household. **~halten** v.i. to keep house; to husband, economize. **~hälterin** f. housekeeper. **~hälterisch** a. economical. **~haltsplan** m. bud-

get. **~herr** m. master. **~hoch** a. (fig.) very high; (of talk) tall. **~hofmeister** m. steward. **~lehrer** m. private tutor. **~macht** f. dynastic power. **~mädchen** n. housemaid. **~mannskost** f. plain fare. **~meister** m. caretaker. **~mittel** n. household remedy. **~rat** m. household furniture. **~sammlung** f. house-to-house collection. **~schuh** m. slipper. **~schwamm** m. dry rot. **~stand** m. household. **~suchung** f. domiciliary visit by police; raid. **~tier** n. domestic animal. **~türe** f. front door. **~wart** m. porter. **~wesen** n. household. **~wirt** m. landlord. **~wirtschaft** f. housekeeping; domestic science. **~wirtschaftlich** a. economical; domesticated. **~zins** m. rent.

Häus-chen n. small house, cottage; aus dem ~chen sein to be beside oneself. **~erkampf** m. house-to-house fighting. **~ler** m. cottager. **~lich** a. household, domestic; economical; domesticated, home-loving. **~lichkeit** f. home; family life; domesticity.

hausen v.i. to dwell, live, reside; fürchterlich ~ to play havoc, ransack.

Hausen² m. (-s, -) sturgeon.

hau'sier-en v.i. to peddle, hawk. **~er** m. pedlar, hawker. **~schein** m. hawker's licence.

Hausse (-o:-) f. (-, -n) advance (of prices), boom. [F]

Haut f. (-, ¨e) skin, hide; coat; membrane; film; ehrliche ~ good fellow; mit ~ und Haar completely, thoroughly; mit heiler ~ safely; sich seiner ~ wehren to defend oneself; aus der ~ fahren to lose one's patience. **~farbe** f. complexion. **~krem** f. skin cream. **~reinigend** a. cleansing. **~schere** f. manicure scissors. **~unreinheit** f. skin blemish. [HIDE]

häuten v.t. to skin; to flay. v.r. to cast one's skin, to slough.

Hava'rie f. (-, -n) damage by sea; average.

Heb-amme f. midwife. **~ebaum**

m. lever, crowbar. ~**ekraft** *f.*
leverage, purchase. ~**el** *m.* lever.
~**er** *m.* siphon. ~**erolle** *f.* register
of dues and taxes. ~**ewerk** *n.*
lifting-tackle, hoisting-gear. ~
ung *f.* raising; lifting; elevation;
(fig.) revival; improvement; encouragement; increase; *(pros.)*
accented syllable.

heben *v.t. st.* to lift, raise; to reduce
(fraction); *(fig.)* to improve. *v.r.*
to rise; to cancel (sum).

Hechel *f.* (·, -n) hackle. ~**n** *v.t.*
to hackle.

Hecht (-çt) *m.* (-es, -e) pike.

Heck *n.* (-es, -e) stern; rear (of
tank). ~**antrieb** *m.* rear drive.

Hecke[1] *f.* (·, -n) hedge. ~**nrose** *f.*
wild rose. ~**nschütze** *m.* sniper.

Hecke[2] *f.* (·, -n) hatch, brood,
breed. ~**n** *v.i. & t.* to hatch,
breed.

Hederich *m.* (-s) field mustard.

Heer (he:r) *n.* (-es, -e) army; mass,
crowd, host. ~**bann** *m.* levies.
~**esbericht** *m.* official army communiqué. ~**esdienst** *m.* military
service. ~**esleitung** *f. Oberste* ~
esleitung Supreme Command
Staff. ~**führer** *m.* general;
army-leader. ~**haufe** *m.,* ~
schar *f.* host. ~**schau** *f.* review,
parade. ~**straße** *f.* highroad,
military road.

Hefe (he:-) *f.* (·) yeast; *(fig.)*
scum.

Heft *n.* (-es, -e) 1. handle; hilt (of
sword). 2. exercise-book, notebook; pamphlet; part, number;
das ~ in der Hand haben to be
master of the situation. ~**el** *m.*
hook; clasp. ~**faden** *m.* basting
thread. ~**klammer** *f.* paper-clip. ~**nadel** *f.* stitching needle.
~**pflaster** *n.* sticking plaster.
~**stich** *m.* tacking stitch. ~
zwecke *f.* drawing-pin.

heften *v.t.* to pin, fasten; to baste,
tack, stitch; to fix. *v.r.* to stick
(to).

heftig *a.* violent, strong; passionate; heavy. ~**keit** *f.* violence;
vehemence; intensity.

hege-n (he:-) *v.t.* to nurse, preserve; to cherish, entertain (a
hope). ~**r** *m.* forester, keeper.

~**zeit** *f.* close season.

Hehl *n. kein ~ machen aus* to
make no secret of. ~**en** *v.t.* to
conceal; to receive stolen goods,
fence. ~**er** *m.* receiver (of
stolen goods). ~**e'rei** *f.* receiving
of stolen goods.

hehr *a.* sublime; high. [HOAR]

Heid-e[1] *f.* (-e, -en) heath. ~
kraut *n.* heather. ~**elbeere** *f.*
bilberry, blueberry. ~**erose** *f.*
wild rose. ~**schnucke** *f.* heath-sheep.

Heid-e[2] *m.* (-en, -en) heathen,
pagan; *(bibl.)* Gentile. ~**enangst**
f. blue funk. ~**engeld** *n.* no end
of money. ~**enlärm** *m.* hullabaloo. ~**enmission** *f.* foreign mission. ~**entum** *n.* heathendom,
paganism. ~**nisch** *a.* heathen-(ish), pagan.

heikel *a.* delicate, ticklish, difficult; dainty, fastidious.

heil *a.* unhurt, intact, unscathed,
safe and sound; healed, cured,
restored. *subst. n.* welfare, happiness; salvation; *im Jahr des ~s*
in the year of grace. *int.* hail!
good luck! *~ dem König* God
save the king; *~ dem, der . . .*
blessed be he who. ~**anstalt** *f.*
hospital, sanatorium, nursing
home. ~**bar** *a.* curable. ~**bringend** *a.* salutary. ~**butt** *m.*
halibut. ~**gymnastik** *f.* remedial
exercises. ~**kräftig** *a.* curative,
restorative. ~**kraut** *n.* medicinal herb. ~**kunde** *f.* medical
science, therapeutics. ~**kundig**
a. skilled in (the art of) medicine.
~**los** *a.* wicked; terrible; hopeless. ~**mittel** *n.* remedy. ~**quelle**
f. mineral spring. ~**sam** *a.* wholesome, salutary; beneficial, good.
~**sarmee** *f.* Salvation Army.
~**serum** *n.* antitoxin. ~**(s)froh**
a. delighted, overjoyed. ~**sgeschichte** *f.* Life and Sufferings of
Christ. ~**stätte** *f.* sanatorium.
~**ung** *f.* healing, cure. ~**verfahren** *n.* medical treatment.
[WHOLE]

Heiland *m.* (-s) Saviour.

heilen *v.t.* to cure; *(also v.i.)* to heal.

heilig (-ç) *a.* holy, godly, saintly;
sacred, hallowed. ~**abend** *m.*

Christmas Eve. ~e(r) m. saint. ~enschein m. halo. ~keit f. holiness, godliness, sanctity; sacredness. ~sprechung f. canonization. ~tum n. sanctuary, shrine; relic. ~ung f. sanctification; consecration.

heiligen v.t. to hallow, sanctify; to keep holy; to justify.

heim adv. home. subst. n. home; hostel; institution, asylum. ~arbeit f. outwork, outdoor work. ~arbeiter m. outdoor worker. ~chen n. cricket. ~fahrt f. return journey. ~fall m. (leg.) reversion. ~führen v.t. to bring home the bride, marry. ~gang m. death. ~gegangen a. deceased. ~isch a. native; indigenous; at home; familiar. ~kehr f. homecoming. ~kunft f. homecoming. ~leiter m. warden. ~leiterin f. matron. ~leuchten v.t. to reprove, (sl.) tell off. ~lich a. secret, furtive; snug, comfortable; private. ~lichkeit f. secrecy; secret. ~stätte f. home. ~suchen v.t. to afflict, plague, trouble; to visit. ~suchung f. trial, misfortune; visitation. ~tücke f. malice. ~tückisch a. malicious, insidious. ~wärts adv. homeward. ~weg m. way home, return. ~weh n. homesickness; ~weh haben to be homesick. ~wehr f. home guard. ~zahlen v.t. to pay out, be revenged on.

Heimat f. (-) native land; home, homeland. ~hafen m. port of registry. ~kunde f. local topography. ~lich a. native, home; home-like. ~los a. homeless. ~vertriebene(r) m. displaced person.

Hein m. Freund ~ Death.

Heinzelmännchen n. brownie.

Heirat f. (-, -en) marriage. ~santrag m. proposal. ~sfähig a. marriageable. ~sgut n. dowry. ~skandidat m. suitor, wooer. ~slustig a. eager to marry. ~svermittler m. matrimonial agent.

heiraten v.t. & i. to marry, get married.

heischen v.t. to demand. [ASK]

heiser (-z-) a. hoarse; ~ sein to be hoarse; to have a sore throat. ~keit f. hoarseness; sore throat.

heiß (-ß-) a. hot; (fig.) burning, ardent. ~blütig a. hot-blooded, choleric. ~hunger m. ravenous hunger. ~luftstrahlantrieb m. (av.) jet propulsion. ~mangel f. pressure roller. ~sporn m. hotspur. ~wasserspeicher m. hot-water tank; geyser.

heißen v.t. st. to call, name; to command, bid; to be called; to mean; es heißt they say.

heiter a. bright, clear, serene; cheerful, gay. ~keit f. brightness, clearness, serenity; cheerfulness.

heiz-bar a. with heating. ~er m. stoker, fireman. ~kissen n. electric pad. ~körper m. radiator. ~material n. fuel. ~raum m. stoke hole. ~rohr n. flue. ~sonne f. electric fire. ~ung f. heating, firing.

heizen v.t. & i. to heat, put on a fire.

hektogra'phieren v.t. to hectograph.

Held (-t) m. (-en, -en) hero. ~enmütig a. heroic. ~isch aa. heroic. ~entat f. heroic deed. ~entum n. heroism. ~in f. heroine.

helf-en v.i. st. to support, help, assist; to be of use, avail. ~er m. helper, assistant. ~ershelfer m. accomplice, abettor.

hell a. bright, shining; clear, distinct, high; light, fair; pale (ale); ~er Wahnsinn sheer madness. ~e, ~igkeit f. brightness, clearness. ~hörig a. keen of hearing. ~(l)icht a. am ~(l)ichten Tage in broad daylight. ~sehen n. clairvoyance. ~seher m., ~seherin f. clairvoyant. ~sichtig a. clairvoyant.

Helle'barde f. (-, -n) halberd.

Heller m. (-s, -) farthing.

Helm m. (-es, -e) helmet; (naut.) helm, rudder. ~busch m. plume, crest.

Hemd n. (-es, -en) shirt, (man's) undervest; (woman's) vest, chemise. ~bluse f. shirt-blouse. ~brust f. shirt-front, dicky. ~hose f. cami-knickers; combinations. **~knopf** m. stud. **~s-ärmelig** a. in one's shirt sleeves.

Hemisphäre f. hemisphere.

hemm-en v.t. to stop; check, slow up; to hinder, restrain. **~nis** n. check, obstruction; hindrance, impediment. **~schuh** m. brake, drag. **~ung** f. check, stoppage, restraint; (med.) inhibition. **~ungslos** a. free, unrestrained, unchecked.

Hengst m. (-es, -e) horse, stallion.

Henkel m. (-s, -) handle.

henk-en v.t. to hang. **~er** m. hangman. **~ersmahl** n. last meal, farewell dinner.

Henne f. (-, -n) hen.

her (he:r) 1. adv. hither, here; since, ago; from; von alters ~ of old, from time immemorial; hin und ~ to and fro; hinter etwas ~ sein to be after something. 2. sep. pref.

he'rab (-p) adv. & sep. pref. down, downwards. **~lassen** v.t. to lower, let down. v.r. to condescend. **~lassung** f. condescension. **~sehen** v.i. to look down (upon). **~setzen** v.t. to lower, degrade; to reduce (price); (fig.) to disparage. **~setzung** f. lowering, degradation; reduction; disparagement. **~würdigen** v.t. to degrade; to abase.

He'raldik f. (-) heraldry.

he'ran adv. & sep. pref. on, up, near, along. **~bilden** v.t. to train, educate. **~kommen** vws.i. to come near; die Dinge an sich ~kommen lassen to bide one's time. **~pirschen** v.r. to stalk up (to). **~reichen** v.i. to reach up to. **~reifen** vws.i. to grow up, grow to maturity. **~wachsen** vws.i. to grow up. **~ziehen** v.t. to draw near; to consult.

he'rauf adv. & sep. pref. up, upwards. **~beschwören** v.t. to conjure up; to bring on, cause. **~setzen** v.t. to put up (price). **~ziehen** v.t. to draw up. vws.i. to approach, draw near.

he'raus adv. & sep. pref. out; from within; forth; from among; ~ damit! out with it! **~bekommen** v.t. to get back (change); to

find out. **~bringen** v.t. to bring out; to get out; to find out. **~fordern** v.t. to challenge; to provoke. **~forderung** f. challenge, provocation. **~gabe** f. giving up, delivering up; setting free; publication; editing. **~geben** v.t. to give up, deliver up; to give change; to publish. **~geber** m. editor; publisher. **~greifen** v.t. to single out, choose. **~kommen** vws.i. to come out; to become known; to appear, be issued; to result (in); auf eins ~kommen to be all the same. **~machen** v.r. to develop well. **~nehmen** v.t. to take out, extract. v.r. to presume, make bold, venture. **~platzen** vws.i. to blurt out. **~putzen** v.t. to dress up. **~reden** v.t. to speak freely. v.r. to make excuses. **~reißen** v.t. to tear out, extract; (fig.) to extricate. **~rücken** v.t. to fork out (money); to come out (with). **~schlagen** v.t. to make a profit. **~stellen** v.r. to turn out, appear. **~streichen** v.t. to extol, praise. **~treten** vws.i. to step out; to protrude.

herb (-p) a. dry (of wine); acrid, tart; (fig.) austere; harsh, bitter. **~heit** f. harshness, bitterness.

her'bei adv. & sep. pref. hither, here, near. **~führen** v.t. to bring about, cause. **~lassen** v.r. to condescend. **~schaffen** v.t. to bring near; to procure, produce.

herbemühen v.t. & r. to trouble to come.

Herberge f. (-, -n) lodging; inn. **~n** v.t. to lodge, shelter. [HARBOUR]

Herbst (herꞏp) m. (-es, -e) autumn. **~lich** a. autumnal. **~zeitlose** f. meadow saffron. [HARVEST]

Herd (heꞏrt) m. (-es, -e) hearth, fire-place, kitchen-range; (fig.) seat, focus; hot-bed. **~platte** f. hot-plate.

Herde (-e:-) f. (-, -n) flock; herd; drove; crowd. **~ntier** n. gregarious animal.

he'rein adv. & sep. pref. in; ~! come in! **~brechen** vws.i. to fall, set in; to befall, overtake. **~fall** m. take-in; sell; failure.

~fallen *vws.i.* (*fig.*) to be taken in; to be disappointed. ~legen *v.t.* (*fig.*) to take in, (*colloq.*) to do. ~schneien *vws.i.* (*fig.*) to arrive unexpectedly, drop in.

her-fallen *vws.i.* to fall (upon). ~gang *m.* course of events. ~geben *v.t.* to deliver, give up, hand over; (*fig.*) to permit. *v.r.* to be a party (to). ~gebracht *a.* traditional; customary. ~gehen *vws.i.* to go on, be going on. ~halten *v.i.* to suffer, bear the brunt.

Hering (he:-) *m.* (-s, -e) herring.

her-kommen *vws.i.* to come near, approach; to come from, originate. *subst. n.* custom; descent, extraction. ~kömmlich *a.* customary; traditional. ~kunft *f.* origin, descent. ~leiten *v.t.* to conduct; to derive, deduce. ~machen *v.r.* to set about; to delete; to fall (upon).

Herme'lin (-i:n) *n.* (-s, -e) ermine.

her'metisch *a.* hermetical.

her'nach *adv.* afterwards, hereafter, after this.

hernehmen *v.t.* to take from, get from.

her'nieder *adv.* down.

He'ro-e *m.* (-en, -en) hero. ~in *f.* (-, -innen) heroine.

Hero'ine (-i:-) *f.* (-, -n) heroine.

he'ro-isch *a.* heroic. ~ismus *m.* heroism.

Herold *m.* (-s, -e) herald.

Heros *m.* (-, He'roen) hero.

Herr *m.* (-n, -en) master; owner; the Lord; gentleman; Sir; Mr.; ~ *werden* to master, overcome; *sein eigener ~ sein* to stand on one's own feet. ~enartikel *m.pl.* gentlemen's outfitting. ~enfahrer *m.* owner-driver. ~enhaus *n.* manor, mansion. ~enlos *a.* without a master, ownerless. ~enschnitt *m.* Eton crop. ~envolk *n.* master race. ~gott *m.* the Lord God. ~in *f.* mistress, lady. ~isch *a.* imperious, dictatorial; domineering. ~je *int.* Goodness! Gracious! ~lich *a.* magnificent, splendid, glorious. ~lichkeit *f.* magnificence, splendour, glory.

~schaft *f.* power, dominion, rule, command; master and mistress; estate, domain. ~schaftlich *a.* belonging to a lord or master; high class.

her richten (he:r-) *v.t.* to arrange, get ready, prepare.

herrsch-en *v.i.* to rule, govern; to prevail, exist, be. ~er *m.* ruler, sovereign. ~sucht *f.* love of power. ~süchtig *a.* fond of power, tyrannical.

her-rühren *v.i.* to come (from), be due to. ~sagen *v.t.* to recite, repeat. ~schaffen *v.t.* to procure, produce. ~schreiben *v.r.* to date (from). ~stellen *v.t.* to put here; to manufacture, produce; to repair; to restore (to health). ~steller *m.* maker, producer. ~stellung *f.* manufacture, production; restoration; recovery.

he'rüber *adv. & sep. pref.* over, across, to this side.

he'rum *adv. & sep. pref.* round; near; about; round about; (*colloq.*) over, finished; *rund ~* all round. ~drehen *v.t.* to turn round. ~drücken *v.r.* to hang about. ~führen *v.t.* to lead round; to show over. ~irren *vws.i.* to wander about. ~kommen *vws.i.* to come round; to travel about; to become known. ~kriegen *v.t.* to talk over, win round. ~lungern *v.i.* to loiter. ~reichen *v.t.* to hand round. ~reiten *vws.i.* (*fig.*) to harp upon. ~treiben *v.r.* to rove, gad about. ~werfen *v.t.* to turn sharply. ~ziehen *vws.i.* to wander about.

he'runter *adv. & sep. pref.* down; off. ~handeln *v.t.* to beat down (price). ~hauen *v.t.* to box (ear). ~holen *v.t.* to fetch down; (*av.*) to shoot down. ~klappen *v.t.* to turn down. ~kommen *vws.i.* to come down; to be pulled down (in health); to go down in the world. ~lassen *v.t.* to let down, lower. ~machen *v.t.* to upbraid. ~reißen *v.t.* to pull down; (*fig.*) to pull to pieces. ~sein *v.i.* (*colloq.*) to be low, feel low. ~setzen v.t. to lower; (fig.) to disparage.

her'vor (-fo:r) adv. & sep. pref. forth, out. ~brechen vws.i. to break through; to rush out. ~bringen v.t. to produce, bring forth; to utter. ~gehen vws.i. to go forth; to result, arise. ~heben v.t. to make prominent; to emphasize, stress; to set off. ~ragen v.i. to stand out, project, jut forth; to be prominent. ~ragend a. prominent, excellent. ~rufen v.t. to call forth; to bring about, cause. ~stechen v.i. to stand out, be conspicuous. ~stechend a. conspicuous. ~stehen v.i. to project. ~treten vws.i. to step forth, come forward, be prominent. ~tun v.r. to distinguish oneself.

her-wärts adv. hither, this way. ~weg m. (the) way here.

Herz (-ts) n. (-ens, -en) heart; mind; feeling; courage; ans ~ legen to urge, enjoin; auf dem ~en haben to have on one's mind; ins ~ schließen to become fond of; sich ein ~ fassen to take courage; sich zu ~en nehmen to take to heart; unterm ~en tragen to be with child; von ~en gern with the greatest of pleasure.

Herz-ader f. aorta. ~beutel m. pericardium. ~blatt n. (fig.) darling. ~bube m. knave of hearts. ~dame f. queen of hearts. ~eleid n. sorrow, grief. ~enseinfalt f. simplicity; simple-mindedness. ~ensergießung f. confidences. ~ensgut a. dear, kind-hearted. ~enslust f. nach ~enslust to one's heart's content. ~erweiterung f. dilatation of the heart. ~fehler m. disease of the heart. ~gegend f. cardiac region. ~grube f. pit of the stomach. ~haft a. brave, stout-hearted; hearty; bold. ~ig a. sweet, lovely. ~innig a. hearty, heartfelt. ~klappe f. valve. ~klopfen n. palpitation. ~leidend a. suffering from heart-trouble. ~lich a. hearty, cordial;

affectionate. ~lichkeit f. heartiness; affection. ~los a. heartless. ~losigkeit f. heartlessness. ~schlag m. heart-beat; (med.) heart failure. ~verfettung f. fatty heart. ~zerreißend a. heart-rending.

herzen (-ts-) v.t. to embrace, caress.

herziehen (-hr-) v.t. to draw near. vws.i. to come to live in a place; ~ über to speak ill of.

Herzog m. (-s, ¨e) duke. ~in f. duchess. ~lich a. ducal. ~tum n. duchy.

her'zu (-tsu:) adv. & sep. pref. up, up to, towards, hither, near.

He'täre f. (-, -n) courtesan. [GK.]

hetero'gen a. heterogeneous.

Hetzblatt n. (newspaper) rag.

Hetz-e f. (-, -en) hunt; hurry, rush; instigation; baiting. ~en v.t. to hunt, drive; to hurry, rush; to incite, agitate; to bait. ~er m. instigator, inciter; baiter. ~jagd f. hunting, hunt; great hurry, rush.

Heu (-oi) n. (-es) hay. ~boden m. hayloft. ~fieber n. hay fever. ~gabel f. pitchfork. ~monat m. July. ~pferd n., ~schrecke f. grasshopper; (bibl.) locust. ~schober m., ~stadel m. hayrick; barn.

Heuche'lei f. (-, -en) hypocrisy.

heuch-eln v.t. to feign, affect, simulate. v.i. to dissemble, play the hypocrite. ~ler m. hypocrite. ~lerisch a. hypocritical, deceitful.

heuen v.i. to make hay.

heu-er¹ adv. this year. ~rig a. this year's.

Heuer² m. (-s, -) haymaker.

heuern v.t. to hire.

heulen v.i. to howl; to cry; to hoot.

heut-e adv. today; ~ e früh this morning; ~ e vor acht Tagen a week ago today. ~ig a. of to-day; of the present time, modern. ~igentags, ~zutage advs. nowadays.

Hexe (hɛksə) f. (-, -n) witch, hag. ~n v.i. to practise witchcraft. ~nkessel m. (fig.) hubbub. ~n-meister m. wizard, magician.

~nprozeß *m.* trial for witch-craft. ~nschuß *m.* lumbago. ~rei *f.* witchcraft, magic. [HAG]

hie(r) *adv.* ~ und da sometimes.

hieb¹ *imperf. of* hauen.

Hieb² (-p) *m.* (-es, -e) blow, stroke, cut; hit, cutting remark. ~fest *a.* proof against blows. ~waffe *f.* weapon; broadsword.

hielt *imperf. of* halten.

hie'nieden *adv.* here below, on earth.

hier (hi:r) *adv.* here; in this place; at this point. ~an *adv.* to that; hereat; by that; hereupon; after that. ~auf *adv.* hereupon; after that. ~aus *adv.* from this, hence. ~bei *adv.* hereby, here-with; enclosed. ~durch *adv.* through this; this way; by this means, thereby. ~für *adv.* for this. ~gegen *adv.* against this. ~her *adv.* hither, here; bis ~her so far, thus far; hitherto, up to now. ~herum *adv.* hereabouts. ~hin *adv.* in this direction, this way; there. ~in *adv.* herein, in this. ~mit *adv.* herewith, with this. ~nach *adv.* after this, hereupon; according to this. ~orts *adv.* here. ~über *adv.* over here; about this; hereat. ~um *adv.* about or round this place. ~unter *adv.* beneath this, under this; among these; by that. ~von *adv.* hereof, of or from this. ~zu *adv.* to this, moreover, in addition to this. ~zulande *adv.* in this country, with us.

Hierar'chie (-çi:) *f.* (-, -n) hierarchy.

Hiero'glyphe *f.* (-, -n) hieroglyph.

hiesig (-ziç) *a.* of this place or country; local.

hieß *imperf. of* heißen.

Hifthorn *n.* hunting-horn.

hilf; hilfst, hilft *imper.* & 2 & 3 *pers. sing. pres. of* helfen.

Hilf-e *f.* (-e, -en) help, assistance, aid; maid, charwoman; support, succour; relief; ~e leisten to help, aid, assist; erste ~e first aid. ~eleistung *f.* help, assistance. ~eruf *m.* cry for help. ~los *a.* helpless, defenceless; destitute. ~losigkeit *f.* helpless-ness. ~reich *a.* helpful; charit-able. ~sarbeiter *m.* temporary worker, temporary hand; assis-tant. ~sbedürftig *a.* needing help; indigent. ~skraft *f.* additional helper, assistant. ~skreuzer *m.* auxiliary cruiser. ~slehrer *m.* assistant teacher. ~slinie *f.* (geom.) auxiliary line; (mus.) ledger line. ~smaßnahme *f.* first-aid; relief measure. ~smittel *n.* remedy; expedient; resource; auxiliary material. ~squelle *f.* resource. ~struppen *f.pl.* auxi-liary troops. ~szeitwort *n.* auxiliary verb.

Himbeere *f.* raspberry.

Himmel *m.* (-s, -) heaven; sky; canopy; aus allen ~n fallen to be bitterly disappointed; gen ~ fahren to ascend to heaven; zum ~ schreien to be scandalous; unter freiem ~ in the open air. ~an *adv.* to the skies, heaven-wards. ~angst *adv.* terribly frightened. ~bett *n.* four-poster. ~fahrt *f.* Ascension; Mariä ~fahrt Assumption. ~hoch *a.* sky-high; (fig.) urgently. ~reich *n.* kingdom of heaven. ~sbahn *f.* celestial space. ~sgegend, ~s-richtung *f.* quarter, direction; point of the compass. ~sgewölbe *n.* canopy or vault of heaven. ~skörper *m.* celestial body. ~sreklame *f.* sky writing. ~sschlüssel *m.* cowslip. ~sstrich *m.* zone, region; climate; lati-tude. ~sstürmend *a.* over-enthusiastic. ~szelt *n.* vault of heaven. ~wärts *adv.* heaven-wards. ~weit *adv.* miles apart, widely.

himmlisch *a.* heavenly; celestial.

hin *adv.* & *sep. pref.* thither, there; along; (colloq.) gone, lost; ex-hausted; ~ und her to and fro; there and back; ~ und her überlegen to turn (an idea) over in one's mind; ~ und wieder now and then; über die ganze Welt ~ all over the world.

hi'nab (-p) *adv.* down, down-ward(s).

hi'nan *adv.* up, up to, upward(s).

hinarbeiten *v.i.* to aim (at).

hi'nauf *adv.* up, up to, upward(s). ~arbeiten *v.r.* to work one's way up.

hi'naus *adv.* out; outside; (*dar*)*über* ~ beyond; further. ~gehen *vws.i.* to go out; ~gehen *über* to go beyond; to surpass, exceed; ~gehen *auf* to look out on, face. ~kommen *vws.i.* to come out; *auf eins* ~kommen to come to the same thing. ~schieben *v.t.* to defer, postpone, put off. ~werfen *v.t.* to throw out, expel. ~wollen *v.i.* to want to go out; to be driving at; *hoch* ~wollen to aim high. ~ziehen *v.t.* to draw out, drag out.

Hin-blick *m.* *im* ~blick *auf* with regard to, with a view to. ~bringen *v.t.* to take, bring, carry (to); to spend, pass (time).

hinder-lich *a.* in the way, hindering, obstructive. ~n *v.t.* to prevent; to hinder; to hamper. ~nis *n.* hindrance, impediment, check, obstacle, bar. ~nisrennen *n.* obstacle race.

hindeuten *v.i.* to point (to), hint (at); to indicate.

Hindin *f.* (-, -nen) hind.

hin'durch *adv.* through, throughout; across.

hi'nein *adv.* into, in. ~gehen *vws.i.* to go into; to be contained; to hold, accommodate.

hin-fahren *v.t.* to convey, carry, drive (to a place). *vws.i.* to drive to, go to; to sail along. ~fahrt *f.* journey there; voyage out. ~fallen *vws.i.* to fall down. ~fällig *a.* frail, weak; (*fig.*) untenable; ~fällig werden to fail, come to nothing. ~fort *adv.* henceforth, in future.

hing *imperf.* of hängen.

Hin-gabe *f.* surrender, abandonment; devotion. ~gang *m.* decease. ~geben *v.t. & r.* to give away; to sacrifice, devote; to indulge in. ~gebend *a.* devoted, self-sacrificing. ~gebung *f.* devotion. ~gegen *conj.* on the contrary; whereas. ~gehen *vws.i.* to go there; to pass; ~gehen lassen to let pass, wink at; ~halten *v.t.* to hold out; to

tender (money); to put off.

hinken *v.i.* to limp, hobble, go lame.

hin-länglich *a.* sufficient, adequate. ~länglichkeit *f.* sufficiency. ~legen *v.t.* to lay down, put down. *v.r.* to lie down. ~nehmen *v.t.* to take, accept; to put up with, suffer.

hinnen *adv. von* ~ away from here, from hence.

hin-raffen *v.t.* to carry off, cut off (by death). ~reichen *v.t.* to hand over, give. *v.i.* to suffice. ~reichend *a.* sufficient. ~reise *f.* journey there; voyage out. ~reißen *v.t.* to carry along; to transport, charm. ~richten *v.t.* to execute, behead. ~richtung *f.* execution. ~scheiden *vws.i.* to pass away, die. ~schlagen *vws.i.* to fall down. ~schwinden *vws.i.* to vanish, dwindle. ~sehen *v.i.* to look at. ~setzen *v.t.* to set down. *v.r.* to sit down. ~sicht *f.* respect; regard; view. ~sichtlich *adv.* with regard to. ~sinken *vws.i.* to sink down, fall, collapse. ~stellen *v.t.* to place; to put down; (*fig.*) to represent. ~strecken *v.t.* to stretch out; to kill, shoot (dead). *v.r.* to lie down.

hin'tan-setzen, ~stellen *v.t.* to set aside; to slight, neglect. ~setzung *f. mit* ~setzung regardless of. ~stehen *v.i.* to stand back.

hinten *adv.* behind, in the rear, at the back; (*naut.*) aft. ~ *adv.* from behind; (*fig.*) secretly. ~nach *adv.* behind, in the rear; afterwards. ~über *adv.* backwards, upside down.

hinter *prep. & insep. pref.* behind, back, at the back of; backwards; after; *sich bringen* to get over; to cover (distance). ~backe *f.* buttock. ~bein *n.* hind leg. ~bliebene(r) *m.* survivor; the bereaved; dependant. ~bliebenenfürsorge *f.* dependants' allowance. ~bringen *v.t.* to inform, bring charge against. ~deck *n.* (*naut.*) poop. ~drein *adv.* behind, at the end. ~einander *adv.* one after the other; *2 Tage ~einander* two days running.

hinter-e *a.* back, hind; at the back; posterior. *subst. m. (vulg.)* bottom, behind. **~fuß** *m.* hind foot. **~gedanke** *m.* mental reservation, ulterior motive. **~gehen** *v.t.* to deceive, impose on. **~grund** *m.* background. **~halt** *m.* ambush. **~hältig** *a.* insidious, malicious. **~hand** *f.* hind quarter (of horse). **~haus** *n.* back of the house, back premises. **~her** *adv.* behind; afterwards. **~kopf** *m.* back of head, occiput. **~lader** *m.* breech-loader. **~lassen** *v.t.* to leave, leave behind. *a.* posthumous. **~lassenschaft** *f.* property left; (*leg.*) estate. **~legen** *v.t.* to deposit. **~legung** *f.* deposition. **~leib** *m.* hindquarters; back; dorsum. **~list** *f.* artifice, fraud. **~listig** *a.* artful, cunning. **~mann** *m.* rear-rank man; backer. **~pfote** *f.* hind paw. **~rad** *n.* backwheel. **~rücks** *adv.* from behind; behind one's back, stealthily.

hinters = hinter das.

hinter-st(e) *a.* hindmost, last. **~steven** *m.* stern post. **~teil** *n.* hind part, back part; buttocks; stern (of ship). **~treffen** *n.* reserve, rearguard; *ins ~treffen geraten* to be handicapped; to have to take a back seat. **~treiben** *v.t.* to hinder, thwart. **~treppe** *f.* backstairs. **~treppenroman** *m.* shilling shocker. **~wäldler** *m.* backwoodsman. **~wärts** *adv.* backwards, behind. **~ziehen** *v.t.* to defraud.

hi'nüber *adv. & sep. pref.* over, across, over there, to the other side.

hi'nunter *adv. & sep. pref.* down, downwards; downstairs. **~gehen** *vws.i.* to go down. **~schauen** *v.i.* to look down. **~schlucken** *v.t.* to swallow.

Hin-weg *m.* the way there. **~weg** *adv. & sep. pref.* away, off. **~wegkommen** (über) *vws.i.* to get over. **~wegsetzen** (über)

v.r. to disregard.

Hinweis *m.* (-es, -e) indication, hint; reference; direction. **~en** *v.t. & i.* to show, refer, direct (to); to point (to).

hin-werfen *v.t.* to throw (down); to make (a remark). **~wieder(um)** *adv.* in return; again. **~ziehen** *v.t.* to draw (to), attract. *v.r.* to drag on, drag out. **~zielen** *v.i.* to aim (at); to be intended (for).

hin'zu (-tsu:) *adv. & sep. pref.* to, near; there; in addition to. **~fügen** *v.t.* to add. **~kommen** *vws.i.* to come up (to); to be added. **~ziehen** *v.t.* to add, include; to consult (specialist).

Hiobspost *f.* bad news.

Hippe *f.* (-, -n) bill-hook; scythe.

Hirn *n.* (-es, -e) brain; brains (*pl.*). **~gespinst** *n.* fancy, whim, bogy. **~hautentzündung** *f.* meningitis. **~schale** *f.* skull, cranium. **~verbrannt** *a.* (*colloq.*) crazy, mad.

Hirsch *m.* (-es, -e) stag, hart. **~fänger** *m.* hunting-knife. **~käfer** *m.* stag-beetle. **~kalb** *n.* fawn. **~keule** *f.* haunch of venison. **~kuh** *f.* hind. **~leder** *n.*, **~ledern** *a.* deer-skin, buckskin.

Hirsebrei *m.* millet gruel.

Hirt *m.* (-en, -en) herdsman, shepherd; pastor. **~enamt** *n.* pastorate. **~enbrief** *m.* pastoral letter. **~in** *f.* shepherdess.

His *n.* (*mus.*) B sharp.

hissen *v.t.* to hoist.

His'tori-ker *m.* (-kers, -ker) historian. **~sch** *a.* historical.

Hitz-e *f.* (-e) heat; (*fig.*) ardour. **~efrei** *a.* days off school because of heatwave. **~ig** *a.* hot. **~kopf** *m.* hot-headed person. **~köpfig** *a.* hot-headed. **~schlag** *m.* heat stroke.

hob *imperf. of* heben.

Hobel (-o:-) *m.* (-s, -) plane. **~bank** *f.* joiner's bench. **~n** *v.t.* to plane. **~späne** *m. pl.* shavings.

Ho'bo-e *f.* (-e, -en) oboe. **~ist** *m.* oboist.

hoch (ho:x) *a.* high, tall, lofty; deep; heavy (fine); (*fig.*) great.

sublime, noble; (*math.*) **vier ~ drei** four to the third (power); *hohes Alter* old age; *hohe See* open sea; *im hohen Norden* in the far North; *Hände ~!* hands up; **~ anrechnen** to value greatly; *es geht ~ her* things are pretty lively; **~ hinaus wollen** to be ambitious; *wenn es ~ kommt* at the most; *lebe!* long live; *leben lassen* to toast, give three cheers for. **subst** *n.* toast, cheer; (*meteor.*) high pressure.

hoch-achten *v.t.* to esteem, respect. **~achtung** *f.* esteem, respect. **~achtungsvoll** *adv.* yours faithfully, yours respectfully. **~amt** *n.* high mass. **~antenne** *f.* overhead aerial. **~bahn** *f.* elevated railway. **~bau** *m.* surface building or engineering. **~betagt** *a.* aged. **~betrieb** *m.* intense activity; hustle, bustle. **~burg** *f.* stronghold. **~deutsch** *n.* High German; standard German. **~druck** *m.* high pressure. **~ebene** *f.* table-land. **~fahrend** *a.* haughty. **~fein** *a.* superfine. **~fliegend** *a.* lofty, ambitious. **~format** *n.* upright size. **~frequenz** *f.* high frequency. **~gebirge** *n.* high mountains; Alps. **~gehen** *vns.i.* to rise, mount; (*colloq.*) to fly into a passion. **~gericht** *n.* place of execution; gallows. **~gespannt** *a.* at high tension; high, great. **~gradig** *a.* to a high degree; intense, extreme. **~halten** *v.t.* to raise; to cherish. **~haus** *n.* skyscraper. **~herzig** *a.* high-minded, magnanimous. **~konjunktur** *f.* (*commerce.*) boom. **~land** *n.* highlands; uplands. **~mut** *m.* pride, arrogance. **~mütig** *a.* proud, arrogant. **~näsig** *a.* supercilious, stuck-up. **~ofen** *m.* blast furnace. **~relief** *n.* alto-relievo. **~rot** *a.* bright red, deep red, crimson. **~schule** *f.* university, college. **~schulreife** *f.* matriculation standard. **~seefischerei** *f.* deep-sea fishing. **~selig** *a.* late, of blessed memory. **~sinnig** *a.*

high-minded. **~sommer** *m.* midsummer. **~spannung** *f.* high tension. **~spannungsanlagen** *f.pl.* high-voltage lines. **~sprache** *f.* standard speech, literary language. **~sprung** *m.* high jump. **~stämmig** *a.* tall; standard (roses). **~stand** *m.* high-water mark; (*fig.*) height, prosperity. **~stapelei** *f.* swindling. **~stapler** *m.* swindler. **~ton** *m.* high pitch; (*gram.*) chief stress. **~tourist** *m.* mountaineer; alpine climber. **~trabend** *a.* high-sounding, bombastic. **~verrat** *m.* high treason. **~wald** *m.* timber forest. **~wasser** *n.* high tide, high water; floods (*pl.*). **~wertig** *a.* of high value; first rate; (*chem.*) of high valence. **~wild** *n.* big game. **~würden** Your Reverence. Reverend Sir. **~würdig** *a.* right reverend.

höchlich *adv.* highly, exceedingly. **höchst** (høːçst) *a.* highest, utmost, extreme; maximum. *adv.* very, most, extremely; *es ist ~e Zeit* it is high time. **~beanspruchung** *f.* maximum stress. **~belastung** *f.* maximum load. **~eigen** *a.* *in ~eigener Person* in person. **~ens** *adv.* at most, at best. **~gebot** *n.* highest bid. **~geschwindigkeit** *f.* top speed; speed limit. **~grenze** *f.* limit. **~kommandierende(r)** *m.* commander-in-chief. **~leistung** *f.* maximum output; record performance. **~temperatur** *f.* peak temperature. **~wahrscheinlich** *a.* most likely.

Hochzeit (hox-) *f.* (-, -en) wedding, marriage. **~er** *m.* bridegroom. **~lich** *a.* bridal, nuptial. **~sreise** *f.* honeymoon trip.

Hocke *f.* (-, -n) heap of sheaves; (*gym.*) squat. **~n** *v.i.* to squat, crouch; (*colloq.*) to sit tight, stick to. **~r** *m.* stool. **~rgrab** *n.* prehistoric grave (with dead in crouching position).

Höcker *m.* (-s, -) protuberance, hump; knot; hunch (back). **~ig** *a.* humpy; hunchbacked.

Hode(n) *m.* & *f.* (-, -n) testicle. **~nsack** *m.* scrotum.

Hof (ho:f) *m.* (-es, ⁀e) yard; court; farm; (*astron.*) halo; *den* ⁀**machen** to pay court to. ⁀**dame** *f.* maid of honour; lady in waiting. ⁀**fähig** *a.* (*colloq.*) presentable. ⁀**haltung** *f.* royal household. ⁀**hund** *m.* watchdog. ⁀**lieferant** *m.* purveyor to royalty. ⁀**mann** *m.* courtier. ⁀**meister** *m.* steward; tutor. ⁀**rat** *m.* Privy Councillor. ⁀**schranze** *f.* courtier, flunkey. ⁀**staat** *m.* princely household; court dress. ⁀**trauer** *f.* court mourning.

Hoffart *f.* (-) haughtiness, pride.
hoffärtig *a.* haughty, arrogant.
hoff-en *v.t. & i.* to hope (for); to expect. ⁀**entlich** *adv.* I hope (so); it is to be hoped. ⁀**nung** *f.* hope; *guter* ⁀**nung** *sein* to be pregnant. ⁀**nungslos** *a.* hopeless. ⁀**nungsvoll** *a.* hopeful; promising.
ho'fieren *v.t.* to court; to flatter.
höf-isch *a.* courtly; courtier-like. ⁀**lich** *a.* a courteous, polite, civil. ⁀**lichkeit** *f.* courtesy, politeness. ⁀**ling** *m.* courtier.
Höhe *f.* (-, -n) height; altitude; latitude; hill; top, summit; amount; dearness (of price); (*mus.*) pitch; *aus der* ⁀ from on high; *auf der* ⁀ *von* in the latitude of; *auf der* ⁀ *sein* to be up to date; to be at the height of one's powers; *auf gleicher* ⁀ on a level; *in die* ⁀ *fahren* to start up; *in die* ⁀ *gehen* to go up, soar; *das ist die* ⁀ that is the limit. ⁀**nkrankheit** *f.* mountain- or air-sickness. ⁀**nkurort,** ⁀**nluftkurort** *m.* mountain health resort. ⁀**nlage** *f.* altitude. ⁀**nlinie** *f.* contour (line). ⁀**nmesser** *m.* altimeter. ⁀**nmotor** *m.* supercharged engine. ⁀**nsonne** *f.* ultra-violet lamp. ⁀**nsteuer** *n.* elevator (rudder); hydrovane. ⁀**nstrahlung** *f.* cosmic rays. ⁀**nzug** *m.* range of hills, mountain chain. ⁀**punkt** *m.* climax; (*astron.*) zenith; (*fig.*) acme.
Hoheit *f.* (-, -en) grandeur, sublimity; Highness. ⁀**sgewässer** *n.pl.* territorial waters. ⁀**svoll**

a. majestic. ⁀**szeichen** *n.* insignia; nationality marking.
Hohe-lied *n.* (*bibl.*) Song of Solomon. ⁀**priester** *m.* high priest.
höher *a.* higher; superior.
hohl *a.* hollow; concave; dull. ⁀**äugig** *a.* hollow-eyed. ⁀**kehle** *f.* hollow, groove, channel. ⁀**kugel** *f.* hollow sphere. ⁀**linse** *f.* concave lens. ⁀**maß** *n.* dry measure. ⁀**raum** *m.* hollow space, cavity. ⁀**saum** *m.* hemstitch. ⁀**schliff** *m.* hollow grinding. ⁀**spiegel** *m.* concave mirror. ⁀**weg** *m.* gorge, narrow pass; sunken road. ⁀**ziegel** *m.* hollow tile. ⁀**zirkel** *m.* spherical compasses. [HOLE]
Höhl-e (-ö:-) *f.* (-e, -en) cave; den; cavern. ⁀**enbewohner** *m.* cave-dweller, cave-man. ⁀**ung** *f.* cavity; hole; excavation.
Hohn *m.* (-es) scorn; sneer, derision, mockery; insult. ⁀**lachen** *v.i.* to jeer, deride. ⁀**sprechen** *v.i.* to flout; to defy.
höhn-en *v.t. & i.* to sneer at, jeer at. ⁀**isch** *a.* scornful, sneering.
Höker *m.* (-s, -) hawker, costermonger. ⁀**n** *v.i.* to hawk.
hold (-t) *a.* lovely, charming, gracious; propitious; *einem* ⁀ *sein* to favour a person, be kind to someone. ⁀**selig** *a.* most charming, lovely. ⁀**seligkeit** *f.* loveliness, charm.
holen *v.t.* to fetch, go for, come for; *sich* ⁀ to catch (cold, &c.); *sich Rat* ⁀ to consult.
Höll-e (-œ-) *f.* (-e, -en) hell. ⁀**enlärm** *m.* infernal noise. ⁀**enmaschine** *f.* infernal machine. ⁀**enrachen** *m.* jaws of hell. ⁀**enstein** *m.* silver nitrate. ⁀**isch** *a.* hellish, infernal.
Holler *m.* (-s, -) elder tree.
Holm[1] *m.* (-es, -e) beam; transom; spar.
Holm[2] *m.* (-es, -e) islet, holm.
holp-ern (-ȯ-) *v.i.* to jolt. ⁀**rig** *a.* rough, uneven; stumbling.
holterdie'polter *adv.* helter-skelter.
Ho'lunder *m.* (-s, -) elder tree.
Holz (-ts) *n.* (-es, ⁀er) wood; timber; thicket, copse. ⁀**apfel** *m.* crab apple. ⁀**blasinstrument**

n. wood-wind instrument. **~bock** *n.* sawing-block; (*zool.*) tick. **~fäller, ~hacker** *m.* wood-cutter. **~faser** *f.* wood fibre. **~fäule** *f.* dry-rot. **~frei** *a.* free from wood-pulp. **~frevel** *m.* damage to a forest; offence against forest laws. **~ig** *a.* woody; ligneous. **~klotz** *m.* block of wood. **~kohle** *f.* charcoal. **~pantine** *f.*, **~pantoffel** *m.* clog. **~schnitt** *m.* woodcut. **~schnitzer** *m.* wood-carver. **~stoß** *m.* wood-pile. **~weg** *m.* cart-track in wood; *auf dem ~weg sein* to be on the wrong tack, be at fault. **~wolle** *f.* wood-wool. **~wurm** *m.* wood worm; death-watch beetle. [HOLT]

holzen *v.i.* to fell wood.

hölzern (-ts-) *a.* wooden; (*fig.*) awkward.

homo'gen *a.* homogeneous.

Homöo'path (-pa:t) *m.* (-en, -en) homoeopath. **~isch** *a.* homoeopathic.

homosexu'ell *a.* homosexual.

Honig (ho:-) *m.* (-s) honey. **~mond** *m.* honeymoon. **~seim** *m.* liquid honey. **~wabe** *f.* honeycomb.

Hono'rar *n.* (-ares, -are) fee, honorarium. **~ieren** *v.t.* to honour, pay.

Honorati'oren *pl.* people of rank, notables, dignitaries.

Hopfen *m.* (-s, -) hop. **~bau** *m.* hop culture. **~stange** *f.* hop-pole; (*fig.*) lamp-post.

hopsen *v.i.* to hop, jump.

hör-bar *a.* audible. **~bild** *n.* sound picture.

horch-en (-ç-) *v.i.* to listen; to spy. **~er** *m.* listener; eavesdropper. **~gerät** *n.* detector, sound locator; intercept receiver. **~posten** *m.* listening sentry, listening post.

Horde *f.* (-, -n) horde, tribe; gang. [TURK.]

hör-en (høː-) *v.t. & i.* to hear; to listen; to obey; to attend (lecture); *London ~en* to listen in to L.; *auf den Namen A. ~en* to answer to the name of A.; *schwer ~en* to be

deaf; *von sich ~en lassen* to give news of oneself; *das läßt sich ~en* that's the thing. **~bericht** *m.* running commentary. **~ensagen** *n.* *vom ~ensagen* by hearsay. **~er** *m.* student; hearer; (*pl.*) audience; (*radio*) listener; (*tel.*) receiver. **~erschaft** *f.* audience; hearers; students. **~fehler** *m.* mistake (in hearing); misapprehension. **~folge** *f.* (*radio*) feature programme. **~gerät** *n.* hearing-aid. **~ig** *a.* bond; a slave to. **~igkeit** *f.* bondage, serfdom. **~muschel** *f.* ear-piece. **~rohr** *n.* ear-trumpet; stethoscope. **~saal** *m.* lecture-room, auditorium. **~spiel** *n.* radio play. **~weite** *f.* earshot.

Hori'zont (-ts-) *m.* (-s, -e) horizon. **~al** *a.* horizontal.

Hor'mon *n.* (-s, -e) hormone.

Horn *n.* (-es, ⸚er) horn; bugle; feeler; *sich die Hörner ablaufen* to learn by experience. **~bläser, ~ist** *m.* horn-blower, bugler. **~brille** *f.* horn-rimmed spectacles. **~haut** *f.* horny skin; cornea. **~signal** *n.* bugle call. **~vieh** *n.* horned cattle; (*fig.*) blockhead.

Hörn-chen *n.* small horn; (*cook.*) crescent. **~ern** *a.* of horn.

Hor'nisse *f.* (-, -n) hornet.

Horo'skop *n.* (-s, -e) *~ stellen* to cast a horoscope.

Horst *m.* (-es, -e) aerie; thicket. **~en** *v.i.* to build an aerie.

Hort *m.* (-es, -e) treasure, hoard; protection, refuge; protector. **~en** *v.t.* to hoard.

Hor'tensie *f.* (-, -n) hydrangea.

Hose (hoːzə) *f.* (-, -n) trousers; shorts; knickers. **~nbandorden** *m.* Order of the Garter. **~nboden** *m.* seat (of trousers). **~nklappe** *f.* nap, flap. **~nnatz** *m.* fly, flap. **~nrolle** *f.* (*theatr.*) man's part. **~nträger** *m.pl.* braces. [HOSE]

Hospi'tal (-a:l) *n.* (-s, ⸚er) hospital.

Hospi't-ant *m.* listener. **~ieren** *v.i.* to attend lectures as guest.

Hos'piz *n.* (-es, -e) hospice; hostel.

Hostie *f.* (-, -n) the Host. **~ngefäß** *n.* pyx.

Ho'tel n. (-s, -s) hotel. **~ier** m. hotel-keeper.

Hub m. (-es) lift, lifting; stroke. **~schrauber** m. helicopter.

hüben adv. on this side, on our side.

hübsch (hypſ) a. pretty, charming; nice; (colloq.) considerable.

huckepack adv. pick-a-back.

hudeln v.t. to scamp.

Huf (hu:f) m. (-es, -e) hoof. **~eisen** n. horseshoe. **~lattich** m. coltsfoot. **~nagel** m. hobnail. **~schlag** m. kick; hoofbeat. **~schmied** m. farrier. **~tier** n. hoofed animal.

Hufe f. (-, -n) hide (of land).

Hüft-bein n. hip bone. **~e** f. hip; haunch. **~gelenk** n. hip joint. **~halter** m. hip-support. **~lahm** a. having a dislocated hip.

Hügel m. (-s, -) hill, hillock, knoll. **~ig** a. hilly.

Huhn n. (-es, ⸚er) hen; pl. poultry; junges ~ chicken, pullet; ein Hühnchen zu pflücken haben to have a crow to pluck (with).

Hühner-auge n. corn. **~augen-operateur** m. chiropodist. **~augenpflaster** n. corn-plaster. **~hof** m. poultry yard. **~hund** m. pointer, setter. **~leiter** f. miniature ladder, hen-roost. **~stall** m. hen house. **~stange** f. perch, roost. **~zucht** f. poultry farming; chicken farm.

Huld (-t) f. (-) grace, favour; charm. **~igen** v.i. to pay homage to; to hold (an opinion); to indulge in. **~igung** f. homage. **~reich**, **~voll** aa. gracious, benevolent.

hülfe and **Hülfe** see **helfen** and **Hilfe**.

Hülle f. (-, -n) cover, wrapper; envelope; case; jacket; veil; (bot.) integument; sterbliche ~ dead body, remains; in ~ und Fülle in abundance. **~n** v.t. to cover, wrap; to envelop.

Hülse f. (-, -n) husk, shell, pod; case. **~nfrucht** f. legume, legumen.

hu'man (-a:n) a. humane.

~ismus m. humanism. **~istisch** a. **~istische Bildung** classical education. **~i'tär** a. humanitarian.

Hummel f. (-, -n) bumble-bee.

Hummer m. (-s, -n) lobster. **~schere** f. claw of lobster.

Hu'mor (-o:r) m. (-s) ♃ comicality, sense of humour. **~eske** f. humorous sketch. **~ist** m. humorous writer; comedian. **~istisch** a. humorous.

humpeln v.i. to limp, hobble.

Humpen m. (-s, -) bumper, tankard.

Humus m. (-) humus, mould.

Hund (-t) m. (-es, -e) dog; junger ~ puppy; auf den ~ kommen to go down in the world; mit allen ~en gehetzt sein to be wily. **~earbeit** f. hard work, drudgery. **~ehütte** f. kennel. **~ekälte** f. bitter cold. **~eleben** n. dog's life. **~emarke** f. dog licence, disk. **~emüde** a. dog-tired. **~ezwinger** m. kennel. **~sfott** m. (vulg.) cur. **~sgemein** a. very low, mean, vulgar. **~sstern** m. dog-star. **~stage** m.pl. dog-days. [HOUND]

hundert a. & subst. n. hundred; zu ~en in or by hundreds. **~er** m. hundred. **~erlei** a. of a hundred kinds. **~fach** a. hundredfold. **~jahrfeier** f. centenary. **~jährig** a. centenary, centenarian.

Hünd-in f. (-in, -innen) bitch. **~isch** a. (fig.) cringing, fawning.

Hüne (hy:-) m. (-n, -n) giant. **~ngrab** n. barrow, cairn. **~nhaft** a. gigantic.

Hunger (-ŋ-) m. (-s) hunger; ~ haben to be hungry; ~s sterben to die of hunger, starve to death. **~kur** f. fasting cure. **~leider** m. poor devil. **~lohn** m. starvation wage. **~snot** f. famine. **~tuch** n. am ~tuch nagen to starve.

hung-ern v.i. to be hungry, to hunger. **~rig** a. hungry.

Hupe (hu:-) f. (-, -n) horn. **~n** v.i. to toot, hoot.

hüpfen vv.s.i. to hop, skip, jump.

Hürde f. (-, -n) hurdle; fold, pen. **~nrennen** n. hurdle-race.

Hure (hu:-) *f.* (-, -n) prostitute; whore, harlot. **~n** *v.i.* to whore; to fornicate. **~r** *m.* whoremonger. **~rei** *f.* prostitution; fornication.

Hu'rrapatriotismus *m.* jingoism.

hurtig *a.* quick, swift. **~keit** *f.* quickness, swiftness.

Hu'sar (-za:r) *m.* (-en, -en) hussar.

huschen *vs.i.* to scurry, whisk.

hüsteln *v.i.* to cough slightly.

husten (hu:-) *v.i.* to cough. *subst. m.* cough. **~bonbon** *n.* cough lozenge. **~stillend** *a.* pectoral.

Hut¹ (hu:t) *m.* (-es, ⸗e) hat; *unter einen ~ bringen* to reconcile (conflicting opinions). **~krempe** *f.* brim. **~macher** *m.* hatter. **~schachtel** *f.* hat-box. **~schnur** *f.; das geht über die ~schnur* that's past a joke.

Hut² (hu:t) *f.* (-) protection; guard; *auf der ~ sein* to be careful.

hüt-en (hy:-) *v.t.* to guard, keep, take care of; *das Zimmer ~en* to be confined to one's room. *v.r.* to take care; to be on one's guard; to beware (of). **~er** *m.* guardian, custodian; herdsman.

Hütte (hytə) *f.* (-, -n) hut, cabin, cottage; foundry, forge, works. **~nkunde** *f.*, **~nwesen** *n.* metallurgy. **~nrauch** *m.* furnace smoke, fumes; white arsenic. **~nwart** *m.* (Alpine) hut-keeper. **~nwerk** *n.* smelting works, foundry.

hutzelig *a.* shrivelled.

Hy'äne (hyɛ:nə) *f.* (-, -n) hyena.

Hy'drat *n.* (-s, -e) hydrate.

Hy'draulik *f.* (-) hydraulics.

hy'draulisch *a.* hydraulic.

Hygi'en-e (-e:-) *f.* (-e) hygiene. **~isch** *a.* hygienic.

Hymne *f.* (-, -n) hymn.

Hy'perbel *f.* (-, -n) hyperbola; hyperbole.

Hyp'no-se (-o:zə) *f.* (-se) hypnosis. **~tisch** *a.* hypnotic. **~ti'seur** *m.* hypnotist. **~ti'sieren** *v.t.* to hypnotize.

Hypo'chond-er *m.* (-ers, -er) hypochondriac. **~rie** *f.* hypochondria.

Hypo'thek (-te:k) *f.* (-, -en) mortgage; **~** *aufnehmen* to raise money on mortgage. **~engläubiger** *m.* mortgagee. **~enschuldner** *m.* mortgagor.

Hypo'the-se (-te:zə) *f.* (-se, -sen) hypothesis. **~tisch** *a.* hypothetical.

Hyst-e'rie (-ri:) *f.* hysteria. **~erisch** (-e:-) *a.* hysterical.

I

I, i (i:) *n.* the letter I, i. *int. i bewahre! i wo!* not at all, nonsense. **~punkt** *m.* i-dot.

ich (iç) *pron.* I. *subst. n.* self; ego.

Ide'al (-a:l) *n.* (-s, -e) ideal. *a.* ideal. **~i'sieren** *v.t.* to idealize. **~'ismus** *m.* idealism. **~'ist** *m.* idealist.

I'dee (-e:) *f.* (-, -n) idea; notion; conception; thought; (*colloq.*) a little, a little bit; *eine fixe ~* a fixed idea.

Iden *pl.* Ides.

identi-fi'zieren *v.t.* to identify. **~sch** *a.* identical. **~tät** *f.* identity.

Idiosynkra'sie *f.* (-, -n) ♧ (abnormal) aversion.

Idi-'ot (-o:t) *m.* (-oten, -oten) idiot. **~o'tie** *f.* idiocy. **~'otisch** *a.* idiotic.

I'dyll *n.*, **~e** *f.* idyll. **~isch** *a.* idyllic.

Igel (i:-) *m.* (-s, -e) hedgehog. **~stellung** *f.* hedgehog defence (position).

Igno'rant *m.* (-anten, -anten) ignoramus. **~anz** *f.* ignorance. **~ieren** *v.t.* to ignore.

ihm *dat.* of *pron.* (to) him; (to) it.

ihn *acc.* of *pron.* him; it. **~en** *dat.* of *pron.* (to) them; *Ihnen* (to) you.

ihr *dat.* of *pron.* (to) her; (to) it; *pl.* you. *poss. pron. & a.* her(s); its; their(s); *Ihr* your(s). **~er** *gen.* of *pron. & a.* of her; of it; of them, of their; of you, of your. ~erseits *adv.* in her (its, their) turn; in your turn. ~esgleichen *adv.* of her (its, their) kind; like her (it, them); of your kind, like you. ~ethalben, ~etwegen, ~etwillen *adv.* on her (its, their) account; for her (its, their) sake; as far as she (it, they) is (are) concerned; on your account. ~ig *pron.* hers (its, their); yours.

illegi'tim (-ti:m) *a.* illegitimate. ~i'tät *f.* illegitimacy.

illo'yal (-ja:l) *a.* disloyal.

illumi'nieren *v.t.* to illuminate.

illu'sorisch (-zo:-) *a.* illusory.

illus'trieren *v.t.* to illustrate.

Iltis *m.* (-ses, -se) polecat.

im = in dem.

imagi'när *a.* imaginary.

Imbiß *m.* bite, snack.

imi'tieren *v.t.* to imitate.

Imker *m.* (-s, -) bee-keeper, bee-master. ~ei *f.* bee-keeping.

immateri'ell *a.* immaterial.

immatriku'lieren *v.t.* to matriculate.

Imme *f.* (-, -n) bee.

immer *adv.* always; ever; every time; *auf* ~ for ever; ~ *mehr* more and more; ~ *wieder* again and again; *wer auch* ~ whoever, whosoever; *wie auch* ~ howsoever; ~dar *adv.* for ever and ever, evermore. ~fort *adv.* continually, constantly, always. ~grün *n.* evergreen. ~hin *adv.* for all that, still, nevertheless. ~während *a.* endless, everlasting, perpetual. ~zu *adv.* all the time, continually; ~ *zu!* forward! go on!

Immo'bilien *pl.* real estate; immovables.

Immor'telle *f.* (-, -n) everlasting flower.

im'mun *a.* immune. ~i'sieren *v.t.* to render immune. ~i'tät *f.* immunity.

Impera'tiv *m.* (-s, -e) imperative.

Imperfekt *n.* (-s, -e) imperfect tense.

Imperia'lismus *m.* (-) imperialism.

imperti'nen·t *a.* impertinent, insolent. ~z *f.* impertinence.

Impf-arzt *m.* inoculator. ~en

v.t. to inoculate, vaccinate. ~stoff *m.* vaccine, lymph. ~ung *f.* inoculation, vaccination. [IMP]

Impondera'bilien *pl.* (*sci.*) imponderable substances.

impo-'nieren *v.t.* to impress. ~nierend, ~sant *aa.* impressive, imposing.

Im'port *m.* (-s, -e) imports; importation. ~e *f.* imported Havana cigar. ~ieren *v.t.* to import.

Impotenz *f.* (-) impotency.

impräg'nieren *v.t.* to impregnate.

improvi'sieren *v.t.* to improvise.

Im'puls *m.* (-es, -e) impulse. ~iv *a.* impulsive.

im'stande *adv.* able, in a position (to).

in *prep.* (*with dat.*) in; (*with acc.*) into; within.

In'angriffnahme *f.* start, setting about.

In'anspruchnahme *f.* laying claim to; being very busy.

inartiku'liert *a.* inarticulate.

inaugu'rieren *v.t.* to inaugurate.

Inbegriff *m.* (-s) embodiment, essence. ~en *adv.* including, inclusive of, included.

Inbe'trieb-nahme, ~setzung *f.* opening, starting, setting to work.

In-brunst *f.* fervour, ardour. ~brünstig *a.* fervent, ardent.

in'dem *conj.* while, whilst; by, on (doing); because, since.

in'des, in'dessen *adv.* while, meanwhile. *conj.* however, while.

Indienststellung *f.* commissioning.

Indikativ *m.* (-s, -e) indicative (mood).

indirekt *a.* indirect.

indiskret *a.* ⚕ inquisitive, prying; tactless. ~i'on *f.* inquisitiveness; tactlessness.

Individu-ali'tät *f.* individuality. ~ell *a.* individual.

Indi'vidu-um *n.* (-ums, -en) individual.

In'dizienbeweis *m.* circumstantial evidence.

industr-iali'sieren *v.t.* to industrialize. ~'ie *f.* industry. ~i'ell *a.* industrial. ~ielle(r) *m.* manufacturer, producer.

inei'nander *adv.* into each other, into one another.

in'fam (-a:m) *a.* infamous. **~ie** *f.* infamy.

In'fant *m.* (-en, -en) ♁ infante.

Infante'rie *f.* (-ie, -ien) infantry. **~ist** *m.* infantryman.

infan'til *a.* infantile.

In'farkt *n.* (-s, -e) infarct.

Infekti'onskrankheit *f.* infectious disease.

In'fel *f.* (-, -n) mitre.

Inferiori'tätskomplex *m.* inferiority complex.

infil'trieren *v.t.* to infiltrate.

Infini'tiv *m.* (-s, -e) infinitive.

infi'zieren *v.t.* to infect.

Inflati'onszeit *f.* inflation period.

Influ'enza *f.* (-) influenza, flu.

in'folge *prep.* in consequence of, as a result of, owing to. **~dessen** *adv.* because of that, hence, consequently.

infor'mieren *v.t.* to inform, to brief.

Infu'sorien *pl.* infusoria.

Ingeni'eur (-ø:r) *m.* (-s, -e) engineer. **~wesen** *n.* engineering.

Ingredi'enz *f.* (-, -en) ingredient.

In'grimm *m.* (-s) anger, wrath. **~ig** *a.* very angry, full of wrath, fierce.

Ingwer (-v-) *m.* (-s) ginger.

In'haber *m.* (-s, -) holder, possessor; proprietor, occupant.

inhaf'tieren *v.t.* to arrest, take into custody.

Inhala'ti'onsapparat *m.* inhaler. **~ieren** *v.i. & t.* to inhale.

In'halt *m.* (-s, -e) contents, content; area, extent; volume, capacity; tenor, subject, purport (of talk). **~lich** *adv.* with regard to the contents. **~sangabe** *f.* summary, contents. **~sleer** *a.* empty, meaningless. **~sreich** *a.* full of meaning; weighty; significant. **~sverzeichnis** *n.* contents, table of contents; index.

Initi'ale *f.* (-, -n) initial.

Initia'tive (-ti:va) *f.* (-) *aus eigener* ~ on one's own initiative.

inji'zieren *v.t.* to inject.

In'jurie *f.* (-n) ♁ insult, slander.

In'kasso *n.* (-s, -s) cashing.

inklu'sive *adv.* including, inclu-

ded.

inkonsequen-t *a.* ♁ inconsistent; contradictory. **~z** *f.* inconsistency; contradiction.

In'krafttreten *n.* coming into force.

Inku'nabel *f.* (-, n) early printed book; (*pl.*) incunabula.

Inland (-t) *n.* interior; inland; home.

Inländ-er *m.* (-ers, -er) native. **~isch** *a.* inland; native, indigenous, home, home-made; home-bred.

In'laut *m.* medial sound.

In'lett *n.* (-s, -e) ♁ bed-tick; ticking.

inliegend *a.* enclosed, herewith.

in'mitten *prep.* in the midst of.

inne *adv. & sep. pref.* within, in. **~haben** *v.t.* to occupy, hold, possess; to know. **~halten** *v.t.* to keep to. *v.i.* to stop; to pause. **~werden** *vws.i.* to perceive, become aware of, learn. **~wohnen** *v.i.* to dwell within, be inherent in.

innen *adv.* within, inside, in. **~architektur** *f.* interior decoration. **~ausstattung** *f.* furnishings. **~fläche, ~seite** *f.* inner surface; inside, inner side; palm (of hand). **~leben** *n.* inner life. **~minister** *m.* Home Secretary. **~politik** *f.* home policy.

inner *a.* interior, internal, inner; intrinsic. **~e(s)** *n.* inside, interior; heart, soul; *Ministerium des ~en* Home Office. **~halb** *adv. & prep.* within; inside. **~lich** *a.* inward, internal, interior; heartfelt; deep (of feelings); intrinsic. **~lichkeit** *f.* inwardness; heartiness, warmth. **~politisch** *a.* of internal policy. **~st** *a.* inmost, innermost. **~ste(s)** *n.* core, heart, intrinsic nature.

innig *a.* hearty, heartfelt; intimate. **~keit** *f.* cordiality, fervour; intimacy.

Innung *f.* (-, -en) guild, corporation.

inoffizi'ell *a.* unofficial.

inquisi'torisch *a.* inquisitorial.

ins = in das. **~besondere** *adv.* particularly, especially. **~geheim** *adv.* secretly. **~gemein**

adv. in common, generally.
~**gesamt** *adv.* all together, collectively.

Insasse *m.* (-n, -n) inmate; inhabitant; passenger.

Inschrift *f.* (-, -en) inscription, legend, caption. ~**lich** *a.* epigraphic. *adv.* by the monuments.

In'sekt (-z-) *n.* (-s, -en) insect. ~**enkunde** *f.* entomology. ~**enpulver** *n.* insect-powder.

Insel (-z-) *f.* (-, -n) island. ~**bewohner** *m.* islander.

Inse'r at *n.* (-ats, -ate) advertisement. ~**ent** *m.* advertiser. ~**ieren** *v.t. & i.* to advertise.

In'signien (-z-) *pl.* insignia.

insinu'ieren *v.t.* to insinuate.

in-sofern, ~soweit *adv.* so far, to that extent. *conjj.* in so far as, inasmuch as, according as. ~**sonderheit, ~sonders** *adv.* especially, particularly.

Insol'venz (-ts) *f.* (-) insolvency.

inspi'rieren *v.t.* to inspire.

Inspiz-i'ent *m.* stage-manager; inspector. ~**ieren** *v.t.* to inspect; to superintend.

Installa'teur (-ø:r) *m.* (-s, -e) fitter; electrician; plumber.

insta'llieren *v.t.* to introduce; to put in, install.

in'stand-halten *v.t.* to keep up, maintain. ~**haltung** *f.* upkeep, maintenance. ~**setzen** *v.t.* to do up, repair; to enable.

inständig *a.* instant, urgent, pressing, earnest.

In'stanz (-ts) *f.* (-, -en) ⚕ stage of a proceeding; court (of justice); *letzte* ~ last resort. ~**enweg** *m.* official channels; stages of appeal.

In'stinkt *m.* (-s, -e) instinct. ~**iv** *a.* instinctive.

Insti'tut (-u:t) *n.* (-s, -e) ⚕ university institute *or* laboratory; (private) school.

instru'ieren *v.t.* to instruct, to brief.

Instru'ment *n.* (-s, -e) instrument. ~**ieren** *v.t.* (*mus.*) to instrument, score.

Insu'laner *m.* (-s, -) islander.

insze'nieren *v.t.* to stage.

Inte'gralrechnung *f.* integral calculus.

integrieren *v.t.* to integrate. ~**d** *a.* integrant.

intell-ektu'ell *a.* intellectual. ~**i'gent** *a.* intelligent. ~**i'genz** *f.* ⚕ intellect; understanding, brains, cleverness; intelligentsia.

Inten'dant *m.* (-en, -en) superintendent; official in charge; (*theatr.*) manager. ~**ur** *f.* office of superintendent; commissariat.

Intensi'tät *f.* (-) intensity.

inten'siv *a.* intensive.

interess-'ant *a.* interesting. ~**e** (-'rɛsə) *n.* interest; advantage. ~**ent** *m.* interested party. ~**ieren** *v.t.* to interest. *v.r.* to be interested (in), take an interest (in).

interimistisch *a.* provisional.

in'tern *a.* internal. ~**at** *n.* boarding-school. ~**ieren** *v.t.* to intern. ~**ierung** *f.* internment. ~**ist** *m.* specialist in internal diseases.

internatio'nal *a.* international.

inter-pe'llieren *v.i.* to interpellate. ~**po'lieren** *v.t.* to interpolate. ~**pret** *m.* interpreter. ~**pre'tieren** *v.t.* to interpret. ~**punk'tieren** *v.t.* to punctuate. ~**punkti'on** *f.* punctuation. ~**punktionszeichen** *n.* punctuation mark. ~**vall** *n.* interval. ~**viewen** *v.t.* to interview.

Inthronisati'on *f.* (-) enthronement.

in'tim (-ti:m) *a.* intimate; close, familiar. ~**i'tät** *f.* intimacy; familiarity.

Intoleranz *f.* (-) intolerance.

into'nieren *v.t.* to intone.

Intri'gant *m.* (-en, -en) intriguer. *a.* ⚕ scheming, plotting, insidious.

In'trig-e *f.* (-, -en) intrigue. ~**ieren** *v.i.* to intrigue, plot.

Inva'lide (-i:də) *m.* (-n, -n) invalid. ~**nversicherung** *f.* old-age insurance.

Inven't-ar (-a:r) *n.* (-ars, -are) inventory, stock. ~**ari'sieren** *v.t.* to take stock; to catalogue. ~**ur(aufnahme)** *f.* stock-taking.

inve'st-ieren *v.t.* to invest. ~**ierung** *f.* investment.

in-wärts (-v-) *adv.* inwards.

~**wendig** *a.* inside, interior, inward. ~**wie'fern,** ~**wie'weit** *adv.* how far, to what extent, in what way.

In'zest (-tsɛst) *m.* (-es, -e) incest.

Inzucht (-ts-) *f.* (-) in-breeding.

in'zwischen (-tsvɪʃ-) *adv.* in the meantime, meanwhile.

Ion *n.* (-s, -en) ion. ~**enspaltung** *f.* ionization. ~**isieren** *v.t.* to ionize.

irden *a.* earthen.

irdisch *a.* earthly; worldly; mortal.

irgend (-t) *adv.* any; some; at all; *wenn ~ möglich* if at all possible. ~**einer,** ~**jemand,** ~**wer** *pron.* anybody; someone. ~**wann** *adv.* at some time or other. ~**wie** *adv.* anyhow; somehow. ~**wo** *adv.* anywhere; somewhere. ~**woher** *adv.* from anywhere; from some place (or other). ~**wohin** *adv.* to any place; to some place (or other).

iri'sierend *a.* iridescent.

Iro'nie (-ï:) *f.* (-) irony.

i'ronisch *a.* ironical.

irre 1. *a.* astray; wrong; confused; insane; ~ *werden an* to lose confidence in, to doubt (a person). **2.** ~**(r)** *subst. m.* madman, lunatic. **3.** *subst. f.* *in die* ~ *gehen* to go astray. ~**führen** *v.t.* to mislead; to lead astray, *gehen rws.i.* to lose one's way, go astray. ~**machen** *v.t.* to confuse, bewilder.

irren *v.i.* to err; to wander, lose one's way. *v.r.* to be mistaken, be wrong.

Irr-enanstalt *f.* lunatic asylum. ~**enarzt** *m.* alienist. ~**fahrt** *f.* wandering; vagary. ~**gang** *m.* maze, labyrinth. ~**garten** *m.* maze. ~**glaube** *m.* heresy, heterodoxy. ~**gläubig** *a.* heretical, heterodox. ~**ig** *a.* erroneous; incorrect, wrong. ~**läufer** *m.* lost letter, letter that has gone to the wrong address. ~**lehre** *f.* false doctrine, heresy. ~**licht** *n.* will-o'-the-wisp. ~**sal** *n.* error. ~**sinn** *m.* madness, insanity. ~**sinnig** *a.* mad, insane. ~**tum** *m.* error, mistake.

~**tümlich** *a.* erroneous, wrong, mistaken. *adv.* by mistake. ~**ung** *f.* error, mistake. ~**wahn** *m.* delusion. ~**weg** *m.* wrong path. ~**wisch** *m.* will-o'-the-wisp, jack-o'-lantern.

irri'tieren *v.t.* to irritate.

Ischias *f.* (-) sciatica.

Iso'l-ator, ~**ierkörper** *m.* insulator. ~**ierband** *n.* insulating tape. ~**ierbaracke** *f.* isolation hospital. ~**ieren** *v.t.* to isolate; (*electr.*) to insulate. ~**ierflasche** *f.* vacuum flask. ~**ierschicht** *f.* insulating layer. ~**ierzelle** *f.* padded cell; cell for solitary confinement.

ißt *3rd pers. sing. pres.* of **essen**.

ist *3rd pers. sing. pres.* of **sein**. ~**stärke** *f.* (*mil.*) actual strength; ~**wert** *m.* true value.

J

J, j (jɔt) *n.* the letter J, j.

ja (ja) *adv. & part.* yes; really, indeed; certainly, by all means, be sure to; ~ *sogar* even. ~**wohl** *adv.* yes, indeed, certainly. ~**wort** *n.* yes; consent.

Jacht (jaxt) *f.* (-, -en) yacht.

Jacke *f.* (-, -n) jacket, jerkin. ~**nkleid** *n.* lady's suit.

Ja'ckett (ʒ-) *n.* (-s, -s) jacket, short coat.

Jagd (ja:kt) *f.* (-, -en) pursuit, chase, hunt; hunting, shooting; *auf die* ~ *gehen* to go hunting or shooting; ~ *machen auf* to hunt, chase. ~**aufseher** *m.* gamekeeper. ~**beute** *f.* booty; quarry. ~**flieger** *m.* fighter pilot. ~**flinte** *f.* sporting-gun. ~**flugzeug** *n.* fighter plane. ~**frevel** *m.* poaching. ~**frevler** *m.* poacher. ~**geschwader** *n.* fighter squadron. ~**hund** *m.* hound; setter. ~**messer** *n.* hunting-knife. ~**schein** *m.* shooting-licence. ~**staffel** *f.* fighter formation. ~**verband** *n.* fighter unit.

jagen (ja:-) *v.t.* to chase, pursue; to hunt; ~ *aus* to turn out (of). *rws.i.* to rush, drive at full speed.

Jäger *m.* (-s, -) hunter, huntsman,

sportsman; (mil.) rifleman; (av.) fighter. ~ei f. hunting. ~latein n. sportsman's slang; tall stories.

jäh (je:) a. sudden; quick; precipitous, steep. ~lings adv. suddenly, abruptly; precipitously. ~zorn m. sudden anger, violent temper. ~zornig a. hot-tempered, irascible.

Jahr n. (-es, -e) year; in die ~ kommen to begin to grow old. ~buch n. almanac, year-book. ~elang a. (lasting) for years. ~esabschluß m. annual balance-sheet. ~eslauf m. course of the year. ~esring m. annual ring (in tree). ~estag m. anniversary. ~eswechsel m., ~eswende f. New Year; turn of the year. ~eszeit f. season. ~gang m. age-class; year of publication or issue (of periodical); year's vintage. ~hundert n. century. ~hundertfeier f. centenary, hundredth anniversary. ~hundertwende f. beginning of a new century. ~markt m. fair. ~tausend n. a thousand years, millennium. ~zehnt n. decade.

jähr-en v.r. to be a year ago (since). ~ig a. a year old, lasting a year. ~lich a. yearly, annual. ~ling m. yearling.

Jalou'sie (žaluzi:) f. (-, -n) (venetian) blind.

Jamb-us m. (-us, -en) iambus. ~isch a. iambic.

Jammer m. (-s) misery; wailing, moaning; was für ein ~! what a pity. ~lappen m. weakling; cry-baby. ~n v.i. to lament, wail, moan. v.t. (pers. & impers.) to pity, feel sorry for. ~schade adv. a thousand pities. ~tal n. vale of tears or woe. ~voll a. lamentable, piteous, wretched.

jämmerlich a. pitiable, miserable, wretched.

Janhagel m. (-s) rabble, mob.

Januar m. (-s, -e) January.

jappen, japsen v.i. to gasp, pant.

Jas'min (-mi:n) m. (-s, -e) jasmine, jessamine.

Jaspis m. (-ses, -se) jasper.

jäten (jɛ:) v.t. & i. to weed.

Jauche (-x-) f. (-, -n) liquid manure.

jauchzen (-tsən) v.i. to exult; to shout; to rejoice.

jaulen v.i. to howl.

Jazzkapelle (jats-) f. jazz band.

je adv. at all times, always; ever; ~ zwei two at a time; sie erhielten ~ ein Pfund they received a pound each; ~ nach according to; ~ nachdem according as; ~ eher, desto (or umso) besser the sooner, the better.

jedenfalls adv. at all events, in any case; however; most probably.

jeder (je:-) pron. every; each; either; any. ~mann pron. everyone, everybody. ~zeit adv. at any time, always.

jedesmal adv. every time; ~ wenn whenever, as often as, ~ig a. in each case, existing, actual.

je'doch adv. however, nevertheless, yet.

jedweder, jeglicher pron. each, every, everyone.

je her adv. von ~ at all times, from time immemorial.

Je'längerje'lieber n. honeysuckle, woodbine.

jemals adv. ever, at any time.

jemand pron. somebody, someone; irgend ~ anyone.

jen-er (je:-) pron. that, that one, the former; the other. ~seitig a. opposite, on the other side. ~seits prep. & adv. beyond, on the other side of, across, yonder. subst. n. the next world, the life to come. [YONDER]

jetz-ig (-iç) a. present, actual, (existing) nowadays. ~t adv. now, at present. ~tzeit f. the present day, these days.

jeweil-ig a. actual, at the moment, for the time being; respective. ~s adv. at times; at any given time.

Joch (jox) n. (-es, -e) yoke; (mountain) ridge; piles (of bridge); cross-beams. ~bein n. cheek-bone.

Jod (jo:t) n. (-s) iodine. ~haltig a. containing iodine. ~kali n. potassium iodide. ~tinktur f. tincture of iodine.

jod-eln v.i. to yodel. ~ler m. yodel.

Jo'hannis-beere f. red currant.

~brot *n.* carob. ~tag *m.* midsummer day. ~würmchen *n.* glow-worm.

johlen *v.i.* to howl, yell.

Jolle *f.* (-, -n) yawl, jolly-boat.

Jong'l-eur *m.* (-eurs, -eure) juggler. ~ieren *v.t. & i.* to juggle.

Joppe *f.* (-, -n) jacket, jerkin.

Jot *n.* letter j. ~a *n.* jot.

Journa'list *m.* (-en, -en) journalist.

Jubel (ju:-) *m.* (-s) rejoicing, jubilation. ~feier *f.* jubilee. ~jahr *n.* alle ~jahre einmal once in a blue moon. ~n *v.i.* to rejoice, shout with joy.

Jubi'l-ar *m.* (-ars, -are) one who celebrates his jubilee. ~äum *n.* jubilee. ~ieren *v.i.* to exult; to shout with joy.

Juchten *n.* (-s) Russia leather. [RUSS.]

Juchzer (-ts-) *m.* (-s, -) shout of joy.

juck-en *v.i. & t.* to itch; to feel itchy. *v.r.* to scratch. *subst. n.,* ~reiz *m.* itching.

Jugend (ju:-) *f.* (-) youth; young people. ~freund *m.* friend of one's youth; school-chum. ~gericht *n.* juvenile court. ~herberge *f.* youth hostel. ~lich *a.* youthful; juvenile. ~liche(r) *m. & f.* boy or girl; (*pl.*) young people. ~liebe *f.* first love, (*iron.*) calf-love; old sweetheart. ~schriften *f. pl.* books for the young. ~zeit *f.* youth, young days. [YOUTH]

Juli (ju:-) *m.* (-s, -s) July.

jung *a.* young, youthful; new, fresh. ~brunnen *m.* fountain of youth.

Junge *m.* (-en, -en) boy, lad; apprentice. *n.* young one; cub. ~nhaft *a.* boyish. ~fer *f.* girl, maid, virgin; lady's maid; *alte ~fer* old maid. ~fernfahrt *f.* (ship's) maiden voyage. ~fernkranz *m.* bridal wreath. ~fernschaft *f.* maidenhood, virginity. ~frau *f.* virgin, maid, maiden. ~fräulich *a.* maidenly, virginal. ~geselle *m.* bachelor. ~vieh *n.* young cattle.

jüng-er *a.* younger, later, junior. *subst. m.* disciple; follower; adherent. ~ferlich *a.* maidenly, coy. ~ling *m.* youth, young man. ~st *a.* youngest; latest; last; recent; *~ster Tag* judgement day, doomsday; *~stes Gericht* the last judgement. *adv.* recently, the other day, lately.

Juni (ju:-) *m.* (-s, -s) June.

Junker *m.* (-s, -) titled landowner; squire; nobleman; aristocrat.

Jupiter *m.* Jove. ~lampe *f.* (*film*) sun lamp.

Jur-a (ju:-) *pl.* ~a studieren to study law. ~ist *m.* jurist; law-student; lawyer. ~istisch *a.* legal, juridical.

just *adv.* just, exactly; just now, only just.

Jus'tiz (-ti:ts) *f.* ♁ administration of the law. ~irrtum *m.* miscarriage of justice. ~minister *m.* Minister of Justice. ~mord *m.* judicial murder. ~rat *m.* King's (Queen's) Counsel.

Jute (ju:-) *f.* (-) jute.

Ju'wel (-ve:l) *n.* (-s, -en) jewel, gem, precious stone; (*pl.*) jewellery. ~ier *m.* jeweller.

Jux (-ks) *m.* (-es, -e) lark, joke. [L]

K

(See also under C)

K, k (ka:) *n.* the letter K, k.

Ka'bale *f.* (-, -n) cabal, intrigue.

Kaba'rett *n.* (-s, -e) cabaret.

Kabel (ka:-) *n.* (-s, -) cable. ~depesche *f.* cablegram. ~n *v.i. & t.* to cable.

Kabeljau *m.* (-s, -e) cod.

Ka'bine (-bi:-) *f.* (-, -n) cabin; cubicle, bathing-box; (*av.*) cockpit.

Kabi'nett *n.* (-s, -e) cabinet; room or section (in museum). ~sfrage *f.* (*fig.*) vital question.

Kabrio'lett *n.* (-s, -e) cabriolet.

Ka'buse *f.* (-, -n) caboose; hut.

Kachel (-x-) *f.* (-, -n) glazed tile, Dutch tile. ~ofen *m.* tiled stove. [L]

Ka'daver (-da:-) *m.* (-s, -) corpse; carcass. [L]

Ka'denz f. (-, -en) cadence.

Ka'dett m. (-en, -en) cadet. **~enanstalt** f. cadet-school.

Käfer m. (-s, -) beetle. [CHAFER]

Kaff n. (-es) chaff; poor village.

Kaffee m. (-s, -s) coffee. n. café. **~grund**, **~satz** m. grounds. **~kanne** f. coffee-pot. **~kränzchen** n. ladies' coffee-party. **~mühle** f. coffee-mill, grinder. **~trichter** m. strainer.

Käfig (kε:-) m. (-s, -e) cage.

kahl a. bare; bald; naked; callow; barren; empty; poor. **~geschoren** a. close-cropped. **~heit** f. baldness; bleakness; barrenness. **~köpfig** a. bald-headed. **~schlag** m. clearing (of forest). [CALLOW]

kahmig a. mouldy.

Kahn m. (-es, ⁼e) boat; punt; barge; skiff.

Kai m. (-s, -e) quay, wharf; embankment.

Kaiser m. (-s, -) emperor. **~in** f. empress. **~lich** a. imperial. **~reich** n. empire. **~schnitt** m. Caesarean operation. **~tum** n. empire; imperial dignity. [L]

Kajak m. & n. (-s, -e) canoe.

Ka'jüte f. (-, -n) cabin; **~ erster Klasse** first-class saloon.

Kakadu m. (-s, -s) cockatoo.

Ka'kao m. (-s) cocoa.

Kakerlak m. (-en, -en) cockroach.

Kaktus m., **Kak'tee** f. (pl. Kakteen) cactus.

Kalauer m. (-s, -) pun; stale joke.

Kalb (-p) n. (-es, ⁼er) calf. **~en** v.i. to calve. **~ern** v.i. to behave foolishly. **~fleisch** n. veal. **~leder** n. calf(-leather). **~sbraten** m. roast veal. **~smilch** f. sweetbread. **~sschnitzel** n. veal cutlet.

Kal'daunen f.pl. intestines; tripe.

Ka'lender m. (-s, -) calendar, almanac. **~block** m. tear-off calendar, block-calendar.

Ka'lesche f. (-, -n) light carriage.

kal'fatern v.t. to caulk.

Kali n. (caustic) potash, potassium hydroxide. **~haltig** a. containing potash. **~nitrat**, **~salpeter** n. potassium nitrate.

Ka'liber n. (-s, -) calibre; (colloq.)

sort, kind.

Ka'lif m. (-en, -en) caliph.

Kalk m. (-s, -e) lime, calcium; gebrannter **~** quicklime; gelöschter **~** slaked lime. **~brennerei** f. lime-kiln. **~düngung** f. liming. **~erde** f. lime, calcium oxide. **~grube** f. lime-pit. **~haltig** a. containing lime, calcareous. [CHALK]

kalku'lieren v.t. to calculate.

Kalo'rie (-ri:) f. (-, -n) calorie.

kalt a. cold; frigid, indifferent; **~ machen** to kill; **~ stellen** to keep cold; (fig.) to shelve; **~er Brand** mortification. **~blütig** a. cold-blooded. **~blütler** m. cold-blooded animal. **~nadeltechnik** f. drypoint. **~schnäuzig** a. impudent. **~wasserheilkur** f. hydropathy.

Kälte f. (-) cold, coldness; frigidity, indifference. **~beständig** a. cold-resisting, anti-freezing. **~welle** f. cold spell.

kalzi'nieren v.t. to calcine. **~um** n. calcium.

kam imperf. of **kommen**.

Kam'büse f. (-, -n) caboose.

Ka'mee f. (-, -n) cameo.

Ka'mel (-e:l) n. (-s, -e) camel.

Ka'melie f. (-, -n) camellia.

Kamera f. (-, -s) camera.

Kame'rad (-ra:t) m. (-en, -en) comrade, mate, chum. **~schaft** f. comradeship, companionship, fellowship; camaraderie. **~schaftlich** a. friendly, companionable. adv. friendly, as comrades, in a spirit of camaraderie.

Ka'mille f. (-, -n) camomile.

Ka'min (-mi:n) m. (-s, -e) chimney; fire-place, fireside. **~aufsatz**, **~sims** m. mantelpiece. **~feger** m. chimney-sweep. **~vorsatz** m. fender. [CHIMNEY]

Kamm m. (-es, ⁼e) comb; crest; ridge; neck (of ox). **~garn** n. worsted (yarn). **~(m)acher** m. comb-maker.

kämmen v.t. to comb; to card (wool).

Kammer f. (-, -n) small room; chamber; board; (mil.) unit clothing stores; (med.) ventricle (of heart). **~diener** m. valet.

~frau. ~jungfer f. chambermaid; lady's maid. ~gericht n. supreme court (in Prussia). ~herr m. chamberlain; gentleman of the bedchamber. ~jäger m. destroyer of vermin. ~musik f. chamber-music. ~ton m. concert-pitch.

Kämmerer m. (-s, -) chamberlain; treasurer.

Kämpe m. (-n, -n) champion.

Kampf m. (-es, ⁼e) fight, combat, battle, conflict; struggle; strife, contest; ~ ums Dasein struggle for existence. ~bahn f. stadium, arena. ~einheit f. fighting unit. ~flieger m. fighter (plane); member of bomber crew. ~flugzeug n. bomber aircraft; fighter. ~geschwader n. fighter squadron; bomber squadron. ~hahn m. fighting cock; (fig.) pugnacious fellow. ~lust f. pugnacity; love of fighting. ~platz m. battle-field, scene of action; arena. ~spiel n. tournament; prize fight; athletic sports. ~unfähig a. disabled; ~unfähig machen to put out of action, knock out. ~wagen m. tank. [L]

kämpf-en v.i. to fight, combat, contend with; to struggle. ~er¹ m. fighter, combatant, warrior; alter ~er (pol.) old Nazi stormtrooper. ~erisch a. warlike; pugnacious.

Kampfer m. (-s) camphor.

Kämpfer² m. (-s, -) (archit.) abutment.

kampieren v.i. to camp.

Ka'nal (-a:l) m. (-s, Kanäle) canal; ditch, drain, channel; the English Channel. ~isati'on f. drainage; canalization; sewerage. ~i'sieren v.t. to drain; to canalize; to sewer.

Kanapee n. (-s, -s) sofa, settee. [GK.]

Ka'narienvogel m. canary.

Kan'dare f. (-, -n) curb, bit.

Kande'laber (-la:-) m. (-s, -) chandelier, candelabrum.

Kandi'd-at m. (-aten, -aten) candidate; applicant; probationer. ~ieren v.i. to be a candidate (for).

kan'd-ieren v.t. to candy. ~is m. candy.

Känguruh n. (-s, -s) kangaroo.

Ka'ninchen n. (-s, -) rabbit. ~bau m. rabbit-burrow. ~stall m. rabbit-hutch.

kann 1st & 3rd pers. sing. pres. of können.

Kanne f. (-, -n) can; tankard; mug; jug, pot. ~gießer m. public-house politician; tub-thumper.

kanne'lieren v.t. to channel, flute.

Kanni'bal-e (-ba:-) m. (-n, -n) cannibal. ~isch a. cannibal.

kannte imperf. of kennen.

Kanon (ka:-) m. (-s, -s) canon. ~isieren v.t. to canonize. ~tafel f. altar card.

Kano'nade f. (-, -n) cannonade.

Ka'non-e (-o:-) f. (-e, -en) cannon, gun. ~enfutter n. cannon-fodder. ~enkugel f. cannon-ball. ~enstiefel m.pl. jack-boots. ~'ier m. gunner.

Kan'tate f. (-, -n) cantata.

Kant-e f. (-e, -en) edge; corner; edging; (cloth) selvage; crust (of bread). ~el n. square ruler. ~en m. (top-)crust (of bread). ~haken m. canthook. ~ig a. edged; angular. [CANT]

kanten v.t. to furnish with edges; to square (a stone).

Kan'tine f. (-, -n) canteen; mess.

Kanto'nist m. (-en, -en) unsicherer ~ (fig.) unreliable fellow.

Kantor m. (-s, -en) precentor; organist; choir-master.

Ka'nu n. (-s, -s) canoe.

Ka'nüle f. (-, -n) cannula.

Kanzel f. (-, -n) pulpit; (av.) cockpit, turret. [L]

Kanz-lei f. (-lei, -leien) chancellery; office. ~leipapier n. foolscap. ~leistil m. official language. ~ler m. chancellor. ~list m. (chancery) clerk.

Kap n. (-s, -s) cape.

Ka'paun m. (-s, -e) capon.

Kapazi'tät f. (-, -en) capacity; authority.

Ka'pell-e f. (-e, -en) chapel; (mus.) band. ~meister m. bandmaster; conductor.

Kaper¹ m. (-s, -) pirate, freebooter; privateer. ~brief m. letter of marque. **~n** *v.t.* to capture (ship).

Kaper² *f.* (-, -n) caper.

ka'pieren *v.t.* (*colloq.*) to understand, take in.

Kapi'tal *n.* (-s, -ien) capital; **~ schlagen aus** (*fig.*) to profit by. **~(s)anlage** *f.* investment. **~i'sieren** *v.t.* to capitalize. **~ismus** *m.* capitalism. **~ist** *m.* capitalist. **~kräftig** *a.* wealthy; (*commerc.*) sound. **~steuer** *f.* capital-profit tax. **~verbrechen** *n.* capital crime.

Kapi'tän *m.* (-s, -e) captain. **~leutnant** *m.* naval lieutenant-commander; naval lieutenant.

Ka'pitel *n.* (-s, -) chapter.

Kapi'tell *n.* (-s, -e) capital.

kapitu'lieren *v.i.* to capitulate.

Kap'lan *m.* (-s, -e) **Kapläne** chaplain.

Kappe *f.* (-, -n) cap; hood, cowl; toe-piece, tip (of shoe); (*archit.*) dome; **etwas auf seine ~ nehmen** to take the responsibility for, answer for.

kappen *v.t.* to cut, sever; to lop, trim, top; to castrate.

Kapri'ole (-o:-) *f.* (-, -n) caper.

kapri'zieren *v.r.* to stick obstinately (to).

Kapsel *f.* (-, -n) capsule; case, box; cover; cap.

ka'putt *a.* broken, in pieces; ruined; done-up. [F]

Ka'puz-e *f.* (-e, -en) hood; cowl. **~iner** *m.* capuchin monk. **~inerkresse** *f.* nasturtium. [IT.]

Kara'biner *m.* (-s, -) carbine, rifle.

Ka'raffe *f.* (-, -n) carafe, decanter.

Karambol'-age (-la:ʒə) *f.* cannon; collision. **~ieren** *v.i.* to cannon; to collide.

Ka'rat (-a:t) *n.* (-s, -e) carat.

Ka'rausche *f.* (-, -n) crucian.

Kara'wane (-va:-) *f.* (-, -n) caravan.

Kar'batsche *f.* (-, -n) scourge, whip. [SLAV.]

Kar'bid (-t) *n.* (-s) carbide.

Kar'bolsäure *f.* carbolic acid.

Karbo'nade *f.* (-, -n) chop, cutlet. [F]

Kar'bunkel *m.* (-s, -) carbuncle.

Kar'dätsche *f.* (-, -n) curry-comb; carding-comb. **~n** *v.t.* to curry (horse); to card (wool).

Kardi'nal (-a:l) *m.* (-s, ~e) cardinal.

Kar-freitag (ka:r-) *m.* Good Friday. **~woche** *f.* Passion Week.

Kar'funkel *m.* (-s, -) carbuncle.

karg (-k) *a.* scanty; poor; sterile. **~en** *v.i.* to be very economical, be stingy. **~heit** *f.* parsimony; scantiness; poverty.

kärglich *a.* scanty, poor.

ka'riert *a.* checked, chequered.

Karika'tur *f.* (-, -en) caricature.

kari'kieren *v.t.* to caricature.

karm-e'sin (-zi:n) *a.* crimson. **~in** *n.* carmine.

Karne'ol *m.* (-s, -e) cornelian.

Karneval *m.* (-s, -e) carnival.

Kar'nickel *n.* (-s, -) rabbit, bunny.

Karo (ka:-) *n.* (-s, -s) square; diamonds (cards).

Ka'rosse *f.* (-, -n) state coach. **~rie** *f.* (*motor.*) body-work.

Ka'rotte *f.* (-, -n) carrot.

Karpfen *m.* (-s, -) carp.

Karre *f.* (-, -n), **Karren** *m.* (-s, -) cart; wheelbarrow; barrow. **~n** *v.t.* to cart.

Ka'rree (-re:) *n.* (-s, -s) square.

Karri'ere (-ɛra) *f.* (-, -n) career, gallop.

Kärrner *m.* (-s, -) carter; carrier.

Karst *m.* (-s, -e) mattock.

Kar'tätsche *f.* (-, -n) case-shot.

Karte *f.* (-, -n) card; (admission) ticket; menu, bill of fare; (*geogr.*) map; (*naut.*) chart; **~n legen** to tell one's fortune. **~nlegerin** *f.* fortune-teller. **~nschlägerin** *f.* fortune-teller. **~nspiel** *n.* game of cards; pack of cards. **~verkauf** *m.* sale of tickets; ticket-office. **~nvorverkauf** *m.* booking.

Kar'tei *f.* (-, -en) card-index, filing cabinet.

Kar'tell *n.* (-s, -e) cartel; ring, syndicate.

Kar'toffel *f.* (-, -n) potato. **~brei** *m.* mashed potatoes. **~käfer** *m.* Colorado beetle. [IT.]

Kar'ton (-tɔ̃) *m.* (-s, -s) cardboard; cardboard *or* pasteboard box; cartoon. **~age** *f.* boarding. **~ieren** *v.t.* to bind in boards.

Karto'thek *f.* (-, -en) card-index.

Kar'tusche *f.* (-, -n) cartridge.

Karu'ssell *n.* (-s, -e) merry-go-round, roundabout. [F]

Karzer m. (-s, -) lock-up; prison.

Kaschemme f. (sl.) low pub, dive.

Kaschmir m. (-s) cashmere.

Käs-e (kɛːzə) m. (-es, -e) cheese. **~eblatt** n. local newspaper, rag. **~eglocke** f. cheese-cover. **~en** v.i. to curdle, curd. **~ig** a. cheesy, caseous, curdy.

Kasel (-z-) f. (-, -n) chasuble.

Kase'matte f. (-, -n) casemate.

Ka'sern-e (-z-) f. (-e, -en) barracks. **~enarrest** m. confinement to barracks. **~ieren** v.t. to quarter in barracks. [IT.]

Ka'sino n. (-s, -s) officers' mess. [IT.]

Kasperletheater n. Punch and Judy show.

Kasse f. (-, -n) cash-box, till; cash-desk; counting-house; pay-office; booking-office; (theatr.) box-office; cash (in hand); gegen ~ for cash. **~narzt** m. panel doctor. **~nbote** m. bankmessenger. **~nerfolg** m. box-office success. **~nführer** m. cashier. **~nprüfer** m. auditor. **~nschein**, **~nzettel** m. receipt, bill; docket; treasury bill. **~nschrank** m. fire-proof safe. **~nsturz** m. cash-audit. [IT.]

Kasse'rolle f. (-, -n) stewpan.

Ka'ssette f. (-, -n) casket; (also archit.) coffer; (phot.) plateholder.

ka'ssier-en v.t. & i. to take in money, receive money; to dismiss; to annul. **~er** m. cashier, teller (in bank).

Kastag'nette f. (-, -n) castanet.

Kas'tanie (-taːniə) f. (-, -n) chestnut.

Kaste f. (-, -n) caste. **~ngeist** m. caste feeling.

kas'tei-en v.t. to castigate, mortify. **~ung** f. castigation, mortification.

Kas'tell n. (-s, -e) castle; citadel; fort. **~'an** m. steward.

Kasten m. (-s, ⁻) box, chest, case.

Kas'trat m. (-aten, -aten) eunuch. **~ieren** v.t. to castrate.

Kasu'ar m. (-s, -e) cassowary.

Kasu'istik f. (-) casuistry.

Kasus m. (-, -) case.

Kata'kombe f. (-, -n) catacomb.

Kata'log m. (-s, -e) catalogue, list.

~i'sieren v.t. to catalogue.

Kataly'sator m. catalyst.

Ka'tarrh m. (-s, -e) catarrh, cold.

Ka'taster m. & n. land-register.

Kata'stroph-e f. (-e, -en) catastrophe. **~al** a. catastrophic.

Kate (kaː-) f. (-, -n) cottage, hut.

Kate'ch-ese (-çeːzə) f. catechizing. **~et** m. catechist. **~ismus** m. catechism.

Kate-go'rie f. category. **~'gorisch** a. categorical.

Kater (kaː-) m. (-s, -) tom-cat; (fig.) hang-over.

Ka'theder (-teː-) n. (-s, -) chair, desk, rostrum (of lecturer, &c.). **~blüte** f. howler.

Kathe'drale (-aːlə) f. (-, -n) cathedral.

Ka'thodenstrahl m. cathode ray.

Katho'lik m. (-en, -en) Roman Catholic.

katho'lisch a. Roman Catholic. **~i'sieren** v.t. to catholicize. **~'zismus** m. Roman Catholicism.

Ka'ttun (-uːn) m. (-s, -e) cotton, calico. [ARAB.]

katz-balgen v.r. to scuffle, fight. **~buckeln** v.i. to cringe, toady. **~e** f. cat. **~enauge** n. cat's-eye; red reflector, rear light. **~enjammer** m. hang-over. **~enmusik** f. caterwauling. **~ensprung** m. (fig.) a stone's throw.

Kätzchen n. (-s, -) kitten; (bot.) catkin.

Kauderwelsch n. gibberish, nonsense.

kau-en v.t. to chew; to masticate. **~tabak** m. tobacco for chewing. **~werkzeuge** n.pl. masticators.

kauern v.i. to cower, crouch.

Kauf m. (-es, ⁻e) buying, purchase; mit in ~ nehmen to put up with; leichten ~es davonkommen to get off lightly. **~brief** m. purchase-deed. **~fahrteischiff** n. merchantman. **~haus** n. stores; warehouse. **~kraft** f. purchasing power. **~kräftig** a. able to buy, wealthy, moneyed. **~laden** m. shop, store. **~lustig** a. keen to buy; (pl.) buyers. **~mann** m. (pl.) **~leute** merchant, shopkeeper. **~männisch** a. mercantile, commercial. **~zwang**

m. obligation to buy. [CHEAP]

kaufen *v.t.* to buy, purchase.

Käuf-er *m.* (-ers, -er) buyer, purchaser. **~lich** *a.* to be bought, marketable; for sale; *(fig.)* venal, corruptible; **~lich erwerben** to buy, acquire by purchase.

Kaulquappe *f.* (-, -n) tadpole.

kaum *adv.* hardly, scarcely, barely, with difficulty; no sooner . . . (than); just; just now.

Kauti'on (-tsio:n) *f.* (-, -en) ♫ security, bail.

Kautschuk *m. & n.* (-s, -e) caoutchouc, rubber.

Kauz (-ts) *m.* (-es, ¨e) (little) owl; *(fig.)* queer fellow.

Kava'lier *m.* (-s, -e) cavalier, gentleman.

Kavalle'r-ie *f.* (-ie, -ien) cavalry. **~ist** *m.* cavalryman, trooper.

Kaviar *m.* (-s) caviare.

Kebs-e **~weib** *n.* concubine.

keck *a.* bold, daring; impudent; dashing. **~heit** *f.* boldness, audacity; pertness.

Kegel (ke:-) *m.* (-s, -) cone; ninepin, skittle; **~schieben** to play at ninepins; *mit Kind und ~* with bag and baggage. **~bahn** *f.* skittle-alley. **~förmig** *a.* conical, tapered. **~rad** *n.* *(motor.)* bevel wheel; bevel pinion. **~schnitt** *m.* conic section. **~stumpf** *m.* truncated cone.

kegeln *v.i.* to play at skittles.

Kehl-e *f.* (-e, -en) throat; gullet; *aus voller ~e* loudly. **~kopf** *m.* larynx. **~kopfbänder** *n.pl.* vocal cords. **~kopfspiegel** *m.* laryngoscope. **~kopfverschluß-laut** *m.* glottal stop. **~laut** *m.* guttural sound. **~leiste** *f.* *(archit.)* moulding.

Kehr-aus *m.* last dance. **~besen** *m.* broom.

Kehre *f.* (-, -n) turn, turning, bend; *(gym.)* flank vault.

kehr-en[1] *v.t. & i.* to sweep. **~icht** *m.* dust, rubbish. **~icht-eimer** *m.* refuse pail, dustbin.

kehr-en[2] *v.t.* to turn; *sich ~en an* to follow, mind, pay attention to. **~reim** *m.* refrain. **~seite** *f.* reverse, back; *(fig.)* drawback.

~t machen *v.i.* to face about. wheel, turn back. **~twendung** *f.* about turn.

keifen *v.i.* to scold.

Keil *m.* (-es, -e) wedge; *(tech.)* key; *(dressm.)* gusset, gore; *(typ.)* quoin; *(pl.)* *(sl.)* thrashing. **~en** *v.t.* to wedge; to win (person) over, *v.r.* *(colloq.)* to fight. **~e'rei** *f.* fight. **~hacke** *f.* pickaxe. **~kissen** *n.* wedge-shaped bolster. **~rahmen** *m.* adaptable *or* adjustable frame. **~schrift** *f.* cuneiform writing.

Keiler *m.* (-s, -) wild boar.

Keim *m.* (-es, -e) germ; embryo; *(bot.)* bud, shoot. **~blatt** *n.* cotyledon. **~frei** *a.* sterile, free from germs. **~ling** *m.* *(bot.)* embryo. **~tötend** *a.* germicidal. **~träger** *m.* *(med.)* carrier. **~zelle** *f.* germ cell.

keimen *v.i.* to germinate; to sprout, bud.

kein *a. & pron.* no, no one, not any, not a, not one, none; **~er von beiden** neither of them. **~erlei** *a.* of no sort. **~esfalls** *adv.* on no account. **~eswegs** *adv.* by no means, not at all. **~mal** *adv.* not once, never.

Keks (ke:-) *m.* (-es, -e) biscuit.

Kelch *m.* (-es, -e) cup, goblet; chalice; communion-cup; *(bot.)* calyx. **~blatt** *n.* sepal. **~glas** *n.* goblet.

Kelle *f.* (-, -n) trowel; (soup) ladle.

Keller *m.* (-s, -) cellar. **~ei** *f.* wine-cellar; cellarage. **~geschoß** *n.* basement. **~meister** *m.* cellarer; butler.

Kellner *m.* (-s, -) waiter; barman; steward (on ship). **~in** *f.* waitress; barmaid.

Kelter *f.* (-, -n) winepress. **~n** *v.t.* to tread *or* press (grapes).

Kem(e)'nate *f.* *(obs.)* bower.

kenn-en *v.t. st.* to know; to be acquainted with; **~en lernen** to get to know, become acquainted with. **~er** *m.* connoisseur. **~erschaft** *f.* connoisseurship. **~karte** *f.* identity card. **~melodie** *f.* signature tune. **~nummer** *f.* car number. **~wort** *n.* password; motto; device; *(commerc.)* code word. **~zeichen** n. characteristic; (distinguishing) mark; identity disk. **~zeichnen** v.t. to characterize; to mark. **~ziffer** f. index (of logarithm); reference number.

kennt-lich a. recognizable, distinguishable. **~nis** f. knowledge; information; *in ~nis setzen* to inform; *zur ~nis nehmen* to take notice of, take note of. **~nisreich** a. well-informed, learned.

kentern v.i.s.i. to capsize, overturn, list, heel over.

Ke'ramik f. (-, -en) ceramics; pottery.

Kerb-e f. (-e, -en) notch; nick; groove. **~en** v.t. to notch; to indent; to mill (coin). **~holz** n. tally; *viel auf dem ~holz haben* to have much to answer for. **~schnitzerei** f. chip-carving. **~tier** n. insect. [CARVE]

Kerbel m. (-s, -) chervil.

Kerker m. (-s, -) prison, jail. **~meister** m. jailer. [L]

Kerl m. (-s, -e) fellow; chap. [CHURL]

Kern m. (-es, -e) kernel, core, stone (of fruit); pith (of wood); nucleus; (*fig.*) heart; core; essence. **~bildung** f. nucleation. **~deutsch** a. thoroughly German. **~gesund** a. thoroughly healthy. **~haus** n. core. **~holz** n. heart-wood. **~ig** a. full of pips or kernels; (*fig.*) pithy. **~ladung** f. (*mil.*) main charge. **~leder** n. best leather, bend-leather. **~obst** n. stone fruit. **~punkt** m. chief point. **~schuß** m. point-blank shot. **~seife** f. best quality soap; washing soap; curd soap. **~spaltung** f. nuclear fission. **~spruch** m. pithy saying. **~truppen** f.pl. picked troops. **~verschmelzung** f. nuclear fusion.

Kerze f. (-, -n) candle; taper; (*motor.*) sparking-plug. **~ngerade** a. bolt upright. **~nhalter** m. candlestick. **~nstärke** f. candle power. [L]

keß a. (*colloq.*) pert, cheeky.

Kessel m. (-s, -) kettle; boiler; cauldron, copper; (*geogr.*) hollow,

valley; (*mil.*) crater; pocket of encircled troops. **~flicker** m. tinker. **~pauke** f. kettledrum. **~schmied** m. coppersmith, boiler-maker. **~stein** m. fur, boiler scale. **~treiben** n. battue. **~wagen** m. tanker; fuel truck.

Kette f. (-, -n) chain; necklace; warp; range (of mountains); series, train; vehicle track. **~nbruch** m. continued fraction. **~nbrücke** f. suspension bridge. **~nfaden** m. warp-thread. **~nfeier** f. *Petri ~nfeier Lammas*, (*R.C.*) St. Peter's chains. **~nglied** n. link, member. **~nhandel** m. black-marketing. **~nhemd** n., **~npanzer** m. coat of mail. **~nhund** m. watchdog. **~nlinie** f. catenary. **~nrad** n. sprocket-wheel. **~nraucher** m. chain-smoker. **~nregel** f. double rule of three. **~nwinde** f. chain jack. **~nwirkung** f. chain reaction. **~nzug** m. pull-chain.

ketten v.t. to chain, to tie (to).

Ketzer m. (-s, -) heretic. **~'ei** f. heresy. **~isch** a. heretical.

keuch-en (-ç-) v.i. to pant, puff. **~husten** m. whooping-cough. [COUGH]

Keule f. (-, -n) club; thigh; leg of veal, &c.).

keusch a. chaste, pure; modest. **~heit** f. chastity, purity; modesty. [L]

Kichererbse f. chick-pea.

kichern (-ç-) v.i. to giggle, titter.

Kiebitz m. (-es, -e) pewit, lapwing.

Kiefer[1] m. (-s, -) jaw, jawbone; (*in compounds*) maxillary.

Kiefer[2] f. (-, -n) Scotch pine or fir. **~nspanner** m. pine-beauty (moth). **~nzapfen** m. pine-cone.

Kiel[1] m. (-s, -e) quill.

Kiel[2] m. (*naut.*) keel. (-s, -e) to careen. **~holen** v.t. to careen. **~raum** m. hold. **~schwein** n. ke(e)lson. **~wasser** n. wake.

Kieme f. (-, -n) gill.

Kien m. (-es) resinous pine-wood. **~apfel** m. pine-cone. **~span** m. splinter of pine-wood.

Kiepe f. (-, -n) basket (carried on back).

Kies (-s) *m.* (-es) gravel. ~**grube** *f.* gravel-pit. ~**ig** *a.* gravelly. ~**weg** *m.* gravel path.

Kiesel *m.* (-s, -) pebble; (*chem.*) silica. ~**säure** *f.* silicic acid.

Kilo-'gramm *n.* kilogram. ~'**meter** *n.* kilometre. ~**meter-zähler** *m.* mileage recorder, hodometer, cyclometer.

Kimme *f.* (-, -n) notch; back-sight V (of rifle).

Kind (-t) *n.* (-es, -er) child; *kleines* ~ baby, infant; *von* ~ *auf* from infancy, from childhood; ~ *des* ~ doomed (man); ~ *der Liebe* illegitimate child. ~**bett** *n.* childbed. ~**bettfieber** *n.* puerperal fever. ~**heit** *f.* childhood. ~**isch** *a.* childish. ~**lich** *a.* childlike; filial. ~**skopf** *m.* stupid, fool. ~**(s)taufe** *f.* christening.

Kinder-arzt *m.* pediatrician. ~**bewahranstalt** *f.* day nursery; children's home. ~**ei** *f.* childishness; nonsense; trifle. ~**frau** *f.*, ~**fräulein** *n.*, ~**mädchen** *n.* nurse, nanny. ~**garten** *m.*, ~**hort** *m.* kindergarten, nursery school. ~**gärtnerin** *f.* kindergarten teacher. ~**lähmung** *f.* infantile paralysis; polio-(myelitis). ~**landverschickung** *f.* transportation *or* evacuation of children to the country. ~**leicht** *a.* child's play. ~**lieb** *a.* fond of children. ~**los** *a.* childless. ~**raub** *m.* kidnapping. ~**schreck** *m.* bogyman. ~**spiel** *n.* (*fig.*) trifle. ~**spott** *m.* laughing-stock. ~**stube** *f.* nursery. ~**wagen** *m.* pram. ~**zulage** *f.* child allowance.

Kindes-beine *pl. von* ~**beinen an** from infancy. ~**kind** *n.* grandchild. ~**mörder** *m.* infanticide.

Kinemato'graph *m.* (-en, -en) cinematograph.

Kinkerlitzchen *pl.* gewgaws, knickknacks.

Kinn *n.* (-es, -e) chin. ~**backen** *m.* jaw, jawbone. ~**bart** *m.* beard on the chin, imperial. ~**haken** *m.* upper cut. ~**lade** *f.* jawbone. ~**riemen** *m.* chin strap.

Kino *n.* (-s, -s) cinema, the

pictures. ~**besucher** *m.* cinema-goer, film-goer, film fan.

Kippe *f.* (-, -n) edge; brink; *auf der* ~ *stehen* (*fig.*) to hang in the balance, be in a critical position. ~**n** *v.t.* to tilt, tip up. *vvs.i.* to lose one's balance. ~**r** *m.* tipper; tipping truck *or* wagon.

Kirch-e (-ça) *f.* (-e, -en) church. ~**gang** *m.* church-going. ~**gänger** *m.* church-goer. ~**hof** *m.* churchyard. ~**lich** *a.* ecclesiastical. ~**spiel** *n.* parish. ~**turm** *m.* church steeple. ~**turmspitze** *f.* spire. ~**weihe** *f.* dedication of a church; country wake.

Kirchen-älteste(r) *m.* churchwarden, elder. ~**bann** *m.* excommunication; interdict. ~**buch** *n.* parish register. ~**diener** *m.* church officer; sacristan; sexton. ~**jahr** *n.* ecclesiastical year. ~**licht** *n.* *kein* ~ *licht sein* to be dull. ~**lied** *n.* hymn. ~**rat** *m.* church committee; consistory. ~**raub** *m.* sacrilege. ~**recht** *n.* canon law. ~**schiff** *n.* nave. ~**spaltung** *f.* schism. ~**staat** *m.* Pontifical State. ~**steuer** *f.* church-rate. ~**stuhl** *m.* pew. ~**vater** *m.* Father of the Church; (*pl.*) the (Early) Fathers.

Kirmes *f.* (*dial.*) = Kirchweihe.

kirre *a.* tame. ~**n** *v.t.* to tame; to allure.

Kirsche *f.* (-, -n) cherry.

Kissen *n.* (-s, -) cushion; pillow. ~**bezug** *m.* cushion cover; pillow-slip.

Kiste *f.* (-, -n) box, chest; packing-case.

Kitsch *m.* (-es) trash, rubbish. ~**ig** *a.* inartistic, trashy. [SKETCH]

Kitt *m.* (-es) putty; lute. ~**en** *v.t.* to cement; to glue.

Kittel *m.* (-s, -) smock; overall; child's frock; Russian blouse.

Kitz *n.*, ~**e** *f.* kid, fawn.

Kitzel *m.* (-s) tickling, tickle; itching; (*fig.*) desire. ~**n** *v.t.* to tickle. ~**ig** *a.* ticklish; difficult.

Kla'bautermann *m.* bogyman.

Kladde *f.* (-, -n) rough copy; daybook; log.

klaffen *v.i.* to yawn, gape.

kläff-en v.i. to yelp, bark; to brawl. **~er** m. yelping dog; (fig.) brawler.

Klafter f. (-, -n) fathom, cord of wood. **~holz** n. cord-wood.

klagbar a. actionable; **~ werden** to go to law, sue.

Klage (-a:-) f. (-, -n) lament, complaint; (leg.) suit, action. **~lied** n. dirge. **~mauer** f. wailing wall. **~sache** f. lawsuit, legal action. **~schrift** f. writ.

klagen (-a:-) v.i. to lament; to complain; (leg.) to go to law. v.t. to complain about.

Kläg-er (-ɛ:-) m. (-ers, -er) plaintiff. **~erisch** a. of the plaintiff. **~lich** a. lamentable, deplorable; poor, miserable, wretched.

klamm a. stiff, numb; tight; short (of money). subst. f. ravine. **~er** f. (tech.) clamp, cramp(-iron); (paper-)clip; (clothes) peg; (typ.) bracket, parenthesis. **~ern** v.t. to fasten; to clasp, clamp. v.r. to cling (to).

Klamotten f.pl. (colloq.) trash; belongings.

Klampf(e) f. (-, -n) guitar.

klang imperf. of klingen.

Klang² (-ŋ) m. (-es, ⁻e) sound; ringing (of bells). **~farbe** f. timbre. **~los** a. soundless; mute; unaccented. **~voll** a. sonorous. [CLANG]

Klappbett n. folding bed, camp-bed.

Klapp-e f. (-e, -en) flap; lid; valve; damper; hatch; (mus.) key, stop; (colloq.) mouth. **~hornvers** m. limerick. **~kragen** m. turn-down collar. **~messer** n. jack-knife. **~sitz** m. tip-up seat. **~stuhl** m. camp-stool or -chair. **~tisch** m. folding table. **~tür** f. trapdoor.

klappen v.i. to bang, rattle, clatter; (fig.) to come off, work well; zum **~ kommen** to come to a head. [CLAP]

Klapper f. (-, -n) rattle; clapper. **~dürr** a. thin as a rake. **~ig** a. rattling; (fig.) shaky, weak. **~kasten** m. old piano. **~schlange** f. rattlesnake. **~storch**

m. stork.

klappern v.i. to clatter, rattle; (of teeth) to chatter.

Klaps m. (-es, -e) smack, slap; einen **~ haben** to be balmy. **~en** v.t. to smack, slap.

klar (kla:r) a. clear; limpid; pure; plain; evident; **~ zum Gefecht** ready for action. **~heit** f. clearness; lucidity. **~legen, ~stellen** v.t. to clear up, explain.

klär-en v.t. to elucidate, explain; to purify, clarify. **~gefäß** n. clarifier. **~mittel** n. clarifying agent. **~ung** f. (fig.) elucidation.

Klari'nett-e f. (-e, -en) clarinet. **~ist** m. clarinet-player.

Klasse f. (-, -n) class, form; order, rank. **~nälteste(r)** m. top boy. **~nbewußt** a. class-conscious. **~nkampf** m. class warfare. **~nlehrer** m. class-teacher, form-master. **~nzimmer** n. class-room, form-room.

klassifi'zieren v.t. to classify.

Klass-ik f. classical art or literature; classical period. **~iker** m. classic, classical author. **~isch** a. classical.

Klatsch m. (-es, -e) smack; crack; (fig.) gossip, tittle-tattle. **~base** f. gossip. **~e** f. fly-flap; gossip. **~e'rei** f. gossip. **~haft** a. gossiping. **~maul** n. gossip. **~mohn** m., **~rose** f. wild poppy. **~naß** a. soaking wet, sopping. **~sucht** f. love of gossiping.

klatschen v.t. & i. to clap; to lash; to applaud; (fig.) to gossip, spread stories; Beifall **~** to applaud.

klauben v.t. to pick; Worte **~** to split hairs.

Klaue f. (-, -n) claw, talon; hoof; paw, jaws (of death); (colloq.) hand. **~n** v.t. (sl.) to pinch. **~nfett** n. neat's-foot oil. **~nseuche** f. foot and mouth disease.

Klaus-e f. (-e, -en) cell, hermitage; mountain pass, defile. **~ner** m. hermit, recluse. **~ur** f. cloister, monastic seclusion; examination.

Klausel f. (-, -n) clause; proviso.

Klavia'tur (-u:r) f. (-, -en) keyboard, keys.

Kla'vier (-vi:r) n. (-s, -e) piano.

~auszug *m.* pianoforte arrangement. ~spieler *m.* pianist. ~stimmer *m.* piano-tuner. [F]

kleb-en *v.t.* to stick, glue, gum, paste. *v.i.* to stick, adhere (to). ~(e)rig *a.* sticky, adhesive, glutinous. ~erolle *f.* adhesive tape. ~mittel *n.* ~stoff *m.* adhesive paste, glue. [CLEAVE]

kleckern *v.i.* to dribble, drop (one's food).

Klecks *m.* (-es, -e) blot, stain, spot. ~en *v.i.* to blot, stain; (*fig.*) to daub.

Klee *m.* (-s) clover, trefoil; shamrock. ~blatt *n.* clover leaf; (*fig.*) trio. ~salz *n.* salt of sorrel.

Kleid (-t) *n.* (-es, -er) dress, frock, gown; (*pl.*) clothes, garments. ~erablage *f.* cloak-room. ~er-bügel *m.* coat-hanger. ~erbürste *f.* clothes-brush. ~erpuppe *f.* lay figure. ~erschrank *n.* wardrobe. ~erständer *m.* hat and coat stand. ~sam *a.* becoming. ~ung *f.* dress, clothes, clothing. ~ungsstück *n.* article of clothing. [CLOTH]

kleiden *v.t.* to dress, clothe; to suit, become; to couch, express (in words).

Kleie *f.* (-) bran. ~nmehl *n.* pollard.

klein *a.* little, small, tiny, minute, diminutive; petty (*mus.*) minor; (*fig.*) narrow-minded, mean; ~ schreiben to write with small letters; ~ schneiden to cut in pieces; ~es Geld small change; im ~en in detail; von ~ auf from infancy; über ein ~es after a little while. ~arbeit *f.* petty work, finicky detail. ~bahn *f.* light railway. ~bauerngut *n.* smallholding. ~bürger *m.* petty bourgeois, little man, philistine. ~gärtner *m.* allotment holder. ~geld *n.* (small) change. ~gläubig *a.* of little faith. ~handel *m.* retail trade. ~heit *f.* littleness, smallness; pettiness, meanness. ~hirn *n.* cerebellum. ~holz *n.* sticks, firewood. ~igkeit *f.* trifle, detail, small matter. ~kaliber *n.* small-or sub-calibre. ~kinderbewahr-

anstalt *f.* day nursery; crèche. ~kram *m.* trifle; bagatelle. ~krieg *m.* guerrilla warfare. ~kunstbühne *f.* cabaret. ~laut *a.* meek, subdued, dejected. ~lich *a.* petty, paltry. ~malerei *f.* miniature painting. ~mut *m.* despondency. ~mütig *a.* despondent. ~rentner *m.* small investor. ~siedler *m.* smallholder. ~staaterei *f.* particularism. ~stadt *f.* small provincial town. ~städtisch *a.* provincial. [CLEAN]

Kleinod (-o:t) *n.* (-s, -ien) jewel, gem; treasure.

Kleister *m.* (-s) paste. ~n *v.t.* to paste.

Klemm-e *f.* (-e, -en) clamp; (*electr.*) terminal; (*fig.*) difficulty, fix. ~en *v.t.* to press, squeeze, pinch. *v.r.* to jam, squeeze. ~er *m.* eye-glasses, pince-nez. ~schraube *f.* terminal.

Klempner *m.* (-s, -) plumber. ~n *v.i.* to do plumbing.

Klepper *m.* (-s, -) nag, hack.

Kler-iker *m.* (-ikers, -iker) cleric, clergyman. ~i'sei *f.* clerical set or tribe. ~us *m.* clergy.

Klette *f.* (-, -n) bur, burdock. ~n *v.r.* to hang on (to).

kletter-n *vws.i.* to climb. ~eisen *n.* climbing iron. ~er *m.* climber. ~pflanze *f.* climber, creeper. ~rose *f.* rambler. ~stange *f.* climbing pole.

Kli'ent *m.* (-en, -en) client.

Klim-a (-i:-) *n.* (-as, -ate) climate. ~aanlage *f.* air-conditioning plant. ~ak'terium *n.* climacteric. ~'atisch *a.* climatic.

Klimbim *m.* (*colloq.*) fuss.

klimm-en *vws.i.* *st.* to climb. ~zug *m.* short-arm stretch.

klimpern *v.i.* to strum.

Klinge *f.* (-, -n) blade, sword; über die ~ springen lassen to put to the sword.

Klingel *f.* (-, -n) bell. ~beutel *m.* collection bag. ~schnur *f.* bell-rope. ~zug *m.* bell-pull.

klingeln *v.i.* to ring; to tinkle; to sound.

klingen *v.i.* *st.* to ring; to sound; to clink; ~de Münze hard cash.

mit ~*dem Spiel* with drums and fifes.

Klini-k (kli:-) *f.* (-k, -ken) ⚕ clinical hospital, nursing home. ~**sch** *a.* clinical.

Klinke *f.* (-, -n) latch; door-handle; (*electr.*) jack, socket-board. ~**n** *v.t.* to press the latch.

Klinker *m.* (-s, -) clinker, brick.

klipp *adv.* ~ *und klar* quite clear.

Klipp-e *f.* (-e, -en) cliff, crag; reef. ~**fisch** *m.* dried cod. ~**ig** *a.* craggy, rocky.

klirren *v.i.* to clink; to jingle; to clank.

Kli'sch-ee (-e:) *n.* (-ees, -ees) stereotype plate; cliché. ~**ieren** *v.t.* to stereotype. [GK.]

Klis'tier *n.* (-s, -e), ~**spritze** *f.* enema. [GK.]

Klitsch-e *f.* (-e, -en) hovel. ~**ig** *a.* doughy, sodden. ~**naß** *a.* sopping wet.

Klo'ake *f.* (-, -n) sewer, sink.

Klob-en *m.* (-ens, -en) log; block, pulley. ~**ig** *a.* clumsy; rude, heavy.

klomm *imperf.* of **klimmen**.

klopf-en *v.t. & i.* to beat; to knock, rap, tap; to break (stones). *subst. n.* beating; knocking; palpitation, throbbing. ~**er** *m.* (carpet-)beater; knocker; sounder. ~**fechter** *m.* rowdy.

Klöppel *m.* (-s, -) bobbin; drumstick; clapper, tongue (of bell). ~**n** *v.t.* to make lace. ~**spitze** *f.* pillow-lace, bone-lace.

Klöpplerin *f.* (-, -nen) lace-maker.

Klops *m.* (-es, -e) meat ball.

Klo'sett *n.* (-s, -s) W.C., toilet, lavatory. ~**papier** *n.* toilet-paper.

Kloß (-o:s) *m.* (-es, -̈e) lump, clod; (*cook.*) dumpling; meat ball.

Kloster (-o:-) *n.* (-s, -̈) monastery; nunnery, convent. ~**bruder** *m.* friar. ~**frau** *f.* nun.

klösterlich (-ö:-) *a.* monastic, conventual.

Klotz *m.* (-es, -̈e) block, log; (*fig.*) blockhead. ~**ig** *a.* heavy; enormous. [CLOT]

Klub (-p-) *m.* (-s, -s) club. ~**sessel** *m.* lounge chair, easy chair.

Klucke *f.* (-, -n) sitting hen.

Kluft *f.* (-, -̈e) chasm, abyss, gulf; ravine, gorge.

klug (klu:k) *a.* intelligent; sensible; clever; prudent; *ich werde nicht ~ aus* I can make neither head nor tail of. ~**heit** *f.* intelligence; good sense; cleverness; prudence.

klüglich *adv.* sensibly, wisely.

Klump-en *m.* (-ens, -en) lump; clod; nugget (of gold). *v.i.* to be lumpy. ~**fuß** *m.* club-foot. [CLUMP]

Klüngel *m.* (-s, -) coterie.

Klunker *m.* (-s, -) tassel; clod.

Kluppe *f.* (-, -n) pincers; die-stock.

Klüse *f.* (-, -n) hawse.

Klüver *m.* (-s, -) jib.

knabbern *v.i. & t.* to nibble, gnaw.

Knabe (-a:-) *m.* (-n, -n) boy, lad. ~**nalter** *n.* boyhood. ~**nkraut** *n.* orchis. [KNAVE]

Knäckebrot *n.* Ryvita, &c.

knack-en *v.t.* to crack; to solve (riddle). *v.i.* to break. ~**mandel** *f.* almond in the shell. ~**s** *m.* cracking noise; crack. ~**wurst** *f.* saveloy. [KNACK]

Knall *m.* (-es, -e) bang, detonation, report; crack, clap; ~ *und Fall* without warning. ~**bonbon** *m. & n.* cracker. ~**effekt** *m.* stage-effect. ~**erbse** *f.* firework cracker. ~**gas** *n.* oxyhydrogen gas. ~**rot** *a.* bright red. [KNELL]

knallen *v.i. & t.* to crack; to fire (gun); to explode, detonate; to bang.

knapp *a.* narrow, tight, close; scanty, poor; barely sufficient; concise, terse; ~ *halten* to keep (one) short; ~ *sitzen* to fit tightly, be close-fitting. ~**heit** *f.* narrowness; scantiness; conciseness.

Knapp-e *m.* (-en, -en) page, esquire; miner. ~**schaft** *f.* body of miners.

Knarr-e *f.* (-e, -en) rattle. ~**en** *v.i.* to creak, squeak; to jar.

Knaster *m.* (-s, -) tobacco; (*fig.*) old man.

knattern *v.i.* to crack; to crackle.

Knäuel *m. & n.* (-s, -) ball, hank, skein; crowd, knot.

Knauf m. (-es, "-e) knob; pommel; (*archit.*) capital.

Knauser m. (-s, -) stingy person. **~ig** a. mean, stingy. **~n** v.i. to be stingy.

knautschen v.t. to crumple, crease.

Knebel (-e:-) m. (-s, -) gag; cudgel; toggle. **~bart** m. turned-up moustache (of old soldier). **~n** v.t. to gag; (*fig.*) to suppress.

Knecht (-çt) m. (-es, -e) servant; farm-hand; slave; (*mach.*) jack. **~en** v.t. to reduce to servitude, enslave. **~isch** a. servile, menial, slavish. **~schaft** f. servitude, slavery, bondage. **~ung** f. enslavement, servitude. [KNIGHT]

kneif-en v.t. st. to pinch, nip. v.i. (*fig.*) to flinch, dodge. **~er** m. eye-glasses, pince-nez. **~zange** f. pincers; tweezers.

Kneipe f. (-, -n) tavern, public house, beer-saloon; pub. **~n** v.i. to pinch; to drink, tipple.

kneten (-e:-) v.t. to knead.

Knick m. (-es, -e) crack; break; bend (of road); quickset hedge. **~en** v.t. to bend; to crack; to break. **~erig** a. niggardly, mean. **~sm** curtsy, bob. **~sen** v.i. to curtsy.

Knie n. (-s, -e) knee; bend; *in die ~e sinken* to go down on one's knees; *übers ~ brechen* to make short work of. **~beuge** f. bend of the knee. **~fall** m. genuflexion. **~fällig** adv. upon one's knees. **~holz** n. dwarf-pine *or* -fir. **~hosen** f.pl. breeches; knickerbockers, plus-fours; shorts. **~kehle** f. hollow of the knee. **~kissen** n. hassock. **~riemen** m. shoemaker's stirrup. **~scheibe** f. knee-pan, patella. **~schützer** m.pl. knee-pads.

knie(e)n v.i. to kneel.

kniff[1] *imperf.* of kneifen.

Kniff[2] m. (-es, -e) pinch; dent, crease; trick, dodge. **~en** v.t. to fold. **~ig** a. difficult, intricate.

knipsen v.t. to punch; (*phot.*) to snap.

Knirps m. (-es, -e) little fellow; dwarf.

knirschen v.i. to crunch; to gnash.

knistern v.i. to rustle; to crackle.

knitter-n v.i. to crackle; to crumple. **~frei** a. uncrushable; crease-resisting.

knobeln (-o:-) v.i. to throw dice.

Knoblauch m. (-[s]) garlic.

Knöchel m. (-s, -) knuckle; ankle-joint.

Knochen m. (-s, -) bone. **~bau** m. frame, skeleton. **~bruch** m. fracture (of bone). **~dürr** a. all skin and bone. **~fraß** m. caries. **~gerüst** n. skeleton. **~mann** m. (*poet.*) Death. **~mehl** n. bone-meal.

knöchern a. of bone, bony.

knochig (-ç) a. bony.

Knödel m. (-s, -) dumpling.

Knoll-e f. (-e, -en) lump; (*bot.*) bulb, tuber. **~en** m. lump; protuberance. **~engewächs** n. bulbous plant. **~ig** a. knobby, bulbous. [KNOLL]

Knopf m. (-es, "-e) button; stud; knob; head. **~loch** n. button-hole.

knöpfen v.t. to button.

Knorpel m. (-s, -) cartilage; gristle. **~ig** a. gristly.

Knorr-en m. (-ens, -en) gnarled branch, tree stump. **~ig** a. gnarled.

Knosp-e f. (-e, -en) bud. **~en** v.i. to bud, sprout. **~ig** a. budding, full of buds.

Knote m. (-n, -n) (*colloq.*) cad.

Knot-en (-o:-) m. (-ens, -en) knot; node, nodule; plot (of play); (*fig.*) difficulty. v.t. to knot. **~enpunkt** m. junction; nodal point. **~enstock** m. knotted stick. **~ig** a. knotty; (*fig.*) coarse, vulgar.

Knöterich m. (-s, -e) knot-grass.

Knuff m. (-es, "-e) cuff, push. **~en** v.t. to cuff, push.

knüllen v.t. to crumple, crease.

knüpfen v.t. to tie, knot, join.

Knüppel m. (-s, -) cudgel, club; round timber; log; (policeman's) truncheon. **~damm** m. corduroy road. **~dick** a. **~dick voll** crammed full.

knurr-en v.i. to growl, grumble, snarl; to rumble. **~ig** a. growling, grumbling.

knusp-ern v.t. to nibble, crunch.
~rig a. crisp.
Knute f. (-, -n) knout.
knutschen (-u:-) v.t. to crumple;
to squeeze, cuddle.
Knüttel m. (-s, -) cudgel, club.
~vers m. doggerel.
Kobaltblau n. cobalt blue, smalt.
Koben, Kofen m. (-s, -) pigsty.
[COVE]
Kober m. (-s, -) basket, hamper.
Kobold (-t) m. (-s, -e) goblin, sprite.
Ko'bolz m. ~ schießen to turn a
somersault.
Koch (-x) m. (-es, ˙˙e) cook. ~buch
n. cookery book. ~er m. cooker.
~gelegenheit f. cooking facilities.
~geschirr n. pots and pans, cooking utensils; (mil.) mess tin. ~
löffel m. ladle. ~salz n. common
salt. ~topf m. saucepan, pot,
casserole.
kochen v.t. to cook, boil; to stew;
gekochtes Obst stewed fruit. v.i.
to be cooking, be boiling.
Köcher (-ç-) m. (-s, -) quiver.
Köchin (-ç-) f. (-, -nen) cook.
Köder (kø:-) m. (-s, -) bait; lure.
~n v.t. to bait; to lure, decoy.
Kod-ex m. (-ex, -ices) code.
~ifi'zieren v.t. to codify. ~i'zill
n. codicil.
Koffe'in (-i:n) n. (-s) caffeine.
Koffer m. (-s, -) trunk; bag,
suitcase. ~radio n. portable
wireless set. ~raum m. boot
(of car). ~zettel m. luggage tag,
label. [F]
Kognak (-ŋ-) m. (-s, -s) cognac, brandy.
Kohä'renz f. (-) coherence.
Kohäsi'on f. (-) cohesion. ~kraft
f. cohesive power.
Kohl m. (-es, -e) cabbage; (fig.)
nonsense, bosh. ~rabi m. kohl-
rabi. ~rübe f. swede (turnip).
~weißling m. cabbage butterfly.
[L]
Kohl-e f. (-e, -en) charcoal; coal;
carbon; auf ~n sitzen to be
on tenterhooks. ~enarbeiter m.
coal-miner, collier. ~enbecken
n. brazier. ~enbergwerk n.
mine, colliery. ~eneimer m.
coal-box, scuttle. ~enfaden-
lampe f. carbon-filament lamp.
~enmeiler m. charcoal-pile.

~enoxyd n. carbon monoxide.
~ensauer a. carbonate of.
~ensäure f. carbonic acid. ~en-
schiff n. collier, barge. ~en-
stoff m. carbon. ~enwasserstoff
m. hydrocarbon. ~epapier n.
carbon paper. ~ezeichnung f.
charcoal drawing. ~meise f.
great tit, titmouse. ~raben-
schwarz a. jet black.
kohlen v.i. to blacken, char; (naut.)
to coal; (fig.) to talk rubbish.
Köhler m. (-s, -) charcoal-burner.
~glaube m. blind faith.
Koitus m. (-) coition.
Koje (ko:-) f. (-, -n) cabin; berth,
bunk. [DU.]
Koka'in (-i:n) n. (-s) cocaine.
Ko'karde f. (-, -n) cockade.
ko'kett a. coquettish. ~e'rie f.
coquetry. ~ieren v.i. to flirt.
Ko'kon (-kõ:) m. (-s, -s) cocoon.
Kokos-baum m. coconut-tree.
~faser f. coir fibre. ~fett n.
coconut-oil. ~nuß f. coconut.
Koks (ko:ks) m. (-es, -e) coke.
Kolben m. (-s, -) club, mace;
flask; alembic; butt (of rifle);
(mach.) piston; soldering iron;
(bot.) spadix. ~hub m. piston
stroke. ~stange f. piston rod.
~triebwerk n. piston engine.
Kolibri m. (-s, -s) humming-bird.
Ko'lik (-i:k) f. (-, -en) colic.
Kolkrabe m. common raven.
kollatio'nieren v.t. to collate,
check.
Ko'lleg (-le:k) n. (-s, -ien) Δ
course of lectures; ~ hören to
attend univ. lectures. ~e m.
colleague. ~i'al a. as a (good)
colleague. ~ium n. council,
board; staff.
Ko'llekt-e f. (-e, -en) collection;
collect. ~iv a. collective.
Koller¹ m. (-s, -) jerkin, doublet;
collar.
Koller² m. (-s,-)staggers; (fig.)rage.
kollern v.i. to rumble; to gobble;
(fig.) to be furious. vvs.i. to roll.
kolli'dieren vvs.i. to collide.
Ko'llodium n. (-s) collodion.
Koloni'alwaren f.pl. groceries.
~händler m. grocer.
Kolo'n-ie f. (-ie, -ien) colony.
~i'sieren v.t. to colonize. ~ist

m. colonist, settler.

Ko'lonne *f.* (-, -n) column.

Kolo'phonium *n.* (-s) colophony.

Kolora'tur *f.* (-, -en) coloratura, grace(-notes).

kolo'r-ieren *v.t.* to colour. ~**it** *n.* colouring, hue, shade.

Ko'loß *m.* (Koloss-es, -e) colossus.

kolo'ssal *a.* colossal, huge. *adv.* very, extremely.

Kolpor't-ageroman *m.* penny dreadful, shocker. ~**ieren** *v.t.* to hawk, sell.

Ko'lumne *f.* (-, -n) ♁ *(typ.)* column. ~**ntitel** *m.* running title.

kombi'nieren *v.t.* to combine.

Kom'büse *f.* (-, -n) caboose; ship's galley.

Ko'met (-me:t) *m.* (-en, -en) comet.

Kom'fort (-for) *m.* (-s) ♁ luxury, ease. ~**wohnung** *f.* luxury flat.

Komi-k (-o:-) *f.* comicality; fun; humour. ~**ker** *m.* comedian, comic actor, comic author. ~**sch** *a.* comical; funny; queer, strange.

Komma *n.* (-s, -s) comma.

Komman'd-ant, -eur *m.* commander. ~**an'tur** *f.* commander's office; garrison H.Q. ~**itgesellschaft** *f.* limited company. ~**o** *n.* command; detachment; (special) squad. ~**obrücke** *f.* *(naut.)* bridge. ~**ostab** *m.* baton. ~**oturm** *m.* conning-tower, control tower.

komman'dieren *v.t. & i.* to command, order; to detach, detail.

kommen *vws.i. st.* to come; to arrive, get to; to approach, draw near; to reach; to arise, result, proceed from; to happen, take place, occur; ~ *auf* to cost; ~ *lassen* to send for; ~ *sehen* to foresee; *auf etwas* ~ to think of, to hit upon (something); *hinter etwas* ~ to discover; *um etwas* ~ to lose; *zu sich* ~ to recover one's senses; *einem gleich* ~ to equal someone; *nicht dazu* ~ to have no time to; *das kommt davon!* that's the result; *wie kommt es, daß . . . ?* how is it that . . .; ~*de Woche* next week.

Kommen't-ar (-a:r) *m.* (-ars, -are)

commentary. ~**ieren** *v.t.* to comment on.

Ko'mmers *m.* students' social gathering, drinking-bout. ~**buch** *n.* students' song-book.

Kommili'tone *m.* (-n, -n) fellow student.

Ko'mmis (-mi:) *m.* (-, -) clerk.

Kommi'ss-ar *m.* (-ars, -are) commissioner, commissary; (police) inspector. ~**arisch** *a.* provisional. ~**io'när** *m.* agent.

Ko'mmiß-brot *n.* army bread. ~**stiefel** *m.pl.* army boots.

Ko'mmode *f.* (-, -n) ♁ chest of drawers.

Kommu'nal-beamte(r) *m.* local or town official. ~**politik** *f.* municipal policy.

Kommuni'kant *m.* ♁ *(theol.)* communicant. ~**on** *f.* *(theol.)* communion. ~**zieren** *v.i.* *(theol. & phys.)* to communicate.

Kommu'n-ismus *m.* communism. ~**ist** *m.* communist. ~**istisch** *a.* communistic.

Komödi'ant *m.* (-en, -en) comedian, actor; *(fig.)* hypocrite.

Ko'mödie (-ø:-) *f.* (-, -n) comedy, play; *(fig.)* farce.

Kompa'(g)nie *f.* (-, -n) company; squadron. ~**chef** *m.* company commander. ~**geschäft** *n.* joint business, partnership.

Kompa'gnon (-jõ:) *m.* (-s, -s) partner.

Kompara'tiv (-ti:f) *m.* (-s, -e) comparative.

Kom'parse *m.* (-n, -n) dumb actor, super.

Kompaß *m.* (-sses, -sse) compass. ~**häuschen** *n.* binnacle. ~**peilung** *f.* compass bearing. ~**strich** *m.* point of the compass.

kom'plett *a.* complete; everything included.

Kom'plex *m.* (-es, -e) block (of houses); *(psych.)* complex, fixation.

Kompli'ment *n.* (-s, -e) compliment; bow.

Kom'plize (-i:tsə) *m.* (-n, -n) accomplice.

kompli'zieren *v.t.* to complicate.

Kom'plott *n.* (-s, -e) plot.

Komponente *f.* component part.

kompo-'nieren v.t. to compose. **∼ist** m. composer. **∼siti'on** f. composition.

Kom'pott n. (-s, -e) stewed fruit. [F]

Kom'pr-esse f. compress. **∼i-'mieren** v.t. to compress.

Kompro'm-iß m. (-isses, -isse) compromise. **∼i'ttieren** v.t. to compromise. v.r. to compromise oneself.

Kom'tesse f. (-, -n) (unmarried) countess.

Konden's-ator m. (-ators, -atoren) condenser. **∼ieren** v.t. to condense. **∼milch** f. tinned milk.

Konditio'nalsatz m. conditional clause.

Kon'ditor (-di:-) m. (-s, -en) pastry-cook, confectioner. **∼ei** f. confectioner's, café. **∼waren** f.pl. cakes, tea-bread, pastries; confectionery. [L]

Kondo'l-enzbesuch m. visit of condolence. **∼ieren** v.i. to condole with, express one's sympathy with.

Konduk'teur m. (-s, -e) ⚠ (bus-or tram-)conductor.

Kon'fekt n. (-s, -e) sweets, chocolates, confectionery.

Konfekti'on (-o:n) f. ready-made clothes. **∼är** m. clothier, outfitter.

Konfe'r-enz f. (-enz, -enzen) conference. **∼ieren** v.i. ⚠ to meet for discussion, confer.

Konfessi'on (-o:n) f. (-, -en) confession (of relig. faith), creed. **∼slos** a. undenominational, unattached.

Konfir'mand (-t) m. (-en, -en) candidate for confirmation.

konfir'mieren v.t. (eccl.) to confirm.

konfis'zieren v.t. to confiscate.

Konfi'türen f.pl. preserves; confectionery, sweets.

Kon'flikt m. (-es, -e) conflict.

konform adv. in conformity (with); **∼ gehen** to be in agreement (with).

konfron'tieren v.t. to confront.

kon'fus (-u:s) a. confused, muddled.

Kon'gre-ß m. (-sses, -sse) congress.

kongru-'ent a. congruent. **∼'enz** f. congruity. **∼'ieren** v.i. to

coincide; to agree.

König (kø:niç) m. (-s, -e) king. **∼in** f. queen. **∼lich** a. royal, regal; kingly, queenly. **∼reich** n. kingdom, realm. **∼skerze** f. mullein. **∼tum** n. royalty, kingship.

konisch a. conical.

Konjugati'on f. (-, -en) conjugation.

konju'gieren v.t. to conjugate.

Konjunktiv m. (-s, -e) subjunctive (mood).

Konjunk'tur f. (-, -en) conjuncture; boom. **∼forschung** f. market research. **∼gewinn** m. market profit. **∼schwankung** f. market vacillation.

kon'kav a. concave.

kon'kret a. ⚠ concrete = real.

Konkubi'nat n. (-s, -e) concubinage.

Konku'rr-ent m. (-enten, -enten) ⚠ competitor, rival. **∼enz** f. competition; opposition. **∼enzkampf** m. (sport.) event. **∼enzlos** a. unrivalled; exclusive. **∼enzunternehmen** n. rival business concern. **∼ieren** v.i. to compete (with).

Kon'kurs m. (-es, -e) bankruptcy; failure. **∼erklärung** f. declaration of insolvency. **∼masse** f. bankrupt's estate. **∼verfahren** n. proceedings in bankruptcy. **∼verwalter** m. liquidator, receiver in bankruptcy.

können (-œ-) irreg. v.t. to know, understand; Deutsch ∼ to know German. v.i. to be able, be capable (of), be in a position (to); to be permitted (to); ich kann I can; I may; das kann sein that may be; das kann nicht sein that is impossible; mehr ∼ to be done (up), be exhausted; er kann nichts dafür he can't help it. subst. n. ability, power, faculty; knowledge.

konse'quen-t a. ⚠ consistent. **∼z** f. consistency; consequence; result; **∼zen ziehen** to draw conclusions.

konserv-a'tiv a. conservative. **∼a'torium** n. academy of music.

Kon'serve f. (-e, -en) tinned food.

~enbüchse f. tin. ~ieren v.t. to preserve, conserve.

Konsis'torium n. (-s, . . . orien) consistory.

konsoli'dieren v.t. to consolidate.

Konso'nant m. (-en, -en) consonant.

Kon'sort-en m.pl. associates; accomplices. ~ium n. group; syndicate.

konspi'rieren v.i. to conspire, plot.

konsta'tieren v.t. to confirm; to state.

konster'niert a. taken aback.

konstitu'ieren v.t. to constitute. ~tio'nell a. constitutional.

konstru'ieren v.t. to construct; to design. ~k'teur m. constructor, designer.

Konsul (-z-) m. (-s, -n) consul. ~at n. consulate. ~ent m. counsel, advocate.

konsul'tieren v.t. to consult.

Kon'sum (-zu:m) m. (-s) consumption, consuming. ~ent m. consumer. ~güter pl. consumer goods, ~ieren v.t. to consume. ~verein n. Co-operative Society.

Kon'takt m. (-s, -e) contact. ~fähig a. able to communicate. ~schlüssel m. ignition key. ~schnur f. flex. ~stöpsel m. (contact) plug.

Konter-admiral m. rear-admiral. ~bande f. contraband. ~tanz m. square dance, quadrille.

Konterfei n. (-s, -e) portrait.

Konti'nent m. (-s, -e) continent. Kontinui'tät f. (-) continuity.

Konto n. (-s, Konten) account. ~auszug m. extract or statement of account. ~korrent n. current account.

Kon'tor (-o:r) n. (-s, -e) office. ~ist m. clerk. [F]

Kontra-baß m. double bass. ~hent m. contracting party. ~punkt m. counterpoint.

Kon'trakt m. (-s, -e) contract, bargain. ~brüchig a. breaking a contract. ~lich a. by contract.

Kon'trast m. (-es, -e) contrast. ~ieren v.t. & i. to contrast.

Kon'troll-e f. (-e, -en) control, examination, supervision. ~abschnitt m. counterfoil. ~eur

m. controller. ~ieren v.t. to control, check; (commerc.) to audit. ~uhr f. control-clock.

Kontroverse f. controversy.

Kon'tur (-u:r) f. (-, -en) contour.

Konventio'nalstrafe f. demurrage; penalty for breach of contract.

konventio'nell a. conventional.

konver'gieren v.i. to converge.

Konversati'onslexikon n. encyclopedia.

Konver'tit m. (-en, -en) convert.

Konvo'lut n. (-s, -e) set of pamphlets; lot.

Konzentr-ati'onslager n. concentration-camp. ~ieren v.t. to concentrate. ~isch a. concentric.

Kon'zept n. (-s, -e) rough copy, draft; aus dem ~ bringen to put out, disconcert. ~papier n. scribbling paper.

Kon'zern n. (-s, -e) (commerc.) combine.

Kon'zert (-ts-) n. (-s, -e) concert. ~flügel m. grand piano. ~ieren v.i. to give a concert.

Konzessi'on f. (-, -en) concession; licence. ~iert a. licensed.

Kon'zil n. (-s, -e) (church) council.

konzi'pieren v.t. to draft, plan.

koordinieren v.t. to co-ordinate.

Köper m. (-s) twill.

Kopf m. (-es, ̈-e) head; top, crown; (fig.) brains; thinker, talented man; (typ.) title, heading; ~ an ~ closely packed; einem den ~ waschen to give a person a dressing-down; sich den ~ zerbrechen to rack one's brains; auf den ~, pro ~ each, a head; auf den ~ gefallen sein to be no fool; auf den ~ zusagen to tell (a person) to his face; auf den ~ stellen to turn upside down; aus dem ~ by heart; sich etwas aus dem ~ schlagen to dismiss something from one's mind; im ~ behalten to remember; sich in den ~ setzen to take into one's head; über den ~ wachsen to be too much (for); es geht um den ~ to be in danger of one's life; vor den ~ stoßen to hurt, offend. [CUP]

Kopf-arbeit f. brain work. ~bahnhof *m.* terminal. ~bedeckung *f.* head-dress, headgear. ~ende *n.* head (of bed). ~hänger *m.* spiritless person. ~haut *f.* scalp. ~hörer *m.* ear-phones. ~kissen *n.* pillow. ~länge *f.* head. ~los *a.* headless; confused. ~nicken *n.* nod. ~rechnen *n.* mental arithmetic. ~salat *m.* garden or cabbage lettuce. ~scheu *a.* shy, timid. ~schmerz *m.*, ~weh *n.* headache. ~schützer *m.* head-protector; Balaclava helmet. ~sprung *m.* header. ~steinpflaster *n.* cobbled pavement. ~steuer *f.* poll-tax. ~tuch *n.* head-shawl, scarf, kerchief. ~über *adv.* head foremost. ~zahl *f.* number of persons. ~zerbrechen *n.* cogitation, rumination.

köpfen *v.t.* to behead.

Ko'p·ie (-i:) *f.* (-ie, -ien) ⚑ copy = reproduction, imitation; transcript. ~ieren *v.t.* to copy. ~ierstift *m.* copying-ink or indelible pencil. ~ist *m.* copyist.

Koppel (-, -n) couple, leash; enclosure, paddock. *n.* (*mil.*) belt. ~n *v.t.* to couple; to link. ~ung *f.* coupling.

kopu'lieren *v.t.* to marry, unite.

Ko'ralle *f.* (-, -n) coral. ~nbank *f.* coral reef. ~nfischer *m.* coral-fisher.

Korb *m.* (-p) (-es, ¨e) basket, hamper; (*fig.*) refusal; *Hahn im ~e sein* to be cock of the walk. ~flasche *f.* carboy. ~flechter *m.* basket-maker. ~möbel *n.pl.* wicker-furniture. ~weide *f.* osier. [L]

Kordel *f.* (-, -n) cord; twine.

Ko'rinthe *f.* (-, -n) currant.

Kork *m.* (-es, -e) cork. ~en *v.t.* to cork. *a.* (of) cork. ~zieher *m.* corkscrew.

Korn *n.* (-es, ¨er) corn; grain; sight (of gun); standard (of metal); type of brandy; *aufs ~ nehmen* to aim at. ~ähre *f.* ear of corn. ~blume *f.* cornflower. ~branntwein *m.* whisky. ~kammer *f.* granary.

körn·en *v.t.* to granulate; to grain (leather). ~ig *a.* granular.

Kor'nett *m.* (-s, -e) cornet, standard-bearer. *n.* (*mus.*) cornet.

Körper *m.* (-s, -) body; (*phys.*) substance, compound; solid. ~bau *m.* bodily structure; build. ~fülle *f.* corpulence. ~größe *f.* stature, size. ~kraft *f.* physical strength. ~lich *a.* physical; bodily, corporeal. ~los *a.* incorporeal. ~maß *n.* cubic measure. ~pflege *f.* physical culture. ~schaft *f.* corporation; body. ~schulung *f.* physical training or culture. ~(teil)chen *n.* particle. ~verletzung *f.* bodily injury. ~wärme *f.* body heat. [CORPSE]

Korpo'ralschaft *f.* section, squad.

Korps (ko:r) *n.* corps. ~geist *m.* team spirit.

Korpu'lenz *f.* (-) corpulence.

ko'rrekt *a.* correct. ~i'onsanstalt *f.* remand home. ~or *m.* press-corrector, proof-reader. ~ur *f.* correction; proof-(sheet). ~urabzug, ~urbogen *m.* proof-sheet.

Korrespon'd·enz *f.* (-enz, -enzen) correspondence. ~enzbüro *n.* news or press agency. ~ieren *v.i.* to correspond.

Korridor *m.* (-s, -e) corridor.

korri'gieren *v.t.* to correct.

korrum'pieren *v.t.* to corrupt.

Kor'sar *m.* (-en, -en) pirate, corsair.

Kor'sett *n.* (-s, -e) corset. ~stange *f.* bone.

Kory'phäe (-fɛ:ə) *m.* (-n, -n) celebrity, star.

koscher (ko:-) *a.* kosher.

kose-n (ko:-) *v.t.* to caress, fondle. *v.i.* to make love, talk amorously. ~name *m.* pet name. [L]

Kosinus *m.* (-) cosine.

Kos'met·ik *f.*, ~isch *a.* cosmetic.

kosm·isch *a.* cosmic. ~opo'lit *m.* cosmopolitan. ~os *m.* cosmos.

Kost *f.* (-) food, victuals, diet; board; *in ~ sein bei* to board with. ~frei *a.* with free board. ~gänger *m.* boarder. ~geld *n.* board, board-wages. ~happen *m.*, ~probe *f.* dainty morsel; taste. ~verächter *m.* *kein ~ sein* to enjoy one's food.

kost·bar *a.* precious, valuable;

costly. **~barkeit** f. preciousness; object of value. **~spielig** a. costly, expensive.

Kosten[1] pl. cost(s), expense(s); **auf** ~ at the expense of; **auf seine ~ kommen** to be satisfied (with a deal). **~anschlag** m. estimate. **~los** a. free, for nothing. **~pflichtig** a. liable for the costs. **~punkt** m. expenses.

kosten[2] v.t. to cost; to require, take.

kosten[3] v.t. to try; to taste.

köstlich a. precious, valuable; tasty, delicious; . excellent, capital.

Kostüm (-ty:m) n. (-s, -e) dress; costume, coat and skirt; fancy-dress. **~fest** n. fancy-dress ball. **~ieren** v.t. to dress; to dress up, disguise. **~probe** f. dress rehearsal.

Kot (ko:t) m. (-es) mud, muck, dirt; excrements, faeces. **~blech** n., **~flügel** m. mudguard, wing, fender. **~ig** a. dirty, muddy.

Ko'tau m. (-s, -s) kotow.

Kote'lett n. (-s, -e) cutlet; chop.

Köter (-ø:-) m. (-s, -) dog; cur.

kotzen v.i. & t. (vulg.) to vomit.

Krabbe f. (-, -n) crab; shrimp.

krabbeln vws.i. to crawl, creep. v.t. to scratch, tickle.

Krach (-ax) m. (-es, -e) crash; noise, din; quarrel; scene; mit Ach und ~ with difficulty, only just. **~en** v.i. to crack; to crash; to burst; to roar.

krächzen (-çts-) v.i. to croak; to caw.

kraft[1] prep. by virtue of, on the strength of.

Kraft[2] f. (-, ¨e) strength; power; force; energy, vigour; faculty; efficacy; (commerc.) worker, professional; nach besten Kräften to the best of one's ability; zu Kräften kommen to regain one's strength; in ~ treten to come into force; außer ~ setzen to annul, abrogate. **~anlage** f. power plant, power station. **~aufwand** m. expenditure of force, exertion, effort. **~ausdruck** m. strong language. **~brühe** f.

clear soup; beef-tea. **~droschke** f. taxi. **~ersparnis** f. saving of strength; economy. **~fahrer** m. motorist; driver. **~fahrzeug** n. motor vehicle. **~feld** n. (phys.) field of force. **~lastwagen** m. motor lorry. **~los** a. weak, feeble, powerless. **~messer** m. dynamometer. **~probe** f. trial of strength. **~rad** n. motor bicycle. **~stoff** m. liquid fuel; petrol. **~verkehr** m. motor-traffic. **~voll** a. vigorous, powerful; pithy. **~wagen** m. motor-car. **~kolonne** f. mechanized supply column. **~werk** n. power station. [CRAFT]

kräftig a. strong, powerful, robust; nourishing; forcible. **~en** v.t. to strengthen, invigorate; to harden, steel. **~ung** f. strengthening.

Kragen (-a:-) m. (-s, -) collar; cape; beim ~ nehmen to collar; ihm den ~ kosten, an den ~ gehen to cost him his life. **~knopf** m. stud. **~spiegel** m. facing, collar patch. **~weite** f. collar size.

Kragstein m. corbel.

Krähe f. (-, -n) crow, rook. **~n** v.i. to crow.

Kra'keel (-ke:l) m. (-s) brawl, squabble, quarrel. **~en** v.i. to brawl; to kick up a row. **~er** m. brawler, rowdy.

Kralle f. (-, -n) claw, talon. **~n** v.r. to claw.

Kram (-a:m) m. (-es) small wares; rubbish, stuff, lumber; (colloq.) affair, business. **~en** v.i. to rummage. **~laden** m. small shop.

Krämer m. (-s, -) small tradesman, grocer. **~seele** f. petty spirit.

Krammetsvogel m. fieldfare.

Krampe f. (-, -n) cramp(-iron), staple.

Krampf m. (-es, ¨e) cramp, spasm; fit. **~ader** f. varicose vein. **~en** v.t. & r. to clench, contract. **~haft** a. convulsive, spasmodic; (fig.) frantic, desperate. **~stillend** a. sedative.

Kran (-a:n) m. (-es, ¨e) crane; hoist.

Kranich (-a:-) *m.* (-s, -e) crane.

krank *a.* ill, sick; ~ *werden* to be taken ill; *sich* ~ *lachen* to split one's sides (with laughter). ~enauto *n.* motor ambulance. ~engeld *n.* sick pay. ~enhaus *n.* hospital. ~enkasse *f.* (National) Health Insurance. ~enlager *n.* sick-bed. ~enpflege *f.* nursing. ~enschein *m.* doctor's certificate. ~enschwester *f.* nurse. ~enstube *f.* sick-room, ward; (*mil.*) sick-bay. ~enträger *m.* stretcher-bearer. ~enwagen *m.* ambulance. ~enwärter *m.* male nurse, attendant; hospital orderly. ~haft *a.* morbid, pathological. ~heit *f.* illness, disease, malady. ~heitserreger *m.* excitant of disease, virus. ~heitshalber *adv.* owing to illness. ~heitsherd *m.* seat of disease.

Kränk-e *f.* (-e) epilepsy. ~eln *v.i.* to be sickly; to be in poor health. ~en *v.t.* to vex, provoke; to offend. *v.r.* to fret, worry. ~lich *a.* sickly. ~ung *f.* insult; offence.

kranken *v.i.* to be ill (with), suffer (from); to lack.

Kranz (-ts) *m.* (-es, ⁓e) wreath, garland. ~gesims *n.* cornice. ~jungfer *f.* bridesmaid. ~spende *f.* funeral wreath.

Kränzchen *n.* (-s, -) small wreath; (*fig.*) ladies' meeting *or* coffee-party.

kränzen *v.t.* to wreathe, crown.

Krapfen *m.* (-s, -) fritter.

Krapp *m.* (-es) madder.

kraß *a.* gross, crass; strong, great.

Krater (-a:-) *m.* (-s, -) crater.

Kratz-bürste *f.* scrubbing-brush; (*fig.*) cross-patch. ~bürstig *a.* irritable, cross; gruff. ~eisen *n.* scraper. ~en *v.t. & i.* to scratch, scrape. ~fuß *m.* bow.

Krätz-e *f.* (-e) itch. ~er *m.* bad wine. ~ig *a.* itchy; mangy.

kraue(l)n *v.t.* to rub gently.

kraus *a.* curly, crinkled, crisp; *die Stirne* ~ *ziehen* to knit one's brow. ~e *f.* ruffle, frill. ~haarig *a.* curly-haired. ~kopf *m.* curly head.

kräuseln (-z-) *v.t.* to curl; to goffer, crimp; to ruffle.

Kraut *n.* (-es, ⁓er) herb; plant; cabbage. **Kräuter-buch** *n.* herbal. ~käse *m.* green cheese. ~tee *m.* infusion of herbs.

Kra'wall *m.* (-s, -e) uproar, row, riot.

Kra'watte *f.* (-, -n) tie, cravat.

kraxeln *vws.i.* (*dial.*) to climb, clamber up.

Krea'tur (-tu:r) *f.* (-, -en) creature.

Krebs (-e:ps) *m.* (-es, -e) crab, crayfish; cancer. ~geschwür *n.* cancerous *or* malignant growth. ~schaden *m.* cancerous sore; (*fig.*) deep-seated evil. ~schere *f.* claw of crayfish.

Kre'denz *f.* sideboard. ~en *v.t.* to serve, offer, present.

Kre'dit (-i:t) *m.* (-s, -e) credit; trust, reputation. ~brief *m.* letter of credit. ~fähig *a.* solvent, sound. ~genossenschaft *f.* mutual loan society. ~ieren *v.t.* to credit. ~iv *n.* credentials; full power. ~seite *f.* creditor's side.

Kreide *f.* (-e, -en) chalk. ~ehaltig *a.* containing chalk, cretaceous. ~eweiß *a.* white as a sheet. ~ig *a.* chalky, cretaceous. [L]

Kreis (-s) *m.* (-es, -e) circle, district, circuit; orbit; (*fig.*) sphere; (*pl.*) set, class; *einen* ~ *ziehen* to describe a circle; *sich im* ~ *drehen* to rotate. ~abschnitt *m.* segment. ~ausschnitt *m.* sector. ~bahn *f.* circular path, orbit. ~förmig *a.* circular, round. ~lauf *m.* circulation; course; revolution, rotation. ~laufstörung *f.* circulatory disturbances. ~säge *f.* circular saw. ~stadt *f.* county town. ~umfang *m.* circumference, periphery.

kreischen *v.i.* to shriek, scream.

Kreisel (-z-) *m.* (-s, -) top; gyroscope. ~pumpe *f.* centrifugal pump.

kreisen (-z-) *v.i.* to revolve; to circle round; to circulate.

kreißen (-s-) *v.i.* to be in labour.

Krema'torium *n.* (-s, ... rien) crematorium.

Krempe f. (-, -n) brim. **~l** m. stuff, rubbish.

kre′pieren vvs.i. (vulg.) to die; to burst. [L]

Krepp m. (-s) crape; crêpe.

Kresse f. (-, -n) cress.

Krethi und Plethi Tom, Dick, and Harry.

kreucht (obs.) = **kriecht**.

Kreuz (-tes) n. (-es, -e) cross; (anat.) small of the back; loins (of horse); (mus.) sharp; (cards) club(s); das ~ schlagen to cross oneself; ans ~ schlagen to nail to the cross; ~ und quer in all directions; über ~ crosswise; zu ~ kriechen to sing small. **~abnahme** f. descent from the cross; (picture of the) deposition. **~band** n. (newspaper) wrapper; unter ~band by book-post. **~bein** n. sacrum. **~brav** a. thoroughly honest. **~erhöhung** f. elevation of the cross. **~esstamm** m. the Holy Rood. **~fahrer**, **~ritter** m. crusader. **~feuer** n. cross-fire. **~fi′del** a. merry as a cricket. **~gang** n. cloisters. **~lahm** a. **~lahm sein** to have backache. **~otter** f. adder. **~schmerzen** m.pl. lumbago. **~schnabel** m. crossbill. **~stich** m. cross-stitch. **~unglücklich** a. downcast, despondent. **~verhör** n. cross-examination. **~weg** m. cross-road(s), crossing; (theol.) way of the cross. **~worträtsel** n. crossword puzzle. **~zug** m. crusade.

kreuz-en (-tes) v.t. to cross. v.i. to cross; (naut.) to cruise. **~er** m. cruiser. **~igen** v.t. to crucify. **~igung** f. crucifixion. **~ung** f. crossing; cross-breeding.

kribbeln v.i. to crawl, swarm; to tickle, itch.

kriech-en (-i:ç-) vvs.i. st. to creep, crawl; (fig.) to cringe, fawn. **~tier** n. reptile. [CROUCH]

Krieg (-:k) m. (-es, -e) war; im ~ in war-time; im ~ sein mit to be at war with; ~ führen to wage war, make war. **~er** m. warrior, soldier. **~erisch** a. warlike, martial. **~führend** a. belligerent. **~führung** f. conduct of

war. **~sbeschädigt** a. disabled on active service. **~sdienst** m. military service. **~sdienstverweigerer** m. conscientious objector. **~sfall** m. case of war. **~sfuß** m. auf ~sfuß on a war-footing; (fig.) hostile. **~sgefangene(r)** m. prisoner of war. **~sgericht** n. court-martial. **~sgewinnler** m. war-profiteer. **~shafen** m. naval port. **~shandwerk** n. military profession. **~shetzer** m. warmonger. **~shinterbliebene(r)** m. dependant of war casualty. **~sknecht** m. mercenary. **~slazarett** n. base hospital. **~slist** f. stratagem. **~slustig** a. bellicose, eager for war. **~srecht** n. martial law. **~sschauplatz** m. seat or theatre of war. **~sschiff** n. battleship, warship. **~sschuld** f. war guilt. **~sstärke** f. war strength. **~sversehrt** a. wounded, disabled. **~svolk** n. forces, troops. **~swichtig** a. of military importance. **~szug** m. military expedition.

kriegen v.i. to wage war. v.t. (colloq.) to get, obtain.

Krimi′nal-polizei (-a:l-) f. criminal investigation department. **~polizist** m. detective. **~roman** m. detective novel.

krimi′nell a. criminal.

Kringel m. (-s, -) ring, circle; biscuit.

Krippe f. (-, -n) crib, manger; crèche. **~nspiel** n. nativity play.

Krise (-i:zə) f. (-, -n) crisis. **~fest** a. panic proof.

Kris′tall m. (-s, -e) crystal. **~en** a. of crystal. **~i′sieren** v.t. to crystallize.

Kri′tik (-ti:k) f. (-, -en) criticism; review; unter aller ~ beneath contempt. **~aster** m. caviller, fault-finder. **~er** m. critic; reviewer. **~los** a. uncritical, undiscriminating.

kriti-sch a. critical. **~sieren** v.t. to criticize; to review.

kritt-eln v.i. to find fault (with). **~ler** m. carping critic.

kritzeln v.t. to scrawl, scribble.

kroch imperf. of **kriechen**.

Kroko′dil n. (-s, -e) crocodile.

Krokus (kro:-) *m.* (-, -se) crocus.

Kron-e (-o:-) *f.* (-e, -en) crown; coronet; top; chandelier; *das setzt der Sache die* ~*e auf* that puts the lid on it. ~**erbe** *n.* heir to the crown. ~**gut** *n.* crown-lands. ~**insignien** *pl.* regalia. ~**leuchter** *m.* chandelier. ~**prinz** *m.* crown prince. ~**zeuge** *m.* chief witness; King's (Queen's) evidence.

krön-en *v.t.* to crown. ~**ung** *f.* coronation; crowning.

Kronsbeere *f.* cranberry.

Kropf *m.* (-es, ⸚e) crop; craw, wen; (*med.*) goitre. ~**ig** *a.* goitrous. ~**taube** *f.* pouter (pigeon).

Kröte (-ö:-) *f.* (-, -n) toad.

Krück-e (-e, -en) crutch. ~**stock** *m.* hooked stick.

Krug (-u:k) *m.* (-es, ⸚e) pitcher, jug, mug; inn, tavern.

Kruke *f.* (-, -n) stone jar or bottle.

Krume (-u:-) *f.* (-, -n) crumb; mould.

krümeln *v.i.* to crumble.

krumm *a.* crooked, bent; curved; ~**nehmen** (*colloq.*) to take offence. ~**beinig** *a.* bandy-legged. ~**holz** *n.* crooked timber; dwarf mountain pine. ~**linig** *a.* curvilinear. ~**nasig** *a.* hook-nosed. ~**säbel** *m.* scimitar. ~**stab** *m.* crosier.

krümm-en *v.t.* to bend. *v.r.* to bend down, stoop; to meander, wind; to cringe, (*fig.*) to cringe, grovel. ~**ung** *f.* bend, curve; winding; contortion; curvature.

Kruppe *f.* (-, -n) crupper.

Krüppel *m.* (-s, -) cripple. ~**haft**, ~**ig** *aa.* crippled, maimed.

Krust-e *f.* (-e, -en) crust; (*med.*) scurf. ~**entier** *n.* crustacean. ~**ig** *a.* crusty; crustacious.

Kruzi'fix *n.* (-es, -e) crucifix.

Krypt-a *f.* (-a, -en) crypt.

Kübel *m.* (-s, -) bucket, pail; tub. [L]

Ku'bik-inhalt *m.* cubic contents. ~**maß** *n.* cubic measure. ~**wurzel** *f.* cube root. ~**zahl** *f.* cube.

Kubus *m.* (-, Kuben) cube.

Küche (kyçǝ) *f.* (-, -n) kitchen;

cooking; *kalte* ~ cold meats. ~**nherd** *m.* range; kitchen-stove. ~**nlatein** *n.* dog-Latin. ~**nzettel** *m.* menu.

Kuchen (ku:x-) *m.* (-s, -) cake, pastry. ~**bäcker** *m.* pastry-cook. ~**blech** *n.* baking tin. ~**form** *f.* cake-tin.

Küchlein[1] *n.* (-s, -) small cake.

Küchlein[2], **Kücken** *n.* (-s, -) chicken.

Kuckuck *m.* (-s, -e) cuckoo; *zum* ~ *!* hang it!

Kufe *f.* (-, -n) vat, barrel; runner (of sledge).

Küfer *m.* (-s, -) cooper; cellarman.

Kugel (ku:-) *f.* (-, -n) ball; globe, sphere; bullet. ~**fang** *m.* butts. ~**fest** *a.* bullet-proof. ~**förmig** *a.* globular; spherical. ~**gelenk** *n.* ball and socket joint. ~**lager** *n.* ball-bearing. ~**schreiber** *m.* ball-pointed pen. ~**stoßen** *n.* putting the weight. [CUDGEL]

kugeln *v.t. & i.* to roll; to bowl.

Kuh *f.* (-, ⸚e) cow; *blinde* ~ blindman's-buff. ~**blume** *f.* marsh marigold. ~**fladen** *m.* cow-dung. ~**stall** *m.* byre, cowshed.

kühl *a.* cool, chilly; fresh. ~**anlage** *f.* cold-storage plant. ~**e** *f.* coolness; freshness. ~**er** *m.* (*motor.*) radiator. ~**erfigur** *f.* radiator mascot. ~**erhaube** *f.* bonnet. ~**haus** *n.* cold-storage depot. ~**ofen** *m.* cooling furnace; annealing oven. ~**raum** *m.* cold-storage chamber. ~**schrank** *m.* refrigerator. ~**ung** *f.* cooling; freshness.

kühlen *v.t. & i.* to cool.

kühn *a.* bold, daring, audacious. ~**heit** *f.* boldness, daring, audacity. [KEEN]

Küken *n.* (-s, -) chicken.

Kuli *m.* (-s) coolie.

Ku'lisse *f.* (-, -n) wing, scene. ~**nmaler** *m.* scene-painter. ~**nschieber** *m.* scene-shifter. [F]

Kult *m.* (-es, -e) cult; worship. ~**usminister** *m.* Minister of Education.

kulti'vier-en *v.t.* to cultivate. ~**t** *a.* cultured.

Kul'tur (-u:r) *f.* (-, -en) culture; cultivation; civilization. ~'**ell a.** *a.* cultural. ~**film** *m.* educational film. **~geschichte** f. history of civilization. **~los** a. uncivilized. **~schicht** f. cultured stratum. **~volk** n. civilized nation. **~zentrum** n. cultural centre.

Kümmel m. (-s, -) caraway (-seed).

Kummer m. (-s) grief, sorrow, worry. **~voll** a. sorrowful, grievous.

kümmer-lich a. miserable; poor, scanty. **~n** v.t. to grieve, trouble, worry; to concern. v.r. (um) to care (for); to worry (about); to mind. **~nis** f. grief, anxiety.

Kum(me)t n. (-s, -e) horse-collar.

Kum'pan m. (-s, -e) companion.

Kumpel m. (-s, -) miner.

kund (-t) pred. a. known, manifest. **~geben**, **~machen**, **~tun** v.t. to notify, inform. **~gebung** f. demonstration, manifestation. **~machung** f. publication; notification. **~schaft** f. intelligence, information; (commerc.) customers.

künd-bar a. recallable; (money) at call; (loan) redeemable. **~en** v.t. to publish, announce. **~igen** v.i. to give notice. v.t. to call in (money); to cancel. **~igung** f. notice, warning.

Kunde 1. m. (-n, -n) customer, client; (sl.) tramp. 2. f. (-) information, news, tidings; knowledge, science. **~nfang** m. touting. **~nsprache** f. thieves' slang.

kundig a. learned, well-informed; experienced.

künftig a. future. **~hin** adv. henceforth, in future.

Kunkel f. (-, n) distaff.

Kunst f. (-, ¨e) art; skill; trick, knack. **~anstalt** f. graphische **~~** fine art printers. **~ausstellung** f. art exhibition. **~blatt** n. art print. **~butter** f. imitation butter, margarine. **~druckpapier** n. art paper. **~dünger** m. artificial manure. **~faser** f. synthetic fibre. **~fertigkeit** f. (artistic or technical) skill. **~flug** m. stunt-flight. **~gerecht** a. skilful, correct. **~geübt** a. skilled; skilful. **~gewerbe** n. arts and crafts. **~griff** m. trick,

knack. **~handel** m. fine art trade. **~händler** m. art dealer. **~harz** m. plastics. **~kenner** m. connoisseur. **~kniff** m. trick, dodge. **~lauf** m. figure-skating. **~maler** m. painter. **~pause** f. pause for effect; awkward pause. **~reich**, **~voll** aa. artistic; ingenious. **~reiter** m. circusrider. **~schlosser** m. art metal worker. **~schreiner** m. cabinetmaker. **~seide** f. artificial silk. **~stickerei** f. art needlework. **~stoff** m. plastics; synthetic material. **~stopferei** f. invisible mending. **~stück** n. feat; trick. **~tischler** m. cabinet-maker. **~werk** n. work of art. **~wissenschaft** f. aesthetics.

Künste'lei f. (-, -en) affectation.

künst-eln v.t. to over-refine, subtilize. **~ler** m. artist. **~lerisch** a. artistic, artist-like. **~lertum** n. artistic gift; genius. **~lich** a. artificial, false; synthetic.

kunterbunt a. higgledy-piggledy.

Kupfer n. (-s) copper. **~chlorid** n. cupric chloride. **~druck** m. copper-plate. **~(geld)** n. coppers. **~n** a. copper. **~stich** m. engraving. **~tiefdruck** m. photogravure.

ku'pieren v.t. to dock (tail).

Kuppe f. (-, -n) rounded hill-top; head (of nail).

Kuppel f. (-, -n) cupola, dome.

Kupp-e'lei f. match-making. **~eln** v.t. to couple, unite, join. v.i. to procure. **~elpelz** m. sich einen **~elpelz verdienen** to bring about a match. **~ler** m. match-maker; procurer. **~lung** f. (tech.) coupling; joint; (motor.) clutch. **~lungshebel** m. clutch-pedal.

Kur¹ (ku:r) f. (-, -en) treatment, cure. **~gast** m. visitor; patient. **~haus** n. pump-room, casino, spa hotel. **~liste** f. list of visitors. **~ort** m. health resort, watering-place. **~pfuscher** m. quack.

Kur² f. die **~ machen**, **~ schneiden** to court, make love to. [F]

Küraß m. (Kürasses, -e) cuirass.

Kura'tel f. (-, -en) guardianship.

Kurbel f. (-, -n) crank; handle; (motor.) starting-handle; winch.

~kasten m. film camera. **~n** v.t. to crank; to reel off. **~stange** f. connecting bar. **~welle** f. crank-shaft. [L]

Kürbis m. (-ses, -se) pumpkin.

küren v.t. (poet.) to elect.

Kurfürst m. elector. **~entum** n. electorate. **~lich** a. electoral.

Kurie (ku:ri:ə) f. (-, -n) curia.

Ku'rier (-ri:r) m. (-s, -e) courier.

ku'rieren v.t. to cure.

kuri'os (-o:s) a. ⚜ odd, strange. **~i'tät** f. a curiosity, rare object.

Kurpfalz f. the Palatine.

Ku'rrentschrift f. running hand.

Kurs m. (-es, -e) course; (commerc.) rate of exchange; außer **~ setzen** to call in. **~bericht** m. market quotations. **~buch** n. time-table, Bradshaw. **~makler** m. stock-broker. **~sturz** m. fall in prices. **~us** m. course. **~zettel** m. stock-exchange list.

Kürschner m. (-s, -) furrier.

kur'sieren v.i. to circulate, be current.

Kur'sivschrift f. italics.

kursorisch a. cursory; summary.

Kurve f. (-, -n) curve, bend; turn.

kurz (-ts) a. short; brief; abrupt. adv. in short, briefly; **~ und bündig** concise(ly); brief(ly); **~ und gut** in short; **~ und klein schlagen** to smash to bits; in **~em** soon, shortly; vor **~em** recently, the other day; über **~ oder lang** sooner or later; zu **~ kommen** to come off badly; **den kürzeren ziehen** to be the loser; to get the worst of it. **~arbeit** f. short-time work. **~atmig** a. short-winded. **~erhand** adv. briefly. **~form** f. abbreviation. **~fristig** a. short-dated. **~gefaßt** a. concise. **~geschichte** f. short story. **~lebig** a. short-lived. **~schluß** m. short circuit. **~schrift** f. shorthand. **~sichtig** a. short-sighted. **~sichtigkeit** f. short-sightedness. **~streckenläufer** m. sprinter. **~um** adv. in short. **~waren** f.pl. haberdashery. **~weil** f. pastime, amusement. **~weilig** a. amusing, entertaining. **~welle** f. short wave. [L]

Kürz-e f. (-e) shortness, brevity. **~en** v.t. to shorten, abridge; to reduce, cut; (math.) to simplify. **~lich** adv. lately, recently. **~ung** f. shortening; abbreviation; reduction, cut.

kuschen v.i. (of dogs) to lie down; (fig.) to crouch.

Ku'sine (-zi:-) f. (-, -n) cousin.

Kuß m. (Kusses, -̈e) kiss. **~fest** a. kiss-proof. **~hand** f. blown kiss.

küssen v.t. to kiss.

Küste f. (-, -n) coast, shore. **~nfahrer** m. coasting-vessel, coaster. **~nhandel** m. coasting trade. **~nstrich** m. coast-line. **~nwache** f. coast-guard; coast-guard station.

Küster m. (-s, -) verger, sexton. [L]

Kustos m. (-, . . . oden) custodian.

Kutsch-bock m. coachman's seat, box. **~e** f. coach, carriage. **~er** m. coachman, driver. **~ieren** v.i. to drive in a carriage, drive a coach.

Kutte f. (-, -n) cowl.

Kutteln f.pl. tripe.

Kutter m. (-s, -) cutter.

Ku'vert (-t) n. (-s, -s) envelope, wrapper; cover (at table). **~ieren** v.t. to put in an envelope. [F]

Kux m. (-es, -e) mining share.

L

L, l (εl) n. the letter L, l.

Lab (la:p) n. (-es, -e) rennet.

labbern v.t. & i. to lap.

Lab-e f., **~sal** n., **~ung** f. refreshment, tonic; comfort. **~en** v.t. & r. to refresh; to enjoy.

la'bil a. unstable; variable.

Labo'r-ant m. (-anten, -anten) laboratory assistant. **~a'torium** n. laboratory.

Lache¹ (la:xa) f. (-, -n) pool, puddle. [LAKE]

Lach-e² f. laugh, laughter. **~er** m. laugher. **~haft** a. ridiculous, laughable. **~krampf** m. .fit of laughter. ~taube f. ring-dove.

läch-eln v.i. to smile; höhnisch ~eln to sneer. subst. n. smile. ~erlich a. laughable, ridiculous; ~erlich machen to ridicule. ~erlichkeit f. ridicule; absurdity.

lachen v.i. to laugh. subst. n. laughter.

Lachs (-ks) m. (-es, -e) salmon. ~farben a. salmon-coloured. ~schinken m. smoked ham.

Lack m. (-es, -e) lacquer, lac; varnish. ~firnis m. varnish, lacquer. ~ieren v.t. to varnish, lacquer. ~leder n. patent leather. ~schuh m. pump, dress shoe.

Lackmus m. (-) litmus.

Lade (la:-) f. (-, -n) box, chest; drawer.

Lade-baum m. derrick. ~fähigkeit f. tonnage. ~gewicht n. service weight. ~hemmung f. jam, stoppage. ~linie f. loadline. ~platz m. loading-place; wharf. ~raum m. (ship's) hold. ~schein m. bill of lading. ~stock m. ramrod; rammer.

laden[1] (la:-) v.t. st. to load; to charge.

laden[2] v.t. st. to invite; to summon, cite.

Laden[3] (la:-) m. (-s, ⸚en) shop, store; shutter. ~besitzer, ~inhaber m. shopkeeper. ~dieb m. shoplifter. ~einbruch m. smash-and-grab raid. ~fenster n. shop-window. ~hüter m. (sl.) white elephant, sticker. ~kasse f. till; cash-desk. ~mädchen n. shop girl. ~preis m. retail price, selling price. ~schild n. shop-sign. ~schluß m. shop closing; closing-time. ~schwengel m. counter-jumper. ~tisch m. counter.

lädieren v.t. to hurt, injure.

Ladung[1] f. (-, -en) load; freight; cargo; charge. ~raum m. hold (of a ship).

Ladung[2] f. (-, -en) summons, citation.

Lafette f. (-, -n) gun-carriage.

Laffe m. (-n, -n) fop.

lag imperf. of liegen.

Lage (la:gə) f. (-, -n) situation, position, site; condition, state,

circumstances; stratum, layer; (mus.) pitch, compass; quire (of paper); round (of beer); (naut.) volle ~ broadside.

Lager (la:-) n. (-s, -) bed, couch; lair, layer, stratum; stock, supply, store; camp, encampment; (fig.) party, side; (mech.) bearing, support; auf ~ on hand, in stock. ~aufnahme f. stock-taking, inventory. ~aufseher m. storekeeper. ~bestand m. stock, inventory. ~buch n. stock-book. ~feuer n. camp-fire. ~gebühr f., ~geld n. storage, warehouse-rent. ~haus n. warehouse, storehouse. ~hütte f. camp-hut, barrack. ~leitung f. camp authorities. ~platz m. resting place; depot. ~schein m. warrant. ~statt, ~stätte f. resting place, bed, couch.

lager-n (la:-) v.i. to lie down; to camp; to be encamped; (fig.) to hang or brood over; (commerc.) to be warehoused, be stored. ~ to store. ~ung f. (recumbent) position; storing, storage; (tech.) support; bearing; (geol.) stratification.

Lagune f. (-, -n) lagoon.

lahm a. lame; paralysed; weak. ~en v.i. to limp. ~heit f. lameness. ~legen v.t. to render useless, bring to a standstill.

lähm-en v.t. to cripple, paralyse; to hinder, stop. ~ung f. lameness, paralysis, palsy.

Laib (-p) m. (-es, -e) loaf.

Laich (-ç) m. (-es, -e) spawn. ~en v.i. to spawn.

Laie (laiə) m. (-n, -n) layman; amateur. ~nbruder m. lay brother. ~nhaft a. amateurish.

Lakai m. (-en, -en) lackey, footman; flunkey.

Lake f. (-, -n) brine, pickle.

Laken (la:-) n. (-s, -) sheet; shroud.

lakonisch a. laconic.

Lakritze f. (-, -n) liquorice.

lallen v.t. & i. to stammer; to babble.

La'melle f. (-, -n) lamella; (electr.) lamina; commutator; (phot.)

leaf, blade. **~nkuppelung** *f.* (*motor.*) plate-clutch.

lamen'tieren *v.i.* to lament.

La'metta *f.* (-) silver tinsel.

Lamm *n.* (-es, "er) lamb. **~braten** *m.* roast lamb. **~en** *v.i.* to lamb. **~fell** *n.* lambskin. **~fromm** *a.* gentle, lamblike.

Lämm-chen, ~lein *n.* little lamb. **~ergeier** *m.* lammergeyer. **~erwolke** *f.* cirrus.

Lampe *f.* (-, -n) lamp. **~ndocht** *m.* wick. **~nfieber** *n.* stagefright. **~nschirm** *m.* lamp-shade.

Lampi'on (-ɔ̃:) *m. & n.* (-s, -s) Chinese lantern.

Lam'prete *f.* (-, -n) lamprey.

lan'cieren *v.t.* to launch; to push.

Land (-t) *n.* (-es, "er & (*poet.*) -e) land, mainland; earth, ground, soil; country; realm; territory; *an ~ gehen* to land, go ashore; *aufs ~ gehen* to go into the country; *außer ~es gehen* to go abroad.

Land-adel *m.* landed gentry. **~arbeiter** *m.* farm-labourer, farm-hand. **~arzt** *m.* country doctor. **~aus** *adv.*, ~aus, landein far afield. **~bau** *m.* agriculture. **~besitz** *m.* land, landed property. **~einwärts** *adv.* inland, up-country. **~enge** *f.* isthmus. **~erziehungsheim** *n.* boarding-school in the country. **~flucht** *f.* migration from the country (to the town). **~flüchtig** *a.* fugitive. **~friede** *m.* public peace. **~gericht** *n.* county court; assizes. **~graf** *m.* landgrave. **~gut** *n.* landed property, manor, country-seat. **~haus** *n.* country-house. **~karte** *f.* map. **~kreis** *m.* rural district. **~läufig** *a.* customary, ordinary. **~leute** *pl.* farmers, peasants; country-people. **~macht** *f.* land-forces, army. **~mann** *m.* farmer, peasant. **~messer** *m.* surveyor. **~nahme** *f.* annexation of territory. **~partie** *f.* picnic, excursion. **~pfleger** *m.* governor. **~plage** *f.* scourge; (*fig.*) calamity. **~pomeranze** *f.* country girl. **~rat** *m.* district magistrate. **~ratte** *f.* landlubber. **~regen** *m.* per-

sistent rain. **~richter** *m.* county-court judge. **~rücken** *m.* ridge of hills. **~schaft** *f.* landscape, scenery; district. **~schaftlich** *a.* of the landscape; provincial. **~schaftsbild** *n.* landscape. **~schulheim** *n.* boarding-school in the country. **~sitz** *m.* country-seat. **~spitze** *f.* cape. **~straße** *f.* highway, highroad. **~streicher** *m.* vagrant, tramp. **~strich** *m.* region, tract of land. **~sturm** *m.* Territorial Reserve. **~tag** *m.* diet. **~transport** *m.* overland transport. **~verschickung** *f.* evacuation to the country. **~vogt** *m.* governor of district. **~wehr** *f.* Territorial Reserve. **~wind** *m.* off-shore wind. **~wirt** *m.* farmer. **~wirtschaft** *f.* farming, agriculture. **~wirtschaftlich** *a.* agricultural. **~zunge** *f.* tongue *or* neck of land. See also **Landes- & Länds-**.

Landauer *m.* (-s, -) landau.

lande-n *v.t.* to land, put ashore. *vvs.i.* to land; to disembark. **~bahn, ~piste** *f.* landing runway. **~zeichen** *n.* landing-signal.

Länd-e'rei *f.* landed property, estates. **~erkampf** *m.* (*sport.*) international contest. **~ler** *m.* slow waltz. **~lich** *a.* rural, rustic.

Landes-angehörigkeit *f.* nationality. **~aufnahme** *f.* ordnance survey; topography. **~brauch** *m.* national custom. **~erzeugnis** *n.* home produce. **~farben** *f.pl.* national colours. **~herr** *m.* sovereign, ruler. **~hoheit** *f.* sovereignty. **~kind** *n.* native. **~kirche** *f.* established church. **~obrigkeit** *f.* government; supreme authority. **~sprache** *f.* vernacular. **~tracht** *f.* national costume. **~trauer** *f.* public mourning. **~üblich** *a.* customary, usual. **~vater** *m.* sovereign. **~vermessung** *f.* ordnance survey. **~verrat** *m.* high treason. **~verräter** *m.* traitor. **~verteidigung** *f.* defence of the country. **~verweisung** *f.* expulsion; banishment; exile. **~verweser** *m.* regent; viceroy; governor. **~verwiesen** *a.* exiled, banished. **~während** f. standard currency.

Lands-knecht m. mercenary, foot-soldier. **~mann** m. (pl. **~leute**) compatriot.

Landung f. (-, -en) landing; disembarkation. **~brücke** f. landing-stage, pier. **~splatz** m. landing-place; pier.

lang (-n) a. long; tall; auf ~e Sicht long-dated (bill); auf die ~e Bank schieben to put off; ~e Finger machen to steal, pilfer; einen ~en Hals machen to crane forward; der ~en Rede kurzer Sinn to cut a long story short; den lieben ~en Tag the livelong day. **~atmig** a. long-winded, lengthy. **~finger** m. thief, pickpocket. **~fristig** a. long-term. **~holz** n. timber, planks. **~jährig** a. of long standing. **~lebig** a. long-lived. **~lebigkeit** f. longevity. **~mut** f. long-suffering, patience. **~mütig** a. patient, forbearing. **~sam** a. slow; tardy. **~samkeit** f. slowness. **~schiff** n. nave. **~schläfer** m. late riser. **~sichtig** a. long-sighted. **~streckenflug** m. long-distance flight. **~(e)weile** f. boredom. **~weilen** v.t. to bore. v.r. to be bored. **~weilig** a. boring, dull; slow. **~welle** f. long wave. **~wierig** a. lengthy, protracted.

lang(-e) adv. long; ~e her long ago; ~e in a long time yet; über kurz oder ~ sooner or later; einen Tag ~ for a day; ~e machen to be long (in) doing something.

Länge (lɛŋə) f. (-, -n) length; size; duration; longitude; (pros.) quantity; zehn Fuß in der ~ ten foot long; auf die ~ in the long run; der ~ nach lengthwise; at full length; longitudinally; in die ~ ziehen to drag on, spin out; ~n haben (lit.) to have tedious passages. **~ngrad** n. degree of longitude. **~nmaß** n. linear measure. **~nunterschied** m. difference in length.

langen v.i. to suffice; ~ nach to reach for; einem eine (Ohrfeige)

~ to box one's ears; ~ Sie zu! help yourself (at table).

länger a. longer; schon ~, seit ~em for some time; je ~ je lieber the longer the better.

Lan'gette f. (-, -n) scallops, scalloping.

länglich (-ç) a. longish, oblong.

längs prep. along. **~achse** f. longitudinal axis. **~schnitt** m. longitudinal section.

längst a. longest. adv. long ago; for a long time; schon ~ long ago; for a long time; noch ~ nicht not nearly; am ~en the longest; **~ens** at the latest; at the most.

Lanze (-tsa) f. (-, -n) lance, spear; eine ~ einlegen für to stand up for.

Lan'zett-e (-tsɛta) f. (-e, -en) lancet. **~förmig** a. lanceolate.

La'ppalie (-paːliə) f. (-, -n) trifle.

Lappen m. (-s, -) rag, cloth, duster; (sci.) lobe; durch die ~ gehen to escape, run away.

Läpper-'ei f. (-ei, -eien) trifle. ~n v.t. to lap, sip; sich zusammen ~n to accumulate, come in driblets. **~schulden** f.pl. petty debts.

lappig (-ç) a. flabby; (sci.) lobed.

läppisch a. foolish, silly, childish.

Lärche (-çə) f. (-, -n) larch.

Lärm m. (-es) noise, din, row; blinder ~ false alarm; ~ schlagen to give the alarm. **~en** v.i. to make a noise, be noisy. **~ig** a. noisy, clamorous, loud. [F]

Larve (-fə) f. (-, -n) mask; (zool.) larva.

las imperf. of **lesen**.

lasch a. limp, flabby; languid.

Lasche f. (-, -n) flap; gusset; tongue (of shoe); (tech.) fishplate; joint; groove.

lassen v.t. & i. st. to let, allow, permit, suffer; to make, cause, order, have done; to leave, let go, abandon, part with, omit; es beim alten ~ to let things remain as they were; aus dem Spiel ~ to leave out of the question; außer Acht ~ to disregard; etwas sein ~ to refrain from doing something; sein Leben ~

to lose one's life; *sagen* ~ to send word; *sich sagen* ~ to be told, take advice; *holen* ~ to send for; *mit sich reden* ~ to be reasonable; *sich Zeit* ~ to take time; *das muß man ihm* ~ one must credit him with that; *warten* ~ to keep waiting; *laß nur!* never mind! *laß das!* don't! *das läßt sich hören* that sounds good. *subst. n. Tun und* ~ commissions and omissions; conduct, behaviour.

lässig (-ç) *a.* lazy, idle; indolent, negligent, careless. ~**keit** *f.* laziness; indolence.

läßlich *a.* venial, pardonable.

Last *f.* (-, -en) load, weight, burden, charge; freight, cargo; tonnage; (*pl.*) taxes; *zur* ~ *fallen* to be a burden to; *zur* ~ *legen* to charge with; *zu* ~ *en von* to the debit of. ~**auto** *n.* motor lorry, van. ~**enaufzug** *m.* goods elevator. ~**enausgleich** *m.* equal distribution of (social) expenditure. ~**enfrei** *a.* tax-free, free of tax. ~**flugzeug** *n.* freightcarrying plane. ~**gebühr** *f.* tonnage. ~**igkeit** *f.* tonnage. ~**kahn** *m.* lighter, barge. ~**kraftwagen** *m.* motor lorry, van. ~**pferd** *n.* pack-horse. ~**schrift** *f.* debit (-item). ~**tier** *n.* beast of burden. ~**träger** *m.* porter. ~**wagen** *m.* cart, truck, lorry, van.

lasten *v.i.* to weigh upon, press heavily upon.

Laster *n.* (-s, -) vice. ~**haft** *a.* vicious, wicked. ~**haftigkeit** *f.* viciousness, wickedness. ~**höhle** *f.* den of iniquity.

Läster-er *m.* (-ers, -er) slanderer; blasphemer. ~**lich** *a.* slanderous; scandalous. ~**maul** *n.* scandalmonger. ~**n** *v.t. & i.* to slander; to blaspheme. ~**ung** *f.* slander; blasphemy. ~**zunge** *f.* slanderous tongue.

lästig (-ç) *a.* troublesome; annoying; irksome.

La'sur *f.* (-) ultramarine; lapis lazuli. ~**farben** *a.* azure, skyblue.

La'tein *n.*, ~**isch** *a.* Latin.

La'terne *f.* (-, -n) lantern, lamp.

~**nanzünder** *m.* lamplighter. ~**npfahl** *m.* lamp-post.

La'trine *f.* (-, -n) latrine.

Latsch-e¹ (la:-) *f.* (-e, -en) old slipper. ~**en** *vns.i.* to shuffle along. ~**ig** *a.* shuffling.

Latsche² *f.* (-, -n) dwarf-pine.

Latte *f.* (-, -n) lath, batten. ~**nverschlag** *m.* wooden partition. ~**nzaun** *m.* wooden fence.

Lattich (-ç) *m.* (-s, -e) lettuce.

Lat'werge *f.* (-, -en) electuary.

Latz *m.* (-es, -"e) bib; flap. ~**schürze** *f.* pinafore, apron.

lau ~**warm** *a.* lukewarm, tepid; mild (weather); (*fig.*) halfhearted. ~**heit**, ~**igkeit** *f.* lukewarmness.

Laub (-p) *n.* (-es) foliage, leaves. ~**dach** *n.* leafy canopy. ~**frosch** *m.* tree-frog. ~**holz** *n.* deciduous wood, wood bearing leaves. ~**hüttenfest** *n.* Feast of Tabernacles. ~**säge** *f.* fret-saw. ~**wald** *m.* deciduous forest. ~**werk** *n.* foliage. [LEAF]

Laub-e *f.* (-e, -en) arbour, summer-house; arcade. ~**enbesitzer** *m.* allotment holder. ~**engang** *m.* arcade.

Lauch (-x) *m.* (-es, -e) leek.

Lauer *f.* (-) ambush; *auf der* ~ on the look-out. ~**n** *v.i.* to wait (for); to lie in wait (for), lurk.

Lauf *m.* (-es, -"e) run, running, pace; race; course; current; way; barrel (of gun); (*mus.*) run; (*zool.*) leg, foot; *in vollem* ~ at full gallop, at top speed; *in full swing; im* ~ *e von* in the course of; *freien* ~ *lassen* to give full scope to; *to give free play to*. ~**bahn** *f.* career; course. ~**band** *n.* tread of tyre. ~**brett** *n.* running board. ~**brücke** *f.* plank bridge; pontoon; gangway. ~**bursche**, ~**junge** *m.* errand boy. ~**e'rei** *f.* running about. ~**feuer** *n.* wildfire; running fire. ~**getriebe** *n.* mechanism; gear. ~**graben** *m.* communication trench. ~**katze** *f.* crane crab. ~**kran** *m.* overhead travelling crane. ~**kundschaft** *f.* passing customers. ~**mantel** *m.* barrel casing. ~**masche** *f.* ladder, slipped

stitch. **~paß** m. dismissal, notice.
~schiene f. guide rail. **~schritt**
m. im **~schritt** at the double.
~stall m. pen. **~steg** m. foot-
bridge; catwalk. **~zeit** f. rutting
season (sport.) time.

laufen vus.i. st. to run; to flow;
to leak, run out; to pass, go by;
to go on; (colloq.) to go; **~**
lassen to let go; to let (things)
slide. **~d** a. running, current;
~den Monats instant; **~de Arbeit**
routine work; **~de Ausgaben**
current expenses; **~de Nummer**
serial number; **~des Band** conveyor belt; **am ~den Band** (fig.)
uninterruptedly; **auf dem ~den**
sein to be up to date, be abreast
(of affairs). [LEAP]

Läufer m. (-s, -) runner; stair-
carpet; drugget; table runner;
(mus.) run; (chess) bishop;
(sport.) half(-back). **~stange** f.
stair-rod.

läufig a. in heat.

Lauge f. (-, -n) lye, buck; leach.
~n v.t. to steep in lye; to leach.
~nhaltig a. containing lye. **~n-**
salz n. alkaline salt.

Laun-e f. (-e, -en) mood; whim,
caprice, fancy; **guter ~e sein** to
be in a good temper. **~enhaft**,
~isch aa. moody; changeable,
capricious. **~enhaftigkeit** f.
moodiness; capriciousness. **~ig**
a. humorous, comical, funny.
[L]

Laus f. (-, ⸚e) louse. **~bube**,
~ejunge m. young rascal, little
devil. **~en** v.t. to delouse.

lausch-en v.i. to listen to; to
eavesdrop. **~er** m. listener.
~ig a. snug, cosy.

Läusepulver n. insect-powder.

laut 1. a. audible; loud, noisy.
adv. aloud; **~ werden** to become
known, get about. 2. prep. according to, in accordance with;
~ Befehl by order, as ordered;
~ Rechnung as per account. 3.
subst. m. (-es, -e) sound, tone;
~ geben to give tongue. **~bar**
a. known. **~gesetz** n. phonetic
law. **~lehre** f. phonetics; phono-
logy. **~lich** a. phonetic. **~los** a.
silent, mute, hushed. **~losigkeit**

f. silence. **~malerei** f. onomatopoeia. **~schrift** f. phonetic
spelling or script. **~sprecher**
m. loudspeaker; megaphone.
~stärke f. intensity of sound; loud-
ness; volume, signal strength.
~tafel f. sound chart. **~ver-**
schiebung f. sound-shift(ing);
Grimm's law. **~verstärker** m.
volume amplifier. **~wandel** m.
sound-change. **~zeichen** n.
phonetic symbol.

Laute f. (-, -n) lute. **~nschläger**
m. lute-player.

lauten v.i. to sound; to say, run,
read; **~ auf** to be issued for; be payable to.

läut-en v.t. & i. to peal, toll,
sound; **etwas ~en hören** to hear
a rumour of. **~(e)werk** n. bell;
alarm-bell.

lauter a. pure, clear; unvarnished; genuine, reliable, honest;
(indecl.) only, nothing but, rank,
mere. **~keit** f. purity; integrity.

läuter-n v.t. to purify; to purge;
to refine; to clarify. **~ung** f.
purification; refining; clarifica-
tion. **~ungsprozeß** m. refining
process.

lau'tieren v.i. to read phonetically.

Lava f. (-, Laven) lava.

La'vendel m. (-s, -) lavender.

la'vieren v.i. to tack.

La'wine (-vi:-) f. (-, -n) avalanche.

lax a. lax, loose. **~ieren** v.i. &
t. to take an aperient; to purge.
~iermittel n. aperient.

Laza'rett n. (-s, -e) hospital.
~wagen m. ambulance.

Lebe-hoch n. cheer; toast. **~mann**
m. man about town; bon vivant.
~männisch a. epicurean. **~**
wesen n. living creature. **~wohl**
n. farewell, good-bye.

leben (le:-) 1. v.i. & t. to live; to
be alive; to dwell, live, stay;
~ von to subsist on, live by;
(hoch) **~ lassen** to drink the
health of, cheer. 2. subst. n.
(-s, -) life, existence; stir,
activity, liveliness; **am ~ sein**
to be alive; **am ~ bleiben** to
survive; **auf ~ und Tod** a
matter of life and death; **ins**
~ rufen to originate; start;

einem Kind das ~ schenken to give birth to; *nach dem ~* from life; *ums ~ bringen* to kill; *ums ~ kommen* to die, perish. *~d a.* living, alive; *~de Bilder* tableaux vivants; *~de Hecke* quickset hedge. **~gewicht** *n.* live weight.

le**'bendig** (-c) *a.* alive, living; lively, vivid. **~keit** *f.* liveliness, animation.

Lebens-abend *m.* old age. **~abriß** *m.* biographical sketch. **~ader** *f.* (*fig.*) life-line. **~alter** *n.* age. **~art** *f.* manners, good breeding. **~bedürfnisse** *n.pl.* necessaries of life. **~bejahend** *a.* optimistic. **~beschreibung** *f.* biography. **~fähig** *a.* capable of living; (*med.*) viable. **~fähigkeit** *f.* vitality. **~frage** *f.* vital question. **~fremd** *a.* unfitted for life; unworldly. **~führung** *f.* manner of living. **~gefahr** *f.* danger to life. **~gefährlich** *a.* highly dangerous, perilous. **~gefährte** *m.* life's companion; husband, wife. **~geister** *m.pl.* (animal) spirits. **~größe** *f.* life-size. **~haltung** *f.* standard of life. **~klugheit** *f.* worldly wisdom. **~kraft** *f.* vital energy. **~lage** *f.* position in life; situation. **~länglich** *a.* for life, perpetual. **~lauf** *m.* curriculum vitae. **~lustig** *a.* gay, fond of life. **~mittel** *n.pl.* food, provisions, victuals. **~mittelversorgung** *f.* food supply. **~müde** *a.* tired of life. **~nerv** *m.* (*fig.*) mainspring. **~notwendig** *a.* vital. **~raum** *m.* living space. **~retter** *m.* life-saver; oxygen breathing apparatus. **~stellung** *f.* social position; appointment for life. **~strafe** *f.* capital punishment. **~trieb** *m.* vital instinct. **~überdrüssig** *a.* weary *or* sick of life. **~unterhalt** *m.* living, livelihood. **~versicherung** *f.* life insurance. **~wahr** *a.* true to life. **~wandel** *m.* life, conduct. **~weise** *f.* mode of life, way of living. **~zeichen** *n.* sign of life. **~zeit** *f.* lifetime, life, age; *auf ~zeit* for life.

~zweck *m.* aim in life.

Leber (le:-) *f.* (-, -n) liver. **~blümchen** *n.* liverwort. **~fleck** *m.* mole. **~tran** *m.* cod-liver oil.

leb-haft *a.* lively, vivacious, spirited, bright; vivid. **~haftigkeit** *f.* liveliness, vivacity. **~kuchen** *m.* gingerbread. **~los** *a.* lifeless, dull, heavy; inanimate. **~tag** *m.* *mein ~tag* all my life. **~zeiten** *f.pl.* lifetime, life.

lechzen (lɛçts-) *v.i.* to be thirsty; to long (for).

Leck *n.* (-es, -e) leak, leakage. *a.* leaky, leaking; *~ werden* to spring a leak. **~en[1]** *v.i.* to leak, run.

leck-en[2] *v.t.* to lick. **~er** *a.* tasty, delicious; dainty, fastidious. **~erbissen** *m.* choice morsel, titbit. **~e'rei** *f.* delicacy, toothsome dainty. **~ermaul** *n.* sweet tooth.

lecken[3] *v.i. wider den Stachel ~* to kick against the pricks.

Leder (le:-) *n.* (-s, -) leather. **~band** *n.* leather binding. **~hose** *f.* leather shorts. **~n** *a.* leather; leathery; (*fig.*) dull.

ledig (-c) *a.* free, exempt; unmarried. **~ensteuer** *f.* bachelor's tax. **~lich** *adv.* solely, merely.

Lee *f.* (-) lee, leeside.

leer *a.* empty; vacant, unoccupied; blank; idle, idleness (talk); *mit ~en Händen* empty-handed; *~ laufen* to run idle. **~e** *f.* emptiness, void, vacuum. **~en** *v.t.* to empty, clear, evacuate. **~gewicht** *n.* dead weight. **~gut** *n.* empty package, empties. **~lauf** *m.* running idle; ticking over; (*fig.*) waste. **~ung** *f.* emptying, clearing.

Lefze (le:-) *f.* (-, -n) lip (of animals).

Le**'gat** (-a:t) *n.* (-s, -e) legacy.

legen (le:-) *v.t.* to lay, put; to sow, plant. *v.r.* to lie down; to die down, abate; to fall (on); *sich auf etwas ~* (*fig.*) to apply oneself to a thing.

Le**'gende** *f.* (-, -n) legend.

le**'gier-en** *v.t.* to alloy; to thicken (soup). **~ung** *f.* alloy(ing).

legi**'tim** (-ti:m) *a.* legitimate. **~ati'on** *f.* legitimation; proof of identity. **~ationspapier** n. identity-card; (pl.) identification papers. **~ieren** v.t. to legitimate. v.r. to prove one's identity. **~i'tät** f. legitimacy.

Leh(e)n n. (-s, -) fief, feudal tenure. **~sherr** m. feudal lord, liege lord. **~smann** m. vassal. **~srecht** n. feudal law. [LOAN]

Lehm m. (-es, -e) clay, loam; mud. **~boden** m. clay soil. **~grube** f. clay- or loam-pit. **~ig** a. clayey, loamy. **~ziegel** m. sun-dried brick.

Lehn-e f. (-e, -en) back (of chair); support, rest; slope, declivity. **~en** v.t., v.i. & r. to lean (against); to lean or rest (upon). **~sessel, ~stuhl** m. easy chair, arm-chair.

Lehn-satz m. lemma. **~wort** n. loan-word.

Lehr-amt n. teaching post, mastership; professorship. **~anstalt** f. educational establishment. **~befähigung** f. qualification to teach. **~beruf** m. teaching profession. **~bogen** m. (archit.) center, centering. **~brief** m. indentures. **~buch** n. text-book. **~fach** n. teaching profession; (special) subject. **~film** m. educational film. **~gang** m. course of instruction. **~geld** n. premium; **~geld zahlen** (fig.) to pay for one's experience. **~haft** a. didactic. **~herr** m. master. **~jahre** n.pl. years of apprenticeship. **~junge** m. apprentice. **~körper** m. teaching staff; professoriate. **~kraft** f. teacher. **~ling** m. apprentice. **~mädchen** f. girl apprentice. **~mittel** n. means of instruction; apparatus. **~plan** m. school curriculum; course of instruction. **~reich** a. instructive. **~saal** m. lecture-room; class-room. **~satz** m. proposition; theorem; doctrine, dogma. **~stelle** f. apprenticeship. **~stuhl** m. (acad.) chair. **~vertrag** m. indentures. **~zeit** f. apprenticeship.

Lehre f. (-, -n) instruction, precept, advice; warning, lesson,

moral; doctrine, dogma; theory, science; apprenticeship; (mach.) gauge; **in die ~ geben** to apprentice to; **in die ~ gehen** to work as an apprentice. [LORE]

lehren v.t. to teach, instruct; to show, prove.

Lehrer m. (-s, -) teacher, instructor, master, tutor. **~in** f. teacher, mistress. **~kollegium** n. staff. **~schaft** f. body of teachers; staff (of school). **~seminar** n. training college.

Leib (-p) m. (-es, -er) body; belly; womb; waist; **~ des Herrn** host, the Bread; **gesegneten ~es** with child; **am ganzen ~e** all over; **bei lebendigem ~e** while alive; **mit ~ und Seele** with heart and soul; **vom ~e bleiben** to keep off; **zu ~e rücken** to become aggressive. **~arzt** m. physician in ordinary. **~binde** f. body-belt; abdominal belt; sash. **~chen** n. vest, bodice, corset. **~eigen** a. in bondage, in thrall. **~eigene(r)** m. bondman, serf. **~eigenschaft** f. bondage, serfdom. **~garde** f. body guard. **~gericht** n., **~speise** f. favourite dish. **~haftig** a. embodied, incarnate; real, true. **~lich** a. corporeal, bodily; material; **sein ~licher Sohn** his own son. **~rente** f. annuity. **~schmerzen** m.pl., **~schneiden**, **~weh** n., **~wäsche** f. stomach-ache, colic. **~wäsche** f. linen, underwear. [LIFE]

Leibes-erbe m. legitimate heir. **~frucht** f. foetus, embryo; offspring. **~kraft** f. physical strength; **aus ~kräften** with all one's might. **~strafe** f. corporal punishment. **~übungen** f.pl. gymnastics, physical jerks. **~visitation** f. bodily search.

leibt (in the phrase) **wie er ~ und lebt** the very image of; his very self.

Leichdorn m. corn.

Leiche (-ça) f. (-, -n) corpse, dead body; carcass; (dial.) funeral.

Leichen-begängnis n. funeral. **~beschauer** m. coroner. **~besorger, ~bestatter** m. undertaker. **~bestattung** f. funeral. **~bittermiene** f. woebegone look.

~blaß *a.* pale as death. ~frau *f.* layer-out. ~geruch *m.* cadaverous smell. ~halle *f.* mortuary. ~hemd *n.* shroud. ~schändung *f.* rape of a dead body. ~schau *f.* inquest. ~starre *f.* rigor mortis. ~stein *m.* tombstone. ~verbrennung *f.* cremation. ~wagen *m.* hearse. ~zug *m.* funeral procession.

Leichnam *m.* (-s, -e) corpse, dead body, remains.

leicht *a.* light; easy; mild (tobacco); insignificant, slight, trifling, little; frivolous, careless. *adv.* easily; ~ *möglich* very probable; ~ *entzündlich* highly inflammable; *etwas* ~ *nehmen* to take it easy, make light of a thing. ~**athletik** *f.* athletics, games. ~**blütig** *a.* sanguine. ~**faßlich** *a.* popular, easily understood. ~**fertig** *a.* thoughtless, frivolous. ~**fertigkeit** *f.* thoughtlessness, frivolity. ~**flüssig** *a.* easily fusible, mobile. ~**fuß** *m.* gay young spark. ~**füßig** *a.* nimble. ~**gewicht** *n.* light weight. ~**gläubig** *a.* credulous. ~**gläubigkeit** *f.* credulity. ~**herzig** *a.* light-hearted. ~**hin** *adv.* lightly, carelessly. ~**igkeit** *f.* lightness; ease. ~**lebig** *a.* easy-going, happy-go-lucky. ~**matrose** *m.* ordinary seaman. ~**sinn** *m.* carelessness, thoughtlessness. ~**sinnig** *a.* careless, thoughtless, frivolous.

Leichter *m.* (-s, -) lighter.

Leid (-t) *n.* (-es) hurt, harm, injury; grief, sorrow; pain; ~ *tragen* to mourn; *sich ein* ~ *antun* to commit suicide. ~ *a. es ist mir* ~ I regret it; *es tut mir* ~ I am sorry about it; *er tut mir* ~ I am sorry for him. ~**tragende(r)** *m.* mourner. ~**voll** *a.* sorrowful. ~**wesen** *n. zu meinem* ~*wesen* to my sorrow.

Leideform *f.* passive voice.

leiden *v.t. & i. st.* to suffer, bear, endure; to allow, permit, tolerate; ~ *mögen*, ~ *können* to like. *subst.n.* (-s, -) suffering; pain; disease, ailment; *Christi* ~ Passion of our Lord. ~**schaft** *f.*

passion. ~**schaftlich** *a.* passionate, vehement. ~**schaftslos** *a.* dispassionate. ~**sgefährte** *m.* companion in misfortune. ~**skelch** *m.* cup of sorrow. ~**sprobe** *f.* trial. ~**swoche** *f.* Passion Week. [LOATH]

leid-er *adv. & int.* unfortunately, I am sorry to say; alas. ~**lich** *a.* tiresome. ~**lich** *a.* tolerable, middling, passable.

Leier *f.* (-, -n) lyre; *die alte* ~ the same old story. ~**kasten** *m.* hurdy-gurdy; barrel-organ. ~**(kasten)mann** *m.* organ-grinder. ~**n** *v.t.* to grind a barrel-organ; to turn (with winch); to drawl.

Leih-bibliothek *f.* lending library, circulating library. ~**en** *v.t. st.* to lend; to borrow. ~**gabe** *f.* loan. ~**haus** *n.* pawnshop. ~**schein** *m.* pawn-ticket; slip (for loan of book). ~**weise** *adv.* as a loan. [LOAN]

Leim *m.* (-es, -e) glue, size; *auf den* ~ *gehen* to fall into a trap; *aus dem* ~ *gehen* to fall to pieces. ~**en** *v.t.* to glue; to paste (paper); (*colloq.*) to cheat. ~**farbe** *f.* distemper. ~**ig** *a.* gluey, glutinous. ~**rute** *f.* lime-twig.

Lein *m.* (-es, -e) flax. ~**e** *f.* line, rope, cord; (dog's) lead. ~**en** *a.* linen. *subst. a.* linen, linen goods. ~**enband** *m.* cloth binding. ~**(en)weberei** *f.* manufacture of linen; linen factory. ~**enzeug** *n.* linen (goods). ~**kuchen** *m.* oilcake. ~**öl** *n.* linseed oil. ~**pfad** *m.* towing-path. ~**samen** *m.* flax-seed, linseed. ~**tuch** *n.* linen cloth; sheet. ~**wand** *f.* linen; canvas; screen.

leise (-za) *a.* low; soft, gentle; slight, faint; ~ *stellen* to tune down (radio). ~**treter** *m.* sneak.

Leiste *f.* (-, -n) ledge, ridge, beading; (*archit.*) fillet; groin. ~**nbruch** *m.* inguinal rupture.

leist-en¹ *v.t.* to perform, do, fulfil, carry out, accomplish; *sich etwas* ~ to treat oneself to; *sich* ~ *können* to be able to afford. ~**ung** *f.* performance, accomplishment, achievement; result, effect; production; output. ~ungsfähig *a.* fit, able; efficient, productive. ~ungsfähigkeit *f.* capacity for work; efficiency; power.

Leisten² *m.* (-s, -) last; boot-tree; *alles über einen ~ schlagen* to treat all alike.

Leit-artikel *m.* leading article, leader. ~faden *m.* manual, text-book, guide. ~fähigkeit *f.* conductivity. ~gedanke *m.* (*fig.*) key-note. ~hammel *m.* bell-wether. ~motiv *n.* leitmotiv. ~satz *m.* motto; guiding principle. ~schiene *f.* (*geom.*) directrix; live rail. ~seil *n.* leash; guiderope. ~stern *m.* pole-star; guiding star. ~tier *n.* leader.

leit-en *v.t.* to lead, conduct; to guide, direct; to oversee; to manage. ~er¹ *m.* leader, conductor, manager, principal, head. **Leiter**² *m.* (-, -n) ladder. ~sprosse *f.* rung of a ladder. ~wagen *m.* cart (with sparred frame).

Leitung *f.* (-, -en) direction, guidance; control, management; conduction, transmission; circuit; wire, lead; line; conduit pipe; tap. ~sdraht *m.* conducting wire, (line) wire. ~sfähigkeit *f.* conductivity, conductive capacity. ~srohr *n.* conducting pipe; conduit; pipe; main. ~sschnur *f.* flex; lead. ~sstörung *f.* defect in line. ~swasser *n.* tap-water.

Lekti'on (-o:n) *f.* (-, -en) lesson. **Lekt-or** *m.* (-ors, -oren) lecturer; (publisher's) reader. ~üre *f.* ◊ reading; books, literature.

Lende *f.* (-, -n) loin, loins; haunch; high. ~nbraten *m.* roast sirloin. ~nschurz *m.* loin cloth. ~nstück *n.* loin; fillet.

lenk-bar *a.* dirigible; (*fig.*) tractable. ~ballon *m.* dirigible balloon. ~er *m.* ruler, guide; driver; pilot. ~rad *n.* steering-wheel. ~sam *a.* tractable, docile. ~säule *f.* steering-column. ~stange *f.* handle-bars. ~ung *f.* steering; driving; controlling; direction.

lenken *v.t. & i.* to drive; to steer, guide, pilot; to turn, direct; to lead; to call (attention to).

Lenz (-ts) *m.* (-es, -e) spring. [LENT]

Lepra *f.* (-) leprosy. ~kranke(r) *m.* leper.

Lerche (-çə) *f.* (-, -n) lark.

lern-begierig *a.* eager to learn, studious. ~behindert *a.* handicapped, unable to learn. ~en *v.t. & i.* to learn; to study.

Les-art *f.* reading; version; variant. ~bar *a.* legible; readable. ~barkeit *f.* legibility; readableness. ~ung *f.* reading (of a bill).

Lese (le:zə) *f.* (-, -n) gleaning; vintage.

Lese-buch *n.* reading-book, reader. ~halle *f.* reading-room. ~kränzchen *n.* reading-circle. ~probe *f.* (*theatr.*) rehearsal. ~ratte *f.* book-worm. ~saal *m.* reading-room. ~welt *f.* reading public. ~zeichen *n.* book-mark.

lesen (le:zən) *v.t. & i. st.* **1.** to glean; to pick; to gather (grapes). **2.** to read; to lecture. ~swert *a.* worth reading.

Leser *m.* (-s, -) reader. ~lich *a.* legible. ~schaft *f.* readers. ~zuschrift *f.* letter to the editor.

Lettner *m.* (-s, -) rood-loft, screen. [ML]

letzen *v.t.* to refresh.

letzt *a.* last; latest; final; extreme; ~en Sonntag last Sunday; in ~er Zeit lately, recently, of late; zu guter ~ finally, in the end; ~e Neuheit latest novelty; sein ~es hergeben to do one's utmost. ~ere(r) *a.* latter. ~ens, ~hin *adv.* lately, of late. ~willig *a.* testamentary.

Leu *m.* (-en, -en) (*poet.*) lion.

Leucht-e *f.* (-e, -en) lamp; (*fig.*) shining light, star. ~er *m.* candlestick; chandelier. ~feuer *n.* beacon lamp or light; (*av.*) flare. ~gas *n.* gas for lighting coal-gas. ~geschoß *n.*, ~granate *f.* star shell. ~käfer *m.* glow-worm, fire-fly. ~kraft *f.* luminosity, illuminating power. ~kugel *f.* Very light. ~pfad *m.*

flare path. **~pistole** f. Very pistol. **~rakete** f. rocket. **~spur** f. tracer (fire). **~turm** m. lighthouse. **~uhr** f. luminous clock or watch. **~zifferblatt** n. luminous dial.

leuchten v.i. to light, give light; to shine; to beam. subst. n. shining; illumination, glow. **~d** a. bright, shining, luminous.

leugnen v.t. to deny; to disavow.

Leuko'plaststreifen m. strip of adhesive tape.

Leumund m. (-s) reputation, character. **~szeugnis** n. testimonial.

Leut-e pl. people, persons, folk, men; the world; servants. **~eschinder** m. slavedriver, sweater. **~selig** a. affable. **~seligkeit** f. affability.

Leutnant m. (-s, -s) second lieutenant; pilot officer; **~ zur See** sub-lieutenant. [F]

Le'vit m. (colloq.) einem die **~en lesen** to lecture a person.

Lev'koje f. (-, -n) stock.

Lexiko'graph m. (-en, -en) lexicographer.

Lexik-on n. (-ons, -a) dictionary, encyclopaedia. [L]

Li'belle f. (-, -n) dragon fly; wateror spirit-level.

Liberalismus m. liberalism.

Licht (-ct) n. (-es, -er) light; (pl. -e) candle; illumination, lighting; eye (of game) (pl.) **~ anmachen** to turn on the light; **bei ~e besehen** to examine closely; **einem ein ~ aufstecken** to open a person's eyes; **mir geht ein ~ auf** it dawns on me; **hinters ~ führen** to dupe, impose upon; **in falsches ~ setzen** to misrepresent. **~ a.** light, shining, bright; clear; thin, sparse; **am ~en Tage** in broad daylight; **~e Augenblicke** sane moments, lucid intervals.

Licht-anlage f. lighting plant. **~bad** n. (med.) insolation. **~bild** n. photograph. **~bildervortrag** m. lantern-slide lecture. **~bildner** m. photographer. **~blick** m. (fig.) ray of hope. **~blond** a. fair. **~bogen** m. arc.

~bündel n. pencil of light. **~druck** m. phototype, photogravure. **~durchlässig** a. translucent; transparent. **~echt** a. fast to light, fadeless. **~empfindlich** a. sensitive to light. **~erglanz** m. brightness (of lights). **~erloh** adv. blazing, in full blaze. **~hof** m. well (of court); (astron.) halo. **~kegel** m. cone of light; beam of searchlight. **~leitung** f. lighting circuit. **~meß** f. Candlemas. **~meßtrupp** m. flash-spotting troop. **~messung** f. photometry. **~pause** f. tracing; blueprint. **~reklame** f. illuminated advertisement; sky-sign. **~schacht** m. light-shaft. **~seite** f. (fig.) bright side. **~spielhaus** n. cinema, picture-house. **~stärke** f. intensity of light. **~strahl** m. light ray, ray of light. **~umflossen** a. bathed in light, radiant. **~undurchlässig** a. opaque to light, light-proof. **~voll** a. luminous; clear, lucid.

licht-en v.t. to thin out; to clear (forest); to weigh (anchor). v.r. to grow thinner; to grow brighter, clear up. **~ung** f. clearing (in forest).

Lichter m. (-s, -) lighter, barge.

Lid (-t) n. (-es, -er) eyelid.

lieb (-p) a. dear, beloved; agreeable; good; **es ist mir ~** I am glad; **es wäre mir ~** I should like. **~äugeln** v.i. to ogle. **~chen** n. darling, love, sweetheart. **~gewinnen** v.t. to grow fond of. **~haben** v.t. to love, like. **~haber** m. lover; fancier; amateur, dilettante. **~haberei** f. fancy; liking; hobby. **~haberpreis** m. fancy price. **~haberrolle** f. role of lover. **~habertheater** n. private theatricals. **~kosen** v.t. to caress, fondle. **~kosung** f. caress, petting. **~lich** a. lovely; charming, sweet. **~ling** m. darling; favourite. **~los** a. unkind. **~reich** a. kind, loving. **~reiz** m. charm, attraction. **~schaft** f. love-affair, amour. **~ste(r)** m. dearest, beloved; lover, sweetheart. See also Liebes-.

Liebe f. (-, -n) love; affection; charity; *aus ~ for* love; *mir zu ~* for my sake. **~dienerei** f. cringing, servility. **~voll** a. loving, kind. [LOVE]

Liebel·ei f. (-ei, -eien) flirtation. **~n** v.i. to flirt.

lieben v.t. to love; to like. v.i. to be in love. **~swert** a. worthy of love. **~swürdig** a. amiable; kind. **~swürdigkeit** f. amiability, kindness.

lieber a. comp. dearer. adv. rather, sooner.

Liebes-abenteuer n. love-affair, intrigue. **~brief** m. love-letter. **~dienst** m. good turn, act of kindness. **~erklärung** f. declaration of love. **~gabe** f. gift, (parcel of) comforts. **~geschichte** f. love-story. **~handel** m. love-affair, intrigue. **~heirat** f. love-match. **~mühe** f. *Verlorene ~mühe* Love's Labour's Lost. **~paar** n. lovers, couple. **~rausch** m. transport of love. **~verhältnis** n. love-affair, liaison. **~werbung** f. courtship. **~werk** n. work of charity.

Lied (li:t) n. (-es, -er) song; air, tune; hymn. **~erabend** m. concert (of songs). **~erbuch** n. song-book; hymn-book. **~erkranz** m. collection of songs. **~ertafel** f. choral society.

liederlich a. slovenly; immoral, dissolute; loose. **~keit** f. slovenliness; loose conduct.

lief imperf. of **laufen**.

Liefe·rant m. (-en, -en) purveyor; contractor; caterer.

liefer-bar a. available (for delivery). **~frist**, **~zeit** f. term of delivery. **~schein** m. receipt, bill of delivery. **~ung** f. delivery, supply; number, part (of book). **~ungsbedingungen** pl. terms of delivery. **~ungsware** n. serial. **~wagen** m. delivery van.

liefern v.t. to deliver; to yield, produce; to furnish, supply; to give (battle); *geliefert sein* (colloq.) to be done for.

Liege-geld n. demurrage. **~kur** f. rest cure. **~stuhl** m. deck-chair.

liegen v.i. st. to lie, rest; to be situated; to be quartered; to be

billeted; to be, stand; *mir liegt daran* I am interested in the matter; *das liegt an mir* it is my fault; *soviel an mir liegt* as far as lies in my power; *es liegt nichts daran* it is of no consequence; *mir liegt nichts daran* I don't care for it; *der Gegenstand liegt mir nicht* the subject does not suit me; **~de Güter** real estate. **~bleiben** vvs.i. to stay in bed; to be left; to lie over, stand over; to break down; to be unsaleable, be left on one's hands. **~lassen** v.t. to let lie; to leave lying (about); to leave behind; to leave off (work).

Liegenschaften f.pl. real estate, landed property; immovables.

lieh imperf. of **leihen**.

ließ imperf. of **lassen**.

liest 2nd & 3rd pers. sing. pres. of **lesen**.

Lift (lift) m. & n. (-es, -e) lift, elevator.

Lig-a f. (-a, -en) league.

Li'guster m. (-s, -) privet.

liiert a. allied.

Li'kör m. (-s, -e) ♣ liqueur.

lila indecl. a. lilac, pale violet.

Lilie (li:lie) f. (-, -n) lily.

Lilipu'taner m. (-s, -) Lilliputian.

Limo'nade (-na:də) f. (-, -n) lemonade.

lind (-t) a. soft, gentle, mild. **~ern** v.t. to soften, mitigate, alleviate, allay, soothe. **~erung** f. alleviation, palliation, relief. **~erungsmittel** n. anodyne, palliative. [LITHE]

Linde f. (-, -n) lime-tree.

Lindwurm m. dragon.

Line'al (-a:l) n. (-s, -e) ruler.

Linie (li:nia) f. (-, -n) line; lineage, descent; branch (of family); *auf gleicher ~ mit* on the same footing as; *in erster ~* first of all, primarily. **~nblatt** n. (sheet with) guide-lines. **~nschiff** n. ship of the line. **~ntreu** a. (pol.) following the party line.

lin(i)'ieren v.t. to rule.

link a. left; wrong side (of cloth); reverse (of coin); (herald.) sinister. **~e** f. left hand, left (side); *Ehe zur ~en* morganatic marriage. **~erhand** adv. on the

left. ~**isch** a. awkward, clumsy.

links adv. to the left; on the left; ~ **sein** to be left-handed; ~ **liegen lassen** to cold-shoulder. ~**außenstürmer** m. outside left. ~**händig** a. left-handed. ~**um** adv. left about turn.

Linnen n. (-s, -) & a. linen.

Linse f. (-, -n) lentil; (opt.) lens.

Lippe f. (-, -n) lip. ~**nlaut** m. labial (sound). ~**nstift** m. lipstick.

Liquid·ati'onsverfahren n. liquidation. ~**ieren** v.t. to liquidate; to charge a fee.

lispeln v.i. & t. to lisp; to whisper.

List f. (-, -en) cunning, craft, artfulness; trick, stratagem. ~**ig** a. cunning, crafty, sly; astute.

Liste f. (-, -n) list, roll, register; catalogue.

Lita'nei f. (-, -en) litany.

Liter (li:-) m. & n. (-s, -) litre.

lite'r·arisch a. literary. ~**at** m. man of letters, writer. ~**a'tur** f. literature, letters. ~**aturgeschichte** f. history of literature. ~**aturnachweis** m. references; bibliography.

Litfaßsäule f. advertisement pillar.

lithogra'phieren v.t. to lithograph.

litt imperf. of **leiden.**

Litur'gie f. (-, -en) liturgy.

li'turgisch a. liturgical.

Litze f. (-, -n) cord, braid, lace; facing; (electr.) flex.

Liv'ree f. (-, -n) livery.

Lizenti'at m. (-en, -en) licentiate.

Li'zenz f. (-, -en) ⚕ permit, licence; (poetic) licence.

Lob (lo:p) n. (-es) praise, commendation. ~**eserhebung** f. high praise, encomium. ~**gesang** m. hymn, song of praise. ~**hudelei** f. fulsome praise, base flattery. ~**preisen** v.t. to extol, praise. ~**rede** f., ~**spruch** m. eulogy.

loben (lo:-) v.t. to praise, commend. ~**swert** a. praiseworthy.

löblich (lø:p-) a. laudable, praiseworthy; commendable.

Loch (-x) n. (-es, ⁻er) hole, gap; (sl.) prison. ~**eisen** m. punch. ~**en** v.t. to punch, perforate. ~**er** m. punch, perforator. ~**karte** f.

punch-card. [LOCK]

löcherig a. full of holes, porous.

Lock·e f. (-e, -en) lock, curl, ringlet. ~**en¹** v.t. to curl. ~**enkopf** m. curly head. ~**enwickler** m. curler. ~**ig** a. curly.

lock·en² v.t. to entice, allure; to decoy. ~**mittel** n. bait; inducement. ~**ruf** m. call (of bird). ~**spitzel** m. agent provocateur. ~**ung** f. attraction, enticement. ~**vogel** m. decoy-bird.

locker a. loose, slack; spongy, light; (fig.) frivolous, dissolute; **nicht ~ lassen** to be firm, insist (upon). ~**n** v.t. to loosen, slacken; to break up (soil).

Loden (lo:-) m. (-s, -) rough woollen cloth. ~**mantel** m. kind of shower-proof Inverness cape.

lodern v.i. to blaze, flame; to burn.

Löffel m. (-s, -) spoon; ear (of hare). ~**n** v.t. to sup. ~**weise** adv. by spoonfuls.

log¹ imperf. of **lügen.**

Log² n. (-s, -e) (naut.) log.

Loga'rith·mus m. (-mus, -men) logarithm.

Loge (lo:ʒə) f. (-, -n) box (in theatre); Freemasons' lodge. ~**nbruder** m. brother mason. ~**nmeister** m. master of a lodge. ~**nschließer** m. (theatr.) attendant.

Lo'gierbesuch (-ʒiːr-) m. visitors, guests. ~**ieren** v.i. to stay, lodge. ~**ierzimmer** n. spare room, guest room. ~**is** n. lodgings, (sl.) digs.

Logi·k f. (-k) logic. ~**sch** a. logical.

Lohe¹ f. (-, -n) flame. ~**n¹** v.i. to blaze up, flare up.

Loh·e² f. (-e, -en) tanning-bark, tan. ~**en¹** v.t. to treat with tan. ~**gerber** m. tanner. ~**gerberei** f. tanning; tannery.

Lohn m. (-es, ⁻e) compensation, reward; wages, pay. ~**abkommen** n. wages agreement. ~**arbeiter** m. workman, labourer. ~**diener** m. extra help, hired servant. ~**drückerei** f. sweating. ~**empfänger** m. wage-earner. ~**kutscher** m. cabman. ~**liste** f. pay-list. ~**steuer** f. tax on wages.

~tag *m.* pay-day. ~tüte *f.* pay-envelope.

lohnen *v.t. & i.* to reward, compensate; to pay; to be worth; *es lohnt sich (der Mühe)* it's worth while. ~d *a.* profitable, advantageous, lucrative.

löhn-en *v.t.* to pay (wages, &c.). ~ung *f.* pay.

lo'kal (-a:l) *a.* local, suburban. *subst. n.* inn, pub; room, premises. ~i'sieren *v.t.* to localize. ~patriotismus *m.* jingoism. ~termin *m.* on the spot-investigation.

Lokomo'tiv-e (-ti:vo) *f.* (-e, -en), **Lok** (*collog.*) *f.* (-, -s) engine. ~führer *m.* engine-driver. ~schuppen *m.* engine shed.

Lokowaren *f.pl.* (*commerc.*) spots.

Lokus *m.* (*collog.*) lavatory.

Lorbeer *m.* (-s, -e) laurel, bay.

Lore *f.* (-, -n), **Lori** *f.* (-, -s) lorry, truck.

Los[1] (lo:s) *n.* (-es, -e) lot; fate, destiny; lottery ticket; *das große* ~ the first prize.

los[2] *a. & sep. pref.* loose, slack; free; flowing. *adv. etwas* ~ *sein* to be rid of; *was ist* ~? what's up; *hier ist viel* ~ there's plenty going on here; *mit ihm ist nicht viel* ~ he's not up to much; *los!* go on, fire away, begin.

los-arbeiten *v.i.* to work away. *v.r.* to extricate oneself. ~binden *v.t.* to untie, loosen. ~brechen *v.t.* to break off. *vvs.i.* to break, burst out. ~bröckeln *v.t. & vvs.i.* to crumble off. ~drücken *v.t. & i.* to fire, fire off. ~eisen *v.t.* to free. ~essen *v.t. darauf* ~ to tuck in. ~fahren *vvs.i.* to depart; (*fig.*) to fly out (at). ~gehen *vvs.i.* to set out; to become loose; to go off; to begin; to attack. ~kaufen *v.t.* to ransom, redeem. ~kommen *vvs.i.* to get away. ~lassen *v.t.* to let loose; to release; to unleash (upon). ~legen *v.i.* (*collog.*) to begin. ~lösen *v.r.* to disengage oneself. ~machen *v.t.* to free, disengage. ~platzen *vvs.i.* to blurt out, explode.

~reißen *v.t.* to tear off; to separate. ~sagen *v.r.* to part from, renounce. ~schießen *v.i.* to fire off; (*collog.*) to fire away. ~schlagen *v.t.* to sell off. *v.i.* to attack. ~schnallen *v.t.* to unbuckle. ~schrauben *v.t.* to unscrew. ~sprechen *v.t.* to absolve, acquit. ~stürmen *vvs.i.* to rush (at), rush forth. ~trennen *v.t.* to undo; to rip off. ~werden *v.t.* to get rid of. ~ziehen *vvs.i.* to set out; (*fig.*) to rail (at one), inveigh (against).

Lösch-blatt, *n.* blotting-paper. ~dienst *m.* fire-fighting service. ~er *m.* extinguisher; blotter. ~gerät *n.* fire-fighting apparatus; extinguisher. ~mannschaft *f.* fire-brigade.

löschen[1] *v.t.* to put out, extinguish, quench; to slake (lime); to blot out; to efface; to discharge, liquidate.

löschen[2] *v.t.* to unload (ship).

lose (lo:za) *a.* loose, slack; disconnected, incoherent; frivolous, dissolute; *~r Mund* malicious tongue; *~r Vogel* wag.

los-en (lo:z-) *v.i.* to draw lots. ~ung *f.* password; watchword; droppings, dung.

lös-en (lø:z-) *v.t.* to loosen, untie; to dissolve, annul; to give up; to relax (limbs); to solve (problem); to fire (shot); to buy (ticket); to receive (money); (*chem.*) to dissolve. ~egeld *n.* ransom. ~lich *a.* soluble. ~lichkeit *f.* solubility. ~ung *f.* solving; (*fig. & chem.*) solution.

Lot (lo:t) *n.* (-es, -e) plummet, plumb-line, perpendicular; solder. See also App. III. ~en *v.i. & t.* to sound, plumb. ~recht *a.* perpendicular. [LEAD]

löt-en (lø:-) *v.t.* to solder. ~kolben *m.* soldering iron. ~rohr *n.* blowpipe.

Lotse (lo:-) *m.* (-n, -n) pilot. ~n *v.t.* to pilot.

Lotter-bett *n.* couch, lounge. ~bube *m.* rascal. ~ig *a.* slovenly, dissolute. ~leben *n.* dissolute life.

Lotte'rielos *n.* lottery ticket.

Löwe (løːvə) *m.* (-n, -n) lion. ~**nanteil** *m.* lion's share. ~**n-grube** *f.* lions' den. ~**nmaul** *n.* (*bot.*) snapdragon. ~**nzahn** *m.* dandelion.

Löwin (-, -nen) lioness.

Loyali'tät *f.* (-) loyalty.

Luch (-x) *f.* (-, ̈e) marsh, bog.

Luchs (luks) *m.* (-es, -e) lynx.

Lücke *f.* (-, -n) opening, hole, gap; blank; omission, deficiency; *eine ~ schließen* (*fig.*) to step into the breach. ~**nbüßer** *m.* stop-gap. ~**nhaft** *a.* full of gaps; defective, incomplete. ~**nlos** *a.* unbroken, uninterrupted, complete.

lud *imperf. of* **laden**.

Luder (luːɐ̯) *n.* (-s, -) carrion; (*vulg.*) wretch; hussy. ~**jan** *m.* rake. ~**leben** *n.* dissolute life.

Luft (-, ̈e) *f.* air; breath; breeze; *frische ~ schöpfen* to take the air; *keine ~ bekommen* not to be able to breathe; *an die ~ setzen* to throw out, turn out; *aus der ~ greifen* to invent; *in die ~ sprengen* to blow up; *in der ~ hängen* to be undecided as yet; *sich ~ machen* to give vent to one's feelings. [LOFT]

Luft-abwehr *f.* air defence, anti-aircraft. ~**amt** *n.* Air Ministry. ~**angriff** *m.* air raid. ~**antenne** *f.* overhead aerial. ~**aufklärung** *f.* air-reconnaissance. ~**bild** *n.* air-photograph. ~**blase** *f.* air-bubble; vesicle. ~**bremse** *f.* air-brake. ~**brücke** *f.* air-lift. ~**dicht** *a.* air-tight. ~**druck** *m.* atmospheric pressure; blast. ~**fahrtministerium** *n.* Air Ministry. ~**feuchtigkeit** *f.* atmospheric humidity. ~**flotte** *f.* air fleet. ~**förmig** *a.* gaseous, aeriform. ~**geräusche** *n.pl.* atmospherics. ~**gespinst** *n.* illusion. ~**hafen** *m.* airport. ~**heizung** *f.* hot-air heating. ~**herrschaft** *f.* air supremacy. ~**hoheit** *f.* freedom of the air. ~**hülle** *f.* atmosphere. ~**kampf** *m.* airbattle. ~**klappe** *f.* air-valve. ~**kurort** *m.* health resort. ~**landetruppen** *f.pl.* air-borne troops. ~**leer** *a.* void of air; *leerer Raum* vacuum. ~**linie** *f.* bee-line. ~**loch** *n.* air

pocket; air-hole. ~**post** *f.* air mail. ~**pumpe** *f.* pneumatic pump. ~**raum** *m.* atmosphere. ~**reifen** *m.* pneumatic tyre. ~**reklame** *f.* sky advertisement. ~**röhre** *f.* wind-pipe. ~**rüstung** *f.* air armament. ~**sack** *m.* wind-sock; wind-direction indicator. ~**schacht** *m.* air-shaft. ~**schaukel** *f.* swing-boat. ~**schicht** *f.* stratum. ~**schiff** *n.* airship. ~**schiffahrt** *f.* aerial navigation, aeronautics. ~**schlange** *f.* paper streamer. ~**schloß** *n.* castle in the air. ~**schutz** *m.* air defence, A.R.P. ~**schutzkeller** *m.* ~**schutzraum** *m.* air-raid shelter. ~**schutzübung** *f.* A.R.P. drill. ~**schwingung** *f.* vibration of air. ~**sperre** *f.* A.A. defences. ~**spiegelung** *f.* mirage. ~**sprung** *m.* leap. ~**störungen** *f.pl.* atmospherics. ~**stoß** *m.* gust of air. ~**strom** *m.* air current. ~**stützpunkt** *m.* air-base. ~**tüchtig** *a.* airworthy. ~**weg** *m.* air route. ~**zufuhr** *f.* air supply. ~**zug** *m.* draught, current of air. See also **Flieger-** & **Flug-**.

Lüft-chen *n.* (-chens, -chen) breeze, zephyr. ~**en** *v.t.* to ventilate; to raise; to reveal, disclose. ~**ung** *f.* airing, ventilation; lifting (of veil); disclosing (of secret).

luftig *a.* airy, breezy; thin, flimsy.

Lug (luː) *m.* (-es) lying, falsehood.

Lüg-e (lyːgə) *f.* (-e, -en) lie, untruth, falsehood; *einen ~en strafen* to give one the lie. ~**engewebe** *n.* tissue of lies. ~**enhaft**, ~**nerisch** *aa.* false, lying, untrue, deceitful. ~**enmaul** *n.* impudent liar. ~**ner** *m.* liar.

lugen (luː) *v.i.* to look out, peep.

lügen (lyː) *v.i. st.* to lie, tell a lie.

Luke (luː) *f.* (-, -n) dormer-window; (*naut.*) hatch; trap door.

lullen *v.t.* to lull.

Lümmel *m.* (-s, -) lout, hooligan, boor. ~**haft** *a.* a loutish, boorish; rude.

Lump *m.* (-en, -en) scamp, rascal. ~**en**[1] *m.* rag, clout. ~**engesindel**, ~**enpack** *n.* riff-raff, rabble. ~**enhändler** *m.* ragman. ~**ensammler** *m.* rag-picker. ~**e'rei**

f. shabby trick. **~ig** a. ragged; shabby; trifling.

lumpen[2] v.i. sich nicht ~ lassen to come down handsomely.

M

Lunge f. (-, -n) lung. **~nentzündung** f. pneumonia. **~nflügel** m. lobe of the lung. **~nkrank** a. consumptive. **~nschwindsucht** f. phthisis.

Lunte f. (-, -n) match (cord); fox's brush; ~ riechen to smell a rat.

Lupe (lu:-) f. (-, -n) magnifying glass; unter die ~ nehmen (fig.) to examine closely.

Lu'pine f. (-, -n) lupine.

Lurch m. (-es, -e) batrachian.

Lust f. (-, ᵉe) pleasure, joy, delight; desire, inclination; ~ haben zu to be inclined, want (to). **~barkeit** f. amusement, entertainment. **~fahrt** f. excursion, drive, trip. **~los** a. dull. **~mord** m. murder and rape. **~seuche** f. venereal disease. **~spiel** n. comedy. **~wandeln** vws.i. to stroll, take a walk.

Lüster m. (-s, -) lustre; chandelier.

lüst-ern a. greedy (for), desirous (of); lascivious, lustful. **~ernheit** f. greediness; lasciviousness, lust. **~ling** m. voluptuary, sensualist.

lustig a. merry, jolly, gay; comical, funny; sich ~ machen über to make fun of. **~keit** f. gaiety; mirth; merriment, fun.

lutschen v.t. & i. to suck.

Luv, **~seite** f. weather-side. **~en** v.i. to luff.

luxuri'ös a. luxurious.

Luxus m. (-) luxury. **~artikel** m. luxury article. **~ausgabe** f. édition de luxe. **~waren** f.pl. fancy goods, luxury articles.

Lymph-e f. (-e, -en) lymph. **~drüse** f. lymphatic gland.

lynch-en v.t. to lynch. **~justiz** f. mob law.

Lyr-a (ly:-) f. (-a, -en) lyre.

Lyri-k (ly:-) f. (-) △ lyric poetry. **~ker** m. lyric poet. **~sch** a. lyric, lyrical.

Ly'zeum (-tse:-) n. (-s, Lyzeen) girls' secondary school.

M, m (ɛm) n. the letter M, m.

Maat m. (-es, -e) (naut.) mate.

Mach-art f. style; description, kind, sort. **~e** f. making; (fig.) pretence, show. **~enschaften** f.pl. machinations. **~erlohn** m. charge for making. **~werk** n. clumsy piece of work.

machen (max-) v.t. to make, do; to manufacture; to cause; to come to, amount to; to tidy, put to rights; ~ zu to appoint; sich ~ an to begin on, start work upon; sich viel ~ aus to care much about; das macht nichts that does not matter; was ~ Sie? how are you; mach' schnell! hurry up; mach', daß du fortkommst! get out of here. v.r. to do well, get on; to come right.

Macht (maxt) f. (-, ᵉe) strength, might, influence; power; authority; forces, army. **~befugnis** f. competency. **~ergreifung, ~übernahme** f. seizure of power. **~haber** m. lord, ruler. **~los** a. powerless. **~spruch** m., **~wort** n. peremptory order, command, word of command. **~stellung** f. strong position, political power. **~vollkommenheit** f. aus eigener ~ on one's own authority. [MIGHT]

mächtig (-ç) a. strong, mighty, powerful; thick. adv. (colloq.) enormously; einer Sache ~ sein to be master of a thing.

Mädchen (mɛːtçən) n. (-s, -) girl; servant; ~ für alles general servant. **~haft** a. girlish, maidenly. **~handel** m. white slave traffic. **~name** m. maiden name. [MAID]

Made (maː-) f. (-e, -en) maggot, worm. **~ig** a. worm-eaten, maggoty.

Mädel n. (-s, -) girl, lass.

mag 1st & 3rd pers. sing. pres. of mögen.

Maga'zin (-tsi:n) n. (-s, -e) storehouse; depot; magazine (of gun); magazine, periodical.

Magd (maːkt) f. (-, ᵉe) maid;

servant. **~lich** *a.* virginal. **~tum** *n.* virginity.

Mägdlein *n.* (-s, -) little girl.

Magen (ma:-) *m.* (-s, ⁺) stomach. **~bitter** *m.* bitters. **~brennen** *n.* heartburn. **~grube** *f.* pit of the stomach. **~knurren** *n.* intestinal rumbling. **~säure** *f.* acidity. **~schmerzen** *m.pl.* stomachache. **~verstimmung** *f.* stomach upset.

mager (ma:-) *a.* thin, lean; scanty, poor, meagre. **~keit** *f.* leanness; poorness. **~milch** *f.* skim milk.

Mag-'ie (-gi:) *f.* (-ie) magic. **~ier**, **~iker** *m.* magician. **~isch** *a.* magic(al).

Ma'gister *m.* (-ers, -er) schoolmaster, tutor. **~rat** *n.* ♣ town *or* borough council.

Mag'nat *m.* (-en, -en) magnate.

Mag'net (-e:t) *m.* (-en, -en) magnet. **~isch** *a.* magnetic. **~i'seur** *m.* mesmerist; magnetist. **~ismus** *m.* magnetism. **~nadel** *f.* magnetic needle. **~zündung** *f.* magneto ignition.

magneti'sieren *v.t.* to magnetize.

Maha'goni (-go:-) *n.* (-s) mahogany.

Mahd (ma:t) *f.* (-) mowing; swath.

mäh-en¹ *v.t. & i.* to mow, cut, reap. **~er** *m.* mower, reaper. **~maschine** *f.* reaper; lawnmower.

mähen² *v.i.* to bleat.

Mahl *n.* (-es, -e) meal. **~zeit** *f.* meal; *gesegnete ~zeit!* God bless this food.

mahl-en *v.t.* to grind; to mill. **~gang** *m.* set of millstones. **~stein** *m.* millstone. **~zahn** *m.* molar.

Mahn-brief *m.* request to pay, dunning letter. **~en** *v.t.* to remind; to admonish, exhort; to warn; to dun. **~er** *m.* admonisher; dun. **~mal** *n.* memorial(-stone). **~ung** *f.* reminder; admonition, warning; dunning.

Mähne *f.* (-, -n) mane.

Mähre *f.* (-, -n) mare.

Mai *m.* (-s, -e) May. **~baum** *m.* maypole. **~feier** *f.* (pol.) Mayday demonstration. **~glöckchen** *n.* lily of the valley. **~käfer** *m.* cockchafer.

Maid *f.* (poet. & colloq.) girl.

Mais *m.* (-es) maize, Indian *or* sweet corn. **~kolben** *m.* corn cob.

Maisch-e *f.* (-e, -en) mash. **~en** *v.t.* to mash.

Maje'stät *f.* (-, -en) majesty. **~isch** *a.* majestic. **~sbeleidigung** *f.* lese-majesty.

Ma'jor (-jo:r) *m.* (-s, -e) major; (av.) squadron leader. **~at** *n.* primogeniture; entail. **~enn** *a.* of age. **~i'tät** *f.* majority.

Majo'ran *m.* (-s, -e) marjoram.

Ma'juskel *f.* (-, -n) capital letter.

Makel (ma:-) *m.* (-s, -) stain, spot; blemish. **~los** *a.* stainless, spotless; faultless, immaculate. [L]

Mäkel-'ei *f.* (-ei, -eien) fault-finding, censoriousness; daintiness. **~ig** *a.* censorious; fastidious, dainty. **~n** *v.i.* to find fault with.

Makka'roni *pl.* macaroni.

Makler (ma:-) *m.* (-s, -) broker; agent. **~gebühr** *f.* brokerage.

Mäkler *m.* (-s, -) fault-finder, caviller.

Ma'krele (-kre:-) *f.* (-, -n) mackerel.

Ma'krone (-o:-) *f.* (-, -n) macaroon.

Makula'tur *f.* waste-paper. **~ieren** *v.t.* to pulp, repulp (paper).

Mal (ma:l) *n.* (-es, -e) **1.** landmark; monument; spot, mole, mark; (sport.) start; goal. **2.** (point of time; turn; *zum ersten ~* for the first time; *zum zweiten ~* at the second time; *mit einem ~* suddenly. **3.** *adv.* once; just. **~nehmen** *v.i.* to multiply. **~zeichen** *n.* multiplication sign.

mal-en (ma:-) *v.t. & i.* to paint; to portray; to represent; *sich ~en lassen* to have one's portrait painted. **~er** *m.* painter, artist. **~e'rei** *f.* painting; picture. **~erisch** *a.* pictorial; picturesque; artistic. **~ermeister** *m.* decorator, house-painter. **~kasten** *m.* paint-box.

Malve *f.* (-, -n) mallow.

Malz (-ts) *n.* (-es) malt. **~bonbon** *m. & n.* cough-lozenge.

Mälzer *m.* (-s, -) maltster.

Ma'ma *f.* (-s) mamma.

Mammut *m. & n.* (-s, -s) mammoth.

Mam'sell f. (-, -en) miss; house-keeper.

man indecl. pron. one, they, people.

manch (-c) pron. & a. many a, many a one; (pl.) **manche** some. **~erlei** indecl. a. various, divers. **~mal** adv. sometimes, now and again. [MANY]

Manchester(samt) m. corduroy.

Man'd-ant m. (-anten, -anten) client. **~at** n. mandate; authorization.

Manda'rine f. (-, -n) mandarin orange, tangerine.

Mandel[1] f (-, -n) almond; (anat.) tonsil. **~entzündung** f. tonsilitis.

Mandel[2] f. set of fifteen (eggs).

Mando'line f. (-, -n) mandolin.

Ma'nege (-e:ʒə) f. (-, -n) riding-school; arena, (circus) ring. [F]

Manen (ma:-) pl. manes.

Man'gan n. (-s) manganese. **~sauer** a. manganate of.

Mangel[1] f. (-, -n) mangle.

Mangel[2] m. (-s, ⸚) need, want (of), dearth (of); absence, lack; fault, defect, flaw; aus ~ an for want of. **~haft** a. faulty; defective; unsatisfactory. **~haftigkeit** f. faultiness, imperfection; defectiveness. **~s** prep. in default of. **~ware** f. goods in short supply.

mangeln[1] v.t. to mangle.

mangeln[2] v.i. to want, be wanting, lack, fail; es mangelt mir an I am short of.

Ma'nie (-ni:) f. (-, -n) mania.

Ma'nier (-ni:r) f. (-, -en) manner, deportment; style. **~iert** a. affected, mannered. **~lich** a. polite, civil, mannerly.

Mani'fest n. (-s, -e) manifesto. **~ieren** v.t. to manifest, declare.

mani'küren v.t. to manicure.

manipulieren v.t. to manipulate.

Manko n. (-s, -s) deficit; deficiency.

Mann m. (-es, ⸚er) man; husband; (pl. -en) vassal; der gemeine ~ the man in the street, the common people; mit ~ und Maus with every soul; an den ~ bringen to dispose of a thing; seinen ~ stehen to hold one's own; wenn Not am ~ ist if the

worst comes to the worst. **~bar** a. marriageable. **~barkeit** f. puberty; manhood, womanhood. **~esalter** n. manhood. **~eskraft** f. manly vigour, virility. **~esstamm** m. male line. **~haft** a. manly. **~haftigkeit** f. manliness. **~heit** f. manhood, virility. **~sbild** n. male. **~schaft** f. personnel; men, ranks; crew; (sport.) team. **~sleute** pl. menfolk, men. **~stoll** a. mad about men. **~weib** n. virago, mannish woman.

Männ-chen n. (-chens, -chen) little man; male; **~chen machen** (of dog) to sit up and beg. **~iglich** pron. everyone, all. **~lich** a. male; manly; (gram.) masculine.

mannig-fach, ~faltig aa. manifold, various. **~faltigkeit** f. variety, multiplicity.

Ma'növer n. (-s, -) manœuvre; trick.

manöv'rieren v.t. to manœuvre.

Man'sarde f. (-, -n) attic. [F]

manschen v.t. & i. to mix; to splash about (in).

Man'schette f. (-, -n) cuff; **~n** h. vor (colloq.) to be afraid of. **~n-knopf** m. cuff-link.

Mantel m. (-s, ⸚) cloak, coat, mantle; jacket, casing, case; outer cover of tyre; den ~ nach dem Wind hängen to trim one's sails according to the wind. **~sack** m. valise, portmanteau. **~tarif** m. skeleton agreement.

Manufak'tur f. (-, -en) manufacture, manufacturing; factory. **~waren** f.pl. manufactured goods, dry goods.

Manu'skript n. (-s, -e) manuscript; copy; script.

Mappe f. (-, -n) document case, portfolio; writing-case; file. [MAP]

Mär f. (-, -en) news, tidings; story. **~chen** n. fairy tale. **~chenhaft** a. fabulous, legendary.

Marder m. (-s, -) marten.

Marga'rine f. (-) margarine.

Marge'rite f. (-, -n) marguerite.

Ma'rien-glas n. mica. **~käfer** m. lady-bird.

Ma'rine (-ri:-) f. (-, -n) marine, shipping, navy. **~flieger** m.

naval airman. **~flugzeug** n. seaplane; plane of the Fleet Air Arm. **~ministerium** n. Admiralty. **~offizier** m. naval officer. **~soldat** m. marine. **~station** f. naval base.

mari'nieren v.t. to pickle.

Mario'nettentheater n. puppet theatre.

Mark[1] f. (-, -stücke) (coin) mark.

Mark[2] n. (-es) marrow; pith; pulp; essence; core; ins ~ treffen to cut to the quick. **~erschütternd** a. blood-curdling. **~ig** a. pithy.

Mark[3] f. (-, -en) frontier, boundary, marches (pl.). **~graf** m. margrave. **~gräfin** f. margravine. **~scheider** m. mine-surveyor. **~stein** m. boundary-stone; (fig.) landmark.

mar'kant a. characteristic; striking; well-marked.

Marke f. (-, -n) mark, sign, token; (postage-)stamp; counter, chip; (commerc.) brand, trade-mark. **~nalbum** n. stamp album. **~nartikel** m., **~nware** f. proprietary article; patent product. **~nschutzgesetz** n. Trade Marks Registration Act.

Marke'tender m. (-s, -) sutler.

mar'kieren v.t. to mark, indicate; to simulate.

Mar'kise (-ki:zə) f. (-, -n) awning, blind.

Markt m. (-es, ̈e) market; marketplace; trade, business. **~bude** f. booth, stall. **~flecken** m. small market-town. **~gängig** a. current. **~halle** f. market-hall. **~helfer** m. packer. **~lage** f. state of the market. **~platz** m. marketplace. **~schreier** m. quack. **~schreierisch** a. charlatan, showy. **~wert** m. current value. **~wirtschaft** f. marketing; freie ~ ~ free enterprise economy.

markten v.i. to bargain, haggle.

Marmel(stein) m. marble.

Marme'lade f. (-, -n) ⚘ jam.

Marmor m. (-s, -e) marble. **~bruch** m. marble quarry. **~ieren** v.t. to marble, grain, vein. **~n** a. marble, of marble. **~platte** f. marble slab. **~schnitt** m. marbled edges (of book).

ma'rod-e a. weary, tired; ill. **~eur** m. marauder. **~ieren** v.i. to pillage.

Ma'rone f. (-, -n) edible chestnut.

Maroquin (-kē:) n. (-s, -e) morocco.

Ma'rotte f. (-, -n) fancy, caprice, whim, fad.

Mars m. (-, -en) top. **~segel** n. topsail.

Marsch[1] m. (-es, ̈e) march. **~ieren** vws.i. to march. **~kolonne** f. marching column. **~mäßig** a. ready for the march, in marching order. **~tempo** n. rate of marching.

Marsch[2] f. (-, -en) marsh, fen. **~boden** m. marshy soil. **~ig** a. marshy.

Marschall m. (-s, Marschälle) marshal. **~stab** m. marshal's baton.

Marstall m. (-es, Marställe) royal stables or stud.

Marter f. (-, -n) torture, torment; agony, pang. **~bank** f. rack. **~holz** n. the Cross. **~pfahl** m. stake.

martern v.t. to torture; to torment.

marti'alisch a. martial.

Märtyrer m. (-s, -) martyr. **~tum**, **Mar'tyrium** n. martyrdom.

März (-ts) m. (-es, -e) March.

Marzi'pan m. & n. (-s, -e) marzipan.

Masch-e f. (-e, -en) mesh; stitch. **~enfest** a. ladder-proof, runproof. **~enwerk** n. network.

Ma'schine f. (-, -n) machine; engine; typewriter. **~'ll** a. mechanical. **~nbauer** m. mechanical engineer. **~ngarn** n. machine-spun yarn, twist. **~ngewehr** n. machine gun. **~nmeister** m. machinist; engine-driver; (theatr.) stage mechanic. **~nöl** n. lubricating oil. **~nschaden** m. engine trouble. **~nschlosser** m. engine fitter. **~nschreiber** m. typist. **~nschrift** f. typescript. **~'rie** f. machinery.

Maschi'nist m. (-en, -en) machinist; engineer; mechanic; artificer.

Maser (ma:-) f. (-, -n) spot, speckle. **~n** (pl.) measles. **~ig** a. mottled, streaked, speckled, grained. ~n v.t. to vein, grain.

Mask-e f. (-e, -en) mask; disguise. ~enball m. fancy-dress ball. ~enverleih m. hire of theatrical properties. ~e'rade f. masquerade. ~ieren v.t. to mask; to disguise.

Masku'linum n. (-s, ... na) masculine (noun).

maß² *imperf. of* **messen**.

Maß² (ma:s) n. (-es, -e) measure; size; extent, dimension; degree; limit, bounds; proportion; standard; (*fig.*) moderation; f. litre (of beer); ~ *nehmen* to measure, take the measurement of; *nach* ~ *gemacht* made to measure; *in verjüngtem* ~e on a reduced scale, in miniature; *in hohem* ~e in a high degree, highly; *in dem* ~e, *daß* to such an extent that; *über die* ~en beyond measure, exceedingly. ~analyse f. volumetric analysis. ~anzug m. tailor-made suit. ~arbeit f. (*dressm.*) made to measure. ~gabe f. *nach* ~*gabe* according to. ~gebend, ~geblich aa. standard, authoritative. ~halten v.i. to observe moderation, keep within limits. ~krug m. tankard, mug. ~liebchen n. daisy. ~los a. boundless; immoderate; extravagant. ~nahme f. measure. ~regel f. measure, step. ~regeln v.t. to reprimand; to inflict disciplinary punishment on. ~schneiderei f. tailoring to measure. ~stab m. yard measure, ruler; measure, scale, standard. ~voll a. moderate. ~werk n. tracery.

Mass-age (-a:ʒə) f. massage. ~eur m. masseur. ~euse f. masseuse. ~ieren v.t. to massage.

Mas'sak-er n. (-ers, -er) massacre. ~rieren v.t. to massacre.

Mass-e f. (-e, -en) quantity; number(s); heap(s); mass, substance, lump, bulk; the multitude, the masses, the people; (*leg.*) assets, property; estate. ~enabsatz m. wholesale. ~enartikel m. wholesale article. ~enaufgebot n. levy en masse, general levy. ~engrab n. com-

mon grave. ~enhaft a. in large quantities, wholesale. ~enmord m. general massacre. ~enquartier n. billets for large numbers. ~enversammlung f. mass-meeting. ~enweise adv. in large numbers, wholesale. ~ig a. bulky, heavy, solid. ~iv a. massive.

mäßig (mɛ:-) a. moderate, frugal; modest, reasonable; middling. ~en v.t. to observe moderation; to assuage, mitigate; to restrain, check; to slacken (one's pace); *gemäßigte Zone* temperate zone. ~keit f. moderation, frugality; temperance. ~ung f. moderation restraint.

Mast¹ m. (-es, -en) mast, pole; pylon. ~korb m. crow's-nest.

Mast² f. (-, -en) mast. ~darm m. rectum. ~kalb n. fatted calf. ~kur f. fattening diet.

mästen v.t. to fatten.

Mastix m. mastic.

Mater (ma:-) f. (-, -n) matrix.

Materi'al (-a:l) n. (-s, -ien) material, substance; stock; *rollendes* ~ rolling stock. ~i'sieren v.t. to materialize. ~ismus m. materialism. ~ist m. materialist. ~istisch a. materialistic. ~waren f.pl. groceries, colonial produce.

Ma'teri-e (-te:ria) f. (-e, -en) matter, stuff, substance. ~ell a. material; materialistic; financial (worries, &c.).

Mathema'tik f. (-) mathematics. **Mathe'mati-ker** m. (-kers, -ker) mathematician. ~sch a. mathematical.

Matjeshering m. white herring.

Ma'tratze f. (-, -n) mattress.

Mä'tresse f. (-, -n) (kept) mistress.

Ma'trikel f. (-, -n) register, roll.

Ma'trize f. (-, -n) matrix; (*mach.*) die.

Ma'trone (-o:-) f. (-, -n) ♀ matron = elderly woman.

Ma'trose (-o:zə) m. (-n, -n) sailor.

Matsch¹ m. (-es) mud, slush. ~ig a. muddy, slushy.

Matsch² m. (-es, -e) loss (in games).

matt a. weak, feeble; dim; mat, dull; (check-)mate; ~ *setzen* to

mate. **~glas** *n.* frosted glass.
~gold *n.* dead gold. **~heit** *f.*
dullness. **~herzig** *a.* faint-
hearted. **~igkeit** *f.* weakness,
feebleness, debility; exhaustion.
~scheibe *f.* (*phot.*) focusing
screen. **~weiß** *a.* dull white;
off-white. [ARAB.]

Matte[1] *f.* (-, -n) alpine meadow.

Matte[2] *f.* (-, -n) mat.

Mätzchen *n.* **~ machen** to play the
fool; to be fussy.

Matze *f.* (-, -n) unleavened bread.

Mauer *f.* (-, -n) wall. **~anschlag**
m. poster. **~blümchen** *n.* wallflower. **~brecher** *m.* battering-
ram. **~polier** *m.* head mason.
~schwalbe *f.* black martin,
swift. **~werk** *n.* stonework,
masonry. [L]

mauern *v.i.* to build (with stone).

Mauke *f.* (-) malanders.

Maul *n.* (-es, "er) mouth; muzzle;
snout; **~- *und* Klauenseuche** foot
and mouth disease. **~affe** *m.*
~affen feilhalten to stand gaping.
~held *m.* braggart. **~korb** *m.*
muzzle. **~schelle** *f.* slap, box on
the ear. **~sperre** *f.* lock-jaw.
~trommel *f.* Jew's harp.

Maulbeerbaum *m.* mulberry tree.

maulen *v.i.* to sulk, pout.

Maul-esel *m.,* **~tier** *n.* mule.

Maulwurf *m.* (-s, ... würfe) mole.
~shügel *m.* molehill.

Maurer *m.* (-s, -) mason, bricklayer.
~geselle *m.* journeyman mason.
~meister *m.* master mason.

Maus *f.* (-, "e) mouse. **~efalle** *f.*
mousetrap. **~en** *v.i.* to catch
mice. *v.t.* (*colloq.*) to steal, pinch.
~etot *a.* stone-dead.

mauscheln *v.i.* to talk sheeny.

mäus-chenstill *a.* quiet as a mouse,
stock-still. **~ebussard** *m.* common buzzard.

Maus-er *f.* moulting. **~ern** *v.r.* to
moult. **~ig** *a. sich ~ig machen*
to put on airs.

Maximal-betrag *m.* maximum
amount. **~gewicht** *n.* maximum
weight.

Ma'xime *f.* (-, -n) maxim.

Mayo'nnäse *f.* (-, -n) mayonnaise.

Mä'zen *m.* (-s, -e) Maecenas.

Me'chan-ik *f.* (-ik) mechanics;

mechanism. **~iker** *m.* mechanic,
fitter, engineer. **~isch** *a.* mechanical. **~i'sierung** *f.* mechaniza-
tion. **~'ismus** *m.* mechanism.

meckern *v.i.* to bleat; (*fig.*) to
grumble, grouse.

Me'daill-e (-dalja) *f.* (-e, -en) medal.
~on *n.* medallion, locket.

Medika'ment *n.* (-s, -e) medica-
ment.

medi'tieren *v.i.* to meditate.

Medium *n.* (-s, Medien) ♀ (*psychic*)
medium.

Medi'zin (-tsi:n) *f.* (-, -en) medicine; physic. **~er** *m.* medical
man; student of medicine. **~
isch** *a.* medical; medicinal.

Meer (me:r) *n.* (-es, -e) sea, ocean.
~busen *m.* gulf, bay. **~enge** *f.*
straits, channel. **~eshöhe** *f.*
~esspiegel *m.* sea-level, surface
of sea. **~katze** *f.* long-tailed
monkey. **~rettich** *m.* horse-
radish. **~schweinchen** *n.* guinea-
pig. **~weib** *n.* mermaid. [MERE]

Me'gäre *f.* (-, -n) termagant,
vixen.

Mehl (me:l) *n.* (-es) flour, meal.
~ig *a.* floury, mealy, farinaceous.
~speise *f.* (milk) pudding. **~
wurm** *m.* meal-worm.

mehr (me:r) *a. & adv.* more; **~
als** more than; **immer ~** more
and more; **je ~ desto** the more
. . . the more; **nicht ~** no more,
no longer; **umso ~ als** all the
more as; **nur ~** only, nothing
but. **~ausgabe** *f.* additional
expenditure. **~bändig** *a.* in
several volumes. **~betrag** *m.*
surplus. **~deutig** *a.* ambiguous.
~fach *a.* manifold, several; re-
peated(ly); multiple. **~farbig** *a.*
multicoloured. **~gewicht** *n.*
excess weight. **~heit** *f.* majority.
~malig *a.* repeated, reiterated.
~mals *adv.* several times, again
and again. **~seitig** *a.* polygonal,
with many sides. **~silbig** *a.*
polysyllabic. **~sprachig** *a.* polyglot. **~stimmig** *a.* part (song);
(music) arranged for several
voices. **~wertsteuer** *f.* high
value tax. **~zahl** *f.* majority;
(*gram.*) plural.

mehr-en *v.t.* to increase, augment.

v.r. to multiply, grow. **~er** *m.*
enlarger, augmenter.

mehrer-e *a.pl.* several; **~es**
several things; sundries. **~lei** *a.*
indecl. various, diverse, divers.

meiden *v.t.* to avoid, shun.

Meier *m.* (-s, -) farmer; steward
(of estate). **~ei** *f.* farm, dairy-
farm. [L]

Meile *f.* (-, -n) mile, league.
~nstein *m.* milestone. **~nweit**
adv. for miles, miles off. See also
App. III.

Meiler *m.* (-s, -) charcoal-pile.

mein *pron. & a.* my, mine; **die ~-
en** my people. **~erseits** *adv.* for
my part, as far as I am concerned. **~esgleichen** *indecl. pron.*
my equals, people like me,
such as I. **~esteils** *adv.* on
my part. **~ethalben**, **~etwegen**
adv. for my sake, for me; for
all I care; I don't mind. **~et-
willen** *adv. um ~etwillen* for my
sake. **~ig** *a.* my, mine.

Meineid *m.* (-s, -e) perjury. **~ig**
a. perjured.

mein-en *v.t. & i.* to think, believe,
suppose; to intend, mean; *wie
~en Sie?* I beg your pardon?
~ung *f.* view, opinion; meaning;
intention; *meiner ~ung nach* to
my mind, in my opinion; *einem
die ~ung sagen* to give a p. a bit
of one's mind. **~ungsbefragung**
f. öffentliche ~~ Gallup poll.
[MEAN]

Meise (-zə) *f.* (-, -n) titmouse.

Meißel *m.* (-s, -) chisel. **~n** *v.t.* to
chisel, carve.

meist *a.* most; *die ~en* most
people. *adv.* most, mostly. **~-
begünstigungsklausel** *f.* most-
favoured-nation clause. **~bie-
tende(r)** *m.* highest bidder. **~-
ens**, **~enteils** *adv.* mostly, for
the most part. **~gebot** *n.* highest bid, best offer.

Meister *m.* (-s, -) master; *(colloq.)*
boss; *(sport.)* champion; **~** *vom
Stuhl* master of the lodge. **~haft**
~lich *aa.* masterly. **~in** *f.*
mistress; (woman) champion.
~schaft *f.* mastery; championship. **~skämpfer** *m.* champion.
~singer *m.* mastersinger. **~-**

stück, **~werk** *n.* masterpiece.

meistern *v.t.* to master; to control.

Melancho'lie (-li:) *f.* (-, -n) melancholy.

Melan'choli-ker *m.* (-kers, -ker)
hypochondriac. **~sch** *a.* melancholy.

Melde-amt *n.* registration office.
~gänger *m.* messenger; runner.
~pflichtig *a.* subject to registration. **~reiter** *m.* dispatch
rider. **~schluß** *m.* closing date
for entries. **~stelle** *f.* local re-
porting office. **~zettel** *m.* registration form.

meld-en *v.t.* to announce, inform;
to report. *v.r.* to report (to
police); to apply for (situation);
to enter (for exam.); *sich ~en
lassen* to send in one's name.
~ung *f.* news, announcement;
advice; notification; report;
notice; *(sport.)* entry.

me'lieren *v.t.* a greying (hair).

Melissengeist *m.* balm(-mint).

melk-en *v.t. st.* to milk. **~er** *m.*
milker. **~e'rei** *f.* dairy(-farm).
~kübel *m.* milking-pail, milking-
tub.

Melo'die *f.* (-, -n) melody, tune, air.

me'lod-isch, **~i'ös** *aa.* melodious.

Me'lone (-lo:-) *f.* (-, -n) melon.

Meltau (me:-) *m.* (-s) mildew, blight.

Mem'bran (-a:-) *f.* (-, -en) membrane; *(tel.)* diaphragm.

Memme *f.* (-, -n) coward, poltroon.

Me'moiren (-mo'a:rən) *n.pl.* ♦mem-
oirs = personal reminiscences.

memo'rieren *v.t.* to memorize.

Menge *f.* (-, -n) quantity, amount,
great deal, lots, a great many;
the masses; crowd, multitude;
in ~n in abundance, plenty of.
~n *v.t.* to mix, blend. *v.r.* to
mingle, mix; to meddle, interfere (with). **~nbestimmung** *f.*
quantitative determination.

Mennig *m.*, **~e** *f.* minium, red
lead, lead oxide.

Mensch *m.* (-en, -en) man, human
being, person, individual. *n.*
(vulg.) hussy; *jeder ~* everybody, everyone; *kein ~* nobody.
~enaffe *m.* anthropoid ape.
~enalter *n.* generation, age.
~enfeindlich *a.* misanthropic.

~entfresser m. cannibal. ~enfreundlich a. philanthropic. ~engedenken n. seit ~ within the memory of man, from time immemorial. ~engeschlecht n. mankind. ~enkenntnis f. knowledge of human nature. ~enmaterial n. manpower. ~enmöglich a. humanly possible. ~enscheu a. unsociable, shy. ~enschinder m. extortioner. ~enschlag m. race of men. ~ensohn m. the Son of Man. ~heit f. human race, mankind. ~lich a. human; (fig.) humane. ~lichkeit f. human nature, humanity; humaneness. ~werdung f. incarnation.

menstru'ieren v.i. to menstruate.

Men'sur (-zu:r) f. (-, -en) students' duel.

Mentali'tät f. (-, -en) mentality.

Menu'ett n. (-s, -e) minuet.

Mergel m. (-s) marl. ~boden m. marly soil. ~grube f. marl-pit. ~n v.t. to manure with marl.

Meridi'an m. (-s, -e) meridian.

merk-bar, ~lich aa. noticeable, perceptible. ~blatt n. leaflet; instructional pamphlet. ~buch n. notebook. ~mal n. characteristic; sign, mark, criterion. ~würdig a. strange, curious; striking; peculiar; remarkable. ~würdigerweise adv. strange to say. ~würdigkeit f. strangeness; peculiarity; sight(s), curiosity. ~zeichen n. characteristic; mark, sign.

merken v.t. to perceive, notice, observe, note. v.r. to bear in mind; sich nichts ~ lassen to appear to know nothing.

Mesner m. (-s, -) sacristan, sexton.

meß-bar a. measurable. ~bild n. scale drawing. ~gerät n. meter; gauge. ~tischblatt n. ordnance survey map; plane table survey. ~trupp m. survey section.

Meß-buch n. missal. ~diener m. acolyte. ~gewand n. vestment; chasuble. ~kelch m. chalice. ~opfer n. (sacrifice of the) mass. Messe f. (-, -n) mass; fair; (officers') mess; ~ lesen to say mass. ~stand m. stall (at a fair).

messen v.t. & i. st. to measure; to survey (land). v.r. to compete (with), try one's strength (with); sich nicht ~ können mit to be no match for; mit Blicken ~ to eye, take stock of. [METE]

Messer n. (-s, -) knife. ~bänkchen n. knife-rest. ~griff m. knife-handle. ~schärfer m. knife-sharpener. ~schmied m. cutler. ~stich m. stab (with a knife).

Messing n. (-s) brass. ~beschlag m. brass mounting. ~schild n. brass plate. [SLAV.]

Met (me:t) m. (-es) mead.

Me'tall n. (-s, -e) metal. ~arbeiter m. metal worker. ~en, ~isch aa. (of) metal, brass; metallic. ~haltig a. containing metal. ~ur'gie f. metallurgy. ~waren f.pl. hardware.

Metamor'phose (-fo:-) f. (-, -n) metamorphosis.

Me'tapher f. (-, -n) metaphor.

Metaphys'ik (-ik) f. metaphysics. ~isch a. metaphysical.

Mete'or n. (-s, -e) meteor. ~o'loge m. meteorologist. ~olo'gie f. meteorology. ~stein m. meteoric stone, aerolite.

Meter (me:-) m. & n. (-s, -) metre. ~maß n. tape-measure.

Me'thod-e f. (-e, -en) method. ~isch a. methodical.

Metr-ik (-ik) f. prosody; versification. ~isch a. metrical. ~um n. (pros.) metre.

Metro'pole f. (-, -n) metropolis.

Mette f. (-, -n) matins.

Mettwurst f. German sausage.

Metze f. (-, -n) prostitute.

Metze'lei f. (-, -en) massacre.

metz-eln v.t. to butcher, massacre. ~ger m. butcher. ~ge'rei f. butcher's shop. [ML]

Meuch-elmord m. assassination. ~elmörder, ~ler m. assassin. ~lerisch a. treacherous, murderous. ~lings adv. treacherously.

meucheln v.t. to assassinate.

Meute f. (-, -n) pack of hounds. ~rei f. mutiny. ~rer m. mutineer. ~risch a. mutinous. ~rn v.i. to mutiny.

mi'auen v.i. to mew, caterwaul.

mich *acc. of pron.* ich me.

mied *imperf. of* meiden.

Mieder *n.* (-s, -) bodice; corset.

Miene *f.* (-, -n) air, countenance, face, mien. **~nspiel** *n.* changing expressions (of face).

mies *a.* (*colloq.*) bad, miserable. **~macher** *m.* alarmist. [HEBR.]

Miesmuschel *f.* mussel.

Miete[1] *f.* (-, -n) stack, rick; shock.

Miet-e[2] *f.* (-e, -en) rent; hire; lease; zur ~e wohnen to live in lodgings, be a tenant. **~er** *m.* tenant, lodger. **~erschaft** *f.* tenantry. **~frei** *a.* rent-free. **~ling** *m.* mercenary, hireling. **~(s)auto** *n.* taxi-cab. **~(s)haus** *n.* tenement house, house with flats to let. **~(s)vertrag** *m.* lease. **~zins** *m.* rent.

mieten *v.t.* to rent, hire; to charter (ship).

Mi'gräne *f.* (-, -n) sick headache. [F]

Mi'krobe *f.* (-, -n) microbe.

Mikro'phon *n.* (-s, -e) microphone.

Mikro'skop *n.* (-s, -e) microscope. **~isch** *a.* microscopic.

Milbe *f.* (-, -n) mite.

Milch (-ç) *f.* (-) milk; roe. **~bart** *m.* downybeard; milksop. **~bruder** *m.* foster-brother. **~geschäft** *n.* dairy (shop). **~gesicht** *n.* baby face. **~glas** *n.* opalescent glass. **~ig** *a.* milky. **~(n)er** *m.* milter. **~pantscher** *m.* adulterator of milk. **~säure** *f.* lactic acid. **~straße** *f.* Milky Way. **~wagen** *m.* milk-float. **~zahn** *m.* milk-tooth. **~zucker** *m.* sugar of milk, lactose.

milchen *v.i.* to give milk.

mild (-t) *a.* mild, soft, gentle, mellow; tender, kind; light; generous, charitable. **~e** *f.* mildness, kindness. **~ern** *v.t.* to soften; to assuage, mitigate, alleviate; ~ernde Umstände extenuating circumstances. **~tätig** *a.* charitable, generous.

Mili'eu (-ø:) *n.* (-s, -s) surroundings, background; local colour.

Mili'tär *n.* (-s) military, soldiery, army. *m.* (-s, -s) military man, soldier. **~arzt** *m.* army surgeon. **~dienst** *m.* (active) service. **~geistliche(r)** *m.* army chaplain.

~isch *a.* military. **~maß** *n.* standard measure. **~musik** *f.* military band. **~vorlage** *f.* army bill.

Milita'rismus *m.* (-) militarism.

Mi'liz *f.* (-, -en) militia. **~soldat** *m.* militiaman.

Milli'arde *f.* milliard. **~'on** *f.* million. **~o'när** *m.* millionaire.

Milz *f.* (-, -en) spleen; milt. **~brand** *m.* anthrax. **~krank** *a.* splenetic.

Mim-e *m.* (-en, -en) actor; mimic. **~en** *v.i.* to act (in plays); to pretend, feign. **~ik** *f.* mimic art; miming. **~isch** *a.* mimic.

Mi'mose (-o:za) *f.* (-, -n) mimosa.

minder *a.* less; minor; inferior. **~begabt** *a.* of inferior ability; subnormal. **~bemittelt** *a.* of moderate means. **~betrag** *m.* deficiency, deficit. **~heit** *f.* minority. **~jährig** *a.* under age, minor. **~jährigkeit** *f.* minority. **~ung** *f.* diminution, decrease. **~wertig** *a.* inferior. **~wertigkeitsgefühl** *n.* inferiority complex. **~zahl** *f.* minority.

mindern *v.t.* to diminish, lessen.

mindest *a.* least, smallest, lowest; nicht im ~ not in the least, not at all, by no means. **~ens** *adv.* at least. **~lohn** *m.* minimum wage. **~maß** *n.* (indispensable) minimum.

Mine (mi:-) *f.* (-, -n) mine; (refill) lead (of pencil). **~nfeld** *n.* mine-field. **~ngang** *m.* gallery, tunnel. **~nleger** *m.* mine-layer. **~nräumer** *m.* mine-sweeper. **~nsperre** *f.* minefield. **~nsucher** *m.*, **~nsuchboot** *n.* mine-sweeper. **~nsuchgerät** *n.* mine detector. **~nwerfer** *m.* (trench) mortar.

Mine'ral (-a:l) *n.* (-s, -e & -ien) mineral. **~isch** *a.* mineral. **~'oge** *m.* mineralogist. **~o'gie** *f.* mineralogy. **~ogisch** *a.* mineralogical. **~quelle** *f.* mineral spring.

Minia'tur *f.* (-, -en) miniature.

mi'nieren *v.t.* to (under) mine, sap.

Minimal-betrag *m.* lowest amount;

minimum. ~satz *m.* minimum rate.

Mi'nister *m.* (-s, -) minister. ~i'alerlaß *m.* ministerial order. ~i'ell *a.* ministerial. ~ium *n.* ministry. ~präsident *m.* Prime Minister. ~rat *m.* Cabinet Council.

Minis'tr-ant *m.* (-anten, -anten) acolyte, ministrant. ~ieren *v.i.* to minister, officiate.

Minn-e *f.* (obs.) love. ~en *v.t.* to love. ~esang *m.* old love song, lyric poem (of 12th to 14th centuries). ~esänger *m.* minnesinger. ~iglich *a.* lovely, charming. [MIND]

mino'r-enn *a.* under age, minor. ~i'tät *f.* minority.

minus *adv.* minus. *subst. n.* deficit. ~kel *f.* minuscule.

Mi'nute *f.* (-nu:-) *f.* (-, -n) minute. ~nlang *a.* for (several) minutes. ~nzeiger *m.* minute hand (of clock).

minuti'ös *a.* minute.

Minze *f.* (-, -n) (bot.) mint.

mir (mi:r) *dat. of pron.* ich me, to me, for me.

Mira'belle *f.* (-, -n) small yellow plum.

Mi'rakel (-a:-) *n.* (-s, -) miracle.

Misch-ehe *f.* mixed marriage. ~ling *m.* mongrel, hybrid, cross; half-caste. ~masch *m.* hotchpotch, medley. ~rasse *f.* mongrel race. ~ung *f.* blend; mixture; compound, combination, composition. ~ungsverhältnis *n.* ratio of components. ~wald *m.* mixed forest.

mischen *v.t.* to mix; to blend; to shuffle (cards). *v.r.* to mix (with people); to join (in); to interfere (with).

mise'rabel *a.* miserable, wretched.

Mispel *f.* (-, -n) medlar.

miß-achten *v.t.* to disregard; to despise. ~achtung *f.* disregard; disdain. ~behagen *v. impers.* to displease. *subst. n.* discomfort. ~bilden *v.t.* to mis-shape. ~bildung *f.* malformation; disfiguration, deformity. ~billigen *v.t.* to disapprove (of). ~billigung *f.* disapproval. ~brauch

m. misuse; abuse. ~brauchen *v.t.* to misuse; to abuse; to take advantage of; to outrage. ~bräuchlich *a.* improper, wrong. ~deuten *v.t.* to misinterpret, misconstrue. ~deutung *f.* misinterpretation.

missen *v.t.* to miss; to do without.

Miß-erfolg *m.* failure. ~ernte *f.* bad harvest, failure of crop.

Misse-tat *f.* misdeed; crime. ~täter *m.* evil-doer; criminal.

miß-fallen *v.i.* to displease. *subst. n.* displeasure, dissatisfaction. ~fällig *a.* unfavourable, disparaging. ~geburt *f.* monster; abortion. ~gelaunt *a.* bad-tempered. ~geschick *n.* bad luck, misfortune. ~gestalt *f.* deformity; monster. ~gestaltet *a.* deformed. ~gestimmt *a.* bad-tempered. ~glücken *vws.i.* to fail. ~gönnen *v.t.* to grudge; envy. ~griff *m.* mistake. ~gunst *f.* envy, jealousy, ill will. ~günstig *a.* envious, jealous. ~handeln *v.t.* to ill-treat. ~handlung *f.* ill treatment. ~heirat *f.* misalliance. ~hellig *a.* dissentient, discordant. ~helligkeit *f.* difference, disagreement, dissension.

Missi'on *f.* (-, -en) mission; innere ~ home mission. ~ar *m.* missionary.

Miß-jahr *n.* bad year. ~klang *m.* dissonance, discord. ~kredit *m.* discredit. ~leiten *v.t.* to mislead. ~lich *a.* unpleasant, awkward; critical, difficult; unfortunate. ~liebig *a.* unpopular. ~lingen *vws.i. st.* to fail. *subst. n.* failure. ~mut *m.* ill humour. ~mutig *a.* bad-tempered, cross. ~raten *vws.i.* to fail, turn out badly. *a.* ill-bred, naughty (child). ~stand *m.* inconvenience, nuisance; grievance. ~stimmen *v.t.* to depress, upset. ~stimmung *f.* ill humour; depression. ~ton *m.* dissonance, discord. ~tönend *a.* discordant, out of tune. ~trauen *v.i.* to distrust, mistrust. *subst. n.* distrust, suspicion. ~svotum *n.* vote of no confidence. ~trauisch *a.* suspicious.

~vergnügen *n.* displeasure; discontent. ~vergnügt *a.* displeased; discontented. ~verhältnis *n.* disproportion, incongruity. ~verständlich *a.* misleading. ~verständnis *n.* misunderstanding, misconception. ~verstehen *v.t.* to misunderstand, mistake. ~wachs *m.* failure of crop. ~wirtschaft *f.* maladministration, mismanagement.

mißt *2nd & 3rd pers. sing. pres. of* messen.

Mist *m.* (-es) dung, manure. ~beet *n.* hotbed. ~fuhre *f.* load of manure. ~gabel *f.* dung-fork. ~haufen *m.* manure heap. ~käfer *m.* dung-beetle.

Mistel *f.* (-, -n) mistletoe.

misten *v.t.* to manure; to clean.

mit *prep., adv., & sep. pref.* with, along with; by, at; at the same time; likewise, also; ~ *Tinte* in ink; ~ *der Post* by post; ~ *zehn Jahren* at the age of ten; ~ *der Zeit* in time, gradually; ~ *dabei sein* to be one of the party, to be there (too).

Mit-angeklagte(r) *m.* co-defendant. ~arbeiten *v.i.* to collaborate; to co-operate (with); to contribute (to). ~arbeiter *m.* collaborator, colleague; contributor; (*pl.*) staff. ~besitzer *m.* joint proprietor. ~bewerber *m.* competitor. ~bewohner *m.* fellow lodger. ~bringsel *n.* souvenir, present. ~bürger *m.* fellow citizen. ~einander *adv.* with one another, together, jointly. ~empfinden *v.t.* to feel for, sympathize with. *subst. n.* sympathy, fellow-feeling. ~erbe *m.* coheir. ~essen *v.t. & i.* to eat with, dine with. ~esser *m.* blackhead. ~geben *v.t.* to give; to give as dowry. ~gefühl *n.* sympathy, fellow-feeling. ~gehen *v.v.s.i.* to go with, accompany. ~gift *f.* dowry. ~giftjäger *m.* fortune-hunter. ~glied *n.* member. ~gliedschaft *f.* membership.

mit-halten *v.i.* to be there, take part (in). *v.t.* to share. ~hilfe *f.* assistance, co-operation. ~hin *conj.* consequently, therefore.

~inhaber *m.* copartner. ~kämpfer *m.* fellow combatant. ~kommen *v.v.s.i.* to accompany; to be able to follow, keep up with. ~läufer *m.* time-server, trimmer; (*pol.*) fellow-traveller. ~laut *m.* consonant. ~leid *n.* sympathy, pity. ~leidenschaft *f.* *in* ~ *ziehen* to affect, involve. ~leidig *a.* compassionate. ~leidslos *a.* pitiless, ruthless. ~machen *v.t. & i.* to take part in, join; to go through. ~mensch *m.* fellow creature. ~nahme *f.* taking, carrying. ~nehmen *v.t.* to take with one; to profit by; to exhaust, tire out. ~nichten *adv.* by no means. ~reißen *v.t.* to tear, drag along with; (*fig.*) to carry (with), sweep along. ~samt *prep.* together with. ~schuldig *a.* implicated (in a crime). ~schuldige(r) *m.* accomplice, accessory. ~schuldner *m.* joint debtor. ~schüler *m.* schoolfellow, fellow pupil. ~spielen *v.t. & i.* to accompany (*mus.*) to play a part; to take part; *übel* ~*spielen* to play a nasty trick. ~spieler *m.* partner. ~sprechen *v.t. & i.* to join in; to come into consideration. ~täter *m.* accomplice. ~täterschaft *f.* complicity.

Mittag (-ta:k) *m.* noon, midday; south. *n.* (*colloq.*) lunch, dinner; *zu* ~*essen* to dine. ~essen *n.* lunch, dinner. ~s *adv.* at noon; at lunch-time. ~spause *f.* lunch hour. ~stisch *m.* table; lunch, dinner.

mittäg-ig, -lich *aa.* noonday, midday; meridional; southern.

Mitte *f.* (-, -n) middle, midst; centre; mean, medium; *das Reich der* ~ Middle Kingdom, China; *goldene* ~ the golden mean; *in die* ~ *nehmen* to take between (us, &c.); ~ *Dreißig* in the middle thirties.

mitteil-en *v.t.* to impart, communicate, inform, notify, tell, pass on. *v.r.* to unbosom oneself. ~sam *a.* communicative. ~ung *f.* information, communication.

news, intelligence; notification; note; notice.

mittel¹ a. see mittler¹.

Mittel² n. (-s, -) means, expedient, way; remedy, medicine; (math.) mean, average; (phys.) medium; (pl.) means, money; sich ins ~ legen to mediate. ~alter n. Middle Ages. ~alterlich a. medieval. ~bar a. indirect, mediate. ~ding n. intermediate thing, something between (. . . and . . .). ~ernte f. average crop. ~finger m. middle finger. ~gewicht n. middle weight. ~hochdeutsch a. Middle High German. ~latein n. Medieval Latin. ~los a. without means, destitute. ~mächte f.pl. Central European Powers. ~mäßig a. average; middling, mediocre, tolerable. ~mäßigkeit f. mediocrity. ~meer n. App. I. ~ohrentzündung f. mastoiditis. ~punkt m. centre.

mittels prep. by means of.

Mittel-smann m., ~sperson f. mediator, go-between; middle-man; (sport.) umpire. ~stand m. middle classes. ~straße f., ~weg m. middle course, compromise, mean. ~stürmer m. centre forward. ~welle f. medium wave. ~wert m. mean value, average.

mitten adv. midway; ~ auf, ~ in in the middle of, in the midst of; ~ unter in the midst of, amidst; ~drin right in the middle of; ~durch right across, right through, through the middle; ~inne in the very centre, in among (them).

Mitternacht f. midnight; north. ~s adv. at midnight.

mitter-nächtig, ~nächtlich aa. midnight.

mittler¹ a. middle, central; mediocre, middling, medium, average; (math.) middle, mean. ~weile adv. meanwhile, (in the) meantime.

Mittler² m. (-s, -) mediator, intercessor; third party.

mittschiffs adv. amidships.

Mittwoch m. (-vɔx) (-s, -e) Wednesday.

mit'unter adv. sometimes, now and then.

Mit-welt f. our age; our contemporaries; our generation. ~wirken v.i. to take a part in, take part; to co-operate. ~wirkende(n) m.pl. (mus., &c.) players; actors, members (of the cast). ~wirkung f. co-operation, assistance. ~wissen n. cognizance, knowledge. ~wisser m. one in the secret, confidant; accessory. ~wisserschaft f. complicity; collusion.

Mix'tur f. (-, -en) mixture.

Möbel (mø:-) n. (-s, -) piece of furniture; (pl.) furniture. ~händler m. furniture dealer. ~spediteur m. furniture remover. ~speicher m. furniture repository. ~tischler m. cabinet-maker, joiner. ~wagen m. furniture van, removal van. [F]

mo'bil (-bi:l) a. active, nimble; mobile. ~e n. perpetuum ~e perpetual motion. ~iar n. furniture. ~ien pl. movables. ~isati'on, ~machung f. mobilization. ~i'sieren v.t. & i. to mobilize.

möb'lieren v.t. to furnish.

mochte, möchte imp rf. & subj. of mögen.

Mode (mo:də) f. (-, -n) fashion, mode, vogue. ~artikel, ~waren pl. fancy goods, novelties. ~dame f. lady of fashion. ~nschau f. fashion show, mannequin parade. ~schriftsteller m. popular writer. ~welt f. fashionable world. ~wort n. vogue-word. ~zeichner m. ~in f. dress designer. ~zeitung f. fashion magazine.

Mo'dell n. (-s, -e) model; pattern; mould; ~ stehen to pose for an artist. ~ieren v.t. & i. to model, mould, fashion.

modeln v.t. to form, to mould.

Moder (mo:-) m. (-s) mould; mud; decay. ~geruch m. musty smell. ~ig a. mouldy, musty.

modern¹ (mo:-) v.i. to moulder, rot, decay.

mo'dern² a. modern, up-to-date;

fashionable, in the latest style. ~i'sieren v.t. to modernize.

modifi'zieren v.t. to modify.

mod-isch a. fashionable, stylish. ~istin f. milliner.

modu'lieren v.t. to modulate.

Modus m. (-, Modi) mode; (gram.) mood.

Moge'lei f. (-, -en) cheating.

mogeln v.i. to cheat.

mögen (mø:-) irreg. v.t. & i. to want, wish, like, be inclined; to be allowed; (v. aux.) may, might; lieber ~ to prefer, like better; das mag sein that may be so; wie dem auch sein mag be that as it may; was ich auch tun mag no matter what I do; das mag ich nicht I don't like that; ich möchte wissen I should like to know; ich möchte nicht I don't want to, I should not like to; er mochte zehn Jahre alt sein he looked about ten years old. [MAY]

möglich (mø:kliç) a. possible, practicable, feasible; alles ~e all kinds of things; everything possible; nicht ~! it can't be, not really; sein ~stes tun to do one's utmost; ~st schnell as quickly as possible. ~enfalls, ~erweise adv. possibly; if possible; perhaps. ~keit f. possibility; potentiality; practicability; feasibility.

Mohn m. (-es, -e) poppy.

Mohr m. (-en, -en) Moor. Negro, darky. ~enknabe m. (obs.) Negro boy. ~enwäsche f. (fig.) vindication. ~in f. negress.

Möhre, Mohrrübe f. carrot.

Moiré f. (-, -s, -s) moiré.

mo'kieren v.r. to mock, sneer at.

Mokka m. (-s, -s) Mocha (coffee).

Molch m. (-es, -e) salamander.

Mole (mo:lə) f. (-, -n) mole.

Mole'kül n. (-s, -e) molecule.

molk imperf. of melken.

Molke f. (-, -n) whey. ~rei f. dairy.

Moll n. (-) & a. (mus.) minor.

mollig a. cosy, snug; soft, rounded.

Mo'lluske f. (-, -n) mollusc.

Molybdän n. (-s) molybdenum.

Mo'ment m. (-es, -e) moment. n.

momentum; impulse, impetus; motive. ~'an a. momentary. adv. just now. ~aufnahme f. snapshot.

Mo'nade f. (-, -n) monad.

Mo'narch (-arç) m. (-en, -en) monarch. ~ie f. monarchy. ~isch a. monarchical.

Monat (mo:-) m. (-s, -e) month. ~elang a. for months. ~lich a. monthly. ~sabschluß m. monthly balance. ~sfluß m., ~sregel f. menses, period. ~skarte f. monthly season-ticket. ~sschrift f. monthly magazine.

Mönch (mœnç) m. (-es, -e) monk, friar. ~isch a. monastic, monkish. ~(s)tum n. monasticism.

Mond (mo:nt) m. (-es, -e) moon; (astron.) satellite; (poet.) month. ~finsternis f. eclipse of the moon. ~gebirge n. mountains of the moon. ~hell a. moonlit. ~hof n. halo round the moon. ~jahr n. lunar year. ~scheibe f. disk of the moon. ~schein m. moonlight. ~sichel f. crescent of the moon, sickle-moon. ~stein m. moonstone. ~süchtig a. moonstruck.

Mo'neten pl. (colloq.) money.

mo'nieren v.t. to remind; to censure, criticize.

Mono-ga'mie f. monogamy. ~'gramm n. monogram. ~kel n. monocle. ~'log m. monologue, soliloquy. ~'pol n. monopoly. ~poli'sieren v.t. to monopolize. ~the'ismus m. monotheism. ~'ton a. monotonous. ~to'nie f. monotony.

Mon'stranz f. (-, -en) monstrance.

mon'strös a. monstrous.

Monstrum n. (-ums, -en) monster.

Mon'sun m. (-s, -e) monsoon.

Montag m. Monday.

Mon'tage (-ta:ʒə) f. setting up, fitting up; erection; assembling. ~eur m. fitter, mechanic, mechanician. ~ieren v.t. to set up, fit, erect, assemble. ~ierung f. setting up, mounting, erection. ~ur f. uniform.

Mon'tanindustrie f. mining industry.

Monu'ment n. (-s, -e) monument.

Moor (mo:r) *n.* (-es, -e) bog, swamp. **~bad** *n.* mud-bath. **~boden** *m.* marshy soil. **~ig** *a.* marshy. [MOOR]

Moos (mo:s) *n.* (-es, -e) moss. **~beere** *f.* cranberry. **~ig** *a.* mossy.

Mop *m.* (-es, -e) mop. **~pen** *v.t.* to mop.

Mops *m.* (-es, ̈e) pug. **~en** *v.t.* (*sl.*) to pinch. *v.r.* to be bored.

Mo'ral (-ra:l) *f.* (-) morality, morals; moral, lesson; morale. **~isch** *a.* moral. **~i'sieren** *v.i.* to moralize. **~i'tät** *f.* morality. **~pauke** *f.* severe reprimand, lecture.

Mo'räne *f.* (-, -n) moraine.

Mo'rast *m.* (-es, . . . äste) morass, bog. **~ig** *a.* marshy.

Morchel *f.* (-, -n) morel, edible fungus.

Mord (mort) *m.* (-es, -e) murder. **~anschlag** *m.* murderous attack. **~brenner** *m.* incendiary. **~bube** *m.* assassin. **~gierig, ~lustig** *aa.* bloodthirsty. **~kommission** *f.* homicide squad. **~skerl** *m.* devil of a fellow. **~smäßig** *a.* awful, terrific. **~sspektakel** *m.* fearful din, hullabaloo.

morden *v.t. & i.* to murder, kill.

Mörder *m.* (-s, -) murderer. **~grube** *f. aus seinem Herzen keine ~grube machen* to be very out-spoken. **~in** *f.* murderess. **~isch** *a.* murderous, bloody. **~lich** *a.* fearful, terrible.

mordio *int.* **~schreien** *v.i.* to cry murder.

Mores *pl.* (*colloq.*) **~ lehren** to teach (one) manners.

Morgen 1. *m.* (-s, -) morning; dawn, daybreak; east; acre (of land); *n.* morrow; **~s, des ~s** in the morning; *früh ~s* early in the morning; *heute ~* this morning; *guten ~* good morning. **2.** *adv.* tomorrow; *~ früh* to-morrow morning. **~dlich** *a.* morning, matutinal. **~gabe** *f.* bridegroom's gift to bride. **~grauen** *n.* dawn of day, break of day. **~land** *n.* the East, the Orient. **~ländisch** *a.* eastern, oriental. **~luft** *f.* **~luft wittern** to scent an advantage. **~rock**

m. dressing-gown. **~rot** *n.* dawn, red morning-sky.

morgig *a.* of tomorrow, next (day).

Morphium *n.* (-s) morphia, morphine. **~spritze** *f.* syringe for injecting morphia; morphia injection.

morsch *a.* rotten.

Mörser *m.* (-s, -) mortar; (*mil.*) heavy howitzer. **~keule** *f.* pestle.

Morse-schrift *f.* Morse code. **~zeichen** *n.* Morse signal.

Mörtel *m.* (-s) mortar. **~trog** *m.* hod.

Mosa'ik (-i:k) *f.* (-, -en) mosaic. **~fußboden** *m.* tessellated pavement.

Mo'schee *f.* (-, -n) mosque.

Moschus *m.* musk. **~tier** *n.* musk-deer.

Mos'kito *m.* (-s, -s) mosquito.

Most (-ɔ-) *m.* (-es, -e) must, new wine.

Mostrich *m.* (-s) mustard.

Mo'tiv (-i:f) *n.* (-s, -e) motive; motif, theme. **~ieren** *v.t.* to motivate.

Motor (mo:-) *m.* (-s, -en) motor; engine. **~boot** *n.* motor boat. **~fahrer** *m.* motorist. **~haube** *f.* bonnet (of car). **~i'sieren** *v.t.* to motorize. **~rad** *n.* motor-cycle. **~schaden** *m.* damage to engine, engine trouble.

Motte *f.* (-, -n) moth. **~nfraß** *m.* damage done by moths. **~npulver** *n.* insect-powder.

mou'ssieren *v.i.* to effervesce, sparkle.

Möwe (mø:və) *f.* (-, -n) sea-gull, mew.

Mucke *f.* (-, -n) whim, idea; mood.

Mücke *f.* (-, -n) midge, gnat. **~nstich** *m.* midge-bite, gnat-bite.

muck-en *v.i.* to stir, move quietly; (*fig.*) to be up in arms. **~er** *m.* hypocrite, bigot. **~ertum** *n.* bigotry, cant.

mucksen *v.i.* to stir (faintly).

müd-e *a.* tired, weary. **~igkeit** *f.* weariness, fatigue.

Muff[1] *m.* (-es, ̈e) (fur) muff. **~e** *f.* (*tech.*) sleeve, socket.

Muff[2] *m.* (-es) musty *or* mouldy smell. **~ig** *a.* musty, fusty, mouldy; (*fig.*) sulky, cross.

Muffel f. (-, -n) muffle.

Müh-e (my:ǝ) f. (-e, -en) labour, toil, trouble, effort; sich ~e geben to take pains; ~e machen to give trouble; der ~e wert worth while; mit ~e und Not only just, barely, with difficulty. ~elos a. easy, effortless. ~evoll a. laborious, difficult, irksome. ~ewaltung f. care, pains, trouble. ~sal n. & f. toil, trouble; hardship; care, distress. ~sam a. troublesome, difficult, intricate. ~selig a. laborious, hard, difficult.

muhen v.i. to low.

mühen v.r. to take pains or trouble.

Mühl-e f. (-e, -en) mill, windmill. ~enflügel m. sail of a windmill. ~rad n. mill-wheel. ~stein m. millstone.

Muhme f. (-, -n) aunt; female relative.

Mu'latt-e m. (-en, -en), ~in f. mulatto.

Mulde f. (-, -n) tray, trough; valley, hollow, depression.

Mull m. (-s) muslin.

Müll m. (-es) dust, rubbish, refuse. ~abfuhr f. removal of refuse. ~eimer m. dustbin. ~grube f. ash-pit. ~kasten m. dustbin, ash-bucket. ~kutscher m. dustman. ~schaufel f. dustpan. ~wagen m. dust-cart.

Müller m. (-s, -) miller. ~in f. miller's wife.

mulmig a. worm-eaten, rotten; (fig.) precarious.

Multipli-kati'on f. multiplication. ~'kator m. multiplier. ~'zieren v.t. to multiply.

Mumi-e (mu:miǝ) f. (-e, -en) mummy. ~fi'zieren v.t. to mummify.

Mummenschanz m., **Mummerei** f. masquerade.

Mumpitz m. (-es) bosh, stuff, nonsense.

Mund (-t) m. (-es, ̈-er) mouth; den ~ halten to hold one's tongue; reinen ~ halten to keep a secret; den ~ vollnehmen to talk big, brag; sich den ~ ver-brennen to put one's foot in it; nicht auf den ~ gefallen sein

to have a ready tongue; im ~e führen to talk constantly about; nach dem ~ reden to flatter; über den ~ fahren to cut short. ~art f. dialect. ~artlich a. dialectical, provincial. ~faul a. taciturn; tongue-tied. ~fäule f. (med.) thrush. ~gerecht a. easy, palatable. ~harmonika f. mouth-organ. ~höhle f. oral cavity. ~schenk m. cup-bearer. ~stück n. mouthpiece; tip (of cigarette); mit ~stück tipped (cigarette); ~tot machen to (reduce to) silence. ~voll m. mouthful. ~vorrat m. victuals, provisions. ~wasser n. mouth-wash. ~werk n. glib tongue, the gift of the gab. ~winkel m. corner of the mouth.

Münd-el n. (-els, -el) ward; minor. ~elsicher a. (of money) absolutely safe. ~ig a. of age; ~ig werden to come of age. ~igkeit f. majority.

munden v.i. to taste good, be appetizing.

münd-en v.i. to flow (into); to run (into). ~lich a. oral. ~ung f. mouth; estuary; muzzle (of gun).

Muniti'on f. (-, -en) ammunition. ~slager n. ammunition dump.

munkeln v.i. & t. to whisper.

Münster n. (-s, -) cathedral, minster.

munter a. wide-awake; alive, lively, gay. ~keit f. liveliness.

Münz-e f. (-e, -en) coin; medal; mint; für bare ~e nehmen to take (words) at their face value, believe implicitly. ~einheit f. monetary unit; standard of currency. ~einwurf m. slot. ~fälscher m. coiner. ~fernsprecher m. telephone-box. ~fuß m. standard (of coinage). ~kunde f. numismatics. ~stempel m. die. ~umlauf m. circulation of money. ~verschlechterung f. debasement of coinage.

münzen v.t. & i. to coin; to mint coin; gemünzt sein auf to be meant for.

mürbe a. tender, soft; mellow; short, crisp; brittle; (fig.) un-nerved, worn-down; ~ machen

to break (a person's) spirit;
(mil.) to soften up; ~ werden to
give in. ~teig m. shortbread,
(short) pastry.

Mure f. (-, -n) landslip.

Murmel m. (-s, -) (toy) marble.

murmel-n v.t. & i. to murmur; to
mutter. ~tier n. marmot.

murren v.i. to murmur, grumble.

mürrisch a. surly, morose, sullen.

Mus (mu:s) n. (-es) purée, stewed
fruit, jam, flan.

Muschel f. (-, -n) mussel; shell;
ear-piece (of phone); conch. ~
kalk m. shell lime or limestone.

Mus-e (mu:zə) f. (-e, -en) muse.
~ensohn m. poet; university
student.

Mu'seum n. (-s, Museen) museum.

Mu'sik (-zi:k) f. (-) music; band.
~alienhandlung f. music shop.
~alisch a. musical. ~ant m.
musician. ~antenknochen m.
funny-bone. ~hochschule f.
academy of music. ~korps n.
band.

Musiker m. (-s, -) musician,
bandsman.

musisch a. fond of, skilled in the
fine arts.

musi'zieren v.i. to play; to have
music.

Mus'kat m., ~blüte f. mace. ~
nuß f. nutmeg.

Muska'teller m. (-s, -) muscatel
(wine).

Muskel m. (-s, -n) muscle. ~band
n. ligament. ~faser f. muscular fibre. ~kater m. stiffness and
soreness. ~kraft f. muscular
strength. ~zerrung f. sprained
muscle.

Mus'ket-e f. (-e, -en) musket.
~ier m. musketeer.

Muskul-a'tur f. muscular system.
~ös a. muscular, sinewy,
brawny.

muß 1. 1st & 3rd pers. sing. pres.
of müssen. 2. subst. n. necessity.

Muße (mu:sə) f. (-) leisure, spare
time; mit ~ at one's leisure, in a
leisurely way.

Musse'lin m. (-s, -e) muslin.

müssen irreg. v.i. to have to, must,
be obliged to.

müßig (my:siç) a. idle, unem-

ployed. ~gang m. idleness.
~gänger m. idler.

Muster n. (-s, -) model; example,
paragon; pattern, design; (commerc.) sample. ~gültig, ~haft
aa. model, exemplary, perfect.
~karte f. pattern card, sample
book. ~klammer f. paper-
fastener. ~knabe m. model boy,
prig. ~koffer m. box of samples.
~schutz m. trade mark, registration of design. [L]

muster-n v.t. to examine; to review (troops), inspect; to figure,
pattern. ~ung f. examination;
inspection, review.

Mut (mu:t) m. (-es) courage, fortitude; state of mind; mood; ~
fassen to summon up courage,
take heart; ~ machen to encourage; guten~es sein to be
full of hope. ~ig a. brave,
courageous. ~los a. despondent.
~losigkeit f. despondency. ~
maßen v.t. to suppose, guess,
surmise. ~maßlich a. probable,
presumable. ~maßung f. surmise, conjecture, suspicion. ~
wille m. wantonness, mischiev-
ousness. ~willig a. mischievous;
malevolent, wanton; roguish.
[MOOD]

Mütchen n. sein ~ kühlen to vent
one's anger (on).

Mutter (mutər) f. (-, ") mother;
(mach.) nut. ~boden m., ~erde
f. native soil. ~gottes f. the
Virgin. ~korn n. ergot. ~
kuchen m. placenta. ~leib f.
womb; vom ~leibe an from birth.
~mal n. birth-mark, mole.
~mord m. matricide. ~schaf
n. ewe. ~schaft f. motherhood,
maternity. ~schlüssel m. wrench-
spanner. ~schwein n. sow. ~
seelenallein pred. a. all alone. ~
sprache f. mother tongue. ~witz
m. mother wit, common sense.

Mütter-chen n. (-chen) m. little
mother; little old woman. ~lich
a. motherly. ~licherseits adv.
on the mother's side.

Mutung f. (min.) claim.

Mütze f. (-, -n) cap. ~nschirm m.
peak of a cap.

Myrrhe f. (-, -n) myrrh.

Myrte f. (-, -n) myrtle.

mysteri'ös a. mysterious.

Mys'ter-ium n. (-iums, -ien) mystery.

mystifi'zieren v.t. to mystify.

Myst-ik f. mysticism. ~iker m., ~isch a. mystic.

Myth-e (-y:-) f., ~us m. (pl. -en) myth. ~isch a. mythical. ~olo'gie f. mythology. ~o'logisch a. mythological.

N

N, n (ɛn) n. the letter N, n.

na! int. well! come now! ~ nu! well I never! hullo? what next? ~ warte! just you wait.

Nabe f. (-, -n) hub, nave; boss.

Nabel (-a:-) m. (-s, -) navel. ~schnur f. umbilical cord.

nach (na:x) prep., adv., & sep. pref. after, behind; for; past; of; at, towards; to; along; by; according to, from, as regards; ~ und ~ gradually; ~ wie vor still, as usual, as (much as) ever.

Nachachtung f. observance.

nachäffen v.t. to ape, mimic.

nachahm-en v.t. to imitate, copy; to mimic; to counterfeit; to emulate. ~enswert a. worthy of imitation. ~er m. imitator. ~ung f. imitation. ~ungstrieb m. imitative instinct.

nacharten v.i. to resemble, take after.

Nachbar (nax-) m. (-s, -n) neighbour. ~lich a. neighbourly; next; adjoining. ~schaft f. neighbourhood. [NEIGHBOUR]

nach-bestellen v.t. to order later; to order some more. ~beten v.t. (fig.) to repeat mechanically. ~bilden v.t. to copy. ~bildung f. copy, imitation. ~bleiben v.i. to remain behind; ~bleiben müssen to be kept in. ~blicken v.i. to gaze after.

nachdem (naxde:m) adv. afterwards. conj. after; je ~ according as.

nach-denken v.i. to reflect,

cogitate, think. subst. n. reflection, meditation. ~denklich a. thoughtful, meditative, pensive. ~dichtung f. imitation; paraphrase; free version. ~drängen v.i. to crowd or press after. ~dringen vws.i. to pursue.

Nachdruck m. stress, emphasis, force; (typ.) reprint, reprinting, reproduction; pirated edition. ~en v.t. to reprint; to pirate. ~svoll, nachdrücklich aa. strong; forcible; emphatic.

nach-eifern v.i. to emulate. ~eiferung f. emulation. ~eilen vws.i. to hasten after. ~einander adv. after each other, successively. ~empfinden v.t. to feel for; to sympathize with.

Nachen m. (-s, -) (poet.) boat, skiff.

Nach-erbe m. next heir. ~ernte f. second crop; gleaning. ~erzählen v.t. to repeat; to adapt.

Nachfahr m. (-en, -en) descendant. ~en vws.i. to drive after.

Nachfeier f. later or extra celebration.

Nachfolge f. succession; ~ Christi Imitation of Christ. ~n vws.i. to follow, succeed. ~r m. successor.

Nachforderung f. extra charge; afterclaim.

nach-forschen v.i. to inquire into; to investigate. ~forschung f. investigation, research. ~frage f. inquiry; demand. ~fragen v.i. to inquire after. ~fühlen v.t. to feel for; to sympathize with.

nach-geben v.i. to yield, give way; einem nichts ~geben to be in no way inferior to a person, be quite as . . . as. ~geboren a. posthumous. ~gebühr f. excess postage, surcharge. ~geburt f. afterbirth.

nach-gehen vws.i. to follow; to investigate, inquire into, trace; to pursue, attend to, be addicted to; (of clock) to be slow. ~gelassen a. posthumous. ~gerade adv. gradually; by this time, by now, after all. ~geschmack m. aftertaste. ~gewiesenermaßen adv. as has been proved. ~giebig a. obliging, easy-going, indulgent; soft; flexible, elastic. ~**giebigkeit** f. indulgence; tractability; softness. ~**grübeln** v.i. to ponder (over). **Nach-hall** m. echo. ~**hallen** v.i. to echo, resound. ~**haltig** a. lasting; effective, persistent. ~**hängen** v.i. to give way to; to be addicted to; Gedanken ~**hängen** to muse. ~**hause** adv. home. ~**heizen** v.i. to make up the fire; to put on coal. ~**helfen** v.i. to help. **nach-her** adv. afterwards, later. ~**herig** a. subsequent, later. ~**hilfe** f. aid, help; coaching. ~**hinken** vws.i. to lag behind. ~**holen** v.t. to make up for; to recover; to take (a lesson) later (on). ~**holbedarf** m. supplementary demand. ~**hut** f. rearguard. **nach-jagen** vws.i. to pursue, chase. ~**klang** m. echo; after-effect; reminiscence. ~**komme** m. descendant. ~**kommen** vws.i. to come later, follow on; to fulfil, comply with. ~**kommenschaft** f. posterity, descendants. ~**kömmling** m. descendant. ~**kriegszeit** f. post-war period. ~**kur** f. rest after treatment. **Nachlaß** m. (-lasses, -lässe) estate; property (of deceased); remission; (commerc.) reduction; literarischer ~ literary remains. ~**verwalter** m. executor. **nach-lassen** v.t. to leave, leave behind; to reduce (price). v.i. to abate, grow less; to stop, cease; to slacken; to temper, anneal (metal, &c.). ~**lassenschaft** f. inheritance, estate. ~**lässig** a. negligent, careless. ~**lässigkeit** f. negligence, carelessness. **nach-laufen** vws.i. to run after. ~**leben** v.i. to live up to. subst. n. after-life. ~**legen** v.t. to put on more (coal), make up the fire. ~**lese** f. gleaning; (lit.) supplement. ~**lesen** v.t. to glean; to look up (passage in book). ~**liefern** v.t. to deliver later. ~**lieferung** f. subsequent or additional delivery. ~**lösen** v.t. to take a supplementary ticket. **nach-machen** v.t. to imitate, copy, mimic; to counterfeit.

~**malig** a. subsequent. ~**mals** adv. afterwards, subsequently. ~**mittag** m. afternoon. ~**mittags** adv. in the afternoon. ~**nahme** f. cash on delivery. ~**name** m. surname. **nach-plappern** v.t. to repeat mechanically. ~**porto** n. excess postage, surcharge. ~**prüfen** v.t. to test; to check; to verify, make sure. **nach-rechnen** v.t. to check, audit. ~**rede** f. epilogue; gossip. ~**reden** v.t. Ubles ~**reden** to speak ill of. **Nachricht** f. (-, -en) news, information; account, report. ~**enbüro** n. news agency. ~**endienst** m. the news (service); (mil.) signals; intelligence service. ~**entruppe** f. Corps of Signals. **nach-rücken** vws.i. to move forward; to follow; to move up. ~**ruf** m. obituary (notice). ~**ruhm** m. posthumous fame. ~**rühmen** v.t. to say to one's credit. **nach-sagen** v.t. to repeat mechanically; to speak or say of. ~**saison** f. off-season. ~**satz** m. postscript; final clause; minor term or proposition. ~**schicken** v.t. to forward (mail). ~**schlag** m. (mus.) grace-note. ~**schlagen** v.t. to look up (word, &c.); to consult (book). vws.i. to take after. ~**schlagewerk** n. reference book. ~**schleichen** vws.i. to creep after. ~**schleppen** v.t. to drag or trail after; to tow. **Nach-schlüssel** m. master-key; skeleton-key. ~**schmecken** v.i. to leave a taste of. ~**schreiben** v.t. to copy; to write or take down. ~**schrift** f. postscript; notes (of lecture); copy, transcript. ~**schub** m. reinforcement, supply, reserves. **nachsehen** v.t. & i. to gaze after; to revise, check, examine; to look up; to see (whether); to overlook, condone, excuse. subst. n. das ~ haben to be too late, have one's trouble for nothing. **nach-senden** v.t. to send after; to redirect, forward. ~**setzen** v.t. to think less of. vws.i. to pursue, hunt after. ~sicht f. indulgence; forbearance, leniency. ~sichtig, ~sichtsvoll aa. indulgent, lenient. ~silbe f. suffix. ~sinnen v.i. to muse, meditate, reflect (on). ~sitzen v.i. – sitzen müssen to be kept in.

Nach-sommer m. Indian summer, mild autumn. ~speise f. sweet; dessert. ~spiel n. epilogue; (mus.) voluntary; (fig.) sequel. ~sprechen v.i. to repeat (a person's words). ~spüren v.i. to track, trace (person, &c.); to spy upon.

nächst (nɛːçst) a. nearest, next; shortest; closest; following. prep. next to, next after. ~beste m. & a. second best. ~dem adv. soon. ~e(r) m. fellow creature, neighbour. ~enliebe f. love for one's fellow men, charity. ~ens adv. shortly, soon. ~folgend a. following, next. ~liegend a. nearest.

nach-stehen v.i. to be inferior to; to make way for. ~stehend a. following, mentioned below. ~stellen v.i. to lie in wait for; to pursue. v.t. to put back (clock). ~stellung f. pursuit, persecution. ~streben v.i. to strive after, aspire to; to emulate. ~suchen v.i. to look for; to petition for, apply for.

Nacht (naxt) f. (-, ⸚e) night; bei ~ des ~s at night; über ~ during the night; über ~ bleiben to stay the night; zu ~ essen to sup. ~essen n. supper. ~falter m. moth. ~geschirr n., ~topf m. chamber-pot. ~gleiche f. equinox. ~hemd n. night-dress; night-shirt (for men). ~jäger m. night-fighter. ~lager n. night's lodging, night quarters. ~mahr m. nightmare. ~schatten m. nightshade. ~schicht f. nightshift. ~schlafend a. zu ~schlafender Zeit when everyone is asleep. ~seite f. (fig.) dismal or seamy side. ~tisch m. bedside table. ~wächter m. nightwatchman. ~wandeln vws.i. to walk in one's sleep. ~wandlerisch a. mit ~wandlerischer

Sicherheit infallibly, with absolute certainty. ~zeug n. nightthings, night-clothes.

Nachteil m. disadvantage; loss, damage, injury; im ~ sein to be at a disadvantage. ~ig a. disadvantageous, detrimental, disparaging, derogatory.

nächt-elang adv. for whole nights. ~igen v.i. to spend the night. ~lich a. nightly.

nachten v.i. to grow dark.

Nachtigall f. (-, -en) nightingale. ~enschlag m. nightingale's song.

Nach-tisch m. dessert. ~tönen v.i. to resound, to (re-)echo. ~trab m. rear(guard). ~trag m. supplement; codicil; postscript. ~tragen v.t. to carry after; to add; (fig.) to bear a grudge against. ~trägerisch a. resentful, vindictive. ~träglich a. additional, further; subsequent, later. ~tragszahlung f. additional payment.

Nach-treter m. follower, adherent. ~trupp m. rearguard. ~tun v.i. to imitate, copy; to emulate. ~urlaub m. additional leave.

nach-wachsen vws.i. to grow again; to grow up. ~wehen pl. after-effects; after-pains; (fig.) evil consequences. ~weinen v.i. to mourn, bewail. ~weis m. evidence, proof; qualification; agency. ~weisbar a. demonstrable, evident. ~weisen v.t. to prove, establish, demonstrate; to get (work, &c.) for (person). ~weislich a. demonstrable, evident, authentic. ~welt f. posterity. ~winter m. second winter. ~wirken v.i. to take effect afterwards; to have an after-effect. ~wirkung f. after-effect. ~wort n. epilogue. ~wuchs m. after-crop; rising generation.

nach-zahlen v.t. to pay in addition. ~zahlung f. additional payment. ~zählen v.t. to check. ~zeichnen v.t. to copy. ~ziehen v.t. to drag along; to pencil (eyebrows). vws.i. to follow, march after. ~zügler m. straggler.

Nacken m. (-s, -) nape of the neck.

neck. **~schlag** m. blow from behind; (fig.) disaster.

nackt (also **nackend**) a. naked, nude; bare; (fig.) plain. **~heit** f. nakedness. **~kultur** f. nudism.

Nadel (na:-) f. (-, -n) needle; pin. **~arbeit** f. needlework. **~baum** m. conifer. **~hölzer** n.pl. conifers. **~kissen** n. pincushion. **~öhr** n. eye of a needle. **~stich** m. prick; stitch; (fig.) pinprick. **~wald** m. coniferous forest.

Nagel (na:-) m. (-s, ⁀) nail; stud; (carpet-)tack; spike, peg; an den ~ hängen to give up; den ~ auf den Kopf treffen to hit the nail on the head; keinen ~ breit not an inch; auf den Nägeln brennen to be urgent. **~bohrer** m. gimlet. **~bürste** f. nail-brush. **~feile** f. nail-file. **~geschwür** n. whitlow. **~kuppe** f. head of nail. **~neu** a. brand-new. **~pflege** f. manicure. **~schere** f. nail-scissors. **~schuh** m. spiked shoe.

nageln v.t. to nail; to spike.

nage-n (-a:-) v.t. & i. to gnaw, nibble; to erode, corrode, eat into; (fig.) to wear out. **~r** m., **~tier** n. rodent.

nah-(e) a. near, close to; close; imminent, approaching. **~aufnahme** f. close-up. **~egehen** vws.i. to affect, grieve. **~ekommen** vws.i. to come near, approach; to get at. **~elegen** v.t. to suggest, urge upon. **~eliegen** v.i. (fig.) to suggest itself; to be obvious. **~estehen** v.i. (fig.) to be closely connected, be friends (with). **~etreten** vws.i. to come into close contact (with); einem zu ~ e treten to hurt a person's feelings. **~ezu** adv. almost, nearly. **~kampf** m. close combat; hand-to-hand fighting; (boxing) clinch. **~verkehr** m. local traffic. [NIGH]

Nähe f. (-) nearness, proximity, vicinity; propinquity; in der ~ near, near to, close at hand.

nahen v.i. & r. to draw near, approach.

näh-en v.t. & i. to sew, stitch. **~e'rei** f. sewing, needlework.

~erin f. needlewoman. **~garn** n. sewing-cotton. **~korb** m. work-basket. **~maschine** f. sewing-machine. **~nadel** f. needle. **~zeug** n. sewing things.

näher a. nearer, closer (to); shorter, more direct; closer, more intimate; more detailed. **~e(s)** n. details, particulars. **~n** v.t. to bring near, place near. v.r. to approach, draw near. **~ungswert** m. approximate value.

nahm imperf. of **nehmen**.

Nähr-boden m. fertile soil; culture medium. **~präparat** n. patent food. **~stand** m. the peasants. **~wert** m. nutritive value.

nähren v.t. to feed, nurse, suckle; (fig.) to cherish, nourish, entertain. v.i. to be nourishing. v.r. to live (on); to maintain oneself.

nahr-haft a. nourishing, nutritive; (fig.) lucrative. **~ung** f. nourishment, food; maintenance, support, sustenance. **~ungsmittel** n.pl. food, food-stuffs, victuals. **~ungssorgen** f.pl. struggle for livelihood.

Naht f. (-, ⁀e) seam; (tech.) join; (med.) suture. **~los** a. seamless.

na'iv (na:i:f) a. naïve, ingenuous, artless, simple. **~i'tät** f. naïvety, simplicity.

Name-(n) (na:-) m. (-ns, -n) name, appellation; character, reputation; dem ~ n nach by name. **~ngebung** f. christening; naming. **~nlos** a. nameless; (fig.) inexpressible, unspeakable. **~ns** adv. named, called, by name of; in the name of. **~nsaufruf** m. roll-call. **~nsfest** m., **~nstag** m. Saint's day; name-day. **~nsvetter** m. namesake. **~ntlich** a. & adv. nominal, by name; especially, particularly.

namhaft a. renowned; considerable; ~ machen to name, specify.

nämlich a. same, very. adv. namely, that is to say, of course.

nannte imperf. of **nennen**.

Napf m. (-es, ⁀e) basin, bowl. **~kuchen** m. kind of sponge-cake.

Narb-e f. (-e, -en) scar; (bot.) stigma; grain. **~en** v.t. to grain (leather) **~ig** a. scarred; grained.

Narde f. (-, -n) spikenard.

Nar'ko-se f. (-se, -sen) narcosis; (med.) anaesthesia. **~tisch** a. narcotic; anaesthetic. **~ti'sieren** v.t. to narcotize; to anaesthetize.

Narr m. (-en, -en) fool; buffoon, jester; **zum ~en halten** to make a fool of; **einen ~en fressen an** to take a great fancy to. **~enhaus** n. madhouse. **~en(s)possen** f.pl. tomfoolery, tricks. **~e'tei** f. folly; madness. **~heit** f. foolishness, craziness.

narren v.t. to fool.

Närr-in f. (-in, -innen) fool. **~isch** a. foolish; peculiar, strange; mad.

Nar'zisse f. (-, -n) narcissus; **gelbe ~** daffodil.

Na'sal(laut) m. nasal sound.

nasch-en v.t. & i. to pilfer (sweets, &c.); to eat sweets on the sly. **~haft** a. fond of sweet things. **~katze** f. sweet-tooth. **~werk** n. sweets.

Näscher m. (-s, -) sweet-tooth. **~'ei** f. eating sweets on the sly; sweets.

Nase (na:zə) f. (-, -n) nose; snout; (fig.) rebuke; **eine ~ drehen** to make a fool of; **auf die ~ binden** to hoax, bamboozle; **auf der ~ liegen** to be ill; **einem etwas unter die ~ reiben** to bring a thing home to a person, rub it in. **~nbein** n. nasal bone. **~nbluten** n. nose-bleeding. **~nflügel** m. side of the nose. **~nloch** n. nostril. **~nrücken** m. bridge of the nose. **~nspitze** f. tip of the nose. **~nstüber** m. (fig.) snubbing; fillip. **~weis** a. pert, saucy, cheeky.

näseln v.i. to nasalize.

nas-führen v.t. to fool, dupe. **~horn** n. rhinoceros.

naß a. wet; damp, moist; rainy. subst. n. liquid; (poet.) water; drink; rain. **~kalt** a. raw.

Nässe f. (-) wetness; dampness; humidity. **~n** v.t. to wet; to moisten.

Nati'on (-tsio:n) f. (-, -en) nation.

natio'nal a. national. **~hymne** f. national anthem. **~i'sieren** v.t. to nationalize. **~i'tät** f. nationality. **~ökonomie** f. political economy. **~sozialismus** m. National Socialism.

Natrium n. (-s) sodium.

Natron n. (-s) soda, sodium hydroxide. **~haltig** a. containing soda. **~salz** n. sodium salt.

Natter f. (-, -n) adder, viper.

Na'tur f. (-, -en) nature; constitution, temperament, disposition; **nach der ~** from the life, from nature; **von ~ aus** by nature; **wider die ~** against the grain; **in ~** in kind. **~bursche** m. child of nature. **~ereignis** n. natural phenomenon. **~erzeugnis** n. produce. **~forscher** m. scientist. **~gemäß** a. natural, in conformity with nature. **~geschichte** f. natural history. **~getreu** a. lifelike, true to nature. **~heilkunde** f. nature cure. **~heilkundige(r)** m. naturopath. **~kunde** f. natural history. **~lehre** f. physics. **~notwendigkeit** f. physical necessity. **~schutzgebiet** n. preserve, national preserved area. **~trieb** m. instinct. **~volk** n. primitive race. **~widrig** a. unnatural, abnormal. **~wissenschaft** f. (natural) science. **~wissenschaftler** m. scientist. **~wissenschaftlich** a. scientific. **~wüchsig** a. natural, original.

Natu'ral-ien pl. natural produce, fruits of the soil; natural-history specimens. **~i'sieren** v.t. to naturalize. **~ismus** m. naturalism. **~istisch** a. naturalistic. **~leistung** f. payment in kind.

Natu'rell n. (-s, -e) nature, disposition, temper.

na'türlich a. natural, innate; genuine, unaffected. adv. of course, certainly. **~keit** f. naturalness; genuineness, simplicity.

Nautik f. (-) nautical science, navigation.

Navig-ati'onsraum m. chart-room. **~ieren** v.t. to navigate.

Nazi m. (-s, -s) follower of Hitler's National Socialism.

Nebel (-e-) m. (-s, -) mist, fog, haze; *künstlicher* ~ smoke-screen. ~**bank** f. fog-bank. ~**fleck** m. nebula. ~**haft** a. nebulous, hazy, dim. ~**ig**, **neblig** aa. misty, foggy, hazy. ~**krähe** f. hooded crow. ~**mond** m. (poet.) November. ~**regen** m. drizzle. ~**schleier** m. veil of mist. ~**schwaden** m. damp fog. ~**streif** m. trail (of mist). ~**werfer** m. smoke mortar. ~**wetter** n. foggy weather.

nebeln v.i. to be foggy.

neben (ne-) adv. & prep. beside, next to, close to, near; besides, in addition to. ~**absicht** f. secondary objective. ~**an** adv. next door, close by. ~**anschluß** m. (electr.) shunt; (tel.) extension. ~**arbeit** f. extra work. ~**bedeutung** f. secondary meaning. ~**bei** adv. adjoining; by the way; besides, moreover. ~**beruf** m. additional occupation; sideline. ~**buhler** m. rival. ~**buhlerschaft** f. rivalry. ~**einander** adv. side by side, abreast. ~**eingang** m. side entrance. ~**einnahme** f. additional income, casual earnings. ~**erzeugnis** n. by-product. ~**fach** n. subsidiary subject. ~**fluß** m. tributary. ~**gebäude** n. adjacent building, annexe. ~**gelaß** n. small room (off), adjoining room, box-room. ~**geleis** n. railway siding, side-track. ~**geräusch** n. (radio) atmospherics. ~**her**, ~**hin** advv. by the side of, along with; by the way. ~**kläger** m. co-plaintiff. ~**linie** f. collateral line; (rail.) branch-line. ~**mann** m. man next to one. ~**mensch** m. fellow creature. ~**niere** f. adrenal gland. ~**person** f. (theatr.) subordinate character. ~**produkt** n. by-product. ~**rolle** f. subordinate part. ~**sache** f. matter of secondary importance. ~**sächlich** a. unimportant, immaterial. ~**satz** m. subordinate clause. ~**stehend** a. accompanying; opposite. ~**straße** f. by-street. ~**umstand** m. minor detail, accessory detail, incident. ~**verdienst** m. casual earnings. ~**zimmer** n. next room.

nebst prep. with, together or along with, in addition to, besides.

neck-en v.t. to tease, chaff. ~**e'rei** f. teasing, banter, raillery. ~**isch** a. roguish; queer, funny.

Neffe m. (-n, -n) nephew.

Nega'tiv n. (-s, -e) & a. negative.

Neger (-e:-) m. (-s, -) Negro. (sl.) nigger. ~**in** f. Negress.

ne'gieren v.t. to deny; to answer in the negative.

nehmen v.t. st. to take, accept, receive; to appropriate; to take away, remove; to seize, capture; *etwas zu sich* ~ to eat something; *es sich nicht* ~ *lassen* to insist on; *es genau* ~ to be pedantic, be very particular; *streng* or *genau genommen* strictly speaking.

Nehrung f. (-) narrow tongue of land.

Neid (-t) m. (-es) envy, jealousy. ~**en** v.t. to envy. ~**er**, ~**hammel** m. envious person. ~**isch** a. envious, jealous.

Neig-e f. (-e, -en) slope; decline; *auf die* ~ *gehen* to be on the decline, come to an end. ~**en** v.t. to lower, tilt; to bow. v.i. to be inclined to. v.r. to slope, dip; to draw (to a close). ~**ung** f. incline, declivity; gradient; dip (of needle); preference; inclination, tendency, taste (for). ~**ungsehe** f. love match. ~**ungsmesser** m. clinometer. ~**ungswinkel** m. angle of incidence.

nein adv. no; denial. adv. no.

Nekrolog m. ♣ necrology = obituary notice.

Nektar m. (-s) nectar.

Nelke f. (-, -n) pink, carnation; clove.

nenn-en v.t. st. to name, call, term. ~**enswert** a. worth mentioning. ~**er** m. denominator. ~**ung** f. naming; nomination; (sport.) entry. ~**wert** m. nominal value. ~**wort** n. noun.

Neonröhre f. neon tube.

Nerv (-f) m. (-s, -en) nerve; *einem auf die* ~**en** *fallen* to drive one mad. **~enheilanstalt** f. clinic for nervous diseases; mental hospital. **~enknoten** m. ganglion. **~enkrank** a. neurotic, neurasthenic. **~enschwäche** f. nervous debility, neurasthenia. **~ensystem** n. nervous system. **~ig** a. nervous; sinewy, pithy. **~ös** a. nervous, nervy. **~osi'tät** f. nervousness, nervosity.

Nerz (-es) m. (-es, -e) mink.

Nessel f. (-, -n) nettle. **~fieber** n. nettle-rash, urticaria. **~tuch** n. unbleached calico.

Nest n. (-es, -er) nest, aerie; (fig.) hole, small provincial town. **~häkchen** n. (fig.) pet, baby.

nesteln v.t. to fasten, lace up.

nett a. nice; neat, pretty; kind. **~igkeit** f. neatness; prettiness; kindness.

netto adv. net. **~gewicht** n. net weight. **~preis** m. net price.

Netz n. (-es, -e) net; network; (hunt.) toils; (opt.) reticle; (electr.) mains; rack (for luggage); (anat.) plexus. **~anschluß** m. connexion to mains. **~antenne** f. mains aerial. **~artig**, **~förmig** aa. reticular. **~empfänger** m. mains operated receiver. **~flügler** m. pl. neuroptera. **~haut** f. retina. **~hemd** n. cellular shirt. **~spannung** f. main voltage. **~werk** n. network; reticulation.

netzen v.t. to wet, moisten.

neu a. new; fresh; recent, modern, latest; aufs **~e**, von **~em** anew, again; in **~ester** Zeit recently, in most recent times; **~ere** Sprachen modern languages.

Neu~ ankömmling m. new-comer. **~artig** a. novel. **~auflage** f. new edition. **~backen**, a. newly baked; just made. **~bau** m. new building, reconstruction. **~bearbeitung** f. revised edition, revision. **~bildung** f. new formation, new growth. **~druck** m. reprint. **~erdings** adv. recently, latterly. **~erer** m. innovator. **~erlich** a. late, recent; renewed, repeated. **~erung** f. innovation. **~erungssüchtig** a. fond of innovations. **~gestaltung** f. re-

organization. **~gier(de)** f. curiosity. **~gierig** a. curious, inquisitive. **~heit** f. novelty; newness. **~hochdeutsch** a. Modern High German. **~igkeit** f. news. **~jahr** n. New Year.

neu-lich adv. the other day, recently. **~ling** m. novice, neophyte, beginner. **~modisch** a. fashionable. **~mond** m. new moon. **~philologe**, **~sprachler** m. student or teacher of modern languages. **~reiche(r)** m. wealthy parvenu. **~silber** n. German silver, argentine. **~vermählt** a. newly married. **~zeit** f. modern times. **~zeitlich** a. modern.

neun a. & subst. f. nine. **~auge** n. lamprey. **~eck** n. nonagon. **~fach** a. ninefold. **~jährig** a. nine years old. **~t** a. ninth. **~zehn** a. nineteen. **~zig** a. ninety.

Neur-al'gie f. neuralgia. **~algisch** a. neuralgic. **~asthe'nie** f. neurasthenia. **~as'theniker** m. neurasthenic. **~ose** f. neurosis.

neu'tral a. neutral. **~i'sieren** v.t. to neutralize. **~i'tät** f. neutrality.

Neutrum n. (-s, Neutren) neuter.

nicht (-çt) adv. not; auch **~** not even; nor; durchaus **~** by no means, in no way; gar **~** not at all; ganz und gar **~** not in the least; noch **~** not yet; **~ einmal** not even; **~ mehr** no longer; **~ wahr?** isn't it? are you not? &c.; mit **~en** not at all; **~** Zutreffendes not to the point, not apt. **~achtung** f. disregard. **~arier** m. non-Aryan, Jew. **~ig** a. null, void; vain, empty; für **~ig** erklären to annul. **~igkeit** f. nullity, invalidity; vanity. **~igkeitsbeschwerde** f. plea of nullity. **~igkeitserklärung** f. annulment. **~raucher** m. non-smoker.

Nichte (-ç-) f. (-, -n) niece.

nichts (-ç-) indecl. pron. nothing, gar **~** nothing at all; **~** als nothing but; **~** anderes nothing else; **~** weniger als anything but; mir **~**, dir **~** quite coolly, bold as brass. subst. n. nothingness; nothing; nonentity; trifle. **~destoweniger** adv. nevertheless,

~nutz *m.* good-for-nothing, ne'er-do-well. ~nutzig *a.* useless, worthless. ~sagend *a.* meaningless, insignificant. ~tuer *m.* idler. ~tun *n.* idling. ~würdig *a.* vile, base. ~würdigkeit *f.* vileness, baseness.

Nickel *n.* (-s, -) nickel.

nick-en *v.i.* to nod, bow; to snooze. ~erchen *n.* snooze, nap.

nie (ni:) *adv.* never.

nieder *a.* low; base, mean. *adv. & sep. pref.* down, low; *auf und* ~ up and down. ~brennen *v.t. & i.* to burn down. ~deutsch *a.* Low German. ~drücken *v.t.* to weigh down; to press down; to depress. ~fahren *v.s.i.* to descend. ~fallen *v.s.i.* to fall down. ~frequenz *f.* low frequency. ~gang *m.* going-down; decline. ~gehen *v.s.i.* to go down; (*av.*) to land; to break out. ~geschlagen *a.* depressed. ~geschlagenheit *f.* depression. ~halten *v.t.* to suppress; to keep down. ~holen *v.t.* to haul down, lower. ~kämpfen *v.t.* to overpower; to silence (enemy's fire). ~kommen *v.s.i.* to be confined. ~kunft *f.* confinement.

Nieder-lage *f.* defeat; depot, warehouse. ~lassen *v.t.* to let down, lower. *v.r.* to sit down; to alight; to establish oneself (in), settle. ~lassung *f.* settling, settlement, establishment; branch (of firm). ~legen *v.t.* to lay down; to give up; to abdicate; to resign; to knock off (work). *v.r.* to lie down. ~machen, ~metzeln *v.t.* to kill, slay. ~reißen *v.t.* to pull down, demolish. ~schlag *m.* rain, precipitation; sediment, deposit; precipitate; knock-out (blow); (*fig.*) outcome, result. ~schlagen *v.t.* to knock down, fell; to cast down (eyes); to suppress; to squash; (*chem.*) to precipitate; *niedergeschlagen* depressed. ~schmettern *v.t.* to strike down; to crush, overwhelm, depress. ~schmetternd *a.* shattering. ~schreiben *v.t.* to write down. ~schrift *f.* writing-down; copy.

~setzen *v.t.* to put *or* set down. *v.r.* to sit down. ~sinken *v.s.i.* to sink down, drop. ~stoßen *v.t.* to knock down. ~strecken *v.t.* to cut down; to knock down. ~tracht *f.* baseness, meanness. ~trächtig *a.* base, mean. ~ung *f.* lowland, marsh, plain. ~wärts *adv.* downwards. ~werfen *v.t.* to throw down; to overcome; to suppress, crush. *v.r.* to prostrate oneself.

niedlich *a.* pretty, nice, neat.

Niednagel (ni:t-) *m.* agnail, hangnail.

niedrig *a.* low; inferior; humble; mean, base. ~keit *f.* lowness; humbleness; baseness.

niemals *adv.* never.

niemand *pron.* nobody, no one.

Niere *f.* (-, -n) kidney. ~nbraten *m.* roast loin of veal. ~nentzündung *f.* nephritis.

nieseln *v.i.* to drizzle.

niesen *v.i.* to sneeze.

Nieß-brauch *m.* usufruct, benefit. ~nutzer *m.* usufructuary.

Niet *n. & m.* (-es, -e) rivet; ~ *und nagelfest* firmly fixed, nailed fast. ~en *v.t.* to rivet. ~nagel *m.* riveting-nail.

Niete *f.* (-, -n) blank; failure. [DU.]

Nihi'lismus *m.* (-) nihilism.

Niko'tin *n.* (-s) nicotine. ~haltig *a.* containing nicotine.

Nilpferd *n.* hippopotamus.

Nimbus *m.* (-) nimbus; prestige.

nimmer, ~mehr *adv.* never, nevermore. ~satt *a.* insatiable. *subst. m.* glutton; wolf. ~wiedersehen *n. auf ~wiedersehen* farewell for ever.

nimmst *2nd sing. pres. of* nehmen.

nippen *v.t. & i.* to sip.

Nippsachen *f.pl.* knick-knacks, trinkets.

nirgend(s) *adv.* nowhere.

Nische (ni:) *f.* (-, -n) niche.

Niß, Nisse *f.* (-, -n) nit.

nist-en *v.i.* to build a nest. ~kasten *m.* nesting-box.

Ni'trat *n.* (-s, -e) nitrate.

Ni'veau (-vo:) *n.* (-s) level, standard.

nive'llier-en *v.t.* to level. ~waage *f.* spirit-level.

Nix *m.* (-es, -e) nix,'water-elf. ~e *f.* water-nymph.

nobel (no:-) *a.* noble, distinguished; generous.

noch (nɔx) *adv.* still, yet; besides, in addition; ~ *immer* still; ~ *nicht* not yet; ~ *nie* never (before); ~ *dazu* into the bargain, in addition; ~ *einer* another, one more; ~ *etwas* some(thing) more, something else; ~ *so* ever so. ~**malig** *a.* repeated. ~**mals** *adv.* once more, again.

Nocke *f.* (-, -n) dumpling. ~**n** *m.* (*motor.*) cam.

No'mad-e *m.* (-en, -en) nomad. ~**isch** *a.* nomadic.

Nomi'nalbetrag *m.* nominal value.

Nominativ *m.* (-s, -e) nominative.

Nonne *f.* (-, -n) nun. ~**nkloster** *n.* convent; nunnery.

Nord (-t) *m.* (-s) north; (*poet.*) north wind. ~**en** *m.* the North. ~**isch** *a.* northern; Norse, Nordic. ~**licht** *n.* aurora borealis. ~**östlich** *a.* north-east(ern). ~**pol** *m.* North Pole. ~**polarkreis** *m.* arctic circle. ~**polfahrt** *f.* arctic expedition. ~**see** *f.* North Sea. ~**wärts** *adv.* northward.

nördlich *a.* northerly, northern; arctic.

Nörg-e'lei *f.* nagging, grumbling. ~**eln** *v.i.* to nag, grumble. ~**ler** *m.* grumbler, fault-finder.

Norm *f.* (-, -en) standard, rule; pattern; measure. ~**al** *a.* normal, standard, regular. ~**ale** *f.* perpendicular (line). ~**algeschwindigkeit** *f.* normal speed. ~**algewicht** *n.* standard weight. ~**alspur** *f.* standard gauge. ~**alzeit** *f.* mean time.

norm-en, ~**ieren** *v.t.* to regulate; to standardize.

Not (no:t) *f.* (-, -̈e) distress; want; need, necessity; trouble, difficulty; danger, emergency; *mit* (*knapper*) ~ only just, narrowly; *ohne* ~ needlessly, without real cause; *zur* ~ if need be, at a pinch; *in Nöten sein* to be hard pressed; ~ *tun, vonnöten sein* to be necessary; *seine liebe* ~ *haben mit* to have no end of trouble with. [NEED]

Nota *f.* (-, -s) memorandum.

Not-anker *m.* sheet-anchor. ~**ausgang** *m.* emergency exit. ~**behelf** *m.* makeshift; expedient. ~**bremse** *f.* emergency brake. ~**durft** *f.* necessity, pressing need; *durft verrichten* to relieve nature. ~**dürftig** *a.* scanty; necessitous, needy; makeshift; *dürftig ausbessern* to make a rough and ready repair. ~**fall** *m.* case of emergency. ~**flagge** *f.* flag of distress. ~**gedrungen** *a.* compulsory, forced. ~**gemeinschaft** *f.* association in aid (of). ~**hafen** *m.* harbour of refuge. ~**helfer** *m.* helper in need. ~**hilfe** *f.* emergency service. ~**lage** *f.* distress, calamity. ~**landen** *vcs.i.* to make a forced landing. ~**landung** *f.* forced landing. ~**leidend** *a.* needy, poor; suffering, distressed; dishonoured (bill). ~**leine** *f.* communication-cord. ~**lüge** *f.* white lie. ~**pfennig** *m.* savings, nest-egg. ~**ruf** *m.* cry of distress; emergency-call. ~**schrei** *m.* cry of distress. ~**schlachtung** *f.* forced slaughter. ~**signal** *n.* distress signal; S.O.S. ~**sitz** *m.* dickey-seat. ~**stand** *m.* state of distress, emergency. ~**standsarbeiten** *f.pl.* relief works. ~**standsgebiet** *n.* distressed area. ~**taufe** *f.* private baptism (in emergency). ~**verband** *m.* temporary dressing, first field dressing. ~**verordnung** *f.* emergency decree. ~**wassern** *v.i,* (*av.*) to make a forced landing on water; (*sl.*) to go into the drink. ~**wehr** *f.* self-defence. ~**wendig** *a.* necessary; urgent. ~**wendigkeit** *f.* necessity; urgency. ~**zeichen** *n.* distress signal. ~**zucht** *f.* rape. ~**züchtigen** *v.t.* to rape, assault.

No'tar *m.* (-s, -e) notary. ~**i'at** *n.* notary's office. ~**i'ell** *a.* notarial, attested by a notary.

Note (no:-) *f.* (-, -n) note; banknote; memorandum; mark, report (in school); (*mus.*) *ganze* ~ semibreve; *halbe* ~ minim; *nach* ~ *n singen* to sing at sight. ~**nausgabe** *f.* issue of bank-notes.

~naustausch *m.* (*pol.*) exchange of notes. ~nblatt *n.* sheet of music. ~nhalter, ~nständer *m.* music-stand. ~nsystem *n.* (*mus.*) staff. ~numlauf *m.* (*commerc.*) circulation of notes.

no'tier-en *v.t.* to note; to quote, state (prices). ~ung *f.* quotation.

nötig (-ç) *a.* necessary, needful; ~ haben to need. ~en *v.t.* to force, urge, compel; to press; sich ~en lassen to need pressing. ~enfalls *adv.* if need be. ~ung *f.* forcing, compulsion; pressing.

No'tiz (-ti:ts) *f.* (-, -en) note; ~ nehmen to take notice of. ~block *m.* jotter, scribbling-pad. ~buch *n.* notebook.

no'torisch *a.* notorious.

No'velle *f.* (-, -n) short story; (*leg.*) supplementary law; amendment.

No'vember *m.* (-s, -) November.

Novi'tät *f.* (-, -en) novelty.

No'viz-e *f.* (-e, -en) novice. ~i'at *n.* novitiate.

Nu *m.* & *n.* im ~ in an instant.

Nuance *f.* shade, minute difference.

nüchtern *a.* empty; sober; clear-headed, sensible; dry; dull, insipid. ~heit *f.* emptiness; sobriety; dryness; dullness.

Nudel *f.* (-, -n) macaroni, vermicelli.

null *a.* nil, null; ~ und nichtig null and void. *subst. f.* zero; nought, cipher. ~punkt *m.* zero. ~strich *m.* zero mark. ~zeit *f.* zero hour.

num-e'rieren *v.t.* to number; ~erierter Platz reserved seat. ~erisch *a.* numerical.

Numis'matik *f.* (-) numismatics.

Nummer *f.* (-, -n) number; part, issue, copy; ticket (in lottery); size (in hats, &c.); (*sport.*) event; eine große ~ sein to be influential; eine gute ~ haben to be well thought of. ~nfolge *f.* numerical order. ~nscheibe *f.* dial (of phone). ~nschild *n.* (*motor.*) number plate.

nun (nu:n) *adv.* now; then, henceforth; (*interrog.*) well?; ~ und nimmer never, nevermore; von ~ an henceforth. ~mehr *adv.* now; by this time; since

then. ~mehrig *a.* present, actual.

Nuntius, Nunzius *m.* (-, Nunzien) nuncio.

nur (nu:r) *adv.* only, solely, merely, alone; except; but; just; ~ mehr still (more), only; wer ~ whoever; wenn ~ if only, would that; ~ zu! go on.

Nuß *f.* (-, Nüsse) nut. ~knacker *m.* nutcracker. ~schale *f.* nut-shell.

Nüstern *f.pl.* nostrils.

Nute *f.* (-, -n) groove, rabbet, slot.

Nutsche *f.* (-, -n) suction filter.

nutz(e), nütz(e) *pred. aa.* useful; zu nichts ~ good for nothing, quite useless; ~ sein to be useful; zu Nutz und Frommen for the good of.

Nutz-anwendung *f.* utilization, practical application; useful lesson. ~bar *a.* useful. ~bringend *a.* profitable, advantageous. ~effekt *m.* efficiency.

Nutz-en *m.* (-ens) use; profit, advantage; usefulness, utility. ~fläche *f.* effective area; (*agric.*) useful acreage. ~garten *m.* kitchen-garden. ~holz *n.* timber. ~last *f.* working or pay load, loading capacity. ~leistung *f.* mechanical power, effective force, efficiency. ~los *a.* useless; unprofitable. ~losigkeit *f.* uselessness, futility. ~nießen *v.t.* to derive the profits from; to have the usufruct of. ~nießer *m.* usufructuary, beneficiary. ~nießung *f.* usufruct. ~ung *f.* yield, produce; revenue.

nütz-en *v.i.* to be of use, be profitable; to serve for. *v.t.* to use, utilize, make use of. ~lich *a.* useful, of use. ~lichkeit *f.* usefulness, utility.

Nymphe *f.* (-, -n) nymph.

O

O, o (o:) *n.* the letter O, o. *int.* oh! ah!

O'ase (o'a:zə) *f.* (-, -n) oasis.

ob (ɔp) *conj.* whether, if; I wonder if; als ~ as if; nicht als ~ not

that; *na* ~ ! rather, I should say
so. *prep.* on account of; above,
over, beyond. ~**gleich**, ~**schon**,
~**zwar** *conj.* although, though.

Obacht (o:-) *f.* heed; care; ~ *geben*
to pay attention (to), take care
(of).

Obdach (op-) *n.* (-es) shelter; lodging. ~**lose(r)** *m.* homeless person, casual.

Obdukti'on *f.* (-, -en) post-mortem
examination.

O-beine *n.pl.* bandy legs.

oben (o:-) *adv.* above, aloft, on
high; at the top; upstairs; on
the surface; *dort* ~ up there;
nach ~ upwards; upstairs; *von*
~ *bis unten* from top to bottom;
wie ~ *erwähnt* (as) mentioned
above; *von* ~ *herab behandeln* to
treat in a condescending manner.
~**an** *adv.* at the top. ~**auf** *adv.*
on the top of; ~*auf sein* to be
in great form. ~**drein** *adv.* into
the bargain, in addition. ~-
hin *adv.* superficially, perfunc-
torily.

ober *a. & pref.* upper, supreme;
higher; senior; leading. *subst. m.*
(head) waiter. ~**e(r)** *m.* head,
chief; superior.

Ober-appellationsgericht *n.* High
Court of Appeal. ~**arm** *m.*
upper arm. ~**arzt** *m.* senior
physician. ~**aufsicht** *f.* super-
intendence. ~**befehl** *m.* supreme command. ~**befehlshaber**
m. commander-in-chief. ~**bett**
n. feather bed. ~**deck** *n.*
upper deck. ~**fläche** *f.* surface;
area. ~**flächlich** *a.* superficial.
~**geschoß** *n.* upper story. ~**gewalt** *f.* sovereignty, supremacy.
~**halb** *adv. & prep.* above. ~-
hand *f.* upper hand. ~**haupt** *n.*
chief, head, sovereign; leader. ~-
haus *n.* House of Lords. ~**hemd**
n. (white) shirt. ~**herrschaft** *f.*
supremacy; sovereignty. ~**hirt**
m. bishop. ~**hofmeister** *m.* Lord
High Steward.

Oberin *f.* (-, -nen) hospital matron;
Mother Superior.

ober-irdisch *a.* surface, above
ground; (*electr.*) overhead. ~-
kellner *m.* head waiter. ~**kiefer**

m. upper jaw. ~**kirchenrat** *m.*
High Consistory. ~**kommando**
n. supreme command. ~**körper**,
~**leib** *m.* upper part of the body.
~**landesgericht** *n.* Provincial
Court of Appeal. ~**lastig** *a.* top-
heavy. ~**lauf** *m.* upper course.
~**leder** *n.* uppers. ~**lehrer** *m.*
senior assistant master. ~**leitung**
f. direction; (*electr.*) overhead
system. ~**leutnant** *m.* (first) lieutenant. ~**licht** *n.* skylight, fan-
light. ~**lippe** *f.* upper lip. ~-
priester *m.* high priest. ~**prima**
f. Upper VI. ~**schenkel** *m.* upper
part of thigh. ~**schicht** *f.* (*fig.*)
upper classes. ~**schwester** *f.* head
nurse, sister. ~**staatsanwalt** *m.*
attorney general. ~**stimme** *f.*
treble, soprano. ~**studienrat** *m.*
senior master. ~**stufe** *f.* senior
class, seniors. ~**wasser** *n.* (*fig.*)
~*wasser haben* to have the upper
hand.

Obers *n.* (*dial.*) whipped cream.

oberst *a.* topmost, highest; chief,
principal; supreme; first, head.
subst. m. colonel.

Obhut (op-) *f.* guardianship; protection, care.

obig (o:-) *a.* above, foregoing.

Ob'jekt *n.* (-s, -e) object. ~'**iv** *a.*
objective; impartial. *subst. n.*
lens. ~**ivi'tät** *f.* objectivity;
impartiality. ~**träger** *m.* (microscope) slide; stand, mount.

Ob'late *f.* (-, -n) wafer.

obliegen *v.i.* to apply oneself to,
be devoted to; to have the task
of. ~**heit** *f.* obligation, duty.

obli'gat *a.* necessary, indispensable. ~**i'on** *f.* bond; obligation. ~**orisch** *a.* obligatory,
compulsory.

Obmann *m.* chairman; foreman
(of jury); umpire.

O'bo-e (-bo:a) *f.* (-e, -en) oboe.
~'**ist** *m.* oboe player.

Obrigkeit *f.* (-, -en) authority;
government; magistrate. ~**lich**
a. official, government(al), magis-
terial.

Observa'torium *n.* (-s, ... rien)
observatory.

obsiegen *v.i.* to triumph over, get
the better of.

Obsorge f. supervision, care.

Obst (o:pst) n. (-es) fruit. ~bau m. fruit-growing. ~ernte f. fruit crop; fruit-picking. ~garten m. orchard.

obs´zön a. obscene.

obwalten v.i. to prevail; to exist, be.

obwohl conj. (al)though.

Ochs(e (ɔks) m. (-en, -en) ox, bull, bullock; (fig.) duffer. ~en v.i. to cram, (sl.) to swot. ~enauge n. fried egg. ~enfleisch n. beef. ~engespann n. ox-team. ~enschwanz m. oxtail.

Ocker m. (-s) ochre.

öd-e (ø:) a. empty, bare, bleak; dreary, dull. subst. f. desert, waste, solitude. ~land n. fallow land.

Odem (o:) m. (-s) (poet.) breath.

O´dem n. (-s, -e) oedema.

oder (o:) conj. or; or else; ~ aber or on the other hand, or instead.

Ofen (o:) m. (-s, ") stove; oven; furnace. ~klappe f. damper, register. ~rohr n. stove-pipe; recess. ~schirm m. fire-screen. ~setzer m. stove-fitter. ~vorsetzer m. fender.

offen a. open; free, vacant; frank, sincere, candid; auf ~er Strecke on the road; ~e Rechnung current account; ~er Wechsel blank cheque; ~e Handelsgesellschaft private firm. ~bar a. obvious, evident, manifest. ~baren v.t. to reveal, disclose; to manifest. ~barung f. revelation; disclosure; manifestation. ~barungseid m. oath of manifestation. ~heit f. frankness, candour. ~herzig a. sincere, frank. ~kundig a. evident; public; notorious. ~sichtlich a. obvious, apparent. ~stehen v.i. to stand open; to remain unpaid; to be allowed, be at liberty (to).

offen´siv a., ~e f. offensive.

öffentlich a. public. ~keit f. publicity; public.

O´fferte f. (-, -n) offer, tender.

offizi´ell a. official.

Offi´zier (-tsi:r) m. (-s, -e) ♣ (mil.)

officer. ~sbursche m. batman. ~smesse f. (naut.) wardroom.

Offi´zin f. (-, -en) workshop; printing-house; chemist's shop.

öffn-en v.t. & r. to open; to dissect (body). ~ung f. opening; dissection; hole, aperture, gap; slot, slit; mouth; outlet.

oft, ofters a. often, frequently. ~er a. & adv. more often, more frequent; ~s, des ~en often, frequent(ly).

Oheim, Ohm m. (-s, -e) uncle.

ohne prep. without; but for, except; ~ daß without; nicht so ~ not bad; ~ weiteres without more ado. ~dies, ~hin adv. apart from this, besides; anyhow, all the same. ~gleichen pred. a. unequalled.

Ohn-macht f. powerlessness, weakness, impotence; (med.) faint, unconsciousness. ~mächtig a. powerless, helpless; faint, unconscious; ~mächtig werden to faint. ~machtsanfall m. fainting-fit.

Ohr n. (-es, -en) ear; hearing; ganz ~ sein to be all ears; ~ übers ~ hauen to cheat a person; bis über die ~en up to the eyes; die ~en steif halten to keep up one's courage; es hinter den ~en haben to be very wily; einem in den ~en liegen to importune a person. ~enarzt m. ear specialist. ~enbeichte f. auricular confession. ~enbläserei f. scandal, slander. ~enklingen n. ringing in the ears. ~enleiden n. disease of the ear. ~ensausen n. buzzing in the ears; (med.) tinnitus. ~enschmalz n. ear-wax. ~enschmaus m. musical treat. ~enschützer m. ear-flap. ~enspeicheldrüse f. parotid gland. ~enzerreißend a. ear-splitting. ~enzeuge m. auricular witness. ~feige f. box on the ear, slap on the face. ~feigen v.t. to box (a person's) ears. ~läppchen n. lobe of the ear. ~muschel f. ear conch, external ear. ~wurm m. earwig.

Öhr n. (-es, -e) eye (of needle).

Okkul´tismus m. occultism.

Öko´nom m. (-en, -en) farmer;

steward. ~'ie f. economy, economics; housekeeping; agriculture. ~isch a. economical.

Okt-a'eder n. octahedron. ~'avband m. octavo (volume). ~'ave f. octave. ~'ett n. octet.

Ok'tober m. (-s, -) October.

Oku'l-ar n. eye-piece. ~ieren v.t. to graft.

öku'menisch a. oecumenical.

Okzident m. (-s) occident.

Öl (ø:l) n. (-es, -e) oil. ~baum m. olive tree. ~berg m. Mount of Olives. ~bild n. oil-painting. ~druck m. oleograph. ~druckbremse f. hydraulic brake. ~farbe f. oil-paint. ~fläschchen n. oil cruet. ~ig a. oily. ~kuchen m. oilcake. ~malerei f. painting in oil. ~papier n. oil-paper. ~quelle f. oil-well. ~schlägerei f. oil-press. ~tuch n. oilcloth. ~ung f. oiling; anointment; (motor.) lubrication; Letzte ~ung extreme unction. ~zweig m. olive branch.

ölen v.t. to oil; to anoint; (mach.) to lubricate.

O'live f. (-, -n) olive.

Omen n. (-s, Omina) omen.

omi'nös a. ominous.

Omnibus m. (-ses, -se) omnibus.

Onanie f. masturbation. ~ren v.i. to masturbate.

ondu'lieren v.t. to wave (hair).

Onkel m. (-s, -) uncle.

opali'sieren v.i. to opalesce.

Oper (o:-) f. (-, -n) opera; operahouse. ~ette f. operetta, musical comedy. ~nglas n. operaglass. ~nsänger m. operatic singer. ~ntext m. libretto, book.

Oper-a'teur m. operator; surgeon. ~ati'on f. operation. ~ationsgebiet n. (mil.) theatre of operations. ~ieren v.t. & i. to operate.

Opfer n. (-s, -) offering, sacrifice; victim, martyr. ~freudig, ~willig aa. self-sacrificing. ~gabe f. offering. ~lamm n. sacrificial lamb; (fig.) victim. ~stock m. poor-box. ~tier n. victim. ~tod m. sacrifice of one's life. ~ung f. sacrificing; sacrifice. [L]

opfern v.t. & i. to sacrifice, offer up.

Opium n. (-s) opium.

oppo'nieren v.i. to oppose.

op'tieren v.i. (pol.) to choose, decide in favour of.

Opt-ik f. (-ik) optics. ~iker m. optician. ~isch a. optic(al); ~ische Täuschung optical illusion.

Opti'mi-smus m. (-smus) optimism. ~stisch a. optimistic.

O'rakel n. (-s, -) oracle. ~haft a. oracular. ~n v.i. to speak in riddles.

O'range (orã:ʒə) f. (-, -n) orange. ~nschale f. orange-peel.

Ora'torium n. (-s, ... rien) oratorio.

Or'chester (-kɛst-) n. (-s, -) orchestra.

orchest'rieren v.t. to orchestrate.

Orchi'dee (-çide:) f. (-, -n) orchid.

Orden m. (-s, -) order; decoration, medal. ~sband n. ribbon of an order. ~sbruder m. member of an order; friar, monk. ~sburg f. castle of (Teutonic, &c.) order. ~skleid n. monastic habit. ~sregel f. statute(s) of an order. ~sschwester f. nun. ~szeichen n. badge, order.

ordentlich a. orderly, tidy; steady, decent; regular, proper, downright, good; ~er Professor university professor in ordinary.

Ordi'n-alzahl f. ordinal number. ~är a. common, ordinary; low, vulgar. ~ariat n. (univ.) professorship; bishopric. ~arius m. professor in ordinary. ~ärpreis m. net or sale price. ~ate f. ordinate. ~ieren v.t. to ordain; ~iert werden to take (holy) orders.

ordn-en v.t. to tidy, put in order; to arrange, sift, classify, sort; to regulate. ~er m. organizer; file, (letter) sorter. ~ung f. order, tidiness; arrangement, classification, class; regulation. ~ungsgemäß a. orderly, regular; according to order. ~ungsstrafe f. fine. ~ungswidrig a. contrary to orders, irregular, illegal. ~ungszahl f. ordinal number, number in a series.

Ordo'nnanz f. (-, -en) orderly.

Or'gan (-ga:n) n. (-s, -e) ♱ organ (of the body); voice; journal, periodical (of a society). ~i'sator *m.* organizer. ~isa'torisch *a.* organizing. ~isch *a.* organic. ~i'sieren *v.t.* to organize. ~ismus *m.* organism.

Orga'nist *m.* (-en, -en) organist.

Orgel *f.* (-, -n) organ. ~n *v.i.* to play the organ; to play a barrel-organ; to strum. ~pfeife *f.* organ-pipe.

Orgie (-gîə) *f.* (-, -n) orgy.

Orient *m.* (-s) orient. ~ale *m.* oriental. ~alisch *a.* oriental, eastern. ~ieren *v.t.* to locate, orientate; to inform. *v.r.* to find one's bearings. ~ierung *f.* orientation; direction; information.

Origi'n-al *n.* (-als, -ale) original. ~alausgabe *f.* first edition. ~ali'tät *f.* originality. ~ell *a.* original; odd, peculiar.

Or'kan (-kaːn) *m.* (-s, -e) hurricane, typhoon.

Orna'mentik *f.* (-) ornamentation.

Or'nat *m.* (-s, -e) official robes.

Ort *m.* (-es, -e) place; spot; locality; village. ~sansässig *a.* resident in the locality. ~schaft *f.* place; village. ~sgespräch *n.* local (telephone) call. ~skenntnis *f.* knowledge of a place, local knowledge. ~skundig *a.* acquainted with a locality. ~ssinn *m.* bump of locality. ~süblich *a.* customary in a place, the local custom. ~sverkehr *m.* local traffic. ~svorsteher *m.* (village) magistrate, mayor.

ort-en *v.i.* to locate. ~ung *f.* orientation, location. ~ungs-gerät *n.* direction-finder.

Ortho-do'xie *f.* orthodoxy. ~gra'phie *f.* orthography. ~phisch *a.* orthographical. ~pä'die *f.* orthopaedy, orthopaedics. ~pädisch *a.* orthopaedic.

örtlich *a.* local. ~keit *f.* locality, place.

Öse (øːzə) *f.* (-, -n) loop; ring; eye (for hook); eyelet (in shoe).

Ost (ɔst) *m.* (-es) east, (poet.) East-wind. ~en *m.* east, orient. ~wärts *adv.* eastward. ~zone *f.* Eastern Zone.

ostenta'tiv *a.* ostentatious.

Oster-fest (oː-) *n.*, ~n *pl.* Easter.

~lamm *n.* paschal lamb.

österlich (øː-) *a.* of Easter, paschal.

östlich (œː-) *a.* eastern, easterly.

Otter[1] *m.* (-s, -) & *f.* otter.

Otter[2] *f.* (-, -n) adder, viper.

Ouver'türe *f.* (-, -n) overture.

O'val *n.* (-s, -e) & *a.* oval.

O'xyd *n.* (-s, -e) oxide. ~ieren *v.t.* & *i.* to oxidize.

Ozean (oːtsɛaːn) *m.* (-s, -e) ocean. ~isch *a.* oceanic.

O'zon (-oːn) *n.* (-s) ozone.

P

P, p (peː) *n.* the letter P, p.

Paar *n.* (-es, -e) pair; couple; brace; *zu ~en treiben* to put to flight, rout. ~a *a.* like, matching, forming a pair; even; some, a few. ~en *v.t.* & *r.* to pair; to couple, copulate, mate; to join. ~ig *a.* in pairs. ~mal *adv. ein ~mal* several times. ~ung *f.* pairing; copulation. ~weise *adv.* in couples, two by two.

Pacht (paxt) *f.* (-, -en) tenure, lease; rent. ~en *v.t.* to lease, rent; to farm; (*fig.*) to monopolize. ~ung *f.* leasing (of); leasehold estate. ~vertrag *m.* lease. ~zins *m.* rent. [ML]

Pächter (-ɛç-) *m.* (-s, -) farmer; tenant; leaseholder.

Pack 1. *m.* (-s, -e) pack; bundle; parcel; packet; bale. 2. *n.* rabble. ~er *m.* packer. ~esel *m.* pack-ass, sumpter mule. ~papier *n.* packing paper, brown paper. ~träger *m.* porter. ~ung *f.* packing, wrapper; (*med.*) (cold-)pack.

Päckchen *n.* (-s, -) small parcel.

packen *v.t.* to seize, grasp; to pack, pack up; (*fig.*) to thrill, affect; to hold. *v.r.* to be gone, clear out. ~d *a.* thrilling, absorbing.

Päda'gog, *m.* (-en, -en) pedagogue. ~ik *f.* pedagogy. ~isch *a.* educational.

Padde *f.* (-, -n) frog; toad.

Paddel-boot n. canoe. **~n** v.i. to paddle.

paff int. **~** sein to be thunderstruck.

paffen v.i. to shoot; (colloq.) to smoke.

Page (pa:ʒə) m. (-n, -n) page. **~nkopf** m. bobbed hair.

pagi'nieren v.t. to paginate, page (book).

Pa'gode f. (-, -n) pagoda.

Pair (pɛːr) m. (-s, -s) peer. **~swürde** f. peerage.

Pa'ket (-keːt) n. (-s, -e) parcel, packet, package. **~annahme** f. parcels-receiving office. **~boot** n. steam-packet, mail-boat. **~karte** f. parcel form.

Pakt m. (-es, -e) pact, agreement. **~'ieren** v.i. to agree (on); to come to terms.

Pa'last m. (-es, Paläste) palace. **~artig** a. palatial. **~dame** f. lady-in-waiting.

Paletot (-toː) m. (-s, -s) overcoat. [F]

Pa'lette f. (-, -n) palette.

Palm-e f. (-e, -en) palm. **~kätzchen** n. catkin. **~wedel** m. palm-branch.

Pampelmuse f. grape-fruit.

Pam'phlet (-fleːt) n. (-s, -e) pamphlet; lampoon. **~ist** m. pamphleteer; lampoonist. [DU.]

Pa'neel n. (-s, -e) panel; wainscot. **~'ieren** v.t. to wainscot, panel.

Pa'nier n. (-s, -e) banner, standard. **pa'nieren** v.t. to dress with breadcrumbs.

Pan-ik (paː-) f., **~isch** a. panic.

Panne f. (-, -n) (motor.) puncture; break-down. [F]

Pa'noptikum n. (-s, . . . ken) waxworks.

Panther m. (-s, -) panther.

Pan'tine f. (-, -n) clog, patten.

Pan'toffel m. (-s, -) (bedroom-) slipper, mule; unter dem **~** stehen to be henpecked. **~held** m. henpecked husband. [IT.]

pan(t)schen v.t. & i. to dabble, splash; to adulterate.

Panzer (-tsər) m. (-s, -) armour; coat of mail; cuirass; tank. **~abwehr** f. anti-tank defence. **~brigade** f. tank brigade. **~**

~faust f. anti-tank bomb. **~granate** f. armour-piercing shell. **~hemd** n. coat of mail. **~jäger** m.pl. anti-tank troops. **~(kampf)wagen** m. tank; armoured car. **~korps** n. armoured corps. **~kreuzer** m. battle-cruiser, pocket-battleship. **~platte** f. armour-plate. **~regiment** n. tank regiment. **~schütze** m. private in a tank unit. **~trupp** m. armoured reconnaissance unit. **~spähwagen** m. armoured car. **~turm** m. armoured turret, gun-turret. **~ung** f. armour-plating. **~zug** m. armoured train.

panzern v.t. to armour; to plate; to arm. v.r. to arm oneself, put on armour.

Pä'onie (-oː-) f. (-, -n) peony.

Papa'gei m. (-s, -en) parrot. **~enkrankheit** f. psittacosis.

Pa'pier (-piːr) n. (-s, -e) paper; (pl.) identity papers; (commerc.) securities, stocks; zu **~** bringen to write down, put on paper. **~abfälle** m.pl. waste-paper. **~bogen** m. sheet of paper. **~en** a. (of) paper. **~fabrik** f. paper-mill. **~fabrikation** f. manufacture of paper. **~geld** n. paper money. **~handlung** f. stationer's shop. **~korb** m. waste-paper basket. **~waren** f. pl. stationery.

Pa'pismus m. (-) popery.

Papp m. (-es, -e) pap; paste. **~band** m. (book bound in) boards. **~e** f. cardboard; paste. **~endeckel** m. pasteboard. **~enstiel** m. (fig.) trifle. **~ig** a. sticky. **~kasten** m., **~schachtel** f. cardboard box. **~schnee** m. soggy snow.

Pappel f. (-, -n) poplar.

päppeln v.t. to feed (child); to coddle.

pappen v.t. & i. to stick, paste.

Paprika m. (-s, -s) red pepper.

Papst (paː-) m. (-es, -̈e) pope. **~tum** n. papacy.

päpstlich a. papal.

Pa'rabel (-raː-) f. (-, -n) parable; (geom.) parabola.

Pa'rad-e f. (-e, -en) parade; review; parry, ward. **~ebett** *n.* *auf dem ~ebett liegen* to lie in state. **~emarsch** *m.* march past. **~eschritt** *m.* goose-step. **~eniform** *f.* gala uniform, full-dress uniform. **~ieren** *v.i.* to parade.

Para'dies *n.* (-es, -e) paradise. **~isch** *a.* paradisiacal, heavenly.

para'dox *a.* paradoxical. **~on** *n.* paradox.

Para'ffin *n.* ♣ paraffin wax. **~öl** *n.* paraffin oil.

Para'llel *a.* parallel. **~e** *f.* parallel. **~i'tät** *f.* parallelism.

Para'ly-se *f.* (-se, -sen) paralysis. **~sieren** *v.t.* to paralyse. **~tiker** *m.*, **~tisch** *a.* paralytic.

Paranuß *f.* Brazil-nut.

Para'sit *m.* (-en, -en) parasite.

Pärchen *n.* (-s, -) couple; lovers.

Pardel, Parder *m.* (-s, -) leopard, panther.

Paren'these *f.* (-, -n) parenthesis.

Par'force-jagd *f.* hunt(ing) with hounds. **~ritt** *m.* steeplechase.

Par'füm *n.* (-fœ) *n.* (-s, -e) perfume, scent. **~e'rie** *f.* perfumery. **~flasche** *f.* scent-bottle. **~ieren** *v.t.* to perfume, scent.

pari *adv.* at par. **~tät** *f.* equality; (*commerc.*) parity.

Paria *m.* (-s, -s) pariah.

pa'rieren *v.t. & i.* to parry, ward off; (*of horse*) to rein in. *v.i.* to obey.

Park *m.* (-es, -e) park; grounds. **~en** *v.t. & i.* to park. **~platz** *m.* car park, parking-place. **~uhr** *f.* parking-meter. **~verbot** *n.* 'no parking'.

Par'kett *n.* (-s, -e) parquet; (*theatr.*) stalls. **~ieren** *v.t.* to parquet.

Parla'ment *n.* (-s, -e) parliament. **~är** *m.* bearer of a flag of truce. **~arier** *m.* parliamentarian. **~ieren** *v.i.* to parley; to negotiate.

Paro'die *f.* (-, -n) parody. **~ren** *v.t.* to parody.

Pa'role *f.* (-, -n) password, parole.

Par'tei *f.* (-, -en) party, faction; side; tenant; *~ nehmen für* to side with. **~abzeichen** *n.* party badge. **~gänger** *m.* partisan. **~geist** *m.*, **~sucht** *f.* faction. **~isch**, **~lich** *aa.* partial, biased; one-sided. **~los** *a.* impartial, neutral. **~nahme** *f.* partisan-

ship. **~ung** *f.* division into parties.

Par'terre *n.* (-s) ground floor; (*theatr.*) pit; *erstes ~* stalls. [F]

Par'tie *f.* (-, -n) part, section; (*commerc.*) lot; game (of cards, &c.); excursion, trip; match.

Par'tikel *f.* (-, -n) particle.

Partikula'rismus *m.* (-) particularism.

Parti'san *m.* (-s, -e) partisan.

Parti'tur *(-tu:r) f.* (-, -en) (*mus.*) score.

Parti'zip *n.* (-s, -ien) participle.

Partner *m.* (-s, -) partner. **~schaft** *f.* partnership.

Parze *f.* (-, -n) goddess of Fate.

Par'zell-e *f.* (-, -en) lot, allotment. **~ieren** *v.t.* to divide into lots.

Pasch *m.* (-es, -e) dice; doublets.

Pascha *m.* (-s, -s) pasha.

pasch-en *v.t. & i.* to smuggle. **~er** *m.* smuggler.

Paspel *f.* (-, -n) piping, edging (on dress).

Paß *m.* (Passes, Pässe) pass; passage; passport; (*of horse*) amble; *zu ~ kommen* to suit well. **~amt** *n.* passport office. **~gänger** *m.* ambling horse. **~kontrolle** *f.* examination of passports.

Passa'gier *(-ʒi:r) m.* (-s, -e) passenger. **~flugzeug** *n.* air liner. **~gut** *n.* passenger's luggage.

Passah *n.* (-s) Passover.

Pa'ssant *m.* (-en, -en) passer-by.

Pa'ssatwind *m.* trade-wind.

passen *v.i.* to fit, suit; to be convenient, be suitable; to pass (at cards); *~ auf* to fit on *or* into; to watch for; *zueinander ~* to go well together, harmonize; to match. *v.r.* to be proper, be seemly. **~d** *a.* suitable, convenient; fit, seemly, appropriate. [F]

Passepar'tout *m.* (-s, -s) master-key; free admission ticket; (*phot.*) mount.

pa'ssier-en *v.t.* to go through, pass; to cross; (*cook.*) to sieve. *vvs.i.* to happen, occur, take place. **~bar** *a.* passable, practicable. **~schein** *m.* permit, pass.

Passi'on *(-o:n) f.* (-, -en) passion;

hobby. **~iert** a. impassioned.

passiv (-i:f) a. passive. subst. n. passive; passive voice; (pl.) liabilities, debts. **~i'tät** f. passivity. **~seite** f. left side (of ledger).

Paste f. paste.

Pa'stell n. (-s, -e) pastel, crayon.

Pa'stete (-e:tə) f. (-, -n) pie; pastry.

pasteuri'sieren v.t. to pasteurize.

Pa'stille f. (-, -n) pastille, lozenge.

Pastor m. (-s, -en) pastor, clergyman, minister. **~in** f. clergyman's wife.

Pat-e (pa:-) m. (-en, -en) godfather. **~enkind** n. godchild. **~enstelle** f. **~enstelle vertreten** to act as godfather to a child. **~in** f. godmother. [L]

Pa'tene f. paten.

Pa'tent n. (-s, -e) letters patent; patent; (mil.) commission; ~ **anmelden** to apply for a patent. **~amt** n. patent office. **~ieren** v.t. to patent.

Pater'noster-aufzug m. continuous lift, hoist. **~werk** n. bucket-chain (of dredger).

pa'thetisch a. ⚕ lofty, elevated, solemn.

Patho'log-e m. (-en, -en) pathologist. **~isch** a. pathological.

Pathos (pa:-) n. (-) ⚕ pathos = solemn or deep feeling.

Patience f. ~ **legen** to play patience.

Pati'ent (-tsi-) m. (-en, -en) patient.

pati'niert a. patinated.

Patri'arch m. (-en, -en) patriarch. **~alisch** a. patriarchal.

Patri'ot m. (-en, -en) patriot. **~isch** a. patriotic. **~ismus** m. patriotism.

Pa'trizier (-tritsiər) m. (-s, -) patrician.

Pa'tron (-o:n) m. (-s, -e) patron; (colloq.) fellow. **~in** f. patroness.

Pa'trone f. (-, -n) cartridge; pattern, model. **~ntasche** f. cartridge pouch.

Pa'trouill-e (-truljə) f. (-, -en) patrol. **~ieren** v.i. to patrol.

Patsch-e f. in der ~ sitzen to be in a fix. **~en** v.i. to splash; to smack, slap. **~hand** f. (tiny) hand. **~naß** a. soaked to the skin.

patz-en v.i. to make blots, spot. **~ig** a. rude, impudent.

Pauk-e f. (-e, -en) kettledrum; (colloq.) lecture, dressing-down. **~en** v.i. to beat the kettledrum; (colloq.) to swot, cram. v.r. to fight a duel. **~enschlag** m. beat of the kettledrum. **~enwirbel** m. roll of the kettledrum. **~er** m. kettledrummer; crammer, teacher. **~e'rei** f. duel; cramming.

pausbäckig a. chubby-faced.

Pau'schal-gebühr f. flat rate. **~summe** f. lump sum.

Paus-e[1] f. (-e, -en) pause; interval, break; (mus.) rest. **~enzeichen** n. (wireless) interval tune. **~ieren** v.i. to pause.

Paus-e[2] f. (-e, -en) tracing; traced design. **~en** v.t. to trace. **~papier** n. tracing paper.

Pavian m. (-s, -e) baboon.

Pavillon (-vilj5) m. (-s, -s) pavilion.

Pazi'fismus m. (-) pacifism.

Pech (-ç) n. (-es) pitch; cobbler's wax; (fig.) bad luck. **~draht** m. shoemaker's thread. **~fackel** f. torch. **~nelke** f. catch-fly. **~schwarz** a. pitch-black. **~strähne** f. run of ill luck. **~vogel** m. unlucky person.

Pe'dal (-a:l) n. (-s, -e) pedal.

Pe'dant m. (-en, -en) pedant. **~e'rie** f. pedantry. **~isch** a. pedantic.

Pe'dell (pe:-) m. (-s, -e) beadle; janitor, porter.

Pegel m. (-s, -) water-gauge. **~stand** m. water mark.

peil-en v.t. to take bearings; to locate; to sound; to gauge. **~funkgerät** n. radio-location instrument, direction-finder. **~ung** f. sounding, measuring; bearings by wireless.

Pein f. (-) pain, agony, torture. **~igen** v.t. to torment, harass. **~iger** m. tormentor. **~igung** f. torment, torture. **~lich** a. painful, embarrassing; exact, careful. **~lichkeit** f. painfulness; exactness, carefulness. [PINE]

Peitsche f. (-, -n) whip, lash, scourge. **~n** v.t. to whip, flog.

~nhieb m. lash, cut with the whip. **~nschnur** f. thong of a whip, lash. [SLAV.]

pekuni′är a. pecuniary.

Pelikan m. (-s, -e) pelican.

Pell-e (dial.) peel, skin. **~en** v.t. to peel. **~kartoffeln** f.pl. potatoes in their jackets.

Pelz (-ts) m. (-es, -e) fur, pelt; skin, hide; fur coat; auf den ~ rücken to importune. **~händler** m. furrier. **~ig** a. furry. **~mantel** m. fur coat. **~werk** n. fur, furs. [L]

Pendel m. & n. (-s, -) pendulum. **~n** v.i. to oscillate, swing; to commute. **~schwingung** f. oscillation, swing. **~uhr** f. pendulum clock. **~verkehr** m. shuttle-traffic.

Pendler m. commuter.

penetrant a. penetrating.

Pe′nn-al n. (-s, -e) (obs.)(secondary) school. **~äler** m. schoolboy. **~e** f. (sl.) (sec.) school.

Penn-bruder m. (sl.) tramp. **~en** v.i. to sleep.

Pensi′on (-o:n) f. (-, -en) (retiring-) pension; boarding-house. **~är** m. pensioner; boarder. **~at** n. boarding-school. **~ieren** v.t. to pension off. **~sberechtigt** a. pensionable.

Pensum n. (-s, Pensen) task, lesson.

Penta′gramm n. (-s, -e) pentacle.

per prep. – Adresse care of, °/o; – Post by post.

pere′nnierend a. perennial.

Perfekt n. (-s, -e) (gram.) perfect tense.

perfo′rieren v.t. to perforate.

Perga′ment n. (-es, -e) parchment. **~papier** n. vellum paper.

Peri′od-e (-o:-) f. (-e, -en) period. **~isch** a. periodic; **~ischer Dezimalbruch** recurring decimal.

Peripetie f. (lit.) dénouement.

Periphe′rie f. (-, -n) periphery, circumference; **~ der Stadt** outskirts (of the town).

Perl-e f. (-e, -en) pearl; bead; bubble. **~en** v.i. to sparkle; to effervesce. **~enkette** f. pearl necklet, string of pearls. **~huhn** n. guinea-fowl. **~mutter** f. mother-of-pearl.

Perpen′dikel m. & n. (-s, -) perpendicular (line); pendulum.

Per′petuum mobile n. perpetual motion.

perplex a. perplexed, dumbfounded.

Pe′rron (-rō) m. (-s, -s) platform.

Per′senning f. (-, -en) tarpaulin.

Per′son (-zo:n) f. (-, -en) person, personage; (theatr.) character, role, part; **in** ~ personally; personified. **~al** n. staff, employees, personnel, officials; servants, attendants. **~alausweis** m. identity card. **~albeschreibung** f. description of a person. **~alchef** m. staff manager. **~alien** pl. particulars about a person. **~enaufzug** m. passenger lift. **~enkraftwagen** m. motor-car. **~enverzeichnis** n. register of persons; dramatis personae. **~enzug** m. local or slow train. **~ifizieren** v.t. to personify; to impersonate.

per′sönlich (-zo:n-) a. personal. adv. in person. **~keit** f. personality.

Perspek′tiv-e f. (-e, -en), **~isch** a. perspective.

Pe′rücke f. (-, -n) wig. [F]

per′vers a. perverse. **~i′tät** f. perversity.

Pessi′m-ismus m. (-) pessimism. **~istisch** a. pessimistic.

Pest f. (-) plague, pestilence; epidemic. **~artig** a. pestilential. **~beule** f. plague-spot.

Peter′silie (-zi:lie) f. (-) parsley.

Petitschrift f. (typ.) brevier.

Pe′troleum n. (-s) ♣ oil, paraffin. **~quelle** f. oil-well.

Petschaft n. (-s, -e) seal, signet.

Petz m. (lit.) Bruin.

petzen v.t. to tell tales, inform.

Pfad (-t) m. (-es, -e) path. **~finder** m. pathfinder; Boy Scout. **~finderin** f. Girl Guide.

Pfaffe m. (-n, -n) priest; parson. **~ntum** n. clericalism.

pfäffisch a. priestlike; priestridden.

Pfahl m. (-es, -̈e) pole, stake, pile, prop, post. **~bau** m. huts built on piles, lake dwelling. **~bürger** m. citizen; Philistine. **~dorf**

n. lake village. ~rost *m.* pile-support. ~werk *n.* paling; palisade. ~wurzel *f.* tap-root.

pfählen *v.t.* to fence in; to impale.

Pfalz *f.* (-, -en) imperial palace. ~graf *m.* Count Palatine.

Pfand *n.* (-es, ̈er) pledge, security; forfeit. ~brief *m.* mortgage (bond). ~gläubiger *m.* mortgagee. ~haus *n.* pawnshop, pawn office. ~leiher *m.* pawnbroker. ~recht *n.* lien. ~schein *m.* pawn-ticket. ~schuldner *m.* mortgagor. ~verschreibung *f.* mortgage deed.

pfänd-bar *a.* (*leg.*) distrainable. ~en *v.t.* to seize, take in pledge. ~erspiel *n.* game of forfeits. ~ung *f.* seizure, distraint, distress. ~ungsbefehl *m.* distress-warrant.

Pfann-e *f.* (-e, -en) pan; (*anat.*) socket. ~kuchen *m.* pancake; (*Berliner*) ~ doughnut.

Pfarr-amt *n.*, ~bezirk *m.*, ~gemeinde *f.* parish. ~e, ~ei *f.* parsonage, vicarage; parish. ~er *m.* pastor, minister, rector, vicar. ~haus *n.* vicarage, rectory, (*Scot.*) manse. ~kind *n.* parishioner. ~kirche *f.* parish church.

Pfau *m.* (-s, -en) peacock. ~enauge *n.* peacock-butterfly. ~enrad *n.* peacock's fan.

Pfeffer *m.* (-s) pepper. ~büchse *f.*, ~streuer *m.* pepper-castor. ~gurke *f.* pickled gherkin. ~kuchen *m.* spiced cake, gingerbread. ~minze *f.* peppermint.

pfeffern *v.t.* to season with pepper; (*sl.*) to throw.

Pfeife *f.* (-, -n) whistle; pipe. ~n *v.t. & i. st.* to whistle; to pipe; (*of wind*) to howl; (*of mice*) to squeak; ~n auf (*fig.*) not to care a straw for. ~nkopf *m.* pipe bowl. ~nspitze *f.* mouthpiece. ~r *m.* piper.

Pfeil *m.* (-es, -e) arrow; dart. ~gerade *a.* straight as an arrow. ~spitze *f.* arrow-head. [L]

Pfeiler *m.* (-s, -) pillar; post, prop, pier.

Pfennig *m.* (-s, -e) See App. III. ~fuchser *m.* stingy fellow.

Pferch (-c) *m.* (-es, -e) fold, pen. ~en *v.t.* to pen, fold; to coop up.

Pferd *n.* (-es, -e) horse; (*gym.*) pommelled horse; *zu* ~ *e* on horseback. ~ebahn *f.* horse-tramway. ~ebremse *f.* horse-fly, cleg. ~edecke *f.* saddle-cloth. ~egeschirr *n.* harness. ~ehändler *m.* horse-dealer. ~eknecht *m.* groom, ostler. ~ekoppel *f.* paddock. ~ekraft *f.* horse-power. ~elänge *f.* length (of a horse). ~erennen *n.* horse-race, horse-racing. ~eschwemme *f.* horse-pond.

pfiff [1] *imperf. of* pfeifen.

Pfiff [2] *m.* (-es, -e) whistle, whistling; trick. ~ig *a.* sly, cunning. ~ikus *m.* sly fellow.

Pfifferling *m.* (-s, -e) chanterelle; *keinen* ~ *wert* not worth a fig or a straw.

Pfingst-en *n.* (-ens, -) & *f.* Whitsuntide. ~montag *m.* Whit Monday. ~rose *f.* peony. ~sonntag *m.* Whitsunday. [GK.]

Pfirsich (-zic) *m.* (-s, -e) peach. ~bowle *f.* peach-cup.

Pflanz-e (-tsə) *f.* (-e, -en) plant. ~enbutter *f.* vegetable butter. ~enfaser *f.* vegetable fibre. ~enfressend *a.* graminivorous, herbivorous. ~enkost *f.* vegetable diet. ~enkunde *f.* botany. ~enleben *n.* vegetable life. ~enreich *n.*, ~enwelt *f.* vegetable kingdom. ~ensaft *m.* sap. ~ensammlung *f.* collection of plants, herbarium. ~er *m.* planter; settler, colonist. ~enschule *f.* nursery. ~enstätte *f.* settlement. (*fig.*) source, nucleus, hotbed. ~ung *f.* planting; plantation; settlement.

pflanzen *v.t.* to plant, to set or lay out.

Pflaster *n.* (-s, -) 1. plaster; *englisches* ~ court plaster. 2. pavement, paving. ~er *m.* paviour, paver. ~n *v.t.* to plaster; to pave. ~stein *m.* paving-stone. ~treter *m.* loafer, loiterer.

Pflaume *f.* (-, -n) plum; *gedörrte* ~ prune. ~nmus *n.* plum jam.

Pflege (-e:-) *f.* (-e, -en) care, attention; nursing; rearing (of child);

cultivation (of arts, &c.). **~e-bedürftig** a. in need of care. **~e-befohlene(r)** m. ward. **~eeltern** pl. foster-parents. **~ekind** n. foster-child. **~er** m., **~erin** f. nurse; guardian, curator. **~lich** a. careful. **~ling** m. foster-child, ward, charge. **~schaft** f. guardianship.

pflegen v.t. to care for, cherish; to nurse; to cultivate, foster. v.i. to be accustomed to, be in the habit of; *Rat* ~ to consult with, deliberate; *Umgang* ~ *mit* to see a good deal of.

Pflicht (-çt) f. (-, -en) duty; obligation. **~beitrag** m. quota. **~eifer** m. zeal. **~gefühl** n. sense of duty. **~gemäß** a. dutiful, conformable to duty; as in duty bound. **~teil** m. lawful share. **~treu** a. dutiful, conscientious. **~vergessen** a. undutiful, disloyal. **~widrig** a. contrary to duty, undutiful. [PLIGHT]

Pflock m. (-es, ⸗e) peg, pin, plug; stake, picket.

pflöcken v.t. to peg, plug.

pflog imperf. of **pflegen**.

pflücken v.t. to pick, gather, pluck.

Pflug (-u:-) m. (-es, ⸗e) plough. **~eisen**, **~messer** n. coulter. **~schar** f. ploughshare.

pflügen v.t. to plough.

Pforte f. (-, -n) gate, door; (*naut.*) porthole; *die Hohe* ~ the Sublime Porte.

Pförtner m. (-s, -) gatekeeper, doorkeeper; (*anat.*) pylorus.

Pfosten m. (-s, -) post; pale, stake; jamb (of door).

Pfote (-o:-) f. (-, -n) paw.

Pfriem m. (-es, -e) awl; puncheon, punch; bodkin.

Pfropf m., **~en** m. (-ens, -en) cork, stopper; wad. **~en** v.t. to cork; to cram (into), to stuff (full of); (*hort.*) to graft. **~enzieher** m. corkscrew. **~messer** n. grafting-knife. **~reis** n. graft, scion.

Pfründ-e f. (-e, -en) prebend, benefice, living; (*fig.*) sinecure. **~ner** m. prebendary; beneficiary, incumbent.

Pfuhl m. (-es, -e) pool, puddle.

Pfühl m. & n. (-es, -e) pillow.

pfui int. fie! shame!

Pfund n. (-es, -e) pound; pound (sterling); (*fig.*) talent.

pfusch-en v.i. & t. to bungle, botch; to meddle with. **~er** m. bungler, botcher. **~e'rei** f. scamped work; bungling.

Pfütze (-ytsə) f. (-, -n) puddle, pool.

Phäno'men (-me:n) n. (-s, -e) phenomenon. **~al** a. phenomenal.

Phanta'sie f. (-, -en) imagination, fancy, inventive faculty; fantastic vision, reverie. **~ren** v.i. to day-dream, imagine (things); (*mus.*) to improvise; (*med.*) to ramble, rave, be delirious.

Phan'tast m. (-en, -en) dreamer, visionary. **~isch** a. fanciful; fantastic.

Phan'tom (-o:m) n. (-s, -e) phantom.

Phari'säer m. (-s, -) Pharisee.

Pharma'zeut m. (-en, -en) pharmacist. **~ik** f. pharmaceutics. **~isch** a. pharmaceutical.

Pharma'zie f. (-) pharmacy.

Phase (-a:-) f. (-, -n) phase.

Philan'throp (-o:p) m. (-en, -en) philanthropist. **~isch** a. philanthropic.

Phi'list-er m. (-ers, -er) Philistine. **~erhaft**, **~rös** aa. narrow-minded.

Philo'log-e (-lo:gə) m. (-en, -en) philologist. **~ie** f. philology. **~isch** a. philological.

Philo'soph (-zo:f) m. (-en, -en) philosopher. **~ie** f. philosophy. **~ieren** v.i. to philosophize. **~isch** a. philosophical.

Phi'ole (-o:-) f. (-, -n) phial.

Phlegm-a n. (-as) ♃ coolness; indolence. **~atiker** m. phlegmatic person. **~atisch** a. slow, indolent.

Pho'netik f. (-) phonetics.

Phosphor m. (-s) phosphorus. **~es'zieren** v.i. to phosphoresce. **~eszierend** a. phosphorescent.

Photo-apparat m. camera. **~graph** m. photographer. **~gra'phie** f. photography; photograph, photo. **~graphisch** a. photographic. **~montage** f. photographic layout.

photogra'phieren *v.t. & i.* to photograph.

Phrase (fra:zə) *f.* (-, -n) phrase. **~ndrescher,** **~nheld** *m.* phrasemonger.

Phy'sik (-si:k) *f.* (-) physics. **~alisch**ɑ. △ **physical** = of physics. **~er** *m.* physicist.

Physio-gno'mie (.. -) *f.* physiognomy. **~lo'gie** *f.* physiology. **~logisch** *a.* physiological.

physisch *a.* physical.

Pia'nist *m.* (-en, -en), **~in** *f.* pianist.

picheln *v.i.* to tipple.

Picke *f.* (-, -n) pickaxe. **~n** *v.t. & i.* to pick; to peck.

Pickel *m.* (-s, -) 1. pimple. 2. pickaxe.

Pickel-flöte *f.* piccolo. **~haube** *f.* spiked helmet. **~hering** *m.* pickled herring.

pick(e)lig *a.* pimply.

Picknick *n.* (-s, -s) picnic.

piecken *v.t.* to prick, sting.

piep-en, **~sen** *v.i.* to chirp, cheep. **~matz** *m.* dicky-bird.

Pie't-ät *f.* (-ät) reverence; piety; love, regard. **~ätlos** *a.* irreverent. **~ätvoll** *a.* reverent. **~ismus** *m.* bigotry, cant. **~istisch** *a.* bigoted, sanctimonious.

Pik (pi:k) *m.* (-s, -s) pique; *(colloq.)* grudge. *n.* spade (at cards). **~ant** *a.* piquant; spicy. **~ante'rie** *f.* spicy joke or story. **~fein** *a.* very smart. **~'iert** *a.* piqued, hurt.

Pike (pi:-) *f.* (-, -n) pike; pique, grudge; *von der* ~ *auf* from the ranks.

Pi'kee *m.* (-s, -s) piqué.

Pikkolo *m.* (-s, -s) boy waiter. **~flöte** *f.* piccolo.

Pi'krinsäure *f.* picric acid.

Pilger *m.* (-s, -) pilgrim. **~fahrt,** **~schaft** *f.* pilgrimage. **~n** *vws.i.* to go on a pilgrimage.

Pille *f.* (-, -n) pill.

Pi'lot (-o:t) *m.* (-en, -en) pilot.

Pilz (-ts) *m.* (-es, -e) mushroom, fungus; *giftiger* ~ toadstool. [L]

pimp(e)lig *a.* soft, flabby; whining.

Pi'nasse *f.* (-, -n) pinnace.

Pingu'in (-i:n) *m.* (-s, -e) penguin.

Pinie (pi:niə) *f.* (-, -n) stone-pine.

pinkeln *v.i.* *(vulg.)* to piddle, make water.

Pinne *f.* (-, -n) drawing-pin, tack; pivot; tiller.

Pinscher *m.* (-s, -) German terrier.

Pinsel *m.* (-s, -) brush, paintbrush; *(fig.)* noodle. **~n** *v.t. & i.* to paint; to daub. **~strich** *m.* stroke of the brush. [L]

Pin'zette *f.* (-, -n) tweezer(s).

Pio'nier *m.* (-s, -e) pioneer, sapper, engineer.

Pips *m.* (-es) *(med.)* pip.

Pi'rat (-a:t) *m.* (-en, -en) pirate.

Pirol *m.* (-s, -e) oriole.

Pirsch *f.* (-) hunting, deer-stalking. **~en** *v.i.* to hunt, stalk deer.

pissen *v.i.* *(vulg.)* to piss.

Pis'tazie *f.* (-, -n) pistachio.

Piste *f.* (-, -n) beaten track or path. [F]

Pis'tole *f.* (-, -n) pistol. **~ntasche** *f.* holster.

pitschnaß *a.* *(colloq.)* wet through.

pittoresk *a.* picturesque.

plack-en *v.t.* to torment. *v.r.* to drudge. **~e'rei** *f.* drudgery.

plä'dieren *v.i.* to plead.

Plage (-a:-) *f.* (-, -n) plague, torment; nuisance. **~geist** *m.* plague, tormentor. **~n** *v.t.* to plague, torment, harass, pester. *v.r.* to drudge, slave.

Plagi'at (-a:t) *n.* (-s, -e) plagiarism, plagiary. **~or** *m.* plagiarist.

plagi'ieren *v.t.* to plagiarize.

Pla'kat (-a:t) *n.* (-s, -e) bill, placard, poster. **~ieren** *v.t.* to stick or post bills. **~künstler** *m.* poster artist. **~säule** *f.* advertisement pillar. **~träger** *m.* sandwich-man.

Pla'kette *f.* (-, -n) plaque.

plan¹ (-a:-) *a.* level, flat; open, clear. *m.* plain; plane; *auf den* ~ *treten* to turn up, appear. **~ime'trie** *f.* planimetry. [L]

Plan² (-a:-) *m.* (-es, ⁓e) plan; map; diagram; design; intention; project, scheme; plot. **~los** *a.* without a fixed plan; desultory. **~mäßig** *a.* according to plan, methodical. **~stelle** *f.* permanent post. **~ung** *f.* planning, plan, **~wirtschaft** *f.* economic planning.

Plan-e f. (-e, -en) awning; tarpaulin. **~wagen** m. covered wagon.

planen v.t. & i. to plan, scheme.

Pläneschmied m. schemer.

Pla'net (-e:t) m. (-en, -en) planet. **~'arium** n. orrery.

pla'nieren v.t. to level, plane; to size (paper).

Planke f. (-, -n) plank, board.

Plänkel-ei f. (-ei, -eien) skirmishing. **~n** v.i. to skirmish.

plan(t)schen v.i. & t. to splash, paddle.

Plan'tage (-a:ʒə) f. (-, -n) plantation.

Plapper-maul n. **~tasche** f. chatterbox. **~n** v.t. & i. to chatter, prattle.

plärren v.t. & i. to cry, blubber; to bawl.

Plasti-k f. (-k, -ken) plastic art; sculpture. **~lin** n. plasticine. **~sch** a. plastic.

Pla'tane f. (-, -n) plane-tree.

Platin n. (-s) platinum.

plätschern v.i. to splash, (poet.) plash; to ripple, murmur.

platt a. flat, level; flattened out; insipid, silly; dull; ~ sein (colloq.) to be dumbfounded. **~deutsch** a. Low German. **~e** f. plate; slab, flag; plateau; (mus.) record, disk; tray, salver; bald head; kalte ~e cold meat(s). **~enabzug** m. stereotyped proof. **~enspieler** m. record player. **~erdings** adv. absolutely, decidedly. **~form** f. platform. **~fuß** m. flat-foot. **~fußeinlage** f. arch-support. **~heit** f. flatness; dullness; platitude.

Plätt-brett n. ironing-board. **~eisen** n. iron. **~erin** f. ironer. **~frau** f. ironer. **~stahl** m. heater (of flat-iron). **~wäsche** f. linen (to be ironed).

plätten v.t. to iron.

pla'ttieren v.t. to plate.

Platz m. (-es, ¨e) place, spot; square; space, room; (theatr., &c.) seat; ~ da! make way! ~ machen to make room; ~ nehmen to sit down; ~ greifen to gain ground, spread; am ~ sein to be pertinent, be opportune.

~angst f. agoraphobia. **~anweiserin** f. usherette. **~karte** f. ticket for reserved seat. **~kommandant** m. military commander. **~mangel** m. lack of space. **~raubend** a. taking up (too) much space.

Plätzchen n. (-s, -) little place; round fancy cake or biscuit; (chocolate) drop.

platz-en vws.i. to burst; to explode. **~patrone** f. blank cartridge. **~regen** m. torrential rain, downpour.

Plauder-'ei f. (-ei, -eien) chat, small talk, talk, conversation. **~er** m. talker, speaker, conversationalist; chatterbox. **~n** v.i. to talk; to chat, gossip. **~tasche** f. chatterbox, gossip. **~ton** m. conversational tone.

Ple'bej-er m., **~isch** a. plebeian.

Plebs m. (-es) & f. mob, rabble.

Pleite f. (-, -n) (sl.) bankruptcy; (fig.) failure. [HEBR.]

Plenum n. (-s) plenary meeting.

Pleuelstange f. connecting rod.

Plissé-e f. (-ees, -ees) pleating. **~ieren** v.t. to pleat.

Plomb-e f. (-e, -en) lead seal; stopping (in tooth). **~ieren** v.t. to seal with lead; to stop (tooth). [L]

Plötze f. (-, -n) roach.

plötzlich (-œ-) a. sudden. adv. suddenly. **~keit** f. suddenness.

Pluderhosen f.pl. wide breeches.

Plu'meau (-o:) n. (-s, -s) feather-bed.

plump (-u-) a. shapeless, heavy; clumsy, unwieldy. **~heit** f. shapelessness, heaviness; clumsiness. **~sen** vws.i. to plump (down).

Plunder (-un-) m. (-s) lumber, trash, rubbish.

Plünder-er m. (-ers, -er) plunderer. **~n** v.t. & i. to plunder, pillage; to strip. **~ung** f. plundering, sack.

Plural m. (-s, -e) plural.

Plus (-us) n. (-, -) plus, surplus. **~quamperfekt** n. pluperfect. **~zeichen** n. plus sign.

Plüsch m. (-es, -e) plush.

Pneu'mati-k *m.* (-ks, -ks) pneumatic tyre. **~sch** *a.* pneumatic.

Pöbel (-ö:-) *m.* (-s) mob, rabble, populace. **~haft** *a.* vulgar, low. **~herrschaft** *f.* mob rule. [F]

poch-en (-x-) *v.i.* to knock, rap; to beat, throb; ~ *auf* (*fig.*) to boast of; to insist on. *v.t.* to crush, pound (ore). **~spiel** *n.* poker. **~werk** *n.* pounding-machine, stamping-mill.

Pocke *f.* (-, -n) pock; (*pl.*) small-pox. **~nimpfung** *f.* vaccination. **~nnarbe** *f.* pock-mark. **~nnarbig** *a.* pock-marked.

Po'dest *m.* landing; stage; platform.

Podium (-o:-) *n.* (-s, Podien) ⚘ rostrum, platform. [L]

Poe'sie (-zi:) *f.* (-, -n) poetry.

Po'et (-e:t) *m.* (-en, -en) poet. **~ik** *f.* poetics. **~isch** *a.* poetic.

Po'kal *m.* (-s, -e) goblet, drinking-cup; cup. **~spiel** *n.* cup-tie.

Pökel-fleisch *n.* salt meat. **~hering** *m.* pickled herring. **~n** *v.t.* to pickle, salt.

poku'lieren *v.i.* to drink, booze.

Pol (po:l) *m.* (-es, -e) (*astron.*) pole.

po'lar *a.* polar, arctic. **~eis** *n.* polar ice. **~forscher** *m.* polar explorer. **~fuchs** *m.* arctic fox. **~gürtel** *m.* frigid zone. **~kreis** *m.* arctic circle. **~licht** *n.* northern lights, aurora borealis. **~meer** *n.* arctic ocean. **~stern** *m.* Pole-star. **~strom** *m.* arctic current.

Po'lemi-k (-le:-) *f.* (-k, -ken) polemics, controversy. **~sch** *a.* polemic. **~sieren** *v.i.* to carry on a controversy.

Po'lice (-li:sa) *f.* (-, -n) (insurance) policy.

Po'lier *m.* (-s, -e) foreman. **~en** *v.t.* to polish. **~wachs** *n.* polish.

Poliklinik *f.* outpatients' department of hospital.

Po'litik *f.* (-, -en) politics; policy.

Po'liti-ker (-kers, -ker) politician. **~sch** *a.* political. **~sieren** *v.i.* to talk politics; to dabble in politics, *v.t.* to make political-minded.

Po'litur *f.* (-, -en) polish.

Po'lizei (-tsai) *f.* (-) police.

~aufsicht *f.* police surveillance; *unter ~aufsicht* on ticket of leave. **~beamte(r)** *m.* police officer. **~kommissar** *m.* inspector of police. **~lich** *a.* police, of the police. **~präsidium** *n.* police headquarters. **~revier** *n.* police station. **~spitzel** *m.* police spy. **~streife** *f.* police raid. **~stunde** *f.* closing-hour; curfew. **~wache** *f.* police station. **~widrig** *a.* contrary to police regulations.

Poli'zist *m.* (-en, -en) policeman, constable.

Polster *n.* (-, -) cushion, pillow; bolster; pad, padding, stuffing. **~möbel** *n.pl.* upholstered furniture. **~n** *v.t.* to upholster; to pad, stuff. **~sessel** *m.* easy chair. **~ung** *f.* upholstery, padding, stuffing.

Polter-abend *m.* wedding-eve (party). **~n** *v.i.* to make a noise; to rumble; to scold.

Polyga'mie *f.* (-) polygamy.

Po'lyp *m.* (-en, -en) polyp; (*med.*) polypus.

Poly'technikum *n.* technical college.

Po'made (-a:-) *f.* (-e, -en) pomade. **~ig** *a.* (*fig.*) phlegmatic.

Pom'eranze *f.* (-, -n) orange.

Pomp *m.* (-es) pomp. **~haft**, **~ös** *aa.* pompous, magnificent.

Pon'ton *m.* (-s, -s) pontoon.

Popanz *m.* (-en, -e) bogy. [cz.]

Po'po *m.* (*vulg.*) behind.

popu'lär *a.* popular. **~ari'sieren** *v.t.* to popularize. **~ari'tät** *f.* popularity.

Po're (-o:-) *f.* (-e, -en) pore. **~ös** *a.* porous. **~osi'tät** *f.* porosity.

Porphyr *m.* (-s, -e) porphyry.

Porree *m.* (-s) leek.

Port *m.* (-es, -e) harbour, port.

Por'tal *n.* (-s, -e) portal.

Porte-feuille (-foej) *n.* portfolio. **~mo'nnaie** *n.* purse. **~pee** *n.* sword-knot.

Porti'er (-e:) *m.* (-s, -s) porter, doorkeeper.

Porti'on *f.* (-, -en) portion, helping; ration.

Porto *n.* (-s, -s) postage. **~frei** *a.* post free, prepaid. **~kasse** *f.* petty cash. **~pflichtig** *a.* liable.

to postage fee. **~satz** m. rate of postage. **~zuschlag** m. surcharge.

Por'trät n. (-s, -s) portrait, likeness. **~ieren** v.t. & i. to portray, paint a portrait of. **~maler** m. portrait painter.

Porze'llan (-la:n) n. (-s, -e) porcelain, china. **~brennerei** f. porcelain manufactory. **~erde** f. porcelain clay, kaolin. **~service** n. set of china.

Posamen'tierwaren f.pl. haberdashery.

Po'saun-e (-z-) f. (-e, -en) trombone; trumpet. **~en** v.t. to play the trombone; (fig.) to trumpet. **~ist** m. trombonist. [F]

Pose¹ f. (-, -n) quill.

Pos-e² (-o:-) f. (-e, -en) pose. **~ieren** v.i. to strike an attitude, pose. **~itiv** a. positive. **~i'tur** f. posture.

Poss-e (-e, -en) jest; farce. **~en** m. trick. **~enreißer** m. jester, buffoon. **~ierlich** a. droll, funny, quaint. [F]

Posse'ssivpronomen n. possessive pronoun.

Post f. (-, -en) post, mail; post office. **~alisch** a. postal. **~amt** n. post office. **~anweisung** f. postal order, money-order. **~auto** n. motorbus (carrying mail & passengers). **~beamte(r)** m. post-office clerk. **~bote** m. postman. **~fach** n. P.O. box. **~karte** f. postcard. **~kasten** m. post-box, letter-box. **~kutsche** f. stage-coach, mail. **~lagernd** a. poste restante. **~leitzahl** f. postal district number. **~scheck** m. postal cheque. **~schließfach** n. post-office box. **~sparkasse** f. post-office savings bank. **~wendend** a. by return of post. **~wertzeichen** n. (postage-) stamp.

Posta'ment n. (-s, -e) pedestal, base.

Posten m. (-s, -e) post, situation, position; outpost, sentry; (commerc.) item, sum; entry; lot, parcel. **~ stehen** to be on sentry duty or on guard; auf dem **~ sein** (fig.) to feel well. **~jäger**

m. place-hunter. **~kette**, **~linie** f. outpost line.

po'stieren v.t. to post, place.

post(h)um a. posthumous.

potenti'ell a. potential.

Po'tenz f. (-, -en) power; (math.) exponent.

Pott-asche f. potash. **~wal** m. sperm-whale.

pou'ssieren v.i. to flirt.

Pracht (-x-) f. (-) splendour, magnificence. **~ausgabe** f. édition de luxe. **~kerl** m. (sl.) sport. **~liebe** f. love of splendour. **~voll** a. splendid, gorgeous, fine.

prächtig (-iç) a. magnificent, splendid; fine, lovely.

Prädi'kat n. (-s, -e) predicate; title; (school) marks.

Präfation (-o:n) f. (R.C.) preface.

Prä'fix n. (-es, -e) prefix.

präg-en v.t. to coin, stamp; (fig.) to impress (on). **~ung** f. shaping; stamping; character.

präg'nant a. ♣ significant, suggestive; exact, precise. **~z** f. terseness.

prähis'torisch a. prehistoric.

prahl-en v.i. to boast, brag; to show off. **~e'rei** f. boasting, bragging. **~erisch** a. boastful, bragging; ostentatious. **~hans** m. boaster, braggart.

Prahm m. (-es, -e) barge, lighter, flat-bottomed boat.

Prakti-k f. (-k, -ken) practice; trick. **~kant** m. probationer. **~ker** m. practical man; expert. **~kus** m. old hand. **~sch** a. clever, handy; experienced; practical, useful; **~scher Arzt** general practitioner; **~sches Wissen** working knowledge. **~zieren** v.t. & i. to practise (as doctor).

Prä'lat m. (-en, -en) prelate.

Prali'né n. (-s, -s) chocolate (-cream). [F]

prall a. taut, tight, tense; plump, chubby; in der **~en Sonne** in the full glare of the sun. subst. m. collision; rebound. **~en** vws.i. to dash (against); (of sun) to shine dazzlingly.

Prä'ludium n. (-s, ...dien) prelude.

Präm-ie (-iə) f. (-ie, -ien) premium;

prize. **~i'ieren** v.t. to award a prize to.

prang-en v.i. to be displayed, exhibited; to boast. **~er** m. pillory.

Pranke f. (-, -n) claw, paw.

pränume'rando adv. in advance.

Präpa'rat (-a:t) n. -s, -e) ♃ (med. & chem.) preparation; compound.

präpa'rieren v.t. to prepare.

Präpositi'on f. (-, -en) preposition.

Prä'rie f. (-, -n) prairie.

Präsen-s n. (-s, -tia) present (tense).

präsen'tieren v.t. to present; to offer.

Prä'senz-bibliothek f. reference library. **~stärke** f. effective strength.

Präsid-ent m. (-enten, -enten) president, chairman. **~i'eren** v.i. to preside. **~ium** n. chair, presidency.

prasseln v.i. to crackle; to hail; (of rain) to patter.

prass-en v.i. to feast, carouse; to revel. **~er** m. glutton; reveller; spendthrift. **~e'rei** f. feasting; revelry, dissipation.

Präten'dent m. (-en, -en) pretender.

Prä'teritum n. (-s, . . . ta) preterite, past tense.

präventiv a. preventive.

Praxis f. (-) practice; experience.

Präze'denzfall m. precedent.

prä'zis (-tsi:s) a. precise, exact; punctual. **~i'on** f. precision.

predig-en (-e:-) v.t. & i. to preach. **~er** m. preacher, minister, clergyman. **~t** f. sermon; lecture.

Preis m. (-es, -e) price, cost, rate; terms; prize; praise, glory; um keinen ~ not at any price. **~abbau** m. reduction of prices. **~angabe** f. quotation of prices. **~ausschreiben** n. prize competition. **~bewerber** m. competitor. **~druckerei** f. close bargaining. **~erhöhung** f. rise in prices. **~frage** f. subject for prize competition. **~gabe** f. surrender, abandonment; exposure. **~geben** v.t. to surrender, give up; to abandon, sacrifice; to expose. **~krönen** v.t. to award a prize to. **~lage** f. price

range. **~nachlaß** m. abatement, reduction. **~richter** m. arbiter, judge. **~schießen** n. shooting competition. **~schleuderei** f. undercutting of prices. **~schrift** f. prize essay. **~senkung** f. reduction. **~sturz** m. fall in prices. slump. **~träger** m. prize-winner. **~treiberei** f. forcing up of prices. **~überwachung** f. price control. **~wert** a. cheap. **~würdig** a. praiseworthy.

Preiselbeere f. cranberry.

preisen v.t. st. to praise; to extol, glorify.

Prell-bock m. buffer-stop. **~en** v.t. to toss; (fig.) to cheat, swindle; **~en auf** to bump against. **~e'rei** f. swindle, fraud. **~stein** m. kerb(-stone).

Premi'ere f. (-, -n) first night.

Presby'terium n. (-s, . . . rien) presbytery.

Presse f. (-, -n) press; crammer, tutorial college. **~attaché,** **~referent** m. press-officer. **~stimme** f. press comment, review.

pressen v.t. to press, squeeze; to urge.

Preß-fehde f. press teud. **~freiheit** f. freedom of the press. **~kohle** f. briquette. **~luft** f. compressed air. **~stoffe** pl. plastics.

prickeln v.i. & t. to prick; to prickle. **~d** a. (fig.) piquant, spicy.

Priem m. quid (of tobacco).

pries imperf. of **preisen**.

Priester m. (-s, -) priest. **~in** f. priestess. **~lich** a. priestly, sacerdotal. **~rock** m. cassock. **~schaft** f., **~tum** n. priesthood. **~weihe** f. ordination of a priest.

Prim-a f. (-a, -en) sixth form, highest class of secondary school. a. prime, first-rate. **~aner** m. sixth-form boy. **~as** m. primate. **~at** n. primacy. **~awechsel** m. first bill of exchange. **~zahl** f. prime number.

Primel f. (-, -n) primrose, primula.

primi'tiv (-i:f) a. primitive. **~i'tät** f. primitiveness.

Prinz m. (-en, -en) prince. **~essin** f. princess. **~gemahl** m. prince consort. **~lich** a. princely.

Prin′zip (-tsi:p) n. (-s, -ien) principle. **~′al** m. principal, head, manager. **~′ell** a. ⌀ on principle. **~ienreiter** m. pedant, stickler for principles.

Prior m. (-s, -en) prior. **~i′tät** f. priority.

Prise (-i:-) f. (-, -n) (naut.) prize; pinch (of snuff).

Prism-a n. (-as, -en) prism.

Pritsche f. (-, -n) iron bed, plank bed; wooden sword.

pri′vat (-va:t) a. private. **~dozent** m. university lecturer. **~im** adv. privately. **~′sieren** v.i. to live on one's means. **~recht** n. civil law.

Privi′leg (-le:k) n. (-s, -ien) privilege. **~ieren** v.t. to privilege.

pro′bat a. proved, tried.

Probe (-o:-) f. (-, -n) trial, experiment; proof, test; probation; (commerc.) sample, specimen; (theatr.) rehearsal; **~ ablegen** to give proof of; **auf die ~ stellen** to put to the test. **~abzug**, **~druck** m. proof(-sheet). **~fahrt** f. trial trip, trial run. **~jahr** n. year of probation. **~nummer** f. specimen number. **~weise** adv. on approval, on trial. **~zeit** f. time of probation.

proben v.t. & i. to rehearse.

pro′bier-en v.t. & i. to try; to taste. **~dame** f. mannequin. **~stein** m. touchstone.

Problem (-e:m) n. (-s, -e) problem. **~atisch** a. problematic.

Pro′dukt n. (-es, -e) produce; product. **~enhandel** m. trade in home produce. **~i′on** f. production. **~ionsleiter** m. works manager; (film) producer. **~ionsmenge** f. output. **~iv** a. productive; prolific. **~ivi′tät** f. productivity.

Produ′z-ent m. (-enten, -enten) grower, producer, manufacturer. **~ieren** v.t. to produce; v.r. to show off, exhibit.

pro′fan (-a:n) a. profane. **~ieren** v.t. to profane. **~ierung** f. profanation.

Pro′feß f. (-) (eccl.) profession, vow.

Profess-i′on f. profession; trade.

~or m. professor. **~ur** f. professorship.

Pro′fil (-i:l) n. (-s, -e) profile; section.

Pro′fit (-fi:t) m. (-s, -e) profit, proceeds. **~ieren** v.i. & t. ⌀ to profit, gain (by). **~macher** m. profiteer.

Prog′nose (-o:-) f. (-, -n) forecast; (med.) prognosis.

Pro′gramm n. (-s, -e) programme. **~ieren** v.t. to instruct computer.

Prohibi′tivzoll m. prohibition duty.

Pro′jekt n. (-es, -e) project. **~i′onsapparat** m. projector. **~ionsschirm** m. screen.

proji′zieren v.t. to project, make projection of.

Proklamati′on f. (-, -en) proclamation.

prokla′mieren v.t. to proclaim.

Pro′kura- f. (-a) (commerc.) procuration; power of attorney. **~ist** m. authorized clerk or manager.

Prole′t (-e:t) m. (-en, -en) proletarian. **~ari′at** n. proletariat. **~arier** m. proletarian. **~arisch** a. proletarian.

Pro′log m. (-s, -e) prologue.

prolon′gieren v.t. to prolong.

Prome′n-ade (-a:-) f. promenade; walk. **~ieren** vrs.i. to take a walk.

Promo-ti′on (-o:n) f. promotion; graduation. **~′vieren** v.t. to promote; to confer a degree. v.i. to graduate, take a degree.

prompt a. prompt, ready; quick.

Pro′nomen (-no:-) n. (-s, -) pronoun.

Propa-′ganda f. propaganda. **~′ieren** v.t. to propagate.

Pro′peller m. propeller; airscrew. **~flügel** m. blade.

Pro′phe-t (-fe:t) m. (-ten, -ten) prophet. **~tie** f. **~zeiung** f. prophecy. **~tin** f. prophetess. **~tisch** a. prophetic. **~zeien** v.t. to prophesy.

Proporti′on f. (-, -en) proportion. **~al** a. proportional. **~iert** a. proportionate; well proportioned.

Propst m. (-es, -e) provost.

Pros-a f. (-a) prose. **~aiker**, **~a′ist** m. prose-writer. **~aisch** a. prosaic.

Prose′lyt m. (-en, -en) proselyte. **~enmacherei** f. proselytism.

prosit, prost *int.* cheers!

Pro'spekt *m.* (-s, -e) prospect, view; prospectus, leaflet.

prostitu-'ieren *v.r.* to prostitute. **~'ierte** *f.* prostitute. **~ti'on** *f.* prostitution.

Pros'zeniumsloge *f.* stage-box.

prote-'gieren (-ʒi:-) *v.t.* to patronize. **~kti'onswirtschaft** *f.* protectionism. **~kto'rat** *n.* protectorate.

Pro'test *m.* (-es, -e) protest; **~ erheben** to protest; **mit ~ zurückkommen** to be dishonoured. **~ant** *m.*, **~antisch** *a.* Protestant. **~an'tismus** *m.* protestantism. **~'ieren** *v.i.* to protest.

Pro'these *f.* (-, -n) artificial limb.

Proto'koll *n.* (-s, -e) minutes; record; register. **~arisch** *a.* upon records; in the minutes. **~buch** *n.* minute-book. **~führer** *m.* keeper of the minutes; recording clerk; registrar. **~ieren** *v.t.* to keep the minutes; to enter, record; to register.

Protz *m.* (-en, -en) snob, swell. **~en** *v.i.* to put on airs; to be purse-proud. **~entum** *n.*, **~e'rei** *f.* snobbism, snobbery. **~ig** *a.* snobbish, purse-proud.

Protze *f.* (-, -n) limber.

Proveni'enz *f.* provenance.

Provi'ant *m.* (-s, -e) provisions, victuals, supplies, stores. **~amt** *n.* supply depot, food-office. **~kolonne** *f.* supply column.

Pro'vinz *f.* (-, -en) province. **~i'ell** *a.* provincial. **~ler** *m.* provincial.

Provisi'on *f.* (-, -en) △ commission; brokerage.

Pro'vis-or (-vi:-) *m.* (-ors, -'oren) △ chemist's assistant. **~'orisch** *a.* provisional, temporary.

Provo-kati'on *f.* provocation. **~'zieren** *v.t.* to provoke.

Proze'dur (-u:r) *f.* (-, -en) procedure; proceeding.

Pro'zent *n.* (-s, -e) per cent. **~satz** *m.* percentage. **~u'al** *a.* expressed in percentage.

Pro'zeß *m.* (Prozess-es, -e) lawsuit; proceedings; process; im **~ liegen** to be involved in a lawsuit; **kurzen ~ machen mit** to make short work of. **~akten**

f.pl. minutes of a law case, pleadings. **~ordnung** *f.* legal procedure. **~vollmacht** *f.* power of attorney.

proze'ssieren *v.i.* to go to law; to be involved in a lawsuit.

Prozessi'on *f.* (-, -en) procession.

prüde *a.* prudish. **~rie** *f.* prudery.

prüf-en (-) *v.t.* to test, investigate; inspect; to examine; to audit, check (account). **~er** *m.* examiner. **~ling** *m.* examinee. **~stein** *m.* touchstone; test. **~ung** *f.* investigation; examination; trial, affliction. **~ungsausschuß** *m.* board of examiners.

Prügel (-) *m.* (-s, -) stick, cudgel; (*pl.*) thrashing. **~ei** *f.* fight, row. **~knabe** *m.* scapegoat. **~n** *v.t.* to thrash. *v.r.* to fight.

Prunk *m.* (-es) splendour; ostentation. **~bett** *n.* bed of state. **~en** *v.i.* to show off. **~sucht** *f.* ostentation. **~süchtig** *a.* ostentatious. **~voll** *a.* gorgeous, splendid.

prusten (-u:-) *v.i.* to snort; to burst out (laughing).

Psalm *m.* (-es, -en) psalm. **~ist** *m.* psalmist.

Pseudo'nym *n.* (-s, -e) pseudonym. *a.* pseudonymous, fictitious.

Psych-i'ater *m.* psychiatrist. **~ia'trie** *f.* psychiatry. **~isch** *a.* psychic(al). **~oana'lyse** *f.* psycho-analysis. **~o'loge** *m.* psychologist. **~o'logisch** *a.* psychological. **~opath** *m.* psychopath. **~ose** *f.* psychosis.

Puber'tät *f.* (-) puberty.

Publi'kum *n.* (-kums) public; audience; public lecture. **~zieren** *v.t.* to publish. **~zistik** *f.* journalism.

Puddingform *f.* pudding-basin.

Pudel (-u:-) *m.* (-s, -) poodle. **~mütze** *f.* fur cap. **~naß** *a.* drenched, sopping.

Puder (-u:-) *m.* (-s, -) toilet powder. **~n** *v.t.* to powder. **~quaste** *f.* powder-puff.

Puff *m.* (-es, -e) push, nudge, thump; report, bang; report; (*sl.*) brothel. **~ärmel** *m.* puffed sleeve. **~bohne** *f.* horsebean. **~er** *m.* buffer; (*cook.*) potato-

cake. **~erstaat** m. buffer state.
~spiel n. backgammon.

puffen v.t. to push, nudge, thump.
v.i. to shoot, pop; to puff.

Pulk m. (-es, -e) regiment; unit.

Pulle f. (-, -n) (dial.) bottle.

Puls (-u-) m. (-es, -e) pulse. **~schlag** m. pulse beat. **~wärmer** m. woollen wristlet.

pulsen, pul'sieren vv.i. to pulsate.

Pult n. (-es, -e) desk. [L]

Pulver n. (-s, -) powder; gunpowder. **~faß** n. auf dem **~faß** sitzen to sit on top of a volcano. **~form** f. in **~form** pulverized. **~ig** a. powdery; powder-like. **~ladung** f. powder charge. **~schnee** m. powdery snow.

pulveri'sieren v.t. to pulverize.

Pump m. (colloq.) auf **~** on tick. **~e** f. pump. **~en** v.t. to pump; (colloq.) to borrow; to lend. **~enschwengel** m. pump-handle. **~hosen** f.pl. wide knickerbockers, plus-fours. **~stiefel** m. top-boot.

Pumpernickel m. Westphalian ryebread.

Punkt m. (-es, -e) point; dot; spot, place; item; (typ.) full stop; matter, subject; **~** ein Uhr at one (o'clock) sharp; der springende **~** the salient point. **~förmig** a. punctiform. **~ieren** v.t. to point; to dot; to punctuate; (med.) to tap. **~roller** m. massage roller. **~sieg** m. winning on points. **~um** n. full stop; end; damit **~um!** there's an end of it! **~ur** f. puncture. **~ziel** n. pin-point target.

pünktlich a. punctual. **~keit** f. punctuality.

Punsch m. (-es, -e) punch.

punzen v.t. to punch.

Pu'pille f. (-, -n) pupil (of eye).

Puppe (pupa) f. (-, -n) doll; puppet; (zool.) chrysalis. **~nspiel** n. puppet-show. **~nwagen** m. doll's pram.

pur (pu:r) a. pure, sheer.

Pü'ree n. (-s, -s) purée, mash (of stewed fruit, &c.).

pur'gier-en v.t. & i. to purge. **~mittel** n. purgative.

Puri'tan-er m., **~isch** a. Puritan.

Purpur m. (-s) purple. **~farben, ~n, ~rot** aa. purple.

Purzel-baum m. somersault. **~n** vws.i. to tumble.

Puste f. (-) breath. **~n** v.t. to puff; to blow.

Pustel f. (-, -n) pustule.

Pute f. (-, -n) turkey-hen. **~r** m. turkey-cock. **~rrot** a. scarlet.

Putsch m. (-es, -e) revolutionary outbreak; riot. **~en** v.i. to riot. **~ist** m. rioter.

Putz m. (-es) trimming, ornaments; dress, finery, attire; (archit.) rough-cast. **~bürste** f. brush. **~frau** f. charwoman. **~ig** a. funny, droll. **~laden** m. milliner's shop. **~lappen** m. duster, flannel, polishing cloth. **~leiste** f. (outer) window-frame. **~macherin** f. milliner. **~pulver** n. polishing powder. **~sucht** f. love of dress. **~süchtig** a. fond of finery. **~waren** f.pl. millinery. **~wolle** f. cotton waste. **~zeug** n. cleaning utensils.

putzen v.t. to clean, polish; to trim (lamp); to groom (horse); to blow or wipe (nose); to brush (teeth); to plaster (wall), roughcast. v.r. to dress up.

Py'jama m. & n. (-s, -s) pyjamas.

Pyra'mide (-mi:-) f. (-, -n) pyramid. **~nförmig** a. pyramidal.

pytha'go'reisch a. Pythagorean.

Q

Q, q (ku:) n. the letter Q, q.

quabbel-ig (kva-) a. flabby. **~n** v.i. to wobble, shake.

Quack-e'lei (kva-) f. silly talk. **~eln** v.i. to shilly-shally. **~salber** m. quack. **~salbern** v.i. to doctor, experiment on.

Quader (kva:-) m. (-s, -) square stone; ashlar.

Quad'rat n. square. **~ratisch** a. quadratic, square. **~ra'tur** f. squaring (of circle). **~rieren** v.t. to square.

quaken (kva:-) v.i. to quack; (of frogs) to croak.

quäken (kvɛ:-) v.i. to squeak.

Quäker (kvɛ:-) *m.* (-s, -) Quaker.

Qual (kva:l) *f.* (-, -en) torment, torture; pain; pang; agony. **~voll** *a.* very painful, agonizing; full of anguish.

quäl-en (kvɛ:-) *v.t.* to torment, worry, harass; to torture; to annoy, pester. *v.r.* to toil hard, drudge. **~er** *m.* tormentor. **~e'rei** *f.* tormenting; torture; worry; annoyance, pestering; drudgery. **~geist** *m.* plague, nuisance.

quali-fi'zieren (kva-) *v.t.* to qualify. **~'tät** *f.* quality. **~ta'tiv** *a.* qualitative. **~'tätsware** *f.* high-class article.

Qualle (kvalə) *f.* (-, -n) jelly-fish.

Qualm (kvalm) *m.* (-s, -e) dense smoke, fumes. **~en** *v.i.* to smoke. **~ig** *a.* smoky.

Quant-entheorie *f.* quantum theory. **~i'tät** *f.* quantity. **~i-ta'tiv** *a.* quantitative. **~um** *n.* quantum, quantity, amount.

Quaran'täne *f.* (-, -n) quarantine; *unter ~ stellen* to quarantine.

Quark *m.* (-s) curds; (*fig.*) rubbish, trifle. **~käse** *m.* sour cream cheese.

quarren *v.i.* to squall.

Quart (kva-) *n.* (-es, -e) quart. **~a** *f.* third form. **~al** *n.* quarter (of year); quarter-day; term. **~aner** *m.* third-form boy. **~är** *n.* quaternary. **~band** *m.* quarto volume. **~e** *f.* quart; (*mus.*) fourth. **~ett** *n.* quartet.

Quar'tier (kva-) *n.* (-s, -e) quarters, billets; quarter, district. **~macher, ~meister** *m.* quartermaster.

Quarz (kvarts) *m.* (-es, -e) quartz.

quasseln *v.i.* (*dial.*) to talk nonsense.

Quast (kvast) *m.* (-es, -e), **~e** *f.* (-e, -en) tassel; brush.

Quä'stur *f.* univ. accounts dept.

Qua'temberfasten *n.* Ember-days.

Quatsch (kva-) *m.* (-es) rubbish, nonsense, bosh. **~en** *v.i.* to talk nonsense. **~kopf** *m.* twaddler.

Quecke *f.* (-, -n) couch-grass.

Quecksilber (kvɛk-) *n.* quicksilver, mercury. **~ig** *a.* (*fig.*) lively, mercurial. **~n** *a.* of quicksilver.

Quell (kvɛl) *m.* (-es, -e), **~e** *f.* (-e, -en) spring, fountain; source, origin. **~en** *vws.i. st.* to gush, well; to flow (from); to swell; (*fig.*) to arise, originate, spring (from). *v.t.* to soak. **~enfor-schung** *f.* critical investigation (of sources, &c.), original research work. **~wasser** *n.* spring-water.

Quengel-'ei (kvɛŋ-) *f.* whining; nagging. **~n** *v.i.* to whine; to nag.

Quent, **~chen** *n.* dram.

quer (kve:r) *a.* cross; lateral; oblique, transverse. *adv.* across, obliquely, athwart. **~achse** *f.* transverse axis. **~balken** *m.*, **~holz** *n.* cross-beam, transom. **~binder** *m.* bow(-tie). **~bolzen** *m.* cross bolt.

Quer-e (kve:rə) *f. der* **~e** *nach* athwart, crosswise; *in die* **~e** *kommen* to thwart, cross (a person's plans). **~feldein** *adv.* across country. **~flöte** *f.* German flute. **~format** *n.* broadsheet. **~kopf** *m.* contrary person; queer fellow. **~leiste** *f.* cross-piece. **~pfeife** *f.* fife. **~schiff** *n.* transept. **~schnitt** *m.* cross-section, cross-cut, profile. **~straße** *f.* cross-road, side road. **~strich** *m.* dash, stroke; cross-line; (*fig.*) *einen* **~strich** *machen durch* to cross (a person's plan). **~summe** *f.* total of the digits of a number. **~treiberei** *f.* intrigue. **~über** *adv.* (*right*) across. **~verbindung** *f.* lateral communication.

queren (kve:-) *v.t.* to traverse.

Queru'l-ant *m.* (-anten, -anten) querulous person, grumbler. **~ieren** *v.i.* to be querulous, grumble.

quetsch-en (kvɛt-) *v.t.* to squeeze, press, squash; to bruise. **~kar-toffeln** *f.pl.* mashed potatoes. **~ung, ~wunde** *f.* contusion; contused wound.

quick (kv-) *a.* lively, brisk. **~born** *m.* (*poet.*) fountain of rejuvenescence.

quieken (kv-) *v.i.* to squeak.

quietschen (kv-) *v.i.* to scream, to squeak; (*of door*) to creak.

quillt 3rd sing. pres. of quellen.

Quint-a f. (-a, -en) second form. ~'aner m. second-form boy. ~'e f. quinte; (mus.) fifth. ~essenz f. quintessence. ~ett n. quintet.

Quirl (kv-) m. (-es, -e) whisk, beater; (bot.) whorl. ~en v.t. to twirl; to whisk, beat.

quitt (kv-) pred. a. free, rid; quits, even. ~ieren v.t. to receipt (a bill); to quit, abandon. ~ung f. receipt.

Quitte (kv-) f. (-, -n) quince.

quoll imperf. of quellen.

Quot-e (kvo:-) f. (-e, -en) quota, share. ~i'ent m. quotient. ~'ieren v.t. to quote.

R

R, r (ɛr) n. the letter R, r.

Ra'batt m. (-s, -e) discount, rebate. ~e f. border, bed; facing (of dress).

Ra'bbiner m. (-s, -) rabbi.

Rabe (ra:-) m. (-n, -n) raven; weißer ~ rare bird. ~nmutter f. cruel mother. ~nschwarz a. raven-black.

rabi'at (-a:t) a. rabid, raving.

Rabu'list m. pettifogger.

Rach-e (raxə) f. (-e) revenge, vengeance. ~eschnaubend a. breathing vengeance. ~gier, ~sucht f. thirst for revenge, vindictiveness. ~süchtig a. revengeful.

Rachen (rax-) m. (-s, -) throat; jaws, mouth (of beasts). ~höhle f. pharynx.

räch-en (rɛç-) v.t. to avenge, revenge. v.r. to take revenge (on); to be brought home (to one); deine Faulheit wird sich ~en you will have to suffer for your laziness. ~er m. avenger.

Ra'chiti-s (raxi:-) f. (-) rickets. ~sch a. rickety.

Racker m. (-s, -) rogue, rascal.

Rad (ra:t) n. (-es, ̈er) wheel; bicycle, trundle; unter die Räder kommen (fig.) to go to the dogs. ~-

bremse f. hub-brake. ~dampfer m. paddle-steamer. ~fahren vws.i. to cycle. ~fahrer, ~ler m. cyclist. ~fahrweg m. cycle track. ~felge f. felloe, felly. ~gestell n. wheel frame. ~kranz m. wheel-rim. ~reifen m. tyre. ~rennbahn f. cycling track. ~rennen n. cycle race. ~schaufel f. sweep (of water-mill), paddle-board. ~schlagen v.i. to turn cart-wheels; (of peacock) to spread the tail. ~speiche f. spoke (of wheel). ~sport m. cycling. ~spur f. rut, wheel track. ~stand m. wheel-base. ~zahn m. cog.

Radar-gerät n. radar-set. ~gesteuert a. radar-guided.

Ra'dau m. (-s) noise, row.

Rade f. (-, -n) cockle.

radebrechen v.i. to mangle, murder (a language).

radeln (a:-) vws.i. to cycle.

Rädelsführer m. ringleader.

räder-n v.t. to break on the wheel; wie gerädert sein to be knocked up. ~werk n. gearing, wheels, clock-work.

ra'dier-en v.t. to etch; to erase, rub out. ~er m. etcher. ~gummi m. india-rubber. ~messer n. eraser, penknife. ~ung f. etching.

Ra'dieschen n. (-s, -) radish.

radi'kal (-a:l) a. radical.

Radio(apparat) m. wireless set. ~hörer m. listener. ~station f. broadcasting station.

Radius (ra:-) m. (-, Radien) radius.

raff-en v.t. to snatch up; to gather up. ~gier f. rapacity.

Raffi'n-ade f. (-) refined sugar. ~e'rie f. refinery.

raffi'niert a. refined; cunning, crafty.

ragen (ra:-) v.i. to tower, tower up.

Rahe f. (-, -n) (naut.) yard.

Rahm m. (-es) cream.

Rahmen m. (-s, -) frame; (fig.) scope; compass; surroundings, milieu. v.t. to frame. ~abkommen n. skeleton agreement. ~antenne f. frame aerial, loop aerial. ~erzählung f. framework story. ~sucher m. view-finder.

Rain m. (-es, -e) balk, ridge; edge.

Ra´kete (-ke:-) f. (-, -n) rocket. **∼nabwehrrakete** f. anti-missile missile. **∼nantrieb** m. rocket propulsion. **∼nflugzeug** n. rocket propelled plane. **∼ngeschoß** n. rocket projectile.

Ra´kett n. (-s, -s) racket.

Ramm´bär m. **∼block** m., **∼e** f. pile-driver, rammer. **∼eln** v.i. to buck; gerammelt voll crammed full. **∼en** v.t. to ram, drive in. **∼ler** m. buck-hare.

Rampe f. (-, -n) ramp, platform; apron (of stage); drive; ascent. **∼nlicht** n. footlights.

rampo´nieren v.t. to damage, bash.

Ramsch m. job lot; rubbish; im **∼ kaufen** to buy in the lump.

ran = heran.

Rand (-t) m. (-es, ⁻er) rim; edge; brim; margin; (fig.) brink, verge; außer **∼ und Band sein** to be out of hand; nicht zu **∼e kommen** to fail to accomplish, make vain efforts. **∼bemerkung** f. marginal note; aside. **∼leiste** f. ledge. **∼siedlung** f. housing estates on the outskirts (of town). **∼staat** m. border state. **∼steller** m. margin stop (of typewriter).

rändern v.t. to edge, border; to mill (coins).

Ranft m. (-es, ⁻e) crust (of bread).

rang¹ imperf. of ringen.

Rang¹ (-g) m. (-es, ⁻e) rank, order; position; quality, class; (theatr.) erster **∼** dress circle; zweiter **∼** upper circle; den **∼ ablaufen** to get the better of; to outdo; ersten **∼es** first-class, first-rate. **∼abzeichen** n. badge of rank. **∼älteste(r)** m. senior officer. **∼liste** f. Army List. **∼ordnung** f. order of precedence. **∼stufe** f. degree.

Range m. (-n, -n) & f. young scamp, tomboy.

Ran´gier-bahnhof m. shunting-station, marshalling-yard. **∼en** v.t. to shunt. v.i. to rank.

rank a. slim, slender. **∼e** f. tendril; shoot, branch. **∼en** v.i. & r. to creep, climb. **∼engewächs** n. creeper. **∼enwerk** n. tendrils; (intertwined) orna-

ment; fleuron.

Ränke m.pl. intrigues, machinations. **∼schmied** m. intriguer, plotter, schemer. [WRENCH]

rann imperf. of rinnen.

rannte imperf. of rennen.

Ra´nunkel f. (-, -n) ranunculus.

Ranzen m. (-s, -) knapsack; satchel, schoolbag.

ranzig a. rancid.

Rappe m. (-n, -n) black horse; auf Schusters **∼n reiten** to go on Shanks's mare.

Rappel m. einen **∼ haben** to be cracked. **∼n** v.i. to rattle; (colloq.) to be cracked.

Raps m. (-es, -e) rape(-seed).

Ra´punzel m. (-s, -n) & f. rampion.

rar (-a:-) a. rare, scarce. **∼i´tät** f. rarity, curiosity.

rasch a. quick, swift, speedy; hasty. [RASH]

rascheln v.i. to rustle.

ras-en¹ (-a:-) v.i. to rave, rage; to be mad; to speed; to scorch. **∼end** a. raving, raging; **∼end machen** to drive one mad; **∼e´rei** f. raving, fury, rage; madness; speeding; scorching. [RACE]

Rasen² (-a:-) m. (-s, -) grass, turf, lawn. **∼mäher** m. lawn-mower. **∼platz** m. grass-plot, green lawn. **∼sprenger** m. lawn-sprinkler.

Ra´sier-apparat m. safety-razor. **∼klinge** f. razor blade. **∼messer** n. razor. **∼pinsel** m. shaving brush. **∼seife** f. shaving soap. **∼wasser** n. after shaving lotion. **∼zeug** n. shaving things.

ra´sieren (-zi:r-) v.t. to shave; sich **∼ lassen** to get shaved.

räso´nieren v.i. to reason; to argue noisily; to grumble.

Raspel f. (-, -n) rasp. **∼n** v.t. to rasp.

Rass-e f. (-e, -en) race, breed. **∼enkampf** m. racial conflict. **∼enkreuzung** f. cross-breeding. **∼enmischung** f. miscegenation. **∼erein** a., **∼ig** a. thoroughbred; racy. **∼isch** a. racial.

rasseln v.i. to rattle; to clank.

Rast f. (-, -en) resting; recreation; rest, repose; (mil.) halt. **∼en** v.i. to rest. **∼los** a. restless;

indefatigable. ~**losigkeit** f. restlessness. ~**tag** m. day of rest.

Raster m. (-s, -) (phot.) screen.

Ra'sur f. (-, -en) erasure.

Rat (ra:t) m. (-[e]s) counsel, advice; consultation, deliberation; remedy, ways and means, expedient; decree; council, board; (-[e]s, ¨e) councillor; ~ **schaffen** to devise means; um ~ **fragen** to ask advice; zu ~ **ziehen** to consult. ~**geber** m. adviser. ~**haus** n. town hall. ~**los** a. at a loss, helpless. ~**losigkeit** f. helplessness, perplexity. ~**sam** a. advisable, expedient. ~**schlag** m. counsel, advice. ~**schlagen** v.i. to deliberate. ~**schluß** m. resolution, decision; decree. See also **Rats-.**

Rate (-a:-) f. (-, -n) instalment. ~**nweise** a. by instalments.

raten (-a:-) v.t. & i. st. to advise, give advice; to guess, solve; sich nicht zu ~ **wissen** to be at one's wit's end.

Räterepublik f. Soviet republic.

ratifi'zieren v.t. to ratify.

Rati'on (-o:n) f. (-, -en) ration. ~**a'lismus** m. rationalism. ~**ell** a. rational, expedient; economical. ~**ieren** v.t. to ration.

rätlich a. advisable.

Rätsel (-ɛ:-) n. (-s, -) conundrum, riddle; enigma, puzzle; es ist mir ein ~ it puzzles me. ~**haft** a. mysterious; enigmatical, puzzling.

Rats-herr m. town-councillor; senator; alderman. ~**keller** m. cellar (restaurant) of town hall. ~**saal** m. council chamber. ~**schreiber** m. town clerk.

Ratte f. (-, -n) rat. ~**nfänger** m. ratcatcher. ~**nkahl, ratzekahl** aa. quite bare. ~**nkönig** m. (fig.) tangle.

rattern v.i. to clatter, rattle.

Raub (-p) m. (-es) robbery; plundering, piracy; rape; prey; auf ~ **ausgehen** to go on the prowl. ~**bau** m. ~**bau treiben** to exhaust (soil); to ruin. ~**gier** f. rapacity. ~**gierig** a. rapacious. ~**mord** m. murder and robbery. ~**ritter** m. robber-knight. ~**tier** n. beast of prey. ~**vogel** m.

bird of prey. ~**zug** m. raid, incursion; depredation.

rauben v.t. & i. to rob, deprive of, plunder.

Räuber m. (-s, -) robber, thief; brigand. ~**bande** f. band of robbers, gang of thieves. ~**ei** f. depredation. ~**höhle** f. den of thieves. ~**isch** a. rapacious, predatory.

Rauch[1] m. (-es) smoke; (poet.) haze. ~**bombe** f. smoke-bomb. ~**er** m. smoker. ~**erabteil** n. smoking compartment. ~**fahne** f. smoke trail, exhaust trail. ~**fang** m. chimney, flue. ~**faß** n. censer. ~**fleisch** n. smoked meat. ~**geschwärzt** a. smoke-stained. ~**ig** a. smoky. ~**säule** f. column of smoke. ~**schwaden** m. wisps of smoke. ~**tabak** m. tobacco. ~**waren** f.pl. tobacco products.

Rauch²-waren f.pl., ~**werk** n. furs.

rauchen v.t. & i. to smoke.

Räucher-faß n. censer. ~**hering** m. kipper. ~**kammer** f. smoke (-curing) room. ~**kerze** f. fumigating pastille. ~**waren** f.pl. smoked meat and fish.

räuchern v.t. to smoke, cure; to burn incense; to fumigate.

Räud-e f. (-e, -en) mange, scab. ~**ig** a. mangy, scabby.

rauf = **herauf.**

Rauf-bold, ~**degen** m. bully, rowdy. ~**en** v.t. to pull out, pluck, v.r. to fight, squabble. ~**e'rei** f. row, scuffle. ~**lust** f. pugnacity.

Raufe f. (-, -n) rack.

rauh a. uneven, rough; raw (skin); hoarse, harsh (voice); inclement, raw (weather); coarse, rude. ~**beinig** a. caddish. ~**haarig** a. wire-haired (terrier). ~**eit,** ~**igkeit** f. roughness; hoarseness; inclemency; harshness. ~**reif** m. hoar-frost.

Raum m. (-es, ¨e) place; room; space; expanse; district, neighbourhood; hold (of ship); capacity; luftleerer ~ vacuum; ~ **geben** to give way to, indulge in. ~**bild** n. space diagram. ~**fahrt** f., ~**flug** m. space-flight.

~inhalt *m.* volume, capacity. ~mangel *m.* lack of room, lack of space. ~meter *m.* cubic metre. ~schiff *n.* space ship. ~~fahrt *f.* astronautics.

räum-en *v.t.* to clear away, remove; to clean; to make room; to leave, evacuate. ~lich *a.* relating to space; spatial; steric. ~lichkeit *f.* room, premises; space, spatiality. ~ung *f.* removal; evacuation; eviction. ~ungsausverkauf *m.* clearance sale.

raunen *v.t. & i.* to whisper.

Raupe *f.* (-, -n) caterpillar. ~nfraß *m.* damage done by caterpillars. ~nschlepper *m.* caterpillar tractor.

raus = heraus.

Rausch *m.* (-es, "e) drunkenness, intoxication; frenzy; transport. ~en *v.i.* to rustle; to rush; to roar; to thunder; to murmur. ~gift *n.* narcotic. ~händler *m.* dope pedlar. ~gold *n.* brass foil; tinsel. ~süchtige(r) *m.* drug addict.

räuspern *v.r.* to clear one's throat.

Raute¹ *f.* (-, -n) (*bot.*) rue.

Raute² *f.* (-, -n) diamond-shaped figure; rhomboid.

Rea'g-enzglas *n.* test-tube. ~ieren *v.i.* to react.

Reakti'on *f.* (-, -en) reaction; backlash. ~är *a.* reactionary.

re'al (-a:l) *a.* real. ~ien *pl.* real facts. ~istisch *a.* realistic. ~ität *f.* reality. ~katalog *m.* subject catalogue. ~lexikon *n.* encyclopaedia. ~politik *f.* realist politics.

Reb-e (re:-) *f.* (-e, -en) grape; vine; tendril. ~engländer *m.* vine trellis. ~enhügel *m.* vine-clad hill. ~ensaft *m.* grape-juice, wine. ~laus *f.* phylloxera. ~ling *m.* vine-shoot. ~stock *m.* vine.

Re'bell *m.* (-en, -en) rebel. ~ieren *v.i.* to rebel, mutiny. ~isch *a.* rebellious.

Rebhuhn *n.* partridge.

Rechen¹ (-ɛç-) *m.* (-s, -) rake. *v.t.* to rake.

Rechen²-aufgabe *f.* sum, problem. ~buch *n.* arithmetic book. ~fehler *m.* miscalculation. ~-

lehrer *m.* arithmetic teacher. ~maschine *f.* calculating machine; computer. ~schaft *f.* account; ~schaft ablegen to account (for); *zur ~schaft ziehen* to call to account. ~schieber *m.* slide-rule.

rechnen (-ɛç-) *v.t. & i.* to count, reckon, do sums, calculate; ~ *zu* to class with, rank amongst; ~ *auf* to count upon.

Rechnung *f.* (-, -en) calculation, sum; account, bill; *auf ~ setzen* to charge, put to one's account; *in ~ ziehen* to take into account; *auf eigene ~ (fig.)* at one's own risk; *auf seine ~ kommen* to profit, benefit (by); ~ *tragen* to allow for. ~sführer *m.* accountant, bookkeeper. ~sjahr *n.* financial year. ~sprüfer *m.* auditor.

recht (reçt) *a.* right, right-hand; correct, proper, fitting; just; genuine; lawful, legitimate. *adv.* right; very, really, quite; ~ *en Zeit* in time, in the nick of time; ~ *und schlecht* not bad, fairly good; *es ist mir* ~ I agree; *es geschieht ihm* ~ that serves him right; ~ *haben* to be (in the) right; ~ *behalten* to be right in the end; ~ *geben* to agree with; *an den ~en kommen* to meet one's match; *nach dem ~en sehen* to see to things; *erst* ~ just, now all the more, now more than ever.

Recht (reçt) *n.* (-es, -e) right; privilege; right (to), title, claim; justice; law; *mit vollem ~* for good reasons; ~ *sprechen* to administer justice; *von ~s wegen* by rights, according to the law; *zu ~ bestehen* to be valid; *die ~e studieren* to study law. ~e *f.* right hand. ~eck *n.* rectangle. ~eckig *a.* rectangular. ~ens *adv.* legally, by law. ~erhand *adv.* on the right-hand side. ~fertigen *v.t.* to justify. ~fertigung *f.* justification. ~gläubig *a.* orthodox. ~haberisch *a.* dogmatic. ~lich *a.* just; lawful, legitimate; legal; honest. ~lichkeit *f.* integrity, honesty. ~mäßig *a.* lawful, legitimate.

schaffen *a.* honest, upright. *adv.* very, exceedingly. **~schreibung** *f.* spelling, orthography. **~sprechung** *f.* administration of justice; jurisdiction. **~winklig** *a.* rectangular. **~zeitig** *a.* in good time, timely. See also **rechts-**.

rechten *v.i.* to dispute; to plead.

rechts (rɛçts) *adv.* on the right, to the right. **~** *a.* legal claim. **~anwalt** *m.* lawyer, solicitor, counsel. **~außenstürmer** *m.* outside right, right winger. **~beistand** *m.* legal adviser. **~beugung** *f.* defeating the ends of justice. **~fall** *m.* suit, law case. **~gelehrte(r)** *m.* jurist, lawyer. **~gültig** & **~kräftig** *aa.* legal, valid. **~handel** *m.* lawsuit, legal action. **~mittel** *n.* legal measure. **~nachfolger** *m.* assign. **~person** *f.* body corporate. **~pflege** *f.* administration of justice. **~spruch** *m.* verdict, sentence. **~staat** *m.* constitutional state. **~um!** *adv.* right turn! **~ungültig** *a.* illegal, invalid. **~verbindlich** *a.* legally binding. **~verdreher** *m.* pettifogger. **~verfahren** *n.* legal procedure. **~verkehr** *m.* right-hand traffic. **~weg** *m.* legal proceedings, law. **~widrig** *a.* illegal. **~wissenschaft** *f.* jurisprudence.

Reck *n.* (-es, -e) (*gym.*) horizontal bar.

Recke *m.* (-n, -n) warrior, hero [WRETCH]

recken *v.t.* to stretch, extend; to crane (neck).

Redak'teur (-tø:r) *m.* (-s, -e) editor.

Redakti'on *f.* (-, -en) editors, editorial staff; editor's office; editing, wording. **~sschluß** *m.* copy dead-line. **~ell** *a.* editorial.

Rede (re:-) *f.* (-, -n) talk, discourse, speech; conversation; address; rumour; *eine ~ halten* to make a speech; *in die ~ fallen* to interrupt; *~ stehen* to answer for; *zur ~ stellen* to call to account; *nicht der ~ wert* not worth mentioning; *davon kann keine ~ sein* that is out of the question; *in ~ stehend* in ques-

tion, material. **~fertig**, **~gewandt** *aa.* glib, fluent, eloquent. **~fluß** *m.* flow of words. **~nsart** *f.* phrase, idiom; empty talk. **~rei** *f.* nonsense, rubbish. **~teil** *m.* (*gram.*) part of speech. **~weise** *f.* manner of speech; style. **~wendung** *f.* phrase, idiom.

reden *v.t.* & *i.* to talk, speak; to converse; to make a speech; *mit sich ~ lassen* to listen to reason; *von sich ~ machen* to cause a stir.

redi'gieren *v.t.* to edit; to revise.

redlich (re:tliç) *a.* honest, just; upright. **~keit** *f.* honesty; uprightness.

Redner *m.* (-s, -) orator, speaker. **~bühne** *f.* platform. **~gabe** *f.* oratorical gift. **~isch** *a.* oratorical, rhetorical.

redselig *a.* talkative. **~keit** *f.* loquacity, talkativeness.

redu'zieren *v.t.* to reduce.

Reede *f.* (-, -n) roadstead. **~r** *m.* owner (of ship). **~rei** *f.* shipping(-line); fitting out of a merchantman.

re'ell (-ɛl) *a.* good, honest, fair.

Reep *n.* (-es, -e) rope.

Refek'torium *n.* (-s, ... rien) refectory.

Refe'rat (-a:t) *n.* (-ats, -ate) report; lecture. **~en'dar** *m.* junior barrister; (junior) assistant teacher. **~ent** *m.* official expert or adviser; reporter; speaker. **~enz** *f.* reference; information. **~ieren** *v.t.* & *i.* to report, relate; to lecture (on).

Reff *n.* (-(e)s, -e) basket; (*naut.*) reef. **~en** *v.t.* to reef.

Reflek'tant *m.* (-en, -en) prospective buyer.

reflek'tieren *v.t.* & *i.* to reflect; *~ auf* to have one's eye on.

Re'flexbewegung *f.* reflex action.

Reflex-i'on *f.* (-ion, -ionen) reflex; reflection. **~iv** *a.* (*gram.*) reflexive.

Re'form *f.* (-, -en) reform. **~ati'on** *f.* reformation. **~'ator** *m.* reformer. **~a'torisch** *a.* reformatory. **~ieren** *v.t.* to reform.

Re'frain (-frɛ̃:) *m.* (-s, -s) refrain.

Re'fraktor *m.* (-s, -en) refractor.

Re'gal (-ga:l) n. (-s, -e) shelf; (book-)shelves; filing-shelves; stand.-

reg-e (re:-) a. active; brisk, lively; nimble, alert. **~sam** a. active, agile, quick. **~samkeit** f. agility, activity, quickness. **~ung** f. movement; emotion; agitation; impulse. **~(ungs)los** a. motionless.

Regel (re:-) f. (-, -n) rule; regulation; precept, principle; (med.) menses; in der **~** as a rule. **~los** a. irregular. **~mäßig** a. regular; proportional. **~recht** a. regular, correct; proper, thorough. **~ung** f. regulation, control. **~widrig** a. irregular; abnormal.

regeln v.t. to arrange; to regulate.

regen¹ v.t. & r. to stir, move.

Regen² (re:-) m. (-s, -) rain; shower. **~bogen** m. rainbow. **~bogenhaut** f. iris. **~decke** f. tarpaulin. **~dicht** a. waterproof. **~fall** m. rainfall. **~fest** a. waterproof. **~haut** f. oilskin coat. **~mantel** m. waterproof. **~messer** m. rain-gauge. **~pfeifer** m. plover. **~schirm** m. umbrella. **~wurm** m. earthworm. **~zeit** f. rainy season.

regene'rieren v.t. to regenerate.

Re'gent (-g-) m. (-en, -en) regent. **~in** f. (female) regent. **~schaft** f. regency; regentship.

Re'gie (-ʒi:) f. (-ie, -ien) administration, management; state monopoly; (theatr.) production. **~i'sseur** m. stage-manager, producer.

re'gier-en (-gi:r-) v.t. to rule, govern. v.i. to govern, reign (over). **~ung** f. reign, rule; government. **~ungsantritt** m. accession to the throne. **~ungsbeamte(r)** m. government official, civil servant. **~ungsbezirk** m. administrative district.

Regi'ment (-gi-) n. (-s, -e & -er) government; (mil.) regiment. **~schef** m. colonel-in-chief; honorary colonel. **~smusik** f. regimental band.

Re'gist-er (-ers, -er) register; index, table of contents; (organ) stop. **~ertonne** f. registered ton.

~rator m. registrar, recorder. **~ra'tur** f. registry. **~rierapparat** m. recording apparatus. **~rieren** v.t. to register, record. **~rierkasse** f. cash register.

Regler m. regulator; controller; governor.

regn-en (re:-) v.i. to rain. **~erisch** a. rainy.

Re'greß m. (Regress-es, -e) recourse, remedy.

regu'l-är a. regular. **~ieren** v.t. to regulate, adjust.

Reh (re:) n. (-es, -e) roe, deer. **~blatt** n. shoulder of a roe. **~bock** m. roebuck. **~braten** m. roast venison. **~braun** a. fawn-coloured. **~kalb** n., **~kitz** n. fawn. **~keule** f., **~schlegel** m. haunch of venison. **~leder** n. doeskin. **~ling** m. chanterelle. **~ziemer** m. loin of venison.

rehabili'tieren v.t. to rehabilitate.

Reib-e f., **~eisen** n. grater. **~en** v.t. to rub; to grate; to grind; wund **~en** to chafe; sich **~en** an (fig.) to vex, irritate. **~e'rei** f. friction. **~fläche** f. rough or striking surface. **~ung** f. friction. **~ungsfläche** f. (fig.) source of irritation. **~ungslos** a. smooth.

reich¹ (-ç) a. rich, wealthy, well off; plentiful, abundant, copious. **~haltig** a. full; rich, abundant, copious; comprehensive. **~haltigkeit** f. fullness; richness, abundance; variety. **~lich** a. plentiful, abundant, copious. **~tum** m. riches, wealth; abundance.

Reich² (-ç) n. (-es, -e) empire, kingdom; realm. **~sadler** m. German Eagle. **~sangehörige(r)** m. German national. **~sanleihe** f. government loan. **~sautobahn** f. State arterial motor-road. **~sfarben** f. pl. national flag or colours. **~sgericht** n. Supreme Court of Justice. **~skanzlei** f. State Chancery. **~skanzler** m. State Chancellor. **~skleinodien** n.pl. crown jewels. **~smark** f. See App. III. **~spost** f. German State Post (Office). **~stag** m. German parliament. **~sunmittelbar** a. subject only to National Government. **~swehr** f. (obs.) German Army and Navy.

reich-en (-ç-) v.t. to give, present, hand; to reach. v.i. to reach (to); to extend (to); to suffice, be enough. **~weite** f. range; reach.

reif[1] a. ripe, mature, mellow. **~e** f. ripeness, maturity, mellowness. **~en** vws.i. to ripen, mature. **~eprüfung** f. leaving examination (in schools). **~ezeugnis** n. leaving certificate. **~lich** a. mature; careful.

Reif[2] m. (-es) hoar-frost. **~en** v.i. to become white with hoar-frost.

Reif[3] m. (-s, -e) ring, circlet. **~rock** m. crinoline.

Reifen m. (-s, -) ring, circlet; hoop; tyre. **~panne** f., **~schaden** m. tyre puncture.

Reigen, Reihen m. (-s, -) round dance.

Reih-e f. (-e, -en) row; range, line; series, succession, sequence, suite; order, rank, file; er ist an der **~e** it is his turn; außer der **~e** out of one's turn; der **~e** nach successively, in rotation; **~ und Glied** rank and file. **~en** v.t. to range, rank; to string. **~enfertigung** f. serial production. **~enfolge** f. succession, sequence, order. **~enhäuserbau** m. ribbon-building. **~entheorie** f. serial theory. **~enweise** adv. in rows. **~um** adv. in turns, by turns.

Reiher m. (-s, -) heron. **~feder** f. aigrette. **~horst** m. heronry.

Reim m. (-es, -e) rhyme. **~en** v.t. & i. to rhyme. v.r. (fig.) to make sense. **~e'rei** f. doggerel. **~schmied** m. rhymester, poetaster.

rein[1] adv. & sep. pref. **~fall** m. failure, let-down, (sl.) sell. See also **herein**.

rein[2] a. pure, genuine; clean, neat, tidy, clear; chaste; unalloyed (metal); undiluted (liquid); mere; (commerc.) net. adv. entirely, quite; **ins ~e kommen** to come to an understanding (with); **ins ~e schreiben** to make a fair copy of; **aus ~em Trotz** out of sheer obstinacy;

~ unmöglich quite impossible. **~druck** m. clean proof. **~gewinn** m. net profit. **~heit** f. purity, pureness, cleanness. **~kultur** f. bacilli culture. **~lich** a. clean, neat, tidy. **~lichkeit** f. cleanliness, neatness, tidiness. **~machefrau** f. charwoman. **~rassig** a. pure-bred. **~schrift** f. fair copy.

reinig-en v.t. to clean, cleanse, purify; to refine (metals); to clarify (liquids); to rectify (spirits); to purge. **~ung** f. cleaning, cleansing; chemische **~ung** dry-cleaning.

Reis[1] m. (-es) rice.

Reis[2] n. (-es, -er) twig, sprig; scion.

Reise (-za) f. (-, -n) journey, tour, trip; (sea) voyage. **~büro** n. tourist office. **~decke** f. travelling-rug. **~führer** m. guide-book. **~lustig** a. fond of travelling. **~scheck** m. traveller's cheque. **~ziel** n. destination.

reisen (-z-) vws.i. to travel, journey, go (to). **~de(r)** m. passenger; traveller; commercial traveller.

Reisig n. (-s) brushwood, twigs. **~bündel** n. bundle of brushwood, faggot, fascine.

Reisige(r) m. (-n, -n) (obs.) horse-soldier, trooper.

Reiß-aus n. **~aus nehmen** to take to one's heels. **~brett** n. drawing-board. **~er** m. thriller; box-office success. **~feder** f. drawing-pen. **~nagel** m., **~zwecke** f. drawing-pin. **~schiene** f. T-square. **~verschluß** m. zip-fastener. **~zeug** n. drawing instruments.

reißen (-s-) v.t. st. to tear; to pull, drag; an sich **~** to seize hold of, snatch up; to monopolize (the conversation); in Stücke **~** to tear to pieces; Witze **~** to crack jokes. vws.i. to tear, tear off; to burst, split. v.r. to get scratched; sich **~ um** to scramble for. subst. n. rheumatic pains. **~d** a. ravenous; rapid; torrential; **~der Strom** torrent. [WRITE]

reit-en *v.t. & vws.i. st.* to ride (a horse, &c.); **~ende** Artillerie horse-artillery. **~er, ~ersmann** *m.* horseman, trooper, cavalryman. **~e'rei** *f.* cavalry. **~erin** *f.* horsewoman. **~erregiment** *n.* cavalry regiment. **~erstandbild** *n.* equestrian statue. **~gerte** *f.* whip, switch. **~hose(n)** *f.* riding-breeches. **~knecht** *m.* groom. **~kunst** *f.* horsemanship. **~schule** *f.* riding-school. **~weg** *m.* bridle-path. **~zeug** *n.* riding equipment.

Reiz (-ts) *m.* (-es, -e) charm, attraction; incentive; stimulus; irritation. **~bar** *a.* sensitive; irritable. **~barkeit** *f.* sensitiveness; irritability. **~los** *a.* unattractive. **~mittel** *n.* incentive; stimulant, stimulus; inducement. **~stoff** *m.* irritant, irritant substance. **~ung** *f.* irritation. **~voll** *a.* charming, attractive.

reizen (-tsən) *v.t.* to excite, stir up; to irritate, provoke; to stimulate; to entice, lure, charm. **~d** *a.* charming.

rekeln, räkeln *v.r.* to loll about.

Reklamati'on *f.* (-, -en) ⌀ claiming back; complaint; protest.

Re'klame (-a:-) *f.* (-, -n) propaganda; advertisement; **~ machen** to advertise, propagate. **~säule** *f.* advertisement pillar. **~schild** *n.* advertisement sign, signboard.

rekla'mieren *v.t.* ⌀ to reclaim; to protest; to exempt (from).

rekognos'zieren *v.t.* to reconnoitre.

rekonstru'ieren *v.t.* to reconstruct.

Rekonvales'zent *m.* (-en, -en) convalescent.

Re'kord *m.* (-s, -e) ⌀ record (performance *or* event).

Re'krut *m.* (-en, -en) recruit. **~ieren** *v.t.* to recruit. *v.r.* to be recruited (from).

Rektor *m.* (-s, -en) ⌀ chancellor (of university); headmaster. **~at** *n.* office of chancellor.

rela'tiv (-ti:f) *a.* relative, relating (to). **~i'tätstheorie** *f.* theory of relativity. **~satz** *m.* relative clause.

Reli'ef (-ɛf) *n.* (-s, -s) ⌀ relief

(design).

Religi'on (-o:n) *f.* (-on, -onen) religion. **~swissenschaft** *f.* theology, divinity, study of religion. **~ös** *a.* religious. **~osi'tät** *f.* religiosity.

Reling *f.* (-, -e) rail (of ship).

Re'liquie (-kviə) *f.* (-, -n) relic. **~ndienst** *m.* worship of relics. **~nschrein** *m.* reliquary.

Remis *n.* (*chess*) drawn game.

Re'mise (-mi:zə) *f.* (-, -n) coach-house; shed.

Remi'tt-enden *f.pl.* remainders. **~ieren** *v.t.* to return, remit.

Re'monte *f.* (-, -n) remount.

Remon'toiruhr (-to'a:r-) *f.* keyless watch.

Remo'u'ladensauce *f.* salad-cream.

Rene'gat (-a:t) *m.* (-en, -en) renegade.

reni'tent *a.* refractory.

Renn-bahn *f.* race-course; cinder track. **~er** *m.* runner; race-horse. **~fahrer** *m.* racing cyclist *or* motorist. **~stall** *m.* racing stable.

rennen *vws.i. st.* to run; to race, run a race. *subst. n.* running; race; *totes* **~** dead heat.

Renntier *n.* reindeer.

reno'mm-ieren *v.i.* to boast, swagger. **~ist** *m.* boaster, bragger.

reno'vieren (-vi:r-) *v.t.* to renovate; to redecorate.

ren'tab-el *a.* profitable, lucrative. **~ili'tät** *f.* profitableness, profits.

Rent-amt *n.* revenue office. **~e** *f.* revenue; pension. **~enempfänger, ~ner** *m.* (old-age) pensioner. **~ier** (rentie:) *m.* man of private means. **~ieren** *v.r.* to yield profit, pay.

reorgani'sieren *v.t.* to reorganize.

Reparat-i'on *f.* (-ion, -ionen) reparation. **~ur** *f.* repair. **~urbedürftig** *a.* out of repair. **~urwerkstätte** *f.* repair shop.

repa'rieren *v.t.* to repair.

repatri'ieren *v.t.* to repatriate.

repe't-ieren *v.t.* to repeat. **~ieruhr** *f.* repeater. **~itor** *m.* coach, tutor. **~itorium** *n.* compendium.

Re'plik *f.* (-, -en) reply; replica.

Re'port m. (-s, -e) (commerc.) contango. ~**age** f. (running) commentary, eyewitness account.

Repräsen't·ant m. (-anten, -anten) representative. ~**ieren** v.t. to represent.

Repre'ssalien f.pl. reprisals; retaliation.

Reproduk'tion (-o:n) f. (-, -en) rendering; reproduction.

reprodu'zieren v.t. to render; to reproduce.

Rep'til (-i:l) n. (-s, -ien) reptile.

Repu'blik (-i:k) f. (-, -en) republic. ~**aner** m., ~**anisch** a. republican.

requi'rieren (-kvi-) v.t. to requisition. ~**siten** n.pl. requisites; (theatr.) properties.

Re'seda f. (-, ... den) mignonette.

Re'serv·e f. (-e, -en) reserve. ~**erad** n. spare wheel. ~**ieren** v.t. to reserve.

Resi'denz f. (-, -en) seat (of the court), (prince's) residence.

resi'dieren v.i. to reside.

Re'siduum n. residue.

resig'nieren v.i. to resign.

Reso'nanz (-ts) f. (-, -en) resonance. ~**boden** m. soundingboard.

Re'spekt m. (-s) respect. ~**abel** a. respectable. ~**ieren** v.t. to respect. ~**los** a. without respect; irreverent. ~**sperson** f. person (to be) held in respect. ~**voll** a. respectful. ~**widrig** a. disrespectful.

Re'ssort n. (-s, -s) department; province; sphere.

Rest m. (-es, -e or -er) rest, remains, remainder, remnant; residue, residuum; (einem) den ~ geben to do for (one), kill; to finish. ~**auflage** f. remainders. ~**bestand** m. remainder; residue. ~**lich** a. remaining. ~**los** a. without a rest, complete. adv. thoroughly, entirely. ~**posten** m. remaining stock.

Restaurati'on f. (-, -en) ♩ restoration, repair; restaurant.

restau'rieren v.t. to repair; to restore.

Resul'tat (-ta:t) n. (-s, -e) result.

Re'torte f. (-, -n) retort (vessel).

rett·en v.t. to save, preserve; to rescue, deliver. v.r. to escape. ~**er** m. rescuer, deliverer; Saviour, Redeemer.

Rettich m. (-s, -e) (white) radish.

Rettung f. (-, -en) rescue, saving; deliverance; escape. ~**sanker** m. sheet-anchor. ~**sboje** f. lifebuoy. ~**sboot** n. lifeboat. ~**sgürtel**, ~**sring** m. lifebelt. ~**skolonne** f. rescue squad. ~**slos** a. irretrievable, past help. ~**smedaille** f. life-saving medal. ~**sstation** f. first-aid post. ~**swerk** n. rescue work.

Re'tusch·e f. (-e, -en) retouching. ~**ieren** v.t. to retouch.

Reu·e f. (-e) repentance; regret; remorse. ~**en** v. impers. to repent; to regret, be sorry for. ~**geld** n. forfeit, penalty. ~**ig**, ~**mütig** aa. repentant, penitent.

Reuse f. (-, -n) wicker-trap.

Re'vanch·e (-vã:ʃə) f. (-e, -en) revenge. ~**ieren** v.r. to take one's revenge; to return a kindness.

revi'dieren v.t. to revise; (commerc.) to audit. ~**si'on** f. revision, revisal, auditing; (leg.) appeal, rehearing of a case. ~**sionsbogen** m. (typ.) revise. ~**sor** m. reviser; auditor.

Re'vier (-vi:r) n. (-s, -e) preserve, hunting-ground; district, quarter; beat (of constable, &c.); (mil.) sick-bay. ~**dienst** m. light mil. duty. ~**krank** a. sick in quarters.

Re'volt·e f. (-e, -en) revolt, insurrection. ~**ieren** v.i. to revolt.

Revoluti'on (-o:n) f. (-, -en) revolution. ~**är** m. & a. revolutionary. ~**ieren** v.t. to revolutionize.

Re'volver m. (-s, -) revolver.

Rezen'sent m. (-enten, -enten) reviewer, critic. ~**ieren** v.t. to review, criticize. ~**i'on** f. review, critique. ~**ionsexemplar** n. reviewer's copy.

Re'zept (-tsɛpt) n. (-s, -e) recipe, prescription; formula.

rezi'prok a. reciprocal.

Rezi'tator (-ta:-) m. (-s, -en) reciter.

rezi'tieren v.t. to recite.

Rha'barber m. (-s) rhubarb.

Rhapso'die f. (-, -n) rhapsody.

rhe'torisch a. rhetorical.

Rheuma n. (-s), ~'tismus m. rheumatism. ~tisch a. rheumatic.

Rhi'nozeros n. (-ses, -se) rhinoceros.

rhythm-isch a. rhythmical. ~us m. (-us, -en) rhythm.

Richt-antenne f. aerial. ~balken m. traverse beam. ~beil n. executioner's axe. ~blei n. plummet, plumb-line. ~block m. executioner's block. ~kanonier m. gun-layer. ~linie f. guiding principle, direction; policy. ~maß n. standard; gauge. ~platz m., ~stätte f. place of execution. ~preis m. standard price. ~scheit n. level, ruler. ~schnur f. plumb-line; (fig.) guiding principle. ~schwert n. executioner's sword. ~strahler m. beam wireless. ~ung f. direction; line, course; bearing; tendency. ~waage f. level.

richten (-ic-) v.t. to set straight, put in order, adjust; to direct, turn; to lay, aim (gun); to address; to prepare (meal); to regulate, set (watch); to judge; to pass sentence (on); sich ~ nach to conform to; to be guided by, depend on; (gram.) to agree with.

Richter m. (-s, -) judge. ~lich a. judicial.

richtig (riçtiç) a. right, accurate, correct; suitable, fit; genuine, real, regular. int. just so! sure enough! quite right! behold! ~gehend a. keeping good time; real, regular. ~keit f. rightness, correctness; accuracy. ~stellung f. rectification.

Ricke f. (-, -n) doe.

rieb imperf. of reiben.

riech-en (-ç-) v.i. & v.t. st. to smell; to scent. ~er m. (fig.) nose. ~fläschchen n. smelling-bottle. ~werkzeuge n.pl. olfactory organs.

Ried (-t) n. (-es, -e) marsh; reed. ~gras n. sedge.

rief imperf. of rufen.

Riefe f. (-, -n) channel, chamfer; flute (of pillar). ~in v.t. to channel; to flute.

Riege f. (-, -n) section.

Riegel m. (-s, -) bolt, sliding bolt; bar (of soap); (mil.) switch line. ~stellung f. switch line.

Riemen¹ m. (-s, -) strap; sling. ~antrieb m. belt drive. ~scheibe f. pulley. ~zeug n. straps, harness.

Riemen² m. (-s, -) oar.

Ries n. (-es, -e) ream (of paper).

Ries-e m. (-en, -en) giant. ~enerfolg m. smash hit. ~enhaft, ~ig aa. gigantic, colossal. ~enschlange f. boa constrictor. ~in f. giantess.

Riesel-feld n. field irrigated with sewage. ~n v.i. to ripple; to trickle; to drizzle.

riet imperf. of raten.

Riff n. (-es, -e) reef.

riffeln v.t. to groove; to ripple (flax).

ri'golen v.t. to trench-plough.

rigo'ros a. rigorous.

Rille f. (-, -n) small groove.

Ri'messe f. (-, -n) remittance.

Rind (-t) n. (-es, -er) ox; cow; (pl.) cattle. ~erbraten m. roast beef. ~fleisch n. beef. ~sledern a. cow-hide. ~vieh n. horned cattle; (fig.) blockhead.

Rinde f. (-, -n) bark; rind of cheese, &c.); crust (of bread).

Ring m. (-es, -e) ring; circle; (commerc.) pool. ~bahn f. circular railway. ~förmig a. cyclic, annular. ~mauer f. city wall. ~richter m. umpire.

Ringel m. (-s, -) small ring. ~locke f. ringlet. ~natter f. ring-snake. ~reigen m. round dance. ~taube f. ring-dove.

ringeln v.r. to curl; to coil.

ring-en v.i. st. to struggle, wrestle (with); ~en nach to strive after or for; to fight for. v.t. to wring; to wrench, wrest (a thing out of). ~er, ~kämpfer m. wrestler, athlete. ~kampf m. wrestling match.

rings adv. round, around. ~um, ~umher advv. round about; all round, all around.

Rinn-e f. (-e, -en) groove, channel;

gutter. **~en** *vws.i. st.* to flow, run; to trickle. *v.i.* to leak. **~sal** *n.* watercourse, rill. **~stein** *m.* gutter.

Ripp **~chen** *n.* cutlet. **~e** *f.* (-, -n) rib; (*archit.*) groin. **~enfell** *n.* pleura. **~nfellentzündung** *f.* pleurisy. **~enspeer** *m.* (smoked) ribs of pork.

Rips *m.* (-es) rep.

Ris-iko *n.* risk. **~kant** *a.* risky. **~kieren** *v.t.* to risk.

Rispe *f.* panicle.

riß¹ *imperf. of* reißen.

Riß² (-s) *m.* (Riss-es, -e) tear, rent, hole, gap, chink, cleft; scratch; sketch, plan; (*fig.*) breach, schism.

rissig *a.* full of rents; cracked (skin).

Rist *m.* (-s, -e) instep; wrist.

ritsch! ratsch! *excl.* snip snap!

ritt¹ *imperf. of* reiten.

Ritt² *m.* (-es, -e) ride (on horse). **~lings** *adv.* astride. **~meister** *m.* captain of cavalry.

Ritter *m.* (-s, -) knight; cavalier; *zum ~ schlagen* to knight; **~arme** (*cook.*) fritters. **~gut** *n.* estate, manor. **~lich** *a.* chivalrous; gallant. **~orden** *m.* order of knighthood. **~schaft** *f.* body of knights; knighthood. **~schlag** *m.* accolade, knighting. **~sporn** *m.* larkspur. **~tum** *n.* chivalry.

ritu'ell *a.* ritual.

Ritus *m.* (-, Riten) rite.

Ritze *f.* (-, -n) chink, crack; scratch, abrasion. **~n** *v.t.* to carve, cut; to scratch, graze.

Ri'val-e (-a:l-) *m.* (-en, -en) rival. **~i'sieren** *v.i.* to rival. **~i'tät** *f.* rivalry.

Rizinusöl (-tsi-) *n.* castor oil.

Robbe *f.* (-, -n) seal.

Robber *m.* (-s, -) ♠ rubber (of whist).

roch *imperf. of* riechen.

Roche *f.* (-ns, -n) ray (fish).

röcheln *v.i.* to rattle (in one's throat).

ro'chieren *v.i. & t.* to castle (at chess).

Rock *m.* (-es, "e) coat; skirt. **~schoß** *m.* coat-tail. [FROCK]

Rocken *m.* (-s, -) (*obs.*) distaff.

Rodel-bahn (ro:-) *f.* toboggan-run. **~n** *v.i.* to toboggan. **~schlitten** *m.* toboggan.

rod-en (ro:-) *v.t. & i.* to root out; to clear (forest); to make arable. **~ung** *f.* cleared woodland.

Rogen (ro:-) *m.* (-s, -) roe, spawn. **~er** *m.* spawner.

Roggen *m.* (-s) rye.

roh *a.* raw; unwrought, crude (iron); coarse, brutal, cruel; *in ~en Bogen* in sheets. **~bau** *m.* rough brickwork. **~bilanz** *f.* trial balance. **~eisen** *n.* pig-iron. **~eit** *f.* raw state, crudeness; rudeness, brutality. **~ertrag** *m.* gross receipts. **~gewicht** *n.* gross weight. **~kost** *f.* uncooked vegetarian food. **~leder** *n.* untanned leather. **~ling** *m.* brute. **~material** *n.*, **~stoff** *m.* raw material. **~metall** *n.* crude metal. **~öl** *n.* crude oil. **~seide** *f.* tussore silk.

Rohr *n.* (-es, -e) reed; cane; pipe, tube; barrel (of gun). **~bruch** *m.* pipe burst. **~dommel** *f.* bittern. **~geflecht** *n.* basketwork, wickerwork. **~kolben** *m.* reed-mace. **~leger** *m.* pipe-fitter, plumber. **~leitung** *f.* pipe lines. **~mündung** *f.* muzzle of a gun. **~netz** *n.* pipes, conduit. **~post** *f.* pneumatic post. **~spatz** *m.* *wie ein ~spatz schimpfen* to scold like a fishwife. **~stock** *m.* cane. **~stuhl** *m.* basket chair, cane-bottomed chair. **~zucker** *m.* cane-sugar.

Röhr-e *f.* (-e, -en) pipe, tube; valve. **~enapparat** *m.* valve set, valve transmitter. **~icht** *n.* reeds.

röhren *v.i.* (*of stag*) to bell.

Rokoko *n.* (-s) rococo.

Roll-e *f.* (-e, -en) roll; roller; reel; cylinder; pulley; mangle; caster; scroll; (*theatr.*) role, part; *aus der ~e fallen* to misbehave; *ins ~en bringen* to set going. **~enbesetzung** *f.* cast. **~er** *m.* rolling sea; canary; scooter (toy). **~feld** *n.* tarmac, runway, landing area. **~film** *m.* roll-film. **~geld** *n.* cartage, transport charges. **~kommando** *n.* raiding-squad, 'murder' squad. **~kutscher** *m.* carter, carrier.

~(l)aden *m.* roll shutter. ~mops *m.* pickled herring. ~schiene *f.* rail. ~schinken *m.* rolled ham. ~schuh *m.* roller-skate. ~sitz *m.* sliding seat. ~splitt *m.* boulders. ~stuhl *m.* Bath-chair, wheel chair. ~treppe *f.* escalator. ~wagen *m.* truck. ~tür *f.* sliding door.

rollen *v.t. & i.* to roll; to mangle; to rumble; (*av.*) to taxi; ~*des Material* rolling-stock.

Ro'man (-ma:n) *m.* (-s, -e) novel; fiction; romance. ~haft *a.* fanciful; fantastic. ~schriftsteller *m.* novelist. [F]

Roma'nist *m.* (-en, -en) teacher *or* student of Romance languages.

Ro'man-tik (-tik) *f.* romantic period; romantic poetry; romanticism. ~tiker *m.* romantic author; romanticist. ~tisch *a.* romantic. ~ze *f.* romance; ballad.

Römer (rø:-) *m.* (-s, -) **1.** large wine-glass. **2.** See App. I.

Rommé *n.* rummy.

Ron'dell *n.* (-s, -e) round (flower-) bed; round tower.

röntgen *v.t.* to X-ray. ~aufnahme *f.,* ~bild *n.* X-ray photograph. ~strahlen *m.pl.* X-rays.

rosa *a.* pink, rose-coloured.

Rose (ro:zə) *f.* (-, -n) rose; (*med.*) erysipelas. ~nkohl *m.* Brussels sprouts. ~nkranz *m.* wreath of roses; rosary. ~nmontag *m.* last Monday before Lent. ~nöl *n.* attar of roses. ~nstock *m.* rose tree.

rosig *a.* rose, rose-coloured, rosy.

Ro'sine *f.* (-, -n) raisin; currant.

Rosma'rin *m.* (-s) rosemary.

Roß (rɔs) *n.* (Ross-es, -e) horse ~händler, ~täuscher *m.* horse-dealer. ~kastanie *f.* horse-chestnut. ~kur *f.* drastic treatment.

Rösselsprung *m.* knight's move.

Rost[1] *m.* (-es) rust. ~fleck(en) *m.* iron-mould. ~frei *a.* stainless (steel). ~ig *a.* rusty. ~schutzmittel *n.* antirust agent.

Rost[2] *m.* (-es, -e) gridiron; grate. ~braten *m.* roast beef, joint.

rosten (rɔs-) *v.i.* to rust.

rösten (rœs-) *v.t.* to roast, grill; to toast.

rot (ro:t) *a.* red, ruddy; ~ *werden* to blush. *subst. n.* red; redness; rouge. ~bäckig *a.* red- *or* rosy-cheeked. ~bart *m.* red-beard. ~blond *a.* auburn. ~buche *f.* copper beech. ~dorn *m.* pink hawthorn. ~fuchs *m.* sorrel *or* bay horse. ~glühend *a.* red-hot. ~haut *f.* redskin. ~käppchen *n.* Red Riding Hood. ~kehlchen *n.* robin. ~kohl *m.* red cabbage. ~lauf *m.* erysipelas; (*vet.*) red murrain. ~schwänzchen *n.* red-start. ~spon, ~wein *m.* claret. ~stift *m.* red pencil. ~welsch *n.* thieves' Latin. ~wild *n.* red deer.

Rotati'onsmaschine *f.* rotary press.

Röt-e (rø:-) *f.* (-e) red, redness; blush. ~el *m.* ruddle, red ochre. ~eln *pl.* German measles. ~lich *a.* reddish.

röten *v.t.* to colour red, redden. *v.r.* to get red, flush.

ro'tieren *v.i.* to rotate.

Rotte *f.* (-, -n) gang, band, troop; (*mil.*) a number of men in file.

Rotz *m.* (-es) mucus; (*vet.*) glanders.

Rou'lade *f.* meat-roll.

Rou'leau (-lo:) *n.* (-s, -s) roller-blind.

routi'niert *a.* experienced, trained.

Rüb-e *f.* (-e, -en) rape; *gelbe* ~*e* carrot; *weiße* ~*e* turnip. ~enzucker *m.* beet-sugar. ~öl *n.* rape-oil. ~samen *m.* rape-seed.

Rubel *m.* (-s, -) rouble.

rüber = **herüber.**

Ru'bin (-i:n) *m.* (-s, -e) ruby.

Ru'bri-k (-i:k) *f.* (-k, -ken) rubric; column. ~'zieren *v.t.* to head; to arrange in columns.

ruch-bar (rux-) *a.* notorious; ~*bar werden* to become known *or* public. ~**los** *a.* wicked, infamous, impious. ~**losigkeit** *f.* wickedness, infamy; wicked act. [RECKLESS]

Ruck (ruk) *m.* (-es, -e) jolt, start, jerk; *sich einen* ~ *geben* to pull oneself together. ~**weise** *adv.* by jerks.

Rück-ansicht f. back view. **~antwort**, **~äußerung** f. reply. **~bezüglich** a. reflexive (verb. &c.); reciprocal. **~blenden** v.t. to flashback. **~blick** m. (a) glance back; retrospect; survey (of past time). **~erinnerung** f. reminiscence. **~erstatten** v.t. to refund. **~fahrkarte** f. return ticket. **~fahrt** f. return journey. **~fall** m. relapse. **~fällig** a. relapsing. **~flug** m. return or homeward flight. **~frage** f. query; checkback. **~gabe** f. return. **~gang** m. retrogression; decline, falling-off. **~gängig** a. **~gängig machen** to cancel, break off. **~halt** m. support; reserve. **~haltlos** a. unreserved, without reserve. **~kauf** m. buying back; redemption. **~kehr**, **~kunft** f. return. **~koppelung** f. (radio) reaction. **~lage** f. reserve (fund). **~läufig** a. retrograde. **~licht** n. rear light. **~lings** adv. backwards; from behind. **~marsch** m. march back; retreat. **~porto** n. return postage. **~reise** f. return, journey home. **~schlag** m. recoil; repercussion; (fig.) reverse, setback; reaction. **~schluß** m. conclusion, inference. **~schritt** m. step back; falling-off, relapse, retrogression. **~seite** f. back, reverse. **~sicht** f. regard, consideration. **~sichtslos** a. inconsiderate, unfeeling, reckless; determined, at all costs. **~sichtsvoll** a. considerate. **~sitz** m. back seat. **~sprache** f. discussion, consultation; **~sprache nehmen** to discuss, talk over. **~stand** m. arrears, residue. **~ständig** a. in arrears; old-fashioned, backward. **~stelltaste** f. back spacer (of typewriter). **~stoßmotor** m. jet propulsion. **~strahler** m. rear reflector. **~strahlung** f. reflection. **~tritt** m. retirement; resignation. **~trittbremse** f. back-pedalling brake. **~vergüten** v.t. to pay, refund. **~versicherung** f. reinsurance. **~wand** f. back wall. **~wärtig** a. rear, rearward; behind the lines. **~wärts** adv.

backwards, back. **~wärtsgang** m. (motor.) reverse gear. **~weg** m. way back, return. **~wirkend** a. retroactive; retrospective. **~wirkung** f. reaction; retroaction. **~zahlung** f. repayment. **~zug** m. withdrawal, retreat.

rücken¹ (ryk-) v.t. to move, push. vws.i. to move away, make room; **ins Feld** ~ to take the field.

Rücken² (ryk-) m. (-s, -) back; rear; ridge; bridge (of nose); ~ **gegen** ~ back to back; **den** ~ **kehren** to turn one's back; **in den** ~ **fallen** to attack in the rear. **~deckung** f. rear cover, protection for the rear. **~flosse** f. dorsal fin. **~flug** m. upside-down flying. **~lehne** f. (chair-)back. **~mark** n. spinal cord. **~schwimmen** n. backstroke. **~titel** m. lettering (on spine of book). **~wirbel** m. dorsal vertebra. [RIDGE]

Rückgrat n. spine, backbone, vertebral column. **~verkrümmung** f. spinal curvature.

Rucksack (ruk-) m. knapsack, rucksack.

Rüde¹ m. (-n, -n) large hound; male dog or fox or wolf.

rüde² a. rude, rough, coarse.

Rudel (ru:-) n. (-s, -) herd, troop, pack; pack (of U-boats).

Ruder (ru:-) n. (-s, -) oar; rudder, helm; **ans** ~ **kommen** to come into power. **~boot** n. rowing-boat. **~er** m. rower, oarsman. **~n** v.i. & t. to row.

Ruf (ru:f) m. (-es, -e) cry; call; summons; reputation; name; **im** ~**e stehen** to be reputed (to be), be generally considered as; **einen** ~ **erhalten** to be offered an appointment. **~mord** m. slander. **~name** m. Christian name. **~nummer** f. telephone number. **~weite** f. **in** ~**weite** within call. **~zeichen** n. exclamation mark; call-signal.

rufen v.t. & i. st. to cry, shout; to call; to summon; to send for; **wie gerufen kommen** to come at the right moment.

Rüffel m. (-s, -) reprimand. **~n** v.t. to reprimand.

Rüge (ry:-) f. (-, -n) censure; reprimand. **~n** v.t. to censure; to reprimand.

Ruhe f. (-) rest, repose; calm, stillness; quiet, silence; peace; *zur ~ gehen* to go to bed; *in aller ~* very calmly; *in ~ lassen* to let or leave alone; *sich zur ~ setzen* to retire. **~gehalt** n. pension. **~los** a. restless. **~stand** m. retirement. **~stätte** f. resting-place. **~stellung** f. stand at ease position. **~störer** m. brawler, rioter.

ruh-en v.i. to rest; to sleep; to stand still; to be idle; *~en auf* to rest on, be based on. **~ig** a. still, quiet, motionless; silent; calm, composed; peaceful, serene. adv. (colloq.) safely; without ado.

Ruhm (ru:m) m. (-es) glory; fame; renown. **~begier** f. thirst for glory. **~eshalle** f. memorial hall. **~los** a. inglorious, obscure. **~redig** a. vainglorious, boastful.

rühm-en (ry:-) v.t. to praise; to extol. v.r. to boast of, brag. **~lich** a. glorious, praiseworthy.

Ruhr f. (-) dysentery.

Rühr-ei n. scrambled eggs. **~faß** n. churn. **~ig** a. active, bustling, quick. **~igkeit** f. activity, nimbleness. **~selig** a. sentimental, emotional. **~stück** n. melodrama; sob-stuff. **~ung** f. emotion; feeling.

rühren v.t. & i. to move; to touch; to stir; to beat (drum). v.r. to stir, move; to bestir oneself; (mil.) to stand at ease. **~d** a. touching, moving, pathetic.

Ru'in (-i:n) m. (-s) ruin, downfall, decay. **~e** f. ruin. **~ieren** v.t. to ruin.

rülpsen v.i. to belch.

Rum[1] m. (-s) rum.

rum[2] = *herum*.

Rummel m. (-s, -) activity; hubbub, tumult; amusement park, fair; *im ~* in the lump.

ru'moren v.i. to make a noise.

Rumpel-kammer f. lumber-room. **~n** v.i. to rumble, lumber, jolt.

Rumpf m. (-es, =e) trunk, body, torso; hull; fuselage. **~beuge** f.

trunk bending. [RUMP]

rümpfen v.t. *die Nase ~* to turn up one's nose.

rund (-) a. round, circulary; plump; spherical; (fig.) frank, plain. **~bau** m. circular building. **~blick** m. view all round; panorama. **~bogen** m. Roman arch. **~e** f. circle; lap, round; beat; *die ~e machen* to go one's rounds. **~fahrt** f. circular tour. **~frage** f. inquiry; questionnaire. **~funk** m. radio, wireless, broadcasting. **~funken** v.t. & i. to broadcast. **~funkgerät** n. wireless set. **~funkhörer** m. listener (-in). **~funksender** m. wireless transmitter. **~funkteilnehmer** m. owner of wireless set. **~gang** m. round, stroll. **~heraus** adv. straight out, flatly. **~(her)um** adv. all around, round about. **~lauf** m. (gym.) giant-stride. **~lich** a. round, rounded; plump. **~reisebillet** n. tourist ticket. **~schau** f. panorama; review. **~schreiben** n. circular (letter). **~schrift** f. round-hand (writing). **~stab** m. round bar. **~ung** f. rounding; curve; roundness. **~weg** adv. plainly, flatly.

runden v.t. & r. to make round; to round (lips).

Rune (ru:-) f. (-, -n) rune.

Runkelrübe f. beetroot.

runter = *herunter*.

Runzel f. (-, -n) wrinkle, pucker. **~ig** a. wrinkled, puckered. **~n** v.t. to wrinkle; *die Stirn ~n* to frown.

Rüpel m. (-s, -) lout. **~'ei** f. rudeness, insolence.

rupfen v.t. to pluck; (fig.) to fleece.

ruppig (-ç) a. shabby; rude.

Rüsche f. (-, -n) ruche, frilling.

Ruß (ru:s) m. (-es) soot. **~en** v.i. to smoke; to blacken. **~ig** a. sooty.

Rüssel m. (-s, -) snout; trunk, proboscis.

rüst-en v.t. & i. to prepare, fit out, equip; to arm; to prepare for war. v.r. to prepare for, get ready. **~ig** a. strong, robust, vigorous. **~igkeit** f. vigour. **~kammer** f. armoury; arsenal.

~ung f. preparation, equipment; arming; armour, armament. **~ungsanlage** f., **~ungsbetrieb** m. armament factory, munition works. **~zeug** n. tools, implements; capacities, knowledge.

Rüster f. (-, -n) elm.

Rute (ru:-) f. (-, -n) rod, twig, switch; tail; penis. **~nbündel** n. bundle of rods, fasces. **~ngänger** m. dowser, water-finder.

Rutsch m. (-es, -e) slide, glide, landslip. **~bahn** f. slide, chute. **~en** vws.i. to slide, slip; to skid; (av.) to side-slip. **~gefahr** f. danger of skidding. **~ig** a. slippery.

rütteln v.t. & i. to shake, jog, jolt.

S

S, s (ɛs) n. the letter S, s.

Saal (za:l) m. (-es, Säle) large room; hall.

Saat f. (-, -en) sowing; seed; standing corn, green crops. **~feld** n. cornfield. **~gut** n. seed-corn. **~korn** n. seed-corn. **~kartoffel** f. seed-potato. **~krähe** f. rook.

Sabbat m. (-s, -e) Sabbath.

sabbern v.i. to slaver.

Säbel m. (-s, -) sabre; sword. **~beine** n.pl. bow-legs. **~hieb** m. sword-cut. **~n** v.t. & i. to sabre.

sabo'tieren v.t. to sabotage.

Sach-angabe f. information, particulars. **~bearbeiter** m. expert. **~dienlich** a. relevant, pertinent. **Sach-e** (zaxə) f. (-e, -en) thing, subject; matter, affair, business, cause; fact, circumstance; (pl.) goods, clothes, &c.; (leg.) case; bei der ~ sein to pay attention to, be intent on; gemeinsame ~ machen to make common cause (with); zur ~e to the point; seine sieben ~en all one's belongings. **~gemäß** a. appropriate, proper. adv. in a suitable manner. **~katalog** m. subject catalogue. **~kunde** f. expert knowledge. **~kundig**, **~verständig** aa. expert, competent. **~lage** f. state of affairs. **~leistung** f. payment

in kind. **~lich** a. to the point, pertinent; objective; material, essential. **~lichkeit** f. reality; objectivity. **~register** n. table of contents, index. **~schaden** m. damage to property. **~verhalt** m. facts of a case. **~walter** m. advocate; attorney, counsel. **~wert** m. real value. **~wörterbuch** n. encyclopaedia. [SAKE]

sächlich a. neuter.

sacht(e) (zaxt) a. soft, gentle; slow.

Sack m. (-es, ⁓e) sack, bag; pocket; purse; mit ~ und Pack with bag and baggage. **~garn** n. sack-thread, twine. **~gasse** f. blind alley, dead end. **~hüpfen** n. sack race. **~landung** f. pancake landing. **~leinwand** f. sackcloth. **~pfeife** f. bagpipe. **~tuch** n. (dial.) handkerchief.

Säckel m. (-s, -) purse, money-bag.

sacken vws.i. to sink, sag.

sä-en v.t. & i. to sow. **~(e)mann** m. sower. **~maschine** f. drill-plough, sowing-machine.

Saffian m. (-s) Morocco leather.

Safran m. (-s) saffron.

Saft m. (-es, ⁓e) juice; sap; fluid, liquid. **~ig** a. juicy, succulent; (fig.) spicy, coarse. **~los** a. dry, sapless; (fig.) insipid.

Sage (za:gə) f. (-, -n) legend, tale; myth. **~nhaft** a. legendary, fabulous, mythical.

Säge (zɛːgə) f. (-, -n) saw. **~bock** m. saw-jack. **~mehl** n. sawdust. **~späne** m.pl. sawdust. **~mühle** f., **~werk** n. sawmill.

sagen v.t. & i. to say, tell; to mean, signify; ~ lassen to send word; sich etwas gesagt sein lassen to be warned; das hat nichts zu ~ that doesn't matter.

sägen v.t. & i. to saw.

Sago m. (-s) sago.

sah imperf. of **sehen**.

Sahne f. (-) cream.

Sai'son (-zɔ̃) f. (-, -s) season. **~ausverkauf** m. clearance sale.

Saite f. (-, -n) string, chord. **~n-instrument** n. stringed instrument. **~nspiel** n. string music; lyre.

Sakko m. (-s, -s) lounge jacket.

Sakra'ment n. (-s, -e) sacrament.

Sakri'st-an m. (-ans, -ane) sacristan, sexton. **~ei** f. vestry.

Säku'lar-feier f. centenary. **~i-'sieren** v.t. to secularize.

Sa'lami f. (-, -) salame (sausage).

Sa'lat (-a:t) m. (-s, -e) salad; grüner ~ lettuce.

sal'badern v.i. to talk nonsense.

Salband n., **Salleiste** f. selvage.

Salb-e f. (-e, -en) salve, ointment. **~en** v.t. to anoint; (fig.) anointing; (fig.) unction. **~ungs-voll** a. unctuous.

Sal'bei m. & f. sage.

Saldo m. (-s, Salden) balance (of account). **~vortrag** m. balance forward.

Sa'line f. (-, -n) salt-works.

Sali'zylsäure f. salicylic acid.

Salm m. (-s, -e) salmon.

Salmiak m. (-s) sal ammoniac. **~geist** m. aqueous or liquid ammonia.

Sa'lon (-lɔ̃) m. (-s, -s) drawing-room; (ship's) saloon. **~löwe** m. ladies' man.

sa'lopp a. slovenly.

Sal'peter m. (-s) saltpetre, sodium nitrate. **~haltig** a. containing saltpetre, nitrous. **~säure** f. nitric acid.

Sa'lut (-lu:t) m. (-s, -e) salute of guns. **~ieren** v.i. & t. to salute.

Salve f. (-, -n) volley (of rifles); salvo (of guns).

Salz (-ts) n. (-es, -e) salt. **~faß** n. salt-cellar; salt-box. **~gurke** f. pickled cucumber. **~haltig** a. containing salt, saliferous. **~ig** a. salty, salt. **~lake** f. brine, pickle. **~säure** f. hydrochloric acid.

salzen v.t. to salt; to season.

Same(-n) (za:-) m. (-ns, -n) seed; sperm. **~nbehälter** m. seed-vessel. **~nbildung** f. seed formation. **~ngehäuse** n. pericarp. **~nhülle** f. seed-case. **~nkapsel** f. seed-pod. **~nkern** m. seed-kernel; endosperm; spermatic nucleus. **~nkorn** n. grain of seed. **~nstaub** m. pollen. **~ntierchen** n. spermatozoon. **~ntragend** a. seed-bearing.

Säme'reien f.pl. seeds.

Sämischleder n. chamois leather.

Sammel-band m. omnibus volume; volume; collected works. **~becken** n. reservoir. **~büchse** f. collecting-box. **~linse** f. convex lens. **~name** m. collective noun. **~platz** m., **~stelle** f. assembly point, rallying point; meeting-place; collecting station; dump; depot. **~surium** n. medley, jumble.

sammeln v.t. to collect, gather; to pick; to amass, accumulate; (fig.) to concentrate. v.r. to assemble, rally; (fig.) to compose oneself.

Sammler m. (-s, -) collector; accumulator. **~batterie** f. storage battery.

Sammlung f. (-, -en) collection (fig.) composure; concentration.

Samstag m. Saturday.

samt[1] prep. & adv. together with; ~ und sonders one and all, jointly and severally.

Samt[2] m. (-es, -e) velvet. **~en, ~ig** aa. velvet, velvety, velvet-like. [ML]

sämtlich a. all, all together; all of them.

Samum m. (-s, -s) simoom.

Sana'torium n. (-s, . . . rien) sanatorium.

Sand (z-t) m. (-es) sand; grit. **~boden** m. sandy soil. **~form** f. sand mould. **~hose** f. gyrating column of sand. **~ig** a. sandy. **~korn** n. grain of sand. **~sack** m. sandbag. **~stein** m. sandstone. **~torte** f. kind of rich madeira cake. **~uhr** f. hourglass.

San'dale (-da:-) f. (-, -n) sandal.

Sandelholz n. sandalwood.

sandte imperf. of senden.

sanft a. soft; tender; delicate; mild; smooth; gentle, slight. **~heit** f. softness; mildness; gentleness. **~mut** f. gentleness, meekness. **~mütig** a. gentle, meek.

Sänfte f. (-, -n) sedan-chair; litter.

Sang[1] (zaŋ) m. (-es, -̈e) song, singing.

sang[2] imperf. of singen.

Sänger (-nər) *m.* (-s, -) singer; minstrel; poet; (*bird*) songster.

Sangu'in-iker *m.* sanguine person. **~isch** *a.* sanguine.

sa'nier-en *v.t.* to restore; to re-organize. **~ung** *f.* renovation; reorganization.

sani'tär *a.* sanitary.

Sani'tät-er *m.* (-ers, -er) ambulance man. **~shund** *m.* first-aid dog. **~soffizier** *m.* medical officer. **~s(kraft)wagen** *m.* motor ambulance, ambulance van.

sank *imperf. of* **sinken**.

Sankt *indecl. a.* Saint.

Sankti'on *f.* (-, -en) sanction. **~-'ieren** *v.t.* to sanction.

sann *imperf. of* **sinnen**.

Saphir *m.* (-s, -e) sapphire.

Sappe *f.* (-, -n) sap (trench).

sapper'-lot, **~'ment** *int.* the dickens!

Sar'delle *f.* (-, -n) sardelle.

Sar'dine *f.* (-, -n) sardine.

Sarg (-k) *m.* (-es, ⸚e) coffin. **~deckel** *m.* coffin-lid. **~tuch** *n.* pall.

Sar'kas-mus *m.* sarcasm. **~tisch** *a.* sarcastic.

Sarko'phag *m.* (-s, -e) sarcophagus.

saß *imperf. of* **sitzen**.

Satan (za:-) *m.* (-s) Satan, devil.

sa'tanisch *a.* satanic.

Sate'llit *m.* (-en, -en) satellite.

Sa'tin (-tɛ̃) *m.* (-s) satin; sateen. **~ieren** *v.t.* to glaze, satin; to calender (paper).

Sa'tir-e (-ti:-) *f.* (-e, -en) satire. **~iker** *m.* satirist. **~isch** *a.* satiric(al).

satt *a.* satisfied, full; saturated, deep, rich (*colour*); *sich ~ essen* to eat one's fill; *nie ~ werden* (*fig.*) never to tire of; *etwas ~ haben* (*sl.*) to be fed up with. **~sam** *adv.* sufficiently, enough. [SAD]

Satte *f.* (-, -n) milk-pan, milk-bowl.

Sattel *m.* (-s, ⸚) saddle; bridge (of nose); ridge (of hill); *aus dem ~ heben* to unhorse; (*fig.*) to supplant, supersede; *in allen Sätteln gerecht sein* to be good at everything. **~fest** *a.* having a good seat; (*fig.*) well up in. **~n** *v.t. & i.* to saddle. **~pferd** *n.*

riding-horse; near horse. **~zeug** *n.* saddle and harness.

sättig-en *v.t.* to satisfy; to saturate; to impregnate. **~ung** *f.* appeasing (of hunger); saturation.

Sattler *m.* (-s, -) saddler. **~ei** *f.* saddlery.

Satz *m.* (-es, ⸚e) jump, bound; set; (*gram.*) sentence, clause; (*math. & phil.*) proposition, theorem; thesis; (*chem.*) deposit, sediment; dregs, grounds; (*mus.*) phrase; movement; (*commerc.*) fixed sum, rate; (*typ.*) composition; matter; *in ~ geben* to give to the printer. **~aussage** *f.* predicate. **~bau** *m.* (*gram.*) construction. **~bild** *n.* (*typ.*) setting. **~fehler** *m.* misprint. **~gefüge** *n.* complex sentence. **~lehre** *f.* syntax. **~spiegel** *m.* (*typ.*) face. **~ung** *f.* rule, ordinance; statute. **~ungsmäßig** *a.* statutory. **~zeichen** *n.* punctuation mark.

Sau (z-) *f.* (-, ⸚e) sow; (*fig.*) slut; (*pl.* -en) wild sow. **~bohne** *f.* broad bean. **~dumm** *a.* very stupid. **~stall** *m.* pigsty. **~wohl** *adv.* (*colloq.*) top-hole.

sauber *a.* clean; neat, tidy; pretty; (*iron.*) fine, nice. **~keit** *f.* cleanness, cleanliness; neatness.

säuber-lich *a.* clean; neat. **~n** *v.t.* to clean; to clear; to mop up; (*fig.*) to purge. **~ung** *f.* cleaning; mopping-up; purge.

Sauc-e (zo:sə) *f.* (-, -en) sauce, gravy. **~iere** *f.* sauce-boat.

sauer *a.* sour, acid; (*fig.*) hard, difficult; morose, surly. **~ampfer** *m.* sorrel. **~kirsche** *f.* morella cherry. **~milch** *f.* curdled milk. **~stoff** *m.* oxygen. **~gerät** *n.* oxygen breathing apparatus. **~haltig** *a.* containing oxygen. **~verbindung** *f.* oxygen compound. **~teig** *m.* leaven, yeast. **~töpfisch** *a.* peevish, sullen.

säuer-lich *a.* sourish, acidulated. **~n** *v.t.* to acidify; to leaven (dough).

Saufbold *m.* (-s, -e) drunkard.

sauf-en *v.t. & i. st.* to drink; to booze. **~e'rei** *f.,* **~gelage** *n.* drinking bout. [SUP]

Säufer *m.* (-s, -) drunkard, toper.

~wahnsinn *m.* delirium tremens.

saug-en *v.t. & i. st.* to suck; to absorb. ~er *m.* sucker; nipple (of bottle). ~fähig *a.* absorbent; absorptive. ~flasche *f.* feeding-bottle. ~heber *m.* siphon. ~kolben *m.* valve-piston. ~pfropfen *m.* rubber teat. ~pumpe *f.* suction pump. ~rohr *n.* induction-pipe. ~rüssel *m.* proboscis.

säug-en *v.t.* to suckle, nurse. ~e-tier *n.* mammal. ~ling *n.* infant, baby. ~lingsheim *n.* crèche, nursery for infants.

Säule *f.* (-, -n) pillar, column; pile; dry battery. ~nfuß *m.* pedestal; plinth. ~ngang *m.* colonnade, arcade. ~nhalle *f.* pillared hall; portico. ~nheilige(r) *m.* stylite. ~nknauf *m.* capital.

Saum *m.* (-es, "e) edge; border, fringe; hem, seam.

säumen[1] *v.t.* to hem; to border.

säum-en[2] *v.i.* to delay; to tarry. ~ig *a.* dilatory, slow.

Saum-esel *m.* sumpter mule. ~pfad *m.* mule track. ~tier *n.* beast of burden.

saumselig *a.* slow, dilatory; negligent. ~keit *f.* tardiness; negligence.

Säure (zoi-) *f.* (-, -n) sourness, tartness; acid; acidity. ~bildung *f.* acidification. ~fest *a.* acid-proof. ~grad *m.* acidity. ~haltig *a.* containing acid.

Sauregurkenzeit *f.* silly season.

Saurier *m.* (-s, -) saurian.

Saus *m.* ~ *und Braus* riotous living. ~en *v.i.* to rush along; to dash; (of wind) to blow hard, bluster.

säuseln *v.i. & t.* to rustle, whisper.

Saxo'phon *n.* (-s, -e) saxophone.

Schabe *f.* (-, -n) cockroach.

Schab-efleisch *n.* scraped meat. ~eisen *n.* scraper. ~en *v.t. & i.* to scrape; to rub. ~kunst *f.* mezzotint.

Schabernack *m.* (-s, -e) trick; hoax; practical joke.

schäbig *a.* shabby, worn; mean. ~keit *f.* shabbiness.

Scha'blon-e (-lo:-) *f.* (-e, -en) model, pattern; stencil; (*fig.*) routine.

~enmäßig *a.* mechanical, stereotyped. ~'ieren *v.t.* to stencil.

Scha'bracke *f.* (-, -n) saddle-cloth.

Schach (ʃax) *n.* (-es) chess; ~ bieten to defy; in ~ halten to keep in check. ~brett *n.* chessboard. ~feld *n.* square. ~figur *f.* chess-man. ~matt *a.* checkmate; (*fig.*) knocked out. ~partie *f.* game of chess. ~spieler *m.* chess-player. ~zug *m.* move (at chess).

Schacher (-ax-) *m.* (-s) petty dealing, higgling and haggling. ~er *m.* haggler. ~n *v.i.* to bargain, haggle.

Schächer (-ɛç-) *m.* (-s, -) robber; (*bibl.*) thief.

Schacht *m.* (-es, "e) pit, shaft; manhole.

Schachtel *f.* (-, -n) box; *alte* ~ (*fig.*) old frump. ~halm *m.* shavegrass. [IT.]

schächten *v.t.* to kill according to Jewish law.

schade *pred. a. es ist* ~ it is a pity; *wie* ~ what a pity; *zu* ~ *für* too good for. *subst. m.* See *Schaden*[2].

Schädel *m.* (-s, -) skull. ~bruch *m.* fracture of the skull. ~decke *f.* scalp. ~haut *f.* pericranium. ~stätte *f.* Golgotha.

schaden[1] (-a:-) *v.i.* to harm, damage; to hurt; to injure; to prejudice; *das schadet nichts* never mind; *das schadet dir nichts* that serves you right. [SCATHE]

Schaden[2] *m.* (-s, "-) damage; harm; injury, hurt; defect; loss; disadvantage, detriment; wrong; ~ *nehmen, zu* ~ *kommen* to come to grief. ~ersatz *m.* compensation; indemnity; damages. ~ersatzklage *f.* action for damages. ~ersatzpflichtig *a.* liable for damages. ~feuer *n.* destructive fire. ~freude *f.* malicious joy. ~froh *a.* rejoicing over another's misfortune.

schad-haft *a.* damaged, defective, faulty; spoilt; dilapidated. ~los *a. sich* ~*los halten* to recoup oneself.

schäd-igen *v.t.* to damage, injure. ~igung *f.* damage; prejudice. ~lich *a.* harmful, noxious, pernicious; detrimental; prejudicial. **~lichkeit** f. harm, perniciousness. **~ling** m. pest; vermin; vile person, social misfit.

Schaf (-a:-) n. (-es, -e) sheep; (fig.) stupid. **~blattern** f.pl. chickenpox. **~bock** m. ram. **~fell** n. sheepskin. **~garbe** f. yarrow. **~hirt** m. shepherd. **~hürde** f. pen, sheep-fold. **~schur** f. sheep-shearing. **~skopf** m. (fig.) blockhead. **~zucht** f. sheep-breeding.

Schäf-chen n. (-chens, -chen) lamb, lambkin; (pl.) cirrus (clouds); sein **~chen ins Trockene bringen** to feather one's nest. **~er** m. shepherd. **~erhund** m. sheep-dog; deutscher **~~** Alsatian wolfhound. **~erin** f. shepherdess. **~erspiel** n. pastoral play. **~erstunde** f. lovers' hour.

Schaff n. (-es, -e) tub, vat.

schaffen v.t. st. to create, produce. v.t. w. to do, make, accomplish; to procure; to provide; to bring; to convey (to); to remove (to). v.i. to be busy, work; sich zu **~ machen** to be busy, potter about; einem zu **~ machen** to give trouble; beiseite **~** to remove; to kill; wie geschaffen für made for. subst. n. creating; (intellectual) work; production, creation. **~d** a. creative; working. **~sdrang** m. creative impulse.

Schäffler m. (-s, -) cooper.

Schaffner m. (-s, -) conductor; guard; (obs.) steward.

Scha'fott n. (-s, -e) scaffold.

Schaft m. (-es, -e) shaft; handle; trunk (of tree); stem or stalk (of flower); rifle stock; leg (of jackboot). **~stiefel** m. knee-boot.

schäften v.t. to fit with a shaft, stock (gun); to put legs to (boots).

Schah m. (-s, -s) shah.

Schakal (-a:l) m. (-s, -e) jackal.

Schäker m. (-s, -) wag, joker. **~n** v.i. to joke, jest; to flirt. [HEBR.]

schal¹ (-a:l) a. flat; stale; insipid.

Schal² m. (-s, -s) shawl; scarf; muffler.

Schal-e (-a:-) f. (-e, -en) 1. skin, peel,

rind; shell; husk; pod; crust; (fig.) outside, surface. 2. dish, bowl, vessel, cup, basin; scale (of balance). **~tier** n. crustacean; shellfish.

schäl-en v.t. to peel, pare, shell; to bark (tree). v.r. to shed the bark; to peel, peel off. **~hengst** m. stallion.

Schalk m. (-es, -e) rogue, wag. **~haft** a. roguish, waggish. **~s-knecht** m. (bibl.) unfaithful servant.

Schall m. (-es, -e) sound. **~auf-nahmegerät** n. sound-recording instrument. **~boden** m. sounding-board. **~dämpfer** m. silencer. **~dicht** a. sound-proof. **~dose** f. sound-box; pick-up. **~lehre** f. acoustics. **~loch** n. sound-hole (in violin); louvre-window (in belfry). **~meßtrupp** m. sound-ranging section. **~platte** f. (gramophone) record. **~trichter** m. bell-mouth; horn; trumpet; megaphone. **~welle** f. sound-wave.

schallen v.i. to sound; to resound; to ring, peal.

Schal'mei f. (-, -en) shawm.

schalt imperf. of schelten.

Schalt-anlage f. switch gear. **~brett** n. switchboard; instrument panel; dashboard. **~er** m. switch; booking-office (window); counter. **~getriebe** n. main gearbox. **~hebel** m. gear lever; switch. **~jahr** n. leap year. **~plan** m. circuit diagram. **~schlüssel** m. ignition key. **~tafel** f. switchboard. **~tag** m. intercalary day. **~ung** f. gearchange; connexion.

schalten v.i. to deal with, use; to rule, direct. v.t. (electr.) to switch; to change gears.

Scha'luppe f. (-, -n) sloop.

Scham (-a:-) f. (-) shame; modesty; (anat.) genitals. **~bein** n. pubic bone. **~gefühl** n. sense of shame. **~haft** a. modest, bashful. **~haftigkeit** f. modesty, bashfulness. **~los** a. shameless; impudent. **~losigkeit** f. shamelessness; impudence. **~rot** a. blushing, red. **~röte** f.

blush. **~teile** *m.pl.* privy parts, genitals.

schämen *v.r.* to be ashamed (of).

Scha'motte *f.* (-, -n) fire-clay.

schampu'nieren *v.t.* to shampoo.

schand-bar *a.* infamous. **~bube** *m.* scoundrel. **~e** *f.* shame, disgrace. **~fleck** *m.* blemish, stain. **~geld** *n.,* **~preis** *m.* scandalous price. **~mal** *n.* stigma, brand. **~maul** *n.* evil tongue; slanderer. **~pfahl** *m.* pillory. **~tat** *f.* crime, misdeed.

schänd-en *v.t.* to spoil, disfigure; to rape; to dishonour. **~er** *m.* violator; ravisher. **~lich** *a.* shameful, disgraceful, infamous; abominable, vile. **~lichkeit** *f.* infamy. **~ung** *f.* disfiguring; violation, rape.

Schank-gerechtigkeit *f.* licence (to sell liquor). **~stätte** *f.* licensed premises; public house. **~tisch** *m.* bar.

Schanzarbeiten *f.pl.* entrenchments.

Schanze-e¹ *f.* (-e, -en) field-work; redoubt. **~en** *v.i.* to dig in, entrench. **~gräber** *m.* sapper. **~korb** *m.* gabion. **~zeug** *n.* entrenching tools.

Schanze² *f. in die ~ schlagen* to risk. [F]

Schar (-a:-) *f.* (-, -en) 1. troop, band; flock; crowd; host, multitude. 2. ploughshare. **~en** *v.t. & r.* to collect, assemble, flock together, rally. **~enweise** *adv.* in bands, in troops. **~führer** *m.* leader, platoon leader. **~wache** *f.* patrol; watch.

Scha'rade (-ra:-) *f.* (-, -n) charade.

Schären *f.pl.* rocky islets; cliffs.

scharf *a.* sharp, pointed; piercing; acute; acrid, pungent, hot, piquant; corrosive; strong, violent; hard, severe; harsh, biting, cutting; keen, quick; (*mil.*) live, primed, armed. **~blick** *m.* penetrating glance, quick eye; acuteness. **~kantig** *a.* sharp-edged. **~macher** *m.* agitator; fire-brand. **~richter** *m.* executioner. **~schießen** *n.* firing with ball *or* live rounds. **~schütze** *m.* sharpshooter, sniper.

~sicht *f.* keenness of sight; perspicacity. **~sichtig** *a.* keen-sighted; penetrating. **~sinn** *m.* sagacity, acumen. **~sinnig** *a.* sagacious, discerning.

Schärfe *f.* (-) sharpness; edge; acidity, acridity, piquancy; severity, rigour; keenness, acuteness. **~n** *v.t.* to sharpen, grind, whet; to set (razor); to increase, strengthen.

Scharlach (-ax) *m.* (-s) scarlet fever. **~farben** *a.* scarlet, vermilion.

Scharlatan *m.* (-s, -e) charlatan, quack. **~e'rie** *f.* quackery.

Schar'mützel *n.* (-s, -) skirmish. [IT.]

Schar'nier *n.* (-s, -e) hinge, joint.

Schärpe *f.* (-, -n) sash.

scharren *v.i. & t.* to scratch; (*of horse*) to paw.

Schart-e *f.* (-e, -en) notch; crack; gap; (*mil.*) loophole; *eine ~ auswetzen* to make amends (for), make up (for). **~ig** *a.* jagged, notched.

Schar'teke (-te:-) *f.* (-, -n) old book; trash.

schar'wenzeln *v.i.* to fawn, toady.

Schatten *m.* (-s, -) shadow, shade; phantom, spirit. **~bild** *n.,* **~riß** *m.* silhouette. **~haft** *a.* shadowy. **~seite** *f.* shady side; (*fig.*) dark side. **~spiel** *n.* shadow-play.

scha'ttier-en *v.t.* to shade; to hatch (on map). **~ung** *f.* shading; shade, tint; hatching.

schattig *a.* shady.

Scha'tulle *f.* (-, -n) cash-box; privy purse.

Schatz *m.* (-es, ¨e) treasure; store; riches; (*fig.*) darling, love. **~amt** *n.* treasury, exchequer. **~anweisung** *f.* treasury-bond, exchequer-bill. **~gräber** *m.* digger for treasure. **~kammer** *f.* treasury. **~meister** *m.* treasurer.

schätz-en *v.t.* to value, estimate; judge; (*fig.*) to respect, esteem; to appreciate. **~enswert** *a.* estimable. **~ung** *f.* estimate; taxation; estimation; esteem. **~ungsweise** *adv.* approximately, roughly (estimated). **~ungswert** *m.* estimated value.

Schau f. (-) sight, view, perception; show, exhibition; review; **zur ~ stellen** to expose, display. **~brot** n. shewbread. **~bude** f. booth (at fair). **~bühne** f. stage, theatre. **~fenster** n. shopwindow. **~fensterdekoration** f. window-dressing. **~fliegen** i. stunt-flying. **~gerüst** n. stage; grand stand. **~haus** n. mortuary. **~kasten** m. showcase. **~lustig** a. curious. (subst. m.) onlooker. **~münze** f. medal, medallion. **~packung** f. dummy. **~platz** m. scene; theatre, seat (of a war). **~spiel** n. spectacle, scene, sight; play, drama. **~spieler** m. actor. **~spielerin** f. actress. **~spielerisch** a. like an actor, histrionic. **~spielern** v.i. to act; to sham. **~spielkunst** f. dramatic art. **~stellung** f. exhibition, show. **~stück** n. show-piece, specimen.

Schauder m. (-s, -) shudder, shuddering, shivering; horror, terror, fright. **~haft** a. horrible, terrible, awful. **~n** v.i. to shiver; to feel creepy; (impers.) to shudder at; **mich ~t vor** or **es ~t mich** I have a horror of.

schauen v.i. & t. to see, behold, look (at), gaze (upon), view. [SHOW]

Schauer m. (-s, -) shivering fit; horror, terror; awe; thrill; shower, storm. **~lich** a. awful; ghastly, gruesome, horrid. **~n** v.i. to shiver; to feel creepy; **mich ~t bei** I shudder at. **~roman** m. thriller, shilling shocker, penny-dreadful.

Schauermann m. docker.

Schaufel f. (-, -n) shovel; scoop; paddle. **~geweih** n. palmed antlers. **~n** v.t. & i. to shovel. **~rad** n. paddle-wheel.

Schaukel f. (-, -n) swing. **~n** v.i. & t. to swing, rock. **~pferd** n. rocking-horse. **~stuhl** m. rocking-chair.

Schaum m. (-es, Schäume) foam; froth; spume; lather (of soap); **zu ~ schlagen** to beat up, whisk. **~gummi** m. foam rubber. **~ig** a. foamy, frothy. **~krone** f. white crest (of wave), white horses.

~löffel m. skimmer. **~schläger** m. (fig.) gas-bag, empty talker. **~wein** m. sparkling wine; champagne.

schäumen v.i. to foam, froth; to sparkle, effervesce; (of soap) to lather; to boil (with rage).

schaurig (-₡) a. awful, horrid, gruesome.

Scheck¹ m. (-s, -e) cheque. **~buch** n. cheque book. **~formular** n. blank cheque. **~inhaber** m. bearer.

Scheck² m. (-en, -en), **~e** f. piebald or dappled horse. **~ig** a. piebald, dappled; spotted, mottled.

scheel (še:l) a. squinting; envious. **~sucht** f. envy.

Scheffel m. (-s, -) bushel. **~n** v.t. to rake in; to heap up. **~weise** adv. in bushels.

Scheibe f. (-, -n) disk; orb; slice (of bread, &c.); (window-)pane; (mil.) practice target; (potter's) wheel. **~ngardine** f. short curtain. **~nhonig** m. honey in the comb. **~nschießen** n. target shooting, target practice. **~nstand** m. butts. **~nwischer** m. windscreen wiper.

Scheich (-₡) m. (-s, -e) sheik.

Scheid-e f. (-e, -en) sheath; boundary, limit; (anat.) vagina. **~ebrief** m. farewell letter; bill of divorce. **~emünze** f. small coin, change. **~ewand** f. dividing-wall, partition. **~eweg** m. cross-road(s). **~ung** f. separation; divorce. **~ungsklage** f. divorce suit.

scheiden v.t. st. to separate, divide; to part; to divorce; to sever; to analyse, decompose. vws.i. to go away, leave, depart; to part; **sich ~ lassen** to get divorced. [SHED]

Schein m. (-es, -e) shine, light, brilliance; air, look; appearance, semblance; pretext, sham; certificate, ticket, receipt; bank-note. **~angrif** m. feint attack. **~argument** n. spurious argument. **~bar** a. apparent; ostensible, pretended. **~bild** n. phantom, illusion. ~blüte *f.* illusory prosperity. ~ehe *f.* mock marriage. ~grund *m.* fictitious reason; sophism. ~heilig *a.* sanctimonious; hypocritical. ~tod *m.* suspended animation; trance. ~werfer *m.* reflector; (*mil.*) searchlight; flood-light; (*motor.*) headlight, head-lamp; (*theatr.*) spotlight.

scheinen *v.i. st.* to shine; to seem, appear, look.

scheißen *v.i. st.* (*vulg.*) to shit.

Scheit *n.* (-es, -e & -er) log. ~erhaufen *m.* funeral pile; stake.

Scheitel *m.* (-s, -) top, crown, apex; (hair-)parting; summit, top (of hill); (*math.*) vertex. ~linie *f.* vertical line. ~n *v.t.* to part the hair. ~punkt *m.* vertex; zenith. ~winkel *m.* vertical angle; opposite angle.

scheitern *vvs.i.* to be wrecked; (*fig.*) to miscarry, fail.

Schellack *m.* (-s, -e) shellac.

Schelle *f.* (-, -n) (little) bell; manacle; (*bibl.*) cymbal; (*cards*) diamonds; (*dial.*) box on the ear. ~n *v.i.* to ring the bell. ~nkappe *f.* fool's cap and bells.

Schellfisch *m.* haddock.

Schelm *m.* (-es, -e) rogue. ~enstreich *m.* prank. ~e'rei *f.* roguery. ~isch *a.* roguish.

Schelt-e *f.* (-e) scolding. ~en *v.t. & i. st.* to scold; to abuse. ~wort *n.* invective.

Schem-a (-e:-) *n.* (-as, -ata) ⊕ order, arrangement; model, pattern; schedule; diagram. ~'atisch *a.* systematic, mechanical.

Schemel (je:-) *m.* (-s, -) footstool.

Schemen (je:-) *m.* (-s, -) phantom, shadow. ~haft *a.* shadowy, unreal.

Schenk *m.* (-en, -en) cup-bearer. ~e *f.* inn, public house, tavern.

Schenkel *m.* (-s, -) thigh; shank; haunch; leg; side (of an angle). ~bruch *m.* fracture of the thigh.

schenk-en *v.t.* to give, present with; to grant; to remit; to forgive; to pour out; to retail, sell (liquor). ~er *m.* donor. ~ung *f.* donation, gift. ~ungsurkunde *f.* deed of gift.

Scherbe *f.* (-, -n) potsherd; fragment. ~ngericht *n.* ostracism.

Scher-e (je:-) *f.* (-e, -en) scissors; shears; clippers; claws (of crabs). ~enfernrohr *n.* stereotelescope. ~enschleifer *f.* knife-grinder. ~enschnitt *m.* silhouette. ~e'rei *f.* trouble, bother. ~messer *n.* razor.

scheren *v.t. st. & w.* to shear, clip; to mow; to shave; (*naut.*) to sheer; (*fig.*) to bother, disturb; *sich fort~* to be off, go away; *sich ~ um* to bother about, care for.

Scherflein *n.* (-s, -) mite; *sein ~ beitragen* to do one's bit.

Scherge *m.* (-n, -n) (*obs.*) constable; executioner; beadle.

Scherz (-ts) *m.* (-es, -e) joke, jest, pleasantry. ~en *v.i.* to joke, jest; to have fun (with); to make fun (of). ~haft *a.* joking, jocular; playful. ~name *m.* nickname. ~wort *n.* joke.

scheu (ʃoi) *a.* shy, timid, bashful; shying (horse). *subst. f.* shyness; awe; aversion. ~klappe *f.,* ~leder *n.* blinker. ~sal *n.* monster.

Scheuche *f.* (-, -n) scarecrow; bugbear.

scheuchen *v.t.* to scare, frighten away.

scheuen *v.t.* to avoid, shun; to spare (no pains). *v.i.* to shy, take fright. *v.r.* to be shy, hesitate; to be afraid (of).

Scheuer *f.* (-, -n) barn, shed.

Scheuer-besen *m.* scrubbing-brush. ~frau *f.* charwoman. ~lappen *m.* dish-cloth; scouring cloth. ~leiste *f.* skirting-board.

scheuern *v.t.* to clean, scour, scrub; to rub, chafe.

Scheune *f.* (-, -n) barn, shed.

scheußlich *a.* horrible, atrocious; ugly, hideous. ~keit *f.* atrocity, horrible deed; hideousness.

Schicht (ʃiçt) *f.* (-, -en) layer, stratum, course, bed; film, coat; class, rank; (working) shift. ~lohn *m.* shift wage. ~meister *m.* foreman; overseer. ~wechsel *m.* change of shift.

schichten *v.t.* to arrange in layers; to stratify; to pile, stack; to classify.

Schick m. (-es) elegance, taste. a. elegant, chic, smart.

schick-en v.t. to send, dispatch; to remit (money); ~en nach to send for, v.r. to happen, come to pass; to be becoming, be proper; sich ~en in to put up with, be resigned to. ~lich a. proper, decent. ~lichkeitsgefühl n. tact; sense of propriety. ~sal n. fate, destiny; fortune; lot. ~salhaft a. ordained by fate, fatal. ~salsschlag m. heavy blow; reverse. ~ung f. dispensation; Providence.

Schieb-efenster n. sash-window. ~er m. slide-rule; (tech.) slide; (fig.) profiteer. ~etür f. sliding door. ~karren m. wheelbarrow. ~ung f. (fig.) profiteering; back-stairs politics.

schieben v.t. st. to shove, push, slide, move; (fig.) to profiteer. ~ auf to lay the blame on.

schied imperf. of scheiden.

Schieds-gericht n. court of arbitration. ~richter m. umpire, referee, arbitrator. ~spruch m. award, arbitration, decision.

schief a. oblique, sloping; crooked; bent; wry; (fig.) false, wrong. adv. askew, awry; der ~e Turm the leaning tower; ~e Ebene inclined plane; ~ ansehen to frown upon; ~ gehen (fig.) to go wrong. ~blatt n. begonia. ~e f. slant; incline; sloping position. ~winklig a. oblique-angled.

Schiefer m. (-s, -) slate, schist; splinter. ~boden m. slaty soil. ~dach n. slate roof. ~decker m. slater. ~tafel f. (school-)slate.

schiefern v.r. to scale off.

schielen v.i. to squint; ~ nach to leer at.

schien imperf. of scheinen.

Schien-bein n. shin-bone. ~e f. rail; iron band (on wheel); splint. ~enleger m. plate-layer. ~ennetz n. railway system. ~enstrang m. railway track. ~enweite f. gauge.

schienen v.t. to put in splints.

schier (fi:r) a. sheer, pure. adv. almost, nearly.

Schierling m. (-s, -e) hemlock.

schiert 3rd pers. sing. pres. of scheren.

Schieß-baumwolle f. gun-cotton. ~bude f. shooting-gallery. ~gewehr n. gun. ~platz m. artillery range. ~prügel m. (colloq.) fire-arm. ~pulver n. gunpowder. ~scharte f. loophole, embrasure, fire-slit. ~scheibe f. practice target. ~stand m. rifle range; butts.

schießen v.t. & i. st. to fire, shoot; to score (goal); ~ lassen (colloq.) to give up. v.i.s.t. to rush along; to rush (to); to flash (through mind); to sweep (down on); to shoot up, spring up.

Schiff n. (-es, -e) ship, boat, vessel; nave (of church); shuttle; zu ~ on board; by ship. ~bar a. navigable. ~bruch m. ship-wreck. ~brüchig a. shipwrecked. ~chen n. small boat, skiff; shuttle. ~er m. sailor, seaman; skipper. ~erklavier n. accordion, concertina. ~(f)ahrt f. navigation. ~sbesatzung f. ship's crew. ~sbrücke f. bridge of boats, pontoon-bridge. ~shinterteil n. poop, stern. ~sjournal n. log (-book). ~sjunge m. cabin-boy. ~skörper m. hull. ~sladung f. cargo. ~smakler m. ship-broker. ~sraum m. hold; tonnage. ~staufe f. naming of a ship. ~swert f. wharf, dock-yard.

schiffen v.w.s.i. to sail. v.t. to ship (goods).

Schi'kan-e f. (-e, -en) vexation, annoyance; refinements (of luxury). ~ieren v.t. to annoy, irritate, torment.

Schild m. (-t) 1. m. (-es, -e) shield; escutcheon, coat-of-arms; auf den ~ heben to choose as leader; im ~e führen to have something up one's sleeve. 2. n. (-es, -er) notice-board; (door-)plate, name-plate; signboard; label; peak (of cap). ~drüse f. thyroid gland. ~erhaus n. sentry-box. ~knappe m. shield-bearer, squire. ~kröte f. tortoise. ~patt n. tortoiseshell. ~wache f. sentry.

schilder-n *v.t.* to describe, depict; to paint. **~ung** *f.* description.

Schilf *n.* (-es, -e) reed, rush; sedge. **~rohr** *n.* reed, reeds.

schillern *v.i.* to change colours.

schilt *3rd pers. sing. pres. of* **schelten**.

Schi'märe *f.* (-, -n) chimera.

Schimmel *m.* (-s, -) 1. mould, mildew. 2. white horse. **~ig** *a.* mouldy, musty. **~n** *v.i.* to turn mouldy. **~pilz** *m.* oidium, vine-mildew.

Schimmer *m.* (-s, -) glitter, glimmer, gleam. **~n** *v.i.* to glitter, glisten, shine.

Schim'panse *m.* (-n, -n) chimpanzee.

Schimpf *m.* (-es, -e) disgrace; affront, insult. **~en** *v.t. & i.* to abuse, revile; to scold; to grumble. **~lich** *a.* disgraceful, infamous. **~wort** *n.* invective, term of abuse.

Schindanger *m.* knacker's yard.

Schindel *f.* (-, -n) shingle, wooden tile. **~n** *v.t.* to roof with shingles.

schind-en *v.t. st.* to exploit; to skin, flay; (*fig.*) to try to get for nothing. **~.r.** to drudge, slave. **~er** *m.* knacker; sweater. **~e-'rei** *f.* (*fig.*) sweating; drudgery. **~luder** *n.* **~luder treiben mit** to treat badly. **~mähre** *f.* miserable hack.

Schinken *m.* (-s, -) ham.

Schinn *m.* (-es, -e) dandruff.

Schipp-e *f.* (-e, -en) spade; shovel. **~en** *v.t.* to shovel. **~er** *m.* soldier on fatigue-duty; sapper.

Schirm *m.* (-es, -e) umbrella; screen; shelter, protection. **~er,** **~herr** *m.* protector, patron. **~futteral** *n.* umbrella-case. **~mütze** *f.* peaked cap. **~ständer** *m.* umbrella-stand.

schirmen *v.t.* to screen; to protect, guard.

Schi'rokko *m.* (-s) sirocco.

schirren *v.t.* to harness.

Schisma *n.* (-s, Schismen) schism.

Schlacht *f.* (-, -en) battle, fight, engagement. **~bank** *f.* slaughter-house. **~beil** *n.* pole-axe. **~feld** *n.* battle-field. **~flieger** *m.* close-support fighter. **~haus** *n.*, **~hof**

m. slaughter-house. **~kreuzer** *m.* battle-cruiser. **~linie,** **~reihe** *f.* line of battle. **~opfer** *n.* sacrifice; victim. **~roß** *n.* charger. **~ruf** *m.* war-cry. **~schiff** *n.* battleship. **~vieh** *n.* fat stock.

schlachten *v.t.* to slaughter, kill; to butcher.

Schlächter *m.* (-s, -) butcher. **~ei** *f.* butcher's shop; (*fig.*) slaughter.

Schlack-e *f.* (-e, -en) slag; dross; dregs, scum. **~en** *v.i.* to slag, form slag. **~ig** *a.* slaggy.

Schlackwurst *f.* German sausage.

Schlaf (fla:-) *m.* (-es) sleep; *im ~ liegen* to be asleep. **~anzug** *m.* pyjamas, sleeping-suit. **~bursche** *m.* night-lodger. **~enszeit** *f.* bedtime. **~krankheit** *f.* sleeping-sickness. **~lied** *n.* lullaby. **~los** *a.* sleepless. **~losigkeit** *f.* insomnia. **~mittel** *n.* narcotic, drug, sleeping-pill. **~mütze** *f.* nightcap; (*fig.*) sleepyhead. **~mützig** *a.* sleepy, slow. **~rock** *m.* dressing-gown. **~saal** *m.* dormitory. **~sack** *m.* sleeping-bag. **~stelle** *f.* night's lodging. **~stube** *f.,* **~zimmer** *n.* bedroom. **~sucht** *f.* somnolence. **~trunk** *m.* sleeping-draught. **~trunken** *a.* overcome with sleep, very drowsy. **~wagen** *m.* sleeping-car, sleeper. **~wandeln** *vws.i.* to walk in one's sleep. **~wandler** *m.* sleep-walker.

Schläf-chen *n.* nap, forty winks, doze. **~er** *m.* sleeper. **~ern** *v. impers.* to feel sleepy. **~rig** *a.* sleepy, drowsy. **~rigkeit** *f.* drowsiness.

Schläfe *f.* (-, -n) temple.

schlafen (fla:-) *v.i. st.* to sleep; **~ gehen** to go to bed.

schlaff *a.* slack, loose, relaxed; limp, feeble, weak; (*fig.*) lax. **~heit** *f.* slackness; (*fig.*) laxity, indolence.

Schla'fittchen *n. am ~ nehmen* to collar (a person).

Schlag[1] (-k) *m.* (-es) race, kind, sort.

Schlag[2] (-k) *m.* (-es, -"e) beating, beat; blow, knock, punch; tap, thud; stroke, striking (of clock) clap (of thunder); (*electr.*) shock (*med.*) apoplectic fit, stroke; song (of birds); carriage-door; pigeon-loft, dovecot; copse; ~ *ein Uhr* sharp one (o'clock). ~ader *f.* artery. ~anfall, ~fluß *m.* stroke, apoplectic fit. ~artig *a.* sudden and violent; surprise (attack); prompt; (*mil.*) in sudden bursts. ~ball *m.* rounders. ~baum *m.* turnpike, barrier. ~bolzen *m.* striker, firing pin. ~er *m.* song-hit. ~fertig *a.* quick at repartee. ~fertigkeit *f.* quickness at repartee; (*mil.*) highest degree of tactical preparedness. ~instrument *n.* percussion instrument. ~kraft *f.* hitting-power, striking-force. ~licht *n.* strong light. ~obers *n.* (*dial.*) whipped cream. ~ring *m.* knuckle-duster; plectrum. ~sahne *f.* whipped cream, ~schatten *m.* cast shadow. ~seite *f.* (*naut.*) list. ~wärter *m.* toll-keeper. ~werk *n.* striking apparatus (of clock). ~wort *n.* catchword, slogan. ~wortkatalog *m.* subject-catalogue. ~zeile *f.* headline. ~zeug *n.* percussion instruments.

schlagen (-a:-) *v.t. st.* to beat, strike, hit; to knock, punch; to fell (tree); to build (bridge); to defeat; to coin (money); ~ *in* or *um* to wrap up. *v.i.* to strike; to throb, beat; to sing, warble; ~ *nach* (*fig.*) to take after. *v.r.* to fight; to fight a duel; *sich* ~ *zu* to side with; *eine geschlagene Stunde* a whole hour. ~d *a.* (*fig.*) striking, conclusive, convincing.

Schläger *m.* (-s, -) hitter, striker; tennis racket; sword, rapier; cricket-bat; golf club. ~ei *f.* fight, scuffle, brawl.

Schla'massel *m.* (-s) (*sl.*) scrape, mess. [HEBR.]

Schlamm *m.* (-es) mud, slime, ooze. ~ig *a.* muddy, slimy, oozy.

schlämm-en *v.t.* to clean, wash. ~kreide *f.* whitening.

Schlamp-e *f.* (-e, -en) slut, sloven, slattern. ~e'rei *f.* untidiness, disorder. (*sl.*) mess. ~ig *a.* slovenly, untidy.

schlang *imperf. of* schlingen.

Schlange *f.* (-, -n) serpent, snake; (*colloq.*) queue; ~ *stehen* to queue up. ~nbeschwörer *m.* snake charmer. ~nbiß *m.* snake-bite. ~nbohrer *m.* spiral drill. ~nlinie *f.* wavy line. ~nmensch *m.* contortionist. ~nwindung *f.* (*fig.*) meandering. ~nzüngig *a.* of spiteful or venomous tongue.

schlängeln *v.r.* to wind (in and out), meander.

schlank *a.* slim, slender. ~heit *f.* slimness, slenderness. ~weg *adv.* flatly, downright.

schlapp *a.* slack, limp, flabby; tired; ~ *machen* to collapse. ~e *f.* reverse; check; defeat; rebuff; blow. ~heit *f.* slackness, indolence. ~hut *m.* slouched hat. ~schwanz *m.* coward, weakling.

Schla'raffen-land *n.* Cockaigne, land of milk and honey. ~leben *n.* life of idleness and luxury.

schlau *a.* sly, cunning, crafty. ~berger, ~kopf, ~meier *m.* sly old fox. ~heit *f.* slyness, cunning.

Schlauch (-x) *m.* (-es, *=*e) hose; leather bottle; (rubber or metal) tube. ~boot *n.* rubber dinghy. ~en *v.t.* to hose; (*colloq.*) to overwork.

Schläue *f.* (-) slyness, cunning.

schlecht *a.* wicked, bad, ill; inferior, poor; wretched; hard (times); ~ *und recht* somehow, after a fashion; ~ *machen* to run down; ~ *werden* to go bad, turn sour; *mir ist* ~ I feel sick or ill. ~erdings *adv.* utterly; absolutely; by all means. ~gelaunt *a.* in a bad temper. ~hin, ~weg *adv.* simply, quite; absolutely. ~igkeit *f.* badness; wickedness. [SLIGHT]

schlecken *v.t. & i.* to lick; to like sweets.

Schlegel (*fle*:-) *m.* (-s, -) clapper (of bell); drumstick; gongstick; mallet, wooden hammer; club; leg (of veal, &c.).

Schleh-dorn *m.* blackthorn. ~e *f.* sloe, wild plum.

Schlei *m.* (-s, -e), ~e *f.* tench.

schleich-en (-ç-) *vws.i. st.* to creep; to slink, steal, prowl; *sich davon ~en* to steal away. **~end** *a.* creeping; furtive; lingering, slow. **~er** *m.* sneak. **~handel** *m.* smuggling; black market. **~weg** *m.* (*fig.*) secret or underhand means.

Schleier *m.* (-s, -) veil; haze; screen; (*mil.*) smoke-screen. **~eule** *f.* barn-owl. **~haft** *a.* mysterious, inexplicable.

Schleife *f.* (-, -n) loop; loop-line; knot; bow; bend, curve; chute, slide; sledge; (*av.*) looping.

schleifen¹ *vt.i. st.* to glide, slide; to pull, drag; to draggle, trail along; to slur (note); to demolish. [SLIP]

schleif-en² *v.t.i. st.* to sharpen, grind, polish; to cut (glass). **~er** *m.* grinder, polisher. **~lack** *m.* grinding-paste; enamel (varnish). **~lackmöbel** *n.pl.* enamelled furniture. **~stein** *m.* grindstone.

Schleim *m.* (-es) slime; phlegm, mucus. **~absonderung** *f.*, **~fluß** *m.* mucous secretion; expectoration; blennorrhoea. **~haut** *f.* mucous membrane. **~ig** *a.* slimy, mucous. **~suppe** *f.* gruel.

schleißen *v.t. st.* to tear, split. *v.t.* to wear out.

schlemm-en *v.i.* to feast; to guzzle. **~er** *m.* gourmand; gourmet. **~e'rei** *f.* feasting; gluttony.

schlend-ern *vws.i. st.* to stroll, saunter. **~rian** *m.* old humdrum way, drift.

schlenkern *v.t. & i.* to swing, dangle; to fling.

Schlepp-dienst *m.* car-tow. **~e** *f.* train (of dress). **~er** *m.* tug(boat); tractor; drag; tout. **~kleid** *n.* dress with a train. **~tau** *n.* hawser; tow-line or -rope. **~zug** *m.* train of barges.

schleppen *v.t. & i.* to carry, lug; to tow; to drag, trail (dress); to tout. **~d** *a.* slow; shuffling; drawling.

Schleuder *f.* (-, -n) sling, catapult; (cream) separator; extractor; centrifugal machine. **~honig** *m.* strained honey. **~preis** *m.* *zu ~preisen* dirt-cheap. **~waren**

f.pl. bargain articles.

schleudern *v.t.* to throw, hurl, fling, toss; to undersell. *v.i.* to skid; (*of ship*) to roll; (*av.*) to catapult.

schleunig (-ç) *a.* quick, speedy, swift, prompt. **~st** *adv.* as quickly as possible; in all haste.

Schleuse *f.* (-, -n) sluice, lock. **~nmeister** *m.*, **~nwärter** *m.* lockkeeper. **~ntor** *n.* lock-gate, flood-gate.

schlich¹ *imperf. of* schleichen.

Schlich² (-ç) *m.* (-es, -e) trick, dodge.

schlicht (-çt) *a.* simple; plain; smooth; sleek; modest, unpretentious; **~er Abschied** dismissal. **~en** *v.t.* to make even, smooth; to dress (yarn); to arrange, adjust, put right, settle. **~er** *m.* mediator, arbitrator. **~heit** *f.* simplicity, plainness; modesty. **~ung** *f.* arrangement, settlement.

Schlick *m.* (-es, -e) mud, slime.

schlief *imperf. of* schlafen.

Schließ-e *f.* (-e, -en) clasp, fastening. **~er** *m.* doorkeeper; turnkey (in prison). **~fach** *n.* locker; safe; post office box. P.O. box. **~feder** *f.* breech-closing spring. **~ung** *f.* closing, close; breaking-up (of meeting, &c.).

schließen *v.t. & i. st.* to shut, close; to lock, bolt; to finish, conclude, stop, end; to break up; to infer (from); to judge (by); *in die Arme ~* to embrace; *in sich ~* to include, imply, involve.

schließlich (-ç) *a.* final; conclusive. *adv.* finally; after all, in the long run, eventually.

Schliff¹ *m.* (-es, -e) cut (of glass); (*fig.*) good manners; (*mil.*) rigid training; hard drill.

schliff² *imperf. of* schleifen.

schlimm *a.* bad; ill, sick; sore; serious; nasty; evil. **~stenfalls** *adv.* if the worst comes to the worst.

Schling-e *f.* (-e, -en) (running) knot, loop, noose; sling; snare; *sich aus der ~e ziehen* to get out of a difficulty. **~gewächs** *n.* creeper, climbing plant.

Schlingel *m.* (-s, -) rascal, naughty boy.

schlingen[1] *v.t. & r. st.* to tie; to wind, twist, twine round.

schlingen[2] *v.t. & st.* to swallow, devour.

schlingern *v.i. (of ship)* to roll.

Schlips *m.* (-es, -e) (neck-)tie, cravat.

Schlitten *m.* (-s, -) sledge, sled, sleigh; toboggan. **~fahrt** *f.* sledge-ride, drive in a sledge. **~kufe** *f.* sledge runner.

schlittern *v.i.* to slide.

Schlittschuh *m.* skate; **~ laufen** to skate. **~läufer** *m.* skater.

Schlitz *m.* (-es, -e) slit; slot; split. **~augen** *n.pl.* slits (of eyes). **~äugig** *a.* almond-eyed. **~en** *v.t.* to slit, slash.

schlohweiß *a.* snow-white.

schloß[1] *imperf. of* schließen.

Schloß[2] *n.* (Schlosses, -̈er) castle, palace; lock; clasp (of necklet); *ins ~ fallen (of door)* to close; to snap to. **~freiheit** *f.* precincts of castle. **~hof** *m.* castle-yard, courtyard. [SLOT]

Schloße *f.* (-, -n) hailstone.

Schlosser *m.* (-s, -) locksmith; fitter, mechanic. **~ei** *f.* locksmith's trade *or* workshop. **~n** *v.i.* to tinker, forge, hammer (at).

Schlot (-o:-) *m.* (-es, -e) chimney, flue. **~feger** *m.* (chimney-)sweep.

schlottern *v.i.* to shake, tremble, wobble; to hang loosely. **~erig** *a.* tottery, wobbly, shaky.

Schlucht (-uxt) *f.* (-, -en) ravine, gorge, gully; glen.

schluchzen (ʃluxtsən) *v.i.* to sob.

Schluck *m.* (-es, -e) gulp, draught. **~en** *v.t. & i.* to gulp, swallow. **~en** *m.*, **~auf** *m.* hiccup. **~er** *m. armer* **~er** poor wretch.

schludrig *a.* botched.

schlug *imperf. of* schlagen.

Schlummer *m.* (-s) slumber. **~lied** *n.* lullaby. **~n** *v.i.* to slumber. **~rolle** *f.* small bolster, cushion (for neck).

Schlumpe *f.* (-e, -en) slattern, slut, sloven. **~ig** *a.* slovenly.

Schlund (-t) *m.* (-es, -̈e) gullet, throat; abyss.

schlüpf-en *vws.i.* to slip, slide. **~er** *m.* knickers. **~rig** *a.* slippery; *(fig.)* obscene, indecent. **~rigkeit** *f.* slipperiness; obscenity.

Schlupf-loch *n.* hiding-place; loophole. **~winkel** *m.* hiding-place, refuge.

schlürfen *v.t.* to sip; to drink (in). *vws.i.* to shuffle.

Schluß *m.* (Schluss-es, -̈e) shutting, closing, upshot; close, end, conclusion; deduction, inference. **~akt** *m.* last act. **~formel** *f.* close, closing phrase, complimentary ending (of letter). **~licht** *n.* tail-light. **~notierung** *f.* final quotation. **~runde** *f.* final round. **~satz** *m.* conclusion, final proposition; *(phil.)* consequent; *(mus.)* finale. **~stein** *m.* keystone. **~vignette** *f.* tail-piece. **~wort** *n.* last word; summary.

Schlüssel (-y-) *m.* (-s, -) key; spanner; code, cipher; *(mus.)* clef. **~bart** *m.* key-bit. **~bein** *n.* collar-bone. **~blume** *f.* cowslip. **~bund** *n.* bunch of keys. **~loch** *n.* keyhole. **~stellung** *f.* key position. **~wort** *n.* key-word, code word.

schlüssig (-ic) *a.* sure, decided, resolved; logical; *sich ~ werden* to decide, make up one's mind.

Schmach (-a:x) *f.* (-) disgrace; dishonour; humiliation. **~voll** *a.* disgraceful; humiliating.

schmachten (-ax-) *v.i.* to languish, pine, long (for).

schmächtig (-ectic) *a.* delicate; slim, slight. **~keit** *f.* delicate health; slimness.

schmackhaft *a.* tasty, savoury, appetizing. **~igkeit** *f.* savouriness.

schmäh-en *v.t.* to abuse; to slander, insult. **~lich** *a.* disgraceful, ignominious, humiliating. **~schrift** *f.* libel; lampoon. **~sucht** *f.* love of slander. **~ung** *f.* defamation, slander; abuse.

schmal (-a:-) *a.* narrow; thin, slender, slim; scanty, poor, meagre. **~film** *m.* 8-mm. film. **~hans** *m. hier ist* **~hans** *Küchenmeister* they are on short commons.

~heit *f.* narrowness; scantiness.
~spur *f.* narrow gauge. ~spurig
a. narrow-gauged. [SMALL]

schmälen (-ɛ:-) *v.i. & t.* to scold;
to abuse.

schmälern (-ɛ:-) *v.t.* to lessen, diminish; to belittle, detract from.

Schmalz (-ts) *n.* (-es) dripping,
lard. ~en *v.t.* to put dripping
or lard into. ~ig *a.* greasy;
(*fig.*) sentimental.

schma'rotz-en *v.i.* to sponge on.
~er *m.* sponger; parasite. ~-
erisch *a.* parasitic(al). ~ertum
n. parasitism.

Schmarr(e)n *m.* (*colloq.*) trash;
(*of book*) shocker.

schmatzen *v.i.* to smack (the lips);
to give a hearty kiss.

schmauchen *v.t. & i.* to smoke,
puff at a pipe.

Schmaus (-s) *m.* (-es, ⁼e) feast,
banquet. ~en *v.i.* to feast.
~e'rei *f.* feasting, banquet.

schmecken *v.t.* to try; to taste.
v.i. to taste nice *or* good; ~
nach to taste of; *wie schmeckt es
dir?* do you like it? are you enjoying it?

Schmeiche'lei *f.* (-, -en) flattery;
adulation; coaxing.

schmeichel-haft *a.* flattering. ~
katze *f.* wheedler.

schmeich-eln *v.i.* to flatter, fawn
upon; to caress, fondle. ~ler
m. flatterer, wheedler. ~lerisch
a. flattering, fawning, wheedling.

schmeißen *v.t. st.* to throw, fling,
hurl.

Schmeißfliege *f.* bluebottle, blow-
fly.

Schmelz (-ts) *m.* (-es, -e) enamel,
glaze; (*fig.*) bloom. ~bar *a.*
fusible, meltable. ~e *f.* melting; melt. ~farbe *f.* enamel
colour. ~hütte *f.* foundry; smelting works. ~ofen *m.* (melting)
furnace. ~punkt *m.* melting-
point. ~sicherung *f.* (*electr.*)
safety fuse. ~tiegel *m.* crucible.

schmelzen *v.t. & i. st.* to melt,
fuse; to smelt; to diminish,
melt away; (*of heart*) to soften.
~d *a.* (*fig.*) melting (glance);
sweet (sound).

Schmerbauch *m.* paunch; (*colloq.*)

corporation.

Schmerle *f.* (-, -n) loach.

Schmerz (-ts) *m.* (-es, -en) pain,
ache, smart; grief, sorrow. ~-
ensgeld *n.* smart-money, compensation. ~enslager *n.* bed of
pain *or* suffering. ~erfüllt *a.*
deeply afflicted. ~haft *a.* painful. ~lich *a.* grievous, painful,
sad. ~los *a.* painless. ~stillend
a. assuaging pain, soothing,
anodyne. [SMART]

schmerzen *v.t. & i.* to hurt, pain,
grieve, afflict.

Schmetterling *m.* (-s, -e) butterfly. ~sblütler *m.pl.* papiliona-
ceous flowers.

schmettern *v.t.* to smash, throw
down. *v.t. & i.* to blare; to warble; to thunder.

Schmied (-t) *m.* (-es, -e) (black-)
smith. ~e *f.* smithy, forge. ~e-
eisen *n.* wrought iron. ~eeisern
a. wrought-iron. ~ehammer *m.*
sledge-hammer.

schmieden *v.t.* to forge, hammer,
strike; to put in irons; (*fig.*) to
plan, scheme, hatch (plot); to
concoct, fabricate.

schmieg-en *v.t.* to bend. *v.r.* to
creep close (to), nestle (against),
cling (to); to twine (round).
~sam *a.* flexible, supple, pliant;
submissive. ~samkeit *f.* flexibility, pliancy.

Schmier-e¹ *f.* (-e) grease; oil;
(*colloq.*) low music-hall; (*sl.*) gaff.
~fink *m.* dirty fellow. ~geld *n.*
tip, bribe. ~ig *a.* greasy; dirty;
(*fig.*) mean, sordid. ~mittel *n.*
lubricant. ~öl *n.* lubricating oil.
~plan *m.* lubrication chart. ~
seife *f.* soft soap.

Schmiere² *f.* ~ *stehen* (*sl.*) to keep
or cave cave. [HEBR.]

schmieren *v.t. & i.* to grease, oil,
lubricate; to smear; to spread
(butter, &c.); to scrawl; to
daub; (*fig.*) to bribe.

schmilzt *3rd pers. sing. pres. of*
schmelzen.

Schmink-dose *f.* rouge-pot. ~e
f. rouge; paint; make-up. ~en
v.t. & r. to rouge, paint the face;
to make up.

Schmirgel *m.* (-s) emery.

Schmiß¹ m. (Schmiss-es, -e) stroke, blow; cut, lash; scar; (fig.) verve, dash, go.

schmiß² imperf. of **schmeißen**.

Schmöker m. (-s, -) old book; trashy book, light novel. **~n** v.i. to read a trashy book; to pore over a book.

schmollen v.i. to pout, be sulky.

Schmollis n. ~ trinken to hobnob (with a person).

schmolz imperf. of **schmelzen**.

Schmorbraten m. stewed steak.

schmoren (-o:-) v.t. & i. to stew.

Schmu m. (colloq.) ~ machen to swindle. [HEBR.]

Schmuck (-u-) m. (-es, -e) ornament, decoration; jewels, jewellery, a, smart, trim; handsome. **~kasten** m. jewel-box. **~los** a. plain, unadorned. **~sachen** f.pl. jewels. **~stück** n. piece of jewellery. **~waren** f.pl. jewellery.

schmücken (-y-) v.t. to adorn, decorate, trim, ornament; to embellish.

Schmuggel m. (-els) smuggling. **~eln** v.t. to smuggle. **~ler** m. smuggler.

schmunzeln v.i. to grin. subst. n. broad smile.

Schmus m. (sl.) cheap talk, soft soap. **~en** v.i. to flatter; to prattle. [HEBR.]

Schmutz m. (-es) dirt, filth, mud. **~blech** n. mudguard. **~fink** m. dirty fellow. **~fleck** m. spot, stain. **~ig** a. dirty, filthy, soiled; (fig.) low, mean, shabby. **~igkeit** f. dirtiness. **~presse** f. gutter press. **~titel** m. (typ.) bastard-title.

schmutzen v.t. & i. to dirty, soil; to get dirty.

Schnabel m. (-s, ‑̈) bill, beak; prow, nose; spout; (colloq.) mouth. **~schuhe** m.pl. pointed shoes. **~tier** n. duck-bill, platypus.

schnäbeln v.r. to bill and coo.

Schnack m. (-es) chatter, gossip. **~en** v.t. & i. to chatter, gossip.

Schnaderhüpfel n. Austrian and Bavarian folk-song.

Schnake¹ f. (-, -n) joke, jest.

Schnake² (-a:-) f. (-, -n) midge.

~nstich m. midge-bite.

Schnalle f. (-, -n) buckle. **~n** v.t. to buckle, fasten, strap up.

~schuh m. shoe with a buckle.

schnalzen (-ts-) v.i. to click one's tongue; to snap one's fingers.

schnapp-en v.i. to gasp, snatch (at); to snap to; nach Luft **~en** to gasp for breath. **~hahn** m. highwayman. **~sack** m. knapsack. **~schloß** n. spring-lock.

Schnäpper m. (-s, -) lancet; catch.

Schnaps m. (-es, ‑̈e) gin, brandy, spirits. **~en** v.i. to tipple.

schnarchen (-arç-) v.i. to snore.

schnarren v.i. to rattle, rasp, jar.

schnatter-haft a. chattering, gabbling. **~n** v.i. to cackle; to chatter, gabble.

schnauben v.i. w. & st. to puff, snort; Rache ~ to breathe vengeance; Wut ~ to foam with rage. v.r. to blow one's nose.

schnaufen v.i. to breathe heavily; to pant.

Schnauz-bart m. moustache. **~bärtig** a. with a moustache. **~e** f. snout; spout; nozzle; (vulg.) jaw. **~en** v.i. to shout (at).

Schnecke f. (-, -n) snail, slug; volute; (anat.) cochlea; spiral, helix. **~nförmig** a. spiral. **~nhaus** n. snail-shell. **~ntempo** n. (fig.) snail's pace.

Schnee (-e:) m. (-s) snow; whipped eggs. **~ball** m. snowball; (bot.) guelder rose. **~ballen** v.t. to snowball. **~brille** f. snow-goggles. **~fall** m. snowfall. **~flocke** f. snowflake. **~glöckchen** n. snowdrop. **~grenze** f. snow-line. **~huhn** n. ptarmigan. **~ig** a. snowy, snow-covered. **~kette** f. (motor.) non-skid chain. **~schläger** m. whisk. **~schuh** m. snowshoe; ski. **~treiben** n. blizzard, heavy snowfall. **~wächte** f. snowdrift. **~wehe** f. snow cornice, snowdrift. **~weiß** a. snow-white. **~wittchen** n. Snow White.

Schneid (-t) m. & f. energy, dash, pluck, spunk. **~ig** a. energetic, dashing; smart.

Schneide f. (-, -n) edge, bit,

blade; *auf des Messers* ~ at a very critical juncture. ~**zahn** *m.* incisor.

schneiden *v.t. st.* to cut, carve; to mow; to trim; to inter-sect, meet; (*fig.*) to be mistaken. ~**d** *a.* (*fig.*) sharp; bitter; bit-ing.

Schneider *m.* (-s, -) tailor. ~**in** *f.* tailoress, dressmaker, cutter. ~**n** *v.i. & t.* to do tailoring or dress-making; to make. ~**puppe** *f.* dummy.

schneien (*ſnaien*) *v.i.* to snow.

Schneise *f.* (-, -n) (forest) aisle, vista; (*av.*) flying lane.

schnell *a.* quick, swift, speedy, fast, rapid; sudden; prompt; mobile. ~**boot** *n.* E-boat; M.T.B. ~**hefter** *m.* rapid letter-file. ~**igkeit** *f.* swiftness, speed, rapidity, velocity. ~**kraft** *f.* elasticity. ~**presse** *f.* steam-press. ~**verfahren** *n.* (*leg.*) summary juris-diction. ~**waage** *f.* steelyard. ~**zug** *m.* express train.

schnellen *v.t.* to let fly, fling; to jerk, dart; to flick, fillip. *vos.i.* to spring, snap, jerk.

Schnepfe *f.* (-, -n) snipe. ~**nstrich** *m.* flight of snipe.

Schneppe *f.* (-, -n) spout; nozzle; peak (of cap).

schneuzen (-*ts-*) *v.r.* to blow one's nose.

Schnickschnack *m.* tittle-tattle.

schniegeln *v.r.* to dress up.

Schnippchen *n. ein* ~ *schlagen* to play a trick on.

Schnipp-el, ~**sel** *m.* (-sels, -sel) bit, scrap, shred. ~**eln**, ~**seln** *v.t.* to cut up.

schnippisch *a.* pert, saucy, im-pertinent.

schnitt[1] *imperf. of* **schneiden**.

Schnitt[2] *m.* (-es, -e) cut; cutting; intersection; section; incision; crop, harvest; shape, contour (of face); edge(s) (of book); fashion; pattern; (*colloq.*) profit; *der goldene* ~ medial section. ~**blumen** *f.pl.* cut flowers. ~**bohne** *f.* French bean. ~**e** *f.* slice (of bread). ~**er** *m.*, ~**erin** *f.* reaper, mower, harvester. ~**fläche** sec-tional area, section. ~**ig** *a.*

smart. ~**kante** *f.* cutting edge. ~**kurve** *f.* intersecting curve. ~**lauch** *m.* chive. ~**linie** *f.* secant. ~**muster** *n.* pattern. ~**punkt** *m.* point of intersection. ~**waren** *f.pl.* haberdashery. ~**wunde** *f.* cut, gash.

Schnitz-arbeit, ~**erei** *f.*, ~**werk** *n.* wood-carving. ~**bank** *f.* cooper's bench. ~**en** *v.t.* to carve, cut (in wood). ~**er** *m.* carver; (*fig.*) blunder.

Schnitzel *n.* (-s, -) chip; (scrap of paper); (*pl.*) parings, shavings; (*cook.*) fillet, cutlet. ~**jagd** *f.* paper-chase. ~**n** *v.t. & i.* to cut, cut up, chip.

schnob *imperf. of* **schnauben**.

schnodderig *a.* pert, cheeky, inso-lent.

schnöde *a.* base, mean; vile; scorn-ful, disdainful.

Schnorchel *m.* snort.

Schnörkel *m.* (-s, -) flourish; (*archit.*) scroll. ~**haft** *a.* full of flourishes; overloaded with orna-ments; (*fig.*) whimsical, capri-cious.

schnorr-en *v.i.* (*sl.*) to cadge. ~**er** *m.* cadger.

schnüff-eln *v.i.* to sniff; (*fig.*) to snoop (around). ~**ler** *m.* spy.

schnull-en *v.i.* to suck. ~**er** *m.* dummy, teat.

Schnupfen[1] *m.* (-s, -) cold in the head, catarrh.

schnupf-en[2] *v.t. & i.* to take snuff. ~**tabak** *m.* snuff. ~**tuch** *n.* handkerchief.

Schnuppe 1. *f.* (-, -n) snuff (of can-dle); shooting star. 2. (*indecl.*) *das ist mir* ~ it is all the same to me; I don't care tuppence.

schnuppern *v.i.* to sniff, nose, smell out.

Schnur (-u:-) *f.* (-, ¨-e) string; cord; flex; *über die* ~ *hauen* to kick over the traces. ~**gerade** *a.* (as) straight as a die. ~**stracks** *adv.* straight; immediately, at once.

Schnür-band *n.* lace (for corset, &c.). ~**boden** *m.* (*theatr.*) grid-iron. ~**chen** *n. wie am* ~**chen** like clock-work. ~**leib** *m.* corset. ~**loch** *n.* eyelet. ~**schuh** *m.* lace-

up shoe. ~senkel m. bootlace.
~stiefel m. lace-up boot.

schnüren v.t. to tie up, tie with
string, cord; to lace, fasten with
a lace. v.r. to tight-lace.

Schnurr-bart m. moustache. ~e
f. jest, joke; funny story. ~en
v.i. to hum, buzz; (of cat) to purr.
~ig a. droll, funny; queer.

Schnute f. (-, -n) snout, nose;
(colloq.) mouth.

schob imperf. of schieben.

Schober (-o:-) m. (-s, -) stack,
rick; barn.

Schock¹ n. threescore.

Schock² m. (-s, -s) shock.

schofel a. shabby, mean. [HEBR.]

Schöffe m. (-n, -n) juror.

Schoko'lade (-la:də) f. (-, -n) chocolate. ~ntafel f. slab or cake of
chocolate.

Scho'lastik f. (-) scholasticism.

Scholl-e f. (-e, -en) 1. clod, sod,
lump; (fig.) land, soil; floe (of
ice). 2. plaice. ~ig a. lumpy,
heavy (soil).

schon (ʃo:n) adv. & part. already;
by this time, so far, as yet; as
early as; the very, even; indeed,
it is true, certainly.

schön (ʃøːn) a. beautiful, lovely,
fair; handsome; fine, noble;
great, considerable; good, sound,
proper; (as answer) certainly,
very well; ~en Dank many
thanks; die ~en Künste the fine
arts; die ~e Literatur belles-
lettres; ~ machen (of dog) to
beg; sich ~ machen to smarten
oneself up, titivate; ~ tun to
coquet, flirt; das wäre noch ~
er! certainly not. ~färberei f.
heightening, colouring. ~geist
m. wit, bel esprit; aesthete.
~geistig a. aesthetic, aesthetical.
~heit f. beauty. ~heitsfehler m.
flaw, disfigurement. ~heitsmittel
n. cosmetic. ~heitspfläscherchen
n. beauty-patch. ~heitspflege f.
beauty treatment. ~redner m.
spouter, speechifier. ~schrift f.
calligraphy. [SHEEN]

schon-en (-o:-) v.t. to spare, save;
to take care of. v.r. to look after
oneself. ~end a. careful; considerate. ~ung f. forbearance,

indulgence; mercy; consideration; nursery for young trees.
~ungsbedürftig a. needing a rest.
~ungslos a. unsparing, pitiless,
relentless. ~zeit f. close season.

Schoner¹ m. (-s, -) schooner.

Schoner² m. (-s, -) antimacassar.

Schopf m. (-es, ⁻e) crown, top (of
the head); tuft, forelock.

Schöpf-brunnen m. draw-well.
~eimer m. bucket. ~er m.
creator. ~erisch a. creative. ~er-
kraft f. creative power. ~kelle
f. ladle. ~löffel m. (bailing-)
scoop, bailer, skimmer, strainer;
ladle. ~rad n. bucket-wheel.
~ung f. creation. ~werk n.
water-engine.

schöpfen v.t. to draw (water); to
scoop (out), ladle; to take
(courage); to draw in (breath);
to conceive (suspicion).

Schoppen m. (-s, -) about half a
pint (of beer, &c.).

Schöps m. wether; (fig.) simpleton.

schor imperf. of scheren.

Schort m. (-es, -e) scab, scurf.

Schornstein m. chimney; funnel
(of steamer, &c.). ~feger m.
chimney-sweep.

schoß¹ imperf. of schießen.

Schoß² (ʃos) m. (Schoss-es, -e) sprig,
shoot.

Schoß³ (ʃo:s) m. (-es, ⁻e) lap;
womb; (fig.) bosom; coat-tail.
~hund m. lap-dog. ~kind n.
pet, darling. [SHEET]

Schößling m. (-s, -e) sprig, shoot.

Schote¹ (-o:-) f. (-, -n) pod, shell,
husk; (pl.) peas.

Schote² f. (-, -n) (naut.) sheet.

Schott n., ~e f. bulkhead.

Schotter m. (-s, -) gravel; road-
metal; (rail.) ballast. ~n v.t.
to metal; to macadamize.

schra'ffieren v.t. to hatch. ~ur
f. hatching, hachures.

schräg a. oblique, slanting, sloping,
transversal, diagonal. ~e f.
slant, slope, bevel; obliquity.
~über adv. across, nearly opposite.

schrak imperf. of schrecken.

Schramm-e f. (-e, -en) scratch,
abrasion, scar. ~en v.t. to

scratch; to graze. **~ig** *a.* scratched.

Schrank *m.* (-es, ⸗e) press, cupboard; wardrobe. **~koffer** *m.* wardrobe trunk.

Schranke *f.* (-, -n) fencing-in, enclosure; railway gate, barrier; toll-bar, turnpike; (*fig.*) limit, bound(s); (*pl.*) lists; *in die ~n fordern* to challenge; *sich in ~n halten* to keep within bounds, restrain oneself. **~nlos** *a.* boundless; unbridled, unrestrained. **~nwärter** *m.* gate-keeper, signalman.

Schranne *f.* (-, -n) shambles; corn-exchange.

Schranze *f.* (-, -n) servile courtier, toady.

Schrap′nell *n.* (-s, -e) shrapnel.

schrappen *v.t. & i.* to scrape.

Schrat *m.* (-es, -e) satyr, faun.

Schraube *f.* (-, -n) screw; propeller; air-screw. **~n** *v.t.* to screw; to turn, twist, wind, spiral. **~ndampfer** *m.* screw-steamer. **~nfeder** *f.* helical spring, coil spring. **~nflugzeug** *n.* helicopter, autogiro. **~nförmig** *a.* screw-shaped, spiral. **~ngang** *m.*, **~ngewinde** *n.* screw-thread. **~nmutter** *f.* nut. **~nschlüssel** *m.* spanner, wrench. **~nzieher** *m.* screwdriver.

Schraubstock *m.* (hand) vice.

Schrebergarten *m.* allotment (garden).

Schreck **~en¹** *m.* (-ens, -en) fright, terror, fear, dread; horror; *in ~en setzen* to terrify. **~ensherrschaft** *f.* reign of terror. **~gespenst** *n.* terrible vision; bogy, bugbear. **~haft** *a.* timid, easily frightened. **~lich** *a.* terrible, dreadful, awful, frightful, horrible. **~schuß** *m.* shot fired in the air; (*fig.*) false alarm.

schrecken² *v.t.* to frighten.

Schrei *m.* (-es, -e) cry, shout, yell, howl, shriek, scream.

schreib-en *v.t. & i. st.* to write; to spell; *Maschine ~en* to type. *subst. n.* writing; letter, note, communication. **~er** *m.* writer; clerk. **~e′rei** *f.* writing; scribbling; correspondence; clerical

work. **~faul** *a.* lazy about writing. **~feder** *f.* pen; nib. **~fehler** *m.* slip of the pen. **~kraft** *f.* typist. **~mappe** *f.* writing-case, blotter, portfolio. **~maschine** *f.* typewriter. **~papier** *n.* notepaper. **~stube** *f.* (*mil.*) orderly room; office. **~tisch** *m.* writing-table. **~unterlage** *f.* writing-pad, blotting-pad. **~waren** *f.pl.* writing materials, stationery. **~warenhändler** *m.* stationer. **~weise** *f.* style. **~zeug** *n.* pen and ink.

schrei-en *v.i. & t. st.* to scream, cry out, shriek, squall, bawl, howl. **~er** *m.* bawler, shouter; cry-baby, noisy brat. **~end** *a.* (*fig.*) glaring, gaudy, loud.

Schrein *m.* (-es, -e) shrine. **~er** *m.* joiner, carpenter. **~e′rei** *f.* joiner's workshop. **~ern** *v.t.* to do joiner's work.

schreiten *vws.i. st.* to stride, stalk; to proceed (to a thing), set about (doing something).

schrie *imperf.* of **schreien**.

schrieb *imperf.* of **schreiben**.

Schrift *f.* (-, -en) writing; handwriting; fount; type; paper, pamphlet, publication, work; *die Heilige ~* The Holy Scriptures. **~band** *n.* scroll. **~bild** *n.* (*typ.*) face; setting. **~deutsch** *n.* literary German. **~führer** *m.* secretary. **~gelehrte(r)** *m.* (*bibl.*) scribe. **~gießerei** *f.* type-foundry. **~grad** *m.* size of letters. **~leiter** *m.* editor. **~leitung** *f.* editorship; editors; newspaper-office. **~lich** *a.* written, in writing; by letter. **~material** *n.* stock of types. **~probe** *f.* specimen of writing *or* of type. **~satz** *m.* composition. **~setzer** *m.* compositor, type-setter. **~sprache** *f.* written *or* literary language. **~steller** *m.* author, writer. **~stellerisch** *a.* literary. **~stellern** *v.i.* to write, do literary work. **~stück** *n.* document. **~tum** *n.* literature. **~wart** *m.* secretary. **~wechsel** *m.* correspondence. **~zeichen** *n.* character, letter. **~zug** *m.* character;

handwriting.

schrill a. shrill. **~en** v.i. to sound or ring shrilly.

Schrippe f. (-, -n) French roll.

schritt[1] imperf. of **schreiten**.

Schritt m. (-es, -e) step, stride, pace; gait, walk; **~ für ~** step by step; **~ halten** to keep pace (with); (fig.) to keep abreast (with); **auf ~ und Tritt** everywhere; all the time; **~ fahren!** dead slow. **~macher** m. pacemaker; pacer. **~weise** adv. step by step. **~zähler** m. pedometer.

schroff a. steep, precipitous; (fig.) rough, gruff; abrupt. **~heit** f. steepness; roughness; bluntness.

schröpfen v.t. to bleed, cup; (fig.) to fleece.

Schrot (-o:-) m. & n. (-es, -e) small shot; crushed grain; weight of coin; von altem **~ und Korn** of the good old type. **~brot** n. wholemeal bread. **~flinte** f. shotgun, fowling-piece. **~korn** n. groats. **~leiter** f. cart-ladder. **~säge** f. pit-saw, great saw.

schroten v.t. to grind small, bruise (corn); to roll down, lower (casks); (naut.) to parbuckle.

Schrott m. (-es) scrap(-iron).

schrubb-en v.t. & i. to scrub. **~er** m. scrubber, scrubbing-brush.

Schrull-e f. (-e, -en) whim, fad, crotchet. **~enhaft**, **~ig** aa. whimsical.

schrump-eln vws.i. to shrink, shrivel. **~lig** a. crumpled, creased; wrinkled.

schrumpf-en vws.i. to shrink, contract, shrivel. **~niere** f. atrophy of kidney. **~ung** f. shrinking, contraction; (med.) stricture.

Schrund m. (-es, **~e**) crack, chink, crevice.

Schub (-p) m. (-es, **~e**) shove, push, thrust; heap; batch. **~er** m. case. **~fach** n., **~lade** f. drawer. **~karren** m. wheelbarrow.

schüchtern (-yç-) a. shy, bashful. **~heit** f. shyness, bashfulness.

schuf imperf. of **schaffen**.

Schuft m. (-es, -e) scoundrel, scamp. **~en** v.i. (colloq.) to drudge, slave. **~ig** a. base,

mean, vile.

Schuh (ʃu:) m. (-es, -e) shoe; boot; foot (of measure); einem etwas in die **~e schieben** to put the blame on someone. **~anzieher** m. shoehorn. **~band** n. bootlace. **~flicker** m. cobbler. **~krem** f. shoe-cream. **~macher** m. shoemaker. **~plattler** m. Bavarian folk-dance. **~putzer** m. shoeblack, shoe-shiner. **~riemen** m. latchet; lace. **~sohle** f. sole. **~spanner** m. boot-tree. **~waren** f.pl. boots and shoes. **~werk**, **~zeug** n. footwear, boots and shoes. **~wichse** f. boot polish.

Schul-arbeit f. lesson; home-work. **~bank** f. form, bench. **~beispiel** n. (fig.) test-case. **~besuch** m. attendance at school. **~bildung** f. schooling, education. **~diener** m. porter, janitor. **~entlassen** a. having left school. **~ferien** pl. school holidays. **~frei** a. having a holiday. **~freund** m. school friend or chum. **~fuchserei** f. pedantry. **~funk** m. schoolbroadcasts. **~geld** n. fees. **~mappe** f. school-bag, satchel. **~meister** m. schoolmaster, teacher. **~meistern** v.t. & i. to teach; to censure. **~pflichtig** a. of school age; bound to attend school. **~rat** m. inspector of schools. **~reiter** m. manège rider. **~schiff** n. training-ship. **~schluß** m. break-up. **~speisung** f. schoolmeals. **~stunde** f. lesson, period. **~vorsteher** m. headmaster. **~wesen** n. public instruction, system of education; school affairs. **~zeugnis** n. school report; certificate. See also **Schule.**

Schuld (-t) f. (-, -en) obligation; debt; cause, fault, blame; offence, sin, guilt; **~en machen** to run into debt; **~ sein to** be to blame (for); **~ geben** to accuse, blame; in jemandes **~ stehen** to be in someone's debt, to be under an obligation to someone. **~bewußt** a. conscious of guilt. **~brief** m. bond, promissory note. **~buch** n. account book, ledger. **~enhalber** adv. owing to debts.

~enmacher m. contractor of debts. **~forderung** f. claim, demand. **~gefängnis** n. debtor's prison. **~haft** f. imprisonment for debt. **~los** a. innocent. **~ner** m. debtor. **~schein** m., **~verschreibung** f. bond; promissory note.

schulden v.t. to owe.

schuldig a. owing; due; obliged, bound; guilty; *Geld ~ sein* to owe money; *Dank ~ sein* to be (greatly) indebted (to); *keine Antwort ~ bleiben* never to be at a loss for an answer. **~(er)** m. culprit; *wie wir vergeben unsern ~ern* as we forgive them that trespass against us. **~keit** f. duty, obligation.

Schul-e (fu:-) f. (-e, -en) school; college; academy; course; (fig.) schooling, training; *Hohe ~e reiten* to put a horse through his paces; *~e machen* to find followers; to form a precedent. **~en** v.t. to school, teach, train. **~ung** f. schooling, training. **~ungslager** n. training-camp.

Schüler (fy:-) m. (-s, -) schoolboy; pupil. **~haft** a. immature. **~in** f. schoolgirl; pupil.

Schulter f. (-, -n) shoulder. **~bein** n. humerus. **~blatt** n. shoulder-blade. **~klappe** f., **~stück** n. (mil.) shoulder-strap. **~n** v.t. to shoulder.

Schultheiß, Schulte m. (obs.) village mayor.

schummeln v.i. (sl.) to cheat.

Schummerstunde f. evening twilight.

Schund (-t) m. (-es) trash. **~literatur** f. worthless or trashy literature.

Schupo m. abbr. of Schutzpolizist.

Schupp-e f. (-e, -en) scale; scurf, dandruff. **~enpanzer** m. coat of mail. **~ig** a. scaly, squamous.

schuppen¹ v.t. to scale; to scrape. v.r. to peel off.

Schuppen² m. (-s, -) shed, coach-house; garage; hangar.

schup(p)sen v.t. to push, shove.

Schur (-u:-) f. (-) shearing; fleece.

schür-en v.t. to poke (the fire); (fig.) to stir up, incite. **~haken**

m. poker.

schürf-en v.t. to scratch; to prospect (for); *tief ~end* (fig.) thorough. **~ung** f. scratch.

Schurk-e m. (-en, -en) rogue, rascal, scoundrel. **~e'rei** f. villainy, dirty trick. **~isch** a. rascally.

Schurz m. (-es, -e) apron. **~fell** n. leather apron.

Schürze f. (-, -n) apron; pinafore. **~n** v.t. to pick up (skirt); to tie. **~njäger** m. man who runs after women. [SHORT]

Schuß m. (Schuss-es, ⁓e) shot; report; round; gunshot wound, bullet wound; (a) dash of (wine, &c.); *~ abgeben* to fire a round; *weit vom ~* wide of the mark; *in ~ kommen* to get into working order. **~bereit** a. ready to fire. **~fest, ~sicher** aa. bullet-proof; shell-proof. **~waffe** f. fire-arm. **~weite** f. range. **~wunde** f. bullet wound, gunshot wound.

Schüssel f. (-, -n) dish; pan; basin, bowl.

Schuster m. (-s, -) shoemaker, cobbler; *auf ~s Rappen* on foot, on Shanks' pony. **~n** v.i. to cobble. **~pech** n. cobbler's wax; heel-ball. [L]

Schute f. (-, -n) barge, lighter.

Schutt m. (-es) rubbish, refuse. **~abladeplatz** m. refuse dump. **~halde** f. scree. **~haufen** m. rubbish heap.

Schüttel-frost m. shivering fit, rigor. **~n** v.t. to shake. v.r. to shiver, tremble. **~reim** m. Spoonerism. [SHUTTLE]

schütten v.t. to pour, pour out. v. impers. (of rain) to pour down.

schütter a. thin, sparse.

Schutz (futs) m. (-es) protection; defence; shelter; refuge, cover; care, keeping; *~ suchen* to take shelter; *in ~ nehmen* to defend, take under one's protection; *im ~ der Nacht* under cover of night. **~anstrich** m. baffle paint; dazzle paint; **~befohlene(r)** m. charge, protégé, ward. **~blech** n. mudguard, wing. **~brief** m. letter of safe-conduct. **~brille** f. protective goggles. **~bündnis**

n. defensive alliance. **~engel** *m.* guardian angel. **~färbung** *f.* protective colouring. **~frist** *f.* term of copyright. **~haft** *f.* protective custody. **~heilige(r)** *m.* patron saint. **~herr** *m.* patron, protector. **~hütte** *f.* shelter, hut. **~impfung** *f.* protective inoculation. **~insel** *f.* street island. **~karton** *m.* case; cardboard; cardboard box. **~los** *a.* defenceless, unprotected. **~mann** *m.* (*pl.* **~männer** *&* **~leute**) policeman. **~marke** *f.* trademark. **~patron** *m.* patron saint. **~pockenimpfung** *f.* vaccination. **~polizei** *f.* (municipal) police. **~polizist** *m.* policeman. **~truppe** *f.* colonial force; force guarding occupied territory. **~umschlag** *m.* wrapper, jacket (of book). **~wehr** *f.* defence work, bulwark. **~zoll** *m.* (protective) duty.

Schütze¹ *f.* sluice-board; shuttle.

Schütze² (ʃytsə) *m.* (**-n**, **-n**) marksman, shot; (*mil.*) rifleman, private; the Archer, Sagittarius. **~nest** *n.* shooting-match. **~feuer** *n.* independent fire. **~graben** *m.* (*mil.*) trench. **~nkette**, **~nlinie** *f.* line of riflemen in extended order.

schütz-en *v.t.* to protect, guard, defend, preserve. **~ling** *m.* protégé.

schwabbeln *v.i.* to babble.

Schwabe¹ *m.* See App. I.

Schwabe² *f.* (**-**, **-n**) cockroach.

schwäbeln *v.i.* to speak in Swabian dialect.

schwach (ʃvax) *a.* weak, frail, feeble, infirm; faint, small, little; sparse, scanty; poor, meagre. **~heit** *f.* weakness, feebleness, frailty. **~kopf** *m.* simpleton, imbecile. **~sinn** *m.* imbecility. **~sinnig** *a.* imbecile. **~strom** *m.* weak *or* low-tension current.

Schwäch-e (ʃvɛçə) *f.* (**-e**, **-en**) weakness, debility; failing, foible. **~en** *v.t.* to weaken, debilitate; to lessen, diminish; to tone down, impair. **~lich** *a.* weak, delicate, sickly, infirm. **~lichkeit** *f.* delicacy; infirmity. **~ling** *m.* weakling. **~ung** *f.* weakening.

Schwaden (**-a:-**) *m.* (**-s**, **-**) vapour; fire-damp; gas cloud; swath.

Schwa'dron (**-o:n**) *f.* (**-**, **-en**) squadron. **~eur** *m.* gas-bag, talker. **~ieren** *v.i.* to jaw.

Schwager *m.* (**-s**, **:̈**) brother-in-law.

Schwäger-in *f.* sister-in-law. **~schaft** *f.* relations by marriage.

Schwalbe *f.* (**-**, **-n**) swallow. **~nschwanz** *m.* swallow-tail; (*carp.*) dovetail; swallow-tail (coat).

Schwall *m.* (**-es**) flood, deluge; torrent (of words).

schwamm¹ *imperf. of* **schwimmen**.

Schwamm² *m.* (**-es**, **:̈e**) sponge; fungus, mushroom; dry rot. **~ig** *a.* fungous, fungoid; bloated.

Schwan (ʃvaːn) *m.* (**-es**, **:̈e**) swan. **~engesang** *m.* swan song. **~enteich** *m.* swannery.

schwand *imperf. of* **schwinden**.

schwanen *v. impers. es schwant mir** I have a presentiment (of).

Schwang¹ *m. im ~ sein* to be in vogue.

schwang² *imperf. of* **schwingen**.

schwanger (**-ŋ-**) *a.* pregnant. **~schaft** *f.* pregnancy. **~sverhütung** *f.* contraception.

schwängern *v.t.* to make pregnant, impregnate.

Schwank¹ (ʃv-) *m.* (**-es**, **:̈e**) prank, hoax; short anecdote; farce.

schwank² *a.* pliable, flexible, wavering, unsteady; slender. **~en** *v.i.* to rock, toss, sway; to roll; to shake; to reel, stagger; to totter; (*commerc.*) to fluctuate (*also fig.*) to hesitate, waver, falter. **~ung** *f.* variation, change; vacillation; fluctuation.

Schwanz *m.* (**-es**, **:̈e**) tail; trail; end. **~ende** *n.* tip of the tail. **~riemen** *m.* crupper. **~sporn** *m.* (*av.*) tail skid.

schwänzeln *v.i.* to wag the tail; (*fig.*) to fawn upon.

schwänzen *v.t. & i.* to play truant.

Schwäre *f.* (**-**) abscess, ulcer. **~n** *v.i.* to suppurate, fester.

Schwarm *m.* (**-es**, **:̈e**) crowd, throng, multitude; swarm (of bees); flock, flight; (*fig.*) idol, hero. **~geist** *m.* enthusiast, fanatic.

schwärm-en *v.i.* to swarm; to riot,

revel; to rove; (mil.) to deploy; (fig.) to enthuse, gush, be enthusiastic (about); to adore, have a crush (on). **~er** m. enthusiast; fanatic; dreamer, visionary; cracker, squib; hawkmoth. **~e'rei** f. enthusiasm; fanaticism. **~erisch** a. enthusiastic; fanatic; gushing.

Schwarte f. (-, -n) rind, skin; crackling (of roast pork); (colloq.) old book.

schwarz (jvarts) a. black; dark, swarthy, sable; negro; dirty, smutty; gloomy, dismal; **~ auf weiß** in black and white; **~ sehen** to look on the dark side; **der ~e Erdteil** Africa; **ins ~e treffen** to hit the bull's-eye. **~arbeit** f. non-union labour. **~brot** n. brown bread; rye bread. **~drossel** f. blackbird. **~e(r)** m. black, negro, nigger. **~handel** m. black market. **~hörer** m. listener-in (without a licence). **~künstler** m. necromancer, magician. **~malerei** f. gloomy picture (of things). **~schlachten** n. illegal slaughtering of cattle. **~seher** m. pessimist. **~wild** n. wild boars. **~wurzel** f. Viper's grass. [SWARTHY]

Schwärz-e f. (-e) blackness; darkness; blacking, blackening; printer's ink; (fig.) baseness, heinousness. **~en** v.t. to blacken, black; to slander, defame. **~lich** a. blackish, darkish, swarthy.

Schwatz (jvats) m. (-es) talk, chat. **~base** f. chatterbox. **~haft** a. talkative. **~haftigkeit** f. talkativeness, loquacity.

schwatzen, schwätzen v.i. & t. to talk, chatter, gossip.

Schwätzer m. (-s, -) babbler, twaddler, gossip.

Schwebe f. in der ~ sein to be undecided, to be trembling in the balance. **~bahn** f. suspension railway. **~bühne** f. suspended platform.

schweben (-e:-) v.i. to be suspended; hang; to hover, soar; (fig.) to move; (fig.) to be undecided, be pending; **auf der Zunge ~** to have on the tip of one's

tongue; **in Gefahr ~** to be in danger.

Schwefel (-e:-) m. (-s) sulphur. **~bad** n. sulphur bath. **~gelb** a. sulphur yellow. **~haltig** a. containing sulphur, sulphurous. **~holz** n. match. **~ig** a. sulphurous; sulphureous. **~sauer** a. sulphate of. **~säure** f. sulphuric acid. **~verbindung** f. sulphur compound. **~wasserstoff** m. hydrogen sulphide.

schwefeln v.t. to sulphurize, to sulphurate.

Schweif m. (-es, -e) tail; train. **~stern** m. comet. **~wedeln** v.i. to wag the tail; (fig.) to fawn upon.

schweifen vws.i. to wander about, roam. [SWEEP]

Schweigegeld n. hush-money.

schweig-en (jv-) v.i. st. to be silent, say nothing, hold one's tongue. **subst.** n. silence. **~epflicht** f. obligation to be silent (about). **~er** m. taciturn person. **~sam** a. silent, taciturn. **~samkeit** f. taciturnity.

Schwein (jv-) n. (-es, -e) hog, pig, swine; **~ haben** (fig.) to be in luck. **~ebraten** m. roast pork. **~efleisch** n. pork. **~ehirt** m. swineherd. **~ehund** m. filthy swine. **~ekoben** m. pigsty. **~e'rei** f. filthiness; dirty thing; dirty trick; obscenity. **~erne(s)** n. pork. **~estall** m. pigsty. **~igel** m. dirty fellow. **~isch** a. swinish; obscene. **~sleder** n. pigskin.

Schweiß (jv-) m. (-es) sweat, perspiration; (fig.) toil, toiling. **~blätter** n.pl. dress-preservers, dress-shields. **~hund** m. bloodhound. **~ig** a. sweaty; (hunting) bloody. **~treibend** a. sudorific. **~tropfen** m. bead of perspiration. **~tuch** n. (bibl.) kerchief, napkin, sudarium.

schweiß-en v.t. to weld. v.i. (hunting) to bleed. **~er** m. welder. **~naht** f. (tech.) weld.

schwelen (-e:-) v.i. to smoulder.

schwelg-en v.i. to feast, to revel (in); to luxuriate (in); indulge (in). **~er** m. sybarite, epicure;

reveller; glutton. **~e'rei** f. feasting, revelry; gluttony. **~erisch** a. luxurious; voluptuous. [SWALLOW]

Schwell-e f. (-e, -en) sill, doorstep, (also fig.) threshold; architrave; beam, joist; railway sleeper. **~en** rws.i. st. to swell, grow fat; (of water) to rise; (fig.) to grow bigger, increase. v.t. to swell; to distend, bloat; to inflate. **~ung** f. swelling; tumour, growth.

Schwemm-e f. (-e, -en) horse-pond, watering-place. **~en** v.t. to water; to wash up. **~land** n. alluvial land.

Schwengel (-ŋ-) m. (-s, -) swingle (of flail); swingletree; clapper; pump-handle.

schwenk-en v.t. to swing (to and fro), wave, shake; to flourish, brandish; to rinse. rws.i. to turn, wheel; to swivel; to traverse; (fig.) to change (sides). **~ung** f. turning or wheeling movement; traversing; change.

schwer (ʃveːr) a. heavy, weighty; oppressive; ponderous, clumsy; difficult, arduous, hard; grave, severe, serious (illness); bad, gross (blunder); heavy, indigestible (food); strong (cigar); **~fallen** or **~halten** to be difficult; etwas **~** nehmen to take something to heart.

Schwer-arbeiter m. manual labourer, navvy. **~blütig** a. melancholic. **~e** f. heaviness, weight; gravity; severity; body (of wine). **~enöter** m. gay Lothario. **~fällig** a. heavy, ponderous, clumsy, slow. **~fälligkeit** f. heaviness, clumsiness. **~gewicht** n. heavy-weight; (fig.) chief stress, emphasis. **~gewichtler** m. (boxing) heavy-weight. **~hörig** a. hard of hearing, deaf. **~hörigkeit** f. deafness. **~kraft** f. (force of) gravity. **~kriegsbeschädigte(r)** m. disabled soldier, crippled soldier. **~lich** adv. hardly, scarcely; with difficulty. **~mut** f. melancholy, sadness, depression. **~mütig** a. melancholy, sad, mournful. **~punkt** m. centre of gravity; (fig.) main

or crucial point; concentration (of power). **~spat** m. heavy spar, barytes. **~verbrecher** m. criminal, gangster; thug. **~wiegend** a. weighty.

Schwert n. (-es, -er) sword; dropkeel, centre-board. **~adel** m. military nobility. **~fisch** m. sword-fish. **~lilie** f. iris.

Schwester (ʃvɛs-) f. (-, -n) sister; hospital nurse. **~lich** a. sisterly. **~npaar** n. couple of sisters.

Schwibbogen (ʃvip-) m. flying buttress; arch(way); pier-arch.

schwieg imperf. of schweigen.

Schwieger-eltern pl. parents-inlaw. **~mutter** f. mother-in-law. **~sohn** m. son-in-law. **~tochter** f. daughter-in-law. **~vater** m. father-in-law.

Schwiel-e f. (-e, -en) callosity; weal. **~ig** a. callous; marked with weals.

schwierig (-ç) a. difficult; complicated; delicate; difficult to deal with; particular. **~keit** f. difficulty; obstacle.

schwillt 3rd pers. sing. present of schwellen.

Schwimm-anstalt f. swimmingbaths. **~bassin** n. swimmingpool. **~blase** f. air-bladder (of fish); waterwings. **~dock** n. floating dock. **~er** m. swimmer; float (of flying boat). **~flosse** f. fin. **~fuß** m. webbed foot. **~gürtel** m. waterwings; lifebelt. **~haut** f. web. **~kraft** f. buoyancy. **~panzer** m. amphibian tank. **~vogel** m. webfooted bird. **~weste** f. 'Mae West', life-jacket.

schwimmen v.i. st. to swim, float; to sail; to be bathed (in), overflow (with); (fig.) to welter, roll.

Schwindel m. (-s, -) dizziness, vertigo, giddiness; (fig.) swindle, fraud, humbug; trick. **~anfall** m. fit of dizziness. **~ei** f. swindle. **~frei** a. not liable to giddiness. **~haft** a. causing giddiness, very high; swindling, fraudulent. **~ig**, schwindlig aa. dizzy, giddy. **~unternehmen** n. bogus concern.

schwind-eln v.i. to swindle, cheat. v. impers. mir **~elt** I feel dizzy *or* giddy. **~ler** *m.* swindler, charlatan.

schwind-en *vws.i. st.* to grow less, dwindle; to decline, shrink, contract; to fade; to disappear, vanish. **~sucht** *f.* consumption, phthisis. **~süchtig** *a.* consumptive.

Schwinge *f.* (-, -n) wing; fan, winnow; swingle (for flax).

schwing-en (šviŋ-) *v.t. & i. st.* to swing, sway, oscillate; to flourish, brandish, wave; to fan (grain); to swingle (flax); (*phys.*) to vibrate. *v.r.* to swing oneself; to vault, leap (over); to soar, ascend. **~achse** *f.* oscillating axle; independent axle. **~ung** *f.* oscillation; vibration; wave. **~ungszahl** *f.* vibration number, vibration frequency.

Schwips *m.* (*colloq.*) einen ~ haben to be tipsy.

schwirren *v.i.* to whiz; to whir; to buzz, hum; (*of rumours*) to fly.

Schwitz-bad *n.* Turkish bath. **~en** *v.i. & t.* to perspire, sweat.

schwoll *imperf. of* **schwellen**.

schwören *v.t. & i. st.* to swear, take an oath; ~ auf to swear by, have absolute confidence in.

schwul *a.* (*sl.*) homosexual, queer.

schwül (-y-) *a.* sultry, close, oppressive. **~e** *f.* sultriness.

Schwulst *m.* (-es) bombast, turgidity (in style). **~ig, schwülstig** *aa.* bombastic, turgid.

Schwund *m.* (-es) falling off; atrophy; loss of (ending); (*wireless*) fading.

Schwung (-ŋ) *m.* (-es, ̈e) swing; bound, vault; vaulting; (*fig.*) impetus, verve, go, dash; flight (of imagination); noble diction; in ~ bringen to set going. **~feder** *f.* pinion. **~haft** *a.* lively, flourishing. **~kraft** *f.* centrifugal force; (*fig.*) liveliness, energy. **~rad** *n.* fly-wheel. **~voll** *a.* energetic, spirited, animated.

schwur *imperf. of* **schwören**.

Schwur² (švu:r) *m.* (-es, ̈e) oath; ~ leisten to take an oath. **~formel** *f.* wording of an oath. **~gericht** *n.* jury.

sechs (zɛks) *a. & subst. f.* six.

~eck *n.* hexagon. **~fach** *a.* sixfold. **~jährig** *a.* six-years-old; sexennial. **~te** *a.* sixth. **~tel** *n.* sixth part. **~tens** *adv.* sixthly.

sechzehn (zɛçtse:n) *a.* sixteen. **~ender** *m.* stag with sixteen points. **~telnote** *f.* semiquaver.

sechzig (zɛçtsiç) *a.* sixty. **~er** *m.* sexagenarian.

sedimentär *a.* sedimentary.

See 1. *m.* (-s, -n) lake. **2.** *f.* (-, -n) sea; *an die ~ gehen* to go to the seaside; *in ~ stechen* to put to sea. **~bad** *n.* seaside resort. **~bär** *m.* (*fig.*) old salt. **~fahrer** *m.* sailor, seafaring man. **~fahrt** *f.* voyage; cruise. **~fest** *a.* ~fest sein to be a good sailor. **~fliegerei** *f.* naval aviation. **~flieger-horst**, **~flughafen** *m.* sea-plane station. **~flugzeug** *n.* sea-plane. **~gang** *m.* heavy sea, swell. **~gefecht** *n.* naval battle *or* action. **~geltung** *f.* prestige at sea. **~gras** *n.* seaweed, green alga. **~herrschaft** *f.* naval supremacy. **~hund** *m.* seal. **~igel** *m.* sea-urchin. **~kadett** *m.* naval cadet. **~karte** *f.* chart. **~klar** *a.* ready to put to sea. **~krank** *a.* seasick. **~löwe** *m.* sea-lion. **~macht** *f.* naval *or* maritime power. **~mann** *m.* (*pl.* **~leute**) seaman, sailor, mariner. **~männisch** *a.* seamanlike. **~meile** *f.* 1·852 km. **~not** *f.* distress. **~platte** *f.* flat country covered with lakes. **~pferdchen** *n.* sea-horse. **~ratte** *f.* old salt, ancient mariner. **~räuber** *m.* pirate. **~rose** *f.* water-lily. **~schlacht** *f.* naval engagement *or* battle. **~schwalbe** *f.* tern. **~stern** *m.* starfish. **~streitkräfte** *f.pl.* naval forces. **~tang** *m.* seaweed, brown alga. **~tüchtig** *a.* seaworthy. **~warte** *f.* naval observatory. **~wasser** *n.* sea-water, salt water. **~weg** *m.* sea-route. **~zunge** *f.* sole.

Seel-e *f.* (-e, -en) soul; mind; heart; spirit; feeling; bore (of gun); *der ~e brennen* to prey on one's mind; *jemandem aus der ~e sprechen* to guess a person's thoughts. **~enamt** *n.*, **~en-**

messe f. office for the dead, requiem. ~**engröße** f. magnanimity. ~**enfroh** a. very glad. ~**enheil** n. spiritual welfare, salvation. ~**enhirt** m. pastor. ~**envergnügt** a. very happy. ~**envoll** a. soulful, tender, sentimental. ~**enwanderung** f. transmigration of souls. ~**isch** a. psychic, mental; spiritual; of the mind; emotional. ~**sorge** f. ministerial work. ~**sorger** m. clergyman, minister.

Segel (ze:-) n. (-s, -) sail, canvas; ~ **einziehen**, ~ **streichen** to strike sail. ~**flieger** m. glider pilot. ~**flug** m. gliding. ~**flugzeug** n. glider. ~**klar** a. ready to sail. ~**klasse** f. rating. ~**schiff** n. sailing-ship. ~**schlitten** m. ice-yacht. ~**stange** f. (naut.) yard. ~**tuch** n. sailcloth, canvas.

segel-n v.i. to sail; to soar; to glide. ~**ler** m. yachtsman; sailing-boat or -vessel.

Segen (ze:-) m. (-s, -) benediction, blessing; luck; grace (for food). ~**sreich** a. blessed; prosperous.

segn-en v.t. to bless, consecrate, give benediction to. ~**ung** f. blessing.

seh-en v.t. & i. st. to see, look, behold; to observe, perceive; to realize; schlecht ~**en** to have poor eyesight; darauf ~**en** to watch, be careful about, see to; ~**en nach** to look after. ~**enswert** a. worth seeing, remarkable. ~**enswürdigkeit** f. sight, object of interest. ~**er** m. seer, prophet. ~**erisch** a. prophetic. ~**feld** n. field of vision. ~**kraft** f. eyesight. ~**nerv** m. optic nerve. ~**schärfe** f. sight; vision; focus. ~**weite** f. range of sight.

Sehn-e f. (-e, -en) sinew, tendon; string (of bow); (math.) chord. ~**enscheide** f. sheath covering tendon. ~**enzerrung** f. wrenching of a tendon. ~**ig** a. sinewy, stringy.

sehn-en v.r. to long, yearn (for). ~**lich** a. ardent, longing, passionate. ~**sucht** f. longing, yearning, desire. ~**süchtig** a. longing, yearning.

sehr adv. very; very much; most. [SORE]

seicht a. shallow; low; flat; superficial; insipid. ~**igkeit** f. shallowness; superficiality.

seid 2nd pers. pl. pres. ind. of **sein**.

Seid-e (zai-) f. (-e, -en) silk. ~**en**, ~**ig** a. silky, silken. ~**enpapier** n. tissue-paper. ~**enraupe** f. ~**enwurm** m. silkworm. ~**enzüchterei** f. breeding of silkworms. [ML]

Seidel m. & n. (-s, -) mug (of beer).

Seidelbast m. daphne; mezereon.

Seife f. (-, -n) soap. ~**nblase** f. soap-bubble. ~**nflocken** f.pl. soap-flakes. ~**nlauge** f. soap solution, soap-suds. ~**npulver** n. soap powder. ~**nschaum** m. lather. ~**nsieder** m. soap-boiler.

seifig a. soapy.

Seih-e f. (-, -n) strainer; dregs. ~**n** v.t. to strain, filter. ~**r** m. strainer, filter.

Seil n. (-es, -e) rope, cord, line; cable. ~**bahn** f. cable railway; funicular. ~**er** m. rope-maker. ~**tänzer** m. tight-rope walker. ~**winde** f. rope winch. ~**zug** m. tackle.

Seim m. (-es) mucilage. ~**ig** a. mucilaginous.

sein¹ (zain) irreg. v.i. to be, exist. subst. n. being, existence.

sein² pron. & a. his; its; her; one's; (rare) of him; of it; die ~**en** his or one's people. ~**erseits** adv. on his side, for his part. ~**erzeit** adv. formerly; one day; in due time, in due course. ~**esgleichen** his equals, people like him, such as he. ~**ethalben**, ~**etwegen**, ~**etwillen** adv. for his sake, on his account, on his behalf. ~**ig** pron. his; his or one's property; his or one's part or duty.

seit prep. & conj. since; for; ~ **kurzem** of late, lately; ~ **langem** for a long time, for some time; ~ **wann**? how long, since when? ~**dem** adv. & conj. since, since then, from that time, ever since. ~**her** adv. since then; up to now.

Seite f. (-, -n) side; flank; page; party; face (of a solid); (math.) member; schwache ~ weakness, foible; ~ an ~ side by side; *auf die* ~e *gehen* to step aside; *zur* ~e *stehen* to stand by, help; *von* ~n on the part of.

Seiten-angriff *m.* flank attack. ~ansicht *f.* side-view; profile. ~blick *m.* side-glance. ~flügel *m.* side-aisle; transept; wing. ~gebäude *n.* wing (of building). ~gewehr *n.* side-arm, bayonet. ~hieb *m.* side-cut; (*fig.*) sarcastic remark, home-thrust. ~lang *a.* filling pages; voluminous. ~lehne *f.* side-rail; arm (of chair). ~linie *f.* branch-line; collateral line. ~schiff *n.* aisle. ~sprung *m.* side-leap, caper; double; (*fig.*) escapade. ~stechen *n.* stitch in the side. ~straße *f.* side-street. ~stück *n.* pendant, companion-picture. ~weg *m.* by-path. ~zahl *f.* number of a page; number of pages.

seitens *prep.* on the part of, on the side of.

seit-lich *a.* lateral, side; collateral. ~ *adv.* at the side. ~wärts *adv.* sideways; aside; laterally; on one side.

Se'kret *n.* (-s, -e) ♂ secretion.

Sekre't-är *m.* (-ärs, -äre), ~ärin *f.* secretary. *m.* (*also*) bureau. ~ari'at *n.* secretary's office.

Sekt (z-) *m.* (-s, -e) champagne.

Sekt-e *f.* (-e, -en) sect. ~ierer *m.* sectarian. ~i'onsbefund *m.* findings of a post-mortem examination.

Sektor *m.* (-s, -en) sector.

Se'kund-a *f.* (-a, -en) fifth form in German school. ~ant *m.* second (in duel). ~awechsel *m.* second (bill) of exchange.

Se'kunde *f.* (-, -n) second. ~nzeiger *m.* second-hand.

sekun'dieren *v.t.* to second.

selb-'ander *adv.* we two. ~dritt *adv.* with two others. ~er *pron.* *ich* ~*er* I myself. ~ig *a.* same, selfsame.

selbst (-pst) *pron.* self; himself, itself, herself, themselves; *von* ~ of one's own accord; voluntarily; automatically. *adv.* even.

selbständig (-ig) *a.* independent. ~keit *f.* independence.

Selbst-anlasser *m.* self-starter. ~anschluß *m.* dial telephone. ~auslöser *m.* self-timer. ~beherrschung *f.* self-control, self-command. ~bekenntnis *n.* voluntary confession. ~bestimmung *f.* self-determination; self-government. ~bewußt *a.* (*phil.*) self-conscious; self-confident. ~bewußtsein *n.* (*phil.*) self-consciousness; self-assurance. ~binder *m.* open-end tie. ~biographie *f.* autobiography. ~erhaltung *f.* self-preservation. ~erkenntnis *f.* knowledge of oneself. ~fahrer *m.* owner-driver. ~gefällig *a.* self-satisfied, complacent. ~gefühl *n.* self-respect, self-confidence; amour propre. ~gerecht *a.* self-righteous. ~gespräch *n.* monologue, soliloquy. ~gezogen *a.* home-grown, home-bred. ~herrlich *a.* autocratic.

selbstisch *a.* selfish.

Selbst-kostenpreis *m.* cost price. ~ladepistole *f.*, ~lader *m.* self-loading pistol. ~laut(er) *m.* vowel. ~los *a.* unselfish, disinterested. ~losigkeit *f.* unselfishness. ~mord *m.* suicide. ~mörder *m.* suicide. ~mörderisch *a.* suicidal. ~redend *a.* self-evident, obvious, natural. ~sicher *a.* self-confident. ~sucht *f.* selfishness, egotism. ~süchtig *a.* selfish, egotistic. ~tätig *a.* automatic, self-acting. ~verlag *m.* im *~verlag* published by the author. ~versorger *m.* small farmer living on the products of his own farm. ~verständlich *a.* self-evident, obvious, natural. ~verständlichkeit *f.* matter of course, foregone conclusion. ~vertrauen *n.* self-confidence. ~wähler *m.* (*tel.*) dial-system. ~fernverkehr *m.* trunk-dialling. ~zucht *f.* self-discipline. ~zufrieden *a.* self-satisfied, complacent. ~zünder *m.* automatic lighter; (*chem.*) pyrophorus. ~zweck *m.* end in itself.

Se'len *n.* (-s) selenium.

selig (ze:lic) *a.* blessed, blest, happy, blissful; late, deceased. ~keit *f.* happiness, bliss. ~

preisung f. (bibl.) Beatitude. ~sprechen v.t. to beatify. ~sprechung f. beatification.

Sellerie m. (-s) celeriac; celery.

selt-en a. rare; unusual. adv. seldom. ~enheit f. rarity, scarcity; curiosity. ~sam a. strange, unusual, odd, curious. ~samkeit f. strangeness, oddness.

Selterwasser n. soda-water.

Se'mester n. (-s, -) term, session, semester, half-year. [L]

Semi'nar (-a:r) n. (-s, -e) training-college; (univ.) seminar; (R.C.) seminary. ~'ist m. pupil of a training-college.

Semmel f. (-, -n) roll. ~blond a. flaxen-haired. [L]

Se'nat (-a:t) m. (-s, -e) senate.

Send-bote m. messenger. ~ebereich m. broadcasting area. ~efolge f. radio programme; feature programme. ~eleiter m. (broadcasting) producer. ~er m. transmitter. ~eraum m. studio. ~espiel n. radio play. ~estation, ~estelle f. broadcasting station. ~ling m. emissary; messenger. ~schreiben n. (open) letter. ~ung f. sending; mission; consignment; transmission.

senden v.t. st. to send; to broadcast, transmit.

Senf m. (-es) mustard. ~gas n. mustard gas. ~korn n. grain of mustard seed. ~pflaster n. mustard plaster. [L]

sengen (-ŋ-) v.t. & i. to singe, scorch; to burn.

senil a. senile.

Senk-blei n. plummet; lead. ~brunnen m. sunk well. ~fuß m. flat foot. ~fußeinlage f. arch-support. ~grube f. cesspool. ~kasten m. caisson. ~rebe f. layer of vine. ~recht a. perpendicular, vertical. ~ung f. sinking; lowering, reduction (of prices); hollow, depression; dip; declivity; (gram.) unaccented syllable. ~waage f. areometer.

Senkel m. (-s, -) lace (of shoe, &c.).

senken (-z-) v.t. to lower, let down; to bow (one's head); to cast down (one's eyes); to sink. v.r. to

sink, subside; to give way; to slope down; to settle, descend upon.

Senn (zɛn) m. (-en, -en) Alpine cowherd, cheesemaker. ~erin f. dairymaid. ~hütte f. chalet; Alpine dairy.

Sennesblätter n.pl. senna leaves.

sensat-io'nell a. sensational, thrilling, exciting. ~i'onslust f. desire to cause a sensation; (lit.) sensationalism.

Sense (zɛnzə) f. (-, -n) scythe. ~nmann m. mower; (fig.) Death.

sen'sibel (zɛnzi:-) a. ♢ sensitive (to). ~ili'tät f. sensibility, sensitiveness, feeling.

Sen'tenz (zɛn-) f. (-, -en) ♢ aphorism, maxim. ~i'ös a. sententious.

Sentimentali'tät f. (-, -en) sentimentality.

Separat-abzug (-a:t-) m. off-print. ~konto n. special account.

Sep'tember m. (-s, -) September.

Sep'tett n. (-s, -e) septet.

Sep'time f. (-, -n) (mus.) seventh.

Se'rail n. (-s, -s) seraglio.

Ser'geant (-ʒ-) m. (-en, -en) sergeant.

Serie (ze:riə) f. (-, -n) series; issue; set. ~nfertigung f. serial manufacture. ~nherstellung f. serial manufacture. ~nschaltung f. connexion in series.

seriös a. serious.

Serpentine (-ti:-) f. winding road.

Serum (ze:-) n. (-s, Seren) serum.

Ser'vice n. (-s, -) service, set.

Ser'vier-brett n. tray. ~en v.t. & i. to serve; to wait (at table).

Servi'ette f. (-, -n) table-napkin.

Sessel m. (-s, -) arm-chair, easy-chair. ~bahn f. passenger rope-way; ski-lift.

seßhaft a. settled, established, resident; sedentary.

Setzei n. fried egg.

setzen (zɛt-) v.t. to put, set, place; to fix; to erect, put up; to stake (money); to plant (tree); (mus. & typ.) to compose; alles daran ~ to risk everything; to do one's utmost. evs.i. to leap (over); to cross (river). v.r. to sit down, take a seat; (of bird) to perch; (chem.) to settle, precipitate, be deposited; *es wird Hiebe ~* it will end in a fight; you will catch it.

Setz-er *m.* compositor. **~e'rei** *f.* compositor's room, composing room. **~kasten** *m.* letter-case. **~ling** *m.* slip, layer. **~reis** *n.* slip. **~waage** *f.* field level.

Seuche (zɔiçə) *f.* (-, -n) epidemic, infectious disease; pestilence. **~nherd** *m.* centre of infection. **~nlazarett** *n.* hospital for infectious diseases.

seufz-en (zɔiftsən) *v.i.* to sigh, heave a sigh. **~er** *m.* sigh.

Sex'tett *n.* (-s, -e) sextet.

sexu'ell *a.* sexual.

se'zier-en (z-) *v.t.* to dissect. **~messer** *n.* scalpel, dissecting knife.

Shawl *m.* See Schal.

sich *pron.* himself, herself, itself; yourself, yourselves; themselves; oneself; one another, each other; *an ~* in itself.

Sichel (ziç-) *f.* (-, -n) sickle; crescent (of moon).

sicher (ziç-) *a.* secure, safe; certain, sure, positive; steady; trustworthy, reliable; *~ gehen* to be on the safe side, make quite sure; *~ stellen* to put in safe keeping; *~ wissen* to know for certain; *seiner Sache ~ sein* to be certain of a thing; *aus ~er Hand* on good authority.

Sicherheit *f.* (-, -en) safety, secureness, security; certainty; trustworthiness; confidence; *~ leisten* to give security; *in ~ bringen* to secure. **~dienst** *m.* security service. **~shalber** *adv.* for safety. **~skette** *f.* door-chain, guard-chain. **~sleistung** *f.* security, bail. **~snadel** *f.* safety-pin. **~schloß** *n.* safety-lock. **~sventil** *n.* safety-valve.

sicher-lich *adv.* surely, certainly, undoubtedly. **~n** *v.t.* to protect, cover; to secure; to set (rifle) at 'safe'. **~stellung** *f.* safeguarding, guarantee. **~ung** *f.* safeguarding, protection; (*electr.*) fuse; safety device; (*mil.*) covering party. **~ungsfahrzeug** *n.* escort vessel.

Sicht (ziçt) *f.* (-) sight; visibility; view; *auf lange ~* long-term. **~bar**, **~lich** *aa.* visible, apparent, obvious. **~barkeit** *f.* visibility. **~bereich** *m.* zone of visibility. **~schutz** *m.* camouflage. **~ung** *f.* sighting; sifting. **~vermerk** *m.* visé, visa. **~wechsel** *m.* bill payable at sight. **~weite** *f.* range of sight; sighting distance.

sichten (ziç-) *v.t.* to sight; to sift; to sort.

sickern (zik-) *vws.i.* to trickle, ooze.

sie (zi:) *pron.* she, her; it; they; them; *Sie* you.

Sieb (zi:p) *n.* (-es, -e) sieve, colander, strainer; sifter, riddle; screen; filter. **~n**[1] *v.t.* to sift, strain, riddle; to weed out; to pick out.

sieben[2] (zi:b-) *a. & subst. f.* seven. **~fach** *a.* sevenfold. **~gestirn** *n.* Pleiades. **~meilenstiefel** *m.pl.* seven-league boots. **~sachen** *f. pl.* goods and chattels, belongings. **~schläfer** *m.* lazybones; dormouse. **~te**, **siebte** *aa.* seventh.

sieb-zehn *a.* seventeen. **~zig** *a.* seventy. **~ziger** *m.* septuagenarian.

siech (zi:ç) *a.* sickly, ailing, infirm, invalid. **~en** *vws.i.* to be a confirmed invalid; to pine away. **~tum** *n.* long illness, invalidism, invalidhood.

Siede-grad *m.* boiling-point. **~punkt** *m.* boiling-point. **~heiß** *a.* scalding hot. **~hitze** *f.* boiling-heat.

sied-eln *v.i.* to settle; to colonize. **~ler** *m.* settler; colonist. **~lung** *f.* settlement; colony; (*pl.*) housing estates. **~lungsgesellschaft** *f.* building-society. **~lungspolitik** *f.* housing- *or* (house-)building-policy.

sieden *v.t. & i. st.* to boil, seethe; to simmer.

Sieg (zi:k) *m.* (-es, -e) victory; triumph. **~er** *m.* victor, conqueror; winner. **~esgewiß** *a.* certain *or* confident of victory. **~estrunken** *a.* elated with victory. **~haft** *a.* triumphant. **~reich** *a.* victorious.

Siegel (zi:g-) *n.* (-s, -) seal. ~**bewahrer** *m.* keeper of the seal, Lord Privy Seal. ~**lack** *m.* sealing-wax. ~**ring** *m.* signet-ring.

siegeln *v.t.* to seal.

siegen (zi:-) *v.i.* to win, conquer, be victorious.

sieht 3rd pers. sing. pres. of **sehen**.

Siel *m. & n.* (-es, -e) sluice; drain, sewer.

Siele *f.* (-, -n) horse-collar, harness.

siezen *v.t.* to address as 'you' (instead of 'thou').

Signal (zïgna:l) *n.* (-s, -e) signal; bugle-call. ~**buch** *n.* code of signals. ~**e'ment** *n.* description (of a person). ~**gast** *m.* signaller. ~**hupe** *f.* siren; klaxon. ~**leine** *f.* bell-rope, communication-cord. ~**mast** *m.* signal mast, signal post; semaphore. ~**pfeife** *f.* (warning-)whistle. ~**scheibe** *f.* signalling-disk.

signali'sieren *v.t. & i.* to signal.

Sign-atarmächte *pl.* signatory powers. ~**atur** *f.* mark, sign; brand; characteristic; signature; conventional sign (on map). ~'**et** *n.* ⚓ printer's *or* publisher's mark. ~'**ieren** *v.t.* to mark, brand; to sign.

Silbe *f.* (-, -n) syllable. ~**nmaß** *n.* quantity. ~**nrätsel** *n.* charade. ~**nstecher** *m.* quibbler.

Silber (zil-) *n.* (-s) silver; plate. ~**fuchs** *m.* silver fox. ~**hell** *a.* silvery. ~**ling** *m.* (*bibl.*) piece of silver. ~**n** *a.* silver. ~**papier** *n.* silver paper. ~**pappel** *f.* white poplar. ~**stift** *m.* silverpoint. ~**weiß** *a.* silvery white. ~**zeug** *n.* silver plate.

Si'lizium *n.* silicon.

Sil'vesterabend *m.* New Year's Eve.

Similistein *m.* artificial stone.

simpel *a.* simple, plain. *subst. m.* simpleton.

Sims (z-) *n.* (-es, -e) ledge; mantel-piece; edge; sill (of window); cornice, moulding.

Simu'lant *m.* (-en, -en) malingerer; (*sl.*) leadswinger.

simu'lieren *v.i.* to malinger; (*sl.*) to swing the lead.

sind 1st & 3rd pers. pl. pres. ind. of **sein**.

Sinekure *f.* cushy job.

Sinfo'nie (-ni:) *f.* (-, -n) symphony. ~**spiel** *n.* operetta, musical comedy. ~**stimme** *f.* singing-voice; vocal part. ~**vogel** *m.* songster, warbler.

sing-en (z-) *v.t. & i. st.* to sing; to warble, carol.

sinken (z-) *vus.i. st.* to sink; to drop, fall; to go down, abate; to decrease; to decline.

Sinn (z-) *m.* (-es, -e) sense, faculty; mind, understanding, intellect; consciousness; tendency; wish; opinion; meaning, interpretation; *im* ~ *haben* to intend; *bei* ~*en sein* to have one's wits about one; *von* ~*en sein* to be out of one's mind, be mad; *anderen* ~*es werden* to change one's mind; *sich etwas aus dem* ~ *schlagen* to dismiss a thing from one's mind.

Sinn-bild *n.* symbol, emblem; allegory. ~**bildlich** *a.* symbolic. ~**enlust** *f.* sensual pleasure, voluptuousness. ~**enmensch** *m.* sensualist. ~**entstellend** *a.* distorting the meaning. ~**enwelt** *f.* material world. ~**esänderung** *f.* change of mind. ~**esart** *f.* character, disposition. ~**esorgan** *n.* sensory organ. ~**eswahrnehmung** *f.* apperception. ~**eswerkzeug** *n.* organ of sense. ~**esstörung** *f.* delusion, mental derangement. ~**estäuschung** *f.* illusion, hallucination. ~**fällig** *a.* obvious. ~**gedicht** *n.* epigram. ~**gemäß** *a.* analogous; equivalent. ~**getreu** *a.* faithful (interpretation). ~**ig** *a.* sensible, thoughtful; ingenious. ~**lich** *a.* sensual; sensuous; material; ~**lichkeit** *f.* sensuality; sensuousness. ~**los** *a.* senseless; mad; foolish. ~**losigkeit** *f.* senselessness, foolishness. ~**reich** *a.* sensible; clever, witty; ingenious. ~**spruch** *m.* epigram; motto. ~**verwandt** *a.* synonymous. ~**voll** *a.* significant, pregnant. ~**widrig** *a.* contrary to sense, nonsensical.

sinnen (z-) *v.i. st.* to think, think over, speculate (upon), reflect, meditate, brood; ~ *auf* to plan, plot, scheme; *gesonnen sein* to be inclined, have a mind to.

sinnieren *v.i.* to meditate.

Sino'loge *m.* (-n, -n) sinologist.

sintemal *conj.* since, whereas.

Sinter *m.* (-s, -) sinter; dross of iron.

Sintflut *f.* Deluge, flood.

Sinus *m.* (-, -e) ♣ (*math.*) sine.

Sipp-e (-e, -en), **~schaft** *f.* kinship; kindred; relatives; kith and kin. **~enforschung** *f.* genealogical research.

Si'rene (-re:-) *f.* (-, -n) siren; klaxon.

Sirup *m.* (-s) treacle; syrup.

si'stieren *v.t.* to stop; to arrest.

Sitt-e (z-) *f.* (-e, -en) custom, habit; usage; (*pl.*) morals, manners. **~engesetz** *n.* moral law, moral code. **~enlehre** *f.* moral philosophy, ethics. **~enlos** *a.* immoral, dissolute, profligate. **~enlosigkeit** *f.* immorality, profligacy. **~enpolizei** *f.* control of prostitutes. **~enrein** *a.* pure, chaste. **~enrichter** *m.* censor. **~ig** *a.* modest, chaste. **~lich** *a.* moral. **~lichkeit** *f.* morality, morals. **~lichkeitsvergehen** *n.* indecent assault. **~sam** *a.* modest. **~samkeit** *f.* modesty.

Sittich *m.* (-s, -e) parakeet.

Situati'on *f.* (-, -en) ♣ site, position, state of affairs, situation.

situ'iert *a. wohl* ~ well-off, well-to-do.

Sitz (z-) *m.* (-es, -e) seat; chair; residence, domicile; place, spot, locus; fit (of dress). **~bad** *n.* hipbath. **~fläche** *f.* seat (of chair). **~fleisch** *n. kein ~fleisch haben* (*fig.*) inability to keep at a thing. **~gelegenheit** *f.* seating accommodation, seat(s). **~platz** *m.* seat. **~stange** *f.* perch. **~streik** *m.* sit-in. **~ung** *f.* sitting; session; meeting. **~ungsbericht** *m.* report, treatise; proceedings.

sitzen *v.i. st.* to sit; (*of bird*) to perch; to hold a meeting; (*of dress, &c.*) to fit; to stick fast, adhere; (*colloq.*) to be imprisoned; **~***de Lebensweise* sedentary life; **~** *bleiben* to remain seated; (*fig.*) to be a wallflower; to remain a

spinster; to be on the shelf; not to get one's remove (in school); **~** *lassen* to leave in the lurch; to jilt, throw over; *etwas auf sich* **~** *lassen* to put up with; to pocket (affront).

Skala (-a:l-) *f.* (-, Skalen) ♣ scale (of thermometer & *mus.*).

Skalp *m.* (-es, -e) scalp. **~'ieren** *v.t.* to scalp.

Skan'dal *m.* (-s, -e) scandal; row, noise. **~ös** *a.* scandalous, shocking.

skan'dieren *v.i.* to scan.

Skat *m.* ~ *dreschen* to play skat (a German card-game). [IT.]

Ske'lett *n.* (-s, -e) skeleton.

Skep-sis *f.* (-sis) scepticism. **~tiker** *m.* sceptic. **~tisch** *a.* sceptical.

Ski (ʃi:) *m.* (-s, -er) ski. **~laufen** *vws.i.* to ski. *subst. n.* skiing. **~läufer** *m.* skier, ski-runner. **~springen** *n.* ski-jumping.

Skizz-e (-tsə) *f.* (-e, -en) sketch; sketch-map. **~enhaft** *a.* sketchy. **~'ieren** *v.t. & i.* to sketch.

Sklav-e (-a:-) *m.* (-en, -en), **~in** *f.* slave. **~enhalter** *m.* slave-owner. **~e'rei** *f.* slavery. **~isch** *a.* slavish, servile.

Skonto *m. & n.* (-s, -s) discount.

Skor'but *m.* (-s) scurvy.

Skorpi'on *m.* (-s, -e) scorpion.

skrofu'lös *a.* scrofulous.

Skrupel *m.* (-s, -) scruple. **~los** *a.* unscrupulous.

skrupulös *a.* scrupulous.

Skulp'tur *f.* (-, -en) sculpture.

sku'rril *a.* ♣ farcical.

Sma'ragd (-rakt) *m.* (-s, -e) emerald. **~en** *a.* emerald.

so (zo:) *adv.* so, thus, in this (that) way, in such a way, like this (that); such; to such a degree; very; anyhow, in any case; already. *int.* indeed? really? *conj.* therefore, then; *so . . . auch* however; *so . . . doch* yet, nevertheless; *so . . . so* though . . . yet, though . . . all the (more, greater, &c.); ~ *groß wie* as big as; ~ *bald* als soon as; ~ *gut wie* as if; practically; *wenn dem* ~ *ist* (if that is) so. *Compounds of* so *appear in alphabet. order below.*

Socke f. (-, -n) sock. **~nhalter** m. suspender.

Sockel m. (-s, -) socle, pedestal, base.

Soda n. (-) soda.

so'dann adv. then; afterwards.

so'daß conj. so that.

Sodbrennen n. heartburn.

so'eben adv. just, just now.

Sofa (zo:) n. (-s, -s) sofa, settee. **~schoner** m. antimacassar.

so'fern conj. so far as; **~** nur if only, as long as.

soff imperf. of saufen.

so'fort adv. at once, immediately, forthwith. **~ig** a. immediate, prompt, instantaneous. **~zahlung** f. cash payment.

Sog¹ (-k) m. (-es, -e) suction; wake (of ship).

sog² imperf. of saugen.

so'gar adv. even. **~genannt** a. so-called. **~gleich** adv. at once, immediately.

Sohle f. (-, -n) sole; bottom (of valley).

Sohn (zo:n) m. (-es, ⁼e) son.

so'lange adv. so or as long as; whilst.

Solawechsel m. bill of exchange, promissory note.

Solbad (zo:-) n. salt-water bath, brine bath.

solch (-ç) pron. & a. such; the same. **~erlei** indecl. a. of such a kind, such. **~ermaßen, ~erweise** adv. in such a way.

Sold (-t) m. (-es) pay, wages. **~buch** n. pay-book.

Sol'dat (-a:t) m. (-en, -en) soldier. **~eska** f. rabble of soldiers. **~isch** a. soldier-like, military, of soldierly bearing.

Söldling (-s, -e), **Söldner** m. (-s, -) mercenary, hireling.

so'lid (-i:t) a. solid, strong, substantial; thorough; sound, reliable, respectable. **~arisch** a. joint; unanimous. **~ari'tät** f. solidarity, unanimity. **~i'tät** f. solidity; respectability.

So'list m. (-en, -en), **~in** f. soloist.

Soll n. (-s, -s) debit. **~bestand** m. nominal balance; (mil.) required strength. **~(l)eistung** f. target.

sollen irreg. v.i. ought, shall, am to,

be bound to, have to, must; to be said to, to be supposed to; Du sollst nicht töten thou shalt not kill; er soll in B. sein they say he is in B; er soll es getan haben he is said to have done it; was soll das (heißen)? what is the purpose (or meaning or use) of that? sollte er kommen? if he should happen to come; sollte er krank sein? can he be ill?

Söller m. (-s, -) balcony; loft.

Solo-stimme f. solo part. **~tänzer** m. principal dancer.

so'mit adv. consequently.

Sommer (zo:-) m. (-s, -) summer. **~fäden** m.pl. gossamer. **~frische** f. health-resort. **~frischler** m. summer visitor, holiday-maker. **~lich** a. summery. **~nachtstraum** m. Mid-summer Night's Dream. **~sonnenwende** f. summer solstice. **~sprosse** f. freckle. **~sprossig** a. freckled.

so'nach adv. consequently.

So'nate f. (-, -n) sonata.

Sonde f. (-, -en) probe; (naut.) plummet. **~ieren** v.t. & i. to probe; to sound; (fig.) to explore the ground.

sonder (z-) prep. without. **~(ab)-druck** m. off-print, separate reprint; extract. **~bar** a. strange, odd, peculiar, curious. **~barerweise** adv. strange to say. **~bündler** m. separatist. **~fall** m. special case, exceptional case. **~friede** m. separate peace. **~gleichen** indecl. a. unequalled, unique, incomparable. **~lich** a. particular, special; remarkable. **~ling** m. quaint character, original, crank. **~meldung** f. special announcement. **~recht** n. privilege. **~zug** m. special train.

sondern¹ conj. but. [SUNDER]

sonder-n² v.t. to separate, sever, segregate. **~ung** f. separation.

sonders adv. samt und **~** all together, each and all.

So'nett n. (-s, -e) sonnet.

Sonnabend m. (-s, -e) Saturday.

Sonne f. (-, -n) sun.

sonnen v.t. to expose to the sun's rays. v.r. (also fig.) to bask.

Sonnen-aufgang m. sunrise. **~bahn** f. orbit of the sun; ecliptic. **~blume** f. sunflower. **~brand** m. sunburn. **~brille** f. sun glasses. **~finsternis** f. eclipse of the sun. **~fleck** m. sun-spot. **~geflecht** n. solar plexus. **~klar** a. clear as daylight, evident. **~schirm** m. sunshade. **~segel** n. awning. **~seite** f. sunny side. **~stand** m. solstitial point. **~stäubchen** n. (dust) mote. **~stich** m. sunstroke. **~strahl** m. sunbeam. **~uhr** f. sun-dial. **~untergang** m. sunset. **~verbrannt** a. sunburnt, tanned. **~wende** f. solstice.

sonnig a. sunny.

Sonntag (-k) m. (-s, -e) Sunday. **~sjäger** m. amateur sportsman. **~skind** n. (child) born under a lucky star. **~sstaat** m. Sunday best.

sonntäglich a. Sunday; every Sunday.

so'nor a. sonorous.

sonst adv. else; moreover; besides, in other respects, otherwise; before, formerly; as a rule; usual(ly); ~ etwas anything else; ~ nichts nothing else; ~ jemand anybody else; ~ ig a. other; remaining; former. **~wie** adv. in some other way. **~wo** adv. elsewhere, somewhere else. **~woher** adv. from some other place. **~wohin** adv. to another place, somewhere else.

Sophiste'rei f. (-, -en) sophistry.

so'phistisch a. sophistical.

So'pran m. (-s, -e) soprano, treble. **~sänger** m. soprano (singer).

Sorg-e f. (-e, -en) grief, sorrow; anxiety, uneasiness, concern, worry, apprehension; care, trouble; ~e tragen to take care of, see to. **~enkind** n. delicate child; problem child. **~enstuhl** m. easy-chair. **~envoll** a. full of cares; careworn, worried, anxious. **~falt** f. carefulness; care, solicitude; accuracy. **~fältig** a. careful; painstaking; accurate, precise. **~lich** a. careful; anxious. **~los** a. carefree, lighthearted; careless, thoughtless.

~losigkeit f. lightheartedness. unconcern; thoughtlessness. **~sam** a. careful, particular. **~samkeit** f. carefulness.

sorgen v.i. ~ für to care for, look after, take care of; to provide for; to see to, attend to. v.r. to be anxious, worry, fear; sich ~ um to be concerned about.

Sort-e f. (-e, -en) kind, sort, species; quality, brand, grade. **~ieren** v.t. to sort, arrange, grade, sift, pick. **~i'ment** n. assortment; retail book-trade; bookshop. **~i'menter** m. bookseller.

sott imperf. of sieden.

Sou'ffl-eur m., **~euse** f. prompter. **~eurkasten** m. prompt-box. **~'ieren** v.i. to prompt.

Souve'rän m. (-s, -e) & a. sovereign. **~i'tät** f. sovereignty.

so-'viel conj. as or so far as. **~weit** conj. as far as. **~wenig** conj. as little as. **~wie** conj. as soon as; as well as; just as, also. **~wie'so** adv. anyhow, in any case. **~wohl** conj. **~wohl ... als auch** as well as ... and ... and.

sozi'al (zotsia:l) a. social. **~demokratie** f. social democracy. **~i'sieren** v.t. to socialize; to nationalize. **~ismus** m. socialism. **~ist** m. socialist. **~istisch** a. socialistic. **~kunde** f. sociology. **~lasten** f. social expenditure. **~leistungen** pl. social insurance benefits. **~wissenschaft** f. sociology; social science.

Sozius (zo:-) m. (-, -se) partner. **~sitz** m. (motor.) pillion seat.

Spachtel (-ax-) f. (-, -n) spatula.

Spagat m. string.

spähen v.i. to be on the look out; to reconnoitre, patrol, scout, explore. **~er** m. scout. **~erblick** m. searching glance. **~trupp** m. patrol.

Spa'lier (-li:r) n. (-s, -e) espalier, trellis; (fig.) lane; ~ stehen to form a lane. **~obst** n. wall-fruit.

Spalt (ʃp-) m. (-es, -e) crack, slit, slot, gap, chink; fissure, crevice; crevasse; (fig.) gulf. **~e** f. 1. = **Spalt. 2.** (typ.) column. **~fläche** f. plane of cleavage. **~holz** n.

firewood, sticks. **~pilz** m. fission-fungus.

spalt-en (ʃp-) v.t. to split; to divide, decompose, ferment. v.r. to split off, cleave; to divide. **~ung** f. splitting, fission; cleavage; decomposition; (fig.) division, dissension; schism.

Span m. (-es, ⸗e) chip, splinter; (pl.) shavings. [SPOON]

Spanferkel n. sucking-pig.

Spange (ʃpaŋə) f. (-, -n) buckle; clasp; strap; brooch; bracelet; bar (to medal, &c.). **~nschuh** m. strap shoe; buckled shoe. [SPANGLE]

spann¹ imperf. of spinnen.

Spann² m. (-es, -e) instep.

Spann-e (ʃp-) f. (-e, -en) span; short space (of time); (commerc.) margin. **~er** m. boot-tree, last; (zool.) butterfly. **~kraft** f. tension, elasticity, spring. **~kräftig** a. elastic. **~ung** f. tension; strain; (archit.) span; (electr.) voltage, potential; (fig.) close attention, intensity; strained relations. **~weite** f. span, width, distance.

spannen v.t. to stretch; to strain; to subject (spring, &c.) to tension; to tighten; to cock (rifle); to bend (bow); an den Wagen **~** to harness (horse). v.i. to be (too) tight; (fig.) to excite. v.r. to exert; gespannt sein (fig.) to be very anxious or curious. **~d** a. thrilling, exciting, absorbing.

Spant n. (-es, -en) rib (of ship).

Spar-büchse f. money-box. **~einlage** f. savings deposit. **~er** m. saver. **~kasse** f. savings-bank. **~pfennig** m. savings, nest-egg. **~sam** a. economical, thrifty, saving. adv. sparingly. **~samkeit** f. economy, thriftiness, thrift.

sparen (ʃp-) v.t. & i. to save, spare; to cut down expenses, economize, use sparingly; to put by money.

Spargel m. (-s, -) asparagus. **~stecher** m. asparagus-knife.

spärlich (ʃp-) a. scanty, meagre, scarce, frugal; sparse, thin. **~keit** f. scantiness; scarcity, rareness, rarity.

Sparren m. (-s, -) spar, rafter; einen **~** haben (fig.) to have a

screw loose. **~werk** n. rafters.

Sparte f. (-, -n) branch; subject.

Spaß (ʃpaːs) m. (-es, ⸗e) jest, joke; fun, amusement, sport; zum **~** for fun. v.i. to joke, jest. **~eshalber** adv. for fun. **~haft**, **~ig** aa. joking, jocular, amusing, funny, odd. **~macher**, **~vogel** m. wag; buffoon. **~verderber** m. spoil-sport. [IT.]

Spat m. (-es, -e) spar; (vet.) spavin.

spät a. late, belated; slow, backward; **~** kommen to be late; wie **~** ist es? what time is it? **~er** comp. a. later, afterwards; **~erhin** later on. **~estens** adv. at the latest. **~ling** m. latest born; late fruit. **~obst** n. late fruit. **~zündung** f. retarded ignition.

Spatel m. (-s, -) spatula; trowel.

Spaten (-aː-) m. (-s, -) spade. **~stich** m. cut with a spade.

Spatz m. (-en, -en) sparrow.

spa'zier-en (-tsiːr-) vws.i. to walk about, stroll, take a walk; **~en** fahren to go for a drive; **~en** gehen to go for a walk. **~fahrt** f. drive. **~gang** m. walk, stroll. **~gänger** m. walker, stroller, promenader. **~stock** m. walking-stick. [IT.]

Specht (-çt) m. (-es, -e) woodpecker.

Speck m. (-es) bacon; fat; blubber; lard. **~ig** a. fat; dirty. **~schwarte** f. rind of bacon. **~seite** f. flitch of bacon. **~stein** m. soapstone, steatite.

spe'd-ieren v.t. to send; to dispatch, forward. **~i'teur** m. forwarding agent, carrier, furniture remover. **~iti'on** f. forwarding; forwarding agency. **~itionsgeschäft** n. forwarding agency; furniture removal business.

Speer m. (-es, -e) spear; lance; javelin.

Speiche (-ç-) f. (-, -n) spoke.

Speichel (-ç-) m. (-s) saliva, spittle. **~drüse** f. salivary gland. **~fluß** m. flow of saliva; salivation. **~lecker** m. toady.

Speicher (-ç-) m. (-s, -) warehouse, storeroom; granary; reservoir; loft. **~n** v.t. to store, warehouse.

spei-en v.t. & i. st. to spit; to vomit;

to belch (fire). **~gatt** n. scupper. **~napf** m. spittoon.

Speise (-za) f. (-, -n) food; meal; dish; (colloq.) sweet, pudding. **~brei** m. chyme. **~eis** n. ice-cream. **~fett** n. cooking fat. **~kammer** f. larder. **~karte** f. menu. **~n-aufzug** m. service lift. **~zettel** m. bill of fare, menu. **~nfolge** f. menu. **~röhre** f. gullet, oesophagus. **~saal** m. dining-room. **~wagen** m. dining-car. [ML]

speisen (-z-) v.t. to feed, give to eat, board; to supply. v.i. to eat, dine, sup.

Spek'takel m. (-s, -) ⚔ noise, row. n. (obs.) show.

Spek'tralanalyse f. spectrum analysis.

Speku'lant m. (-en, -en) speculator.

speku'lieren v.i. to speculate.

Spe'lunke f. (-, -n) den; low gin-shop.

Spelz (-ts) m. spelt. **~e** f. glume (of grains); awn, beard.

Spend-e f. (-e, -en) gift, present; contribution, donation; alms, charity. **~en** v.t. to administer, dispense; to bestow; to contribute (to); to give. **~er** m. giver, donor; benefactor. **~'ieren** v.t. to stand, pay for, treat.

Spengler m. (-s, -) plumber; tin-smith.

Sperber m. (-s, -) sparrow-hawk.

Spe'renzchen pl. mach' keine ~ don't make a fuss.

Sperling m. (-s, -e) sparrow.

Sperma n. sperm.

sperr'angelweit adv. ~ offen wide open.

Sperrdruck m. spaced type.

Sperr-e (jp-) f. (-e, -en) shutting, closing; blockade; ban; barricade; barrier; block; embargo; **~e verhängen** to closure, block, ban. **~feuer** n. (mil.) barrage (fire); curtain fire. **~flieger** m. patrol aircraft. **~gebiet** n. prohibited area; blockade zone. **~gut** n. bulky goods. **~guthaben** n. blocked account. **~haken** m. catch. **~holz** n. plywood. **~ig** a. protruding; unwieldy. **~kette** f. drag-chain. **~-**

schicht f. insulating layer. **~sitz** m. (theatr.) stall, reserved seat. **~ung** f. barricade; blocking. **~vorrichtung** f. locking device, lock.

sperren v.t. to close, shut, bar, block, barricade; to cut off (gas, &c.); to straddle (legs); to space (type); ins Gefängnis ~ to put in prison. v.r. (fig.) to struggle, resist.

Spesen f.pl. charges, expenses.

Speze'rei f. (-, -en) spice.

Spezi'al-arzt (-tsia:l-) m. specialist. **~fall** m. special case. **~'sieren** v.t. to specialize. **~i'tät** f. speciality.

spezi'ell a. special, particular.

spe'zifisch a. specific. **~i'zieren** v.t. to specify.

Sphär-e f. (-e, -en) sphere. **~isch** a. spherical.

Spick-aal m. smoked eel. **~en** v.t. to lard.

spie imperf. of speien.

Spiegel m. (-s, -) looking-glass, mirror; (med.) speculum; (naut.) stern; facing, tab. **~bild** n. reflected image. **~blank** a. shining. **~ei** n. fried egg. **~fechte'rei** f. sham fight, humbug; **~glas** n. plate glass. **~glatt** a. smooth as a mirror, glassy. **~pfeiler** m. (archit.) pier. **~scheibe** f. pane of plate glass. **~schrank** m. wardrobe with mirror. **~schrift** f. mirror writing. **~ung** f. reflection; mirage. [L]

spiegeln v.i. to shine, glitter, sparkle. v.t. to reflect. v.r. to be reflected.

Spiel n. (-es, -e) play, game, sport; (mus.) touch, manner of playing; (theatr.) playing, acting, performance; set, suit, pack (of cards); gambling; motion, working; (fig.) plaything, sport; mit klingendem ~ with drums and trumpets sounding; aufs ~ setzen to stake; auf dem ~ stehen to be at stake; das ~ verloren geben to throw up the sponge; leichtes ~ haben to have no difficulty; seine Hand im ~ haben to have a finger in the pie; sein ~ treiben mit to make game of; im ~ sein to be involved in the case; *aus dem ~ lassen* to leave out of the question, let alone.

Spiel-art f. variety. **~automat** m. slot-machine; juke-box. **~ball** m. ball; (*fig.*) plaything, sport. **~bank** f. gaming-table. **~dose** f. musical box. **~er** m. player, actor, performer; gambler. **~e'rei** f. (*fig.*) trifle. **~feld** n. ground, field; (tennis-)court. **~film** m. feature-film. **~hahn** m. heath-cock, black-cock. **~hölle** f. gambling-hell. **~leiter** m. stage-manager, producer. **~mann** m. (*pl.* **~leute**) musician; minstrel; bandsman. **~marke** f. counter, chip. **~plan** m. programme; repertory, repertoire. **~platz** m. playground. **~raum** m. (free) play; elbow-room, latitude, scope; (*mach.*) clearance. **~sachen**, **~waren** f.pl. toys. **~schar** f. (*theatr. & mus.*) amateur company *or* players. **~uhr** f. musical box (with clock). **~verderber** m. spoil-sport, killjoy, wet blanket. **~werk** n. chime (of clock). **~zeug** n. toy.

spielen v.t. & i. to play, sport; to act, take the part of; to perform; to gamble; to trifle (with), toy *or* coquet (with); to simulate, feign, pretend; to take place, (*of scene*) be laid; to glitter, sparkle, flash. **~d** adv. (*fig.*) with the utmost ease.

Spiere f. (-, -n) spar, boom.

Spieß m. (-es, -e) lance, spear, pike; spit. **~bürger** m. 'bourgeois', narrow-minded townsman, Philistine. **~bürgerlich** a. 'bourgeois', narrow-minded, commonplace. **~er** m. (*colloq.*) Philistine. **~geselle** m. accomplice. **~glanz** m. antimony. **~ig** a. narrow-minded, uncultured. **~ruten** f.pl. **~ruten laufen** to run the gauntlet.

spießen v.t. to spear; to pierce, transfix, impale.

Spill n. (-es, -e) capstan, winch; windlass.

Spi'nat (-a:t) m. (-s) spinach.

Spind m. & n. (-es, -e) wardrobe, press; locker.

Spindel f. (-, -n) spindle; distaff; pinion, mandrel. **~dürr** a. lean as a rake.

Spi'nett n. (-s, -e) spinet.

Spinn-e f. (-e, -en) spider. **~e-feind** a. bitterly hostile. **~e'rei** f. spinning; spinning-mill. **~erin** f. spinner. **~fäden** m.pl. gossamer. **~faser** f. synthetic fibre. **~gewebe** n., **~webe** f. cobweb. **~rad** n. spinning-wheel. **~rocken** m. distaff. **~stoffindustrie** f. textile industry.

spinnen v.t. & st. to spin; (*of cat*) to purr; (*fig.*) to be crazy.

spintisieren v.i. to muse.

Spi'on (-o:n) m. (-s, -e) spy; mirror (fixed to outside of window). **~age** f. espionage, spying. **~ageabwehr** f. counter-espionage service. **~ieren** v.i. to spy, play the spy; to spy upon, pry into.

Spi'ral-e (-a:l-) f. (-e, -en) spiral; coil. **~bohrer** m. twist-drill; auger. **~feder** f. spiral spring.

Spiri'tismus m. (-) spiritualism.

Spiritu'osen pl. spirituous liquors.

Spiritus m. (-) spirit, spirits; methylated spirit. **~brennerei** f. distillery. **~kocher** m. spirit-stove.

Spi'tal (-a:l) n. (-s, "er), **Spittel** n. (-s, -) hospital.

Spitz m. (-es, -e) Pomeranian dog; (*fig.*) einen **~ haben** to be slightly tipsy.

spitz[2] a. pointed, peaked, sharp, tapering; acute; sarcastic, caustic, biting. **~bart** m. pointed beard. **~bogen** m. pointed *or* Gothic arch. **~bube** m. rogue, rascal; swindler. **~bübisch** a. roguish; rascally.

Spitz-e f. (-e, -en) point; tip (*of* tongue); top, summit; head; peak; toe; extremity; apex, vertex; lace; pointed remark, sarcastic observation; *einem die ~e bieten* to defy a person; *etwas auf die ~e treiben* to carry to extremes. **~enfilm** m. top film. **~enklöppelei** f. pillow-lace(-making). **~enleistung** f. record; maximum output *or* performance. **~enlohn** m. maximum pay. **~entanz** m. toe dance.

~enverband *m.* head organization. ~feile *f.* tapered file. ~findig *a.* subtle, sharp; shrewd; cavilling. ~findigkeit *f.* subtlety, sophistry. ~hacke *f.* pickaxe. ~ig *a.* pointed, sharp; sarcastic. ~marke *f.* (*typ.*) heading. ~maus *f.* shrew-mouse. ~name *m.* nickname. ~winklig *a.* acute-angled.

Spitzel *m.* (-s, -) police spy *or* agent; informer. ~n *v.i.* to spy upon.

spitzen *v.t.* to point, sharpen; *seine Ohren* ~ to prick up one's ears; *den Mund* ~ to purse the lips; *sich* ~ *auf* to hope for, count on.

spleißen *v.t. st.* to split.

Splint *m.* peg; sap(-wood).

Splitter *m.* (-s, -) splinter, chip, fragment; (*bibl.*) mote. ~n *v.i.* to splinter, split. ~bombe *f.* fragmentation bomb. ~(faser-)nackt *a.* stark naked. ~richter *m.* fault-finder, carper, caviller. ~sicher *a.* splinter-proof, non-splintering.

spon'tan *a.* spontaneous.

Spore *f.* (-, -n) spore.

Sporn *m.* (-es, Sporen) spur; (*av.*) tail skid; tail spade; (*fig.*) stimulus, incentive. ~en *v.t.* to spur. ~streichs *adv.* post-haste, immediately.

Sport (-ɔ-) *m.* (-es) sport; ~ *treiben* to go in for sports. ~abzeichen *n.* sports badge. ~funk *m.* radio sports news. ~ler, ~smann *m.* sportsman. ~lich *a.* sporting, athletic; sportsmanlike. ~s-mütze *f.* tweed cap. ~swagen *m.* sports car; folding pram.

Sporteln *f.pl.* perquisites, fees.

Spott (-ɔ-) *m.* (-es) mockery, ridicule, derision, scorn, banter; butt, laughing-stock. ~bild *n.* caricature. ~billig *a.* dirt-cheap. ~drossel *f.* mocking-bird. ~geburt *f.* abortion, monstrosity. ~geld *n.,* ~preis *m.* trifling sum, a mere song. ~name *m.* nickname. ~vogel *m.* mocking-bird; mocker.

Spötte'lei *f.* (-, -en) banter, chaff, raillery.

spött-eln *v.i.* to laugh, jeer (at), sneer (at). ~er *m.,* ~erin *f.*

mocker, scoffer, jeerer. ~isch *a.* mocking, jeering, scoffing.

spotten *v.i.* to mock, jeer (at), deride; *jeder Beschreibung* ~ to beggar description.

sprach *imperf.* of **sprechen.**

Sprache (-a:xə) *f.* (-, -n) speech, talk; language, tongue; diction; voice; *alte* ~ classical languages; *neuere* ~n modern l.; *einem die* ~ *benehmen* to strike one dumb; *mit der* ~ *herausrücken* to speak freely; *zur* ~ *bringen* to broach (a subject); *zur* ~ *kommen* to be mentioned, be touched on; *in der* ~ in terms (of).

Sprach-fehler *m.* grammatical mistake; speech defect. ~fertigkeit *f.* fluency. ~forscher *m.* linguist, philologist. ~gebrauch *m.* usage. ~gefühl *n.* feeling for what is correct *or* idiomatic in a language. ~gewandt *a.* fluent. ~grenze *f.* linguistic frontier. ~insel *f.* isolated district speaking a dialect of its own. ~kundig *a.* proficient in languages. ~lehre *f.* grammar. ~lich *a.* linguistic, grammatical. ~los *a.* speechless, dumb. ~rohr *n.* speaking-tube; (*fig.*) mouthpiece. ~schatz *m.* vocabulary. ~schnitzer *m.* blunder, mistake, solecism. ~störung *f.* speech defect, impediment. ~tum *n.* language. ~unterricht *m.* teaching of languages. ~werkzeug *n.* organ of speech. ~widrig *a.* ungrammatical, incorrect. ~wissenschaft *f.* linguistics, philology; *vergleichende* ~ comparative philology.

sprang *imperf.* of **springen.**

sprechen (-ç-) *v.t. & i. st.* to speak, talk; to converse; to talk over, discuss; to say; to pronounce; (*fig.*) to be evident; to be written in (one's face); *dafür* ~ to speak in favour of, support (theory); *nicht zu* ~ *sein* to be engaged; *gut zu* ~ *sein auf* to be kindly disposed to; *sich herum* ~ to be the talk (of the town, &c.). ~d *a.* (*fig.*) speaking, striking (likeness); conclusive.

Sprech-er *m.* (-ers, -er) speaker; spokesman; announcer. ~film *m.* talkie. **~melodie** *f.* intonation, speech-melody. **~stunde** *f.* consulting hour; office hour. **~stundenhilfe** *f.* receptionist at a doctor's. **~trichter** *m.* mouthpiece (of telephone, &c.). **~weise** *f.* manner of speaking; diction. **~zimmer** *n.* consulting room.

spreiten *v.t.* to spread.

Spreiz-e *f.* (-e, -en) strut, stay. **~en** *v.t.* to spread out, stretch out; to straddle. *v.r.* to boast; to be affected; to resist.

Spreng-bombe *f.* H.E. bomb. **~er** *m.* (lawn-)sprinkler, spray. **~geschoß** *n.* projectile, shell. **~granate** *f.* H.E. shell. **~kapsel** *f.* detonator. **~kommando** *n.* bomb disposal unit; demolition party. **~körper** *m.* explosive slab. **~kraft** *f.* explosive force. **~ladung** *f.* explosive charge. **~pulver** *n.* blasting-powder. **~stoff** *m.* high explosive. **~trichter** *m.* mine crater. **~ung** *f.* blowing up, blasting. **~wagen** *m.* sprinkler.

Sprengel *m.* (-s, -) diocese; parish.

sprengen *v.t.* to burst (open); to blow up, blast; to spring (mine); to break (bank); to break up (a meeting); to sprinkle, spray; to water. *vws.i.* to gallop, ride hard.

sprenkeln *v.t.* to speckle, spot.

Spreu *f.* (-) chaff.

spricht *3rd pers. sing. pres. of* **sprechen**.

Sprich-wort *n.* proverb, adage; saying. **~wörtlich** *a.* proverbial.

sprießen *v.i. st.* to sprout, bud, shoot up.

Spring-brunnen *m.* fountain; jet (of water). **~er** *m.* jumper, vaulter; (*chess*) knight. **~feder** *f.* spring. **~flut** *f.* spring-tide. **~insfeld** *m.* young harum-scarum. **~quell** *m.* fountain, spring. **~seil** *n.* skipping-rope.

springen *vws. & v.i. st.* to leap, jump, hop, skip, spring; to run; (*of fountain*) to gush, play. *vws.i.* to crack, split, snap; *in die Augen ~* to be obvious; *etwas ~ lassen* to stand, treat (one to).

Sprit *m.* (-s, -e) spirit, alcohol.

Spritz-e *f.* (-e, -en) fire-engine;

spray, sprayer; (*med.*) syringe; injection. **~enhaus** *n.* fire-station. **~er** *m.* squirt; splash; spot. **~fahrt** *f.* trip, excursion. **~ig** *a.* prickling; lively. **~kuchen** *m.* fritter. **~leder** *n.* splash leather. **~wand** *f.* dashboard.

spritzen *v.t.* to squirt, spray, sprinkle; to splash, bespatter. *v.i.* to gush forth, spurt up; to splutter.

spröd-e *a.* brittle; rough (skin); reserved, shy, prim. **~igkeit** *f.* brittleness; reserve, shyness, coldness.

sproß[1] *imperf. of* **sprießen**.

Sproß[2] (-o-) *m.* (Spross-es, -e) shoot, sprout; offspring, scion; antler (of stag).

Sprosse *f.* (-, -n) rung (of ladder).

sprossen *v.i.* to sprout, shoot.

Sprößling *m.* (-s, -e) sprout, shoot; offspring, scion.

Sprotte *f.* (-, -n) sprat.

Spruch (-x) *m.* (-es, ⸚e) aphorism, maxim, saying, (bible-)text; sentence, verdict. **~band** *n.* banderol, scroll. **~kammer** *f.* Court of Judicature. **~reif** *a.* ripe for decision.

Sprudel (-u:-) *m.* (-s, -) (hot) spring, bubbling well. **~n** *v.i.* to gush forth, bubble up; (*fig.*) to sparkle (with), brim over (with).

sprüh-en *v.i. & t.* to spark, emit sparks; to fly; to spray; to drizzle; (*fig.*) to sparkle (with wit), flash (with anger). **~regen** *m.* drizzle, drizzling rain.

Sprung *m.* (-es, ⸚e) spring, bound, leap, jump; dive; dash; (horse's) curvet; crack, fissure, split; *auf dem ~ sein zu* . . . to be on the point of; *hinter jemandes Sprünge kommen* to find a person out. **~bein** *n.* ankle-bone. **~brett** *n.* springboard. **~feder** *f.* spring. **~haft** *a.* by leaps and bounds; (*fig.*) unsteady; desultory, disconnected. **~schanze** *f.* ski-jump. **~weise** *a.* in jerks, by leaps and bounds.

Spuck-e (-uk-) *f.*(-e) spittle, saliva. **~en** *v.i. & t.* to spit, expectorate. **~napf** *m.* spittoon.

Spuk (-u:k) *m.* (-es, -e) ghost,

spectre, apparition, spook; mischief. **~en** *v.i.* to haunt; to be haunted. **~geist** *m.* hobgoblin. **~geschichte** *f.* ghost-story. **~haft** *a.* ghostly, ghostlike.

Spul-e (-u:-) *f.* (-e, -en) spool, bobbin; quill; (*electr.*) coil. **~en** *v.t.* to wind, spool, reel. **~maschine** *f.* bobbin-frame, spooling machine. **~rad** *n.* spooling-wheel. **~wurm** *m.* mawworm.

spül-en (-y:-) *v.t.* to rinse, wash, flush. **~faß** *n.* wash-tub. **~icht** *n.* dish-water; slops; swill. **~ung** *f.* cleansing, rinsing; flushpipe. **~wasser** *n.* dish-water; slops.

Spund *m.* (-es, -e) bung, plug; stopper. **~en** *v.t.* to bung. **~loch** *n.* bung-hole.

Spur *f.* (-, -en) trace, trail, track; footprint, footstep; scent; mark, sign; vestige; remains, clue; (*tech.*) groove, channel; (*collog.*) small quantity; *keine ~ !* not a bit, not at all; *einem auf die ~ kommen* to be on a person's tracks. **~los** *a.* trackless. *adv.* without a trace. **~weite** *f.* gauge (of rails); track (between wheels).

spür-en *v.t.* to feel, to be conscious of, perceive, experience; **~en nach** to track, follow the track of, scent out. **~hund** *m.* pointer; (*fig.*) spy. **~nase** *f.* good nose, keen sense of smell. **~sinn** *m.* sagacity, shrewdness; **~sinn haben** to have a scent *or* flair (for).

sputen *v.r.* to hurry, hurry up, make haste. [SPEED]

Staat *m.* (-es, -en) state, commonwealth; government; pomp, show, parade; finery, dress; *in vollem ~* in full dress; **~ machen (mit)** to show off; to boast (of). **~enlos** *a.* having no nationality. **~lich** *a.* state-; public; political.

Staats-akt *m.* state ceremony. **~aktion** *f.* political event. **~angehörige(r)** *m.* subject, national. **~angehörigkeit** *f.* nationality; citizenship. **~anwalt** *m.* public prosecutor. **~archiv** *n.* public record office. **~beamte(r)** *m.* civil servant, government official. **~bürger** *m.* citizen; national.

~bürgerkunde *f.* training in citizenship, civics. **~bürgerlich** *a.* civic. **~bürgerschaft** *f.* citizenship. **~dienst** *m.* civil service. **~form** *f.* form of government. **~gewalt** *f.* supreme power. **~haushalt** *m.* budget, finances. **~hoheit** *f.* sovereignty. **~kasse** *f.* treasury; exchequer. **~kerl** *m.* fine fellow. **~kleid** *n.* gala dress. **~klug** *a.* diplomatic, politic. **~körper** *m.* body politic. **~kunst** *f.* political science, statecraft, politics. **~mann** *m.* statesman, politician. **~männisch** *a.* statesmanlike; political. **~papiere** *n.pl.* government securities, stocks. **~recht** *n.* constitutional law. **~streich** *m.* coup d'état. **~verfassung** *f.* constitution. **~wesen** *n.* state, commonwealth. **~wirtschaft** *f.* political economy. **~wissenschaft** *f.* political science. **~wohl** *n.* common weal. **~zugehörigkeit** *f.* nationality.

Stab (-a:p) *m.* (-es, -̈e) stick, rod, staff; (iron bar; crosier; mace; pole; baton; (magic wand; (*mil.*) staff, headquarters personnel; **den ~ brechen über** (*fig.*) to condemn. **~(hoch)sprung** *m.* polejump. **~reim** *m.* alliteration. **~sarzt** *m.* medical officer. **~schef** *m.* Chief of Staff. **~soffizier** *m.* field officer. **~squartier** *n.* headquarters.

Stäbchen *n.* (-s, -) rodlet, rod.

sta'bil (-i:l) *a.* stable. **~i'sieren** *v.t.* to stabilize.

stach *imperf. of* stechen.

Stachel (-x-) *m.* (-s, -n) thorn, prickle, prick; sting; quill; spike; prong; goad; (*fig.*) sting; stimulus, spur. **~beere** *f.* gooseberry. **~draht** *m.* barbed wire. **~halsband** *n.* spiked dog-collar. **~ig** *a.* prickly, thorny. **~schwein** *n.* porcupine.

stacheln *v.t.* to goad; to stimulate, spur on.

Stadel *m.* (-s, -) barn, shed.

Stadion *n.* (-s, Stadien) stadium, arena.

Stadium (-a:-) *n.* (-s, Stadien) ♦ phase, stage (of development).

Stadt f. (-, ¨e) town; city. **~bahn** f. city railway; metropolitan railway. **~bekannt** a. known or notorious all over the town. **~bezirk**, **~teil** m. quarter, district, ward. **~bild** n. panorama of the town; plan or site (of town). **~gespräch** n. talk of the town. **~koffer** m. suitcase. **~randsiedlung** f. settlement on the outskirts of a town. **~rat** m. alderman. **~schreiber** m. town-clerk. **~väter** m.pl. city-fathers. **~verordnete(r)** m. town-councillor, **~verwaltung** f. municipality. [STEAD]

Städt-er m. (-ers, -er) townsman, citizen. **~erin** f. townswoman. **~isch** a. municipal, urban.

Sta'fette f. (-, -n) courier, express. **~nlauf** m. relay race.

Sta'ffage f. (-, -n) (paint.) decorative figures; decoration.

Staffel f. (-, -n) step, rung; (mil.) echelon; detachment, party; (av.) squadron; (sport.) relay. **~ei** f. easel. **~lauf** m. relay race. **~n** v.t. to graduate. **~tarif** m. adjustable tariff; graded wage scale. **~ung** f. graduation; gradation; (mil.) echelon formation; stagger of aircraft wings.

Stag n. (-es, -e) (naut.) stay.

stag'nieren v.i. to stagnate.

stahl imperf. of **stehlen**.

Stahl² m. (-es, -e) steel. **~bad** n. chalybeate bath or spa; (fig.) (mil.) barrage. **~beton** m. reinforced concrete. **~feder** f. pen-nib; steel spring. **~guß** m. cast steel. **~helm** m. steel helmet. **~kammer** f. strong-room. **~stich** m. steel engraving. **~waren** f.pl. cutlery, hardware. **~werk** n. steelworks.

stähl-en v.t. to convert into steel; (fig.) to harden, steel. **~ern** a. steel; steely.

stak imperf. of **stecken**.

Staken m. (-s, -) stake. v.t. to pole, punt.

Sta'ket n. (-s, -e) palisade, fence.

Stall m. (-es, ¨e) stable; sty; kennel. **~dienst** m. stable-work. **~knecht** m. ostler, groom, stable-

boy. **~magd** f. dairy maid. **~meister** m. riding-master, equerry, master of the horse. **~ung** f. stabling; stables; mews.

Stamm m. (-es, ¨e) stem; root; stalk; trunk; race, family, clan; stock, breed; tribe; (fig.) main part, main body.

Stamm-aktie f. ordinary share. **~baum** m. genealogical tree; pedigree. **~buch** n. album. **~eltern** pl. first parents, ancestors. **~folge** f. line of descent. **~gast** m. regular customer. **~gut** n. family estate. **~halter** m. eldest son, son and heir. **~kapital** n. original capital. **~kneipe** f., **~lokal** n. favourite pub. **~land** n. mother country. **~linie** f. lineage. **~(m)utter** f. ancestress. **~rolle** f. (mil.) nominal roll. **~silbe** f. root syllable. **~tafel** f. genealogical table. **~tisch** m. table reserved for regular customers. **~vater** m. ancestor. **~verwandt** a. cognate, kindred. **~wort** n. root word, stem.

stamm-eln v.t. & i. to stammer, stutter. **~ler** m. stammerer, stutterer.

stammen rvs.i. to spring (from), come (from), originate; (gram.) to be derived (from).

stämmig a. sturdy, strong, vigorous. **~keit** f. sturdiness, strength.

stampf-en v.t. & i. to stamp; to pound; to mash; to crush; to beat; to trudge; (of horse) to paw the ground; (naut.) to pitch. **~kartoffeln** f. pl. mashed potatoes.

stand¹ imperf. of **stehen**.

Stand² m. (-es, ¨e) standing; upright position; stand, position; constellation (of stars); stall, pitch, booth; (pol.) estate; (obs.) guild, corporation; level (of prices); condition; state; social standing, rank, class; profession; einen schweren ~ haben to have a hard fight, have a tough job; in gutem ~ sein to be in good condition. See also **imstande**, **instand**, and **zustande**.

Stand-bild n. statue. **~esamt** n. registrar's office. **~esbeamte(r)**

m. registrar. ~esdünkel *m.* pride of place. ~esehe *f.* marriage for position *or* rank. ~esehre *f.* professional honour. ~esgemäß *adv.* in accordance with one's rank. ~esgenosse *m.* equal in rank, compeer. ~esregister *n.* register of births, &c. ~esunterschied *m.* difference of rank, class distinction. ~esvorurteil *n.* class prejudice. ~geld *n.* stallage. ~gericht *n.* court martial. ~haft *a.* steadfast, constant, firm, steady. ~haftigkeit *f.* steadfastness, constancy, firmness. ~halten *v.i.* to hold out, stand firm; to withstand, resist. ~lager, ~quartier *n.* permanent quarters; station. ~ort *m.* station; position; garrison. ~pauke *f.* severe reprimand, (*sl.*) telling-off. ~punkt *m.* point of view, standpoint. ~recht *n.* martial law. ~rechtlich *a.* according to martial law. ~rede *f.* harangue. ~uhr *f.* grandfather clock.

Stan'darte *f.* (-, -n) standard; unit.

Länd-chen *n.* (-chens, -chen) serenade. ~er *m.* stand; post, pillar. ~ig *a.* permanent; fixed; constant. *adv.* continuously.

Stange (-ŋə) *f.* (-, -n) pole; (iron) bar; stake; perch; stick (of sealing-wax, &c.); *eine ~ Gold* (*fig.*) a mint of money; *bei der ~ bleiben* to persevere (with task); *einem die ~ halten* to take a person's part; *von der ~* ready-made (suit), (*sl.*) reach-me-down. ~bohne *f.* runner bean. ~nsellerie *f.* celery. ~nspargel *m.* asparagus.

stank *imperf. of* stinken

Stänker *m.* (-s, -) quarrelsome person. ~ei *f.* squabble. ~n *v.i.* to squabble.

Stanni'ol *n.* (-s) tinfoil.

Stanze *f.* (-, -n) stanza; (*tech.*) stamp, die. ~n *v.t.* to stamp, punch.

Stapel (-a:-) *m.* (-s, -) pile, heap; (*naut.*) stocks; depot, dump; *vom ~ lassen* to launch; *vom ~ laufen* to be launched. ~lauf *m.* launching. ~n *v.t.* to pile up, stack up.

~platz *m.* depot, dump.

stapfen *vws.i.* to plod.

Star¹ (-a:r) *m.* (-es, -e) cataract (on the eye); *einem den ~ stechen* to operate on a person for cataract; (*fig.*) to open a person's eyes.

Star² (-a:r) *m.* (-es, -e) starling. ~kasten *m.* nesting-box.

starb *imperf. of* sterben

stark *a.* strong; stout; considerable, numerous; voluminous; heavy (rain); intense, great; *das ist ~ !* that's a bit thick; *~ auftragen* (*fig.*) to exaggerate, boast. ~strom *m.* (*electr.*) power current. ~stromleitung *f.* (*electr.*) power-line, power-circuit. [STARK]

Stärke *f.* (-, -n) strength, force, vigour; power, energy; violence, intensity; stoutness, corpulence; thickness; (*fig.*) strong point, forte; (*chem.*) starch. ~grad *m.* degree of strength; intensity. ~haltig *a.* containing starch, starchy. ~mehl *n.* starch-flour.

stärk-en *v.t.* to strengthen; to invigorate; to fortify; to confirm; to starch. ~ung *f.* strengthening; invigoration; refreshment. ~ungsmittel *n.* tonic.

starr *a.* fixed, rigid; stiff; staring (eyes); (*fig.*) obstinate, stubborn; *~ vor Staunen* dumbfounded. ~heit *f.* rigidity; stiffness; obstinacy. ~köpfig *a.* stubborn, pigheaded. ~krampf *m.* tetanus. ~sinn *m.* obstinacy.

starren *v.i.* to stare; to be numb; to tower up; *~ vor* to be covered with, bristle with (dirt).

Start *m.* (-es, -e) start. ~bahn *f.* (*av.*) runway. ~en *v.i.* to start. ~klar *adv.* (*av.*) ready for the take-off. ~zeichen *n.* starting signal.

Statik *f.* (-) statics.

statisch *a.* static.

Stati'on *f.* (-o:n) *f.* (-, -en) station, stop; ward (in hospital); *freie ~* free board and lodging. ~sarzt *m.* resident physician, house physician. ~svorsteher *m.* station-master.

Sta'tist *m.* (-en, -en) (*theatr.*) walker-on, supernumerary actor; mute (figure); (film) extra.

Sta′tist·ik f. (-ik, -iken) statistics. **~iker** m. actuary. **~isch** a. statistical.

Sta′tiv n. (-s, -e) stand; tripod.

statuieren v.t. to maintain, establish.

Statt f. (-) place, stead; *an Eides ~* in lieu of an oath; *an Kindes ~ annehmen* to adopt a child. *prep. & conj.* instead of; in lieu of.

finden, ~haben v.i. to take place. **~geben** v.i. to permit, allow. **~haft** a. admissible, allowable, legal. **~halter** m. governor. **~halterschaft** f. governorship. **~lich** a. imposing, commanding, stately; magnificent, grand; considerable. **~lichkeit** f. stateliness, dignity; magnificence. See also **zustatten** and **zustatten**.

Stätte f. (-, -n) place, abode.

Statue (-a:tua) f. (-, -n) statue.

Sta′tur (-u:r) f. (-, -en) figure; height, stature.

Sta′tut n. (-s, -en) statute, regulations; (pl.) articles (of an association). **~enmäßig** a. statutory.

Stau-becken n. reservoir; static tank. **~damm** m. dam. **~see** m. reservoir. **~ung** f. stowing; damming up (of water); (traffic) block; obstruction. **~wasser** n. dammed-up water; static water. **~werk** n. lock.

Staub (-p) m. (-es) dust; powder; pollen; *~ aufwirbeln* (fig.) to cause a flutter; *sich aus dem ~ machen* to make off, abscond; *in den ~ ziehen* to degrade, depreciate. **~beutel** m. (bot.) anther. **~blatt** n. (bot.) stamen. **~faden** m. (bot.) stamen; filament. **~fänger** m. dust collector, dust trap. **~gefäß** n. stamen. **~ig** a. dusty. **~kamm** m. small-tooth comb. **~korn** n. dust particle. **~lappen** m., **~tuch** n. duster. **~sauger** m. vacuum cleaner. **~wedel** m. feather-duster. **~zucker** m. castor sugar.

stauben v.i. to be dusty, give off dust.

stäuben v.t. to dust. v.i. to raise dust; to throw off spray.

stauchen v.t. to stook (corn, &c.); (mach.) to upset.

Staude f. (-, -n) shrub.

stauen v.t. to stow (goods); to dam up (water). v.r. to be banked up; to jam (up), block.

staunen v.i. to be astonished, amazed (at). *subst.* n. astonishment, amazement.

Staupe[1] f. flogging.

Staupe[2] f. (-, -n) (vet.) distemper.

stäupen v.t. to flog.

Stea′rinkerze f. stearin-candle.

Stech-apfel m. thorn-apple. **~bahn** f. tilt-yard. **~becken** n. bed-pan. **~er** m. hair-trigger (of gun). **~fliege** f. cleg, horse-fly. **~heber** m. siphon. **~mücke** f. gnat. **~palme** f. holly, ilex. **~schritt** m. goose-step. **~uhr** f. control clock.

stechen (-c-) v.t. & i. st. to prick; to pierce; to sting, bite; to stab; to stick (pig), kill; to cut (peat, &c.); to engrave; to trump (card), take (trick); (of sun) to burn, scorch; *in die Augen ~* to take one's fancy.

Steck-brief m. warrant. **~dose** f. (electr.) wall plug; socket.

Steck-en[1] m. (-ens, -en) stick; staff. **~enpferd** n. hobby-horse; hobby, fad. **~er** m., **~dose** f. (electr.) plug. **~kissen** n. cushion for carrying infant. **~kontakt** m. plug point. **~ling** m. cutting (of plant). **~nadel** f. pin. **~rübe** f. turnip. **~schlüssel** m. box-spanner.

stecken[2] v.t. to stick, put (in); to pin up, fasten together; to fix; to plant. v.i. (also st.) to be; to be hiding; to be stuck; to be involved (in); to be in(side); to stick fast; *dahinter steckt etwas* there's something at the bottom of it. **~bleiben** v.v.s.i. to be stuck, come to a standstill, break down. **~lassen** v.t. to leave (key in door).

Steg (-k) m. (-es, -e) footpath; foot-bridge; strap; (mus.) bridge. **~reif** m. *aus dem ~reif sprechen* to speak extempore.

Steh-bierhalle f. pub, public bar. **~er** m. stayer. **~kragen** m. stand-up collar. **~lampe** f. standard lamp. **~leiter** f. step-ladder. **~platz** m. standing-room.

stehen v.i. st. to stand; to stop,

stand still; to be; to suit, become; ~ **auf** (of clock, &c.) to point to, be at, show; ~ **für** to guarantee, vouch for; **zu** ~ **kommen** to cost; **geschrieben** ~ to be written; **es steht bei dir** it rests with you. ~ **bleiben** vws.i. to stop; to remain standing. ~**d** a. standing; stationary; upright; permanent; regular; stagnant (water); ~**den Fußes** at once, on the spot; ~**de Redensart** hackneyed phrase. ~ **lassen** v.t. to leave (standing).

stehlen v.t. & i. st. to steal, rob, take away. subst. n. stealing, robbery, larceny.

steif a. stiff, rigid, inflexible; numb; thick; formal. ~**en** v.t. to stiffen. ~**heit** f. stiffness, rigidity; formality. ~**leinen** n. buckram.

Steig (-k) m. (-es, -e) path. ~**bügel** m. stirrup. ~**eisen** n. crampon, climbing iron. ~**er** m. mine inspector. ~**flug** m. ascent. ~**höhe** f. (av.) ceiling. ~**ung** f. ascent; incline, gradient.

steigen vws.i. st. to climb, ascend, go up, mount; to rise; to increase; **zu Kopf** ~ to go to one's head; ~ **lassen** to fly (kite). ~**d** a. growing, increasing. [STY]

steiger-n v.t. to raise; to increase, intensify, heighten; (gram.) to compare; to bid (at auction). v.r. **sich** ~**n** in to work up, intensify (feelings). ~**ung** f. raising, increase; gradation, climax; (gram.) comparison.

steil a. steep, precipitous. ~**feuer** n. high-angle fire. ~**hang** m. steep slope. ~**heit** f. steepness. ~**kurve** f. (av.) steep turn.

Stein m. (-es, -e) stone, flint, rock; memorial, gravestone; precious stone; (at draughts) piece; kernel; ~ **des Anstoßes** stumbling-block; **einen** ~ **im Brett haben bei** to be in a person's good books; ~ **und Bein frieren** to freeze hard; ~ **und Bein schwören** to swear by all the Gods. ~**adler** m. golden eagle. ~**alt** a. old as the hills. ~**bock** m. ibex; Capricorn. ~**bruch** m. quarry. ~**butt** m. turbot. ~**druck** m. lithography. ~**eiche** f. holm-oak. ~**ern** a. stone,

of stone. ~**garten** m. rock-garden. ~**gut** n. stoneware, earthenware. ~**hart** a. hard as stone. ~**hauer**, ~**metz** m. stonemason. ~**klopfer** m. stonebreaker. ~**kohle** f. coal, pit-coal. ~**obst** n. stone-fruit. ~**pilz** m. edible mushroom. ~**reich** a. (fig.) very wealthy. ~**schlag** m. avalanche of stones. ~**setzer** m. paviour, paver. ~**zeichnung** f. lithography. ~**zeit** f. Stone Age.

steinig a. stony, rocky. ~**en** v.t. to stone.

Steiß m. (-es, -e) backside, buttocks. ~**bein** n. coccyx.

Stell-'age (-la:ʒə) f. stand. ~**bock** m. trestle. ~**dichein** n. rendezvous; place of meeting.

Stell-e f. (-e, -en) place; spot; situation; passage (in book); job; post; office ~**e** vacancy; **auf der** ~**e** immediately; **auf der** ~**e treten** (fig.) to mark time; **von der** ~**e kommen** to make progress, get on; **zur** ~**e sein** to be present; **an** ~**e von** instead of, in place of. ~**enangebot** n. vacancy. ~**engesuch** n. application for a post; (pl.) situations wanted. ~**enjäger** m. place-hunter. ~**enlos** a. unemployed. ~**ennachweis** m., ~**envermittlung** f. employment agency; Labour Exchange. ~**enweise** adv. in places, sporadically, here and there. ~**macher** m. wainwright; wheelwright. ~**mutter** f. lock-nut; adjusting nut. ~**netz** n. anchored net. ~**schlüssel** m. adjusting spanner or key. ~**schraube** f. adjusting screw. ~**vertretend** a. vicarious; delegated; vice-. ~**vertreter** m. deputy; representative; substitute; proxy. ~**vorrichtung** f. adjusting gear or mechanism. ~**wagen** m. coach. ~**werk** n. signal-box.

stellen v.t. to put, place, set; to arrange; to regulate; to provide, furnish; to challenge; to corner; to arrest. v.r. to station oneself, take up one's stand, stand; to present oneself; to give oneself up; (mil.) to enlist; to feign, pretend, sham; **sich** ~ **auf** to cost;

sich ~ *mit* to get on with, be on
(good) terms with; *sich* ~ *zu* to
behave towards; *auf sich selbst
gestellt sein* to be dependent on
oneself; *gut gestellt sein* to be well
off; *nach dem Leben* ~ to attempt
(a person's) life.

Stellung f. (-, -en) position, situation; posture, attitude; (*mil.*)
line; ~ *nehmen zu* to express one's
opinion on; ~ *beziehen zu* to move
into a position. ~**nahme** f. opinion expressed, comment, attitude (regarding a thing). ~**s-
befehl** m. enlisting order, calling-
up. ~**gesuch** n. application for a
post. ~**skrieg** m. static warfare,
positional warfare. ~**swechsel**
m. change of position.

Stelz-bein n., ~**fuß** m. wooden leg.
~**e** f. stilt. ~**en** vws.i. to stalk
along.

Stemm-eisen n. chisel; crow-bar.
~**en** v.t. to support, lever up,
prop; to stem, dam up (water).
v.r. to lean firmly (against); to
resist, oppose.

Stempel m. (-s, -) rubber stamp;
die; stamp; postmark; brand;
mark; hallmark (on plate); ~
(*tech.*) piston; (*bot.*) pistil. ~
gebühr f. stamp duty. ~**geld** n.
unemployment relief. ~**kissen**
n. ink-pad. ~**schneider** m.
stamp-cutter, die-sinker.

stempeln v.t. to stamp; to mark;
~ *gehen* to be on the dole.

Stengel m. (-s, -) stalk, stem.

Steno-´gramm n. shorthand note;
~*gramm aufnehmen* to take down
in shorthand. ~**gra´phieren** v.t.
& i. to write in shorthand, write
shorthand. ~**graphisch** a. shorthand, stenographic. ~**ty´pist** m.,
~**typistin** f. typist.

Stepp-decke f. quilt. ~**en** v.t. to
quilt. ~**stich** m. back-stitch,
lock-stitch.

Steppe f. (-, -n) steppe. ~**nwolf** m.
prairie wolf.

Sterbe-bett n. death-bed. ~**fall** m.
a death. ~**kasse** f. burial fund or
club. ~**nskrank** a. dangerously
ill. ~**nswort** n. *kein* ~**nswort**
not a syllable. ~**sakramente** n.
pl. last sacraments.

sterben vws.i. st. to die. *subst. n.*
dying; death; *im* ~ *liegen* to be
dying. [STARVE]

sterblich a. mortal; ~ *verliebt* head
over ears in love. ~**keit** f. mor-
tality. ~**keitsziffer** f. death-rate.

Stereo-me´trie f. stereometry. ~
´**skop** n. stereoscope. ~**typ** a.
stereotype; (*fig.*) stereotyped. ~
ty´pieren v.t. to stereotype.

ste´ril a. sterile. ~**isieren** v.t. to
sterilize.

Stern m. (-es, -e) star; (*typ.*) asterisk. ~**bild** n. constellation. ~
deuter m. astrologer. ~**enbanner**
n. star-spangled banner. ~**(en)-
himmel** m., ~**enzelt** n. (*poet.*)
starry sky. ~**hagelbesoffen** a.
dead drunk. ~**schnuppe** f. shooting star. ~**warte** f. observatory.

Sterz m. (-es, -e) tail; handle of
plough.

stet, ~ig (-e:-) aa. steady; constant,
continual. ~**igkeit** f. steadiness;
constancy; continuity.

stets (-e:-) adv. always, for ever;
continually, constantly.

Steuer¹ n. (-s, -) rudder, helm;
(steering) wheel; controls. ~
bord n. starboard. ~**knüppel** m.
(*av.*) control column, (joy-)stick.
~**mann** m. helmsman, man at
the wheel; (*naut.*) mate; (*sport.*)
coxswain. ~**rad** n. steering-
wheel. ~**ruder** n. rudder, helm.
~**ung** f. steering; driving;
piloting; steering-gear.

Steuer² f. (-, -n) tax. ~**anschlag** m.
assessment. ~**einnehmer** m. tax-
collector. ~**erhebung** f. collection of taxes. ~**erlaß** m. tax-
provision. ~**frei** a. exempt from
taxation; free of duty. ~**hinter-
ziehung** f. evasion of taxes. ~
nachlaß m. remission of taxes.
~**pflichtig** a. subject to taxation;
dutiable. ~**satz** m. rate of
assessment). ~**zahler** m. tax-
payer, rate-payer. ~**zuschlag** m.
surtax, supertax.

steuern v.t. & i. to steer; to drive;
to pilot; *einer Sache* ~ to check
or repress a thing; ~ *zu* to contribute to.

Steven m. (-s, -) (*naut.*) stem.

sti´bitzen v.t. to pilfer, purloin.

Stich (-ç) *m.* (-es, -e) sting; prick; stitch; cut (with spade); (*fencing*) stab, thrust; (*med.*) puncture; stitch, sharp pain; engraving; (*card*-)trick; (*mil.*) knot, hitch; (*fig.*) gibe, taunt, pointed remark; *ein ~ ins Grüne* a tinge or touch of green; *einen ~ haben* to have gone bad, turned sour; *~ halten* to hold good, stand the test; *im ~ lassen* to leave in the lurch, forsake. *~blatt* n. guard (of sword); (*at cards*) trump; (*fig.*) butt. *~el* m. graving tool, graver. *~e'lei* f. (*fig.*) gibe, taunt. *~flamme* f. darting flame. *~haltig* a. that will stand the test; sound. *~probe* f. test or sample taken at random. *~tag* m. fixed day. *~waffe* f. sword, foil. *~wahl* f. final ballot. *~wort* n. catchword; key-word; caption; (*theatr.*) cue; code word; party-cry. *~wortverzeichnis* n. list of subjects; index. *~wunde* f. stab.

sticheln v.t. & i. to stitch, sew; (*fig.*) to taunt, jeer (at).

Stichling m. (-s, -e) stickleback.

sticht 3rd pers. sing. pres. of **stechen.**

stick-en v.t. to embroider. *~e'rei* f. embroidery. *~garn* n. embroidery cotton. *~muster* n. pattern.

Stick-gas n. suffocating gas. *~ig* a. suffocating, close, stuffy. *~luft* f. stuffy air. *~stoff* m. nitrogen. *~stoffhaltig* a. nitrogenous.

stieben vvs.i. st. to scatter, disperse, fly about.

Stief-bruder m. stepbrother. *~mutter* f. stepmother. *~mütterchen* n. pansy. *~mütterlich* a. like a stepmother. *~schwester* f. stepsister. *~vater* m. stepfather.

Stiefel m. (-s, -) boot. *~anzieher* m. shoe horn. *~knecht* m. bootjack. *~putzer* m. (hotel) boots; shoeshiner, shoeblack. *~wichse* f. blacking. [IT.]

stiefeln vvs.i. to walk, march along.

stieg imperf. of **steigen.**

Stiege f. (-, -n) staircase, stairs.

Stieglitz m. (-es, -e) goldfinch, thistle-finch.

stiehlt 3rd pers. sing. pres. of **stehlen.**

Stiel (-i:l) m. (-es, -e) handle; stick; stalk. *~äugig* a. stalk-eyed.

stier[1] a. staring, fixed. *~en* v.i. to stare, look fixedly (at).

Stier[2] m. (-es, -e) bull. *~fechter* m. bull-fighter. *~nackig* a. bull-necked. [STEER]

stieß imperf. of **stoßen.**

Stift[1] m. (-es, -e) peg, pin, nail; pencil; (*colloq.*) apprentice. *~zahn* m. china crown (tooth).

Stift[2] n. (-es, -e) charitable institution; Eventide home (for old people); religious establishment or training college. *~er* m. founder, donor. *~sdame* f. canoness. *~sherr* m. canon, prebendary. *~shütte* f. (*bibl.*) tabernacle. *~ung* f. foundation; establishment; charitable endowment, bequest. *~ungsfest* n. founder's day.

stiften v.t. to give, donate; to found, establish; to bring about, make, cause.

Stigma n. stigma. *~tisieren* v.t. to stigmatize.

Stil m. (-es, -e) ☿ style = manner, distinctive manner, way; kind. *~blüte* f. pun, (Irish) bull. *~gerecht, ~voll* aa. in good style or taste. *~i'sieren* v.t. to write, compose; to stylize. *~istik* f. ☿ art of composition. *~istisch* a. stylistic, in the matter of style. *~möbel* pl. period furniture.

Sti'lett n. (-s, -e) stiletto.

still a. still, calm, motionless; silent, quiet; soft; peaceful; *~er Freitag* Good Friday; *~er Gesellschafter* sleeping partner; *~er Ozean* Pacific Ocean.

Stille f. (-. (-e) stillness, calm; silence, quietness; peace; *in aller ~* quietly; privately; secretly. *~halten* v.t. & i. to keep still; to stop, pause. *~leben* n. (*painting*) still life. *~legen* v.t. to shut down. *~legung* f. shutting-down. *~schweigen* v.i. to be silent. *subst. n.* silence. *~schweigend* a. silent; tacit. *~stand* m. standstill, stop; stoppage, cessation; deadlock. *~stehen* v.i. to stand still; stop,

~gestanden! Attention! **~vergnügt** a. quietly enjoying.

stillen v.t. to quiet; to appease, allay, satisfy, gratify; to quench (thirst); to staunch (blood); to nurse, suckle (child).

Stimm-abgabe f. voting, vote. **~band** n. vocal cord. **~berechtigt** a. entitled to vote. **~bruch** m. breaking of the voice.

Stimm-e f. (-e, -en) voice; (mus.) part; (newspaper) comment; vote; **~e abgeben** to vote. **~enfang** m. canvassing. **~engleichheit** f. same number of votes. **~enmehrheit** f. majority of votes. **~enprüfung** f. scrutiny of votes. **~enthaltung** f. abstention from voting. **~er** m. tuner. **~führer** m. spokesman. **~gabel** f. tuning-fork. **~haft** a. voiced. **~lage** f. register, pitch. **~lich** a. vocal. **~los** a. voiceless. **~recht** n. right to vote, suffrage. **~ung** f. tuning; pitch, key; mood, frame of mind, humour, temper, disposition; atmosphere, impression; **~ung machen für** to canvass, make propaganda for. **~ungsmensch** m. moody person. **~ungsvoll** a. appealing to the emotions; impressive. **~wechsel** m. breaking of the voice. **~zettel** m. ballot-paper.

stimmen v.t. to tune; (fig.) to prejudice (person in favour of or against a thing); to put (person) in a (good, bad, &c.) humour; to make (glad, sad, &c.). v.i. to vote; to be all right, to be correct; to suit; to tally (with), agree (with), correspond (to).

Stink-bombe f. tear-gas bomb. **~en** v.i. st. to stink. **~faul** a. (colloq.) bone-lazy. **~tier** n. skunk.

Stint f. (-es, -e) smelt (fish).

Sti'pendi-um n. (-ums, -ien) scholarship, exhibition.

stippen v.t. to dip, steep.

Stippvisite f. short visit.

stirbt 3rd pers. sing. pres. of **sterben**.

Stirn f. (-, -en) forehead, brow; (archit.) front; (fig.) impudence, cheek; **einem die ~ bieten** to show a bold front, defy. **~höhle** f.

frontal cavity. **~höhlenentzündung** f. sinusitis. **~locke** f. forelock. **~riemen** m. frontlet of bridle. **~runzeln** n. frowning.

stob imperf. of **stieben**.

stöbern v.i. to hunt, search, rummage about; (of snow) to blow about, drift.

stochern v.t. & i. to poke about (in), pick (one's teeth).

Stock m. (-es, "e) stick, staff, cane, baton, rod, wand; stem (of plant); story, floor; **über ~ und Stein** up hill and down dale. **~dumm** a. utterly stupid. **~dunkel** a. pitch-dark. **~engländer** m. typical Englishman, regular John Bull. **~finster** a. pitch-dark. **~fisch** m. stockfish, dried cod. **~fleck** m. damp stain; mildew. **~fleckig** a. stained by damp. **~ig** a. fusty; decayed. **~schnupfen** m. chronic nasal catarrh. **~steif** a. stiff as a poker. **~taub** a. stone-deaf. **~ung** f. standstill, cessation; stoppage; check; (traffic) block, congestion. **~werk** n. story, floor.

Stöckelschuh m. high-heeled shoe.

stocken v.i. to stop, stand still, pause; to hesitate, falter; to turn mouldy; to curdle. **~d** a. stagnant; faltering (voice).

Stockung f. stoppage, standstill; jam; (fig.) deadlock.

Stoff m. (-es, -e) matter, substance; stuff, fabric, material; subject, theme, topic; subject-matter. **~lich** a. material; with regard to the subject-matter. **~wechsel** m. metabolism.

stöhnen v.i. to groan.

Stoiker m. (-s, -) Stoic.

Stola f. (-, Stolen) stole.

Stolle f. (-, -n) rich fruit loaf.

Stollen m. (-s, -) mine gallery; tunnel; (mil.) deep dug-out; calk (in horseshoe).

stolpern vws.i. to stumble, trip (over).

stolz (-ts) a. proud; haughty, arrogant; stately. subst. m. pride; glory; haughtiness, arrogance. **~ieren** vws.i. to strut.

stopf-en v.t. to stuff, cram; to fill (pipe); to plug, stop up; to darn, mend; (*mil.*) to cease (firing); (*med.*) to bind, constipate. *v.i.* to fill up, be filling; to be constipating; **einem den Mund ~** to silence a person; **gestopft voll** crammed full. **~ei** *n.* darner. **~garn** *n.* darning cotton. **~nadel** *f.* darning-needle.

Stoppel *f.* (·, -n) stubble. **~bart** *m.* stubbly beard. **~feld** *n.* stubble-field. **~ig** *a.* stubbly, like stubble.

stopp-en *v.t.* to stop. **~uhr** *f.* stop-watch.

Stöpsel *m.* (-s, -) stopper; cork, plug; bung. **~n** *v.t.* to cork, stopper.

Stör *m.* (-es, -e) sturgeon.

Storch (-c) *m.* (-es, ¨e) stork **~schnabel** *m.* stork's bill; cranesbill; (*tech.*) pantograph.

stör-en (-o:-) *v.t. & i.* to disturb, trouble, inconvenience; to intrude, interrupt; to be in the way; (*mil.*) to harass; (*wireless*) to jam, interfere. **~angriff** *m.* nuisance raid. **~enfried** *m.* mischief-maker. **~ung** *f.* disturbance, upset; intrusion, interruption; perturbation; break-down; (*wireless*) jamming, atmospherics, interference; *geistige* **~ung** mental disorder. **~ungsstelle** *f.* (*tel.*) faults section. **~ungssucher** *m.pl.* break-down squad; linemen. [STIR]

stor'nieren *v.t.* to countermand; to stop (cheque).

störrig, störrisch *aa.* stubborn, headstrong.

Stoß (-o:-) *m.* (-es, ¨e) push, shove, thrust; blow, knock, stroke, punch; kick; jerk, jolt; shock, percussion; (*tech.*) impact; pile, heap, bundle; seam. **~dämpfer** *m.* shock-absorber. **~fänger** *m.* bumper on vehicle. **~gebet** *n.* short fervent prayer. **~klinge** *f.* small-sword blade. **~kraft** *f.* impetus, impulsive force; (*tech.*) impact. **~seufzer** *m.* deep sigh or groan. **~stange** *f.* buffer-bar; push rod. **~trupp** *m.* assault detachment; raiding party; (*pl.*) assault troops, shock troops. **~verkehr** *m.* heavy traffic (during rush hours). **~weise** *adv.* by jerks; by fits and starts. **~zahn**

m. tusk. **~zeit** *f.* rush hour.

Stößel *m.* (-s -) pestle; (*tech.*) tappet.

stoßen (-o:-) *v.t. st.* to push, shove, thrust; to strike, hit, punch, knock; to kick; to butt; to buffet; to nudge, jog; to jostle; to push away; to expel, oust, drive out; to stab; to pound, crush. *v.r.* to knock (oneself) against, hurt oneself; (*fig.*) to take offence. *v.i.* (*fencing*) to thrust; (*of goat*) to butt; to jolt, bump; *in die Trompete* **~** to sound the trumpet; **~ an** to knock against, run against; (*fig.*) to border on, adjoin; **~ auf** to pounce on, shoot down upon; to meet with, come across, chance upon; **~ zu** to join, join up with.

Stotterer *m.* (-s, -) stutterer, stammerer.

stottern *v.t. & i.* to stutter, stammer.

stracks *adv.* direct(ly), straight (ahead); immediately; exactly.

Straf-anstalt *f.* penitentiary, reformatory; prison. **~arbeit** *f.* imposition, lines (in school) **~bar** *a.* liable to punishment, punishable, criminal, culpable. **~aufschub** *m.* reprieve.

Straf-e (-a:-) *f.* (-e, -en) punishment; penalty, fine; *bei* **~** *von* on pain of. **~entlassene**(r) *m.* ex-convict. **~erlaß** *m.* remission of punishment; amnesty. **~fällig** *a.* punishable, liable to be fined. **~frei, ~los** *aa.* exempt from punishment, unpunished. **~gefangene**(r) *m.* convict. **~gericht** *n.* tribunal, criminal court; judgment. **~gesetz** *n.* penal law. **~gesetzbuch** *n.* penal code. **~losigkeit** *f.* impunity. **~mandat** *n.* penalty. **~mündig** *a.* (of a) responsible (age). **~porto** *n.* extra postage, surcharge. **~predigt**, **~rede** *f.* lecture, reprimand. **~prozeß** *m.* criminal case. **~punkt** *m.* (*sport.*) point deducted, penalty. **~recht** *n.* criminal law. **~rechtlich** *a.* criminal, penal. **~verfahren** *n.* criminal procedure. **~vollzug** *m.* execution of a punishment. **~würdig** *a.* punishable, deserving punishment.

strafen (-a:-) v.t. to punish; to chastise. ~d a. reproachful (look, &c.).

straff a. stretched, tense, tight; taut; straight, erect; strict, severe, stern. ~en v.t. to tighten, stretch. ~heit f. tightness; tautness, strictness.

sträf‖lich a. criminal, punishable; unpardonable. ~ling m. convict.

Strahl m. (-es, -en) ray, beam; flash; jet; radius; (vet.) frog (of hoof). ~antrieb m. jet propulsion. ~enbrechung f. refraction. ~enbündel n. pencil of rays. ~enkrone f. glory, halo.

strahlen v.i. to radiate, emit rays, beam, shine. ~d a. radiant, beaming, shining.

strählen v.t. to comb.

Strähn‖e f. (-e, -en) lock, strand (of hair); hank, skein (of yarn). ~ig a. in strands; of strands.

Stra'min m. (-s) fine canvas.

stramm a. tight, close, taut; robust, strong, strapping; erect. ~stehen v.i. to stand at attention.

strampeln v.i. to kick; sich bloß ~ to kick the bed-clothes off.

Strand m. (-es) sea-shore, beach, strand. ~bad n. seaside resort. ~gut n. flotsam, jetsam, wreckage. ~hafer m. bent, lyme-grass. ~korb m. canopied beach-chair. ~läufer m. sand-piper. ~räuber m. wrecker. ~schuhe m.pl. sandshoes, beach-shoes. ~wächter m. coast-guard.

stranden v.s.i. to run aground or ashore; to beach.

Strang (-n) m. (-es, ˮe) rope, cord, halter; trace, strap; hank (of yarn); track, rail; vein, artery; zum ~ verurteilen to condemn to the gallows; am gleichen ~ ziehen to act in concert; über die Stränge schlagen to kick over the traces; wenn alle Stränge reißen if the worst comes to the worst. ~u'lieren v.t. to strangle.

Stra'paz‖e f. (-e, -en) exertion, fatigue. ~ieren v.t. to tire, knock up; to wear hard. ~ierfähig a. hard-wearing. ~iös a. tiring. [tr.]

Straße (-a:-) f. (-, -n) street; high-

way, road; water-way; strait(s); an der ~ by the wayside; auf der ~ in the street; auf die ~ setzen to turn out, send packing.

Straßen‖arbeiter m. roadman, navvy. ~bahn f. tramway. ~bau m. road construction. ~damm m. causeway, roadway. ~dirne f. street-walker, prostitute. ~dorf n. village built on either side of main road. ~feger, ~kehrer m. scavenger. ~graben m. roadside ditch. ~handel m. street hawking. ~junge m. street arab, ragamuffin. ~laterne f. street-lamp. ~netz n. road net. ~räuber m. highwayman. ~schild n. street-sign. ~überführung f. viaduct. ~unterführung f. subway. ~zug m. line of streets, row.

Stra'teg‖e (-te:gə) m. (-en, -en) strategist. ~ie f. strategy. ~isch a. strategic.

Strato'sphärenflugzeug n. stratocruiser.

sträuben v.t. to ruffle up, bristle. v.r. to stand on end; to struggle against, resist (a thing).

Strauch (-x) m. (-es, ˮer) shrub, bush. ~dieb m. footpad, highwayman. ~werk n. shrubs, brushwood, underwood.

straucheln (-x-) v.w.i. to stumble.

Strauß¹ m. (-es, ˮe) bouquet.

Strauß² m. (-es, ˮe) combat.

Strauß³ m. (-es, -e) ostrich.

Strazze (-tsa) f. (-, -n) daybook.

Strebe f. (-, -n) support; strut. ~balken m. strut, buttress. ~bogen m. flying buttress. ~pfeiler m. buttress.

streb‖en (-e:-) v.i. to endeavour (to get), seek or strive (after); to aspire (to); to tend (toward). subst. n. striving, endeavour, effort; aspiration, tendency, aim. ~er m. pushing person, place-hunter. ~ertum n. place-hunting. ~sam a. industrious, zealous. ~samkeit f. industry, zeal.

Streck-balken m. stretcher(bridging). ~bett n. orthopaedic bed.

Streck‖e f. (-, -en) stretch, length, distance; tract (of land); section (of railway line); (geom.) straight line; auf freier ~e (rail., &c.) on the open track, on the road; *eine* ~*e Weges* some distance; *zur* ~*e bringen* to kill, bag. ~**enapparat** *m.* portable *or* lineman's telephone. ~**enarbeiter** *m.* platelayer. ~**enwärter** *m.* linekeeper, lineman. ~**enweise** *adv.* here and there. ~**grenze** *f.* yielding point. ~**muskel** *m.* extensor muscle. ~**verband** *m.* appliance for stretching fractured limb.

strecken *v.t.* to extend, stretch, stretch out; (*fig.*) to make (something) last, go slow (with something); *zu Boden* ~ to fell to the ground; *die Waffen* ~ to lay down (one's) arms; *in gestrecktem Lauf* at full speed.

Streich (-ç) *m.* (-es, -e) stroke, blow; trick, prank; *einem einen* ~ *spielen* to play a trick on a person. ~**holz**, ~**hölzchen** *n.* match. ~**instrument** *n.* stringed instrument. ~**musik** *f.* string music. ~**orchester** *n.* string band. ~**quartett** *n.* string quartet.

streicheln *v.t.* to stroke, caress.

streichen *v.t. st.* to pass lightly (over), rub, touch gently, stroke; to strike (match); to play (violin); to spread (on bread); to paint; to make (bricks); to strike out, erase, cancel; to strike (flag); to furl *or* lower (sails); (*sport.*) to scratch. *vws.i.* to wander, stroll, ramble; to fly, migrate; to cut *or* plough (through waves); to run, extend; to stroke *or* pass hand (over); *frisch gestrichen!* wet paint! *gestrichen voll* full to the brim.

Streif *m.* = **Streifen**. ~**band** *n.* wrapper, cover.

Streif-e *f.* (-e, -en) patrol; raid, razzia. ~**en** *m.* streak; stripe, band; strip, sector; slip (of paper). ~**ig** *a.* striped. ~**jagd** *f.* shoot, shooting expedition. ~**kolonne** *f.*, ~**kommando** *n.* raiding party, flying column. ~**licht** *n.* sidelight. ~**schuß** *m.* grazing shot. ~**zug** *m.* expedition; scouting raid.

streifen *v.t.* to touch slightly, scrape, graze, brush; to strip off; to turn up, turn down (sleeve);

to take off ring; to put on; to touch upon (subject); ~ *an* to border on. *vws.i.* to wander, rove, stroll, roam; (*mil.*) to patrol, reconnoitre. See also **gestreift**.

Streik *m.* (-es, -e) strike; *in den* ~ *treten* to go on strike. ~**brecher** *m.* blackleg. ~**en** *v.i.* to strike. ~**posten** *m.* picket; ~**en stehen** to picket.

Streit *m.* (-es, -e) fight; quarrel; dispute; controversy; (*leg.*) litigation. ~**axt** *f.* battle-axe. ~**bar** *a.* pugnacious; valiant. ~**er** *m.* fighter, combatant; disputant. ~**fall** *m.* quarrel; controversy. ~**frage** *f.* matter in dispute, point at issue. ~**ig** *a.* debatable, moot; in dispute; *einem etwas* ~*ig machen* to contest a person's right to a thing. ~**igkeit** *f.* quarrel, difference; dispute, controversy. ~**kräfte** *f.pl.* troops, military forces. ~**lustig** *a.* pugnacious. ~**schrift** *f.* polemical pamphlet. ~**süchtig** *a.* quarrelsome; disputatious.

streiten *v.i. & r. st.* to fight; to quarrel.

streng (-ŋ) *a.* severe, stern, hard; strict; stringent; sharp; harsh, austere. ~**e** *f.* severity, sternness; strictness; stringency; sharpness; harshness, austerity. ~**genommen** *adv.* strictly speaking. ~**gläubig** *a.* orthodox. [STRONG]

Streu *f.* (-) bed of straw. ~**büchse** *f.*, ~**er** *m.* (sugar-, &c.) castor; dredger. ~**garbe** *f.* cone of dispersion. ~**mine** *f.* uncontrolled mine. ~**sand** *m.* (blotting-)sand. ~**zucker** *m.* castor sugar.

streu-en *v.t.* to strew; to scatter; to sprinkle; to spread (manure); to litter (cattle). ~**feuer** *n.* searching and sweeping fire.

streunen *v.i.* to roam about.

strich[1] *imperf.* of **streichen**.

Strich[2] *m.* (-es, -e) dash, stroke; line; compass point; (*mil.*) graticule; tract, region, district; flight (of birds); grain, (right) way (of fabric); *einen* ~ *machen durch* (*fig.*) to frustrate, thwart; *einen* ~ *machen unter* (*fig.*) to put an

end to; *jemanden auf dem ~ haben*
to bear someone a grudge; *auf
den ~ gehen* to walk the streets;
gegen den ~ against the grain;
nach ~ und Faden thoroughly,
properly. **~ätzung** *f.* line etching. **~einteilung** *f.* graduation
(in mils). **~punkt** *m.* semicolon.
~regen *m.* local shower. **~vogel**
m. bird of passage. **~weise** *a.*
local. *adv.* here and there.
stricheln *v.t.* to mark with little
lines, hatch.

Strick *m.* (-es, -e) cord, rope; halter;
snare; (*fig.*) young rascal, rogue.
~arbeit *f.* knitting. **~en** *v.t. & i.*
to knit. **~leiter** *f.* rope ladder.
~strumpf *m.* knitting (of stocking). **~zeug** *n.* knitting; knitting
things.

Striegel *m.* (-s, -) curry-comb. **~n**
v.t. to curry (horse); to ill-use.

Striem-e *f.*, **~en** *m.* (-ens, -en)
wale, weal. **~ig** *a.* covered with
weals.

strikt *a.* strict.

Strippe *f.* (-, -n) string; (trouser-)
strap; (boot-)tab.

stritt *imperf. of* streiten.

strittig *a.* debatable; in dispute.

Stroh *n.* (-es) straw; thatch; *leeres
~ dreschen* to waste one's words
or labour. **~dach** *n.* thatched roof.
~feuer *n.* short-lived passion. **~-
halm** *m.* (a) straw. **~ig** *a.* strawy.
~mann *m.* man of straw; lay
figure; (*at whist*) dummy. **~sack**
m. straw mattress, palliasse. **~-
wisch** *m.* wisp of straw. **~wit-
we** *f.* grass widow. **~witwer** *m.*
grass widower.

Strolch (-c) *m.* (-es, -e) tramp, vagabond. **~en** *vus.i.* to roam about;
to idle.

Strom (-o:m) *m.* (-es, "e) large
river; stream; (*electr.*) current;
flow, torrent (of words). **~ab-
leitung** *f.* shunt. **~abwärts** *adv.*
down stream. **~aufwärts** *adv.*
up stream. **~erzeuger** *m.* dynamo; current generator. **~kreis**
m. circuit. **~linienform** *f.*
streamlined shape. **~messer** *m.*
ammeter. **~prüfer** *m.* current
tester. **~schiene** *f.* live rail.
~schnelle *f.* rapid. **~spannung**

f. voltage. **~stärke** *f.* intensity
of current. **~strahler** *m.* electric beam transmitter. **~unter-
brecher** *m.* circuit-breaker;
(*electr.*) cut-out. **~versorgung** *f.*
current supply. **~wender** *m.*
commutator; current reversing
key. **~zähler** *m.* electric meter.

ström-en (-ö:-) *vus.i.* to stream,
flow; to pour (down); to rush;
to flock, crowd. **~ung** *f.* current,
stream, flow, flood, drift; (*fig.*)
spirit, tendency.

Stromer *m.* (-s, -) tramp, vagabond.

Strophe (-o:-) *f.* (-, -n) stanza, verse.

strotzen *v.i.* **~ von** to superabound
with, be full of. **~d** *a.* robust,
vigorous (health).

Strudel (-u:-) *m.* (-s, -) whirlpool,
eddy, vortex; stream, rush, crush.
~n *v.i.* to whirl, swirl; to boil,
bubble.

Strumpf *m.* (-es, "e) stocking, sock;
(gas) mantle; *sich auf die Strümpfe
machen* to make off. **~band** *n.*
garter. **~halter** *m.* suspender. **~-
waren** *f.pl.* hosiery. **~wirke'rei**
f. manufacture of stockings.

Strunk *m.* (-es, "e) stalk; stump.

struppig (-c) *a.* bristly; unkempt;
shaggy.

Strych'nin *n.* (-s) strychnine.

Stube (-u:-) *f.* (-, -n) room, chamber,
apartment; *gute ~* drawing-room.
~nälteste(r) *m.* senior soldier of a
barrack room. **~narrest** *m.* confinement to quarters. **~nfliege** *f.*
common fly. **~ngelehrte(r)** *m.*
bookworm. **~ngenosse** *m.* fellow
lodger, room-mate. **~nhocker** *m.*
stay-at-home. **~nmädchen** *n.*
housemaid. **~nrein** *a.* house-
trained (dog, &c.). [STOVE]

Stuck (-uk) *m.* (-es) stucco. **~-
atur** *f.* stucco work. **~decke** *f.*
stuccoed ceiling.

Stück (-yk) *n.* (-es, -e) piece; bit;
morsel, fragment; lump (of
sugar); passage, extract; head
(of cattle); play; *ein ~ Arbeit* a
stiff job; *ein starkes ~* a bit thick;
aus einem ~ all of a piece; *aus
freien ~en* of one's own accord;
in allen ~en in every respect; *in
~e gehen* to break in pieces;
große ~e halten auf to think

much of (a person). ~arbeit f. piece-work. ~enzucker m. lump sugar. ~gut n. goods in packets or bales. ~lohn m. wages for piece-work. ~weise adv. piece by piece, piecemeal. ~werk n. imperfect work, bungled work. ~zahl f. number of pieces.

stückeln v.t. to cut into pieces.

stücken v.t. to patch.

Stu'dent m. (-en, -en) student, undergraduate. ~enschaft f. students, undergraduates. ~in f. woman student. ~isch a. student-like.

Stud-ie (-ia) f. (-ie, -ien) study, sketch, essay. ~iengang m. course of study. ~ienhalber adv. for the purpose of studying. ~ienrat m. assistant master. ~'ieren v.t. & i. to study; to be at college. ~ierstube f. study. ~ium n. study, (university) education.

Stufe (-u:-) f. (-, -n) step, stair; rung (of ladder); shade, nuance; degree; grade; stage; auf gleicher ~ mit on a level with. ~nfolge f., ~ngang m. gradation; gradual development; succession. ~nleiter f. scale, gradation. ~nweise adv. by degrees, gradually.

Stuhl m. (-es, ⁻e) chair; seat; pew; (med.) evacuation of the bowels; der Heilige ~ The Holy See; einem den ~ vor die Tür setzen to turn a person out; sich zwischen zwei Stühle setzen, to fall between two stools. ~bein n. leg of a chair. ~bezug m. chair-cover. ~drang m. need to relieve bowels. ~feier f. Petri ~feier St. Peter's Day. ~gang m. evacuation of the bowels. [STOOL]

Stuka = Sturzkampfflugzeug n. dive bomber.

Stulle f. (-, -n) slice of bread and butter; sandwich.

Stulp-e f. (-e, -en) (boot-)top; cuff (of sleeve). ~handschuh m. gauntlet glove. ~stiefel m. top-boot.

stülp-en v.t. to put on, clap on; to turn up; to turn upside down. ~nase f. snub-nose, turned-up nose.

stumm a. dumb; speechless; silent; mute. ~heit f. dumbness.

Stummel m. (-s, -) stump, (cigar-)end.

Stumpen m. (-s, -) stump; (Swiss) cigar.

Stümper m. (-s, -) bungler. ~haft a. bungling. ~n v.t. to bungle.

stumpf a. blunt; obtuse; dull; indifferent; apathetic. subst. m. stump; mit ~ und Stiel root and branch. ~heit f. bluntness; obtuseness; dullness. ~nase f. snub-nose, turned-up nose. ~sinn m. stupidity. ~sinnig a. stupid, dull. ~winklig a. obtuse-angled.

Stunde f. (-, -n) hour; lesson; period. ~nbuch n. prayer-book, book of hours. ~nglas n. hour-glass. ~nlang a. for hours. ~nplan m. time-table. ~nschlag m. striking of the hour. ~nzeiger m. hour-hand.

stund-en v.t. to grant a respite; to allow time to pay. ~ung f. respite, delay of payment.

stündlich a. hourly; every hour.

stups-en v.t. to nudge. ~nase f. snub-nose, turned-up nose.

stur a. stubborn, obdurate.

Sturm m. (-es, ⁻e) storm, gale; assault; (fig.) fury; tumult, turmoil; ~ laufen to assault, storm; ~ läuten to ring the alarm; im ~e nehmen to take by storm. ~bataillon n. shock battalion. ~flut f. high tide raised by a storm. ~glocke f. alarm bell. ~leiter f. scaling-ladder. ~riemen m. chinstrap (of cap, &c.). ~schritt m. quickened step for assault. ~trupp m. assault party. ~vogel m. petrel. ~wind m. heavy gale, hurricane.

stürm-en v.t. to take by storm. v.i. to be stormy (weather). vus.i. to dash, rush along. ~er m. (football) forward. ~isch a. stormy; (fig.) impetuous; frantic.

Sturz (-ts) m. (-es, ⁻e) fall, tumble, crash; dive, plunge; overthrow; ruin, downfall, collapse; zum ~ bringen to overthrow. ~acker m. newly ploughed field. ~bach m. torrent, waterfall. ~flug m. n.

nose-dive. **~helm** m. crash helmet. **~kampfflieger** m. divebomber pilot. **~see** f. heavy sea. **~wellen** f.pl. breakers.

stürzen (-tsən) v.t. to throw, throw down; to overthrow; to hurl (down or into); to tilt (box) over. vws.i. to fall, fall down; to fall (into); plunge (into); to fall (upon); to rush, dash, hurry; to stream (from); (av.) to dive; to crash.

Stute f. (-, -n) mare. **~nfüllen** n. foal, filly.

Stützbalken m. joist, supporting beam.

Stutzbart m. trimmed beard.

Stütz-e f. (-e, -en) prop, stay, support; help; lady help. **~mauer** f. buttress; retaining wall. **~pfeiler** m. pillar; support. **~punkt** m. base; strong point.

stutz-en (ʃtuts-) **1.** v.t. to cut (short), curtail; to trim (beard); to crop (ears); to dock (tail); to clip (wings). v.i. to stop short, be taken aback. **2.** subst. m. short rifle; (tech.) nozzle. **~er** m. fop, dandy. **~flügel** m. baby grand (piano). **~ig** a. puzzled, taken aback. **~uhr** f. timepiece, mantelpiece clock.

stützen (ʃtyts-) v.t. to support, prop up; to base, found. v.r. to lean upon, rest (one's arms) on; to be based upon, be founded on.

Subjekt n. (-s, -e) ♀ (gram. & phil.) subject; verkommenes ~ (a) bad lot. **~iv** a. subjective. **~ivi'tät** f. subjectivity.

subku'tan a. subcutaneous.

Subli'mat n. (-s, -e) sublimate. **subli'mieren** v.t. to sublimate.

Subskri'b-ent m. (-enten, -enten) subscriber. **~ieren** v.t. to subscribe (to).

Subskripti'on f. (-, -en) subscription.

substanti'ell a. substantial.

Substantiv (-ti:f) n. (-s, -e) substantive, noun.

Sub'stanz f. (-, -en) substance, matter, stuff.

Sub'strat n. (-s, -e) substratum.

sub'til a. subtle, subtile, fine.

subtra'hieren v.t. to subtract.

subventio'nieren v.t. to subsidize.

Suche (-u:-) f. (-) search; quest; auf der ~ nach in search for, on the lookout for, on the hunt for; auf die ~ gehen to go in search of. **~n** v.t. & i. to search or hunt for, try to find, look for, seek; to desire, want; to try to; das Weite ~ to run away; nach Worten ~ to be at a loss for words; hier nichts zu ~n haben to have no business here. **~r** m. seeker; (opt.) finder; (mil.) spot-light.

Sucht f. (-, ̈e) passion, mania, rage; sickness, disease; addiction; fallende ~ epilepsy. **~krauke(r)** m. drug-taking person.

süchtig a. addicted.

Sud (zu:t) m. (-es, -e) boiling; decoction. **~earbeit, ~e'lei** f. dirty, slovenly work; daubing; scribbling. **~eln** v.t. to do in a dirty, slovenly way. **~ler** m. bungler.

Süd (zy:t) m. (-s) south; (poet.) south-wind. **~en** m. (-ens) south. **~früchte** f.pl. tropical fruit, fruits from the south. **~kreuz** n. the Southern Cross. **~länder** m. southerner. **~lich** a. southern, southerly, lying towards the south. **~ost** m. south-east wind. **~osten** m. south-east. **~östlich** a. south-east. **~pol** m. South Pole. See also App. I.

Suff m. (vulg.) tippling.

süffig a. delicious, nice (to drink).

sugge'rieren v.t. to suggest.

Suhle f. (-, -n) muddy pool.

Sühn-e (-e, -en), **~ung** f. expiation, atonement. **~en** v.t. to expiate, atone for.

Sultan m. (-s, -e) sultan. **~ine** f. sultana (raisin).

Sülze f. (-, -n) jelly; jellied meat, brawn. **~n** v.t. to jelly (meat).

su'mmarisch a. summary, succinct.

Summ-e f. (-e, -en) sum; sum-total; amount; ~e ziehen to sum up. **~ieren** v.t. to add up. v.r. to amount to.

summ-en v.i. & t. to hum; to buzz. **~er** m. buzzer.

Sumpf m. (-es, ̈e) marsh, swamp, fen, bog, moor, morass; (mining & motor.) sump. **~en** v.i. (sl.) to lead a dissolute life. **~fieber** *n.* malaria, marsh-fever. **~huhn** *n.* moorhen. **~ig** *a.* marshy.

Sund *m.* (-es, -e) sound, strait(s).

Sünd-e *f.* (-e, -en) sin, transgression, trespass, offence. **~enbock** *m.* scapegoat. **~enfall** *m.* the Fall (of man), Adam's sin. **~er** *m.*, **~erin** *f.* sinner. **~flut** see Sintflut. **~haft, ~ig** *aa.* sinful.

sündigen *v.i.* to sin, transgress.

Superlativ *m.* (-s, -e) superlative.

Superoxyd *n.* peroxide.

Suppe *f.* (-, -n) soup, broth. **~n-kräuter** *n. pl.* pot-herbs. **~nter-rine** *f.* soup-tureen. **~nwürfel** *m.* soup cube.

Supposi'torium *n.* (-s, . . . rien) (*med.*) suppository.

Supre'mat *n.* (-s, -e) supremacy.

surren *v.i.* to hum, buzz.

Surro'gat *n.* (-s, -e) substitute.

suspen-'dieren *v.t.* to suspend. **~sorium** *n.* (*med.*) suspensory.

süß (-y:-) *a.* sweet; fresh; lovely. **~e** *f.* sweetness. **~holz** *n.* liquorice; **~holz raspeln** to say soft nothings, flirt. **~igkeit** *f.* sweetness; suavity; (*pl.*) sweets. **~lich** *a.* sweetish, mawkish. **~speise** *f.* sweet, pudding. **~stoff** *m.* saccharin. **~wasser** *n.* fresh water.

süßen *v.t.* to sweeten.

Sym'bol (-o:l) *n.* (-s, -e) symbol. **~ik** *f.* symbolism. **~isch** *a.* symbolical.

Symme'trie *f.* (-) symmetry. **sy'mmetrisch** *a.* symmetrical.

Sympa'thie *f.* (-, -n) sympathy. **sym'path-isch** *a.* ♃ congenial; likeable. **~i'sieren** *v.i.* to sympathize (with); to like.

Sympho'nie *f.* (-, -n) symphony.

Symp'tom *n.* (-s, -e) symptom. **~atisch** *a.* symptomatic.

Syna'goge (-go:ga) *f.* (-, -n) synagogue.

synchronisieren *v.t.* to synchronize; (*film*) to dub.

Syndi'kat *n.* (-s, -e) syndicate.

Syndikus *m.* (-, . . . ken) syndic.

synko'pieren *v.t.* to syncopate.

Sy'node (-o:-) *f.* (-, -n) synod.

syno'nym *a.* synonymous. *subst. n.* synonym.

syn'taktisch *a.* syntactical.

Syntax *f.* (-) syntax.

Syn'the-se *f.* (-se, -sen) synthesis. **~tisch** *a.* synthetic.

Syphilis *f.* (-) syphilis.

syphi'litisch *a.* syphilitic.

Sys'tem *n.* (-s, -e) system; method; doctrine.

syste'matisch *a.* systematic.

Szen-e (stse:na) *f.* (-e, -en) scene; *in ~e setzen* to stage (play). **~e-'rie** *f.* scenery, décor. **~isch** *a.* scenic.

Szepter see Zepter.

T

T, t (te:) *n.* the letter T, t

Tabak *m.* (-s, -e) tobacco. **~s-beutel** *m.* tobacco-pouch. **~s-dose** *f.* snuff-box.

tabe'llarisch *a.* tabular, tabulated.

Ta'belle *f.* (-, -n) table, index; schedule.

Taber'nakel *m. & n.* (-s, -) tabernacle.

Ta'blett *n.* (-s, -e) ♃ tray, salver. **~e** *f.* tablet, lozenge.

Tabu'rett *n.* (-s, -e) stool.

Tacho'meter *n.* speedometer.

Tadel (-a:-) *m.* (-s, -) blame, reprimand, reproof; fault, bad mark. **~los** *a.* irreproachable; excellent, perfect. **~n** *v.t.* to blame, find fault with, reprimand. **~sucht** *f.* censoriousness. **~süchtig** *a.* censorious.

Tadler *m.* (-s, -) faultfinder, critic.

Tafel (-a:-) *f.* (-, -n) board; blackboard; slate; slab, plaque, tablet; cake (of chocolate); (dinner-)table; table; chart; index; diagram; *die ~ aufheben* to rise from table. **~aufsatz** *m.* centre-piece. **~be-steck** *n.* knife, fork, and spoon. **~butter** *f.* best butter. **~obst** *n.* dessert (fruit). **~runde** *f.* guests (at table). **~werk** *n.* book with full-page plates.

tafeln *v.i.* to dine, sup, feast.

täfel-n *v.t.* to floor, inlay, wainscot. **~ung** *f.* inlaying (of floors); panelling; wainscoting.

Taf(fe)t *m.* (-s, -e) taffeta.

Tag (ta:k) *m.* (-es, -e) day; daylight; light; life, lifetime; *alle* ~*e* every day; *den ganzen* ~ all day long; *einen um den andern* ~ every other day; day about; ~ *um* ~ or ~ *für* ~ day by day, day after day; *dieser* ~*e* one of these days, recently; *bei* ~*e* in the day-time; by daylight; *in acht* ~*en* within *or* in a week; *eines* ~*es* one (fine) day; ~*s darauf* the next day; *an den* ~ *bringen* to bring to light; *in den* ~ *hinein-leben* to live for the present; to live from hand to mouth; *auf seine alten* ~*e* in his old age; *unter* ~*e arbeiten* (*mining*) to work underground.

tag-aus, ~**ein** *adv.* day in day out, every day. ~**ebau** *m.* surface-mining. ~**ebuch** *n.* diary, journal; daybook; log. ~**edieb** *m.* idler. ~**egeld** *n.* day travelling allowance. ~**elang** *a.* for days (on end). ~**elöhner** *m.* day-labourer. ~**esanbruch** *m.* daybreak. ~**es-befehl** *m.* order of the day; routine order. ~**esgespräch** *n.* topic of the day. ~**eskurs** *m.* day's rate of exchange, quotation. ~**es-licht** *n.* daylight. ~**esordnung** *f.* agenda; *zur* ~ *übergehen* to deal with the agenda, get down to business. ~**espresse** *f.* daily press. ~**eszeitung** *f.* daily paper. ~**ewerk** *n.* day's work, daily task. ~**falter** *m.* butterfly. ~**hell** *a.* as light as day, clear. ~**süber** *adv.* during the day. ~**täglich** *a.* daily, every day. ~**undnachtgleiche** *f.* equinox.

tag-en *v.i.* to dawn, get light; to confer, sit, meet. ~**ung** *f.* conference, session, meeting.

täglich *a.* daily, everyday; ~*es Geld* call-money.

Tai'fun *m.* (-s, -e) typhoon.

Taille (taljə) *f.* (-, -n) waist; bodice. [F]

Takel *n.* (-s, -) tackle. ~**age** *f.* ~**ung** *f.*, ~**werk** *n.* rigging, tackle. ~**n** *v.t.* to rig (ship).

Takt *m.* (-es, -e) time, measure; (*fig.*) tact; *im* ~ in time; in step; ~ *halten* to keep time; ~ *schlagen* to beat time; ~**fest** *a.* keeping

good time; sound, reliable. ~**gefühl** *n.* tact. ~**los** *a.* tactless. ~**losigkeit** *f.* tactlessness, want of tact; indiscretion. ~**stock** *m.* baton. ~**strich** *m.* bar. ~**voll** *a.* tactful, discreet.

tak'tieren *v.t. & i.* to beat time.

Takt-ik *f.* (-, -iken) tactics. ~**iker** *m.* tactician. ~**isch** *a.* tactical.

Tal (ta:l) *n.* (-es, "er) valley. ~**(ab)-wärts** *adv.* down hill; valleywards. ~**aufwärts** *adv.* up hill; up stream. ~**fahrt** *f.* descent. ~**kessel** *m.* ~**mulde** *f.* hollow (of valley); basin-shaped valley. ~**senke** *f.* hollow (of valley). ~**sohle** *f.* bed *or* bottom of a valley. ~**sperre** *f.* river dam.

Ta'lar (-a:r) *m.* (-s, -e) teacher's, clergyman's, *or* lawyer's gown.

Ta'lent *n.* (-s, -e) talent, ability, faculty, gift, attainments; talented person. ~**iert**, ~**voll** *aa.* talented.

Taler *m.* (-s, -) thaler.

Talg (-k) *m.* (-es) tallow; suet. ~**drüse** *f.* sebaceous gland. ~**ig** *a.* tallowy. ~**licht** *n.* tallow candle.

Talje *f.* (-, -n) tackle.

Talk *m.* (-es) talcum. ~**erde** *f.* magnesia.

Tambour *m.* (-s, -e) drummer. ~**major** *m.* drum-major.

Tambu'rin *n.* (-s, -e) tambourine.

tamponieren *v.t.* to plug (wound).

Tand (-t) *m.* (-es) trifle, gew-gaw, bauble, trinket; toy. [L]

Tände'lei *f.* (-, -en) trifling, dallying; dawdling.

tänd-eln *v.i.* to trifle, dally; to dawdle. ~**ler** *m.* trifler, dawdler; second-hand dealer.

Tang (-ŋ) *m.* (-es, -e) seaweed. [SCAND.]

Tan'gente *f.* (-, -n) (*math.*) tangent.

Tank *m.* (-s, -s) tank. ~**abwehr** *f.* anti-tank defence. ~**anlage** *f.* fuel tank. ~**stelle** *f.* petrol station, refuelling-point, filling-station. ~**wagen** *m.* petrol tender, tank lorry. ~**wart** *m.* petrol-pump attendant; (*mil.*) petrol-point orderly.

tanken *v.i.* to take in petrol *or* fuel; to fill up.

Tann *m.* = Tannenwald pine forest.

Tanne *f.* (-, -n) fir. ~nbaum *m.* fir-tree. ~nnadeln *f.pl.* fir-needles. ~nzapfen *m.* fir-cone.

Tante *f.* (-, -n) aunt.

Tanti'eme (-ε:ma) *f.* (-, -n) percent-age, share, royalty.

Tanz (-ts) *m.* (-es, ⸗e) dance; ball. ~bein *n.* das ~bein schwingen to dance. ~boden *m.* dance-hall. ~e'rei *f.* dance, hop.

tänz-eln *vws.i.* to trip along; (*of horse*) to amble. ~er *m.*, ~erin *f.* dancer; partner.

tanzen *v.t. & i.* to dance; to rock; to go round, spin.

Ta'pet (-pe:t) *n.* aufs ~ bringen to start or broach (a subject). ~e *f.* wallpaper. ~entür *f.* hidden door, jib-door.

Tape'zier, ~er (-tsi:r-) *m.* (-ers, -er) paper-hanger; decorator; uphol-sterer. ~en *v.t.* to paper.

tapfer *a.* brave, gallant. ~keit *f.* bravery, gallantry. [DAPPER]

Tapisse'riewaren *f.pl.* tapestry goods.

tappen *v.i.* to grope one's way; to fumble.

täppisch *a.* awkward, clumsy.

Ta'rantel *f.* (-, -n) tarantula; von der ~ gestochen in a frenzy.

Ta'rif (-ri:f) *m.* (-s, -e) tariff, rate, scale of prices, list of charges, list of fares. ~lich, ~mäßig *aa.* in ac-cordance with the tariff. ~lohn *m.* standard wages. ~vertrag *m.* tariff treaty; wage-agreement.

tarn-en *v.t.* to camouflage, screen, disguise. ~kappe *f.* magic hood, invisible cap. ~ung *f.* camou-flage.

Tasche *f.* (-, -n) pocket; pouch, bag; handbag; purse; jemandem auf der ~ liegen to be a (financial) drain on a person. ~nbuch *n.* pocket-book. ~ndieb *m.* pick-pocket. ~nformat *n.* pocket-size. ~nkrebs *m.* common crab. ~nlampe *f.* electric torch. ~n-messer *n.* pocket-knife. ~n-spieler *m.* conjurer, juggler. ~n-tuch *n.* handkerchief. ~nuhr *f.* watch.

Taschner *m.* (-s, -) purse-maker.

Täßchen *n.* (-s, -) little cup.

Tasse *f.* (-, -n) cup (and saucer). ~nkopf *m.* cup. [F]

Tasta'tur *f.* (-, -en) keys, keyboard.

Taste *f.* (-e, -en) (*mus. & telegr.*) key. ~en *v.t. & i.* to touch, feel; to grope; (*mil.*) to key. ~sinn *m.* sense of touch. ~werkzeug *n.* organ of touch, feeler.

tat¹ *imperf. of* tun.

Tat² (ta:t) *f.* (-, -en) deed, act, action; fact; achievement, feat; auf frischer ~ in the very act; in der ~ indeed, as a matter of fact. ~bestand *m.* facts (of a case). ~einheit *f.* (*leg.*) coincidence. ~endrang, ~endurst *m.* thirst for action, desire to do great things. ~enlos *a.* inactive, idle. ~form *f.* (*gram.*) active voice. ~kraft *f.* energy. ~kräftig *a.* energetic. ~sache *f.* fact. ~sächlich *a.* real, actual. *adv.* in fact.

Tät-er *m.* (-ers, -er) doer; per-petrator; culprit. ~erschaft *f.* guilt; perpetration (of crime). ~ig *a.* active; busy; employed, engaged. ~igkeit *f.* activity; action; function; occupation, profession. ~igkeitswort *n.* verb. ~lich *a.* ~lich werden to assault (person), become violent. ~lichkeit *f.* violence, assault (and battery).

tätigen *v.t.* to effect, conclude.

täto'wieren *v.t.* to tattoo.

tätscheln *v.t.* to stroke, caress.

Tatze *f.* (-, -n) paw, claw.

Tau¹ *m.* (-es) dew. ~en *v.i.* to fall (as dew); to thaw, melt. ~feucht *a.* wet with dew. ~perle *f.* dew-drop. ~wetter *n.* thaw.

Tau² *n.* (-es, -e) rope, cable. ~werk *n.* cordage, rigging. ~ziehen *n.* (*sport.*) tug of war.

taub (-p) *a.* deaf; empty, hollow; numb; dead, barren. ~heit *f.* deafness. ~nessel *f.* dead-nettle. ~stumm *a.* deaf and dumb. ~stumme(r) *m.* deaf-mute.

Taube *f.* (-, -n) pigeon; dove. ~n-schlag *m.* dovecot. ~nzüchter *m.* pigeon-fancier.

Täuber(ich) *m.* cock-pigeon.

Tauchboot *n.* submarine.

tauch-en *v.t.* to dip, steep, duck. *v.i.* to dive, plunge, submerge.

~er *m.* diver. **~erglocke** *f.* diving-bell. **~sieder** *m.* immersion heater. [DUCK]

Tauf-akt *m.* baptism; christening ceremony. **~becken** *n.*, **~stein** *m.* baptismal font. **~buch** *n.* parish register.

Tauf-e *f.* (-e,-en) baptism; christening; *aus der ~e heben* to be godfather *or* godmother to a child; (*fig.*) to initiate, originate. **~kapelle** *f.* baptistry. **~name** *m.* Christian name. **~pate** *m.* godfather. **~patin** *f.* godmother. **~schein** *m.* certificate of baptism. **~zeuge** *m.* sponsor.

taufen *v.t.* to baptize; to christen.

Täuf-er *m.* (-ers) *Johannes der ~er* John the Baptist. **~ling** *m.* infant to be christened; candidate for baptism.

taug-en *v.i.* to be of use; to be worth (something); to be good *or* fit (for); to answer, do, serve. **~e-nichts** *m.* good-for-nothing. **~lich** *a.* suitable; capable; useful; (*mil.*) fit. **~lichkeit** *f.* suitability; fitness.

Taumel *m.* (-s) reeling, staggering; giddiness; (*fig.*) passion; frenzy; transport. **~ig** *a.* reeling; giddy. **~n** *vns.i.* to reel, stagger; to be giddy.

Tausch *m.* (-es, -e) exchange, barter. **~en** *v.t.* to exchange, barter, (*sl.*) swop. **~handel** *m.* barter.

täusch-en *v.t.* to delude, deceive; to disappoint. *v.r.* to be mistaken; to deceive oneself; **~end** *ähnlich* indistinguishable, as like as two peas. **~ung** *f.* mistake; deception, fraud; illusion.

tausend *a. & subst.* a. thousand; *~ und eine Nacht* the Arabian Nights. **~er** *m.* thousand; figure marking the thousands. **~erlei** *a.* of a thousand kinds. **~fach**, **~fältig** *aa.* thousandfold. **~füßler** *m.* millepede. **~jährig** *a.* of a thousand years; thousand years old; millennial. **~künstler** *m.* Jack of all trades; conjurer. **~mal** *adv.* a thousand times. **~schönchen** *n.* daisy.

Taxa'meter *m.* taximeter.

Ta'xator *m.* (-s, -en) valuer.

Tax-e *f.* (-e, -en) valuation; authorized charge; tax, rate, duty. **~ieren** *v.t.* to appraise, value, estimate.

Taxus *m.* (-) yew.

Techn-ik *f.* (-ik, -iken) technics; industry; engineering; technology; technique, skill, execution. **~iker** *m.* technician; engineer. **~ikum** *n.* technical school. **~isch** *a.* technical; mechanical; engineering.

Teckel *m.* (-s, -) dachshund.

Tee (te:) *m.* (-s) tea. **~brett** *n.* tea-tray. **~büchse**, **~dose** *f.* tea-caddy. **~haube** *f.* tea-cosy. **~löffel** *m.* tea-spoon. **~rose** *f.* tea-rose. **~sieb** *n.* tea-strainer. **~wagen** *m.* tea-trolley.

Teer *m.* (-es) tar. **~en** *v.t.* to tar.

Teich *m.* (-c) *m.* (-es, -e) pond, pool.

Teig *m.* (-es) dough, paste; batter. **~ig** *a.* doughy.

Teil *m. & n.* (-es, -e) part; section, division; share, portion, party; (*fig.*) due; *edle ~e* vital parts; *ich für mein ~* I for one, as for me, for my part; *sich seinen ~ denken* to have one's own ideas; *zum ~* in part, partly, to some extent; *zum größten ~* for the most part. See also **zuteil**. [DEAL]

teil-bar *a.* divisible. **~chen** *n.* particle. **~haben** *v.i.* to have a share (in), participate (in). **~haber** *m.* participant, sharer; participator; partner. **~haber-schaft** *f.* partnership. **~haftig** *a.* **~haftig werden** participating in, sharing in. **~nahme** *f.* participation; share; co-operation; interest; sympathy, condolence. **~nahmslos** *a.* apathetic, indifferent. **~nahmsvoll** *a.* sympathetic, full of sympathy. **~neh-men** *v.i.* to take part (in); to interest oneself (in). **~nehmer** *m.* participant, sharer; member; subscriber; accomplice. **~s** *adv.* partly. **~strecke** *f.* section. **~ung** *f.* division; partition; graduation, scale. **~weise** *a. adv.* partial. *adv.* in part, partly, to some extent. **~zahlung** *f.* part-payment, instalment.

teilen v.t. to divide, share out, portion, distribute, deal out; to share. v.r. to share in; to give a share of; to branch off, divide, diverge; *geteilte Gefühle* mixed feelings; *geteilter Meinung sein* to be of a different opinion.

Teint (tɛ̃) m. (-s) complexion.

Tele-'funken pl. wireless telegraphy. ~**gramm** n. telegram, wire. ~**grammformular** n. telegraph form. ~'**graphenstange** f. telegraph pole. ~**gra'phie** f. telegraphy. ~**gra'phieren** v.t. & i. to telegraph, wire; to cable. ~'**graphisch** a. by telegram. ~**pa'thie** f. telepathy.

Tele'phon (-'fo:n) n. (-s, -e) telephone; ~ *haben* to be on the telephone. ~**anruf** m. telephone call. ~**anschluß** m. telephone extension. ~**buch** n. directory. ~**ieren** v.t. & i. to telephone, to ring up. ~**isch** a. telephonic; by telephone. ~'**ist** m., ~'**istin** f. telephone operator. ~**zelle** f. callbox. ~**zentrale** f. telephone exchange.

Tele'skop (-ko:p) n. (-s, -e) telescope.

Teller m. (-s, -) plate, dish. ~**mine** f. A.T. mine. ~**mütze** f. flat-peaked cap. ~**tuch** n. dishcloth. [F]

te'llur-isch a. tellurian. ~**ium** n. tellurium.

Tempel m. (-s, -) temple. ~**herr**, **Templer** m. Knight Templar. ~**raub** m. sacrilege.

Tempera f. (*paint.*) distemper; tempera.

Tempera'ment n. (-s, -e) temperament, temper, character, constitution, disposition, humour; spirits, vivacity. ~**los** a. wanting in vivacity, spiritless. ~**voll** a. vivacious, high-spirited; ardent, passionate, eager.

Tempera'tur (-u:r) f. (-, -en) temperature. ~**schwankungen** f.pl. variations of temperature.

Tempe'renzler m. (-s, -) teetotaller.

tempe'rieren v.t. to temper.

Tempo n. (-s, -s & Tempi) time, measure; speed, pace.

Tempus n. (-, Tempora) (*gram.*) tense.

Ten'denz f. (-, -en) tendency, inclination, propensity, trend. ~**i-'ös** a. tendencious; not impartial, biased. ~**roman** m. novel calculated to advance a cause.

tendieren v.i. to tend to.

Tender m. (-s, -) tender.

Tenne f. (-, -n) threshing-floor.

Tennis n. (-) (lawn-)tennis. ~**platz** m. tennis-court. ~**schläger** m. tennis-racket.

Te'nor (-o:r) m. (-s, ̈e) (*mus.*) tenor.

Teppich (-ç) m. (-s, -e) carpet. ~**kehrmaschine** f. carpet sweeper. ~**schoner** m. drugget. [L]

Ter'min (-i:n) m. (-s, -e) time; fixed day; (*leg.*) term; summons. ~**gerecht** a. in due time, to schedule. ~**geschäft** n. (*comm.*) (dealing in) futures. ~**ologie** f. terminology.

Ter'mite f. (-, -n) white ant.

Terpen'tin (-ti:n) n. (-s, -e) turpentine.

Te'rrain (-rɛ̃:) n. (-s, -s) ground.

Te'rrasse f. (-, -n) terrace.

Te'rrine (-i:nə) f. (-, -n) tureen.

Terri'torium n. (-s, Territorien) territory.

terrori'sieren v.t. to terrorize.

Tertia (-tsia) f. (-, Tertien) fourth form. ~**ner** m. fourth-form boy.

Terti'är n. & a. tertiary.

Terz (-ts) f. (-, -en) third; (*fencing*) tierce; *große* ~ major third; *kleine* ~ minor third. ~'**ett** n. trio.

Tesching n. (-s, -s) small rifle.

Testa'ment n. (-s, -e) testament, will. ~'**arisch** a. testamentary, by will. ~**svollstrecker** m. executor.

Tes'tat n. (-s, -e) certificate. ~'**ieren** v.t. to make a will; to bequeath; to testify.

teuer a. dear, expensive, costly; (*fig.*) dear, beloved, cherished. ~**ung** f. dearness; scarcity, dearth; high cost of living.

Teufel m. (-s, -) devil, deuce, Old Nick, dickens; fiend; *pfui* ~ *!* how disgusting! *zum* ~ *gehen* to go to rack and ruin; *des* ~*s sein* to be mad *or* possessed; **den ~ an die Wand malen** talk of the devil and he will appear. **~ei** f. devilry. **~saustreibung** f. exorcism. **~sdreck** m. asafoetida. [GK.]

teuflisch a. devilish, diabolical, fiendish.

Text m. (-es, -e) text; words, wording; libretto; (*film*) caption; *aus dem ~kommen* to lose the thread, be put out; *einem den ~ lesen* to give a person a good talking-to. **~buch** n. words; libretto. **~lich** a. textual.

Tex'tilien, Tex'tilwaren pl. textiles.

The'ater (-a:-) n. (-s, -) theatre; stage. **~besuch** m. playgoing. **~besucher** m. playgoer. **~direktor** m. manager of a theatre. **~kasse** f. box-office. **~stück** n. play, drama. **~zettel** m. playbill.

thea'tralisch a. theatrical.

Theke (te:-) f. (-, -n) counter (in a shop).

Thema (te:-) n. (-s, -ta & Themen) theme, subject, topic.

Theo'log-e m. (-en, -en) theologian. **~ie** f. theology. **~isch** a. theological.

Theo'r-etiker m. theorist. **~etisch** a. theoretical. **~eti'sieren** v.i. to theorize. **~ie** f. theory.

Theoso'phie f. (-, -n) theosophy.

Thera'p-eutik f. therapeutics. **~ie** f. therapy.

Thermo'meter n. & m. thermometer. **~stand** m. thermometer reading.

Thermosflasche f. thermos flask.

These (te:za) f. (-, -n) thesis.

Thrombose f. thrombosis.

Thron (tro:n) m. (-es, -e) throne. **~besteigung** f. accession to the throne. **~erbe** m. heir to the throne. **~folger** m. successor to the throne. **~himmel** m. canopy. **~saal** m. throne room. **~sessel** m. chair of state, canopied chair.

thronen v.i. to be enthroned; to reign.

Thunfisch m. tunny.

Thymian m. (-s, -e) thyme.

ticken v.i. to tick.

tief 1. a. deep, profound; low; dark; far; (*fig.*) innermost; extreme, utmost, utter; *in ~er*

Nacht far into the night; *zu ~ singen* to sing flat; *~er stimmen* to lower the pitch; *das läßt ~blicken* that tells a tale. **2.** *subst.* n. barometric depression.

Tief-angriff m. low-flying attack. **~bau** m. underground building *or* engineering. **~blau** a. dark blue. **~blick** m. insight. **~bohrer** m. auger. **~druck** m. low pressure; (*typ.*) intaglio printing; photogravure.

Tief-e f. (-e, -en) depth; deepness; profundity; low altitude; (*bibl.*) the deep. **~ebene** f. plain, lowland(s). **~enmesser** m. bathometer. **~gang** m. draught (of boat, &c.). **~gebeugt** a. (*fig.*) deeply afflicted. **~gekühlt** a. deep-freeze. **~greifend** a. profound, far-reaching; radical. **~gründig** a. deep, profound. **~kühltruhe** f. deep-freezer. **~land** n. lowland(s). **~liegend** a. (of eyes) sunken; low-lying; deep-seated. **~punkt** m. lowest point; rockbottom. **~schlag** m. hit below the belt. **~schürfend** a. thorough, profound. **~see** f. deep sea. **~sinn** m. deep thought; melancholy. **~sinnig** a. profound; pensive; melancholy. **~stand** m. lowness, low level; (*fig.*) low-water mark.

Tiegel m. (-s, -) saucepan; crucible; (*typ.*) platen. [L]

Tier n. (-es, -e) animal; beast; brute. **~art** f. species of animal. **~arzneikunde** f. veterinary science. **~arzt** m. veterinary surgeon. **~bändiger** m. tamer of wild beasts. **~garten** m. zoological gardens. **~geographie** f. zoogeography. **~isch** a. animal, animal-like; brutish, bestial. **~kreis** m. (*astron.*) zodiac. **~kunde** f. zoology. **~reich** n. animal kingdom. **~schutzverein** m. society for the prevention of cruelty to animals. [DEER]

Tiger m. (-s, -) tiger. **~in** f. tigress.

tilg-en v.t. to extinguish; to efface, obliterate, blot out; to destroy; to eradicate; to cancel, annul; to pay off (debt); to redeem. **~ung** f. effacement, blotting out;

destruction; cancelling; repayment; redemption. **~ungsfonds**
m. sinking-fund.

Tingeltangel m. & n. low music-hall.

Tink'tur f. (-, -en) tincture.

Tinte f. (-, -n) ink; tint; *in der ~ sitzen* to be in the soup. **~nfaß**
n. inkstand. **~nfisch** m. cuttle-fish. **~nfleck, ~nklecks** m. blot.
~nstift m. indelible pencil. **~n-wischer** m. pen-wiper. [ML]

tippeln *vws.i.* to tramp, walk the roads.

tipp-en *v.t.* to touch lightly, tap; to type(write); *(fig.)* to tip. **~fräulein** n. typist.

Tisch m. (-es, -e) table; meal, dinner, supper; *bei ~* during the meal, at dinner or supper; *am grünen ~* by red tape; *reinen machen* to make a clean sweep; *unter den ~ fallen* to be ignored, not come under consideration.
~dame f., **~herr** m. partner at table. **~decke** f. table-cover.
~karte f. place card. **~klopfen**
n. table-rapping. **~lade** f. table-drawer. **~platte** f. table-top. **~rede** f. after-dinner speech. **~rücken** n. table-turning. **~tennis**
n. table tennis, ping-pong. **~tuch**
n. table-cloth. **~zeit** f. meal-time, dinner-time. [DISK]

Tischler m. (-s, -) joiner, carpenter, cabinet-maker. **~ei** f. carpentry, joiner's work, woodwork;
joiner's workshop, carpenter's shop. **~leim** m. strong glue. **~n**
v.t. & i. to carpenter, do joiner's work.

ti'tanisch a. titanic.

Titel (ti:-) m. (-s, -) title; claim;
heading. **~bild** n. frontispiece.
~blatt n. title-page. **~halter,**
~verteidiger m. title-holder. **~sucht** f. mania for titles.

titu'l-ar a. titulary. **~a'tur** f.
titles. **~ieren** *v.t.* to give the title of; to call.

Toast (to:st) m. (-es, -e) toast,
health; toasted bread. **~en** *v.i.*
to drink toasts; to propose toasts.

tob-en (to:-) *v.i.* to storm, rage,
roar; to rave; to be wild, romp.
~sucht f. raving madness. **~**

süchtig a. raving mad.

Tochter (·x·) f. (-, -ö) daughter.
~gesellschaft f. subsidiary company.

töchter-lich a. daughterly. **~schule** f. *höhere* **~~** high-school
for girls, ladies' college.

Tod (to:t) m. (-es) death; decease;
des ~es sein to be doomed. **~feind** m. deadly enemy. **~geweiht** a. doomed. **~krank**
a. dangerously ill. **~müde** a.
dead tired, knocked-up. **~sicher**
a. dead certain. **~sünde** f. mortal
sin. **~wund** a. mortally wounded. See also **tot-.**

Todes-angst f. death-agony; mortal
fear. **~anzeige** f. death notice,
obituary. **~fall** m. death; *(mil.)*
casualty. **~furcht** f. fear of
death. **~gefahr** f. imminent
danger, peril of one's life. **~kampf** m. death-agony. **~kandidat** m. a doomed man, dying
man. **~schweiß** m. cold sweat
of death. **~stoß** m. death-blow.
~strafe f. capital punishment;
death penalty. **~tag** m. day of
anniversary of (a person's) death.
~urteil n. death sentence.

tödlich a. fatal; deadly; mortal;
murderous.

Toi'lette f. (-, -n) toilet; dress;
dressing-table; lavatory, W.C.;
~ machen to dress, get dressed.
~npapier n. toilet-paper.

tole'r-ant a. tolerant. **~anz** f.
toleration; tolerance. **~ieren** *v.t.*
to tolerate.

toll a. mad, insane; frantic, raving;
wild; awful; excessive; wanton.
~haus n. lunatic asylum. **~häusler** m. madman, lunatic. **~heit** f. madness, frenzy; rage,
fury; piece of folly. **~kirsche** f.
deadly nightshade. **~kopf** m.
madcap. **~kühn** a. foolhardy,
rash. **~kühnheit** f. foolhardiness.
~wut f. hydrophobia, rabies.
[DULL]

Tolle f. (-, -n) tuft; topknot.

tollen *v.i.* to romp; to fool about.

Tolpatsch, Tölpel m. lout, clumsy
fellow.

tölpisch a. clumsy.

To'mate f. (-, -n) tomato.

Tombola f. raffle.

Ton¹ (to:n) m. (-es, ⸚e) sound; note; timbre; stress, accent; tone; colour, shade, tint; (fig.) tone, fashion; **den ~ angeben** to give the note; (fig.) to set the fashion. **~angebend** a. setting the fashion, leading. **~art** f. key. **~band** n. **~streifen** m. tape recorder; (film) sound track. **~bandaufnahme** f. tape recording. **~dichtung** f. musical composition; symphonic poem. **~fall** m. intonation, speech-melody; (mus.) inflexion; cadence. **~film** m. talkie, sound film. **~fixierbad** n. (phot.) toning and fixing bath. **~folge** f. scale, succession of tones; melody. **~führung** f. modulation. **~funksystem** n. Audion wireless system. **~höhe** f. pitch. **~kunst** f. music, musical art. **~lage** f. compass, pitch. **~leiter** f. scale, gamut. **~los** a. soundless; voiceless; unaccented. **~malerei** f. onomatopoeia. **~setzer** m. composer. **~stufe** f. pitch. **~verstärker** m. sound amplifier.

Ton² (to:n) m. (-es) clay. **~erde** f. alumina; **essigsaure ~erde** aluminium acetate. **~gefäß** n. earthen vessel. **~waren** f.pl. pottery.

tön-en v.i. to sound, resound; to ring. v.t. to shade, shade off. **~ung** f. tinge; shading.

tönern a. of clay, earthen.

Tonika f. (-, Toniken) (mus.) tonic.

Tonne f. (-, -n) tun, butt; cask, barrel; bin; (naut.) ton; buoy. **~ngehalt** m. tonnage. **~ngewölbe** n. barrel-vault.

Ton'sur f. (-, -en) tonsure.

To'pas m. (-es, -e) topaz.

Topf m. (-es, ⸚e) pot; jar, crock. **~gucker** m. inquisitive person, Nosy Parker. **~lappen** m. kettle-holder, oven-cloth.

Töpfer m. (-s, -) potter. **~ei** f. potter's trade or workshop. **~scheibe** f. potter's wheel. **~waren** f.pl. pottery, crockery, earthenware.

topp¹ int. done! agreed! (sl.) right oh!

Topp² m. (-es, -e) top, head. **~mast** m. topmast. **~reep** n. guy.

~segel n. topsail.

Tor¹ (to:r) n. (-es, -e) gate; (football) goal. **~hüter** m. gate keeper, porter. **~schluß** m. closing of the gate(s); **kurz vor ~schluß** (fig.) at the eleventh hour. **~stoß** m. (football) goal-kick. **~wächter**, **~wart** m. (football) goalkeeper. **~weg** m. gateway. [DOOR]

Tor² (to:r) m. (-en, -en) fool. **~heit** f. folly, foolishness.

Torf m. (-es, -e) peat. **~boden** m. peat-soil. **~moor** n. peat-bog. **~mull** m. peat-dust. **~stecher** m. peat-cutter. **~stich** m. peat-cutting. **~streu** f. peat-litter. [TURF]

tör-icht a. foolish, silly. **~in** f. foolish woman.

torkeln vus.i. to reel, stagger.

Tor'nister m. (-s, -) knapsack; (mil.) pack.

torpe'dieren v.t. to torpedo.

Tor'pedo m. (-s) torpedo.

Tort (-t) m. (-es) wrong, injury.

Torte f. (-, -n) iced cake, layer cake. **~nheber** m. cake server.

Tor'tur f. (-, -en) torture.

tosen (to:-) v.i. to rage, roar.

tot (to:t) a. dead; lifeless, inanimate; dull, lustreless; stagnant; idle; **~e Hand** mortmain; **~er Punkt** dead centre; (fig.) deadlock; **~es Rennen** dead heat; **~e Zeit** dead season. **~e(r)** m. dead person, deceased, corpse, defunct. **~arbeiten** v.r. to kill oneself with work. **~geboren** a. still-born. **~lachen** v.r. to split one's sides (with laughter). **~schlag** m. homicide, manslaughter. **~schlagen** v.t. to kill; (fig.) to waste (time). **~schläger** m. murderer, one guilty of manslaughter. **~schweigen** v.t. to hush up (a matter). **~sicher** a. cocksure. **~stellen** v.r. to feign death.

Total-i'sator m. totalizer, totalizator. **~i'tär** a. totalitarian.

töt-en (to:-) v.t. to kill, slay, put to death; to deaden; to mortify (the flesh). v.r. to commit suicide. **~ung** f. killing, slaying.

Toten-acker m. graveyard, churchyard. **~bett** n. death-bed. **~blaß**, **~bleich** aa. pale as death.

~glocke f. funeral bell, passing-bell, knell. ~gräber m. grave-digger. ~hemd n. shroud, wind-ing-sheet. ~kopf, ~schädel m. death's head; skull. ~liste f. death-roll. ~marsch m. funeral march. ~maske f. death-mask. ~messe f. mass for the dead. ~schau f. coroner's inquest; post-mortem examination. ~schein m. death certificate. ~starre f. rigor mortis. ~still a. still as death. ~stille f. (fig.) dead silence. ~tanz m. the dance of death. ~uhr f. (zool.) death-watch (beetle).

Toto n. football pool.

Tour f. (-, -en) tour, excursion, trip, journey; (dance-)figure, set; re-volution (of engine, &c.); turn; round (of knitting); in einer ~ without stopping, at a stretch. ~enrad n. roadster. ~enwagen m. touring-car. ~enzahl f. revo-lutions per minute. ~enzähler m. speed indicator. ~'ist m. tour-ist. ~nee f. (theatr.) tour.

Trab m. (-es) trot; im ~ at a trot; einen auf den ~ bringen to make a person speed up. ~en vcs.i. to trot. ~er m. trotter. ~reiten n. trot. ~rennen n. trotting-race.

Tra'bant m. (-en, -en) satellite.

Tracht f. (-axt) f. (-, -en) dress, costume; national costume; fash-ion; uniform (of nurse); load; eine ~ Prügel a sound thrash-ing.

trachten v.i. to strive, seek after, aspire to; einem nach dem Leben ~ to make an attempt on a person's life.

trächtig a. pregnant.

traditio'nell a. traditional.

traf imperf. of **treffen**.

Trag-altar m. portable altar. ~bahre f. stretcher, litter. ~balken m. beam, transom. ~bar a. portable; wearable; bearable.

Trag-e (-a:-) f. (-e, -en) barrow; lit-ter. ~fähig a. capable of bearing or carrying. ~fähigkeit f. carrying capacity; tonnage (of ship); load-limit (of bridge); productiveness (of soil). ~fläche f., ~flügel m. wing of aircraft. ~himmel m.

canopy. ~korb m. pannier. ~last f. load; hand-luggage, pan-nier. ~riemen m. carrying strap. ~sessel m. sedan-chair. ~tier n. pack-animal. ~weite f. range; bearing, importance.

träg-e (-e:-) a. slow, sluggish; lazy, idle; indolent. ~heit f. slowness; laziness, idleness; inertia. ~heitsgesetz n. law of inertia.

tragen v.t. st. to carry, bear; to con-vey, transport, take; to endure, suffer; to support; to yield; to produce; to have; to wear, have on; bei sich ~ to have about one. v.i. to reach, carry. v.r. to dress; sich ~ mit to be thinking of, intending to. [DRAW]

Träger m. (-s, -) bearer; porter, carrier; (archit.) beam, girder.

Trag-ik f. (-ik) tragic art; calamity. ~isch a. tragic, tragical; sad, calamitous. ~öde m. tragic actor. ~ödie f. tragedy; tragic drama; sad event, calamity. ~ödin f. tragic actress.

train-'ieren v.t. & i. to train. ~ingsanzug m. training suit, track-suit; (mil.) smock.

Tra'jekt n. (-s, -e) (train-)ferry.

Trakt-at (-a:t) m. & n. (-ats, -ate) treatise; (theol.) tract; treaty. ~ieren v.t. to treat (to).

Traktor m. (-s, -en) tractor.

trällern v.t. & i. to hum, warble.

trampel-n v.i. to trample, stamp. ~tier n. dromedary.

Tran (-a:n) m. (-es) train-oil; blubber. ~ig a. oily; tasting of oil.

tran'chier-en v.t. to carve, cut up. ~besteck n. carvers, carving-knife and fork. ~messer n. carving-knife.

Träne (-e:-) f. (-, -n) tear. ~n v.i. (of eyes) to water; to be full of tears. ~ndrüse f. lachrymal gland. ~n-gas n. tear gas. ~nreiz m. eye irritation. ~nsack m. lachrymal sac.

trank[1] imperf. of **trinken**.

Trank[2] m. (-s, -̈e) drink; draught. ~opfer n. libation.

Tränk-e f. (-e, -en) watering-place, horse-pond. ~en v.t. to give to drink; to water (cattle); to soak, steep, saturate, impregnate.

trans-fe'rieren *v.t.* to transfer. ~for'mator *m.* (*electr.*) transformer.

transitiv *a.* transitive.

Trans-missionsapparat *m.* transmitter. ~missionswelle *f.* connecting-shaft. ~pa'rent *n.* transparency. *a.* transparent.

transpi'rieren *v.i.* to perspire.

trans-po'nieren *v.t.* to transpose. ~'port *m.* transport, carriage; shipment. ~por'teur *m.* transporter, carrier; (*geom.*) protractor. ~portflugzeug *n.* transport; troop-carrying plane. ~por'tieren *v.t.* to transport, convey; to ship. ~portschiff *n.* transport; troop-transport. ~zendent *a.* transcendental.

Tra'pez (-pe:ts) *n.* (-es, -e) trapeze; (*math.*) trapezium, trapezoid. ~künstler *m.* trapeze artiste, acrobat.

Trappe *f.* (-, -n) bustard.

trappeln *v.i.* to patter, toddle; (*o horse*) to trot.

tra'ssieren *v.i.* to draw (bill).

trat *imperf.* of treten.

Tratsch *m.* (-es) (*colloq.*) tittle-tattle, gossip.

Tratte *f.* (-, -n) (*commerc.*) draft.

Trau-altar *m.* marriage-altar. ~ring *m.* wedding-ring. ~schein *m.* marriage lines, certificate of marriage. ~ung *f.* marriage ceremony, wedding. ~zeuge *m.* witness to a marriage.

Traube *f.* (-, -n) grape; bunch of grapes; cluster, bunch. ~nlese *f.* grape-harvest; grape-gathering; vintage. ~nmost *m.* grape-juice, new wine, must. ~npresse *f.* winepress. ~nzucker *m.* grape-sugar.

trauen *v.t.* to marry, give in marriage, join together in wedlock; *sich ~ lassen* to get married. *v.i.* to trust, trust in, rely upon, have confidence in, believe in. *v.r.* to dare, venture. [TRUTH]

Trauer *f.* (-) sorrow, grief, affliction, pain; mourning. ~anzeige *f.* announcement of a death. ~botschaft *f.* sad news. ~fall *m.* a death. ~feier *f.* funeral service.

~flor *m.* crape. ~mantel *m.* (*zool.*) Camberwell Beauty. ~marsch *m.* funeral march. ~rand *m.* black edge. ~spiel *n.* tragedy. ~weide *f.* weeping willow.

trauern *v.i.* to mourn, grieve (for); to wear mourning.

Trauf-e *f.* (-e, -en) gutter; eaves; *vom Regen in die ~* out of the frying-pan into the fire. ~rinne *f.* gutter (of roof).

träufeln *v.t.* to drop, let fall in drops. *v.i.* to drip, trickle.

traulich *a.* intimate; homely; cosy, snug, comfortable. ~keit *f.* cosiness, comfort.

Traum *m.* (-es, ⁼e) dream; fancy, illusion. ~bild, ~gesicht *n.* vision. ~deuter *m.* interpreter of dreams. ~haft *a.* dreamlike. ~verloren *a.* lost in dreams.

träum-en *v.i. & i.* to dream; to muse, think deeply; to day-dream; to imagine; to believe. ~er *m.* dreamer. ~e'rei *f.* reverie, brown study. ~erisch *a.* dreamy; given to dreaming.

traurig *a.* sad, sorrowful, mournful, dismal. ~keit *f.* sadness, sorrow, melancholy. [DREARY]

traut *a.* dear, beloved; cosy, comfortable.

Treber *pl.* draff, grains; skins of grapes.

treck-en *v.i.* to emigrate, wander. ~er *m.* tractor.

Treff *n.* (-s, -s) club (card).

treffen 1. *v.t. & i. st.* to hit, strike; to concern, affect, touch; to find; to meet; to meet with; to fall in with; to strike, fall upon; to strike (the right note); to take (measures); to make (preparations); (*phot. & paint.*) to achieve a good likeness; *empfindlich ~* (*fig.*) to cut to the quick. *v.r* to happen; *sich gut ~* to be lucky; *sich getroffen fühlen* to feel hurt. 2. *subst. n.* meeting; encounter, battle. ~d *a.* well-aimed; right, appropriate; pertinent; to the point; striking (resemblance).

Treff-er *m.* (-ers, -er) hit; winning ticket, prize; luck, lucky chance; *einen ~er erzielen* to score a hit. ~lich *a.* excellent, admirable. ~

lichkeit f. excellence. ~punkt m. rendezvous; (mil.) point of impact. ~sicher a. accurate; (fig.) pertinent; sound.

Treib-eis n. drift-ice. ~er m. driver; drover; beater. ~haus n. hot-house, conservatory. ~holz n. drift-wood. ~jagd f. battue. ~kraft f. motive power; moving force. ~rad n. fly-wheel. ~riemen m. driving-belt. ~sand m. quicksand. ~stoff m. petrol, fuel; propellent.

treiben v.t. st. to drive, set in motion, propel; to drive out, expel (from); to whip (top); to put forth (leaves, &c.); (of plant) to force; (med.) to produce, promote; (fig.) to urge on, incite; to do, carry on; to study, practise; to chase or emboss (metal); vor sich her ~ to dribble (football). v.i. to float, drift; to blossom forth. subst. n. doings; life; activity; stir.

treidel-n v.t. (naut.) to tow. ~weg m. tow-path.

tremu'lieren v.t. & i. to shake, quaver; to sing tremolo.

trennbar a. separable; divisible.

trenn-en v.t. to separate, divide, sever; to disunite, dissolve; to undo (seam); (tel.) to interrupt, disconnect. v.r. to part, separate; to divide, branch off. ~schärfe f. discrimination; (radio) selectivity. ~ung f. separation; dissolution; parting. ~ungslinie f. line of demarcation; (mil.) formation boundary. ~ungsstrich m. dash.

Trense f. (-, -n) snaffle.

trepp-'ab adv. downstairs. ~'auf adv. upstairs.

Treppe f. (-, -n) staircase, stairs, flight of stairs; steps; eine ~ hoch wohnen to live on the first floor. ~nabsatz m. landing. ~ngeländer n. banisters, railing. ~nhaus n. hall; well of staircase. ~nläufer m. stair-carpet. ~nwitz m. witty (but too late) comment, esprit de l'escalier.

Tre'sor m. (-s, -e) treasury; safe.

Tresse f. (-, -n) braid, galloon.

tret-en (-e:-)vws.i. st. to tread, step,

walk, go; to pedal; to treadle. v.t. to tread, trample; to push (pedal); to work (treadle); (fig.) to press, dun; mit Füßen ~en to trample under foot. ~anlasser m. kick-starter; foot-starter. ~mine f. contact mine. ~mühle f. treadmill. ~rad n. treadwheel. ~schemel m. treadle (of loom).

treu a. faithful, true, loyal, constant; accurate; retentive (memory). ~bruch m. breach of faith; perfidy; disloyalty. ~brüchig a. faithless; perfidious; disloyal.

Treu-e f. (-) fidelity, faithfulness, loyalty; accuracy. ~händer m. trustee, executor. ~handgesellschaft f. trust company. ~herzig a. frank; guileless; trusting. ~herzigkeit f. frankness; naivety. ~lich adv. faithfully, truly, loyally. ~los a. faithless, perfidious; treacherous. ~losigkeit f. faithlessness; perfidy; treacherous deed.

Tri'bun m. (-s, -en) tribune.

Tri'büne f. (-, -n) platform; (grand-)stand; gallery.

Tri'but m. (-s, -e) tribute. ~pflichtig a. tributary.

Tri'chine f. (-, -n) trichina.

Trichter m. (-s, -) funnel; crater; horn (of gramophone). ~feld n. shell-torn or -pitted ground.

Trick m. (-s, -s) trick, dodge, stunt. ~film m. stunt film.

trieb[1] imperf. of treiben.

Trieb[2] m. (-es, -e) sprout, shoot; motive power; spur, impetus; instinct, impulse. ~feder f. spring; (fig.) motive. ~haft a. instinctive; unbridled; (psychoan.) instinctual. ~kraft f. motive power. ~sand m. quicksand. ~stange f. push-rod. ~stoff m. petrol, fuel; propellent. ~wagen m. rail-motor, motor-carriage. ~werk n. gearing; machinery, mechanism; driving unit.

Trief-auge n. watering eye, blear eye. ~äugig a. bleary, blear-eyed. ~en v.i. st. & w. to drop, drip, trickle, run; vor Nässe ~en to be soaking wet. ~naß a. sopping, dripping wet.

triezen v.t. (colloq.) to vex.

trifft 3rd pers. sing. pres. ind. of **treffen**.

Trift f. (-, -en) drift; floating (of wood); pasture land.

triftig a. weighty, cogent, good, strong.

Trigonome'trie f. (-) trigonometry.

Tri'kot (-ko:) n. (-s, -s) stockinet; tights. **~agen** pl. knitted goods, hosiery.

Triller m. (-s, -) trill, shake; quaver. **~n** v.i. & t. to trill, shake; (of birds) to warble.

Trini'tät f. (-) Trinity.

trinkbar a. drinkable.

trink-en v.t. & i. st. to drink; to tipple; to imbibe, absorb; **~en auf** to drink to, toast. **~er** m. drunkard. **~gelage** n. drinking-bout, carouse. **~geld** n. tip, gratuity. **~spruch** m. toast. **~wasser** n. drinking-water.

Trio n. (-s, -s) trio.

Tri'ole f. (-, -n) (mus.) triplet.

trippeln vvs.i. to trip.

Tripper m. (-s, -) (med.) gonorrhoea.

tritt¹ 3rd pers. sing. pres. ind. of **treten**.

Tritt² m. (-es, -e) step, pace; kick; footstep, track; small step-ladder; **~ halten** to keep in step, keep pace (with). **~brett** n. running-board, footboard. **~leiter** f. step-ladder, pair of steps. **~rad** n. spinning-wheel (with treadle).

Tri'umph m. (-es, -e) triumph, victory. **~al** a. in triumph. **~'ator** m. victor, conquering hero. **~bogen** m. triumphal arch. **~'ieren** v.i. to triumph; to boast, exult (in); to vanquish, conquer.

trocken a. dry, dried up; arid, parched; (fig.) boring, dull; **im ~en sein** to be under cover; **auf dem ~en sitzen** (fig.) to be in low water. **~apparat** m. desiccator. **~boden** m. drying-loft. **~dock** n. dry dock. **~element** n. dry cell, dry battery. **~futter** n. fodder. **~gestell** n., **~ständer** m. towel-horse, clothes-horse. **~heit** f. dryness, drought; aridity; (fig.) dullness. **~legen** v.t. to drain (land); to change (baby's) napkins. **~milch** f. milk pow-

der, dried milk.

trocknen v.t. & vws.i to dry, dry up, desiccate.

Troddel f. (-, -n) tassel.

Tröd-el (-ə.:) m. (-els) lumber, rubbish; second-hand goods. **~eln** v.i. to deal in second-hand goods; to dawdle, loiter, be slow. **~el-waren** f. pl. second-hand goods. **~ler** m. dealer in second-hand goods; dawdler.

troff imperf. of **triefen**.

Trog¹ (-k) m. (-es, "e) trough.

trog² imperf. of **trügen**.

trollen v.r. to stroll away, toddle off, saunter on.

Trommel f. (-, -n) drum; tympanum; tympanic membrane. **~feuer** n. drum fire, intense bombardment. **~schlag** m. beat of drum. **~schläger** m. drummer. **~schlegel** m. drumstick. **~wirbel** m. roll of drums.

tromm-eln v.t. & i. to drum, beat the drum. **~ler** m. drummer.

Trom'pete (-pe:-) f. (-, -n) trumpet. **~n** v.i. to trumpet (forth); to blow the trumpet. **~nschall** m. sounding of trumpets. **~nstoß** m. flourish of trumpets. **~r** m. trumpeter.

Trop-en (-o:-) pl. tropics. **~enhelm** m. sun-helmet, pith helmet. **~isch** a. tropical.

Tropf m. (-es, "e) simpleton; (poor) wretch.

tröpfeln v.t. & i. to drop, drip, trickle.

tropf-en v.t. & i. to drop, drip, trickle. **~en** subst. m. drop; bead (of perspiration); (fig.) drip. **~enweise** adv. by drops, drop by drop. **~naß** a. dripping wet. **~stein** m. stalactite.

Tro'phäe f. (-, -n) trophy.

Troß (-s) m. (Tross-es, -e) baggage, transport; gang, followers.

Trosse f. (-, -n) cable, hawser.

Trost (-o:-) m. (-es) comfort, consolation, solace; nicht bei **~e sein** to be off one's head. **~bedürftig** a. in need of consolation. **~los** a. disconsolate, sad; hopeless; cheerless; bleak, desolate. **~losigkeit** f. despair; hopelessness;

dreariness. **~reich** *a.* comforting, consoling. [TRUST]

tröst-en (-ø:-) *v.t.* to console, comfort, solace. *v.r.* to be comforted, consoled; to take comfort (in), console oneself (with). **~er** *m.* comforter. **~lich** *a.* consoling, comforting; cheering. **~ung** *f.* consolation.

Trott *m.* (-es) trot; jog-trot. **~en** *vus.i.* to trot. **~oir** (-toʹaːr) *n.* pavement.

Trottel *m.* (-s, -) idiot, fool.

trotz[1] *prep.* in spite of, notwithstanding. **~dem** *adv. & conj.* nevertheless, in spite of that.

Trotz[2] *m.* (-es) obstinacy, stubbornness; defiance; insolence; **~ bieten** to defy; *einem zum* **~** in defiance of a person, in spite of. **~en** *v.i.* to defy; to be obstinate or stubborn. **~ig** *a.* defiant; obstinate; refractory; sulky. **~kopf** *m.* stubborn or pigheaded person.

trüb (-yːp) *a.* muddy, turbid; dull, dim; cloudy; dark, sad, gloomy; *im ~en fischen* to fish in troubled waters. **~en** *v.t.* to make muddy or turbid; to dim, trouble; to spoil, ruffle, upset; *der Himmel trübt sich* the sky is clouding over or becoming overcast. **~heit** *f.* muddy or turbid state; dimness; opaqueness; gloom. **~sal** *f.* affliction, trouble, distress, misery; **~sal blasen** to be in the dumps, mope. **~selig** *a.* sad; woeful. **~sinn** *m.* melancholy, gloom. **~sinnig** *a.* melancholy, sad, dejected, gloomy. **~ung** *f.* making turbid; dimming, darkening, tarnishing; (*fig.*) ruffling.

Trubel (-uː-) *m.* (-s) turmoil, confusion, excitement.

Truchseß *m.* (Truchsess-es, -e) high steward.

trudeln *vws.i.* (*av.*) to spin, go into a spin.

Trüffel *f.* (-, -n) truffle.

trug[1] *imperf. of* tragen.

Trug[2] (-uːk) *m.* (-es) delusion, illusion, deception; fraud, imposture. **~bild** *n.* phantom, vision; optical illusion, mirage. **~schluß** *m.* false conclusion, fallacy.

trüg-en (-yː-) *v.t. & i. st.* to deceive, delude, mislead; to prove fallacious; to be deceptive. **~erisch** *a.* deceitful, deceptive, delusive; insidious; treacherous.

Truhe *f.* (-, -n) chest, trunk.

Trümmer *pl.* ruins; wreckage; debris; fragments, pieces. **~haft** *a.* in ruins, decayed.

Trumpf *m.* (-es, ¨e) trump, trumpcard. **~en** *v.i. & t.* to play trumps, to trump.

Trunk *m.* (-es, ¨e) drink; draught; drinking. **~en** *a.* drunk, intoxicated. **~enbold** *m.* drunkard. **~enheit** *f.* drunkenness, intoxication. **~sucht** *f.* dipsomania. **~süchtig** *a.* dipsomaniac.

Trupp *m.* (-s, -s) troop, band, gang; (*mil.*) section, party, squad. **~e** *f.* troupe, company; (*mil.*) unit; (*pl.*) troops, forces. **~enaushebung** *f.* levy of troops. **~engattung** *f.* arm, branch of the service. **~enkörper** *m.* corps. **~enschau** *f.* military review. **~enteil** *m.* unit. **~enübungsplatz** *m.* training area, permanent military camp. **~enverband** *m.* formation of various arms. **~enverbandplatz** *m.* regimental aid post.

Trut-hahn *m.* turkey(-cock). **~henne** *f.* turkey-hen.

Trutz *m.* (-es) defiance; offensive. **~waffen** *f.pl.* weapons for attack.

Tube (tuː-) *f.* (-, -n) ♁ tube (with screw cap).

Tu'berk-el *f.* (-el, -eln) tubercle. **~elbildung** *f.* tuberculation. **~u-'lös** *a.* tubercular, tuberculous. **~u'lose** *f.* tuberculosis.

Tuch (tuːx) *n.* 1. (-es, -e) cloth, fabric, stuff, material. 2. (-es, ¨er) shawl, scarf. **~fabrik** *f.* cloth-mill, cloth factory. **~fühlung** *f.* close touch, close drill formation. **~händler** *m.* cloth-merchant, draper. **~waren** *f.pl.* drapery.

tüchtig *a.* fit, qualified, able; capable, efficient; good, excellent; sound, hard, proper, thorough. **~keit** *f.* fitness, ability; efficiency. [DOUGHTY]

Tück-e *f.* (-e, -en) malice, spite;

mischievous trick. ~isch *a.* malicious, spiteful; malignant (disease); vicious (dog).

Tuff(stein) *m.* tuff.

Tüfte|lei *f.* (-, -en) hair-splitting, subtlety.

tüfteln *v.i.* to puzzle (over); to split hairs.

Tugend (tu:-) *f.* (-, -en) virtue. ~haft, ~sam *aa.* virtuous. ~richter *m.* moralist, censor.

Tüll *m.* (-s) tulle. ~spitze *f.* net lace.

Tülle *f.* (-, -n) socket; spout.

Tulpe *f.* (-, -n) tulip.

tummel|n *v.t.* to exercise horse. *v.r.* to hurry, make haste; to bustle about; to romp. ~platz *m.* playground; (*fig.*) scene.

Tümpel *m.* (-s, -) pool, puddle.

Tu'mult *m.* (-s, -e) tumult, uproar, riot, hubbub, commotion. ~u'ant *m.* rioter. ~u'arisch *a.* riotous.

tun (tu:n) *irreg. v.t. & i.* to do, make, act, perform, execute; to work; to put; to send (to school); to hurt, harm; ~ *als ob* to pretend to, sham; *das tut nichts* that doesn't matter; *mir ist darum zu* = I care about it, I attach great importance to it, I feel very anxious about it; *des Guten zuviel* ~ to overdo a thing; *es zu* ~ *bekommen mit* to have trouble with. *subst. n.* action, doings. Other idioms connected with tun will be found under the respective nouns or compounds with **tun**.

Tünche *f.* (-, -n) whitewash; (*fig.*) veneer, varnish. ~n *v.t.* to whitewash.

Tunichtgut *m.* (-es, -e) ne'er-do-well.

Tunika *f.* (-, Tuniken) tunic.

Tunke *f.* (-, -n) gravy; sauce. ~n *v.t.* to dip, steep.

tunlich *a.* feasible, practicable; advisable, expedient. ~st *a.* utmost. *adv.* if possible.

Tunnel *m.* (-s, -) tunnel.

Tüpfel *m.* (-s, -) dot; spot. ~n *v.t.* to dot; to spot; to stipple.

tupfen *v.t. & i.* to dot; to touch lightly; to dab. *subst. m.* dot, spot.

Tür (ty:r) *f.* (-, -en) door; *vor der* ~ *stehen* (*fig.*) to be imminent; *mit der* ~ *ins Haus fallen* to blurt out. ~einfassung *f.* door-frame. ~flügel *m.* leaf of door. ~füllung *f.* door-panel. ~griff *m.* door-handle. ~hüter *m.* doorkeeper, porter. ~klinke *f.* latch. ~klopfer *m.* knocker. ~sturz *m.* lintel.

Turban *m.* (-s, -e) turban.

Tur'bine *f.* (-, -n) turbine.

Tür'kis *m.* (-es, -e) turquoise.

Turm *m.* (-es, "e) tower; turret; steeple; (*chess*) rook, castle. ~fahne *f.* vane. ~falke *m.* kestrel. ~hoch *adv.* (*fig.*) very high; miles above; beyond. ~luke *f.* louvre-window; (*naut.*) turret door or hatch. ~schwalbe *f.* swift. ~spitze *f.* spire. ~uhr *f.* church-clock.

türm|en *v.t.* to pile up. *v.r.* to tower up, rise high. *vvs.i.* (*sl.*) to scamper off. ~er *m.* watchman, warder of a tower.

turn|en *v.i.* to do gymnastics; to drill. *subst. n.* gymnastics, drill. ~er *m.* gymnast. ~erisch *a.* gymnastic, athletic. ~erschaft *f.* athletic club; the gymnasts. ~gerät *n.* gymnastic apparatus. ~halle *f.* gymnasium. ~hose *f.* shorts. ~unterricht *m.* physical training. [L]

Tur'nier *n.* (-s, -e) tournament. ~platz *m.* the lists.

Turteltaube *f.* turtle-dove.

Tusch *m.* (-es, -e) (*mus.*) flourish.

Tusch|e *f.* (-e, -en) Indian ink. ~en *v.t.* to wash, paint with Indian ink. ~kasten *m.* paint-box.

tuscheln *v.i. & t.* to whisper.

Tüte *f.* (-, -n) paper-bag.

tuten *v.t. & i.* to toot, honk.

Tüttelchen *n.* (-s, -) dot; jot.

Twist *m.* twist; cotton waste.

Typ *m.* ~us *m.* (*pl.* Typen) type. ~isch *a.* typical.

Type *f.* (-, -en) type. ~enhebel *m.* type bar. ~ogra'phie *f.* typography. ~o'graphisch *a.* typographical.

typh-'ös *a.* typhoid. ~us *m.* ♁ typhoid.

Ty'rann *m.* (-en, -en) tyrant. ~-
'ei *f.* tyranny. ~isch *a.* tyrannical. ~i'sieren *v.t.* to tyrannize
over.

U

U, u (uː) *n.* the letter U, u.

übel (yː-) *a.* evil, wrong, bad; sick,
ill; ~ *daran sein* to be in a bad
way; *nicht* ~ not bad, rather nice;
mir ist ~ I feel sick. *subst.* ~ *n.* evil;
injury; ailment, malady; disease;
misfortune; inconvenience. ~-
befinden *n.* indisposition. ~ge-
launt, ~launig *aa.* cross, grumpy.
~gesinnt *a.* evil-minded. ~keit
f. sickness, nausea. ~nehmen
v.t. to take amiss. ~nehmerisch
a. touchy, easily offended. ~-
stand *m.* inconvenience, drawback, defect, abuse. ~täter *m.*
evil-doer, criminal. ~wollend *a.*
malevolent.

üb-en (yː-b-) *v.t. & r.* to exercise; to
practise; to train; *geübt sein* to
be skilled (at). ~lich *a.* usual,
usual, customary, in use. ~ung *f*
exercise, practice; training, drill;
use ~ungsflug *m.* practice flight.

über (yːbər) *prep.* over, above, on
top of; higher than, superior to;
beyond, on the other side of;
across; on, upon; more than;
during, while; about, concerning.
adv. wholly, completely; over, in
excess. *pref.* over-, super-, per-,
hyper-, supra-; ~ *Berlin nach Rom*
to Rome via Berlin; ~ *alles* beyond everything, more than anything; *Fehler* ~ *Fehler* mistake
after mistake, error upon error;
einmal — *das andere Mal* time after
time, again and again; *heute* ~ *acht
Tage* this day week; ~*s Jahr*
next year; *die ganze Zeit* ~ all
along; *den Sommer* ~ the whole
summer; ~ *und* ~ over and over;
quite, completely; *etwas* ~ *haben*
to be tired of a thing; *einem* ~
sein to surpass or beat someone.

über|all *adv.* everywhere; all over;
throughout.

über|'altert *a.* too old; dated.

Über|angebot *n.* excessive supply.

über|'anstrengen *v.t.* to overwork,
overstrain.

über|'antworten *v.t.* to deliver up,
surrender.

über|'arbeit-en *v.t.* to revise, go
over, touch up. *v.r.* to overwork
oneself. ~ung *f.* revision, touching up; overwork, overstrain.

über|'aus *adv.* exceedingly, ex-
tremely.

Überbau *m.* superstructure.

überbeanspruchen *v.t.* to over-
stress; to overload.

Überbein *n.* node, exostosis.

überbelichten *v.t.* (*phot.*) to over-
expose.

über'bieten *v.t.* to excel, surpass;
(*commerc.*) to outbid.

überbleib-en *vvs.i.* to remain, be
left over. ~sel *n.* remainder;
residue; relic.

überblenden *v.t.* to fade over.

Über-blick *m.* survey; view; synopsis, summary. ~blicken *v.t.* to
survey, glance over.

Überbrettl *n.* small variety theatre,
cabaret.

über'bring-en *v.t.* to deliver, bring.
~er *m.* bearer.

über'brück-en *v.t.* to bridge, span;
(*fig.*) to bridge over. ~ungs-
kredit *m.* stop-gap loan.

über'bürd-en *v.t.* to overload, overburden. ~ung *f.* overburdening.

Überchlorsäure *f.* perchloric acid.

über'dachen *v.t.* to roof.

über'dauern *v.t.* to outlast.

über'denken *v.t.* to think over, consider.

über'dies *adv.* besides, moreover.

über'drehen *v.t.* to overwind
(watch).

Überdruck *m.* overprint; surcharge
(on stamp); (*tech.*) excess pressure.

Über-druß *m.* (-drusses) boredom;
satiety; ennui; disgust; *zum* ~
druß werden to become boring or
a bore. ~drüssig *a.* tired of, sick
of, bored with, weary of; disgusted with.

Über|eifer *m.* overgreat zeal.

über|'eignen *v.t.* to transfer, assign,
convey.

über|'eil-en *v.t.* to hurry too much;
to precipitate; to scamp (work).
v.r. to be in too great a hurry, be

precipitate, act rashly. ~ung f. hastiness, precipitancy, rashness.

über|ei'nander adv. one upon another; die Beine ~ schlagen to cross one's legs.

über|'ein-kommen vws.i. to agree (about a thing), come to an agreement. subst. n. agreement, settlement, contract. ~kunft f. agreement, arrangement. ~stimmen v.i. to agree, coincide, correspond. ~stimmung f. agreement, harmony, conformity.

über'essen v.r. to overeat.

über-fahren v.t. to pass over, traverse, cross; to run over (person); to overrun (signal); to ferry or convey over. vws.i. to pass over, cross.

Überfahrt f. crossing; passage; ferrying over.

Über-fall m. surprise attack; raid. ~'fallen v.t. to attack suddenly, surprise; to overtake. ~fällig a. overdue. ~fallkommando n. flying squad (of police); (mil.) raiding party.

über'fliegen v.t. to fly over; (fig.) to glance over, skim through.

überfließen vws.i. to overflow; to flow over.

über'flügeln v.t. (mil.) to outflank; (fig.) to surpass, outstrip.

Über-fluß m. abundance, plenty; profusion; exuberance; im ~fluß abundantly; zum ~fluß needlessly, unnecessarily. ~flüssig a. superfluous, unnecessary; left over, surplus.

über'fluten v.t. to inundate, flood, swamp.

über'fordern v.t. to overcharge; to overtax.

Überfracht f. excess freight, overweight.

Überfremdung f. foreign influence; infiltration of foreigners or foreign money.

über'führ-en v.t. to convey, transport from one place to another; to convict (of); to convince (of); (chem.) to transform, convert. ~ung f. conveying; transfer; crossing; viaduct; (leg.) conviction; (chem.) conversion.

Über-fülle f. excess, superabun-

dance, repletion. ~'füllen v.t. to load, overload, cram; to crowd; to overfill; to overstock. ~'füllung f. overloading, cramming; overcrowding; glut.

über'füttern v.t. to overfeed.

Übergabe f. handing over, delivery, surrender.

Übergang m. passage; crossing; going over; transition; change. ~szeit f. transition period.

über'geben v.t. to hand over, deliver up; (mil.) to surrender. v.r. to vomit, be sick.

übergehen[1] vws.i. to cross, pass over; to go over; to change (into), change over (to); to overflow; to turn (sour).

über'geh-en[2] v.t. to pass over, pass by; to omit. ~ung f. passing over; omission, neglect.

übergeordnet a. higher, superior.

Übergewicht n. overweight, excess weight; (fig.) preponderance; das ~ bekommen to lose one's equilibrium; to get top-heavy; (fig.) to get the upper hand (of).

übergießen v.t. to pour over; to spill; mit Licht übergossen bathed in light; von Schweiß übergossen wet with perspiration.

über-greifen v.i. to overlap; to encroach (on), infringe. ~griff m. encroachment, infringement.

Über'hand-nahme f. increase, prevalence. ~nehmen v.i. to increase, spread.

Überhang m. overhanging rock, projecting ledge; curtain, hanging(s). ~en, überhängen v.i. to hang over.

über'häufen v.t. to load (with); to swamp (with); to overwhelm (with).

über'haupt adv. in general; at all; altogether.

über'heb-en v.t. to save, spare; to exempt from; to relieve of. v.r. to strain oneself (by lifting); (fig.) to be overbearing. ~lich a. presumptuous, overbearing. ~ung f. presumption.

über'hitzen v.t. to overheat; to superheat.

überholen[1] v.t. to fetch over, haul over.

über'holen[2] *v.t.* to overtake, outdistance; to outstrip, surpass; to overhaul; *überholt* (*fig.*) antiquated, out of date.

über'hören *v.t.* to miss, not to hear; to ignore; to hear (lesson).

über'irdisch *a.* supernatural.

überkippen *vws.i.* to tilt over; to lose one's equilibrium.

über'kleben *v.t.* to paste over.

Überkleid *n.* overdress; overall.

überkochen *vws.i.* to boil over.

über'kommen *v.t.* to be seized with; to get, receive; *~e Sitten* traditional customs, customs transmitted to.

über'laden *v.t.* to overload; to overdo, adorn profusely.

Über'land-flug *m.* cross-country flight. **~zentrale** *f.* long-distance power station.

über'lass-en *v.t.* to leave; to give up, relinquish, cede, make over; to let have. *v.r.* to give way to, give oneself up to. **~ung** *f.* leaving; cession; abandonment.

über'lasten *v.t.* to overload; (*fig.*) to overburden.

überlaufen[1] *vws.i.* to run or flow over; (*mil.*) to go over, desert.

über'laufen[2] *v.t. & v. impers.* to be seized with, be overcome with; *~ sein von* to be deluged with, besieged by.

Überläufer *m.* deserter.

über'leben *v.t.* to survive, outlive; *sich überlebt haben* to be antiquated or old-fashioned or out-of-date. **~de(r)** *m.* survivor. **~s-groß** *a.* bigger than life-size.

überlegen[1] *v.t.* to lay over, cover; (*colloq.*) to whip (boy).

über'leg-en[2] *v.t.* to reflect upon, consider. **~ung** *f.* reflection, consideration.

über'legen[3] *a.* superior. **~heit** *f.* superiority.

überleiten *v.t. & i.* to lead over or across; to form a transition; to transfuse (blood).

überlesen *v.t.* to read through, run over; to overlook.

über'liefer-n *v.t.* to deliver; to transmit, hand down; to surrender. **~ung** *f.* delivery; tradition; surrender.

über'listen *v.t.* to outwit.

überm = über dem.

über'machen *v.t.* to transmit; to remit; to bequeath.

Über-macht *f.* superior force(s), predominance. **~mächtig** *a.* too powerful, overwhelming; paramount.

über'malen *v.t.* to paint over, paint out.

übermangansauer *a.* permanganate of.

über'mannen *v.t.* to overcome, overpower.

Über-maß *n.* excess; *im ~maß* to excess, excessively. **~mäßig** *a.* excessive; immoderate; exorbitant.

Übermensch *m.* superman. **~lich** *a.* superhuman.

über'mitt-eln *v.t.* to convey; to transmit. **~lung** *f.* transmission.

übermorgen *adv.* the day after tomorrow.

über'müd-en *v.t.* to overtire. **~ung** *f.* over-fatigue.

Über-mut *m.* wantonness; presumption, insolence; high spirits. **~mütig** *a.* wanton, presumptuous, insolent; in high spirits.

über'nachten *v.i.* to pass the night, stay over night.

übernächtig *a.* seedy, blear-eyed.

Übernahme *f.* (-) taking over, taking possession of; taking in hand, undertaking (work).

übernatürlich *a.* supernatural.

über'nehmen *v.t.* to take over, seize, take possession of; to take upon oneself; to undertake (work), accept or assume (responsibility). *v.r.* to overwork; to overeat.

überordnen *v.t.* to place over, set over.

Überproduktion *f.* surplus output.

überquellen *vws.i.* to flow over.

über'quer *adv.* across, crossways. **~en** *v.t.* to cross.

über'ragen *v.t.* to overtop, rise above; (*fig.*) to surpass.

über'rasch-en *v.t.* to surprise. **~ung** *f.* surprise.

über'red-en *v.t.* to persuade. **~ung** *f.* persuasion.

überreich *a.* abounding (in), overflowing (with). ~**lich** *a.* superabundant.

über'reich-en *v.t.* to hand over, present. ~**ung** *f.* presentation.

überreif *a.* overripe.

über'reiten *v.t.* to overtake in riding; to outride; to ride over, run down.

über'reizen *v.t.* to over-excite; to overstrain.

Überrest *m.* remainder, remnant; remains; relics.

Überrock *m.* overcoat, top-coat.

über'rumpel-n *v.t.* to surprise, take by surprise. ~**ung** *f.* surprise, sudden attack.

übers = über das.

übersät *a.* dotted or strewn (with); studded (with stars).

über'sättigen *v.t.* to surfeit; (*chem.*) to supersaturate.

Überschall *m.* supersonics. ~**geschwindigkeit** *f.* supersonic speed.

über'schatten *v.t.* to overshadow.

über'schätzen *v.t.* to overrate, overestimate.

über'schauen *v.t.* to overlook; to survey.

überschäumen *vws. & h.,* i. to foam over, froth over; (*fig.*) to exuberate, abound.

Überschicht *f.* extra shift.

über'schießen *v.i.* to fire beyond the target; (*fig.*) to overshoot (mark). *v.r.* to turn head over heels; ~*de Summe* surplus.

Überschlag *m.* estimate, rough calculation; (*gym.*) somersault. ~**laken** *n.* top sheet.

über'schlagen *v.t.* to cross (legs); (*fig.*) to estimate; to skip (pages). *v.r.* to go head over heels, turn a somersault; (*av.*) to turn over, loop the loop; (*of voice*) to break.

überschnappen *vws.i.* mit der Stimme ~ to squeak; (*fig.*) to turn crazy.

über'schneiden *v.t. & r.* to intersect; to overlap.

über'schreiben *v.i.* to transfer; to superscribe; to head, entitle.

über'schreien *v.t.* to cry down. *v.r.* to overstrain one's voice.

über'schreit-en *v.t.* to cross; to exceed, overstep; to transgress; to

infringe (law); to overdraw (one's account). ~**ung** *f.* crossing; excess; transgression.

Über-schrift *f.* superscription, heading, title. ~**schuh** *m.* overshoe, galosh. ~**schuß** *m.* surplus, excess, balance. ~**schüssig** *a.* surplus; excess.

über'schütten *v.t.* to cover (with); to overwhelm, load (with).

Überschwang *m.* exuberance, rapture.

über'schwemm-en *v.t.* to inundate, flood. ~**ung** *f.* inundation, flood.

überschwenglich *a.* exuberant, rapturous.

Übersee *f.* overseas. ~**isch** *a.* transoceanic, oversea.

über'sehen *v.t.* to survey; to overlook, not to notice.

über'send-en *v.t.* to send, transmit. ~**er** *m.* sender. ~**ung** *f.* transmission.

übersetzen[1] *v.t.* to ferry across. *vws.i.* to pass over, cross.

über'setz-en[2] *v.t.* to translate. ~**er** *m.* translator. ~**ung** *f.* translation; gear (of bicycle).

Übersicht *f.* view; review; survey; summary, synopsis; control. ~**lich** *a.* clear, easily visible. ~**lichkeit** *f.* clearness; lucidity. ~**s-karte** *f.* large map; general plan.

übersied-eln *vws.i.* to remove (to); to emigrate. ~**lung** *f.* removal; emigration.

übersinnlich *a.* transcendental.

über'spann-en *v.t.* to stretch over, span; to cover (with); to overstrain; (*fig.*) to exaggerate. ~**t** *a.* eccentric. ~**theit** *f.* eccentricity.

überspitzt *a.* (*fig.*) too subtle.

überspringen *v.t.* to jump across, leap over; to omit, skip. *v.i.* (*of sparks*) to flash across.

übersprudeln *v.i.* to bubble over.

über'stechen *v.t.* to overtrump (at cards).

überstehen[1] *vws.i.* to stand out, project.

über'stehen[2] *v.t.* to endure, go through; to survive, get over.

über'steigen *v.t.* to cross; (*fig.*) to pass, exceed.

über'steigern *v.t.* to overbid, outbid.

über'stimmen *v.t.* to outvote.

über'strahlen v.t. to shine upon; to outshine.

überströmen vws.i. to overflow, abound.

überstülpen v.t. to put on, cover with.

Überstunden f.pl. overtime.

über'stürzen v.t. to hurry, do in a hurry, precipitate. v.r. to act rashly or hastily or precipitately; to press upon each other.

über'täuben v.t. to deafen; to stifle; to drown.

über'teuern v.t. to overcharge.

über'tölpeln v.t. to dupe, take in.

über'tönen v.t. to drown (sound).

Über-trag m. carrying over; sum brought forward. ~'tragbar a. transferable; (med.) catching. ~-'tragen v.t. to transfer, give up to; to entrust with (work); (commerc.) to carry over, enter; to translate; to transcribe; (radio) to transmit, relay; (med.) to spread, infect with, communicate (disease); ~tragene Bedeutung figurative sense. ~'tragung f. transfer; carrying over; conferring; translation; transcription; transmission, relaying; spreading, infection; transference.

über'treffen v.t. to excel, surpass.

über'treib-en v.t. to exaggerate; to overdo. ~ung f. exaggeration; excess.

übertreten¹ vws.i. to go over, change over (to); to change (one's religion); to turn (Roman Catholic, &c.).

über'tret-en² v.t. to violate, transgress, trespass. ~ung f. violation, transgression, trespass.

über'trieben a. excessive, exaggerated, extravagant, extreme.

Übertritt m. going over (to); change (of religion).

über'trumpfen v.t. to overtrump; (fig.) to outdo.

über'tünchen v.t. to whitewash.

über'völkert a. over-populated.

über'vorteilen v.t. to take advantage of, take in; to defraud.

über'wach-en v.t. to watch over, supervise, superintend. ~ung f. observation; supervision. ~-ungsstelle f. control office.

über'wältig-en v.t. to overwhelm; to overpower, conquer. ~end a. overwhelming. ~ung f. overwhelming, conquering, subjugation.

über'weis-en v.t. to transfer, remit. ~ung f. transfer, remittance.

über'wendlich a. whipped.

überwerfen¹ v.t. to throw over.

über'werfen² v.r. to fall out (with).

über'wiegen v.i. to outweigh; to preponderate, predominate. ~d a. preponderant, predominant. adv. chiefly, mainly.

über'wind-en v.t. to overcome, vanquish, conquer. v.r. to bring oneself to. ~er m. conqueror. ~lich a. conquerable; surmountable. ~ung f. overcoming, conquest, triumph (over); self-control.

über'wintern v.i. to winter (at); to hibernate.

über'wölben v.t. to arch or vault over.

über'wuchern v.t. to overgrow, overrun.

Überwurf m. wrap, cloak, shawl.

Überzahl f. numerical superiority; superior forces; majority.

über'zählen v.t. to count over.

überzählig a. surplus, supernumerary.

über'zeichnen v.t. to oversubscribe.

über'zeug-en v.t. to convince. ~ung f. conviction, belief; der ~ung sein to be convinced.

überzieh-en¹ v.t. to put on; to pull over. ~er m. overcoat, greatcoat.

über'zieh-en² v.t. to cover (cushion); Bett ~ to put fresh sheets on; to overdraw (account); to invade, overrun. v.r. to become overcast.

über'zuckern v.t. to sugar (over), to ice; to gild (pill).

Überzug m. cover, slip, case; covering, coating, coat; plating, crust.

über'zwerch adv. across, athwart.

üblich see **üben**.

U-Boot see **Unterseeboot**.

übrig (y:-) a. (left) over, remaining, other; nichts ~ haben für (fig.) to care little for, think little of; ein ~es tun to do more than is necessary, go out of one's way to

show a kindness; *zu wünschen* ~
lassen to leave much to be desired; *im* ~*en* for the rest, in
other respects; *im* ~ *lassen* to leave.
~ens *adv.* by the way; after all.
Übung see üben.
Ufer (u:-) *n.* (-s, -) shore, beach;
bank (of river). ~damm *m.* embankment, quay. ~los *a.* (*fig.*)
extravagant; leading nowhere.
Uhr *f.* (-, -en) clock; timepiece;
watch; time of day; hour; *wieviel*
~ *ist es?* what time is it? *um*
wieviel ~? when? at what time?
um halb zwei = at half past one.
~feder *f.* watch-spring. ~ge-
hänge *n.* trinkets. ~gehäuse *n.*
case. ~kette *f.* chain. ~macher
m. watchmaker. ~werk *n.*
works. ~zeiger *m.* hand.
Uhu *m.* (-s, -s) eagle-owl.
U'lan *m.* (-en, -en) uhlan, lancer.
Ulk *m.* (-es, -e) fun, lark, joke. ~en
v.i. to lark, joke. ~ig *a.* funny,
amusing.
Ulme *f.* (-, -n) elm.
Ultimo *m.* last day of the month.
~abrechnung *f.* monthly settlement.
Ultraschall *m.* ultrasonics.
um 1. *prep.* round, about; at,
about, toward(s); because of, for;
in exchange for; by (so much);
~ *sechs Uhr* at six o'clock; *die*
Hälfte mehr half as much again;
~ *ein Jahr älter* a year older; *so*
besser all the better, so much the
better; *so weniger* all the fewer,
all the less; *Tag* = *Tag* every day;
einen Tag ~ *den andern* every
other day. 2. *conj.* = *zu* in order
to. 3. *adv. & pref.* ~ *und* ~
round about; from or on all sides;
~ *sein* to be over, expire, be gone.
um|ackern *v.t.* to plough up.
um|adressieren *v.t.* to redirect
(letter).
um|änder-n *v.t.* to change, alter.
~ung *f.* change, alteration.
um|arbeit-en *v.t.* to recast; to re-
model. ~ung *f.* recasting; re-
modelling.
um'arm-en *v.t.* to embrace, hug.
~ung *f.* embrace, hug.
Umbau *m.* rebuilding; reconstruction, alterations. ~en *v.t.* to

rebuild; to reconstruct, make
alterations (in).
umbehalten *v.t.* to keep on.
Umbesetzung *f.* reshuffle, change.
umbetten *v.t.* to put into another
bed.
umbiegen *v.t.* to bend; to turn
down or back.
umbilden *v.t.* to remould; to transform; to reform; to reconstruct;
to reshuffle (Cabinet).
umbinden *v.t.* to tie round, put
on.
umblasen *v.t.* to blow down or over.
umblättern *v.t.* to turn over (a leaf).
umblicken *v.i. & r.* to look about
one; to look round.
um'brechen¹ *v.t.* to break down; to
break up (field).
um'brechen² *v.t.* (*typ.*) to make up.
umbringen *v.t.* to kill, murder.
Umbruch *m.* radical change, revolution; (*typ.*) making up into
pages; page-proof.
umdreh-en *v.t.* to turn, turn round;
to wring (a fowl's neck); to twist.
~*v.r.* to turn round, rotate, revolve. ~ung *f.* turning round,
rotation; revolution (of engine).
Umdruck *m.* reprint, transfer.
um'düster-n *a.* dark, gloomy.
umfahren¹ *v.t.* to run down or over.
um'fahren² *v.t.* to drive or sail
round.
Umfahrt *f.* circular tour (of).
umfallen *vus.i.* to fall down; to be
upset or overturned.
Umfang *m.* circumference; periphery, perimeter; extent; size;
radius, range, compass; volume,
bulk. ~reich *a.* comprehensive;
extensive; voluminous.
um'fang-en *v.t.* to surround, enclose; to embrace.
um'fass-en *v.t.* to clasp; to embrace; to enclose, surround; to
comprise, comprehend, include;
(*mil.*) to outflank, envelop. ~end
a. comprehensive; extensive. ~
ung *f.* enclosure; fence. ~ungs-
bewegung *f.* outflanking movement.
um'flort *a.* muffled (voice); dim
(with tears).
umform-en *v.t.* to transform; to reform; to remodel, recast; (*electr.*)

to transform, convert. **~er** *m.* transformer, converter.

Umfrage *f.* inquiry; poll.

um'fried-en *v.t.* to enclose, fence in. **~ung** *f.* enclosure, fence.

umfüllen *v.t.* to transfuse, decant.

Umgang *m.* circular passage; (ambulatory) procession; intercourse, relations (with), association. **~s-formen** *f.pl.* manners. **~ssprache** *f.* colloquial speech; *niedere* **~s-sprache** slang.

umgänglich *a.* sociable, companionable.

um'garnen *v.t.* to ensnare, enmesh, trap.

um'gaukeln *v.t.* to flit *or* hover around.

um'geb-en *v.t.* to surround. **~ung** *f.* surroundings, environs; society, company, associates; environment; background.

Umgegend *f.* neighbourhood, vicinity, environs.

umgehen[1] *vws.i.* to go a roundabout way; to circulate; (*of ghost*) to haunt (a place); **~ mit** to deal with, treat; to associate with; *mit etwas* **~** to be occupied with; to contemplate, plan to; **~d ant-worten** to answer by return.

um'geh-en[2] *v.t.* to go round; to outflank; (*fig.*) to evade, elude. **~ungsbewegung** *f.* flanking movement. **~ungsweg** *m.* by-pass.

umgekehrt *a.* opposite, reverse, contrary. *adv.* on the contrary; vice versa.

umgestalten *v.t.* to alter, transform; to reform; to reorganize.

umgießen *v.t.* to decant; to recast.

umgraben *v.t.* to dig, dig up; to break up (soil).

um'grenzen *v.t.* to encircle, enclose, bound; to limit, circumscribe.

umgruppieren *v.t.* to regroup, redistribute.

um'gürten *v.t.* to gird (up).

umhaben *v.t.* to have round one, have on.

um'halsen *v.t.* to embrace, hug.

Umhang *m.* cape, wrap; shawl.

umhängen *v.t.* to put on. **~tasche** *f.* shoulder bag.

umhauen *v.t.* to fell, cut down.

um'her *adv.* around, about, here

and there. **~blicken** *v.i.* to glance round, look about one. **~gehen** *vws.i.* to walk about. See also Compp. of *herum.*

um'hin *adv. ich kann nicht* **~** I cannot help.

um'hüll-en *v.t.* to wrap, cover, case, veil. **~ung** *f.* wrapping, covering, casing, veil.

Umkehr *f.* return, turning back; change, revulsion (of feeling). **~en** *vws.i.* to turn back, return. *v.t.* to turn round; to turn inside out; to turn upside down; (*mus., &c.*) to invert; (*electr.*) to reverse. **~ung** *f.* inversion; reversal.

umkippen *v.t.* to overturn, upset. *vws.i.* to tilt over; to lose one's equilibrium.

um'klammer-n *v.t.* to clasp, embrace; (*mil.*) to encircle. **~ung** *f.* encirclement; (*boxing*) clinch.

umklappen *v.t.* to turn down (collar).

umkleide-n *v.t. & r.* to change (dress). **~raum** *m.* dressing-room.

umkommen *vws.i.* to die, perish; (*of food*) to go bad, spoil; to be wasted.

Umkreis *m.* circle, circumference; circuit; radius; vicinity.

um'kreis-en *v.t.* to revolve or circle round; to encircle. **~ung** *f.* encirclement.

umkrempeln *v.t.* to tuck up, turn up.

umladen *v.t.* to tranship; to reload.

Umlage *f.* assessment, rates.

um'lagern *v.t.* to surround; to besiege.

Umland *n.* outskirts.

Umlauf *m.* rotation; revolving; revolution, turn; circulation; circular; *in* **~** *setzen* to circulate; to spread (rumour).

umlaufen *vws.i.* to circulate; to take a roundabout way.

Umlaut *m.* modification (of vowel).

umleg-en *v.t.* to put on; to put round; to lay down; to change the position (of); to shift; to apportion; (*sl.*) to kill. **~(e)kragen** *m.* turn-down collar.

umleit-en *v.t.* to divert (traffic). **~ung** *f.* diversion (of traffic).

umlenken *v.t.* to turn round or back.

umlernen *v.i.* to readjust one's views.

umliegend *a.* surrounding, neighbouring.

um'mauern *v.t.* to wall in.

ummodeln *v.t.* to remodel, alter.

um'nachtet *a.* wrapped in darkness; (*fig.*) deranged.

um'nebeln *v.t.* to cloud.

umpflanzen[1] *v.t.* to transplant.

um'pflanzen[2] *v.t.* to plant round.

umpflügen *v.t.* to plough up.

umquartieren *v.t.* to remove to other quarters.

um'rahmen *v.t.* to frame, surround.

um'randen, **um'rändern** *v.t.* to surround, border, edge.

um'ranken *v.t.* to twine round.

umrechn-en[1] *v.t.* to change, convert. **~ungskurs** *m.* rate of exchange. **~ungszahl** *f.* conversion factor.

umreißen[1] *v.t.* to pull down.

um'reißen[2] *v.t.* to outline.

um'ringen *v.t.* to surround.

Umriß *m.* sketch; outline, contour.

umrühren *v.t.* to stir.

ums = **um das**.

umsatteln *v.t.* to resaddle (horse). *v.i.* (*fig.*) to change one's studies or profession.

Umsatz *m.* sale, turnover; returns. **~steuer** *f.* purchase tax.

umsäumen[1] *v.t.* to hem.

um'säumen[2] *v.t.* to enclose, surround.

umschalt-en *v.t.* to switch over; to reverse. **~er** *m.* switch, commutator; (*typewriter*) shift-key. **~hebel** *m.* change-lever. **~stöpsel** *m.* switch-plug.

Umschau *f.* looking round; **~ halten** to look round. **~en** *v.i. & r.* to look round.

umschichtig *adv.* in layers; (*fig.*) alternately, in turns.

um'schiffen *v.t.* to circumnavigate; to sail round; to double (a cape).

Umschlag *m.* cover, wrapper; envelope; hem; cuff; poultice, compress; (*commerc.*) transfer or reshipment of load; (*fig.*) change, turn. **~en** *v.t.* to fell, knock down; to put on (shawl); to turn up (hem); to turn down (collar); to turn over (page). *vvs.i.* to fall

over, tilt over; (*of boat*) to capsize; (*of wind*) to change; (*of voice*) to break. **~papier** *n.* wrapping paper. **~shafen** *m.* port of reshipment. **~tuch** *n.* shawl, wrap.

um'schließen *v.t.* to enclose, surround; to clasp.

um'schlingen *v.t.* to embrace, clasp round.

umschmelz-en *v.t.* to remelt, recast, refound. **~ung** *f.* (*fig.*) reorganization; *sich in einem ~ungsprozeß befinden* to be in the melting-pot.

umschnallen *v.t.* to buckle on.

umschreiben[1] *v.t.* to rewrite; to transfer, make over; to reindorse (bill).

um'schreib-en[2] *v.t.* to circumscribe; (*fig.*) to paraphrase. **~ung** *f.* (*fig.*) paraphrase.

Umschrift *f.* inscription, legend; transcription.

umschulen *v.t.* to remove from one school to another; to train on different lines.

umschütten *v.t.* to upset, spill; to pour into another vessel.

um'schwärmen *v.t.* to swarm round; to beset; (*fig.*) to adore.

Umschweif *m.* digression; circumlocution; *ohne ~e* bluntly, plainly, point-blank.

umschwenken *v.i.* to wheel round; (*fig.*) to change one's mind.

Umschwung *m.* change, revulsion (of feeling); revolution.

umsehen *v.r.* to look back or round; to look about; to take a look round; to look out (for); *im ~* in a twinkling.

umseitig *a.* on the other page, overleaf.

umsetzen *v.t.* to transplant; (*mus.*) to transpose; (*commerc.*) to sell, dispose of, realize; to transform, convert.

Umsicht *f.* circumspection, caution, prudence. **~ig** *a.* circumspect, cautious, prudent.

umsiedeln *vvs.i.* to change one's quarters, settle somewhere else.

umsinken *vvs.i.* to drop, sink down.

um'sonst *adv.* gratis, for nothing;

in vain, to no purpose; without a reason.

umspannen[1] v.t. to change horses; to reharness; (electr.) to transform.

um'spannen[2] v.t. to enclose; to encompass; to comprise.

umspringen[1] vws.i. to veer (round), change; ~ mit to treat, manage (person).

um'springen[2] v.t. to jump round (a person, &c.).

um'spülen v.t. to wash; (poet.) to lave.

Umstand m. circumstance; fact; (pl.) particulars; ceremonies, formalities; difficulty; fuss, trouble. ado; ohne Umstände without ceremony; unter Umständen in certain circumstances, circumstances permitting; unter allen Umständen in any case, at all events; unter keinen Umständen on no account; mildernde Umstände (leg.) extenuating circumstances; in andern Umständen sein to be pregnant. ~skleid n. maternity dress. ~skrämer m. fussy person. ~swort n. adverb.

umstand-ehalber adv. owing to circumstances. ~lich a. laborious; involved, intricate; circumstantial; formal; fussy. ~lichkeit f. formality; fussiness.

um'stehen v.t. to stand round or about, surround. ~d a. next, following (page); die ~den the bystanders.

Umsteige-billet n., ~fahrkarte f. transfer-ticket.

umsteigen vws.i. to change (trains, &c.).

umstell-en[1] v.t. to put into a different place, rearrange; to change position; to transpose; to invert; to convert (to). v.r. to assume a different attitude (to); to adapt oneself (to new conditions). ~ung f. change; inversion; conversion.

um'stellen[2] v.t. to surround, encircle.

umstimmen v.t. (mus.) to tune to another pitch; (fig.) to make (person) change his mind, talk (person) over.

umstoßen v.t. to upset, overturn,

knock down; (fig.) to annul, invalidate.

um'stricken v.t. to ensnare, entangle.

um'stritten a. disputed, controversial.

umstülpen v.t. to turn upside down, tilt over.

Umsturz m. downfall, overthrow; revolution.

umstürz-en v.t. to throw down, overturn. vws.i. to fall down. ~ler m. revolutionary. ~lerisch a. revolutionary.

umtaufen v.t. to rename.

Umtausch m. exchange. ~en v.t. to change (for).

umtopfen v.t. to repot (plants).

Umtriebe m.pl. machinations, intrigues.

umtun v.t. to put on. v.r. to put oneself about (for), look (for).

umwälz-en v.t. to roll round; (fig.) to revolutionize. ~ung f. revolution.

umwand-eln v.t. to change, transform; to convert (stocks, &c.). ~lung f. change, transformation; conversion.

umwechseln v.t. to exchange (for); to change (money).

Umweg m. roundabout way, detour.

umwehen v.t. to blow down.

Umwelt f. surrounding world; environment.

umwenden v.t. to turn; to turn over. v.r. to turn round or back.

um'werben v.t. to court; umworben sein (fig.) to be sought after.

umwerfen v.t. to upset, overturn; to overthrow; to throw round or over, put on (coat).

umwert-en v.t. to revalue. ~ung f. revaluation.

um'wickeln v.t. to wrap up (in).

um'winden v.t. to wind round.

um'wittern v.t. (fig.) to envelop, surround.

Umwohner m.pl. neighbours, inhabitants of the vicinity.

um'wölken v.t. to overcast; (fig.) to darken.

um'zäunen v.t. to enclose, fence round.

umziehen[1] v.t. to change (person's

clothes). *v.r.* to change (one's clothes). *vws.i.* to remove, move (to).

um'ziehen[2] *v.t.* to walk round; to surround; *umzogen* overcast.

um'zingeln *v.t.* to surround, encircle.

Umzug *m.* procession; (*pol.*) demonstration; removal.

um'züngeln *v.t.* (*of flames*) to envelop, play around.

un-ab'änderlich *a.* unalterable, irrevocable. ~ab'dingbar *a.* unalterable, final. ~abhängig *a.* independent; ~*abhängig von* irrespective of. ~abhängigkeit *f.* independence. ~abkömmlich *a.* indispensable, reserved. ~abläs-sig *a.* incessant, unremitting. ~ab'sehbar *a.* immeasurable; incalculable, unbounded, immense. ~absichtlich *a.* unintentional, involuntary. ~ab'weisbar, ~ab'-weislich *aa.* unavoidable; pressing, imperative. ~ab'wendbar *a.* inevitable.

un'achtsam *a.* inattentive, careless. ~keit *f.* inattention, carelessness.

un'ähnlich *a.* unlike, dissimilar; ~keit *f.* dissimilarity.

un-an'fechtbar *a.* indisputable, incontestable. ~angebracht *a.* out of place, unsuitable. ~angefoch-ten *a.* undisputed; unhindered, unhampered. ~angemessen *a.* inadequate, unsuitable, improper. ~angenehm *a.* unpleasant, disagreeable. ~angreifbar *a.* unassailable. ~an'nehmbar *a.* unacceptable. ~annehmlichkeit *f.* annoyance, inconvenience; trouble. un-ansehnlich *a.* poor-looking, mean; plain; insignificant. ~ansehnlichkeit *f.* meanness (of appearance); plainness. ~an-ständig *a.* improper; indecent. ~an'ständigkeit *f.* impropriety, indecency. ~anstößig *a.* inoffensive, harmless. ~an'tastbar *a.* inviolable, unimpeachable, unassailable.

un'appetitlich *a.* not appetizing; uninviting, repellent.

Un'art *f.* bad behaviour; ill breeding, rudeness. *m.* naughty child; rude person. ~ig *a.* badly be-

haved, naughty; rude.

un'artikuliert *a.* inarticulate.

un'ästhetisch *a.* not aesthetic; repellent.

un-auf'dringlich, ~auffällig *a.* unobtrusive, inconspicuous.

un-auf'findbar *a.* not to be found; undiscoverable. ~aufgefordert *a.* unasked, unbidden. ~aufhaltsam *a.* irresistible; impetuous; incessant; without stopping. ~auf'hörlich *a.* incessant. ~auf'lösbar, ~auf'löslich *aa.* insoluble; inexplicable. ~aufmerksam *a.* inattentive. ~aufmerksamkeit *f.* inattention. ~aufrichtig *a.* insincere. ~aufrichtigkeit *f.* insincerity. ~auf'schiebbar *a.* pressing, urgent.

un-aus'bleiblich *a.* unfailing, certain; inevitable. ~aus'führbar *a.* impracticable, not feasible. ~ausgesetzt *a.* constant, uninterrupted. ~aus'löschlich *a.* inextinguishable; indelible. ~aus'sprechlich *a.* inexpressible, unspeakable, ineffable. ~aus'steh-lich *a.* insufferable, intolerable. ~aus'weichlich *a.* inevitable, unavoidable.

Un-band *m.* unruly child *or* person. ~bändig *a.* unruly, intractable; excessive, tremendous.

unbarmherzig *a.* unmerciful, pitiless. ~keit *f.* unmercifulness, mercilessness.

un-beabsichtigt *a.* unintentional, undesigned. ~beachtet *a.* unnoticed; disregarded. ~bean-standet *a.* not objected to; unopposed, unhampered; unimpeached. ~beantwortet *a.* unanswered. ~bearbeitet *a.* raw (material); not yet dealt with; not treated before. ~bebaut *a.* uncultivated.

un-bedacht(sam) *a.* inconsiderate, thoughtless; indiscreet; rash. ~bedenklich *a.* unhesitating; harmless. *adv.* without hesitation, without scruples. ~bedeutend *a.* insignificant, trifling.

unbedingt *a.* unconditional, unquestioning; absolute; implicit; *du mußt ~ dabei sein* you must be there whatever happens.

un-beeinflußt *a.* unbiased, unprejudiced. ~befähigt *a.* incompetent. ~befahrbar *a.* impassable; impracticable. ~befangen *a.* impartial, unprejudiced; unembarrassed; natural. ~befangenheit *f.* impartiality; unaffectedness. ~befleckt *a.* unsullied, unspotted; *(fig.)* immaculate. ~befriedigend *a.* unsatisfactory. ~befriedigt *a.* unsatisfied, dissatisfied; disappointed. ~befugt *a.* unauthorized.

un-begabt *a.* not gifted, not clever. ~begreiflich *a.* incomprehensible, inconceivable. ~begreiflichkeit *f.* incomprehensibility, incomprehensible thing. ~begrenzt *a.* unbounded, unlimited. ~begründet *a.* unfounded, groundless.

Un-behagen *n.* discomfort; uneasiness. ~behaglich *a.* uncomfortable; uneasy. ~behauen *a.* unhewn. ~behelligt *a.* unmolested, undisturbed. ~beherrscht *a.* lacking self-control. ~behilflich *a.* helpless. ~behindert *a.* unimpeded; unrestrained. ~beholfen *a.* clumsy, awkward. ~beholfenheit *f.* clumsiness; awkwardness.

un-be|irrbar *a.* imperturbable, not to be put out. ~be|irrt *a.* imperturbable, unflinching. ~bekannt *a.* unknown; unacquainted (with), ignorant (of), a stranger (to). ~bekehrbar *a.* inconvertible. ~bekümmert *a.* unconcerned, carefree; careless. ~bekümmertheit *f.* carelessness.

un-belästigt *a.* unmolested. ~belebt *a.* lifeless, inanimate; dull; empty. ~belehrbar *a.* unteachable. ~beliebt *a.* disliked; unpopular. ~beliebtheit *f.* unpopularity.

un-bemannt *a.* unmanned. ~be-'merkbar *a.* imperceptible. ~bemerkt *a.* unnoticed, unperceived. ~bemittelt *a.* poor, without means. ~benommen *pred. a.* permitted; free (to do).

un-bequem *a.* uncomfortable; inconvenient; disagreeable; awkward. ~bequemlichkeit *f.* discomfort; inconvenience. ~be'rechenbar *a.* incalculable. ~berechtigt *a.* unauthorized, not entitled (to); unlawful; unjustified. ~berufen *a.* uncalled for; unauthorized; ~berufen! touch wood! ~berührt *a.* untouched; intact; innocent, chaste.

un-beschadet *prep.* without prejudice to, without detriment to. ~beschädigt *a.* undamaged, intact; uninjured, safe and sound. ~bescheiden *a.* immodest; arrogant, presumptuous; exorbitant. ~bescheidenheit *f.* lack of modesty; arrogance. ~bescholten *a.* blameless, irreproachable. ~bescholtenheit *f.* blameless reputation; integrity. ~beschränkt *a.* unlimited, boundless; absolute. ~be'schreiblich *a.* indescribable. ~beschrieben *a.* blank, not written upon. ~beschwert *a.* unburdened, light.

un-beseelt *a.* inanimate. ~besehen *adv.* without inspection, without hesitation. ~be'siegbar, ~be'sieglich *aa.* invincible, unconquerable. ~besonnen *a.* thoughtless; ill-advised; rash. ~besonnenheit *f.* thoughtlessness; imprudence; indiscretion; rashness. ~besorgt *a.* unconcerned; carefree, easy; *sei ~besorgt* don't worry, don't trouble yourself (about).

Un-bestand *m.* instability, inconstancy; changeableness. ~beständig *a.* unstable, unsteady, inconstant; unsettled (weather). ~beständigkeit *f.* instability, inconstancy; fickleness. ~bestechlich *a.* incorruptible. ~bestechlichkeit *f.* incorruptibility; integrity. ~be'stellbar *a.* not deliverable; dead (letter). ~be-'stimmbar *a.* undefinable, nondescript. ~bestimmt *a.* undetermined, undefined, indeterminate; uncertain; undecided; vague, indistinct; *(gram.)* indefinite. ~bestimmtheit *f.* indeterminateness; indefiniteness; uncertainty; vagueness. ~be'streitbar *a.* incontestable, indisputable. *adv.*

surely. ~be'stritten a. uncontested, undisputed.

un-beteiligt a. not concerned, not participating; indifferent. ~betont a. unstressed, unaccented. ~beträchtlich a. inconsiderable, trifling. ~beugsam a. unbending, inflexible; stubborn. ~beugsamkeit f. inflexibility; stubbornness.

un-bewacht a. unguarded, unwatched. ~bewaffnet a. unarmed; naked (eye). ~bewandert a. unversed (in), inexperienced. ~beweglich a. immovable, motionless; real (property). ~bewehrt a. unarmed, defenceless. ~beweibt a. unmarried, bachelor. ~be'wohnbar a. uninhabitable. ~bewohnt a. uninhabited. ~bewußt a. unconscious; involuntary.

un-be'zahlbar a. priceless. ~bezahlt a. be'zähmbar a. untamable; indomitable. ~be'zwingbar, ~be'zwinglich aa. invincible; indomitable.

un-biegsam a. inflexible, unbending. ~bildung f. lack of education, illiteracy.

Unbill f. (-, Unbilden) wrong, injustice; inclemency (of weather). ~ig a. unfair, unjust. ~igkeit f. unfairness, injustice.

un-blutig a. bloodless; (R.C. theol.) unbloody. ~botmäßig a. unruly, refractory. ~botmäßigkeit f. insubordination. ~brauchbar a. useless, of no use, unserviceable. ~brauchbarkeit f. uselessness. ~bußfertig a. impenitent, unrepentant.

unchristlich a. unchristian.

und conj. and; und? and then? and afterwards? well?

Undank m. ingratitude. ~bar a. ungrateful; thankless. ~barkeit f. ingratitude.

un-datiert a. undated, bearing no date. ~dekli'nierbar a. indeclinable. ~denkbar a. unthinkable, inconceivable. ~denklich a. immemorial. ~deutlich a. indistinct; vague; obscure; unintelligible; inarticulate. ~dicht a. not tight; leaky. ~ding n. absurdity; impossibility. ~duldsam a.

intolerant. ~duldsamkeit f. intolerance. ~durchdringlich a. impenetrable; impermeable, impervious. ~durchführbar a. impracticable. ~durchlässig a. impermeable, waterproof, lightproof. ~durchsichtig a. not transparent, opaque.

un|eben a. uneven, rough, rugged; nicht ~ not bad. ~bürtig a. of inferior rank, inferior. ~heit f. unevenness; roughness, ruggedness.

un|echt a. not genuine, sham, false, spurious; adulterated; imitation, artificial; not fast (colour); (math.) improper.

un-ehelich a. illegitimate. ~ehrbar a. immodest, immodest. ~ehre f. dishonour, disgrace, discredit. ~ehrenhaft a. dishonourable. ~ehrerbietig a. disrespectful, irreverent. ~ehrlich a. dishonest; insincere, underhand, false. ~ehrlichkeit f. dishonesty; insincerity.

un-eigennützig a. disinterested, unselfish. ~eigentlich a. not literal, figurative. ~einbringlich a. irrecoverable, irretrievable. ~einig a. disunited; at variance (with). ~einigkeit f. discord, disagreement; disunion; dissension. ~ein'nehmbar a. impregnable. ~eins adv. ~eins sein to disagree, be at variance (with).

un|empfänglich a. insusceptible, unreceptive.

un|empfindlich a. insensible; insensitive (to); indifferent (to). ~keit f. insensibility; unfeelingness, indifference.

un|endlich a. infinite; endless; vast; ~ klein infinitesimal. ~keit f. infinity; infinite space.

un-entbehrlich a. indispensable. ~ent'geltlich a. free, gratis, gratuitous. ~enthaltsam a. intemperate; incontinent. ~entrinnbar a. inescapable.

un|entschieden a. undecided; drawn (game); (fig.) irresolute. un|entschlossen a. irresolute, undecided. ~heit f. irresolution, indecision.

un|entschuldbar a. inexcusable.

un-entwegt *a.* unflinching; steadfast. **~ent′wirrbar** *a.* inextricable. **~ent′zifferbar** *a.* indecipherable.

un-erachtet *prep.* notwithstanding, in spite of. **~er′bittlich** *a.* inexorable. **~erfahren** *a.* inexperienced. **~er′findlich** *a.* undiscoverable; incomprehensible. **~er′forschlich** *a.* impenetrable, inscrutable. **~erfreulich** *a.* unpleasant, unsatisfactory. **~er′füllbar** *a.* unrealizable; impossible to fulfil.

un-ergiebig *a.* unproductive, sterile. **~ergründlich** *a.* unfathomable, abysmal; impenetrable. **~erheblich** *a.* insignificant, irrelevant, inconsiderable, trifling. **~erhört** *a.* unheard; unheard of, unprecedented; scandalous, shocking; exorbitant. **~er′klärlich** *a.* inexplicable; unaccountable. **~er′läßlich** *a.* indispensable. **~erlaubt** *a.* illicit, unlawful. **~erledigt** *a.* not finished, not settled.

un-er′meßlich *a.* immense, immeasurable; boundless, infinite; vast, huge, untold. **~er′müdlich** *a.* untiring, indefatigable, unflagging. **~erquicklich** *a.* unpleasant, uncomfortable, unedifying. **~e′rreichbar** *a.* unattainable; inaccessible; out of reach. **~erreicht** *a.* unrivalled, unequalled; record (performance).

un-er′sättlich *a.* insatiable. **~erschlossen** *a.* not opened up, undeveloped. **~er′schöpflich** *a.* inexhaustible. **~erschrocken** *a.* intrepid, fearless. **~erschrockenheit** *f.* intrepidity. **~er′schütterlich** *a.* unshakeable, imperturbable, firm. **~er′schwinglich** *a.* unattainable, beyond one's means; exorbitant. **~er′setzlich** *a.* irreplaceable; irretrievable, irreparable. **~er′sprießlich** *a.* unprofitable; unpleasant.

un-er′träglich *a.* intolerable. **~erwartet** *a.* unexpected. **~er′weislich** *a.* indemonstrable. **~erwidert** *a.* unanswered; unrequited, unreturned. **~erwiesen** *a.* not proved. **~erwünscht** *a.* undesired, unwished for, unwelcome.

~erzogen *a.* uneducated; illbred.

unfähig *a.* incapable (of); unable (to); unfit, incompetent. **~keit** *f.* incapacity, inability; inefficiency.

Unfall *m.* accident. **~station** *f.* ambulance station, first-aid post. **~versicherung** *f.* insurance against accidents.

un′faß-bar, **~lich** *aa.* inconceivable, incomprehensible.

un-′fehlbar *a.* unfailing; infallible. *adv.* certainly, surely. **~fehlbarkeit** *f.* infallibility. **~fein** *a.* coarse, unmannerly, impolite. **~fern** *adv.* not far off, near. *prep.* not far from, near. **~fertig** *a.* unfinished; immature.

Unflat *m.* (-s) filth, dirt.

unflätig *a.* filthy, dirty.

un-folgsam *a.* disobedient. **~folgsamkeit** *f.* disobedience. **~förmig**, **~förmlich** *aa.* deformed, mis-shapen, shapeless; monstrous. **~förmigkeit** *f.* deformity; monstrosity. **~frankiert** *a.* not prepaid. **~frei** *a.* not free; embarrassed, constrained. **~freiwillig** *a.* involuntary; compulsory.

unfreundlich *a.* unfriendly, unkind; harsh; inclement (weather). **~keit** *f.* unfriendliness; inclemency.

Unfriede(n) *m.* discord, dissension.

unfruchtbar *a.* unfruitful, unproductive; barren, sterile. **~keit** *f.* barrenness, sterility. **~machung** *f.* sterilization.

Unfug *m.* wrong, offence, misdemeanour; mischief; nonsense.

un-gangbar *a.* impassable; not current; unsaleable. **~gastlich** *a.* inhospitable. **~geachtet** *a.* not esteemed. *prep.* notwithstanding, in spite of. **~geahndet** *a.* unpunished. **~geahnt** *a.* unexpected, not anticipated, never dreamt of.

un-gebärdig *a.* unruly, wild. **~gebeten** *a.* uninvited. **~gebeugt** *a.* unbent, uncurbed. **~gebildet** *a.* uneducated; ill-bred. **~gebleicht** *a.* unbleached. **~gebräuchlich** *a.* unusual. **~gebrochen** *a.* unbroken; not refracted (rays).

Ungebühr f. indecency, impropriety. **~lich** a. indecent, improper; undue.

ungebunden a. unbound; (of book) in sheets; in paper-backs; (fig.) free, unrestrained, loose. **~heit** f. freedom, lack of restraint.

ungedeckt a uncovered, without cover; not yet laid (table); dishonoured (cheque).

Ungeduld f. impatience. **~ig** a. impatient.

ungeeignet a. unsuitable, unfit.

ungefähr a. approximate; vague; casual. adv. about, near, nearly; von ~ by chance. subst. n. chance, accident.

un-gefährdet a. safe, not endangered. **~gefährlich** a. not dangerous, harmless. **~gefällig** a. disobliging, unkind. **~gefälligkeit** f. discourtesy. **~gefalzt** a. (of book) in sheets. **~gefüge** a. misshapen, monstrous. **~gefügig** a. unwieldy; unmanageable.

ungegerbt a. untanned.

un-gehalten a. angry; indignant. **~geheißen** a. unasked. adv. spontaneously. **~gehemmt** a. unchecked, unhampered. **~geheuchelt** a. unfeigned, sincere. **~geheuer** a. enormous, huge, colossal; monstrous. adv. exceedingly. subst. n. monster. **~geheuerlich** a. monstrous. **~geheuerlichkeit** f. monstrosity; enormity (of crime). **~gehobelt** a. unplaned; (fig.) unpolished, rude. **~gehörig** a. undue; improper; impertinent. **~gehörigkeit** f. impropriety. **~gehorsam** a. disobedient. subst. m. disobedience, insubordination.

ungeklärt a. unsolved.

un-gekünstelt a. unaffected, simple, natural. **~gekürzt** a. unabridged. **~geladen** a. uninvited; unloaded (gun). **~gelegen** a. inconvenient, inopportune. **~gelegenheit** f. inconvenience; trouble. **~gelenk** a. stiff, clumsy. **~gelernt** a. unskilled. **~gelöscht** a. unquenched; unslaked (lime).

Ungemach n. discomfort; trouble, hardship.

un-gemein a. uncommon; extra-

ordinary. **~gemessen** a. (fig.) unlimited. **~gemütlich** a. uncomfortable; unpleasant.

un-genannt a. anonymous. **~genau** a. inexact, inaccurate. **~genauigkeit** f. inexactitude, inaccuracy. **~genießbar** a. uneatable; unpalatable; unbearable. **~genügend** a. insufficient; unsatisfactory, below standard. **~genügsam** a. insatiable. **~genügsamkeit** f. greediness. **~genutzt** a. unused; unutilized, not made use of.

ungepflegt a. neglected, untidy.

un-gerächt a. unavenged. **~gerade** a. not straight, uneven; odd (number). **~geraten** a. spoiled, undutiful (child). **~gerechnet** a. not included, not taken into account. **~gerecht** a. unjust, unfair. **~gerechtfertigt** a. unjustified. **~gerechtigkeit** f. injustice. **~gereimt** a. unrhymed; (fig.) absurd. **~gern** adv. unwillingly, reluctantly.

un-gesäuert a. unleavened. **~gesäumt** a. 1. seamless. 2. prompt, immediate. adv. without delay. **~geschehen** a. undone. **~geschick** n. misfortune. **~geschicklichkeit** f. awkwardness, clumsiness. **~geschickt** a. awkward, clumsy; stupid. **~geschlacht** a. uncouth; clumsy. **~geschliffen** a. unpolished; uncut; (fig.) ill-bred, uncouth. **~geschmälert** a. undiminished, whole. **~geschminkt** a. not rouged or made up; (fig.) plain, unvarnished. **~geschoren** a. unshorn; (fig.) unmolested; **~geschoren lassen** to leave alone.

un-gesellig a. unsociable. **~gesetzlich** a. illegal. **~gesittet** a. unmannerly; uncivilized. **~gestalt** a. deformed, mis-shapen. **~gestillt** a. unquenched; unappeased. **~gestört** a. undisturbed; uninterrupted. **~gestraft** a. unpunished. adv. with impunity. **~gestüm** a. impetuous; violent. subst. m. & n. impetuosity; violence. **~gesund** a. unhealthy; unwholesome.

un-getreu a. faithless. **~getrübt** a. unclouded; clear; untroubled. **~getüm** n. monster. **~geübt** a. untrained, inexperienced.

un-gewandt a. awkward, clumsy, unskilful. **~gewaschen** a. unwashed; slanderous (tongue). **~gewiß** a. uncertain. **~gewißheit** f. uncertainty. **~gewitter** n. violent storm, thunderstorm. **~gewöhnlich** a. unusual, uncommon; strange. **~gewohnt** a unaccustomed, unfamiliar; unusual.

un-gezählt a. unnumbered, untold, innumerable. **~gezähmt** a. untamed. **~geziefer** n. vermin. **~geziemend** a. unseemly; improper. **~gezogen** a. ill-bred, rude; naughty. **~gezogenheit** f. rudeness, impertinence; naughtiness. **~gezügelt** a. unbridled, unrestrained. **~gezwungen** a. unaffected, natural; unconstrained. **~gezwungenheit** f. unaffectedness; ease.

Un-glaube m. disbelief; unbelief. **~gläubig** a. incredulous; unbelieving; infidel. **~gläubigkeit** f. incredulity; unbelief. **~glaublich** a. incredible. **~glaubwürdig** a. untrustworthy; unreliable; unauthenticated.

ungleich a. unequal; unlike, dissimilar; odd, uneven; different, varying. adv. incomparably; much, a great deal. **~artig** a. dissimilar, different; heterogeneous. **~förmig** a. not uniform, unequal; irregular. **~heit** f. inequality; dissimilarity; difference. **~mäßig** a. uneven; disproportionate; unsymmetrical.

Unglimpf m. (-s) harshness; wrong; injustice; insult. **~lich** a. harsh; unfair; insulting.

Unglück n. (-s, -e) misfortune; distress, misery, disaster, reverse, calamity; bad luck; accident. **~lich** a. unfortunate, unlucky; unhappy, miserable; ill-starred; unrequited (love). **~licherweise** adv. unfortunately. **~selig** a. unfortunate; miserable; disastrous. **~sfall** m. accident, casualty. **~srabe** m. croaker. **~svogel** m. bird

of ill omen; (fig.) unlucky person.

Ungnade f. disgrace; displeasure; in ~ fallen bei to incur a person's displeasure.

ungnädig a. ungracious; ill-humoured.

ungültig a. invalid; not current; not available; ~ erklären to annul. **~keit** f. invalidity, nullity.

Ungunst f. unpropitiousness; disadvantage; inclemency (of weather).

ungünstig a. unfavourable; disadvantageous.

ungut a. unfriendly, unkind; nichts für ~! no harm meant.

un-'haltbar a. not durable; untenable. **~handlich** a. unwieldy. **~harmonisch** a. inharmonious, discordant.

Unheil n. mischief, harm; disaster, calamity. **~bar** a. incurable; irreparable. **~bringend** a. fatal, ominous, unlucky. **~schwanger** a. fraught with disaster. **~stifter** m. mischief-maker. **~voll** a. disastrous, calamitous; pernicious.

un-heilig a. unholy; profane; unhallowed. **~heimlich** a. uncanny; sinister. adv. tremendously; awfully. **~höflich** a. impolite, rude. **~höflichkeit** f. impoliteness, rudeness. **~hold** a. ungracious; ill-disposed. subst. m. monster; fiend, demon. **~hörbar** a. inaudible. **~hygienisch** a. insanitary.

Uni'form f. (-, -en) uniform. **~iert** a. uniformed; uniform.

Unikum n. (-s, Unika) unique object or example; original (person).

Univer'sal-erbe m. sole heir, residuary legatee. **~mittel** n. universal remedy, panacea.

Universi'tät f. (-, -en) university.

Uni'versum n. (-s) universe.

Unke f. (-, -n) toad. **~n** v.i. to prophesy evil.

un-kenntlich a. unrecognizable. **~kenntlichkeit** f. unrecognizable condition. **~kenntnis** f. ignorance. **~keusch** a. unchaste, lewd. **~keuschheit** f. unchastity, lewdness. **~klar** a. not clear; turbid, muddy; hazy, indistinct; (fig.) obscure. **~klarheit** f. want of

clearness; obscurity. ~klug a.
imprudent, unwise. ~klugheit f.
imprudence, foolish action. ~
körperlich a. incorporeal; immaterial; spiritual.

Unkosten pl. charges, expenses,
costs; laufende ~ overheads.

Unkraut n. weed(s).

un'kündbar a. unredeemable; con-
solidated.

un-kundig a. ignorant of, unac-
quainted with.

un-längst adv. not long ago, recently, the other day. ~lauter a.
impure; insincere; unfair, mean.
~leidlich a. unbearable, intolerable. ~leserlich a. illegible. ~
'leugbar a. undeniable. ~liebens-
würdig a. unamiable, unkind.
~liebsam a. unpleasant, disagreeable. ~lin(i)iert a. unruled,
without lines. ~logisch a. illogical. ~lösbar, ~löslich aa.
insoluble.

Unlust f. dislike, disinclination;
aversion; indifference; dullness.
~ig a. listless; disinclined, reluctant.

un-manierlich a. unmannerly. ~
männlich a. unmanly.

Un-maß n. excessive amount, immense number. ~masse f. vast
quantity, enormous number.
maßgeblich a. without authority,
open to correction. ~mäßig a.
immoderate; intemperate; excessive. ~mäßigkeit f. immo-
deration; intemperance; excess.

Un-menge f. vast quantity or
number. ~mensch m. monster.
~menschlich a. inhuman, barbarous; (colloq.) tremendous,
terrible. ~menschlichkeit f. in-
humanity, cruelty. ~'merklich
a. imperceptible. ~'meßbar a.
immeasurable.

un-mittelbar a. immediate, direct.
~möbliert a. unfurnished. ~
modern a. old-fashioned, antiquated. ~möglich a. impossible.
~möglichkeit f. impossibility. ~
moralisch a. immoral. ~moti-
viert a. without motive; not sufficiently motivated; unfounded.
~mündig a. minor, not of age.
~mündigkeit f. minority. ~

musikalisch a. unmusical.

Unmut m. ill humour; displeasure.
~ig a. annoyed, angry.

un-nachahmlich a. inimitable. ~
nachgiebig a. unyielding, relentless; uncompromising. ~nach-
sichtig a. unrelenting; strict,
severe. ~nahbar a. unapproach-
able, inaccessible. ~natürlich a.
unnatural; affected. ~natürlich-
keit f. unnaturalness; affectation.
~nennbar a. unutterable, inexpressible, ineffable. ~nötig a.
unnecessary, needless. ~nütz a.
useless, unprofitable, idle, vain.

un-ordentlich a. disorderly, untidy,
confused. ~ordnung f. disorder,
untidiness, confusion. ~orga-
nisch a. inorganic.

un-paar a. not even (number); odd
(glove, &c.). ~parteiisch a. impartial, disinterested. ~partei-
lichkeit f. impartiality. ~pas-
send a. improper, unbecoming;
inopportune. ~päßlich a. indisposed, ailing. ~päßlichkeit f. indisposition. ~patriotisch a. un-
patriotic. ~persönlich a. impersonal. ~pfändbar a. unseizable.
~politisch a. unpolitical. ~
praktisch a. unpractical; inex-
pert, unskilful. ~pünktlich a.
unpunctual.

unqualifiziert a. unqualified.

unrasiert a. unshaven.

Unrast f. restlessness.

Unrat m. rubbish, refuse; ~ wittern
to smell a rat.

unrationell a. wasteful.

un-rätlich, ~ratsam aa. inadvis-
able.

unrecht a. not right, wrong; unjust, unfair; evil, bad; unsuitable; inopportune. an den ~en
kommen to catch a Tartar; am
~en Ort sein to be out of place.
subst. n. wrong; injustice; ~
haben to be in the wrong, be
mistaken; zu ~ unlawfully, ille-
gally; einem ~ geben to decide
against a person. ~mäßig a. unlawful, illegal.

un-redlich a. dishonest. ~red-
lichkeit f. dishonesty. ~reell a.
unfair, dishonest. ~regelmäßig
a. irregular; anomalous.

~regelmäßigkeit f. irregularity; anomaly. ~reif a. unripe, green; immature. ~reife f. unripeness; immaturity. ~rein a. unclean; impure; dirty; ins ~reine schreiben to jot down, make a rough copy. ~reinlich a. unclean; dirty. ~rettbar a. past saving, past help. ~richtig a.wrong; incorrect; erroneous. ~richtigkeit f. incorrectness.

Unruh f. balance (of watch).

Unruh-e f. (-e, -en) unrest, restlessness; noise; disturbance; riot; alarm, anxiety, uneasiness. ~ig a. restless; turbulent; uneasy; restive (horse). ~stifter m. agitator; trouble-maker.

unrühmlich a. inglorious.

uns acc. & dat. of pron. wir us, to us; ourselves. ~er pron. & a. our, ours; of us. ~ere, ~rige a. ours; (pl.) our people. ~ereins indecl. pron. people like us, such as we. ~ererseits adv. as for us, for our part. ~eresgleichen indecl. a. people like us. ~erethalben, ~eretwegen, ~eretwillen advv. for our sakes, on our behalf, because of us.

un-sachlich a. not objective, personal, subjective; not pertinent, not to the point. ~sagbar, ~säglich aa. unspeakable, unutterable; (fig.) immense. ~sauber a. dirty, filthy; (fig.) unfair. ~sauberkeit f. dirt, filth.

un-schädlich a. harmless, innocuous; ~schädlich machen to render harmless, prevent from doing harm; to disarm; to neutralize (poison). ~scharf a. blurred, hazy; poorly defined. ~schätzbar a. inestimable, invaluable. ~scheinbar a. insignificant; plain, homely. ~schicklich a. improper, indecent, unseemly. ~schicklichkeit f. impropriety.

Unschlitt n. (-es, -e) tallow.

un-schlüssig a. wavering, irresolute. ~schlüssigkeit f. irresolution, indecision. ~schön a. plain, unpleasant, ugly; unfair. ~schuld f. innocence. ~schuldig a. innocent; harmless. ~schwer a. not difficult, easy.

Unsegen m. adversity, misfortune; curse.

un-selbständig a. dependent, helpless. ~selbständigkeit f. dependence (on others), helplessness. ~selig a. unfortunate; accursed; fatal. ~sicher a. unsafe, insecure; unsteady; irresolute; precarious; uncertain, dubious. ~sicherheit f. insecurity; precariousness; uncertainty. ~sichtbar a. invisible. ~sichtbarkeit f. invisibility.

Unsinn m. nonsense. ~ig a. nonsensical, absurd.

Unsitt-e f. bad habit; abuse. ~lich a. immoral; indecency. ~lichkeit f. immorality; indecency.

unsolide a. dissipated; unreliable.

unsozial a. unsociable; antisocial.

un-statthaft a. inadmissible; illicit, illegal. ~sterblich a. immortal. ~sterblichkeit f. immortality.

Unstern m. unlucky star; misfortune.

un-stet a. changeable; unsteady; inconstant; restless. ~stetigkeit f. unsettled condition; inconstancy; restlessness. ~stillbar a. unquenchable; insatiable; unappeasable. ~stimmigkeit f. discrepancy; inconsistency. ~sträflich a. irreproachable, blameless. ~streitig a. incontestable, unquestionable. ~summe f. enormous sum. ~sympathisch a. unpleasant, disagreeable, distasteful.

un-'tadelhaft, ~'tadelig aa. blameless.

Untat f. crime, outrage.

un-tätig a. inactive; idle. ~tätigkeit f. inactivity. ~tauglich a. useless; unsuitable; unfit, disabled. ~tauglichkeit f. uselessness; unfitness. ~teilbar a. indivisible.

unten adv. below; beneath, underneath; at the foot; at the bottom; downstairs; von oben bis ~ from top to bottom; von ~ auf dienen to rise from the ranks.

unter 1. prep. under, below, beneath, underneath; among, amongst; during; by; ~ uns among ourselves, between ourselves; *nicht ~ zwei Pfund* not less than two pounds. **2.** *a.* lower, under, inferior. **3.** *pref.* under, below, beneath; among; amid.

Unter-abteilung *f.* subdivision; sub-unit. **~arm** *m.* forearm. **~arzt** *m.* junior surgeon; surgeon-ensign.

Unter-bau *m.* substructure; foundation (of road); formation level (of railway). **~bauen** *v.t.* to lay a foundation for, establish, found. **~beamte(r)** *m.* subordinate official. **~beinkleider** *n.pl.* knickers; pants. **~belichten** *v.t.* to under-expose. **~bett** *n.* feather-bed. **~bewußtsein** *n.* the subconscious. **~bieten** *v.t.* to undercut, undersell; to lower (record). **Unter-bilanz** *f.* deficit. **~binden** *v.t.* to tie up; to neutralize (attack); (*fig.*) to cut off, paralyse. **~bleiben** *vns.i.* to be left undone; not to take place; to cease, be discontinued. **~brechen** *v.t.* to interrupt; to cut short; to break (journey); to discontinue; to stop. **~brechung** *f.* interruption, break; stop. **~breiten** *v.t.* to lay before, submit to.

unterbringen *v.t.* to shelter, accommodate, lodge; to billet (troops); to provide (a place) for; to dispose of, sell; to store (goods); to invest (money).

Unterdeck *n.* lower deck. **unterder'hand** *adv.* secretly, in secret.

unter-'des, ~'dessen *advv.* meanwhile, in the meantime.

unter'drück-en *v.t.* to oppress; to repress; to suppress, crush, quell. **~er** *m.* oppressor. **~ung** *f.* oppression; repression; suppression.

unterei'nander *adv.* (with) each other; among themselves; together; mutually, reciprocally.

unter-ernährt *a.* underfed, undernourished. **~ernährung** *f.* underfeeding. **~'fangen** *v.r.* to dare, venture (to), presume (to). *subst. n.* undertaking, enterprise, venture. **~'fertigen** *v.t.* to sign. **~'fertige(r)** *m.* (the) undersigned. **~'führung** *f.* subway; (*motor.*) underpass. **~futter** *n.* lining.

Unter-gang *m.* setting, going down, sinking, decline; destruction, fall, ruin; foundering (of a ship). **~'gebene(r)** *m.* subordinate, subaltern. **~gehen** *vns.i.* (*of sun*) to set; to founder, sink; to perish. **~geschoß** *n.* ground floor. **~gestell** *n.* chassis; undercarriage. **~gewicht** *n.* underweight. **~'graben** *v.t.* to undermine, sap. **~grund** *m.* subsoil. **~grundbahn** *f.* underground, tube. **unterhaken** *v.t.* (*colloq.*) to take a person's arm.

unterhalb *prep.* below.

Unterhalt *m.* maintenance; livelihood.

unter'halt-en *v.t.* to support; to maintain, sustain; to keep up; to entertain, amuse. *v.r.* to converse (with); to enjoy oneself. **~end, ~sam** *aa.* entertaining, amusing. **~ung** *f.* keeping up, maintenance, support; conversation, talk; entertainment, amusement. **~ungsliteratur** *f.* light reading or fiction.

under'hand-eln *v.i.* to negotiate; to treat (with), parley. **~lung** *f.* negotiation; *in ~lungen stehen* to carry on negotiations (with).

Unter-händler *m.* negotiator, agent, mediator, go-between. **~haus** *n.* Lower House, House of Commons. **~hemd** *n.* vest. **~höhlen** *v.t.* to undermine. **~holz** *n.* undergrowth, brushwood, copse. **~hosen** *f.pl.* pants. **~irdisch** *a.* underground, subterraneous, subterranean. **~jacke** *f.* undervest. **~jochen** *v.t.* to subjugate, subdue.

unter'kellern *v.t.* to provide with a cellar.

Unter-kiefer *m.* lower jaw. **~kleid** *n.* slip. **~kleidung** *f.* underwear.

unter-kommen *vns.i.* to find accommodation; to find a situation, get employment. *subst. n.* accommodation, lodging; billet; employment. **~körper** *m.* lower part of the body. **~kriegen** *v.t.* to get the better of; *sich nicht ~kriegen lassen* to hold one's ground. **~kunft** *f.* accommodation, lodging; billet.

Unterlage f. foundation, support, rest; evidence; basis; record, document; (pl.) data; blotting-pad.

Unterlaß m. ohne ~ without intermission, incessantly.

unter'lass-en v.t. to omit, neglect (doing), fail (to do). ~**ung** f. omission, neglect.

Unterlauf m. lower course (of river).

unterlaufen[1] vws.i. to occur, creep in.

unter'laufen[2] a. mit Blut ~ suffused with blood, bloodshot.

unterlegen v.t. to lay or put under; to attach (new meaning to); to set (words to music).

Unterleib m. abdomen.

unter'liegen vws.i. to succumb; to be defeated; keinem Zweifel ~ to admit of no doubt.

Unterlippe f. lower lip.

unterm = unter dem.

unter-'malen v.t. to prepare the canvas, put on the ground colour.

'mauern v.t. to build a foundation to, underpin. ~**mengen** v.t. to mix with, mingle. ~**mensch** m. gangster. ~**mieter** m. subtenant. ~**mi'nieren** v.t. to undermine.

unter'nehm-en v.t. to undertake; to attempt; subst. n. undertaking; enterprise. ~**end** a. enterprising, lively. ~**er** m. contractor; employer. ~**ung** f. undertaking; enterprise. ~**ungsgeist** m. spirit of enterprise. ~**ungslustig** a. enterprising.

Unteroffizier m. N.C.O., corporal.

unterordn-en v.t. to subordinate. v.r. to submit to; von untergeordneter Bedeutung sein to be of secondary importance. ~**ung** f. subordination.

Unter-pfand n. pledge; security ~**prima** f. lower sixth (form).

unter'red-en v.r. to converse, confer (with). ~**ung** f. conversation, talk; conference.

Unterricht m. (-s) instruction, tuition, teaching, education; lesson. ~**sbriefe** pl. correspondence course. ~**swesen** n. education, public instruction, educational matters. ~**ung** f. information.

unter'richten v.t. to teach, instruct, educate, train; to give a lesson; to inform, acquaint (with).

Unterrock m. petticoat.

unters = unter das.

unter'sagen v.t. to forbid, prohibit.

Untersatz m. support; base; saucer.

unter'schätzen v.t. to underrate.

unter'scheid-en v.t. to distinguish, discriminate, differentiate. v.r. to differ (from). ~**ung** f. distinction, discrimination, differentiation. ~**ungsmerkmal** n. distinctive mark.

Unterschenkel m. shank.

unterschieben v.t. to push under; to substitute; to foist on, father upon; (fig.) to impute to, insinuate.

Unterschied m. (-s, -e) difference, distinction. ~**en**, ~**lich** aa. different, distinct. ~**slos** adv. indiscriminately; without exception.

unterschlächtig a. undershot.

unter'schlag-en v.t. to embezzle; to intercept; to suppress. ~**ung** f. embezzlement; interception; suppression.

Unter-schleif m. embezzlement; fraud. ~**schlupf** m. shelter, refuge. ~**schreiben** v.t. to sign; to subscribe to. ~**schrift** f. signature; (film) caption; subtitle.

unterschwellig a. subliminal.

Unter-seeboot n. submarine. ~**seeisch** a. submarine. ~**sekunda** f. lower fifth (form). ~**setzen** v.t. to mix (with), intermix. ~**setzer** m. stand; (table) mat. ~**setzt** a. thick-set, dumpy. ~**sinken** vws.i. to go down, sink.

Unter'staatssekretär m. Under-Secretary of State.

Unterstand m. (mil.) dug-out.

unterstehen[1] vws.i. to stand under, shelter under.

unter'stehen[2] v.i. to be under (someone), be subordinate to. v.r. to dare, venture.

unterstellen[1] v.t. to put under; to put under cover.

unter'stell-en[2] v.t. to place under command; (fig.) to impute to, insinuate. ~**ung** f. imputation, insinuation.

unter'streichen v.t. to underline.

Unterstufe f. lower grade, lower forms (of school).

unter'stütz-en v.t. to support; to aid, assist. **~ung** f. support; aid, help, assistance, relief.

unter'such-en v.t. to examine, inspect; to investigate, inquire into; to explore. **~ung** f. examination; investigation; inquiry. **~ungsgefangene(r)** m. prisoner upon trial. **~ungshaft** f. imprisonment on remand. **~ungsrichter** m. examining magistrate.

Untertagebau m. underground mining.

Unter-tan m. (-tans, -tanen) subject. **~tänig** a. subject; submissive, humble. **~tänigkeit** f. submission; humility. **~tasse** f. saucer. **~tauchen** v.t. to dip, v.i. to dive, plunge, dip; (fig.) to be lost, disappear. **~teil** m. lower part, base, bottom. **~titel** m. subtitle, subheading. **~ton** m. undertone.

untervermieten v.t. to sublet.

unterwandern v.t. to infiltrate.

unter-wärts adv. downwards; underneath. **~wäsche** f. underwear, underclothing. **~wasserbombe** f. depth charge. **~wegs** adv. on the way. **~'weisen** v.t. to instruct. **~weisung** f. instruction. **~welt** f. lower regions, Hades; underworld.

unter'werf-en v.t. to subjugate, bring into subjection. v.r. to submit, yield, resign oneself to. **~ung** f. subjection; submission, surrender; resignation (to), acquiescence (in).

unter-'winden v.r. to venture (upon), presume (to do). **~wühlen** v.t. to undermine. **~würfig** a. submissive; obsequious, servile. **~würfigkeit** f. submissiveness; obsequiousness, servility.

unter'zeichn-en v.t. to sign, ratify (treaty). **~er** m. signatory. **~ete(r)** m. (the) undersigned. **~ung** f. signing; signature; ratification.

Unter-zeug n. underwear, underclothing. **~ziehen¹** v.t. to put on (underneath). **~'ziehen²** v.t. to

subject to. v.r. to undergo; to go in for (examination); to undertake.

un-tief a. shallow. **~tiefe** f. shallow (place); shoal; bottomless depth. **~tier** n. monster. **~'tilgbar** a. indelible; irredeemable. **~tragbar** a. unbearable, intolerable. **~trennbar** a. inseparable. **~treu** a. unfaithful, faithless. **~treue** f. unfaithfulness; (leg.) breach of trust. **~tröstlich** a. disconsolate. **~trüglich** a. infallible, unerring. **~tüchtig** a. incapable; unfit, incompetent. **~tüchtigkeit** f. incapacity, incompetence. **~tugend** f. vice, bad habit. **~tunlich** a. impracticable, not feasible.

unüber-legt a. thoughtless, inconsiderate, ill-advised, rash. **~sehbar** a. immense, vast; incalculable. **~setzbar** a. untranslatable. **~steigbar** a. insurmountable. **~'tragbar** a. not transferable; not negotiable. **~trefflich** a. unequalled, unrivalled, incomparable. **~troffen** a. unsurpassed; unexcelled. **~windlich** a. invincible, unconquerable, insurmountable (difficulty).

unum-'gänglich a. indispensable, absolutely necessary. **~schränkt** a. unlimited; absolute. **~stößlich** a. irrefutable; irrevocable. **~wunden** a. candid, frank, plain.

ununter-'brochen a. uninterrupted; continuous, incessant. **~'scheidbar** a. indistinguishable.

un-veränderlich a. unchangeable, unalterable; invariable. **~verantwortlich** a. irresponsible; inexcusable. **~verantwortlichkeit** f. irresponsibility; inexcusable action. **~ver'äußerlich** a. inalienable. **~ver'besserlich** a. incorrigible. **~verbindlich** a. not obligatory; without obligation, not binding; unkind, disobliging. **~verblümt** a. plain, blunt. **~verbrennbar** a. incombustible. **~ver'brüchlich** a. inviolable; absolute. **~verbürgt** a. unwarranted; unconfirmed (news).

un-verdaulich a. indigestible. **~verdaulichkeit** f. indigestibleness;

indigestion. **~verdaut** *a.* not digested. **~verdient** *a.* unmerited, undeserved. **~verdorben** *a.* unspoiled; pure. **~verdrossen** *a.* indefatigable, unwearied.

un-verehelicht *a.* unmarried, single. **~ver'einbar** *a.* incompatible, irreconcilable.

un-verfälscht *a.* unadulterated; genuine, real, pure. **~verfänglich** *a.* harmless. **~verfroren** *a.* unabashed, imperturbable, impudent.

un-ver'gänglich *a.* imperishable; immortal. **~ver'geßlich** *a.* unforgettable. **~ver'gleichlich** *a.* incomparable, matchless, unique.

un-verhältnismäßig *a.* disproportionate. **~verheiratet** *a.* unmarried. **~verhofft** *a.* unexpected, unforeseen. **~verhohlen** *a.* unconcealed, open, frank.

un-verkäuflich *a.* unsaleable; not for sale. **~ver'kennbar** *a.* unmistakable. **~verkürzt** *a.* not curtailed; unabridged (text).

un-ver'letzbar, ~ver'letzlich *aa.* invulnerable; inviolable; sacred. **~verletzt** *a.* unhurt, uninjured. **~ver'lierbar** *a.* that cannot be lost; immortal; unforgettable.

un-vermählt *a.* unmarried. **~ver'meidlich** *a.* unavoidable, inevitable. **~vermerkt** *a.* unperceived, unnoticed. **~vermindert** *a.* undiminished, unabated. **~vermischt** *a.* unmixed; unalloyed. **~vermittelt** *a.* sudden, abrupt. **~vermögen** *n.* inability; incapacity, impotence. **~vermögend** *a.* powerless, unable; impotent; poor, penniless. **~vermutet** *a.* unexpected.

un-vernehmlich *a.* inaudible, indistinct; unintelligible. **~vernunft** *f.* unreasonableness; folly. **~vernünftig** *a.* unreasonable; foolish.

unverpflichtend *a.* non-committal.

unverrichtet *a.* **~er Sache** without having achieved one's purpose, unsuccessfully.

unverrückt *adv.* immovably; fixedly.

un-verschämt *a.* impudent; exorbitant (price). **~verschämtheit** *f.* impudence, cheek. **~verschuldet**

a. undeserved, unmerited; not in debt, unencumbered. **~versehens** *adv.* unawares, unexpectedly. **~versehrt** *a.* uninjured, intact, safe. **~ver'siegbar, ~ver'sieglich** *aa.* inexhaustible. **~versöhnlich** *a.* irreconcilable; implacable. **~versorgt** *a.* unprovided for, destitute.

Un-verstand *m.* want of sense; folly. **~verständig** *a.* injudicious, unwise, foolish. **~verständlich** *a.* unintelligible, incomprehensible. **~verstellt** *a.* undissembled, unfeigned. **~versucht** *a.* untried, unattempted; **nichts ~versucht lassen** to leave no stone unturned.

unverträglich *a.* unsociable; quarrelsome; incompatible. **~keit** *f.* unsociableness; quarrelsome disposition.

unverwandt *a.* steadfast, unmoved, fixed.

unverwehrt *a.* **es ist Ihnen ~** you are quite free to.

un-verweilt *adv.* without delay. **~verwelklich** *a.* unfading; immortal. **~verweslich** *a.* incorruptible. **~verwundbar** *a.* invulnerable. **~ver'wüstlich** *a.* indestructible; indefatigable, inexhaustible; evergreen; irrepressible (humour).

un-verzagt *a.* intrepid, undaunted. **~ver'zeihlich** *a.* unpardonable. **~ver'zinslich** *a.* paying no interest. **~verzollt** *a.* duty unpaid. **~ver'züglich** *a.* immediate.

un-vollendet *a.* unfinished, uncompleted. **~vollkommen** *a.* imperfect. **~vollkommenheit** *f.* imperfection. **~vollständig** *a.* incomplete, defective. **~vollständigkeit** *f.* incompleteness.

un-vorbereitet *a.* unprepared; extempore (speech). **~vor'denklich** *a.* immemorial. **~vor'hergesehen** *a.* unforeseen. **~vorsätzlich** *a.* unintentional, undesigned. **~vorsichtig** *a.* imprudent; incautious; careless. **~vorsichtigkeit** *f.* imprudence, carelessness. **~vorstellbar** *a.* unimaginable. **~vorteilhaft** *a.* unprofitable; disadvantageous; unbecoming (dress); ~~ aussehen not to look one 's best.

un'wägbar a. imponderable.

unwahr a. untrue, false. ~haftig a. untruthful, insincere. ~heit f. untruth, falsehood. ~scheinlich a. improbable, unlikely. ~scheinlichkeit f. improbability.

un'-wandelbar a. immutable, unchangeable. ~wegsam a. pathless. ~weib n. virago. ~weiblich a. unwomanly. ~'weigerlich a. unresisting; unquestioning; strict. adv. without fail. ~weise a. unwise, imprudent.

unweit adv. not far off, near. prep. not far from, near, close to.

unwert a. unworthy.

Unwesen n. mischief, tricks; nuisance; abuse; sein ~ treiben to be up to one's tricks; to haunt (a place). ~tlich a. unessential, immaterial; unimportant, insignificant; das ist (ganz) ~tlich that doesn't matter.

Unwetter n. thunderstorm, storm.

unwichtig a. unimportant, insignificant. ~keit f. insignificance.

un-wider'legbar, ~wider'leglich aa. irrefutable. ~wider'ruflich a. irrevocable. ~widersprochen a. uncontradicted; undisputed. ~wider'stehlich a. irresistible.

unwieder'bringlich a. irretrievable.

Unwill-e m. indignation; reluctance. ~ig a. indignant; reluctant. ~kommen a. unwelcome, unpleasant. ~kürlich a. involuntary; instinctive.

un-wirklich a. unreal. ~wirksam a. ineffectual, inefficacious, ineffective; inefficient; null, void. ~wirksamkeit f. inefficacy; inefficiency. ~wirsch a. cross; morose, surly. ~wirtlich a. inhospitable; dreary. ~wirtschaftlich a. uneconomic.

unwissen-d a ignorant. ~heit f. ignorance. ~schaftlich a. unscientific. ~tlich adv. unknowingly, unconsciously.

un-wohl a. unwell, indisposed. ~wohlsein n. indisposition. ~wohnlich a. uninhabitable; uncomfortable. ~würdig a. unworthy ~würdigkeit f. unworthiness.

Un'zahl f. endless number (of). ~'zählig a. countless, innumerable. ~'zählbar a. untamable; indomitable. ~zart a. indelicate; rude.

Unze f. (-, -n) ounce.

Unzeit f. wrong time; zur ~ inopportunely. ~gemäß a. inopportune; behind the times; out of season. ~ig a. untimely; unripe; premature.

un-zerbrechlich a. unbreakable. ~zer'legbar a. indivisible; elementary. ~zer'reißbar a. untearable. ~zer'störbar a. indestructible; imperishable. ~zertrennlich a. inseparable.

un-ziemend, ~ziemlich aa. unseemly, improper. ~zivilisiert a. uncivilized, barbarous. ~zucht f. unchastity; prostitution. ~züchtig a. unchaste; lewd.

un-zufrieden a. discontented, dissatisfied. ~zufriedenheit f. discontent, dissatisfaction. ~zugänglich a. inaccessible; (fig.) reserved. ~zulänglich a. insufficient, inadequate. ~zulänglichkeit f. insufficiency, inadequacy; shortcoming. ~zulässig a. inadmissible; forbidden. ~zumutbar a. unreasonable. ~zurechnungsfähig a. irresponsible. imbecile. ~zurechnungsfähigkeit f. irresponsibility; imbecility. ~zureichend a. insufficient, inadequate.

un-zusammenhängend a. disconnected, disjointed; incoherent. ~zuträglich a. unwholesome, unhealthy, not good (for). ~zuträglichkeit f. discord, dissension. ~zutreffend a. incorrect. ~zuverlässig a. unreliable, untrustworthy; treacherous. ~zuverlässigkeit f. unreliability, untrustworthiness.

un-zweckmäßig a. unsuitable, inexpedient. ~zweckmäßigkeit f. unsuitableness, inexpediency. ~zweideutig a. unequivocal, unambiguous. ~zweifelhaft a. undoubted, indubitable.

üppig a. luxuriant; abundant, plentiful; sumptuous; voluptuous; well-developed (figure). ~keit f.

luxuriant growth; plenty; luxury.
Ur-abstimmung (u:r-) *f.* plebiscite. **~ahn** *m.* great-grandfather; ancestor. **~ahne** *f.* great-grandmother; ancestress. **~alt** *a.* very old; ancient, primeval.

Uran (-a:n) *n.* (-s) uranium. **~erz** *n.* uranite. **~haltig** *a.* uraniferous. **~vorkommen** *n.* uranium deposit.

ur-anfänglich (u:r-) *a.* original, primeval. **~aufführung** *f.* first performance (of play, &c.), first night.

urbar *a.* arable; **~ machen** to bring into cultivation, cultivate, till.

Ur-bewohner *m.pl.* aborigines. **~bild** *n.* original; prototype. **~christentum** *n.* primitive Christianity; the early Church. **~eigen** *a.* original; innate. **~einwohner** *m.* original inhabitant. **~eltern** *pl.* first parents, ancestors. **~enkel** *m.* great-grandson *or* -child. **~enkelin** *f.* great-granddaughter.

Ur-fehde *f.* oath to refrain from vengeance. **~fidel** *a.* very jolly. **~form** *f.* original form, prototype.

ur-gemütlich *a.* exceedingly comfortable; very pleasant. **~geschichte** *f.* earliest history, prehistory. **~geschichtlich** *a.* prehistoric. **~gestalt** *f.* original shape; prototype, archetype. **~gestein** *n.* primitive rock. **~großeltern** *pl.* great-grandparents.

Urheber *m.* (-s, -) author, originator, creator. **~recht** *n.* copyright. **~schaft** *f.* authorship.

U'rin *m.* (-s, -e) urine. **~ieren** *v.i.* to urinate.

Ur-kirche *f.* primitive *or* early Church. **~komisch** *a.* very funny, screamingly funny. **~kraft** *f.* original force; moving principle; elementary power.

Urkund-e *f.* deed, document; title; record; charter. **~enfälscher** *m.* forger of documents. **~enlehre** *f.* palaeography. **~lich** *a.* documentary; authentic.

Urlaub *m.* (-s, -e) leave, furlough. **~er** *m.* soldier on leave.

Urmensch *m.* primitive man.

Urne *f.* (-, -n) urn; casket.

ur-plötzlich *a.* very sudden. **~quell** *m.* fountain-head; primary source, origin. **~sache** *f.* cause, motive, ground, reason; *keine ~ sache* don't mention it. **~sächlich** *a.* causal, causative. **~schrift** *f.* original (text). **~schriftlich** *a.* (in the) original. **~sprache** *f.* original language. **~sprung** *m.* source, origin, beginning, initial; cause. **~sprünglich** *a.* original, primitive; natural. **~stoff** *m.* primary matter; element.

Urteil *n.* (-s, -e) judgement, decision; sentence, verdict; view, opinion. **~seröffnung** *f.* pronouncement of a decree, publication of a judgement. **~sfähig** *a.* competent to judge, judicious. **~sfällung** *f.* passing of sentence. **~skraft** *f.*, **~svermögen** *n.* power of judgement, discernment. **~slos** *a.* without judgement, injudicious. **~sspruch** *m.* sentence; verdict. [ORDEAL]

urteilen *v.i.* to pass sentence; to judge, give one's opinion.

Ur-text *m.* original text. **~tier** *n.* protozoon. **~tümlich** *a.* original, native. **~ureltern** *pl.* forefathers, early ancestors. **~väterzeit** *f.* olden times. **~volk** *n.* primitive people; aborigines. **~wahl** *f.* preliminary election. **~wald** *m.* primeval forest. **~welt** *f.* primeval world. **~weltlich** *a.* primeval. **~wort** *n.* wise saying. **~wüchsig** *a.* original, native; rough, blunt. **~zeit** *f.* primitive times. **~zelle** *f.* primitive cell, ovum. **~zeugung** *f.* abiogenesis. **~zustand** *m.* primitive state, original condition.

U'sance *f.* (-, -n) (*commerc.*) usage.

Usur'p-ator *m.* (-ators, -atoren) usurper. **~ieren** *v.t.* to usurp.

Uten'silien *pl.* utensils.

Utili'tarier *m.* (-s, -) utilitarian.

Uto'pie (-pi:) *f.* (-, -n) utopian scheme.

u'topisch *a.* utopian.

uzen *v.t.* (*colloq.*) to chaff, tease.

V

V, v (fau) *n.* the letter V, v.

vag *a.* vague.

Vaga'bund *m.* (-en, -en) vagabond, vagrant, tramp. **~entum** *n.* vagabondage, vagabondism; vagrancy. **~ieren** *v.i.* to lead a vagabond life; to tramp, roam.

va'kant-a *a.* vacant. **~z** *f.* vacancy; vacation, holidays.

Vakuumreiniger *m.* vacuum cleaner.

Va'luta *f.* (-, Valuten) value, rate (of exchange); currency; standard.

Vampir *m.* (-s, -e) vampire.

Van'dal-e *m.* (-en, -en), **-isch** *a.* vandal. **~ismus** *m.* vandalism.

Va'nille (-nilje) *f.* (-) vanilla.

Vari-'ante *f.* variant. **~ati'on** *f.* variation. **~e'tät** *f.* variety. **~eté** *n.* music-hall. **~ieren** *v.i. & t.* to vary.

Va'sall *m.* (-en, -en) vassal. **~enstaat** *m.* tributary state, satellite.

Vase (va:zə) *f.* (-, -n) vase.

Vase'lin *n.* (-s) vaseline.

Vater (fa:-) *m.* (-s, ⸚) father; male parent, sire (of animals). **~haus** *n.* parental house, home. **~land** *n.* native land or country, fatherland. **~ländisch** *a.* national; patriotic. **~landsliebend** *a.* patriotic. **~los** *a.* fatherless. **~mord** *m.* parricide. **~mörder** *m.* parricide; (*obs.*) old-fashioned high collar. **~schaft** *f.* paternity; fatherhood. **~sname** *m.* surname. **~stadt** *f.* native town. **~stelle** **~stelle vertreten bei** *or* **an** to be a father to. **~unser** *n.* The Lord's Prayer.

Väter-chen *n.* daddy. **~lich** *a.* fatherly; paternal. **~licherseits** *adv.* on the father's side. **~sitte** *f.* manners *or* customs of our forefathers.

Vegeta'bil-ien *pl.* vegetables. **~isch** *a.* vegetable.

Vege't-arier *m.*, **~arisch** *a.* vegetarian. **~ati'on** *f.* vegetation. **~ieren** *v.i.* to vegetate.

Vehe'menz *f.* (-) vehemence.

Ve'hikel *n.* (-s, -) vehicle.

Veilchen *n.* (-s, -) violet.

Veitstanz *m.* St. Vitus's dance.

Ve'linpapier *n.* vellum.

Vene (ve:-) *f.* (-, -n) vein. **~nentzündung** *f.* phlebitis.

ve'nerisch *a.* venereal.

Ven'til (-i:l) *n.* (-s, -e) valve; (*fig.*) outlet. **~ati'on** *f.* ventilation. **~'ator** *m.* ventilator; fan. **~ieren** *v.t.* to ventilate. **~steuerung** *f.* valve timing.

ver-'abfolgen *v.t.* to deliver, hand over, let (a person) have (something).

ver-'abred-en *v.t. & r.* to agree upon; to make an appointment, fix (a date, &c.). **~etermaßen** *adv.* as agreed upon. **~ung** *f.* agreement; appointment; engagement.

ver-'abreichen *v.t.* to give; to dispense (medicine). **~absäumen** *v.t.* to neglect, omit; to fail. **~abscheuen** *v.t.* to abhor, abominate, detest. **~abscheuenswert** *a.*, **~abscheuenswürdig** *aa.* abominable, detestable. **~abschieden** *v.t.* to dismiss, discharge; to disband (troops); to pass (law). **~v.r.** to say good-bye (to), take leave (of). **~abschiedung** *f.* dismissal, discharge.

ver-'acht-en *v.t.* to despise, scorn, disdain. **~ung** *f.* contempt, scorn, disdain.

Ver-'ächt-er *m.* (-ers, -er) despiser, scorner. **~lich** *a.* contemptuous, disdainful; contemptible, despicable.

ver-allge'meiner-n *v.t.* to generalize. **~ung** *f.* generalization.

ver-'alt-en *vvs.i.* to become obsolete. **~et** *a.* old, antiquated; obsolete.

Ve'randa *f.* (-, Veranden) veranda(h).

ver-'änder-lich *a.* changeable, variable; inconstant, unstable; unsettled; fickle, vacillating. **~lichkeit** *f.* changeableness, variability; instability, fickleness. **~n** *v.t.* to change, alter; to vary. **v.r.** to change, alter; to take another situation. **~ung** *f.* change, alteration; variation.

ver-'ängstigt *a.* intimidated, cowed.

ver|'ankern v.t. to moor, anchor; (fig.) to establish firmly.

ver|'anlag-en v.t. to assess (taxes). **~t** a. (fig.) gut **~t** sein to be cut out (for), be talented. **~ung** f. assessment; predisposition; (fig.) talent, turn (for).

ver|'anlass-en v.t. to cause, occasion, give rise to; to induce (person to do). **~ung** f. cause, occasion; motive, inducement; suggestion; request; order; instigation.

ver|'anschaulichen v.t. to illustrate, make clear.

ver|'anschlagen v.t. to estimate (at); zu hoch **~** to overrate.

ver|'anstalt-en v.t. to arrange, organize, get up. **~er** m. organizer; promoter. **~ung** f. arrangement; organization; (sporting) event; show, entertainment, performance.

ver|'antwort-en v.t. to answer or account for; to defend. v.r. to justify oneself. **~lich** a. responsible. **~ung** f. responsibility; auf seine **~ung** at his own risk; zur **~ung** ziehen to call to account. **~ungslos** a. irresponsible. **~ungsvoll** a. involving great responsibility, responsible.

ver|'arbeit-en v.t. to use, work up, manufacture, fashion; (fig.) to assimilate, digest. **~et** a. toil-worn (hands, &c.). **~ung** f. working up, manufacturing, fashioning; assimilation, digestion.

ver-'argen v.t. to blame, reproach (one for). **~ärgert** a. angry, annoyed. **~armen** vws.i. to grow poor, become impoverished. **~'armung** f. impoverishment, pauperization. **~arzten** v.t. (colloq.) to doctor, physic.

ver-'ästeln v.r. to branch out, ramify. **~auktio'nieren** v.t. to sell by auction. **~ausgaben** v.t. to spend. v.r. to run short of money; to expend, exhaust oneself. **~'äußerlich** a. alienable; saleable. **~'äußern** v.t. to alienate; to sell. **~'äußerung** f. alienation; sale.

Verb (-p) n. (-s, -en) verb. **~al-injurie** f. insult.

ver-'bal(l)hornen v.t. to bowdlerize.

Ver-'band m. (-s, "e) (med.) surgical dressing, bandage; society, union; formation, unit. **~kasten** m. first-aid box. **~päckchen** n. field-dressing. **~platz** m. dressing-station, first-aid post. **~smit-glied** n. member of a society. **~stoff** m., **~zeug** n. dressings and bandages, bandaging material.

ver-'bann-en v.t. to banish, exile. **~te(r)** m. exile. **~ung** f. banishment, exile.

ver-barrika'dieren v.t. to barricade, block. **~'bauen** v.t. to build up; to block up, obstruct; to spend in building; to build badly. **~'bauen** vws.i. to become countrified. **~'beißen** v.t. to stifle, suppress; sich **~beißen** in to stick obstinately to, to be set on (a thing). **~'bergen** v.t. to conceal, hide.

Ver-'besser-er m. (-ers, -er) improver, reformer. **~n** v.t. to improve; to correct. **~ung** f. improvement; correction.

ver-'beug-en v.r. to bow, make a bow. **~ung** f. bow.

ver-'beult a. battered.

ver-'biegen v.t. to bend, twist. **~-'bieten** v.t. to forbid, prohibit. **~-'bilden** v.t. to spoil; to educate badly. **~'billigen** v.t. to reduce in price.

ver-'bind-en v.t. to tie, bind up; to bandage, dress (wound); to join, unite; to connect; (tel.) to put through; (chem.) to combine; to pledge (to), oblige (to do); sich zu Dank verbunden fühlen to feel indebted to. **~lich** a. binding, obligatory; courteous, obliging. **~lichkeit** f. liability, obligation; civility, courtesy; compliment. **~ung** f. union, combination, blending; association, club; alliance; communication, connexion, contact; (chem.) compound; sich in **~ung** setzen mit to get into touch with. **~ungsgang** m. connecting passage. **~ungsgraben** m. communication trench. **~ungslinie** f. line of communication. **~ungsmann** m. mediator. **~ungsoffizier** m. liaison officer. **~ungsstück** n. tie, coupling, joint.

ver-'bissen *a.* obstinate, grim, dogged. ~'bissenheit *f.* obstinacy, grimness, doggedness. ~'bitten *v.r.* not to permit, not to stand; not to put up with. ~'bittern *v.t.* to embitter. ~'bitterung *f.* bitterness (of heart). ~'blassen *v.i.* to fade, lose colour; to turn pale. ~'blättern *v.t.* to lose one's place (in a book).

Ver'bleib *m.* (-s) place, abode; whereabouts. ~en *vvs.i.* to remain; to persist (in).

ver-'bleichen *vvs.i.* to grow pale; to fade. ~blenden *v.t.* to face (with bricks, &c.); to screen (lights); (*fig.*) to delude. ~'blendung *f.* delusion. ~blichen *a.* faded; deceased. ~'blüffen *v.t.* to disconcert, flabbergast. ~'blüffung *f.* stupefaction, amazement. ~'blühen *vvs.i.* to fade, wither. ~blümt *a.* figurative; allusive; veiled. ~bluten *vvs.i.* & *r.* to bleed to death.

ver'bohr-en *v.r.* to be mad (on a thing), to persist (in). ~t *a.* obdurate, stubborn.

ver'borgen¹ *v.t.* to lend (out).

ver'borgen² *a.* hidden, secret, concealed. ~heit *f.* concealment; secrecy; retirement, seclusion.

Ver'bot *n.* (-s, -e) prohibition. ~en *a.* prohibited, forbidden; illicit.

ver'brämen *v.t.* to border, edge, trim.

Ver'brauch *m.* (-es) consumption; expenditure. ~en *v.t.* to consume, use up; to wear out; to spend. ~er *m.* consumer. ~steuer *f.* excise duty.

ver'brech-en *v.t.* to commit a crime. *subst. n.* crime. ~er *m.* criminal. ~erisch *a.* criminal. ~erkolonie *f.* penal or convict settlement. ~ertum *n.* delinquency, criminality.

ver'breit-en *v.t.* to spread, diffuse; to circulate, spread abroad, disseminate; *sich ~en über* (*fig.*) to expatiate, enlarge upon (a theme). ~ung *f.* spreading, diffusion; circulating; dissemination; propagation.

ver'breitern *v.t.* to widen, broaden.

ver'brenn-bar *a.* combustible. ~en *v.t.* & *vvs.i.* to burn; to scorch; to cremate. ~ung *f.* burning; combustion; burn, scald; cremation. ~ungsmotor *m.* internal combustion engine.

ver-'briefen *v.t.* to confirm *or* guarantee by a document. ~'bringen *v.t.* to spend, pass (time). ~'brüdern *v.r.* to fraternize. ~'brüderung *f.* fraternization. ~'brühen *v.t.* to scald.

ver-'buchen *v.t.* to book (order, &c.). ~'buhlt *a.* amorous, wanton. ~'bummeln *v.t.* to forget; to waste (time). *vvs.i.* to come down in the world. ~'bunden *a.* united; connected; obliged. ~'bundenheit *f.* bond, tie; connexion, relationship. ~'bünden *v.r.* to ally oneself (with). ~'bündete(r) *m.* ally, confederate. ~'bürgen *v.t.* & *r.* to guarantee, vouch for. ~'büßen *v.t.* to serve one's time.

ver'chromen *v.t.* to plate with chromium.

Ver'dacht (-axt) *m.* (-es) suspicion. ~'dächtig *a.* suspected; suspicious. ~en *v.t.* to cast suspicion on; to distrust. ~ung *f.* insinuation; false charge.

ver'damm-en *v.t.* to condemn; to damn. ~enswert *a.* damnable, execrable. ~nis *f.* damnation; perdition. ~ung *f.* condemnation; damnation.

ver'dampf-en *vvs.i.* to evaporate. ~er *m.* vaporizer.

ver'danken *v.t.* to owe (something to).

verdarb *imperf.* of verderben.

ver'dattert *a.*(*colloq.*)flabbergasted.

ver'dau-en *v.t.* to digest. ~lich *a.* digestible. ~lichkeit *f.* digestibility. ~ung *f.* digestion. ~ungsbeschwerden *f.pl.* indigestion.

Ver'deck *n.* deck; (*motor.*, *&c.*) hood; top. ~en *v.t.* to cover; to hide, conceal.

ver'denken *v.t.* to blame.

Ver'derb *m.* (-s) ruin. ~en 1. *v.t. st.* to ruin; to destroy; to spoil; to demoralize, corrupt; *sich den Magen ~en* to upset one's stomach. *vvs.i.* to go bad, be spoiled; to perish; *es ~en mit* to incur another's displeasure. **2.** *subst. n.* ruin, destruction; *jemanden ins ~en stürzen* to ruin a person. **~er** *m.* destroyer; corrupter. **~lich** *a.* pernicious; perishable. **~lichkeit** *f.* perniciousness; corruptibility; perishable nature. **~nis** *f.* ruin; depravity, corruption. **~t** *a.* depraved, corrupt. **~theit** *f.* depravity, corruption.

ver-'deutlichen *v.t.* to elucidate, make clear. **~'deutschen** *v.t.* to translate into German. **~'dichten** *v.t.* to condense; to compress; to consolidate; to solidify. **~dichtung** *f.* condensation. **~dicken** *v.t.* to thicken, concentrate.

ver'dien-en *v.t.* to earn; to gain; to win; to merit, deserve. **Ver'dienst** *m.* (-es) gain, profit; earnings. *n.* (-es, -e) merit; deserts. **~lich** *a.* meritorious, deserving. **~spanne** *f.* margin of profits.

ver'dient *a.* deserving; well deserved; *sich ~ machen um* to deserve well of. **~ermaßen** *adv.* deservedly, according to one's deserts.

Ver'dikt *n.* (-es, -e) verdict.

ver'dingen *v.t.* to hire out. *v.r.* to take a situation.

ver-'dolmetschen *v.t.* to interpret. **~'doppeln** *v.t.* to double; to redouble. **~'dopplung** *f.* doubling; duplication. **~'dorben** *a.* spoiled; tainted (meat); depraved. **~'dorren** *vvs.i.* to dry up, wither.

ver'dräng-en *v.t.* to displace; to push away, push aside; to repress, suppress; (*psychoanal.*) to inhibit. **~ung** *f.* displacement; forcing out; repression, suppression; inhibition.

ver'dreh-en *v.t.* to twist; to roll (one's eyes); to contort (limbs); to sprain; to distort, misrepresent; *einem den Kopf ~en* to turn someone's head. **~t** *a.* distorted; (*fig.*) cracked, mad, (*sl.*) barmy. **~theit** *f.* craziness. **~ung** *f.* distortion, contortion; misrepresentation.

ver'dreifachen *v.t.* to treble.

ver'drieß-en *v.t. st.* to annoy, vex; *es sich nicht ~en lassen* not to be discouraged by; not to shrink from; *sich keine Mühe ~en lassen* to spare no pains. **~lich** *a.* cross, bad-tempered, peevish; annoyed, vexed; annoying; tiresome, unpleasant. **~lichkeit** *f.* bad temper, peevishness; annoyance, vexation, irksomeness.

ver'drossen *a.* sulky, sullen; cross; annoyed.

ver'drucken *v.t.* to misprint.

ver'drücken *v.t.* (*colloq.*) to eat up, polish off. *v.r.* to slink away.

Ver'druß *m.* (Verdruss-es) annoyance, trouble, chagrin.

ver'duften *vvs.i.* to evaporate; (*sl.*) to make off, slip away.

ver'dummen *v.t.* to make stupid, stupefy. *vvs.i.* to grow stupid.

ver'dunkel-n *v.t.* to darken, obscure; to blackout; (*astron.*) to eclipse. **~ung** *f.* darkening; obscuration; blackout; eclipse. **~ungsgefahr** *f.* (*leg.*) danger of prejudicing the course of justice.

ver'dünn-en *v.t.* to thin; to attenuate; to dilute (liquids); to rarefy (gases). **~ung** *f.* thinning; attenuation; dilution; rarefaction.

ver'dunst-en *vvs.i.* to evaporate. **~ung** *f.* evaporation.

ver-'dursten *vvs.i.* to die of thirst. **~'düstern** *v.t.* to darken, cloud. **~'dutzen** *v.t.* to bewilder, disconcert.

ver'ebben *v.i.* to ebb; to subside.

ver'edel-n *v.t.* to ennoble; to improve; to cultivate; to graft; to refine; to finish. **~ung** *f.* ennobling; improvement; cultivation; refinement; finishing.

ver'ehelich-en *v.t. & r.* to marry. **~ung** *f.* marriage.

ver'ehr-en *v.t.* to respect, revere; to worship, adore; *einem etwas ~en* to present someone with something. **~er** *m.* worshipper; admirer, lover. **~lich** *a.* honourable; esteemed. **~ung** *f.* respect, veneration; worship, adoration. **~ungswürdig** *a.* venerable.

ver-'eidig-en *v.t.* to swear in, put on

oath. **~ung** f. swearing in; taking the oath.

Ver|'ein m. (-s, -e) union; association, society, club; *im ~ mit* together with; (published) jointly by. **~bar** a. compatible, consistent. **~baren** v.t. to agree upon; to reconcile. **~barkeit** f. compatibility. **~barung** f. agreement, arrangement.

ver|'ein-en, ~igen v.t. & r. to unite, join; to combine; to ally (oneself) with; to reconcile (with). **~igung** f. union; combination; junction; alliance, confederation; fusion; amalgamation.

ver-|'einfachen v.t. to simplify. **~'einheitlichen** v.t. to unify, standardize. **~'einnahmen** v.t. to receive (money). **~'einsamen** vws.i. to become isolated, live more and more alone. **~'einzelt** a. single, solitary; sporadic.

ver-|'eisen vws.i. to turn to ice, freeze. **~'eisung** f. ice-formation; (av.) icing up. **~'eiteln** v.t. to frustrate, thwart. **~'eitern** vws.i. to fester, suppurate. **~'ekeln** v.t. to disgust with; to spoil (a thing for one).

ver-|'elenden vws.i. to sink into poverty or wretchedness. **~'enden** vws.i. to die, perish. **~'engern** v.t. to narrow, contract.

ver|'erb-en v.t. to bequeath, leave (to); to transmit (disease); to hand down. v.r. to be hereditary, run in the family; to devolve upon. **~ung** f. heredity; hereditary transmission. **~ungsforschung** f. genetics. **~ungstheorie** f. law of heredity.

ver|'ewig-en v.t. to perpetuate; to immortalize. **~t** a. deceased, departed, (the) late.

ver|'fahren 1. v.i. & vws.i. to proceed, act; to treat, use. v.t. to spend (time or money in driving about). v.r. to lose one's way, take the wrong road; (fig.) to be on the wrong tack. 2. a. bungled, hopeless. 3. subst. n. proceeding; procedure; (chem.) process; method; dealing.

Ver|'fall m. (-es) decay, ruin, decline, deterioration; maturity (of

bill); foreclosure; *in ~ geraten* to go to ruin, decay. **~en** vws.i. to decay, go to ruin; to decline, grow weaker, lose flesh; to fall due; to expire; to lapse, be forfeited; to incur (penalty); to fall (into); slip back (into); to hit (upon an idea); *einem ~en* to become a person's slave; *~ene Züge* worn features. **~serscheinung** f. symptom of decline. **~tag** m. day of payment (for bill).

ver-'fälsch-en v.t. to falsify; to adulterate. **~ung** f. falsification; adulteration.

ver|'fangen v.t. to take effect, tell, avail. v.r. to be caught, become entangled.

ver|'fänglich a. insidious; captious; risky; embarrassing, awkward.

ver|'färben v.r. to change colour, grow pale.

ver|'fass-en v.t. to compose, write (book, &c.), draw up (document). **~er** m. author, writer. **~erin** f. authoress. **~erschaft** f. authorship. **~ung** f. condition, state; disposition, frame of mind; constitution. **~ungsmäßig** a. constitutional. **~ungsurkunde** f. charter of the constitution. **~ungswidrig** a. unconstitutional.

ver|'faulen vws.i. to rot.

ver|'fecht-en v.t. to stand up for, defend; to advocate, champion (a cause). **~er** m. defender; advocate, champion (of cause).

ver|'fehl-en v.t. & i. to miss, not to meet or find; to fail (to). **~t** a. wrong, false; spoiled, bungled. **~ung** f. mistake; lapse, offence.

ver-'feinden v.r. to fall out with. **~'feinern** v.t. to refine; to polish; to improve. **~'femen** v.t. to outlaw.

ver|'fertig-en v.t. to make, manufacture. **~er** m. maker, manufacturer. **~ung** f. making, manufacture, fabrication.

Ver|'fettung f. (-) fatty degeneration.

ver-'feuern v.t. to burn, consume; to waste fuel; to use up. **~'filmen** v.t. to film. **~'filzen** v.t. to felt; to mat. **~'filzt** a. entangled. **~'finstern** v.t. & r. to darken, grow dark; to eclipse. **~'fitzen** v.t. to entangle

ver'flachen *vws.i.* to become flat; (*fig.*) to become shallow, decline intellectually.

ver'flechten *v.t.* to entwine, interlace; (*fig.*) to implicate, involve.

ver'fliegen *vws.i.* to fly away; to disappear, vanish; (*of time*) to pass, fly; (*chem.*) to volatilize; *v.r.* (*av.*) to lose one's way.

ver'fließen *vws.i.* to run (into), blend; (*of time*) to pass, elapse.

ver'flixt *a.* (*colloq.*) confounded. **~flossen** *a.* past; late. **~fluchen** *v.t.* to curse. **~flucht** *a.* cursed, confounded. **~flüchtigen** *v.t.* to volatilize. *v.r.* to evaporate. **~flüssigen** *v.r.* to become liquid, liquefy.

Ver'folg *m.* course, progress; pursuance. **~en** *v.t.* to follow; to pursue; to follow up; to persecute; (*leg.*) to prosecute; **~en** to shadow. **~er** *m.* pursuer; persecutor. **~ung** *f.* pursuit; persecution; prosecution. **~ungswahn** *m.* persecution mania.

ver'frachten *v.t.* to charter; to load *or* ship (goods).

verfremd-en *v.t.* to alienate. **~ung** *f.* alienation.

ver'früht *a.* premature.

ver'füg-bar *a.* available. **~en** *v.t.* to decree, ordain, order, arrange. *v.i.* **~en über** to dispose of, be master of, have at one's disposal. *v.r.* to betake oneself (to), proceed (to). **~ung** *f.* order, instruction, arrangement; disposal; (*leg.*) enactment; *zur ~ung stellen* to place at one's disposal.

ver'führ-en *v.t.* to induce, prevail upon, entice, tempt; to seduce. **~er** *m.* tempter; seducer. **~erisch** *a.* tempting, seductive, alluring. **~ung** *f.* temptation; seduction.

ver'füttern *v.t.* to use as fodder.

Vergabe *f.* allocation.

ver'gaffen *v.r.* to fall in love (with).

ver'gällen *v.t.* to embitter; to mar; to make loathsome; (*chem.*) to denature.

vergalo'ppieren *v.r.* to make a blunder.

ver'gangen *a.* past, last, bygone. **~heit** *f.* the past; (*gram.*) past tense.

ver'gänglich *a.* transitory, transient, fleeting; perishable. **~keit** *f.* transitoriness; perishableness.

ver'gas-en *v.t.* to gasify; to gas; (*motor.*) to carburet. **~er** *m.* carburettor. **~ermotor** *m.* petrol engine.

ver'geb-en *v.t.* to give away, dispose of; to confer, bestow upon; to give in marriage; to forgive, pardon; to misdeal (cards); *Auftrag* **~en** to commission; *sich etwas* **~en** to degrade oneself; **~en sein** to be engaged, have a previous engagement. **~ens** *adv.* in vain, vainly. **~lich** *a.* vain, idle, futile. **~ung** *f.* bestowal; giving (of work); placing (of order); appointing (to office); pardon, forgiveness.

ver'gegenwärtigen *v.t.* to represent, figure. *v.r.* to imagine, realize.

ver'gehen *vws.i.* to go away; to pass, elapse; to stop, disappear, go; to pine, waste away; to perish, die; *~ vor* to die of. *v.r.* to trespass, offend (against); injure; to assault. *subst. n.* offence, crime; sin; transgression.

ver'geistigen *v.t.* to spiritualize.

ver'gelt-en *v.t.* to repay, pay back, return; to reward; to render; to retaliate. **~ung** *f.* requital, return, recompense; retaliation, reprisal. **~ungswaffe** *f.* flying bomb, V 1.

vergesellschaften *v.t.* to socialize; to nationalize.

ver'gess-en *v.t. st.* to forget; to neglect. **~enheit** *f.* oblivion. **~(ß)lich** *a.* forgetful. **~(ß)lichkeit** *f.* forgetfulness.

ver'geud-en *v.t.* to waste, squander, dissipate. **~er** *m.* spendthrift. **~ung** *f.* squandering; waste, wastefulness; extravagance.

verge'waltig-en *v.t.* to offer violence, use force; to rape, violate. **~ung** *f.* assault; rape; violation.

ver'gewissern *v.r.* to make sure of, ascertain.

ver'gießen *v.t.* to shed; to spill.

ver'gift-en *v.t.* to poison. **~ung** *f.* poisoning; (*gas*) contamination.

ver'gilbt *a.* yellowed.

Ver'gißmeinnicht n. (-s, -e) forget-me-not.

ver'gittern v.t. to enclose with lattice-work; to grate up, wire in.

ver'glast a. glazed.

Ver'gleich m. (-s, -e) comparison; agreement, arrangement; settlement, composition. ~bar a. comparable. ~en v.t. to compare; to collate, check; to adjust, settle; sich ~en mit to come to terms with. ~sverfahren n. adjustment procedure; (leg.) settlement sub judice. ~sweise adv. by way of comparison. ~swert m. relative value.

ver-'gletschern vws.i. to turn into glacier-ice. ~'glimmen vws.i. to cease glowing, go out, die. ~'glühen vws.i. to cease glowing; to die out.

ver'gnüg-en v.t. to amuse. v.r. to enjoy oneself, delight (in). subst. n. pleasure, fun; diversion; amusement. ~t a. pleased, glad; joyous, gay, cheerful. ~ung f. pleasure, amusement, recreation. ~ungsreise f. pleasure trip. ~ungssüchtig a. pleasure-seeking, pleasure-loving.

ver'gold-en v.t. to gild. ~er m. gilder. ~ung f. gilding.

ver'gönnen v.t. to allow; not to grudge.

ver'gotten v.t. to deify.

ver'götter-n v.t. to deify; to idolize, adore, worship. ~ung f. deification; idolizing, worship.

ver'graben v.t. to bury, hide in the ground.

ver'grämt a. care-worn.

ver'greifen v.r. to touch by mistake; to touch the wrong note; sich ~ an to seize hold of, violate; to steal.

ver'greisen vws.i. to become senile; to decay.

ver'griffen a. sold out; out of print.

ver'gröbern v.t. to reproduce too crudely.

ver'größer-n v.t. to enlarge; to increase; to extend; to magnify; (fig.) to aggravate; to exaggerate. ~ung f. enlargement; increase; extension; exaggeration. ~ungsapparat m. enlarging camera.

~ungsglas n. magnifying glass.

Ver'günstigung f. (-, -en) privilege, favour; concession; reduction (in price).

ver'güt-en v.t. to compensate, indemnify; to refund, pay back; to refine (metal). ~ung f. compensation, indemnification; reimbursement; allowance.

ver'haft-en v.t. to arrest, take into custody, give in charge; ~et sein (fig.) to be dependent on, be closely connected with. ~ung f. arrest; capture. ~ungsbefehl m. warrant (of arrest).

ver'hageln vws.i. to be damaged by hail.

ver'hallen vws.i. to die or fade away.

ver'halt-en v.t. to keep back, stop, retain; to restrain, suppress. v.r. to be, be the case; to stand; to behave, keep; (math.) to be in the ratio of; sich ~en zu to be in proportion to. subst. n. behaviour, conduct; attitude. ~ungsweise f. (typical) behaviour. ~ungsmaßregeln f.pl. rules of conduct; instructions, orders.

Ver'hältnis n. (-ses, -se) relation, rate, ratio; proportion; love-affair, liaison; mistress; (pl.) circumstances, condition, situation. ~mäßig a. relative, comparative; proportional. ~widrig a. disproportionate. ~wort n. preposition. ~zahl f. proportional figure.

ver'hand-eln v.i. to negotiate, parley; to plead, try (a case). v.t. to discuss; to sell, barter away, dispose of. ~lung f. negotiation; transaction; discussion; pleading, trial, hearing. ~lungstermin m. day fixed for trial.

ver'häng-en v.t. to cover; to inflict (punishment), impose (a penalty); mit ~tem Zügel at full speed. ~nis n. fate, destiny; unseliges ~nis disaster. ~nisvoll a. fatal, fateful; disastrous.

ver'härmt a. care-worn.

ver'harren v.i. to remain; to persist (in); to hold out, persevere.

ver'harscht a. (of wound) closed, healed; crusted (with snow).

ver'härt-en v.t. & r. to harden, grow hard. **∼ung** f. hardening; callosity; hardness.

ver'haspeln v.r. to tangle up; (fig.) to break down or get muddled (in speech).

ver'haßt a. hated, hateful, odious.

ver'hätscheln v.t. to spoil, coddle, pamper.

Ver'hau m. (-s, -e) abat(t)is.

ver'hauen v.t. to thrash. v.r. to blunder.

ver'heben v.r. to strain oneself.

ver'heer-en v.t. to devastate, lay waste. **∼end** a. devastating; (colloq.) awful. **∼ung** f. devastation.

ver'hehlen v.t. to hide, conceal.

ver'heilen vvs.i. to heal up.

ver'heimlich-en v.t. to conceal, keep secret. **∼ung** f. concealment.

ver'heirat-en v.t. to marry, give in marriage. v.r. to marry, get married. **∼ung** f. marriage.

ver'heiß-en v.t. to promise. **∼ung** f. promise. **∼ungsvoll** a. promising.

ver'helfen v.i. to help (a person) to get.

ver'herrlich-en v.t. to glorify. **∼ung** f. glorification.

ver'hetzen v.t. to stir up, instigate. **∼hexen** v.t. to bewitch, enchant. **∼himmeln** v.t. to praise up to the skies. **∼hindern** v.t. to hinder, prevent. **∼hinderung** f. hindrance, impediment.

ver'hohlen a. hidden, concealed.

ver'höhn-en v.t. to deride, jeer gibe. **∼ung** f. derision, mockery.

verhökern v.t. (colloq.) to sell (dirt-cheap).

Ver'hör n. (-s, -e) examination, trial. **∼en** v.t. to examine, interrogate. v.r. to hear wrongly, misunderstand (words).

ver'hüll-en v.t. to cover, veil; to wrap up; to disguise. **∼ung** f. covering, veiling; disguise.

ver-'hundertfachen v.t. to centuple. **∼hungern** vvs.i. to die of hunger, starve. **∼hunzen** v.t. to spoil, bungle. **∼hüten** v.t. to prevent, ward off; to preserve

(from). **∼hütten** v.t. to work, smelt (ores). **∼hütung** f. prevention. **∼smittel** n. preventive; prophylactic; contraceptive. **∼hutzelt** a. shrivelled, wizened.

verinnerlicht a. deep-feeling.

ver'irr-en v.r. to lose one's way, go astray. **∼ung** f. losing one's way; aberration; error, mistake.

ver'jagen v.t. to drive away, expel.

ver'jähr-en vvs.i. to become superannuated, grow obsolete. **∼t** a. old, obsolete; superannuated; prescriptive. **∼ung** f. superannuation; prescription; (leg.) limitation.

ver-'jubeln, **∼juxen** vv.t. to squander, (sl.) to blue (money).

ver'juden vvs.i. to become Jewish; to come under Jewish influence.

ver'jüng-en v.t. to rejuvenate; to taper. v.r. to be rejuvenated, grow young again; to taper; in **∼tem Maßstab** on a reduced scale. **∼ung** f. rejuvenescence; tapering.

ver'kalk-en vvs.i. to calcify; (chem.) to calcine. **∼ung** f. calcification; calcination; (med.) arteriosclerosis.

ver-kalku'lieren v.r. to miscalculate. **∼kappen** v.t. to disguise. **∼kapseln** v.r. to become encysted. **∼katert** a. suffering from a hang-over.

Ver'kauf m. (-s) sale. **∼en** v.t. & r. to sell; zu **∼en** for sale. **∼spreis** m. selling price. **∼sschlager** m. best-seller.

Ver'käuf-er m. seller; shop assistant, salesman. **∼erin** f. shop girl, shop assistant, saleswoman. **∼lich** a. saleable; for sale.

Ver'kehr m. (-s) traffic; (train, &c.) service; trade, commerce; communication; connexion; circulation; (social or sexual) intercourse. **∼sader** f. arterial road. **∼sampel** f. traffic light. **∼sandrang** m. rush. **∼sinsel** f. island. **∼sminister** m. Minister of Transport. **∼sordner** m. traffic warden. **∼sreich** a. crowded, pointsman. **∼sschwach** a. slack (period). **∼ssicherheit** f. road

safety. ~ssignal n. traffic signal.
~stark a. busy; ~starke Zeit
rush hours. ~stockung a., ~störung f. traffic block; break-down.
~sunfall m. street accident. ~swesen n. traffic, (train-)service.
~zeichen n. traffic sign, road
sign.

ver'kehr-en v.t. to the wrong
way, turn upside down; to invert; to transform, convert,
change (into); to pervert. v.i. to
frequent, visit; (of buses, &c.) to
ply (between), run regularly;
~en mit to associate with, see a
good deal of; to have sexual intercourse with. ~t a. inverted,
upside down, reversed; wrong;
absurd. ~theit f. absurdity, folly.

ver'kenn-en v.t. to fail to recognize;
to mistake, misunderstand, misjudge; to undervalue. ~ung f.
mistaking, misunderstanding;
lack of appreciation.

ver'kett-en v.t. to chain or link
together. ~ung f. chain, concatenation; coincidence.

ver'ketzern v.t. to calumniate.

ver'kitten v.t. to cement; to fasten
with putty.

ver'klagen v.t. to accuse; to sue,
bring an action against.

ver'klär-en v.t. to make bright; to
transfigure, to glorify. ~t a.
radiant; transfigured; glorified.
~ung f. transfiguration; glorification.

ver-'klatschen v.t. to slander; to
inform against.

ver'klausu'lieren
v.t. to stipulate, limit by provisos.

~kleben v.t. to paste over; to
plaster up; to glue, gum up; to
stick together.

ver'kleid-en v.t. to disguise, mask,
camouflage; to wainscot; to
revet; to line (with planks). ~ung
f. disguise, camouflage; wainscoting; revetment.

ver'kleiner-n v.t. to make smaller;
to diminish; to reduce; (fig.) to
belittle. ~ung f. diminution; reduction. ~ungswort n. diminutive.

ver'kleistern v.t. to paste up; to
patch up.

ver'klingen vws.i. to die away.

Ver'knappung f. (-) shortage,
scarcity.

ver-'kneifen v.r. to forgo; to stifle.
~kniffen a. wry; pinched. ~'-
knöchern vws.i. to ossify; (fig.)
to become narrow-minded or
pedantic. ~'knorpeln vws.i. to
become cartilaginous. ~'knoten
v.t. to knot, tie up; to knit together.

ver'knüpf-en v.t. to tie, bind, connect, join, link, unite; to
entail, involve. ~ung f. connexion; combination.

ver'kohlen vws.i. to carbonize. v.t.
(joc.) to hoax.

ver'kommen vws.i. to be ruined;
to become bad; to come down in
the world. a. ruined; gone to the
bad; depraved, degenerate. ~heit f. depravity; degeneracy.

ver'korken v.t. to cork, cork up.

verkorksen v.t. to bungle, upset.

ver-'körper-n v.t. to embody; to
personify; to incarnate. ~ung
f. embodiment; personification;
incarnation.

ver-'köstigen v.t. to board, feed.
~krachen vws.i. to go bankrupt, fail. v.r. to fall out (with).
~krampft a. cramped. ~kriechen v.r. to hide, creep away. ~
krümeln v.t. to crumble away;
to fritter away. v.r. (fig.) to make
off, disappear.

ver'krümm-t a. crooked, bent. ~
ung f. crookedness; curvature.

ver'krüppelt a. crippled; deformed;
stunted.

ver'krustet a. covered with a crust.

ver'kühlen v.r. to catch cold.

ver'kümmern vws.i. to become
stunted, atrophy, shrink, shrivel
up; to pine away; to perish. v.t.
to spoil, embitter.

ver'künd-en, ~igen vv.t. to announce, make known; to publish,
proclaim; to pronounce (sentence); to preach (the gospel).
~(ig)ung f. announcement; publication, proclamation; preaching; Mariä ~igung Annunciation or Lady-day.

ver'kuppeln v.t. to couple; to procure, pander.

ver'kürz-en *v.t.* to shorten; to diminish, lessen; to abridge; to beguile (time); to curtail, cut. **~ung** *f.* shortening; foreshortening.

ver'lachen *v.t.* to laugh at, deride.

ver'lad-en *v.t.* to load (on to); to ship; to entrain. **~ung** *f.* loading, shipping, entraining.

Ver'lag (-k) *m.* (-s, -e) publication; publishing-firm *or* -house. **~ert** *a.* displaced; (*med.*) dislocated. **~sartikel** *m.* publication. **~sbuchhandel** *m.* publishing business *or* trade. **~sbuchhändler** *m.* publisher. **~skatalog** *m.* publisher's catalogue. **~srecht** *n.* copyright. **~szeichen** *n.* publisher's mark *or* monogram.

ver'langen *v.t.* to demand; to require; to desire. *v.i.* **~ nach** to long for, hanker after. *subst. n.* demand; request; desire, wish; longing; *auf* **~** by request, on demand; **~ tragen nach** to long for.

ver'länger-n *v.t.* to lengthen; to extend, prolong. **~ung** *f.* lengthening; extension, prolonging.

ver'langsamen *v.t.* to slow down, retard.

ver'läppern *v.t.* to fritter away.

Ver'laß *m.* *auf ihn ist kein* **~** he cannot be relied on.

ver'lassen *v.t.* to leave, quit; to forsake, abandon, desert. *v.r.* to rely *or* depend (upon). *a.* forsaken; lonely; deserted. **~heit** *f.* loneliness.

ver'läßlich *a.* reliable.

Ver'laub *m.* *mit* **~** by your leave, with your permission.

Ver'lauf *m.* course, lapse; expiration; progress, development; *nach* **~** *von* after the lapse of; *einen schlimmen* **~** *nehmen* to take a bad turn.

ver'laufen *vws.i.* to pass, elapse; to take its course, proceed, develop, turn out. *v.r.* to take a wrong road, get lost; to be scattered, disperse; to run off. *a.* stray, lost.

ver'laut-baren *v.t.* to make known, notify. **~en** *v. impers.* to become known; *es* **~et** it is said; **~en** *lassen* to give to understand,

hint.

ver'leb-en *v.t.* to spend, pass. **~t** *a.* worn out; decrepit.

ver'legen¹ *v.t.* to lay somewhere else, move to another place; to transfer; to mislay, put in a wrong place; to locate (a scene); to put off, postpone; to adjourn (a meeting); to obstruct, bar; to publish, bring out. *v.r. sich* **~** *auf* to take up, go in for; to apply *or* devote oneself to.

ver'legen² *a.* embarrassed, self-conscious, confused; *um etwas* **~** *sein* to be at a loss for; *um Geld* **~** *sein* to be short of money. **~heit** *f.* embarrassment; difficulty, dilemma.

Ver'leger *m.* (-s, -) publisher.

Ver'legung *f.* transfer, removal; postponement, adjournment.

ver'leiden *v.t.* to disgust (one with), spoil.

Ver'leih *m.* hire; distribution. **~en** *v.t.* to lend out, let out; to give; to confer, bestow, endow, grant; to invest with. **~er** *m.* lender. **~ung** *f.* lending; conferring; grant; investiture.

ver'leiten *v.t.* to mislead; to lead astray, seduce; to induce.

ver'lernen *v.t.* to unlearn, forget (how to).

ver'lesen *v.t.* to read out; to pick. *v.r.* to make a slip in reading.

ver'letz-bar, **~lich** *aa.* vulnerable; susceptible. **~en** *v.t.* to hurt, injure; to offend; to infringe (law). **~end** *a.* offensive. **~ung** *f.* injury; offence; infringement, violation.

ver'leugn-en *v.t.* to deny, disavow; to renounce; *sich* **~en** *lassen* to refuse to see visitors, to be 'not at home'. **~ung** *f.* denial; disavowal; renunciation.

ver'leumd-en *v.t.* to calumniate, slander. **~er** *m.* slanderer. **~erisch** *a.* slanderous, defamatory. **~ung** *f.* calumny, slander, defamation, libel.

ver'lieb-en *v.r.* to fall in love (with). **~t** *a.* in love; enamoured; amorous. **~theit** *f.* amorousness, being in love.

ver'lieren *v.t. & i. st.* to lose; to

waste (time); to shed (leaves, &c.); to give up (hope). *v.r.* to lose one's way, get lost; to disperse; (*fig.*) to disappear.

Ver′lies *n.* (-es, -e) dungeon.

ver′lob-en *v.t.* to affiance (to), betroth (to). *v.r.* to get engaged (to). ~**te(r)** *m.* fiancé. ~**te** *f.* fiancée. ~**ung** *f.*, **Verlöbnis** *n.* engagement, betrothal.

ver′lock-en *v.t.* to entice, allure, tempt. ~**end** *a.* enticing, tempting. ~**ung** *f.* enticement, allurement, temptation.

ver′logen *a.* mendacious, untruthful. ~**heit** *f.* mendacity, untruthfulness.

ver′lohnen *v. impers.* **es verlohnt (sich) der Mühe** it is worth while.

ver′loren *a.* lost; lonely; ~ **e Eier** devilled eggs; *der* ~ **e Sohn** the Prodigal Son; ~ **gehen** *vws.i.* to get up for lost. ~ **gehen** *vws.i.* to get lost, be lost.

ver′löschen *v.t.* to extinguish. *vws.i.* to go out.

ver′los-en *v.t.* to dispose of by lot, raffle. ~**ung** *f.* lottery, raffle.

ver′löten *v.t.* to solder.

ver′-lottern, ~**lumpen** *vv.t.* to waste, squander; to ruin. *vws.i.* to go to the dogs.

Ver′lust *m.* (-es, -e) loss, privation; bereavement; waste; leak, escape (of gas); forfeiture; (*pl.*) casualties. ~**ig** *a.* ~**ig gehen** to lose, forfeit. ~**liste** *f.* list of casualties.

ver′-machen *v.t.* to bequeath. ~**mächtnis** *n.* will, testament; bequest, legacy.

ver′mähl-en *v.t.* to marry, give in marriage. *v.r.* to marry, get married (to). ~**ung** *f.* marriage, wedding.

ver′mahnen *v.t.* to admonish, warn.

ver′male′deien *v.t.* to curse. ~**′manschen** *v.t.* to make a mess of. ~**′massung** *f.* submerging of individuality. ~**′mauern** *v.t.* to wall up.

ver′mehr-en *v.t. & r.* to increase, multiply, augment; to enlarge; to propagate. ~**ung** *f.* increase, multiplying; propagation.

ver′meid-en *v.t.* to avoid, elude,

evade; to escape (from). ~**lich** *a.* avoidable. ~**ung** *f.* avoidance.

ver′mein-en *v.t.* to think, believe, suppose, imagine. ~**tlich** *a.* supposed, alleged; pretended; imaginary.

ver′melden *v.t.* to announce, notify, inform. ~**mengen** *v.t.* to mix, mix up. ~**menschlichen** *v.t.* to represent in a human form; to humanize.

Ver′merk *m.* (-s, -e) note, entry. ~**en** *v.t.* to observe, remark; to note down; **übel** ~**en** to take amiss.

ver′mess-en *v.t.* to measure; to survey. *v.r.* to measure wrong; (*fig.*) to dare (to), presume (to). *a.* bold; presumptuous; impudent. ~**enheit** *f.* boldness, daring, audacity; presumption; insolence. ~**ung** *f.* measurement; survey (-ing).

ver′miet-en *v.t.* to let; to hire out ~**er** *m.* landlord. ~**ung** *f.* letting; hiring out.

ver′minder-n *v.t.* to lessen, diminish, decrease; to impair; to reduce, abate. ~**ung** *f.* lessening, diminution, decrease; reduction.

ver′misch-en *v.t.* to mix, mingle; to blend. ~**t** *a.* mixed; miscellaneous. ~**ung** *f.* mixing, mixture; alloy.

ver′missen *v.t.* to miss; *vermißt werden* to be missing; to be greatly missed.

ver′mitt-eln *v.t.* to obtain, secure, get; to arrange, establish; to bring about, negotiate, mediate. ~**els**, ~**elst** *prepp.* by means of, through. ~**ler** *m.* mediator; agent; go-between. ~**lung** *f.* procuring; supplying, providing, finding; mediation, negotiation; intervention; intercession. ~**lungsstelle** *f.* agency; (telephone) exchange, operator.

ver′möbeln *v.t.* (*joc.*) to thrash.

ver′modern *vws.i.* to mould, rot, decay.

ver′möge *prep.* by virtue of, by dint of.

ver′mögen *v.t.* to be able, have the power (to do); to have influence (over); to induce, prevail upon (one to do a thing). *subst. n.* ability, power; capacity, faculty; fortune, means, wealth, property. ~d *a.* well off; wealthy, rich. ~s-abgabe *f.* capital levy. ~steuer *f.* property tax. ~zuwachs *m.* increment value.

ver'morscht *a.* rotten.

ver'mottet *a.* moth-eaten.

ver'mummen *v.t.* to muffle up, wrap up; to disguise.

ver'mut-en *v.t.* to suppose, presume, suspect. ~lich *a.* presumable. probable. *adv.* probably; I suppose. ~ung *f.* supposition, conjecture, surmise, guesswork.

ver'nachlässig-en *v.t.* to neglect. ~ung *f.* neglect(ing).

ver-'nageln *v.t.* to nail up. ~-'nähen *v.t.* to sew up. ~'narben *vws.i.* to heal up. ~'narren *v.r.* to become infatuated (with). ~-'naschen *v.t.* to spend (money) on sweets.

ver'nehm-en *v.t.* to perceive, become aware of; to learn, understand; to hear; (*leg.*) to interrogate, examine; *sich ~en lassen* to speak, declare, express an opinion. *subst. n. dem ~nach* from what we hear. ~lich *a.* audible, distinct. ~ung *f.* interrogation, examination, trial.

ver'neig-en *v.r.* to bow; to curtsy. ~ung *f.* bow; curtsy.

ver'nein-en *v.t.* to answer in the negative; to deny, disavow. ~end *a.* negative. ~ung *f.* negation; denial; negative.

ver'nicht-en *v.t.* to annihilate, destroy. ~ung *f.* annihilation, destruction; extermination.

ver'nickeln *v.t.* to plate with nickel.

ver'nieten *v.t.* to rivet.

Ver'nunft *f.* (-) reason; understanding; intelligence; good sense, judgement; *~ annehmen* to listen to reason; *zur ~ bringen* to bring (one) to his senses. *~ehe f.* marriage arranged in view of position, money, &c.; *mariage de convenance.* ~gemäß *a.* reasonable; rational. ~widrig *a.* contrary to reason; unreasonable.

ver'nünft-eln *v.i.* to subtilize. ~-

ig *a.* reasonable; sensible, wise; rational.

ver'öd-en *vws.i.* to become desolate. ~et *a.* desolate, deserted, waste. ~ung *f.* desolation; devastation.

ver'öffentlich-en *v.t.* to publish. ~ung *f.* publication.

ver'ordn-en *v.t.* to order, decree; (*med.*) to prescribe. ~ung *f.* order, decree; prescription.

ver'pacht-en *v.t.* to lease. ~ung *f.* leasing.

ver'pack-en *v.t.* to pack up, wrap up. ~ung *f.* packing up, wrapping up; packing (material).

ver'päppeln *v.t.* to pamper, spoil.

ver'passen *v.t.* to miss (train); to let slip (opportunity); to fit *or* adjust (clothing).

ver-'patzen *v.t.* to bungle, spoil. ~-'pesten *v.t.* to poison, infect, taint. ~'petzen *v.t.* to inform against, tell tales.

ver'pfänd-en *v.t.* to pawn, pledge; to mortgage. ~ung *f.* pawning, pledging; mortgaging.

ver'pflanz-en *v.t.* to transplant. ~-ung *f.* transplantation.

ver'pfleg-en *v.t.* to feed, board; to cater for. ~ung *f.* feeding, board, maintenance; food; food supply; (*mil.*) messing; (*pl.*) rations. ~-ungsamt *n.* food office.

ver'pflicht-en *v.t.* to oblige, bind; to engage. *v.r.* to bind *or* commit oneself (to do a thing). ~ung *f.* obligation, duty; commitment, engagement.

ver'pfuschen *v.t.* to make a mess of, bungle.

ver'pimpeln *v.t.* to coddle.

ver-'plappern, ~'plaudern *vv.r.* to let the cat out of the bag; to give oneself away.

ver'plempern *v.t.* to waste (money, &c.).

ver'pönt *a.* in bad taste; tabooed.

ver-'prassen *v.t.* to waste, dissipate. ~provian'tieren *v.t.* to supply, provision. ~prügeln *v.t.* to thrash soundly. ~puffen *vws.i.* to explode; (*fig.*) to produce no effect (upon), be lost (upon). ~-'pulvern *v.t.* to waste (money). ~pumpen *v.t.* to lend. ~pup-

pen *v.r.* to change into a chrysalis.
~pusten *v.r.* to recover breath.
~putzen *v.t.* to plaster; to rough-cast; (*colloq.*) to squander (money).
ver'qualmt *a.* filled with smoke.
ver'quer *adv. das geht mir* ~ that upsets my plans.
ver'quick-en *v.t.* to amalgamate. **~ung** *f.* amalgamation, fusion.
ver'quollen *a.* bloated (face), swollen; warped (wood).
ver'ramme(l)n *v.t.* to bar, barricade.
ver'ramschen *v.t.* (*commerc. sl.*) to sell below cost price.
ver'rannt *a.* adhering stubbornly (to); obstinate. **~heit** *f.* stubbornness, stubborn adherence (to).
Ver'rat *m.* (-es) treason; betrayal; treachery. **~en** *v.t.* to betray; to disclose, reveal, show.
Ver'räter *m.* (-s, -) traitor; betrayer, informer. **~ei** *f.* treason; treachery. **~in** *f.* traitress. **~isch** *a.* treacherous; perfidious, faithless; revealing; suspicious.
ver'rauchen *vns.i.* to go up in smoke; to evaporate; (*fig.*) to pass away. *v.t.* to spend (money) on tobacco.
ver'räuchert *a.* filled or black with smoke.
ver'rauschen *vns.i.* (*fig.*) to die away.
ver'rechn-en *v.t.* to reckon up, charge to account. *v.r.* to make a mistake, miscalculate. **~ung** *f.* reckoning up, charging to account, settling of account. **~ungsscheck** *m.* non-negotiable cheque; crossed cheque.
ver'recken *vns.i.* (*vulg.*) to die, perish.
ver'regnen *v.t.* to spoil by rain.
ver'reisen *vns.i.* to go on a journey, go away.
ver'reißen *v.t.* to pull to pieces, criticize sharply.
ver'renk-en *v.t.* to dislocate, sprain. **~ung** *f.* dislocation, sprain.
ver'rennen *v.r.* (*fig.*) to adhere stubbornly (to).
ver'richt-en *v.t.* to execute, do, perform, accomplish. **~ung** *f.*

execution, doing, performance; function; duty, work.
ver-'riegeln *v.t.* to bolt, bar, lock; (*mil.*) to cut off, barricade. **~ringern** *v.t.* to diminish, lessen, reduce. **~rinnen** *vns.i.* to run off or away; to elapse. **~rohen** *vns.i.* to become brutal. **~rosten** *vns.i.* to rust. **~rotten** *vns.i.* to rot.
ver'rucht *a.* infamous, vile; atrocious. **~heit** *f.* infamy; villainy; atrocity.
ver'rück-en *v.t.* to displace, shift, remove. **~t** *a.* mad, crazy; *einen* ~ *machen* to drive one mad. **~te(r)** *m.* lunatic, madman. **~theit** *f.* madness, craziness.
Ver'ruf *m. in* ~ *kommen* to get into bad odour. **~en** *v.t.* to condemn, decry. *a.* ill-reputed, notorious, disreputable.
ver'rühren *v.t.* to stir, stir into.
ver'rußt *a.* sooty.
Vers (fɛrs) *m.* (-es, -e) verse; stanza, strophe; *sich keinen* ~ *machen können aus* not to make head or tail of. **~bau** *m.* versification. **~fuß** *m.* metrical foot. **~lehre** *f.* prosody, metrics. **~zählung** *f.* scanning, scansion.
ver'sacken *vns.i.* to sink, give way; to get bogged or ditched.
ver'sag-en *v.t.* to deny, refuse. *v.i.* to fail, break down; to miss fire. *v.r.* to forgo, deny oneself; **~t** *sein* to have another engagement. *subst. n.* failure, break-down. **~er** *m.* failure, unsuccessful person; (*mil.*) misfire; dud shell. **~ung** *f.* denial, refusal.
Ver'salien *pl.* capital letters.
ver'salzen *v.t.* to oversalt; (*fig.*) to spoil.
ver'samm-eln *v.t.* to assemble, bring together, collect; to convene. *v.r.* to meet, assemble. **~lung** *f.* assembly, meeting, gathering.
Ver'sand *m.* (-es) dispatch; export (-ation). **~geschäft** *n.* export business; distributing house.
ver'sanden *vns.i.* to get choked up with sand; (*fig.*) to break down, stick.

Ver'satz *m.* pledging, pawning. **~amt** *n.* pawnshop. **~stück** *n.* (*theatr.*) set (scene).

ver'sauern *vws.i.* (*fig.*) to become morose.

ver'saufen *v.t.* (*vulg.*) to spend or waste on drink.

ver'säum-en *v.t.* to neglect, omit; to miss. **~nis** *f. & n.* neglect, omission; loss of time, delay.

ver-'schachern *v.t.* to barter away. **~'schaffen** *v.t.* to procure, get, obtain. **~'schalen** *v.t.* to board up or over, cover with planks. **~'schämt** *a.* bashful, shamefaced. **~'schandeln** *v.t.* to spoil, disfigure.

ver'schanz-en *v.t.* to entrench.. *v.r.* to shelter (behind). **~t** *a.* dug in. **~ung** *f.* entrenchment.

ver'schärf-en *v.t.* to aggravate, increase, sharpen, make worse; to tighten up (regulations); to intensify. **~ung** *f.* increase, sharpening; tightening up; intensification.

ver'scharren *v.t.* to bury.

ver'scheiden *vws.i.* to die, expire. *subst. n.* death.

ver-'schenken *v.t.* to give away, make a present of. **~'scherzen** *v.t.* to lose, forfeit. **~'scheuchen** *v.t.* to scare away, drive off; (*fig.*) to banish.

ver'schick-en *v.t.* to send away, dispatch, forward; to transport; to deport (criminals). **~ung** *f.* dispatch; transportation; evacuation.

Ver'schiebebahnhof *m.* marshalling yard.

ver'schieb-en *v.t.* to shift, displace; to shunt (train); to postpone, put off; (*sl.*) to sell through the black market. *v.r.* to get out of place. **~ung** *f.* displacement; postponement.

verschieden[1] *pp.* of verscheiden.

ver'schieden[2] *a.* different (from), distinct (from); (*pl.*) divers, sundry, various. **~artig** *a.* various. heterogeneous. **~erlei** *indecl. a.* of various kinds, divers. **~tarbig** *a.* variegated. **~heit** *f.* difference; diversity, variety. **~tlich** *a.* different; repeated. *adv.* repeatedly, more than once.

ver'schießen *v.t.* to use up (ammunition). *vws.i.* to fade, lose colour.

ver'schiffen *v.t.* to ship; to export.

ver'schimmeln *vws.i.* to get mouldy.

ver'schlacken *vws.i.* to be reduced to slag, be turned into dross.

ver'schlafen *v.t.* to miss or neglect by sleeping; to spend in sleeping; to sleep too long, oversleep. *a.* sleepy, drowsy.

Ver'schlag *m.* wooden partition; shed; box.

ver'schlagen *v.t.* to nail up; *mit Brettern* ~ to board up; to lose one's place (in book); to drive (ship) out of her course; to drive (on to); ~ *werden* to land (in); *einem den Atem* ~ to take away one's breath. *v.i.* *es verschlägt nichts* it doesn't matter. *a.* lukewarm; (*fig.*) sly, cunning, crafty. **~heit** *f.* slyness, cunning, craftiness.

ver'schlammen *vws.i.* to get choked with mud; to silt up.

ver'schlampen *v.t.* to bring into disorder; to lose; to take no care of. *vws.i.* to neglect oneself.

ver'schlechter-n *v.t.* to make worse, impair. *v.r.* to deteriorate, get worse. **~ung** *f.* deterioration.

ver'schleier-n *v.t.* to veil; to conceal; *Bilanz* ~n to cook accounts (*sl.*). **~t** *a.* hazy, slightly clouded (sky); husky (voice); veiled (glance). **~ung** *f.* veiling; concealment.

ver'schleifen *v.t.* to slur.

ver'schleimen *v.t.* to choke up with mucus.

Ver'schleiß *m.* (-es) wear and tear; retail trade. **~en** *v.t.* to wear out; to sell by retail.

ver'schlemmen *v.t.* to squander in feasting.

ver'schlepp-en *v.t.* to carry off; to deport; to take to a wrong place, misplace; to spread (disease); to protract, delay, put off. **~ung** *f.* carrying off; deportation; spreading; procrastination, obstruction.

ver'schleuder-n *v.t.* to waste, dissipate; to throw away, sell dirt-cheap. **~ung** f. wasting, squandering; selling at ruinous prices.

ver'schließen v.t. to shut; to lock; *sich einer Sache* **~** to keep aloof from a thing; to close one's mind to.

ver'schlimmer-n v.t. to make worse, aggravate. *v.r.* to get worse. **~ung** f. change for the worse, deterioration.

ver'schlingen v.t. to twist, intertwine, entangle; to devour, swallow up.

ver'schlissen a. worn-out, threadbare.

ver'schlossen a. closed; locked; (*fig.*) reserved, taciturn. **~heit** f. reserve, taciturnity.

ver'schlucken v.t. to swallow. *v.r.* to choke, swallow the wrong way.

Ver'schluß m. lock, fastener, zipper, clasp, seal, plug; (*phot.*) shutter; *unter* **~** under lock and key. **~laut** m. (*gram.*) plosive, stop. **~stück** n. plug, stopper.

ver'schlüsseln v.t. to (en)code.

ver'schmachten vws.i. to languish, pine away, die (of).

ver'schmähen v.t. to disdain, despise, scorn.

ver'schmelzen v.t. to melt, melt together, fuse; to blend; to amalgamate. *vws.i.* to melt, melt away; to blend, merge, coalesce.

ver'schmerzen v.t. to get over (the loss of); to put up with, make the best of.

ver'schmieren v.t. to smear, daub; to waste (paper) in writing; to cover with writing; (*chem.*) to lute.

ver'schmitzt a. wily, sly, cunning. **~heit** f. wiliness, slyness, cunning.

ver'schmutzt a. dirty, filthy.

Verschmutzung f. pollution.

ver'schnappen v.r. to give the show away.

ver'schnaufen v.r. to recover one's breath.

ver'schneiden v.t. to cut, clip, prune; to cut badly, spoil; to mix *or* adulterate (wine); to castrate.

ver'schneit a. snowed up, covered with snow.

Ver'schnitt m. mixed *or* adulterated wine; blend. **~ene(r)** m. eunuch.

ver'schnörkeln v.t. to adorn with flourishes.

ver'schnupft a. stuffed up (with a cold); (*fig.*) annoyed.

ver'schnüren v.t. to tie up, cord up; to lace.

ver'schollen a. lost, missing; long past, forgotten.

ver'schonen v.t. to spare; to exempt (from).

ver'schöner-n v.t. to beautify, embellish, adorn. **~ung** f. embellishment.

ver'schossen a. faded, discoloured; **~** *in* madly in love with, smitten.

ver'schränken v.t. to cross, fold (one's arms).

ver'schreiben v.t. to use up in writing; to order, write for; (*med.*) to prescribe; (*leg.*) to make over (to). *v.r.* to make a slip (in writing); (*fig.*) to sell oneself to; to set one's heart upon.

ver'schreien v.t. to decry. **~schroben** a. confused, intricate; queer, eccentric. **~'schrotten** v.t. to break up, scrap. **~'schrumpelt** a. wrinkled, shrivelled. **~'schüchtert** a. intimidated.

ver'schuld-en v.t. to be guilty of, commit; **~et** *sein* to be in debt. *subst.* n. fault. **~ung** f. fault, offence; indebtedness, being in debt.

ver'schütten v.t. to spill; to fill, fill up (with earth, &c.), bury; *es* **~** *bei* to get into someone's bad books.

ver'schwägert a. related by marriage.

ver'schweig-en v.t. to keep secret, conceal, suppress. **~ung** f. concealment, suppression.

ver'schwend-en v.t. to squander, waste, lavish. **~er** m. spendthrift; extravagant person. **~erisch** a. wasteful, prodigal, extravagant, lavish. **~ung** f. wastefulness, extravagance.

ver'schwiegen a. discreet, close, reticent. **~heit** f. secrecy; discretion; reticence.

ver'schwimmen vws.i. to dissolve, fade away; to grow hazy, become blurred.

ver'schwinden *vws.i.* to disappear, vanish, be lost. *subst. n.* disappearance.

ver-'schwistert *a.* (*fig.*) like brothers or sisters; closely united. **~'schwitzt** *a.* wet through (with perspiration); (*colloq.*) forgotten. **~schwommen** *a.* indistinct, vague.

ver-schwör-en *v.t.* to forswear, abjure. *v.r.* to conspire, plot; to protest with oaths. **~er** *m.* conspirator. **~ung** *f.* conspiracy, plot.

ver'sehen *v.t.* to provide, furnish, supply (with); to fill (post); to discharge, perform (duty); to administer last sacrament; to keep, look after (house); to overlook, neglect. *v.r.* to make a mistake; *sich einer Sache ~* to expect, look for; *ehe man sich's versieht* unexpectedly, suddenly. *subst. n.* oversight; mistake, slip. **~t-lich** *adv.* inadvertently, by mistake.

ver'sehr-en *v.t.* to hurt, injure. **~t** *a.* disabled. **~tengeld** *n.* disablement pension.

ver'send-en *v.t.* to send off, dispatch, forward; to export, ship. **~ung** *f.* dispatch, forwarding; exportation; transport.

ver'sengen *v.t.* to singe; to burn, scorch; to parch.

ver'senk-en *v.t.* to sink; to lower, let down; to submerge. *v.r.* to become absorbed (in). **~ung** *f.* sinking; (*theatr.*) trap-door.

ver'sessen *a.* **~** *auf* bent on, mad about.

ver'setz-en *v.t.* to put (into some state), set; to displace; to transplant (tree); to transfer (official); to move (pupil up); (*typ.*) to transpose; to pawn, pledge; to mix (with); to alloy; to give, deal (blow); (*colloq.*) to leave in the lurch. *v.i.* to reply, rejoin. *v.r.* to imagine *or* place oneself (in a position). **~ung** *f.* transfer, transference; moving *or* transposition; mixing; alloy. **~ungs-zeichen** *n.* (*mus.*) accidental.

ver'seuch-en *v.t.* to infect, contaminate. **~ung** *f.* infection,
contamination.

ver'sicher-n *v.t.* to insure; to affirm, assert, aver; *sei ~t* be assured, depend on. *v.r.* to make sure of, ascertain. **~ung** *f.* insurance; assurance; affirmation. **~ungs-nehmer** *m.* insured person; policy holder. **~ungsprämie** *f.* insurance premium.

ver-'sickern *vws.i.* to trickle away. **~siegeln** *v.t.* to seal (up). **~siegen** *vws.i.* to dry up, be exhausted. **~silbern** *v.t.* to plate, silver over; to convert into money. **~sinken** *vws.i.* to sink, founder; to immerse. **~sinn-bildlichen** *v.t.* to symbolize. **~'sinnlichen** *v.t.* to render perceptible to the senses, illustrate. **~sippt** *a.* closely related. **~'sittlichen** *v.t.* to civilize.

ver'sklaven *v.t.* to enslave.

ver'soffen *a.* (*vulg.*) drunk, drunken.

ver'sohlen *v.t.* (*colloq.*) to thrash.

ver'söhn-en *v.t.* to reconcile, conciliate; to propitiate, appease. **~lich** *a.* forgiving, conciliatory. **~ung** *f.* reconciliation. **~ungstag** *m.* Day of Atonement.

ver'sonnen *a.* lost in thought.

ver'sorg-en *v.t.* to provide, supply, furnish (with); to provide for, maintain; to nurse, care for, look after. **~er** *m.* mainstay, support; bread-winner. **~ung** *f.* supply, provision; maintenance, care (for).

ver'sparen *v.t. sich etwas ~* to defer *or* put off something.

ver'spät-en *v.t.* to delay. *v.r.* to be late, be behind time. **~et** *a.* belated, late. **~ung** *f.* delay, lateness.

ver'speisen *v.t.* to eat up.

verspeku'lieren *v.r.* to lose by speculation; (*fig.*) to be out in one's calculations.

ver'sperren *v.t.* to block, obstruct; to close, lock up.

ver'spielen *v.t. & i.* to lose, gamble away; to spend in playing; *es bei einem ~* to lose a person's favour, get into a person's bad books.

versponnen *a.* (to be) wrapt up (in); dreamy.

ver'spott-en *v.t.* to deride, ridicule,

scoff at. ~ung *f.* derision, ridicule; scoffing.

ver'sprech-en *v.t.* to promise, bind oneself; to give promise of; *sich etwas ~en von* to expect much of. *v.r.* to make a slip of the tongue. *subst. n.*, ~ung *f.* promise.

ver'spreng-en *v.t.* to scatter, disperse. ~te(r) *m.* straggler; (*mil.*) man separated from his unit in action.

ver'spritzen *v.t.* to shed; to spill.

versprochenermaßen *adv.* as promised.

ver'spüren *v.t.* to feel, perceive, be aware of.

ver'staatlich-en *v.t.* to nationalize. ~t *a.* nationalized; taken over by the government. ~ung *f.* nationalization.

ver'städtern *vns.i.* to become urban in appearance, &c.

Ver'stand *m.* (-es) understanding, mind, intellect; brains, intelligence, sense; judgement; *den ~ verlieren* to go out of one's mind; *zu ~ kommen* to arrive at the age of discretion. ~esmensch *m.* matter-of-fact person. ~esschärfe *f.* sagacity.

ver'ständ-ig *a.* intelligent, sensible; prudent, cautious, wise. ~igen *v.t.* to inform. *v.r* to come to an understanding (with). ~igkeit *f.* (good) sense, insight, prudence. ~igung *f.* information; agreement, arrangement; understanding; (*tel.*) reception; quality of reception. ~lich *a.* intelligible; distinct, clear; comprehensible; *sich ~lich machen* to make oneself understood. ~lichkeit *f.* intelligibility; clearness. ~nis *n.* comprehension; understanding, sympathy; ~nis haben für to appreciate. ~nisinnig *a.* full of deep understanding. ~nislos *a.* devoid of understanding; unappreciative; imbecile. ~nisvoll *a.* understanding, sympathetic, appreciative.

ver'stärk-en *v.t.* to strengthen, reinforce; to intensify; to amplify. ~er *m.* amplifier. ~ung *f.* strengthening; reinforcement(s), support(s).

ver-'statten *v.t.* to allow, permit, grant. ~'stauben *vns.i.* to get dusty. ~'stauchen *v.t.* to sprain. ~'stauen *v.t.* to stow away.

Ver'steck *n.* (-s, -e) hiding-place. ~en *v.t.* to hide, conceal. ~spiel *n.* hide-and-seek. ~t *a.* hidden, concealed; (*fig.*) veiled, covert; secretive, sly; ~te Absichten ulterior motives.

ver'stehen *v.t. st.* to comprehend, understand; to hear; to see; to know (how); to know well; *zu ~ geben* to intimate (to one); *falsch ~ to* misunderstand; *Spaß ~* to see a joke; *was ~ Sie darunter?* what do you mean by it? *v.r.* to understand one another, agree; *sich von selbst ~* to be a matter of course, go without saying; *sich ~ auf* to be skilled in, understand, know well; *sich ~ zu* to accede, agree, consent to.

ver'steifen *v.t.* to stiffen; to strut, stay; *sich ~ auf* to insist upon, make a point of.

ver'steigen *v.r.* to lose one's way (in the mountains); (*fig.*) to go too far, have the presumption to, go so far as to.

ver'steiger-n *v.t.* to sell by auction. ~ung *f.* auction.

ver'steiner-n *v.t. & i.* to turn (in)to stone, petrify; to fossilize. ~ung *f.* petrifaction; fossil.

ver'stell-bar *a.* adjustable. ~en *v.t.* to change order *or* position (of a thing); to put in the wrong place; to block, bar; to disguise; *v.r.* to sham, feign. ~ung *f.* pretence, make-believe; disguise; dissimulation; hypocrisy.

ver'steuern *v.t.* to pay duty on.

ver'stiegen *a.* (*fig.*) high-flown, eccentric.

ver'stimm-en *v.t.* (*fig.*) to annoy, upset. ~t *a.* out of tune; upset (stomach); in a bad mood, cross. ~ung *f.* ill humour, bad temper; discord, ill feeling.

ver'stockt *a.* obdurate; impenitent, hardened; stubborn. ~heit *f.* obduracy; hardness of heart; stubbornness.

ver'stohlen *a.* stealthy, furtive, secret; surreptitious.

ver'stopf-en *v.t.* to block, stop up; (*med.*) to constipate. ~ung *f.* obstruction; stopping, stoppage; constipation.

ver'storben *a.* deceased, defunct, late.

ver'stört *a.* troubled, disconcerted; haggard, wild; disordered (mind). ~heit *f.* consternation, confusion, discomposure.

Ver'stoß *m.* offence; mistake, fault. ~en *v.t.* to reject, cast off, expel, put away. *v.i.* to offend (against), transgress. ~ene(r) *m.* outcast. ~ung *f.* rejection; expulsion; repudiation.

ver-'streben *v.t.* to strut, stay, brace. ~streichen *vws.i.* to pass, slip by, elapse. ~streuen *v.t.* to scatter, disperse. ~stricken *v.t.* (*fig.*) to ensnare. ~stümmeln *v.t.* to mutilate. ~stümmelung *f.* mutilation. ~stummen *vws.i.* to grow dumb; to become silent.

Ver'such (-x) *m.* (-s, -e) experiment, attempt; trial, test, practice. ~en *v.t.* to try, attempt; to taste, sample; to tempt, entice; *es ~en mit* to put to the test. ~er *m.* tempter, seducer. ~sanstalt *f.* research institute. ~sballon *m.* (*fig.*) kite. ~skaninchen *n.* (*fig.*) guinea-pig. ~sreihe *f.* series of experiments. ~sweise *adv.* by way of experiment; tentatively. ~ung *f.* temptation.

ver'sumpfen *vws.i.* to become marshy *or* boggy; (*fig.*) to go to the bad, grow dissolute.

ver'sündig-en *v.r.* to sin (against), offend. ~ung *f.* sin, offence.

ver'sunken *a.* sunk, lost.

ver'süßen *v.t.* to sweeten.

ver'tag-en *v.t.* to adjourn. ~ung *f.* adjournment.

ver-'tändeln *v.t.* to trifle away. ~'täuen *v.t.* to moor (boat). ~'tauschen *v.t.* to exchange; to mistake; (*math.*) to substitute, permute. ~tausendfachen *v.t.* to increase a thousandfold; to multiply by a thousand.

ver'teidig-en *v.t.* to defend. ~er *m.* defender; advocate; barrister. ~ung *f.* defence. ~ungsanlagen *f.pl.* defence works, defences.

~ungsrede *f.* counsel's speech, plea, defence.

ver'teil-en *v.t.* to distribute; to dispense; to apportion; to assign; to divide. *v.r.* to disperse; to spread. ~ung *f.* distribution.

ver'teuern *v.t.* to make dearer, r ise the price of.

ver'teufelt *a.* devilish; the devil of a. *adv.* awfully.

ver'tief-en *v.t.* to deepen, make deeper. *v.r.* (*fig.*) to become absorbed (in), bury oneself (in), be engrossed (in). ~ung *f.* deepening; depression, hollow, cavity; recess, niche; (*fig.*) absorption.

ver'tiert *a.* brutish.

verti'kal *a.* vertical.

ver'tilg-en *v.t.* to exterminate; to destroy; to annihilate; to consume. ~ung *f.* extermination, destruction.

ver'tippen *v.r* to make a typing error.

ver'ton-en *v.t.* to set to music, compose ~ung *f.* composition; melody; musical arrangement.

ver'trackt *a.* difficult; confounded.

Ver'trag (-a:k) *m.* (-es, -̈e) contract, agreement; treaty. ~en *v.t.* to carry away; to bear, stand, endure, tolerate; to digest; *ich kann diese Speise nicht ~en* this food doesn't agree with me. *v.r.* to agree, harmonize, get on well (together); to be compatible, be consistent; *sich wieder ~en* to settle one's differences, make it up. ~lich *a.* contractual; stipulated, agreed (upon). ~brüchig *a.* defaulting (in a contract). ~smäßig *a.* stipulated, agreed (upon). ~swidrig *a.* contrary to an agreement.

ver'träglich *a.* sociable, peaceable; good-natured; compatible (with). ~keit *f.* peaceable disposition; good nature.

ver'trau-en *v.i.* to trust, rely (upon), have confidence (in), put one's trust (in). *subst. n.* confidence; trust, reliance; *im ~en* confidentially, in confidence, between ourselves; *im ~en auf* relying on, trusting to. ~ensmann *m.* reliable *or* trustworthy person. ~ensselig *a.* too trusting, gullible. ~ensvoll *a.* full of confidence, confident. ~enswürdig *a.* trustworthy, reliable. ~lich *a.* confidential, private; intimate. ~lichkeit *f.* intimacy; familiarity. ~t *a.* intimate, familiar; conversant (with), versed (in). ~te(r) *m.* intimate friend; confidant. ~theit *f.* intimacy, familiarity; thorough knowledge (of), acquaintance (with).

ver'trauern *v.t.* to spend in sorrow, mourn away (one's life)

ver'träumen *v.t.* to dream away.

ver'treib-en *v.t.* to drive away, expel, banish; to sell, distribute (goods); (*sich*) *die Zeit* ~en to while away the time. ~ung *f.* expulsion; banishment.

ver'tret-en *v.t.* to represent; to deputize (for); to act as substitute; to defend, answer for; to plead *or* intercede for; *einem den Weg* ~en to stand in a person's way, stop a person; *sich den Fuß* ~en to sprain one's foot; *sich die Beine* ~en to stretch one's legs. ~er *m.* representative; deputy, proxy, substitute, locum; advocate; champion; agent. ~ung *f.* representation; replacement; *eine* ~ung übernehmen to deputize (for); take the place of; *in* ~ung signed for.

Ver'trieb *m.* sale; distribution.

ver-'trinken *v.t.* to spend (money) on drink. ~'trocknen *vws.i.* to dry up, wither. ~'trödeln *v.t.* to waste, fritter away (time). ~'trösten *v.t.* to put (one) off (with), give hope to; to console. ~'trusten *v.t.* (*commerc.*) to pool. ~'tun *v.t.* to waste, squander. ~'tuschen *v.t.* to hush up.

ver-'übeln *v.t.* to take amiss; to blame (one) for. ~'üben *v.t.* to commit, perpetrate. ~'ulken *v.t.* to make fun of, tease. ~'unehren *v.t* to dishonour, disgrace. ~'uneinigen *v.t.* to set at variance. *v.r.* to fall out, quarrel. ~'unglimpfen *v.t.* to dishonour; to disparage; to revile.

ver|'unglücken *vws.i.* to meet with an accident; to perish, be killed; to fail.

ver|'unreinig-en *v.t.* to dirty, soil; to pollute. ~ung *f.* dirtying, soiling; pollution.

verunsichern *v.t.* to make unsafe; to weaken.

ver-'unstalten *v.t.* to disfigure, deface. ~'untreuen *v.t.* to embezzle, misappropriate. ~'unzieren *v.t.* to disfigure, mar. ~'ursachen *v.t.* to cause, occasion, bring about, produce; to provoke; to give rise to; to involve, entail.

ver|'urteil-en *v.t.* to sentence, condemn. ~ung *f.* sentence; condemnation.

ver|'vielfältig-en *v.t.* to multiply; to duplicate, copy; to reproduce. ~ung *f.* multiplication; duplication, copying; reproduction. ~ungsmaschine *f.* duplicating machine, duplicator, hectograph.

ver'vollkommn-en *v.t.* to perfect. ~ung *f.* perfecting; perfection.

ver'vollständig-en *v.t.* to complete; to replenish. ~ung *f.* completion.

ver'wachs-en *vws.i.* to grow together; to heal up, close; to be tied (to), engrossed (in). *a.* deformed. ~ung *f.* growing together; healing up; deformity.

ver'wahr-en *v.t.* to keep, put away; to preserve. *v.r.* to resist; to protest (against). ~ung *f.* keeping; custody; care; ~ung einlegen to protest (against).

ver'wahrlos-en *v.t.* to neglect. *vws.i.* to be ruined by neglect; to go to the bad, degenerate. ~t *a.* neglected, unkempt; overrun with weeds; depraved, degenerate. ~ung *f.* neglect; demoralization.

ver'wais-en *vws.i.* to become an orphan. ~t *a.* orphaned; (*fig.*) deserted.

ver'walt-en *v.t.* to administer, manage, conduct, superintend; to govern, rule; to hold (office). ~er *m.* administrator, manager; steward. ~ung *f.* administration, management. ~ungsbeamte(r) *m.* administrative official.

~ungsbehörde *f.* government board, board of management.

~ungsdienst *m.* civil service. ~ungskosten *pl.* costs of administration or management.

ver'wand-eln *v.t.* to transform; to change; to convert, turn; to commute. ~lung *f.* transformation; change; conversion; metamorphosis; transubstantiation.

~lungskünstler *m.* quick-change artist. ~lungsszene *f.* transformation scene.

ver'wandt *a.* related; similar, kindred; allied; cognate. ~e(r) *m.* relation, relative. ~schaft *f.* relationship; family, relations; (*chem.*) affinity. ~schaftlich *a.* kindred; as (among) relatives.

ver'wanzt *a.* infested with bugs.

ver'warn-en *v.t.* to warn, caution; to admonish. ~ung *f.* warning, caution; admonition.

ver'waschen *v.t.* to wash out; to use up in washing. a. faded; (*fig.*) vague, indistinct.

ver'wässern *v.t.* to dilute, weaken; (*fig.*) to water down.

ver'weben *v.t.* to interweave.

ver'wechs-eln *v.t.* to take for, mistake for; to change; to confuse, mix up. ~lung *f.* mistake; confusion.

ver'wegen *a.* bold, daring, audacious. ~heit *f.* boldness, audacity, temerity.

ver'wehen *v.t.* to blow away; to drift; to cover up. *vws.i.* to be scattered (in all directions).

ver'wehren *v.t.* to hinder, prevent; to forbid, prohibit; to refuse.

ver'weichlichen *v.t.* to coddle. *vws.i.* to grow flabby or soft, become effeminate.

ver'weiger-n *v.t.* to deny (someone something), refuse. ~ung *f.* denial, refusal.

ver'weilen *v.i.* to stay, linger; to stop, stay (at); (*fig.*) to dwell upon.

ver'weint *a.* red or swollen with weeping.

Ver'weis *m.* (-es, -e) reproof, rebuke, reprimand; reference. ~en *v.t.* to reprove, rebuke, reprimand; ~en *auf* to refer (one) to;

des Landes ~en to exile, banish. ~ung *f.* exile, banishment.

ver'welken *vws.i.* to fade, wither.

ver'weltlich-en *v.t.* to secularize. ~ung *f.* secularization.

ver'wend-en *v.t.* to use, utilize, employ; to spend, expend; to apply; *nützlich* ~en to turn to account. *v.r.* to intercede (on behalf of). ~ung *f.* use, utilization, employment; application; *zur* ~ung kommen to be used.

ver'werf-en *v.t.* to reject, refuse. *v.r.* to become warped; (*geol.*) to (show a) fault. ~lich *a.* objectionable; reprehensible.

ver'wert-en *v.t.* to utilize, turn to account; to realize, sell (shares, &c.). ~ung *f.* utilization, use; realization.

ver'wes-en¹ *v.t.* to administer; to manage. ~er *m.* administrator; regent. ~ung *f.* administration.

ver'wes-en² *vws.i.* to rot, decay, decompose. ~lich *a.* liable to decay. ~ung *f.* decay, putrefaction, decomposition.

ver'wichen *a.* past, former.

ver'wick-eln *v.t.* to entangle; to complicate; to involve. ~elt *a.* (*fig.*) complicated, intricate. ~lung *f.* entanglement; tangle; complication; intricacy.

ver'wilder-n *vws.i.* to grow wild or savage; to become depraved; to run wild; to be neglected. ~ung *f.* return to a wild state or to barbarism; degeneration.

ver'winden *v.t.* to get over, overcome; (*av.*) to warp, twist.

ver'wirk-en *v.t.* to forfeit; to incur (punishment). ~ung *f.* loss, forfeiture.

ver'wirklich-en *v.t.* to realize, materialize. ~ung *f.* realization, materialization.

ver'wirr-en *v.t.* to tangle; to confuse, bewilder, embarrass. ~ung *f.* entanglement; disorder; confusion, embarrassment.

ver'wischen *v.t.* to efface, blot out, obliterate.

ver'witter-n *vws.i.* to weather; to crumble away; to disintegrate. ~t *a.* weather-beaten; dilapidated.

ver′witwet *a.* widowed.

ver′wöhn-en *v.t.* to spoil, pamper, coddle. **~t** *a.* spoiled, pampered; dainty, fastidious; **~ung** *f.* spoiling, pampering; indulgence.

ver′worfen *a.* depraved, vile. **~heit** *f.* depravity.

ver′worren *a.* confused.

ver′wund-en *v.t.* to wound, injure. **~ung** *f.* wound, injury.

ver′wunder-lich *a.* astonishing, surprising. **~n** *v.r.* to wonder, be surprised (at). **~ung** *f.* astonishment, surprise.

ver′wunschen *a.* enchanted, bewitched.

ver′wünsch-en *v.t.* to curse, wish ill to; to bewitch, cast a spell on. **~t** *a.* cursed, confounded. **~ung** *f.* curse, imprecation, malediction.

ver′wurzeln *vws.i.* to become firmly or deeply rooted.

ver′wüst-en *v.t.* to devastate, lay waste; to ruin. **~ung** *f.* devastation.

ver′zag-en *v.i.* to lose heart, be despondent, despair. **~t** *a.* despondent, disheartened; faint-hearted. **~theit** *f.* despondency, despair.

ver′zählen *v.r.* to count wrongly, miscount.

ver′zahn-en *v.t.* to tooth, cog; to dovetail (joint). **~ung** *f.* toothed gearing.

ver′zapfen *v.t.* to join by mortise; to sell on draught.

ver′zärtel-n *v.t.* to coddle, pet. **~ung** *f.* coddling, pampering; effeminacy.

ver′zauber-n *v.t.* to enchant, bewitch, charm. **~ung** *f.* enchantment.

ver′zehr-en *v.t.* to eat (up), consume. *v.r.* to waste away, pine away. **~ung** *f.* consumption.

ver′zeichnen *v t.* to write down, make a list (of); to book, enter; to report; to draw badly. **~nis** *n.* list, catalogue; inventory; index; specification.

ver′zeih-en *v.t.* to pardon, forgive; **~en Sie!** excuse me! I beg your pardon. **~lich** *a.* excusable; pardonable. **~ung** *f.* pardon;

forgiveness; **um ~ung bitten** to beg pardon, to apologize.

ver′zerr-en *v.t.* to distort. **~ung** *f.* distortion, contortion, grimace.

ver′zettel-n *v.t.* to waste, squander, dissipate; to catalogue, make catalogue of.

Ver′zicht *m.* (**-s, -e**) renunciation; resignation; **~ leisten** to renounce. **~en** *v.i.* to renounce, forgo, give up, resign, waive (claim).

ver′zieh-en *v.t.* to distort, contract; to spoil (child). *vws.i.* to remove, go away; to delay; to be slow. *v.r.* to warp; to be twisted; to pucker; to make off; to vanish, disappear; to disperse.

ver′zier-en *v.t.* to decorate, adorn, ornament; to embellish. **~ung** *f.* decoration, ornament; ornamentation; embellishment; (*mus.*) flourish(es).

ver′zinken *v.t.* to galvanize.

ver′zinnen *v.t.* to tin (-plate).

ver′zins-en *v.t.* to pay interest on. *v.r.* to bear or yield interest. **~lich** *a.* bearing interest. **~ung** *f.* (payment of) interest.

ver′zöger-n *v.t.* to delay, retard; to procrastinate. *v.r.* to be late, be deferred. **~ung** *f.* delay, retardation.

ver′zoll-en *v.t.* to pay duty on; **haben Sie etwas zu ~en?** have you anything to declare? **~ung** *f.* (payment of) duty; clearance.

ver′zucker-n *v.t.* to sweeten; to sugar over, ice; (*fig.*) to sugar or gild (the pill).

ver′zück-t *a.* in raptures, enraptured, ecstatic. **~ung** *f.* ecstasy, rapture.

Ver′zug *m.* delay; **ohne ~** at once, immediately; **Gefahr ist im ~** there is imminent danger.

ver′zweif-eln *vws.i.* to despair. **~elt** *a.* desperate; despairing. **~lung** *f.* despair, desperation; **zur ~lung bringen** to drive (one) mad.

ver′zweig-en *v.r.* to ramify, branch (out). **~ung** *f.* ramification, branching.

ver′zwickt *a.* complicated, intricate, awkward.

Vesper (f-) f. (-, -n) vespers. ~**glocke** f. evening bell. ~**n** v.i. to have a light meal in the afternoon.

Ves'talin f. (-, -nen) vestal (virgin).

Vesti'bül n. (-s, -e) vestibule, hall.

Vete'ran (-a:n) m. (-en, -en) veteran (soldier).

Veteri'närarzt m. veterinary surgeon, (sl.) vet

Veto n. ~ **einlegen** to veto a thing.

Vettel f. (-, -n) slut.

Vetter m. (-s, -n) (male) cousin. ~**nwirtschaft** f. nepotism.

Ve'xier-bild n. picture-puzzle. ~**en** v.t. to tease; to puzzle, mystify. ~**schloß** n. puzzle-lock. ~**spiegel** m. distorting mirror.

Via'dukt m. (-es, -e) viaduct.

vi'brieren v.i. to vibrate.

Vieh (fi:) n. (-es) cattle; beast. ~**bestand** m. live-stock. ~**futter** n. fodder, forage. ~**händler** m. cattle-dealer. ~**isch** a. brutal, bestial. ~**knecht** m. farm-hand, herdsman. ~**magd** f. farm-servant, dairymaid. ~**markt** m. cattle-market. ~**salz** n. cattle salt. ~**schwemme**, ~**tränke** f. watering-place, horse-pond. ~**seuche** f. murrain; foot-and-mouth disease. ~**wagen** m. cattle-truck. ~**weide** f. pasture. ~**zucht** f. cattle-breeding. [FEE]

viel (fi:l) a. & adv. much, a great deal; numerous; often; (as pref.) multi-, poly-; ~e many; sehr ~e many (people), very many, a great many; ein bißchen ~ a little too much; noch einmal so ~ as much again; mehr als zu ~ more than enough; das ~e Geld all that money; in ~em in many respects. ~**artig** a. manifold, various, multifarious. ~**ästig** a. with many branches. ~**deutig** a. ambiguous. ~**eck** n. polygon. ~**erlei** a. indecl. many (kinds of), divers, different, various. ~**erorts** adv. in many places. ~**fach** a. manifold, multifarious; repeated. adv. frequently, in many cases. ~**fältig** a. manifold, various. ~**fraß** m. glutton. ~**gestaltig** a. of many shapes, multiform. ~**götterei** f. polytheism. ~**heit** f.

multiplicity; great number or quantity, multitude. ~**köpfig** a. polycephalous, many-headed; numerous. ~**liebchen** n. philippina. ~**mals** adv. many times, often, frequently; very much. ~**mehr** adv. rather; much more. conj. rather, on the contrary. ~**sagend** a. very significant; highly suggestive; full of meaning, expressive. ~**schichtig** a. multiple; multilayered. ~**schreiber** m. prolific writer, quill-driver. ~**seitig** a. many-sided; versatile; (geom.) polyhedral. ~**silbig** a. polysyllabic. ~**sprachig** a. polyglot. ~**stimmig** a. polyphonic. ~**verheißend**, ~**versprechend** aa. very promising, of great promise. ~**weiberei** f. polygamy. ~**wisser** m. erudite man, (colloq.) walking encyclopedia. ~**zellig** a. multicellular.

vie'lleicht adv. perhaps.

vier (fi:r) a. & subst. f. four; unter ~ Augen tête-à-tête; privately; auf allen ~en on all fours; zu ~en, zu ~t four of (us); zu je ~en in fours. ~**blättrig** a. four-leaved. ~**eck** n. square; quadrangle; quadrilateral figure. ~**eckig** a. four-cornered, square, quadrangular. ~**er** m. (rowing) four. ~**erlei** indecl. a. four kinds of. ~**fach** a. fourfold, quadruple. ~**fürst** m. tetrarch. ~**füß(l)er** m. quadruped. ~**gestrichen** a. four-tailed (note). ~**händig** a. four-handed; ~händig spielen to play a duet. ~**jährig** a. of four years; lasting four years. ~**linge** pl. quadruplets. ~**mal** adv. four times. ~**malig** a. repeated four times. ~**schrötig** a. square-built, thick-set. ~**seitig** a. four-sided, quadrilateral. ~**sitzer** m. (motor.) four-seater. ~**spänner** m. carriage and four, four-in-hand. ~**stellig** a. of four places, of four digits. ~**stimmig** a. for four voices. ~**stöckig** a. four-storied. ~**taktmotor** m. four-stroke engine.

vierte a. fourth.

vierteilen v.t. to divide into four parts; to draw and quarter.

Viertel n. (-s, -) fourth part, quarter; ward, quarter; ein ~ (auf) zwei a quarter past one; drei ~ (auf) zwei a quarter to two. ~jahr n. quarter, three months. ~jahresschrift f. quarterly (periodical). ~jährlich a. quarterly. ~note f. crotchet; ~stunde f. quarter of an hour. ~stündlich a. every quarter, every fifteen minutes.

viertens adv. fourthly, in the fourth place.

Vier-ung f. (archit.) crossing, intersection of the nave. ~vierteltakt m. common time. ~zehn a. fourteen; ~zehn Tage a fortnight. ~zehnte a. fourteenth. ~zeiler m. poem consisting of four lines. ~zig a. forty. ~zigste a. fortieth.

Vigilie (-gi:lie) f. (-, -n) vigil.

Vi'kar m. (-s, -e) ⚕ curate.

Viktu'alien pl. victuals, provisions.

Vill-a f. (-a, -en) villa. ~enkolonie f. garden-city.

Vi'ol-a f. (-a, -en) viola. ~'ine f. violin. ~i'nist m., ~i'nistin f. violinist. ~inkasten m. violin-case. ~inschlüssel m. treble-clef. ~on'cello n. cello.

Vi'ol-e f. (-e, -en) violet; (bot.) viola. ~'ett a. violet.

Viper f. (-, -n) viper.

virtu'os a. masterly. ~e m., ~in f. virtuoso. ~i'tät f. virtuosity, mastery.

Vi'sier (-zi:r) n. (-s, -e) visor; sight; backsight. ~en v.t. to aim at; to gauge; to visé, endorse, examine (passport). ~fernrohr n. telescopic sight. ~klappe f. leaf of backsight (on gun). ~linie f. line of sight. ~weite f. range of sight.

Visi'on (-o:n) f. (-, -en) ⚕ vision = dream, phantom; phantasm. ~är a. visionary.

Visitati'on f. ⚕ search; (visit of) inspection.

Vi'sit-e f. (-e, -en) visit, call. ~enkarte f. visiting-card. ~ieren v.t. to search, inspect.

Visum n. (-s, Visa) visa.

Vitalität f. vitality.

Vita'min n. (-s, -e) vitamin.

Vi'trine (-i:na) f. (-, -n) show-case, glass case.

vitri'olhaltig a. containing vitriol, vitriolic.

Vivat n. cheer. int. long live . . .! hurrah!

Vize-admiral m. vice-admiral. ~könig m. viceroy.

Vlies n. (-es, -e) fleece.

Vogel (fo:-) m. (-s, ⸚) bird; einen ~ haben to have a bee in one's bonnet; den ~ abschießen to carry off the prize. ~bauer n. bird-cage. ~beerbaum m. mountain ash, rowan. ~dunst m. small shot. ~fänger m., ~steller m. bird-catcher, fowler. ~frei a. outlawed. ~futter n. bird-seed. ~haus n. aviary. ~hecke f. breeding-cage. ~herd m. fowling place. ~kirsche f. bird-cherry. ~kunde f. ornithology. ~miere f. chickweed. ~perspektive f. bird's-eye view. ~schau f. bird's-eye view. ~schauer m. augur. ~scheuche f. scarecrow. ~strich, ~zug m. flight or migration of birds of passage. ~warte f. ornithological station. ~zucht f. breeding of birds.

Vogt (fo:kt) m. (-es, ⸚e) steward; overseer; bailiff; governor. [ML]

Vo'kabel f. (-, -n) word. ~schatz m. vocabulary, range of language.

Vo'kal (-a:l) m. (-s, -e) vowel.

Vokativ m. (-s, -e) vocative.

Vo'lant m. (-s, -s) frill, flounce; (motor.) steering-wheel.

Volk n. (-es, ⸚er) people, nation, tribe; the common people, crowd, lower classes; swarm (of bees); covey (of partridges); das arbeitende ~ the working classes; das gemeine ~ the rabble, the mob; der Mann aus dem ~ the man in the street. ~reich a. populous. [FOLK]

Völk-chen n. tribe; set; young folk. ~erbund m. League of Nations. ~erkunde f. ethnology. ~errecht n. international law. ~errechtlich a. relating to international law; international. ~erschaft f. people; tribe. ~erwanderung f. migration of nations. ~isch a. national.

Volks-abstimmung f. plebiscite. ~**aufstand** m. revolution, rising. ~**befragung** f. referendum. ~**beschluß** m. plebiscite. ~**bibliothek** f. free library. ~**deutsche** m.pl. German ethnic group. ~**dichte** f. density of population. ~**dichter** m. national or popular poet. ~**eigen** a. belonging to the people. ~**empfänger** m. people's radio set. ~**entscheid** m. plebiscite. ~**epos** n. national epic. ~**fest** n. national festival. ~**genosse** m. fellow countryman; comrade. ~**glaube** m. popular belief. ~**haufe** m. mob, crowd. ~**hochschule** f. (adult) evening classes. ~**justiz** f. mob-justice; lynch-law. ~**küche** f. soup-kitchen. ~**kunde** f. folk-lore. ~**lied** n. folk-song. ~**mund** m. popular tradition. ~**redner** m. popular speaker; agitator, stump orator. ~**schicht** f. social class. ~**schlag** m. race. ~**schule** f. elementary or primary school. ~**sprache** f. popular tongue; vernacular. ~**stamm** m. race, tribe. ~**tracht** f. national costume. ~**tum** n. nationality; national characteristics. ~**tümlich** a. national, popular. ~**verbunden** a. closely bound up with one's nation. ~**versammlung** f. public meeting. ~**wagen** m. people's car. ~**weise** f. popular air. ~**wirt** m. political economist. ~**wirtschaft** f. political economy. ~**zählung** f. census.

voll a. full, filled; replete; rounded; complete, whole, entire; (colloq.) drunk; full up; aus dem ~en schöpfen to draw freely from the store of (one's ideas); to have plenty of (money, &c.); aus ~em Herzen from the bottom of one's heart, heartily; aus ~er Kehle at the top of one's voice; in ~er Fahrt at full speed; für ~ nehmen to take seriously; den Mund ~ nehmen to boast, brag; es schlägt ~ it's striking the hour.

voll-auf adv. in abundance, abundantly, plentifully. ~**bad** n. (full) bath. ~**bart** m. beard. ~**besitz** m. full possession. ~**bild** n. full-page illustration. ~**blut** n. thoroughbred. ~**blütig** a. full-blooded, plethoric; sanguine. ~'**bringen** v.t. to accomplish, achieve, complete, carry out; to fulfil. ~**bürtig** a. full, born of the same parents. ~**busig** a. full-bosomed. ~**dampf** m. full steam.

voll'end-en v.t. to finish, terminate; to accomplish, complete; to perfect. ~**ung** f. finishing, termination; completion; perfecting, perfection; consummation.

vollends adv. wholly, entirely, completely; finally; altogether; quite.

voller indecl. a. full of. comp. a. fuller.

Völle'rei f. (-) gluttony, intemperance.

voll-'führen v.t. to execute, carry out. ~**führung** f. execution. ~**gas** n. full throttle. ~**gefühl** n. (full) consciousness. ~**genuß** m. full enjoyment. ~**gepfropft** a. crammed (full). ~**gummi** m. solid rubber.

völlig a. full, entire, complete; thorough. adv. quite.

voll-jährig a. of age. ~**jährigkeit** f. majority; full age. ~'**kommen** a. perfect. ~'**kommenheit** f. perfection. ~**kornbrot** n. wholemeal bread. ~**körnig** a. full-grained. ~**kraft** f. full vigour, prime. ~**machen** v.t. to fill up; to complete; (colloq.) to dirty. ~**macht** f. full power; power of attorney; warrant, authority. ~**matrose** m. able-bodied seaman. ~**mensch** m. complete personality. ~**milch** f. full-cream milk. ~**mond** m. full moon. ~**reifen** m. solid tyre. ~**saftig** a. juicy, succulent. ~**schiff** n. full-rigged ship. ~**schlank** a. well developed (figure). ~**spurbahn** f. standard gauge railway. ~**spurig** a. broad-gauged. ~**ständig** a. complete, entire, whole, integral. adv. quite, perfectly. ~**ständigkeit** f. completeness; integrity. ~**stimmig** a. full-voiced.

voll'streck-en v.t. to execute, carry out. ~**er** m. executor. ~**ung** f. execution. ~**ungsbefehl** m. warrant, writ of execution.

voll-tönend a. sonorous, full-toned. **~treffer** m. direct hit. **~versammlung** f. plenary meeting. **~wertig** a. perfect; of high quality; up to standard. **~wichtig** a. of full weight; weighty. **~zählig** a. complete, full. **~zähligkeit** f. completeness. **~ziehen** v.t. to accomplish, carry out, execute. v.r. to take place. **~zug** m. accomplishment, execution.

Volon't-är m. (-ärs, -äre) voluntary helper; unsalaried clerk. **~ieren** v.i. to volunteer; to work as voluntary helper.

Volt-e f. (-e, -en) volt; sleight of hand. **~i'gieren** v.i. to vault.

Voltmesser m. voltmeter.

Vo'lumen (-lu:-) n. (-s, -) ♩ tome, volume; bulk, size, volume; capacity, content, volume.

volumi'nös a. voluminous.

vom = von dem.

von prep. from; of; about; by; in; on, upon; **~ . . . ab** from . . . onwards; **~ mir aus** I don't mind, if you like; **~ selbst** of itself, automatically. **~ein'ander** adv. apart, separate; from each other; of each other. **~'nöten** adv. **~nöten sein** to be needful or necessary. **~'statten** adv. **~statten gehen** to proceed, progress.

vor (fo:r) prep. before, previous, prior to; in front of, ahead of; in the presence of; for or with (joy, &c.); against; from; for; of. pref. fore-, pre-, pro-, preliminary, previous, prior, first; zehn Minuten **~** zwei Uhr ten minutes to two; **~** einer Woche a week ago; **~** Zeiten formerly; **~** der Zeit prematurely; **~** allem above all, especially; nach wie **~** as usual; **~** sich gehen to occur, take place; **~** sich hin to oneself.

vorab adv. above all, first of all.

Vor'abdruck m. (novel, &c.) published in a newspaper before issue in book-form.

vor'ahn-en v.t. to have a presentiment. **~ung** f. presentiment.

Voralpen pl. the lower Alps.

vo'ran adv. before; at the head, in front; on, onwards; voran! go

on, go ahead! **~gehen** rws.i. to walk at the head of, lead the way; to precede; mit gutem Beispiel **~gehen** to set a good example. **~kommen** rws.i. to get on, progress, advance; (fig.) to make progress.

Vor-anmeldung f. (tel.) personal call. **~anschlag** m. estimate. **~anzeige** f. preliminary announcement or advertisement.

Vor'arbeit f. preliminary work, ground work, preparation. **~en** v.i. to prepare the ground (for); to prepare (work); einem **~en** to pave the way for a person. **~er** m. foreman. **~erin** f. forewoman.

vo'rauf adv. before, in front, ahead.

vo'raus adv. on ahead, in front; im 'voraus in advance, beforehand; etwas **~** haben vor to have an advantage over (a person).

vo'raus-bedingen v.t. to stipulate beforehand. **~bestellen** v.t. to order or book beforehand, or in advance. **~bezahlen** v.t. to pay in advance, prepay. **~gehen** rws.i. to lead the way, walk in front; to precede. **~gehend** a. preceding; previous. **~nehmen** v.t. to anticipate, forestall. **~sage, ~sagung** f. prediction; prophecy; (weather-)forecast; tip; (sport.) selection(s). **~sagen** v.t. to foretell, predict; to prophesy; to forecast. **~sehen** v.t. to foresee. **~setzen** v.t. to (pre)suppose, assume, surmise. **~setzung** f. supposition, hypothesis, assumption. **~sicht** f. foresight, prudence. **~sichtlich** a. presumable, probable, to be expected. **~truppe** f. vanguard; advanced detachment. **~zahlung** f. prepayment.

Vor-bau m. front (of building); projecting structure; porch. **~bauen** v.t. to build in front of; to build out. v.i. (fig.) to guard against, prevent; to provide for (the future). **~bedacht** m. forethought, premeditation; mit **~bedacht** deliberately, on purpose. **~bedeutung** f. foreboding, omen, augury.

Vorbehalt m. (-es, -e) reservation;

proviso; *ohne* ~ unconditionally; *unter* ~ *aller Rechte* all rights reserved. ~**en** v.t. sich ~**en** to reserve to oneself. ~**lich** prep. with the proviso that, on condition that. ~**los** a. unconditional.

vor'bei adv. by, along, past; past, over, gone, done. ~**gehen** vvs.i. to pass by, go past, walk along; to pass, stop, cease; to miscarry, go wrong; to miss the mark. ~**lassen** v.t. to let pass. ~**marschieren** vvs.i. to march past. ~**reden** v.i. *aneinander* ~**reden** to be at cross purposes. ~**schießen** v.i. to miss (target).

Vorbemerkung f. preliminary remark; preamble; prefatory notice.

Vorberge pl. foot-hills.

vorbereit-en v.t. to prepare, make ready. ~**ung** f. preparation.

Vorbescheid m. preliminary decision.

Vorbesprechung f. preliminary discussion.

vorbestraft a. previously convicted.

vorbeten v.i. to lead in prayer; *das Tischgebet* ~ to say grace.

vorbeug-en v.i. to hinder, prevent, obviate; v.r. to bend forward, crane (forward). ~**end** a. preventive. ~**ungsmaßregel** f. preventive measure. ~**ungsmittel** n. preservative; preventive; prophylactic.

Vorbild n. model, pattern, standard; example; prototype, original. ~**en** v.t. to train; to prepare. ~**lich** a. model; ideal; exemplary; typical, representative. ~**ung** f. preparatory training; education.

vorbinden v.t. to tie on, put on.

Vorbote m. forerunner, precursor, harbinger.

vorbringen v.t. to bring forward; to produce; to state, express (a wish); to make (an excuse, &c.); to propose, put forward, say.

vorbuchstabieren v.t. to spell out (for).

vorchristlich a. pre-Christian.

vordatieren v.t. to antedate.

vordem adv. formerly, in former

times, of old.

vorder a. fore, forward, anterior, front.

Vorder-achse f. front-axle. ~**ansicht** f. front-view. ~**arm** m. forearm. ~**bein** n. foreleg. ~**deck** n. fore-deck. ~**front** f. front. ~**fuß** m. forefoot. ~**gebäude** n. front building. ~**grund** m. foreground. ~**hand** f. forehand.

vorderhand adv. for the present, in the meantime.

Vorder-haus n. front part of house. ~**lader** m. muzzle-loader. ~**lastig** a. (av.) nose-heavy. ~**mann** m. man in front; front-rank man. ~**mast** m. foremast. ~**rad** n. front-wheel. ~**radantrieb** m. front-wheel drive. ~**satz** m. protasis; antecedent; premiss. ~**seite** f. front; façade; face (of coin). ~**steven** m. stem of ship. ~**teil** n. front; (naut.) prow. ~**zähne** m.pl. front teeth.

vorderst a. foremost, first.

vor-drängen v.t. & r. to rush forward. ~**dringen** vvs.i. to advance; to gain ground. ~**dringlich** a. urgent. ~**druck** m. form, schedule.

vorehelich a. prenuptial.

vor-eilig a. hasty, rash, precipitate, premature. ~**keit** f. precipitancy, rashness, overhaste.

voreingenommen a. prejudiced, biased. ~**heit** f. prejudice, bias.

Vor-eltern pl. ancestors, forefathers.

vorenthalten v.t. to keep back, withhold (from a person).

vorerst adv. first of all; for the time being, in the meantime.

Vorfahr m. (-en, -en) ancestor.

vorfahr-en vvs.i. to drive up to, stop at (a person's door). ~**tsrecht** n. priority (in traffic). ~**tszeichen** n. priority sign (on a vehicle).

Vorfall m. occurrence; event, incident; case; (med.) prolapsus. ~**en** vvs.i. to occur, happen, take place.

Vor-fechter m. (fig.) pioneer. ~**feier** f. preliminary celebration. ~**finden** v.t. to find, meet with, come upon. ~**freude** f. joy of anticipation. ~**frühling** m. early spring; premature spring.

vorführ-en v.t. to demonstrate; to present; to produce; to trot out (horse). ~**dame** f. mannequin. ~**ung** f. demonstration; presentation; production.

Vorgabe f. (sport.) points given; handicap.

Vorgang m. occurrence, event, incident; process; precedent.

Vorgänger m. (-s, -) predecessor.

Vorgarten m. front garden.

vorgaukeln v.t. to buoy up with false hopes; to lead (a person) to believe (that).

vorgeb-en v.t. to give points (to), allow (a person) points; (fig.) to pretend; ~**lich** a. pretended; ostensible; so-called, would-be.

Vorgebirge n. foot-hills; promontory, cape.

vorgefaßt a. preconceived.

Vorgefühl n. presentiment; anticipation.

vorgehen vws.i. to go on, go forward, advance; to go first, lead, take the lead; to be first; to proceed, act; to proceed (against); to take place, occur, happen; to have the precedence; to be of special importance; to take precedence (of). subst. n. advance; proceedings; procedure.

vorgerückt a. advanced (age).

Vorgeschicht-e f. prehistory; prehistoric times; history of a preceding period; antecedents. ~**lich** a. prehistoric.

Vorgeschmack m. foretaste.

Vorgesetzte(r) m. (-n, -n) chief, superior; senior (officer).

vorgestern adv. the day before yesterday.

vorgreifen v.i. to anticipate; to forestall.

vorhaben v.t. to have on, wear (apron); to intend, purpose, have in mind; to be engaged on, be busy with. subst. n. intention, project, purpose, design.

Vorhalle f. vestibule; (entrance-) hall.

vorhalt-en v.t. to hold before (one), hold out; (fig.) to reproach (one)

with. v.i. to hold out, last. ~**ung** f. reproach, remonstrance.

Vorhand f. lead (at cards); forehand; (commerc.) precedence.

vor'handen a. present, existing, existent; on hand, in stock; ~ **sein** to exist; to be in stock. ~ **sein** n. presence, existence.

Vorhang m. curtain.

vorhäng-en v.t. to hang before. ~**eschloß** n. padlock.

Vorhaut f. foreskin, prepuce.

Vorhemd n. shirt-front; dickey.

vorher adv. before, beforehand, in advance, previously. ~**gehen** vws.i. to precede. ~**gehend** a. preceding, previous. ~**ig** a. previous, preceding, former. ~**sagen** v.t. to foretell, predict. ~**sehen** v.t. to foresee.

vorherrschen v.i. to predominate, to prevail. ~**d** a. predominant; prevailing, prevalent.

vorhin adv. before; a short time ago.

Vorhof m. forecourt.

Vorhut f. (-, -en) vanguard.

vorig a. last; preceding, former, previous; die ~**en** (theatr.) the same.

Vorinstanz f. lower court.

Vor-jahr n. preceding year. ~**jährig** a. of last year, last year's.

Vorkämpfer m. (fig.) pioneer.

vorkauen v.t. to chew (for); (fig.) to spoon-feed.

Vorkaufsrecht n. right of pre-emption; first refusal.

Vorkehrung f. (-, -en) precaution, provision, arrangement; (pl.) (preventive) measures.

Vorkenntnis f. previous knowledge; (pl.) rudiments (of a subject).

vorkomm-en vws.i. to come forward; to occur, happen, take place; to be found; to appear, seem. subst. n. presence, existence. ~**nis** n. occurrence, event.

Vorkriegszeit f. pre-war days.

vorlad-en v.t. to summon (witness). ~**ung** f. summons, citation.

Vorlage f. model, pattern, copy; (parl.) bill.

vorlagern v.r. to extend in front of.

vorlängst adv. long ago.

vorlassen *v.t.* to let pass before, give precedence (to); to admit, show in.

Vor-lauf *m.* start; (*chem.*) first runnings. **~läufer** *m.* forerunner, precursor; harbinger; pioneer. **~läufig** *a.* preliminary, preparatory, introductory; provisional. *adv.* (in the) meantime, for the present, provisionally.

vorlaut *a.* pert, forward.

Vorleben *n.* former life; antecedents.

Vorlege-besteck *n.* carvers. **~schloß** *n.* padlock.

vorlegen *v.t.* to lay *or* put before; to put on (padlock); to help (to), serve (with) food; to exhibit, display, show; to submit (for inspection). *v.r.* to lean forward.

Vorleger *m.* (*-s, -*) mat, rug.

vorles-en *v.t.* to read (to), read aloud. **~er** *m.* reader (to others). **~ung** *f.* lecture; recital.

vorletzt *a.* last but one, penultimate.

Vorliebe *f.* predilection; preference; partiality; special liking (for).

vor'liebnehmen *v.i.* to put up (with).

vorliegen *v.i.* to lie before (one), be submitted to, be put forward; to be; to be present, exist. **~d** *a.* in question; present, in hand.

vorlügen *v.t.* to tell lies (to one).

vorm = **vor dem**.

vormachen *v.t.* to put *or* place before; to show (how to do); to humbug (one), impose upon (a person).

Vormacht *f.* leading power; supremacy.

vormal-ig *a.* former. **~s** *adv.* formerly; once upon a time.

Vormarsch *m.* advance.

Vormarssegel *n.* fore-topsail.

vormerken *v.t.* to make a note of, put down; *sich ~ lassen* to have reserved for one; to book.

Vormittag *m.* forenoon. **~s** *adv.* in the forenoon, in the morning.

Vormund *m.* guardian. **~schaft** *f.* guardianship; tutelage. **~schaftlich** *a.* tutelary, as a guardian, of a guardian.

vorn *adv.* in front; in the front, in the forepart; at the beginning, on the front (page); *nach ~* forward; *von ~* from the front; facing; *von ~ anfangen* to start afresh; *nach ~e heraus wohnen* to live in the front part of a house; *von ~(e)herein* from the first, from the outset, to begin with. **~über** *adv.* forward, bent forward. **~weg** *adv.* at the beginning, from the outset.

Vornahme *f.* taking up, doing, taking in hand.

Vorname *m.* Christian name.

vornehm *a.* of high rank, of gentle birth; noble, distinguished; *~ tun* to put on airs; *die ~ste Pflicht* the first *or* principal duty. **~heit** *f.* distinction; high rank; distinguished bearing. **~lich** *adv.* principally, chiefly, especially.

vornehmen *v.t.* to put on (apron). *v.r.* to resolve, intend, make up one's mind (to); to take up, occupy oneself with; *sich einen ~* to take a person to task.

Vor ort *m.* suburb. **~verkehr** *m.* suburban traffic.

Vorplatz *m.* court; hall, vestibule.

Vorposten *m.* outpost. **~gefecht** *n.* outpost skirmishes.

Vorrang *m.* precedence, priority, pre-eminence, superiority.

Vorrat *m.* store, stock, provision, supply stores. **~skammer** *f.* store-room, pantry.

vorrätig *a.* in stock, on hand; *nicht mehr ~* out of stock.

vorrechnen *v.t.* to reckon up; to give an account of.

Vorrecht *n.* privilege, prerogative.

Vorred-e *f.* preface, introduction, prologue. **~en** *f.* to tell a plausible tale; to talk (person) into. **~ner** *m.* previous speaker.

vorreit-en *v.s.i.* to ride before. *v.t.* to put (a horse) through its paces. **~er** *m.* outrider.

vorricht-en *v.t.* to prepare, get ready. **~ung** *f.* preparation, arrangement; contrivance, appliance, apparatus; mechanism, device.

vorrücken *v.t.* to push *or* move forward; to put (clock) on. *v.s.i.* to advance, move on.

Vorrunde f. preliminary round.

vors = **vor das**.

Vorsaal m. ante-room, entrance-hall.

vorsagen v.t. & i. to dictate; to say (to a person); to prompt.

Vorsaison f. early season.

Vorsänger m. leader of a choir; precentor.

Vorsatz m. purpose, intention, plan; resolution. **~papier** n. end-paper.

vorsätzlich a. intentional, deliberate.

Vorschau f. trailer; preview (of film).

Vorschein m. zum ~ bringen to produce; zum ~ kommen to appear.

vorschieben v.t. to shove or push forward; to slip (bolt); to plead as an excuse, pretend.

vorschießen v.t. to lend, advance (money).

Vorschlag m. proposal, proposition; motion, offer; (mus.) grace-note, appoggiatura. **~en** v.t. to propose; to offer; to move (resolution).

Vor-schlußrunde f. semi-final. **~schmack** m. foretaste. **~schneiden** v.t. to carve. **~schnell** a. precipitate, hasty, rash.

vorschreiben v.t. to set a copy (of a thing to a person); to prescribe; to order, command; to dictate (to).

vorschreiten vws.i. to advance; to march on; to step forward.

Vorschrift f. copy; direction, instruction(s), regulation(s); (med.) prescription. **~smäßig** a. according to instructions.

Vorschub m. help, aid, support; (mach.) feed; ~ leisten to further; to abet.

vorschuhen v.t. to new-front (shoe).

Vorschule f. preparatory school; elementary course.

Vorschuß m. payment in advance.

vorschützen v.t. to pretend, blead.

vorschweben v.i. to hover before; mir schwebt (etwas) vor I have in mind; I have a recollection of.

Vorsegel n. foresail.

vorseh-en v.t. to provide for, consider. v.r. to take care, be cautious, be careful, mind, beware (of). **~ung** f. providence.

vorsetzen v.t. to put or set before; to serve (food); to offer; to prefix; to set over (another). v.r. to resolve, determine (to).

Vorsicht f. foresight; caution, prudence; discretion; providence; Vorsicht! take care! beware! look out! ~, Stufe! mind the step! **~ig** a. cautious, prudent; careful; wary; guarded. **~shalber** adv. as a precaution. **~smaßregel** f. precaution, precautionary measure.

Vorsilbe f. prefix.

vorsingen v.t. to sing to. v.i. to lead the choir.

vorsintflutlich a. antediluvian.

Vorsitz m. presidency, chairmanship, the chair; den ~ führen to preside, be in the chair. **~ende(r)** m. president, chairman.

Vorsorg-e f. foresight; precaution. **~en** v.i. to take precautions; to take care (that), provide for. **~lich** a. careful, provident.

Vorspann m. trace horses; ~ leisten to help. **~en** v.t. to put (horses, &c.) to; to stretch in front of.

Vorspeise f. hors-d'œuvre, relish.

vorspiegel-n v.t. to deceive, delude; to awake false hopes. **~ung** f. deceiving, shamming; sham, pretence, false pretences.

Vorspiel n. prelude; overture; (theatr.) curtain-raiser. **~en** v.t. to play to or before (a person).

vorsprechen v.t. to pronounce (to), teach how to pronounce; to recite. v.i. ~ bei to call on.

vorspringen vws.i. to leap forward; to project, jut out. **~d** a. projecting; prominent; der Winkel salient.

Vorsprung m. projection, projecting part; salient; ledge; advantage, lead, start.

Vor-stadt f. suburb. **~städter** m. suburbanite. **~städtisch** a. suburban.

Vorstand m. board of directors; executive committee; director.

vorsteck-en *v.t.* to pin on (brooch, &c.); to poke out *or* forward ~**nadel** *f.* scarf pin.

vorsteh-en *v.i.* to project; to manage, direct, administer; to be at the head of. ~**er** *m.* principal, chief; director, manager; superintendent; headmaster. , ~**erdrüse** *f.* prostate gland. ~**hund** *m.* pointer, setter.

vorstellbar *a.* conceivable, imaginable.

vorstell-en *v.t.* to place before, put in front of; to put on (clock); to present, introduce; to demonstrate; to represent, act; to pose (as); to signify, mean; to explain, make clear; to remonstrate, protest, expostulate (with). *v.r.* to imagine, suppose, fancy, conceive. ~**ig** *a.* ~**ig werden** to present a case *or* petition; to protest. ~**ung** *f.* introduction, presentation; performance; remonstrance, expostulation; conception, idea, notion, imagination. ~**ungsvermögen** *n.* imagination, imaginative faculty.

Vorstoß *m.* push forward; attack, thrust. ~**en** *vws.i.* to push forward; to attack.

Vorstrafe *f.* previous conviction.

vorstreck-en *v.t.* to stretch out *or* forward; to stick out; to advance, lend (money).

Vorstufe *f.* first step(s); introduction; preliminary stage.

Vortänzer *m.* leader of the dance .

vortäuschen *v.t.* to feign, simulate.

Vorteil *m.* advantage; profit; benefit. ~**haft** *a.* advantageous; profitable; lucrative; favourable; ~**haft aussehen** to look one's best.

Vortrab *m.* vanguard.

Vortrag *m.* (-s, ̈e) reciting; elocution, delivery; (*mus.*) execution; recitation; performance; lecture; discourse, report, statement; (*commerc.*) balance carried forward. ~**en** *v.t.* to carry forward (*also commerc.*); to carry before *or* in front of; to recite, declaim; to perform, execute, play (piece of music); to give a lecture, lecture; to report on; to express (one's opinion). ~**ende(r)** *m.*

lecturer; speaker; performer. ~**skünstler** *m.* elocutionist; performer.

vor'trefflich *a.* excellent, admirable, splendid. ~**keit** *f.* excellence.

Vortritt *m.* precedence.

Vortrupp *m.* vanguard.

vo'rüber *adv.* past, over, by, along; past, gone, over. ~**gehen** *vws.i.* to go by, pass, go past; to pass by, pass over, neglect; to pass away, be over, cease, stop. ~**gehend** *a.* passing, temporary, transitory, transient. ~**gehende(r)** *m.* passer-by.

Vor|untersuchung *f.* preliminary examination.

Vor|urteil *n.* prejudice. ~**slos** *a.* unprejudiced, unbiased.

Vor-väter *m.pl.* ancestors, forefathers. ~**vergangenheit** *f.* pluperfect. ~**verkauf** *m.* (*theatr.*) booking in advance; advance sale. ~**vorgestern** *adv.* three days ago. ~**vorig** *a.* last but one, penultimate. ~**walten** *v.i.* to prevail.

Vorwand *m.* (-es, Vorwände) pretext, pretence, excuse, plea.

vorwärts *adv.* forward, onward, on; forwards; *vorwärts!* go on! go ahead! ~**gehen** *vws.i.* to go on, advance, progress. ~**kommen** *vws.i.* to get on; to make headway; to advance; to prosper. ~**treiben** *v.t.* to drive on; to propel.

vor'weg *adv.* beforehand; to begin with. ~**nehmen** *v.t.* to anticipate.

vorweisen *v.t.* to show, produce, exhibit.

Vorwelt *f.* former ages, antiquity; prehistoric times.

vorwerfen *v.t.* to cast before; to throw to; (*fig.*) to reproach *or* upbraid with.

Vorwerk *n.* farm-steading.

vorwiegen *v.i.* to preponderate, prevail; to predominate. ~**d** *a.* predominant, prevalent. *adv.* principally, chiefly, mostly.

Vorwissen *n.* previous knowledge.

Vorwitz *m.* curiosity, inquisitiveness; forwardness, pertness.

ig *a.* prying, inquisitive; forward, pert.

Vorwort *n.* foreword, preface.

Vorwurf *m.* reproach, reproof, blame; motif, subject. ∼**frei** *a.* irreproachable. ∼**svoll** *a.* reproachful.

Vorzeichen *n.* omen; (*mus.*) signature; (*math.*) sign.

vorzeichnen *v.t.* to draw sketch (for); to trace out; to mark, indicate.

vorzeig-en *v.t.* to show, produce, exhibit, display; to present (a bill). ∼**ung** *f.* showing, production; exhibition.

Vorzeit *f.* antiquity; olden times. ∼**en** *adv.* once upon a time; formerly. ∼**ig** *a.* premature; precocious.

vorziehen *v.t.* to draw, draw forward; to prefer.

Vorzimmer *n.* ante-room, antechamber.

Vorzug *m.* preference; precedence; priority; superiority; excellence; (*pl.*) good qualities; privilege, advantage. ∼**saktien** *f.pl.* preference shares. ∼**sdruck** *m.* édition de luxe. ∼**spreis** *m.* special price. ∼**sweise** *adv.* preferably, pre-eminently, chiefly.

vor'züglich *a.* excellent, superior, first-rate; choice. *adv.* particularly, above all. ∼**keit** *f.* excellence, superiority; choiceness.

Vo'tivbild *n.* votive picture.

Votum *n.* (-s, Voten) vote, suffrage.

vul'gär *a.* vulgar, common.

Vul'kan (-a:n) *m.* (-s, -e) volcano. ∼**fiber** *f.* vulcanized fibre. ∼**isch** *a.* volcanic. ∼**i'sieren** *v.t.* to vulcanize.

W

W, w (ve:) *n.* the letter W, w.

Waag-e *f.* (-e, -en) balance, scales; weighing-machine; (*astron.*) the Scales, Libra; (*gym.*) horizontal position (on parallel bars); *jmm die* ∼*e halten* to be a match for; *sich die* ∼*e halten* to counterbalance each other. ∼**ebalken** *m.*

(scale-)beam. ∼**emeister** *m.* inspector of weights and measures. ∼**(e)recht** *a.* horizontal, level. ∼**schale** *f.* scale; scales, balance.

wabbelig *a.* flabby.

Wabe (va:bə) *f.* (-, -n) honeycomb.

wabern *v.i.* to flicker.

wach (vax) *a.* awake, astir; brisk, alive; on the alert. ∼**dienst** *m.* guard duty. ∼**e** *f.* guard, watch, sentry; watchman; guard room, police station; ∼**e** *ablösen* to relieve the guard; *auf* ∼*e* to mount guard; *auf* ∼*e ziehen* to mount guard; ∼*e stehen* to stand sentry. ∼**habend** *a.* on duty. ∼**posten** *m.* sentry. ∼**rufen** *v.t.* to wake; (*fig.*) to call forth, rouse. ∼**sam** *a.* vigilant, watchful; alert, wideawake, sharp. ∼**samkeit** *f.* vigilance. ∼**traum** *m.* day-dream. See also **Wacht**.

wachen (vax-) *v.i.* to be awake, remain awake; to be on guard, keep watch; ∼ *über* to watch over, keep an eye on.

Wa'cholder *m.* (-s, -) juniper.

Wachs (-ks) *n.* (-es, -e) wax. ∼**bild** *n.* wax image. ∼**figurenkabinett** *n.* waxworks. ∼**kerze** *f.* candle, taper. ∼**leinwand** *f.*, ∼**tuch** *n.* oilcloth. ∼**stock** *m.* taper. ∼**zieher** *m.* wax-chandler.

wachsen[1] *v.t.* to wax.

wachs-en[2] *vws.i. st.* to grow; to thrive; to increase, extend; *ans Herz* ∼*en* to get fond of, become attached to; *einem gewachsen sein* to be a match for one; *einer Sache gewachsen sein* to be equal to a task. ∼**tum** *n.* growth; increase.

wächsern (vɛks-) *a.* waxen, of wax; pale.

Wacht *f.* (-, -en) guard, watch. ∼**dienst** *m.* guard duty. ∼**feuer** *n.* watch-fire. ∼**habend** *a.* on duty. ∼**mannschaft** *f.* guard, picket. ∼**meister** *m.* sergeant-major. ∼**stube** *f.* guard room.

Wächte *f.* (-, -n) snow cornice.

Wachtel *f.* (-, -n) quail. ∼**hund** *m.* spaniel. ∼**könig** *m.* corn-crake.

Wächter *m.* (-s, -) watchman; caretaker; warder, keeper; look-out man.

wack-eln *v.i.* to shake, rock, wobble; to totter, reel, stagger; to be loose. ~**(e)lig** *a.* shaky, tottering; loose; wobbly.

wacker *a.* brave. *adv.* bravely; soundly; heartily.

Wade (va:-) *f.* (-, -n) calf (of leg). ~**nbein** *n.* fibula.

Waffe *f.* (-, -n) weapon, arm. ~**n-bruder** *m.* brother in arms, comrade; ally. ~**ndienst** *m.* military service. ~**nfähig** *a.* capable of bearing arms. ~**ngang** *m.* passage of arms; armed conflict. ~**n-gattung** *f.* arm or branch of the service. ~**ngewalt** *f.* force of arms. ~**nglück** *n.* fortune of war. ~**nrock** *m.* tunic. ~**nruhe** *f.* suspension of hostilities, truce. ~**nschein** *m.* gun-licence. ~**n-schmied** *m.* armourer. ~**n-schmuck** *m.* full armour. ~**n-schmuggel** *m.* gun-running. ~**n-stillstand** *m.* armistice. ~**ntat** *f.* feat of arms. ~**nübung** *f.* military exercise; army manœuvres.

Waffel *f.* (-, -n) waffle. ~**eisen** *n.* waffle-iron.

waffnen *v.t.* to arm.

Wage see **Waage.**

Wag-ehals *m.* dare-devil. ~**(e)hal-sig** *a.* reckless, foolhardy. ~**(e)-halsigkeit** *f.* foolhardiness. ~**e-mut** *m.* daring, gallantry. ~**e-stück** *n.* dangerous enterprise, risk. ~**nis** *n.* risk, bold venture.

wagen[1] (va:-) *v.t.* to venture, risk; to presume; to dare; *gewagt* daring, risky, perilous.

Wagen[2] (va:-) *m.* (-s, -) carriage, coach; vehicle, conveyance; cart; lorry, truck, van; wag(g)on; (motor-)car; *der Große* ~ the Plough, Great Bear. ~**burg** *f.* barricade of wagons; laager. ~**decke** *f.* tarpaulin, cover, tilt. ~**heber** *m.* jack. ~**lenker** *m.* driver. ~**park** *m.* car park. ~**schlag** *m.* carriage-door. ~**schmiere** *f.* grease; lubricant.

wägen (vɛ:-) *v.t. st. & w.* to weigh; to consider.

Wa:gon *m.* (-s, -s) railway carriage; truck. [F]

Wahl *f.* (-, -en) choice, selection, option; election; *seine* ~ *treffen*

to make one's choice; *vor die* ~ *stellen* to let one choose; *in engere* ~ *kommen* to be on the short list; *geheime* ~ (secret) ballot. ~**berechtigt** *a.* entitled to vote. ~**bezirk** *m.* constituency; ward. ~**fach** *n.* optional subject. ~**gang** *m.* ballot. ~**heimat** *f.* country of one's choice. ~**kampf** *m.* election contest. ~**kreis** *m.* constituency; ward. ~**liste** *f.* register of electors. ~**lokal** *n.* polling-place. ~**los** *adv.* indiscriminately; without guiding principle. ~**recht** *n.* right to vote, franchise. ~**rede** *f.* election speech. ~**spruch** *m.* motto, device. ~**stimme** *f.* vote. ~**urne** *f.* ballot-box. ~**versammlung** *f.* election meeting. ~**verwandt-schaft** *f.* elective affinity; congeniality. ~**zelle** *f.* polling-booth. ~**zettel** *m.* voting-paper.

wähl-en *v.t.* to choose, elect; to pick out; (*tel.*) to dial. ~**er** *m.* elector; selector. ~**erisch** *a.* particular; fastidious. ~**erschaft** *f.* body of electors, constituency ~**scheibe** *f.* dial.

Wahn *m.* (-es) delusion, illusion; error; fancy; madness; folly; hallucination. ~**bild** *n.* chimera, phantom, delusion. ~**sinn** *m.* insanity; frenzy; madness, craziness. ~**sinnig** *a.* insane, mad; frantic; (*colloq.*) terrific. ~**witz** *m.* insanity; madness; absurdity. ~**witzig** *a.* mad; absurd.

wähnen *v.t.* to believe, think, suppose, imagine.

wahr (va:r) *a.* true; sincere; genuine; real, proper, veritable; *so* ~ *ich lebe* as sure as I live; *nicht* ~? isn't it? don't you think so? *etwas nicht* ~ *haben wollen* not to admit a thing; ~ *werden* to come true.

wahr-en *v.t.* to keep, look after, preserve, watch over; to keep up; to maintain. ~**ung** *f.* preservation, maintenance.

währ-en *v.i.* to last, continue. ~**ung** *f.* standard, currency.

während *prep.* during, in the course of, for. *conj.* while, whilst; whereas.

wahr-haft, **~haftig** *aa.* true, genuine; sincere; truthful; real, actual. *adv.* truly, really, actually. **~heit** *f.* truth; *einem (gehörig) die ~heit sagen* to give a person a piece of one's mind. **~heitsgetreu** *a.* truthful, true. **~heitsliebend** *a.* truthful, veracious. **~lich** *adv.* truly; verily.

wahrnehm-bar *a.* perceptible, noticeable. **~en** *v.t.* to notice, observe, perceive; to make use of, avail oneself of; to look after, protect. **~ung** *f.* perception; observation; maintenance, protection. **~ungsvermögen** *n.* power of observation, perceptive faculty.

wahr-sagen *v.t.* to tell fortunes; to prophesy. **~sager** *m.*, **~sagerin** *f.* fortune-teller; soothsayer. **~sagung** *f.* fortune-telling; prediction; prophecy. **~scheinlich** *a.* probable, likely. **~scheinlichkeit** *f.* probability; likelihood. **~scheinlichkeitsrechnung** *f.* theory of probabilities. **~spruch** *m.* verdict. **~zeichen** *n.* landmark; mark, token, sign.

Waidmann see **Weidmann**.

Waise *f.* (-, -n) orphan. **~nhaus** *n.* orphanage. **~nknabe** *m.* orphanboy.

Wal, **~fisch** *m.* whale. **~fischfahrer** *m.* whaler. **~fischtran** *m.* train-oil. **~rat** *m. & n.* spermaceti. **~roß** *n.* walrus.

Wald (valt) *m.* (-es, ²e) wood, forest; woodland **~brand** *m.* forest fire. **~erdbeere** *f.* wild strawberry. **~gegend** *f.* wooded country. **~horn** *n.* French horn; bugle. **~hüter** *m.* keeper, ranger. **~ig** *a.* wooded, woody. **~lichtung** *f.* clearing, glade. **~meister** *m.* woodruff. **~reich** *a.* well-wooded, rich in forests. **~saum** *m.* fringe of a wood. **~schneise** *f.* forest lane, aisle, or vista. **~schrat** *m.* forest-sprite. **~ung** *f.* wood; woodland. **~wiese** *f.* glade.

walk-en *v.t.* to full (cloth). **~erde** *m.* fuller's earth. **~mühle** *f.* fulling-mill. **~müller** *m.* fuller.

Wall *m.* (-es, ²e) rampart; embank-

---

ment; dike. **~graben** *m.* moat, ditch of rampart.

Wallach *m.* (-s, -e) gelding.

wall-en¹ *vws.i.* to wander, travel; to go on a pilgrimage. **~fahrer** *m.* pilgrim. **~fahrt** *f.* pilgrimage. **~fahr(t)en** *vws.i.* to go on a pilgrimage.

wall-en² *v.i.* to undulate; to bubble, boil; to float, flow, flutter; to be agitated. **~ung** *f.* undulation; ebullition; flow; flutter; agitation.

Walnuß *f.* walnut.

Walstatt *f.* battle-field.

walten *v.i.* to rule, govern, hold sway; to execute, carry out. *subst. n.* working; rule, government.

Walzblech *n.* rolled plate, sheet-iron.

Walz-e *f.* (-e, -en) cylinder; platen, roller; roll; barrel. **~en** *v.t.* to roll; to roll out. *v.i.* to waltz. **~er** *m.* waltz. **~werk** *n.* rolling-mill.

wälz-en *v.t.* to roll, turn about. *v.r.* to roll; to wallow; to welter; *die Schuld ~en auf* to throw the blame upon. **~er** *m.* heavy tome, tome.

Wamme *f.* (-, -n) paunch; belly; (*vet.*) dewlap.

Wams *n.* (-es, ²er) doublet, jerkin, jacket.

wand¹ *imperf.* of **winden**.

Wand² *f.* (-, ²e) wall (of room); side; partition; (*med.*) coat. **~bekleidung** *f.* wainscot(ing). **~gemälde** *n.*, **~malerei** *f.* fresco, mural painting. **~karte** *f.* wall-map. **~leuchter** *m.* sconce, bracket. **~schirm** *m.* screen. **~schrank** *m.* cupboard. **~tafel** *f.* blackboard. **~ung** *f.* wall, partition.

Wan'dale see **Vandale**.

Wandel *m.* (-s) change, alteration, mutation; conduct, behaviour; habits, mode of life; *Handel und ~* trade, commerce. **~bar** *a.* changeable, variable; fickle; perishable. **~gang** *m.* lobby, corridor. **~stern** *m.* planet.

wand-eln *vws.i.* to wander, walk, travel. *v.r.* to change; to turn (into). ~lung f. change, transformation; (theol.) transubstantiation.

Wander-bühne f. travelling theatre. ~bursche m. travelling journeyman. ~er m. wanderer, traveller; hiker. ~heuschrecke f. migratory locust. ~jahre n.pl. years spent in travel (by artisan, &c.). ~leben n. roving life. ~niere f. floating kidney. ~prediger m. itinerant preacher. ~preis m. challenge trophy. ~ratte f. brown rat, sewer rat. ~schaft f. travelling, travels, journey, tour, trip; migration. ~smann m. traveller; wayfarer. ~stab m. walking-stick. ~trieb m. roving spirit; migratory instinct. ~ung f. walking tour; travelling; excursion, trip; hike; migration. ~vogel m. bird of passage; member of German youth movement.

wandern vws.i. to wander, travel, hike.

wandte imperf. of wenden.

Wange f. (-ŋa) f. (-, -n) cheek.

Wankel-mut m. inconstancy, fickleness. ~mütig a. inconstant, fickle.

wanken v.i. to stagger, reel, totter, sway; (fig.) to waver, be irresolute.

wann (van) adv. when; dann und ~ now and then; sometimes; von ~en whence.

Wanne f. (-, -n) tub; bath. ~nbad n. sponge-bath; tub, bath.

Wanst m. (-es, ⁼e) belly, paunch.

Wanten f.pl. (naut.) shrouds.

Wanze f. (-, -n) bug.

Wappen n. (-s, -) (coat of) arms, armorial bearings; crest. ~bild n. heraldic figure. ~buch n. book of heraldry. ~könig m. King of Arms. ~kunde f. heraldry. ~schild n. escutcheon. ~schmuck m. blazonry. ~spruch m. heraldic motto, device. ~tier n. heraldic animal.

wappnen v.t. to arm.

war imperf. of sein.

warb imperf. of werben.

ward (poet.) imperf. of werden.

Ware (va:-) f. (-, -n) article, commodity; (pl.) goods, merchandise.

~nballen m. bale of goods. ~nhaus n. department store. ~nlager n. stock-in-trade; assortment of goods. ~niederlage f. warehouse, magazine. ~nprobe f. sample. ~nzeichen n. trade mark.

wart imperf. of werfen.

warm a. warm; hot; ~ stellen to keep (food) hot; sich ~ laufen to run hot; ~ laufen lassen to warm up (engine). ~blüter m. warm-blooded animal. ~herzig a. warm-hearted. ~wasserheizung f. central heating. ~wasserspeicher m. geyser. ~wasserversorgung f. hot-water supply.

Wärm-e f. (-e) warmth; heat; warmness. ~eabgabe f. loss of heat. ~eaufnahme f. absorption of heat. ~eeinheit f. heat unit. ~egrad m. degree of heat; temperature. ~ehaltig a. heat-retaining. ~elehre f. theory of heat. ~eleiter m. conductor of heat. ~emesser m. calorimeter; thermometer. ~eflasche f. hot-water bottle.

wärmen v.t. to warm; to heat. v.r to warm oneself, bask.

warn-en v.t. to warn, caution. ~ruf m. warning cry. ~ung f. warning; caution, admonition. ~ungssignal n. danger signal; alert. ~ungstafel f. notice-board.

Warte f. (-, -n) look-out; watch-tower.

Warte-frau f. nurse, attendant. ~geld n. half-pay. ~saal m. waiting-room (at station). ~zimmer n. (doctor's) waiting-room.

wart-en v.t. to nurse; to attend to; to look after. v.i. to wait, stay; ~en auf to wait for; ~en lassen to keep waiting. ~ung f. attendance, nursing; grooming; servicing.

Wärter m. (-s, -) attendant; nurse; keeper; care-taker; (prison-)warder; (park-)keeper; signalman, pointsman. ~in f. nurse; care-taker.

wa'rum adv. why, for what reason.

Warze f. (-, -n) wart; nipple.

was pron. what; whatever; that

which; which, that; something;
~ *für ein!* what a; ~ *für ein?*
what sort of a? ; ~ *mich anlangt* as
for me; ~ *auch immer* whatever,
no matter what; *ach* ~ *!* stuff
and nonsense; *nein, so* ~ *!* well, I
never; ~ *haben wir gelacht!* how
we laughed.

Wasch-anstalt f. laundry. **~bär**
m. racoon. **~becken** n. hand-
basin. **~blau** n. washing-blue.
~echt a. fast (colour); (*fig.*) real.
~faß n. wash-tub. **~frau** f.
washerwoman, laundress. **~ge-
schirr** n. washstand set. **~kessel**
m. boiler, copper. **~kleid** n. cotton frock, print dress. **~korb**
m. clothes-basket. **~küche** f.
wash-house, laundry. **~lappen**
m. face-cloth; (*fig.*) molly-coddle.
~leder n. wash-leather, chamois-
leather. **~leine** f. clothes-line.
~raum m. cloak-room, lavatory,
ladies' room. **~schüssel** f. hand-
basin. **~tisch** m. washstand. **~-
ung** f. washing; lotion, wash;
ablution. **~wasser** n. water for
washing. **~zettel** m. laundry
list; (*fig.*) publisher's note, blurb.

Wäsche f.(-.-n) washing; linen; underclothing; *schmutzige* ~ soiled
linen, dirty clothes; *große* ~
haben to have washing-day; *in
die* ~ *geben* to send to the
laundry. **~beutel** m. soiled-linen
bag. **~geschäft** n. linen warehouse, lingerie. **~klammer** f.
clothes-peg. **~leine** f. clothes-
line. **~mangel** f. mangle. **~-
rei** f. laundry. **~rin** f. washerwoman, laundress. **~schrank** m.
linen-cupboard. **~ständer** m.
clothes-horse.

waschen v.t., v.i. & r., st. to
wash.

Wasen m. (-s, -) turf, grass.

Wasser n. (-s, -°) water; *unter* ~
setzen to submerge, flood; *zu* ~
und zu Lande by land and sea; ~
ziehen to leak; *ins* ~ *fallen*,
zu ~ *werden* (*fig.*) to come to
naught, end in smoke; *von rein-
stem* ~ (*fig.*) of the first water;
mit allen ~*n gewaschen sein* to be
cunning; *sich über* ~ *halten* (*fig.*)
to keep one's head above water.

Wasser-armut f. scarcity of water.
~ball m. water-polo. **~behälter**
m. reservoir, tank, cistern. **~
blase** f. bubble; vesicle. **~blau**
a. sea-blue. **~bombe** f. depth-
charge. **~dicht** a. watertight;
waterproof. **~fall** m. waterfall.
~farbe f. water-colour; distemper. **~fläche** f. surface of water;
water-level; sheet of water. **~
flugzeug** n. sea-plane. **~glas**
n. water-glass; glass, tumbler.
~hahn m. tap; water-cock.
~haltig a. containing water,
aqueous; hydrous, hydrated.
~heilanstalt f. hydropathic.
~jungfer f. mermaid, water-
nymph. **~kanne** f. water-jug;
ewer. **~kante** f. (North Sea
and Baltic) sea-side. **~kessel** m.
kettle; cauldron, copper, tank;
boiler. **~kopf** m. hydrocephalus.
~kraft f. water power, hydraulic
power. **~kunst** f. artificial fountain; hydraulics; hydraulic engine. **~lache** f. pool. **~lauf** m.
watercourse. **~leitung** f. water
supply, water pipes, piping;
aqueduct. **~linse** f. duckweed.
~mangel m. scarcity of water.
~mann m. (*astron.*) Aquarius.
~messer m. water-gauge, hydrometer. **~mühle** f. water-mill. **~
ratte** f. water-rat; (*fig.*) old salt,
sea-dog. **~reich** a. rich in water;
of high humidity. **~schaden** m.
damage caused by water or
floods. **~scheide** f. watershed.
~scheu f. hydrophobia. **~snot**
f. inundation, floods. **~speicher**
m. reservoir, tank. **~speier** m.
gargoyle. **~spiegel** m. water-
surface, water-level. **~sport** m.
aquatic sports. **~stand** m. water-
level, state of the tide. **~stands-
messer** m. water-gauge. **~stiefel**
m.pl. rubber boots. **~stoff** m.
hydrogen. **~stoffhaltig** a. containing hydrogen. **~stoffsuper-
oxyd** n. hydrogen peroxide. **~
strahl** m. jet of water. **~straße** f.
waterway, navigable river. **~
sucht** f. dropsy. **~süchtig** a.
dropsical. **~suppe** f. gruel. **~
vögel** m.pl. water-fowl. **~waage**
f. water-level, gauge. **~werk** n.

waterworks. ~zeichen *n.* watermark.

Wässer-chen *n.* rivulet, brook. ~ig *a.* watery, aqueous, serous; *einem den Mund ~ig machen* to make a person's mouth water.

wassern *v.i. (av.)* to alight on water.

wässer-n *v.t.* to water, irrigate; *(phot.)* to wash; to soak; to dilute. ~ung *f.* watering, irrigation; soaking; hydration.

waten *vvs.i.* to wade.

watscheln *vvs.i.* to waddle.

Watt[1] *n.* (-s, -) *(electr.)* watt.

Watt[2] *n.* (-es, -e) mud flat, shore belt. ~enmeer *n.* shallows, shallow sea.

Watt-e *f.* (-e, -en) wadding, cotton-wool. ~ebausch *m.* pad of cotton-wool, tuft of cotton-wool. ~'ieren *v.t.* to pad, line with wadding; to wad, quilt. ~ierung *f.* padding.

Web-ebaum *m* weaver's beam, warp-beam. ~ekante *f.* selvage (of cloth). ~er *m.*, ~erin *f.* weaver. ~e'rei *f.* weaving; weaver's trade; weaving-mill; texture, woven material. ~erknecht *m.* (*zool.*) daddy-long-legs. ~erschifchen *n.* shuttle. ~ervogel *m.* weaver-bird. ~stuhl *m.* weaver's loom. ~waren *f.pl.* textiles.

weben (ve:-) *v.t. & i. st.* to weave; *(poet.)* to float; to move, be active.

Wechsel (vck-) *m.* (-s, -) change, alteration; succession, turn, alternation, rotation; fluctuation; vicissitude; exchange; relay (of horses); *(hunt.)* runway; *(commerc.)* bill of exchange; *eigener ~* note of hand; *gezogener ~* draft.

Wechsel-balg *m.* changeling. ~beziehung *f.* correlation. ~fälle *m.pl.* vicissitudes, ups and downs. ~fälscher *m.* forger of bills. ~fälschung *f.* forgery of bills. ~fieber *n.* malaria, intermittent fever. ~folge *f.* alternation. ~geld *n.* change; small change. ~gesang *m.* amoebaean song, antiphony. ~geschäft *n.* banking business; exchange office. ~gespräch *n.*, ~rede *f.* dialogue. ~getriebe *n.* change (speed) gear. ~haft *a.*

changing. ~jahre *n.pl.* climacteric. ~kurs *m.* rate of exchange. ~makler *m.* bill-broker. ~ordnung *f.* codified law of bills of exchange. ~rede *f.* dialogue. ~reiterei *f.* bill-jobbing. ~schaltung *f.* alternating switch. ~seitig *a.* reciprocal, mutual; alternate. ~spiel *n.* interplay. ~streit *m.* conflict, dispute. ~strom *m.* alternating current. ~stube *f.* exchange office. ~tierchen *n.* amoeba. ~weise *adv.* alternately; reciprocally, mutually. ~wirkung *f.* reciprocal action, mutual effect.

wechs-eln (vck-) *v.t. & i.* to change, exchange; to vary; to alternate (with); to shift (scene); to cut (new teeth); *seinen Wohnort ~eln* to remove, go elsewhere. ~ler *m.* money-changer.

Weck(en) *m.* (-ens, -en) (bread) roll.

weck-en *v.t.* to wake, awaken, rouse, call. *subst. n.* reveille. ~er *m.*, ~uhr *f.* alarm-clock. ~ruf *m.* reveille; call.

Wedel (ve:-) *m.* (-s, -) fan; feather-duster; tail, brush; (*bot.*) frond; palm-leaf. ~n *v.i.* to fan; (*of dog*) to wag (its tail).

weder (ve:-) *conj.* neither.

Weg[1] (ve:k) *m.* (-es, -e) way, path; road, street; route, course; walk; errand; manner, means; *am ~e* by the roadside; *auf halbem ~e* half-way, midway; *sich auf den ~ machen* to set out, start; *seiner ~e gehen* to go one's way; *woher des ~es?* where do you come from; *aus dem ~e gehen* to make way for, stand aside; (*fig.*) to evade, shirk; *im ~e sein* to be in the way; *aus dem ~e räumen* to remove; to kill, bump off; *in die ~e leiten* to pave the way for, prepare for; *auf gütlichem ~e* in a friendly way, amicably; *das hat gute ~e* there is no hurry. ~bereiter *m.* forerunner, pioneer. ~ebau *n.* road-making. ~egabel *f.* road fork. ~elagerer *m.* highwayman. ~enge *f.* narrow defile. ~sam *a.* practicable, passable (road). ~scheide *f.* cross-roads.

WEG

road fork. **~strecke** f. stretch of road; length of way; distance. **~stunde** f. league. **~warte** f. chicory. **~weiser** m. signpost, (direction) indicator; guide (book). **~zehrung** f. provisions or food taken on a journey.

weg² (vɛk) adv. & sep. pref. away; gone, lost; disappeared; beyond; ~ da! be off! get out! Hände ~! hands off! ganz ~ sein (colloq.) to be in raptures (about). **~bleiben** vws.i. to stay away; to be omitted. **~bringen** v.t. to take away, remove. **~eilen** vws.i. to hurry off, hasten away. **~fahren** v.t. to remove, cart away. vws.i. to drive off. **~fall** m. cessation; omission; abolition; in ~fall kommen to be abolished. **~gang** m. departure. **~geben** v.t. to give away. **~gehen** vws.i. to go away, depart, leave. **~haben** v.t. to have received; (fig.) to have got the knack of. **~jagen** v.t. to drive away. **~kommen** vws.i. to get away; to get lost; gut ~kommen to come off well. **~lassen** v.t. to leave out, omit; to let go. **~legen** v.t. to put away. **~nahme** f. seizure, capture, confiscation. **~nehmen** v.t. to take away, carry off; to confiscate; to take up, occupy (space, &c.). **~räumen** v.t. to clear away, remove. **~schaffen** v.t. to remove. **~scheren** v.r. to decamp, be off. **~schnappen** v.t. to snatch away. **~stehlen** v.r. to steal away. **~treten** vws.i. to step aside; (mil.) to break the ranks. **~tun** v.t. to put away, remove. **~werfen** v.t. to throw away. **~werfend** a. disparaging, contemptuous. **~ziehen** v.t. to pull away. vws.i. to remove, go somewhere else. **~zug** m. removal, departure.

wegen (ve:-) prep. on account of, because of, for, for the sake of; in consideration of; with regard to; regarding; in consequence of, owing to.

Wegerich m. (-s, -e) (bot.) plantain.

weh (ve:) int. alas! O dear! a. pain-ful, sore, aching; ~ tun to ache, hurt. subst. n. woe; pain; grief. **~en** pl. labour pains, travail. **~geschrei** n. lamentations, wailings. **~klage** f. lamentation, wail. **~klagen** v.i. to lament, wail. **~leidig** a. woebegone, plaintive. **~mut** f. sadness, melancholy. **~mütig** a. sad, melancholy. **~mutter** f. midwife. [WOE]

Wehe f. (-, -n) (snow-)drift. **~n** v.t. & i. to blow, blow away; to flutter, wave.

Wehr¹ (ve:r) n. (-es, -e) weir; dam, dike.

Wehr² (ve:r) f. (-) weapon, arm; equipment; bulwark; defence, resistance; sich zur ~ setzen to offer resistance, resist, show fight. **~bezirk** m. military district subarea. **~dienst** m. service with the colours. **~fähig** a. fit to bear arms, able-bodied. **~gehenk** n. sword-belt. **~haft** a. strong, full of fight. **~kraft** f. armed forces. **~los** a. unarmed; defenceless, weak. **~losigkeit** f. defencelessness. **~macht** f. the Armed Forces. **~machtbericht** m. official army communiqué. **~ordnung** f. conscription regulations. **~pflicht** f. compulsory military service, conscription. **~pflichtig** a. liable to military service. **~sport** m. army sports. **~stand** m. the military profession, the army. **~vorlage** f. army bill. **~wille** m. desire for military preparedness. **~wissenschaft** f. military science.

wehren v.t. & i. to hinder, forbid, keep from, restrain; to arrest, check. v.r. to defend oneself, resist; sich seiner Haut ~ to fight for one's life.

Weib (vaip) n. (-es, -er) woman, female; wife. **~chen** n. little woman; (zool.) female, she-, -hen. **~erfeind** m. woman-hater, misogynist. **~isch** a. womanish; effeminate. **~lich** a. female; feminine, womanly. **~lichkeit** f. womanliness; womanhood; feminine nature. **~sbild** n. female, hussy. **~svolk** n. womenfolk.

weich (-ç) a. soft, mild, mellow; tender; smooth; supple, pliant;

yielding; sensitive; ~es Ei lightly boiled egg; ~ werden to soften, relent, be moved. ~heit f. softness; mellowness; tenderness; gentleness. ~herzig a. tenderhearted. ~lich a. soft; flabby, sloppy; effeminate, weak. ~lichkeit f. softness; flabbiness; effeminacy, weakness. ~ling m. weakling, molly-coddle. ~teile m.pl. belly, abdomen. ~tier n. mollusc. [WEAK]

Weichbild n. outskirts (of a town); precincts; municipal area.

Weiche¹ f. (-, -n) softness; flank, side; weak part; groin.

Weiche² f. (-, -n) (rail.) points; switch, shunt. ~nhebel m. switchlever. ~nschiene f. movable rail, switch-rail. ~nsignal n. switchsignal. ~nsteller m. pointsman.

weichen¹ v.t. to make soft, soften; to soak, steep. vvs.i. to become soft.

weichen² vvs.i. st. to give ground, fall back, retreat; to give in, yield; zum ~ bringen to push back, repel.

Weichselkirsche f. morello cherry.

Weide¹ f. (-, -n) pasture; pasturage. ~land n. pasture-land.

Weide² f. (-, -n) willow, osier. ~n a. willow. ~ngeflecht n. wickerwork. ~ngerte, ~nrute f. willow-twig, osier switch. ~nkätzchen n. catkin. ~nkorb m. wicker basket. ~nröschen n. willow-herb.

weiden v.t. & i. to graze, drive to pasture; (fig.) to delight (in), feast (one's eyes on).

weidlich a. brave, valiant. adv. very much, thoroughly, properly.

Weid-mann m. huntsman, sportsman. ~männisch a. sportsmanlike. ~messer n. hunting-knife. ~werk n. chase, sport, hunt. ~wund a. shot in the intestines.

weiger-n v.r. to refuse, decline. ~ung f. refusal.

Weih m. (-es, -e) (zool.) kite.

Weih-altar m. holy altar. ~bischof m. suffragan bishop.

Weih-e f. (-e, -en) consecration; dedication; ordination; initiation;

inauguration; solemn mood. ~en v.t. to consecrate; to dedicate; to ordain; to bless. v.r. to devote oneself (to). ~evoll a. solemn, holy, hallowed. ~gabe f. votive offering. ~nacht &c. see below. ~rauch m. incense. ~rauchfaß n. censer. ~wasser n. holy water. ~wasserbecken n. font; stoup. ~wasserkessel m. aspersorium, font. ~(wasser)wedel m. aspergillum.

Weiher m. (-s, -) (fish-)pond. [L]

Weihnacht-en f.pl. Christmas. ~lich a. Christmas, of Christmas. ~sabend m. Christmas Eve. ~sbaum m. Christmas tree. ~sbescherung f. distribution of Christmas presents. ~slied n. carol. ~smann m. Father Christmas.

weil conj. because, since.

weiland adv. formerly, of old; late, deceased.

Weile f. (-) while, (space of) time; leisure; damit hat es gute ~ there's no hurry; eile mit ~ more haste, less speed. ~n v.i. to stay, stop; to linger.

Weiler m. (-s, -) hamlet.

Wein m. (-es, -e) wine; vine; grapes; wilder ~ Virginia creeper. ~bau m. wine-growing. ~bauer m. vine-grower, vine-dresser. ~beere f. grape. ~berg m. vineyard. ~bergschnecke f. edible snail. ~ernte f. vintage. ~essig m. wine vinegar. ~faß n. winecask. ~geist m. (ethyl) alcohol, spirit of wine. ~händler m. wine-merchant. ~karte f. winelist. ~laub n. vine leaves or foliage. ~lese f. vintage. ~leser m., ~leserin f. vintager. ~probe f. sample of wine; tasting of wine. ~ranke f. vine branch or tendril. ~rebe f., ~stock m. vine. ~reisende(r) m. traveller for a wine-firm. ~schenk m. cupbearer. ~stein m. tartar. ~traube f. grape; bunch of grapes. ~zwang m. obligation to order wine (with a meal).

wein-en v.i. & t. to weep, cry. ~erlich a. inclined to weep; whining. ~krampf m. crying-fit, convulsive sobbing.

weise¹ *a.* wise; prudent. *subst. m.* wise man.

Weise² (-za) *f.* (-, -n) manner, way, method, fashion; habit, custom; tune, melody; *auf diese* ~ in this way; *in der* ~, *daß* in such a way that; so that.

weis-en (-zan) *v.t. & i. st.* to show; to indicate, point out; to direct; to refer (to); to point at; ~*en aus* to expel; *von sich* ~*en* to refuse, decline, reject. ~**er** *m.* pointer, indicator. ~**ung** *f.* order, instruction.

Weisheit *f.* (-, -en) wisdom; prudence.

weislich *adv.* wisely, prudently.

weis-machen *v.t.* to make one believe (a thing), hoax. ~**sagen** *v.t.* to prophesy, predict. ~**sager** *m.*, ~**sagerin** *f.* prophet; prophetess; fortune-teller. ~**sagung** *f.* prophecy, prediction.

weiß¹ *1st & 3rd pers. sing. pres. of* **wissen**.

weiß² *a.* white; clean; blank; hoary; ~*er Sonntag* Sunday after Easter, Low Sunday; *die* ~ *en* the white races. ~**bäckerei** *f.* baker and confectioner's shop. ~**bier** *n.* pale ale. ~**blech** *n.* tinplate. ~**brot** *n.* white bread. ~**buche** *f.* hornbeam. ~**dorn** *m.* hawthorn. ~**fisch** *m.* whitebait. ~**fluß** *m.* leucorrhoea. ~**gerber** *m.* tawer. ~**glühend** *a.* white-hot; incandescent. ~**glut** *f.* white heat. ~**kohl** *m.* white cabbage. ~**lich** *a.* whitish. ~**näherin** *f.* needlewoman. ~**tanne** *f.* silver fir. ~**waren** *f.pl.* linen goods, drapery. ~**wein** *m.* white wine, hock. ~**wurst** *f.* Bavarian sausage. ~**zeug** *n.* (household-)linen.

weißen *v.t.* to whiten; to whitewash.

weit *a.* distant, far away, remote; long (way); far; wide, broad, extensive, spacious; capacious; immense, vast; loose; ~ *und breit* far and wide; *drei Meter* ~ a distance of three metres; *bei* ~*em* by far, much; *bei* ~*em nicht* by no means; *von* ~*em* from a distance, from afar; *es* ~ *bringen* to get on (well); *nicht* ~ *her sein* not

to be worth much; ~ *gefehlt!* you are quite wrong; *wenn alles so* ~ *ist* when everything is ready; *das* ~ *e suchen* to decamp. ~**ab** *adv.* far away. ~**aus** *adv.* by far, much. ~**blick** *m.* foresight, far-sightedness.

Weit-e *f.* (-e, -en) width, size; capacity; extent; distance, length; *(fig.)* range; comprehensiveness; breadth. ~**gehend** *a.* far-reaching; full (understanding), much. ~**her** *adv.* from afar. ~**hin** *adv.* far away, far off. ~**läufig** *a.* distant; wide, extensive, roomy, spacious, vast; detailed, circumstantial; complicated. ~**maschig** *a.* with wide meshes. ~**schweifig** *a.* long-winded; detailed, circumstantial; tedious. ~**schweifigkeit** *f.* verbosity. ~**sichtig** *a.* long-sighted; *(fig.)* far-sighted. ~**sichtigkeit** *f.* long-sightedness. ~**sprung** *m.* long jump. ~**verbreitet** *a.* widespread, prevalent, general.

weiten *v.t.* to widen, expand, enlarge; to stretch (shoe). *v.r.* to broaden out; *(fig.)* to broaden.

weiter *comp. a.* farther; further, additional; wider, more extensive. *adv.* farther, further; more, else; forward, on; *und so* ~ and so on; *nichts* ~ nothing more; *was* ~? what else?; ~ *niemand* no one else; *nur* ~! go on! proceed; *des* ~*en* furthermore; moreover; *bis auf* ~*es* until further notice, for the present; *ohne* ~*es* without more ado, immediately. ~**befördern** *v.t.* to forward. ~**bestehen** *v.i.* to continue to exist, go on. ~**bringen** *v.t.* to help on. *v.i. es* ~*bringen* to get on, make progress. ~**führen** *v.t.* to continue, carry on. ~**geben** *v.t.* to pass on (to next person). ~**gehen** *vws.i.* to walk on; to go on, continue. ~**hin** *adv.* in future, after that. ~**kommen** *vws.i.* to get on; to progress, advance. ~**leiten** *v.t.* to transmit; to forward. ~**lesen** *v.t. & i.* to continue reading, go on reading. ~**reise** *f.* continuation of a journey. ~**sagen** *v.t.* to tell (others), repeat. **~ungen** f.pl. difficulties; complications; formalities.

Weizen (-tsən) m. (-s) wheat; corn. **~mehl** n. wheaten flour.

welch (-ç) pron. & a. which, what; who, which, that; some, any; *~er auch immer* whosoever. **~erart, ~ergestalt** advr. in what way or manner; by what means, how. **~erlei** indecl. a. of what kind.

welk a. withered; limp, flabby. **~en** vws.i. to wither, fade.

Wellblech n. corrugated iron.

Well-e (v-) f. (-e, -en) wave, billow, surge; frequency, wave(-length); (mach.) axle, shaft, spindle; bundle (of brushwood); *~en schlagen* to rise in waves. **~enbad** n. bathe; swimming-bath with artificial waves. **~enbewegung** f. undulation. **~enbrecher** m. breakwater. **~enförmig** a. wave-like, undulating. **~enlänge** f. wave-length. **~enlinie** f. wavy line. **~enreiter** m. surf rider. **~enschlag** m. dashing or breaking of waves. **~ensittich** m. budgerigar. **~entheorie** f. undulatory theory. **~enfleisch** n. boiled pork. **~ig** a. undulating; wavy. **~pappe** f. corrugated pasteboard. **~sand** m. shifting sand.

wellen v.t. to wave (hair).

Welpe f. (-, -n) whelp.

Wels m. (-es, -e) sheat-fish.

welsch see App. I.

Welt (v-) f. (-, -en) world; universe; people; *alle* ~ everybody, everyone, all the world; *auf der* ~ on earth; *auf die* ~ *kommen* to come into the world, be born; *aus der* ~ *schaffen* to put out of the way; *in die* ~ *setzen, zur* ~ *bringen* to give birth to, bring into the world. **~all** n. universe. **~alter** n. age, period in history. **~anschaulich** a. ideological. **~anschauung** f. (philosophical) conception of the world; world outlook, (one's) views, (one's) creed. **~ball** m. globe. **~bekannt** a. known everywhere, world-famous. **~bild** n. conception of the world. **~bummler** m. globe-

trotter. **~bürger** m. citizen of the world, cosmopolitan. **~dame** f. woman of the world; fashionable lady. **~eislehre** f. glacial cosmogony. **~entrückt** a. isolated, detached. **~ereignis** n. event of world-wide importance. **~erschütternd** a. world-shaking. **~fremd** a. secluded, solitary; ignorant of the world. **~geistliche(r)** m. secular priest. **~gericht** n. last judgement. **~geschichte** f. universal history. **~gewandt** a. knowing the (ways of the) world. **~handel** m. international trade, world commerce. **~händel** pl. political struggles. **~kind** n. worldling. **~klug** a. worldly-wise; prudent. **~körper** m. heavenly body, sphere. **~kugel** f. globe. **~lage** f. general political situation; state of political affairs. **~lauf** m. course of the world.

weltlich a. worldly; mundane; secular; profane; temporal. **~keit** f. worldliness.

Welt-macht f. world power. **~mann** m. man of the world, society man. **~männisch** a. well-bred; society (man). **~meister** m. world champion. **~meisterschaft** f. world championship. **~politik** f. foreign policy on the grand scale. **~postverein** m. Postal Union. **~priester** m. secular priest. **~raum** m. space; universe. **~ruf** m. world-wide reputation. **~schmerz** m. pessimistic outlook on life in general. **~sprache** f universal language. **~stadt** f. metropolis. **~teil** m. continent; quarter of the globe; part of the world. **~umseglung** f. circumnavigation of the world. **~umspannend** a. world-wide, universal. **~untergang** m. end of the world. **~verloren** a. cut off from the world, lonely. **~wende** f. turning-point in world history. **~wunder** n. wonder of the world.

wem dat. of **wer** to whom. **~fall** m. dative case.

wen acc. of **wer** whom. **~fall** m. accusative case.

Wend-e f. (-e, -en) turn; turning-point; change; new epoch or era; (gym.) face vault. **~ehals** m. wryneck (bird). **~ekreis** m. tropic. **~epunkt** m. turning-point, crisis; solstitial point. **~ig** a. nimble; manœuvrable; (fig.) versatile. **~ung** f. turn; turning; (mil.) wheeling, facing (about); turning-point, change, crisis; phrase, saying, idiomatic expression.

Wendeltreppe f. spiral staircase.

wenden v.t. st. & w. to turn, turn round; sich ~ an to turn to, apply to; Geld ~ an to spend money on; bitte ~ ! please turn over.

wenig (ve:nıç) a. little; (pl.) few, a few. **~er** comp. a. less; vier ~ zwei four minus two; nichts ~er als anything but; nicht ~er als no less than. **~keit** f. small quantity; trifle; meine ~keit my humble self. **~st** sup. a. least; nicht zum ~sten last not least; die ~sten only a few (people). **~stens** adv. at least.

wenn (vɛn) conj. when; if, in case jedesmal ~ whenever; ~ anders if indeed, provided that, if at all, if really; ~ auch although, even if; ~ auch noch so if ever so; ~ nicht, außer ~ unless, except when or if; selbst ~ even if, even supposing that, though. **~gleich**, **~schon** conjj. though, although.

wer (ve:r) pron. who; which; he who; that; (colloq.) somebody, anyone; ~ auch immer whoever; ~ da? who goes there? **~fall** m. (gram.) nominative.

Werbefunk m. commercial radio.

werb-en v.t. st. to recruit, levy, enrol, enlist. v.i. ~en um to court, woo; to sue for; to ask for (hand in marriage); to enlist a person's sympathy); to engage a person for something); **~en für** to make propaganda for; to canvass for; to advertise for. **~ekosten** pl. advertising expenses. **~eleiter** m. manager of the advertising department. **~etexter** m. propaganda text writer. **~etrommel** f. die **~etrommel rühren**

to beat up recruits; (fig.) to make propaganda. **~ung** f. recruiting, levying; wooing, courting; propaganda.

Werdegang m. development; growth, process; evolution; career.

werden vws.i. irreg. to become, grow; to turn out, prove; to happen; (fut.) shall, will; (pass.) be, is, are, &c.; ~ zu to change into, turn into; **~de Mutter** expectant mother. subst. n. growing, developing; development; evolution, formation, rise, genesis, growth, origin.

Werder m. (-s, -) river islet, holm.

werfen v.t. st. to throw, hurl, cast, fling, toss, pitch; to bring forth (young). v.r. to warp; sich ~ auf to throw oneself upon, engage vigorously in, apply oneself to.

Werft f. (-, -en) wharf; shipyard, dockyard; workshops (of airfield). **~arbeiter** m. dock labourer, docker. **~besitzer** m. wharfinger.

Werg (-k) n. (-es) tow, oakum.

Werk n. (-es, -e) work, labour; workmanship; production; performance; action; deed; undertaking, factory, workshops, works; mechanism; clock-work; ans ~! go to it; ins ~ setzen to set going; zu ~e gehen to set about, begin. **~führer**, **~meister** m. foreman, overseer. **~heilige(r)** m. hypocrite. **~leute** pl. workmen, hands, workpeople. **~spionage** f. industrial spying system. **~statt**, **~stätte** f. workshop. **~stein** m. freestone. **~stoff** m. material. **~student** m. student who earns his living. **~tag** m. working-day; week-day. **~tags** adv. on week-days. **~tätig** a. active; working; **~tätige Bevölkerung** working classes. **~zeug** n. tool, implement, instrument; organ. **~zeugmaschine** f. machine tool.

Wermut m. wormwood; vermouth.

wert a. valuable; worth; worthy; dear; honoured, esteemed; nichts ~ sein to be no good, be worthless. subst. m. (-es, -e) value, worth; use; price, rate; importance, stress; appreciation, merit; (chem.) valence; *gleicher* ~ equivalent; *im* ~ *e von* at a price of; to the value of; ~ *legen auf* to attach great importance to, set great store by. ~**angabe** *f.* declaration of value. ~**beständig** *a.* stable, of fixed value. ~**brief** *m.* registered letter, letter containing money. ~**gegenstände** *m.pl.* valuables. ~**igkeit** *f.* (chem.) valence. ~**los** *a.* worthless. ~**messer** *m.* standard (of value). ~**paket** *n.* registered parcel, parcel containing valuables. ~**papier** *n.* security, bond. ~**sachen** *f.pl.* valuables. ~**schätzen** *v.t.* to value, esteem highly. ~**schätzung** *f.* esteem, value; appreciation (of). ~**sendung** *f.* parcel containing money or valuables. ~**urteil** *n.* judgement as to value. ~**voll** *a.* valuable, precious. ~**zeichen** *n.* paper money; stamp. ~**zuwachssteuer** *f.* 'increased value' tax.

werten *v.t.* to value, appraise.

wes = **wessen**. ~**fall** *m.* (gram.) genitive case. ~**halb**, ~**wegen** *adv. & conjj.* why, wherefore; on account of which; therefore, so.

Wesen *n.* (-s, -) being, creature; essence; reality, substance, nature, intrinsic virtue; character, disposition; system, organization; conduct, manners; way, air, demeanour, bearing; *sein* ~ *treiben* to go about; to haunt (a place); *viel* ~*s machen von* to make a fuss about. ~**haft** *a.* real; substantial. ~**los** *a.* incorporeal; unreal, shadowy. ~**seigen** *a.* characteristic. ~**seinheit** *f.* consubstantiality. ~**sgleich** *a.* consubstantial; homogeneous. ~**szug** *m.* characteristic feature.

wesentlich *a.* essential, substantial; real, intrinsic; important, material, vital.

Wesir *m.* vizier.

Wespe *f.* (-, -n) wasp. ~**nstich** *m.* wasp's sting.

wessen (gen. of pron. **wer**) whose.

West (v-) *m.* west; (poet.) west wind. ~**en** *m.* the west, the oc-

cident. ~**lich** *a.* west, westerly, western, occidental, westward. ~**mächte** *f.pl.* Western Powers. ~**wärts** *adv.* westward.

Weste *f.* (-,-n) waistcoat, vest. ~**ntasche** *f.* waistcoat-pocket.

wett *a.* equal; ~ *sein* to be quits. ~**bewerb** *m.* competition; (sport.) event. ~**bewerber** *m.* competitor.

Wett-e *f.* (-e, -en) wager, bet; *was gilt die* ~*e?* what do you bet; *eine* ~*e eingehen* to make a bet; *um die* ~*e laufen* to race someone; *um die* ~*e . . .* to vie with one another in. ~**eifer** *m.* emulation, rivalry, competition. ~**eifern** *v.i.* to emulate; to vie, contend (with). ~**fahrt** *f.* (boat, &c.) race. ~**flug** *m.* air race. ~**kampf** *m.* match, contest, prize-fighting. ~**kämpfer** *m.* champion, athlete; prizefighter. ~**lauf** *m.* race, foot-race, running match. ~**läufer** *m.* runner. ~**machen** *v.t.* to make up for. ~**rennen** *n.* race, racing. ~**rüsten** *n.* armaments race. ~**spiel** *n.* match, tournament. ~**streit** *m.* competition, contest, match.

wett-en *v.t. & i.* to bet, wager; to bet (on), back (a horse). ~**er**[1] *m.* better, backer.

Wetter[2] *n.* (-s, -) weather; bad weather, storm, tempest; *schlagende* ~ fire-damp; *alle* ~! my word! by Jove! ~**bericht** *m.* meteorological report, weather forecast. ~**beständig** *a.* weatherproof. ~**dienst** *m.* meteorological service. ~**fahne** *f.* vane, weathercock. ~**fest** *a.* weatherproof. ~**glas** *n.* barometer. ~**hahn** *m.* weathercock. ~**karte** *f.* meteorological chart, weather chart. ~**lage** *f.* weather conditions, atmospheric conditions. ~**läuten** *n.* ringing of bells as storm-signal. ~**leuchten** *n.* sheet-lightning. ~**schacht** *m.* air-shaft. ~**seite** *f.* weather side. ~**stein** *m.* belemnite. ~**sturz** *m.* sudden fall of temperature. ~**umschlag**, ~**wechsel** *m.* change of weather. ~**vorhersage** *f.* weather forecast. ~**warte** *f.* meteorological station. ~**wendisch** *a.* fickle, changeable, capricious. ~**wolke** *f.*

thundercloud. **~zeichen** n. sign of storm.

wettern v.i. to thunder and lighten, storm, be stormy; (fig.) to curse and swear.

wetz-en v.t. to whet, grind, sharpen. **~stein** m. whetstone, hone.

wich imperf. of **weichen**.

Wichs (viks) m. full dress, (sl.) glad rags. **~bürste** f. blacking-brush. **~e** f. blacking, polish; (fig.) thrashing. **~en** v.t. to black, polish; (fig.) to thrash.

Wicht (-çt) m. (-es, -e) creature; child, chit, chap; wight. **~el-männchen** n. brownie, pixie, goblin.

wichtig (viçtiç) a. important, momentous; sich ~ machen to give oneself airs, assume an air of importance. **~keit** f. importance, moment. **~tuer** m. pompous individual. **~tuerei** f. pomposity, self-importance. [WEIGHTY]

Wicke f. (-, -n) vetch; sweet peas.

Wickel m. (-s, -) (ice-)pack; curler; beim ~ nehmen to catch hold of, collar. **~band** n. baby's binder. **~gamasche** f. puttee. **~kind** n. infant, baby in long clothes. **~n** v.t. to wind (round), roll (up); to wrap up; to make, roll (cigarette); to put (hair) in curlers; to put on a baby's clothes.

Widder (vi-) m. (-s, -) ram; (astron.) Aries.

wider (vi:-) prep. against, contrary to; versus. pref. counter-, contra-, re-, anti-, with-. **~borstig** a. cross-grained, intractable. **~druck** m. counterpressure, reaction. **~fahren** vvs.i. to happen, befall; to meet with. v.t. ~fahren lassen to mete out to. **~haarig** a. cross-grained, perverse. **~haken** m. barb, barbed hook. **~hall** m. echo; response. **~hallen** v.i. to echo, resound. **~halt** m. hold, support, prop. **~lager** n. abutment. **~legen** v.t. to refute, confute. **~legung** f. refutation.

wider-lich a. repulsive, disgusting, loathsome, repugnant, nauseous. **~lichkeit** f. repulsiveness, loathsomeness. **~natürlich** a. un-

natural, monstrous. **~part** m. adversary, opponent; opposition. **~raten** v.t. to dissuade (from). **~rechtlich** a. unlawful, illegal. **~rede** f. contradiction, objection. **~rist** m. withers. **~ruf** m. revocation; recantation, disavowal; (leg.) disclaimer; bis auf ~ruf until recalled. **~rufen** v.t. to revoke, recant, retract, withdraw, disavow. **~ruflich** a. revocable. **~sacher** m. adversary, opponent. **~schein** m. reflection. **~setzen** v.r. to oppose, resist. **~setzlich** a. refractory, insubordinate. **~setzlichkeit** f. refractoriness, insubordination. **~sinn** m. nonsense; absurdity. **~sinnig** a. nonsensical, absurd, contradictory.

wider-spenstig a. refractory; obstinate. **~spenstigkeit** f. refractoriness; obstinacy. **~spiegeln** v.t. to reflect; to mirror. v.r. to be reflected. **~spiel** n. contrary, reverse. **~sprechen** v.i. to contradict; to oppose. **~sprechend** a. contradictory; contrary to. **~spruch** m. contradiction; opposition; conflict. **~stand** m. resistance, opposition. **~stähig** a. resistant. **~stehen** v.i. to resist, withstand; to be repugnant to. **~streben** v.i. to struggle against; to resist; to be repugnant to, go against the grain. subst. n. reluctance, repugnance; opposition. **~strebend** a. reluctant. **~streit** m. opposition; conflict. **~streiten** v.i. to conflict, clash with, be contrary to; to militate against. **~wärtig** a. disagreeable; annoying; disgusting. **~wärtigkeit** f. nuisance; adversity, calamity, loathsomeness. **~wille** m. repugnance, aversion, disgust; reluctance. **~willig** a. reluctant, unwilling.

widm-en v.r. to dedicate. v.r. to devote oneself to. **~ung** f. dedication. **~ungsexemplar** n. presentation copy, inscribed copy.

widrig a. contrary; adverse; hostile, inimical; unfavourable; repugnant, disgusting. **~enfalls** adv. failing which. **~keit** f. adversity.

wie (vi:) *adv.* how. *conj.* as, such as, like; ~ *auch* (*immer*) however; ~ *bitte?* what did you say? I beg your pardon; ~ *gesagt* as has been said. ~'*so adv.* why. ~*viel adv.* how much; (*pl.*) how many; *der* ~*vielte ist heute?* what day of the month is it? ~*wohl conj.* although.

Wiedehopf *m.* (-es, -e) hoopoe.

wieder (vi:-) *adv. & pref.* again, anew, afresh; back, in return for; *immer* ~ again and again; *hin und* ~ now and then, from time to time.

wieder-abdrucken *v.t.* to reprint. ~**anfang** *m.* recommencement; reopening. ~**anknüpfen** *v.t.* to renew (acquaintance). ~**aufbau** *m.* reconstruction. ~**aufbauen** *v.t.* to reconstruct. ~**auffinden** *v.t.* to find, recover. ~**aufnahme** *f.* resumption. ~**aufnehmen** *v.t.* to resume, take up again. ~**beginn** *m.* recommencement. ~**bekommen** *v.t.* to get back, recover. ~**beleben** *v.t.* to revive, reanimate. ~**belebungsversuch** *m.* attempt at resuscitation. ~**bringen** *v.t.* to bring back; to restore, return to. ~**einnehmen** *v.t.* to recapture. ~**einsetzen** *v.t.* to reinstate; to replace. ~**erkennen** *v.t.* to recognize. ~**erlangen** *v.t.* to get back, recover. ~**erobern** *v.t.* to reconquer. ~**erstatten** *v.t.* to return, restore; to refund. ~**erstattung** *f.* restitution; repayment. ~**erzählen** *v.t.* to repeat; to retell. ~**finden** *v.t.* to find, recover. ~**gabe** *f.* return, giving back; rendering, reading; reproduction; translation. ~**geben** *v.t.* to give back, return; to render; to reproduce; to translate. ~**geburt** *f.* rebirth, regeneration. ~**gewinnen** *v.t.* to regain, recover, retrieve. ~**gutmachen** *v.t.* to make amends for; to compensate. ~**gutmachung** *f.* reparation. ~**haben** *v.t.* to have (got) back, have recovered. ~**herstellen** *v.t.* to restore; to repair; to cure; to re-establish. ~**herstellung** *f.* restoration; recovery.

wiederholen[1] *v.t.* to fetch or bring back.

wieder'hol-en[2] *v.t.* to repeat; to reiterate; to renew. *v.r.* to say (over and over) again; to recur. ~**t** *adv.* repeatedly, often, again and again. ~**ung** *f.* repetition; reiteration; *im* ~*ungsfalle* if it should happen again. ~**ungszeichen** *n.* (*mus.*) repeat; dittomarks.

wieder-hören *v.t.* to hear again; (*radio*) *auf* ~*hören!* good-bye, good night (everybody)! ~**instandsetzen** *v.t.* to recondition, repair. ~**instandsetzung** *f.* reconditioning. ~**käuen** *v.t.* to ruminate. ~**käuer** *m.* ruminant. ~**kehr** *f.* return, coming back, coming home; repetition, recurrence. ~**kehren** *vws.i.* to return, come back. ~**kunft** *f.* return, coming back; (second) advent (of Christ). ~**sagen** *v.t.* to repeat, tell again. ~**sehen** *v.t.* to see or meet again. *subst. n.* meeting (again), reunion; *auf* ~*sehen!* good-bye! so long! au revoir! ~**taufe** *f.* anabaptism. ~**täufer** *m.* anabaptist. ~**um** *adv.* again, anew, afresh; on the other hand. ~**vereinigen** *v.t.* to reunite; to reconcile. ~**vereinigung** *f.* reunion; reconciliation. ~**vergelten** *v.t.* to requite, retaliate. ~**vergeltung** *f.* retaliation. ~**verheiraten** *v.r.* to marry again, remarry. ~**verkäufer** *m.* retailer. ~**verwertung** *f.* reutilization, further utilization. ~**wahl** *f.* re-election. ~**zustellen** *v.t.* to return.

Wiege *f.* (-, -n) cradle. ~**messer** *n.* mincing-knife. ~**ndruck** *m.* incunabulum, early printed book. ~**nfest** *n.* birthday. ~**nkind** *n.* infant. ~**nlied** *n.* lullaby, cradle song.

wiegen[1] *v.t. & ist.* to weigh.

wiegen[2] *v.t.* to rock, move to and fro; to sway; to shake; to mince, chop up (meat). *v.r.* (*fig.*) to imagine, delude oneself (with), indulge (in hopes, &c.).

wiehern *v.i.* to neigh; ~*des Gelächter* horse-laugh, roaring laughter. *subst. n.* neighing.

wies *imperf. of* weisen.

Wiese (-zə) f. (-, -n) meadow. ~n-grund m. grassy valley, meadow-land. ~nschaumkraut n. lady's smock, cuckoo-flower.

Wiesel n. (-s, -) weasel.

wieviel and **wiewohl** see **wie-**.

wild (vilt) **1.** a. wild; rough, impetuous; savage, uncivilized; unruly, intractable; fierce, ferocious; angry, furious; untidy, dishevelled, unkempt; ~er Wein Virginia creeper; ~es Fleisch proud flesh; ~e Ehe unlawful marriage, concubinage; ~e Flucht headlong flight, rout; ~ werden to get furious; (of horse) to shy. **2.** subst. n. (-es) game, deer; venison.

Wild-bach m. torrent. ~bad n. hot springs. ~bahn f. preserve, hunting-ground. ~braten m. (roast) venison. ~bret n. venison, game. ~dieb m. poacher. ~erer m. poacher. ~dieberei f. poaching. ~e(r) m. savage. ~ente f. wild duck. ~fang m. wild boy; tomboy. ~fremd a. quite strange. ~gehege n. preserve, park. ~heit f. wildness; barbarity; ferocity. ~hüter m. gamekeeper. ~leder n., ~ledern a. deerskin, buckskin, doeskin; chamois-leather. ~ling m. wild tree; wild beast. ~nis f. wilderness; desert. ~schaden m. damage done by game. ~schütz(e) m. poacher. ~schwein n. wild boar. ~wasser n. torrent.

wildern v.i. to poach.

will 1st & 3rd pers. sing. pres. of **wollen**.

Wille m. (-n) will, volition, determination; wish; purpose, design, intention; guter ~ kind intention; letzter ~ last will, last testament; aus freiem ~n of one's own accord, voluntarily; mit ~n on purpose, intentionally; wider ~n unwillingly; involuntarily, unintentionally; in spite of oneself; einem zu ~n sein to do as a person wishes; um ... ~n for ... sake; ~ns sein to be willing or ready to. ~nlos a. lacking will-power, irresolute; weak-minded. ~nlosigkeit f. lack of will-power,

indecision. ~nsakt m. act of volition. ~nsfreiheit f. free will, freedom of will. ~nskraft f. will-power, strength of mind; faculty of volition. ~ntlich a. intentional, wilful.

will-'fahren v.i. to gratify, grant (wish); to please or humour (person); to accede or comply with. ~fährig a. accommodating, compliant. ~fährigkeit f. compliance. ~ig a. willing, ready. ~igen v.i. see **einwilligen**. ~igkeit f. willingness, readiness. ~kommen n. welcome, reception. a. welcome; acceptable, opportune; ~kommen heißen to welcome. ~kür f. discretion; choice; arbitrary action; despotism. ~kürlich a. arbitrary, despotic. ~kürlichkeit f. arbitrariness; arbitrary act.

wimmeln v.i. to swarm, teem (with).

wimmern v.i. to whimper, moan.

Wimpel m. (-s, -) pennon, pendant, pennant.

Wimper f. (-, -n) eyelash.

Wind (-t) m. (-es, -e) wind, breeze; (med.) flatulence; wind; guter ~ fair wind; bei ~ und Wetter in storm and rain, in all weathers; vor dem ~ segeln to run before the wind; in den ~ reden to talk in vain; in den ~ schlagen to disregard, make light of.

Wind-beutel m. éclair, cream puff; (fig.) windbag. ~ei n. wind-egg. ~eseile f. lightning speed. ~fahne f. weather vane. ~fang m. ventilator. ~harfe f. Aeolian harp. ~hose f. whirlwind. ~hund m. greyhound; whippet; borzoi; (fig.) wind-bag. ~ig a. windy, breezy; (fig.) unreliable; vain, empty. ~jacke f. waterproof jerkin, windproof jacket. ~licht n. storm lantern. ~messer m. anemometer. ~mühle f. windmill. ~mühlenflugzeug n. autogiro. ~pocken f.pl. chicken-pox. ~röschen n. anemone. ~rose f. compass card. ~sack m. wind-sleeve. ~sbraut f. gale, hurricane, whirlwind. ~schatten m. lee. ~schief a. twisted.

warped. ~(schutz)scheibe f. wind-screen. ~seite f. weather side. ~spiel n. whippet. ~stärke f. force of wind. ~still a. calm. ~stille f. calm. ~stoß m. gust of wind. ~strich m. point of the compass, rhumb. ~winkel m. (av.) angle of drift. ~zug m. draught, current of air; gust.

Winde f. (-, -n) winch; windlass; capstan; lifting-jack; (bot.) bindweed, wild convolvulus.

Windel f. (-, -n) baby's napkin; pilch. ~kind n. infant. ~n v.t. to swaddle. ~weich a. soft, yielding, compliant; ~weich schlagen to beat to a jelly.

wind-en v.t. st. to wind (on); to make (wreath); to reel; to hoist; to wrest or wrench (from). v.r. to writhe; to meander, wind; to twine (round). ~ung f. winding, twisting; turn, bend; convolution; coil; spire, whorl; worm (of screw).

Wink m. (-es, -e) sign; nod; wink; beckoning, wave; (fig.) hint, suggestion; tip. ~en v.i. to wave; to wink; to nod; to beckon; to make signs; (mil.) to signal, flag, semaphore. ~er m. flag or disk signaller; (motor.) trafficator. ~zeichen n.pl. manual signals.

Winkel m. (-s, -) corner; angle; anglepiece; nook, secret spot; (mil.) stripe on sleeve. ~advokat m. pettifogger, inferior legal practitioner. ~blatt n. local rag, obscure newspaper. ~eisen n. angle-iron. ~funktion f. trigonometric function. ~haken m. square, rule; composing-stick. ~ig, winklig aa. angular; crooked. ~kneipe f. low pub. ~maß n. square; rule. ~messer m. clinometer, goniometer. ~messung f. goniometry. ~zug m. trick, dodge.

winseln v.i. to whine.

Winter (v-) m. (-s, -) winter; im ~, ~s in winter(-time). ~frische f. winter resort. ~frucht f. winter crop. ~garten m. conservatory. ~hart a. hardy. ~lich a. wintry. ~märchen n. winter's tale. ~saat f. winter corn; winter crop. ~schlaf m. hibernation. ~schlußverkauf m. winter clearance sale. ~sport m. winter sports. ~süber adv. during winter(-time).

wintern v.i. to grow wintry.

Winzer m. (-s, -) vine-dresser, vine-grower; vintager.

winzig (vintsic) a. tiny, diminutive; minute. ~keit f. tininess, diminutive size; minuteness.

Wipfel m. (-s, -) tree-top.

Wippe f. (-, -n) see-saw. ~n v.i. to see-saw; to flap (wings).

wir (vi:r) pron. we.

wirb imper. of werben.

Wirbel m. (-s, -) eddy, whirlpool, vortex; wreath, curl (of smoke); (cervical) vertebra; crown (of head); roll (of drum); peg, pin (of violin); vom ~ bis zur Zeh from top to toe. ~ig a. whirling; giddy; wild, impetuous. ~kasten m. neck for pegs (of violin). ~knochen m. vertebra. ~los a. spineless, invertebrate. ~säule f. spine, vertebral column. ~sturm m. cyclone, tornado, hurricane. ~tier n. vertebrate animal. ~wind m. whirlwind.

wirbeln v.i. to whirl, eddy, whirl round, swirl round; (of drum) to roll; mir wirbelt der Kopf my head is swimming.

wirbt 3rd pers.sing.pres.of werben.

wird 3rd pers. sing. pres. of werden.

wirf, wirft imper. & 3rd pers. sing. pres. of werfen.

wirken v.t. to act, do, work, effect, produce, bring about; to weave (stocking); to knead (dough). v.i. to be active, work; ~ auf to have an effect on; to influence; to impress.

wirklich a. real, actual; true, genuine. adv. really, actually, truly. ~keit f. reality, actuality. ~snah a. realistic; naturalistic. ~sfremd a. (fig.) starry-eyed.

wirk-sam a. active; effective, efficient. ~samkeit f. activity; effectiveness, efficacy; effect; in ~samkeit treten to come into operation or force, take effect.

~ung f. action; working, operation, agency; efficacy; effect; impression; influence. **~ungsbereich** m. range, radius of action; zone of fire. **~ungskreis** m. sphere of activity, sphere of influence. **~ungslos** a. ineffectual, inefficient. **~ungsvoll** a. effective, striking. **~waren** f.pl. knitwear.

wirr a. dishevelled; confused; chaotic; wild. **~en** f.pl. disturbances, disorders. **~kopf** m. muddle-headed fellow. **~nis** f., **~sal** n., **~ung** f. confusion, disorder; error. **~warr** m. disorder, confusion, jumble, chaos.

Wirsing(kohl) m. savoy.

Wirt m. (-es, -e) host; innkeeper; proprietor, landlord. **~in** f. hostess; innkeeper; proprietrix, landlady. **~lich** a. hospitable; habitable. **~shaus** n. inn, public house. **~sleute** pl. host and hostess; innkeeper and innkeeper's wife; landlord and landlady. **~sstube** f. inn parlour, coffeeroom.

Wirtschaft f. (-, -en) housekeeping, domestic economy; household; economic system; industry and trade; husbandry; inn, public house; goings-on, to-do. **~en** v.i. to keep house; to economize, manage (well); (colloq.) to rummage about. **~er** m., **~erin** f. manager, manageress; steward, housekeeper. **~lich** a. economic; economical; profitable; thrifty. **~sbuch** n. housekeeping book. **~sgebäude** n. farm-buildings, outhouses. **~sgeld** n. housekeeping money. **~sgruppe** f. corporation; trust. **~sjahr** n. financial year. **~skrise** f. economic crisis. **~slage** f. economic situation. **~sprüfer** m. chartered accountant; (a firm's) general adviser. **~swissenschaft** f. political economy, science of production.

Wisch (v-) m. (-es, -e) scrap of paper, slip, note. **~en** v.t. to wipe. **~er** m. (drawing) stump; (motor.) windscreen-wiper. **~lappen** m. duster, cloth, rag.

Wisent (vi:z-) m. (-s, -e) bison.

Wismut m. (-s) bismuth.

wispern v.i. & t. to whisper.

Wißbegier, ~de f. thirst for knowledge, (intellectual) curiosity. **~ig** a. anxious to know or learn, inquisitive.

wissen irreg. v.t. & i. to know; to be aware of; to understand, be acquainted with; ich daß ich wußte not that I am aware of. subst. n. knowledge, erudition, learning, scholarship; meines ~s as far as I know, to the best of my belief; nach bestem ~ und Gewissen most conscientiously; wider besseres ~ against (one's) better judgement. **~schaft** f. science, knowledge, learning, scholarship. **~schaftler** m. scientist; scholar. **~schaftlich** a. scientific; scholarly, learned. **~sdrang, ~strieb** m. thirst for knowledge. **~swert** a. worth knowing, interesting. **~szweig** m. branch of knowledge. **~tlich** a. knowing; conscious; wilful, deliberate. adv. deliberately, on purpose.

wittern v.t. to scent, smell, perceive, suspect. **~ung** f. weather; scent. **~ungsumschlag** m. change of weather. **~ungsverhältnisse** n.pl. atmospheric conditions.

Witw-e (vitva) f. (-e, -en) widow; Königin **~e** queen dowager. **~enstand** m. widowhood. **~entracht** f. widow's weeds. **~enverbrennung** f. suttee. **~er** m. widower.

Witz m. (-es, -e) wit, wittiness; mother wit, common sense; witticism, joke, pun; **~e** machen or reißen to crack jokes. **~blatt** n. comic paper. **~bold** m. wit, wag. **~e'lei** f. witty chaffing. **~ig** a. witty; facetious, funny; smart, clever. **~sprühend** a. sparkling with wit.

witzeln v.i. to joke mildly; to poke fun (at).

wo (vo:) adv. where, in which; when; **~** auch immer wherever, whithersoever; von **~** whence, from which; **~** nicht if not, unless. **~anders** adv. somewhere else, elsewhere.

wob *imperf. of* **weben.**

wo'bei *adv.* whereat, whereby; where, in which, in the course of which; through which, by doing which; 'and here', 'in saying which'.

Woche (voxǝ) *f.* (-, -n) week; *heute in einer ~* today week, this day week; (*pl.*) childbed; *in die ~n kommen* to be delivered of; *in den ~n liegen* to be confined. **~n-bett** *n.* childbed. **~nblatt** *n.* weekly paper. **~nende** *n.* week-end. **~nfieber** *n.* puerperal fever. **~nlang** *a.* for weeks. **~nlohn** *m.* weekly wage. **~nschau** *f.* review of the week, weekly review; (*film*) news-reel. **~ntag** *m.* week-day, day of the week. **~ntags** *adv.* on week-days.

wöch-entlich (vœç-) *a.* weekly, every week, a week; by the week. **~nerin** *f.* woman in childbed.

wo'durch *adv.* by which, whereby, by which means. **~'fern** *conj.* (in) so far as; if, provided that; **~'fern nicht** unless. **~'für** *adv.* for which, for what, what for.

wog *imperf. of* **wiegen.**

Woge (vo:gǝ) *f.* (-, -n) wave, billow. **~n** *v.i.* to surge; to wave; to undulate; to heave; *hin und her ~n* to fluctuate.

wo'gegen *adv.* in return for what; in return for which; against what. *conj.* whereas, whilst, on the other hand. **~her** *adv.* whence, from what place; **~her wissen Sie das?** how do you know that? **~'hin** *adv.* whither, where (. . . to), to what place. **~hi'naus** *adv.* which way; to what place; where.

wohl (vo:l) **1.** *adv.* well; *~ bekomm's!* may it do you good! your health! *sich ~ sein lassen* to enjoy oneself; to have a good time; *~ dem, der . . .* happy he who; *~ oder übel* willy-nilly, come what may. **2.** (*particle*) about; possibly, probably; perhaps; very likely; to be sure; indeed. **3.** *subst. n.* good health; well-being, weal, welfare; prosperity; *auf Ihr ~!* your health! good luck! cheers!

wohl-'an *int.* now then! come on! well! **~'auf** *adv.* well, in good health. *int.* come on! now then! **~bedacht** *a.* well-considered. **~befinden** *n.* good health; well-being. **~behagen** *n.* (feeling of) comfort, ease. **~behalten** *a.* safe and sound. **~bekannt** *a.* well-known, familiar. **~beschaffen** *a.* in good condition. **~bestallt** *a.* duly appointed or installed. **~ergehen** *n.* well-being, welfare, health and happiness. **~erzogen** *a.* well-bred, well brought up. **~fahrt** *f.* welfare, weal. **~fahrtspflege** *f.* welfare work. **~feil** *a.* cheap. **~feilheit** *f.* cheapness. **~geartet** *a.* well-bred. **~geboren** *a.* (*obs.*) Esquire; Sir, Madam. **~gefallen** *n.* pleasure, satisfaction; (*bibl.*) good will. **~gefällig** *a.* pleasant, agreeable; complacent. **~gelitten** *a.* much liked, popular. **~gemeint** *a.* well-meant. **~gemut** *a.* cheerful, gay. **~genährt** *a.* well-fed. **~geruch** *m.* fragrance, sweet perfume. **~geschmack** *m.* pleasant taste or flavour. **~gesetzt** *a.* well-worded. **~gestalt** *a.* handsome, fine. **~gestaltet** *a.* well-made, finely shaped. **~habend** *a.* wealthy, well-off. **~habenheit** *f.* wealth, affluence, opulence.

wohlig *a.* comfortable; content, happy.

Wohl-klang, ~laut *m.* melodious sound; euphony, harmony, melody. **~klingend** *a.* harmonious, melodious. **~leben** *n.* good living, luxury, life of pleasure. **~riechend** *a.* fragrant, sweet-scented. **~schmeckend** *a.* tasty, palatable, savoury. **~sein** *n.* well-being; good health; *zum ~sein!* your health! cheers! **~stand** *m.* well-being, prosperity; wealth, fortune. **~tat** *f.* benefit; comfort, blessing; kindness; charity, benefaction. **~täter** *m.* benefactor. **~täterin** *f.* benefactress. **~tätig** *a.* beneficent; salutary; charitable. **~tätigkeit** *f.* charity. **~tuend** *a.* beneficial; comforting, pleasant. **~tun** *v.i.* to do good, dispense charity; to be comforting *or* pleasant. **~unterrichtet** *a.* well-informed. **~verdient** *a.* well-deserved *or* -merited. **~verhalten** *n.* good conduct. **~verstanden** *a.* well-understood. **~weislich** *adv.* prudently, wisely. **~wollen** *i.* good will, kind feeling, kindness, benevolence. *v.i.* to wish (one) well. **~wollend** *a.* kind, benevolent.

wohn-en *v.i.* to live, dwell, reside, stay; *zur Miete ~en* to lodge. **~haft** *a.* living, dwelling, resident. **~haus** *n.* dwelling-house. **~küche** *f.* parlour-kitchen. **~lich** *a.* comfortable, snug, cosy, warm. **~ort** *m.* place of residence, domicile. **~stube** *f.*, **~zimmer** *n.* sitting-room. **~ung** *f.* house, dwelling, residence; flat, rooms. **~ungsnachweis** *m.* house-agency. **~ungsnot** *f.* housing shortage. **~ungswechsel** *m.* change of residence. **~viertel** *n.* residential quarter *or* district. **~wagen** *m.* caravan.

wölb-en *v.t.* to vault, arch (over). *v.r.* to arch (over). **~ung** *f.* vault, vaulting; arch; dome.

Wolf *m.* (-es, ⁻e) wolf. **~eisen** *n.* wolf trap. **~shund** *m.* Alsatian dog. **~smilch** *f.* spurge.

Wölf-in *f.* (-in, -innen) she-wolf. **~isch** *a.* wolfish.

Wolfram *m.* tungsten, wolframite.

Wolk-e *f.* (-e, -en) cloud; *aus allen ~en fallen* to be thunderstruck. **~enbruch** *m.* cloud-burst. **~enkratzer** *m.* skyscraper. **~enlos** *a.* cloudless. **~enschicht** *f.* stratum of cloud. **~enwand** *f.* bank of clouds. **~ig** *a.* cloudy, clouded. [WELKIN]

Wolldecke *f.* blanket.

Woll-e *f.* (-e, -en) wool; *in der ~e gefärbt* dyed in the grain. **~en**¹ *a.* woollen; worsted. **~faser** *f.* wool fibre. **~ig** *a.* woolly. **~stoff** *m.* woollen material. **~waren** *f.pl.* woollens.

wollen² *irreg. v.t. & i.* to will; to be willing; to want, desire, wish; to like, choose; to intend; to be on the point of, be about to; to mean; *das will ich meinen!* I

should think so! rather!; *das will etwas heißen* that means something; *dem sei, wie ihm wolle* be that as it may; *er mag ~ oder nicht* whether he likes it or not; *er will gehört haben* he pretends *or* maintains he has heard; *wir ~ singen* let us sing; *lieber ~ to* prefer; *(das) wollte Gott!* I would to God. *subst. n.* will, volition; intention.

Wollust *f.* voluptuousness; lust.

wollüst-ig *a.* voluptuous. **~ling** *m.* voluptuary, debauchee.

wo-'mit *adv.* wherewith, with what; wherewith, by which, with which. **~'möglich** *adv.* if possible, possibly. **~'nach** *adv.* after which *or* what; whereupon, whereafter.

Wonn-e *f.* (-e, -en) joy, delight, bliss, rapture. **~emonat** *m.*, **~emond** *m.* month of May. **~esam** *a.* delightful, blissful. **~etrunken** *a.* enraptured. **~ig** *a.* delightful, delicious, blissful.

wo-'rauf *adv.* whereon; whereat; by what; of what; at which; by which; **~ran** *liegt es?* how is it that? **~'rauf** *adv.* whereupon; upon what, upon which. **~'raus** *adv.* out of which *or* what; from which, whence. **~'rein** *adv.* into which *or* what; with which.

Worfel *f.* (-, -n) winnowing-shovel. **~n** *v.t.* to winnow, fan.

wo-'rin *adv.* in which *or* what; wherein.

Wort (vort) *n.* (-es, -e; (*gram.*) Wörter) word; expression; term; saying; word of honour, promise; *kein ~ mehr!* not another word; *das ~ ergreifen* to (begin to) speak; *einem das ~ erteilen* to allow a person to speak; *ums ~ bitten* to ask leave to speak; *zu ~ kommen lassen* to let (one) have one's say; *das ~ führen* to be spokesman; *das große ~ führen* to swagger, brag; to monopolize the conversation; *das ~ haben* to have leave to speak; *viele ~e machen* to talk too much; to make a fuss; *einer Sache das ~ reden* to speak for *or* in favour of; *aufs ~ gehorchen* to obey implicitly; *einen beim ~ nehmen* to take one at one's word; *ins* ~ *fallen* to interrupt, cut short.

Wort-ableitung *f.* derivation of words; etymology. ~**arm** *a.* deficient in vocabulary. ~**armut** *f.* poverty of language. ~**aufwand** *m.* verbosity. ~**bildung** *f.* word-formation. ~**bruch** *m.* breach of one's word. ~**brüchig** *a.* having broken one's word; disloyal, treacherous. ~**emacher** *m.* idle talker, verbose speaker. ~**fechter** *m.* stickler for words. ~**feld** *n.* semantic field. ~**folge**, ~**stellung** *f.* word-order. ~**fügung** *f.* construction. ~**lehre** *f.* syntax. ~**führer** *m.* speaker; spokesman. ~**gefecht** *n.* dispute. ~**geklingel** *n.* jingle of words. ~**getreu** *a.* word for word, literal. ~**karg** *a.* laconic, taciturn. ~**kargheit** *f.* taciturnity. ~**klauberei** *f.* hair-splitting. ~**kunst** *f.* (good) literary style. ~**laut** *m.* wording, text. ~**reich** *a.* abundant in words; verbose, wordy. ~**schatz** *m.* vocabulary. ~**schwall** *m.* torrent of words; long rigmarole; verbosity, bombast. ~**sinn** *m.* meaning of a word; literal sense. ~**spiel** *n.* play upon words, pun. ~**wechsel** *m.* (high) words, dispute. ~**witz** *m.* pun. ~**wörtlich** *adv.* word for word, exactly (like that), literally.

Wört-erbuch *n.* dictionary. ~**lich** *a.* verbal, verbatim; literal; word for word

wo-'rüber *adv.* of what, about which *or* what; whereof, whereat; over which *or* what. ~**rum** *adv.* about what *or* which. ~**runter** *adv.* among what *or* which. ~**'selbst** *adv.* where. ~**von** *adv.* about what *or* which; whereof, of which. ~**'vor** *adv.* before what *or* which; of what *or* which. ~**zu** *adv.* for what, what . . . for; why; to which.

Wrack (vrak) *n.* (-es, -e) wreck.

wring-en *v.t. st.* to wring. ~**ma-schine** *f.* wringer.

Wruke *f.* (-, -n) Swedish turnip.

Wucher (vu:x-) *m.* (-s) usury; profiteering; (*bibl.*) interest. ~**ei**

f. usury; profiteering. ~**er** *m.* money-lender, usurer; profiteer. ~**gewinn** *m.* inordinate profit. ~**isch** *a.* usurious; profiteering. ~**ung** *f.* rank growth, exuberance; (*med.*) growth, tumour. ~**zins** *m.* usurious interest.

wuchern *v.i.* to practise usury, profiteer; (*fig.*) to make the most of; (*bot.*) to grow rankly *or* luxuriantly.

Wuchs[1] (vu:ks) *m.* (-es) growth; shape, figure, form.

wuchs[2] *imperf. of* **wachsen.**

Wucht (vuxt) *f.* (-) burden, weight; force; impetus. ~**en** *v.i.* to weigh heavy *or* heavily. *v.t.* to lever up. ~**ig** *a.* weighty, heavy.

Wühlarbeit *f.* subversive activity.

wühl-en *v.i. & t.* to dig, turn up (ground); to rummage, rake about (in); to burrow; to tear, gnaw (at); to be rolling (in money); (*fig.*) to agitate, stir up. ~**er** *m.* agitator. ~**e'rei** *f.* agitation. ~**maus** *f.* vole.

Wulst *m.* (-es, -̈e) roll, fold, pad; (*archit.*) torus. ~**ig** *a.* padded, stuffed; swelled. ~**lippen** *f.pl.* thick lips, blubber lips.

wund (v-t) *a.* sore; chafed; wounded; *sich* ~ *liegen* to get bed-sores; (*fig.*) ~**er** *Punkt* sore point. ~**arzneikunst** *f.* surgery. ~**arzt** *m.* surgeon.

Wund-e *f.* (-e, -en) wound. ~**fieber** *n.* wound fever. ~**gelaufen** *a.* footsore. ~(**en**)**mal** *n.* scar. ~**male** *n.pl.* (*theol.*) stigmata. ~**salbe** *f.* ointment for wounds.

Wunder *n.* (-s, -) miracle; wonder, marvel; *es nimmt mich* ~ *I* wonder at it; ~ *tun* to work wonders *or* miracles; *sein blaues* ~ *erleben* to be amazed; *sich* ~ *was einbilden* to be full of conceit, be very cocky.

wunder-bar *a.* wonderful, wondrous, marvellous; strange; miraculous. ~**barerweise** *adv.* strange to say. ~**bild** *n.* miracle-working image. ~**ding** *n.* wonderful thing, marvel. ~**doktor** *m.* quack. ~**glaube** *m.* belief in miracles. ~**horn** *n.* *des Knaben* ~*horn* The Boy's Magic Horn. ~**hübsch**

a. lovely. **~kind** *n.* infant prodigy. **~lich** *a.* strange, odd; eccentric. **~lichkeit** *f.* strangeness, oddness; eccentricity. **~sam** *a.* wonderful, wondrous; strange. **~schön** *a.* beautiful, lovely, exquisite. **~süchtig** *a.* longing for miracles. **~täter** *m.* miracle-worker. **~tätig** *a.* working wonders, miraculous. **~tier** *n.* monster; (*fig.*) prodigy. **~voll** *a.* wonderful, marvellous. **~zeichen** *n.* miraculous sign.

wundern *v.r.* to wonder (at), marvel (at); to be surprised.

Wunsch *m.* (**-es**, **⁺e**) wish, desire; *auf ~* by request; if desired; *nach ~* as one desires. **~bild** *n.* ideal. **~form** *f.* optative mood. **~gemäß** *adv.* according to one's wishes. **~konzert** *n.* request performance. **~traum** *m.* wish (-fulfilment) dream; wishful thinking. **~zettel** *m.* list of things desired, 'letter to Santa Claus'.

Wünschelrute *f.* divining-rod.

wünschen *v.t.* to wish, desire, wish for, long for; *Glück ~* to congratulate; to wish (a person) luck. **~swert** *a.* desirable.

wurde *imperf. indic.*, **würde** *condit. & subj. of* **werden**.

Würde (vyr-) *f.* (**-**, **-n**) dignity; honour, title, rank; (academic) degree; office; *in Amt und ~n* holding (high) office; *unter aller ~* beneath contempt. **~los** *a.* undignified. **~nträger** *m.* dignitary. **~voll** *a.* dignified, full of dignity.

würdig *a.* worthy of, deserving of; dignified; respectable. **~en** *v.t.* to value, appreciate; to deign; *nicht eines Wortes ~en* not to vouchsafe a word (to). **~keit** *f.* worth, merit. **~ung** *f.* appreciation; estimation; valuation.

Wurf *m.* (**-es**, **⁺e**) throw, cast, throwing; litter, brood; (*tech.*) projection; *zum ~ ausholen* to get ready to throw. **~bahn** *f.* trajectory. **~geschoß** *n.* projectile, missile. **~granate** *f.* mortar bomb. **~linie** *f.* line of projection. **~scheibe** *f.* discus; quoit. **~sendung** *f.* mass of circulars sent out. **~weite** *f.* range (of projection).

Würfel *m.* (**-s**, **-**) die; cube; hexahedron; *der ~ ist gefallen* the die is cast. **~becher** *m.* dice-box. **~bude** *f.* booth for dice-throwing (at fair). **~förmig** *a.* cubic, cuboidal, cube-shaped. **~ig** *a.* cubic; checkered. **~inhalt** *m.* cubic contents. **~muster** *n.* checkered pattern. **~spiel** *n.* game at dice. **~spieler** *m.* dice-player. **~zucker** *m.* lump sugar, cube sugar.

würfeln *v.i.* to play at dice, throw (dice).

würg-en *v.t.* to choke, strangle, throttle. *v.i.* to choke, stick in one's throat; to retch. **~engel** *m.* destroying angel. **~er** *m.* murderer, slayer; (*zool.*) butcher-bird. [WORRY]

Wurm *m.* (**-es**, **⁺er**) worm; maggot, grub; (*obs. & poet.*) dragon; (*colloq.*) poor little thing, little mite. **~abtreibend** *a.* **~abtreibendes Mittel** vermifuge. **~artig** *a.* worm-like, vermiform. **~fortsatz** *m.* appendix. **~ig** *a.* maggoty, worm-eaten. **~mehl** *n.* worm-dust. **~stichig** *a.* worm-eaten.

wurmen *v.t.* to vex, annoy; *es wurmt mich* it annoys me.

Wurst *f.* (**-**, **⁺e**) sausage; *~ wider ~* tit for tat; *das ist mir ~* it's all one to me. **~eln** *v.i.* (*colloq.*) to muddle along. **~ig** *a.* (*sl.*) quite indifferent. **~igkeit** *f.* complete indifference. **~kessel** *m.* sausage-boiler. **~waren** *f.pl.* sausages.

Würz-e (vyrtsə) *f.* (**-e**, **-en**) seasoning, flavour; spice; wort; (*fig.*) zest. **~en** *v.t.* to season, spice. **~ig** *a.* spicy, well-seasoned; piquant; aromatic, fragrant.

Wurzel *f.* (**-**, **-n**) root; (*math.*) radical; *~ schlagen* to take root. **~exponent** *m.* radical index. **~faser** *f.* root-fibre; rootlet. **~keim** *m.* radicle. **~knollen** *m.* tuber, bulb. **~los** *a.* without roots. **~schößling** *m.* sucker, runner, layer. **~ständig** *a.* radical. **~werk** *n.* roots. **~zeichen** *n.* radical sign.

wurzeln *v.i.* to root, take root, be rooted.

wusch *imperf.* of waschen.

wußte *imperf.* of wissen.

Wust (vu:-) *m.* (-es) confusion, chaos.

wüst (vy:-) *a.* waste, desert, desolate, deserted; disorderly, wild; coarse, vulgar, rude; dissolute. ~e *f.* desert, wilderness. ~e'nei *f.* desert place, wilderness. ~enschiff *n.* camel. ~ling *m.* libertine, dissolute person.

wüsten *v.i.* to squander, waste; to ruin, spoil.

Wut (vu:t) *f.* (-) rage, fury; *in* ~ *geraten* to fly into a rage. ~anfall *m.* fit of rage. ~entbrannt *a.* infuriated, enraged, furious. ~schäumend, ~schnaubend *aa.* foaming with rage, in a towering passion.

wüt-en (vy:-) *v.i.* to rage, be furious. ~end, ~ig *aa.* enraged, furious; mad. ~erich *m.* savage fellow; cruel tyrant.

X

X, x (iks) *n.* the letter X, x; *einem ein X für ein U machen* to bamboozle a person. ~beine *n.pl.* knock-knees. ~beinig *a.* knock-kneed. ~beliebig *a.* any, whoever, whatever (you like). ~mal *adv.* ever so often, hundreds of times. ~Strahlen *m.pl.* X-rays.

Xenie (kse:niə) *f.* (-, -n) (satirical) epigram.

Xylo'graph (ksy-) *m.* (-s, -en) xylographer.

Xylo'phon (ksy-) *n.* (-s, -e) xylophone.

Y

(See also under **J**)

Y, y (ypsilon) *n.* the letter Y, y.

Ysop (i:z-) *m.* (-s, -e) hyssop.

Z

(See also under **C**)

Z, z (tsɛt) *n.* the letter Z, z.

Zack-e (ts-) *f.* (-e, -en) peak, point; tooth (of comb); prong (of fork); scallop; (*bot.*) crenature. ~en *v.t.* to tooth, indent, notch; to scallop. ~ig *a.* jagged, pointed; notched, indented, toothed; pronged; branched; scalloped; serrate, crenate; (*sl.*) smart.

zag-en (tsa:-) *v.i.* to be afraid, hesitate. *subst. n.* fear, timidity, hesitation. ~haft *a.* timid, timorous. ~haftigkeit *f.* timidity, fear.

zäh (-e) (tsɛ:) *a.* tough; viscous; tenacious, stubborn. ~flüssig *a.* viscous. ~igkeit *f.* toughness, tenacity; viscosity. ~lebig *a.* tenacious of life.

Zahl (ts-) *f.* (-, -en) figure, digit, numeral; number; cipher. ~bar *a.* payable, due. ~brett *n.* money-tray. ~enmäßig *a.* numerical. ~er *m.* payer. ~karte *f.* money-order form. ~kellner *m.* head waiter. ~los *a.* countless, innumerable. ~meister *m.* paymaster. ~reich *a.* numerous. ~stelle *f.* pay-office, cashier's office. ~tag *m.* pay-day. ~ung *f.* payment; *an* ~*ungs Statt* in lieu of cash. ~ungsbefehl *m.* writ of execution. ~ungseinstellung *f.* suspension of payment. ~ungsempfänger *m.* payee. ~ungsfähig *a.* solvent. ~ungsmittel *n.* (legal) tender. ~ungsunfähig *a.* insolvent. ~wort *n.* numeral. [TALE]

zahlen *v.t. & i.* to pay

zähl-en *v.t. & i.* to count, number, reckon, calculate; to belong (to); to scan (metre); to score (points); ~*en auf* to count on, rely upon. ~er *m.* meter; counter; numerator; speedometer. ~ung *f.* counting, computation, numeration, census.

zahm (tsa:m) *a.* tame; domestic; tractable. ~heit *f.* tameness.

zähm-en (ts-) *v.t.* to tame; to break in; to subdue, check, restrain. ~ung *f.* taming.

Zahn (tsa:n) *m.* (-es, ⸗e) tooth; fang; tusk; cog (of wheel); *einem auf den ⸗ fühlen* to sound a person; *Haare auf den Zähnen haben* to be a Tartar.

Zahn-arzt *m.* dentist, dental surgeon. **⸗bein** *n.* dentine. **⸗bürste** *f.* toothbrush. **⸗ersatz** *m.* artificial teeth. **⸗fäule** *f.* caries. **⸗fleisch** *n.* gum. **⸗füllung** *f.* stopping, filling. **⸗geschwür** *n.* gumboil, abscess. **⸗heilkunde** *f.* dentistry. **⸗höhle** *f.* socket of a tooth. **⸗los** *a.* toothless. **⸗lücke** *f.* gap between teeth. **⸗pasta** *f.* tooth-paste, dentifrice. **⸗pulver** *n.* toothpowder. **⸗rad** *n.* cog-wheel, gear (-wheel). **⸗radbahn** *f.* cog-wheel railway. **⸗reißen** *n.*, **⸗schmerz** *m.*, **⸗weh** *n.* toothache. **⸗schnitt** *m.* (*archit.*) denticulation. **⸗stein** *m.* tartar. **⸗stocher** *m.* toothpick. **⸗wechsel** *m.* teething, dentition, cutting of teeth. **Zähne-fletschen** *n.* showing one's teeth. **⸗klappern** *n.* chattering of teeth.

zahnen *v.i.* to cut teeth, to teethe.

zähnen *v.t.* to indent, notch, tooth.

Zähre *f.* (-, -n) (*poet.*) tear.

Zander *m.* (-s, -) pike-perch.

Zange (tsaŋə) *f.* (-, -n) pincers; tongs; tweezers; pliers; forceps; (*zool.*) claw.

Zank (ts⸗) *m.* (-es) quarrel, quarrelling, row, brawl. **⸗apfel** *m.* bone of contention. **⸗sucht** *f.* quarrelsomeness. **⸗süchtig** *a.* quarrelsome. **⸗teufel** *m.* quarrelsome person; shrew.

zanken *v.i. & r.* to quarrel, wrangle, have words (with), fall out. *v.t.* to scold.

zänkisch *a.* quarrelsome.

Zäpfchen *n.* (-s, -) uvula; (*med.*) suppository.

Zapfen[1] *m.* (-s, -) plug, peg, pin, gudgeon; tap; pivot; cone; trunnion. **⸗lager** *n.* trunnion bed. **⸗loch** *n.* mortise. **⸗streich** *m.* tattoo.

zapf-en[2] *v.t.* to tap. **⸗stelle** *f.* petrol station, refuelling-point.

zapp-eln *v.i.* to fidget; to struggle; **⸗eln lassen** to keep in suspense.

⸗e)lig *a.* fidgety, restless.

Zar *m.* (-en, -e) czar. **⸗in** *f.* czarina.

zart (ts⸗) *a.* tender; soft, delicate; fragile, frail; fine, slender; pale; sensitive; fond, loving; fresh, young. **⸗besaitet** *a.* sensitive. **⸗fühlend** *a.* tactful, sensitive, of delicate feeling. **⸗gefühl** *n.*, **⸗sinn** *m.* delicacy of feeling. **⸗heit** *f.* tenderness; softness; delicacy; delicateness, frailty.

zärtlich *a.* affectionate, fond, loving, tender. **⸗keit** *f.* tenderness, fondness; caress.

Zä'sur *f.* (-, -en) caesura.

Zauber (tsau-) *m.* (-s, -) magic, charm, spell, enchantment. **⸗ei** *f.* magic, witchcraft, black magic. **⸗er** *m.* magician, sorcerer, wizard; conjurer, juggler. **⸗flöte** *f.* magic flute. **⸗formel** *f.* incantation, magic formula. **⸗haft** *a.* magical, bewitching, enchanting. **⸗in** *f.* sorceress, witch. **⸗kräftig** *a.* magical. **⸗kunst** *f.* magic art, black magic. **⸗künstler** *m.* conjurer, juggler. **⸗kunststück** *n.* conjuring trick. **⸗lehrling** *m.* magician's apprentice. **⸗spruch** *m.* incantation. **⸗trank** *m.* magic potion.

zaubern *v.i.* to practise magic; to do by magic. *v.t.* to conjure (up).

zaudern *v.i.* to hesitate; to delay; to temporize. *subst. n.* hesitation; delay; temporizing.

Zaum (ts⸗) *m.* (-es, ⸗e) bridle; *im ⸗ halten* to keep a tight rein on, restrain. **⸗zeug** *n.* horse's bridle, &c.

zäumen *v.t.* to bridle; to restrain.

Zaun (tsaun) *m.* (-es, ⸗e) hedge, fence; *Streit vom ⸗e brechen* to pick a quarrel. **⸗gast** *m.* nonpaying spectator, looker-on, dead-head. **⸗könig** *m.* wren. **⸗latte** *f.* pale, stake. **⸗pfahl** *m.* fence-post; *mit dem ⸗pfahl winken* to give a broad hint. [TOWN]

zausen (tsauzən) *v.t.* to tug, pull about; to tousle (hair).

Zebra (tse:-) *n.* (-s, -s) zebra.

Zechbruder *m.* boon companion; tippler, toper.

Zech-e f. (-e, -en) bill; mine; mining-company. **~en** v.i. to drink, tipple. **~er** m. toper; reveller. **~gelage** n. drinking-party, spree. **~preller** m. guest who evades paying bill. **~prellerei** f. evading payment of bill.

Zecke f. (-, -n) (zool.) tick.

Zeder f. (-, -n) cedar.

ze'dieren v.t. to cede, transfer.

Zehe f. (-, -n) toe. **~nspitze** f. tiptoe, point of the toe.

zehn (tse'n) a. & subst. f. ten. **~ender** m. stag with ten points. **~er** m. ten, the ten. **~fach** a. tenfold. **~pfennigstück** n. See App. III. **~te** a. tenth. subst. m. tithe. **~tel** n. tenth (part). **~tens** adv. tenthly, in the tenth place.

zehr-en (tse-) v.i. to live on, feed on, enjoy (memories); to consume; to waste; (fig.) to gnaw (at), prey (upon). **~pfennig** m. travelling-allowance. **~ung** f. expenses; consumption; waste; provisions; letzte **~ung** extreme unction.

Zeichen¹ (tsaiç-) n. (-s, -) sign, signal; token, (distinguishing) mark; brand, stamp; badge; indication; symptom; proof; omen; zum **~**, daß as a proof that; seines **~s** ein Bäcker sein to be a baker by trade. **~deutung** f. interpretation of signs; astrology. **~erklärung** f. key; explanation of symbols used. **~setzung** f. punctuation. **~sprache** f. language of signs. [TOKEN]

Zeichen²-brett n. drawing-board. **~saal** m. drawing-office; art-room. **~stift** m. pencil, crayon. **~stunde** f. drawing-lesson. **~vorlage** f. drawing-copy.

zeichn-en v.t. & i. to draw; to design; to mark; to brand; to sign; to subscribe. **~er** m. designer, draughtsman; subscriber. **~erisch** a. **~erische Begabung** talent for drawing. **~ung** f. drawing, sketch, design; subscription. **~ungsberechtigt** a. authorized to sign.

Zeigefinger m. forefinger, index.

zeig-en (tsâi-) v.t. to show, point (at), point out; to exhibit, manifest,

display; to indicate; to demonstrate; to prove. v.r. to appear, be found; to show itself; to turn out; to be noticeable. **~er** m. hand (of clock); pointer. **~estab**, **~estock** m. pointer.

zeihen v.t. to accuse (of), charge (with).

Zeile (ts-) f. (-, -n) line; row. **~n-gußmaschine** f. linotype.

Zeisig m. (-s, -e) siskin.

Zeit f. (-, -en) time, term, space of time, duration, period, age, epoch, era; season; days, times; (gram.) tense; höchste **~**! high time; du liebe **~**! good heavens; es ist an der **~** it is (high) time; damit hat es **~** there is no hurry; auf **~** (commerc.) on credit, on account; eine **~** lang for a time; in jüngster **~** quite recently; mit der **~** gradually; in the course of time; vor der **~** prematurely; vor **~en** once upon a time, formerly, in olden times; zu **~en** now and then; zu gleicher **~** at the same time; zur **~** now, at present; in the time of; in time; zur rechten **~** in the nick of time. prep. **~** seines Lebens during life, as long as he lives. [TIDE]

Zeit-abschnitt m. epoch, period. **~abstand** m. interval or period (of time). **~alter** n. age; generation, era. **~angabe** f. time; date. **~aufnahme** f. time exposure. **~aufwand** m. loss of time; time spent (on). **~einheit** f. unit of time. **~einteilung** f. time-table; timing. **~enfolge** f. sequence of tenses. **~folge** f. chronological order. **~form** f. tense. **~geist** m. spirit of the age. **~gemäß** a. timely; seasonable; opportune; up to date, modern. **~genosse** m. contemporary. **~genössisch** a. contemporary. **~geschichte** f. contemporary history.

zeitig a. early; timely; ripe, mature. adv. early, in time. **~en** v.t. to mature, ripen; to produce, effect.

Zeit-karte f. season-ticket. **~lage** f. juncture, state of affairs. **~lang** f. while, time. **~lauf** m. course of time, period. **~läufte**

(pl.) conjunctures, times. ~lebens adv. during life, for life.

zeitlich a. temporary; in time; temporal; das ~e segnen to die.

Zeit-lupe f. time-lens. ~lupen-aufnahme f. slow-motion picture. ~maß n. measure of time; (pros.) quantity; (mus.) time. ~messer m. chronometer, metronome. ~messung f. measurement of time; timing; prosody. ~punkt m. time, moment. ~raffer m. quick-motion apparatus, time accelerator. ~raubend a. taking up much time; protracted. ~raum m. space of time, period, interval. ~rechnung f. chronology; era. ~schrift f. journal, periodical, magazine. ~spanne f. period of time. ~tafel f. chronological table. ~umstände m.pl. times, circumstances (of the time). ~vertreib m. pastime, amusement. ~weilig a. temporary. ~weise adv. for a time; from time to time. ~wort n. verb. ~zeichen n. time-signal. ~zünder m. time-fuse.

Zeitung (ts-) f. (-, -en) newspaper, paper. ~sablage f. newspaper stand. ~sausschnitt m. press cutting. ~sbeilage f. supplement. ~sente f. canard, hoax. ~sexpedition f. newspaper office. ~skiosk m. news-stall. ~snotiz f. notice, item, paragraph. ~sschreiber m. journalist. ~sver-käufer m. newsvendor; news-agent. ~swesen n. journalism; the (daily) press.

zele'brieren v.t. to celebrate.

Zell-e f. (-, -en) cell. ~enförmig a. cellular. ~gewebe n. cellular tissue. ~horn n. celluloid. ~kern m. nucleus. ~schicht f. layer of cells. ~stoff m., ~ulose f., ~wolle f. cellulose, wood fibre. ~wand f. cell wall.

Ze'lot m. (-en, -en) zealot.

Zelt (tsɛlt) n. (-es, -e) tent; marquee. ~bahn f. canvas sheet, bivouac sheet. ~dach n. awning, canvas roof. ~en v.i. to camp. ~lager n. tent camp; camping. ~leinwand f. canvas, tent-cloth. ~pflock m. tent-peg. ~schnur f.

tent guy-rope. ~stange f. tent-pole.

Zelter m. (-s, -) palfrey.

Ze'ment m. (-s, -e) cement. ~'ieren v.t. to cement. ~stahl m. cementation steel.

Ze'nit (-ni:t) m. (-s) zenith.

zen'sieren v.t. to censor; to examine; to give marks.

Zens-or m. (-ors, -'oren) censor. ~'ur f. censoring, censorship; (school) report; certificate; marks.

Zenti'meter m. & n. (-s, -) centi-metre. See App. III.

Zentner m. (-s, -) hundredweight, fifty kilograms. ~last f. (fig.) heavy weight. ~schwer a. very heavy.

Zen'tral-e f. (-e, -en) central office; central station; telephone ex-change. ~heizung f. central heating. ~isati'on f. centraliza-tion. ~i'sieren v.t. to centralize.

Zentrifu'galkraft f. centrifugal power.

Zentrum n. (-s, Zentren) centre; bull's-eye; Centre party.

Zephir (tse:-) m. (-s, -e) zephyr.

Zepter n. (-s, -) sceptre.

zer'beißen v.t. to bite into pieces; to crunch.

zer'bersten vws.i. to burst, split in pieces.

zer'bomben v.t. to destroy by bombs.

zer'brech-en v.t. & vws.i. to break, shatter, smash; sich den Kopf ~en to rack one's brains. ~lich a. fragile; brittle; breakable. ~lichkeit f. fragility; brittleness.

zer'bröckeln v.t. to crumble. vws.i. to crumble away.

zer'drücken v.t. to crush; to crumple.

Zeremon-ie (-ni:) f. (-ie, -ien) cere-mony. ~i'ell a. ceremonial, for-mal. ~i'ös a. ceremonious.

zer'fahren v.t. to crush, destroy (by driving over). a. careless, scatter-brained. ~heit f. carelessness, absent-mindedness.

Zer'fall m. ruin, decay; decadence; decomposition, disintegration. ~en vws.i. to fall to pieces; decay; to decompose, disintegrate; to be divided (into); ~en sein mit to be on bad terms with, be at variance with.

zer·'fetzen *v.t.* to tear in pieces, tear up; to slash; to mutilate. ~fleischen *v.t.* to lacerate; to mangle. ~fließen *vws.i.* to melt, dissolve; to run (out); to disperse. ~fressen *v.t.* to eat *or* gnaw away; to corrode. ~furcht *a.* wrinkled, furrowed.

zer·'gehen *vws.i.* to melt; to dissolve; to dwindle.

zer·'glieder-n *v.t.* to dissect; to dismember, cut up; (*fig.*) to analyse. ~ung *f.* dissection; analysis.

zer·'hacken *v.t.* to hack, mince, chop. ~hauen *v.t.* to cut, cut up. ~kleinern *v.t.* to reduce to small pieces; to chop up; to chew. ~klopfen *v.t.* to beat to pieces. ~klüftet *a.* cleft, riven.

zer·'knautschen, ~knüllen *vv.t.* to crush, crumple.

zer·'knirsch-t *a.* contrite. ~ung *f.* contrition.

zer·'knittern *v.t.* to crumple. ~'kratzen *v.t.* to scratch. ~lassen *v.t.* to melt.

zer·'leg-bar *a.* collapsible (boat). ~en *v.t.* to part, divide, separate; to cut up; to carve (meat); to split up; to dissect; to dismantle (machine); to strip (a weapon); to analyse. ~ung *f.* splitting up; dissection; dismantling; analysis.

zer·'lesen *a.* well-thumbed (book). ~löchert *a.* full of holes. ~lumpt *a.* ragged, tattered. ~malmen *v.t.* to crush, grind. ~martern *v.t.* to torment, torture; to rack (one's brains). ~'mürben *v.t.* to wear down. ~mürbung *f.* attrition. ~nagen *v.t.* to eat away; to erode; to corrode. ~pflücken *v.t.* to pluck to pieces. ~'platzen *vws.i.* to burst. ~quetschen *v.t.* to crush, squash.

Zerrbild *n.* caricature.

zer·'reiben *v.t.* to rub away; to grind down, pound.

zer·'reiß-bar *a.* tearable. ~en *v.t.* to tear (into pieces); to lacerate; to sever. *vws.i.* to tear, wear, split; to break. ~fest *a.* tear-

proof. ~probe *f.* breaking test.

zerren *v.t.* to drag, pull, pull about.

zer·'rinnen *vws.i.* to melt away; to disappear, vanish away.

Zer·'rissenheit *f.* torn *or* tattered condition; lack of unity, disunion; (inner) strife.

zer·'rütt-en *v.t.* to throw into confusion; to shatter; to ruin; to unhinge (mind). ~ung *f.* disorder, confusion; ruin; derangement.

zer·'sägen *v.t.* to saw (in pieces).

zer·'schellen *v.t.* to smash, break in pieces. *vws.i.* to be battered to pieces, be smashed; to be wrecked.

zer·'schießen *v.t.* to shoot to pieces.

zer·'schlagen *v.t.* to batter; to smash, break; to beat. *v.r.* (*fig.*) to be broken off, come to nothing. *a.* battered, shattered, broken.

zer·'schmettern *v.t.* to smash, shatter, destroy, crush.

zer·'schneiden *v.t.* to cut, cut up, sever.

zer·'setz-en *v.t.* to decompose, dissolve; (*fig.*) to undermine. ~end *a.* (*fig.*) undermining; demoralizing. ~ung *f.* decomposition.

zer·'spalten *v.t.* to cleave, split.

zer·'splitter-n *v.t. & vws.i.* to splinter; to split (up); to disperse; (*fig.*) to dissipate. *v.r.* to fritter away one's energy. ~ung *f.* splintering; dissipation.

zer·'sprengen *v.t.* to blow up, burst; to rout; to disperse.

zer·'springen *vws.i.* to explode, burst; to crack; to split.

zer·'stampfen *v.t.* to pound; to trample down.

zer·'stäub-en *v.t.* to pulverize; to reduce to dust; to atomize; to scatter, spatter; to spray. ~er *m.* atomizer, spray.

zer·'stieben *vws.i. st.* to scatter as dust; to vanish.

zer·'stör-en *v.t.* to destroy; to demolish; to devastate; to ruin, shatter. ~er *m.* destroyer; (*av.*) two-engined fighter, pursuit fighter; devastator. ~ung *f.* destruction; demolition; ruin.

zer·'stoßen *v.t.* to pound; to bruise, break.

zer·'streu-en *v.t.* to disperse, scatter,

disseminate; to dissipate, dispel; to divert. *v.r.* to divert, distract, amuse oneself. **~t** *a.* dispersed; diffused; absent-minded, preoccupied. **~theit** *f.* absent-mindedness. **~ung** *f.* dispersion; diversion, distraction, amusement.

zer'stückel-n *v.t.* to dismember; to cut (into small pieces), cut up; to partition, parcel out. **~ung** *f.* cutting up; dismembering; partition, parcelling out.

zer'teilen *v.t.* to divide; to cut up; to separate, resolve; to disperse.

zer'treten *v.t.* to crush, trample under foot.

zer'trümmer-n *v.t.* to destroy, wreck, smash, break, demolish, ruin; to split (atoms). **~ung** *f.* destruction, ruin; splitting (of atoms).

Zerve'latwurst *f.* saveloy.

Zer'würfnis *n.* (-ses, -se) difference, disagreement, dissension, quarrel.

zer'zausen *v.t.* to crumble; to dishevel (hair).

Zeter-geschrei *n.* shouting (for help); cry of 'murder!'; outcry. **~n** *v.i.* to shout, cry 'murder!'

Zettel *m.* (-s, -) scrap of paper; slip; note; label; ticket; poster, bill, placard. **~ankleber** *m.* billsticker, bill-poster. **~kasten, ~katalog** *m.* box for slips; filing-cabinet. [L]

zeuch (*obs.*) *imper. of* ziehen.

Zeug (tsoik) *n.* (-es) stuff, material, cloth, fabric; textiles; matter; utensils, things; implements, tools; rubbish; nonsense; all sorts of things; *das ~ haben zu* to have it in one (to); *sich ins ~ legen* to set to work with a will; *arbeiten was das ~ hält* to work with might and main; *einem am ~ flicken* to pick holes in. **~haus** *n.* arsenal, armoury. **~meister** *m.* master of ordnance. **~schuhe** *m.pl.* cloth shoes.

Zeuge *m.* (-n, -n), **Zeugin** *f.* witness.

zeug-en[1] *v.i.* to bear witness, testify; to give evidence (of); to prove. **~enaussage** *f.* evidence, deposition. **~envernehmung** *f.* hearing of witnesses. **~nis** *n.*

proof, evidence, testimony; certificate; (servant's) character; testimonial; school report.

zeug-en[2] *v.t.* to beget, procreate, generate, produce. **~ung** *f.* begetting, procreation, generation. **~ungsfähig** *a.* procreative, able to beget. **~ungsglied** *n.* penis. **~ungstrieb** *m.* sexual instinct. **~ungsunfähig** *a.* impotent.

Zi'chorie (tsiço:rie) *f.* (-, -n) chicory.

Zicklein *n.* (-s, -) kid.

Zickzack *m.* zigzag.

Ziege (tsi-) *f.* (-, -n) goat; she-goat. **~nbart** *m.* goatee. **~nbock** *m.* he-goat, billy-goat. **~nfell** *n.* goat-skin. **~nleder** *n.* kid. **~npeter** *m.* (*med.*) mumps.

Ziegel *m.* (-s, -) brick; tile. **~arbeiter, ~brenner** *m.* brickmaker. **~brennerei, Ziege'lei** *f.* brickworks; brickyard. **~dach** *n.* tiled roof. **~ofen** *m.* brickkiln. **~stein** *m.* brick. [L]

Ziehbrunnen *m.* draw-well.

ziehen (tsi:en) *v.t. st.* to pull, draw, haul, tug; to tow (boat); to pull out, extract (tooth); (*chess*) to move (piece); to rear; to cultivate; to dig (trench, &c.); to make (a comparison). *vvs.i.* to move; to wander, stroll; to march along; to go; to move (to), remove; to migrate. *v.i.* (*of tea*) to draw. *v. impers.* to be draughty; to ache; (*fig.*) to attract, draw; to be of value, weigh. *v.r.* to warp; to extend, stretch; *nach sich ~* to have consequences; *den kürzeren ~* to get the worst of it; *Wasser ~* to absorb water; to leak. Other usages will be found under the respective nouns.

Zieh-harmonika *f.* accordion, concertina. **~mutter** *f.* foster-mother. **~tag** *m.* moving day. **~ung** *f.* drawing (of lottery ticket). **~ungsliste** *f.* list of prize-winners (in lottery).

Ziel (tsi:l) *n.* (-es, -e) destination; goal; end, aim, object; objective, target; winning-post; limit, boundary; (*commerce*) term; *sich ein ~ setzen* to aim at; *einem ein ~ setzen* to check, put a stop to.

~band n. (sport.) tape. ~bewußt a. systematic, methodical; with an object in view; resolute. ~fernrohr n. telescopic sight. ~los a. aimless. ~scheibe f. practice target; ~scheibe des Spottes sein to be a laughing-stock. ~setzung f. fixing of an aim. ~sicher a. sure of one's aim; steady. ~strebig a. purposive. [TILL]

ziel-en v.i. to aim (at), take aim; (fig.) to drive (at); to allude to, refer (to).

ziem-en (tsi:-) v.i. & r. to be seemly, become; to be suitable, be fitting, be proper. ~lich a. suitable; fit; fair, good, moderate; passable, middling. adv. fairly, rather, tolerably, pretty.

Ziemer m. (-s, -) hind quarter, haunch; whip, cat.

ziepen v.i. to tug (hair).

Zier (tsi:r) f. (-) ornament, decoration, embellishment. ~affe m. affected person, dressy woman. ~at m. ornament, decoration. ~de f. ornament, decoration; honour. ~e'rei f. affectation, airs. ~garten m. flower-garden, ornamental garden. ~leiste f. vignette; border, edging. ~lich a. elegant; neat; dainty, delicate. ~lichkeit f. grace; elegance. ~pflanze f. ornamental plant. ~puppe f. dressy woman. ~strauch m. ornamental shrub.

zieren v.t. to ornament, adorn, be an ornament to; to decorate, embellish. v.r. to be affected; to be prim or coy; to need pressing (to eat).

Ziffer (tsif-) f. (-, -n) figure, numeral, digit, number; cipher. ~blatt n. dial, face. ~nmäßig a. numerical, by figures.

Ziga'rette (tsigarɛtə) f. (-, -n) cigarette. ~netui n. cigarette-case. ~nhülse f. ~nspitze f. cigarette-holder.

Zi'garre (tsigarə) f. (-, -n) cigar. ~nabschneider m. cigar-cutter. ~ndeckblatt n. wrapper. ~nhändler m. cigar merchant, tobacconist. ~nkiste f. cigar-box. ~nspitze f. cigar-holder; tip (of cigar). ~nstummel m. cigar-end.

Zi'geuner m. (-s, -). ~in f. gipsy. ~wagen m. caravan.

Zi'kade f. (-, -n) cicada.

Zimbel f. (-, -n) cymbal.

Zimmer (tsimər) n. (-s, -) room, apartment, chamber. ~antenne f. indoor aerial. ~decke f. ceiling. ~flucht f. suite (of rooms). ~gymnastik f. indoor gymnastics. ~herr m. lodger. ~mädchen n. chambermaid; housemaid. ~pflanze f. indoor plant. ~vermieterin f. landlady. [TIMBER]

zimmer-n v.t. & i. to carpenter, make, build (of wood). ~arbeit f. carpentry, timber-work. ~geselle f. journeyman carpenter. ~mann m. (pl. ~leute) carpenter.

Zimmet, Zimt m. (-s) cinnamon.

zimperlich a. supersensitive; prim, prudish; affected. ~keit f. supersensitiveness; primness, prudery; affectation.

Zink n. & m. (-es) zinc. ~ätzung f. zincography, zinc etching. ~blech n. sheet zinc, zinc-plate. ~haltig a. containing zinc. ~salbe f. zinc ointment.

Zinke f. (-, -n) prong; tooth; spike; tenon, dovetail; (mus.) cornet; secret mark (on cards).

Zinn (tsin) n. (-es) tin; pewter. ~bergwerk n. tin-mine. ~e(r)n a. of tin, tin, pewter. ~gießer m. tin-founder. ~kraut n. horsetail. ~soldat m. tin soldier.

Zinne f. (-, -n) battlement; pinnacle.

Zi'nnober m. (-s, -) cinnabar. ~rot a. vermilion.

Zins (tsins) m. (-es, -en) tax, duty; rent; (bibl.) tribute; (pl.) interest; auf ~en ausleihen to lend (money) on interest; mit ~ und ~eszins (fig.) in full measure. ~eszins m. compound interest. ~fuß, ~satz m. rate of interest. ~pflichtig a. subject to tax; tributary. ~rechnung f. calculation of interest. ~schein m. coupon; dividend-warrant. [L]

Zipfel m. (-s, -) tip, end, point, corner; tongue. ~ig a. pointed, peaked. ~mütze f. jelly-bag cap, tasselled cap, nightcap.

Zipperlein n. (-s) gout.

Zirbel-drüse f. pineal gland. ~**kiefer** f. stone-pine.

Zirkel (ts-) m. (-s, -) circle; compasses. ~**schluß** m. vicious circle.

Zirku'l-ar n. (-ars, -are) circular, pamphlet. ~**ati'on** f. circulation. ~**ieren** v.i. to circulate.

Zirkum'flex m. (-es, -e) circumflex.

Zirkus m. (-, -se) circus.

zirpen v.i. to chirp; to cheep.

zischeln v.i. to whisper.

zisch-en v.i. to hiss; to whiz. ~**laut** m. hissing sound; (gram.) sibilant.

Zise'lier-arbeit f. chasing, chiselled work. ~**en** v.t. to chase, chisel, engrave.

Zi'sterne f. (-, -n) cistern.

Zita'delle f. (-, -n) citadel.

Zi't-at (-ta:t) n. (-ats, -ate) quotation. ~**ieren** v.t. to quote, cite; to call up, summon.

Zither f. (-, -n) zither.

Zitro'nat n. candied lemon peel.

Zi'trone (-ro:-) f. (-, -n) lemon. ~**nfalter** m. brimstone butterfly. ~**nlimonade** f. lemon squash. ~**npresse** f. lemon-squeezer. ~**nsaft** m. lemon juice. ~**nschale** f. lemon peel. ~**nwasser** n. still lemonade.

Zitter-aal m. electric eel. ~**gras** n. quaking-grass. ~**ig** a. trembling, shaky. ~**pappel** f. aspen. ~**rochen** m. electric ray, torpedo fish.

zittern v.i. to tremble, shake, shiver, quake, quiver.

Zitze f. (-, -n) teat, nipple.

zi'vil (tsivi:l) a. civil; moderate, reasonable (price). subst. n. civilians (pl.); in ~ in mufti, in plain clothes, (sl.) in civvies. ~**bevölkerung** f. civilian population. ~**isati'on** f. civilization. ~**isa'tor** m. civilizer. ~**isa'torisch** a. civilizing. ~**i'sieren** v.t. to civilize. ~**ist** m. civilian. ~**trauung** f. marriage at a registry office.

Zobel (-o:-) m. (-s, -) sable.

Zofe f. (-, -n) lady's maid.

zog imperf. of **ziehen**.

zögern (tsø:-) v.i. to hesitate; to delay, loiter, linger. subst. n. hesitation; delay.

Zögling (ts:ø-) m. (-s, -e) pupil.

Zöli'bat m. & n. (-s) celibacy.

Zoll¹ (tsol) m. (-es, -e) inch. ~**stock** m. yard-stick, rule.

Zoll² (tsol) m. (-es, "e) duty; toll; tariff; customs, custom-house; (also fig.) tribute. ~**abfertigung** f. clearing of the customs. ~**amt** n. custom-house. ~**beamte** m. custom-house officer, customs officer. ~**einnehmer** m. toll-collector; customs receiver. ~**frei** a. free of duty. ~**gebühr** f. duty. ~**pflichtig** a. dutiable. ~**revision** f. customs examination. ~**schein** m. customs receipt; certificate of clearance. ~**schranke** f. customs barrier. ~**verein** m. tariff union. ~**verschluß** m. customs seal. [L]

zollen v.t. (fig.) to pay, give; to show (respect).

Zöllner m. (-s, -) customs collector; (bibl.) publican.

Zone (tso:no) f. (-, -n) zone.

Zoo'log-e (-lo:ga) m. (-en, -en) zoologist. ~**ie** f. zoology. ~**isch** a. zoological.

Zopf m. (-es, "e) pigtail; plait, tress; (fig.) pedantry; red tape. ~**ig** a. (fig.) pedantic; old-fashioned. [TOP]

Zorn (ts-) m. (-es) anger, wrath, rage. ~**entbrannt**, ~**schnaubend** aa. boiling with rage. ~**ig** a. angry, in a passion. ~**röte** f. angry flush, flush of anger.

Zot-e (tso:ta) f. (-e, -en) obscenity, smutty joke. ~**enreißer** m. obscene talker. ~**ig** a. obscene, filthy, smutty.

Zott-e f. (-e, -en) tuft, lock. ~**ig** a. shaggy; matted.

zotteln vws.i. to shuffle along.

zu (tsu:) prep. in, at; to; by; on; up to; for; as; with; ~ zweien by twos, in twos, in couples; two of us (of them). adv. & pref. too; towards; to; shut, closed; ab und ~ now and then; nur ~! go on!

zu-allererst adv. first of all. ~**allerletzt** adv. last of all.

Zubehör m. & n. (-s, -e) accessories; fittings; belongings; trimmings;

appendages; conveniences. **~teile** *m.pl.* accessories.

zubeißen *v.i.* to snap (at), bite; to tuck in, eat away.

Zuber *m.* (-s, -) tub.

zubereit-en *v.t.* to prepare; to cook; to mix (drink). **~ung** *f.* preparation; dressing; cooking; mixing (of drinks).

zu-billigen *v.t.* to grant, allow, concede. **~binden** *v.t.* to tie up; to bind up; *Augen ~binden* to blindfold. **~bleiben** *vws.i.* to remain shut. **~blinzeln** *v.i.* to wink at. **~bringen** *v.t.* to bring to, take to; to pass, spend (time). **~bringerdienst** *m.* feeder service.

Zubuße *f.* additional contribution.

Zucht (tsuxt) *f.* (-) breeding, rearing; breed, race, stock; growing; cultivation; culture; education; drill; discipline; training; decorum, propriety; *in ~ halten* to keep strict discipline. **~haus** *n.* convict prison. **~häusler** *m.* convict. **~hausstrafe** *f.* penal servitude. **~hengst** *m.* stallion. **~los** *a.* insubordinate; undisciplined; dissolute. **~losigkeit** *f.* insubordination; want of discipline; licentiousness. **~meister** *m.* taskmaster, disciplinarian. **~rute** *f.* rod, scourge. **~stier** *m.* bull. **~stute** *f.* brood-mare. **~wahl** *f.* natural selection.

zücht-en *v.t.* to breed; to grow, cultivate; to train. **~er** *m.* breeder; grower, cultivator. **~ling** *m.* convict. **~ung** *f.* breeding; growing, cultivation.

züchtig *a.* chaste, modest. **~en** *v.t.* to chastise, discipline, punish, correct; *körperlich ~en* to flog. **~keit** *f.* chastity, modesty. **~ung** *f.* chastisement, punishment, correction.

zuck-en *v.i.* to twitch; (*of lightning*) to flash; (*fig.*) *es ~te ihm in allen Gliedern* he was itching (to do something). *v.t.* to shrug (one's shoulders). **~ung** *f.* convulsion, twitch.

zücken *v.t.* to draw (sword).

Zucker (tsukar) *m.* (-s) sugar. **~bäcker** *m.* confectioner. **~dose**

f. sugar-basin. **~erbse** *f.* small green pea. **~guß** *m.* icing. **~haltig** *a.* containing sugar. **~hut** *m.* sugar-loaf. **~ig** *a.* sugary. **~krank** *a.*, **~kranke(r)** *m.* diabetic. **~krankheit** *f.* diabetes. **~rohr** *n.* sugar-cane. **~rübe** *f.* beetroot, sugar-beet. **~süß** *a.* sweet as sugar. **~werk** *n.* confectionery; sweets. **~zange** *f.* sugar-tongs.

zuckern *v.t.* to sugar, sweeten.

zudecken *v.t.* to cover up; to put a lid on; to conceal.

zu'dem *adv.* besides, moreover, in addition.

zudenken *v.t.* to intend (as a present) for.

Zudrang *m.* rush (to), run (on).

zudrehen *v.t.* to turn off; *einem den Rücken ~* to turn one's back on a person.

zudringlich *a.* forward; obtrusive; importunate; officious. **~keit** *f.* forwardness; obtrusiveness; importunity.

zudrücken *v.t.* to shut, close; *ein Auge ~* (*fig.*) to wink at (a thing), let it pass, connive at.

zu'eign-en *v.t.* to dedicate. **~ung** *f.* dedication.

zu'eilen *vws.i.* to run towards or up to; to hasten to.

zu'ei'nander *adv.* to each other.

zu'erkennen *v.t.* to award; to adjudicate; to confer on; to sentence (person) to.

zu'erst *adv.* firstly, in the first place; first; at first; first of all.

zu'erteilen *v.t.* to allow, apportion (a thing); to confer upon, bestow on.

zufahren *vws.i.* to drive on, go on; *~ auf* to drive towards; to rush at.

Zufahrt *f.* 'Drive In'. **~sstraße** *f.* approach, approach road.

Zufall *m.* chance, accident; event, occurrence; *durch ~* by accident, accidentally. **~streffer** *m.* chance hit.

zufallen *vws.i.* to close, fall to; to fall to (one's lot), devolve on.

zufällig *a.* chance, accidental; casual. *adv.* by chance. **~erweise** *adv.* by chance; as chance would have it. **~keit** f. chance; contingency.

zufassen v.i. to lend a hand, set to work.

zufliegen vws.i. to fly (to or towards); (of door) to slam, shut with a bang.

zufließen vws.i. to flow towards; to flow into; to flow in; (of words, &c.) to come readily (to).

Zuflucht f. refuge, shelter; recourse; seine ~ nehmen zu to take refuge with, have recourse to.

Zufluß m. tributary; flowing in, influx; supply (of goods).

zuflüstern v.t. to whisper to; to prompt.

zu'folge prep. in consequence of, owing to; on the strength of; according to.

zu'frieden a. content, satisfied; sich ~ geben to acquiesce (in), rest content (with); ~ lassen to let alone, leave in peace. **~heit** f. contentment, satisfaction. **~stellen** v.t. to content, satisfy. **~stellend** a. satisfactory. **~stellung** f. satisfaction.

zufrieren vws.i. to freeze up or over.

zufügen v.t. to add (to); to do, cause.

Zufuhr f. (-, -en) supply; provisions; bringing up of supplies.

zuführ-en v.t. to bring to, lead to; to procure, supply; to conduct, convey, feed, lead in. **~ung** f. supply; provision; feed.

Zug (tsu:k) m. (-es, ¨e) drawing, pulling; pull, tug; stress; draught, gulp; whiff, pull, pull (at a pipe); move (in chess); draught, current of air; march, marching; expedition; procession; band, gang; (mil.) platoon; troop; section; groove (of a rifle barrel); flight (of birds), migration; drift (of clouds); range (of hills); row (of houses); (railway) train; stroke (of pen); outline, line; (fig.) feature, trait; characteristic; impulse, bent, inclination; auf einen ~ at one draught; in einem ~ (fig.) at one stroke, straight off; uninterruptedly; im ~e sein to be in full swing; in ~ bringen to

set going, start; ~ um ~ without delay, uninterruptedly; ~ der Ereignisse train of events; in vollen Zügen (fig.) deeply, very, thoroughly; in den letzten Zügen liegen to be dying, be at one's last gasp. [TUG]

Zugabe f. extra, addition; repetition, 'encore'.

Zug-abteil n. railway compartment. **~artikel** m. popular article, (a) 'draw'. **~brücke** f. drawbridge. **~führer** m. guard (of train); (mil.) platoon or section commander. **~ig** a. draughty. **~kraft** f. tensile force; tractive power; attraction. **~kräftig** a. attractive. **~leine** f. towing-rope, drag-rope. **~luft** f. draught, current of air. **~mittel** n. attraction, draw, means of attracting (crowd). **~ochse** m. draught ox. **~pflaster** n. blister. **~stiefel** m.pl. elastic-sided boots. **~stück** n. popular play, draw. **~tier** n. draught animal. **~verkehr** m. railway traffic. **~vogel** m. bird of passage. **~weise** adv. (mil.) by platoons or sections. **~wind** m. draught.

Zugang m. entrance, door; access; approach; increase; (of books) accession.

zugänglich a. accessible; approachable; open to; affable.

zugeben v.t. to add; to give into the bargain; (fig.) to allow, permit; to admit; to confess.

zugegebenermaßen adv. admittedly.

zu'gegen pred. a. present.

zugehen vws.i. to close; to go on, go faster; ~ auf to go towards or up to; to be sent to (a person), reach (a person); to take place, happen; einem etwas ~ lassen to forward or send something to a person.

zugehör-en v.i. to belong to. **~ig** a. belonging to; accompanying; proper. **~igkeit** f. forming part of; membership (of club, &c.); (fig.) relationship.

zugeknöpft a. (fig.) reserved, uncommunicative.

Zügel (tsy:-) m. (-s, -) rein, bridle; check, curb; mit verhängtem ~ at full speed; *die ~ schießen lassen* to let loose (one's passions, &c.).

~los *a.* unbridled, unrestrained; licentious. **~losigkeit** *f.* impetuosity; licentiousness. **~n** *v.t.* to bridle, check, curb.

zugesellen *v.t. & r.* to associate with, join.

Zugeständnis *n.* concession; compromise; admission.

zugestehen *v.t.* to concede, grant; to admit.

zugetan *pred. a.* attached to, devoted to.

zugewanderte(r), zugezogene(r) *m. & a.* immigrant; newcomer.

zu'gleich *adv.* at the same time, together, also.

zu-greifen *v.i.* to take a hand (at), help; to take hold of; to grasp at; to grab; to take the opportunity; to help oneself (at table). **~griff** *m.* grip, clutch.

zu'grunde *adv.* **~ gehen** to perish, be ruined; **~ legen** to take as a basis, base upon; **~ liegen** to underlie, be based upon, be at the root of; **~ richten** to destroy, ruin, wreck.

zu'gunsten *adv.* in favour of, for the benefit of.

zu'gute *adv.* **~ halten** to allow for, take into consideration; **~ kommen** to stand (one) in good stead, be an advantage to; **~ kommen lassen** to give (a person) the benefit of; *sich etwas ~ tun auf* to be proud of, pique oneself on a thing.

zuguterletzt *adv.* in the end, at long last.

zuhalten *v.t.* to keep shut; to close. *v.i. ~ auf* to make for, proceed towards.

Zuhälter *m.* (-s, -) souteneur.

zu'handen *adv.* at hand, ready.

zuhängen *v.t.* to hang (curtain, &c.) over.

zuhauen *v.t.* to hew. *v.i.* to strike (at).

zu'hauf *adv.* (*poet.*) together.

zuheilen *vvs.i.* to heal up.

Zu'hilfenahme *f. unter ~ von* with the help of.

zu'hinterst *adv.* at the very end, last of all.

zuhör-en *v.i.* to listen to. **~er** *m.*

hearer, listener. **~erschaft** *f.* audience.

zuinnerst *adv.* innermost, deeply.

zujauchzen, zujubeln *vv.i.* to cheer, hail.

zukehren *v.t.* to turn to or towards; to turn (one's back) on (a person).

zuklappen *v.t.* to slam, bang; to close, *vvs.i.* to slam to.

zuklatschen *v.t.* to applaud (a person).

zukleben *v.t.* to paste or glue up; to gum, fasten down.

zuklinken *v.t.* to latch.

zuknöpfen *v.t.* to button up.

zukommen *vvs.i.* to belong to, fall to one's share; to be due to; to befit; *es kommt dir nicht zu, so zu sprechen* it's not for you to talk like that; **~ auf** to approach, come to; *einem etwas ~ lassen* to let a person have something; to make a present of.

zukorken *v.t.* to cork, cork up.

Zukost *f.* vegetables, &c. (eaten along with meat or bread).

Zukunft *f.* (-) future, time to come.

zukünftig *a.* future; *meine ~e* my intended. *adv.* in future, for the future.

zulächeln *v.i.* to smile at.

Zulage *f.* addition; increase; extra pay or allowance.

zu'lande *adv. bei uns ~* in my country.

zulangen *v.t.* to hand, give. *v.i.* to help oneself (at table); to be sufficient.

zulänglich *a.* sufficient, adequate.

zulass-en *v.t.* to leave closed; to admit; to permit, grant; to allow, admit of. **~ung** *f.* admission; permission; licence.

zulässig *a.* admissible, permissible, allowable.

Zulauf *m.* crowd, rush, run; **~ haben** to be popular, be run after, draw crowds. **~en** *vvs.i.* to run to; to run (towards or up to); to run on; to run faster; *spitz ~en* to taper (off).

zulegen *v.t.* to put more (to), add (to), increase; *sich etwas ~* to get, buy, procure something.

zu'leide *adv.* **~ tun** to hurt, harm, do harm to.

zuleit-en *v.t.* to lead to, direct to. **~ung** *f.* lead; supply.

zu'letzt *adv.* finally, ultimately; last, for the last time; at last, in the end; **~ kommen** to arrive last.

zu'liebe *adv.* **einem ~** to please someone.

zum = **zu dem.**

zumachen *v.t.* to close, shut, fasten. *v.i.* to hurry, make haste.

zu'mal *adv.* especially (as); all the more, particularly (because).

zumauern *v.t.* to wall or brick up.

zu'meist *adv.* mostly, for the most part.

zumessen *v.t.* to measure out, mete out; to allot, assign (task); to apportion (share).

zu'mindest *adv.* at least.

zu'mute *adv.* **mir ist wohl ~** I feel well.

zumut-en *v.t.* to expect of (a person); **sich zu viel ~en** to attempt too much. **~ung** *f.* (unreasonable) demand; imputation.

zu'nächst *adv.* first, first of all; above all; in the first instance, to begin with. *prep.* next to, close to.

zunageln *v.t.* to nail up, nail down.

zunähen *v.t.* to sew up, sew together.

Zunahme *f.* (-,-n) increase; growth.

Zuname *m.* surname.

Zündapparat *m.* magneto; ignition apparatus.

zünd-en (-yn-) *v.i.* to catch fire; to ignite; *(fig.)* to arouse enthusiasm, inflame. **~er** *m.* fuse; igniter. **~holz** *n.* match. **~holzschachtel** *f.* match-box. **~hütchen** *n.* percussion cap. **~kabel** *n.* ignition lead. **~kapsel** *f.* detonator. **~kerze** *f.* sparking-plug. **~leine** *f.* slow-match. **~loch** *n.* vent. **~nadelgewehr** *n.* needlegun. **~schnur** *f.* fuse, match. **~stoff** *m.* combustible matter, fuel; *(fig.)* inflammable material. **~ung** *f.* priming; ignition.

Zunder (-un-) *m.* (-s, -) tinder; touchwood.

zunehmen *v.i.* to grow, grow larger, increase; to grow heavier; to put on flesh; to grow heavier; **~der Mond** waxing moon; **~de Jahre** advancing years.

zuneig-en *v.i.* to lean toward; to incline to; **sich dem Ende ~en** to draw to a close. **~ung** *f.* liking, affection; sympathy, inclination.

Zunft *f.* (-, ¨e) guild; corporation.

zünftig *a.* belonging to a guild; skilled, competent; *(colloq.)* thorough, proper.

Zunge (tsuŋə) *f.* (-, -n) tongue; language; *(zool.)* sole; **eine belegte ~** a dirty tongue; **eine feine ~ haben** to be a gourmet; **sein Herz auf der ~ tragen** to wear one's heart on one's sleeve; **das Wort schwebt mir auf der ~** I have the word on the tip of my tongue. **~nfertig** *a.* glib. **~nfertigkeit** *f.* glib tongue. **~nrücken** *m.* dorsal surface of tongue.

züngeln *v.i.* to dart or shoot out the tongue; *(of flame)* to leap up, lick.

zu'nichte *adv.* **~ machen** to destroy; to frustrate.

zunicken *v.i.* to nod to.

zu'nutze *adv.* **sich ~ machen** to profit by, turn to account.

zu'oberst *adv.* at the top, uppermost.

zuordnen *v.t.* to attach to, appoint to.

zupacken *v.i.* to set to (work); to grasp at.

zu'paß *adv.* **~ kommen** to come at the right moment **or** in the nick of time.

zupf-en *v.t.* to pull, tug; to pull out, pluck, pick. **~geige** *f.* guitar.

zur = **zu der.**

zuraten *v.i.* to advise, recommend.

zurechn-en *v.t.* to add; to attribute, ascribe, to impute; to include, class. **~ung** *f.* addition, attribution. **~ungsfähig** *a.* responsible, of sound mind. **~ungsfähigkeit** *f.* responsibility, sound state of mind; accountability.

zu'recht *adv.* right, in order; rightly, with reason; in time, in good time. **~finden** *v.r.* to find one's way (about); to begin to know. **~kommen** *vvs.i.* to arrive in time; to get on well (with something). **~legen** *v.t.* to put out,

put ready; *sich etwas ~legen*
to figure out something. **~machen** *v.t.* to prepare. *v.r.* to get
ready, dress. **~setzen** *v.t. einem
den Kopf ~setzen* to bring one to
reason. **~weisen** *v.t.* to direct,
show the way; to reprimand. **~weisung** *f.* reprimand, reproof.

zureden *v.i.* to advise, urge on, persuade. *subst. n.* encouragement;
persuasion.

zureichen *v.t.* to reach, hand to.
v.i. to suffice. **~d** *a.* sufficient.

zureiten *v.t.* to break in (a horse).
vws.i. to ride on; *~ auf* to ride
up to.

zurichten *v.t.* to prepare, get ready;
to cook; *übel ~* to ill-treat,
handle roughly.

zuriegeln *v.t.* to bolt.

zürnen *v.i.* to be angry (with).

zurück *adv. & sep. pref.* back;
backwards; backward, behind;
in arrears; late. *int.* stand back!
~beben *vws.i.* to start back, recoil. **~begeben** *v.r.* to return.
~behalten *v.t.* to keep back, retain. **~bekommen** *v.t.* to get
back, recover. **~bleiben** *vws.i.* to
stay behind; to be left behind; to
lag behind; to be backward; to
be slow. **~bringen** *v.t.* to bring
back; to recall; to retard. **~datieren** *v.t.* to antedate. **~denken** *v.i.* to think back. **~drängen** *v.t.* to press back, force back;
to repress. **~erobern** *v.t.* to reconquer. **~fahren** *vws.i. & v.t.*
to drive back; to return. *vws.i.*
(fig.) to start back. **~fallen** *v.i.*
to fall back; to relapse. **~fordern**
v.t. to reclaim. **~führen** *v.t.* to
lead back; to attribute (to), trace
back (to); to reduce (to). **~gabe**
f. giving back; return; restoration. **~geben** *v.t.* give back; return.

zurückgehen *vws.i.* to go back, return; to retreat; to decrease; to
get smaller; to subside; to fall, go
down, decline; to fall off; to be
broken off, be cancelled; *~ auf*
to trace back (to); to have its
source *or* origin in, originate in
(something) *or* from *or* with (a
person).

zurück-gezogen *a.* retired, secluded, lonely. **~gezogenheit** *f.*
retirement, seclusion, privacy,
solitude. **~greifen** *v.i.* to go
back (to); to refer (to).

zurückhalt-en *v.t.* to hold back,
delay; to keep in, detain; to prevent, restrain, curb, check, repress. *v.i. ~en mit* to refrain
from; to reserve (judgement); to
conceal, hide, keep back (something). *v.r.* to keep to oneself,
be reserved. **~end** *a.* reserved,
uncommunicative. **~ung** *f.* reserve; retention.

zurück-kehren *vws.i.* to return,
go back; to come back. **~kommen** *vws.i.* to come back, return;
to get behindhand (with work);
to become reduced (in circumstances); *~kommen von (fig.)* to
alter (one's) opinion, change
(one's mind). **~kunft** *f.* return.
~lassen *v.t.* to leave behind. **~legen** *v.t.* to lay aside; to save, put
by; to traverse; to complete,
attain (age); to go through
(course). *v.r.* to lie back. **~liegen**
v.i. to belong to the past. **~nahme** *f.* (the) taking back; withdrawal; revocation; recantation.
~nehmen *v.t.* to take back; to
withdraw; to revoke; to recall;
to cancel. **~prallen** *vws.i.* to
rebound; to start back. **~rufen**
v.t. to call back, recall; to call (to
mind).

zurück-schauen *v.i.* to look back.
~schlagen *v.t.* to repel, repulse
(enemy); to return (ball); to
throw off; to throw open. *v.i.*
to strike back. **~schrecken** *v.t.*
to frighten away, deter. *vws.i.*
to shrink (from); to start back. **~sehnen** *v.t.* to sigh for. *v.r.* to long
to return. **~setzen** *v.t.* to put
back, replace; to reduce, lower
(price); *(fig.)* to slight, neglect;
Verkauf ~gesetzter Waren bargain-sale. **~setzung** *f.* neglect,
slight. **~springen** *vws.i.* to jump
back; to rebound; *(archit.)* to
recede. **~stehen** *vws.i.* to stand
back; *(fig.)* to be inferior (to).
~stellen *v.t.* to put back, replace;
to reserve; to put aside, shelve;

(*mil.*) to defer. **~stoßen** *v.t.* to push back; to repel, repulse. **~strahlen** *v.t.* to reflect. *v.i.* to be reflected. **~treten** *vws.i.* to step back; to recede; to withdraw; to retire; to resign.

zurück-versetzen *v.t.* to put back, restore; *sich in eine Zeit ~versetzen* to go back (in imagination) to a time. **~verweisen** *v.t.* to refer back (to). **~weichen** *vws.i* to retreat, fall back; to recede; to give in, yield. **~weisen** *v.t.* to send away, send back; to repulse, repel; to decline, refuse; to reject. *v.i.* to refer back (to). **~weisung** *f.* rejection; refusal; repulse. **~werfen** *v.t.* to throw back; to repulse; to reflect (rays). **~wirken** *v.i.* to react (upon). **~zahlen** *v.t.* to pay back, repay, refund. **~zahlung** *f.* repayment. **~ziehen** *v.t.* to draw back, take back; to withdraw; to retract. *vws.i.* to return; to move *or* march back; to retreat, fall back. *v.r.* to retire; to withdraw; to retreat.

Zuruf *m.* acclamation, shout, call. **~en** *v.i. & t.* to call to, shout to.

zurüst-en *v.t.* to fit out, equip; to prepare, get ready. **~ung** *f.* fitting out, equipment; preparation.

Zusage *f.* acceptance; promise. **~n** *v.t.* to promise; *einem etwas auf den Kopf ~n* to tell a person something plainly *or* to his face. *v.i.* to accept (invitation); to please, suit; (*of food*) to agree with. **~nd** *a.* suitable.

zu'sammen (-z-) *adv.* together; in all, all told, all together; in a body. **~arbeit** *f.* co-operation. **~ballen** *v.t.* to roll into a ball; to clench (fist); to concentrate; to mass. *v.r. (of clouds)* to gather; (*fig.*) to draw near. **~beißen** *v.t. die Zähne ~beißen* to set one's teeth. **~binden** *v.t.* to tie up, tie together. **~brechen** *vws.i.* to collapse, break down. **~bringen** *v.t.* to collect; to amass (fortune); to raise (money); to bring together (people). **~bruch** *m.* collapse, break-down. **~drängen** *v.t. & r.*

to crowd together; to compress; to condense; to concentrate. **~drücken** *v.t.* to compress. **~fahren** *vws.i.* to collide (with); to start, wince. **~fallen** *vws.i.* to collapse; to coincide (with). **~falten** *v.t.* to fold, fold up. **~fassen** *v.t.* to sum up, summarize, recapitulate; to collect; to unite, combine; to concentrate. **~fassend** *a.* comprehensive. **~fassung** *f.* summing up, summary, recapitulation; concentration. **~fließen** *vws.i.* to flow together, join their waters, meet. **~fluß** *m.* confluence, junction, conflux. **~fügen** *v.t.* to join, unite, combine. **~führen** *v.t.* to bring together.

zusammen-gehen *vws.i.* to go together; to suit one another, match; to be attended (with). **~gehören** *v.i.* to belong together; to match; to be correlated. **~gehörig** *a.* belonging together; correlated; homogeneous. **~gehörigkeit** *f.* intimate connexion; unity; homogeneousness. **~geraten** *vws.i.* to fall out, quarrel, have words with. **~gesetzt** *a.* composed; compound; composite; complex. **~gewürfelt** *a.* motley. **~halt** *m.* holding together; cohesion; consistency; unity. **~halten** *v.t.* to hold together; to support, maintain, keep going; to compare. *v.i.* to stick together, be staunch friends. **~hang** *m.* connexion; coherence; correlation; context; cohesion; continuity. **~hängen** *v.i.* to be connected with; to cohere. **~d** *a.* coherent; continuous. **~hanglos** *a.* disconnected; incoherent; rambling, desultory. **~klang** *m.* accord, harmony. **~klappbar** *a.* folding, collapsible. **~klappen** *v.t.* to fold up, fold together. *vws.i.* to break down. **~kleben** *v.t.* to agglutinate. **~kommen** *vws.i.* to meet, assemble; to come together. **~kunft** *f.* meeting, reunion; assembly; interview; conference.

zusammen-laufen *vws.i.* to run together; to congregate, collect; (*math.*) to converge; to curdle; to shrink; (of colours) to run. ~leben v.i. to live together. ~legen v.t. to put together (in a heap), pile up; to unite, combine; to fuse; to club together; to fold. ~nehmen v.r. to make an effort; to take care, watch, look out; to control oneself. ~passen v.t. to fit, adapt, adjust, match. v.i. to be well matched, go well together. ~pferchen v.t. to pack, crowd, squeeze (together), pen up (cattle). ~raffen v.t. to seize, collect hurriedly; to amass (fortune). v.r. to make an effort, pull oneself together. ~rechnen v.t. to reckon up, add up. ~reimen v.t. to understand, make out. v.r. to fit in, make sense. ~reißen v.r. to make a desperate effort. ~rotten v.r. to form a gang, band together. ~rottung f. riot; riotous mob. ~rücken vws.i. to move closer together, sit closer, move nearer to.

zusammen-schießen v.t. & i. to shoot down; to knock out; to club together. ~schlagen v.t. to smash, smash up; to clap (hands); to click (heels). v.i. (of waves) to close (over a person), engulf (person). ~schließen v.r. to join, unite, amalgamate; to close the ranks. ~schluß m. union, federation; amalgamation; merger. ~schnüren v.t. to lace up; to cord, tie up; to wring (heart). ~schrumpfen vws.i. to shrink, shrivel up. ~schweißen v.t. to weld together. ~setzen v.t. to put together; to compose, make up; to join; to pile (arms). v.r. to sit together; to consist of, be composed of. ~setzung f.composition; combination; synthesis; structure; construction, formation. ~spiel n. (the) playing together; (theatr. & sport.) team-work. ~stecken v.t. to put together. v.i. to be very thick with someone; to conspire together. ~stehen vws. & h. i. to stand together; to stick together. ~stellen v.t. to put together; to collate, compile; to group; to make up; to compose, compare. ~stellung f.

combination; compilation; summary; list; inventory; grouping, classification; juxtaposition; comparison. ~stimmen v.i. to agree; to accord, harmonize. ~stoß m. collision; clash, encounter; (mil.) engagement. ~stoßen v.t. to smash; to clink (glasses). vws.i. to collide; to clash, conflict; to adjoin.

zusammen-treffen vws.i. to meet, meet each other; to coincide. subst. n. meeting; coincidence. ~treten vws.i. to meet. ~tun v.r. to associate, unite, join, combine. ~wirken v.i. to work together, co-operate. ~zählen v.t. to count up, add up. ~ziehen v.t. to draw together; to contract; to concentrate; to oppress, wring (heart). v.r. to gather; (fig.) to draw near. ~ziehung f. contraction; concentration.

Zu-satz m. addition; adjunct; supplement; appendix; postscript; codicil; (chem.) admixture; alloy. ~sätzlich a. additional.

zu schanden adv. ~ jagen to work (a horse) to death; ~ machen to foil, thwart, ruin; ~ werden to come to nothing, be ruined.

zuschanzen v.t. to secure, (sl.) wangle.

zuscharren v.t. to fill up (hole).

zuschau-en v.i. to look on, watch. ~er m. spectator, onlooker; (pl.) audience, public. ~erraum m. (theatr.) house; auditorium; seats (pl.).

zuschaufeln v.t to fill up (hole).

zuschicken v.t. to send on, forward; to remit (money).

zuschieben v.t. to push towards; to shut (drawer); to put the (blame) on; to give a person the oath.

zuschießen v.t. to rush (at); to supply, contribute; to add to, subsidize.

Zuschlag m. addition; increase (in price), additional charge; additional tax, surtax; bonus; knocking down (to bidder at auction); (metal) flux. ~en v.t. to slam (door); to knock down to (bidder). v.i. to strike hard, hit out. ~

gebühr *f.* additional fee; excess fare. ~karte *f.* additional ticket. ~porto *n.* excess postage, surcharge. ~spflichtig *a.* liable to additional payment.

zuschließen *v.t.* to lock, lock up.

zuschmeißen *v.t.* to slam, bang (door); to throw to.

zuschnallen *v.t.* to buckle, fasten.

zuschnappen *v.i.* to snap up. *vws.i.* to snap to.

zuschneid-en *v.t.* to cut out. ~er *m.* (tailor's) cutter.

Zuschnitt *m.* cut; style.

zuschnüren *v.t.* to lace; to tie up; to strangle; to choke.

zuschrauben *v.t.* to screw up; to screw down.

zuschreiben *v.t.* to attribute to; to blame, thank, owe (it) to; (*commerc.*) to transfer to, place to credit of. *v.i.* to accept an invitation (by letter).

zuschreien *v.t. & i.* to shout to.

zuschreiten *vws.i.* to walk along, step out.

Zuschrift *f.* letter, communication.

zu'schulden *adv. sich etwas ~ kommen lassen* to be guilty of doing something.

Zuschuß *m.* extra allowance; rise (in salary); subsidy.

zuschütten *v.t.* to pour on to, add to; to fill up (hole).

zusehen *v.i.* to look on, watch; to wait; to take care, look out for; to see to (it). ~ds *adv.* visibly, noticeably.

zusenden *v.t.* to send on to; to forward to.

zusetzen *v.t.* to add to; to lose (money). *v.i.* to importune, press (a person) hard; to wear out (health).

zusicher-n *v.t.* to assure of, promise. ~ung *f.* assurance, promise.

zusiegeln *v.t.* to seal up.

zusperren *v.t.* to lock, close, bar.

zuspielen *v.t.* to pass (ball) to; *einem etwas ~* to play into a person's hands.

zuspitzen *v.t.* to point, sharpen (pencil). *v.r.* (*fig.*) to get critical, come to a crisis.

zusprechen *v.t. & i.* to encourage; *Trost ~* to comfort, console;

dem Essen ~ to eat heartily; *dem Glas ~* to imbibe freely. *v.t.* to award, adjudge.

zuspringen *vws.i.* to run towards; to jump up (at); (*of lock*) to snap to.

Zuspruch *m.* consolation, encouragement; custom, clientele, customers; praise, approval.

Zustand *m.* state, condition; situation, position; state of things, state of affairs; (*pl.*) attack (of nerves), fit (of hysteria).

zu'stande *adv. ~ bringen* to accomplish, achieve, bring about; *~ kommen* to come about, happen, take place; *nicht ~ kommen* not to come off.

zuständig *a.* belonging to, appertaining to; responsible; authorized, competent; proper. ~keit *f.* competence.

zu'statten *adv. ~ kommen* to prove useful, come in useful.

zustecken *v.t.* to pin up; *einem etwas ~* to slip something into one's hand; to provide a person secretly with something.

zustehen *v.i.* to behove; to become, suit; to be due to, belong to.

zustell-en *v.t.* to forward to, deliver to; to obstruct, block up, barricade. ~ung *f.* delivery; forwarding, sending on; writ.

zusteuern *v.t.* to contribute. *v.i. ~ auf* to steer for; (*fig.*) to aim at.

zustimm-en *v.i.* to assent, consent, agree to. ~ung *f.* consent, approval.

zustopfen *v.t.* to stop up; to darn.

zustoßen *v.t.* to push (door) to, shut, close. *v.i.* to thrust forward. *vws.i.* to happen to, meet with, befall.

zustreben *vws.i.* to hasten towards; to strive for, make for.

Zustrom *m.* influx; crowd, multitude, run (on bank); flow.

zuströmen *vws.i.* to flow into; to throng to, stream towards.

zustürzen *vws.i.* to rush (towards).

zustutzen *v.t.* to cut, trim; to adapt.

zu'tage *adv.* to light; *~ fördern* to bring to light; *~ liegen* to be manifest.

Zutat f. ingredient, seasoning; (dressm.) trimmings.

zu'teil adv. ~ werden to fall to one's share: ~ werden lassen to allot to.

zuteil-en v.t. to assign to, allot to; to apportion; to distribute; (mil.) to attach to, appoint, post to. ~ung f. apportioning, distribution; appointment, posting, attachment.

zu'tiefst adv. at bottom; deeply.

zutragen v.t. to carry to; to tell, repeat, report. v.r. to happen, take place.

Zuträge'rei f. (-, -en) talebearing, gossip.

zuträglich a. advantageous, useful; wholesome.

zutrau-en v.t. to believe (one) capable of; to give (one) credit for. subst. n. confidence, trust. ~lich a. confiding, trusting, friendly. ~lichkeit f. trustfulness, friendliness.

zutreffen vws.i. to prove true, come true. ~d a. correct, right, to the point.

zutrinken v.i. to drink to.

Zutritt m. admission, entrance, (free) access.

zutun v.t. to add; to close, shut. subst. n. help, assistance. ~lich a. confiding, friendly.

zuverlässig a. reliable, trustworthy, dependable; authentic. ~keit f. reliability, trustworthiness; authenticity.

Zuversicht f. (-) confidence, trust. ~lich a. confident. ~lichkeit f. confidence, trust; assurance; self-assurance.

zuviel (-fi:l) adv. too much.

zu'vor (-fo:r) adv. before, previously; first, beforehand; formerly. ~kommen vws.i. to come first, forestall, anticipate; to prevent. ~kommend a. obliging, polite. ~kommenheit f. politeness, kindness. ~tun v.i. es einem ~tun to surpass, outdo a person.

Zuwachs m. growth, increase, increment; auf ~ allowing for growth. ~en vws.i. to grow together, close up; to heal up; to

become overgrown; to accrue to, fall to one's lot.

zuwandern vws.i. to immigrate.

zuwarten v.i. to wait.

zu'wege adv. ~ bringen to bring about, accomplish.

zu'weilen adv. sometimes, at times, now and then, occasionally.

zuweisen v.t. to allot to; to attribute to.

zuwend-en v.t. to turn towards; to give, make a present of; to bestow upon; to devote to. ~ung f. gift, donation.

zuwerfen v.t. to throw to; to slam (door); to fill up (hole).

zu'wider a. repugnant, offensive. prep. against, contrary to. ~handeln v.i. to contravene, infringe (regulations). ~handlung f. contravention; transgression. ~laufen vws.i. to run counter to, be contrary to. ~sein v.i. to be repugnant to; das ist mir ~ I hate or loathe it.

zuwinken v.i. to beckon to, wave to; to nod to.

zuzahlen v.t. to pay extra.

zu'zeiten adv. at times.

zuzieh-en v.t. to draw together; to draw (curtain); to call in, invite; to consult (doctor). v.r. to incur; to catch (illness). vws.i. to move in, immigrate. ~ung f. calling in (of doctor); consulting (of doctor); unter ~ung von with the help of; including (expenses).

Zuzug m. immigration; increase (of population); arrival; (mil.) reinforcements. ~sgenehmigung f. permit of residence.

zuzüglich prep. with the addition of, including, plus.

zwacken (tsvak-) v.t. to pinch.

zwang¹ imperf. of **zwingen**.

Zwang² (tsvaŋ) m. (-es) compulsion, coercion; force; constraint; (moral) obligation; pressure; sich ~ antun to restrain oneself; sich keinen ~ antun to be quite free and easy. ~los a. free and easy, natural; unconventional; occasional, indefinite. ~losigkeit f. freedom; ease; informality. ~s-anleihe f. forced loan. ~sarbeit f. hard labour. ~sjacke f. strait jacket. ~slage f. sich in einer ~slage befinden to be hard pressed; to be under the necessity (of doing something). ~släufig adv. necessarily, inevitably, automatically. ~neurose f. obsession. ~svergleich m. forced settlement. ~svollstreckung f. distraint, distress. ~svorstellung f. hallucination. ~sweise a. compulsory, forcible. ~swirtschaft f. government control.

zwängen v.t. to press (into), force (into).

zwanzig (tsvantsiç) a. twenty, a score. ~er m. man of twenty; in den ~ern sein to be in one's twenties. ~st a. twentieth.

zwar (tsva:r) adv. indeed, although; und ~ in fact, namely, that is.

Zweck (tsvɛk) m. (-es, -e) purpose, design, aim, object, end, goal; zu welchem ~? why? what for? keinen ~ haben to be of no use, be pointless. ~bau m. functional building. ~dienlich, ~entsprechend, ~mäßig aa. expedient, suitable, appropriate, conformable with the purpose. ~los a. useless; purposeless; aimless. ~losigkeit f. uselessness; aimlessness. ~widrig a. inexpedient, unsuitable, inappropriate.

Zwecke f. (-, -n) drawing-pin; tack; nail.

zwecks prep. for the purpose of.

zwei (tsvai) a. & subst. f. two; zu ~en in twos, in pairs, two by two. ~beinig a. two-legged. ~bettig a. with two beds. ~decker m. biplane. ~deutig a. ambiguous, equivocal; doubtful; smutty, obscene. ~deutigkeit f. ambiguity. ~erlei a. of two kinds; different. ~fach a. twofold, double; in ~facher Ausführung in duplicate. ~farbendruck m. two-colour print(ing). ~gestrichen a. (mus.) twice accented. ~gleisig a. double-tracked. ~händig a. (mus.) for two hands. ~jährig a. two-years-old; (bot.) biennial. ~kampf m. duel. ~mal adv. twice. ~malig a. done twice, repeated, reiterated. ~rad n.

bicycle. ~reihig a. with two rows; double-breasted (coat). ~röhrenapparat m. two-valve (radio) set. ~schläfrig a. double (-bed). ~schneidig a. two-edged; (fig.) cutting both ways, ambiguous. ~silbig a. disyllabic. ~sitzer m. two-seater. ~spännig a. drawn by two horses. ~sprachig a. bilingual. ~stimmig a. for two voices. ~stündig a. of two hours, lasting two hours. ~stündlich a. every two hours. ~taktmotor m. two-stroke engine. ~teilig a. two-piece bipartite. ~unddreißigstelnote f. demisemiquaver. ~viertelnote f. minim. ~vierteltakt m. two-four time. ~wertig a. bivalent. ~zeiler m. couplet. See also zweit-.

Zweifel m. (-s, -) doubt, suspicion, misgiving. ~haft a. doubtful, uncertain, dubious, questionable; suspicious; equivocal. ~los a. doubtless, indubitable. adv. undoubtedly, without doubt, decidedly. ~sfall m. im ~sfall in case of doubt. ~s|ohne adv. without doubt, doubtless. ~sucht f. scepticism. ~süchtig a. sceptical.

zweifeln v.i. to doubt, waver, question; to be distrustful, suspect; to be in doubt (about).

Zweifler m. (-s, -) sceptic, doubter.

Zweig (tsvaik) m. (-es, -e) branch, bough, twig; section. ~geschäft n., ~niederlassung f. branch (of shop, &c.). ~stelle f. branch office.

zweit (tsvait) a. second; next; zu ~ two (of us), two by two. ~ältest a. second eldest. ~ens adv. secondly, in the second place. ~letzt a. last but one, penultimate.

zwerch adv. über~ across. ~fell n. diaphragm. ~fellerschütternd a. side-splitting.

Zwerg m. (-es, -e) dwarf, pygmy, midget. ~enhaft a. diminutive, tiny; undersized, dwarfish, stunted. ~kiefer f. dwarf pine.

Zwetsch(g)e (tsvɛtʃgǝ) f. (-, -n) plum.

Zwickel m. (-s, -) wedge; gusset; gore; clock (of stocking); (*archit.*) spandrel.

zwick-en v.t. to pinch, nip; to gripe. ~**er** m. eye-glasses, pince-nez. ~**mühle** f. (*fig.*) dilemma.

Zwieback m. (-s, -e) rusk.

Zwiebel f. (-, -n) onion; bulb. ~**gewächs** n. bulbous plant. ~ v.t. to season with onions; (*fig.*) to give one a rough handling. ~**turm** m. onion-shaped dome. [L]

zwie-fach, ~**fältig** aa. twofold, double. ~**gespräch** n. dialogue, conversation, talk. ~**licht** n. twilight, dusk. ~**spalt** m. dissension, discord; schism. ~**spältig** a. disunited, divided, conflicting. ~**sprache** f. conversation, dialogue. ~**tracht** f. discord, dissension. ~**trächtig** a. discordant.

Zwiesel f. (-, -n) forked branch; bifurcation.

Zwilch, Zwillich m. (-s, -e) ticking.

Zwilling m. (-s, -e) twin; (*pl. astron.*) Gemini, the Twins. ~**s-achse** f. twin-axis. ~**bruder** m. twin-brother.

Zwingburg f. fortified castle, stronghold.

Zwinge f. (-, -n) ferrule; clamp; (hand-screw) cramp; vice.

zwing-en v.t. st. to compel, force; to get through, finish. v.r. to force oneself (to). ~**end** a. forcible, cogent. ~**er** m. outer courtyard, court; cage, den; arena; (bear-)pit. ~**herr** m. despot, tyrant. ~**herrschaft** f. despotism, tyranny.

zwinkern v.i. to blink, wink, twinkle.

Zwirn m. (-es, -e) thread, sewing-cotton, yarn. ~**en** a. of thread, of yarn. v.t. to twine, twist. ~(**s**)**faden** m. thread. ~(**s**)**rolle** f. reel of thread.

zwischen (tsvi∫ən) prep. between; among, amongst. ~**akt** m. entr'acte, interval. ~**bemerkung** f. aside, digression. ~**bilanz** m. interim statement. ~**deck** n. lower deck, steerage. ~**ding** n. mixture; combination. ~**durch** adv. through, in the midst; at times, in between. ~**fall** m. in-

cident, episode. ~**frage** f. question (interjected in speech). ~**gericht** n. entrée. ~**glied** n. connecting link. ~**handel** m. middleman's business. ~**händler** m. middleman; agent, intermediary; commission-agent. ~**landung** f. intermediate landing *or* stop (during flight). ~**pause** f. interval; break, interlude. ~**raum** m. space (between), interstice, gap; interval. ~**ruf** m. interruption. ~**schaltung** f. interposition. ~**spiel** n. intermezzo, interlude. ~**staatlich** a. international. ~**stecker** m. adapter. ~**stellung** f. intermediate position. ~**stock** m. entresol, mezzanine. ~**stufe** f. intermediate stage. ~**trägerei** f. talebearing. ~**vorhang** m. drop-scene. ~**wand** f. partition-wall. ~**zeit** f. intervening time, interval; *in der* ~**zeit** in the mean time, meanwhile.

Zwist m. (-es, -e) dissension, discord; quarrel. ~**ig** a. in dispute. ~**igkeit** f. dissension, quarrel. [TWIST]

zwitschern (tsvit∫-) v.i. to twitter, chirp, warble.

Zwitter m. (-s, -) mongrel; hybrid; hermaphrodite. ~**bildung** f. hybridization, hermaphroditism. ~**haft** a. hybrid; hermaphrodite.

zwo = **zwei**.

zwölf (tsvœlf) a. & subst. f. twelve. ~**eck** n. dodecagon. ~**finger-darm** m. duodenum. ~**t** a. twelfth. ~**tel** n. a twelfth (part). ~**tens** adv. twelfthly.

Zy'ane f. (-, -n) (*bot.*) corn-flower, bluebottle.

Zyan'kali n. (-s) cyanide of potassium.

Zy'klon m. (-s, -e) cyclone.

Zy'klop m. (-en, -en) Cyclops; (*pl.*) Cyclopes. ~**isch** a. cyclopean.

Zyklus (tsy:klus) m. (-, Zyklen) cycle; course, series (of lectures).

Zy'linder m. (-s, -) cylinder; lamp-chimney; silk hat, top-hat. ~**förmig**, **zy'lindrisch** aa. cylindrical. ~**presse** f. roller-press.

Zyn-iker (tsy:-) m. (-ikers, -iker) Cynic (philosopher); cynic. ~**isch**

a. cynical, shameless, sneering.
~**ismus** *m.* Cynicism; cynicism,
shamelessness.

Zy′presse *f.* (-, -n) cypress.
Zyste *f.* (-, -n) cyst.

APPENDIXES

I. LIST OF NAMES

Aachen *n.* Aix-la-Chapelle.
Abe'ssinien *n.* Abyssinia.
A'bruzzen *pl.* (the) Abruzzi.
A'dele *f.* Adela.
Adelheid *f.* Adelaide.
Adriatische(s) Meer *n.* the Adriatic Sea, the Adriatic.
Afrik-a *n.* Africa. ∼'aner *m.*, ∼'anisch *a.* African.
Ä'gäische(s) Meer *n.* the Aegean Sea.
Ä'gypt-en *n.* Egypt. ∼er *m.*, ∼isch *a.* Egyptian.
Al'ban-ien *n.* Albania. ∼er *m.*, ∼isch *a.* Albanian.
Algier *n.* Algeria; Algiers (town).
Alpen *pl.* the Alps.
A'malie *f.* Amelia.
A'merik-a-n *n.* America. ∼'aner *m.*, ∼'anisch *a.* American.
Anden *pl.* the Andes.
An'dreas *m.* Andrew.
Angel-sachse *m.*, ∼'sächsisch *a.* Anglo-Saxon.
An'tillen *pl.* the Antilles.
Anti'ochien *n.* Antioch.
Anton *m.* Anthony.
Ant'werpen *n.* Antwerp.
Ape'nnin *m.* (-s, -en) (the) Apennines.
Arab-er *m.*, Arab. ∼isch *a.* Arabian. ∼ien *n.* Arabia.
Argen'tinien *n.* the Argentine.
Ar-ier *m.*, ∼isch *a.* Aryan.
Ar'menien *n.* Armenia.
Aschenbrödel, Aschenputtel *n.* Cinderella.
Asi-'ate *m.*, ∼'atisch *a.* Asiatic.
Asien *n.* Asia.
A'ssyr-er *m.*, ∼isch *a.* Assyrian. ∼ien *n.* Assyria.
A'then *n.* Athens. ∼er *m.*, ∼isch *a.* Athenian.
Äthi'opien *n.* Ethiopia.
At'lantische(r) Ozean *m.* the Atlantic Ocean.
Ätna *m.* Mount Etna.
August *m.* Augustus.

Augu'stin *m.* Augustine, Austin.
Aus'tral-ien *n.* Australia. ∼ier *m.*, ∼isch *a.* Australian.
A'zoren *pl.* (the) Azores.

Bale'aren *pl.* the Balearic Isles.
Balt-e *m.* inhabitant of the Baltic provinces. ∼ikum *n.* (the) Baltic provinces.
Basel *n.* Basle.
Bayer *m.*, ∼isch, bayrisch *aa.* Bavarian. ∼n *n.* Bavaria.
Bedu'ine *m.* Bedouin.
Belg-ien *n.* Belgium. ∼ier *m.*, ∼isch *a.* Belgian.
Belgrad *n.* Belgrade.
Ben'galen *n.* Bengal.
Bern *n.* Berne.
Berner Oberland *n.* Bernese Alps.
Bernhard *m.* Bernard.
Birma *n.* Burma. ∼nisch *a.* Burmese.
Bis'kaya *n.* Biscay.
Bodensee *m.* Lake of Constance.
Böhm-en *n.* Bohemia. ∼isch *a.* Bohemian.
Bozen *n.* Bolzano.
Brasili'an-er *m.*, ∼isch *a.* Brazilian. **Bra'silien** *n.* Brazil.
Braunschweig *n.* Brunswick.
Bre'tagne *f.* Brittany.
Bri'gitte *f.* Bridget.
Bri'tann-ien *n.* Britain. ∼isch *a.* British, Britannic.
Brit-e *m.* British subject. ∼isch *a.* British.
Brügge *n.* Bruges.
Brüssel *n.* Brussels.
Bukarest *n.* Bucharest.
Bul'gar-en *m.*, ∼isch *a.* Bulgarian. ∼ien *n.* Bulgaria.
Buren *pl.* Boers. ∼krieg *m.* Boer War.
Bur'gund *n.* Burgundy.
By'zanz *n.* Byzantium.

Cä'cilie *f.* Cecilia.
Chi'len-e *m.*, ∼isch *a.* Chilian.

Chin-a *n.* China. **~'ese** *m.* Chinese, Chinaman. **~'esisch** *a.* Chinese.
Christ *m.,* **~in** *f.,* **~lich** *a.* Christian.
Christoph *m.* Christopher.
Christus *n.* Christ; *vor Christi Geburt* before Christ, B.C.

Dal'matien *n.* Dalmatia.
Dän-e *m.* Dane. **~emark** *n.* Denmark. **~isch** *a.* Danish.
Darda'nellen *pl.* the Dardanelles.
deutsch *a.,* **~e(r)** *m.,* **~e** *f.* German. **~land** (*n.*) Germany. **~tum** *n.* German nationality; German tradition.
Dolo'miten *pl.* the Dolomites.
Donau *f.* (the) Danube.
Dornröschen *n.* the Sleeping Beauty.
Dünkirchen *n.* Dunkirk.

Eberhard *m.* Everard.
Eduard *m.* Edward.
Eismeer *n.* Polar Sea; *Nördliches* **~** Arctic Ocean; *Südliches* **~** Antarctic Ocean.
Eleo'nore *f.* Eleanor.
E'lisabeth *f.* Elizabeth.
Elsaß *n.* Alsace.
Elsäss-er *m.,* **~isch** *a.* Alsatian.
Emil *m.* Emil.
E'milie *f.* Emily.
Engländer *m.* Englishman. **~in** Englishwoman.
englisch *a.* English; **~e** *Krankheit* rickets.
Erich *m.* Eric.
Ernst *m.* Ernest.
Est-e *m.,* **~nisch** *a.* Esthonian. **~land** *n.* Esthonia.
Etsch *f.* (River) Adige.
Eu'rop-a *n.* Europe. **~'äer** *m.,* **~'äisch** *a.* European.

Feuerland *n.* Tierra del Fuego.
Fidschi-Inseln *pl.* Fiji Islands.
Finn-e, **~länder** *m.* Finn, Finlander. **~isch** *a.* Finnish. **~land** *n.* Finland.
Flame *m.* Fleming.
flämisch *a.* Flemish.
Fland-ern *n.* Flanders. **~risch** *a.* Flemish.
Floren'tin-er *m.,* **~isch** *a.* Florentine.

Flo'renz *n.* Florence.
Franken *n.* Franconia.
Frankfurt *n.* Frankfort.
Frankreich *n.* France.
Franz *m.* Frank, Francis. **~'iska** *f.* Frances.
Fran'z-ose *m.* Frenchman. **~ösin** *f.* Frenchwoman. **~ösisch** *a.* French.
Frida *f.* Freda.
Friede'rike *f.* Frederica.
Friedrich *m.* Frederic(k).
Fries-e *m.,* **~isch** *a.* Frisian. **~land** *n.* Frisia.
Fritz *m.* Fred, Freddie.

Galater *pl.* Galatians.
Gali'lä-a *n.* Galilee. **~er** *m.,* **~isch** *a.* Galilean.
Ga'lizien *n.* Galicia.
Gallen, *St.* *n.* St. Gall.
Gall-ien *n.* Gaul. **~ier** *m.* Gaul.
Genf *n.* Geneva. **~er** *m.,* **~erisch** *a.* Genevese.
Gent *n.* Ghent.
Genua *n.* Genoa.
Georg *m.* George.
Gerhard *m.* Gerard, Gerald.
Ger'man-e *m.* German, Teuton. **~isch** *a.* Germanic, Teutonic.
Gertrud *f.* Gertrude.
Gi'braltar *n.* *Straße von* **~** Straits of Gibraltar.
Golgatha *n.* Golgotha.
Got-e *m.* Goth. **~isch** *a.* Gothic.
Gottfried *m.* Godfrey, Geoffrey.
Gotthard *m.* Goddard; *St.* **~** St. Gotthard.
Grau'bünden *pl.* the Grisons.
Gregor *m.* Gregor. **~i'anisch** *a.* Gregorian.
Griech-e *m.* Greek. **~enland** *n.* Greece. **~entum** *n.* Hellenism. **~isch** *a.* Greek, Hellenic.
Grönland *n.* Greenland.
Großbri'tannien *n.* Great Britain.
Große(r) Ozean *m.* Pacific Ocean.
Gustav *m.* Gustavus, Guy.

Haag *m.* The Hague.
Habsburg *n.* Hapsburg.
Hameln *n.* Hamelin; *der Rattenfänger von* **~** the Pied Piper of H.
Ha'nnover *n.* Hanover.
Hans *m.* John, Jack.
Hansestädte *pl.* Hanseatic towns.

Ha'vanna *n.* Havana.
He'brä-er *m.*, ~isch *a.* Hebrew.
He'briden *pl.* Hebrides.
Heinrich *m.* Henry, Harry.
Helena, He'lene *f.* Helen.
Helgoland *n.* Heligoland.
Helsingör *n.* Elsinore.
Henri'ette *f.* Henrietta, Harriet.
He'rodes *m.* Herod.
Hess-e *m.*, ~isch *a.* Hessian. ~en *n.* Hesse.
Hildegard *f.* Hilda.
Hinterindien *n.* Farther India, Indo-China.
Hiob *m.* Job.
Holland *n.* the Netherlands.
Holländ-er *m.* Dutchman. ' ~isch *a.* Dutch.
Ho'raz *m.* Horace.
Hugo *m.* Hugh.
Hunne *m.* Hun.

Ilse *f.* Elsie.
Ind-er *m.*, ~isch *a.* Indian. ~ien *n.* India.
Indi'aner *m.* Red Indian.
Irak *m.* Iraq.
Ir-e, ~länder *m.* Irishman. ~isch *a.* Irish; ~ische Sprache Erse. ~land *n.* Ireland, Eire.
Is-land *n.* Iceland. ~länder *m.* Icelander. ~ländisch *a.* Icelandic.
Israe'lit *m.*, ~isch *a.* Israelite.
I'talien *n.* Italy.
Itali'en-er *m.*, ~isch *a.* Italian.

Jakob *m.* James, Jacob.
Japan *n.* Japan.
Ja'pan-er *m.*, ~isch *a.* Japanese.
Jere'mias *m.* Jeremiah.
Je'saias *m.* Isaiah.
Johann, Jo'hannes *m.* John.
Jo'hanna *f.* Joan, Joanna, Johanna.
Jordanien *n.* Jordan.
Jude *m.* Jew. ~nhetze *f.* Jew-baiting. ~ntum *n.* Judaism.
Jüd-in *f.* Jewess. ~isch *a.* Jewish.
Jugo'slawien *n.* Jugoslavia.
Julie *f.* Julia, Juliet.
Jütland *n.* Jutland.

Kali'fornien *n.* California.
Kal'varienberg *m.* Mount Calvary.
Kanada *n.* Canada.

Ka'nad-ier *m.*, ~isch *a.* Canadian.
Ka'nal *m.* the English Channel.
Ka'narische(n) Inseln *pl.* the Canaries, the Canary Islands.
Kapstadt *n.* Cape Town.
Karl *m.* Charles.
Kärnten *n.* Carinthia.
Kar'pathen *pl.* the Carpathians.
Kaspar *m.* Jasper.
Käte *f.* Kate, Kitty.
Katha'rina *f.* Katherine, Kathleen.
Klein'asien *n.* Asia Minor.
Köln *n.* Cologne.
Ko'losser *m. pl.* Colossians.
Konstanti'nopel *n.* Constantinople.
Ko'sak *m.* Cossack.
Krakau *n.* Cracow.
Kreml *m.* the Kremlin.
Kreta *n.* Crete.
Krim *f.* Crimea.
Kro'at-e *m.*, ~isch *a.* Croatian. ~ien *n.* Croatia.

Lapp-e *m.* Lapp ~land *n.* Lapland.
La'tein *n.*, ~isch *a.* Latin; ~ische Buchstaben Roman characters.
Lett-e *m.*, ~isch *a.* Latvian. ~land *n.* Latvia.
Libanon *n.* Mount Lebanon.
Libyen *n.* Libya.
Lilli *f.* Lilian, Lilias, Lily.
Lissabon *n.* Lisbon.
Litau-en *n.* Lithuania. ~er *m.*, ~isch *a.* Lithuanian.
Livius *m.* Livy.
Liv-land *n.* Livonia. ~länder *m.*, ~ländisch *a.* Livonian.
Li'vorno *n.* Leghorn.
Lom'bard-e *m.*, ~isch *a.* Lombard. ~ei *f.* Lombardy.
Lorenz *m.* Laurence, Lawrence.
Lothring-en *n.* Lorraine. ~er *m.*, ~isch *a.* Lothringian.
Löwen *n.* Louvain.
Ludwig *m.* Lewis, Louis.
Lu'ise *f.* Louisa, Louise.
Lukas *m.* Luke.
Lüttich *n.* Liège.
Lu'zern *n.* Lucerne.

Maas *f.* (River) Meuse.
Mähr-en *n.* Moravia. ~isch *a.* Moravian.

Mai-land *n.* Milan. ~länder *m.*, ~ländisch *a.* Milanese.

Mainz *n.* Mayence.

ma'laiisch *a.* Malayan.

Mandschu'rei *f.* Manchuria.

Marga'rete *f.* Margaret, Margery, Marjory.

Ma'ria *f.* Mary.

Mark *f.* March.

Markus *m.* Mark.

Ma'rokko *n.* Morocco.

Ma'thilde *f.* Matilda.

Ma'tthäus *m.* Matthew.

Maur-e *m.* Moor. ~isch *a.* Moorish.

Maze'don-ien *n.* Macedonia. ~ier *m.*, ~isch *a.* Macedonian.

Mer'kur *m.* Mercury.

Mesopo'tamien *n.* Mesopotamia.

Me'ssias *m.* Messiah.

Mittel-eu'ropa *n.* Central Europe. ~ländische(s) **Meer**, ~meer *n.* the Mediterranean (Sea).

Moldau *f.* Moldavia.

Mon'gol-e *m.*, ~isch *a.* Mongolian. ~ei *f.* Mongolia.

Moritz *m.* Maurice, Morris.

Mosel *f.* Moselle.

Mosk-au *n.* Moscow. ~owiter *m.*, ~owitisch *a.* Muscovite.

München *n.* Munich.

Ne'apel *n.* Naples.

Neu'fundland *n.* Newfoundland.

Neu'seeland *n.* New Zealand.

Nieder-lande *pl.* (the) Netherlands. ~länder *m.* Dutchman. ~ländisch *a.* Dutch.

Niederrhein *m.* Lower Rhine.

Nil *m.* the Nile.

Nizza *n.* Nice.

Nordsee *f.* the North Sea.

Norman'die *f.* Normandy.

Nor'mann-e *m.*, ~isch *a.* Norman.

Norweg-en *n.* Norway. ~er *m.*, ~isch *a.* Norwegian.

Nub-ier *m.*, ~isch *a.* Nubian.

Nürnberg *n.* Nuremberg.

Ober-bayern *n.* Upper *or* South Bavaria. ~italien *n.* North Italy. ~pfalz *f.* Upper Palatinate.

Ölberg *m.* Mount of Olives.

Os'manische(s) **Reich** *n.* Ottoman Empire.

Ost-'asien *n.* Eastern Asia, Far East. ~indien *n.* the East Indies. ~see *f.* the Baltic (Sea).

Österreich *n.* Austria. ~er *m.*, ~isch *a.* Austrian.

Palä'stin-a *n.* Palestine. ~ensisch *a.* Palestinian.

Pa'ris-er *m.*, ~er, (~isch) *aa.* Parisian.

Par'naß *m.* Parnassus.

Parzival *m.* Percival.

Paulus *m.* Paul.

Pers-er *m.*, ~isch *a.* Persian. ~ien *n.* Persia.

Pfalz *f.* the Palatinate.

Phari'sä-er *m.* Pharisee. ~isch *a.* Pharisaical.

Philipper *m. pl.* Philippians.

Phö'niz-ier *m.*, ~isch *a.* Phoenician.

Pol-e *m.* Pole. ~en *n.* Poland. ~nisch *a.* Polish.

Pommer *m.* Pomeranian. ~n *n.* Pomerania.

Portu'gies-e *m.*, ~isch *a.* Portuguese.

Posen *n.* (the province) Posnania, (the town) Posnan.

Prag *n.* Prague.

Preuß-e *m.*, ~isch *a.* Prussian. ~en *n.* Prussia. ~entum *n.* Prussianism.

Pyre'näen *pl.* the Pyrenees.

Rhein *m.* the Rhine.

Rho'desien *n.* Rhodesia.

Rom *n.* Rome.

Röm-er *m.*, ~isch *a.* Roman.

Ru'män-e *m.*, ~isch *a.* Roumanian. ~ien *n.* Roumania.

Ruprecht *m.* Rupert.

Russ-e *m.*, ~isch *a.* Russian.

Rußland *n.* Russia.

Sachse *m.*, sächsisch *a.* Saxon.

Sachsen *n.* Saxony.

Salomo(n) *m.* Solomon.

Sar'dinien *n.* Sardinia.

Schlesi-en *n.* Silesia. ~er *m.*, ~sch *a.* Silesian.

Schott-e *m.* Scot, Scotsman. ~isch *a.* Scottish, Scotch. ~land *n.* Scotland.

Schwabe *m.*, schwäbisch *a.* Swabian.

Schwaben n. Swabia.

Schwarze(s) Meer n. the Black Sea.

Schwarzwald m. the Black Forest.

Schwed-e m., ~isch a. Swede. ~en n. Sweden.

Schweiz f. Switzerland. ~er m., ~erisch a. Swiss; ~er Garde Papal body-guard.

Se'mit m. (-en, -en) Semite. ~isch a. Semitic.

Serb-e m., ~isch a. Serbian. ~ien n. Serbia.

Si'bir-ien n. Siberia. ~isch a. Siberian.

Sieben'bürgen n. Transylvania.

Simson n. Samson.

Si-zili'aner m., ~zil(i'an)isch a. Sicilian. ~'zilien n. Sicily.

Slaw-e m. Slav. ~isch a. Slavonic.

Slo'wak-e m., ~isch a. Slovak. ~ei f. Slovakia.

Sowjet m. Soviet. ~union f. Union of Soviet Socialist Republics (U.S.S.R.).

Span-ien n. Spain. ~ier m. Spaniard. ~isch a. Spanish.

Stambul n. Constantinople.

Steier-mark f. Styria. ~märker m., ~märkisch a. Styrian.

Stille(r) Ozean m. the Pacific Ocean.

Su'deten pl. the Sudetes.

Südsee f. the South Sea.

Su'sanne f. Susan.

Syra'kus n. Syracuse.

Syrien n. Syria.

Theben n. Thebes.

Themse f. the Thames.

The'rese f. Teresa.

The'ssalien n. Thessaly.

Thrazien n. Thrace.

Thüring-en n. Thuringia; ~er Wald Thuringian Forest.

Ti'motheus m. Timothy.

Ti'rol n. Tyrol. ~er m., ~isch a. Tyrolese.

Tizian m. Titian.

Tos'kana n. Tuscany.

Tri'ent n. Trent.

Trier n. Treves.

Tripolis n. Tripoli.

Troj-a n. Troy. ~aner m., ~a-nisch a. Trojan.

Tschech-e m., ~isch a. Czech. ~ei, ~oslowa'kei f. Czechoslovakia.

Tu'nesisch a. Tunisian.

Türk-e m. Turk. ~ei f. Turkey. ~isch a. Turkish.

Tyr'rhenische(s) Meer n. Tyrrhenian Sea.

Ungar m., ~isch a. Hungarian. ~n n Hungary.

Vati'kan n. Vatican.

Ve'ne-dig n. Venice. ~zi'aner m., ~zi'anisch a. Venetian.

Vereinigte Staaten pl. the United States.

Vergil m. Virgil.

Ve'suv m. Vesuvius.

Vierwaldstätter See m. Lake of Lucerne.

Vlissingen n. Flushing.

Vo'gesen pl. Vosges (Mountains).

Vorder-asien n. the Near East. ~indien n. India.

Wa'lach-e m. Wallachian. ~ei f. Wallachia.

Wall-is n. the Canton of Valais. ~iser m., ~iserin f. Welshman. ~isisch a. Welsh.

Warschau n. Warsaw.

Weichsel f. Vistula.

welsch a. Italian; French. ~land n. Italy; France.

West-'fale m., ~'fälisch a. Westphalian. ~'falen n. Westphalia.

West'indien n. West Indies.

Wien n. Vienna. ~er m., ~erisch a. Viennese.

Wilhelm m. William. ~ine f. Wilhelmina.

Württemberg n. Wurtemberg.

Xaver m. Xavier.

Zacha'rias m. Zachariah.

Zebaoth m. Sabaoth.

Zuidersee m., f. Zuyder Zee.

Zürich n. Zurich.

Zyp-ern n. Cyprus. ~risch a. Cyprian, Cypriot(e).

II. GERMAN ABBREVIATIONS

For abbreviations of weights and measures see App. III.

a. *an, am* on; *aus* from, of.
A. A. *Auswärtiges Amt* Foreign Office.
a. a. O. *am angeführten Orte* loco citato.
Abb. *Abbildung* illustration, figure, fig.
abds. *abends* at night, p.m.
Abg. *Abgeordnete(r)* Member of Reichstag, Bundestag, & c.
Abh. *Abhandlung* treatise.
Abk. *Abkürzung* abbreviation.
Abs. 1. *Absatz* paragraph. 2. *Absender* sender.
Abt. *Abteilung* department.
a. Chr. *ante Christum* (*natum*) B.C.
a. d. *an der* on.
a. D. *außer Dienst* retired, on half-pay.
ADAC *Allgemeiner Deutscher Automobilklub* German Automobile Club.
Adr. *Adresse* address.
A. G. *Aktiengesellschaft* Limited Company.
ahd. *althochdeutsch* Old High German.
a. L. *an der Lahn* on the Lahn.
allg. *allgemein* general.
a. M. *am Main* on the Main.
amtl. *amtlich* official.
Ang., Angeb. *Angebot* offer.
Anm. *Anmerkung* note.
a. O. *an der Oder* on the Oder.
a. o. Prof. *außerordentlicher Professor* assistant professor.
a. Rh. *am Rhein* on the Rhine.
a. S. *an der Saale* on the Saale.
A. T. *Altes Testament* Old Testament.
Aufl. *Auflage* edition.
Ausg. *Ausgabe* edition.

b. *bei, beim* near; care of.
bayr. *bayrisch* Bavarian.
Bd. (*pl.* **Bde.**) *Band* (*Bände*) volume.

BDR *Bundesrepublik Deutschland* Federal Republic of Germany.
bearb. *bearbeitet* revised.
Beibl. *Beiblatt* supplement.
beif. *beifolgend* herewith.
beil. *beiliegend* enclosed.
Bem. *Bemerkung* note, annotation.
bes. *besonders* especially.
betr. *betreffend, betreffs* concerning; with reference (to).
bez. *bezahlt* paid; *beziehungsweise* respectively, or; *bezüglich* with reference (to).
Bez. *Bezirk* district.
BGB *Bürgerliches Gesetzbuch* Civil Code.
Bhf. *Bahnhof* station.
Bl. *Blatt* leaf (of paper); (weekly *or* monthly) paper, magazine.
Bln. *Berlin.*
br., brosch. *broschiert* paper-bound, sewn.
b.w. *bitte wenden* please turn over, p.t.o.
bzw. *beziehungsweise* respectively; or.

ca. *circa* about.
cand. phil. *candidatus philosophiae* student preparing for his finals.
CDU *Christlich demokratische Union.*
Chr. *Christus* Christ.
Co. *Companie* (*commerc.*) company.
CSU *Christlich Soziale Union* Christian Social Union.
c. t. *cum tempore* (*univ.*) a quarter past.

D. Doctor of Divinity.
d. Ae. *der Ältere* the elder, senior.
DDR *Deutsche Demokratische Republik* German Democratic Republic.
dgl. *dergleichen, desgleichen* likewise, ditto.

d. Gr. *der Große* the Great.

d. h. *das heißt* that is, i.e.

d. i. *das ist* i.e.

DIN *Deutsche Industrie Normen* German Industry Standards.

Dipl.-Ing. *Diplom-Ingenieur* fully certificated engineer, engineer with an Honours Degree.

Diss. *Dissertation* thesis.

d. J. *dieses Jahres* of this year.

DM *Deutsche Mark.*

d. M. *dieses Monats* of this month, inst.

DNB *Deutsches Nachrichtenbüro* German News Agency.

do. *dito* ditto.

DRGM *Deutsches Reichsgebrauchsmuster* German registered trade mark.

DRP *Deutsches Reichspatent* German patent.

Dr. phil. *Doctor philosophiae* Ph.D.

dt., dtsch. *deutsch* German.

d. Vf. *der Verfasser* the author.

dz *Doppelzentner* 100 kilogrammes

D-Zug *Durchgangszug* express, through-train; corridor-train.

ebd. *ebenda* in the same place, ib., ibid.

ehem. *ehemals* formerly.

Einl. *Einleitung* introduction

einschl. *einschließlich* inclusive.

E. K. *Eisernes Kreuz* Iron Cross

em. *emeritus* retired.

enth. *enthaltend* containing.

ev. *evangelisch* Protestant.

ev. *eventuell* perhaps.

e. V. *eingetragener Verein* registered association *or* club.

Expl. *Exemplar* copy.

Fa. *Firma* firm.

FDP *Freie demokratische Partei.*

FD-Zug *Fern D-Zug* long-distance express.

ff. 1. *folgende* the following. **2.** *hochfein* extra fine.

Folio *Folio* page, folio.

Forts. *Fortsetzung* continuation.

fr. *frei* post free, post paid.

Fr. *Frau* Mrs.

Frhr. *Freiherr* Baron.

Frl. *Fräulein* Miss.

g *Gramm* gramme.

geb. 1. *geboren* born; *geborene* née. **2.** *gebunden* bound.

Gebr. *Gebrüder* Brothers.

gegr. *gegründet* founded.

geh. *geheftet* sewn, paper-bound.

gen. *genannt* mentioned.

ges. gesch. *gesetzlich geschützt* registered trade mark.

gest. *gestorben* died.

gez. *gezeichnet* signed.

Gldr. *Ganzleder* leather.

G. m. b. H. *Gesellschaft mit beschränkter Haftung* Limited Liability Company.

gr. *groß* great, large; **gr. 8°** large 8°.

ha *Hektar* hectare

Hbf. *Hauptbahnhof* Central Station.

h. c. *honoris causa* honorary.

HGB *Handelsgesetzbuch* commercial law code.

hl *Hektoliter* 22 gallons.

Hldr. *Halbleder* half morocco; half calf.

Hlw. *Halbleinwand* half cloth.

hrsg. *herausgegeben* edited.

Hs. (*pl.* **Hss.**) *Handschrift* manuscript.

i. *in,* im in.

i. A. *im Auftrag* by order, on behalf of.

i. Br. *im Breisgau.*

Ing. *Ingenieur* engineer

Inh. *Inhaber* proprietor.

i. R. *im Ruhestand* emeritus, retired.

i. Ü. *im Üchtland (Schweiz).*

i. V. *in Vertretung* on behalf of; by proxy.

Jhrb. *Jahrbuch* annual.

jun., jr. *junior* junior.

Juso *Jungsozialisten*

kart. *kartonniert* (bound in) boards.

kath. *katholisch* Roman Catholic.

Kgl. *königlich* Royal.

km *Kilometer* kilometre.

KP *Kommunistische Partei* Communist Party.

Kripo *Kriminalpolizei* Criminal Investigation Department.

KZ *Konzentrationslager* concentration camp.

1 *Liter* litre.
Ldrbd. *Lederband* leather binding.
lfd. *laufend* current, instant, inst.
Lfrg. *Lieferung* instalment, part.
Lwd. *Leinwand* cloth.

m *Meter* metre.
M. d. L. *Mitglied des Landtags* Member of the Diet.
M.d.B. *Mitglied des Bundestages* Member of the Bundestag.
MEZ *Mitteleuropäische Zeit* Central European Time.
mg *Milligramm* milligramme.
mhd. *mittelhochdeutsch* Middle High German.
mm *Millimeter* millimetre.
möbl. *möbliert* furnished.
Ms. *Manuskript* manuscript.

Nachf. *Nachfolger* successor.
n. Chr. *nach Christus* after Christ, A.D.
nhd. *neuhochdeutsch* New High German.
nm. *nachmittags* in the afternoon.
N. N. *nomen nescio* unknown; so-and-so.
No., Nr. *Nummer* number, no.
N. T. *Neues Testament* New Testament.

o. *oben* above.
Obb. *Oberbayern* South Bavaria.
o. J. *ohne Jahr* no date.
o. O. *ohne Ort* not stated where published.
o. Prof. *ordentlicher Professor* Professor in ordinary.

p. A. *per Adresse* care of, c/o.
part. *parterre* ground floor.
Pf. *Pfennig.*
Pkw. *Personenkraftwagen* car, taxi.
p. p., ppa. *per procura (commerc.)* by proxy, per pro.
Ppbd. *Pappband* (bound in) boards.
prakt. *praktisch(er) Arzt* general practitioner.
Prof. *Professor* Professor.

prot. *protestantisch* Protestant.
Prov. *Provinz* province.
PS *Pferdestärke* horse-power.

qm *Quadratmeter* square metre.

R *Réaumur* Réaumur.
Reg.-Bez. *Regierungsbezirk* administrative district.
Rel. *Religion* religion.
Rh. *Rhein* Rhine.
R. P. *Reichspatent* state patent.

s. *siehe!* see.
S. *Seite* page.
Sa. *summa* sum, total.
SED *Sozialistische Einheitspartei Deutschlands.*
sel. *selig* deceased, late.
s. o. *siehe oben* see above.
sog. *sogenannt* so-called.
SPD *Sozialdemokratische Partei Deutschlands.*
S.S. *Sommersemester* summer term.
s. t. *sine tempore (univ.)* sharp.
St. 1. *Sankt* Saint. **2.** *Stück* piece.
StGB *Strafgesetzbuch* penal code.
StPO *Strafprozeßordnung* Code of Criminal Procedure.
Str. *Straße* street.
s. u. *siehe unten* see below.

t *Tonne* ton.
teilw. *teilweise* partly.
Tel. *Telephon* telephone
Tel.-Adr. *Telegramm-Adresse* telegraphic address.
T. H. *Technische Hochschule* technical (university) college.

u. 1. *und* and. **2.** *unter* among.
u. a. *unter anderm* amongst other things.
u. a. m. *und andres mehr* and other things, and so forth, and so on.
u. A. w. g. *um Antwort wird gebeten* an answer is requested, R.S.V.P.
U-Bahn *Untergrundbahn* underground.
übers. *übersetzt* translated.
u. (ü.) d. M. *unter (über) dem Meeresspiegel* below (above) sea-level.
UKW *Ultrakurzwelle* ultra-short wave.

usf. *und so fort* and so forth.

usw. *und so weiter* and so on, &c.

u. U. *unter Umständen* on occasion, under certain conditions.

v. *von, vom* by, from, of; prefix of nobility.

v. Chr. *vor Christus* before Christ, B.C.

verb. *verbessert* revised, improved.

Verf. *Verfasser* author.

vergl., vgl. *vergleiche* see, compare.

verh. *verheiratet* married.

v. H. *vom Hundert* per cent.

v. J. *vorigen Jahres* (of) last year.

v. M. *vorigen Monats* ult., of last month.

vorm. 1. *vormals* formerly. 2. *vormittags* forenoon, a.m.

Westf. *Westfalen* Westphalia.

W. S. *Wintersemester* winter term.

Württ. *Württemberg.*

Wwe. *Witwe* widow.

z. B. *zum Beispiel* for instance, e.g.

z. H. *zu Händen* care of, c/o.

ZPO *Zivilprozeßordnung* Civil Procedure Code.

z. S. *zur See* naval, of the navy.

Zs., Ztschr. *Zeitschrift* magazine, periodical.

z. T. *zum Teil* partly.

z. Z. *zur Zeit* for the time being, at present.

III. GERMAN WEIGHTS, MEASURES, AND MONEY

1. WEIGHTS AND MEASURES

Weight

1 Milligramm (1,000 mg. = 1 g.) = 0·015 grain
1 Zentigramm (100 cg. = 1 g.) = 0·154 grain
1 Dezigramm (10 dg. = 1 g.) = 1·543 grains
1 Gramm (1,000 g. = 1 kg.) = 15·432 grains
1 Dekagramm (100 dkg. = 1 kg.) = 5·644 drams
1 Hektogramm (10 hg. = 1 kg.) = 3·527 oz.
1 Kilogramm (1,000 kg. = 1 t.) = 2·205 lb.
1 Zentner (1 ztr. = 50 kg.) = 110·23 lb.
1 Doppelzentner (1 dz. = 100 kg.) = 220·46 lb.
1 Tonne (1 t. = 1,000 kg.) = 19 cwt. 12 oz. 5 dwt.

Linear Measure

1 Millimeter (1,000 mm. = 1 m.) = 0·039 inch
1 Zentimeter (100 cm. = 1 m.) = 0·394 inch
1 Dezimeter (10 dcm. = 1 m.) = 3·937 inches
1 Meter (1,000 mm. = 1 m.) = 39·37 inches *or* 1·094 yards
1 Dekameter (100 dkm. = 1 km.) = 10·937 yards
1 Hektometer (10 hm. = 1 km.) = 109·361 yards
1 Kilometer (1 km. = 1,000 m.; 7½ km. = 1 (German) mile) = 1093·614 yards
1 (deutsche) Meile (land mile) = 4·6 miles

Square Measure

1 Quadratzentimeter (10,000 qcm. = 1 qm.) = 0·116 sq. inch
1 Quadratmeter (100 qm. = 1 a.) = 1·196 sq. yards
1 Ar (100 a. = 1 ha.) = 119·6 sq. yards
1 Morgen = 0·631 acre
1 Hektar (100 ha. = 1 qkm.) = 2·471 acres

Cubic Measure

1 Kubikzentimeter (1 c.cm. = 1,000,000th cb.m.) = 0·061 cub. inch
1 Kubikmeter (cb.m.) = 1·308 cubic yards

Measure of Capacity

1 Schoppen (2 Schpp. = 1 l.) = 0·88 pint
1 Liter (100 l. = 1 hl.) = 1·76 pints
1 Hektoliter (hl.) = 2·75 bushels

Piece Goods

1 Dutzend = 12 pieces
1 Mandel = 15 pieces
1 Schock = 60 pieces
1 Schober = 60 pieces
1 Gros = 144 pieces = 12 dozen, 1 gross

Paper

 1 Bogen = 16 pages
 1 Heft = 10 sheets
 1 Buch = 100 sheets
 1 Ries = 1,000 sheets

Thermometer

   0° Celsius (freezing-point) 32° Fahrenheit
 100° Celsius (boiling-point) 212° Fahrenheit
   0° Réaumur   32° Fahrenheit
  80° Réaumur   212° Fahrenheit

Some convenient approximate conversions:

Centimetres to inches: multiply by 4 and divide the product by 10.
Kilograms to cwts.: divide by 50.
Kilograms to pounds: double and add 1/10 of the figure arrived at.
Kilometres to miles: divide the number of kilometres by 8 and
  multiply by 5.
Litres to pints: add 75 per cent. to the number of litres.
Metres to yards: add 10 per cent. to the number of metres.

2. MONEY

Germany

 100 Pfennige = 1 DM = Deutsche Mark
  10 Pfennige = (*colloq.*) Groschen

Austria

 100 Groschen = 1 Schilling

Switzerland

 100 Centimes = 1 Franc

LIST OF STRONG AND IRREGULAR VERBS

* Sometimes weak.

Infinitive	3rd Pers. Sing. Present	Imperfect	Past Participle	English
backen	bäckt	buk (backte)	gebacken	bake
befehlen	befiehlt	befahl	befohlen	command
beginnen		begann	begonnen	begin
beißen		biß	gebissen	bite
biegen		bog	gebogen	bend
bieten		bot	geboten	offer
binden		band	gebunden	bind
bitten		bat	gebeten	beg, ask
blasen	bläst	blies	geblasen	blow
bleiben		blieb	ist geblieben	remain
brechen	bricht	brach	hat, ist gebrochen	break
brennen		brannte	gebrannt	burn
bringen		brachte	gebracht	bring
denken		dachte	gedacht	think
dringen		drang	gedrungen	press
dürfen	darf	durfte	gedurft	may, be allowed
empfehlen	empfiehlt	empfahl	empfohlen	recommend
erschrecken	erschrickt	erschrak	ist erschrocken	be frightened
essen	ißt	aß	gegessen	eat
fahren	fährt	fuhr	ist, hat gefahren	go, drive
fallen	fällt	fiel	ist gefallen	fall
fangen	fängt	fing	gefangen	catch
finden		fand	gefunden	find
fliegen		flog	ist geflogen	fly
fliehen		floh	ist geflohen	flee
fließen		floß	ist geflossen	flow
fressen	frißt	fraß	gefressen	devour
frieren		fror	gefroren	freeze
gebären	gebiert	gebar	geboren	bear
geben	gibt	gab	gegeben	give

Infinitive	3rd Pers. Sing. Present	Imperfect	Past Participle	English
gehen		ging	ist gegangen	go, walk
gelingen	es gelingt + dat.	gelang	ist gelungen	succeed
genießen		genoß	genossen	enjoy
geschehen	es geschieht	geschah	ist geschehen	happen
gewinnen		gewann	gewonnen	win
gießen		goß	gegossen	pour
gleichen		glich	geglichen	resemble
gleiten		glitt	ist geglitten	glide
graben	gräbt	grub	gegraben	dig
greifen		griff	gegriffen	seize
haben	hat	hatte	gehabt	have
halten	hält	hielt	gehalten	hold
hängen*		hing	gehangen	hang
heben	hebt	hob	gehoben	lift
heißen		hieß	geheißen	bid, be called
helfen	hilft	half	geholfen	help
kennen		kannte	gekannt	know
klingen		klang	geklungen	sound
kommen		kam	ist gekommen	come
können	kann	konnte	gekonnt	be able, can
kriechen		kroch	ist gekrochen	creep
laden	lädt, ladet	lud	geladen	load, invite
lassen	läßt	ließ	gelassen	let
laufen	läuft	lief	ist gelaufen	run
leiden		litt	gelitten	suffer
leihen		lieh	geliehen	lend
lesen	liest	las	gelesen	read
liegen		lag	gelegen	lie
lügen		log	gelogen	(tell a) lie
meiden		mied	gemieden	avoid
messen	mißt	maß	gemessen	measure
mögen	mag	mochte	gemocht	like, may
müssen	muß	mußte	gemußt	must

Infinitive	3rd Pers. Sing. Present	Imperfect	Past Participle	English
nehmen	nimmt	nahm	genommen	take
nennen		nannte	genannt	call, name
pfeifen		pfiff	gepfiffen	whistle
preisen		pries	gepriesen	praise
raten	rät	riet	geraten	advise
reißen		riß	hat, ist gerissen	tear
reiten		ritt	hat, ist geritten	ride
rennen		rannte	ist gerannt	run
riechen		roch	gerochen	smell
rufen		rief	gerufen	call
saugen		sog	gesogen	suck
schaffen	schafft	schuf	geschaffen	create
(er)schallen	erschallt	erscholl	ist erschollen	sound
scheiden		schied	hat, ist geschieden	separate
scheinen		schien	geschienen	shine
schieben		schob	geschoben	shove, push
schießen		schoß	geschossen	shoot
schlafen	schläft	schlief	geschlafen	sleep
schlagen	schlägt	schlug	geschlagen	strike
schleichen		schlich	ist geschlichen	creep, sneak
schließen		schloß	geschlossen	shut, close
schmeißen		schmiß	geschmissen	throw, fling
schneiden		schnitt	geschnitten	cut
schrecken	schreckt	schreckte	geschreckt	frighten
schreiben		schrieb	geschrieben	write
schreien		schrie	geschrieen	cry, shriek
schreiten		schritt	ist geschritten	step, stride
schweigen		schwieg	geschwiegen	be silent
schwellen	schwillt	schwoll	ist geschwollen	swell
schwimmen		schwamm	ist geschwommen	swim
schwinden		schwand	ist geschwunden	disappear
sehen	sieht	sah	gesehen	see
sein	ist	war	ist gewesen	be

Infinitive	3rd Pers. Sing. Present	Imperfect	Past Participle	English
senden*		sandte	gesandt	send
singen		sang	gesungen	sing
sinken		sank	ist gesunken	sink
sitzen		saß	gesessen	sit
sollen	soll	sollte	gesollt	shall
sprechen	spricht	sprach	gesprochen	speak
springen		sprang	ist gesprungen	spring
stehen		stand	gestanden	stand
stehlen	stiehlt	stahl	gestohlen	steal
steigen		stieg	ist gestiegen	climb
sterben	stirbt	starb	ist gestorben	die
stoßen	stößt	stieß	gestoßen	push
streichen		strich	gestrichen	stroke
tragen	trägt	trug	getragen	carry, bear
treffen	trifft	traf	getroffen	meet, hit
treiben		trieb	getrieben	drive
treten	tritt	trat	hat, ist getreten	tread, step
trinken		trank	getrunken	drink
tun		tat	getan	do
verderben	verdirbt	verdarb	hat, ist verdorben	spoil
vergessen	vergißt	vergaß	vergessen	forget
verlieren		verlor	verloren	lose
wachsen	wächst	wuchs	ist gewachsen	grow
waschen	wäscht	wusch	gewaschen	wash
weisen		wies	gewiesen	show
wenden*		wandte	gewandt	turn
werden	wird	wurde (ward)	ist geworden	become
werfen	wirft	warf	geworfen	throw
wiegen*		wog	gewogen	weigh
wissen	weiß	wußte	gewußt	know
wollen	will	wollte	gewollt	wish, want, will
ziehen		zog	hat, ist gezogen	draw, pull
zwingen		zwang	gezwungen	compel

THE
POCKET OXFORD
ENGLISH-GERMAN
DICTIONARY

THE
POCKET OXFORD
ENGLISH-GERMAN
DICTIONARY

INTRODUCTION

THIS dictionary has been planned on the same general lines as the second part of the *Concise Oxford French Dictionary* and is intended as a complement to the *Pocket Oxford German–English Dictionary*.

It is designed primarily for the convenience of English-speaking users who wish to speak and write German, and in this respect it differs from most English–German dictionaries which contain many words and phrases needed by German-speaking readers of English. Fuller treatment than usual has therefore been given to the vocabulary of everyday usage and to those 'functional words' which bulk so largely in word-frequency lists. Archaic and literary words and technical terms have not been included, but recent scientific neologisms which have become generally current have been given a place.

For facility of reference compound expressions are listed as a rule under the first of their elements. The gender of nouns is given, but in a list of nouns of the same gender it is indicated only once at the end of the list. The abbreviations indicating parts of speech, e.g. *adv.*, *sb.*, are added only when the same words are used as different parts of speech.

The appendix contains a list of names of countries and other proper names.

ST. ANDREWS   C. T. C.

PREFACE TO THE
SECOND EDITION

The dictionary, first published in 1951, has now been revised and brought up to date. Many words which have become current since 1951 have been added.

C. T. C.

ABBREVIATIONS

a., adjective
acc., accusative
adv., adverb
agric., agriculture
anat., anatomy
archaeol., archaeology
art., article
astron., astronomy
attrib., attributive
av., aviation

bibl., biblical
biol., biology
bot., botany

chem., chemistry
colloq., colloquial
commerc., commercial
comp., comparative
conj., conjunction

dat., dative
def., definite
dem., demonstrative
dial., dialect

eccles., ecclesiastical
econ., economics
electr., electricity

f., feminine
fig., figuratively
fut., future

geol., geology
gen., genitive
gram., grammatical

i., intransitive
imper., imperative
imperf., imperfect
impers., impersonal
insep., inseparable
int., interjection

m., masculine
math., mathematics
med., medicine
mil., military
mus., music

n., neuter
naut., nautical
nom., nominative
num., numeral

parl., parliament
part., participle
pass., passive
photog., photography
phys., physics
pl., plural
pol., political
poss., possessive
pred., predicative
pref., prefix
prep., preposition
pres., present
pron., pronoun

refl., reflexive

sb., substantive
sculp., sculpture
sep., separable
sing., singular
sup., superlative

t., transitive
tech., technical
theatr., theatrical
theol., theology

v., verb
v.i., verb intransitive
v.t., verb transitive

zool., zoology

ENGLISH-GERMAN DICTIONARY

a, an, ein(e).

aback, taken ∼, verblüfft, bestürzt.

abandon, v.t. aufgeben; verlassen, preisgeben; sb. Ausgelassenheit, f.; ∼ed, verlassen; lasterhaft, verworfen; ∼ment, Aufgabe, Verlassenheit, f.

abase, erniedrigen; ∼ment, Erniedrigung, f.

abate, (sich) vermindern; (storm) nachlassen, sich legen; ∼ment, Verminderung, f.; (commerc.) Rabatt, m.

abattoir, Schlachthaus, n.

abbess, Äbtissin, f.

abbey, Abtei, f.

abbot, Abt, m.

abbreviat|e, abkürzen; ∼ion, Abkürzung, f.

abdicat|e, abdanken; ∼ion, Abdankung, f.

abdomen, Unterleib, Bauch, m.

abduct, entführen; ∼ion, Entführung, f.

aberration, Abirrung, f.

abet, aufhetzen; unterstützen; ∼tor, Anstifter, m.

abhor, verabscheuen; ∼rence, Abscheu, m.; ∼rent, abscheulich, widerlich.

abide, bleiben; (tolerate) ausstehen; ∼ by, sich halten an.

ability, Fähigkeit, f.; to the best of one's ∼, nach bestem Vermögen.

abject, ∼ly, verächtlich.

ablaze, in Flammen.

abl|e, ∼y, fähig, geschickt; to be ∼e to, instande sein; ∼e-bodied, rüstig; (mil.) diensttauglich; ∼e-bodied seaman, Vollmatrose, m.

abnormal, abnorm, regelwidrig; ∼ity, Regelwidrigkeit; Abweichung, f.

aboard, an Bord.

abode, Wohnort; Aufenthalt, m.

abol|ish, abschaffen; ∼ition, Abschaffung, f.

A-bomb, Atombombe, f.

abomin|able, ∼ably, abscheulich; ∼ate, verabscheuen; ∼ation, Greuel, m.

aborigines, Ureinwohner, m.pl.

abor|tion, Fehlgeburt, f.; ∼tive, (fig.) mißlungen, fruchtlos.

abound, reich sein (with an).

about, prep. um, herum; (fig.) über; adv. herum; (nearly) etwa, ungefähr; to be ∼ to, im Begriff sein; bring ∼, zustande bringen; round ∼, ringsum; what is it all ∼?, was soll das alles heißen?

above, prep. (exceeding) über, mehr als; adv. oben; ∼ all, vor allem.

abreast, nebeneinander; keep ∼ with, Schritt halten mit.

abridge, abkürzen; ∼ment, Abkürzung, f.

abroad, im Auslande, ins Ausland; (out of doors) draußen; get ∼, bekannt werden.

abrupt, ∼ly, plötzlich, jäh; (manner) schroff, kurz angebunden; ∼ness, Steilheit; Schroffheit, f.

abscess, Geschwür, n.

abscond, durchbrennen, ausreißen.

absen|ce, Abwesenheit, f.; on leave of ∼ce, auf Urlaub; ∼ce of mind, Zerstreutheit, f.; ∼t, a. abwesend; v. sich entfernen, ausbleiben; ∼t-minded, zerstreut; ∼tee, Abwesende(r).

absinth, Absinth, m.

absolute, ∼ly, unumschränkt, unbedingt.

absol|ution, Lossprechung, f.; Sündenerlaß, m.; ∼ve, freisprechen; entbinden (from von).

absorb, auf-, ein- saugen; (fig.) in Anspruch nehmen.

abstain, sich enthalten (with gen.); ∼er, Abstinenzler, m.

abstemious, ~ly, enthaltsam; ~ness, Enthaltsamkeit, f.

abstract, a. abstrakt; sb. Auszug, m.; v.t. abziehen, abstrahieren; ~ion, Abstraktion, f.

abstruse, ~ly, schwerverständlich, dunkel.

absurd, albern, ungereimt; ~ity, Ungereimtheit, f.

abundan|ce Überfluß (of an), m.; ~t(ly), überflüssig, reichlich.

abus|e, sb. Mißbrauch, m.; (insult) Beschimpfung, f.; v.t. mißbrauchen; beschimpfen; ~ive(ly), schimpfend, schmähend, Schimpf-, Schmäh-.

abyss, Abgrund, m.

acacia, Akazie, f.

academ|ical, akademisch; ~y, Akademie, f.

accede, beitreten, beipflichten; einwilligen (in).

accelerat|e, beschleunigen; ~ion, Beschleunigung, f.; ~or, Gashebel, m.

accent, (mark) Akzent, m., Tonzeichen, n.; (tone) Betonung, f.; ~uate, akzentuieren, betonen; ~uation, Betonung, f.

accept, annehmen; ~able, annehmbar, willkommen; ~ance, Annahme, f.

access, Zutritt, Zugang, m.; ~ible, zugänglich; ~ion (to the throne) Thronbesteigung, f.; ~ory, sb. Mitschuldige(r); (thing) Zubehör, n.; a. hinzukommend, Ersatz-.

accident, (chance) Zufall, m.; (mischance) Unfall, m.; by ~, zufällig; ~al(ly), zufällig.

acclaim, (einem) Beifall zurufen.

acclamation, Zuruf, Beifall, m.

acclimatize, akklimatisieren.

accommodat|e, anpassen; (lodge) unterbringen; ~ing, willfährig; ~ion, Anpassung, Einrichtung, f.; (quarters) Unterkommen, n., Unterkunft, f.

accompan|iment, Begleitung, f.; ~y, begleiten.

accomplice, Mitschuldige(r), m.

accomplish, vollbringen, ausführen; ~ed, gebildet; (finished) zu Ende geführt; ~ment, (completion) Vollendung, f.; (attain-

ment) Fertigkeit, f.; Talent, n.

accord, sb. Übereinstimmung, f.; v.t. zugestehen; of his own ~, aus eigenem Antriebe; with one ~, einmütig; ~ance, Übereinstimmung, f.

according, prep. & conj.: ~ as, je nachdem; ~ to, gemäß, nach; ~ly, demgemäß.

accordion, Ziehharmonika, f.

account, sb. (bill) Rechnung, f.; (narrative) Bericht, m., Schilderung, f.; (banking) Konto, n.; (of conduct) Rechenschaft, f.; on ~ of, wegen, um ... willen; of no ~, unbedeutend; call to ~, zur Rechenschaft ziehen; take ~ of, in Betracht ziehen, berücksichtigen; turn to ~, ausbeuten, verwenden; ~-book, Rechnungs-, Konto-buch, n.; ~-day, Zahltag, m.; ~-s, Rechnungen, f.pl.; ~, v.t. betrachten als, halten für; ~ for, erklären, Rechenschaft ablegen; ~able, verantwortlich; ~ancy, Buchführung, f.; ~ant, Rechnungsführer, Bücherrevisor, m.

accredit, bevollmächtigen.

accretion, Zuwachs, m.

accrue, zuwachsen; entstehen (from aus).

accumulat|e, (sich) aufhäufen; ~ion, Anhäufung, f.; ~or, Sammler, Akku(mulator), m.

accura|cy, Genauigkeit, f.; ~te(ly), genau, pünktlich.

accus|ation, Anklage, f.; ~e, anklagen, beschuldigen; ~er, (An)kläger(in).

accusative, Akkusativ, m.

accustom, gewöhnen (to an); ~ed, gewohnt, gewöhnlich.

ace, As, n.; (dice) Eins, f.; within an ~ of, um ein Haar, beinahe.

acetic, essigsauer; ~ acid, Essigsäure, f.

acetylene, Azetylen, n.

ache, sb. Schmerz, m.; v.i. schmerzen, weh tun.

achieve, ausführen, vollenden; (victory) gewinnen; ~ment, (completion) Vollendung, f.; (act) Tat, Leistung, f.

acid, a. sauer; sb. Säure, f.; ~ity Säure, f.

acknowledge, anerkennen; (*fault*) bekennen; (*letter*, &c.) antworten auf (*with acc.*); bestätigen; ~**ment,** Anerkennung, Empfangsbestätigung, *f.*; Dank, *m.*

acme, Höhepunkt, Gipfel, *m.*

acolyte, Altardiener, Ministrant, *m.*

aconite, Eisenhut, *m.*

acorn, Eichel, *f.*

acoustic, akustisch; ~**s,** Akustik, Schallehre, *f.*

acquaint, bekannt machen (mit); ~**ance,** Bekanntschaft, *f.*

acquiesce, einwilligen, zustimmen; ~**nce,** Einwilligung, *f.*

acquire, erwerben, erlangen; ~**ment,** Erwerbung, Fertigkeit *f.*; ~**ments,** Kenntnisse, *f.pl.*

acquisi|tion, Erwerb, *m.*; Erwerbung, Errungenschaft, *f.*; ~**tive,** erwerbsüchtig.

acquit, freisprechen; ~**tal,** Freisprechung, *f.*

acre, Acker, *m.*; ~**age,** Ackerfläche, *f.*

acrid, beißend, scharf.

acrimonious, ~**ly,** beißend, bitter.

acrobat, Akrobat, *m.*

across, *adv.* kreuzweise; *prep.* (quer) durch; (quer) über; come ~, zufällig treffen.

act, *sb.* Handlung, Tat, *f.*; (*play*) Akt, Aufzug, *m.*; (*parliament*) Akte, *f.*, Gesetz, *n.*; ~**s of the** *Apostles,* die Apostelgeschichte; in the ~ of, im Begriff zu; in the very ~ of, auf frischer Tat; ~, *v.i.* handeln, sich benehmen; (*work*) wirken; *v.t.* spielen, darstellen.

acting, *sb.* Spiel, *n.*; *a.* (*effective*) wirkend; (*temporary*) stellvertretend.

action, Handlung, Wirkung, *f.*; (*law*) Klage, *f.*; (*mil.*) Gefecht, *n.*; bring an ~ against, verklagen; ~**able,** klagbar.

active, ~**ly,** tätig, wirksam; (*gram.*) aktiv; on ~e service, im Wehrdienst; ~**ity,** Wirksamkeit, Tätigkeit, *f.*

act|or, Schauspieler, *m.*; ~**ress,** Schauspielerin, *f.*

actual, ~**ly** tatsächlich, wirklich; ~**ity,** Wirklichkeit, *f.*

actuary, Versicherungsstatistiker, *m.*

acumen, Scharfsinn, *m.*

acute, ~**ly** (*angle*) spitz; (*pain*, *sense*, &c.) scharf; (*mind*, &c.) scharfsinnig; ~**ness,** (*fig.*) Scharfsinn, *m.*

adage, Sprichwort, *n.*

adapt, anpassen; ~**able,** anwendbar; anpassungsfähig; ~**ation,** Anpassung, *f.*; (*of a book*, &c.) Bearbeitung, *f.*

add, hinzutun, zufügen; (*remark*, &c.) hinzufügen; ~ **up,** addieren.

adder, Natter, *f.*

addict, *v.t.* sich ergeben (*with dat.*); *sb.* Süchtige(r).

addition, Zusatz, *m.*; (*arith.*) Addition, *f.*; in ~, außerdem; in ~ to, außer; ~**al,** hinzukommend; Zusatz-.

addled, unfruchtbar; (*egg*) faul.

address, *sb.* (*speech*) Anrede, Ansprache, *f.*; (*letter*) Adresse, Anschrift *f.*; (*skill*) Gewandtheit, *f.*; *v.t.* anreden; (*letter*) adressieren; ~**ee,** Adressat, Empfänger, *m.*

adduce, beibringen, anführen.

adequate, ~**ly,** angemessen; hinreichend.

adhere, (*to a person*) anhängen; (*stick*) ankleben; ~ **to one's opinion,** auf seiner Meinung bestehen; ~**nt,** Anhänger, *m.*

adhes|ion, Anhaften, *n.*; Adhäsion, *f.*; ~**ive,** *a.* anhaftend, anklebend; gummiert; *sb.* Klebstoff, *m.*

adjacent, anliegend, angrenzend.

adjective, Adjektiv, Eigenschaftswort, *n.*

adjoin, angrenzen.

adjourn, vertagen; ~**ment,** Vertagung, *f.*

adjust, (an)ordnen; berichtigen; anpassen (*with dat.*); ~**ment,** Berichtigung, Regulierung, *f.*

adjutant, Adjutant, *m.*

administ|er, verwalten; darreichen; verabreichen; ~**ration,** Verwaltung, *f.*; ~**rative,** verwaltend; ~**rator,** Verwalter, *m.*

admirab|le, ~**y,** bewunderungswürdig.

admiral, Admiral, *m.*; rear-~, Konteradmiral, *m.*; ~**ty,** Admiralität, *f.*

admir|ation, Bewunderung, *f.*; ~e, bewundern; ~er, Verehrer, *m.*; (*lover*) Liebhaber(in); ~ingly, mit Bewunderung.

admiss|ible, zulässig; ~ion, Zulassung, *f.*; Eintritt, Zutritt, *m.*; (*confession*) Zugeständnis, *n.*

admit, (*let in*) zulassen; (*reason, &c.*) zugestehen, gelten lassen; ~tance, Zulassung *f.*; no ~tance! Eintritt verboten!

admonish, ermahnen.

adolescen|ce, Jünglingsalter, *n.*; ~t, *a.* jugendlich; *sb.* Jüngling, *m.*, junges Mädchen, *n.*

adopt, annehmen; (*child*) adoptieren; ~ed, Adoptiv-; ~ion, Annahme; Adoption, *f.*

ador|able, anbetungswürdig; ~ation, Anbetung, *f.*; ~e, anbeten.

adorn, schmücken, zieren; ~ment, Ausschmückung, Verzierung, *f.*

adroit, ~ly, gewandt; ~ness, Gewandtheit, *f.*

adult, *a.* erwachsen; *sb.* Erwachsene(r).

adulterat|e, verfälschen; ~ion, Verfälschung, *f.*

adulter|er, Ehebrecher, *m.*; ~ous, ehebrecherisch; ~y, Ehebruch, *m.*

advance, *sb.* (*mil.*) Vorrücken, *n.*; (*progress*) Fortschritt, *m.*; (*loan*) Vorschuß, *m.*; (*of prices*) Steigen, *n.*; ~ booking, Vorausbestellung, *f.*, Vorverkauf, *m.*; in ~, im voraus; *v.t.* (*a cause*) fördern; (*money*) vorschießen; *v.i.* (*mil.*) vorrücken; (*progress*) Fortschritte machen; ~d, vorgeschritten; ~ment, Beförderung, *f.*; Fortschritt, *m.*

advantage, Vorteil, Vorzug, *m.*; take ~ of, sich etwas zunutze machen; (*unfairly*) übervorteilen; ~ous(ly), vorteilhaft.

advent, (*festival*) Advent, *m.*; (*arrival*) Ankunft, *f.*

adventur|e, Abenteuer, *n.*; ~er, Abenteurer, Glücksritter, *m.*; ~ous(ly), abenteuerlich.

adverb, Adverb, Umstandswort, *n.*

advers|ary, Gegner, *m.*; ~e(ly), widrig, entgegengesetzt; ~e

balance, Unterbilanz, *f.*; ~ity, Unglück, *n.*

advertise, annoncieren, anzeigen, werben für; ~ment, Annonce, Anzeige, *f.*; Inserat, *n.*; ~r, Inserent, Anzeiger, *m.*

advice, Rat, *m.*

advis|able, ratsam; ~e, raten; (*inform*) benachrichtigen; ~edly mit Bedacht; ~er, Ratgeber, *m.*

advocate, *sb.* Advokat, *m.*; (*fig.*) Fürsprecher, *m.*; *v.t.* verfechten; befürworten.

adze, Krummaxt, *f.*

aerated, kohlensauer.

aerial, *a.* Luft-; *sb.* (*wireless*) Antenne, *f.*

aero|drome, Flugplatz, Flughafen, *m.*; ~plane, Flugzeug, *n.*

aesthetic, ~ally, ästhetisch; ~s, Ästhetik, *f.*

affab|le, ~ly, leutselig; ~ility, Leutseligkeit, *f.*

affair, Angelegenheit, *f.*, Geschäft, *n.*; love ~, Liebeshandel, *m.*

affect, (*concern*) berühren, betreffen; (*influence*) beeinflussen; (*feign*) affektieren; ~ation, Affektiertheit, Geziertheit, *f.*; ~ed(ly), (*feigned*) erkünstelt, affektiert; (*touched*) gerührt; (*disease*) befallen (von); ~ing, rührend; ~ion, Zuneigung, Liebe, *f.* (*disease*) Krankheit, *f.*; ~ionate(ly), zärtlich, liebevoll.

affinity, Verwandtschaft, *f.*

affirm, bestätigen, behaupten; ~ative, bejahend.

afflict, betrüben, plagen; *to be* ~ed *with*, leiden an; ~ion, Kummer, *m.*; Leiden, *n.*

afford, gewähren; *I cannot* ~ *it*, meine Mittel erlauben es nicht.

affront, *sb.* Beschimpfung, *f.*; *v.t.* beschimpfen.

afloat, flott, schwimmend.

afraid, bange; *I am* ~ *that*, ich fürchte, daß . . .

aft, *adv.* achter, hinten.

after, *prep.* nach, hinter; ~ *all*, am Ende; *conj.* nachdem; *adv.* hernach, hinterher; *the day* ~, am folgenden Tage; ~math, Nachernte, *f.* (*also fig.*);

noon, Nachmittag, *m.*; ~wards, nachher.

again, wieder, nochmals; ~ *and* ~, immer wieder.

against, gegen, wider.

agate, Achat, *m.*

age, *sb.* Alter, Zeitalter, *n.*; *of* ~, mündig; *under* ~, minderjährig; *middle* ~*s*, Mittelalter, *n.*; *old* ~, hohes Alter; *v.i.* altern; ~**d**, bejahrt.

agen|cy, (*medium*) Wirkung, *f.*; (*commerc.*) Agentur, *f.*; ~**t**, Agent, Vertreter, *m.*

agenda, Tagesordnung, *f.*

aggrandize, vergrößern; ~**ment**, Vergrößerung, *f.*

aggravat|e, verschlimmern; (*provoke*) reizen, ärgern; ~**ion**, Verschlimmerung; Reizung, *f.*

aggregate, *sb.* Aggregat, Ganze(s), *n.*; *a.* angehäuft, gesamt.

aggress|ion, Angriff, Anfall, *m.*; ~**ive**, aggressiv, angreifend; ~**or**, Angreifer, *m.*

aghast, erschrocken, bestürzt.

agil|e, flink, behend; ~**ity**, Behendigkeit, *f.*

agitat|e, aufregen, beunruhigen; erschüttern; ~**ion**, Erschütterung; Hetzerei, *f.*; ~**or**, Agitator, Hetzer, *m.*

agnostic, *a.* agnostisch; *sb.* Agnostiker, *m.*

ago, vor; *long* ~, vor langer Zeit; *a year* ~, vor einem Jahre.

agony, Todeskampf, *m.*; Pein, *f.*; ~ *column*, Suchspalte, *f.*

agree, übereinstimmen; zustimmen, zugeben; (*come to agreement*) sich vergleichen; ~**able**, angenehm; einverstanden; ~**ment**, Übereinstimmung, *f.*; (*contract*) Vertrag, Kontrakt, *m.*

agricultur|e, Landwirtschaft, *f.*; ~**al**, landwirtschaftlich.

agrimony, Ackermennig, *m.*

aground, gestrandet.

ah, ah! ach!

ahead (nach) vorn; *go* ~*!* vorwärts!

ahoy, ahoi.

aid, *sb.* Hilfe, Unterstützung, *f.*, Beistand, *m.*; *first* ~, Erste Hilfe; *v.t.* helfen, unterstützen.

ail, schmerzen; ~**ing**, kränklich; ~**ment**, Krankheit, *f.*

aim, *sb.* Ziel, *n.*, Zweck, *m.*; *v.t.* zielen (*at* auf); (*fig.*) trachten (*at* nach); ~**less**(ly), ziellos.

air, *sb.* Luft, *f.*; (*manner*) Miene, *f.*; (*tune*) Melodie, Weise, *f.*; *give oneself* ~*s*, großtun; *v.t.* lüften; ~**base**, Luftstützpunkt, *m.*; ~**conditioned**, klimatisiert; ~ conditioning, Klimatisierung, *f.*; ~**craft**, Flugzeug, *n.*; ~**craft-carrier**, Flugzeugträger, *m.*; ~**field**, Flugplatz, *m.*; ~ **force**, Luftmacht, Luftwaffe, *f.*; ~**hostess**, Luftstewardeß, *f.*; ~**letter**, Luftbrief, *m.*; ~**mail**, Luftpost, *f.*; ~**man**, Flieger, *m.*; ~**port**, Flughafen, *m.*; ~ **raid**, Fliegerangriff, *m.*; ~**raid shelter**, Luftschutzraum, *m.*; ~**ship**, Luftschiff, *n.*; ~**sick**, luftkrank; ~**tight**, luftdicht; ~**way**, Luftlinie, *f.*; ~**y**, ~**ily**, luftig; (*fig.*) lebhaft; leichtfertig.

aisle, Seitenschiff, *n.*, Gang, *m.*

ajar, angelehnt.

a-kimbo, in die Seite gestemmt.

alabaster, *sb.* Alabaster, *m.*

alacrity, Bereitwilligkeit, *f.*

alarm, *sb.* Alarm; (*noise*) Lärm, *m.*; (*trouble*) Besorgnis, *f.*; *v.t.* alarmieren; (*fig.*) beunruhigen; ~**clock**, Wecker, *m.*; ~**ist**, Schwarzseher, *m.*

alas, ach! o weh!

albatross, Albatros, *m.*

album, Album, *n.*

albumen, Eiweiss, *n.*

alchem|ist, Alchimist, *m.*; ~**y**, Alchimie, *f.*; ~**ic**, alkoholisch.

alcohol, Alkohol, *m.*; ~**ic**, alkoholisch.

alcove, Alkoven, *m.*, Nische, *f.*

alder, Erle, *f.*

ale, Ale, *n.*

alert, *a.* (*watchful*) wachsam; (*brisk*) flink, behend; *sb.* (*mil.*) Alarmbereitschaft, *f.*; Fliegeralarm, *m.*; *on the* ~, auf der Hut, wach.

algebra, Algebra, *f.*

alias, sonst ... genannt; angenommene(r) Name.

alibi, Alibi, *n.*

alien, *a.* fremd; *sb.* Ausländer(in,
f.), *m.*; ~ate, entfremden.

alight ¹, *v.i.* aussteigen; (*bird*) sich
niederlassen; (*aircraft*) landen.

alight ², *a.* brennend, in Flammen.

alike, gleich, ähnlich.

alimony, Unterhaltsgeld, *n.*

alive, lebendig; (*fig.*) munter, lebhaft; *be* ~ *with*, wimmeln von;
keep ~, (*fig.*) nähren.

alkali, Alkali, *n.*; ~ne, alkalisch.

all, *a.* alle(r, s); (*entire*) ganz; *adv.*
gänzlich; *after* ~, am Ende,
schließlich; *at* ~, durchaus,
überhaupt; ~ *at once*, auf einmal; ~ *but*, fast; *by* ~ *means*,
auf jeden Fall; *not at* ~, gar
nicht; ~ *the better*, desto besser;
~ *right*, schon gut; *for* ~ *I know*,
soviel ich weiß; ~ *told*, im
ganzen; All Saints' Day, Allerheiligen, *n.*; All Souls' Day,
Allerseelen, *n.*

allay, beruhigen, beschwichtigen.

allege, behaupten, vorbringen;
~ation, Behauptung, f., Vorgeben, *n.*

allegiance, Treue, f., Gehorsam, *m.*

allegory, Allegorie, f.; ~ical(ly),
allegorisch.

alleviate, erleichtern; ~ion, Erleichterung, f.

alley, Gasse, f., Gäßchen, *n.*;
blind ~, Sackgasse, f.

alliance, Bündnis, *n.*

allied, verbündet; (*related*) verwandt.

alligator, Alligator, *m.*

alliterate, alliterieren; ~ion, Stab-
reim, *m.*; ~ive, alliterierend,
stabreimend.

allocate, zuteilen, anweisen; ~ion,
Zuteilung, Anweisung, f.

allot, zuteilen, zuerkennen; ~ment,
Anteil, *m.*; Zuteilung, f.; (*land*)
Parzelle, f., Schrebergarten, *m.*

allow, erlauben, gestatten; (*admit*)
zugeben; (*grant*) bewilligen;
~able, zulässig; ~ance, (*money*)
Taschengeld, *n.*, Zulage, f.;
(*food*) Ration, f.; *make* ~ *for*,
Rücksicht nehmen auf.

alloy, *sb.* Legierung, f.; *v.t.* legieren.

allude, anspielen (*to auf*).

allure, anlocken; ~ement, An-
lockung, Verführung, f.;

~ing(ly), verführerisch.

allusion, Anspielung, f.; ~ive,
anspielend.

ally, *sb.* Verbündete(r); *v.t.* sich
verbünden (*with* mit).

almanac, Kalender, *m.*

almighty, allmächtig.

almond, Mandel, f.

almost, beinahe, fast.

alms, Almosen, *n.*; ~-house,
Armenhaus, *n.*

aloe, Aloe, f.

alone, allein; *let* ~, in Ruhe lassen.

along, *prep.* entlang (*m.*); *adv.* entlang,
weiter; ~side, längsseits.

aloof, abseits; *keep* ~ *from*, sich
fern halten von.

aloud, laut.

alpaca, Alpaka, *n.*

alphabet, Alphabet, *n.*; ~ical(ly),
alphabetisch.

Alpine, alpin, Alpen-.

already, schon, bereits.

also, auch, ebenfalls.

altar, Altar, *m.*; ~-cloth, Altar-
decke, f.; ~piece, Altarge-
mälde, *n.*

alter, *v.t.* (ver)ändern; *v.i.* sich
ändern; ~ation, Veränderung, f.

alternate, *v.t.* abwechseln; ~ing
current, Wechselstrom, *m.*; ~ion,
Abwechselung, f.; ~ive, *sb.*
Alternative, Wahl, f.; *a.* alter-
nativ.

although, obgleich, obschon.

altitude, Höhe, f.

altruism, Altruismus, *m.*

alum, Alaun, *m.*

aluminium, Aluminium, *n.*

always, immer, stets.

a.m., vormittags.

amalgamate, vereinigen, fusionie-
ren; ~ion, Vereinigung, Fusion,
f.

amass, anhäufen.

amateur, Liebhaber, Dilettant, *m.*

amaze, in Erstaunen setzen;
~ement, Erstaunen, *n.*; ~ing,
erstaunlich.

Amazon, Amazone, f.

ambassador, Botschafter, *m.*

amber, Bernstein, *m.*

ambiguity, Zweideutigkeit, f.;
~ous(ly), zweideutig.

ambition, Ehrgeiz, *m.*; ~ious(ly),
ehrgeizig.

amble, *sb.* Paßgang, *m.*; *v.i.* den Passgang gehen, bedächtig gehen.

ambulance, Krankenwagen, *m.*, Feldlazarett, *n.*; ~man, Krankenträger, *m.*; ~station, Unfallstation, *f.*

ambush, *sb.* Hinterhalt, *m.*; *v.i.* im Hinterhalt liegen (lauern); *v.t.* auflauern (*dat.*).

amenable, zugänglich (*with dat.*).

amend, *v.t.* verbessern; ~s, Ersatz, *m.*: *make* ~*s for*, entschädigen für; ~ment, Verbesserung, *f.*; (*parl.*) Verbesserungsantrag, *m.*

amenity, Annehmlichkeit, *f.*

amethyst, Amethyst, *m.*

amiab|le, ~ly, liebenswürdig; ~ility, Liebenswürdigkeit, *f.*

amicab|le, ~ly, freundschaftlich.

amid(st), mitten in, mitten unter; ~ships, mittschiffs.

amiss, unrecht, verkehrt; *take it* ~, es übelnehmen.

ammonia, Ammoniak, *n.*

ammunition, Munition, *f.*, Kriegsvorrat, *m.*

amnesty, Amnestie, *f.*

among(st), unter, zwischen.

amorous, ~ly, verliebt.

amount, *sb.* Betrag, *m.*; *v.i.* sich belaufen (*to* auf).

amphibi|an, *sb.* Amphibie, *f.*; *a.* amphibisch; ~ous, amphibisch, Amphibien-.

ample, ~y, umfassend, weit; reichlich.

amplif|y, erweitern; verstärken; ~ication, Erweiterung, Verstärkung, *f.*;~ier,Verstärker,*f.*

amputat|e, amputieren; ~ion, Amputation, *f.*

amulet, Amulett, *n.*

amus|e, unterhalten, belustigen; ~ement, Unterhaltung, *f.*; Vergnügen, *n.*; ~ing, unterhaltend, ergötzlich.

an: see a.

anachronism, Anachronismus, *m.*

anaemi|a, Anämie, Blutarmut, *f.*; ~c, blutarm.

anaesthetic, Betäubungsmittel, *n.*

analys|is, Analyse, Auflösung, *f.*; ~e, analysieren, auflösen; ~t, Analytiker, *m.*

anarch|y, Anarchie, *f.*; ~ist, Anarchist, *m.*; ~ic(al), anarchisch.

anathema, Kirchenbann, Fluch, *m.*; ~tize, in den Kirchenbann tun.

anatom|y, Anatomie, *f.*; ~ical(ly), anatomisch; ~ist, Anatom(iker) *m.*

ancest|or, Ahnherr, Vorfahr, *m.*; ~ral, angestammt; ~ress, Ahnfrau, *f.*; ~ry, Abstammung, *f.*, Ahnen, *pl.*

anchor, *sb.* Anker, *m.*; *at* ~, vor Anker; *v.t.* ankern, vor Anker legen; ~age, Ankergrund, *m.*

anchovy, Anschovis, *f.*

ancient, alt.

and, und.

anecdote, Anekdote, *f.*

anemone, Anemone, *f.*

angel, Engel, *m.*; ~ic, engelhaft.

angelica, Engelwurz, *f.*

anger, *sb.* Zorn, *m.*; *v.t.* erzürnen.

angina, Halsbräune, *f.*

angl|e, *sb.* Winkel; Angelhaken, *m.*; *v.i.* angeln; ~er, Angler, *m.*; ~ing-rod, Angelrute, *f.*

Anglican, anglikanisch.

Anglo-, Anglo-; ~Saxon, *sb.* Angelsachse, *m.*; *a.* angelsächsisch.

angr|y, ~ily, zornig, aufgebracht.

anguish, Angst, Qual, *f.*

angular, winkelig, eckig.

aniline, Anilin, *f.*

animal, *sb.* Tier, *n.*; *a.* animalisch.

animat|e, beleben, beseelen; ~ion, Beseelung; Lebhaftigkeit, *f.*

animosity, Feindseligkeit, *f.*

aniseed, Anis(samen), *m.*

ankle, Fußknöchel, *m.*

annals, Jahrbücher, *n.pl.*

annex, *v.t.* anhängen, beifügen; (*territory*) annektieren; *sb.* Nachtrag, Anhang, *m.*; (*building*) Nebengebäude, *n.*; ~ation, Annektierung, *f.*

annihilat|e, vernichten; ~ion, Vernichtung, *f.*

anniversary, Jahrestag, *m.*

annotat|e, kommentieren; ~ion, Anmerkung, *f.*

announce, ankündigen, anzeigen; ~ment, Anzeige, Ankündigung. *f.*; ~r, (*wireless*) Ansager, *m.*

annoy, ärgern, belästigen; ~ance, Belästigung, f., Verdruß, m.

annual, a., ~ly, jährlich; sb. Jahrbuch, n.; (plant) einjährige Pflanze.

annuity, Jahresrente, f.

annul, aufheben, annullieren; ~ment, Aufhebung, f.

annunciation, Verkündigung, f.; (eccles.) Mariä Verkündigung.

anoint, salben; ~ment, Salbung, f.

anonymous, ~ly, anonym, ungenannt.

another, ein anderer; noch einer; one ~, einander.

answer, sb. Antwort, f.; v.t. antworten; (letter) beantworten; (suit) entsprechen (with dat.); ~ for, bürgen, einstehen, für; ~able, verantwortlich.

ant, Ameise, f.; ~hill, Ameisenhaufen, m.

antagonist, Gegner, m.; ~ic to, gegen.

antarctic, antarktisch; Antarctic Circle, südlicher Polarkreis; ~ Ocean, das Südliche Eismeer.

antecedent, sb. (gram.) Antezedens, n.; (logic) Vordersatz, m.; a. vorhergehend.

antechamber, Vorzimmer, n.

antediluvian, vorsintflutlich.

antelope, Antilope, f.

anthem, Chorgesang, m.; Hymne, f.

anthology, Anthologie, f.

anthracite, Anthrazit, m.

anthropolog|y, Anthropologie, f.; ~ist, Anthropolog, m.

anti-aircraft, Fliegerabwehr-.

antic, Posse, f.

anticipat|e, (forestall) vorwegnehmen, zuvorkommen; (expect) voraussehen; ~ion, Vorwegnahme, f.; Zuvorkommen, n.; Erwartung, f.; Vorgeschmack, m.

anticyclone, Antizyklon, m., Hoch, n.

antidote, Gegengift, n.

antimony, Antimon, n.; Spießglanz, m.

antipath|y, Abneigung, f.; ~etic, antipathisch, (pred.) zuwider.

antipodes, Antipoden, m.pl.

antiqu|arian, sb. Altertumskenner, Altkunsthändler, m.; a. alter-

tümlich; ~ated, veraltet; ~e, sb. Antike, f.; a. altertümlich; ~ity, Altertum, n., Vorzeit, f.

antiseptic, a. antiseptisch; sb. antiseptisches Mittel.

anti-submarine, Ubootsabwehr-.

anti-tank, Panzerabwehr-.

antithesis, Gegensatz, m.

antler, Geweih(ende), n.

anvil, Amboß, m.

anx|iety, Angst, Besorgnis, f.; ~ious(ly), ängstlich, besorgt.

any, jede(r,s), irgend ein(e); not ~, keiner, niemand, nichts; ~body, ~one, irgend jemand; ~thing, (irgend) etwas; ~how, irgendwie, immerhin; jedenfalls; ~where, irgendwo.

apart, beiseite, für sich; ~ from, abgesehen von; set ~, beiseitelegen.

apartment, Zimmer, n.

apath|y, Apathie, Gleichgültigkeit, f.; ~etic, apathisch, stumpf.

ape, sb. Affe, m.; v.t. nachäffen.

aperient, a. abführend; sb. Abführmittel, n.

apex, Spitze, f.; Gipfel, m.

aphorism, Aphorismus, Denkspruch, m.

apiary, Bienenstand, m.

Apocalypse, die Offenbarung Johannis.

apocrypha, die apokryphen Schriften, f.pl.

apolog|ize, sich entschuldigen; ~y, Entschuldigung, f.

apoplexy, Schlaganfall, m.

aposta|sy, Abtrünnigkeit, f.; Glaubensabfall, m.; ~te, abtrünnig.

apost|le, Apostel, m.; ~olic, apostolisch.

appal, erschrecken; ~ling, entsetzlich.

apparatus, Apparat, m.; Gerät, n.

apparel, sb. Kleidung, f.; v.t. ankleiden.

apparent, ~ly (evident) augenscheinlich, sichtbar; (seeming) scheinbar.

apparition, Erscheinung, f.; Gespenst, n.

appeal, sb. Appellation, Berufung, f.; v.i. sich berufen (to auf).

(*attract*) gefallen; (*law*) appellieren (*to* an).

appear, erscheinen; (*seem*) scheinen; *it* ~s *that*, es stellt sich heraus, daß; ~ance, Erscheinung, *f.*; Anschein, *m. keep up* ~s, den Schein wahren; *put in an* ~, erscheinen, sich zeigen.

appease, beruhigen; ~ment, Beruhigung, *f.*

append, beifügen, anhängen.

appendicitis, Blinddarmentzündung, *f.*

appendix, Anhang; (*med.*) Blinddarm, *m.*

appeti|te, Appetit, *m.*, Eßlust, *f.*; ~sing, appetitlich.

applaud, applaudieren, Beifall spenden.

applause, Beifall, *m.*

apple, Apfel, *m.*; ~-pie, Apfeltorte, -speise, *f.*; *in* ~-*pie order*, in schönster Ordnung.

appliance, Gerät, *n.*, Vorrichtung, *f.*

applic|able, anwendbar; ~ant, Bewerber, *m.*; ~ation, Anwendung, *f.*; (*request*) Gesuch, *n.*; (*diligence*) Fleiß, *m.*

apply, *v.t.* anwenden, gebrauchen; *v.i.* sich bewerben (*for* um); sich wenden (*to* an); sich beziehen auf.

appoint, ernennen; bestimmen; ~ment, Ernennung, *f.*; (*meeting*) Verabredung, *f.*

apposite, ~ly, angemessen.

appreciat|e, *v.t.* würdigen; schätzen; *v.i.* (*in price, value*) im Preise (Werte) steigen; ~ion, Würdigung; Schätzung, *f.*; (*in price, value*) Zunahme, *f.*; Steigen, *n.*; ~ive, verständnisvoll, anerkennend.

apprentice, *sb.* Lehrling, *m.*; *v.t.* in die Lehre tun; ~ship, Lehrlingsausbildung, *f.*; Lehrjahre, *n.pl.*

approach, *sb.* Annäherung, *f.*; (*place*) Zugang, *m.*; *v.* sich nähern; anrücken; ~able, zugänglich.

appropriat|e, *a.* angemessen, schicklich; *v.t.* sich aneignen; ~ion, Aneignung, *f.*

approv|al, Billigung, *f.*; *on* ~, auf Probe; ~e, billigen.

approximat|e, *a.* annähernd; *v.t.*

nähern; ~ion, Annäherung, *f.*

apricot, Aprikose, *f.*

April, April, *m.*; ~-fool, Aprilnarr, *m.*

apron, Schürze, *f.*; ~-string, Schürzenband, *n.*; *in* ~-strings, (*fig.*) am Gängelbande.

apse, Apsis, *f.*

apt, ~ly, geschickt; fähig; (*suitable*) angemessen; ~itude, *f.*; ~ness, Befähigung; Tauglichkeit; Neigung, *f.*

aqu|arium, Aquarium, *n.*; ~atic, Wasser-, ~educt, Wasserleitung, *f.*; ~eous, wässerig.

Arab, Araber, *m.*; *street* ~, Straßenjunge, *m.*; ~ian, arabisch; *the* ~*ian Nights*, Tausendundeine Nacht; ~ic, arabisch.

arabesque, Arabeske, *f.*

arable, pflüg-, ur-bar.

arbitrar|y, ~ily, willkürlich; ~iness, Willkürlichkeit, *f.*

arbitrat|e, entscheiden, schlichten; ~ion, Schiedsspruch, *m.*; Entscheidung, *f.*; ~or, Schiedsrichter, *m.*

arbour, Laube, *f.*

arc, Bogen, *m.*; ~-lamp, Bogenlampe, *f.*

arcade, Arkade, *f.*; Bogengang, *m.*

arch[1], *sb.* Bogen, *m.*, Gewölbe, *n.*; *v.i.* sich wölben.

arch[2], *a.*, ~ly, schalkhaft.

arch[3], *pref.* Erz-.

archaeolog|y, Altertumskunde, *f.*; ~ist, Altertumsforscher, *m.*

archaic, altertümlich, veraltet.

archer, Bogenschütze, *m.*; ~y, Bogenschießen, *n.*

archipelago, Archipel, *m.*; Inselmeer, *n.*

architect, Architekt, *m.*; ~ure, Baukunst, *f.*

archives, Archiv, *n.*

arctic, arktisch, nördlich; **Arctic Circle**, nördlicher Polarkreis; ~**Ocean**, das Nördliche Eismeer.

ard|ent, ~ently, brennend; eifrig; ~our, Eifer, *m.*

arduous, ~ly, schwierig; mühsam; ~ness, Schwierigkeit, *f.*

area, Flächenraum, *m.*

arena, Kampfplatz, *m.*; Arena, *f.*

argue, *v.t.* erörtern; *v.i.* streiten; disputieren; ~ment, Beweis, *m.*, Beweisführung, *f.*; **~menta-tive**, streitsüchtig.

arid, **~ly**, dürr; **~ity**, Dürre, *f.*

arise, aufstehen; *(result)* her-rühren.

aristocra|cy, Aristokratie, *f.*; **~tic**, aristokratisch.

arithmetic, Rechenkunst, *f.*; **~al**, arithmetisch.

ark, Arche, *f.*

arm[1], *sb.* Arm, *m.*; **~-chair**, Lehn-stuhl, *m.*; **~let**, Armbinde, *f.*; **~pit**, Achselhöhle, *f.*

arm[2], *v.t.* bewaffnen; *v.i.* sich rüsten.

armament, Kriegsausrüstung; *(fortress, tank, &c.)* Armierung; *(nav.)* Bestückung, *f.*

armature, *(mil.)* Bewaffnung, *f.*; *(nav.)* Panzer, *m.*; *(dynamo, &c.)* Anker, *m.*

armistice, Waffenstillstand, *m.*

armour, Rüstung, *f.*, Panzer, *m.*; Panzertruppen, *f.pl.*; **~ed**, Panzer-; **~er**, Waffenschmied, Waffenwart, *m.*; **~y**, Zeughaus, ' *n.*, Rüstkammer, *f.*

arms, Waffen, *f.pl.*; *(heraldry)* Wappen, *n.*; **~ ground ~**, Gewehr ab; *shoulder ~*, Gewehr auf.

army, Heer, *n.*, Armee, *f.*

aroma, Wohlgeruch, *m.*; **~tic**, aromatisch, würzig.

around, rings herum; umher.

A.R.P. Luftschutz, *m.*

arrange, ordnen, einrichten; **~ment**, Anordnung, Einrich-tung; *(agreement)* Übereinkunft, *f.*

arrears, *in* **~**, rückständig.

arrest, *sb.* Verhaftung, *f.*; *v.t.* verhaften.

arriv|e, ankommen; gelangen; **~al**, Ankunft, *f.*

arrogan|ce, Anmaßung, Vermes-senheit, *f.*; **~t(ly)**, anmaßend.

arrow, Pfeil, *m.*; **~root**, Pfeil-wurz, *f.*

arsenal, Zeughaus, *n.*

arsenic, Arsen(ik), *n.*

arson, Brandstiftung, *f.*

art, Kunst, *f.*; *(trickery)* List, *f.*; **~ful(ly)**, listig, verschlagen; **~less(ly)**, rein, arglos.

arter|y, Arterie, Pulsader, *f.*; **~ial**, Pulsader-; **~ial road**,

Verkehrsader, *f.*

artichoke, Artischocke, *f.*

article, *(gram. & literary)* Artikel, *m.*; *(object)* Gegenstand, *m.*; *(commerc.)* Ware, *f.*

artific|e, Kunstgriff, *m.*; **~er**, *(nav. & mil.)* Handwerker, *m.*; **~ial(ly)**, künstlich.

artillery, Artillerie, *f.*

artisan, Handwerker, *m.*

artist, Künstler, *m.*; **~ic(ally)**, künstlerisch.

Aryan, *sb.* Arier, *m.*; *a.* arisch.

as, *conj.* *(comparison)* als, so; *(time)* indem, während; *(cause)* da, weil; *(in proportion)* je nachdem; **~** *big* **~**, so groß wie; **~** *for*, **~** *to*, was . . . betrifft; **~** *it were*, gleichsam, so zu sagen; **~** *soon* **~**, sobald wie; **~** *yet*, noch, bisher.

asbestos, Asbest, *m.*

ascend, *v.i.* hinaufsteigen; *v.t.* *(hill, throne)* besteigen; *(river)* hinauffahren; **~ancy**, Über-legenheit, Oberhand, *f.*; Ein-fluß, *m.*

ascension, *(of Christ)* Himmel-fahrt, *f.*

ascent, Hinaufsteigen, *n.*; *(moun-tain)* Besteigen, *f.*; *(rise)* An-höhe, *f.*

ascertain, ermitteln, feststellen.

ascetic, *a.* asketisch; *sb.* Asket, *m.*

ascribe, zuschreiben.

ash, *(residue of fire)* Asche, *f.*; *(tree)* Esche, *f.*; **~en**, asch-farbig; **~pit**, Aschengrube, *f.*; **~tray**, Aschenbecher, *m.*

Ash-Wednesday, Aschermitt-woch, *m.*

ashamed, *be* **~**, sich schämen *(with gen.)*

aside, beiseite, abseits.

ask, *(request)* bitten *(for* um); *(interrogate)* fragen; *(a question)* stellen; **~** *after*, fragen nach.

askance, schief.

asleep, schlafend; *be* **~**, schlafen; *fall* **~**, einschlafen.

asparagus, Spargel, *m.*

aspect, Anblick, *m.*; Ansicht, Aussicht, *f.*

aspen, Espe, *f.*

asphalt, Asphalt, *m.*

asphyxia, Erstickung, *f.*; ~te, ersticken.

aspir|ate, *sb.* Aspirata, *f.*; *v.t.* aspirieren; ~ation, Streben, *n.*; Sehnsucht, *f.*; ~e, streben (*to* nach).

ass, Esel, *m.*; Eselin, *f.*

assail, angreifen, anfallen; ~ant, Angreifer.

assassin, Meuchelmörder, *m.*; ~ate, ermorden; ~ation, Meuchelmord, *m.*

assault, Angriff, Sturm, *m.*; (*criminal*) Überfall, *m.*; *v.t.* angreifen; ~craft, Landungsfahrzeug, *n.*; ~ troops, Stoßtruppen, *f.pl.*

assembl|e, *v.t.* sammeln; (*machines*) montieren; *v.i.* sich versammeln ~y, Versammlung; (*machines*) Montage *f.*; ~y line, Montagerampe, *f.*; Fließband, *n.*

assent, *sb.* Genehmigung, Zustimmung, *f.*; *v.i.* zustimmen (*with dat.*).

assert, behaupten; ~ion, Behauptung, *f.*

assess, einschätzen; ~ment, Einschätzung, *f.*

assets, (*commerc.*) Aktiva, *pl.*

assidu|ity, Emsigkeit, *f.*; ~ous(ly), emsig.

assign, anweisen; ~ation, Anweisung, *f.*; (*meeting*) Stelldichein, *n.*; ~ment, Anweisung, *f.*

assimilat|e, assimilieren, angleichen; ~ion, Assimilation, *f.*

assist, helfen; beistehen (*with dat.*); ~ance, Beistand, *m.*; ~ant, Helfer, Gehilfe, *m.*

associat|e, *sb.* Genosse; Teilhaber, *m.*; *v.t.* verbinden, in Verbindung bringen; *v.i.* verkehren, umgehen (*with mit*); ~ion, Verein, *m.*, Gesellschaft, Vereinigung, *f.*

assort, assortieren; ~ment, Sortiment, *n.*, Auswahl, *f.*

assum|e, *v.t.* annehmen; sich anmaßen; ~ing, anmaßend; ~ption, Annahme, Voraussetzung, *f.*

assur|e, versichern; sicher stellen; ~ance, Versicherung, *f.*

aster, Aster, *f.*

asterisk, Sternchen, *n.*

astern, achteraus.

asthma, Asthma, *n.*; ~tic, asthmatisch.

astonish, in Erstaunen setzen; ~ing, erstaunlich; ~ment, Erstaunen, *n.*

astray, *go* ~, sich verirren; verloren gehen; *lead* ~, irreführen.

astride, rittlings.

astrolog|er, Astrolog, *m.*; ~y, Astrologie, *f.*

astronaut, Astronaut, *m.*

astronom|er, Astronom, *m.*; ~ical, astronomisch; ~y, Astronomie, Sternkunde, *f.*

astute, ~ly, schlau; ~ness, Schlauheit, *f.*

asylum, Asyl, *n.*, Zufluchtsort, *m.*; *lunatic* ~, Irrenhaus, *n.*

at, zu, an, bei, auf, in; ~ *all*, überhaupt; *not* ~ *all*, durchaus nicht; ~ *first*, zuerst; ~ *last*, endlich; ~ *least*, wenigstens; ~ *length*, schließlich; ~ *once*, (*at the same time*) auf einmal; (*immediately*) sofort, sogleich; ~ *hand*, bei der (*or zur*) Hand; ~ *home*, zu Hause; ~ *sea*, auf der See; ~ *war*, im Kriege.

atheis|m, Atheismus, *m.*; ~t, Atheist, *m.*; ~tic, atheistisch.

athlet|e, Athlet, *m.*; ~ic, athletisch; ~ics, Körperübungen, *f.pl.*, (*Leicht*)athletik, *f.*

atlas, Atlas, *m.*

atmospher|e, Atmosphäre, *f.*; ~ic, atmosphärisch; ~ics, (*wireless*) Luftstörungen, *f.pl.*

atom, Atom, *n.*; ~ic, Atom-; ~ pile, Atommeiler, *m.*

atone, sühnen, büßen; ~ment, Sühne, *f.*

atro|cious, ~ciously, scheußlich; gräßlich; ~city, Scheußlichkeit, *f.*; Greuel, *m.*

atrophy, Atrophie, *f.*

attach, anhängen, anheften; *be* ~*ed to*, jemandem ergeben sein; ~ment, Anhänglichkeit, Ergebenheit, *f.*

attack, *sb.* Angriff, *m.*; *v.t.* angreifen.

attain, erreichen, erlangen; ~ment, Erlangung, *f.*; ~ments, Kenntnisse, *f.pl.*

attempt, *sb.* Versuch, *m.*; *v.t.* versuchen.

attend, *v.t.* aufwarten, pflegen; (*med.*) behandeln; beiwohnen (*with dat.*), besuchen; *v.i.* achten, achtgeben, merken (*to* auf); sorgen für; zugegen sein; ~ance, Bedienung, *f.*; (*med.*) Behandlung, *f.*; Besuch, *m.*; ~ant, Diener, Aufwärter, *m.*

attention, Aufmerksamkeit, *f.*; (*mil.*) stillgestanden!; ~ive(ly), aufmerksam.

attest, bezeugen, beglaubigen.

attic, Dachstube, *f.*

attire, *sb.* Kleidung, *f.*; *v.t.* (an)kleiden.

attitude, Stellung; Haltung, *f.*

attorney, Anwalt, *m.*; *power of* ~, (schriftliche) Vollmacht, *f.*

attract, anziehen, reizen; ~ion, Anziehung, *f.*, Reiz, *m.*; ~ive(ly) anziehend.

attribute, *sb.* (*gram.*) Attribut, *n.*; Eigenschaft, *f.*; *v.i.* zuschreiben.

attrition, Abreibung, Abnutzung, *f.*

auburn, nuß-, kastanien- braun.

auction, *sb.* Versteigerung, *f.*; *v.t.* versteigern; ~eer, Versteigerer, Auktionator, *m.*

audacious, ~iously, kühn, verwegen; ~ity, Kühnheit, Verwegenheit, *f.*

audible, hörbar; ~ility, Hörbarkeit, *f.*

audience, Zuhörer, *m.pl.*; (*reception*) Audienz, *f.*

audit, *sb.* Rechnungsprüfung, *f.*; *v.t.* (Rechnungen) prüfen; ~ion, Hörprobe, *f.*; ~or, Buchprüfer, *m.*

augment, vermehren.

august[1], *a.* erhaben.

August[2], *sb.* August, *m.*

aunt, Tante, *f.*

aurora, Morgenröte, *f.*; ~ *borealis*, Nordlicht, *n.*

auspices, Vorbedeutung, *f.*; Wahrzeichen, *n.*; Schutz, *m.*; ~ious(ly), günstig.

austere, ely, streng, herb; ~ity, Strenge, Härte, *f.*

authentic, echt, glaubwürdig; ~ate, beurkunden; als echt beweisen; ~ity, Echtheit, *f.*

author, Verfasser; (*fig.*) Urheber, *m.*; ~ship, Autorschaft, *f.*

authoritative, bevollmächtigt; gebieterisch; ~ity, (Voll)macht, *f.*; Autorität, *f.*, Ansehen, *n.*; (*official*) Behörde, *f.*; ~ize, bevollmächtigen, ermächtigen; ~ization, Bevollmächtigung, *f.*

autobiography, Selbstbiographie, *f.*

autocracy, Selbstherrschaft, *f.*; ~t, Autokrat, Selbstherrscher, *m.*; ~tic, autokratisch, selbstherrlich.

automatic, ~ically, automatisch, selbsttätig; ~ic telephone, Selbstanschluß, *m.*; ~on, Automat, *m.*

automobile, Automobil, *n.*, Kraftwagen, *m.*

autonomous, autonom; ~y, Selbstregierung, *f.*

autopsy, Leichenschau, *f.*

autumn, Herbst, *m.*; ~al, herbstlich.

auxiliary, Hilfs-; ~ies, (*mil.*) Hilfstruppen, *f.pl.*; (*nav.*) Hilfsschiffe, *n.pl.*

avail, *v.t.* sich zunutze machen; sich bedienen (*with gen.*); *of no* ~, vergeblich; ~able, verfügbar; erhältlich, vorrätig.

avalanche, Lawine, *f.*

avarice, Geiz, *m.*, Habsucht, *f.*; ~ious(ly), geizig, habsüchtig.

avenge, rächen, *f.*; ~r, Rächer, *m.*

avenue, Allee, *f.*; Zugang, *m.*

average, Durchschnitt, *m.*; *on an* ~, durchschnittlich.

averse, ely, abgeneigt (*with dat.*); ~ion, Widerwille, *m.*

avert, abwenden.

aviary, Vogelhaus, *n.*

aviation, Fliegen, Flugwesen, *n.*; ~or, Flieger, *m.*

avid, gierig (*for* nach); ~ity, Gier, Begierde, *f.*

avoid, vermeiden, *f.*; ~ance, Vermeidung, *f.*

await, erwarten.

awake, *a.* wach; *v.i.* aufwachen.

award, *sb.* Preis, *m.*; Urteil, *n.*, Entscheidung, *f.*; *v.t.* zuerkennen; gewähren.

aware, *to be* ~ *of*, sich (einer Sache) bewußt sein; *I wasn't* ~ *of it*, ich wußte es nicht.

away, weg, fort; (*distance*) entfernt; ~ *from home*, von Hause abwesend; ~*match*, auswärtiges Spiel.

awe, Ehrfurcht, *f.*; ~ful(ly). (*solemn*) feierlich; (*colloq.*) schrecklich.

awhile, eine Zeitlang.

awkward, ~ly, ungeschickt, linkisch; ~ness, Ungeschicklichkeit, *f.*

awl, Pfriem, *m.*

awning, Zeltdecke, *f.*; (*naut.*) Sonnensegel, *n.*

awry, schief; verkehrt.

axe, Axt, *f.*, Beil, *n.*

axiom, Axiom, *n.*, Grundsatz, *m.*

axis, Achse, *f.*

axle, Achse, *f.*

azalea, Azalie, *f.*

azure, himmelblau.

B

babble, lallen; (*water*) murmeln; ~r, Schwätzer, *m.*

baboon, Pavian, *m.*

baby, kleines Kind, Baby, *n.*, Säugling, *m.*; ~hood, erste Kindheit; ~ish, kindisch; ~linen, Kinderzeug, *n.*; ~sitter, Babysitter, *m.*

bachelor, Junggeselle, *m.*

back, *sb.* Rücken, *m.*; Rückseite, *f.*; (*football*) Verteidiger, *m.*; *put one's* ~ *up*, jemanden reizen; *v.t.* (*bet on*) wetten auf; (*support*) unterstützen; *v.i.* rückwärts gehen; *adv.* zurück; ~bite, verleumden; ~bone, Rückgrat, *n.*; ~door, Hintertür, *f.*; ~er, Unterstützer, *m.*; ~fire, *v.i.* frühzünden; *sb.* Frühzündung, *f.*; ~gammon, Puffspiel, *n.*; ~ground, Hintergrund, *m.*; ~hand, (*tennis*) Rückhand, *f.*; ~handed, mit dem Handrücken; ~ing, Unterstützung, *f.*; ~pedal, rückwärts treten; ~pedalling brake, Rücktrittbremse, *f.*; ~side, Rückseite, *f.*; ~slide, (*fig.*) abfallen; rückfällig werden; ~stairs, Hintertreppe, *f.*; ~ward, rückwärts; (*un-*

developed) zurückgeblieben; ~wards, rückwärts; ~water, Stauwasser, *n.*; ~woodsman, Hinterwälder, *m.*

bacon, Speck, *m.*

bacteria, Bakterien, *f.pl.*; ~ology, Bakterienkunde, *f.*; ~ologist, Bakteriolog, *m.*

bad, ~ly, schlecht, schlimm, böse; *be* ~*ly off*, schlecht dran sein; *go to the* ~, zu Grunde gehen; *go* ~, verderben; ~ *debt*, uneinbringliche Schuld; ~ *language*, Fluchen, *n.*; ~ness, Schlechtigkeit; Bosheit, *f.*

badge, Abzeichen, *n.*

badger, *sb.* Dachs, *m.*; *v.t.* plagen.

baffle, *sb.* (*wireless*) Dämpfer, *m.*; *v.t.* vereiteln; verwirren.

bag, *sb.* Beutel, Sack, *m.*; (*game killed*) Beute, *f.*; *paper* ~, Tüte, *f.*; *v.i.* (sich) bauschen; *v.t.* erlegen.

baggage, Gepäck, *n.*; (*mil.*) Troß, *m.*

bagpipe, Dudelsack, *m.*

bail, *sb.* Bürgschaft, *f.*; *v.t.* sich verbürgen für.

bait, *sb.* Köder, *m.*; *v.t.* ködern; (*fig.*) hetzen, quälen, reizen.

bake, backen; ~er, Bäcker, *m.*; ~ery, Bäckerei, *f.*; ~ingpowder, Backpulver, *n.*

balance, *sb.* (*scales*) Waage, (*account*) Bilanz, *f.*; (*poise*) Gleichgewicht, *n.*; *v.t.* balancieren; erwägen; bilanzieren; ~sheet, Rechnungsabschluß, *m.*

balcony, Balkon, *m.*

bald, ~ly, kahl; ~ness, Kahlheit, *f.*

bale[1], *sb.* Ballen, *m.*

bale[2], *v.* : ~ *out*, (*naut.*) (leer) schöpfen; (*av.*) abspringen.

ball, (*games, dance*) Ball, *m.*; (*billiards, shot, machinery*) Kugel, *f.*; (*wool, &c.*) Knäuel, *m.* or *n.*; ~bearing, Kugellager, *n.*; ~point pen, Kugelschreiber, *m.*

ballad, Ballade, *f.*

ballast, *sb.* Ballast, *m.*; *v.t.* (*naut.*) mit Ballast versehen.

ballet, Ballett, *n.*; ~dancer, Balletttänzer(in).

balloon, (Luft)ballon, *m.*; ~barrage, Ballonsperre, *f.*

ballot, *sb.* Wahlkugel, *f.*; Stimm-
zettel, *m.*; *v.i.* ballotieren, losen,
abstimmen; ~box, Wahlurne, *f.*

balm, Balsam, *m.*

balust|ers, Treppengeländer, *n.*;
~rade, Geländer, *n.*

bamboo, Bambus, *m.*

ban, *sb.* Bann, *m.*; *v.t.* in den Bann
tun.

banana, Banane, *f.*

band, *sb.* Band, *n.*; (*mus.*) Kapelle,
f.; (*company*) Bande, *f.*; ~age,
sb. Bandage, *f.*; Verband, *m.*;
v.t. verbinden; ~box, Hutschachtel, *f.*; ~master, Kapell-
meister, *m.*; ~stand, Musik-
pavillon, *m.*

bandit, Bandit, *m.*

bandy, *v.t.* hin und her schlagen;
(*words*) sich zuwerfen, aus-
tauschen.

bandy-legged, krummbeinig.

bang, *sb.* Schlag; Knall, *m.*; *v.i.*
knallen; *v.t.* (*door*) zuschlagen;
(*int.*) bums.

bangle, Armring, *m.*

banish, verbannen; ~ment, Verbannung, *f.*

banister, Treppengeländer, *n.*

banjo, Banjo, *n.*

bank, *sb.* (*river*) Ufer, *n.*; (*earth*)
Damm, *m.*; (*commerc.*) Bank, *f.*;
savings-~, Sparkasse, *f.*; *v.t.*
eindämmen; (*money*) depo-
nieren; ~ account, Bankkonto,
n.; ~bill, Bankwechsel, *m.*;
~book, Kontobuch, *n.*; ~er,
Bankier, *m.*; ~ing, Bank-
geschäft, *n.*; ~note, Banknote,
f.; ~rate, Bankdiskont(o), *m.*;
~rupt, *a.* bankrott; *go* ~,
bankrott werden; *sb.* Bank-
rotteur, Zahlungsunfähig(er);
v.t. bankrott machen; ~ruptcy,
Bankrott, Konkurs, *m.*

banner, Banner, *n.*; Fahne, *f.*

banns, Aufgebot, *n.*; *publish the* ~,
aufbieten.

banquet, Festessen, *n.*

bantam, Bantam-, Zwerg-huhn,
n.; ~weight, Bantamgewicht, *n.*

banter, *sb.* Neckerei, *f.*; *v.t.* necken,
hänseln.

bapt|ism, Taufe, *f.*; ~ist, Baptist,
m.; ~ize, taufen.

bar, *sb.* (*iron*, *&c.*) Stange, *f.*;

Riegel, *m.*; (*metal*, *sand*, *&c.*);
Barre, *f.*; (*mus.*) Takt, *m.*;
(*obstacle*) Hindernis, *n.*;
Schranke, *f.*; (*court of law*)
Schranke, *f.*; Gericht, *n.*;
(*counter for drinks*) Bar, *f.*;
Ausschank, *m.*; *v.t.* (*ver*)hin-
dern, verriegeln; ~maid, Kellnerin, Bardame, *f.*

barb, Widerhaken, *m.*; ~ed wire,
Stacheldraht, *m.*

barbar|ian, *sb.* Barbar, *m.*; *a.*
barbarisch; ~ous(ly), roh, barbarisch.

barber, Barbier, Friseur, *m.*

barberry, Berberitze, *f.*

bare, *a.* bloß; nackt; (*empty*) leer;
v.t. entblößen; ~faced, frech,
schamlos; ~footed, barfuß;
~headed, barhaupt; ~legged,
mit entblößten Beinen; ~ly,
kaum; ~ness, Nacktheit; Dürf-
tigkeit, *f.*

bargain, *sb.* Geschäft, *n.*; Handel,
m.; Spottpreis, *m.*; *into the* ~,
obendrein; *it's a* ~!, abgemacht!, es bleibt dabei!; *v.i.*
handeln, feilschen (*for* um).

barge, Leichter, *m.*, Schute, *f.*;
~e, Schiffer, *m.*

baritone, Bariton, *m.*

barium, Barium, *n.*

bark[1], *sb.* (*tree*) Rinde, Borke,
(*ship*) Barke, *f.*

bark[2], *sb.* (*of dog*) Bellen, *n.*; *v.i.*
bellen.

barley, Gerste, *f.*; ~corn, Gerstenkorn, *n.*; ~water, Gersten-
trank, *m.*

barm, Hefe, *f.*

barn, Scheune, *f.*; ~owl, Schleier-
eule, *f.*

barometer, Barometer, *n.*

baron, Baron, Freiherr, *m.*; ~ess,
Baronin, Freifrau, *f.*; ~ial,
Barons-.

baroque, *a.* barock; *sb.* Barock,
n.

barracks, Kaserne, *f.*

barrage, Damm, *n.*; Wehr, *n.*;
(*mil.*) Sperrfeuer, *n.*; (*nav.*)
Sperre, *f.*

barrel, Faß, *n.*; (*gun*) Lauf, *m.*;
~organ, Drehorgel, *f.*

barren, ~ly, unfruchtbar; ~ness,
Unfruchtbarkeit, *f.*

barricade, sb. Barrikade, f.; v.t. versperren, verrammeln.

barrier, Schranke, f.; (fig.) Hindernis, n.

barrister, Rechtsanwalt, m.

barrow, Schiebkarren, m.; (mound) Hügel, m.; Hünengrab, n.

barter, sb. Tauschhandel, m.; v.t. um-, vertauschen.

basalt, Basalt, m.; ~ic, basaltisch.

base¹, sb. (arch.) Basis, f.; (chem.) Base, f.; (mil.) Operationsbasis, f.; (nav.) Stützpunkt, m.; (air) Einsatzhafen, m.; (fig.) Grund, m.; v.t. gründen (on auf); ~less, grundlos; ~-line, Grundlinie, f.; ~ment, Grundmauer, f.; Kellergeschoß, n.

base², ~ly, niedrig, schlecht; (metal) unedel; ~ness, Niedrigkeit, Niederträchtigkeit, f.

bashful, ~ly, schüchtern; ~ness, Schüchternheit, f.

basin, Becken, n.; Hafenbecken, Flußbecken, n.

basis, Grundlage, f.

bask, sich sonnen.

basket, Korb, m.; ~-ball, Korbspiel, n.

bass¹, sb. (voice) Baß, m.

bass², sb. (fish) Seebarsch, m.

bassoon, Fagott, n.

bast, Bast, m.; Bastmatte, f.

bastard, sb. Bastard, m.; a. unehelich.

bastion, Bastion, Bastei, f.

bat, (cricket) Schläger, m.; (zool.) Fledermaus, f.; ~man, Offiziersbursche, m.; ~sman, Schläger, m.

batch, (bread) Schub, m.; (mil.) Trupp, m.; (quantity) Menge, Partie, f.

bath, sb. Bad, n.; v.t. baden; ~-chair, Rollstuhl, m.; ~-room, Badezimmer, n.

bathe, baden; ein Bad nehmen; ~er, Badende(r); ~ing-trunks, Badehose; f.; ~ing-dress, Badeanzug, m.; ~ing-resort, Badeort, m.

bathos, Bathos, n.

baton, (mil.) (Kommando) Stab, m.; (mus.) Taktstock, m.

battalion, Bataillon, n.

batter, v.t. zerschlagen, zer-

trümmern; v.i. klopfen, stoßen, gegen; sb. dünner Teig.

battery, Batterie, f.

battle, sb. Schlacht, f.; v.i. kämpfen (with mit); ~-array, Schlachtordnung, f.; ~-cruiser, Schlachtkreuzer, m.; ~-field, Schlachtfeld, n.; ~ment, Zinne, f.

bawl, laut schreien.

bay¹, sb. (geog.) Bai, Bucht, f.; (arch.) Lücke, Nische, f.; (bot.) Lorbeer(baum), m.; ~-window, Erkerfenster, n.

bay², a. (colour) rotbraun; ~ horse, Braune(r).

bay³, v.i. bellen; stand at ~, sich stellen.

bayonet, sb. Bajonett, Seitengewehr, n.; v.t. bajonettieren.

bazaar, Basar, m.

be, v.i. (pass. aux.) werden (followed by a verb, am, is, are to ... &c.) sollen, e.g. he is to come, er soll kommen (followed by past part. in the passive) werden, e.g. he was arrested, er wurde verhaftet (followed by a pres. part. indicating a continuous action, not usually indicated in German, e.g. he is sleeping, er schläft.

beach, Strand, m.; ~-head, Landekopf, m.

beacon, Leuchtfeuer, n.; Bake, f.

bead, Perle, f.; ~s, (necklace) Halsband, n.; (rosary) Rosenkranz, m.

beagle, Spürhund, m.

beak, Schnabel, m.

beaker, Becher, m.

beam, sb. (timber) Balken, m.; (light) Strahl, m.; v.i. strahlen.

bean, Bohne, f.; broad ~, Saubohne, f.; French, haricot ~, grüne Bohne.

bear¹, sb. (stock exchange) Baissier, m.; polar ~, Eisbär, m.

bear², v.t. tragen; (suffer) ertragen, leiden; (children) gebären; (fruit) tragen; ~ oneself, sich betragen; ~ away, off, wegtragen, davontragen; ~ down, überwinden; ~ in mind, nicht vergessen; ~ denken; ~ on, Bezug haben, wirken auf; ~ with, Geduld haben mit; ~ witness, Zeugnis ablegen; ~able, erträglich; ~er, Träger; Überbringer, m.; ~ing, Tragen, n.; (of person) Haltung, f.; (machinery) Lager, n.; (relation) Beziehung, f. (naut.) Peilung, f.; takes (one's) ~s, peilen; sich orientieren.

beard, sb. Bart, m.; v.t. Trotz bieten, ~ed, bärtig; ~less, bartlos.

beast, Tier, Vieh, n.; ~ of prey, Raubtier, n.; ~liness (fig., colloq.) Gemeinheit, f.; ~ly, viehisch; (fig.) scheußlich.

beat, sb. Schlag, m.; (pulse) Klopfen, n.; (round) Runde, f.; v.t. (conquer) schlagen, besiegen; (hit) schlagen, klopfen; dreschen; that ~s everything, da hört alles auf; ~ time, den Takt schlagen; dead ~, erschöpft; ~ing, Schlagen, n.; (thrashing) Prügel, pl.; give a person a good ~ing, durchprügeln.

beatitudes, Seligpreisungen, f.pl.

beau, Stutzer, m.

beauti|ful, ~ifully, schön; ~ify, schön machen; ~y, Schönheit, f.

beaver, Biber, m.

because, weil; ~ of, wegen.

beckon, (zu)winken.

become, v.i. werden; v.t. (suit) stehen, kleiden; ~ing, passend; kleidsam.

bed, Bett, n.; (garden) Beet; (geol.) Lager, n.; go to ~, schlafen gehen, zu Bett gehen; ~clothes, Bettzeug, n.; ~ding, Bettzeug, n.; (litter) Lagerstreu, f.; ~ fellow, Schlafgenosse, m.; ~ridden, bettlägerig; ~room, Schlafzimmer, n.; ~spread, Bettdecke, f.; ~ stead, Bettstelle, f.; ~time, Schlafenszeit, f.

bee, Biene, f.; ~hive, Bienenkorb, m.; ~keeper, Imker, m.; ~keeping, Bienenzucht, f.; ~line, Luftlinie, f.; in a ~line, auf dem geraden Wege.

beech, Buche, f.

beef, Rindfleisch, n.; ~steak,

Beefsteak, n.; ~tea, Rindfleischsaft, m.

beer, Bier, n.

beet, ~root, rote Rübe, f.; sugar ~, Zuckerrübe, f.; ~sugar, Rübenzucker, m.

beetle, Käfer, m.

befall, sich ereignen.

befitting, schicklich, passend.

befool, betören.

before, prep. vor; conj. bevor, ehe; adv. vorn; früher; the day ~, am Tage vorher; the day ~ yesterday, vorgestern; ~ long, in kurzem; ~hand, (im) voraus.

beg, v.t. betteln; (ask) bitten; I ~ your pardon, bitte um Verzeihung; wie meinen Sie?; v.i. betteln gehen; sich erlauben.

beget, (er)zeugen.

beggar, sb. Bettler, m.; v.t. zum Bettler machen; to ~ description, jeder Beschreibung spotten; ~ly, armselig, verächtlich.

begin, anfangen, beginnen; ~ner, Anfänger, m.; ~ning, Anfang, m.

begonia, Begonie, f.

begrudge, mißgönnen.

beguile, hintergehen; (time) vertreiben.

behalf, on ~ of, im Namen; zu Gunsten.

behave, sich betragen, sich benehmen; ~iour, Betragen; Verhalten, n.

behead, enthaupten.

behind, prep. hinter; adv. hinten, zurück; ~hand, im Rückstande (with mit).

behold, v.t. erblicken; (int.) Siehe!; ~en, verpflichtet, verbunden (with dat.); ~er, Zuschauer, m.

being, Wesen, Dasein, n.; for the time ~, einstweilen; in ~, wirklich vorhanden.

belated, verspätet.

belch, rülpsen.

beleaguer, belagern.

belfry, Glockenturm, m.

belie, Lügen strafen; im Widerspruch stehen.

belief, Glaube, m. (in an).

believe, glauben (in an); (a person) vertrauen auf; glauben (with *dat.*); ~able, glaublich; ~er, Gläubige(r).

belittle, verkleinern, herabsetzen.

bell, Glocke, Schelle (*electric*) Klingel, *f.*; ~-founder, Glockengießer, *m.*; ~-metal, Glockenspeise, *f.*; ~-shaped, glockenförmig; ~-wether, Leithammel, *m.*

belladonna, Tollkirsche, *f.*

bellicose, kriegerisch.

belligerent, kriegführend.

bellow, brüllen; ~ing, Brüllen, *n.*

bellows, Blasebalg, *m.*

belly, *sb.* Bauch, *m.*; *v.i.* sich ausbauschen.

belong, gehören (*with dat.*); ~ings, Besitz, *m.*; Habe, *f.*

beloved, geliebt.

below, *prep.* unter; *adv.* unten.

belt, *sb.* Gürtel; Treibriemen, *m.*; *v.t.* umgürten.

bench, Bank, *f.*; (*for work*) Arbeitstisch, *m.*; (*court*) Gerichtsbank, *f.*

bend, *sb.* Biegung, *f.*; *v.t.* biegen; (*a bow*) spannen; (*body*) beugen; *v.i.* sich biegen; ~ down, sich niederbeugen.

beneath, *prep.* unter; *adv.* unten.

benediction, Segen, *m.*

benefac|tion, Wohltat, *f.*; ~or, Wohltäter, *m.*

benefice, Pfründe, *f.*

beneficen|ce, Wohltätigkeit, *f.*; ~t(ly), wohltätig.

beneficial, ~ly, heilsam, nützlich.

benefit, Vorteil, Nutzen, *m.*; (*insurance*) Unterstützung, *f.*; *v.t.* nützen, gut tun; *v.i.* ~ from, Nutzen ziehen aus.

benevolen|ce, Wohlwollen, *n.*; ~t(ly), wohlwollend.

benign, ~ly, gütig, mild; ~ity, Güte, Milde, *f.*

bent, gebogen; ~ on, erpicht auf, entschlossen zu.

benumb, betäuben, starr machen.

benz|ine, Benzin, *n.*; ~ol, Benzol, *n.*

bequeath, vermachen.

bequest, Vermächtnis, *n.*

bereave, berauben (*with gen.*); ~d, leidtragend, hinterblieben; ~ment, Verlust, *m.*; Beraubung, *f.*

berry, Beere, *f.*; (*coffee*) Bohne, *f.*

berth, (Schiffs)bett, *n.*; (Schlaf) koje, *f.*; (*anchorage*) Liegeplatz, Ankerplatz, *m.*; *give a wide* ~ *to*, jemandem weit aus dem Wege gehen.

beseech, anflehen, bitten.

beset, bedrängen, bestürmen; ~ting sin, Gewohnheitssünde, *f.*

beside, neben; ~ *oneself*, außer sich; ~ *the mark*, weit vom Ziel; ~s, außerdem.

besiege, belagern.

besmear, beschmieren.

besotted, versoffen; betört.

bespeak, (*order*) bestellen; (*indicate*) verraten.

besprinkle, besprengen.

best, *a.* (der, die, das) beste; *adv.* aufs beste; am besten; *do one's* ~, sein Möglichstes tun; *the* ~ *of one's abilities*, nach besten Kräften; *have the* ~ *of it*, dabei am besten wegkommen; *make the* ~ *of it*, sich damit abfinden, sich so gut wie möglich daraus ziehen; ~man, Brautführer, *m.*; ~seller, Bestseller, *m.*

bestial, ~ly, viehisch.

bestir, sich rühren, sich regen.

bestow, verleihen.

bet, *sb.* Wette, *f.*; *v.* wetten (*on* auf); ~ting, Wetten, *n.*

betake, sich begeben.

betray, verraten; ~al, Verrat, *m.*

betroth, verloben; ~al, Verlobung, *f.*

better, *a.* and *adv.* besser, lieber, mehr; *get the* ~ *of*, besiegen, überwinden; *think* ~ *of it*, sich eines Bessern besinnen; *be* ~ *off*, in besseren Verhältnissen sein; *v.t.* verbessern; ~ *oneself*, sich verbessern.

between, zwischen; ~ *ourselves*, unter uns gesagt.

beverage, Getränk, *n.*

bevy, Schar, *f.*

bewail, beklagen.

beware, sich hüten (*of* vor).

bewilder, verwirren, bestürzen; ~ment, Bestürzung, *f.*

beyond, *prep.* über, jenseits; *adv.* darüber hinaus.

bias, Neigung, *f.*; Vorurteil, *n.*; *free from ~*, vorurteilsfrei.

bib, Kinderlätzchen, *n.*

bib|le, Bibel, *f.*; ~ical, biblisch.

bibliograph|er, Bibliograph, *m.*; ~y, Bücherkunde, Bibliographie, *f.*

bicarbonate, *~ of soda*, doppeltkohlensaures Natron.

biceps, Bizeps, *m.*

bicker, zanken; ~ing, Zank, *m.*

bicycl|e, Zweirad, Fahrrad, *n.*; ~ist, Radfahrer, Radler, *m.*

bid, *sb.* Gebot, *n.*; *v.t.* (*order*) befehlen; (*offer*) bieten; ~der, Bietende(r); *highest~der*, Meistbietende(r); ~ding, Befehl, *m.*; Einladung, *f.*; (*auction*) Bieten, Gebot, *n.*

bier, Totenbahre, *f.*

big, groß; *talk ~*, prahlen; ~ness, Größe, *f.*; Umfang, *m.*; ~wig, großes Tier, *n.*; Bonze, *m.*

bigam|ist, Bigamist, *m.*; ~ous, bigamistisch; ~y, Doppelehe, Bigamie, *f.*

bigot|ed, bigott; ~ry, Bigotterie, *f.*

bikini, Bikini, *m.*

bilberry, Heidelbeere, *f.*

bil|e, Galle, *f.*; ~ious, Gallen-; (*fig.*) gallig.

bilge, Bilge, *f.*, Kimm, *m.*; ~-water, Schlagwasser, *n.*

bilingual, zweisprachig.

bilk, beschwindeln.

bill, (*bird*) Schnabel, *m.*; (*account*) Rechnung, *f.*; (*banker's*) Wechsel, *m.*; (*parliament*) Vorlage, *f.*; (*poster*) Anschlagzettel, *m.*; *~ of fare*, Speisekarte, *f.*; *~ of lading*, Frachtbrief, *m.*; ~-hook, Hippe, *f.*

billet, *sb.* Klotz, *m.*; (*mil.*) Quartier, *n.*; Quartierzettel, *m.*; *v.t.* einquartieren.

billiard|s, Billardspiel, *n.*; ~-cue, (Billard)queue, *n.*; ~-marker, Markeur, *m.*; ~-table, Billard, *n.*

billow, *sb.* Woge, *f.*; *v.i.* schwellen.

bin, Kasten, *m.*

bind, binden; (*compel*) verpflichten, zwingen; ~ing, *sb.* Binden, *n.*; (*book*) Einband, *m.*; *a.* bindend; ~weed, Winde, *f.*

binnacle, Kompaßhäuschen, *n.*

binocular, Feldglas, *n.*; Operngucker, *m.*

biochem|ical, biochemisch; ~ist, Biochemiker, *m.*; ~istry, Biochemie, *f.*

biograph|er, Biograph, *m.*; ~ical, biographisch; ~y, Biographie, *f.*

biolog|ist, Biologe, *m.*; ~y, Biologie, *f.*

biped, Zweifüßler, *m.*

biplane, Doppeldecker, *m.*

birch, (*bot.*) Birke, *f.*; (*rod*) Rute, *f.*

bird, Vogel, *m.*; *~ of passage*, Zugvogel, *m.*; *~ of prey*, Raubvogel, *m.*; ~-cage, Vogelbauer, *n.*; ~-lime, Vogelleim, *m.*; *~'s-eye view*, Vogelperspektive, *f.*; *~'s-nest*, Vogelnest, *n.*

birth, Geburt, *f.*; ~-control, Geburtenbeschränkung, *f.*; ~day, Geburtstag, *m.*; ~-place, Geburtsort, *m.*; ~-rate, Geburtenziffer, *f.*

biscuit, Keks, *m.*

bisect, halbieren.

bishop, Bischof, *m.*; (*chess*) Läufer, *m.*; ~ric, Bistum, *n.*

bismuth, Wismut, *m.* or *n.*

bison, Bison, *m.*

bit, Bissen, *m.*; Bißchen, Stück, *n.*; (*bridle*) Gebiß, *n.*; *not a ~ of it*, nicht im geringsten.

bitch, Hündin, *f.*

bit|e, Biß, *m.*; (*of insect*) Stich, *m.*; (*fishing*) Anbeißen, *n.*; *v.t.* beißen; (*insects*) stechen; (*tool, &c.*) greifen; ~ing, beißend.

bitter, ~ly, bitter; erbittert; ~ness, Bitterkeit, *f.*

bittern, Rohrdommel, *f.*

bitum|en, Erdpech, *n.*; ~inous, bituminös.

bivouac, *sb.* Feldwache, *f.*; Biwak, *n.*; *v.i.* biwakieren.

bizarre, bizarr.

black, *sb.* (*colour*) Schwarz, *n.*; Schwärze, *f.*; (*person*) Neger, *m.*; *a.* schwarz; *v.t.* schwärzen; (*shoes*) wichsen; ~ball, hinausballotieren; ~beetle, Schabe, *f.*; ~berry, Brombeere, *f.*; ~bird, Amsel, *f.*; ~board, Schul-Wand-tafel, *f.*; ~currant, schwarze Johannisbeere, *f.*; *~ eye*, blaues Auge; ~guard,

Lump, Schuft, *m.*; ~ish, schwärzlich; ~ lead, Graphit, *m.*; Reißblei, *n.*; (*pencil*) Bleistift, *m.*; ~leg, Streikbrecher, *m.*; ~mail, *sb.* Erpressung, *f.*; *v.t.* Geld erpressen; ~ market, der schwarze Markt; ~ness, Schwärze, *f.*; ~out, *sb.* Verdunklung, *f.*; *v.t.* verdunkeln; ~ pudding, Blutwurst, *f.*; ~ sheep, (*person*) Taugenichts, *m.*; ~smith, (Grob)schmied, *m.*; ~thorn, Schlehdorn, *m.*

bladder, Blase, *f.*

blade, (*knife*) Klinge, *f.*; (*oar*) Blatt, *n.*; (*grass*) Halm, *m.*; (*propeller*) Flügel, *m.*

blame, *sb.* Tadel, *m.*; Schuld, *f.*; *v.t.* tadeln; ~less, untadelhaft; ~worthy, tadelnswert.

blancmange, Flammeri, *m.*

bland, ~ly,sanft; einschmeichelnd.

blandishment, Schmeichelei, *f.*

blank, *a.* leer, unausgefüllt; point-~, geradezu; *sb.* (*commerc.*) Blanko, Blankett, *n.*; leerer Raum, *m.*; ~ cartridge, Platzpatrone, *f.*; ~ cheque, Blankscheck, *m.*; ~ verse, Blankvers, *m.*

blanket, (Bett)decke, *f.*

blare, schmettern.

blaspheme, *v.t.* Gott lästern; ~er, Gotteslästerer, *m.*; ~ous(ly), gotteslästerlich; ~y, Gotteslästerung, *f.*

blast, *sb.* (*wind*) Windstoß, *m.*; (*trumpet*) Schall, *m.*; (*explosive*) Explosion, Luftdruckwirkung, *f.*; *v.t.* sprengen, vernichten; ~furnace, Hochofen, *m.*

blaze, *sb.* Flamme, Lohe, *f.*; (*on a tree*) Marke, *f.*; (*outburst*) Ausbruch, *m.*; *v.i.* lodern, flammen; *v.t.* (*tree*) markieren; ~r, Sportjacke, *f.*

bleach, bleichen; ~er, Bleicher,*m.*; ~ing-powder, Bleichpulver, *n.*

bleak, ~ly, öde, verödet; ~ness, Öde, *f.*

blear-eyed, triefäugig.

bleat, *sb.* Blöken, *n.*; *v.i.* blöken.

bleed, *v.i.* bluten; *v.t.* (jemanden) zur Ader lassen.

blemish, *sb.* Makel, Fehler, *m.*; *v.t.* beflecken, entstellen.

blench, zurückweichen, zurückfahren.

blend, *sb.* Mischung, *f.*; *v.t.* vermischen; *v.i.* sich mischen, verschmelzen.

bless, segnen; ~ed, gesegnet, selig; ~ing, Segen, *m.*

blight, *sb.* Meltau, Brand, Rost, *m.*; *v.t.* verderben.

blind, *sb.* Rouleau, *n.*; *Venetian* ~, Jalousie, *f.*; (*fig.*) Vorwand, *m.*, Ausflucht, *f.*; *a.* blind; *v.t.* blind machen; (*fig.*) (ver)blenden; ~ alley, Sackgasse, *f.*; ~fold, *v.t.* die Augen verbinden; *a.* mit verbundenen Augen; ~ing, blendend; ~ly, blindlings; ~man's-buff, Blindekuh, *f.*; ~ness, Blindheit, *f.*; ~worm, Blindschleiche, *f.*

blink, *sb.* Blinzeln, *n.*; (*light*) Schimmer, *m.*; *v.i.* blinken; blinzeln; (*light*) schimmern; ~ers, Scheuklappen, *f.pl.*

bliss, Wonne, Seligkeit, *f.*; ~ful(ly), wonnevoll, selig.

blister, *sb.* Blase, *f.*; *v.i.* Blasen ziehen (*or* bilden).

blizzard, Schneesturm, *m.*

bloated, aufgedunsen, aufgeblasen.

bloater, geräucherter Hering, *m.*

block, *sb.* (*stone, pulley, buildings*) Block, *m.*; (*wood*) Klotz, *m.*; (*stoppage*) Versperrung, Stokkung, *f.*; *v.t.* versperren, blockieren, verstopfen; ~ade, *sb.* Blockade, *f.*; *v.t.* blockieren; ~head, Dummkopf, *m.*; ~house, Blockhaus, *n.*

blond, *sb.* Blondine, *f.*; *a.* blond.

blood, Blut, *n.*; ~ count, Blutbild, *n.*; ~curdling, haarsträubend; ~ heat, Blutwärme,*f.*; ~horse, Vollblut, *n.*; ~hound, Schweiß-Blut- hund, *m.*; ~poisoning, Blutvergiftung, *f.*; ~shed, Blutvergießen, *n.*; ~shot, mit Blut unterlaufen, blut-~stained, blutbefleckt; ~sucker, Blutsauger, *m.*; ~thirsty, blutdürstig; ~ transfusion, Blutübertragung, *f.*; ~vessel, Blutgefäß, *m.*; ~y, blutig; blutdürstig.

bloom, *sb.* Blüte, *f.*; (*on fruit*) Flaum, *m.*; *v.i.* blühen.

blossom, *sb.* Blüte, *f.*; *v.i.* blühen.

blot, *sb.* Klecks, *m.*; *v.t.* beklecksen; ~ out, auslöschen; ~ter, Löscher, *m.*; ~ting-paper, Löschpapier, *n.*

blouse, Bluse, *f.*

blow, *sb.* Schlag, Stoß, *m.*; *v.i.* wehen; *v.t.* blasen; ~ one's nose, sich schneuzen; ~ one's brains out, sich eine Kugel durch den Kopf jagen; ~ up, sprengen; (*scold*) auszanken; (*tyre*) aufpumpen; ~lamp, Lötlampe, *f.*; ~pipe, Lötrohr, *n.*

blubber, Tran, *m.*

bludgeon, Knüttel, *m.*

blue, *a.* blau; *sb.* Blau, *n.*; ~ blood, blaues Blut; ~book, Blaubuch, *n.*; ~bottle, Schmeißfliege, *f.*; ~jacket, Blaujacke, *f.*; ~ness, Blau, *n.*; ~ print, Blaupause, *f.*; ~stocking, Blaustrumpf, *m.*; ~ish, bläulich.

bluff, *a.* derb, barsch; *sb.* Renommisterei, *f.*; Bluff, *m.*

blunder, *sb.* Fehler, *m.*; *v.i.* (einen) Fehler machen; ~er, Stümper, Tölpel, *m.*

blunt, ~ly, (*edge*) stumpf; (*answer*) offen; (*person*) grob, plump; *v.t.* abstumpfen; ~ness, Stumpfheit; Plumpheit, *f.*

blur, trüben, verwischen.

blurt, ~ out, herausplatzen.

blush, *sb.* Erröten, *n.*; *v.i.* erröten.

bluster, toben groß tun; ~er, Prahlhans, *m.*

boa, Boa, Riesenschlange, *f.*

boar, Eber, *m.*

board, *sb.* Brett, *n.*; (*plank*) Bohle, *f.*; (*book-cover*) Pappe, *f.*; (*food*) Kost, Pension, *f.*; (*naut.*) Bord, *m.*; on ~, an Bord; (*directors, &c.*) Direktorium, *n.*, Behörde, *f.*; *v.t.* (*plank*) dielen; (*ship*) an Bord gehen; (*enemy's ship*) entern; (*train, &c.*) einsteigen; (*feed*) in die Kost geben; beköstigen; ~er, Kostgänger, Pensionär, *m.*; (*school*) Internatsschüler(in, *f.*), *m.*; ~inghouse, Pension, *f.*; ~ing-school, Internat, *n.*

boast, prahlen, sich rühmen; ~er, Prahler, *m.*; ~ful, prahlerisch.

boat, Boot, Schiff, *n.*; ~ing,

Rudern, *n.*; Rudersport, *m.*; ~race, Wettrudern, *n.*; ~swain, Bootsmann, *m.*; ~train, Schiffszug, *m.*

bobbed, ~ hair, Bubikopf, *m.*

bobbin, Spule, *f.*; Haspel, *m.*

bodice, Mieder, *n.*

bodily, körperlich.

bodkin, Pfriem, *m.*

body, Körper, Leib, *m.*; (*troops*) Abteilung, *f.*; (*number of persons*) Körperschaft, *f.*; in a ~, sämtlich, insgesamt; ~guard, Leibgarde, *f.*

bog, Sumpf, *m.*, Moor, *n.*; ~gy, sumpfig.

bogie, bewegliches Radgestell.

bogus, falsch, unecht.

bogy, Kobold, *m.*; Schreckgespenst, *n.*

boil, *sb.* Furunkel, *m.*; Geschwür, *n.*; *v.* kochen, sieden; ~ over, überkochen; ~er, (Dampf)kessel, *m.*; ~er-maker, Kesselschmied, *m.*; ~ing-point, Siedepunkt, *m.*

boisterous, ~ly, stürmisch, ungestüm.

bold, ~ly, kühn, dreist; make ~ to, sich erkühnen; ~ness, Kühnheit, Dreistigkeit, *f.*

bolster, Kissen, Polster, *n.*

bolt, *sb.* Bolzen, Riegel, *m.*; *v.t.* verriegeln; (*swallow*) hinunterschlingen; *v.i.* (*horse, person*) durchgehen, durchbrennen; ~ upright, kerzengerade.

bomb, *sb.* Bombe, *f.*; *v.t.* mit Bomben belegen, Bomben werfen auf; ~ed out, ausgebombt; ~er, Bombenflugzeug, *n.*; Bomber, *m.*; ~ing-raid, Bombenangriff, *m.*; ~proof, bombenfest; ~shell, Bombe (*also fig.*), *f.*

bombard, bombardieren, beschießen; ~ment, Bombardement, *n.*, Beschießung, *f.*

bond, (*security*) Obligation, *f.*; in ~, unter Zollverschluß; ~age, Knechtschaft, *f.*

bone, Knochen, *m.*; (*fish*) Gräte, *f.*; ~ of contention, Zankapfel, *m.*

bonfire, Freudenfeuer, *n.*

bonnet, Mütze, Haube; (*motorcar*) (Motor)haube, *f.*

bonn|y, ~ily, hübsch, nett.

bonus, Prämie, Extradividende, f.; Zuschlag, m.

booby, Tölpel, m.; ~ prize, Trostpreis, m.; ~trap, Falle, f.; (school) Schabernack, m.

book, sb. Buch, n.; v.t. eintragen; (ticket) lösen; (seat) bestellen; ~binder, Buchbinder, m.; ~case, Bücherschrank, m.; ~ing-office, (railway) Fahrkartenausgabe; (theatre) Kasse, f.; ~keeping, Buchführung, f.; ~maker, bookie, Buchmacher, m.; ~post, als Drucksache, f.; ~seller, Buchhändler, m.; second-hand ~seller, Antiquar, m.; ~shop, Buchhandlung, f.; second-hand ~shop, Antiquariat, n.; ~stall, Bücherstand, m.; ~trade, Buchhandel, m.; ~worm, Bücherwurm, m.

boom, sb. (roar) Donner, Dröhnen, n.; (naut.) Spiere, f.; (harbour) Sperre, f.; (commerc.) Aufschwung, m.; Hausse, f.; v.i. dröhnen; (commerc.) einen Aufschwung nehmen; v.t. große Reklame machen für.

boomerang, Bumerang, m.

boon, Gabe, Wohltat, f.; ~ companion, lustiger Genosse.

boor, Bauer; (fig.) Lümmel, m.; ~ish, bäurisch, grob.

boost, große Reklame machen für.

boot, Stiefel, Schuh; (of a car) Kofferraum, m.; to ~, obendrein; ~black, Stiefelputzer, m.; ~lace, Schuhriemen, m.; ~legger, Alkoholschmuggler, m.; ~tree, Leisten, Stiefelspanner, m.; boots, Hausknecht, m.

booth, Bude, f.

booty, Beute, f.

booze, saufen.

bora|x, Borax, m.; ~cic, Borsäure.

border, Rand, Saum, m.; Grenze, f.; v.i. grenzen (on an); v.t. einfassen; ~er, Grenzbewohner, m.

bore, Bohrloch, n.; (gun) Kaliber, n.; (tube, etc.) Bohrung, f.; (person) langweiliger Mensch; (fig.) Plage, f.; v.t. bohren, m.; (weary) langweilen.

borrow, borgen, leihen.

bosom, Busen; (fig.) Schoß, m.

boss, Herr, Meister, m.

botan|ical, botanisch; ~ist, Botaniker, m.; ~y, Botanik, Pflanzenkunde, f.

botch, (ver)pfuschen.

both, beide, v.t.; ~ ... and, sowohl ... als auch.

bother, Plage, f.; v.t. plagen, quälen.

bottle, sb. Flasche, f.; v.t. auf Flaschen ziehen (or füllen); ~neck, (fig.) Engpaß, m.; Stauung, f.

bottom, sb. Boden; Grund, m.; (of stairs, hill, page, &c.) Fuß, m, unten; (posterior) Hintere, m.; a. unterst, letzt; ~less, bodenlos.

bough, Ast, m.

boulder, Steinblock, m.

bounce, sb. Aufprall, m.; v.i. (auf)springen; v.t. springen machen.

bound[1], Sprung, m.; v.i. springen.

bound[2], a. bestimmt, auf der Reise (nach).

bound[3], v.t. begrenzen; sb. Grenze, f.; ~less, grenzenlos.

boundary, Grenze, f.

bount|iful, ~eous, freigebig, wohltätig; ~y, Freigebigkeit, f.; Prämie, f.

bouquet, Strauß, m.; (of wine) Blume, f.

bourgeois, sb. Bürger, Bourgeois, m.; a. bürgerlich.

bout, Wettstreit, Kampf, m.; drinking~, Trinkgelage, n.

bow[1], sb. (curtsy) Verbeugung, f.; v.i. sich verbeugen; ~ to, grüßen; (submit to) sich unterwerfen (with dat.).

bow[2], sb. (weapon, saddle) Bogen, m.; (knot) Schleife, f.; cross-~, Armbrust, f.; ~legged, krummbeinig; ~window, Erkerfenster, n.

bow[3], sb. (naut.) Bug, m.; ~sprit, Bugspriet, n.

bowlderize, verballhornen.

bowels, Eingeweide, n.pl.; ~ of the earth, das Innere der Erde.

bower, Laube, f.

bowl, sb. (dish) Schüssel, f.; (pipe)

BOX [22] BREAST

Pfeifenkopf, *m.*; (*ball*) Kugel, *f.*; *v.t.* rollen; schieben; **~er**, (*cricket*) Ballmann, *m.*; **~er-hat**, steifer (Filz)hut.

box, *sb.* Büchse, *f.*, (*wooden*) Kasten, *m.*; (*match, cardboard*) Schachtel, *f.*; (*theatre*) Loge, *f.*; (*cab*) Bock, *m.*; (*tree*) Buchsbaum, *m.*; **~ on the ear**, Ohrfeige, *f.*; *v.i.* boxen; *v.t.* (*compass*) den Kompaß bestimmen; (*person's ears*) jemandem eine Ohrfeige geben; **~er**, Boxer, *m.*; **~ing**, Boxen, *n.*; **Boxing-day**, zweiter Weihnachtstag; **~ing-gloves**, Boxhandschuhe, *m.pl.*; **~ing-match**, Boxkampf, *m.*; **~office**, Kasse, *f.*

boy, Knabe, Junge, *m.*; **~hood**, Knabenalter, *n.*; **~ish**, knabenhaft; **~ scout**, Pfadfinder, *m.*

boycott, *sb.* Boykott, *m.*; *v.t.* boykottieren.

bra, see **brassière**.

brac|e, *sb.* (*pair*) Paar, *n.*; (*arch.*) Strebe, Stütze, *f.*; (*naut.*) Brasse, *f.*; *v.t.* **~ up**, stärken; (*naut.*) brassen; **~es**, Hosenträger, *m. pl.*; **~ing**, stärkend, gesund.

bracelet, Armband, *n.*

bracken, Farnkraut, *n.*

bracket, *sb.* Klammer, *f.*; (*gas, electr., &c.*) Arm, *m.*; (*arch.*) Stütze, *f.*; *v.t.* einklammern; (*fig.*) auf eine Stufe stellen.

brackish, salzig.

brag, prahlen; **~gart**, Prahler, **m.**

brahmin, Brahmane, *m.*

braid, *sb.* Litze, *f.*; *v.t.* flechten.

brain, Gehirn, *n.*; (*fig.*) Verstand, *m.*; *v.t.* den Schädel einschlagen; *rack one's* **~s**, sich den Kopf zerbrechen; **~fever**, Gehirnentzündung, *f.*; **~less**, hirnlos; unvernünftig; **~washing**, Gehirnwäsche, *f.*; **~wave**, glücklicher Einfall; **~y**, klug.

brake, *sb.* (*on wheel*) Bremse, *f.*; (*thicket*) Gebüsch, *n.*; *v.* bremsen.

bramble, Brombeerstrauch, *m.*

bran, Kleie, *f.*

branch, *sb.* Zweig, Ast, *m.*; (*subject*) Fach, *n.*; (*commerc.*) Filiale, *f.*; *v.i.* sich abzweigen; **~line**, Zweigbahn, *f.*

brand, *sb.* (*fire*) (Feuer) brand, *m.*;

(*mark*) Brandmal, *n.*; (*commerc.*) Sorte, *f.*; *v.t.* brandmarken; **~ing-iron**, Brandeisen, *n.*; **~new**, nagelneu.

brandish, schwingen.

brandy, Branntwein, Kognak, *m.*

brass, Messing, *n.*; **~band**, Blechmusikkapelle, *f.*; **~founder**, Gelbgießer, *m.*; **~ plate**, Messingschild, *n.*

brassard, Armbinde, *f.*

brassière, Büstenhalter, BH, *m.*

brat, Balg, *m.*

brave, tapfer; *v.t.* trotzen (*with dat.*); **~ry**, Tapferkeit, *f.*

brawl, *sb.* Streit, Zank, *m.*; *v.i.* zanken.

brawn, Sülze, *f.*; **~y**, sehnig.

bray, *sb.* Eselsgeschrei, *n.*; *v.i.* schreien.

brazen, ehern; (*fig.*) unverschämt.

brazier, Kohlenpfanne, *f.*

Brazil nut, Paranuß, *f.*

breach, Bruch, *m.*; (*mil.*) Bresche, *f.*; **~ of promise**, Verlöbnisbruch, *m.*

bread, Brot, *n.*; **~ and butter**, Butterbrot, *n.*

breadth, Breite, *f.*

break, *sb.* Bruch, *m.*; Unterbrechung, Pause, *f.*; (*billiards*) Serie, *f.*; **~ of day**, Tagesanbruch, *m.*; *v.t.* brechen; *v.i.* entzweigehen; (*storm*) sich brechen; (*bank*) fallieren; bankrott werden; (*weather*) sich ändern; (*voice*) umschlagen; **~ away**, sich losmachen; ausbrechen; **~ down**, *v.t.* abbrechen; *v.i.* (*carriage*) umwerfen; stecken bleiben; (*health*) versagen; (*fail*) scheitern; **~ in**, einbrechen; (*horse*) zureiten; **~ off**, abbrechen; **~ up**, zerstören; (*school*) die Ferien antreten; **~able**, zerbrechlich; **~age**, Bruch, *m.*; **~down**, Zusammenbruch, *m.*; (*motor*) Panne, *f.*; **~ers**, Brandung, *f.*; **~fast**, *sb.* Frühstück, *n.*; *v.i.* frühstücken; **~neck**, *at a pace*, Hals über Kopf; **~water**, Buhne, *f.*; Hafendamm, *m.*

bream, Brassen, *m.*

breast, Brust, *f.*; **~plate**, Brustharnisch, *m.*; **~stroke**, Brustschwimmen, n.; ~work, Brustwehr, f.

breath, Atem; (fig.) Hauch, m.; take ~, Atem schöpfen; ~e, atmen; not to ~e a word, kein Wort verlauten lassen; ~less, atemlos.

breeches, Kniehosen, f.pl.

breed, sb. Rasse, Zucht,; (birds) Brut, f.; v.t. züchten; erzeugen; v.i. sich paaren; fruchtbar sein; ~ing, (animals) Züchten, n.; (pers.) Bildung, f.

breez|e, Lüftchen, n.; (naut.) Brise, f.; ~y, luftig, windig.

brevity, Kürze, f.

brew, sb. Gebräu, n.; v.t. brauen; ~er, Brauer, m.; ~ery, Brauerei, f.

briar: see brier.

bribe, ~ry, Bestechung, f.; v.t. bestechen.

brick, Back-, Ziegel- stein, m.; v.t., ~ up, zumauern; ~-kiln, Ziegelofen, m.; ~-layer, Maurer, m.

bridal, hochzeitlich, bräutlich.

bride, Braut, f.; (after the ceremony) junge Frau, f.; ~groom, Bräutigam, m.; ~smaid, Brautjungfer, f.

bridge, sb. Brücke, f.; (game) Bridge, n.; v.t. überbrücken; ~-head, Brücken- Lande-kopf, m.

bridle, Zaum, m.; ~-path, Reitweg, m.

brief, ~ly, kurz; bündig; ~ness, Kürze, f.

brier, Dornstrauch, m.; ~ pipe, Holzpfeife, Bruyèrepfeife, f.

brigad|e, Brigade, f.; ~ fire ~e, Feuerwehr, f.; ~ier, Brigadier, m.

brigand, Räuber, m.; ~age, Räuberei, f.

bright, ~ly, hell; klar; intelligent; ~en, hell werden, glänzen; glänzend machen; ~en up, aufheitern; ~ness, Glanz, m.; Klarheit, f.

brillian|ce, Glanz, m.; Pracht, f.; ~t(ly), glänzend, prachtvoll; (pers.) geistreich.

brim, Rand, m.; (hat) Krempe, f.; ~ming over with, vor . . . überschäumend.

brimstone, Schwefel, m.

brine, Salzwasser, n.; Sole, f.

bring, bringen; holen; führen; ~ about, verursachen, herbeiführen; ~ forth, hervorbringen, gebären; ~ in, einbringen; ~ round, wieder zu sich bringen; ~ up, erziehen.

brink, Rand, m.

brisk, ~ly, frisch; lebhaft; ~ness, Lebhaftigkeit, f.

bristl|e, sb. Borste, f.; v.i. starren (with vor); ~y, borstig.

brittle, zerbrechlich; (glass, metal) spröde; ~ness, Zerbrechlichkeit; Sprödigkeit, f.

broach, (cask) anzapfen; (subject) aufs Tapet bringen, vorbringen.

broad, breit, weit, groß; (views) liberal; ~ bean: see bean; ~ day, heller Tag; ~cast, sb. Rundfunk, m., Radio, n.; v. rundfunken; ~casting station, (Rundfunk)-sender, m.; ~en, breiter machen (werden); ~-minded, liberal, weitherzig; ~side, (guns) Salve, f.; ~sword, Säbel, m.

brocade, Brokat, f.

broccoli, Brokkoli, pl.

broker, Makler, m.; ~age, Maklergebühr, f.

brom|ide, Bromid, n.; ~ine, Brom, n.

bronchitis, Luftröhrenentzündung, f.

bronze, Bronze, f.

brooch, Brosche, Spange, f.

brood, sb. Brut, f.; v.i. brüten.

brook, Bach, m.

broom, Besen; (bot.) Ginster, m.; ~stick, Besenstiel, m.

broth, Brühe, f.

brothel, Bordell, n.

brother, Bruder, m.; ~hood, Bruderschaft, f.; ~-in-law, Schwager, m.; ~ly, brüderlich.

brow, Augenbraue, f.; (forehead) Stirn, f.; (hill) Rand, m.; ~beat, einschüchtern.

brown, a. braun; v.t. bräunen; ~ish, bräunlich; ~ paper, Packpapier, n.

browse, weiden.

bruise, sb. Beule, f.; v.t. quetschen, zerstoßen.

brunt, Anprall, Stoß, m.; (fig.) Heftigkeit, f.

brush, sb. Bürste, f.; (paint) Pinsel, m.; (broom) Besen, m.; v.t. bürsten, fegen; (touch) streifen; ~wood, Gestrüpp, Unterholz, n.

brusque, ~ly, barsch, brüsk, kurz angebunden.

Brussels, ~ carpet, Brüsseler Teppich, m.; ~ sprouts, Rosenkohl, m.

brut|al, ~ally, viehisch; roh; ~ality, Brutalität, Roheit, f.; ~e, Tier; (person) Vieh, n.; by ~ force, durch rohe Gewalt.

bubble, sb. (Seifen-, Wasser-)blase, f.; v.i. (auf)wallen, sprudeln.

buccaneer, Seeräuber, m.

buck, Bock, m.; (dandy) Stutzer, m.; ~shot, Rehposten, m.; ~skin, Wildleder, n.; ~wheat, Buchweizen, m.

bucket, Eimer, m.

buckle, sb. Schnalle, f.; v.t. schnallen; v.i. sich biegen, einknicken; ~r, Schild, m.

bud, sb. Knospe, f.; v.i. knospen, sprossen; v.t. pfropfen.

budge, sich rühren.

budget, Budget, n.

buff, sb. Lederfarbe, f.; Braungelb, n.; a. braungelb.

buffalo, Büffel, m.

buffer, Puffer, m.

buffet, sb. (blow) Faustschlag, m.; (stool) Fußschemel, m.; (sideboard, bar) Büfett, n.; Schenktisch, m.; v.t. stoßen, puffen.

buffoon, Possenreißer, Hanswurst, m.; ~ery, Possen, f.pl.

bug, Wanze, f.; ~bear, Popanz, m.

bugle, (Wald-, Signal-)horn, n.; ~r, Hornist, m.

build, sb. (of person) Wuchs, m.; (building) Bauart, f.; Stil, m.; v.t. bauen; ~er, Baumeister, m.; ~ing, (act) Bauen, m.; (structure) Gebäude, n.

bulb, Zwiebel, Knolle, f.; (electric light) Birne, f.; ~ous, knollenförmig.

bulge, sb. Ausbauchung, f.; v.i. sich ausbauchen, hervorstehen.

bulk, Masse, Größe, f.; Hauptteil, m.; (naut.) Schiffsladung, f.; ~head, Schott, n.; ~y, groß, dick; unhandlich.

bull, Stier, m.; (pope's) Bulle, f.; (stock exchange) Haussier, m.; ~dog, Bullenbeißer, m.; Bulldogge, f.; ~dozer, Planiermaschine, f.; ~finch, Gimpel, m.; ~frog, Ochsenfrosch, m.; ~ock, Ochs(e), m.; ~'s-eye, (target) Zentrum, Schwarze, n.; (in window) Butzenscheibe, f.

bullet, Kugel, f.; ~-proof, kugelfest.

bulletin, Tagesbericht, m.; Bulletin, n.

bullion, Gold-, Silber-barren, m.

bully, sb. (school) Tyrann, m.; v.t. tyrannisieren, einschüchtern.

bulrush, Binse, f.

bulwark, Bollwerk, n.; (naut.) Reling, f.

bumble-bee, Hummel, f.

bump, sb. (hit) Schlag, m.; (lump) Beule, f.; v.t. stoßen (gegen); ~er, (motor-car) Stoßfänger, m.; ~kin, Tölpel, m.; ~y, holperig, uneben.

bumptious, ~ly, aufgeblasen.

bun, kleiner Kuchen.

bunch, Büschel, m.; Bündel, n.; (flowers) Strauß, m.; ~ of grapes, Weintraube, f.

bundle, sb. Bündel, n.; v.t. einpacken.

bungalow, Bungalow, m.

bungle, sb. Stümperei, f.; v.t. verpfuschen; ~r, Stümper, m.

bunk, (naut.) Koje, f.

bunker, (naut.) Bunker, m.

bunting, Flaggentuch, n.; (zool.) Ammer, f.

buoy, sb. Boje, Tonne, f.; life~, Rettungsgürtel, m.; v.t. flott machen; ~ up, (fig.) aufmuntern; ~ancy, Schwimmkraft; (fig.) Schwungkraft, f.; ~ant, schwimmend; (fig.) heiter.

burbot, Quappe, f.

burden, sb. Last, Bürde, f.; (of song) Refrain, m.; v.t. belasten, beladen; ~some, beschwerlich.

burdock, Klette, f.

bureau, Büro, n.; Schreibtisch, m.; ~cracy, Bürokratie, f.; ~crat, Bürokrat, m.

burgher, Bürger, m.

burgl|e, einbrechen; ~ar, Einbrecher, m.; ~ary, Einbruch, m.

burgomaster, Bürgermeister, *m.*

burgundy, (*wine*) Burgunder, *m.*

burial, Begräbnis, *n.*

burlesque, *a.* possenhaft; *sb.* Burleske, Posse, *f.*; *v.t.* travestieren.

burly, stämmig, dick.

burn, *sb.* Brandmal, *n.*, Brandwunde, *f.*; (*brook*) Bach, *m.*; *v.t.* and *i.* brennen; **~er,** Brenner, *m.*

burrow, *sb.* Kaninchenbau, *m.*; *v.i.* sich eingraben, wühlen.

bursar, Schatzmeister; Stipendiat, *m.*; **~y,** Stipendium, *n.*

burst, *sb.* Ausbruch; Riß, *m.*; *v.i.* bersten, platzen; *v.t.* sprengen; **~ into tears,** in Tränen ausbrechen.

bury, begraben, (*hide*) verbergen.

bus, (Omni)bus, *m.*

bush, Busch, Strauch, *m.*; **~y,** buschig; (*beard*) struppig.

business, Geschäft, *n.*; Handel, *m.*; (*affairs*) Angelegenheiten, *f.pl.*

bust, Büste, *f.*

bustard, Trappe, *f.*

bustle, *sb.* Lärm, Auflauf, *m.*; *v.i.* sich rühren, geschäftig sein.

bus|y, ~ily, geschäftig; beschäftigt; *to be* **~,** zu tun haben; *v. reflex.* sich beschäftigen (*with mit*).

but, *conj.* aber; (*after negative*) sondern; *adv. & prep.* (*only*) nur; (*except*) außer; *nothing* **~,** nichts als.

butcher, *sb.* Fleischer, Metzger, *m.*; *v.t.* schlachten, niedermetzeln; **~bird,** Würger, *m.*; **~y,** (*fig.*) Metzelei, *f.*

butt, *sb.* dickes Ende, *n.*; (*gun*) Kolben, *m.*; (*push*) Stoß, *m.*; (*shooting*) Scheibenstand, *m.*; (*laughing-stock*) Zielscheibe, *f.*; *v.t.* stoßen (*at* gegen).

butter, *sb.* Butter, *f.*; *v.t.* mit Butter bestreichen; **~cup,** Butterblume, *f.*; **~fly,** Schmetterling, *m.*; **~milk,** Buttermilch, *f.*

buttock, Hinterteil, *n.*

button, *sb.* Knopf, *m.*; *v.t.* zuknöpfen; **~hole,** Knopfloch, *n.*; **~hook,** Knöpfer, *m.*

buttress, *sb.* Strebepfeiler, *m.*; *v.t.* stützen.

buxom, drall, kräftig.

buy, kaufen; **~er,** Käufer, *m.*

buzz, *sb.* Summen, *n.*; *v.i.* summen; **~er,** Summer, *m.*

buzzard, Bussard, *m.*

by, *prep.* (*means*) durch; (*near*) bei, neben; (*via*) über; (*author*) von; (*according to*) nach; *adv.* nahe; (*past*) vorbei; **~ the ~,** beiläufig gesagt; **~ day,** am Tage; **~ night,** bei Nacht; *day* **~ day,** Tag für Tag; *one* **~ one,** der eine nach dem andern; **~ degrees,** nach und nach; **~ far,** bei weitem; **~ all means,** auf jeden Fall; **~ no means,** keineswegs; **~ heart,** auswendig; **~ turns,** abwechselnd; *lay* **~,** beiseite legen, sparen; **~election,** Nachwahl, *f.*; **~gone,** vergangen; **~law,** Ortsstatut, *n.*; **~name,** Beiname, *m.*; **~pass,** (*gas*) Kleinsteller, *m.*; (*road*) Umgehungsstraße, *f.*; **~play,** Pantomime, *f.*; Nebenspiel, *n.*; **~product,** Nebenprodukt, *n.*; **~stander,** Zuschauer, *m.*; **~way,** Seitenweg, *m.*; **~word,** Sprichwort, *n.*

byre, Kuhstall, *m.*

C

cab, Droschke, *f.*; (*taxi*) Taxe, *f.*, Taxi, *n.*; **~driver,** Droschkenkutscher, *m.*; **~stand,** Taxenstand, *m.*

cabbage, Kohl, *m.*

cabin, (*hut*) Hütte; (*ship*) Kajüte, Kabine, *f.*; **~trunk,** Kabinenkoffer, *m.*

cabinet, Kabinett, *n.*; (*furniture*) Schrank, *m.*; **~maker,** Kunsttischler, *m.*

cable, *sb.* Kabel, Ankertau, *n.*; (*telegram*) Depesche, *f.*; *v.* kabeln, telegraphieren.

cackle, gackern, schnattern.

cactus, Kaktus, *m.*

cad, gemeiner Kerl, Flegel, *m.*

caddie, (*golf*) Golfjunge, *m.*

caddy, Teebüchse, *f.*

cadence, Tonfall, *m.*

cadet, Kadett, *m.*

cadge, (*sl.*) schnorren.

cadmium, Kadmium, *n.*

caesura, Zäsur, *f.*

café, Café, Kaffeehaus, *n.*

cage, *sb.* Käfig, *m.*; *v.t.* einsperren.

cairn, Steinhügel, *m.*

caisson, Senkkasten, *m.*

cajole, schmeicheln, bereden.

cake, Kuchen, *m.*; (*soap, chocolate, &c.*) Stück, *n.*

calamit|ous, unglückselig; ~y, Unglück, Unheil, *n.*

calcium, Kalzium, *n.*

calcul|ate, *v.t.* berechnen; *v.i.* rechnen (*on* auf); ~able, berechenbar; ~ation, Berechnung, *f.*; ~ator, Rechenmaschine, *f.*

calendar, Kalender, *m.*

calf, Kalb, *n.*; (*of leg*) Wade, *f.*

calibre, Kaliber, *n.*

calico, Kaliko, Kattun, *m.*

caliph, Kalif, *m.*

call, *sb.* Ruf, *m.*; (*duty*) Berufung, *f.*; (*claim*) Anspruch, *m.*; (*visit*) Besuch, *m.*; *v.t.* rufen; nennen; (*summon*) auffordern; (*awaken*) wecken; ~ *for*, abholen; (*require*) erfordern; ~ *on* besuchen, bei jemandem vorsprechen; ~ *out*, (*troops*) aufbieten; *to be* ~*ed*, heißen; ~-box, Fernsprechzelle, *f.*; ~er, Besucher, *m.*; ~ing, Beruf, *m.* Gewerbe, *n.*; ~-sign, Rufzeichen, *n.*

callous, ~ly, schwielig; (*fig.*) verhärtet, unempfindlich; ~ness, Unempfindlichkeit, *f.*

callow, nicht flügge; (*fig.*) unreif.

calm, *a.*, ~ly, ruhig; *sb.* Ruhe; Windstille, *f.*; *v.t.* beruhigen, besänftigen; ~ness, Stille, Ruhe, *f.*

calorie, Kalorie, Wärmeeinheit, *f.*

calumn|iate, verleumden; ~y, Verleumdung, *f.*

calve, kalben.

calyx, Blumenkelch, *m.*

cambric, Batist, *m.*

camel, Kamel, *n.*

cameo, Kamee, *f.*

camera, Kamera, *f.*, Fotoapparat, *m.*

camomile, Kamille, *f.*

camouflage, *sb.* Tarnung, *f.*; *v.t.* tarnen.

camp, *sb.* Lager, *n.*; *v.i.* lagern; ~-bed, Feldbett, *n.*; ~-stool, Klappstuhl, *m.*

campaign, *sb.* Feldzug, *m.*; *v.i.* einen Feldzug mitmachen; ~er, alter Soldat.

campanula, Glockenblume, *f.*

camphor, Kampfer, *m.*

can¹, *sb.* Kanne; Konservenbüchse, *f.*; *v.t.* einmachen.

can², *aux. v.* kann, können.

canal, Kanal, *m.*; ~ize, kanalisieren.

canary, Kanarienvogel, *m.*

cancel, ungültig machen, aufheben, widerrufen; ~lation, Aufhebung, Abbestellung, *f.*

cancer, Krebs, *m.*; ~ous, krebsartig.

candelabrum, Armleuchter, *m.*

candid, ~ly, offen, aufrichtig.

candidat|e, Kandidat, Bewerber, *m.*; ~ure, Kandidatur, *f.*

candle, Licht, *n.*; Kerze, *f.*; Candlemas, Lichtmeß, *f.*; ~power, Kerzenstärke, *f.*; ~stick, Leuchter, *m.*

candour, Offenheit, Aufrichtigkeit, *f.*

candy, *sb.* Kandis(zucker), *m.*; *v.t.* kandieren.

cane, *sb.* Rohr, *n.*; (*stick*) Stock, *m.*; *v.t.* durchprügeln; ~ing, Prügel, *m.pl.*

canine, Hunds-; ~ tooth, Eckzahn, *m.*

canister, (Blech)büchse, *f.*

canker, Brand, Rost; (*fig.*) Wurm, Kummer, *m.*

cannibal, Kannibale, Menschenfresser, *m.*

cannon, *sb.* Kanone; (*billiards*) Karambolage, *f.*; *v.i.* karambolieren; ~ade, Kanonade, *f.*; ~-ball, Kanonenkugel, *f.*

canoe, Kanu, Paddelboot, *n.*

canon, Domherr, *m.*; (*rule*) Regel, *f.*; ~ize, heilig sprechen; ~ law, Kirchenrecht, *n.*

canopy, Traghimmel; (*bed*) Betthimmel, *m.*; (*parachute*) Schirmhülle, *f.*

cantankerous, streitsüchtig.

canteen, Kantine, *f.*

canter, *sb.* leichter Galopp; *v.i.* im leichten Galopp reiten.

canting, scheinheilig.

canton, Kanton, *m.*

canvas, Kanevas, *m.*; (*sail*) Segeltuch, *n.*; (*painting*) Leinwand, *f.*

canvass, um Stimmen werben; ~**er**, Stimmenwerber, *m.*

cap, Mütze, *f.*; (*lid*) Deckel, *m.*; *v.t.* übertreffen, übertrumpfen.

capab|le, fähig; ~**ility**, Fähigkeit, *f.*

capac|ious, geräumig; ~**ity**, Rauminhalt, Umfang, *m.*; (*fig.*) Fähigkeit; Eigenschaft, *f.*

cape, (*geog.*) Vorgebirge, *n.*; (*cloak*) Umhang, *m.*, Cape, *n.*

caper[1], *sb.* Luftsprung, *m.*; *v.i.* umherspringen.

caper[2], Kapernstrauch, *m.*; ~**s**, Kapern, *f.pl.*

capital, *sb.* (*arch.*) Kapitell, *n.*; (*commerce.*) Kapital, *n.*; (*town*) Hauptstadt, *f.*; (*letter*) großer Anfangsbuchstabe, *m.*; *a.* Haupt- (*excellent*) vortrefflich; ~ **punishment**, Todesstrafe, *f.*; ~ **ship**, Schlachtschiff, *n.*; ~**ism**, Kapitalismus, *m.*; ~**ist**, Kapitalist, *m.*

capitulat|e, kapitulieren; ~**ion**, Kapitulation, *f.*

capric|e, Grille, Launenhaftigkeit, *f.*; ~**ious(ly)**, launenhaft, grillenhaft.

capsize, kentern.

capstan, Gangspill, *n.*

capsule, Kapsel, *f.*

captain, *sb.* (*mil.*) Hauptmann, *m.* (*naut.*) Kapitän; (*games*) Führer, *m.*; *v.t.* anführen, befehligen.

caption, (*film*) Bildtext, *m.*

captious, ~**ly**, tadelsüchtig.

captivate, einnehmen, gewinnen, bezaubern; ~**ing**, bezaubernd, einnehmend.

captiv|e, *sb.* Gefangene(r); *a.* gefangen; ~**ity**, Gefangenschaft, *f.*

capture, *sb.* Raub, *m.*; Beute, *f.*; *v.t.* erbeuten.

car, Auto, *n.*; Wagen, *m.*; ~**park**, Parkplatz, *m.*

caramel, Karamel, *m.*

carat, Karat, *n.*

caravan, Karawane, *f.*; Reise-, Wohn- wagen, *m.*

caraway, Kümmel, *m.*

carbide, Karbid, *n.*

carbine, Karabiner, *m.*

carbohydrates, Kohlenwasserstoffe, *m.pl.*

carbolic, ~ **acid**, Karbolsäure, *f.*

carbon, Kohlenstoff, *m.*; ~**ate**, kohlensaures Salz; ~ **copy**, Durchschlag, *m.*; ~ **dioxide**, Kohlensäure, *f.*; ~**paper**, Kohlepapier, Kopierpapier, *n.*

carbuncle, Karbunkel, *m.*

carburettor Vergaser, *m.*

carcass, Leichnam, *m.*; Aas, *n.*; ~ **meat**, frisches Fleisch.

card, Karte, *f.*; ~**board**, Pappe, *f.*; ~**index**, Kartei, *f.*; ~**table**, Spieltisch, *m.*

cardigan, Wolljacke, *f.*

cardinal, *sb.* Kardinal, *m.*; *a.* Kardinal-, Haupt-; ~ **number**, Grundzahl, *f.*; ~ **point**, Himmelsrichtung, *f.*

care, *sb.* (*anxiety*) Sorge; (*caution*) Vorsicht, *f.*; take ~!, Achtung!; take ~ of, auf etwas achtgeben, sorgen für; take ~ to, sorgen dafür, daß; *v.i.* sorgen; sich kümmern; I don't ~, meinetwegen; I don't ~ much for it, ich mache mir sehr wenig daraus; ~**ful(ly)**, vorsichtig; sorgfältig; ~**fulness**, Vorsicht, Sorgfalt, *f.*; ~**less(ly)**, sorglos; nachlässig; ~**lessness**, Sorglosigkeit; Nachlässigkeit, *f.*; ~**taker**, Wächter, Hauswart, *m.*; ~**worn**, abgehärmt.

career, Laufbahn, *f.*; rascher Lauf, *m.*

caress, *sb.* Liebkosung, *f.*; *v.t.* liebkosen.

cargo, Schiffsladung, *f.*

caricature, *sb.* Karikatur, *f.*; Zerrbild, *n.*; *v.t.* karikieren.

car|ies, Knochenfraß, *m.*; ~**ious**, kariös, angefressen.

carmine, Karmin, *n.*; *a.* karminrot.

carnage, Gemetzel, *n.*

carnal, ~**ly**, fleischlich.

carnation, Gartennelke, *f.*

carnival, Karneval, Fasching, *m.*

carnivorous, fleischfressend.

carol, Lobgesang, *m.*; Christmas ~ Weihnachtslied, *n.*

carous|al, Trinkgelage, n.; ~e, zechen.

carp, sb. Karpfen, m.; v.i. kritteln (at an).

carpent|er, Zimmermann, m.; ~ry, Zimmerhandwerk, n.

carpet, sb. Teppich, m.; v.t. mit Teppichen belegen; ~bag, Reisetasche, f.; ~sweeper, Teppichkehrmaschine, f.

carriage, Wagen, m.; (gun) Lafette, f.; (typewriter, aeroplane, &c.) Gestell, n.; (freight) Fracht, f.; (conveying) Spedieren, n.; (behaviour) Benehmen, n.; Haltung, f.; ~ paid, franko.

carrier, Fuhrmann, m.; (med.) Bazillenträger; (on bicycle, &c.) Gepäckhalter, m.

carrion, Aas, n.

carrot, gelbe Rübe, Möhre, f.

carry, v.t. tragen; bringen; ~ oneself, sich betragen; ~ forward, übertragen; ~ a motion, einen Antrag durchbringen; ~ on, weiterführen; (colloq.) Umstände machen; ~ out, ausführen; ~ through, durchführen, durchsetzen.

cart, sb. Karren, m.; v.t. karren; put the ~ before the horse, das Pferd beim Schwanze aufzäumen; ~er, Fuhrmann, m.; ~horse, Zugpferd, n.; ~load, Karrenladung, f.; ~road, Fahrweg, m.; ~wheel, Wagenrad, n.

cartel, Kartell, n.

Carthusian, Kartäuser(mönch), m.

cartilage, Knorpel, m.

cartoon, Karikatur, f.

cartridge, Patrone, f.

carv|e, (wood) schnitzen; (meat) tranchieren; vorschneiden; ~ing, Schnitzerei, f.; ~ingknife, Vorlegemesser, n.

cascade, Wasserfall, m.; Kaskade, f.

case, sb. (event, instance) Fall, m.; (container) Behälter, m.; (for machinery) Gehäuse, n.; (packing) Kiste, f.; (typog.) Setzkasten, m.; (law) Sache, m.; (med.) Krankheitsfall, m.; (gram.) Fall, m.; in ~, im Falle, falls; in any ~, auf jeden Fall; if that is the ~, wenn das der

Fall ist; v.t. überziehen, beschlagen (with mit).

casement, Fensterflügel, m.

cash, sb. bares Geld, n., Barschaft, f.; (book-keeping) Kasse, f.; v.t. einwechseln; zu Gelde machen; ~book, Kassabuch, n.; ~ier, sb. Kassierer, m.; v.t. (mil.) kassieren, entlassen.

casing, Futteral, Gehäuse, n.

casino, Kasino, n.

cask, Faß, n.; Tonne, f.

casket, Schmuckkästchen, n.

cassock, Soutane, f.

cassowary, Kasuar, m.

cast, sb. (throw) Wurf, m.; (theatr.) Rollenbesetzung, Rollenverteilung, f.; (shade) Nuance, f.; (metal, &c.) Guß, m.; Form, f.; v.t. (throw) (aus-, weg-) werfen; (metal, &c.) gießen; (theatr.) (Rollen) verteilen; ~ aside, away, wegwerfen; ~down, niederwerfen; ~ off, (naut.) losmachen; (clothes) ablegen; ~ out, austreiben, verstoßen; ~ anchor, Anker werfen; ~ lots, das Los ziehen; ~away, Schiffbrüchige(r); Verworfene(r); ~ing, (metal) Gießen, n., Guß, m.; ~ing-vote, entscheidende Stimme, f.; ~ iron, Gußeisen, n.; ~off, abgeworfen, abgelegt.

castanet, Kastagnette, f.

caste, Kaste, f.

castigat|e, züchtigen; ~ion, Züchtigung, f.

castle, Schloß, n.; Burg, f.; (chess) Turm, m.

castor[1], (pharm.) Bibergeil, n.

castor[2], (for sugar, salt, &c.) Streubüchse; (wheel) Laufrolle, f.; ~sugar, Streuzucker, m.

castor oil, Rizinusöl, n.

castrat|e, kastrieren; ~ion, Verschneidung, f.

casual, ~ly, zufällig, gelegentlich; ~ labourer, Gelegenheitsarbeiter, m.; ~ties, Verluste, m.pl.; ~ty, Todesfall, Unfall, m.

cat, Katze, f.; tom~, Kater, m.; ~burglar, Fassadenkletterer, m.; ~fish, Seewolf, m.; ~gut, Darmsaite, f.; ~'s-paw, (fig.) Gefoppte(r); Werkzeug, n.

cataclysm, Überschwemmung, *f.*; Sintflut, *f.*

catacomb, Katakombe, *f.*

catalep|sy, Katalepsie, Starrsucht. *f.*; ~tic, starrsüchtig.

catalogue, *sb.* Katalog, *m.*; Verzeichnis, *n.*; *v.t.* katalogisieren.

catapult, Katapult. *m.* or *n.*; *v.t.* abschießen, abschleudern.

cataract, Wasserfall; (*med.*) Star, *m.*

catarrh, Katarrh. *m.*

catastroph|e, Katastrophe, *f.*; ~ic, katastrophal.

catch, *sb.* (*ball*) Fang, *m.*; (*fish*) Zug, Fang, *m.*; (*fastening*) Klinke, *f.*; Haken. *m.*; (*trick*) Falle, Schlinge. *f.*; (*marriage*) gute Partie; *v.t.* fangen; (*disease*) bekommen; ~ cold, sich erkälten; ~ a train, den Zug erreichen; ~ up, einholen; ~ing, ansteckend; ~word, Schlagwort, *n.*

catechism, Katechismus, *m.*

categor|y, Kategorie, Klasse, *f.*; ~ical(ly), kategorisch, unbedingt.

cater, Lebensmittel anschaffen, einkaufen; (*fig.*) sorgen für; ~er, Lieferant, *m.*

caterpillar, Raupe, *f.*; ~-wheel, Raupenrad, *n.*

cathedral, Dom, *m.*

cathode, Kathode, *f.*

catholic, *a.* katholisch; *sb.* Katholik, *m.*; ~ism, Katholizismus, *m.*

catkin, (*bot.*) Kätzchen, *n.*

cattle, Vieh, Rindvieh, *n.*; ~-breeding, Viehzucht, *f.*; ~-dealer, Viehhändler, *m.*; ~-plague, Rinderpest, *f.*; ~-show, Viehausstellung, *f.*; ~-truck, Viehwagen, *m.*

cauldron, Kessel, *m.*

cauliflower, Blumenkohl, *m.*

caus|e, *sb.* Ursache, *f.*; Grund, *m.*; *v.t.* verursachen; ~al, ursächlich.

causeway, Bürgersteig. *m.*; Chaussee, *f.*

caustic, ätzend; (*fig.*) beißend; ~ potash, Ätzkali, *n.*; ~ soda, Ätznatron, *n.*

cauterize, ausbrennen, ätzen.

caution, *sb.* Vorsicht; Warnung, *f.*; *v.t.* warnen.

cautious, ~ly, vorsichtig, behutsam; ~ness, Vorsicht; Behutsamkeit, *f.*

cavalcade, Reiterzug. *m.*, Kavalkade, *f.*

cavalier, Kavalier, Ritter, *m.*

cavalry, Kavallerie, Reiterei, *f.*; ~ soldier, Kavallerist, *m.*

cave, *sb.* Höhle, *f.*; *v.i.* ~ in, einsinken; weichen; ~rn, Höhle. *f.*

caviar, Kaviar, *m.*

cavil, ~ at, spitzfindig tadeln; ~ling, Spitzfindigkeit, *f.*

cavity, Höhlung, *f.*

caw, krächzen.

cease, aufhören, nachlassen; ~less, unaufhörlich.

cedar, Zeder, *f.*

cede, abtreten (*to* an).

ceiling, Decke; (*av.*) Steighöhe; (*weather*) Wolkenhöhe, *f.*; (*price*) Höchstpreis, *m.*

celandine, Schellkraut, *n.*; *lesser* ~, Feigwurz, *f.*

celebrat|e, feiern, preisen; ~ed, berühmt; ~ion, Feier, *f.*

celebrity, Berühmtheit; berühmte Person *f.*

celery, Sellerie, *m.* or *f.*

celestial, himmlisch.

celiba|te, unverheiratet; ~cy, Zölibat, *m.* or *n.*

cell, Zelle, *f.*; (*electr.*) Element, *n.*

cellar, Keller, *m.*

cello, Cello, *n.*

cellular, zellig, zellenförmig.

celluloid, Zelluloid, *n.*

cellulose, Zellulose, *f.*; Zellstoff, *m.*

Celt, Kelte, *m.*; ~ic, keltisch.

cement, *sb.* Zement, Kitt, *m.*; *v.t.* verkitten.

cemetery, Friedhof, Kirchhof, *m.*

cenotaph, Ehren(grab)mal, *n.*

censer, Rauchfaß, *n.*

censor, *sb.* Zensor, *m.*; *v.t.* zensieren; ~ious(ly), tadelsüchtig; ~ship, Zensur, *f.*

censure, *sb.* Verweis, Tadel, *m.*; *v.t.* tadeln, verurteilen.

census, Volkszählung, *f.*

centenary, Hundertjahrfeier, Zentenarfeier, *f.*

centi|gramme, Zentigramm. *n.*;

~metre, Zentimeter, n.; ~pede, Tausendfuß, m.

central, ~ly, zentral; im Mittelpunkte befindlich; ~ heating, Zentralheizung, f.; ~ize, zentralisieren.

centre, sb. Zentrum, n.; Mittelpunkt, m.; v.i. im Mittelpunkte ruhen; sich gründen auf; ~forward, Mittelstürmer, m.; ~ of gravity, Schwerpunkt, m.

centri|fugal, zentrifugal; ~petal, zentripetal.

century, Jahrhundert, n.

ceramic, keramisch; ~s, Keramik, f.

cereal, Getreide-; ~s, Zerealien, pl.; Kornfrüchte, f.pl.

ceremon|ial, ~ially, förmlich, zeremoniell; ~ious(ly), feierlich, zeremoniös; ~y, Zeremonie, Feierlichkeit, Förmlichkeit, f.

certain, ~ly, gewiß, sicher; ~ty, Gewißheit, f.

certificate, Bescheinigung, f.; Zeugnis, n.

certify, bezeugen, bescheinigen.

cesspool, Senkgrube, f.; (fig.) Sündenpfuhl, m.

chafe, wund reiben; (fig.) sich ärgern (at über).

chaff, sb. Spreu; (banter) Neckerei, f.; v.t. necken.

chaffinch, Buchfink, m.

chain, sb. Kette f.; v.t. anketten; ~smoker, Kettenraucher, m.

chair, Stuhl, Sessel, m. (professorship) Lehrstuhl, m.; ~lift, Sesselbahn, f.; ~man, ~woman, Vorsitzende(r).

chalice, Kelch, m.

chalk, Kreide, f.; ~y, kreidig.

challenge, sb. Herausforderung, f.; (mil.) Anruf, m.; v.t. herausfordern; (mil.) anrufen; ~r, Herausforderer, m.

chamber, Zimmer, n.; Kammer, f.; ~lain, Kammerherr, m.; ~maid, Zimmermädchen, n.

chameleon, Chamäleon, n.

chamois, Gemse, f.; ~(leather), Sämischleder, n.

champagne, Champagner, m.

champion, sb. Verfechter; (sport) Meister, m.; v.t. verteidigen;

~ship, Meisterschaft, f.

chance, sb. Zufall, m., Glück, n.; Aussicht, f.; by ~, zufällig, von ungefähr; v.i. sich ereignen, sich zutragen; v.t. versuchen, wagen.

chancel, Chor, m. or n.

chancellery, chancery, Kanzlei, f.

chancellor, Kanzler, m.

chandelier, Arm-, Kron- leuchter, m.

change, sb. Veränderung, f.; Wechsel, m.; (cash) Kleingeld, n.; v.t. (ver)ändern; wechseln; v.i. sich ändern; (trains) umsteigen; ~able. veränderlich.

channel, Kanal, m., Fahrwasser, n.

chant, sb. Gesang, m.; v.t. singen.

chao|s, Chaos, n., Wirrwarr, m.; ~tic, chaotisch.

chap, sb. (person) Kerl; (in the skin) Riß, m.; v.i. Risse bekommen, aufspringen.

chapel, Kapelle, f.

chaperon, sb. Anstandsdame, f.; v.t. begleiten, (colloq.) bemuttern.

chaplain, Kaplan; (mil.) Feldprediger, m.

chapter, Kapitel, n.

char, verkohlen.

char(woman), Scheuerfrau, f.

character, Charakter, m.; (letter) Buchstabe, m.; (role) Rolle, f.; (testimonial) Zeugnis, n.; ~istic, sb. Merkmal, n.; a. charakteristisch; ~ize, charakterisieren, bezeichnen; ~ization, Charakterisierung, f.

charade, Scharade, f.

charcoal, Holzkohle, f.; ~burner, Köhler, m.

charge, sb. (price) Preis, m.; (gun, electr.) Ladung, f.; (attack) Angriff, m.; (legal) Anklage, f.; (care) Aufsicht, f.; free of ~, unentgeltlich; v.t. (load) laden; (accuse) anklagen; (commission) beauftragen; (prices) fordern, verlangen; (commerc.) anrechnen, debitieren; (mil.) angreifen.

chariot, Triumphwagen, m.; ~eer, Wagenlenker, m.

charit|able, ~ably, wohltätig, milde; ~y, Mildtätigkeit, f.; Almosen, n.

charlatan, Scharlatan, Markt-schreier, *m.*

charm, *sb.* Zauber, Reiz, *m.*; Zauber -mittel, *n.*, -formel, *f.*; *v.t.* bezaubern, entzücken; ~ing, reizend.

charnel-house, Beinhaus, *n.*

chart, Seekarte; Tabelle, *f.*

charter, *sb.* Urkunde, *f.*; *v.t.* (*ship, aircraft*) chartern; ~-flight, Charterflug, *m.*

charly, ~ily, sorgsam; karg.

chase, *sb.* Jagd, *f.*; (*typ.*) Rahmen, *m.*; *v.t.* jagen, verfolgen; (*metals*) ziselieren.

chasm, Kluft, *f.*; Abgrund, *m.*

chassis, (Fahr)gestell, *n.*

chaste, ~ly, keusch.

chasten, züchtigen; reinigen.

chastise, züchtigen, bestrafen; ~ment, Züchtigung, *f.*

chastity, Keuschheit, *f.*

chat, *sb.* Plauderei, *f.*; *v.i.* plaudern.

chatter, *sb.* Geschwätz, Geschnatter, *n.*; *v.i.* schwatzen, schnattern; (*birds*) zwitschern; (*teeth*) klappern; ~box, Plappermaul, *n.*; ~er, Schwätzer, *m.*

chauffeur, Chauffeur, Fahrer, *m.*

cheap, ~ly, billig; ~ness, Billig-keit, *f.*

cheat, *sb.* (*act*) Betrug; (*person*) Betrüger, *m.*; *v.t.* betrügen.

check, *sb.* Hindernis, *n.*, Ein-schränkung, *f.*; Kontrolle, *f.*; (*chess*) Schach, *n.*; *v.t.* hemmen, aufhalten; kontrollieren, nach-prüfen; (*chess*) Schach bieten; ~(ed), (*pattern*) kariert; ~mate, *sb.* Schachmatt, *n.*; *v.t.* matt setzen.

cheek, Backe, Wange, *f.*; (*fam.*) Frechheit, *f.*; ~y, frech.

cheer, *sb.* (*applause*) Beifallsruf, *m.*; Lebehoch, *n.*; (*hospitality*) Be-wirtung, *f.*; *of good* ~, guten Mutes; *v.t.* aufmuntern; (*applaud*) mit Beifall begrüßen; *v.i.* Beifall rufen; ~ful(ly), ~y, fröhlich, munter; ~fulness, ~iness, Munterkeit, Heiterkeit, *f.*; ~less, mutlos; freudlos.

cheese, Käse, *m.*; ~monger, Käse-händler, *m.*; ~paring, knau-serig.

chef, (Küchen)chef, *m.*

chemical, chemisch; ~s, Chemi-kalien, *pl.*

chemise, Damenhemd, *n.*

chemist, (*scientist*) Chemiker; (*druggist*) Apotheker, *m.*; ~ry, Chemie, *f.*; ~'s shop, Apotheke, *f.*

cheque, Scheck, *m.*; ~-book, Scheckbuch, *n.*

cherish, pflegen, hegen.

cherry, Kirsche, *f.*; ~-brandy, Cherry Brandy, Kirschlikör, *m.*; ~-tree, Kirschbaum, *m.*

cherub, Cherub, *m.*; ~ic, Engel(s)-, engelhaft.

chess, Schach(spiel), *n.*; ~-board, Schachbrett, *n.*; ~-man, Schachfigur, *f.*

chest, (*box*) Kiste; (*person*) Brust, *f.*; ~ *of drawers*, Kommode, *f.*

chestnut, *sb.* Kastanie, *f.*; *a.* kastanienbraun.

chew, kauen; ~ing-gum, Kau-gummi, *n.*

chick(en), Hühnchen, Küken, *n.*; ~-pox, Windpocken, *f.pl.*

chicory, Zichorie, *f.*

chide, schelten, tadeln.

chief, *sb.* (*of tribe*) Häuptling, *m.*; (*official*) Chef, *m.*; *a.* (*person*) Ober-; (*things*) hauptsächlich; ~ly, hauptsächlich; ~tain, Häuptling, *m.*

chilblain, Frostbeule, *f.*

child, Kind, *n.*; *with* ~, schwanger; ~birth, Gebären, *n.*; Nieder-kunft, *f.*; ~hood, Kindheit, *f.*; ~ish(ly), kindisch; ~less, kin-derlos; ~like, kindlich; ~'s play, Kinderspiel, *n.*

chill, *sb.* Erkältung, *f.*; Schauer, *m.*; *a.* frostig; kühl; *v.t.* kalt machen; mutlos machen; ~y, frostig, etwas kalt; ~iness, Kälte, *f.*; Schauer, *m.*

chime, *sb.* Glockenspiel, Glocken-geläute, *n.*; *v.i.* läuten; *v.i.* klingen.

chimera, Hirngespinst, *n.*; ~ical, schimärisch, eingebildet.

chimney, Schornstein; Kamin; (*lamp*) Zylinder, *m.*; ~-piece, Kaminsims, *m.* or *n.*; ~-pot, Schornsteinaufsatz, *m.*; ~-sweep, Schornsteinfeger, *m.*

chimpanzee, Schimpanse, *m.*

chin, Kinn, *n.*

china, Porzellan, *n.*

Chinese, *a.* chinesisch; *sb.* (*person*) Chinese, *m.*; Chinesin, *f.*; (*language*) Chinesisch, *n.*; ~lantern, Lampion, *m.*

chink, Ritze, *f.*

chintz, Zitz, Möbelkattun, *m.*

chip, *sb.* Span, *m.*; Schnitzel, *m.* or *n.*; *v.t.* schnitzeln; ~ped, (*china*, &c.) angeschlagen.

chiropod|y, Hand- und Fußpflege, *f.*; ~ist, Hühneraugenoperateur, *m.*

chirp, *sb.* Gezwitscher, *n.*; *v.i.* zwitschern.

chisel, *sb.* Meißel, *m.*; *v.t.* meißeln.

chivalr|ous, ritterlich; ~y, Ritterschaft; Ritterlichkeit, *f.*

chive, Schnittlauch, *m.*

chlor|ate, Chlorat, *n.*; ~ide, Chlorid, *n.*; ~ine, Chlor, *n.*; ~oform, *sb.* Chloroform, *n.*; *v.t.* chloroformieren.

chocolate, Schokolade, *f.*; Praline, *f.*; Praliné, *n.*

choice, *sb.* Wahl; (*assortment*) Auswahl, *f.*; *a.* auserlesen; (*language*) gewählt.

choir, Chor, *m.*

choke, ersticken, (er)würgen.

cholera, Cholera, *f.*

choose, wählen; vorziehen.

chop, *sb.* (*piece*) Stück, *n.*, Scheibe, *f.*; (*meat*) Kotelett(e, *f.*), *n.*; *v.t.* hauen, hacken, spalten; ~ up, kleinhacken; ~per, Hackmesser, *n.*; ~stick, Eßstäbchen, *n.*

chord, (*string*) Saite, *f.*; (*mus.*) Akkord, *m.*

chorister, Chorsänger, *m.*

chorus, Chor, *m.*

Christ, Christus, *m.*

christen, taufen; ~ing, Taufe, *f.*

Christendom, Christenheit, *f.*

Christian, *sb.* Christ, *m.*; *a.* christlich; ~ity, Christentum, *n.*; ~ize, zum Christentum bekehren; ~ name, Vorname, *m.*; ~ Science, Christliche Wissenschaft.

Christmas, Weihnacht(en), *f.*; ~-box, Weihnachtsgeschenk, *n.*; ~ carol, Weihnachtslied,

n.; ~ Day, Weihnachtstag, *m.*; ~ Eve, heiliger Abend; ~ tree, Weihnachtsbaum, *m.*

chromium, Chrom, *n.*

chronicle, *sb.* Chronik, *f.*; *v.t.* aufzeichnen; Chronicles, (O.T.) Chronika, *f.*

chronolog|y, Chronologie, Zeitrechnung, *f.*; ~ical(ly), chronologisch.

chronometer, Chronometer, *n.*

chrysalis, Puppe, *f.*

chrysanthemum, Chrysanthemum, *n.*

chubby, pausbäckig.

chuckle, kichern.

chum, Kamerad, *m.*

chunk, Klumpen, *m.*

church, Kirche, *f.*; Church of England, die anglikanische Kirche; ~warden, Kirchenvorsteher, *m.*; ~yard, Kirchhof, *m.*

churl, Grobian, *m.*; ~ish(ly), grob; ~ishness, Grobheit, *f.*

churn, *sb.* Butterfaß, *n.* *v.t.* buttern; schütteln.

cicada, Zikade, *f.*

cider, Apfelwein, *m.*

cigar, Zigarre, *f.*; ~ette, Zigarette, *f.*

cinder, ausgebrannte Kohle, *f.*

cine-, Film-, Kino-.

cinema, Kino, *n.*; ~tograph, Kinematograph, *m.*

cinnamon, Zimt, *m.*

cipher, *sb.* Ziffer; Null; Geheimschrift, *f.*; *v.t.* chiffrieren.

circle, *sb.* Kreis, Ring, *m.*; *v.t.* umkreisen.

circuit, Umkreis, Kreislauf, *m.*; (*electr.*) Stromkreis, *m.*; Schaltung, *f.*; short ~, Kurzschluß, *m.*; ~ous, weitschweifig; einen Umweg machend.

circular, *a.* kreisförmig; *sb.* Rundschreiben, *n.*; ~ize, durch Rundschreiben benachrichtigen (*or* bekanntmachen).

circulat|e, *v.t.* verbreiten, in Umlauf bringen; *v.i.* sich verbreiten; (*blood*) kreisen; ~ing library, Leihbibliothek, *f.*; ~ion, Umlauf, *m.*; (*blood*) Kreislauf, *m.*; (*newspaper*) Auflage, *f.*

circumcis|e, beschneiden; ~ion, Beschneidung, *f.*

circumference, (Kreis)umfang, Umkreis, *m.*

circumflex, Zirkumflex, *m.*

circumlocution, Umschreibung, *f.*

circumspect, ~ly, vorsichtig, behutsam; ~ion, Vorsicht, *f.*

circumstance, Umstand, *m.*; (*pl.*) Verhältnisse, *n.pl.*; ~tial, umständlich.

circus, Zirkus, *m.*

cistern, Zisterne, *f.*; Wasserbehälter, *m.*

citadel, Festung, *f.*

cit|e, anführen; ~ation, Zitat, *n.*; Anführung, *f.*; (*law*) Vorladung, *f.*

citizen, Bürger, *m.*; ~ship, Bürgerrecht, *n.*

citron, Zitrusfrucht, *f.*

city, Stadt, *f.*

civet, Zibetkatze, *f.*

civic, bürgerlich.

civies, Zivilkleidung, *f.*

civil, ~ly, (*polite*) höflich; (*not mil.*) Zivil-; ~ servant, Staatsbeamte(r); ~ service, Staatsdienst, *m.*; ~ war, Bürgerkrieg, *m.*; ~ian, Zivilist, *m.*; ~ity, Höflichkeit, *f.*

civiliz|e, zivilisieren; ~ation, Zivilisation, Kultur, *f.*

claim, *sb.* Anspruch, *m.*; Forderung, *f.*; *v.t.* beanspruchen; fordern; reklamieren; ~ant, Anspruchsteller, Kläger, *m.*

clairvoyant, Hellseher(in, *f.*), *m.*

clamber, klettern.

clammy, kaltfeucht.

clamo|ur, *sb.* Geschrei, *n.*; *v.i.* schreien (*for* um, nach); ~rous, lärmend.

clamp, *sb.* Klammer, *f.*; *v.t.* mit Klammern befestigen.

clan, Stamm, *m.*; Sippe, *f.*

clandestine, ~ly, heimlich.

clang, Klang, Schall, *m.*

clap, *sb.* (of hands) Klatschen, *n.*; ~ of thunder, Donnerschlag, *m.*; *v.i.* klatschen.

claret, Rotwein, Bordeaux, *m.*

clarify, aufklären.

clari(o)net, Klarinette, *f.*

clash, *sb.* Geklirr, Gerassel, *m.*; (*fig.*) Widerstreit, *m.*; *v.i.* klirren; widerstreiten.

clasp, *sb.* Haken, *m.*; Spange, *f.*;

(*embrace*) Umarmung, *f.*; *v.t.* zuhaken; umarmen; ~-knife, Taschenmesser, *n.*

class, *sb.* Klasse, *f.*; ~ification, Einteilung (in Klassen), *f.*; ~ify, *v.t.* klassifizieren.

classic, ~al, *a.* klassisch; *sb.* Klassiker, *m.*; ~ism, Klassizismus, *m.*

clatter, *sb.* Gerassel, Getrappel, *n.*; *v.i.* klappern, rasseln.

clause, Klausel, *f.*; (*gram.*) Nebensatz, *m.*

claw, Klaue, Kralle, *f.*

clay, Ton, *m.*

clean, *a.* rein; sauber; *v.t.* reinigen; (*boots*) putzen; ~ly, reinlich; ~liness, Reinlichkeit, *f.*; ~se, reinigen; ~shaved, glatt rasiert.

clear, *a.* ~ly, klar, hell, rein; deutlich; (*free from*) frei; *keep* ~ *of,* sich fernhalten von; *v.t.* reinigen; (*weg*)räumen; springen über; (*prisoner*) freisprechen, lossprechen; (*debt*) tilgen, abtragen; *v.i.* hell, frei, werden; ~ *away,* wegräumen; ~ *out,* (*cupboard, &c.*) ausräumen; (*person*) ausreißen; ~ance, Aufräumung, *f.*; Bodenabstand, *m.*; (*customs*) Verzollung, *f.*; ~ance *sale,* Ausverkauf, *m.*; ~ing, (*in forest*) Lichtung, *f.*; ~ing *house,* Abrechnungsstelle, *f.*; ~ness, Klarheit, *f.*; (*distinctness*) Deutlichkeit, *f.*

cleav|e, *v.t.* spalten; *v.i.* festhängen (*to* an); ~age, Spalten, *n.*; Spalte, *f.*

clematis, Klematis, Waldrebe, *f.*

clemen|cy, Gnade, Milde, *f.*; ~t, gnädig, mild.

clench, fest zusammenpressen; (*teeth*) aufeinanderbeißen; (*fist*) ballen.

clergy, Geistlichkeit, *f.*; ~man, Geistliche(r).

clerical, (*eccles.*) geistlich; Schreib-; ~ *error,* Schreibfehler, *m.*

clerk, (*commerc.*) Kommis, *m.* (*law*) Schreiber, *m.*; *town*-~, Stadtsyndikus, *m.*

clever, ~ly, gescheit, gewandt; ~ness, Geschicklichkeit, Gewandtheit, *f.*

cliché, Klischee, *n.*

click, *sb.* Ticken, Knipsen, Einschnappen, *n.*; *v.i.* ticken, knacken, klappen.

client, Klient, Kunde, *m.*

cliff, Klippe, *f.*

climat|e, Klima, *n.*; **~ic**, klimatisch.

climax, Klimax, *f.*; Gipfelpunkt, *m.*

climb, klimmen, klettern, (er)steigen; **~** *down*, (*fig.*) nachgeben; **~er**, Kletterer, Steiger, *m.*; **~ing plant**, Schlingpflanze *f.*

cling, haften, hangen (*to* an).

clinic, Klinik, *f.*; **~al**, klinisch.

clip, *sb.* Klammer, *f.*, Halter, *m.*; (*for cartridges*) Einsteckmagazin, *n.*; *v.t.* beschneiden, scheren; (*ticket*) lochen; **~per**, Klipper, *m.*; **~ping**, Abfall; Ausschnitt, *m.*

cloak, *sb.* Mantel; Deckmantel, *m.*; *v.t.* bemänteln; **~-room**, Garderobe, *f.*; (*at railway station*) Gepäckaufbewahrungsraum, *m.*

clock, Uhr, *f.*; (*stocking*) Zwickel, *m.*; **~-dial**, **~-face**, Zifferblatt, *n.*; **~-maker**, Uhrmacher, *m.*; **~-work**, Uhrwerk, *n.*; *like* **~-work**, pünktlich wie eine Uhr.

clod, Kloß, Klumpen, *m.*; **~-hopper**, Tölpel, *m.*

clog, *sb.* (*wooden shoe*) Holzschuh, *m.*; *v.t.* hemmen, überladen; *v.i.* stocken, sich klemmen.

cloister, (*convent*) Kloster, *n.*; (*arch.*) Kreuzgang, *m.*

close[1], *sb.* Schluß, *m.*; *v.t.* (ver)schließen, zumachen; beendigen; *v.i.* sich schließen; endigen.

close[2], *a.*, **~ly**, eng; dicht; (*weather*) drückend, schwül; (*secret*) verschwiegen, verschlossen; (*miserly*) knauserig, geizig; (*attention*) gespannt; **~** *by*, dicht bei; **~** *time*, Schonzeit, *f.*; **~-fisted**, karg, filzig; **~ness**, Nähe; Verschlossenheit; Schwüle; Kargheit, *f.*; **~-up**, (*cinema*) Großaufnahme, *f.*

closet, Kabinett, *n.*; Abort, *m.*

clot, *sb.* Klümpchen, *n.*; *v.i.* gerinnen.

cloth, Zeug, Tuch, *n.*; Leinwand, *f.*; *lay the* **~**, den Tisch decken; *the* **~**, die Geistlichkeit.

clothe, (be-, ein-)kleiden.

clothes, Kleider, *n.pl.*; *bed-* **~**, Bettzeug, *n.*; *suit of* **~**, Anzug, *m.*; **~-line**, Wäscheleine, *f.*; **~-press**, Kleiderschrank, *m.*

clothing, Kleidung, *f.*

cloud, *sb.* Wolke, *f.*; *v.t.* verdunkeln; **~** *over*, sich bewölken; **~less**, unbewölkt; **~y**, (*sky*) bewölkt, bedeckt; (*liquid*) trüb.

clove, Gewürznelke, *f.*

clover, Klee, *m.*

clown, Clown, Hanswurst, *m.*; **~ish**, grob, bäuerisch.

cloy, überladen, sättigen.

club, *sb.* (*stick*) Keule, *f.*; (*society*) Klub, Verein, *m.*; (*golf*) Schläger, *m.*; *v.i.* sich vereinigen; beitragen; **~-foot**, Klumpfuß, *m.*; **~s**, (*cards*) Treff, Kreuz, *n.*

cluck, glucken.

clue, Spur, *f.*; Schlüssel, *m.*

clump, Klumpen, *m.*

clums|y, **~ily**, plump, ungeschickt; **~iness**, Plumpheit, Ungeschicklichkeit, *f.*

cluster, *sb.* Büschel, *m.* or *n.*; Traube, *f.*; Haufen, *m.*; *v.i.* in Büscheln wachsen; sich zusammenhäufen.

clutch, *sb.* Griff, *m.*; (*motor.*) Kuppelung, *f.*; *v.t.* greifen, packen.

coach, *sb.* Kutsche, *f.*; (*tutor*) Einpauker, *m.*; (*sport*) Trainer, *m.*; *v.t.* einpauken; (*sport*) trainieren; **~-box**, Kutschersitz, Bock, *m.*; **~-maker**, Wagenbauer, *m.*; **~-man**, Kutscher, *m.*

coagulate, gerinnen.

coal, *sb.* Kohle, *f.*; *v.i.* Kohlen einnehmen, bunkern; **~-face**, Streb, *m.*; **~-field**, Kohlen(-gebiet), *n.*; **~-mine**, **~-pit**, Kohlengrube, *f.*; **~-scuttle**, Kohlenkasten, *m.*; **~-seam**, Kohlenflöz, *n.*; **~-tar**, Kohlenteer, *m.*

coalesce, sich vereinigen, verschmelzen.

coarse, ~ly, grob; roh; ~ness, Grobheit, Roheit, f.

coast, Küste, f.; ~guard, Küstenwache, f.

coat, sb. Rock, m.; (animal's) Fell, n.; (paint) Überzug, m.; dress-~, Frack, m; ~ of arms, Wappenschild, n.; ~ of mail, Panzerhemd, n.; v.t. bekleiden; (be)streichen (with mit); ~hanger, Kleiderbügel, m.; ~ing, Anstrich, Überzug, m.; ~tail, Rockschoß, m.

coax, beschwatzen, schmeicheln.

cobalt, Kobalt, m.

cobbler, Schuster, m.

cobweb, Spinn(en)gewebe, n.

cocaine, Kokain, n.

cock, sb. Hahn; (hay) Haufen, m.; weather~, Wetterfahne, f.; v.t. (gun) spannen; (ears) spitzen; (tail) aufrichten; ~crow, Hahnenschrei, m.; ~fight, Hahnenkampf, m.; ~pit, Kampfplatz (m.) für Hähne (naut.) Raumdeck, n.; Lazarett, n.; (aeroplane) Führersitz, m.; ~sure, bombensicher, anmaßlich.

cockade, Kokarde, f.

cock-a-doodle-do, Kikeriki.

cockatoo, Kakadu, m.

cockchafer, Maikäfer, m.

cocked, aufgekrempelt; ~ hat, Dreimaster, m.

cockerel, junger Hahn.

cockle, sb. Herzmuschel, f. (bot.) Kornrade, f.; v.i. sich runzeln, sich falten.

cockroach, (Küchen)schabe, f.

cocktail, Cocktail, m.

coco|a, Kakao, m.; ~nut, Kokosnuß, f.

cocoon, Kokon, m.; Puppe, f.

cod, ~fish, Kabeljau, m.; ~liver oil, Lebertran, m.

coddle, verzärteln, verhätscheln.

code, sb. (laws) Gesetzbuch, n.; Schlüssel, m.; v.t. chiffrieren; ~word, Schlüsselwort, n.

coerc|e, zwingen; ~ion, Zwang, m.; ~ive, zwingend.

coffee, Kaffee, m.; ~berry, Kaffeebohne, f.; ~pot, Kaffeekanne, f.

coffer, Koffer, Kasten, m.

coffin, Sarg, m.

cog, Zahn, m.; ~wheel, Zahnrad, n.

cogen|t, zwingend; ~cy, Triftigkeit, f.

cogitat|e, erwägen, überlegen; ~ion, Überlegung, f.

cognate, verwandt.

cognizance, Erkenntnis, f.

cognomen, Beiname, m.

cohabit, zusammenleben, zusammenwohnen.

coheir, Miterbe, m.

coher|e, zusammenhängen; ~ence, Zusammenhang, m.; Kohäsion, f.; ~ent(ly), zusammenhängend.

cohesion, Zusammenhang, m.; Kohäsion, f.

coil, sb. Rolle, Spule; Windung, f.; ~ of rope, Rolle, f.; Tauwerk, n.; v.t. aufwickeln; (naut.) aufschießen.

coin, sb. Münze, f.; v.t. münzen, prägen; (words) erdenken; ~age, Geld, n.; Münzen, f.pl.; Prägung, f.; ~er, Münzer; Falschmünzer, m.

coincid|e, zusammentreffen, übereinstimmen; ~ence, Zusammentreffen, n., Übereinstimmung, f.

coke, Koks, m.

colander, Durchschlag, m.

cold, a., ~ly, kalt; gefühllos; sb. Kälte, Erkältung, f. Schnupfen, m. catch ~, sich erkälten; ~blooded, kaltblütig; gefühllos; ~ness, Kälte, f.; ~ storage, Lagerung (f.) im Kühlraum; put into ~ storage, kalt stellen, kühl lagern; ~ war, der kalte Krieg.

collaborat|e, zusammenarbeiten; ~ion, Mitwirkung, f.; ~or, Mitarbeiter, m.

collaps|e, sb. Zusammenfallen, n. Zusammenbruch, Einsturz, m.; v.i. zusammenfallen, einfallen; zusammenbrechen; ~ible, Falt-.

collar, Kragen, m.; (dog's) Halsband, n.; (horse's) Kumt, n.; ~bone, Schlüsselbein, n.

collate, vergleichen.

colleague, Kollege, m.

collect, sammeln; (taxes) erheben; ~ion, Sammlung, f.; (money)

Kollekte, *f.*; ~ive, gesamt; ~ive *noun*, Kollektiv, *n.*; ~ively, insgesamt; ~or, Sammler, Steuereinnehmer, *m.*

college, Kollegium, *n.*; Hochschule, *f.*; Gymnasium, *n.*

collide, zusammenstoßen.

collier, Grubenarbeiter, *m.*; (*naut.*) Kohlenschiff, *n.*; ~y, Kohlenbergwerk, *n.*; Zeche, *f.*

collision, Zusammenstoß, *m.*

colloquial, in der Umgangssprache, Gesprächs-.

colon, Doppelpunkt, *m.*

colonel, Oberst, *m.*

colon|ial, Kolonial-; ~ist, Kolonist, *m.*; ~ize, kolonisieren, besiedeln; ~y, Kolonie, *f.*

colonnade, Säulengang, *m.*

colour, *sb.* Farbe, *f.*; (*fig.*) Vorwand, *m.*; *v.t.* färben, anstreichen; *v.i.* ~ up erröten; ~blind, farbenblind; ~ed, gefärbt; (*negro, &c.*) farbig; (*stary*) ausgeschmückt; ~ing, Färbung, *f.*; ~ing matter, Farbstoff, *m.*; ~less, farblos; ~s, (*mil.*) Fahne, (*naut.*) Flagge, *f.*; the national ~s, die Nationalfarben; with the ~s, unter der Fahne.

colt, Füllen, *n.*

columbine, Akelei, *f.*

column, Säule; (*type*) Spalte; (*mil.*) Kolonne, *f.*

coma, Schlafsucht, *f.*; ~tose, schlafsüchtig.

comb, *sb.* Kamm, *m.*; (*honey*) Wabe, Scheibe, *f.*; *v.t.* kämmen; (*horse*) striegeln.

combat, *sb.* Kampf, *m.*; Gefecht, *n.*; *v.t.* bekämpfen; ~ant, Kombattant, *m.*

combin|e, *sb.* Kartell, *n.*, Trust, *m.*; *v.t.* verbinden; *v.i.* sich verbinden; ~ation, Verbindung, *f.*; ~ations, (*garment*) Hemdhose, *f.*

combust|ible, *a.* brennbar, verbrennlich; *sb.* Brennstoff, *m.*; ~ion, Verbrennung, *f.*

come, kommen; (*become*) werden; ~ about, sich ereignen; ~ across, treffen; ~ by, erlangen, erwerben; ~ down, herunter-, herab-kommen; ~ for, abholen;

~ from, herkommen; herstammen; ~ in! Herein!; ~ off, herabfallen, loskommen; stattfinden, zustande kommen; ~ round, sich erholen; sich anders besinnen; ~ to, nach (*place*), zu (*person*)...kommen; (*amount to*) betragen; (*a decision*) einen Entschluß fassen; (*one's senses*) wieder zum Bewußtsein kommen; ~ under, unter den Titel (in die Rubrik) kommen; ~ undone, sich lösen, aufgehen; ~ up, heraufkommen; (*plants*) aufgehen; (*naut.*) Flagge, *f.*; ~r, Kommende(r); new ~r, Ankömmling, *m.*

comed|ian, Komödiant, *m.*; Komödiantin, *f.*; ~y, Komödie, *f.*, Lustspiel, *n.*; musical ~y, Operette, *f.*

comel|y, hübsch, anmutig; ~iness, Schönheit, Anmut, *f.*

comet, Komet, *m.*

comfort, *sb.* Trost, *m.*; Bequemlichkeit, *f.*; *v.t.* trösten; ~able, bequem; ~er, (*child's*) Lutscher, Schnuller, *m.*

comic(al), ~ly, komisch.

coming, *sb.* Ankunft, *f.*; ~-of-age, Mündigwerden, *n.*; *a.* künftig.

comma, Komma, *n.*; inverted ~s, Anführungszeichen, *n.pl.*

command, *sb.* Befehl, *m.*; (*of troops*) Oberbefehl, *m.*; *v.t.* befehlen; beherrschen; (*troops*) befehligen, anführen; ~ant, Kommandant, *m.*; ~eer, requirieren; ~er, Befehlshaber; (*nav.*) Fregattenkapitän, *m.*; ~er-in-chief, Oberbefehlshaber, *m.*; ~ing, (*mil.*) befehlshabend; dominierend; beherrschend; ~ment, Gebot, *n.*; ~o, Kommando, *n.*

commemorat|e, feiern; ~ion, Feier, *f.*

commence, anfangen; ~ment, Anfang, *m.*

commend, empfehlen, loben; ~able, empfehlenswert, lobenswert; ~ation, Empfehlung, *f.*, Lob, *n.*

comment, *sb.* Bemerkung, *f.* (*on* über); *v.i.* Bemerkungen machen; ~ary, Kommentar, *m.*; ~ator, Kommentator, *m.*

commerc|e, Handel, *m.*; ~ial,

Handels-; ~ial traveller, (Geschäfts)reisende(r).

commiserat|e, bemitleiden; ~ion, Mitleid, n.

commission, sb. (order) Auftrag, m.; (of crime, &c.) Begehung, Verübung, f.; (on sales) Provision, f.; (committee, inquiry, &c.) Kommission, f.; (mil.) Offiziers-patent, n.; (of ship) Indienst-stellung, f.; v.t. beauftragen, bevollmächtigen; in Dienst stellen; ein Offizierspatent erteilen; ~ of enquiry, Untersuchungs-kommission, f.; ~er, Kommissar, m.

commit, (give over to) übergeben; (crime) begehen; ~ to memory, sich einprägen; ~ to writing, zu Papier bringen; ~ment, Verhaftung; Begehung; Verpflichtung, f.

committee, Komitee, n., Ausschuß, m.

commode, Kommode, f.

commodious, ~ly, geräumig, bequem.

commodity, Ware, f.

common, a., ~ly, (person) gemein; (ordinary) gewöhnlich; (belonging to more than one) gemeinsam; ~market, der Gemeinsame Markt; ~ sense, gesunder Menschenverstand; ~ sb. Gemeindeweide, f.; ~ness, Gewöhnlichkeit, f.; ~place, sb. Gemeinplatz, m.; a. abgedroschen; ~s, die Gemeinen, m.pl.; House of C~s, Unterhaus, n.

commotion, Aufruhr, m.

commun|e, Kommune; Gemeinde; f.; ~al, Kommunal-; Gemeinde-.

communicant, Kommunikant, m.

communicat|e, v.t. mitteilen; v.i. (of rooms, etc.) in Verbindung stehen; (sacraments) das Abendmahl nehmen; ~ion, Mitteilung; Verbindung, f.; ~ive, gesprächig, mitteilsam.

communion, (sacraments) Abendmahl, n.; (religious body) Glaubensgemeinde, f.; ~ table, Abendmahlstisch, m.

commun|ism, Kommunismus, m.;

~ist, sb. Kommunist, m.; a. kommunistisch.

community, Gemeinde, f.

commute, v.t. (aus-, um-) tauschen; (a sentence) herabsetzen; v.i. (between two places) pendeln; ~er, Pendler, m.

compact, sb. Vertrag, m.; Puderdose, f.; a. kompakt, dicht, fest; ~ness, Dichtigkeit, Festigkeit; Bündigkeit, f.

companion, Gefährte, Genosse, m.; ~ship, Gesellschaft; Begleitung, f.; ~ladder, Kajütentreppe, f.

company, Gesellschaft; (mil.) Kompanie, Abteilung; (ship's) Mannschaft, f.

comparative, a. vergleichend; sb. Komparativ, m.

compar|e, vergleichen; ~able, vergleichbar; ~ison, Vergleich, m. Vergleichung, f.

compartment, Abteilung, f.; (railway) Abteil, n.

compass, Umkreis; (mariner's) Kompaß; (of voice) Umfang, m.; point of the ~, Kompaßstrich, m.; pair of ~es, Zirkel, m.

compassion, Mitleid, n.; ~ate, mitleidig; ~ate leave, Sonder-urlaub, m.

compatible, vereinbar (with mit).

compatriot, Landsmann, m.

compel, zwingen.

compensat|e, entschädigen; ~ion, Entschädigung, f. (for für).

compete, konkurrieren, sich mitbewerben (for um).

competen|ce, Fähigkeit, f.; (income) Auskommen, n.; (law) Kompetenz, f.; ~t(ly), zuständig, kompetent; zulänglich.

competit|ion, Wettbewerb, m.; Konkurrenz, f.; Preisbewerbung, Preisausschreibung, f.; ~ive, wetteifernd; Konkurrenz-; ~or, Mitbewerber, Konkurrent, m.

compil|e, zusammentragen; ~ation, Sammlung, f.; Sammelwerk, n.; ~er, Kompilator, m.

complacen|t, selbstgefällig, selbstzufrieden; ~cy, Willfährigkeit, Nachgiebigkeit, f.

complain, sich beklagen; ~t,

Klage, Beschwerde, f.; (*illness*) Krankheit, f.

complement, Ergänzung,; (*mil., &c.*) volle Zahl, f.; ~ary, ergänzend.

complet|e, *a.*; ~ely, vollständig; vollkommen; vollendet; *v.t.* vollenden; vollständig machen; ~ion, Vollendung, f.

complex, *sb.* Komplex, *m.*; *a.* verwickelt; zusammengesetzt.

complexion, Gesichtsfarbe, f.; Teint, *m.*; (*fig.*) Aussehen, *n.*; Färbung, f.

complian|ce, Willfährigkeit, f.; *in* ~ *with*, gemäß; ~t, willfährig.

complicat|e, verwickeln; ~ion, Verwickelung, f.

complicity, Mitschuld, f.

compliment, *sb.* Gruß, *m.*, Kompliment, *n.*; *v.t.* beglückwünschen, gratulieren (*on* zu); ~ary, höflich; schmeichelhaft; ~ary ticket, Freikarte, f.

comply, nachgeben, sich fügen (*with dat.*).

component, Bestandteil, *m.*

compos|e, zusammensetzen; verfassen; (*type*) setzen; (*music*) komponieren; (*differences*) schlichten; ~ *oneself*, sich beruhigen; ~ed, (*person*) gelassen, ruhig; ~er, Verfasser, *m.*; (*music*) Komponist, *m.*; ~ing-machine, Setzmaschine, f.; ~ing-stick, Winkelhaken, *m.*; ~ite, zusammengesetzt; ~ition, Zusammensetzung, f.; (*essay*) Aufsatz, *m.*; (*mus.*) Komposition, f.; ~itor, (Schrift) setzer, *m.*

composure, Fassung, Gemütsruhe, f.

compound, *sb.* Zusammensetzung, f.; (*chem.*) Verbindung, f.; *v.t.* zusammensetzen; *a.* zusammengesetzt; ~ *interest*, Zinseszins, *m.*

comprehen|d, (*understand*) begreifen; (*include*) in sich begreifen; ~sion, Fassungskraft, f.; Begreifen, *n.*; ~sive, umfassend.

compress, *sb.* Kompresse, f.; *v.t.* zusammen -drücken, -pressen;

~ed air, Preßluft, f.; ~ion, Zusammendrückung, Pressung, f.; ~or, Preßluftmaschine, f.

comprise, umfassen.

compromise, *sb.* Kompromiß, *m.* or *n.*, Vergleich, *m.*; *v.t.* durch Vergleich beilegen (schlichten); ~ *oneself*, sich kompromittieren.

compuls|ion, Zwang, *m.*; ~ory, zwingend, Zwangs-.

compunction, Gewissensbisse, *m. pl.*

comput|e, berechnen; ~ation, Berechnung, f.; ~er, (Rechen)-gerät, *n.*, -maschine, f.

comrade, Kamerad, *m.*

concave konkav, hohl.

conceal, verbergen, verhehlen; ~ment, Verbergung, f.

concede, zugestehen; zugeben.

conceit, Dünkel, *m.*, Eingebildetheit, f.; ~ed, eingebildet.

conceiv|e, (*imagine*) begreifen; (*child*) empfangen, schwanger werden; ~able, begreiflich.

concentrat|e, *v.t.* zusammenziehen, konzentrieren, massieren, verdichten; *v.i.* sich konzentrieren (auf); ~ion, Konzentrierung, Konzentration, f.; ~ion camp, Konzentrationslager, *n.*

conception, (*idea*) Begriff, *m.*, Vorstellung, f.; (*of women*) Empfängnis, f.

concern, *sb.* (*matter*) Angelegenheit, f.; (*anxiety*) Sorge, f.; (*share*) Anteil, *m.*; (*importance*) Belang, *m.*, Wichtigkeit, f.; (*business*) Geschäft, *n.*, Firma, f.; *v.t.* betreffen, angehen; ~ed, besorgt, bekümmert; interessiert; ~ing, betreffend.

concert, *sb.* Verabredung, f.; (*mus.*) Konzert, *n.*; *v.t.* verabreden.

concertina, Ziehharmonika, f.

concerto, Konzert, *n.*

concession, Erlaubnis, Bewilligung; (*govt.*) Konzession, f.

conciliat|e, versöhnen; ~ion, Versöhnung, f.

concise, ~ly, kurz, gedrängt; ~ness, Kürze, Gedrängtheit, f.

conclude, schließen; folgern.

conclus|ion, (*end*) Schluß, *m.*;

(logical) Folgerung, *f.;* ~ive, entscheidend.

concord, Eintracht; *(mus.)* Harmonie; *(gram.)* Kongruenz, *f.*

concrete, *sb.* Beton, *m.; a.* konkret; fest, dicht.

concur, übereinstimmen; ~rence, Übereinstimmung, *f.;* ~rent, übereinstimmend.

concussion, Erschütterung, *f.*

condemn, verdammen, verurteilen *(to zu);* ~ation, Verdammung, Verurteilung, *f.*

condens|e, *v.t.* verdichten, kondensieren; abkürzen; *v.i.* sich verdichten; ~ation, Verdichtung, Kondensation, *f.;* ~er, Kondensator, *m.*

condescen|d, sich herablassen, geruhen *(to zu);* ~sion, Herablassung, *f.*

condiment, Würze, *f.*

condition, *(state)* Zustand, *m.; (stipulation)* Bedingung, *f.;* ~al(ly), bedingt.

condol|e, Mitleid bezeigen, kondolieren *(with dat.);* ~ence, Kondolenz, *f.*

condone, verzeihen, vergeben.

conduc|e, dienen *(to zu),* förderlich sein *(to für);* ~ive, förderlich *(to* für).

conduct, *sb.* Benehmen, *n.; safe* ~, sicheres Geleit; *v.t.* führen *(liquids, electr., &c.)* leiten; *(escort)* begleiten; ~ion, Leitung, *f.;* ~or, Begleiter, *m.; (mus.)* Dirigent, *m.; (tram)* Schaffner, *m.; (electr.)* Leiter, *m.; lightning-*~or, Blitzableiter, *m.*

cone, Kegel, *m.; (fir)* Tannenzapfen, *m.*

confectioner, Zuckerbäcker, Konditor, *m.;* ~y, Zuckerwerk, *n.;* Konditorei, *f.*

confeder|acy, Bündnis, *n.;* Bund, *m.;* ~ate, Verbündete(r); ~ation, Bund, *m.*

confer, *v.t.* verleihen; *v.i.* sich besprechen; ~ence, Konferenz, Tagung, Versammlung, *f.;* ~ment, Verleihung, *f.*

confess, bekennen, gestehen; *(eccles.)* beichten; ~ion, Bekenntnis, Geständnis, *n.;*

Beichte, *f.;* ~ional, Beichtstuhl, *m.;* ~or, *(priest)* Beichtvater, *m.*

confid|e, (an)vertrauen; ~ant, Vertraute(r); ~ence, Vertrauen, *n.;* Zuversicht, *f.;* ~ent(ly), zuversichtlich; ~ential(ly), vertraulich, geheim.

confine, begrenzen, beschränken; einsperren; *to be* ~d, *(med.)* in den Wochen liegen; ~ment, Einsperrung, *f.,* Arrest, *m.; (woman)* Niederkunft, *f.*

confirm, bestätigen; *(eccles.)* konfirmieren, einsegnen; ~ation, Bestätigung, *f.; (eccles.)* Konfirmation, Firm(el)ung, *f.;* ~ed, unverbesserlich.

confiscat|e, beschlagnahmen, einziehen; ~ion, Beschlagnahme, Einziehung, *f.*

conflict, *sb.* Kampf, Streit, Konflikt, *m.; v.i.* in Widerspruch stehen *(with* mit); ~ing, (sich) widersprechend.

confluence, Zusammenfluß, *m.*

conform, sich richten *(to* nach), sich fügen *(dat.);* ~ity, Übereinstimmung, *f.;* in ~ity *with,* gemäß.

confound, verwirren; vernichten; verwechseln.

confront, gegenüber -stehen, -stellen; ~ation, Gegenüberstellung, *f.*

confus|e, verwirren; *(mistake)* verwechseln; ~ed, verwirrt; ~ion, Verwirrung; Unordnung, *f.*

confute, widerlegen.

congeal, gefrieren; gerinnen.

congenial, sympathisch, zusagend; gleichartig; angemessen.

congenital, angeboren.

conger, Meeraal, *m.*

congest|ed, verstopfen; überfüllen; ~ion, *(med.)* Blutandrang, *m.; (traffic)* Verkehrsstauung, *f.*

congratulat|e, gratulieren, beglückwünschen *(on zu);* ~ion, Glückwunsch, *m.*

congregat|e, sich versammeln; ~ion, Gemeinde, *f.*

congress, Kongreß, *m.*

congruous, angemessen, schicklich.

conic|al, konisch, kegelförmig; ~ section, Kegelschnitt, m.

conifer, Nadelholzbaum, m.

conjectur|e, sb. Mutmaßung, f.; v.t. mutmaßen; ~al, mutmaßlich.

conjugal, ehelich.

conjunction, (gram.) Konjunktion, f., Bindewort, n.

conjur|e, zaubern; jonglieren; ~er, Zauberer, Jongleur, m.; ~ing trick, Zauberstück, n.

connect, verbinden, vereinigen; ~ed, verbunden, verwandt; ~ingrod, Kuppel-, Treibstange, f.; ~ion, Zusammenhang, m.; Verbindung, f.; (pers.) Verwandte(r); (railway) Anschluß, m.

conning-tower, Kommandoturm, m.

conniv|e, übersehen, ein Auge zudrücken; ~ance, Nachsicht, f.; Einvernehmen, n.

connoisseur, Kenner, m.

conquer, (country) erobern; (enemy) besiegen; (fig.) überwinden; ~or, Eroberer, m.

conquest, Eroberung, f.; (fig.) Sieg, m.

consanguinity, Blutsverwandtschaft, f.

conscien|ce, Gewissen, n.; ~tious(ly), gewissenhaft; ~tious objector, (mil.) Dienstverweigerer, m.; ~tiousness, Gewissenhaftigkeit, f.

conscious, ~ly, bewußt; ~ness, Bewußtsein, n.

conscript, a. (mil.) ausgehoben, eingezogen; sb. Eingezogene(r); ~ion, Aushebung, Wehrpflicht, f.

consecrat|e, weihen; (ein)segnen; ~ion, Einsegnung, Einweihung, f.

consecutive, aufeinanderfolgend; (gram.) konsekutiv; ~ly, nacheinander.

consent, sb. Einwilligung (to zu) f.; v.i. einwilligen.

consequence, (result) Folge; (importance) Bedeutung, f.; in ~, folglich.

consequent, folgend; ~ly, folglich.

conservative, konservativ.

conservatory, Gewächshaus, n.

consider, überlegen, bedenken; berücksichtigen; ~able, beträchtlich; ~ate, rücksichtsvoll; ~ation, Betrachtung, Überlegung, Erwägung; Rücksichtnahme; (reward) Belohnung, f.; in ~ation of, mit Rücksicht auf; take into ~ation, in Erwägung ziehen; ~ing, in Anbetracht (with gen.).

consign, überweisen, übergeben; (goods) übersenden, konsignieren; ~ment, Übersendung, Konsignation, f.

consist, bestehen (of aus); ~ency, Festigkeit, Dichtigkeit; Folgerichtigkeit, Konsequenz, f.; ~ent(ly), konsequent; übereinstimmend (with mit).

consol|e, trösten; ~ation, Trost, m.

consonant, sb. Konsonant, Mitlaut, m.; a. übereinstimmend, harmonierend.

consort, sb. Gemahl(in, f.), m.; v.i. sich gesellen (with zu).

conspicuous, ~ly, deutlich, sichtbar; auffallend; hervorragend.

conspira|cy, Verschwörung, f.; ~tor, Verschwörer, m.

conspire, sich verschwören (against gegen).

constab|le, Schutzmann, Polizist, m.; ~ulary, Polizei, f.

constan|cy, Standhaftigkeit, Beständigkeit, ; f. ~t(ly), (faithful) treu; (continuous) anhaltend.

constellation, Konstellation, f.; Sternbild, n.

consternation, Bestürzung, f.

constipat|ed, verstopft; ~ion, Verstopfung, f.

constituency, Wahlkreis, m.

constituent, sb. (voter) Wähler; (part) Bestandteil, m.; a. ausmachend, wesentlich.

constitut|e, ausmachen, bilden; (appoint) ernennen; ~ion, (govt.) Verfassung; (body) (Körper-) beschaffenheit, Konstitution, f.; ~ional(ly), verfassungsmäßig.

constrain, zwingen; ~t, Zwang, m.

construct, erbauen, errichten; ~ion, Bau, m.; (gram.) Konstruktion, Wortfügung, f.; (math.) Zeichnung, f.

consul, Konsul, *m.*; ~ar, konsularisch; ~ate, Konsulat, *n.*

consult, *v.i.* sich beraten; *v.t.* zu Rate ziehen; (*doctor*) konsultieren; (*book*) nachschlagen (in); ~ation, (*med.*) Konsultation, Beratung, *f.*; ~*ation hours*, Sprechstunden, *f.pl.*; ~*ing room*, Sprechzimmer, *n.*

consume, verzehren; verbrauchen; ~r, Abnehmer, *m.*

consummat|e, *a.* vollendet; ~ion, Vollendung, *f.*

consumpt|ion, (*use*) Verbrauch, *m.*; (*med.*) Schwindsucht, *f.*; ~ive, schwindsüchtig.

contact, Berührung, *f.*; (*electr.*) Kontakt, *m.*

contagi|on, Ansteckung, *f.*; ~ious, ansteckend.

contain, enthalten; ~er, Behälter, *m.*

contaminat|e, verunreinigen, vergiften, besudeln; ~ion, Verunreinigung, Vergiftung, Besudelung, *f.*

contemplat|e, betrachten; beabsichtigen; ~ion, Betrachtung, *f.*; ~ive, beschaulich.

contemporary, *sb.* Zeitgenosse, *m.*; *a.* gleichzeitig, zeitgenössisch.

contempt, Verachtung, *f.*; ~ible, verächtlich; ~uous, verachtend.

contend, streiten; behaupten.

content, *a.* zufrieden (*with* mit); *v.t.* befriedigen; ~ment, Zufriedenheit, *f.*

content|ion, Streit, *m.*; *bone of* ~ion, Zankapfel, *m.*; ~ious, streitsüchtig; streitig.

contents, Inhalt, *m.*

contest, *sb.* Kampf, Streit, *m.*; *v.t.* bestreiten.

context, Zusammenhang, Wortlaut, *m.*

contigu|ity, Berührung, Nähe, *f.*; ~ous, angrenzend, nahe.

continen|ce, Enthaltsamkeit, *f.*; ~t(ly)[1], enthaltsam.

continent[2], Kontinent, *m.*, Festland, *n.*; ~al, kontinental.

continual, ~ly, fortwährend, ununterbrochen, anhaltend.

continuance, Fortdauer, *f.*

continuation, Fortsetzung, *f.*;

~ *school*, Fortbildungsschule, *f.*

continu|e, *v.t.* fortsetzen; *v.i.* fortfahren; beharren (*in* bei); ~ed, fortgesetzt; *to be* ~ed, (*story*) Fortsetzung folgt; ~ous(ly), ununterbrochen; fortlaufend.

contort|ed, (*features*) verzerrt; ~ion, Verzerrung, *f.*

contour, Umriß, *m.*; ~ *lines*, Konturlinien, *f.pl.*

contra, gegen, wider.

contraband, Schmuggelware, Konterbande, *f.*

contracept|ion, Empfängnisverhütung, *f.*; ~ive, empfängnisverhütendes Mittel.

contract, *sb.* Kontrakt, Vertrag, *m.*; *v.t.* (*shorten*) zusammenziehen; abkürzen; (*debts*) (Schulden) machen; (*marriage*) schließen; (*disease*) sich zuziehen; *v.i.* sich zusammenziehen; ~ion, Zusammenziehung, Abkürzung, *f.*; ~or, Bauunternehmer; Lieferant, *m.*

contradict, widersprechen; ~ion, Widerspruch, *m.*; ~ory, widersprechend.

contralto, Alt, *m.*, Altistin, *f.*

contrary, *sb.* Gegenteil, *n.*; *on the* ~, im Gegenteil; *a.* entgegengesetzt; ~ *to*, gegen; unvereinbar mit.

contrast, *sb.* Kontrast, Gegensatz, *m.*; *v.t.* (etwas einer Sache) entgegenstellen; *v.i.* abstechen (*with* gegen).

contravene, übertreten; ~tion, Übertretung, *f.*

contribut|e, beitragen; beisteuern; ~ion, Beitrag, *m.*; Beisteuer, *f.*; ~ive, beitragend; ~or, Beitragende(r), Mitarbeiter, *m.*; ~ory, beitragend.

contrit|e, zerknirscht, reuig; ~ion, Zerknirschung, Reue, *f.*

contriv|e, *v.t.* ersinnen, erdenken; *v.i.* fertig bringen (*to* zu); ~ance, Erfindung; Vorrichtung, Vorkehrung, *f.*

control, *sb.* Kontrolle, Aufsicht; Beherrschung, *f.*; *v.t.* kontrollieren, beaufsichtigen; beherrschen; ~ler, Kontrolleur,

Aufseher, Leiter, *m.*; ~s, Kontrollgestänge, *n.*

controvers|y, Streit, *m.*; Streitfrage, *f.*; ~ial, streitig; polemisch.

conundrum, Scherzrätsel, *n.*

convalescen|ce, Genesung, *f.*; ~t, *a.* genesend; *sb.* Genesende(r), Rekonvaleszent, *m.*

convene, *v.t.* zusammenberufen; vorladen; *v.i.* zusammenkommen.

convenien|ce, Bequemlichkeit; (*thing*) Annehmlichkeit, *f.*; ~t(ly), bequem, passend, gelegen; *if* ~t, wenn es . . . paßt.

convent, Nonnenkloster, *n.*

convention, Zusammenkunft, *f.*; (*treaty*) Vertrag, *m.*; (*custom*) Herkommen, *n.*, Brauch, *m.*; ~al(ly), herkömmlich, konventionell.

converge, zusammenlaufen (*on* auf); ~nt, konvergierend.

conversant, vertraut (mit); bewandert (in).

convers|e¹, *v.i.* sich unterhalten; reden; ~ation, Gespräch, *n.*, Unterhaltung, *f.*; ~ational, Unterhaltungs-.

converse², *a.*; ~ly, umgekehrt; *sb.* Gegenteil, *n.*

conversion, Umwandlung, Verwandlung, *f.* (*from* von ; *into* in); (*eccles.*) Bekehrung, *f.*

convert, *sb.* (Neu)bekehrte(r); umändern, verwandeln; umsetzen; (*eccles.*) bekehren; ~er, Umformer, *m.*; ~ible, umwandelbar; umsetzbar.

convex, konvex.

convey, führen, befördern; übertragen, übersenden; mitteilen; ~ance, Transport, *m.*; (*vehicle*) Wagen, *m.*, Fuhrwerk, *n.*; (*by deed*) Übertragung, *f.*; ~or, laufendes Band, Fließband, *n.*

convict, *sb.* Sträfling, Zuchthäusler, *m.*; *v.t.* überführen; für schuldig erklären; ~ion, Überzeugung, *f.*; (*prisoner*) Überführung, *f.*

convince, überzeugen.

convivial, festlich, gesellig.

convolvulus, Winde, *f.*

convoy, *sb.* Geleit, *n.*, Geleitzug,

m.; *v.t.* geleiten.

convuls|e, erschüttern; ~ion, Krampf, *m.*, Zuckung, *f.*; ~ive, krampfhaft.

coo, girren.

cook, *sb.* Koch, *m.*, Köchin, *f.*; *v.t.* kochen, zubereiten; ~er, (*stove*) Kocher, Herd, *m.*; ~ery, Kochkunst, *f.*

cool, *a.*, ~ly, kühl; kaltblütig; *v.t.* kühlen; *v.i.* erkalten; ~ness, Kühle; Kaltblütigkeit, *f.*

coop, *sb.* Hühnerkorb, *m.*; *v.t.* einsperren.

cooper, Böttcher, Küfer, *m.*

co-operat|e, mitwirken; ~ion, Mitwirkung, *f.*; ~ive society, Konsumverein, *m.*

co-ordinate, *a.* beigeordnet; *v.t.* beiordnen.

coot, Wasserhuhn, *n.*

cope¹, *sb.* Chorrock, *m.*

cope², *v.i.* ~ *with*, gewachsen sein (*with dat.*), fertigwerden mit.

copious, ~ly, reichlich, häufig.

copper, Kupfer, *n.*; Kupferkessel, *m.*; ~münze, *f.*; ~plate, Kupferstich, *m.*; ~smith, Kupferschmied, *m.*

coppice, copse, Unterholz, Gebüsch, *n.*

copulat|e, sich begatten; ~ion, Begattung, *f.*; Beischlaf, *m.*

copy, *sb.* Abschrift, Kopie, *f.*, Abdruck, *m.*; (*of book*) Exemplar, *n.*; *v.t.* kopieren, abschreiben; nachahmen; ~book, Schreibheft, *n.*; ~hold, Lehnsbesitz, *m.*; ~ing-ink, Kopiertinte, *f.*; ~right, Verlagsrecht, Urheber- recht, *n.*

coquet|te, kokettieren; ~ry, Gefallsucht, *f.*; ~te, Kokette, *f.*; ~tish, kokett.

coral, Koralle, *f.*

cord, Strick, *m.*, Schnur, *f.*; ~age, Tauwerk, *n.*; ~ed, geschnürt; gerippt.

cordial, *a.*, ~ly, herzlich; *sb.* Kräuterlikör, *m.*; ~ity, Herzlichkeit, *f.*

cordon, Ordensband, *n.*, Kordon, *m.*; Truppen-kordon, *m.*, -kette, *f.*

corduroy, Kord, *m.*; ~s, Manchesterhosen, *f. pl.*

core, Kern, *m.*, Mark, *n.*, Herz, *n.*

cork, *sb.* Kork, Stöpsel, *m.*; *a.* Kork-; *v.t.* verkorken; ~screw, Korkzieher, *m.*

cormorant, Kormoran, *m.*, Scharbe, *f.*

corn, Korn, Getreide, *n.*; (*on foot*) Hühnerauge, *n.*, Leichdorn, *m.*; ~crake, Wachtelkönig, *m.*; ~ed, eingesalzen; ~ed beef, Büchsenfleisch, *n.*; ~flour, Maismehl, *n.*; ~flower, Kornblume, *f.*

cornea, Hornhaut, *f.*

corner, *sb.* Ecke, *f.*, Winkel, *m.*; *v.t.* in die Enge treiben; aufkaufen; ~seat, Eckplatz, *m.*

cornet, (*mus.*) Kornett, *n.*; (*mil.*) Fähnrich, *m.*

cornice, Karnies, *n.*, Fries, *m.*; Schneewächte, *f.*

corollary, Folgesatz, *m.*

coronation, Krönung, *f.*

coronet, Adelskrone, *f.*

corporal, *sb.* Korporal, Unteroffizier, *m.*; *a.* körperlich, leiblich.

corporation, Körperschaft, Stadtbehörde, Innung, *f.*; (*slang, abdomen*) Schmerbauch, *m.*

corps, Korps, *n.*

corpse, Leichnam, *m.*

corpulen|ce, Beleibtheit, *f.*; ~t, beleibt.

correct, *v.t.* berichtigen, korrigieren; *a.*, ~ly, richtig, fehlerfrei; ~ion, Berichtigung; Verbesserung *f.*; *a.* ~ive, verbessernd; *sb.* Milderungsmittel, *n.*; ~ness, Richtigkeit, Genauigkeit, *f.*

correspond, korrespondieren; einen Briefwechsel führen (mit); entsprechen (*to, with dat.*); ~ence, Briefwechsel, *m.*; Übereinstimmung, *f.*; ~ent, Korrespondent, *m.*; ~ing, entsprechend.

corridor, Gang, Korridor, *m.*

corroborat|e, bestätigen; ~ion, Bestätigung, *f.*

corro|de, zerfressen; ~sion, Zerfressen, *n.*; ~sive, *a.* zerfressend, ätzend; *sb.* Ätzmittel, *n.*

corrugated, gewellt; ~ iron, Wellblech, *n.*

corrupt, *v.t.* verderben, bestechen,

verführen; *a.* verdorben, lasterhaft; bestechlich; ~ion, Verdorbenheit, Fäulnis, Bestechung, *f.*

corset, Schnürleib, *m.*, Korsett, *n.*

corundum, Korund, *m.*

corvette, Korvette, *f.*

cosmetic, *sb.* Schönheitsmittel, *n.*; *a.* kosmetisch.

cosmopolitan, *sb.* Weltbürger, *m.*; *a.* weltbürgerlich, kosmopolitisch.

Cossack, Kosak, *m.*

cost, *sb.* Kosten, *pl.*, Preis, *m.*; Aufwand, *m.*; *v.i.* kosten; ~ly, kostspielig; ~liness, Kostspieligkeit, *f.*

costermonger, Straßenverkäufer, *m.*

costume, Kostüm, *n.*

cos|y, ~ily, behaglich.

cot, Kinderbettchen, *n.*

cottage, (Bauern)hütte, *f.*; Landhaus, *n.*

cotton, Baumwolle, *f.*, Kattun, *m.*; ~mill, Baumwollspinnerei, *f.*; ~wool, Watte, *f.*

couch, *sb.* Lager; Liegesofa, *n.*

cough, *sb.* Husten, *m.*; *v.i.* husten.

council, Rat, *m.*; Ratsversammlung, *f.*; ~lor, Ratsherr, Stadtverordnete(r), *m.*

counsel, *sb.* Rat, *m.*; Beratschlagung, *f.*; (*lawyer*) Anwalt, Sachwalter, *m.*; *v.t.* raten; ~lor, Ratgeber; Sachwalter, *m.*

Count[1], *sb.* Graf, *m.*; ~ess, Gräfin, *f.*

count[2], *sb.* Summe, *f.*, Zählen, *n.*, Anklagepunkt, *m.*; *v.t.* zählen, rechnen; ~ on, auf jemanden zählen.

countenance, *sb.* Gesicht, *n.*; (*favour*) Gunst, *f.*; *v.t.* begünstigen, zulassen.

counter[1], *sb.* Ladentisch, Zahltisch, *m.*; (*in a game*) Spielmarke, *f.*

counter[2], *adv.* and *pref.* gegen.

counteract, entgegenwirken.

counter-attack, Gegenangriff, *m.*

counter-espionage, Abwehrdienst, *m.*

counterfeit, *v.t.* nachmachen, (*coin*) fälschen; *a.* nachgemacht, gefälscht.

counterfoil, Kontrollabschnitt, *m.*

countermand, sb. Gegenbefehl, m.; v.t. widerrufen; abbestellen.

counterpane, Steppdecke, f.

counterpart, Gegenstück, Gegenbild, n.

counterpoint, Kontrapunkt, m.

countersign, sb. Gegenzeichnung; Losung, f.; v.t. gegenzeichnen.

countless, unzählig.

country, sb. Land, n.; Gegend, Landschaft, f.; Vaterland, n.; a. ländlich, Land-; ~-house, ~-seat, Landhaus, n., Landsitz, m.; ~man, Landmann; (compatriot) Landsmann, m.

county, Grafschaft, f.

coupl|e, sb. Paar, n.; v.t. koppeln; verbinden; v.i. sich paaren; ~et, Reimpaar, n.; ~ing, Kupp(e)lung, f.; (electr.) Kopp(e)lung, f.

coupon, Coupon, Abschnitt, m.

courage, Mut, m., Tapferkeit, f.; ~ous(ly), mutig, tapfer.

course, (way) Lauf, Gang, m.; (naut., lectures, &c.) Kurs, m.; (at a meal) Gang, m.; (turn) Reihe, f.; in due ~, zu seiner Zeit, zur rechten Zeit; in the ~ of time, mit der Zeit; of ~, natürlich, selbstverständlich; take it's ~, seinen Lauf nehmen; ~r, Rennpferd, n.

court, sb. Hof, m.; (law) Gericht, n., Gerichtshof, m.; v.t. den Hof machen, freien, sich bewerben um; ~eous(ly), höflich, gefällig; ~esan, Kurtisane, f.; ~esy, Höflichkeit, f.; ~ier, Höfling, m.; ~ly, höfisch, vornehm; ~-martial, sb. Kriegsgericht, n.; v.t. vor ein Kriegsgericht stellen; ~ship, Liebeswerbung, f.; ~yard, Hof, m.

cousin, Vetter, m., Cousine, f.

covenant, Bündnis, n., Vertrag, m.

cover, sb. Decke, f.; (lid, book-cover, &c.) Deckel, m.; (knife and fork, &c.) Gedeck, n.; (mil.) Deckung, f.; (for chair, &c.) Überzug, m.; (shelter) Obdach, n.; (thicket) Gehölz, n.; (fig.) Vorwand, m.; v.t. bedecken; verbergen; schützen; (with a

gun) aufs Korn nehmen; ~let, Bettdecke f.

covet, begehren; ~ous(ly), begierig, habsüchtig; ~ousness, Begierde, f.

covey, Brut, f.; (of partridges) Volk, n.

cow, sb. Kuh, f.; v.t. einschüchtern; ~herd, Kuhhirt, m.; ~hide, Kuhhaut, f.; ~slip, Schlüsselblume, f.

coward, Feigling, m.; ~ice, Feigheit, f.; ~ly, feig(e).

cower, kauern.

cowl, Kapuze, Kutte, f.; (chimney) Schornsteinaufsatz, m.

coxcomb, Stutzer, m.

coxswain, Bootsführer, m.

coy, ~ly, schüchtern, spröde; ~ness, Sprödigkeit, f.

crab, Krabbe, f.; (apple) Holzapfel, m.; ~bed, mürrisch; (writing) unleserlich.

crack, sb. Riß, m., Spalte, f.; (noise) Knall, m.; v.t. spalten; (nuts) knacken; (whip) knallen; v.i. krachen, bersten, springen; a. ausgezeichnet, schneidig; ~ a joke, einen Witz machen; ~ regiment, schneidiges Regiment; ~ shot, ausgezeichneter Schütze; ~ up, anpreisen; ~-brained, verrückt; ~er, Knallbonbon, m.

crackl|e, knattern; knistern; ~ing, Geknister, n.

cradle, sb. Wiege, f.; v.t. einwiegen.

craft, (skill) Kunstfertigkeit, f.; (trade) Gewerbe, n.; (cunning) List, f.; (naut.) Schiff, Fahrzeug, n.; ~iness, Verschlagenheit, f.; ~sman, Handwerker, m.; ~y, ~ily, listig.

crag, Klippe, f., Fels, m.; ~gy, felsig.

cram, vollstopfen; (pupil) einpauken; ~mer, Einpauker, m.

cramp, Krampf, m.; ~ed, (for room) beengt.

cranberry, Krons-, Preisel- beere, f.

crane, sb. (bird) Kranich, m.; (hoist) Kran, m.; v.t. den Hals recken; ~'s-bill, (bot.) Storchschnabel, m.

cranium, Schädel, m.

crank, *sb.* (*mach.*) Kurbel, *f.*; (*person*) Original, *n.*; *v.t.* (*motor*) ankurbeln; ~-shaft, Kurbelwelle, *f.*; ~y, verschroben; exzentrisch.

cranny, Riß, *m.*

crape, Flor, Krepp, *m.*

crash, *sb.* Krach, *m.*; (*aircraft*) Absturz, *m.*; *v.i.* krachen; (*aircraft*) abstürzen; ~ helmet, Sturzhelm, *m.*; ~-landing, Bruchlandung, *f.*

crass, grob, kraß.

crate, Packkorb, *m.*

crater, Krater, *m.*

crav|e, *v.t.* flehen (*for* um), verlangen; ~ing, Verlangen (*for* nach), *n.*

craw, Kropf *m.*

crawl, kriechen; (*swimming*) kraulen; ~ with, wimmeln von.

crayfish, Krebs *m.*

crayon, Zeichenstift, *m.*

craz|e, Grille, Manie, *f.*; ~iness, Verrücktheit, *f.*; ~y, ~ily, verrückt.

creak, knarren.

cream, Rahm, *m.*, Sahne, *f.*; (*fig.*) das Beste; ~ery, Molkerei, *f.*; ~-laid, gelblichweißgerippt; ~y, sahnig.

crease, *sb.* Falte, *f.*; *v.t.* falten, kniffen.

creat|e, *v.t.* erschaffen; verursachen; ernennen; ~ion, Schöpfung, *f.*; ~ive, schöpferisch; or, Schöpfer, *m.*; ~ure, Geschöpf, *n.*; (*animal*) Tier, *n.*; (*pejorative*) Kreatur, *f.*

creden|ce, Glaube, *m.*; Beglaubigung, *f.*; ~tials, Empfehlungsschreiben, *n.*

credib|le, ~ly, glaubwürdig; ~ility, Glaubwürdigkeit, *f.*

credit, *sb.* Glaube, *m.*, Ehre, *f.*; (*commerc.*) Kredit, *m.*; *v.t.* glauben, trauen; kreditieren, gutschreiben; on ~, auf Kredit; to his ~, zu seinen Gunsten; letter of ~, Kreditbrief, *m.*; ~able, ~ably, lobenswert, rühmlich; ~or, Gläubiger, *m.*

credul|ity, Leichtgläubigkeit, *f.*; ~ous, leichtgläubig.

creed, Glaubensbekenntnis, *n.*, Glaube, *m.*

creek, kleine Bucht, *f.*

creel, Weiden-, Fisch- korb, *m.*

creep, kriechen, schleichen; *it makes one's flesh ~*, man bekommt eine Gänsehaut davon; ~er, Schlingpflanze, *f.*; ~y, gruselig.

cremat|e, einäschern, verbrennen; ~ion, Leichenverbrennung, *f.*; ~orium, Krematorium, *n.*

creosote, Kreosot, *n.*

crescent, Mondsichel, *f.*; (*fig.*) Halbmond, *m.*

cress, Kresse, *f.*

crest, Helmbusch, Helmschmuck, *m.*; (*bird's*) Haube, *f.*; (*cock's*) Kamm, *m.*; (*ridge*) Bergrücken, *m.*; ~fallen, niedergeschlagen.

crevasse, Gletscherspalte, *f.*

crevice, Riß, *m.*

crew, Mannschaft, Besatzung, *f.*

crib, *sb.* Krippe, *f.*; Kinderbett, *n.*; *v.i.* entwenden, (*colloq.*) klemmen.

cricket, (*zool.*) Grille, *f.*, Heimchen, *n.*; (*game*) Kricket, *n.*

crim|e, Verbrechen, *n.*; ~inal, *sb.* Verbrecher, *m.*; *a.* verbrecherisch, Kriminal-; ~inal law, Strafrecht, *n.*

crimson, *sb.* Karmesin, *n.*; *a.* karmesinrot.

cringe, sich krümmen, kriechen.

cripple, *sb.* Krüppel, *m.*; *v.t.* lähmen.

crisis, Krise, *f.*

crisp, (*pastry*) knusperig; (*hair*) kraus; (*air*) frisch.

criss-cross, kreuz und quer laufend.

criterion, Kennzeichen, Merkmal, *n.*

critic, Kritiker, *m.*; ~al, kritisch; tadelsüchtig; entscheidend; ~ism, Kritik, Rezension, *f.*; ~ize, kritisieren, (*books*) rezensieren.

croak, quaken, krächzen.

crochet, *sb.* Häkelei, *f.*; *v.i.* häkeln.

crockery, Töpferware, *f.*, Geschirr, *n.*

crocodile, Krokodil, *n.*; ~ tears, Krokodil(s)tränen, *pl.*

crocus, Krokus, *m.*

cron|e, altes Weib; ~y, Busenfreund, *m.*

crook, Haken; Hirtenstab; (*cheat*)

Schwindler, *m.*; ~ed, krumm, gewunden, schief.

crop, *sb.* (*bird's*) Kropf, *m.*; (*harvest*) Ernte, *f.*; *v.t.* abschneiden, ernten; (*feed*) abweiden; ~ **up**, *v.i.* auftauchen; ~**per**, Sturz, *m.*

croquet, Krocket, *n.*

cross, *sb.* Kreuz, *n.*; (*breed*) Kreuzung, *f.*; *a. and adv.* quer, kreuzweise; (*bad-tempered*) böse, verdrießlich; *v.t.* kreuzen; widersprechen; ~ **out**, ausstreichen; ~**bar**, Querholz, *n.*; (*football*) Torlatte, *f.*; ~**bow**, Armbrust, *f.*; ~**breed**, Mischrasse, *f.*; ~**country**, Gelände-; ~**examination**, Kreuzverhör. *n.*; ~**examine**, einem Kreuzverhör unterziehen; ~**grained**, querfaserig; (*fig.*) störrisch; ~**ing**, (*street, railway*) Übergang, *m.*; (*of animals*) Kreuzung, *f.*; (*by sea*) Überfahrt, *f.*; ~**purposes**, Mißverständnis, *n.*; *to be at* ~*purposes*, aneinander vorbeireden; ~**road**, Kreuzweg, *m.*; ~**roads**, Straßenkreuzung, *f.*; ~**ways**, ~**wise**, kreuzweise; ~**word** **puzzle**, Kreuzworträtsel, *n.*

crouch, sich (nieder)ducken; sich zusammenkauern.

croup, (*horse*) Kruppe, *f.*; (*med.*) Halsbräune, *f.*

crow, Krähe, *f.*; ~**bar**, Brecheisen, *n.*; ~**'s-feet**, Krähenfüße, *m.pl.*

crowd, *sb.* Haufen, *m.*, Gedränge, *n.*; *v.* (sich) drängen.

crown, *sb.* Krone, *f.*; (*of head*) Scheitel, *m.*; (*of hat*) Kopf, *m.*; *v.t.* krönen; ~**prince**, Kronprinz, *m.*

crucial, kritisch, entscheidend.

crucible, Schmelztiegel, *m.*

crucif|ix, Kruzifix, *n.*; ~**ixion**, Kreuzigung, *f.*; ~**y**, kreuzigen.

crude, ~**ly**, roh, unreif; ~**ness**, Rohheit, Unreife, *f.*

cruel, ~**ly**, grausam; ~**ty**, Grausamkeit, *f.*

cruet, Menage, *f.*

cruis|e, *sb.* Seefahrt, *f.*; *v.* kreuzen; (*nav.*) marschieren; ~**er**, Kreuzer, *m.*; ~**ing-speed**, (*nav.*) Marschfahrt, *f.*

crumb, Krume, *f.*

crumble, zerbröckeln.

crumple, zerdrücken, zerknüllen.

crunch, zerkauen; zermalmen.

crusade, Kreuzzug, *m.*; ~**r**, Kreuzfahrer, *m.*

crush, (zer)quetschen, zerdrücken; unterdrücken.

crust, (*bread*) Kruste; (*earth*) Erdrinde, *f.*; ~**y**, (*person*) mürrisch.

crutch, Krücke, *f.*

cry, *sb.* Geschrei, *n.*, Aus-, Zu-ruf, *m.*; *v.* (*shout*) schreien; (*weep*) weinen; ~ **down**, in schlechten Ruf bringen; ~ **off**, sich lossagen (von).

crypt, Gruft, Krypta, *f.*

crystal, *sb.* Kristall, *m.*; *a.* kristallen; ~**lize**, kristallisieren; ~**lization**, Kristallisation, *f.*

cub, Junge, *n.*

cub|e, Würfel, Kubus, *m.*; ~**e** **root**, Kubikwurzel, *f.*; ~**ic**, kubisch.

cubicle, Schlafraum, *m.*

cuckold, Hahnrei, *m.*

cuckoo, Kuckuck, *m.*

cucumber, Gurke, *f.*

cud, *chew the* ~, wiederkäuen.

cuddle, herzen, liebkosen.

cudgel, Knüttel, *m.*

cue, (*billiards*) Queue, *n.*, Billardstock, *m.*; (*theat.*) Stichwort, *n.*

cuff, (*blow*) Faustschlag, *m.*; (*dress*) Manschette, *f.*, Aufschlag, *m.*

culinary, zur Küche gehörig, Koch-.

cull, aussuchen, auslesen.

culminat|e, kulminieren, gipfeln; ~**ion**, Gipfelpunkt, *m.*

culpab|le, strafbar, schuldig; ~**ility**, Strafbarkeit, Schuld, *f.*

culprit, Verbrecher, *m.*, Schuldige(r), Angeklagte(r).

cult, Kultus, *m.*

cultivat|e, (*land*) anbauen; (*flowers*) ziehen; (*fig.*) ausbilden, pflegen; ~**ion**, Anbau, *m.*; Ziehen, *n.*; Pflege, *f.*

culture, Anbau, *m.*, Kultur, Bildung, *f.*; ~**al**, kulturell, Kultur-.

culvert, Abzugskanal, *m.*

cumbersome, **cumbrous**, lästig, beschwerlich.

cumulative, (an)häufend ; Zusatz-.

cunning, *sb.* List, Schlauheit ; Geschicklichkeit, *f.*; *a.*, ~ly, listig, schlau ; geschickt.

cup, Tasse, *f.*; (*goblet*) Becher, *m.*; (*bot. and fig.*) Kelch, *m.*; (*sports prize*) Pokal, *m.*; ~**board**, Schrank, *m.*

cupidity, Begierde, Habgier, *f.*

cupola, Kuppel, *f.*

curable, heilbar.

cura|cy, Hilfsgeistlichenstelle, *f.*; ~te, Hilfsgeistliche(r).

curator, Kurator, Aufseher, *m.*

curb, *sb.* Kinnkette, *f.*; (*fig.*) Beschränkung, *f.*; *v.t.* im Zaume halten ; bändigen.

curd, geronnene Milch, *f.*; (*Käse*)quark, *m.*; ~le, gerinnen ; gerinnen machen.

cure, *sb.* Heilung, Kur, *f.*; (*Heilmittel, n.*; *v.t.* heilen ; (*salt*) einsalzen, einpökeln ; (*smoke*) räuchern.

curfew, Abendglocke, *f.*; (*abendliches*) Ausgehverbot, *n.*

curiosity, Neugierde, *f.*; (*thing*) Kuriosität, Rarität, *f.*

curious, ~ly, neugierig ; seltsam, sonderbar.

curl, *sb.* Locke, *f.*; (*of wave, smoke, &c.*) Kräuseln, *n.*; *v.t.* kräuseln, winden ; *v.i.* sich locken, sich kräuseln ; ~er, Lockenwickler, *m.*; ~y, lockig, kraus.

curlew, Brachvogel, *m.*

currant, (*dried*) Korinthe, *f.*; *black, red* ~, schwarze, rote, Johannisbeere, *f.*

curren|cy, Umlauf, *m.*; Vorherrschen, *n.*; Währung Münze, *f.*; ~t, *sb.* (*water, air, electricity, &c.*) Strom ; (*fig.*) Lauf, *m.*; *a.* gangbar, gültig, geläufig ; ~t *price*, Marktpreis, *m.*

curriculum, Lehrplan, *m.*

curry, *sb.* Curry, *m.* or *n.*; *v.t.* (*horse*) striegeln ; (*leather*) gerben ; ~ *favour*, sich (bei jemandem) einschmeicheln.

curse, Fluch, *m.*; Verwünschung, *f.*; *v.t.* verfluchen, verwünschen ; *v.i.* fluchen.

cursor|y, ~ily, flüchtig, oberflächlich.

curt, ~ly, kurz, kurz angebunden ;

~ness, Barschheit, *f.*

curtail, abkürzen, einschränken.

curtain, (*theatr., &c.*) Vorhang, *m.*; (*bed, window*) Gardine, *f.*; ~lecture, Gardinenpredigt, *f.*

curt|sy, ~sey, *sb.* Verneigung, *f.* Knicks, *m.*; *v.i.* sich verneigen, knicksen.

curve, *sb.* Kurve ; Krümmung, *f.*; *v.* (sich) krümmen, (sich) biegen ; ~d, krumm, gebogen.

cushion, Kissen, Polster, *n.*

custard, Eierkrem, *m.*

custod|ian, Kustos, *m.*; ~y, Verwahrung ; (*imprisonment*) Haft, *f.*; *take into* ~y, verhaften.

custom, Gebrauch, *m.*; Gewohnheit, *f.*; (*tradesman's*) Kundschaft, *f.*; ~s, Zoll, *m.*; ~ary, ~arily, gebräuchlich, üblich ; ~er, Kunde, *m.*; ~-house, Zollamt, *n.*

cut, *sb.* (*incision, fashion*) Schnitt, *m.*; (*sword, whip, &c.*) Hieb, *m.*; (*piece*) Schnitte, *f.*, Stück, *n.*; (*cards*) Abheben, *n.*; (*woodcut*) Holzschnitt, *m.*; *short* ~, Richtweg, *m.*; *v.t.* schneiden ; (*cards*) abheben ; (*in price*) zu Schleuderpreisen verkaufen ; (*person*) schneiden, ignorieren ; (*diamonds, glass, &c.*) schleifen ; (*meat, &c.*) vorschneiden ; ~ *down*, abhauen ; (*expenses*) einschränken ; (*abbreviate*) verkürzen ; ~ *off*, abschneiden ; (*telephone*) trennen ; ~ *out*, ausschneiden ; ausschalten ; ~ *teeth*, zahnen ; ~ *one's throat*, den Hals abschneiden ; ~ *a*, geschnitten ; geschliffen ; (*prices*) herabgesetzt ; ~ *and-dry*, fix und fertig ; ~**purse**, Taschendieb, *m.*; ~**throat**, *sb.* Halsabschneider, Mörder, *m.*; *a.* mörderisch.

cutlass, (*naut.*) Entermesser, *n.*; (*hunting*) Hirschfänger, *m.*

cutler, Messerschmied, *m.*; ~y, Messerwaren, *f.pl.*

cutlet, Kotelett(e,) *f., n.*

cutter, (*tool*) Schneidewerkzeug, *n.*; (*naut.*) Kutter, *m.*

cutting, *sb.* (*plant*) Steckling, Ableger, *m.*; (*railway, &c.*) Durchstich, *m.*; (*from news-*

paper, *&c.*) Ausschnitt, *m.*;
a. schneidend; beißend.

cuttle-fish, Tintenfisch, *m.*

cwt., Zentner, *m.*

cyanide, Zyanid, *n.*

cycl|e, *sb.* (*of years*) Zyklus, *m.*;
(*bicycle*) Fahrrad, *n.*; (*electr.*)
Periode, *f.*; *v.i.* radfahren,
(*colloq.*) radeln; ~ist, Rad-
fahrer, *m.*

cyclone, Zyklon, Wirbelsturm, *m.*

cygnet, junger Schwan.

cylind|er, Zylinder, *m.*; Walze, *f.*;
~rical, zylindrisch, walzen-
förmig.

cymbals, (Schall)becken, *n.pl.*

cynic, Zyniker, *m.*; ~al(ly),
zynisch; ~ism, Zynismus, *m.*

cypress, Zypresse, *f.*

cyst, Zyste, Blase, *f.*

czar: *see* Tsar.

D

dab, *sb.* Fleck, Klecks, *m.*; (*fish*)
Plattfisch, *m.*, Flunder, *f.*; *v.t.*
antippen; beschmieren.

dabble, ~ *in*, (*fig.*) herumstümpern
in, hineinpfuschen in, sich
mengen in.

dad, daddy, Papa, Vati, *m.*

daffodil, gelbe Narzisse.

dagger, Dolch, *m.*; *be at* ~s
drawn, auf sehr gespanntem
Fuße stehen (*with* mit).

dahlia, Dahlie, *f.*

daily, *a.* täglich; *sb.* Tageszeitung,
f.

dainty, *sb.* Leckerbissen, *m.*; *a.*,
~ily, fein, nett, elegant, niedlich; lecker; ~iness, Feinheit,
Niedlichkeit, *f.*

dairy, Molkerei, Milchwirtschaft,
f.; ~maid, Milchmädchen, *n.*

dais, Estrade, *f.*

daisy, Gänseblümchen, *n.*

dale, Tal, *n.*

dall|iance, Tändelei, *f.*; ~y,
tändeln.

dam, *sb.* (*barrier*) Damm, Deich,
m.; Talsperre, *f.*; (*animals*)
Muttertier, *f.*; *v.t.* dämmen,
stauen.

damage, *sb.* Schaden, Nachteil, *m.*;
v.t. beschädigen; ~s, Schaden-
ersatz, *m.*

damask, Damast, *m.*

damn, verdammen; verwerfen;
~ation, Verdammung, *f.*

damp, *sb.* Feuchtigkeit, *f.*; *a.*
feucht; *v.t.* befeuchten; (*fire*)
dämpfen; ~er, Dämpfer, *f.*;
(*oven, &c.*) Klappe, *f.*; ~ness =
damp, *sb.*

damson, Damaszenerpflaume, *f.*

danc|e, *sb.* Tanz, *m.*; *v.i.* tanzen;
~r, Tänzer(in, *f.*), *m.*; ~ing-
master, Tanzlehrer, *m.*

dandelion, Löwenzahn, *m.*

dandruff, Schinn, *m.*

dandy, Stutzer, Gigerl, *m.*

Dan|e, Däne, *m.*, Dänin, *f.*; ~ish,
dänisch.

danger, Gefahr, *f.*; ~ous(ly), gefährlich.

dangle, baumeln.

dank, dumpfig, feucht.

dapper, schmuck; flink, gewandt.

dapple, scheckig, gesprenkelt;
~-grey, Apfelschimmel, *m.*

dar|e, wagen, sich erkühnen; *I dare
say*, ich glaube wohl; ~e-devil,
Wagehals, *m.*; ~ing, *sb.* Kühnheit, *f.*; *a.* kühn, vermessen.

dark, *sb.* Dunkelheit, *f.*; *a.* dunkel,
finster; *after* ~, bei Einbruch
der Nacht; ~en, verdunkeln;
dunkel werden; ~ness = dark,
sb.; ~-room, Dunkelkammer, *f.*

darling, *sb.* Liebling, *m.*; *a.* lieb,
teuer.

darn, stopfen, ausbessern; ~ing-
needle, Stopfnadel, *f.*

dart, *sb.* Wurfspieß, *m.*; *v.i.*
fliegen; (*persons*) sich stürzen auf.

dash, *sb.* Schlag, Stoß, *m.*; (*mil.*)
Vorstoß, *m.*; (*of pen*) Feder-
strich, *m.*; (*stroke*) Gedanken-
strich, *m.*; (*vigour*) Schneid,
Elan, *m.*; (*liquor*) Zusatz, *m.*;
v.t. schlagen; (*water*) besprengen, bespritzen; (*hopes*)
vereiteln; ~ *off*, hastig hin-
schreiben; *v.i.* sich stürzen,
sich schlagen; ~ *off*, weg-
stürzen; fortlaufen; ~-board,
Spritzbrett; Instrumentenbrett,
Schaltbrett, *n.*; ~ing, schneidig,
flott.

dastard, Feigling, *m.*; ~ly, feige;
(heim)tückisch.

data, Angaben, Tatsachen, *f.pl.*

date, *sb. (time)* Datum, *n.; (fruit)* Dattel, *f.; out of* ~, veraltet, aus der Mode; *up to* ~, modern; *v.* datieren.

dative, Dativ, *m.*

daub, *sb. (painting)* Sudelei, Schmiererei, *f.; v.t.* beschmieren, beschmutzen; besudeln.

daughter, Tochter, *f.;* ~**in-law**, Schwiegertochter, *f.*

daunt, entmutigen, *f.;* ~**less**, unerschrocken.

davit, Davit, Bootskran, *m.*

dawdle, schlendern, bummeln.

dawn, *sb.* Tagesanbruch, *m.,* Morgendämmerung, *f.; v.i.* dämmern, Tag werden.

day, Tag, *m.; ~ after ~,* von Tag zu Tag; *the ~ before yesterday,* vorgestern; *by* ~, bei Tage; *every other* ~, jeden zweiten Tag; *one* ~, einst, eines Tages; *this ~ week,* heute über acht Tage; *heute vor acht Tagen; carry (gain, win) the* ~, den Sieg davontragen; ~**break**, Tagesanbruch, *m.;* ~**labourer**, Tagelöhner, *m.;* ~**light**, Tageslicht, *n.;* ~**time**, Tageszeit, *f.*

daze, betäuben, blenden.

dazz|le, blenden, *f.;* ~**ing**, blendend.

deacon, Diakon(us), *m.;* ~**ess**, Diakonissin, *f.*

dead, tot; *(sound)* dumpf; *(fig.)* untätig, unnütz; *(absolutely)* vollständig, total; *(insensible)* abgestumpft *(to* gegen); *the* ~, die Toten, *pl.;* ~ *against*, absolut entgegen; ~ *body*, Leichnam, *m.;* ~ *calm*, gänzliche Windstille; ~ *certain*, absolut sicher; ~ *drunk*, total betrunken; *in* ~ *earnest*, in vollem Ernst; ~ *heat*, totes Rennen; ~*march*, Totenmarsch, *m.;* ~*reckoning*, *(naut.)* Gissung, *f.;* Besteck, *n.;* ~ *shot*, ausgezeichneter Schütze; ~ *wall*, blinde Mauer; ~ *weight*, totes Gewicht; *stop* ~, plötzlich stehen bleiben; ~**alive**, äußerst langweilig; ~**beat**, todmüde; ~**en**, *(pain)* abstumpfen, töten; *(sound)* dämpfen; ~**liness**, Tödlichkeit,

Todesgefahr, *f.;* ~**lock**, Stockung, *f.,* Stillstand, *m.;* ~**ly**, tödlich; ~*ly sin*, Todsünde, *f.;* ~**ness**, Leblosigkeit, Erstarrung, Flauheit, *f.;* **The Dead Sea**, das Tote Meer.

deaf, taub; ~ *and dumb*, taubstumm; ~**en**, betäuben, *f.;* ~**ness**, Taubheit, *f.*

deal[1], *sb.* Teil, *m.,* Menge, *f.; (trading)* Handel, *m.,* Geschäft, *n.; (cards)* Geben, *n.; a good* ~, sehr viel; *v.t.* austeilen; *(cards)* geben; *v.i.* handeln *(in* mit); Karten geben; sich beschäftigen *(with* mit); ~**er**, Händler, *m.; (cards)* Geber, *m.;* ~**ing**, Handeln, Geschäft, *n.;* Umgang, Verkehr, *m.; double* ~**ing**, Doppelzüngigkeit, *f.*

deal[2], *sb. (wood)* Tannen-, Kiefernholz, *n.*

dean, Dekan, *m.*

dear, ~**ly**, lieb; *(expensive)* teuer; *my* ~, mein Liebster, meine Liebste; ~ *me! ach Gott!* ~**ness**, Zärtlichkeit, *f.; (prices)* Kostspieligkeit, *f.,* hoher Preis.

dearth, Mangel, *m. (of* an).

death, Tod, *m.,* Todesfälle, *m.pl.; at* ~*'s door,* dem Tode nahe; *at the point of* ~, im Sterben; *put to* ~, töten, hinrichten; ~**bed**, Sterbebett, *n.;* ~**blow**, Todesstoß, *m.;* ~**duty**, Erbschaftssteuer, *f.;* ~**less**, unsterblich; ~ **penalty**, Todesstrafe, *f.;* ~**rate**, Sterblichkeitsziffer, *f.;* ~**rattle**, Todesröcheln, *n.;* ~**roll**, Totenliste, *f.;* ~**warrant**, Todesurteil, *n.;* ~**watch**, *(beetle)* Totenuhr, *f.*

debar, ausschließen; *(jemandem etwas)* versagen.

debase, erniedrigen; *(coinage)* verfälschen; ~**ment**, Erniedrigung; Verfälschung, *f.*

debate, *sb.* Debatte, *f.; v.t.* diskutieren; *v.i.* beratschlagen *(on* über).

debauch, *sb.* Ausschweifung, *f.; v.t.* verführen, verderben; ~**ery** = **debauch**, *sb.*

debenture, Obligation, Schuldverschreibung, *f.*

debilit|ate, schwächen, entkräften; **~y**, Schwäche, f.

debit, sb. Debet, Soll, n.; v.t. debitieren, belasten.

debris, Trümmer, pl.

debt, Schuld, f.; **~or**, Schuldner, m.

decade, Jahrzehnt, n.

decaden|ce, Verfall, m.; **~t**, dekadent.

decalogue, die zehn Gebote, n.pl.

decamp, ausreißen.

decant, abgießen; **~er**, Karaffe, f.

decapitate, enthaupten.

decarboniz|e, entkohlen; **~ation**, Entkohlung, f.

decay, sb. Verfall, m., Verwesung, f.; v.i. verfallen, verfaulen; **~ed**, (of teeth) brüchig, hohl.

decease, sb. Hinscheiden, n.; v.i. sterben; **~d**, verstorben.

deceit, Betrug, m.; List, f.; **~ful**(ly), betrügerisch; listig; **~fulness**, Hinterlist, f.

deceive, betrügen, täuschen; **~r**, Betrüger, m.

December, Dezember, m.

decen|cy, Anstand, m., Schicklichkeit, f.; **~t**(ly), anständig, schicklich.

decentraliz|e, dezentralisieren; **~ation**, Dezentralisation, f.

decept|ion, Betrug, m.; **~ive**(ly), trügerisch.

decide, (sich) entscheiden, bestimmen; **~d**, entschieden, entschlossen.

decimal, sb. Dezimalbruch, m.; a. dezimal.

decimat|e, dezimieren; **~ion**, Dezimierung, f.

decipher, entziffern.

decis|ion, Entscheidung, f.; (firmness) Entschlossenheit, f.; **~ive**, entscheidend.

deck, sb. (Ver)deck, n.; v.t. schmücken; **~-chair**, Liegestuhl, m.

decla|im, deklamieren; **~mation**, Deklamation, f.; **~matory**, deklamatorisch.

declar|e, erklären; behaupten; (customs) deklarieren; **~ation**, Erklärung, f.; (customs) Deklaration, f.; **~ation of war**, Kriegserklärung, f.

declension, Abnahme, f.; (gram.) Deklination, f.

decline, sb. Abnahme, f., Verfall, Rückgang, m.; v.t. (refuse) ablehnen, verweigern; (gram.) deklinieren; v.i. abnehmen, (ver)fallen.

declivity, Abhang, m.

decoction, Absud, m.

decode, entziffern.

decompos|e, v.t. auflösen; v.i. verfaulen, verwesen; **~ition**, Auflösung, Zersetzung, Verwesung, f.

decontaminat|e, entgiften, entgasen; **~ion**, Entgiftung, Entgasung, f.

decontrol, freigeben.

decorat|e, verzieren, schmücken; **~ion**, Verzierung, f.; (order) Orden, m.; **~ive**, schmückend; **~or**, Dekorateur, m.

decor|um, Anstand, m.; **~ous**(ly), anständig.

decoy, sb. (bait) Köder; (bird) Lockvogel, m.; v.t. locken, ködern.

decrease, sb. Abnahme, f.; v.t. vermindern; v.i. abnehmen.

decree, sb. Beschluß, m.; Verordnung, f.; v.t. beschließen, verordnen.

decrepit, abgelebt; **~ude**, Abgelebtheit, Altersschwäche, f.

decry, tadeln, in Verruf bringen.

dedicat|e, widmen; **~ion**, Widmung, f.

deduce, folgern, herleiten.

deduct, abziehen, abrechnen; **~ion**, Abzug, m.; (logic) Schlußfolgerung, f.

deed, Tat, Handlung; (law) Urkunde, f.

deep, **~ly**, tief; (thorough) gründlich; (secret) geheim; (crafty) schlau; (colour) dunkel; **~en**, (sich) vertiefen; **~ness**, Tiefe, f.

deer, Hirsch, m., Reh, n.; **~-stalking**, Pirschen, f.

deface, entstellen; **~ment**, Entstellung, f.

defam|e, verleumden; **~ation**, Verleumdung, f.; **~atory**, verleumderisch.

default, sb. Versäumnis, f.; Nichterscheinen, n.; in ~ of. mangels; v.i. fallieren; fehlen.

defeat, *sb.* Niederlage, *f.*; *v.t.* schlagen, besiegen; vereiteln; ~**ism**, Defätismus, *m.*; ~**ist**, Defätist, *m.*

defect, Mangel, *m.*; Gebrechen, *n.*; ~**ion**, Abfall, *m.*, Abtrünnigkeit, *f.*; ~**ive**, mangelhaft, schadhaft.

defence, Verteidigung, *f.*; Schutz, *m.*; ~**less**, wehrlos.

defend, verteidigen; ~**ant**, Angeklagte(r); ~**er**, Verteidiger, *m.*

defensive, *sb.* Defensive, *f.*; *a.* Verteidigungs-, Abwehr-.

defer, aufschieben; ~**ence**, Rücksicht, Ehrerbietung, *f.*; ~**ential(ly)**, ehrerbietig.

defian|ce, Herausforderung, *f.*, Trotz, *m.*; ~**t(ly)**, herausfordernd.

deficien|cy, Mangel, *m.* (*of an*); Unzulänglichkeit, *f.*; ~**t**, mangelhaft, unzulänglich; *be ~t in* (*einer Sache*) ermangeln, Mangel haben an.

deficit, Defizit, *n.*, Fehlbetrag, *m.*

defile[1], *sb.* Engpaß, *m.*; *v.i.* defilieren.

defile[2], *v.t.* beflecken, verunreinigen; schänden; ~**ment**, Befleckung; Schändung, *f.*

defin|e, erklären, definieren; ~**ite(ly)**, bestimmt; ~**ition**, Erklärung; Begriffsbestimmung, *f.*; ~**itive**, endgültig.

defiat|e, die Luft herauslassen; ~**ion**, Deflation, *f.*

deflect, ablenken; abweichen; ~**ion**, Abweichung, *f.*

deform|**ed**, entstellt, mißgestaltet; ~**ity**, Mißgestaltung, *f.*, Gebrechen, *n.*

defraud, betrügen.

defray, bestreiten, bezahlen.

deft, *ly*, geschickt, gewandt.

defunct, verstorben.

degenerat|e, *v.i.* entarten; *a.* entartet; ~**ion**, Entartung, *f.*

degrad|e, herabsetzen, erniedrigen; (*mil.*) degradieren; ~**ation**, Herabsetzung, Absetzung, Erniedrigung; Degradation, *f.*

degree, Grad, *m.*; (*rank*) Rang, *m.*; *by ~s*, allmählich, nach und nach; *take one's ~*, promovieren.

deif|y, vergöttern; ~**ication**, Vergötterung, *f.*

deign, sich herablassen, geruhen.

de|ism, Deismus, *m.*; ~**st**, Deist, *m.*

deity, Gottheit, *f.*

deject|**ed**, niedergeschlagen; ~**ion**, Niedergeschlagenheit, *f.*

delay, *sb.* Aufschub, Verzug, *m.*; Verzögerung, *f.*; *without ~*, unverzüglich; *v.t.* aufschieben; hindern; *v.i.* zögern.

delectable, ergötzlich.

delegat|e, *sb.* Abgeordnete(r); *v.t.* abordnen; ~**ion**, Abordnung, Delegation, *f.*

delet|e, auslöschen, tilgen; ~**ion**, Streichung, Tilgung, *f.*

deliberat|e, *v.t.* überlegen; *v.i.* beratschlagen; *a.* ~**ely**, absichtlich; vorsichtig; ~**ion**, Überlegung, *f.*

delica|cy, Zartgefühl, *n.*; (*weakness*) Schwächlichkeit, *f.*; (*food*) Leckerbissen, *m.*; ~**te(ly)**, zart, fein, empfindlich; (*weak*) schwächlich; (*question*) heikel.

delicious, ~*ly*, köstlich.

delight, *sb.* Vergnügen, *n.*; Wonne, *f.*; *v.t.* erfreuen, entzücken; *v.i.* sich an etwas ergötzen; ~**ful(ly)**, ergötzlich, entzückend.

delineat|e, zeichnen, entwerfen; ~**ion**, Entwurf, *m.*, Schilderung, *f.*

delinquen|cy, Vergehen, *n.*; Missetat, *f.*; Kriminalität, *f.*; ~**t**, Missetäter, *m.*

deliri|um, Fieberwahnsinn, *m.*; ~**ous(ly)**, irreredend; (*fig.*) wahnsinnig.

deliver, befreien (*from* von); (*message*) besorgen; (*goods*) (ab)liefern; (*speech*) halten; (*letters*) ausgeben, bestellen; ~ *over*, *up*, übergeben; *be ~ed*, (*woman*) niederkommen, entbunden werden (*of* von); ~**ance**, Befreiung, *f.*; ~**er**, Befreier, Erretter, *m.*; ~**y**, (*goods*) Ablieferung, *f.*; (*message*) Überbringung, *f.*; (*letters*) Bestellung, *f.*; (*birth*) Niederkunft, *f.*; (*speech*) Halten, *n.*; (*style of speaking*) Vortragsart, *f.*

delphinium, Rittersporn, *m.*

delta, Delta, n.

delu|de, betrügen, täuschen; ~sion, Betrug, m.; Täuschung, f.; Wahn, m.; ~sive(ly), trügerisch, täuschend.

deluge, sb. Überschwemmung (Noah's) Sintflut, f.; v.t. überschwemmen.

demagogue, Demagog, m.

demand, sb. Forderung, f.; (claim) Anspruch, m.; (pol. econ.) Nachfrage, f.; on ~, auf Verlangen; v.t. fordern; verlangen; (need) erfordern.

demarcat|e, abgrenzen; ~ion, Grenzlinie, f.

demean, ~ oneself, sich erniedrigen; ~our, Betragen, n.

demented, toll, verrückt.

demi-, halb-.

demobiliz|e, demobilisieren, demobilmachen; ~ation, Demobilisierung, Demobilmachung, f.

democra|cy, Demokratie, f.; ~t, Demokrat, m.; ~tic(ally), demokratisch.

demol|ish, zerstören, niederreißen; ~ition, Zerstörung, f.

demon, Dämon, Teufel, m.; ~iac, Besessene(r).

demonstrat|e, beweisen, demonstrieren; ~ion, Beweis, m.; Kundgebung, f.; ~ive, beweiskräftig; (gram.) hinweisend; überschwenglich; laut; ~or, Beweisführer; Demonstrierende(r); (Laboratoriums)assistent, m.

demoraliz|e, demoralisieren; ~ation, Demoralisation, f.

demot|e, degradieren; ~ion, Degradierung, f.

demure, ~ly, sittsam, spröde, zimperlich; ~ness, Sprödigkeit, Zimperlichkeit, f.

den, Höhle, Grube, f.

denial, Verneinung, Ablehnung, f.

denominat|e, benennen; ~ion, Benennung; Klasse; Konfession, f.; ~or, Nenner, m.

denote, bezeichnen; bedeuten.

denounce, anklagen, denunzieren, anzeigen; ~ment, Denunziation, Anzeige, f.

dens|e, ~ely, dicht, fest; (stupid)

dumm; ~ity, Dichtigkeit, f.

dent, Beule, Eindruck, m.

dental, a. Zahn-; sb. Zahnlaut, m.

dentifrice, Zahnpulver, n., Zahnpasta, f.

dentist, Zahnarzt, m.; ~ry, Zahnheilkunde, f.

denud|e, entblößen; ~ation, Entblößung, f.

denunciation, Denunziation, Anzeige, f.

deny, (ab)leugnen, abschlagen; ~ oneself, sich versagen.

depart, abreisen; abweichen; ~ment, Abteilung, f.; Bezirk, m.; Fach, n.; ~ure, Abreise; Abweichung, f.

depend, abhängen (on von); (rely) sich verlassen (on auf); it ~s, es kommt darauf an; ~able, verlässig; ~ant, Abhängige(r), Untergebene(r); ~ence, Vertrauen, n.; Abhängigkeit, f.; ~ency, (überseeische) Besitzung, Kolonie, f.; ~ent, abhängig.

depict, beschreiben, schildern.

deplete, entleeren; erschöpfen.

deplor|e, beklagen, beweinen; ~able, kläglich, beklagenswert.

deploy, aufmarschieren lassen, (Truppen) entwickeln; ~ment, Aufmarsch, m.

depopulat|e, entvölkern, aussiedeln; ~ion, Entvölkerung, f.

deport, ausweisen, deportieren; ~ation, Ausweisung, Deportation, f.

deportment, Haltung, f.; Betragen, n.

depos|e, v.t. absetzen; v.i. bezeugen; ~ition, Absetzung; eidliche Aussage, f.

deposit, sb. (pledge) Pfand, n.; (bank) Depot, Depositum, n.; (payment) Anzahlung, f.; (geol.) Ablagerung, f.; v.t. niederlegen; einzahlen; v.i. sich ablagern; ~or, Einzahler, m.; ~ory, Verwahrungsort, m.

depot, Depot, n., Niederlage, f.; ~ ship, Mutterschiff, n.

deprav|ed, verdorben; ~ity, Verderbtheit, f.

deprecat|e, sich verbitten, mißbilligen; ~ory, mißbilligend.

depreciat|e, v.t. (prices) herabsetzen; (fig.) geringschätzen; v.i. sinken; ~**ion**, Entwertung; Herabsetzung; Geringschätzung, f.

depredat|ion, Plünderung, f.; ~**or**, Räuber, m.

depress, (nieder)drücken, deprimieren; ~**ed**, niedergeschlagen; gedrückt, ~**ion**, (mental) Niedergeschlagenheit, f.; (barometric) Tief, n.; (trade) Depression, Flauheit, f.

depriv|e, berauben, entziehen; ~**ation**, Beraubung, f., Verlust, m.

depth, Tiefe, f.; in the ~ of winter, mitten im Winter; ~**-charge**, Wasserbombe, f.

deput|e, abordnen, ~**ation**, Deputation, Abordnung, f.; ~**ize**, jemandes Stelle vertreten; ~**y**, Stellvertreter, m.; (parl.) Abgeordnete(r); a. Vize-.

derail, entgleisen (lassen); ~**ment**, Entgleisung, f.

derange, in Unordnung bringen; ~**d**, (insane) geistig gestört; ~**ment**, Unordnung; Geistesstörung, f.

derelict, verlassen, herrenlos.

deride, verlachen.

deris|ion, Verspottung, f.; ~**ive**, höhnisch.

deriv|e, ableiten, herleiten; ~**ation**, Ableitung, Herleitung, f.; ~**ative**, a. abgeleitet; sb. Ableitung, f.

derogatory, beeinträchtigend, nachteilig.

derrick, Ladebaum, Hebelkran, m.

dervish, Derwisch, m.

descend, hinab- herab- steigen; sich senken; abstammen (from von); ~**ant**, Nachkomme, m.

descent, Abstieg, Abhang; (attack) Einfall, m.; Abstammung, f.

descri|be, beschreiben; ~**ption**, Beschreibung, f.; (kind) Sorte, f.; ~**ptive**, beschreibend.

desecrat|e, entweihen; ~**ion**, Entweihung, f.

desert, sb. Wüste, Einöde, f.; a. öde, wild; v.t. verlassen; (mil.) desertieren; ~**er**, Deserteur, Fahnenflüchtige(r), m.;

~**ion**, Verlassen, n.; (mil.) Fahnenflucht, f.

deserts, Verdienst, n.

deserv|e, verdienen; ~**ing**, verdient, verdienstlich.

design, sb. (plan) Entwurf, Plan, m.; (sketch) Zeichnung, f.; (on materials, &c.) Muster, n.; (intention) Vorhaben, n.; v.t. entwerfen; vorhaben; ~**er**, Entwerfer; Zeichner, m.; ~**ing**, hinterlistig.

designat|e, bezeichnen; ~**ion**, Bezeichnung, f.

desir|e, sb. Wunsch, m., Verlangen, n.; Begierde, f.; v.t. verlangen; ~**able**, wünschenswert; ~**ability**, Erwünschtheit, f.; ~**ous**, begierig.

desist, abstehen (from von).

desk, Pult, n.

desolat|e, v.t. verheeren, verwüsten; a. öde, (sad) trostlos; ~**ion**, Verwüstung; Trostlosigkeit, f.

despair, sb. Verzweiflung, f.; v.i. verzweifeln.

despatch: see **dispatch**.

desperat|e, ~**ely**, verzweifelt: verwegen; ~**ion**, Verzweiflung, f.

despicabl|e, ~**y**, verächtlich.

despise, verachten, verschmähen.

despite, trotz.

despoil, plündern.

desponden|cy, Verzagtheit, Verzweiflung, f.; ~**t(ly)**, verzweifelnd.

despot, Despot, Selbstherrscher, m.; ~**ic**, despotisch; ~**ism**, Gewaltherrschaft, f.

dessert, Nachtisch, m.; ~**-spoon**, Dessertlöffel, m.

destin|e, bestimmen; ~**ation**, Bestimmungsort, m.; Ziel, n.; ~**y**, Schicksal, n.

destitut|e, mittellos hilflos; ~**ion**, Not, Mittelosigkeit, f.

destroy, zerstören, vernichten; ~**er**, Zerstörer, m.

destruct|ion, Zerstörung, Vernichtung, f.; ~**ive**, zerstörend.

desultor|y, planlos; oberflächlich; abschweifend; ~**iness**, Planlosigkeit, f.

detach, trennen, absondern; (mil.) abkommandieren; ~**able**, ab-

nehmbar; ~ed, (house) allein-
stehend; ~ment, Abtrennung,
f., (mil.) Kommando, n.

detail, sb. Einzelheit, f.; v.t.
umständlich erzählen (or darstellen); ~ed, ausführlich.

detain, zurückhalten, abhalten; in
Haft behalten.

detect, entdecken; ~ion, Entdeckung, f.; ~ive, Detektiv, m.;
~or Detektor m.

detention, Vorenthaltung; (law)
Haft, f.

deter, abschrecken, abhalten.

deteriorat|e, verderben, schlechter
werden; ~ion, Verschlechte-
rung f.

determin|e, bestimmen, entschei-
den; ~ation, Entschluß, m.;
(resolution) Entschlossenheit, f.;
~ed entschlossen.

detest, verabscheuen; ~able, abscheulich; ~ation, Abscheu, m.

dethrone, entthronen; ~ment,
Entthronung f.

detonat|e, explodieren; ~ion,
Detonation, Explosion, f.,
Knall, m.; ~or, Zünder, m.

detour, Umweg, m.

detract, abziehen (from von);
herabsetzen, verleumden; ~ion,
Herabsetzung, Verleumdung, f.

detriment, Nachteil, m.; ~al,
nachteilig.

deuce, (devil) Teufel, m.; (cards)
Zwei, f.; (tennis) gleich(e
Punkte).

devastat|e, verwüsten; ~ion, Ver-
wüstung, f.

develop, entwickeln; (mine, land,
&c.) ausbeuten, ausbauen;
~ment, Entwick(e)lung, Ent-
faltung, f.

deviat|e, abweichen; ~ion, Ab-
weichung, f.

device, (motto) Devise, f., Wahl-
spruch, m.; (plan) Kunstgriff, m.

devil, Teufel, m.; ~ish(ly), teuflisch; ~ry, Teufelei, f.

devise, ersinnen, erdenken.

devoid, ~ of, leer (an) ohne (with
acc.).

devot|e, widmen; (auf)opfern;
~ed(ly), ergeben; ~ion, Hin-
gabe, Widmung, f.; Andacht, f.

devour, verschlingen.

devout, ~ly, andächtig; ~ness,
Andacht, f.

dew, Tau, m.; ~lap, Wamme, f.;
~y, betaut, tauig.

dexter|ity, Geschicklichkeit, f.;
~ous(ly), geschickt, gewandt.

diabet|es, Zuckerkrankheit, f.,
Diabetes, m.; ~ic, zuckerkrank.

diabolical, ~ly, teuflisch.

diadem, Diadem, n.

diagnos|e, die Diagnose stellen;
~is, Diagnose, f.

diagonal, a. schräg, diagonal;
sb. Diagonale, f.

diagram, Plan, m. Figur, f.
graphische Darstellung, f.;

dial, sb. (clock, watch) Zifferblatt,
n.; (gauge, &c.) Zeigerblatt, n.;
(telephone) Nummernscheibe, f.;
sun-~, Sonnenuhr, f.; v.t.
(telephone) drehen, wählen.

dialect, Dialekt, m., Mundart, f.,
~al, mundartlich.

dialogue, Zwiegespräch, n.

diamet|er, Durchmesser, m.;
~rically opposed, grade entgegengesetzt.

diamond, Diamant, m.; ~s,
(cards) Karo, n.

diaphragm, (anat.) Zwerchfell, n.;
(telephone, &c.) Membran(e), f.;
(optics) Blende, f.

diarrhoea, Durchfall, m.

diary, Tagebuch, n.

dice, sb. Würfel, m.pl.; v.i.
würfeln; ~-box, Würfelbecher,
m.

dicky, Rücksitz, m.

dictaphone, Diktaphon, n.

dictat|e, diktieren; befehlen;
~ion, Diktat, m.; ~or, Dik-
tator, m.; ~orial, diktatorisch;
~orship, Diktatur, f.

diction, Ausdrucksweise, f.

dictionary, Wörterbuch, n.

didactic, didaktisch.

die¹, sb. Stempel, Würfel, m.

die², sterben; ~ away, verlöschen,
ersterben; ~ out, aussterben,
erlöschen; ~hard, Unent-
wegte(r).

Diesel; ~ engine, Dieselmotor, m.

diet, sb. Kost, Diät, f.; (parl.)
Reichstag, m.; v.t. jemandem
Diät vorschreiben; v.i. Diät
leben, Diät halten.

differ, verschieden sein, sich unterscheiden; anderer Meinung sein; ~ence, Unterschied, *m.*; ~ent, verschieden, anders; ~entiate, unterscheiden.

difficult, schwierig; ~y, Schwierigkeit; Verlegenheit, *f.*

diffiden|ce, Schüchternheit, *f.*; ~t(ly), schüchtern.

diffract, (Lichtstrahlen usw.) ablenken, brechen; ~ion, Ablenkung, Brechung, *f.*

diffus|e, *v.t.* verbreiten, zerstreuen; *a.* verbreitet; (*verbose*) weitschweifig; ~ion, Verbreitung, Ausstreuung, *f.*

dig, graben.

digest, *sb.* Übersicht, *f.*; *v.t.* verdauen; ~ible, verdaulich; ~ion, Verdauung, *f.*; ~ive, Verdauungs-.

digit, Finger, *m.*; Ziffer, *f.*

digitalis, Digitalis, *f.*

dignif|y, ehren; ~ied, würdevoll.

dignity, Würde, *f.*; Rang, *m.*

digress, abschweifen; ~ion, Abschweifung, *f.*

dike, Deich, Damm, *m.*

dilapidat|ed, verfallen; ~ion, Verfall, *m.*

dilat|e, erweitern, ausdehnen; ~ion, Ausdehnung, *f.*

dilator|y, ~ily, (ver)zögernd, langsam; ~iness, Zögern, *n.*, Saumseligkeit, *f.*

dilemma, Dilemma, *n.*, Klemme, *f.*; *on the horns of a* ~, in der Klemme.

diligen|ce, Fleiß, *m.*; ~t(ly), fleißig, emsig.

dilut|e, verdünnen; ~ion, Verdünnung, *f.*

dim, *a.*, ~ly, dunkel, trübe; *v.t.* verdunkeln, abblenden; ~ness, Dunkelheit, Trübheit, *f.*

dimension, Ausdehnung, *f.*, Maß, *n.*

dimin|ish, *v.t.* vermindern; *v.i.* abnehmen; ~ution, Verminderung, Abnahme, *f.*; ~utive, *a.* (auffallend, ganz) klein; *sb.* Verkleinerungswort, *n.*

dimple, Grübchen, *n.*

din, Getöse, *n.*

din|e, (zu Mittag) essen, speisen; ~er, ~ing-car, Speisewagen,

m.; ~ing-room, Speise -zimmer, *n.*, -saal, *m.*

dinghy, Dingi, Schlauchboot, *n.*

dingy, schmutzig.

dinner, Mittagessen; (*public*) Festmahl, *n.*; ~ jacket, Smoking, *m.*

diocese, Diözese, *f.*; Sprengel, *m.*

dip, *v.t.* eintauchen, eintunken; (*flag*) dippen (*v.i.*) sich senken.

diphtheria, Diphtherie, *f.*

diphthong, Diphthong, *m.*

diploma, Diplom, *n.*

diploma|cy, Diplomatie, *f.*; ~t, Diplomat, *m.*

dire, gräßlich.

direct, *v.t.* richten; (*show the way*) weisen; (*command, manage*) befehlen, leiten; (*letters, &c.*) adressieren; *a.*, gerade, direkt; ausdrücklich; ~ current, Gleichstrom, *m.*; ~ hit, Volltreffer, *m.*; ~ion, Richtung, *f.*; (*leading*) Führung, Leitung, *f.*; (*instruction*) Anweisung, *f.*; ~ly, gleich, sofort; ~or, Direktor, Leiter, *m.*; ~ory, Adreßbuch, *n.*

dirge, Grab-, Trauer- lied, *n.*

dirt, Schmutz, Dreck, Kot, *m.*; ~-cheap, spottbillig; ~iness, Schmutzigkeit, *f.*; ~y, *a.* schmutzig, dreckig; *v.t.* besudeln.

disability, Unvermögen, *n.*, Unfähigkeit, *f.*

disable, unfähig machen; außer Gefecht setzen; ~d, (*ship*) seeuntüchtig; (*mil.*) kriegsversehrt, schwerverletzt.

disadvantag|e, Nachteil, *m.*; ~eous, nachteilig.

disagree, nicht übereinstimmen; streiten; (*food*) schlecht bekommen; ~able, unangenehm; (*pers.*) unhöflich; ~ment, Meinungsverschiedenheit, *f.*, Zerwürfnis, *n.*

disallow, nicht gestatten, verwerfen.

disappear, verschwinden; ~ance, Verschwinden, *n.*, Schwund, *m.*

disappoint, enttäuschen; ~ment, Enttäuschung, *f.*

disapprov|e, mißbilligen (*with acc.*); ~al, Mißbilligung, *f.*

disarm, *v.t.* entwaffnen; *v.i.*

abrüsten; ~ament, Abrüstung, f.

disarrange, verwirren, in Unordnung bringen; ~ment, Unordnung, f.

disaster, Unglück, n.; Katastrophe, f.; ~rous(ly), unheilvoll, verhängnisvoll.

disavow, ableugnen; nicht anerkennen.

disband, (sich) auflösen, entlassen.

disbelief, Unglaube, m.

disbelieve, nicht glauben; ~r, Ungläubige(r).

disburse, auszahlen.

disc = disk.

discard, verwerfen, beiseitelegen; (cards) weglegen.

discern, wahrnehmen, unterscheiden; ~ing, scharfsichtig, verständig; ~ment, Verstand, m., Urteilsfähigkeit, f.

discharge, (dismissal) Entlassung, f.; (gun) Abschuß, m., Abfeuern, n.; (cargo) Löschung, f.; (debt) Tilgung, f.; (duty) Erfüllung, f.; (med.) Ausfluß, m.; v.t. (dismiss) entlassen; (gun) abfeuern, entladen; (cargo) löschen; (debt) tilgen, bezahlen; (duty) erfüllen; v.i. abfließen, sich ergießen.

disciple, Jünger, Schüler, m.

discipline, sb. Zucht, Disziplin, f.; (learning) Wissenszweig, m.; (punishment) Züchtigung, f.; v.t. disziplinieren; bestrafen; ~ary, Disziplinar-.

disclaim, verleugnen, entsagen; ~er, Widerruf, m.

disclose, entdecken, enthüllen; ~ure, Enthüllung, f.

discolour, (sich) entfärben; ~ration, Entfärbung, f.

discomfort, Unbehagen, n.

disconcert, außer Fassung bringen.

disconnect, trennen; (mech.) abstellen, ausschalten; ~ed(ly), abgestellt; (fig.) unzusammenhängend.

disconsolate, trostlos.

discontent, Unzufriedenheit, f.; ~ed(ly), unzufrieden.

discontinue, unterbrechen, aufgeben; ~ance, Aufhören, Aufgeben, n.

discord, Uneinigkeit, f.; (mus.) Dissonanz, f., Mißklang, m.; ~ant(ly), uneinig, widerspruchsvoll; mißklingend.

discount, sb. Diskont, Rabatt, m.; v.t. (bill) diskontieren; (fig.) vermindern; unberücksichtigt lassen.

discourage, entmutigen, abschrecken; mißbilligen; ~ment, Entmutigung, Mißbilligung, f.

discourse, sb. Gespräch, n., Rede, f.; v.i. sich unterreden (about über), sprechen (about von).

discourtesy, Unhöflichkeit, f.; ~ous, unhöflich.

discover, entdecken; offenbaren; ~er, Entdecker, m.; ~y, Entdeckung, f.

discredit, sb. übler Ruf, m.; v.t. in schlechten Ruf bringen; bezweifeln.

discreet, ~ly, vorsichtig, verschwiegen.

discrepancy, Widerspruch, m.; ~t, widersprechend.

discretion, Klugheit, Verschwiegenheit, f., Takt, m.; at ~, nach Belieben; age of ~, mündiges Alter; ~ary, uneingeschränkt.

discriminate, unterscheiden; ~ion, Unterscheidung, f.; Scharfsinn, m.

discursive, abschweifend, sprunghaft.

discuss, erörtern, besprechen; ~ion, Erörterung, Diskussion, f.

disdain, sb. Verachtung, f.; v.t. verachten, verschmähen.

disease, Krankheit, f.; ~d, krank.

disembark, ausschiffen, ausbooten; landen; ~ation, Ausschiffung, Landung, f.

disengage, befreien; absetzen.

disentangle, entwirren.

disestablish, entstaatlichen; ~ment, Entstaatlichung, f.

disfavour, Ungnade, f., Mißfallen, n.

disfigure, entstellen; ~ation, Entstellung, f.

disfranchise, das Wahlrecht entziehen.

disgorge, ausspeien, wiederherausgeben.

disgrace, sb. Ungnade, Schande, f.;
v.t. entehren; **~ful(ly),** schändlich.

disguise, sb. Verkleidung, f.; v.t.
verkleiden.

disgust, sb. Ekel, Widerwille, m.;
v.t. Ekel erregen; **~ing(ly),**
ekelhaft, abscheulich.

dish, Schüssel, f.; (food) Gericht,
n.; **~cloth,** Tellertuch, n.; **~-
washer,** Geschirrspüler, m.

dishearten, verzagt machen.

dishevelled, aufgelöst, in Unordnung.

dishonest, ~ly, unehrlich; **~y,**
Unredlichkeit, f.

dishonour, sb. Unehre, Schande, f.;
v.t. entehren; (bill) nicht
honorieren; **~able,** schändlich,
ehrlos.

disillusion, sb. Enttäuschung, f.;
v.t. enttäuschen.

disinclin|ed, abgeneigt; **~ation,**
Abneigung, f.

disinfect, desinfizieren; **~ant,**
Desinfektionsmittel, n.; **~ion,**
Desinfizierung, f.

disinherit, enterben.

disintegrat|e, sich auflösen; **~ion,**
Auflösung, f.

disinterested, unparteiisch, un-
eigennützig.

disjointed, ~ly, unzusammenhängend.

disk, Scheibe, (Grammophon)-
platte, f.

dislike, sb. Abneigung, f., Miß-
fallen, n.; v.t. nicht gern haben.

dislocat|e, verrenken; verwirren;
~ion, Verrenkung; Unordnung,
f.

dislodge, vertreiben.

disloyal, ~ly, treulos, verräterisch;
~ty, Untreue, f.

dismal, ~ly, trübe, traurig.

dismantle, abmontieren; (naut.)
abtakeln.

dismay, sb. Schrecken, m., Bestürzung, f.; v.t. erschrecken;
entmutigen.

dismember, zerstückeln.

dismiss, entlassen, wegschicken;
imp. Weggetreten!; **~al,** Entlassung, f.

dismount, absteigen, absitzen.

disobedien|ce, Ungehorsam, m.;

~t(ly), ungehorsam.

disobey, nicht gehorchen; ungehorsam sein.

disorder, Unordnung, Verwirrung,
f.; (med.) Unpäßlichkeit, f.;
(disturbance) Aufruhr, m.; **~ed,**
verworren; (mind) zerrüttet;
(stomach) verdorben; **~ly,** un-
ordentlich, aufrührerisch; liederlich.

disorganiz|e, auflösen, zerrütten,
in Unordnung bringen; **~ation,**
Auflösung, Zerrüttung, Be-
triebsstörung, f.

disown, verleugnen, verwerfen.

disparage, erniedrigen, herabsetzen; **~ment,** Herabsetzung, f.

disparity, Ungleichheit, f.

dispatch, sb. (speed) Eile, Erledi-
gung, f.; (goods, &c.) Absen-
dung, Abfertigung f.; Depesche,
f., Telegramm, n.; v.t. absenden,
expedieren; (kill) umbringen;
~ boat, Aviso, m.; **~box,**
Dokumententasche, f.; **~rider,**
Melde-reiter, -fahrer, m.

dispel, vertreiben, zerstreuen.

dispensary, Apotheke, f.

dispens|e, austeilen; (med.) be-
reiten; **~ with,** entbehren
können, nicht missen; **~ation,**
Erlassung, f.; (eccles.) Dispens,
m.; (of providence) Fügung, f.

dispers|e, (sich) zerstreuen; **~al,
~ion,** Zerstreuung, f.

displace, versetzen, verlegen, ver-
rücken; **~ment,** Verrückung,
Verlegung, f.; (naut.) Wasser-
verdrängung, f.

display, sb. Schaustellung, Darstellung, f.; Aufwand, m.; v.t.
zur Schau stellen, zeigen, entfalten.

displease, mißfallen; **~ure,** Miß-
fallen, n.

dispos|e, (arrange) anordnen; **~ of,**
beseitigen; verfügen über; absetzen, verkaufen; erledigen;
~al, Verfügung; Anordnung,
f.; Verkauf, m.; **~ed,** geneigt;
~ition, (arrangement) Anordnung; (temper) Gemütsart, f.

dispossess, berauben.

disprove, widerlegen.

disput|e, sb. Streit, Wortwechsel,

m.; *v.t.* bestreiten; *v.i.* streiten;
~able, streitig.

disqualif|ication, Ausschließung, *f.*;
~y, unfähig machen (or er-
klären), ausschließen.

disquiet, Unruhe, *f.*; *v.t.*
beunruhigen.

disregard, *sb.* Mißachtung, Vernachlässigung, *f.*; *v.t.* unbeachtet lassen.

disreputable, verrufen; schimpflich.

disrespect, Unehrerbietigkeit, *f.*;
~ful(ly), unehrerbietig.

disrupt, zum Bruch bringen,
spalten; ~ion, Bruch, *m.*;
Spaltung, *f.*

dissatisf|action, Unzufriedenheit,
f.; ~y, nicht befriedigen.

dissect, zerschneiden; *(anat.)*
sezieren; ~ing, Sezier-; ~ion,
Zerschneiden; *(anat.)* Sezieren,
n., Sektion, *f.*

dissemble, sich verstellen; ~r,
Heuchler, *m.*

disseminat|e, (aus)säen, aus-
streuen, verbreiten; ~ion, Ausstreuen, *n.*, Verbreitung, *f.*

dissension, Uneinigkeit, Zwie-
tracht, *f.*

dissent, *sb.* abweichende Meinung;
v.i. anderer Meinung sein;
~er, Dissident, *m.*; ~ient,
andersdenkend.

dissertation, Dissertation, Abhandlung, *f.*

dissimilar, ~ly, ungleichartig,
verschiedenartig; ~ity, Ungleichheit, Verschiedenheit, *f.*

dissimulat|e, sich verstellen; ~ion,
Verstellung, *f.*

dissipat|e, zerstreuen; verschwen-
den; ~ed, ausschweifend;
~ion, Ausschweifung, *f.*

dissociat|e, trennen, absondern;
~ion, Trennung, Absonderung, *f.*

dissolub|le, löslich, (auf)lösbar;
trennbar; ~ility, Auflösbar-
keit, *f.*

dissolut|e, ~ely, ausschweifend;
~ion, Auflösung, Zerstörung, *f.*

dissolve, (sich) auflösen, schmelzen.

dissonan|ce, Mißklang, *m.*, Dis-
sonanz, *f.*; ~t, mißtönend.

dissua|de, abraten; ~sion, Ab-
raten, *n.*

distaff, Spinnrocken, *m.*

distan|ce, Entfernung, *f.*, Abstand,
m.; ~t(ly), entfernt, weit;
(manner) kühl, fremd; ~t
relations, entfernte Verwandte.

distaste, Ekel, Widerwille, *m.*;
~ful(ly), ekelhaft, widrig.

distemper, *sb. (dogs)* Staupe, *f.*;
(paint) Tempera-, Wasser-farbe,
f.; *v.t.* mit Tempera bemalen.

distend, ausdehnen, aufblasen.

distil, destillieren; ~lation, Destillieren, *n.*; ~ler, Destillateur,
m.; ~lery, Brennerei, *f.*

distinct, ~ly, *(clear)* deutlich;
(different) verschieden; *(decided)*
ausdrücklich; ~ion, *(difference)*
Unterschied, *m.*; *(fame)* Ruhm,
m., *(honour)* Auszeichnung, *f.*;
~ive, unterscheidend; ~ness,
Deutlichkeit, *f.*

distinguish, unterscheiden; ~one-
self, sich auszeichnen; ~ed,
vornehm.

distort, verdrehen, verzerren;
~ion, Verdrehung, Verzerrung,
f.

distract, ablenken; zerstreuen;
~ed, zerstreut, verwirrt, außer
sich.

distress, Not, *f.*, Elend, *n.*; ~ed,
bedrängt, notleidend; über-
anstrengt; ~ful(ly), elend, unglücklich, jämmerlich.

distribut|e, aus-, ver- teilen; ~ion,
Aus-, Ver- teilung, *f.*

district, Gegend, *f.*, Bezirk, Kreis,
m.

distrust, *sb.* Mißtrauen, *n.*; *v.t.*
mißtrauen *(with dat.)*; ~ful(ly),
mißtrauisch.

disturb, stören, in Unordnung
bringen; ~ance, Störung, *f.*;
Aufruhr, *m.*

disun|ion, ~ity, Uneinigkeit, *f.*

ditch, Graben, *m.*

ditty, Lied, *n.*

divan, Diwan, *m.*

dive, *sb.* Kopfsprung; Sturzflug,
m.; *v.i.* tauchen; ~ bomber,
Sturzkampfflugzeug, Stuka,
n.; ~r, Taucher, *m.*

diverge, auseinander -gehen,
-laufen; ~nce, Auseinander-
laufen, *n.*, Abweichung, *f.*;
~nt, abweichend.

divers|e, verschieden, mannigfaltig; **~ion**, Ablenkung, *f.*, Zeitvertreib, *m.*; **~ity**, Verschiedenheit, *f.*

divert, ablenken; unterhalten, amüsieren.

divest, entkleiden, berauben.

divide, teilen, trennen.

dividend, Dividende, *f.*

divin|e, *v.t.* wahrsagen, weissagen; erraten; *sb.* Geistliche(r); *a.* **~ely**, göttlich; **~e service**, Gottesdienst, *m.*; **~ing-rod**, Wünschelrute, *f.*; **~ity**, Gottheit; Theologie, *f.*

division, Teilung, Spaltung; *(mil. and arith.)* Division; *(voting)* Abstimmung, *f.*

divorce, *sb.* Ehescheidung, *f.*; *get a ~*, sich scheiden lassen; *v.t.* *(one's wife)* verstoßen; *~ oneself from*, sich scheiden lassen von.

divulge, ausplaudern, verbreiten.

dizz|y, schwind(e)lig; **~iness**, Schwindel, *m.*

do, *v.t.* and *i.*, tun, machen; *(suit)* passen, gehen; *(suffice)* genügen; *(get on, manage)* gut gehen; *(cheat)* betrügen; *that will ~*, das genügt; *that won't do*, das geht nicht; *how do you do?*, wie geht es Ihnen?; *~ away with*, abschaffen; *~ in*, töten; *~ up*, *(pack)* einpacken, zuschnüren; instandsetzen; *~ without*, ohne . . . fertig werden, entbehren.

docil|e, gelehrig; **~ity**, Gelehrigkeit, Gefügigkeit, *f.*

dock, *sb.* Dock, *n.*; *(law-court)* Anklagebank, *f.*; *v.t.* *(ship)* docken; *(tail)* stutzen; **~er**, Hafen-, Dock- arbeiter, *m.*; **~yard**, Werft, *f.*

docket, Etikette, *f.*; Aktenschwanz, *m.*; *(for commodities)* Bezugsschein, *m.*

doctor, *sb.* Doktor, Arzt, *m.*; *v.t.* ärztlich behandeln; fälschen.

doctrine, Lehre, *f.*

document, Dokument, *n.*, Urkunde, *f.*; **~ary**, urkundlich; **~ary film**, Kulturfilm, *m.*

dodge, *sb.* Seitensprung; Kniff, Schlich, *m.*; *v.t.* jemandem aus dem Wege gehen; *v.i.* ausweichen; schwindeln.

doe, Reh *(rabbit, &c.)* Weibchen, *n.*

dog, *sb.* Hund, *m.*; *(fire)* Feuerbock, *m.*; *(colloq., of person)* Kerl, Bursche, *m.*; *v.t.* jemandem auf den Fersen sein; *go to the ~s*, auf den Hund kommen; **~biscuit**, Hundekuchen, *m.*; **~days**, Hundstage, *m.pl.*; **~fish**, Katzenhai, *m.*; **~kennel**, Hundehütte, *f.*; **~Latin**, Küchenlatein, *n.*; **~rose**, Heckenrose, *f.*; **~'s-ear**, *(in a book)* Eselsohr, *n.*; **~tired**, totmüde.

dogged, **~ly**, halsstarrig, verbissen.

doggerel, Knüttelvers, *m.*

dogma, Glaubenssatz, *m.*; **~tic (ally)**, dogmatisch; **~tism**, Dogmatismus, *m.*; **~tize**, dogmatisieren.

doing, Tun, *n.*, Verrichtung, Handlung, *f.*

doldrums, Kalmengürtel, *m.*; *(fig.)* Niedergeschlagenheit, *f.*

dole, *sb.* Austeilung; Arbeitslosenunterstützung, *f.*; *go on the ~*, stempeln gehen; *v.t.* austeilen.

doleful, **~ly**, traurig, kummervoll.

doll, Puppe, *f.*

dolphin, Delphin, *m.*

dolt, Tölpel, *m.*; **~ish**, tölpelhaft.

domain, Gebiet, *n.*

dome, Kuppel, *f.*

domestic, *a.* häuslich, Haus-; einheimisch; zahm; *sb.* Dienstbote, *m.*; **~ animal**, Haustier, *n.*; **~ate**, zähmen; heimisch machen; **~ated**, häuslich.

domicile, Wohnsitz, *m.*; **~d**, wohnhaft.

domin|ant, (vor)herrschend; **~ate**, beherrschen; **~ation**, (Ober)herrschaft, *f.*; **~eer**, tyrannisieren; **~eering**, herrisch, anmaßend; **~ion**, Herrschaft, *f.*; Dominion, *n.*

Dominican, Dominikaner, *m.*

domino, Domino, *m.*; **~es**, *(game)* Domino(spiel), *n.*

donation, Schenkung, *f.*

done, see also **do**; *(cooking)* gar; *(finished)* fertig; *(exhausted)* erschöpft; *~ for*, zugrunde gerichtet, fertig.

donkey, Esel, *m.*; ~-engine, Hilfsmaschine, *f.*

donor, Geber, Schenker, *m.*

doom, *sb.* Schicksal, Verhängnis, *n.*; *v.t.* verurteilen, verdammen (*to* zu); ~sday, der Jüngste Tag.

door, Tür, *f.*; *next* ~, nebenan; *out of* ~s, im Freien; ~keeper, Pförtner, *m.*; ~post, Türpfosten, *m.*; ~way, Türöffnung, *f.*, Torweg, *m.*

dope, *sb.* Rauschgift, Betäubungsmittel, *n.*; *v.t.* betäuben.

dormant, schlafend, unbenutzt.

dormitory, Schlafsaal, *m.*

dormouse, Haselmaus, *f.*

dorsal, Rücken-.

dose, *sb.* Dosis, *f.*; *v.t.* jemandem Arznei verordnen (*or* geben).

dot, *sb.* Punkt, *m.*; *v.t.* tüpfeln.

dotage, *in his* ~, im Altersschwachsinn, wieder kindisch geworden.

dote, närrisch verliebt sein (*on* in).

double, *sb.* das Doppelte; (*person*) Doppelgänger, *m.*; *a.* doppelt; zweideutig; (*increase*) verdoppeln; (*fold*) umfalten (*naut.*) umschiffen; (*fist*) ballen; ~ barrelled, doppelläufig; ~ breasted, zweireihig; ~-dealing, Doppelzüngigkeit, Falschheit, *f.*; ~ entry, doppelte Buchführung; ~ march, Sturmschritt, *m.*; ~ meaning, Doppelsinn, *m.*; ~s, (*tennis*) Doppel(spiel).

doubt, *sb.* Zweifel, *m.*; *v.t.* zweifeln an, bezweifeln; *v.i.* zweifeln; ~er, Zweifler, *m.*; ~ful(ly), zweifelhaft; ~less, zweifellos.

douche, Dusche, *f.*

dough, Teig, *m.*

douse, (aus)löschen.

dove, Taube, *f.*; ~cot, Taubenschlag, *m.*; ~tail, *sb.* Schwalbenschwanz, *m.*; *v.t.* (ein)schwalben, fest einfügen.

dowdy, schlampig.

down¹, *sb.* Daune, *f.*

down², *prep. and adv.* hinab, herunter, nieder; *go* ~, (*of sun*) untergehen; *go* ~stairs, nach unten gehen; *knock* ~, zu Boden schlagen; *run* ~, (*clock*) abge-

laufen; (*person*) erschöpft; *up and* ~, auf und ab; ~ *with fever*, am Fieber daniederliegend; *v.t.* (*tools*) niederlegen; ~cast, niedergeschlagen; ~fall, Sturz, Untergang, *m.*; ~hearted, verzagt; ~hill, bergab; abschüssig; ~pour, Platzregen, *m.*; ~right, gerade heraus, ohne Umstände; offenherzig, bieder; ~stairs, (nach) unten; ~stream, stromab; ~trodden, niedergetreten, unterdrückt; ~wards, abwärts, hinab.

dowry, Mitgift, *f.*

doze, *sb.* Schläfchen, *n.*; *v.i.* schlummern.

dozen, Dutzend, *n.*

draft, (*banker's*) Wechsel, *m.*; (*sketch*) Skizze, *f.*; (*mil.*) Detachement, *n.*; *v.t.* (*document*) aufsetzen; (*sketch*) entwerfen; (*mil.*) detachieren, abkommandieren.

drag, *sb.* (*brake*) Hemmschuh, *m.*; (*aeronaut.*) Luftwiderstand, *m.*; *v.t.* ziehen, schleppen; ~ *anchor*, vor Anker treiben.

dragon, Drache, *m.*; ~-fly, Libelle, *f.*

dragoon, Dragoner, *m.*

drain, *sb.* Abzugs -graben, -kanal, *m.*; *v.t.* dränieren, trocken legen; (*drink*) ausleeren; (*deprive*) entblößen; ~age, Entwässerung. Dränierung, *f.*; ~-pipe, Abzugsrohr, *n.*

drake, Enterich, *m.*

drama, Drama, *n.*; ~tic(ally), dramatisch; ~tist, Dramatiker, *m.*

drape, drapieren, schmücken; ~r, Tuchhändler, *m.*; ~ry, Tuch, Zeug, *n.*; Tuchgeschäft, *n.*; (*art*) Drapierung, *f.*

drastic, ~ally, drastisch, kräftig.

draught, (*hauling*) Zug, *m.*; (*air*) Luftzug, *m.*; (*fishes*) Fischzug, *m.*; (*drink*) Trunk, *m.*; (*sketch*) Entwurf, *m.*, Skizze, *f.*; (*ship*) Tiefgang, *m.*; *on* ~, vom Faß; ~ *animal*, Zugtier, *n.*; ~-board, Dam(e)brett, *n.*; ~s, (*game*) Damenspiel, *n.*; ~sman, (Muster)zeichner, *m.*

draw, *sb.* Ziehen, Los, *n.*, Aus-

losung, f.: unentschiedenes
Spiel, n.; Zugstück, n.; v.t.
ziehen; (liquids) abziehen,
schöpfen; (teeth) ausziehen;
(sketch) zeichnen; (attract) anziehen; (bow) spannen; ~ back,
(sich) zurückziehen; ~ near,
sich nähern; ~ off, abziehen;
~ on, anziehen, heranrücken;
~ up, in die Höhe ziehen;
(document) abfassen; (mil.) aufstellen; (carriage) vorfahren;
~back, Kehrseite, f., Nachteil,
m.; ~bridge, Zugbrücke, f.;
~er, Schublade, f.; ~ers,
Unterhose, f.; ~ing, Zeichnung,
f.; ~ing-board, Reißbrett, n.;
~ing-room, Gesellschaftszim-
mer, n., Salon, m.

drawl, (die Worte) dehnen.

dread, sb. Schrecken, m.; v.t.
(sich) sehr fürchten (vor);
~ful(ly) schrecklich, furchtbar;
~nought, Dreadnought, m.

dream, sb. Traum, m.; v.i.
träumen; ~er, Träumer, m.;
~y, träumerisch.

drear, ~y, ~ily, traurig, trostlos,
öde; langweilig; ~iness,
Traurigkeit; Langweiligkeit, f.

dredge, baggern; ~r, Bagger, m.

drench, durchnässen.

dress, sb. Kleidung, f.; Anzug, m.,
Kleid, n.; in full ~, in vollem
Staat; v.t. ankleiden; (wound)
verbinden; (cooking) zurichten;
(hair) frisieren; (skins) zurichten; v.i. sich anziehen;
(mil.) sich richten; ~circle,
erster Rang; ~coat, Frack, m.;
~er, (kitchen) Anrichte, f.;
~ing, Ankleiden, n.; (for
wounds) Verband(stoff), m.;
(skins) Zurichten, n.; (food)
Zutat, Füllung, Sauce, f.; ~ing-
gown, Schlafrock, m.; ~ing-
room, (sport) Umkleideraum, m.;
~ing-station, Verbandplatz, m.;
~ing-table, Toilettentisch, m.;
~maker, Damenschneiderin, f.;
~making, Damenschneiderei,
f.; ~suit, Gesellschaftsanzug,
m.; ~y, putzsüchtig, modisch.

dribble, tröpfeln, geifern; (football)
dribbeln.

drift, sb. (naut.) Abtrift, f.; (snow)

Schneewehe; (fig.) Tendenz, Absicht, f.; a. Treib-; v.i. treiben;
(snow) sich aufhäufen; ~er,
(Fisch)logger, m.; ~ice, Treib-
eis, n.

drill, sb. (tool) Dreh-, Drill- bohrer,
m.; (agric.) Furche, f.; (mil.)
Exerzieren, n., Drill, m.; (cloth)
Drillich, m.; v.t. drillen, bohren;
einexerzieren; v.i. exerzieren;
~ground, Exerzierplatz, m.

drink, sb. (geistiges) Getränk, n.;
a ~, ein Trunk, Schluck, m.;
v.t. trinken; (of animals and
vulg.) saufen; ~ing-bout, Trinkgelage, n.; ~ing-water, Trink-
wasser, n.

drip, tröpfeln; ~dry, bügelfrei;
~ping, Bratenfett, n.

drive, sb. Fahrweg, m.; Ausfahrt,
f.; (tennis, &c.) Drive, Flach-
schlag, m.; (mech.) Antrieb, m.;
v.t. (train, motor, &c.) fahren
(nails, &c.) einschlagen; (bargain) (ein gutes Geschäft) zum
Abschluß bringen; ~ in, fahren;
~ away, weg-, fort- treiben;
~ back, zurücktreiben; zurückfahren; ~ off, wegtreiben; fortfahren; ~er, Kutscher,
Fuhrmann, (Lokomotiv)führer,
Fahrer, Chauffeur, m.; ~ing-
band, -belt, Treibriemen, m.;
~ing-box, Kutschbock, m.

drivel, sb. Geifer; (fig.) Unsinn, m.;
v.i. geifern; (fig.) faseln.

drizzle, sb. Sprühregen, m.; v.i.
rieseln, nieseln.

dromedary, Dromedar, n.

drone, sb. Drohne, f.; (pers.)
Faulenzer, m.; v.i. summen.

drop, sb. Tropfen; Fall, m.; Sinken,
n.; (sweet) Plätzchen, n.; v.t.
fallen lassen, aufgeben, absetzen; (bombs) abwerfen; v.i.
(nieder)fallen, sinken; ~ in,
zufällig vorsprechen; ~ off,
abfallen; ~ out, wegfallen, ausscheiden; ~scene, (Theater)
vorhang, m.; Schlussszene, f.

drops|y, Wassersucht, f.; ~ical,
wassersüchtig.

dross, Schlacke, f.; Abfall, m.

drought, Dürre, Trockenheit, f.

drove, Herde, f.; ~r, Viehtreiber,
m.

drown, v.t. ertränken; (sounds) übertönen; to be ~ed, ertrinken.

drowsy, schläfrig; ~iness, Schläfrigkeit, f.

drudgery, Plackerei, f.

drug, sb. (pharm.) Droge, f.; Rauschgift, n.; v.t. betäuben; ~addict, Rauschgiftsüchtige(r); ~gist, Drogist, Drogenhändler, m.

drum, sb. Trommel, f.; (of ear) Trommelfell, n.; (of oil, &c.) Faß, n.; v.i. trommeln; ~major, Tambourmajor, m.; ~mer, Trommler, m.; ~stick, Trommelstock, m.

drunk, betrunken; ~ard, Trunkenbold, m.; ~enness, Trunkenheit, f.

dry, a. trocken, dürr, ausgetrocknet; (pers.) trocken, langweilig; (wine) herb; v.t. trocknen; (fruit) dörren; v.i. dürr werden, austrocknen; ~ cell, Trockenelement, n.; ~clean, chemisch reinigen; ~dock, Trockendock, n.; ~ing, Trocken-; ~ness, Trockenheit, f.; ~nurse, Kinderwärterin, f.; ~shod, trockenen Fußes.

dryad, Dryade, Waldnymphe, f.

dual, Zwei-, Doppel-.

dub, ernennen; (film) nachsynchronisieren.

dubbing, Lederschmiere, f.

dubious, ~ly, zweifelhaft.

duchess, Herzogin, f.; ~y, Herzogtum, n.

duck, sb. Ente, f.; v.t. untertauchen; v.i. sich ducken; ~board, Holzrost, Plankenweg, m.; ~ing, Tauchen, n.; ~ling, junge Ente.

duct, Kanal, Gang, m., Röhre, f.

dud, Blindgänger, m.

due, sb. das Gebührende; Gebühr, Abgabe, f.; a., fällig, zustehend, schuldig; ~ to, veranlaßt durch, die Folge von.

duel, Zweikampf, m.

duffer, Tölpel, Pfuscher, m.

dug-out, (mil.) Unterstand, Bunker, m.

duke, Herzog, m.; ~dom, Herzogtum, n.

dull, a. (colour) matt; (sound) dumpf; (weather) trüb; (business) flau; (edge) stumpf; (pers.) dumm, plump; (wearisome) langweilig; v.t. stumpf machen; abstumpfen; trüben; ~ness, Dumpfheit; Stumpfheit; Glanzlosigkeit; Trübheit; Dummheit; Langweiligkeit; Flauheit, f.

duly, gehörig, pünktlich.

dumb, ~ly, stumm; ~bells, Hanteln, f.pl.; ~founded, verblüfft; ~ness, Stummheit, f.; ~ show, Gebärdenspiel, n.; ~waiter, Drehtisch, m.

dummy, (tailor's) Kleiderpuppe, f.; (baby's) (Gummi)lutscher, m.; (whist, &c.) Strohmann, m.; Attrappe, f.; ~ cartridge, Exerzierpatrone, f.; ~ signal, Scheinfunk, m.

dump, sb. Ablade-, Sammel-stelle, f.; (Munitions)lager, Depot, n.; v.t. hinwerfen, abladen; auf den Markt werfen; ~heap, Schutthaufen, m.

dumpling, Mehlkloß, m.

dumpy, kurz und dick, untersetzt.

dun, a. falb, braungelb; v.t. drängen (um).

dunce, Dummkopf, m.

dune, Düne, f.

dung, sb. Mist, Dünger, m.; v.t. düngen; ~fork, Mistgabel, f.; ~heap, Misthaufen, m.

dungeon, Kerker, m.

dupe, sb. Betrogene(r), Gimpel, m.; v.t. anführen, täuschen.

duplicate, sb. Duplikat, n.; a. doppelt; v.t. verdoppeln, vervielfältigen; ~or, Vervielfältigungsapparat, m.

duplicity. Zweideutigkeit, f.

durable, dauerhaft; ~ility, Dauerhaftigkeit, f.

duration, Dauer, f.

during, während.

dusk, Dämmerung, f.; ~y, dämmerig, dunkel.

dust, sb. Staub, m.; v.t. abstäuben; ~bin, Müllkasten, m.; ~cart, Müllwagen, m.; ~er, Wischlappen, Staubbesen, m; ~jacket, Schutzumschlag, m.; ~man, Kehrichtfuhrmann, m.; ~sheet, Staubdecke, f.; ~storm, Sandsturm, m.; ~y, staubig.

dut|y, Pflicht, *f.*; (*tax, &c.*) Zoll, *m.*, Steuer, *f.*; **on ~**, im Dienst; **auf Wache**; **~iful(ly)**, pflichttreu, gehorsam; **~-free**, zollfrei.

dwarf, *sb.* Zwerg, *m.*; *v.t.* (*fig.*) in den Schatten stellen; **~ed**, zwerghaft; verkümmert.

dwell, wohnen; verweilen; **~ on**, betonen, sich aufhalten (bei); **~ing**, Wohnung, *f.*; **~ing-place**, Wohnort, *m.*

dwindle, abnehmen, sich vermindern.

dye, *sb.* Farbstoff, *m.*; *v.t.* färben; **~ing**, Färben, *n.*; **~r**, Färber, *m.*; **~-works**, Färberei, *f.*

dynam|ic, dynamisch; **~ics**, Dynamik, *f.*; **~o**, Dynamo, *m.*

dynamite, Dynamit, *n.*

dynast|y, Dynastie, *f.*; **~ic**, dynastisch.

dysentery, Ruhr, *f.*

dyspepsia, Dyspepsie, *f.*

E

each, jede(r, s); **~ other**, einander, sich.

eager, **~ly**, eifrig; **~ness**, Eifer, *m.*, Begierde, *f.*

eagle, Adler, *m.*

ear, Ohr, *n.*; (*wheat, &c.*) Ähre, *f.*; **lend an ~**, jemandem Gehör schenken; *prick up one's ~s*, die Ohren spitzen; **~-ache**, Ohrenschmerzen, *m.pl.*; **~-lap**, Ohrläppchen, *n.*; **~-mark**, *sb.* Kennzeichen, *n.*; *v.t.* vormerken; **~-phones**, Kopfhörer, *m.pl.*; **~-piece**, (*telephone*) Hörmuschel, *f.*; **~-shot**, Hörweite, *f.*; **~-wax**, Ohrenschmalz, *n.*; **~-wig**, Ohrwurm, *m.*

earl, Graf, *m.*; **~dom**, Grafenwürde, *f.*

early, früh, zeitig.

earn, verdienen; **~ings**, Verdienst, Lohn, *m.*

earnest, **~ly**, ernstlich; **~ness**, Ernsthaftigkeit, *f.*

earth, *sb.* Erde, *f.*; (*radio*) Erdung, *f.*, Erdschluß, *m.*, Erdleitung *f.*; *v.t.* (*radio*) erden; **~en**, irden; **~enware**, Töpferware, *f.*, Steingut, *n.*; **~ly**, irdisch; **~quake**, Erdbeben, *n.*; **~worm**, Regenwurm, *m.*

ease, *sb.* Ruhe, Gemächlichkeit, Erleichterung, *f.*; *at ~*, bequem, gemächlich; *stand at ~!*, (*mil.*) rührt euch!; *v.t.* erleichtern, lindern.

easel, Staffelei, *f.*

easiness, Leichtigkeit, Bequemlichkeit, *f.*

east, *sb.*, *a.* Osten, Orient, *m.*; *a.*, **~erly**, **~ern**, östlich; **~ward**, ostwärts.

Easter, Ostern, *n. or pl.*; **~ Sunday**, Ostersonntag, *m.*

easy, **eas|ily**, leicht; bequem; ungezwungen; **~ chair**, Lehnstuhl, *m.*; **~-going**, lässig, gutmütig.

eat, essen; (*animals*) fressen; **~able**, eßbar; **~ables**, Eßwaren, Lebensmittel, *pl.*; **~ing-house**, Restaurant, Speisehaus, *n.*

eau-de-Cologne, Kölnisches Wasser.

eaves, Dachtraufe, *f.*; **~dropper**, Horcher, *m.*

ebb, *sb.* Ebbe, *f.*; *v.i.* ebben.

ebony, Ebenholz, *n.*

eccentric, exzentrisch; **~ity**, Exzentrizität, *f.*

ecclesiastic, *sb.* Geistliche(r); *a.*, **~al**, geistlich, kirchlich.

echelon, *sb.* Staffel, *f.*; *v.t.* staffeln.

echo, *sb.* Widerhall, *m.*, Echo, *n.*; *v.* widerhallen.

éclat, Aufsehen, *n.*

eclipse, *sb.* Verfinsterung, *f.*; **~ of the moon**, Mondfinsternis, *f.*; **~ of the sun**, Sonnenfinsternis, *f.*; *v.t.* verfinstern; (*fig.*) verdunkeln.

econom|ical, **~ly**, sparsam, wirtschaftlich; **~ics**, Volkswirtschaft, *f.*; **~ist**, Ökonom, *m.*; **~ize**, (er)sparen; **~y**, Sparsamkeit, *f.*; *political ~y*, Volkswirtschaft, *f.*

ecsta|sy, Verzückung, Ekstase, *f.*; **~tic**, ver-, ent- zückt.

eczema, Ekzem, *n.*

eddy, *sb.* Wirbel, *m.*; *v.i.* wirbeln.

edge, *sb.* (*blade*) Schärfe, Schneide, *f.*; (*rim, border*) Rand, *m.*, Kante, *f.*; *v.t.* einfassen, säumen; ~ing, Besatz, *m.*, Einfassung, *f.*

edible, eßbar.

edict, Verordnung, *f.*

edif|y, erbauen; ~ication, Erbauung, *f.*; ~ice, Gebäude, *n.*; ~ying, erbaulich.

edit, herausgeben; ~ion, Ausgabe, Auflage, *f.*; ~or, Herausgeber, Redakteur, *m.*; ~orial, Leitartikel, *m.*

educat|e, erziehen; ~ed, gebildet; ~ion, Erziehung, *f.*; ~ive, bildend, Unterrichts-.

eel, Aal, *m.*

eerie, unheimlich.

efface, austilgen.

effect, *sb.* Wirkung, *f.*; *v.t.* bewirken, ausführen; ~ive, wirksam; ~s, Habe, *f.*, Effekten, *pl.*

effemina|cy, Weichlichkeit, *f.*; ~te, weibisch, weichlich.

effervesce, aufbrausen; ~nce, Aufbrausen, *n.*; ~nt, Brause-.

effete, abgebraucht, schwächlich.

effica|cious, wirksam; ~y, Wirksamkeit, *f.*

efficien|cy, Leistungsfähigkeit, Tüchtigkeit, Wirksamkeit, *f.*; ~t(ly), (leistungs)fähig, tüchtig, wirksam.

effigy, Bild(nis), *n.*

effort, Anstrengung, *f.*

effrontery, Frechheit, *f.*

efful|gence, Glanz, Schimmer, *m.*; ~t, glänzend, strahlend.

effu|sion, Ausgießung, *f.*; Erguß, *m.*; ~ive, überschwenglich.

egg, Ei, *n.*; *boiled* ~, gekochtes Ei; *fried* ~, Spiegelei, *n.*; *new-laid* ~, frisch gelegtes Ei; *scrambled* ~, Rührei, *n.*; *v.t.* ~ *on*, aufhetzen; anreizen; ~cup, Eierbecher, *m.*; ~shell, Eierschale, *f.*

ego|ism, Egoismus, *m.*; ~ist, Egoist, *m.*

Egyptian, *sb.* Ägypter, *m.*; *a.* ägyptisch.

eider|-duck, Eidergans, *f.*; ~down, Eiderdaune; Bettdecke, *f.*

eight, acht; ~een, achtzehn; ~eenth, achtzehnte; ~h, achte; ~hly, achtens; ~ieth, achtzigste; ~y, achtzig; *the*

~ies, die achtziger Jahre.

either, *pron.* eine(r, s) von beiden; jede(r, s) von beiden; beide; *conj.* entweder.

ejaculat|e, ausrufen; ~ion, Ausruf, *m.*

eject, ausstoßen, vertreiben; ~ion, Ausweisung, Vertreibung, *f.*

elaborate, *a.*, ~ly, ausgearbeitet, kunstvoll; umständlich; *v.t.* ausarbeiten, verfeinern.

elapse, verfließen, verlaufen.

elastic, *a.* elastisch; *sb.* Gummiband, *n.*; ~ity, Federkraft, Elastizität, *f.*

elat|ed, gehoben, erhaben, stolz; ~ion, gehobene Stimmung, *f.*

elbow, *sb.* Ellbogen, *m.*; (*mech.*) Knie, *n.*; *v.t.* ~ *out*, verdrängen; ~-room, (*fig.*) Spielraum, *m.*

elder¹, *sb.* (*bot.*) Holunder, Flieder, *m.*

elder², *a.* älter; *sb.* (*church*) Älteste(r); ~ly, ältlich, bejahrt.

elect, *v.t.* wählen; *a.* erwählt; ~ion, Wahl, *f.*; ~ive, ~oral, Wahl-; ~or, Wähler, *m.*; ~orate, Wählerschaft, *f.*

electric, ~al, elektrisch; ~al *engineer*, Elektrotechniker, *m.*; ~ *razor*, Trockenrasierer, *m.*; ~ian, Elektriker, *m.*; ~ity, Elektrizität, *f.*

electrif|y, elektrisieren; elektrifizieren; ~ication, Elektrisieren, *n.*; Elektrifizierung, *f.*

electron, Elektron, *n.*

electro, ~cute, elektrisch hinrichten; (*accident*) durch Strom töten; ~cution, elektrische Hinrichtung, *f.*; ~magnetic, elektromagnetisch; ~plate, (*galvanisch*) versilberte Ware; ~plated, (galvanisch) versilbert; ~type, Galvano, *n.*

elegan|ce, Eleganz, Zierlichkeit, *f.*; ~t(ly), elegant, zierlich.

eleg|y, Elegie, *f.*; ~iac, elegisch.

element, Element, *n.*; ~ary, elementar, einfach; ~ary *school*, Volksschule, *f.*

elephant, Elefant, *m.*

elevat|e, erhöhen, erheben; (*host*) emporheben; ~ion, Erhöhung, *f.*; (*height*) Höhe, *f.*; (*drawing*) Aufriß, *m.*; (*of host*) Emporheben, *n.*; ∼or, (*lift*) Lift, *m.*; (*on aircraft*) Höhenruder, *n.*

eleven, elf; ∼th, elfte; ∼thly, elftens.

elf, Kobold, *m.*. Elf(e, *f.*), *m.*

elicit, herauslocken, hervorrufen.

elide, elidieren; auslassen.

eligib|le, wählbar; wünschenswert, passend; ∼ility, Wählbarkeit, *f.*

eliminat|e, ausscheiden, entfernen; ∼ion, Ausscheidung, Wegschaffung, *f.*

elision, Weglassung, Ausstoßung, Elision, *f.*

elixir, Elixir, *n.*

elk, Elentier, *n.*

ellip|sis, Ellipse, *f.*; ∼tical, elliptisch.

elm, Ulme, *f.*

elocution, Redekunst; Vortragsweise, *f.*

elongate, verlängern.

elope, entlaufen, sich entführen lassen; ∼ment, Entlaufen, *n.*

eloquen|ce, Beredsamkeit, *f.*; ∼t(ly), beredt, beredsam.

else, sonst; *anyone* ∼, irgend ein anderer; *everybody* ∼, jeder andere; *nobody* ∼, sonst niemand; ∼where, anderswo.

elucidate, erläutern.

elude, ausweichen, entgehen.

elusive, ∼ly, ausweichend; flüchtig; täuschend, trügerisch.

emaciat|ed, abgemagert; ∼ion, Abmagerung, *f.*

emanat|e, austrahlen; herrühren; ∼ion, Ausströmung, Ausstrahlung, *f.*

emancipat|e, befreien; ∼ion, Emanzipation, Freimachung, *f.*

embalm, einbalsamieren.

embankment, Eindämmung, *f.*; (*railway, &c.*) Damm, *m.*

embargo, Embargo; (Handels)verbot, *n.*

embark, (sich) einschiffen; (*fig.*) sich einlassen (auf); ∼ation, Einschiffung, *f.*

embarrass, verlegen machen, hindern; ∼ment, Verlegenheit, *f.*

embassy, Gesandtschaft, Botschaft, *f.*

embedded, eingebettet, eingelagert

(*in* in).

embellish, verschönern; ∼ment, Verschönerung, *f.*

embers, glühende Kohlen, *f.pl.*

embezzle, unterschlagen, veruntreuen; ∼ment, Unterschlagung, *f.*

embitter, verbittern.

emblem, Sinnbild, *n.*; ∼atical, sinnbildlich.

embod|y, verkörpern, einverleiben; umfassen, enthalten; ∼iment, Verkörperung, *f.*

embrace, *sb.* Umarmung, *f.*; *v.t.* umarmen; (*fig.*) umfassen, enthalten.

embrasure, Schießscharte; Fenster-, Tür- vertiefung, *f.*

embrocation, Einreibungsmittel, *n.*

embroider, sticken; ausschmücken; ∼y, Stickerei, *f.*

embryo, Embryo, *m.*

emend, verbessern; ∼ation, Verbesserung, *f.*

emerald, Smaragd, *m.*

emerge, auftauchen, emporkommen.

emergency, *sb.* Notfall, *m.*; *a.* Not-.

emery, Schmirgel, *m.*

emetic, Brechmittel, *n.*

emigr|ate, auswandern; ∼ant, émigré, Emigrant *m.*; ∼ation, Auswanderung, *f.*

eminen|ce, Anhöhe; (*title*) Eminenz, *f.*; ∼t, hervorragend, ausgezeichnet.

emissary, Abgesandte(r).

emission, Ausströmung, Ausstrahlung, *f.*

emit, aussenden, ausströmen lassen; verbreiten.

emolument, Gewinn, *m.*; Gehalt, *n.*; ∼s, Einkünfte, Sporteln, *f.pl.*

emotion, Gemütsbewegung, *f.*; ∼al, erregbar, leicht bewegt.

emperor, Kaiser, *m.*

empha|sis, Nachdruck, *m.*; ∼size, Nachdruck auf . . . legen; ∼tic, nachdrücklich.

empire, Reich, *n.*

empiric, empirisch, erfahrungsmäßig.

employ, *v.t.* (*use*) anwenden; (*person*) beschäftigen; ∼ee, Arbeitnehmer, *m.*; Angestellte, *m.* or *f.*; ~er, Arbeitgeber, *m.*; ~ment, Arbeit, Beschäftigung, *f.*; (*position*) Amt, *n.*, Stelle, *f.*

emporium, Stapelplatz, *m.*; (*shop*) Warenhaus, *n.*

empower, ermächtigen.

empress, Kaiserin, *f.*

empt|iness, Leere; Nichtigkeit, *f.*; ~y, *a.* leer: *on an* ~ *stomach*, auf nüchternen Magen; *v.t.* (aus)leeren.

emu, Emu, *m.*

emulat|e, wetteifern (*with* mit); ~ion, Wetteifer, *m.*

emulsion, Emulsion; (*photog.*) Schicht, *f.*

enable, in den Stand setzen; möglich machen.

enact, verordnen; (*laws*) erlassen.

enamel, Emaille, *f.*; Schmelz, *m.*; *v.t.* emaillieren.

enamoured, verliebt.

encamp, (sich) lagern; ~ment, Lager, *n.*

enchant, bezaubern; ~er, Zauberer, *m.*; ~ment, Bezauberung, *f.*

encircle, umringen.

enclos|e, einhegen, einschließen; (*in a letter, &c.*) beischließen; ~ure, Einhegung, *f.*, Zaun, *m.*; (*letter, &c.*) Einlage, *f.*

encore, *adv.* noch einmal! da capo!; *sb.* Dacaporuf, *m.*; *v.t.* da capo verlangen.

encounter, *sb.* Zusammentreffen; Gefecht, *n.*; *v.t.* zusammentreffen mit; stoßen auf.

encourage, ermutigen, aufmuntern; fördern; unterstützen; ~ment, Ermutigung; Unterstützung, *f.*

encroach, einen Eingriff tun, übergreifen; ~ment, Eingriff, *m.*

encumb|er, beschweren, belasten; ~rance, Bürde, Belastung, *f.*

encyclopedia, Enzyklopädie, *f.*; Konversationslexikon, *n.*

end, *sb.* Ende, *n.*; (*aim*) Absicht, *f.*; *v.t.* beenden, beendigen; *v.i.* enden, aufhören; *at an* ~, zu Ende; *in the* ~, schließlich; *no* ~ *of*, unendlich viel; *to no* ~, vergebens; *make both* ~*s meet*, sich durchschlagen; auskommen; *his hair stood on* ~, die

Haare standen ihm zu Berge; ~ing, Schluß *m.*, Ende, *n.*; Endung, *f.*; ~less(ly), unendlich, endlos.

endanger, gefährden.

endear, lieb machen; ~ment, Liebkosung, *f.*

endeavour, *sb.* Bestreben, *n.*; *v.i.* sich bemühen, sich bestreben.

endemic, endemisch.

endorse, indossieren; (*fig.*) billigen; ~ment, Indossierung; (*fig.*) Billigung, *f.*

endow, begaben, ausstatten; ~ment, Stiftung, *f.*

endur|e, aushalten, erdulden; ~able, erträglich; ~ance, Ausdauer, *f.*; Erdulden, *n.*; (*attrib.*) Dauer-.

enemy, Feind, *m.*; (*attrib.*) feindlich, Feind-.

energ|etic, ~etically, energisch, kraftvoll; ~y, Energie, Kraft, *f.*

enervat|e, entnerven, schwächen; ~ing, schwächend.

enfilade, *sb.* Längsbestreichung, *f.*; *v.t.* der Länge nach bestreichen.

enforce, erzwingen, durchsetzen; geltend machen; ~ment, Durchsetzung, Erzwingung, *f.*

enfranchise, das Wahlrecht erteilen; (*slaves*) befreien.

engage, *v.t.* (*rooms, &c.*) mieten, bestellen; (*employee*) in Dienst nehmen, anstellen; (*enemy*) angreifen; (*mech.*) einrücken, in Gang setzen; *v.i.* (*pledge*) sich verpflichten (*to* zu); ~d, (*occupied*) beschäftigt (*in* mit); (*betrothed*) verlobt (*to* mit); (*pledged to*) zu jemandem verpflichtet; (*seat, room, &c.*) besetzt, bestellt, gemietet; ~ment, Verpflichtung, *f.*; (*betrothal*) Verlobung, *f.*; (*fight*) Gefecht, *n.*; (*appointment*) Engagement, *n.*, Anstellung, *f.*; *I have an* ~*ment for this evening*, ich bin heute abend schon anderweitig in Anspruch genommen.

engine, Maschine, *f.*; Motor, *m.*; (*railway*) Lokomotive, *f.*; (*fire*) Feuerspritze, *f.*; ~-driver, Lokomotivführer, *m.*; ~man,

Maschinist, *m.*; ~room, Maschinenraum, *m.*; ~shed, Lokomotivschuppen, *m.*; ~trouble, Motorstörung, *f.*

engineer, *sb.* Ingenieur, Techniker; (*mil.*) Pionier, *m.*; *v.t.* (*fig.*) durchsetzen, einrichten; ~ing, Ingenieurwesen, *n.*; *electrical* ~ing, Elektrotechnik, *f.*

English, *a.* englisch; *sb.* (*language*) Englisch, *n.*; ~man, Engländer, *m.*; ~woman, Engländerin, *f.*

engrav|e, gravieren, stechen; ~ing, Kupfer-, Stahl- stich, Holzschnitt, *m.*

enhance, erhöhen, steigern.

enigma, Rätsel, *n.*; ~tical, rätselhaft.

enjoy, genießen; ~ *oneself*, sich amüsieren; ~able, angenehm; ~ment, Genuß, *m.*

enlarge, erweitern, vergrößern; ~ment, Erweiterung, Vergrößerung, *f.*

enlighten, aufklären, belehren; ~ment, Aufklärung, *f.*

enlist, *v.t.* (an)werben; *v.i.* sich anwerben lassen; ~ment, Anwerbung, *f.*

enliven, beleben, ermuntern.

enmity, Feindschaft, *f.*

ennoble, veredeln.

enorm|ity, Ungeheuerlichkeit, *f.*; ~ous(ly), ungeheuer.

enough, genug, genügend.

enquire = inquire.

enrage, in Wut versetzen.

enrich, bereichern.

enrol, einschreiben; (*mil.*) anwerben.

ensign, Fahne, Flagge, *f.*; (*person*) Fähnrich, *m.*

enslave, knechten.

ensnare, fangen, verstricken.

ensue, (er)folgen, sich ergeben.

entail, *sb.* Fideikommiss, *n.*; *v.t.* zu einem Fideikommiss machen; (*involve*) zur Folge haben, nach sich ziehen.

entangle, verwickeln, verwirren; ~ment, Verwicklung, Verwirrung, *f.*; (*mil.*) Verhau, *m.*

enter, *v.i.* ein -fahren, -laufen, -treten, hineingehen; (*exam.*) sich stellen (*for* zu); *v.t.* be-

treten, ein -fahren, -laufen, -treten in; (*one's name*) sich einschreiben, eintragen; ~ *into* (*subject*) eindringen; (*agreement*) ein Abkommen schließen.

enterpris|e, Unternehmung, *f.*; Unternehmungsgeist, *m.*; ~ing, unternehmend.

entertain, unterhalten; bewirten; (*hopes*) hegen; ~ment, Unterhaltung, *f.*; Schauspiel, *n.*

enthral, (*fig.*) fesseln; ~ling, (*fig.*) bezaubernd, fesselnd.

enthusias|m, Begeisterung, *f.*; ~t, Schwärmer, Begeisterte(r), *m.*; ~tic(ally), begeistert, schwärmerisch.

entic|e, reizen, verführen; ~ement, Reiz, *m.*; Verführung, *f.*; ~ing(ly), verführerisch.

entire, ~ly, ganz, vollständig; ~ty, Ganzheit, *f.*

entitle, berechtigen.

entity, Wesen, *n.*

entomolog|ist, Entomolog, Insektenkenner, *m.*; ~y, Insektenkunde, *f.*

entrails, Eingeweide, *n.pl.*

entrain, *v.t.* verladen; *v.i.* (in einen Zug) einsteigen.

entrance[1], *sb.* Eingang; Eintritt, *m.*; ~fee, Eintrittsgeld, *n.*; ~hall, Vorhalle, *f.*

entrance[2], entzücken.

entrant, (*sport*) Bewerber (in, *f.*), *m.*

entreat, ersuchen, anflehen; ~y, Bitte, *f.*

entrench, (*mil.*) verschanzen; ~ment, Verschanzung, Grabenstellung, *f.*

entrust, anvertrauen.

entry, Eingang, Eintritt, *m.*; (*of a name, &c.*) Eintragung, *f.*; (*book-keeping*) Posten, *m.*

enumerat|e, aufzählen; ~ion, Aufzählung, *f.*

envelop, einhüllen, einwickeln.

envelope, *sb.* Hülle, *f.*; (*letter*) Briefumschlag, *m.*

envi|able, beneidenswert; ~ous (ly), neidisch.

environ|ment, Umgebung, *f.*; Milieu, *n.*; ~s, Umgebung, *f.*

envoy, Gesandte(r), *m.*

envy, *sb.* Neid, *m.*; *v.t.* beneiden.

ephemera, Eintagsfliege, *f.*; ~l, eintägig; (rasch) vorübergehend.

epic, *sb.* Epos, *n.*; *a.* episch.

epicure, Feinschmecker, *m.*

epidemic, Epidemie, Seuche, *f.*

epigram, Epigramm, Sinngedicht, *n.*

epilep|sy, Epilepsie, Fallsucht, *f.*; ~tic, epileptisch, fallsüchtig.

epilogue, Epilog, *m.*; Schlußwort, *n.*

Epiphany, Dreikönigsfest, *n.*

episcopa|cy, Episkopat, *n.*; ~l, bischöflich; ~te, Bistum, *n.*

epitaph, Grabschrift, *f.*

epithet, Beiwort, *n.*

epoch, Epoche, *f.*

equable, gleichförmig; ruhig.

equal, *a.*, ~ly, gleich, gleichmässig; (*fig.*) gewachsen (*dat.*); *v.t.* jemandem gleich sein, gleichen; ~ity, Gleichheit, *f.*; ~ize, gleichmachen; ~ization, Gleichstellung, *f.*

equanimity, Gleichmut, *m.*

equation, Gleichung, *f.*

equator, Äquator, *m.*; ~ial, äquatorial.

equestrian, *sb.* (Kunst)reiter, *m.*; *a.* reitend, Reiter-.

equilateral, gleichseitig.

equilibrium, Gleichgewicht, *n.*

equino|x, Tag- und Nachtgleiche, *f.*; ~ctial, äquinoktial.

equip, ausrüsten; versehen (*with* mit); ~ment, Ausrüstung, *f.*

equitable, billig; ~y, Billigkeit, *f.*

equivalent, *a.* gleichwertig; *sb.* Gegenwert, *m.*, Äquivalent, *n.*

equivocal, zweideutig.

era, Zeit(rechnung), Ära, *f.*

eradicate, ausrotten.

eras|e, ausradieren; ~er, Radiermesser, *n.*, -gummi, *m.*; ~ure, Ausradierung, *f.*

erect, *a.* aufrecht, grade; *v.t.* aufrichten, errichten, aufstellen; ~ion, Aufrichtung, *f.*; Gebäude, *n.*

ermine, (*animal*) Hermelin, *n.*; (*fur*) Hermelin, *m.*

erosion, Zerfressung; Wegschwemmung, *f.*

erotic, erotisch, Liebes-.

err, (sich) irren; umherschweifen.

errand, Auftrag, *m.*; ~-boy, Laufjunge, *m.*

erratic, (umher)wandernd; seltsam, exzentrisch; unregelmäßig; (*geol.*) erratisch.

erratum, Druckfehler, *m.*

erroneous, ~ly, irrig, irrtümlich.

error, Irrtum, Fehler, *m.*

erudit|e, gelehrt; ~ion, Gelehrsamkeit, *f.*

eruption, (*volcano*) Ausbruch, *m.*; (*skin*) Hautausschlag, *m.*

erysipelas, Rotlauf, *m.*; Rose, *f.*

escalator, Rolltreppe, *f.*

escapade, Seitensprung, Streich, *m.*

escape, *sb.* Flucht, *f.*, Entrinnen, *n.*; (*gas, fluids, &c.*) Ausströmen, *n.*; *v.i.* entlaufen, entrinnen, davonkommen; ~ *by the skin of one's teeth*, mit knapper Not davonkommen; ~ *one's notice*, seiner Aufmerksamkeit entgehen.

escort, *sb.* Bedeckung, Sicherung, *f.*, Geleit, *n.*; *v.t.* geleiten, decken.

escutcheon, Wappenschild, *m.* or *n.*

especial, besonder, ~ly, besonders.

espionage, Spionage, *f.*

esplanade, Esplanade, *f.*

espous|al, Vermählung, *f.*; ~e, verheiraten; (*a cause*) Partei nehmen (für).

essay, *sb.* Versuch; Aufsatz, *m.*; *v.t.* versuchen, prüfen.

essen|ce, Wesen, *n.*; (*extract*) Essenz, *f.*; ~tial(ly), wesentlich.

establish, errichten, (be)gründen; ~ed Church, die Staatskirche; ~ment, Gründung, Niederlassung; Organisation, *f.*; Bestand, *m.*

estate, (*condition*) Stand, *m.*; (*property*) (Land)gut, Besitztum, Vermögen, *n.*; ~ agent, Landagent, *m.*

esteem, *sb.* Achtung, *f.*; *v.t.* achten, schätzen.

estimable, achtungswert.

estimat|e, *sb.* Schätzung, *f.*; Voranschlag, *m.*; *v.t.* schätzen, berechnen; veranschlagen; ~ion, Schätzung; Meinung; Achtung, *f.*

estrangement, Entfremdung, *f.*

estuary, Mündung, *f.*

etch, ätzen, radieren; ~ing, Radierung, *f.*

etern|al, ~ally, ewig; ~ity, Ewigkeit, *f.*

ether, Äther, *m.*; ~eal, ätherisch.

ethic|al, ~ally, ethisch, sittlich; ~s, Ethik, Sittenlehre, *f.*

ethnography, Völkerkunde, *f.*.

etiquette, Etikette, gute Sitte, *f.*; Standesbrauch, *m.*

etymolog|ical, etymologisch; ~y, Etymologie, Wortforschung, *f.*

eucharist, (heiliges) Abendmahl, *n.*

eulog|ize, loben; ~y, Lobrede, *f.*

eunuch, Eunuch, Verschnittene(r), *m.*

euphemism, Euphemismus, *m.*

euphon|ious, wohlklingend; ~y, Wohlklang, *m.*

Eurasian, *a.* eurasisch; *sb.* Eurasier, *m.*

Europe, Europa, *n.*; ~an, *a.* europäisch; *sb.* Europäer, *m.*

evacuat|e, ausleeren; (*mil.*) räumen; (*med.*) abführen; ~ion, Ausleerung; Räumung, *f.*; Stuhlgang, *m.*

evade, ausweichen, umgehen.

evangelical, evangelisch.

evaporat|e, verdunsten, verdampfen; ~ion, Verdunstung, *f.*

evas|ion, Ausflucht, *f.*, Umgehen, *n.*; ~ive, ausweichend, Ausweich-.

eve, (Vor)abend, *m.*; *Christmas* ~, der heilige Abend.

even, *a.*, ~ly, eben, gleich; (*smooth*) glatt; (*sum*) rund; (*number*) gerade; (*equal*) quitt; *adv.* selbst, sogar; *not* ~, nicht einmal; ~ness, Gleichheit; Glätte, *f.*

evening, Abend, *m.*; ~ dress, Gesellschaftsanzug, *m.*

event, Ereignis, *n.*, Vorfall, *m.*; *at all* ~s, auf alle Fälle; ~ful, ereignisreich; ~ual(ly), etwaig, möglich; schließlich; ~uality, Möglichkeit, *f.*

ever, je, jemals; (*always*) immer; ~green, Immergrün, *n.*; ~lasting(ly), ewig, immerwährend; ~more, immerfort.

every, jede(r, s); ~one, ~body,

jedermann; ~day, alltäglich; ~thing, alles; ~where, überall.

evict, (*eines Besitzes*) entsetzen, vertreiben; ~ion, Entsetzung, Austreibung, *f.*

eviden|ce, Beweis, *m.*, Zeugnis, *n.*; ~t(ly), augenscheinlich, klar.

evil, *sb.* Böse, Übel, *n.*; *a.*, ~ly, böse, übel; ~doer, Übeltäter, *m.*

evince, zeigen, an den Tag legen.

evoke, beschwören, hervorrufen.

evolution, Evolution, Entwicklung, *f.*

evolve, (sich) entwickeln.

ewe, Mutterschaf, *n.*

ewer, Wasserkanne, *f.*

exact[1], *a.*, ~ly, genau, pünktlich; ~ness, Genauigkeit, Pünktlichkeit, *f.*

exact[2], *v.t.* erpressen, fordern; ~ing, strenge, genau; ~ion, Erpressung, *f.*

exaggerat|e, übertreiben; ~ion, Übertreibung, *f.*

exalt, erhöhen, erheben; ~ation, Erhöhung, Erhebung, *f.*

examin|ation, Prüfung, Untersuchung, *f.*; Examen, *n.*; (*customs*) Zollrevision, *f.*; ~e, prüfen, untersuchen; (*law*) verhören; (*customs*) revidieren; ~er, Examinator, Prüfer, *m.*

example, Beispiel, *n.*; *for* ~, zum Beispiel.

exasperat|e, reizen, erbittern; ~ion, Reizung, Erbitterung, *f.*

excavat|e, aushöhlen, ausgraben; ~ion, Aushöhlung, Ausgrabung, *f.*; ~or, Trockenbagger, *m.*

exceed, übertreffen; (*instructions*) überschreiten; ~ing(ly), äußerst, außerordentlich.

excel, *v.t.* übertreffen; *v.i.* sich auszeichnen.

excellen|ce, Vortrefflichkeit, *f.*; ~cy, (*title*) Exzellenz, *f.*; ~t(ly), vortrefflich.

except, *prep.* ausgenommen, außer; *v.t.* ausnehmen; ~ion, Ausnahme, *f.*; ~ional, außergewöhnlich; ~ionally, ausnahmsweise.

excess, Übermaß, *n.*; ~ fare, Zuschlag, *m.*; ~ luggage, Übergewicht, *n.*; ~ive(ly), übermäßig.

exchange, *sb.* (Aus)tausch, *m.*; (*stock exchange*) Börse, *f.*; (*telephone*) Fernsprechamt, *n.*; *bill of* ~, Wechsel, *m.*; *rate of* ~, Wechselkurs, *m.*; *v.t.* wechseln (*for* gegen), umtauschen.

exchequer, Staatskasse, *f.*; *Chancellor of the* ~, Finanzminister, *m.*

excise, Akzise, Steuer, *f.*

excit|e, erregen, aufregen; reizen; ~able, reizbar; ~ed, erregt, aufgeregt; ~ement, Aufregung, *f.*

exclaim, ausrufen.

exclamation, Ausruf, *m.*; ~mark, Ausrufungszeichen, *n.*

exclu|de, ausschließen; ~sion, Ausschließung, *f.*; ~sive(ly), ausschließend, ausschließlich; exklusiv.

excommunicat|e, in den Bann tun; ~ion, (Kirchen)bann, *m.*

excrement, Auswurf, Kot, *m.*

excrescence, Auswuchs, *m.*

excretion, Absonderung, *f.*

excruciating, qualvoll, sehr schmerzhaft.

exculpat|e, rechtfertigen; ~ion, Rechtfertigung, *f.*

excursion, Ausflug, Abstecher, *m.*; ~train, Sonderzug, *m.*

excuse, *sb.* Entschuldigung, *f.*; *v.t.* entschuldigen, verzeihen.

execrable, abscheulich.

execut|e, (*order, work*) ausführen; (*document*) vollziehen; (*criminal*) hinrichten, erschießen; ~ion, Ausführung; Vollziehung; Hinrichtung, *f.*; ~ioner, Scharfrichter, *m.*

executive, *sb.* Exekutive, *f.*; *a.* Exekutiv-, vollziehend.

executor, Testamentsvollstrecker, *m.*

exemplary, musterhaft.

exempt, *v.t.* ausnehmen; (*from mil. service*) befreien, zurückstellen; *a.* frei, ausgenommen; befreit, zurückgestellt; ~ion, Befreiung, Zurückstellung, *f.*

exercise, *sb.* Übung, *f.*; (*of rights, power*) Ausübung, *f.*; (*mil.*) Exerzieren, *n.*; (*school*) Aufgabe, *f.*; *v.t.* (aus)üben; einexerzieren.

exert, anstrengen; (*influence, &c.*) geltend machen; ~ oneself, sich anstrengen; ~ion, Anstrengung, *f.*

exhale, ausdünsten; ~ation, Ausdünstung, *f.*

exhaust, *sb.* Auspuff, Auslaß, *m.*; *v.t.* erschöpfen; ~ gas, Abgas, *n.*; ~ing, ermüdend; ~ion, Erschöpfung, *f.*; ~ pipe, Auspuffrohr, *n.*; ~ steam, Abdampf, *m.*; ~ valve, Auslaßventil, *n.*

exhibit, *sb.* Ausstellung(sgegenstand, *m.*), *f.*; *v.t.* ausstellen; zeigen, aufweisen; ~ion, Ausstellung, *f.*; (*scholarship*) Stipendium, *n.*; ~or, Aussteller, *m.*

exhilarat|e, aufheitern; ~ion, Aufheiterung, *f.*

exhort, ermahnen; ~ation, Ermahnung, *f.*

exhum|e, exhumieren, wiederausgraben; ~ation, Wiederausgrabung, *f.*

exile, *sb.* Verbannung, *f.*; Verbannte(r); *v.t.* verbannen.

exist, existieren, vorhanden sein; leben; ~ence, Dasein, *n.*; ~ent, vorhanden; ~ing, wirklich, bestehend.

exit, Ausgang, *m.*

exodus, Auszug, *m.*; (*Bible*) das zweite Buch Mosis.

exonerat|e, lossprechen; ~ion, Lossprechung, *f.*

exorbitan|ce, Übermaß, *n.*; ~t(ly), übermäßig.

exorcize, beschwören.

exotic, exotisch, ausländisch.

expand, (sich) ausdehnen.

expans|e, Ausdehnung, *f.*; ~ive, ausgedehnt, weit.

expatriat|e, verbannen; ~ion, Verbannung, *f.*

expect, erwarten; (*suppose*) glauben; ~ation, Erwartung, *f.*

expedien|cy, Ratsamkeit, Tunlichkeit, *f.*; ~t, *a.* tunlich, ratsam, zweckdienlich; *sb.* Notbehelf, Ausweg, *m.*

expedit|e, befördern, beschleunigen; ~ion, (*speed*) Eile, (*f.*); (*journey*) Forschungsreise, (*f.*); (*mil.*) Expedition, *f.*, Feldzug, *m.*; ~ious, eilig; förderlich.

expel, austreiben, ausschließen.

expend, ausgeben, auslegen; verbrauchen; ~iture, (Geld)ausgabe, f.; (strength, &c.) Aufwand, m.

expens|e, Kosten, pl.; ~ive(ly), kostspielig, teuer.

experience, sb. Erfahrung, f.; v.t. erfahren.

experiment, sb. Experiment, n., Versuch, m.; v.i. experimentieren, versuchen; ~al, Erfahrungs-; Versuchs-.

expert, sb. Fachmann, Sachverständige(r), m.; a., ~ly, geschickt, erfahren (at, in, in); ~ness, Erfahrenheit; Sachkunde, f.

expiat|e, sühnen; ~ion, Sühne, f.

expir|e, sterben; (end) ablaufen, fällig werden; ~ation, (breathing) Aushauchen, n.; (end) Ablauf, m.

explain, erklären, erläutern.

explanat|ion, Erklärung, f.; ~ory, erklärend.

expletive, Füllwort, n.; Fluch, m.

explicit, ~ly, ausdrücklich, deutlich.

explode, v.t. sprengen; v.i. explodieren, bersten.

exploit, sb. Heldentat, Großtat, f.; v.t. ausbeuten, ausnutzen.

explor|e, erforschen, untersuchen; ~ation, Erforschung, Untersuchung, f.; ~er, Erforscher, Forschungsreisende(r), m.

explos|ion, Explosion, f.; (fig.) Ausbruch, m.; ~ive, sb. Sprengstoff, m.; a. Spreng-.

exponent, Exponent, m.

export, sb. Export, m., Ausfuhr, f.; Ausfuhrware, f.; v.t. exportieren, ausführen; ~er, Exporteur, m.

expos|e, aussetzen; (photog.) belichten; (person) bloßstellen; (misdeeds) enthüllen, aufdecken; ~ure, Ausstellung; Bloßstellung; Belichtung; Aufdeckung, f.

exposition, Erklärung, Auslegung, f.

expound, auslegen.

express, sb. Schnellzug, m.; a.

Schnell-, Eil-; v.t. (opinion) ausdrücken, äußern; (luggage) als Eilgut expedieren; (squeeze out) auspressen; ~ion, Ausdruck, m.; Redensart, f.; ~ionism, Expressionismus, m.; ~ive, ausdrucksvoll; ~ly, deutlich, bestimmt, genau.

expropriat|e, enteignen; ~ion, Enteignung, f.

expulsion, Vertreibung, f.

expunge, ausstreichen, tilgen.

expurgate, reinigen, ausmerzen.

exquisite, ~ly, vorzüglich, ausgezeichnet, köstlich.

extant, vorhanden, bestehend.

extempore, aus dem Stegreif, unvorbereitet.

extend, v.t. ausdehnen; hinausschieben, verlängern; (mercy, &c.) erweisen; v.i. sich erstrecken.

extens|ion, Ausdehnung, Erweiterung; Fristverlängerung; Prolongierung, f.; ~ive(ly), ausgedehnt, sehr groß.

extent, Ausdehnung, f.; Umfang, m.

extenuat|e, mildern; ~ion, Beschönigung, f.

exterior, sb. das Äußere; a. äußerlich, Außen-.

exterminat|e, ausrotten; ~ion, Ausrottung, f.

external, ~ly, äußerlich; ~s, Äußerlichkeiten, f.pl.

extinct, erloschen, ausgestorben; ~ion, Erlöschen, n.; (debt) Tilgung, f.

extinguish, auslöschen; (debt) tilgen.

extirpat|e, ausrotten; ~ion, Ausrottung, f.

extol, preisen.

extort, erpressen, abzwingen; ~ion, Erpressung, f.; ~ionate, erpresserisch; (prices) übermäßig.

extra, Extra-, Sonder-, Neben-; ~s, Nebenkosten, pl.

extract, sb. Auszug (spirits, &c.) Extrakt, m.; v.t. (chem., teeth, &c.) ausziehen; ~ion, Ausziehen, n.; (descent) Abkunft; (of flour) Ausmahlung, f.

extradit|e, ausliefern; **~ion**, Auslieferung, *f.*

extraneous, fremd, nicht zur Sache gehörig.

extraordinar|y, **~ily**, außerordentlich.

extravagan|ce, Überspanntheit, Verschwendung, Übertriebenheit, *f.*; **~t(ly)**, überspannt, verschwenderisch, übermäßig.

extrem|e, *sb.* das Äußerste, Extrem, *n.*; *a.*, **~ely**, äußerst, höchst; übertrieben; **~e** *unction*, die letzte Ölung; **~ity**, das Äußerste, *n.*; äußerste Not, *f.*; **~ities**, Gliedmaßen, *pl.*

extricate, herausziehen.

extrinsic, **~ally**, äußerlich, von außen.

extru|de, ausstoßen, verdrängen; **~sion**, Ausstoßung, Verdrängung, *f.*

exuberan|ce, Überfluß, *m.*, Fülle, *f.*; **~t(ly)**, üppig; überschwenglich.

exult, frohlocken; **~ant**, frohlockend; **~ation**, Frohlocken, *n.*

eye, *sb.* Auge, *n.*; (*needle*) Öhr, *n.* (*bud*) Knospe, *f.*; *v.t.* ansehen, betrachten; beäugeln; *have in one's* **~**, im Auge haben; *keep a (close)* **~** *on*, ein wachsames Auge haben auf; **~ball**, Augapfel, *m.*; **~brow**, Augenbraue, *f.*; **~lash**, Wimper, *f.*; **~let**, Öse, *f.*; **~lid**, Augenlid, *n.*; **~opener**, Überraschung, *f.*; **~piece**, (*optics*) Okular, *n.*; (*gas mask, &c.*) Augenfenster, *n.*; **~sight**, Gesicht(ssinn, *m.*), *n.*; *good* **~sight**, gute Augen; **~sore**, *it's an* **~sore**, es beleidigt das Auge; **~witness**, Augenzeuge, *m.*

F

fable, Fabel, *f.*

fabric, Bau, *m.*, Gebäude, *n.*; Gewebe, *n.*, Stoff, *m.*; **~ate**, verfertigen; erdichten; **~ation**, Erdichtung, *f.*

fabulous, fabelhaft.

façade, Fassade, *f.*

face, *sb.* Gesicht, *n.*; (*things*) Vorderseite, Front, *f.*; (*clock, &c.*) Zifferblatt, *n.*; (*of cloth*) rechte Seite; (*geom.*) Fläche, *f.*; (*type*) Bild, *n.*; (*impudence*) Unverschämtheit, *f.*; (*fig.*) das Äußere, *n.*, Anschein, *m.*; **~** *to* **~**, von Angesicht zu Angesicht; *in the* **~** *of*, angesichts, in Gegenwart (*with gen.*); *make* **~** *at*, Grimassen (*or* Fratzen) schneiden; *on the* **~** *of it*, allem Anschein nach; *show one's* **~**, sich sehen lassen; *shut the door in a person's* **~**, jemandem die Tür vor der Nase zumachen; *v.t.* (*person*) jemandem entgegentreten (*or* Trotz bieten); (*opposite to*) gegenüberstehen (*with dat.*); (*direction*) nach ... liegen; (*cover*) besetzen; (*difficulty, &c.*) begegnen; *v.i.* **~** *about*, (*mil.*) kehrtmachen.

facet, Facette, *f.*

facetious, **~ly**, scherzhaft; **~ness**, *f.*; **~t(ly)**, üppig; Scherzhaftigkeit, *f.*

facial, Gesichts-.

facil|e, leicht; gewandt; **~itate**, erleichtern; **~ity**, Leichtigkeit, Fertigkeit, *f.*; **~ities**, Vorteile, *m. pl.* (*for* für).

facing, *sb.* Besatz, Aufschlag, *m.*; *prep.* gegenüber.

facsimile, Faksimile, *n.*

fact, Tat(sache), *f.*; *in* **~**, in der Tat; *as a matter of* **~**, zwar, wirklich.

fact|ion, Partei, *f.*; **~ious(ly)**, aufrührerisch.

factitious, erkünstelt.

factor, (*pers.*) Verwalter, Vertreter; (*math.*) Faktor; (*fig.*) Umstand, *m.*

factory, Fabrik, *f.*; **~shop**, **~shed**, Werkhalle, *f.*

factual, Tatsachen-.

faculty, Fähigkeit, *f.*, Vermögen, *n.*; (*university*) Fakultät, *f.*

fad, Marotte, Liebhaberei, *f.*; **~dy**, launenhaft.

fade, (*colours*) verschießen; (*plants*) verwelken; (*wireless*) schwinden; **~** *away*, verschwinden; dahinsiechen; **~** *in*, (*radio*) aufkommen lassen, einblenden; **~** *out*, (*radio*) abklingen lassen, abblenden.

fading, *sb.* (*radio*) Schwund, *m.*,

Fading, *n.*; *a.* schwindend, verwelkend.

fag, *sb.* (*school slang*) Fuchs, *m.*; (*slang*) (schlechte) billige Zigarette, *f.*; *v.t.* ermüden; **~end,** letztes Ende; **~ged out,** ganz erschöpft.

faggot, Reisig-, Holz- bündel, *n.*

fail, fehlen, Mangel haben (*an with dat.*); mißlingen, fehlschlagen; (*harvest*) mißraten; (*commerc.*) bankrott werden, fallieren; (*in exam.*) durchfallen; *without* **~,** unfehlbar; **~ing,** *sb.* Fehler, *m.*, Schwäche, *f.*; *prep.* in Ermangelung (*with gen.*); **~ure,** Mangel, *m.*; Mißlingen, Versagen, *n.*, Mißerfolg, *m.*; Bankrott, *m.*; **~ure** *of harvest*, Mißernte, *f.*

faint, *v.i.* in Ohnmacht fallen; *a.* **~ly,** schwach, matt; **~hearted,** mutlos, verzagt; **~ing,** Ohnmacht, *f.*; **~ness,** Schwäche, *f.*

fair, *sb.* (Jahr)markt, *m.*; Messe, *f.*

fair[2], *a.* (*beautiful, weather*) schön; (*complexion*) hell; (*hair*) blond; (*just*) billig, ehrlich; (*sport*) fair; **~** *play*, ehrliches Spiel; **~ly,** ziemlich; leidlich; billig; **~ness,** Billigkeit, Ehrlichkeit; Schönheit, *f.*; heller Teint, helle Farbe; **~way,** Fahrwasser, *n.*; (*golf*) Spielfläche, *f.*

fairy, *sb.* Fee, *f.*; *a.* feenartig, Feen-; **~tale,** Märchen, *n.*

faith, Glaube, *m.*; Vertrauen; Versprechen, *n.*; **~ful[1]y,** gläubig; treu; *yours* **~fully,** hochachtungsvoll; **~fulness,** Treue, *f.*; **~healing,** Gesundbeterei, *f.*; **~less,** treulos; **~lessness,** Treulosigkeit, *f.*

fake, *sb.* Schwindel, Betrug, *m.*; *v.t.* betrügen; betrügerisch nachmachen.

falcon, Falke, *m.*

fall, *sb.* Fall, Sturz, *m.*; (*prices, &c.*) Sinken, *n.*; (*slope*) Abhang, *m.*; (*fig.*) Abnahme, *f.*, Verfall, *m.*; *the* **~** (*of man*), der Sündenfall; **~s,** Wasserfall, *m.*; *v.i.* fallen, stürzen; abnehmen, sinken; **~** *into a passion*, in Zorn geraten; **~** *asleep*, einschlafen; **~** *away*, abfallen;

~ *due*, fällig werden; **~** *in*, (*mil.*) antreten; **~** *in with*, begegnen; (*agree*) übereinstimmen mit; **~** *off*, abfallen; sich vermindern; **~** *on*, (*attack*) überfallen; (*devolve on*) zufallen (*with dat.*); **~** *out*, ausfallen; (*happen*) sich ereignen; (*quarrel*) sich zanken, in Streit geraten; (*mil.*) austreten; **~** *through*, durchfallen; mißlingen; **~** *to*, jemandem zuteil werden; (*begin*) zugreifen; sich machen an.

fallac[1]y, Trugschluß, *m.*; **~ious[1]y,** trügerisch, irreleitend.

fallib[1]e, fehlbar; trüglich; **~ility,** Fehlbarkeit, *f.*

fallow, (*land*) brach; (*colour*) falb, braungelb.

false, **~ly,** falsch, unecht; treulos; **~** *step*, Fehltritt, *m.*; **~hood,** Lüge, *f.*; **~ness,** Falschheit, *f.*

falsetto, Fistel(stimme), *f.*

falsif[1]y, fälschen; **~ication,** (Ver)fälschung, *f.*

falter, (*stumble*) straucheln; (*in speech*) stammeln; **~ing,** (*steps*) schwankend; (*voice*) zitternd.

fame, Ruhm, Ruf, *m.*; **~d,** berühmt.

familiar, **~ly,** vertraut (*with* mit); intim; **~ity,** Vertraulichkeit, *f.*; **~ize,** vertraut machen.

family, Familie, *f.*; (*species*) Gattung, *f.*; **~** *allowance*, Familienbeihilfe, *f.*

famine, Hungersnot, *f.*; Mangel, *m.*

famish, verhungern.

famous, **~ly,** berühmt (*for* für, *wegen*).

fan, *sb.* Fächer, *m.*; (*threshing*) Schwinge, Wanne, *f.*; Ventilator, *m.*; begeisterte(r) Anhänger, Fan(atiker), *m.*; *v.t.* (*fire and fig.*) anfachen; *v.i.* **~** *out*, (*mil.*) ausschwärmen; **~light,** Fächerfenster, *n.*; **~mail,** Verehrerbriefe, *m.pl.*

fanatic, *sb.* Fanatiker, Schwärmer, *m.*; **~al[1]y,** fanatisch; **~ism,** Fanatismus, *m.*, Schwärmerei, *f.*

fancier, Liebhaber, Züchter, *m.*; **~iful[1]y,** phantastisch; **~y,** *sb.* Einbildung, Phantasie, *f.*; (*desire*) Lust (*for* nach), *f.*; (*whim*) Grille, *f.*; *a.* bunt; *v.t.* sich einbilden; gern mögen; *just ~*. Denken Sie sich nur!; **~ dress,** (Masken)kostüm, *n.*; **~ goods,** Luxus-, Mode- waren, *f.pl.*

fanfare, Fanfare, *f.*

fang, Fangzahn, *m.*; *(of tooth)* Wurzel, *f.*

fantastic, ~ally, phantastisch, wunderlich.

far, *a.* fern, entfernt; *adv.* weit, fern; *(with comparatives)* viel; *by ~,* bei weitem; *go too ~,* zu weit gehen; **~-fetched,** bei den Haaren herbeigezogen.

farc|e, Posse, *f.*; **~ical,** possenhaft.

fare, *sb.* Fahrgeld, *n.*; Fahrpreis, *m.*; *(person)* Fahrgast, *m.*; *(food)* Kost, *f.*; *bill of ~,* Speisekarte, *f.*; *v.i.* einem (er)gehen; **~well,** *sb.* Abschied, *m.*, Lebewohl, *n.*; *int.* lebe wohl!

farm, *sb.* Pachtgut, *n.*, Bauernhof, *m.*, Meierei, *f.*; *v.t.* (ver)pachten; bebauen; **~er,** Landwirt, Bauer, *m.*; **~yard,** Hof, *m.*

farrier, Hufschmied; Roßarzt, *m.*

farth|er, *a. and adv.* weiter, ferner; **~est,** *a.* weitest; *adv.* am weitesten.

farthing, Heller, *m.*

fascinat|e, bezaubern; **~ion,** Bezauberung, *f.*

Fascis|m, Faschismus, *m.*; **~t,** Faschist, *m.*

fashion, *sb.* Mode; Sitte; Form, Gestalt, *f.*; *v.t.* bilden, gestalten; *after a ~,* gewissermaßen; **~able, ~ably,** elegant, modisch, modern.

fast[1], *sb.* Fasten, *n.*, Fasttag, *m.*; *v.i.* fasten.

fast[2], *a. and adv.* *(firm)* fest, befestigt; *(shut)* verschlossen; *(quick)* schnell; *(clock)* vorgehend; *(colours)* waschecht; *(manners)* flott, leichtlebig; *the clock is 10 mins. ~,* die Uhr geht 10 Minuten vor; **~ asleep,** fest eingeschlafen; **make ~,** festmachen.

fasten, befestigen, verschließen; **~er, ~ing,** Verschluß, Beschlag, *m.*

fastidious, ~ly, wählerisch.

fat, *sb.* Fett, Schmalz, *n.*; *a.* *(person)* dick; *(meat, pasture, &c.)* fett.

fatal, ~ly, verhängnisvoll, tödlich; **~ism,** Fatalismus, *m.*; **~ist,** Fatalist, *m.*; **~istic,** fatalistisch; **~ity,** Unglück, *n.*, Unglücksfall, *m.*

fate, Schicksal, Verhängnis, *n.*; **~ful,** verhängnisvoll.

father, Vater, *m.*; **~hood,** Vaterschaft, *f.*; **~-in-law,** Schwiegervater, *m.*; **~land,** Vaterland, *n.*; **~less,** vaterlos; **~ly,** väterlich.

fathom, *sb.* Faden, *m.*, Klafter, *f.*; *v.t.* *(fig.)* ergründen.

fatigue, *sb.* Müdigkeit, *f.*; *v.t.* ermüden; *(mil.)* **~ duty,** Arbeitsdienst, *m.*; **~ party,** Arbeitskommando, *n.*

fatness, Fettheit, Wohlbeleibtheit, *f.*

fatten, *v.t.* mästen, fett machen; *v.i.* fett (dick) werden.

fatty, fettig, ölig, Fett-.

fatuity, Albernheit, *f.*; **~ous(ly),** albern, einfältig.

fault, *(error, tennis, &c.)* Fehler, *m.*; *(geol.)* Verwerfung, *f.*; *find ~ with,* tadeln; *whose ~ is it?* Wer ist schuld daran?; **~-finder,** Tadler, *m.*; **~less(ly),** fehlerfrei; **~y, ~ily,** fehlerhaft, mangelhaft.

favour, *sb.* Gunst, Begünstigung, *f.*; *in ~ of,* zu Gunsten von; *do one the ~,* jemandem den Gefallen tun; *v.t.* begünstigen; **~able, ~ably,** günstig; **~ed,** begünstigt; **~ite,** *sb.* Günstling, Liebling, *m.*; *a.* Lieblings-.

fawn, *sb.* Rehkalb, *n.*; Rehfarbe, *f.*; *v.i.* **~ on,** kriechend schmeicheln.

fear, *sb.* Furcht, *f.* *(of vor)*; *v.i. and t.* fürchten, sich fürchten *(vor)*; **~ful(ly),** furchtsam; fürchterlich; **~less(ly),** unerschrocken, furchtlos; **~lessness,** Furchtlosigkeit, *f.*

feasible, möglich, tunlich.

feast, *sb.* Fest, *n.*, Schmaus, *m.*; *v.i.* schmausen; *(fig.)* sich weiden *(on an)*.

feat, Großtat, Leistung, *f.*; Kunststück, *n.*

feather, Feder, *f.*; *show the white ~,*

sich feige zeigen; ~-brained, töricht; ~ed, gefiedert; ~y, federartig.

feature, *sb.* (Gesichts)zug, *m.;* Merkmal, *n.; v.t.* darstellen.

febrile, fieberhaft.

February, Februar, *m.*

fecund, fruchtbar; ~ity, Fruchtbarkeit, *f.*

federa|l, *a.* Bundes-; ~tion, (Staaten)bund, Verband, *m.*

fee, Gebühr, *f.*, Honorar, *n.*

fee|**ble**, ~**bly**, schwach; ~**ble-minded**, geistesschwach, schwach begabt; ~**bleness**, Schwäche, *f.*

feed, *sb.* Futter, *n.;* (*tech.*) Zuleitung, *f.; v.t.* füttern; speisen; *v.i.* sich nähren (*on von*); ~back, Rückkoppelung, *f.;* ~er, (*eater*) Esser, *m.;* (*water, &c.*) Zufluß, *m.;* (*child's*) Latz, *m.;* ~ing-bottle, Saugflasche, *f.;* ~ing-stuffs, Futter, *n.;* ~pipe, Speiseröhre, *f.*, Zufuhrschlauch, *m.;* ~water, Speisewasser, *n.*

feel, *sb.* Gefühl, *n.; v.t.* fühlen, empfinden; (*touch*) betasten; ~er, (*zool.*) Fühler, *m.*, Fühlhorn, *n.*, -faden, *m.;* ~Antenne, *f.*, Fühler, *m.;* ~ing, Gefühl, *n.;* ~ingly, gefühlvoll.

feign, heucheln, sich stellen (als ob); ~ed, erdichtet.

feint, (*fencing and fig.*) Finte, *f.;* (*mil.*) Scheinangriff, *m.*

felicit|**ate**, beglückwünschen; ~ion, Beglückwünschung, *f.*

felicit|**ous**, glücklich; ~y, Glückseligkeit, *f.*

feline, katzenartig, Katzen-.

fell, fällen, niederschlagen.

fellow, Kamerad, Gefährte; Bursche, *m.;* ~ citizen, Mitbürger, *m.;* ~ countryman, Landsmann, *m.;* ~ creature, Mitmensch, *m.;* ~ship, Gemeinschaft, Genossenschaft, *f.*

felon, Verbrecher, *m.;* ~ious(ly), verbrecherisch; ~y, schweres Verbrechen.

felt, Filz, *m.*

female, *sb.* weibliche Person, *f.;* (*zool.*) Weibchen, *n.; a.* weiblich; ~ screw, Schraubenmutter, *f.*

femin|**ine**, weiblich; ~**ine gender**,

weibliches Geschlecht; ~ism, Frauenbewegung, *f.;* ~ist, Frauenrechtler(in, *f.*), *m.*

fen, Moor, *n.*, Sumpf, *m.*

fenc|**e**, *sb.* Umzäunung, *f.*, Zaun, *m.;* (*receiver of stolen goods*) Hehler, *m.;* (*mach.*) Schutzvorrichtung, *f.; v.t.* einzäunen, einhegen; *v.i.* fechten; ~er, Fechter, *m.;* ~ing, Fechten, *n.;* Fechtkunst, *f.*

fend, abwehren; ~er, Kamingitter, *n.;* (*nav.*) Fender, *m.*

fennel, Fenchel, *m.*

ferment, *sb.* Gärungsstoff, *m.;* (*fig.*) Gärung, *f.; v.t.* in Gärung bringen; *v.i.* gären; ~ation, Gärung, *f.*

fern, Farnkraut, *n.*

feroc|**ious**, ~**iously**, wild, grimmig; ~ity, Wildheit, Grausamkeit, *f.*

ferret, *sb.* Frettchen, *n.; v.t.* ~ out, ausspüren.

ferro-concrete, Eisenbeton, *m.*

ferrule, Zwinge, *f.*

ferry, *sb.* Fähre, *f.; v.t.* übersetzen, überführen; ~man, Fährmann, *m.*

fertil|**e**, fruchtbar; ~ity, Fruchtbarkeit, *f.;* ~ization, Befruchtung, *f.;* ~ize, fruchtbar machen, befruchten; ~izer, Düngemittel, *n.*

fervent, ~ly, heiß, inbrünstig.

fervour, Eifer, *m.*, Inbrunst, *f.*

fester, schwären, eitern.

festiv|**al**, *sb.* Fest(tag, *m.*), *n.; a.* festlich; ~ity, Festlichkeit, *f.*

festoon, *sb.* Girlande, *f.; v.t.* bekränzen.

fetch, holen, bringen; einbringen.

fetid, stinkend.

fetish, Fetisch, *m.*

fetlock, Köten-haar, -gelenk, *n.*

fetter, *sb.* Fessel, *f.; v.t.* fesseln.

feud, Fehde, *f.;* ~al, lehnbar, Lehns-; ~alism, Lehnswesen, *n.*

fever, Fieber, *n.;* ~ish, fieberhaft, fieberkrank.

few, wenig(e); *a* ~, einige.

fiancé, Verlobte(r), Bräutigam, *m.;* ~e, Verlobte, Braut, *f.*

fiasco, Fiasko, *n.*, Fehlschlag, *m.*

fib, *sb.* (unbedeutende) Lüge, *f.;* *v.i.* flunkern.

fibr|e, Faser, *f.*; **~ous**, faserig.

fickle, wankelmütig, unbeständig; **~ness**, Wankelmut, *m.*

fict|ion, (*novel*) Prosadichtung, (*invention*) Erdichtung, *f.*; **~itious**(**ly**), erdichtet.

fiddle, *sb.* Geige, *f.*; *v.i.* geigen; (*trifle*) tändeln; **~r**, Geiger, *m.*; **~sticks**, Unsinn, *m.*

fidelity, Treue, *f.*

fidget, *sb.* Unruhe, *f.*; *v.i.* unruhig sein; **~y**, unruhig, nervös.

field, Feld, *n.*, Acker, *m.*; (*meadow*) Wiese, *f.*; **~glass**, Feld -glas, *n.*, -stecher, *m.*; **~marshal**, Feldmarschall, *m.*; **~ officer**, Stabsoffizier, *m.*

fiend, Teufel, Unhold, *m.*; **~ish**(**ly**), teuflisch.

fierce, *ly*, wild, grimmig.

fier|y, **~ily**, feurig; jähzornig.

fife, (Quer)pfeife, *f.*

fifteen, fünfzehn; **~th**, fünfzehnte.

fifth, fünfte; **~ly**, fünftens.

fiftieth, fünfzigste.

fifty, fünfzig; *in the fifties*, in den fünfziger Jahren; *fifty-fifty*, halb und halb.

fig, Feige, *f.*; **~tree**, Feigenbaum, *m.*

fight, *sb.* Kampf, *m.*, (*mil.*) Gefecht, *n.*; *v.t. and i.* kämpfen, streiten, fechten; **~er**, (*aircraft*) Jagdflugzeug, *n.*, Jäger, *m.*; **~er bomber**, Jagdbomber, Jabo, *m.*; **~er escort**, Jagdschutz, *m.*; **~er pilot**, Jagdflieger, *m.*; **~ing**, Kampf, *m.*

figment, Erdichtung, *f.*

figurative, **~ly** bildlich.

figure, *sb.* (*form*) Figur, Gestalt, *f.*; (*arith.*) Ziffer, Zahl, *f.*; *v.t.* sich vorstellen; **~d**, gemustert, *f.*; **~head**, (*fig.*) Strohmann, *m.*

filament, Faser, *f.*, Fädchen, *n.*, Glühdraht, *m.*

file, *sb.* (*for papers*) Papierhalter, Ordner, *m.*; (*list*) Verzeichnis, *n.*; (*tool*) Feile, *f.*; (*mil.*) Reihe, *f.*; *rank and* **~**, die große Masse; *in single* **~**, im Gänsemarsch; *v.t.* (*papers*) ordnen, heften; (*metals*) abfeilen; *v.i.* defilieren.

filial, **~ly**, kindlich.

filigree, Filigranarbeit, *f.*

filings, Feilspäne, *m.pl.*

fill, *sb.* Fülle, Genüge, *f.*; *v.t.* füllen; (*stuff*) stopfen; (*position*) bekleiden; *v.i.* voll werden; **~ in**, **up**, (*form*) ausfüllen; **~ing**, Füllung, *f.*

fillet, (Kopf)binde, *f.*; (*of meat*) Lendenstück, Filet, *n.*; (*of fish*) Schnitte, *f.*

film, *sb.* Häutchen, *n.*; (*photog., cinema*) Film, *m.*; *v.t.* verfilmen; **~star**, Filmstar, *m.*

filter, *sb.* Filter, *m.* or *n.*; *v.t.* filtern, filtrieren; *v.i.* durchsickern.

filth, Schmutz, Kot; (*fig.*) Unflat, *m.*; **~iness**, Schmutzigkeit, Unflätigkeit *f.*; **~y**, schmutzig, kotig; (*fig.*) unflätig.

fin, Flosse, *f.*

final, *sb.* (*sport*) Schlußrunde, *f.*; (*exam.*) Abschlußprüfung, *f.*; *a.*; **~ly**, schließlich, endlich; (*decisive*) entscheidend.

financ|e, *sb.* Finanzwesen, *n.*; *v.t.* finanzieren; **~es**, Finanzen, *pl.*; **~ial**(**ly**), finanziell; **~ier**, Finanzmann, *m.*

finch, Fink, *m.*

find, *sb.* Fund, *m.*; *v.t.* finden; (*person*) auffinden; (*discover*) entdecken, erfinden; (*provide*) versehen, versorgen (mit); **~ fault with**, tadeln; **~ out**, ermitteln, raten, entdecken; **~er**, Finder, Entdecker, *m.*; (*optics*) Sucher, *m.*; **~ing**, Urteil, *n.* Urteilsspruch, *m.*

fine[1], *sb.* Geldstrafe, *f.*; *v.t.* jemanden mit (*amount*) bestrafen.

fine[2], *a.*, **~ly**, schön, prachtvoll, fein, zart; **~ness**, Feinheit, Schönheit, *f.*; (*metals*) Feingehalt, *m.*; **~ry**, Staat, Putz, *m.*

finger, *sb.* Finger, *m.*; *v.t.* betasten; **~ing**, (*wool*) Wollgarn, *n.*; **~post**, Wegweiser, *m.*; **~print**, Fingerabdruck, *m.*

finish, *sb.* Fertigstellung, *f.*; Vollendung, *f.*, Schliff, *m.*; Appretur, *f.*; (*sport*) Endkampf, *m.*; *v.t.* beendigen, vollenden, ausschmücken; *v.i.* enden; **~ed**, fertig.

finite, endlich.

Finn, Finne, Finnländer, *m.*; ~ish, finnisch.

fir, Tanne, Kiefer, *f.*

fire, *sb.* Feuer, *n.*, Feuersbrunst, *f.*; catch ~, in Brand geraten; miss ~, versagen; set ~ to, in Brand stecken; *v.t.* anstecken, in Brand setzen; (*gun*) abschießen; (*dismiss*) hinauswerfen; *v.i.* in Brand geraten; schießen (*at* auf); Feuer, ~alarm, Feuermelder, *m.*; ~arms, Feuerwaffen, *f.pl.*; ~brand, Feuerbrand; Aufwiegler, *m.*; ~brick, Schamottestein, *m.*; ~brigade, Feuerwehr, *f.*; ~damp, schlagende Wetter, *n.pl.*, Grubengas, *n.*; ~dog, Feuerbock, *m.*; ~engine, Feuerspritze, *f.*; ~escape, Rettungsleiter, *f.* -apparat, *m.*; ~fly, Leuchtkäfer, *m.*; ~guard, Schutzgitter, *n.*; ~man, Feuerwehrmann, *m.*; ~place, Herd, Kamin, *m.*; ~proof, feuerfest; ~side, Herd, Kamin, *m.*; ~wood, Brennholz, *n.*; ~works, Feuerwerk, *n.*

firing, Schießen, Feuern, *n.*; ~line, Feuerlinie, *f.*; ~party, Erschießungskommando, *n.*

firm, *sb.* Firma, *f.*; *a.*, ~ly, fest; entschlossen; ~ness, Festigkeit, *f.*

firmament, Firmament, *n.*

first, der, die, das, erste; *a.* zuerst, anfangs; ~ of all, vor allen Dingen; ~ aid, erste Hilfe; ~born, erstgeboren; ~ly, erstens; ~rate, vorzüglich.

fish, *sb.* Fisch, *m.*; *v.t.* and *i.* fischen; ~bone, Gräte, *f.*; ~er(man), Fischer, *m.*; ~ery, Fischerei, *f.*; ~ing-boat, Fischerboot, *n.*; ~ing-line, Angelschnur, *f.*; ~ing-net, Fischnetz, *n.*; ~ing-rod, Angelrute, *f.*; ~monger, Fischhändler, *m.*; ~y, (*slang*) verdächtig.

fission, Spaltung, *f.*

fissure, Spalte, *f.*

fist, Faust, *f.*

fit¹, *sb.* (*med.*) Anfall, *m.*; (*whim*) Laune, *f.*; ~ful(ly), launisch.

fit², *v.t.* anpassen; zurechtmachen;

(*tech.*) montieren; ~ out, ausrüsten; ~ up, einrichten, ausstatten; *v.i.* passen; *a.*, ~ly, passend, geeignet, tauglich; ~ness, Tauglichkeit, *f.*; Schicklichkeit, *f.*; ~ter, (*mach.*) Monteur, Schlosser, *m.*; ~ting, *a.* passend; schicklich; ~tings, *sb.* Armaturen, Einrichtungen, *f.pl.*

five, fünf.

fix, *sb.* Klemme, Verlegenheit, *f.*; *v.t.* befestigen; festsetzen, bestimmen; (*photog.*) fixieren; ~ed, fest; festgesetzt, bestimmt; ~ed star, Fixstern, *m.*; ~ture, unbewegliches (Haus)gerät, *n.*; (*date*) Abmachung, *f.*

fizz, zischen, brausen.

fjord, Fjord, *m.*

flabbergast, verblüffen.

flabby, schlaff; fig.); ~iness, Schlaffheit, *f.*

flaccid, schlaff (*fig.*) welk.

flag¹, *sb.* Fahne, (*naut.*) Flagge, *f.*; (*paving*) Steinplatte, *f.*; ~ship, Flaggschiff, *n.*; ~staff, Flaggenstange, *f.*

flag², *v.i.* erschlaffen, matt werden.

flagon, Flasche, *f.*

flagrant, ~ly, offenkundig.

flail, Dreschflegel, *m.*

flak|e, *sb.* (*layer*) Schicht, *f.*; *v.i.* sich abblättern; ~y, flockig; geschichtet.

flame, *sb.* Flamme, *f.*; *v.i.* flammen; ~thrower, Flammenwerfer, *m.*

flange, Flansche, *f.*

flank, Flanke, Seite, *f.*; (*mil.*) Flügel, *m.*

flannel, Flanell, *m.*

flap, *sb.* Lappen, *m.*, Klappe, *f.*; Rockschoß, *m.*; *v.i.* baumeln.

flare, *sb.* (*mil.*) Leucht-bombe, -kugel, *f.*; *v.i.* flackern, lodern; ~ up, auflodern.

flash, *sb.* Aufblitzen, *n.*, Blitz, *m.*; (*gun*) Mündungsfeuer, *n.*; (*on uniform, &c.*) Abzeichen, *n.*; *v.i.* aufblitzen, auflodern; *a.* falsch, Gauner-; ~back, Rückblende, *f.*; ~light, (*photog.*) Blitzlicht, *n.*; ~point, Flammpunkt, *m.*

flask, Flasche, f.

flat, sb. Fläche, f.; (naut.) Untiefe, f.; (story) Etage, f., Stockwerk, n.; (suite of rooms) Wohnung, f.; (mus.) B, n.; a. flach; (tasteless) schal, abgestanden, geschmacklos; (colours) matt; (commerc.) flau; (mus.) zu tief; (tyre) platt; ~-footed, plattfüßig; ~-iron, Plätteisen, n.; ~ly, flach; rundweg; ~ness, Flachheit, f.; ~ race, Flachrennen, n.; ~ spin, flach trudeln; ~ten, flach machen (or werden); ~ten out, (aircraft) ausschweben, abfangen.

flatter, schmeicheln (with dat.); ~er, Schmeichler, m.; ~ing(ly), schmeichelhaft; ~y, Schmeichelei, f.

flatulen|ce, Blähung, f.; ~t, blähend.

flaunt, prunken, sich aufblähen.

flavour, sb. Geschmack, m.; (wine) Bouquet, n.; (fig.) Beigeschmack, m.; v.t. würzen (with mit).

flaw, Riß, Fehler, Flecken, m.; ~less, fehlerlos, makellos.

flax, Flachs, m.; ~-comb, Hechel, f.; ~en, flachsen, Flachs-.

flay, schinden.

flea, Floh, m.; ~-bite, (fig.) Kleinigkeit, f.

fledge|d, flügge; ~ling, flügger junger Vogel.

flee, fliehen.

fleec|e, sb. Vlies, n.; v.t. scheren; (fig.) rupfen; ~y, flockig, wollig.

fleet, sb. Flotte, f.; a. schnell; ~ing, flüchtig, vergänglich.

flesh, Fleisch, n.; ~ly, fleischlich; ~y, fleischig.

flex, Litze, f.; ~ible, ~ibly, biegsam; ~ibility, Biegsamkeit, f.; ~ion, Biegung, f.; (gram.) Beugung, f.

flicker, flackern, flimmern.

flight, Flucht, f.; (bird, aircraft, &c.) Flug, m.; (group of aircraft) Kette, f.; (of stairs) (Treppen)flucht f.; ~-deck, Abflugdeck, n.; ~ mechanic, Bordmechaniker, m.; ~y, flüchtig, phantastisch.

flimsy, a. dünn, locker; sb. Durch-

schreibblatt, n.; ~iness, Dünnheit, f.; (fig.) Geringfügigkeit, f.

flinch, zurück-schaudern, -weichen.

fling, Wurf, m.; v.t. werfen, schleudern.

flint, Feuerstein, Kiesel, m.

flip, schnellen.

flippan|cy, Leichtfertigkeit; Zungenfertigkeit, f.; ~t(ly), leichtfertig; zungenfertig; (adv.) leichthin.

flirt, sb. Kokette, f.; v.t. schnellen; v.i. kokettieren, flirten; ~ation, Flirt, m.

flit, flattern, huschen.

fitch, Speckseite, f.

float, sb. Floß, n.; (aircraft) Schwimmer, m.; v.t. flott machen; (company) gründen; v.i. schwimmen, flott sein; (fig.) schweben, wehen; ~ing, Flottmachen, n.; Gründung, f.; a. schwimmend; schwebend; ~ing capital, Umlaufkapital, n.; ~ing debt, schwebende Schuld; ~ing-dock, Schwimmdock, n.

flock, (sheep and fig.) Herde, f.; (birds) Flug, Schwarm, m.; Schar, f.; (fleece) Flocke, f.; v.i. strömen, sich scharen.

floe, Eisscholle, f.

flog, peitschen, züchtigen; ~ging, Züchtigung, Prügelstrafe, f.

flood, sb. Flut, Überschwemmung, f.; (of tears) Tränenstrom, m.; v.t. überschwemmen; v.i. fluten; ~gate, Schleusentor, n.; ~light, Scheinwerferlicht, n.; ~tide, Flut, f.

floor, sb. Fußboden, m.; (story) Stockwerk, n.; v.t. zu Boden werfen; ~ing, Dielung, f.

flop, (hin)plumpsen.

floral, Blumen-.

florid, ~ly, blühend, frisch.

florist, Blumenhändler, m.

flotilla, Flottille, f.

flotsam, Treibgut, n.

flounder, sb. Flunder, f.; v.i. zappeln, umhertappen.

flour, feines Mehl; ~-mill, Mahlmühle, f.

flourish, sb. Schnörkel, m., Verzierung, f.; Trompetenstoß, m.; v.t. (brandish) schwingen; v.i.

blühen, gedeihen; ~ing, blühend.

flout, (ver)spotten.

flow, *sb.* Fluß, Strom, Erguß, *m.*; *v.i.* fließen, strömen.

flower, *sb.* Blume, Blüte, *f.*; *v.i.* blühen; ~pot, Blumentopf, *m.*; ~y, blumig; (*style*) blumenreich.

fluctuat|e, schwanken; ~ion, Schwankung, *f.*

flue[1], Rauchfang, *m.*; Feuerrohr, *n.*

flue[2], (*med.*) Grippe, *f.*

fluen|cy, (Rede)fluß, *m.*; Geläufigkeit, *f.*; ~t(ly), fließend.

fluid, *sb.* Flüssigkeit, *f.*; *a.* flüssig.

fluke, (*of anchor*) Schaufel, *f.*; (*fish*) Plattfisch, *m.*; (*chance*) Dusel, *m.*

flunkey, Lakai, *m.*

flurry, beunruhigen, verwirren.

flush, *sb.* Erröten, *n.*, Glut, Aufwallung, *f.*; *v.t.* ausspülen; *v.i.* erröten; ~deck, Glattdeck, *n.*

fluster, verwirren, aufregen.

flute, Flöte, *f.*; (*groove*) Kannelierung, Rinne, *f.*

flutter, *sb.* Geflatter, *n.*; Aufregung, Unruhe, *f.*; Spekulation, *f.*; *v.i.* flattern.

flux, Fluß, *m.*; (Löt)flußmittel, *n.*

fly[1], *sb.* Fliege, *f.*; ~catcher, Fliegenfänger, *m.*

fly[2], *v.i.* fliegen; ~leaf, Vorsetzblatt, *n.*; ~weight, Fliegengewicht, *n.*; ~wheel, Schwungrad, *n.*

flying, fliegend; ~boat, Flugboot, *n.*; ~bomb, fliegende Bombe; ~ buttress, Strebebogen, *m.*; ~ machine, Flugzeug, *n.*; ~officer, Oberleutnant, *m.*

foal, *sb.* Fohlen, *n.*; *v.i.* fohlen.

foam, Schaum, *m.*; *v.i.* schäumen, geifern; ~y, schaumig.

focus, *sb.* Brennpunkt, *m.*; in ~, scharf (eingestellt); out of ~, unscharf (eingestellt); *v.t.* (*photog.*) einstellen.

fodder, Futter, *n.*

foe, Feind, *m.*

fog, (dicker) Nebel, *m.*; ~gy, neblig; ~horn, Nebelhorn, *n.*; ~signal, Nebelsignal, *n.*

foible, Schwäche, *f.*

foil, *sb.* (*metal and fig.*) Folie, *f.*,

Hintergrund, *m.*; (*fencing*) Florett, *n.*; tin~, Stanniol, *n.*; *v.t.* vereiteln.

foist, unterschieben (*upon*, with *dat.*).

fold, *sb.* Falte, *f.*, Falz, *m.*; (*for sheep*, &c.) Pferch, *m.*, Hürde, *f.*; *v.t.* falten; ~er, Umschlag, *m.*; ~ing-chair, Klappstuhl, *m.*; ~ing-door, Flügeltür, *f.*; ~seat, Klappsitz, *m.*

foliage, Laubwerk, *n.*

folio, (*size*) Folio, *n.*; (*volume*) Foliant, *m.*

folk, Volk, *n.*, Leute, *pl.*; ~lore, Volkskunde, *f.*; ~song, Volkslied, *n.*

follow, *v.t.* folgen (with *dat.*); (*pursue*) verfolgen; (*business*) nachgehen (with *dat.*); as ~s, wie folgt: *that does not* ~, das folgt nicht daraus: ~ *suit*, (*cards*) bedienen, Farbe bekennen; ~er, Anhänger, *m.*; ~ing, folgend; ~ing wind, Rückenwind, *m.*

folly, Torheit, *f.*

foment, bähen; (*fig.*) anstiften; ~ation, Bähung, *f.*

fond, ~ly, zärtlich; vernarrt; *be* ~ *of*, gern haben, lieben; ~le, liebkosen, verzärteln; ~ness, Zärtlichkeit; (*liking*) Vorliebe, *f.*

font, Tauf-becken, -stein, *m.*

food, Speise, *f.*, Lebensmittel, *n.pl.*, Nahrung, *f.*; ~stuffs, Nährstoffe, *m.pl.*

fool, *sb.* Tor, Narr, *m.*; *v.t.* zum besten haben, betrügen; ~ery, Narrheit, *f.*; ~hardiness, Tollkühnheit, *f.*; ~hardy, tollkühn; ~ish(ly), töricht, närrisch; ~ishness, Torheit, *f.*; ~proof, kinderleicht, betriebssicher; ~scap, Kanzleiformat, Kanzleipapier, *n.*

foot, Fuß, *m.*; on ~, zu Fuß; set on ~, in Gang setzen; ~ball, Fußball, *m.*; Fußballspiel, *n.*; ~bridge, Steg, *m.*; ~fault, (*tennis*) Fußfehler, *m.*; ~hold, Halt, *m.* (für die Füße); ~ing, Halt, *m.*; (*fig.*) Fuß, *m.*; *obtain a* ~ing, festen Fuß fassen; *on an equal* ~ing, auf gleichem

Fuß; ~lights, Rampenlichter,
n.pl.; ~man, Lakai, *m.*; ~note,
Anmerkung, Fußnote, *f.*; ~
pad, Straßenräuber, *m.*; ~path,
Fußweg, *m.*; (*in a street*)
Trottoir, *n.*, Bürgersteig, *m.*;
~plate, Heizerstand, *m.*;
~print, Fuß(s)tapfe, *f,.*; ~sore,
wundgelaufen; ~step Schritt,
m.; ~stool, Fußbank, *f.*;
Schemel, *m.*; ~wear, Schuh-
zeug, *n.*

fop, Geck, *m.*; ~pery, Ziererei, *f.*;
~pish, geckenhaft, geziert.

for, *prep.* für, zu; (*on account of*)
wegen; (*for a period*) während,
seit; (*as*) als; ~ *all that*, trotzdem; *as* ~ *me*, meinetwegen;
word ~ *word*, Wort für Wort.

forage, *sb.* Furage, *f.*; *v.i.* fura-
gieren; ~~cap, Feldmütze, *f.*

forbear, unterlassen; sich enthalten (*with gen.*); ~ance,
Geduld, Nachsicht; Unter-
lassung, *f.*

forbid, verbieten; *God* ~, Gott
behüte!; ~ding, abstoßend.

force, *sb.* Kraft, Gewalt; (*mil.*)
Kriegsmacht; (*validity*) Gültigkeit, *f.*; *v.t.* zu zwingen, überwältigen; erstürmen; (*plants*)
künstlich züchten; ~ *back*,
zurückdrängen; ~ *open*
aufbrechen; ~d landing, Not-
landung, *f.*; ~d march, Eil-
marsch, *m.*; ~ful(ly), kräftig,
wirkungsvoll; ~meat, ge-
hacktes Füllsel; ~s, Truppen,
Streitkräfte, *f.pl.*

forceps, Zange, *f.*

forcible, ~y, gewaltsam; wirksam.

ford, *sb.* Furt, *f.*; *v.t.* durchwaten.

fore, *a.* vorder; *adv.* vorn; *to the* ~,
voran, im Vordergrund.

forebode, ahnen.

forecast, *sb.* Prophezeiung;
(*weather*) (Wetter)vorhersage, *f.*;
v.t. vorhersehen; voraussagen.

forefather, Vorfahr, *m.*

forefinger, Zeigefinger, *m.*

forefoot, Vorderfuß, *m.*

for(e)go, verzichten (auf *with acc.*);
~ne, vorweggenommen.

foreground, Vordergrund, *m.*

forehand, Vorhand, *f.*

forehead, Stirn, *f.*

foreign, ausländisch, fremd;
Foreign Office, das Auswärtige
Amt; ~ *policy*, auswärtige
Politik; ~er, Ausländer, *m.*

forelock, Schopf, *m.*

foreman, Vorarbeiter, Werk-
meister, *m.*

foremast, Fockmast, *m.*

foremost, vorderst; vornehmst.

forenoon, Vormittag, *m.*

forensic, gerichtlich.

forepart, Vorderteil, *m.*

forerunner, Vorläufer, *m.*

foresee, vorhersehen.

foreshadow, vorher andeuten.

foreshore, Strand, *m.*

foresight, Vorsicht, Klugheit, *f.*

foreskin, Vorhaut, *f.*

forest, Wald, Forst, *m.*; ~er,
Förster, *m.*; ~ry, Forstwirt-
schaft, *f.*

forestall, zuvorkommen (*with dat.*).

foretaste, Vorgeschmack, *m.*

foretell, vorhersagen.

forethought, Vorbedacht, *m.*

foretop, Fockmars, *m.*

forewarn, vorher warnen.

forfeit, *sb.* Verwirkung, Geldbuße,
f.; *v.t.* verwirken, verlieren; ~s,
(*game*) Pfänderspiel, *n.*

forge, *sb.* Schmiede, Esse, *f.*; *v.t.*
(*hammer*) schmieden; (*coin,
signature*) fälschen, nach-
machen; ~r, Fälscher, Falschmünzer, *m.*; ~ry, Fälschung,
f.

forget, vergessen; ~ful, vergeß-
lich; ~fulness, Vergeßlichkeit,
f.; ~me-not, Vergißmein-
nicht, *n.*

forgivl|e, vergeben, verzeihen;
~ing, versöhnlich.

fork, *sb.* Gabel; (*road, river*)
Gabelung, *f.*; *v.i.* sich gabeln;
~ed, gabelförmig; (*lightning*)
zickzackförmig.

forlorn, verloren, verlassen;
~ *hope*, verlorener Posten, *m.*,
Todespatrouille, *f.*

form, *sb.* (*shape*) Form, Gestalt, *f.*;
Formular, *n.*, Fragebogen, *m.*;
Bank, *f.*; Klasse, *f.*; *good* ~,
guter Ton; *bad* ~, gegen den
guten Ton; *in* ~, (*sport*) tüchtig;
out of ~, (*sport*) in schlechter

Verfassung; *v.t.* bilden, einrichten; **~al**, förmlich, steif; **~ally**, der Form gemäß; **~ity**, Förmlichkeit, *f.*; **~ation**, Bildung, *f.*; (*geol. and mil.*) Formation, *f.*; (*aircraft*) Verband, *m.*; Anordnung, *f.*; **~ative**, bildend; **~less**, formlos, ungestaltet.

former, vorig, vorhergehend; (*previous*) ehemalig, früher; **~ly**, ehemals.

formic acid, Ameisensäure, *f.*

formidabl|e, **~y**, furchtbar.

formula, Formel, *f.*; **~te**, formulieren; **~tion**, Formulierung, *f.*

fornicat|e, huren; **~ion**, Hurerei, *f.*

forsake, verlassen.

forswear, abschwören.

fort, Fort, Festungswerk, *n.*

forth, vorwärts, heraus, hinaus; *and so* **~**, und so weiter; **~coming**, bevorstehend, bereit; **~with**, sogleich.

fortieth, vierzigste.

fortif|ication, Befestigung, *f.*; **~y**, befestigen; (*fig.*) ermutigen.

fortitude, (Geistes)stärke, Standhaftigkeit, *f.*, Mut, *m.*

fortnight, vierzehn Tage, *m.pl.*

fortress, Festung, *f.*

fortuitous, **~ly**, zufällig.

fortunate, **~ly**, glücklich; günstig.

fortune, (*wealth*) Vermögen, *n.*; (*luck*) Glück, *n.*; **~-teller**, Wahrsager(in, *f.*), *m.*

forty, vierzig.

forum, Marktplatz, Gerichtshof, *m.*

forward, *sb.* (*football*) Stürmer, *m.*; *a.* frühzeitig; (*person*) vorlaut, keck; *adv.* vorwärts; *look* **~** *to*, entgegensehen (*with dat.*), sich freuen auf; **~** *to*, befördern, absenden, spedieren; **~ness**, Frühreife; Voreiligkeit, *f.*; **~s**, vorwärts, weiter.

fossil, Fossil, *n.*; **~ize**, versteinern.

foster, ernähren, pflegen; (*fig.*) hegen; **~-father**, **-mother**, **-brother**, &c., Pflege -vater, *m.*, -mutter, *f.*; -bruder, *m.*

foul, **~ly**, unrein, schmutzig; (*muddy*) trübe; (*deed*) gemein; (*play*) faul, falsch; (*weather*)

schlecht; (*air*) verdorben; (*breath*) übelriechend; **~** *play*, unehrliches Spiel, *n.*; Schwindel, *m.*, Verbrechen, *n.*; *v.t.* verunreinigen; (*naut.*) anfahren gegen; **~ness**, Unreinigkeit; Schändlichkeit, Gemeinheit, *f.*

found, gründen, stiften; (*metals*) gießen; **~ation**, Gründung, Grundmauer, Stiftung, *f.*; **~ation-stone**, Grundstein, *m.*; **~er¹**, *sb.* Gründer, Stifter, Gießer, *m.*; **~ling**, Findelkind, *n.*; **~ry**, Gießerei, *f.*

founder², *v.i.* (*ship*) sinken, untergehen; (*fig.*) scheitern.

fount, Schriftguß, *m.*

fountain, Quelle, *f.*; Springbrunnen, *m.*; **~-head**, Urquell, *m.*; **~-pen**, Füllfeder, *f.*

four, vier; **~-barrelled gun**, Vierling, *m.*; **~-fold**, vierfach; **~-footed**, vierfüßig; **~-seater**, Viersitzer, *m.*; **~-some**, Vierer(spiel, *n.*), *m.*; **~teen**, vierzehn; **~teenth**, vierzehnte; **~th**, vierte; **~thly**, viertens; **~-wheeler**, vierrädriger Wagen.

fowl, Vogel, *m.*, (*hen*) Huhn, *n.*; **~er**, Vogelsteller, *m.*; **~ing-piece**, Vogelflinte, *f.*

fox, Fuchs, *m.*; **~-glove**, Fingerhut, *m.*; **~-hole**, Fuchsbau, *m.*; (*mil.*) Schlupfloch, *n.*; **~-hunt**, Fuchsjagd, *f.*; **~-trot**, Foxtrott, *m.*

fracas, Lärm, *m.*

fraction, Bruch(teil), *m.*

fracture, *sb.* Bruch, *m.*; *v.t.* brechen.

fragil|e, zerbrechlich, schwach; **~ity**, Zerbrechlichkeit, *f.*

fragment, Fragment, Bruchstück, *n.*; **~ary**, fragmentarisch; **~ation**, Splitterwirkung, *f.*

fragran|ce, Wohlgeruch, Duft, *m.*; **~t(ly)**, wohlriechend.

frail, gebrechlich, schwach; **~ty**, Gebrechlichkeit, Schwachheit, *f.*

frame, *sb.* Rahmen, *m.*; Gerüst, Gestell, *n.*; (*human*) Körperbau, *m.*; (*of mind*) Gemütsverfassung, *f.*; *v.t.* bilden; einrahmen; ersinnen; **~-up**, Komplott, *n.*; **~-work**, Rahmen, *m.*

franchise, Wahlrecht, *n.*

frank, *a.,* **~ly,** aufrichtig; freimütig; *v.t.* frankieren; **~incense,** Weihrauch, *m.;* **~ness,** Offenheit, Aufrichtigkeit, *f.*

frantic, ~ally, wahnsinnig.

fratern|al, ~ally, brüderlich; **~ity,** Brüderschaft; Brüderlichkeit, *f.;* **~ize,** (brüderlich) verkehren (mit).

fratricide, Brudermord; Brudermörder, *m.*

fraud, Betrug, Schwindel, *m.;* **~ulent(ly),** betrügerisch.

fray, *sb.* Schlägerei, *f.; v.i.* ausfransen, sich abnützen.

freak, Einfall, *m.;* Grille, *f.;* Mißbildung, Mißgeburt, *f.;* **~ish,** launisch; wunderlich.

freckle, Sommersprosse, *f.;* **~d,** sommersprossig.

free, *a.,* **~ly,** frei; unabhängig; *(gratis)* unentgeltlich; *(frank)* offenherzig; *set* **~,** freilassen; *v.t.* befreien; **~-board,** Freibord, *m.;* **~-booter,** Freibeuter, *m.;* **~dom,** Freiheit, *f.;* **~ fight,** Handgemenge, *n.;* **~-hand,** Freihand-; **~-hold,** freier Grundbesitz; **~-holder,** Eigner *(m.)* freien Grundbesitzes; **~-kick,** Freistoß, *m.;* **~mason,** Freimaurer, *m.;* **~-masonry,** Freimaurerei, *f.;* **~-thinker,** Freidenker, Freigeist, *m.;* **~trade,** Freihandel, *m.;* **~-wheel,** *sb.* Freilauf, *m.; v.i.* das Rad frei laufen lassen; **~-will,** *a.* freiwillig.

freez|e, (ge)frieren; **~ing-mixture,** Kältemischung, *f.;* **~ing-point,** Gefrierpunkt, *m.*

freight, Fracht, Ladung, *f.;* **~er,** Frachtschiff, *n.*

French, *a.* französisch; *sb.* Französisch, *n.; the* **~,** die Franzosen, *pl.;* **~ beans,** grüne Bohnen, *f.pl.;* **~man,** Franzose, *m.;* **~ polish,** Möbelpolitur, *f.;* **~ window,** Flügelfenster, *n.;* **~woman,** Französin, *f.*

frenzied, wahnsinnig.

frequen|cy, Häufigkeit; *(electr.)* Frequenz, *f.;* **~t(ly),** häufig; **~t,** *v.t.* oft besuchen.

fresco, Fresko, *n.*

fresh, ~ly, frisch; neu; *(water)* süß; *(eggs)* frischgelegt; *(tipsy)* angeheitert **~en,** *v.i.* (*wind*) auffrischen; *v.t.* erfrischen; **~er, ~man,** Fuchs, *m.;* **~ness,** Frische; Neuheit, *f.;* **~water,** Süßwasser-.

fret, *v.t.* abreiben, (zer)fressen; *v.i.* sich ärgern, sich grämen; **~ful(ly),** ärgerlich, verdrießlich; **~fulness,** Verdrossenheit, *f.;* **~-saw,** Laubsäge, *f.;* **~-work,** Laubsägearbeit, *f.,* Schnitzwerk, *n.*

friar, Mönch, Frater, *m.; black* **~,** Dominikaner, *m.; grey* **~,** Franziskaner, *m.*

friction, Reibung, *f.*

Friday, Freitag, *m.; Good* **~,** Karfreitag, *m.*

fried: see **fry.**

friend, Freund(in, *f.*), *m.;* **~less,** freundlos; **~liness,** Freundlichkeit, *f.;* **~ly,** freundlich; **~ship,** Freundschaft, *f.*

frieze, Fries, *m.*

frigate, Fregatte, *f.*

fright, Schrecken, *m.;* **~en,** erschrecken; **~ful(ly),** schrecklich, entsetzlich; **~fulness,** Schrecklichkeit, *f.*

frigid, kalt, eisig; **~ity,** Kälte, *f.;* Kaltsinn, *m.*

frill, ~ing, Krause, *f.; v.t.* kräuseln.

fringe, *sb.* Franse, *f.;* (*fig.*) Rand, Saum, *m.; v.t.* (*fig.*) umsäumen.

frisk, springen, hüpfen; **~y,** ausgelassen; hüpfend; mutwillig.

fritter, *sb.* kleiner Pfannkuchen; *v.t.* **~ away,** (*time*) vertändeln; (*money*) vergeuden.

frivol|ity, Leichtsinn(igkeit, *f.*), *m.;* **~ous(ly),** leichtsinnig, frivol.

fro, *to and* **~,** hin und her, auf und ab.

frock, Frauen-, Kinder- kleid, *n.;* (*monk's*) Mönchskutte, *f.;* **~coat,** Gehrock, *m.*

frog, Frosch, *m.*

frolic, *sb.* Scherz, *m.; v.i.* scherzen; **~some,** lustig.

from, von, aus; (*according to*) nach; (*as a result of*) aus, vor, wegen; **~** *above,* von oben; **~** *behind,* von hinten; **~** *below,* von unten; **~** *outside,* von außen; ~ *time to time*, von Zeit zu Zeit; ~ *top to bottom*, von oben bis unten; ~ *morning till night*, von früh bis spät; ~ *my experience*, aus eigener Erfahrung.

frond, Wedel, *m.*

front, *sb.* Vorderseite; (*mil.*) Front, *f.*; (*shirt*) Vorderhemdchen, *n.*; *in*, ~ *of*, vor: *go in* ~ vorangehen; *a.* vorder; *v.t.* gegenüberstehen; ~**age**, Fassade, Vorderfront, *f.*; ~ **door**, Haustür, *f.*; ~ **line**, (*mil.*) Front(linie) *f.*; ~ **room**, Vorderzimmer, *n.*; ~ **stairs**, Vordertreppe, *f.*

frontier, Grenze, *f.*

frontispiece, Titelbild, *n.*

frost, Frost, Reif, *m.*; ~**bite**, Frostbeule, Erfrierung, *f.*; ~**bitten**, erfroren; ~**ed**, ~*ed glass*, Eisglas, *n.*; ~**y**, frostig.

froth, *sb.* Schaum, *m.*; *v.i.* schäumen; ~**y**, schaumig.

frown, Stirnrunzeln, *n.*; *v.i.* die Stirn runzeln; finster blicken.

frozen, gefroren; ~ *meat*, Gefrierfleisch, *m.*

fructif|y, befruchten; ~**ication**, Befruchtung, *f.*

frugal, ~**ly**, mäßig, genügsam, sparsam; ~**ity**, Mäßigkeit, *f.*

fruit, Obst, *n.*; Frucht, *f.*; Ertrag, *m.*; ~**erer**, Obsthändler, *m.*; ~**ful(ly)**, fruchtbar; ~**fulness**, Fruchtbarkeit, *f.*; ~**less**, unnütz, fruchtlos.

fruition, Verwirklichung, *f.*; ersehnter Erfolg.

frustrat|e, vereiteln; ~**ion**, Vereitelung, *f.*

fry, braten, backen; *fried eggs*, Spiegeleier, *n.pl.*; *fried fish*, gebackener Fisch; *fried potatoes*, Bratkartoffeln, *f.pl.*; ~**ing-pan**, Bratpfanne, *f.*

fuchsia, Fuchsie, *f.*

fuel, Brenn-, Treib-, Kraft- stoff, *m.*

fugitive, *sb.* Flüchtling, *m.*; *a.* flüchtig.

fugue, Fuge, *f.*

fulcrum, Stützpunkt, *m.*

fulfil, erfüllen, vollziehen; ~**ment**,

Erfüllung, Vollziehung, *f.*

full, *a.* voll, angefüllt (mit); besetzt; (*detailed*) ausführlich; *adv.*, ~**y**, gänzlich, völlig; *to the* ~, völlig; *in* ~, vollständig; ausgeschrieben; ~**blown**, in voller Blüte; ~**dress**, Gala-; ~**grown**, erwachsen; ~**length**, *a.* in Lebensgröße; ~ *moon*, Vollmond, *m.*; ~ *stop*, Punkt, *m.*

fuller, Tuchwalker, *m.*

fullness, Fülle, *f.*; Überfluß, *m.*

fulmar, Sturmvogel, *m.*

fulminate, (*fig.*) donnern, wettern (*against* gegen).

fulsome, ~**ly**, ekelhaft, widerlich.

fumble, umhertappen, tasten.

fume, *sb.* Dampf, Rauch, *m.*; *v.i.* rauchen; (*fig.*) zornig sein; *v.t.* räuchern.

fumigat|e, (aus)räuchern; ~**ion**, Räuchern, *n.*; ~**or**, Räucherapparat, *m.*

fun, Scherz, Spaß, *m.*; *make* ~ *of*. sich über . . . lustig machen.

function, *sb.* Verrichtung, Tätigkeit; (*ceremony*) Feier; (*duty*) Pflicht; (math) Funktion, *f.*; *v.i.* funktionieren, wirksam sein; ~**ary**, Beamte(r), *m.*

fund, Kapital, *n.* Fonds, *m.*; Schatz, Vorrat, *m.*; *public* ~*s*, Staatsschulden, *f.pl.*

fundamental, ~**ly**, wesentlich, Grund-.

funeral, Begräbnis, Leichenbegängnis, *n.*

fung|us, Schwamm, Pilz, *m.*; ~**ous**, schwammig.

funicular, Drahtseil-.

funk, *sb.* (*person*) Feigling, *m.*; *be in a* ~, große Angst haben; *v.t. and i.* fürchten, sich drücken.

funnel, Trichter; (*of steamer*, &c.) Schornstein, *m.*

funn|y, ~**ily**, komisch, spaßhaft, seltsam.

fur, Fell, *n.*, Pelz; (*in boiler*, &c.) Kesselstein; (*on tongue*) Belag, *m.*; ~**lined**, mit Pelz gefüttert; ~**s**, Rauchwaren, *f.pl.*

furious, ~**ly**, wütend, rasend.

furl, aufrollen, aufziehen.

furlough, Urlaub, *m.*

furnace, Ofen, *m.*; *blast* ~, Hochofen, *m.*

furnish, versehen (*with* mit); (*house*) möblieren; ~ed rooms, möblierte Zimmer, *n.pl.*

furniture, Möbel, *n.pl.*

furrier, Kürschner, *m.*

furrow, *sb.* Furche; Runzel, *f.*; *v.t.* furchen.

further, *a. and adv.* ferner, weiter; *v.t.* befördern; ~**more**, ferner, außerdem.

furthest, *a.* weiteste, fernste; *adv.* am weitesten, am fernsten.

furtive, ~**ly**, verstohlen.

fury, Wut, *f.*

furze, Stechginster, *m.*

fus|e, *sb.* Zünder, *m.*; (*electr.*) Sicherung, *f.*; *v.t.* schmelzen; *v.i.* abschmelzen, durchbrennen; ~**ible**, schmelzbar.

fuselage, (*aircraft*) Rumpf, *m.*

fusilier, Füsilier, *m.*

fusion, Schmelzen, *n.*; (*fig.*) Verschmelzung, Fusion, *f.*

fuss, Lärm, *m.*, Getue, *n.*; ~**y**, viel Aufhebens machend.

fust|y, muffig, moderig; ~**iness**, Modergeruch, *m.*

futile, nutzlos, nichtig; ~**ity**, Nutzlosigkeit, *f.*

futur|e, *sb.* Zukunft, *f.*; *a.* künftig; ~**ism**, Futurismus, *m.*; ~**ist**, Futurist, *m.*

G

gabble, *sb.* Geschwätz, Geschnatter, *n.*; *v.i.* schwatzen, schnattern.

gable, Giebel, *m.*

gadget, Zubehörteil, *m.*, Vorrichtung, *f.*; (*fig.*) Kniff, *m.*

gag, *sb.* Knebel, *m.*; Improvisation, *f.*; *v.t.* knebeln.

gaiety, Munterkeit, Fröhlichkeit, *f.*

gaily, lustig, munter; bunt.

gain, *sb.* Gewinn, Vorteil, *m.*; *v.t.* gewinnen, erlangen; ~**er**, Gewinner, *m.*; ~**ful(ly)**, einträglich; ~**ings**, Gewinn, *m.*

gait, Gang, *m.*

gaiters, Gamaschen, *f.pl.*

gala, Gala, Fest, *n.*

galaxy, Milchstraße, *f.*

gale, Sturm, *m.*

gall, Galle, *f.*, (*fig.*) Bitterkeit, *f.*

gallant, *sb.* Stutzer, feiner Herr, *m.*; *a.*, ~**ly**, tapfer; höflich, galant; ~**ry**, Tapferkeit; Galanterie, *f.*

gallery, Galerie; Tribüne, Empore, *f.*; (*mining*) Stollen, *m.*; (*sport*) Zuschauer, *m.pl.*

galley, (*kitchen*) Kombüse, *f.*; ~**proof**, Fahnenabzug, *m.*

galling, ärgerlich.

gallop, *sb.* Galopp, *m.*; *v.i.* galoppieren.

gallows, Galgen, *m.*

galoshes, Überschuhe, Gummischuhe, *m.pl.*

galvan|ic, galvanisch; ~**ize**, galvanisieren, verzinken.

gamble, spielen; ~**r**, Spieler, *m.*

gambol, *sb.* Luftsprung, *m.*; *v.i.* springen, hüpfen.

game, Spiel, *n.*; (*animals*) Wild, *n.*; ~**keeper**, Wildhüter, *m.*

gamut, Tonleiter, *f.*; (*fig.*) Umfang, *m.*

gander, Gänserich, *m.*

gang, Bande, *f.*, Trupp, *m.*; ~**ster**, Gangster, *m.*; ~**way**, (*naut.*) Fallreep, *n.*; (*in bus, &c.*) Gang, *m.*

gangrene, Brand, *m.*

gaol, Gefängnis, *n.*

gap, Lücke, Bresche, *f.*

gape, gaffen; (*fig.*) klaffen.

garage, *sb.* Garage, *f.*; *v.t.* in einer Garage unterbringen.

garb, Tracht, Kleidung, *f.*

garbage, Abfall, *m.*

garble, (*fig.*) verstümmeln, entstellen.

garden, *sb.* Garten, *m.*; *v.i.* Gartenbau treiben; ~**er**, Gärtner, *m.*; ~**ing**, Gartenarbeit, *f.*

gardenia, Gardenie, *f.*

gargle, *sb.* Gurgel-, Mund- wasser, *n.*; *v.i.* gurgeln.

gargoyle, Wasserspeier, *m.*

garish, grell.

garland, Girlande, *f.*, Blumenkranz, *m.*

garlic, Knoblauch, *m.*

garment, Kleid, Gewand, *n.*

garner, aufspeichern, sammeln.

garnet, Granat, *m.*

garnish, garnieren, verzieren.

garret, Dachstube, *f.*, Boden, *m.*

garrison, *sb.* Garnison, Besatzung;

f.; *v.t.* mit einer Garnison belegen.

garrul|ity, Schwatzhaftigkeit, *f.*; ~ous, schwatzhaft.

garter, Strumpfband, *n.*

gas, Gas; (*slang*) Geschwätz, *n.*; *v.t.* vergasen; ~ attack, Gasangriff, *m.*; ~ burner, Gasbrenner, *m.*; ~eous, gasartig; ~lamp, Gaslaterne, *f.*; ~light, Gaslicht, *n.*; ~ mask, Gasmaske, *f.*; ~meter, Gasmesser, *m.*; ~ometer, Gasbehälter, *m.*; ~pipe, Gasrohr, *n.*; ~sed, vergast, gaskrank; ~stove, Gasherd, *m.*; ~works, Gasanstalt, *f.*

gash, *sb.* Schmarre, klaffende Wunde, *f.*; *v.t.* tief verwunden.

gasp, keuchen.

gastric, gastrisch, Magen-.

gastronomy, Feinschmeckerei, Gastronomie, *f.*

gate, Tor, *n.*, Pforte, *f.*; ~crasher, ungebetener Gast; ~money, Eintrittsgeld, *n.*; ~way, Torweg, *m.*

gather, *v.t.* sammeln; pflücken; (*needlework*) in Falten legen, kräuseln; (*conclude*) schließen, folgern; *v.i.* sich sammeln; (*med.*) eitern; ~ing, Versammlung, *f.*; Sammeln, *n.*; (*med.*) Geschwür, *n.*; (*needlework*) Falte, *f.*

gaud|y, ~ily, prunkend, geputzt; bunt; ~iness, Flitterstaat, *m.*

gauge, *sb.* Eichmaß, *n.*; Messer, *m.*; (*railway*) Spurweite, *f.*; *v.t.* eichen; (*fig.*) abschätzen.

gaunt, ~ly, hager, dünn.

gauntlet, (*hist.*) Panzerhandschuh; Automobilhandschuh, *m.*; *run the* ~, Spießruten laufen.

gauze, Gaze, *f.*

gay, lustig, munter; bunt.

gaze, *sb.* starrer Blick; *v.i.* starren; ~ at, anstarren.

gazelle, Gazelle, *f.*

gazette, Zeitung, *f.*, Amtsblatt, *n.*; ~er, geographisches Lexikon.

gear, *sb.* (*mech.*) Getriebe, *n.* Übersetzung, *f.*, Gang, *m.*; (*naut.*) Takelage, *f.*, Gerät, *n.*; *in* ~, im Gange; *out of* ~, nicht im Gange; *v.t.* in Gang

setzen; mit Getriebe versehen; ~box, Getriebegehäuse, *n.*; ~ lever, Schalthebel, *m.*; ~wheel, Zahnrad, *n.*

gelatine, Gelatine, *f.*, Gallert(e, *f.*), *n.*

gelding, Wallach, *m.*

gem, Edelstein, *m.*, (*fig.*) Perle, *f.*

gender, Geschlecht, *n.*

genealog|y, Genealogie, *f.*; ~ical, genealogisch, Stamm-.

general, *sb.* General, *m.*; (*servant*) Mädchen für alles, *n.*; *a.*, allgemein, gewöhnlich; *in* ~, im allgemeinen; ~ity, Allgemeinheit, *f.*; ~ization, Verallgemeinerung, *f.*; ~ize, verallgemeinern; ~ly, gewöhnlich, im allgemeinen; ~ship, Strategie; Leitung, *f.*

generat|e, erzeugen; ~ion, Erzeugung, *f.*; Geschlecht, Menschenalter, *n.*; ~or, Erzeuger; (*mach.*) Generator, *m.*

gener|osity, Freigebigkeit, *f.*; Edelmut, *m.*; ~ous(ly), freigebig; großmütig.

genesis, Entstehung(sgeschichte); (*bible*) Genesis, *f.*

genial, ~ly, munter, lustig; freundlich.

genitals, Geschlechtsteile, *m.pl.*

genitive, Genitiv, *m.*

genius, Genie, *n.*; Schutzgeist, *m.*

genteel, ~ly, vornehm, fein.

gentian, Enzian, *m.*

gentile, *sb.* Heide, *m.*; *a.* heidnisch.

gentle, vornehm; artig, fein; sanft; (*slope*) allmählich; ~man, Herr, Gentleman, *m.*; ~ness, Sanftmut; Artigkeit, *f.*; ~woman, vornehme Dame; gently, sanft, mild.

gentry, die oberen Klassen, *f.pl.*

genuflexion, Kniebeugung, *f.*

genuine, ~ly, echt, rein; ~ness, Echtheit, *f.*

geography, Erdkunde, Geographie, *f.*; ~er, Geograph, *m.*; ~ical, geographisch.

geolog|y, Geologie, *f.*; ~ical, geologisch; ~ist, Geolog(e), *m.*

geometr|y, Geometrie, *f.*; ~ical(ly), geometrisch.

geopolitics, Geopolitik, *f.*

geranium, Geranium, *n.*

germ, Keim, *m.*

German, *a.* deutsch; *sb.* (*person*) Deutsche(r); (*lang.*) Deutsch, *n.*; ~measles, Röteln, *pl.*; ~silver, Neusilber, *n.*

germane, verwandt.

germinat|e, keimen, sprossen; ~ion, Keimen, Sprossen, *n.*

gerund, Gerundium, *m.*

gestation, Schwangerschaft; (*animals*) Trächtigkeit, *f.*

gesticulat|e, Gesten machen; ~ion, Gestikulation, *f.*, Gesten, *f.pl.*

gesture, Gebärde, *f.*

get, (*become*) werden; (*obtain*) bekommen, erhalten, erwerben; besorgen; finden; (*acquire*) erlangen; (*gain*) gewinnen; (*beget*) erzeugen; ~ about, herumkommen; ~ abroad, bekannt werden; ~ at, kommen an; ~ away, sich davon machen; weggehen; ~ back, zurückerhalten; zurückkommen; ~ better, besser werden; ~ done, machen lassen; ~ down, herunterkommen; ~ dressed, sich anziehen; ~ in, einsteigen; hineinbringen; ~ into, geraten; ~ married, sich verheiraten; ~ off, davonkommen; sich entziehen; ~ on, weiterkommen, vorwärtskommen, Erfolg haben; ~ on with, mit (jemandem) auskommen; ~ out, aussteigen; herausbekommen; ~ over, überwinden, hinwegkommen über; zu Ende bringen; ~ ready, sich bereit machen; ~ rid of, loswerden; von ~ loskommen; ~ through, durchkommen; (*exam.*) bestehen; ~ to, ankommen in; ~ together, zusammenbringen; zusammenkommen; ~ up, aufstehen; (*arrange*) veranstalten, vorbereiten; ~-up, *sb.* Aufmachung, Ausstattung, *f.*

geyser, Geiser; Wassererhitzer, *m.*

ghastl|y, gräßlich; totenblaß; ~iness, Gräßlichkeit; Totenblässe, *f.*

ghost, Geist, *m.*, Gespenst, *n.*; ~ly, geister-, gespensterhaft; ~story, Gespenstergeschichte, *f.*

giant, *sb.* Riese, *m.*; *a.* Groß-,

Riesen-; ~ess, Riesin, *f.*

gibberish, Kauderwelsch, *n.*

gibe, *sb.* Hohn, Spott, *m.*; *v.* spotten (*at* über).

giblets, Gänseklein, *n.*

gidd|y, ~ily, schwindelig; schwindelerregend; (*fig.*) leichtsinnig; ~iness, Schwindel; Leichtsinn, *m.*

gift, Gabe, *f.*, Geschenk, *n.*; ~ed, begabt.

gigantic, riesenhaft, riesig.

giggle, kichern.

gild, vergolden; ~ing, Vergoldung, *f.*

gills, (of *fish*) Kiemen, *f.pl.*

gilt, Vergoldung, *f.*; ~-edged, (*securities*) mündelsicher.

gimlet, Bohrer, *m.*

gin[1], (*liquor*) Gin, Wacholderschnaps, Steinhäger, *m.*

gin[2], (*trap*) Schlinge, *f.*

ginger, Ingwer, *m.*; ~bread, Lebkuchen, *m.*

gipsy, Zigeuner(in, *f.*), *m.*

giraffe, Giraffe, *f.*

gird, (um)gürten; ~er, Träger, Tragbalken, *m.*; ~le, Gürtel, *m.*

girl, Mädchen, *n.*; ~hood, Mädchenjahre, *n.pl.*; ~ish(ly), mädchenhaft.

girth, (Sattel)gurt; Umfang, *m.*

gist, Kern, *m.*, Wesen, *n.*

give, *v.t.* geben, schenken, erteilen; übergeben, überreichen; *v.i.* nachgeben; sich dehnen lassen; ~ away, verschenken; ~ back, zurückgeben; ~ in, *v.t.* einreichen; *v.i.* nachgeben; ~ offence, Anstoß erregen; ~ out, *v.t.* bekannt machen; austeilen; *v.i.* verbraucht sein, zu Ende gehen; ~ over, *v.i.* aufhören; *v.t.* aufgeben; ~place, Platz machen; ~ thanks, Dank abstatten; ~ up, aufgeben; ~ way, nachgeben, weichen; sich überlassen, sich hingeben (*to*, *with dat.*); ~n, bestimmt, gegeben.

gizzard, Kropf, *m.*

glac|ial, eisig, Eis-; ~ier, Gletscher, *m.*

glad, ~ly, froh, heiter; ~den, erfreuen; ~ness, Freude, *f.*

glade, Lichtung, *f.*

gladiolus, Gladiole, *f.*

glamo|ur, Zauber, Reiz, *m.*; ~rous, zauberhaft, reizend.

glance, *sb.* Blick, *m.*; *v.i.* einen Blick werfen (*at auf*); ~ through, flüchtig durchsehen.

gland, Drüse, *f.*

glar|e, *sb.* blendender Glanz, Schimmer; durchdringender Blick, *m.*; *v.i.* blenden; starren (*at auf*); ~ing, blendend; grell; offenkundig.

glass, *sb.* Glas, *n.*; *looking*-~, Spiegel, *m.*; *plate*-~, Spiegelglas, *n.*; *stained* ~, buntes Glas; *weather*-~, Wetterglas, *n.*; *a.* gläsern, Glas-; ~-blower, Glasbläser, *m.*; ~-shade, Glasglocke, *f.*; ~es, Brille *f.*; ~-works, Glashütte, *f.*; ~y, glasig.

glaz|e, *sb.* Glasur, Glätte, *f.*; *v.t.* verglasen; (*paper*) glätten; ~ier, Glaser, *m.*

gleam, *sb.* Schein, Schimmer, *m.*; *v.i.* schimmern, glänzen.

glean, nachlesen, sammeln; ~er, Ährenleser, *m.*

glee, Fröhlichkeit, Freude, *f.*; ~ful(ly), fröhlich.

glen, Bergschlucht, *f.*, Tal, *n.*

glib, ~ly, zungenfertig; ~ness, Zungenfertigkeit, *f.*

glide, gleiten, einen Gleitflug machen; ~r, Segelflugzeug, *n.*; Segelflieger, *m.*

glimmer, *sb.* Schimmer, *m.*; *v.i.* schimmern.

glimpse, Schimmer; Blick, *m.*

glint, *sb.* Glanz, *m.*; *v.i.* glänzen, funkeln.

glisten, funkeln, glitzern.

glitter, *sb.* Glanz, *m.*; *v.i.* glitzern, glänzen.

gloaming, Dämmerung, *f.*

gloat, glotzen; ~ over, sich weiden an.

globe, Kugel, *f.*; ~-trotter, Weltbummler, *m.*

globul|e, Kügelchen, *n.*; ~ar, kugelförmig.

gloom, ~iness, Dunkel, *n.*; (*fig.*) Trübsinn, *m.*; ~y, ~ily, düster, dunkel; schwermütig.

glorif|ication, Verherrlichung, *f.*; ~y, verherrlichen.

glor|ious, ~iously, herrlich, glor-reich; ~y, *sb.* Ruhm, *m.*, Herrlichkeit, *f.*; Stolz, *m.*; *v.i.* sich rühmen.

gloss[1], (*shine*) Glanz, *m.*, Politur, *f.*; ~y, glänzend, glatt; ~iness, Glätte, Politur, *f.*

gloss[2], (*note*) Glosse, *f.*; ~ary, Glossar, *n.*

glove, Handschuh, *m.*

glow, *sb.* Röte, Glut, *f.*; *v.i.* glühen; ~-worm, Glühwurm, Leuchtkäfer, *m.*

glucose, Glykose, *f.*

glue, *sb.* Leim, *m.*; *v.t.* leimen.

glum, finster, mürrisch.

glut, *sb.* Überfüllung, Übersättigung, *f.*; *v.t.* überladen; sättigen.

glutton, (*person*) Fresser; (*zool.*) Vielfraß, *m.*; ~ous(ly), gefräßig; ~y, Gefräßigkeit, *f.*

glycerine, Glyzerin, *n.*

gnarled, knorrig.

gnash, ~ one's teeth, mit den Zähnen knirschen.

gnat, Mücke, *f.*

gnaw, nagen.

gnome, Gnom, Erdgeist, *m.*

go, gehen, fahren; weggehen; verschwinden; ~ against, widerstreiten; ~ bad, verderben; ~ between, vermitteln; ~ by, vorbeigehen; (*be guided by*) sich richten nach; ~ down, fallen, heruntergehen, (*ship, sun*) untergehen; ~ for, (*fetch*) holen; (*walk*) spazierengehen; (*pass for*) gelten für; (*attack*) sich auf jemanden stürzen; ~ in for, sich befassen mit; ~ into, sich bewerben um; ~ into, eintreten; (*fig.*) untersuchen; ~ off, losgehen, sich entladen; ~ on, vor sich gehen; fortfahren; weiterfahren; sich benehmen; ~ out, ausgehen; (*fire, light*) ausgehen, erlöschen; ~ over, durchgehen; ~ through, übertreten (*to zu*); ~ through, durchgehen; ~ up, hinaufgehen; (*price, &c.*) steigen; ~ with, begleiten; übereinstimmen mit; ~ without, entbehren.

goad, *sb.* Stachelstock, *m.*; (*fig.*) Stachel, Ansporn, *m.*; *v.t.* (an)treiben, reizen.

go-ahead, unternehmend, energisch, strebsam.

goal, Ziel; *(football)* Tor, *n.;* ~-keeper, Torwart, *m.;* ~-kick, Torstoß, *m.;* ~-post, Torpfosten, *m.*

goat, Ziege, *f.; he-*~, Ziegenbock, *m.*

gobble, verschlingen.

go-between, Vermittler, Unterhändler, *m.*

goblet, Becher, *m.*

goblin, Kobold, *m.*

God, Gott, *m.;* ~child, Patenkind, *n.;* ~dess, Göttin, *f.;* ~father, Pate, *m.;* ~fearing gottesfürchtig; ~head, Gottheit, *f.;* ~less, gottlos; ~lessness, Gottlosigkeit, *f.;* ~like, göttlich; ~liness, Gottseligkeit, *f.;* ~ly, gottselig, fromm; ~mother, Patin, *f.;* ~send, Gottesgabe, *f.,* unerwarteter Fund.

goggle, *v.i.* glotzen; ~s, Schutzbrille, *f.*

goitre, Kropf, *m.*

gold, Gold, *n.;* ~en, golden; ~finch, Stieglitz, *m.;* ~fish, Goldfisch, *m.;* ~ lace, Goldtresse, *f.;* ~leaf, Blattgold, *n.;* ~smith, Goldschmied, *m.*

golf, Golfspiel, *n.;* ~club, Schläger, *m.;* ~er, Golfspieler, *m.;* ~links, Golfplatz, *m.*

golliwog, Groteskpuppe, *f.*

goloshes = galoshes.

gondol|a, Gondel, *f.;* ~ier, Gondelführer, *m.*

gone, weg, fort; *(time)* vergangen; *(lost)* verloren.

gong, Gong, *m.*

gonorrhoea, Tripper, *m.*

good, *sb.* das Gute; *a.* gut, recht, geeignet; *for* ~, für immer; *for the* ~ *of,* zum Besten von; *it is no* ~, es nützt nichts; ~ *day,* guten Tag; *a.* ~ *deal,* viel(es); ~ *Friday,* Karfreitag, *m.;* ~ *luck,* Glück, *n.;* ~ *morning,* guten Morgen; *a* ~ *while,* ziemlich lange, ~-bye, Lebewohl, Auf Wiedersehen; ~-fornothing, Taugenichts, *m.;* ~looking, schön, hübsch; ~ly, schön, anmutig; ~-natured,

gutmütig; ~ness, Güte, Gütigkeit, *f.; for* ~ness' *sake,* um Himmels willen; ~will, Wohlwollen, *n.;* Geschäftswert, *m.*

goods, Waren, Güter, *pl.;* ~ station, Güterbahnhof, *m.;* ~ train, Güterzug, *m.*

goose, Gans, *f.;* ~berry, Stachelbeere, *f.;* ~step, Paradeschritt, *m.*

gore, *sb.* (geronnenes) Blut; *v.t.* durchbohren.

gorge, *sb.* *(throat)* Kehle, *f.;* *(between mountains)* Bergschlucht, *f.; v.t.* verschlucken.

gorgeous, ~ly, prächtig, prachtvoll.

gorilla, Gorilla, *f.*

gormandize, fressen, schlemmen.

gorse, Stechginster, *m.*

gory, blutig.

gosling, Gänschen, *n.*

gospel, Evangelium, *n.*

gossip, *sb.* Schwätzer, *m.,* Klatschbase, *f.;* Klatsch, *m.,* Geschwätz, *n.; v.i.* klatschen.

Goth, Gote, *m.;* ~ic, gotisch.

gouge, *sb.* Hohlmeißel, *m.; v.t.* ausmeißeln.

gourd, Kürbis, *m.*

gourmand, Feinschmecker, *m.*

gout, Gicht, *f.;* ~y, gichtisch.

govern, regieren, beherrschen; ~ess, Gouvernante, *f.;* ~ment, Regierung, *f.,* Staat, *m.;* ~or, Gouverneur, Direktor, *m.;* *(mech.)* Regulator, *m.*

gown, Überwurf; *(scholastic, etc.)* Talar, *m.*

grab, packen, ergreifen.

grace, *sb.* Gnade, Gunst, *f.;* *(charm)* Anmut, Grazie, *f.;* *(before meal)* Tischgebet, *n.;* *Your* ~, Euer Gnaden; *v.t.* schmücken; ~ful(ly), anmutig; ~fulness, Anmut, *f.*

gracious, ~ly, gnädig; anmutig; ~ness, Güte, Freundlichkeit, *f.*

gradation, Steigerung, Abstufung, *f.*

grad|e, *sb.* Grad, Rang, *m.; v.t.* abstufen, einteilen; ~ing, Eingruppierung, Einstufung, *f.*

gradient, Steigung, *f.,* Gefälle, *n.*

gradual, ~ly, allmählich, stufenweise.

graduat|e, *sb.* (*university*) Graduierte(r); *v.t.* abstufen; staffeln;

graduieren, *v.i.* (*university*) promovieren; ~ion, Promotion, *f.*

graft, *sb.* (*horticulture*) Pfropfreis, *n.*; (*fig.*) Schiebung, *f.*; *v.t.* pfropfen.

grain, Korn, Getreide; (*Troy weight*) Gran, Grän; (*sand, &c.*) Korn, *n.*; (*wood*) Faser; (*fig.*) Richtung, Natur, *f.*; against the ~, (*fig.*) gegen den Strich; *v.t.* (*leather*) narben; (*painting*) ädern; ~s, Treber, *pl.*

gramm|ar, Grammatik, Sprachlehre, *f.*; ~arian, Grammatiker, *m.*; ~atical(ly), grammatisch.

gramme, Gramm, *n.*

gramophone, Grammophon, *n.*

granary, Kornspeicher, *m.*

grand, groß, erhaben; ~child, Enkel(in, *f.*), *m.*; ~daughter, Enkelin, *f.*; ~duke, Großherzog, *m.*; ~eur, Größe, Pracht, *f.*; ~father, Großvater, *m.*; ~iloquent, großsprecherisch; ~iose, großartig; hochtrabend; ~mother, Großmutter, *f.*; ~son, Enkel, *m.*

granite, Granit, *m.*

grant, *sb.* Bewilligung, *f.*; Unterstützung, *f.*, Zuschuß, *m.*; *v.t.* bewilligen, verleihen; zugestehen. [körnig.

granul|e, Körnchen, *n.*; ~ar,

grape, Weinbeere, *f.*; Traube, *f.*; bunch of ~s, Weintraube, *f.*; ~fruit, Pampelmuse, Grapefruit, *f.*

graph, graphische Darstellung, *f.*, Diagramm, *n.*; ~ic, graphisch, anschaulich.

graphite, Graphit, *m.*

grapnel, Enterhaken, *m.*

grapple, packen, ergreifen; ~ with, sich ernstlich an (etwas) machen.

grasp, *sb.* Griff, *m.*; Fassungskraft, *f.*; *v.t.* ergreifen, fassen; begreifen; ~ing, habgierig.

grass, Gras, *n.*; ~hopper, Heuschrecke, *f.*; ~-plot, Rasenplatz. *m.*; ~-widow, Strohwitwe, *f.*; ~y, grasig.

grate, *sb.* Gitter, *n.*; (*for fire*) Feuerrost, *m.*; *v.i.* knirschen; *v.t.* reiben.

grateful, ~ly, dankbar; ~ness, Dankbarkeit, *f.*

grater, Reibeisen, *n.*

gratif|ication, Befriedigung, *f.*; ~y, befriedigen.

grating, Vergitterung, *f.*; (*noise*) Knirschen; Reiben, *n.*

gratis, unentgeltlich.

gratitude, Dankbarkeit, *f.*

gratuit|ous, ~ously, freiwillig; grundlos; unentgeltlich; ~y, Geschenk, Trinkgeld, *n.*

grave¹, *sb.* Grab, *n.*; ~digger, Totengräber, *m.*; ~stone, Grabstein, *m.*

grave², *a.* ~ly, ernst, feierlich.

gravel, Kies, *m.*

gravitat|e, gravitieren, zuneigen; ~ion, Schwerkraft, *f.*

gravity, Ernst, *m.*, Schwere, *f.*; centre of ~, Schwerpunkt, *m.*

gravy, (Braten)sauce, *f.*

gray = grey.

graze, weiden, grasen; (*rub*) streifen.

grease, *sb.* Fett, *m.*, Schmiere, *f.*; *v.t.* schmieren; ~-proof, fettdicht.

great, groß, berühmt; ~coat, Überzieher, *m.*; ~ly, sehr; ~ness, Größe, *f.*

greed, Gier(igkeit), *f.*; ~y, ~ily, gierig.

Greek, *sb.* (*person*) Grieche, *m.*; Griechin, *f.*; (*lang.*) Griechisch. *n.*; *a.* griechisch.

green, *sb.* (*colour*) Grün, *n.*; (*grass*) Rasenplatz, *m.*; *a.* grün; ~ery, Laub, *n.*; ~fly, Blattlaus, *f.*; ~gage, Reneklode (Reineclaude), *f.*; ~grocer, Gemüsehändler, *m.*; ~horn, Grünschnabel, Neuling, *m.*; ~house, Gewächshaus, *n.*; ~ish, grünlich; ~ness, Grüne; Unreife; Unerfahrenheit, *f.*; ~s, Gemüse, *n.*

greet, grüßen; ~ing, Gruß, *m.*

grenad|e, Granate, *f.*; ~ier, Grenadier, *m.*

grey, *sb.* Grau, *n.*, *a.* grau; ~hound, Windhund, *m.*; ~ish, etwas grau.

grid, Bratrost, *m.*; (*electric*) Überlandzentrale, *f.*; (*radio*) Gitter, *n.*

grief, Gram, Kummer, *m.*

griev|ance, Beschwerde, *f.*; Mißstand, *m.*; **~e**, *v.t.* kränken; *v.i.* sich grämen; **~ous(ly)**, schmerzlich; schlimm; drükkend.

grill, *sb.* Bratrost, *m.*; *v.t.* rösten.

grim, **~ly**, grimmig.

grimace, *sb.* Grimasse, *f.*; *v.i.* Grimassen schneiden.

grim|e, Schmutz, Ruß, *m.*; **~y**, schmutzig, rußig.

grin, *sb.* Grinsen, *n.*; *v.i.* grinsen.

grind, mahlen; (*teeth*) knirschen; (*sharpen*) schleifen; **~stone**, Schleifstein, *m.*

grip, *sb.* Griff, Handdruck, *m.*; Gewalt, *f.*; *v.t.* greifen, packen.

gristl|e, Knorpel, *m.*; **~y**, knorp(e)lig.

grit, Grieß, Kies, *m.*; (*fig.*) Entschlossenheit, *f.*, Mut, *m.*; **~ty**, kiesig, sandig.

groan, *sb.* (schwerer) Seufzer, *m.*; *v.i.* seufzen, ächzen, stöhnen.

grocer, Kolonialwarenhändler, *m.*; **~ies**, Kolonialwaren, *f.pl.*

grog, Grog, *m.*

groin, (*anat.*) Leiste(ngegend), *f.*; (*arch.*) Rippe, *f.*

groom, *sb.* Pferdeknecht, *m.*; Bräutigam, *m.*; *v.t.* pflegen, putzen.

groove, Rinne, Furche, Rille, *f.*

grope, tappen, tasten.

gross, *sb.* Gros, *n.*; *a.* **~ly**, dick; grob; (*total*) brutto; **~ weight**, Bruttogewicht, *n.*; **~ness**, Grobheit, *f.*

grotesque, **~ly**, wunderlich, grotesk.

grotto, Grotte, *f.*

ground, *sb.* Grund, *m.*; (*earth*) Boden, *m.*; (*fig.*) Grund, *m.*, Ursache, *f.*; *v.t.* gründen; (*electr.*) erden; (*arms*) niederlegen; **~ed**, (*aircraft*) abgestellt; **~floor**, Erdgeschoß, *n.*; **~less**, grundlos; **~ mechanic**, Wart, *m.*; **~plan**, Grundriß, *m.*; **~rent**, Grundrente, *f.*; **~s**, Bodensatz, *m.*; **~sel**, Kreuzkraut, *n.*; **~sheet**, Zeltbahn, *f.*; **~ staff**, Bodenpersonal, *n.*; **~ swell**, Grundsee,

f.; **~ troops**, Erdtruppen, *f. pl.*; **~work**, (*fig.*) Grundlage, *f.*

group, *sb.* Gruppe, *f.*; (*aircraft*) Geschwader, *n.*; *v.t.* gruppieren; **~captain**, Oberst, *m.*

grouse[1], Birk-, Schnee- huhn, *n.*

grouse[2], *v.i.* (*slang*) murren.

grove, Gehölz, *n.*, Hain, *m.*

grovel, kriechen.

grow, *v.i.* wachsen, werden; zunehmen; *v.t.* (*plant*) ziehen; (*hair*, &c.) wachsen lassen; **~n-up**, erwachsen; **~th**, Wachstum, *n.*, Wuchs, *m.*; (*fig.*) Zunahme, *f.*

growl, *sb.* Knurren, *n.*; *v.i.* knurren, brummen.

groyne, Buhne, *f.*

grub, Made, Larve, *f.*; (*slang*) Futter, *n.*

grudg|e, *sb.* Groll, Neid, *m.*; *v.t.* mißgönnen; ungern tun; **~ingly**, ungern, widerwillig.

gruel, Schleimsuppe, *f.*

gruesome, grausig.

gruff, **~ly**, mürrisch, barsch.

grumble, murren (*at* über).

grumpy, mürrisch, böse.

grunt, *sb.* Grunzen, *n.*; *v.i.* grunzen.

guarantee, *sb.* (*person*) Bürge, *m.*; Bürgschaft, Garantie, *f.*; *v.t.* Bürgschaft (Gewähr) leisten (für); verbürgen, sichern.

guard, *sb.* (*mil.*) Wache, *f.*; (*railway*) Schaffner, *m.*; (*on sword*) Stichblatt, *n.*; (*on watch*) Sicherheitskette, *f.*; Schutzvorrichtung, *f.*; Schutz, *m.*; Vorsicht, *f.*; *on* **~**, auf Wache; *v.t.* bewachen, beschützen, hüten (*against* vor); **~ed(ly)**, vorsichtig; **~ian**, Wächter, Vormund, Beschützer, *m.*; **~ian angel**, Schutzengel, *m.*; **~ianship**, Vormundschaft, *f.*; **~ room**, Wach(t)stube, Wache, *f.*; **~ship**, Wachtschiff, *n.*; **~sman**, Gardist, *m.*

guerrilla warfare, Guerrilla-, Partisanenkrieg, *m.*

guess, *sb.* Vermutung, *f.*; *v.t.* (er)raten, vermuten; **~work**, Mutmaßen, *n.*

guest, Gast, *m.*; *paying* **~**, Pensionsgast, *m.*

guffaw, rohes Gelächter.

guid|e, *sb.* Führer, *m.*; *v.t.* führen, leiten; ~ance, Führung, Leitung, *f.*; ~ing, lenkend, leitend.

guild, Gilde, Innung, *f.*

guile, Arglist, *f.*, Betrug, *m.*; ~ful(ly), arglistig; ~less(ly), arglos.

guillotine, *sb.* Guillotine, *f.*, Fallbeil, *n.*; *v.t.* guillotinieren.

guilt, Schuld, *f.*; ~less, schuldlos; ~y, schuldig.

guinea[1], Guinee, *f.*

guinea[2], ~fowl, Perlhuhn, *n.*; ~pig, Meerschweinchen, *n.*

guise, Gestalt, Form, *f.*

guitar, Gitarre, *f.*

gulf, Meerbusen, *m.*; *(fig.)* Abgrund, *m.*; ~ stream, Golfstrom, *m.*

gull, *sb.* Möwe, *f.*; *v.t.* betrügen.

gullet, Gurgel, *f.*, Schlund, *m.*

gullib|le, leichtgläubig; ~ility, Leichtgläubigkeit, *f.*

gulp, *sb.* Schluck, *m.*; *v.t.* (hinunter)schlucken.

gum, *sb.* Gummi; Zahnfleisch, *n.*; *v.t.* gummieren; ~boots, Gummistiefel, *m.pl.*

gun, *(rifle)* Gewehr, *n.*; *(canon)* Geschütz,*n.*; ~boat, Kanonenboot, *n.*; ~carriage, Lafette, *f.*; ~cotton, Schießbaumwolle, *f.*; ~layer, Richtkanonier, *m.*; ~metal, Geschützmetall, *n.*; ~ner, Kanonier, *m.*, *(air)* Schütze, *m.*; ~nery, Schießkunst, *f.*; ~powder, Schießpulver, *n.*; ~room, *(naut.)* Kadettenmesse, *f.*; ~running, Waffenschmuggel, *m.*; ~shot Schußweite, *f.*; ~sight, (Richt) aufsatz, *m.*; ~smith, Büchsenmacher, *m.*

gunwale, Bordwand, *f.*

gurgle, glucksen, rieseln.

gush, strömen, *(fig.)* schwärmen; ~ing, *(fig.)* überschwenglich.

gusset, Zwickel, *m.*

gust, Bö, *f.*; ~y, böig.

gusto, Eifer; Genuss, *m.*

gut, *sb.* Darm, *m.*, Eingeweide, *n.*; *v.t.* ausweiden, ausplündern; ~ted, ausgebrannt.

gutta-percha, Guttapercha, *f.*

gutter, Rinne, Gosse, *f.*; ~ press, Skandalpresse, *f.*; ~snipe,

Straßenkind, *n.*

guttural, *sb.* Kehllaut, *m.*; *a.* Kehl-.

guzzle, schlemmen, schwelgen; verschlingen.

gymnas|ium, Turnhalle, *f.*; ~t, Turner, *m.*; ~tics, Turnkunst, *f.*, Leibesübungen, *f.pl.*

gynaecolog|y, Gynäkologie, *f.*; ~ist, Gynäkolog(e), Frauenarzt, *m.*

gypsum, Gips, *m.*

gyrat|e, kreiseln; ~ion, Kreisbewegung, *f.*

gyro-compass, Kreiselkompaß, *m.*

H

haberdasher, Kurzwarenhändler, *m.*; ~y, Kurzwaren, *f.pl.*

habit, Gewohnheit; Lebensweise, *f.*; *(plants)* Habitus, *m.*

habitable, bewohnbar.

habitation, Wohnung, *f.*

habitual, ~ly, gewohnt, (an)gewöhnt, Gewohnheits-.

hack, *sb.* Mietspferd, *n.*; Skribent, *m.*; *v.t.* hacken.

hackneyed, abgedroschen.

haddock, Schellfisch, *m.*

haemorrhage, Blutung, *f.*

haemorrhoids, Hämorrhoiden, *f.pl.*

hag, Hexe, häßliche Alte, *f.*

haggard, hager, abgehärmt.

haggle, feilschen.

hail[1], *sb.* Hagel, *m.*; *v.i.* hageln; ~stone, Hagelkorn, *n.*

hail[2], *sb.* Gruß, Ruf, *m.*; *within* ~, in Hörweite; *v.t.* anrufen.

hair, Haar, *n.*; ~brush, Haarbürste, *f.*; ~dresser, Friseur, *m.*; ~dye, Haarfärbemittel, *n.*; ~less, haarlos, kahl; ~oil, Haaröl, *n.*; ~pin, Haarnadel, *f.*; ~raising, haarsträubend; ~splitting, Wortklauberei, *f.*; ~trigger, Stecher, *m.*; ~y, haarig.

hake, Seehecht, *m.*

half, *sb.* Hälfte, *f.*; *a.* halb; ~back, Läufer, *m.*; ~blood, Halbblut, *n.*; ~bound, in Halbfranzband; ~caste, Mischling, *m.*; ~hearted, lau, gleichgültig; ~mast, halb-

mast; ~pay, Halbsold, *m.*;
on ~-pay, zur Disposition;
~-price, zum halben Preise;
~-time, Halbzeit, *f.*; ~-way,
halbwegs; ~-witted, einfältig.

halibut, Heilbutt, *m.*

hall, Saal, *m.*; (*mansion*) Herren-
haus, *n.*; (*entrance*) Hausflur, *m.*;
~-mark, Feingehaltsstempel,
m.; ~-stand, Flurständer, *m.*

halloo, hallo.

hallow, weihen, heiligen.

hallucination, Halluzination, Sin-
nestäuschung, *f.*

halo, (*sun and moon*) Hof, *m.*;
(*painting and fig.*) Heiligen-
schein, *m.*

halt, *sb.* Halt, *m.*, Haltestelle, *f.*;
v.i. haltmachen, anhalten;
(*limp*) hinken.

halter, Halfter, *f.* or *m.*

halve, halbieren.

halyard, Fall, *n.*

ham, Schinken, *m.*

hamlet, Dörfchen, *n.*

hammer, *sb.* Hammer, *m.*; *v.t.*
hämmern, schmieden.

hammock, Hängematte, *f.*

hamper, *sb.* Packkorb, *m.*; *v.t.*
hemmen, behindern.

hand¹, *sb.* Hand, *f.*; (*writing*)
Handschrift, *f.*; (*clock, &c.*)
Zeiger, *m.*; (*cards*) Karten, *f.pl.*;
(*side*) Seite, *f.*; (*workman*)
Arbeiter, *m.*; (*help*) Hilfe, *f.*;
at ~, zur Hand, nahe; by ~,
mit der Hand; in ~, im Gange;
(*balance*) in Kasse; on ~, vorrätig, bei der Hand; out of ~,
unlenkbar; ~ to ~, hand-
gemein; from ~ to mouth, von
der Hand in den Mund; get the
upper ~ of, die Oberhand gewinnen; lay ~s on, sich (einer
Sache) bemächtigen; shake ~s
with, jemandem die Hand
geben; ~-bag, Handtasche, *f.*;
~ball, (Handball, *m.*) spiel, *n.*;
~bill, Plakat, *n.*; Zettel, *m.*;
~book, Handbuch, *n.*; ~cuff(s),
sb. Handschellen, *f.pl.*; *v.t.*
jemandem die Handschellen
anlegen; ~ful, Handvoll, *f.*;
~kerchief, Taschentuch, *n.*;
~made, Hand-, mit der Hand
gemacht; ~rail, Geländer, *n.*;

~writing, Handschrift, *f.*

hand², *v.t.* reichen, geben; ~ in,
abgeben; ~ over, übergeben;
~ out, ausliefern.

handicap, *sb.* Handikap, *n.*; *v.t.*
ausgleichen; (*fig.*) hemmen, aufhalten.

handicraft, Handarbeit, *f.*; Hand-
werk, *n.*

handiness, Geschicklichkeit, *f.*

handiwork, (Hand)arbeit, *f.*

handle, *sb.* Griff, *m.*; (*brush, &c.*)
Stiel, *m.*; (*cup, jug*) Henkel, *m.*;
(*door*) Knopf, *m.*, Klinke, *f.*;
v.t. handhaben; (*subject*) be-
behandeln; (*touch*) befühlen;
~-bar, Lenkstange, *f.*

handsome, ~ly, schön; beträchtlich; ~ness, Schönheit, *f.*

hand|y, ~ily, geschickt, gewandt;
(*convenient*) handlich, bequem.

hang, *v.t.* hängen; *v.i.* hängen,
hängen, schweben; ~ fire, auf
sich warten lassen; ~ up, aufhängen; ~er-on, Anhänger,
m.; ~man, Henker, *m.*; ~over,
Katzenjammer, *m.*

hangar, Hangar, *m.*, Flugzeug-
halle, *f.*

hank, Knäuel, *m.*; Docke, *f.*

hanker, sich sehnen (nach).

haphazard, zufällig.

happen, geschehen, sich ereignen,
stattfinden; (*with infin.*) zufällig.

happ|iness, Glück, *n.*, Glückselig-
keit, *f.*; ~ily, ~y, glücklich.

harangue, *sb.* Ansprache, *f.*; *v.t.*
anreden.

harass, ärgern, quälen; (*mil.*)
stören.

harbour, *sb.* Hafen, *m.*; (*fig.*)
Zuflucht, Herberge, *f.*; *v.t.*
beherbergen; (*revenge, &c.*)
hegen.

hard, hart; mühsam, schwer;
(*cash*) bar; (*rain, frost, &c.*)
stark, heftig; (*stingy*) geizig;
~ up, mittellos, in Not; look
~ at, scharf ansehen; ~en,
v.t. härten; *v.i.* hart werden;
~-earned, schwer erworben; ~
of hearing, harthörig; ~-hearted,
hartherzig; ~ labour, Zwangs-
arbeit, *f.*; ~ness, Härte; Grausamkeit; Schwierigkeit, *f.*

~ship, Beschwerde, Not, *f.*;
~ware, Metall-, Eisen- waren,
f.pl.; ~working, fleißig, arbeitsam.

hardihood, Kühnheit, Dreistigkeit, *f.*

hardiness, Festigkeit, Ausdauer,
Körperkraft, *f.*

hardly, schwerlich; (*scarcely*)
kaum; ~ ever, fast nie.

hardy, kühn, stark; (*plants*)
winterhart.

hare, Hase, *m.*; ~bell, (wilde)
Glockenblume, *f.*; ~brained,
gedankenlos, unüberlegt; ~lip,
Hasenscharte, *f.*

harem, Harem, *m.*

haricot, Hammelragout, *n.*;
~ bean, weiße Bohne.

harlequin, Harlekin, *m.*

harlot, Hure, *f.*

harm, *sb.* Schaden, *m.*; *v.t.*
schädigen, verletzen; ~ful(ly),
schädlich, nachteilig; ~less(ly),
unschädlich, harmlos.

harmonic, *sb.* (*physics*) Ober-
schwingung, *f.*

harmonious, ~ly, harmonisch,
wohlklingend.

harmonium, Harmonium, *n.*

harmonize, *v.t.* in Einklang
bringen; *v.i.* übereinstimmen.

harmony, Harmonie, *f.*, Einklang, *m.*

harness, *sb.* Geschirr, *n.*; *v.t.*
anschirren, einspannen; (*water
power*) nutzbar machen.

harp, Harfe, *f.*

harpoon, *sb.* Harpune, *f.*; *v.t.*
harpunieren.

harpy, Harpyie, *f.*

harrow, *sb.* Egge, *f.*; *v.t.* eggen;
~ing, (*fig.*) herzzerreißend.

harry, plündern, verheeren.

harsh, ~ly, hart, streng; (*taste*)
herb; (*voice*) rauh; (*colour*)
grell; (*manner*) barsch; ~ness,
Herbheit, Barschheit, *f.*

hart, Hirsch, *m.*; ~shorn,
Hirschhorn, *n.*

harvest, *sb.* Ernte, *f.*; *v.t.* ernten;
~er, Schnitter, *m.*

hash, *sb.* Haschee, gehacktes
Fleisch, *n.*; make a ~ of, ver-
hunzen; *v.t.* zerhacken.

hasp, Haspe, *f.*

hassock, Kniekissen, *n.*

haste, Eile, *f.*; ~en, *v.i.* eilen;
v.t. beschleunigen; ~iness,
Hastigkeit; Übereilung, *f.*; ~y,
~ily, hastig; (*temper*) hitzig.

hat, Hut, *m.*; put on one's ~, den
Hut aufsetzen; take off one's ~,
den Hut abnehmen; ~-box,
Hutschachtel, *f.*; ~-pin, Hut-
nadel, *f.*

hatch, *sb.* (*naut.*) Luke, *f.*; *v.t.*
aushecken; (*plot*) anzetteln;
~way, Luke, *f.*

hatchet, Beil, *n.*, Axt, *f.*

hate, *sb.* Haß, *m.*; *v.t.* hassen;
~ful(ly), verhaßt; gehässig.

hatred, Haß, *m.*

haught|iness, Hochmut, *m.*; ~y,
~ily, hochmütig.

haul, *sb.* Zug, *m.*; *v.t.* ziehen,
schleppen; ~ down, (*flag*)
streichen; ~ in, einholen; ~ up,
hissen; aufholen; ~ier, Fuhrmann, *m.*

haunt, *sb.* Aufenthaltsort, *m.*; *v.t.*
umgehen, spuken in; ver-
folgen; this house is ~ed, in
diesem Hause spukt es.

have, haben; (*get*) bekommen;
~ to, müssen; ~ done, ~ made,
&c., tun lassen, machen lassen.

haversack, Tornister, Brotbeutel,
m.

havoc, Verwüstung, Zerstörung, *f.*

hawk[1], *sb.* Habicht, Falke, *m.*

hawk[2], *v.t.* hausieren; ~er,
Hausierer, *m.*

hawse, (*nav.*) Klüse, *f.*; ~r,
Trosse, *f.*, Schlepptau, *n.*

hawthorn, Hagedorn, *f.*

hay, Heu, *n.*; ~box, Kochkiste,
f.; ~cock, Heuhaufen, *m.*;
~fever, Heufieber, *m.*; ~loft,
Heuboden, *m.*; ~rick, Heu-
schober, *m.*

hazard, *sb.* Gefahr, *f.*; *v.t.* wagen;
~ous, gefährlich.

haze, Dunst, leichter Nebel, *m.*;
~y, dunstig.

hazel, *sb.* Haselstaude, *f.*; *a.*
nußbraun; ~nut, Haselnuß, *f.*

he, er; he-, männlichen.

head[1], *sb.* Kopf, *m.*, Haupt, *n.*;
(*of a firm*) Chef, Prinzipal, *m.*;
(*procession, spear*) Spitze, *f.*;
(*bed*) Kopfende, *n.*; (*river*)

Quelle, *f.*; (*cattle*) Stück, *n.*; (*chief*) Haupt-, Ober-; (*title*) Titel, *m.*; bring, come to a ~, zur Reife bringen, kommen; ~ first, Kopf voran; lose one's ~, den Kopf verlieren; off his ~, verrückt; take it into one's ~, sich in den Kopf setzen; I can't make ~ or tail of it, ich kann daraus nicht klug werden; ~ache, Kopfweh, *n.*; ~dress, Kopfputz, *m.*; ~er, Kopfsprung, *m.*; (*football*) Kopfball, ~ing, Überschrift, *f.*; Brief-, Titel- kopf, *m.*; ~land, Vorgebirge, *n.*; ~light, Scheinwerfer, *m.*; ~line, Kopf-, Schlag- zeile, *f.*; ~long, unbesonnen; Hals über Kopf; ~man, Häuptling, *m.*; ~master, Direktor, *m.*; ~mistress, Direktorin, *f.*; ~phone, Kopfhörer, *m.*; ~quarters, Hauptquartier, *n.*; ~rest, Kopfstütze, *f.*; ~stone, Grabstein, *m.*; ~strong, halsstarrig, eigensinnig; ~waiter, Oberkellner, *m.*; ~way, Fortschritt, Erfolg, *m.*; ~wear, Kopfbedeckung, *f.*; ~y, hitzig, berauschend.

head², *v.* anführen, befehligen; mit einem Titel versehen; (*football*) köpfen; ~ed, betitelt.

heal, heilen.

health, Gesundheit, *f.*; ~ resort, Kurort, *m.*; ~y, ~ily, gesund; heilsam.

heap, *sb.* Haufen, *m.*; *v.t.* häufen.

hear, hören; Nachricht bekommen; erfahren; ~er, Zuhörer, *m.*; ~ing, Gehör, *n.*; Gehörsinn, *m.*; Hörweite, *f.*; ~say, Hörensagen, *n.*

hearse, Leichenwagen, *m.*

heart, Herz, *n.*; (*courage*) Mut, *m.*; ~s, (*cards*) Herz, Coeur, *n.*; at ~, im Grunde; by ~, auswendig; take ~, Mut fassen; ~breaking, herzbrechend; ~broken, mit gebrochenem Herzen; ~felt, innig empfunden; ~iness, Herzlichkeit, *f.*; ~less(ly), herzlos, grausam; ~y, ~ily, herzlich; (*meal*) tüchtig.

hearth, Herd, *m.*; ~rug, Kamin-

vorleger, *m.*

heat, *sb.* Hitze; Heftigkeit, *f.*; (*animals*) Brunst, *f.*; (*sport*) einzelnes Rennen; dead ~, totes Rennen; *v.t.* heizen, erhitzen, heiß machen; ~er, (*water*) Vorwärmer, *m.*; ~resisting, feuerfest; ~wave, Hitzewelle, *f.*

heath, Heide, *f.*

heathen, *sb.* Heide, *m.*; *a.* heidnisch.

heather, Heidekraut, *n.*

heave, *sb.* Heben, *n.*, Stoß, *m.*; *v.t.* (er)heben; *v.i.* sich erheben; ~ to, (*naut.*) beidrehen.

heaven, Himmel, *m.*; ~ly, himmlisch.

heav|iness, Schwere; Schwermut, *f.*; ~y, ~ily, schwer, stark.

Hebrew, *sb.* Hebräer, Jude, *m.*; (*language*) Hebräisch, *n.*; *a.* hebräisch; jüdisch.

hectic, hektisch.

hedge, *sb.* Hecke, *f.*, Zaun, *m.*; *v.t.* einhegen; *v.i* Ausflüchte machen; ~hog, Igel, *m.*; ~row, Hecke, *f.*

heed, *sb.* Achtung, Aufmerksamkeit, *f.*; *v.t.* achtgeben, Achtung geben; ~less(ly), unachtsam.

heel, *sb.* Ferse, *f.*; (*of boot*) Absatz, *m.*; take to one's ~s, ausreißen; *v.t.* (*boots*) mit Absätzen versehen; *v.i.* ~ over, (*naut.*) krängen.

hefty, stramm, stämmig, schwer.

hegemony, Hegemonie, Vorherrschaft, *f.*

heifer, junge Kuh.

height, Höhe, *f.*; Höhepunkt, Gipfel, *m.*; in ~, hoch; in the ~ of, mitten in; ~en, erhöhen.

heir, Erbe, *m.*; ~ess, Erbin, *f.*; ~loom, Erbstück, *n.*

helicopter, Hubschrauber, Helikopter, *m.*

heliotrope, *sb.* (*bot. and min.*) Heliotrop, *n.*; *a.* heliotropfarben.

hell, Hölle, *f.*; ~ish, höllisch.

helm, (Steuer)ruder, *m.*; ~sman, Steuermann, *m.*

helmet, Helm, *m.*

help, *sb.* Hilfe, Unterstützung, *f.*; *v.t.* helfen; (*at table*) bedienen; I cannot ~ it, ich kann nichts dafür; ~ yourself, bedienen Sie sich; ~er, Helfer, Gehilfe, *m.*; ~ful(ly), nützlich, behilflich; ~ing, (*food*) Portion, *f.*; ~less(ly), hilflos; ~mate, Gehilfe, *m.*, Gehilfin, *f.*

hem, *sb.* Saum, *m.*; *v.t.* säumen; ~*med in*, umringt; ~stitch, *sb.* Hohlsaum, *m.*; *v.t.* mit Hohlsaum versehen.

hemisphere, Hemisphäre, Halbkugel, *f.*

hemlock, Schierling, *m.*

hemp, Hanf, *m.*; ~en, hänfen.

hen, Henne, *f.*; ~coop, Hühnerkorb, -stall, *m.*; ~roost, Hühnerstange, *f.*

hence, von hier; von nun an; so, deshalb; ~forth, von nun an.

hen-pecked, unter dem Pantoffel stehend.

her, sie, ihr; (*poss.*) ihr(e).

herald, *sb.* Herold; (*fig.*) Vorläufer, *m.*; *v.t.* verkünden; ~ry, Wappenkunde, *f.*

herb, Kraut, *n.*; ~aceous, krautartig; ~age, Gras, *n.*; ~alist, Kräuter-kenner, -händler, *m.*; ~ivorous, pflanzenfressend.

herd, *sb.* Herde, *f.*; *v.i.*, ~ *together*, sich zusammenscharen; ~sman, Hirt, *m.*

here, hier, her; ~after, hiernach; ~by, hierdurch, hiermit.

hereditary, erblich, vererbt; ~y, Erblichkeit, *f.*

heresy, Ketzerei, *f.*

heretic, Ketzer, *m.*; ~al(ly), ketzerisch.

heritage, Erbschaft, *f.*

hermaphrodite, Zwitter, *m.*

hermetic, ~ally, luftdicht.

hermit, Einsiedler, *m.*; ~age, Einsiedelei, *f.*

hernia, Bruch, *m.*

hero, Held, *m.*; ~ic(ally), heroisch, heldenhaft; ~ine, Heldin, *f.*; ~ism, Heldenmut, *m.*, Tapferkeit, *f.*

heroin, Heroin, *n.*

heron, Reiher, *m.*

herring, Hering, *m.*

hers, für (die, das) ihrige; ~elf, sie (ihr) selbst; *refl.* sich.

hesitat|e, zögern, unschlüssig sein; ~ion, Zögern, *n.*, Unschlüssigkeit, *f.*

heterodox, andersgläubig, ~y, Irrlehre, *f.*

heterogeneous, verschiedenartig.

hew, hauen, fällen.

hexagon, Sechseck, *n.*; ~al, sechseckig.

hexameter, Hexameter, *m.*

hibernat|e, überwintern; ~ion, Winterschlaf, *m.*

hiccup, hiccough, *sb.* Schlucken, *m.*; *v.i.* den Schlucken haben.

hide¹, Haut, *f.*; ~bound, starr, beschränkt; engherzig.

hid|e², *v.t.* verstecken; *v.i.* sich verbergen, sich verstecken; ~ing-place, Schlupfwinkel, *m.*

hideous, ~ly, scheußlich.

hierarchy, Hierarchie, *f.*

hieroglyphics, Hieroglyphen, *f.pl.*

hi-fi, (*in compounds*) Hi-Fi-.

higgledy-piggledy, alles durcheinander.

high, hoch; (*sublime*) erhaben; (*wind*) stark; (*game, &c.*) angegangen, pikant; ~born, hochgeboren; ~brow, Intellektuelle(r); ~class, erstklassig; ~explosive, Brisanz, *f.*; ~explosive bomb, Sprengbombe, *f.*; ~flown, bombastisch; ~frequency, Hochfrequenz, *f.*; ~grade, Qualitäts-; ~handed, hochfahrend; ~heeled, mit hohen Absätzen; ~jump, Hochsprung, *m.*; ~lands, Hochland, *n.*; ~ life, vornehme Welt; ~light, *sb.* Höhepunkt, *m.*; *v.t.* (stark) hervorheben; ~ly, hoch, höchst; *think* ~*ly of*, eine hohe Meinung von . . . haben; ~ness, (*title*) Hoheit, *f.*; ~pressure, Hochdruck-; ~priest, Hohe(r)priester, *m.*; ~road, Landstraße, *f.*; ~ seas, hohe See. ~Hochsee-; ~speed, Schnell-; ~spirited, mutig; ~strung, nervös; ~tension, Hochspannungs-; ~treason, Hochverrat, *m.*; ~water, Hochwasser, *n.*; ~way, Landstraße, *f.*; ~wayman, Wegelagerer, *m.*

hijack, *v.t.* (ein Flugzeug) entführen.

hike, *sb.* Wanderung, *f.*; *v.i.* wandern.

hilar|ious, heiter; ~ity, Heiterkeit, f.

hill, Hügel, Berg, m.; ~ock, kleiner Hügel; ~y, hügelig.

hilt, Griff, m., Heft, n.

him, ihn, ihm; ~self, er (ihn, ihm) selbst; refl. sich.

hind¹, sb. Hirschkuh, f.

hind², a. hinter; ~most, hinterst; ~quarters, Hinterteil, m. or n.

hinder, hindern, stören.

hindrance, Hindernis, n., (Be)hinderung, f.

hinge, sb. Türangel, Haspe, f.

hint, sb. Wink, Fingerzeig, m., Andeutung, f.; v.i. einen Wink geben; ~ at, auf . . . anspielen.

hip, (anat.) Hüfte; (berry) Hagebutte, f.; ~bath, Sitzbad, n.

hippopotamus, Nilpferd, n.

hippy, Beatnik, m.

hire, sb. Miete, f.; v.t. (ver)mieten; ~purchase, Ratenkauf, m.

his, sein(e); der (die, das) seinige.

hiss, zischen.

histor|ian, Geschichtschreiber, m.; ~ical(ly), geschichtlich; ~y, Geschichte, f.

hit, sb. Schlag, Stoß, m.; (on target and fig.) Treffer; (theatr., &c.) Schlager, m.; v.t. schlagen, stoßen; treffen.

hitch, sb. Hindernis, n.; Schwierigkeit, f.; v.t. festmachen, anbinden; ~hike, Autostop machen, trampen, hitchen; ~hiker, Anhalter, m.

hither, hierher; ~to, bis jetzt.

hive, Bienenkorb, Schwarm, m.

hoard, sb. Vorrat, Schatz, m.; v.t. aufhäufen, hamstern; ~ing, Bauzaun, m.

hoar-frost, Reif, m.

hoarse, ~ly, heiser; ~ness, Heiserkeit, f.

hoary, eisgrau, altersgrau.

hoax, sb. Fopperei, f., Streich, m.; v.t. foppen.

hobble, humpeln.

hobby, Steckenpferd, n.

hock, (weisser) Rheinwein.

hockey, Hockey(spiel), n.

hoe, sb. Hacke, f.; v.t. (be)hacken.

hog, Schwein, n.

hoist, sb. Aufzug, m.; v.t. hissen; aufwinden.

hold, sb. Griff, Halt, m.; Macht, f.; (naut.) Laderaum, m.; (support) Stütze, f.; v.t. halten, haben, besitzen; (celebrate) feiern, (think) meinen; v.i. sich halten; ~ forth, vortragen, reden; ~ good, gültig sein; ~ in, einhalten, sich zurückhalten; ~ off, abhalten, sich fern halten; ~ office, ein Amt bekleiden; ~ out, aushalten; in Aussicht stellen; ~ one's tongue, schweigen; ~all, Reisetasche, f.; ~er, (owner) Inhaber, Besitzer, m.; (for things) Halter, m.; ~ing, Pachtgut, n.; Besitz, m.

hole, Loch, n., Höhle, f.

holiday, Feiertag, freier Tag, m.; ~s, Ferien, pl.

holiness, Heiligkeit, f.

hollo, hallo.

hollow, sb. Höhle, Höhlung, f.; a. hohl; v.t. aushöhlen.

holly, Stechpalme, f.; ~hock, Stockrose, f.

holster, (Pistolen)halfter, f.

holy, heilig; the Holy Ghost, der Heilige Geist; the Holy Land, das Heilige Land; ~ water, Weihwasser, n.; ~ week, Karwoche, f.

homage, Huldigung, f.; do ~ to, huldigen (with dat.).

home, Heimat, Wohnung, f., Heim, n.; a. häuslich, heimisch; at ~, zu Hause; go ~, nach Hause gehen; Home Office, Ministerium des Innern; Home Rule, Selbstverwaltung, f.; ~less, heimatlos; ~liness, Einfachheit, f.; ~ly, einfach; ~made, zu Hause (or im Lande) gemacht; ~sickness, Heimweh, n.; ~wards, nach Hause, heimwärts.

homicide, Totschlag, m.

homily, Predigt, f.

homing-pigeon, Brieftaube, f.

homogeneous, gleichartig.

homosexual, homosexuell.

hone, sb. Wetzstein, m.; v.t. abziehen.

honest, ~ly, ehrlich, redlich, aufrichtig; ~y, Ehrlichkeit, Redlichkeit, f.

honey, Honig, m.; ~comb, Honigwabe, f.; ~combed,

durchlöchert; ~moon, Flitterwochen, *f.pl.*; ~suckle, Geißblatt, *n.*

honorary, Ehren-.

honour, *sb.* Ehre, *f.*; Auszeichnung, *f.*; Ehrenzeichen, *n.*; *v.t.* ehren; *(cheque, &c.)* honorieren; ~able, ~ably, ehrenvoll, ehrenwert; ~s, *(position)* Würde, *f.*; *(cards)* Honneurs, *pl.*

hood, Kapuze, Kappe, *f.*; *(motor)* Haube, *f.*; ~wink, täuschen.

hoof, Huf, *m.*

hook, *sb.* Haken, *m.*; *(reaping)* Sichel, *f.*; by ~ or by crook, so oder so; *v.t.* anhaken, angeln; ~ed, gebogen, gekrümmt.

hooligan, Straßenlümmel, Rowdy, *m.*

hoop, Reif(en), *m.*

hooping-cough, Keuchhusten, *m.*

hoot, *sb.* Geschrei, *n.*; *v.i.* schreien; hupen, tuten; ~er, Hupe, *f.*, Horn, *n.*

hop¹, *(bot.)* Hopfen, *m.*

hop², *sb.* Sprung, *m.*, Hüpfen, *n.*; *v.i.* hüpfen.

hope, *sb.* Hoffnung, *f.*; *v.i.* hoffen *(for* auf*)*; ~ful(ly), hoffnungsvoll; ~less(ly), hoffnungslos.

horde, Horde, *f.*

horizon, Horizont, *m.*; ~tal(ly), waagerecht, horizontal.

horn, Horn, *n.*; *(motor)* Hupe, *f.*

hornet, Hornisse, *f.*

horoscope, Horoskop, *n.*

horrib|le, ~ly, abscheulich, schrecklich.

horrid, schrecklich.

horrify, entsetzen.

horror, Entsetzen, *n.*

horse, Pferd; Roß, *n.*; Gaul, *m.*; ~on ~back, zu Pferde; ~box, Pferdewagen, *m.*; ~boy, Pferdeknecht, *m.*; ~chestnut, Roßkastanie, *f.*; ~dealer, Pferdehändler, *m.*; ~hair, Roßhaar, *n.*; ~man, Reiter, *m.*; ~manship, Reitkunst, *f.*; ~play, derber Spaß; ~power, Pferdekraft, *f.*; ~race, Pferderennen, *n.*; ~radish, Meerrettich, *m.*; ~shoe, Hufeisen, *n.*

horticulture, Gartenbau, *m.*

hose, *(stocking)* Strümpfe, *m.pl.*; ~pipe, Schlauch, *m.*

hosier, Strumpfwarenhändler, *m.*; ~y, Strumpfwaren, *f.pl.*

hospitab|le, ~ly, gastfreundlich.

hospital, Krankenhaus, *n.*; *(mil.)* Lazarett, *n.*; ~ nurse, Krankenpflegerin, *f.*

hospitality, Gastfreundschaft, *f.*

host¹, Wirt, Gastgeber, *m.*; ~ess, Wirtin, Gastgeberin, *f.*

host², *(army)* Schar, *f.*, Heer, *n.*

host³, *(wafer)* Hostie, *f.*

hostage, Geisel, *m.*

hostel, Gasthof, *m.*, Wohnheim, *n.*

hostile, ~ely, feindlich; ~ity, Feindseligkeit, *f.*

hot, ~ly, heiß; heftig, hitzig; ~bed, *(fig.)* Brutstätte, *f.*; ~head, Hitzkopf, *m.*; ~house, Treibhaus, *n.*; ~water bottle, Wärmflasche, *f.*

hotch-potch, Mischmasch, *m.*

hotel, Hotel, *n.*; Gasthof, *m.*; ~keeper, Hotelier, *m.*

hound, *sb.* Jagdhund, *m.*; *(fig. and contempt.)* Hund, *m.*; *v.t.* hetzen, verfolgen.

hour, Stunde, *f.*; ~glass, Sanduhr, *f.*; ~hand, Stundenzeiger, *m.*; ~ly, stündlich.

house, *sb.* Haus, *n.*, Wohnung, *f.*; *v.t.* unterbringen, beherbergen; ~breaking, Einbruch, *m.*; ~hold, Haushalt, *m.*; Familie, *f.*; ~holder, Haushalter, *m.*; ~keeper, Haushälterin, *f.*; ~keeping, Haushaltung, *f.*; ~maid, Zimmermädchen, *n.*; ~wife, Hausfrau, *f.*; ~wifery, Hauswesen, *n.*

hovel, elende Hütte.

hover, schweben; ~craft, Schwebe-, Luftkissenfahrzeug, *n.*

how, wie; ~ever, dennoch; wie auch.

howitzer, Haubitze, *f.*

howl, *sb.* Geheul, *n.*; *v.i.* heulen; ~er, grober Fehler.

hub, Nabe, *f.*; *(fig.)* Mittelpunkt, *m.*

hubbub, Tumult, Lärm, *m.*

huddle, ~together, sich zusammendrängen.

hue, Farbe; Schattierung, *f.*

hug, *sb.* Umarmung, *f.*; *v.t.* umarmen.

huge, ungeheuer, sehr groß; ~ly, außerordentlich.

hulk, Hulk, Rumpf, *m.*

hull, (*husk*) Hülse, *f.*; (*naut.*) Rumpf, *m.*

hum, *sb.* Gesumme, *n.*; *v.i.* summen, brummen.

human, ~ly, menschlich; ~ being, Mensch, *m.*; ~ism, Humanismus, *m.*; ~ist, Humanist, *m.*; ~itarian, Menschenfreund, *m.*; *a.* Humanitäts-; ~ities, klassische Wissenschaft, *f.*; Humaniora, *pl.*; ~ity, Menschheit; Menschlichkeit, *f.*; ~kind, Menschengeschlecht, *n.*

humane, ~ly, menschenfreundlich, barmherzig.

humb|le, *a.*, ~ly, demütig; (*lowly*) niedrig; *v.t.* demütigen.

humbug, *sb.* Humbug, Schwindel, *m.*; Schwindler, *m.*; *v.t.* foppen, betrügen.

humdrum, uninteressant.

humid, feucht, ~ity, Feuchtigkeit, *f.*

humiliat|e, erniedrigen; ~ion, Erniedrigung, *f.*

humility, Demut, Unterwürfigkeit, *f.*

humming-bird, Kolibri, *m.*

humor|ist, Humorist, *m.*; ~ous(ly), humoristisch.

humour, *sb.* Humor, *m.*; (*mood*) Laune, Grille, *f.*; *v.t.* willfahren (*with dat.*); good-~ed, gut gelaunt.

hump, Buckel, (*camel's*) Höcker, *m.*; ~back, Buck(e)lige(r).

Hun, Hunne, *m.*

hunchback = humpback.

hundred, hundert, *n.*; ~weight, Zentner, *m.*

hung|er, *sb.* Hunger, *m.*; *v.i.* hungern; ~ry, ~ily, hungrig.

hunt, *sb.* Jagd, *f.*; *v.* jagen; ~ up, nachsuchen; ~er, Jäger, *m.*; Jagdpferd, *n.*; ~ing, Jagd, *f.*; ~ing-box, Jagdhäuschen, *n.*; ~sman, Jäger, *m.*

hurdle, Hürde, *f.*; ~race, Hindernisrennen, *n.*

hurdy-gurdy, Drehorgel, *f.*

hurl, schleudern, werfen.

hurrah, hurra.

hurricane, Orkan, *m.*

hurry, *sb.* Eile, Unruhe, *f.*; *v.t.* beeilen, beschleunigen; *v.i.* eilen, sich beeilen.

hurt, *sb.* Verletzung, *f.*; Schaden, *m.*; *v.t.* verletzen; *v.i.* schmerzen, weh tun; ~ful. schädlich.

husband, *sb.* Mann, Gatte, *m.*; *v.t.* (*resources*) sparen; ~man, Landwirt, *m.*; ~ry, Landwirtschaft, *f.*

hush, *int.* still! *v.t.* zum Schweigen bringen; ~ up, vertuschen, unterdrücken; *v.i.* schweigen; ~money, Schweigegeld, *n.*

husk, *sb.* Hülse, *f.*; *v.t.* schälen.

husky, heiser.

hussar, Husar, *m.*

hustle, drängen, stoßen.

hut, Hütte, (*mil.*) Baracke, *f.*

hutch, Kaninchenkasten, *m.*

hyacinth, Hyazinthe, *f.*

hybrid, *sb.* Hybride, *f.*; *a.* Zwitter-.

hydrangea, Hortensie, *f.*

hydrant, Wasserhahn, *m.*

hydraulic, hydraulisch.

hydro, Wasserheilanstalt, *f.*: ~carbon, Kohlenwasserstoff, *m.*; ~chloric acid, Salzsäure, *f.*; ~electric plant, Wasserkraftwerk, *n.*; ~gen, Wasserstoff, *m.*; ~genation, Hydrierung, *f.*; ~meter, Hydrometer, *n.*; ~pathic, hydropathisch; ~pathy, Wasserheilkunde, *f.*; ~phobia, Wasserscheu, *f.*; ~phone, Hydrophon, *n.*

hyena, Hyäne, *f.*

hygien|e, Hygiene, Gesundheitslehre, *f.*; ~ic, hygienisch.

hymn, Hymne, *f.*

hyperbol|e, Hyperbel, Übertreibung, *f.*; ~ical, übertrieben.

hyphen, Bindestrich, *m.*

hypnot|ic, einschläfernd, hypnotisch; ~ism, Hypnotismus, *m.*; ~ize, hypnotisieren.

hypochondriac, schwermütig.

hypocri|sy, Heuchelei, *f.*; ~te, Heuchler, *m.*; ~tical(ly), heuchlerisch.

hypothe|sis, Hypothese, Annahme, *f.*; ~tical, hypothetisch, angenommen, unterstellt.

hysteric|al, hysterisch; ~s, Hysterie, *f.*

I

I, ich; *it is* ~, ich bin es.

iambic, *a.* iambisch; *sb.* iambischer Vers.

ibex, Steinbock, *m.*

ice, *sb.* Eis, *n.*; *v.t.* mit Eis kühlen; überzuckern; ~**axe,** Eispickel *m.*; ~**berg,** Eisberg, *m.*; ~**bound,** eingefroren; ~**box,** Eisschrank, *m.*; ~**breaker,** Eisbrecher, *m.*; ~**cream,** (Speise)eis, Gefrorenes, *n.*; ~**hockey,** Eishockey, *n.*; ~**pack,** Packeis, *n.*; (*med.*) Eisbeutel,*m.*

icicle, Eiszapfen, *m.*

icing, Zuckerguß, *m.*

iconoclast, Bilderstürmer, *m.*

icy, ~**ily,** eisig; (*fig.*) kühl.

idea, Idee, *f.*, Begriff, *m.*; *I have no* ~, ich habe keine Ahnung.

ideal, *a.*, ~**ly,** ideal, mustergültig, vorbildlich; *sb.* Ideal, *n.*; ~**ism,** Idealismus, *m.*; ~**ist,** Idealist, *m.*; ~**ize,** idealisieren.

identical, ~**ly,** identisch; ebender-(die-, das-)selbe.

identification, Identifizierung, Erkennung, *f.*; ~**y,** identifizieren.

identity, Identität, Gleichheit, *f.*; ~ **card,** Ausweiskarte, *f.*

idiocy, Blödsinn, *m.*

idiom, Redensart; Mundart, *f.*; ~**atic,** idiomatisch, mundartlich.

idiosyncrasy, Idiosynkrasie, *f.*

idiot, Blödsinnige(r); ~**ic,** blödsinnig; verrückt.

idle, *a.* müßig; faul, träge; unnütz; *v.i.* müßig gehen; (*mach.*) leer laufen, anlaufen; *v.t.* vertändeln; ~**ness,** Müßiggang, *m.*; Trägheit, Faulheit, *f.*; ~**r,** Müßiggänger, *m.*

idol, Götzenbild, *n.*; Abgott, *m.*; ~**ater,** Götzendiener, *m.*; ~**atrous,** abgöttisch; ~**atry,** Götzendienst, *m.*; ~**ize,** vergöttern.

idyll, Idylle, *f.*; ~**ic,** idyllisch.

if, wenn, ob.

ignite, *v.t.* anzünden; *v.i.* sich entzünden; ~**ion,** (Ent)zündung, *f.*

ignoble, ~**ly,** gemein; niedrig.

ignominious, ~**iously,** schimpflich; ~**y,** Schmach, Schande, *f.*

ignoramus, Ignorant, Dummkopf, *m.*; ~**ance,** Unwissenheit, *f.*; ~**ant(ly),** unwissend.

ignore, unbeachtet lassen, absehen von.

ill, *sb.* Übel, *n.*; *a.* übel, böse; (*sick*) unwohl, krank; ~**bred,** unmanierlich; ~**fated,** unglücklich; ~ **feeling,** Abneigung, *f.*; ~ **natured,** bösartig; ~**ness,** Krankheit, *f.*; ~**tempered,** mürrisch; ~**treat,** schlecht behandeln; ~ **will,** Groll, *m.*, Übelwollen, *n.*

illegal, ~**ly,** gesetzwidrig; ~**ity,** Gesetzwidrigkeit, *f.*

illegible, ~**ly,** unleserlich.

illegitimacy, Unrechtmäßigkeit, uneheliche Geburt, *f.*; ~**ate,** unrechtmäßig; unehelich.

illicit, unerlaubt; Schwarz-.

illiterate, *sb.* Analphabet, *m.*; *a.* ungebildet.

illogical, ~**ly,** unlogisch.

illuminate, erleuchten; ~**ion,** Erleuchtung, *f.*

illusion, Täuschung, *f.*; ~**ive,** ~**ory,** täuschend, trüglich.

illustrate, illustrieren; erläutern; ~**ion,** Illustration, Abbildung; Erläuterung, *f.*; ~**ive,** erläuternd.

illustrious, ~**ly,** berühmt, erhaben.

image, Bild, *n.*; ~**ry,** bildliche Rede.

imagine, sich denken, sich einbilden; ersinnen; ~**able,** denkbar; ~**ary,** eingebildet; ~**ation,** Einbildung, Phantasie, *f.*; ~**ative,** erfinderisch, phantasiereich.

imbecile, schwachsinnig; ~**ity,** Geistesschwäche, *f.*

imbibe, einsaugen.

imitate, nachahmen; ~**ion,** Nachahmung, *f.*; Kunst-; ~**ive,** nachahmend; ~**or,** Nachahmer, *m.*

immaculate, unbefleckt.

immanent, innewohnend.

immaterial, unwesentlich.

immature, unreif; ~**ity,** Unreife,*f.*

immeasurable, unermeßlich.

immediate, unmittelbar; ~ly, sogleich.

immemorial, undenklich.

immense|e, ~ely, unermeßlich; ungeheuer; ~ity, Unermeß-lichkeit, f.

immers|e, eintauchen, versenken; ~ion, Eintauchen, n.; ~ion heater, Tauchsieder, m.

immigr|ant, Einwanderer, m.; ~ate, einwandern; ~ation, Einwanderung, f.

imminent, bevorstehend.

immobil|e, unbeweglich; ~ity, Unbeweglichkeit, f.

immoderate, ~ly, unmäßig.

immodest, ~ly, unanständig, un-bescheiden; ~y, Unanständig-keit, Unbescheidenheit, f.

immoral, ~ly, unsittlich; ~ity, Unsittlichkeit, f.

immortal, ~ly, unsterblich; ~ity, Unsterblichkeit, f.; ~ize, ver-ewigen, unsterblich machen.

immun|e, frei, geschützt; (med.) immun (from gegen); ~ity, Freiheit (from von); (med.) Immunität, f.; ~ize, immuni-sieren.

immutable, unveränderlich.

imp, Kobold; kleiner Schelm, m.

impact, Stoß, Aufschlag, m.

impair, beeinträchtigen, vermin-dern.

impart, mitteilen, erteilen.

impartial, ~ly, unparteiisch; ~ity, Unparteilichkeit, f.

impass|able, ungangbar; ~e, Sackgasse, f.

impassive, unempfindlich.

impatien|ce, Ungeduld, f.; ~t(ly), ungeduldig.

impeccable, tadellos.

imped|e, verhindern; ~iment, Hindernis, n.; ~imenta, (mil.) Gepäck, n.

impel, antreiben.

impend, bevorstehen.

impenetrable, undurchdringlich.

impeniten|ce, Unbußfertigkeit, f.; ~t(ly), unbußfertig, verstockt.

imperative, sb. Imperativ, m.; a. befehlend; dringend nötig.

imperceptible, unmerklich.

imperfect, sb. (gram.) Imperfek-tum, n.; a., ~ly, unvollkommen;

~ion, Unvollkommenheit, f.

imperial, ~ly, kaiserlich; Reichs-; ~ism, Imperialismus, m.; ~ist, Imperialist, m.

imperil, gefährden.

imperious, ~ly, gebieterisch.

imperishable, unvergänglich.

impermeable, undurchdringlich.

impersonal, ~ly, unpersönlich.

impersonat|e, verkörpern; (theatr.) darstellen; ~ion, Verkör-perung; Darstellung, f.

impertinen|ce, Anmaßung, Frech-heit, f.; ~t(ly), unverschämt, frech.

imperturbable, unerschütterlich.

impervious, unzugänglich, un-durchdringlich; ~ to air, water, luftdicht, wasserdicht.

impetu|osity, Ungestüm, n., Heftigkeit, f.; ~ous(ly), un-gestüm, heftig.

impetus, Antrieb, m., Triebkraft, f.

impi|ety, Gottlosigkeit, f.; ~ous, gottlos.

implement, Gerät, Werkzeug, n.

implicat|e, verwickeln; ~ion, Ver-wick(e)lung; Folgerung, f.

implicit, ~ly, unbedingt; (still-schweigend) einbegriffen.

implore, anflehen.

imply, in sich schließen, voraus-setzen.

impolite, ~ly, unhöflich; ~ness, Unhöflichkeit, f.

import, sb. Einfuhr, f.; v.t. ein-führen; ~er, Einführer, Im-porteur, m.

importan|ce, Wichtigkeit, f.; ~t, wichtig.

importun|e, belästigen; ~ity, Zudringlichkeit, f.

impos|e, auferlegen, aufbürden; ~e upon, mißbrauchen, täu-schen; ~ing, imponierend; ~ition, Betrügerei; (school) Strafarbeit, f.

impossib|le, unmöglich; ~ility, Unmöglichkeit, f.

impostor, Betrüger, m.

impoten|ce, Unvermögen, n.; ~t, ~ly, unvermögend; zeugungs-unfähig.

impracticable, untunlich.

impregnable, unbezwinglich.

impregnate, schwängern; sättigen.

impress, *sb.* Eindruck, *m.*; *v.t.* eindrücken; Eindruck machen auf; ~ion, Eindruck, *m.* (*book, &c.*) Abdruck, *m.*; ~ionable, empfänglich; ~ionism, Impressionismus, *m.*; ~ionist, Impressionist, *m.*; ~ive(ly), Eindruck machend, ergreifend.

imprint, Impressum, *n.*

imprison, gefangensetzen; ~ment, Haft, *f.*

improbab|le, ~ly, unwahrscheinlich; ~ility, Unwahrscheinlichkeit, *f.*

impromptu, *a.* Stegreif-; *sb.* Improvisation, *f.*

improp|er, ~erly, ungeziemend, ungehörig, unanständig; ~riety, Unanständigkeit, *f.*

improve, *v.t.* (ver)bessern; *v.i.* sich bessern, besser werden; ~ment, (Ver)besserung, *f.*

improviden|ce, Sorglosigkeit, *f.*; ~t(ly), sorglos, unbedachtsam.

improvise, improvisieren; ~d, behelfsmäßig; improvisiert.

impruden|ce, Unvorsichtigkeit, *f.*; ~t(ly), unvorsichtig, unklug.

impuden|ce, Unverschämtheit, *f.*; ~t(ly), unverschämt.

impuls|e, Impuls, Antrieb, *m.*; ~ive(ly), erregbar, impulsiv.

impunity, Straflosigkeit, *f.*; *with* ~, ungestraft.

impur|e, ~ely, unrein; unkeusch; ~ity, Unreinheit; Unreinigkeit, *f.*

imput|e, zurechnen, beimessen; ~ation, Anschuldigung, Beimessung, *f.*

in, *prep.* in, an, zu, bei, unter, während; *adv.* darin, herein, hinein; zu Hause; ~ *fashion*, nach der Mode, ~ *time*, mit der Zeit; zur rechten Zeit.

inability, Unfähigkeit, *f.*

inaccessible, unzugänglich.

inaccura|cy, Ungenauigkeit, *f.*; ~te(ly), ungenau.

inact|ion, Untätigkeit, *f.*; ~ive, untätig.

inadequa|cy, Unzulänglichkeit, *f.*; ~te(ly), unzulänglich.

inadmissible, unzulässig.

inadvertent, unachtsam; ~ly, unversehens.

inan|e, ~ely, geistlos, fad(e); ~ity, Geistlosigkeit, Fadheit, *f.*

inanimate, leblos.

inapplicable, unanwendbar.

inappropriate, unpassend.

inapt, ungeschickt, untauglich, unpassend; ~itude, Untauglichkeit, *f.*

inarticulate, ~ly, unvernehmlich, unverständlich, undeutlich.

inatten|tion, Unaufmerksamkeit, *f.*; ~ive, unaufmerksam.

inaudible, unhörbar.

inaugur|al, Antritts-; ~ate, einweihen, einführen.

inauspicious, ~ly, ungünstig.

inborn, angeboren.

incandescent, weißglühend, Glüh-; ~ *lamp*, Glühlampe, *f.*

incantation, Zauberspruch, *m.*

incap|able, unfähig; ~ability, Unfähigkeit, *f.*; ~acitate, unfähig machen.

incarnation, Menschwerdung, *f.*

incautious, ~ly, unvorsichtig.

incendiar|ism, Brandstiftung, *f.*; ~y, *sb.* Brandstifter, *m.*; *a.* Brand-; ~y bomb, Brandbombe, *f.*

incense[1], Weihrauch, *m.*

incense[2], *v.t.* erzürnen.

incentive, Antrieb, Anreiz, *m.*

incessant, ~ly, unablässig, unaufhörlich.

incest, Blutschande, *f.*; ~uous, blutschänderisch.

inch, Zoll, *m.*; *by* ~, allmählich.

incidence, Vorkommen; Fallen, *n.*

incident, Vorfall, *m.*, Ereignis, *n.*; ~al(ly), zufällig; beiläufig, Begleit-.

incis|ion, Einschnitt, *m.*; ~ive, schneidend, scharf; ~or, Schneidezahn, *m.*

incite, anreizen, antreiben; ~ment, Anreiz, Antrieb, *m.*

incivility, Unhöflichkeit, *f.*

inclemen|cy, (*weather*) Unfreundlichkeit, *f.*; ~t, unfreundlich.

inclin|ation, Neigung, *f.*; ~e, *sb.* Abhang, *m.*; *v.t.* neigen; *v.i.* sich neigen; geneigt sein.

inclu|de, einschließen; ~sion, Einschließung, *f.*; ~sive, einschließlich, einschließend.

incognito, inkognito, unter frem-
dem Namen.

incoheren|ce, Inkonsequenz, f.;
Mangel (m.) an Zusammen-
hang; ~t(ly), unzusammen-
hängend, inkonsequent.

incombustible, unverbrennlich.

income, Einkommen, n.; Einkünfte, f.pl.; ~-tax, Ein-
kommensteuer, f.

incomparable, unvergleichlich.

incompatib|le, ~ly, unverträglich,
unvereinbar; ~ility, Unver-
träglichkeit, Unvereinbarkeit, f.

incompeten|ce, Untauglichkeit, f.;
(law) Unzuständigkeit, f.;
~t(ly), untauglich, unzulänglich; (law) unzuständig.

incomplete, unvollständig; un-
vollendet.

incomprehensib|le, ~ly, unbe-
greiflich.

inconceivab|le, ~ly, unvorstellbar.

inconclusive, nicht überzeugend.

incongru|ity, Inkongruenz, Un-
angemessenheit, f.; ~ous,
unangemessen; nicht übereinstimmend.

inconsiderable, unbedeutend, unwichtig.

inconsiderate, ~ly, rücksichtslos,
unbedachtsam.

inconsisten|cy, Unvereinbarkeit,
Inkonsequenz, f.; ~t(ly), unvereinbar, inkonsequent.

inconspicuous, ~ly, unauffällig.

inconstan|cy, Unbeständigkeit, f.;
~t, unbeständig.

incontestable, unbestreitbar.

incontinen|ce, Unenthaltsamkeit,
f.; ~t(ly), unenthaltsam, un-
keusch.

inconvenien|ce, Unbequemlich-
keit, Unzuträglichkeit, f.;
~t(ly), unbequem; ungelegen.

incorrect, ~ly, unrichtig.

incorrigible, unverbesserlich.

increase, sb. Zunahme, f.; Wachstum, n.; v.t. vergrößern; v.i.
zunehmen.

incred|ible, ~ibly, unglaublich;
~ulous, ungläubig.

increment, Zuwachs, m.; Zunahme, f.

incriminate, beschuldigen.

incubat|e, (aus)brüten; ~ion,

Ausbrütung; (med.) Inkuba-
tion, f.; ~or, Brut -apparat,
-ofen, m.

incubus, Alpdrücken, n.

inculcate, einschärfen.

incunabula, Wiegendrucke, m.pl.;
Inkunabeln, f.pl.

incur, sich zuziehen, auf sich laden.

incurab|le, ~ly, unheilbar.

incursion, Einfall, m.

indebted, verschuldet; (beholden)
verpflichtet.

indecen|cy, Unanständigkeit, f.;
~t(ly), unanständig.

indecisive, unschlüssig; unentschieden.

indeclinable, undeklinierbar.

indeed, in der Tat; freilich.

indefensible, unhaltbar.

indefinite, ~ly, unbestimmt.

indelible, unauslöschlich; ~ ink,
Kopiertinte, f.

indelicate, unzart, grob.

indemni|fy, schadlos halten; ~ty,
Schadloshaltung, Entschädigung, f.

indentation, Einschnitt, m.; Kerbe,
Vertiefung, f.

independen|ce, Unabhängigkeit, f.;
~t(ly), unabhängig.

indescribable, unbeschreiblich.

indestructible, unzerstörbar.

index, sb. Inhaltsverzeichnis,
Register, n.; (finger) Zeigefinger, m.; v.t. mit einem
Inhaltsverzeichnis versehen,
registrieren.

Indian, sb. Indianer, m.; a.
indianisch; indisch; ~ corn,
Mais, m.; ~ file, Gänsemarsch,
m.; ~ summer, Nachsommer,
m.

indiarubber, (Radier)gummi, m.

indicate, anzeigen, bezeichnen;
~ion, Anzeichen, Merkmal, n.;
~ive, sb. Indikativ, m.; a.
anzeigend; ~or, Anzeiger, m.

indifferen|ce, Gleichgültigkeit, f.;
~t(ly), gleichgültig.

indigenous, eingeboren, boden-
ständig.

indigent, dürftig, arm.

indigest|ible, unverdaulich; ~ion,
Verdauungsstörung, f.

indign|ant, ~antly, empört, un-
willig (at über); ~ation, Ent-

rüstung, *f.*, Unwille, *m.*; ~ity, Beschimpfung, *f.*

indigo, Indigo, *m.*

indirect, ~ly, indirekt, mittelbar.

indiscre|et, ~etly, indiskret; unbedachtsam; ~tion, Indiskretion; Unbedachtsamkeit, *f.*

indiscriminate, ~ly, verwirrt, unterschiedslos.

indispensable, unentbehrlich, unabkömmlich.

indispos|ed, unpäßlich; ~ition, Unpäßlichkeit, *f.*

indisputab|le, ~ly, unbestreitbar.

indistinct, ~ly, undeutlich.

indistinguishable, ununterscheidbar.

individual, *sb.* Individuum, *n.* Einzelne(r); *a.* einzeln, persönlich; ~ity, Individualität; Eigenart, *f.*

indivisible, unteilbar.

indolen|ce, Trägheit, *f.*; ~t(ly), träge.

indomitable, unbezähmbar.

indoors, zu, im, Hause.

indubitab|le, ~ly, unzweifelhaft.

induce, veranlassen, überreden; ~ment, Anlaß, Beweggrund, *m.*

induct|ion, Induktion, *f.*; ~ive, induktiv, folgerungsmäßig.

indulge, befriedigen, frönen; ~nce, Nachsicht, *f.*; (*theol.*) Ablaß, *m.*; ~nt(ly), nachsichtig.

industr|ial, industriell, Gewerbe-; ~ious(ly), fleißig; ~y, Fleiß, *m.*; (*trade*) Gewerbe, *n.*, Industrie, *f.*

ineffective, ineffectual, ~ly, unwirksam.

inefficien|cy, Unfähigkeit, *f.*; ~t, unfähig, nicht voll leistungsfähig, unwirksam.

inelegant, geschmacklos.

ineligible, ungeeignet, untauglich.

inequality, Ungleichheit, *f.*

inert, träge; ~ia, Trägheit, *f.*

inestimab|le, ~ly, unschätzbar.

inevitab|le, ~ly, unvermeidlich.

inexhaustible, unerschöpflich.

inexorab|le, ~ly, unerbittlich.

inexpedient, unzweckmäßig, unpassend.

inexpensive, wohlfeil.

infallib|le, ~ly, unfehlbar; ~ility, Unfehlbarkeit, *f.*

infam|ous, verrufen, schändlich; ~y, Schande, *f.*

infan|cy, Kindheit; (*law*) Minderjährigkeit, *f.*; ~t, Kind, *n.*; (*law*) Minderjährige(r); Säugling, *m.*; ~tile, kindlich.

infantry, Infanterie, *f.*; ~man, Infanterist, Grenadier, *m.*

infatuat|e, betören; ~ion, Betörung, *f.*

infect, anstecken; ~ion, Ansteckung, *f.*; ~ious, ansteckend.

infer, schließen, folgern; ~ence, Folgerung, *f.*

inferior, untergeordnet, niedriger, geringer; *to be* ~ *to*, nachstehen (*with dat.*); ~ity, Minderwertigkeit, *f.*; untergeordneter Zustand.

infern|al, höllisch; ~o, die Hölle.

infest, plagen, versuchen, belästigen.

infidel, Ungläubige(r).

infidelity, Untreue, *f.*; Unglaube, *m.*

infiltrate, einsickern, eindringen.

infinit|e, ~ely, unendlich; ~ive, Infinitiv, *m.*; ~y, Unendlichkeit, *f.*

infirm, gebrechlich, schwach; ~ary, Krankenhaus, *n.*; ~ity, Schwäche, Krankheit, *f.*

inflam|e, entflammen; (*med.*) entzünden; ~mable, entzündlich; ~mation, Entzündung, *f.*; ~matory, Entzündungs-; (*fig.*) aufreizend.

inflat|e, aufblasen, aufblähen; ~ion, Inflation, *f.*; ~ionary, Inflations-.

infle|ct, flektieren, biegen; ~xion, Flexion, *f.*

inflexib|le, ~ly, unbiegsam; (*fig.*) unbeugsam.

inflict, zufügen, auferlegen, verhängen; ~ion, Strafverhängung; Heimsuchung, *f.*

influen|ce, *sb.* Einfluß, *m.*; *v.t.* beeinflussen; ~tial, einflußreich.

influenza, Influenza, Grippe, *f.*

influx, Zufluß, *m.*

inform, unterrichten, benachrichtigen; *~ against*, angeben, denunzieren; ~al(ly), nicht formell; ~ality, Ungezwungenheit, *f.*; ~ant, Gewährsmann, *m.*; Anzeigende(r); ~ation, Auskunft, Nachricht, *f.*; ~er, Angeber, *m.*

infra-red, infrarot.

infringe, übertreten, verletzen; ~ment, Übertretung, *f.*

infuriate, wütend machen.

ingen|ious, ~iously, erfinderisch, klug; ~uity, Scharfsinn, *m.*

ingot, Barren, *m.*

ingrained, eingefleischt.

ingratitude, Undankbarkeit, *f.*

ingredient, Bestandteil, *m.*

inhabit, bewohnen; ~able, bewohnbar; ~ant, Einwohner, *m.*

inhale, einatmen.

inherent, anhaftend, eigen.

inherit, erben; ~ance, Erbschaft, *f.*

inhospitab|le, ~ly ungastlich.

inhuman, unmenschlich; ~ity, Unmenschlichkeit, *f.*

inimical, feindselig.

iniquit|ous, ungerecht, unbillig; ~y, Ungerechtigkeit, Unbilligkeit, *f.*

initial, *sb.* Anfangsbuchstabe, *m.*; *a.*, ~ly anfänglich, Anfangs-; *v.t.* paraphieren.

initiat|e, einführen, einweihen; ~ion, Einführung, Einweihung, *f.*

inject, einspritzen; ~ion, Einspritzung, *f.*

injudicious, ~ly, unverständig, unüberlegt.

injur|e, verletzen, beeinträchtigen; ~ious, schädlich, nachteilig; ~y, Verletzung, Beschädigung, *f.*, Nachteil, *m.*

injustice, Unrecht, *n.*; Ungerechtigkeit, *f.*

ink, Tinte, *f.*; ~pot, ~stand, Tintenfaß, *n.*; ~y, tintig, tintenschwarz.

inland, inländisch, Binnen-.

inlay, einlegen.

inlet, Einlaß, Zugang, *m.*; (kleine) Bucht, *f.*

inmate, Insasse, Hausgenosse, *m.*

inmost, innerst.

inn, Wirtshaus, *n.*, Gasthof, *m.*; ~keeper, Wirt, *m.*

innate, angeboren.

inner, innerlich, Innen-; ~ tube,

Luftschlauch, *m.*

innocen|ce, Unschuld, *f.*; ~t(ly), unschuldig.

innocuous, unschädlich.

innovation, Neuerung, *f.*

innuendo, Andeutung, *f.*

innumerable, unzählig.

inoculat|e, einimpfen; ~ion, (Ein)impfung, *f.*

inoffensive, harmlos.

inopportune, ungelegen.

inorganic, (*chem.*) anorganisch.

inquest, gerichtliche Untersuchung, Leichenschau, *f.*

inquire, sich erkundigen, fragen (*after, for,* nach); ~y, Erkundigung, Nachfrage, *f.*

inquisit|ion, Inquisition, *f.*; ~ive, neugierig.

inroad, Einfall, Eingriff, *m.*

insan|e, geisteskrank, verrückt; ~ity, Geistesstörung, *f.*, Irrsinn, *m.*

insatiab|le, ~ly, unersättlich.

inscri|be, einschreiben; widmen; ~ption, Inschrift, *f.*

inscrutable, unerforschlich.

insect, Insekt, *n.*

insecur|e, ~ly, unsicher; ~ity, Unsicherheit, *f.*

insensible, unempfindlich, gefühllos; bewußtlos.

inseparable, unzertrennlich.

insert, einsetzen, einfügen; einschalten; ~ion, Einfügung, Einschaltung, *f.*

inset, Beilage, Einlage, *f.*

inside, *sb.* das Innere; *a.* inner; *adv.* darin, im Innern; ~ left, right, (*football*) Linkssinnen, Rechtsinnen, *m.*

insidious, ~ly, hinterlistig.

insight, Einblick, *m.*, Einsicht, *f.*

insignia, Insignien, *pl.*

insignifican|ce, Unwichtigkeit, Geringfügigkeit, *f.*; ~t, unbedeutend.

insincer|e, ~ely, unaufrichtig; ~ity, Unaufrichtigkeit, *f.*

insinuat|e, einflüstern, andeuten; sich einschmeicheln; ~ion, Einflüsterung, Andeutung, *f.*

insipid, ~ly, unschmackhaft, fade; ~ity, Abgeschmacktheit, *f.*

insist, bestehen (*on* auf); ~ence, Beharren, *n.*

insolen|ce, Frechheit, *f.*; **~t(ly),** frech, unverschämt.

insoluble, unlöslich.

insolvent, zahlungsunfähig.

insomnia, Schlaflosigkeit, *f.*

inspect, besichtigen, beaufsichtigen; **~ion,** Besichtigung, Aufsicht, *f.*; **~or,** Aufseher, Inspektor, *m.*

inspir|e, begeistern, eingeben; **~ation,** Begeisterung, Eingebung, *f.*

install, einsetzen, einbauen, montieren, aufstellen; **~ation,** Bestallung; Aufstellung, Installierung, *f.*

instalment, Ratenzahlung, Teilzahlung, Teillieferung, *f.*

instance, *sb.* Beispiel, *n.*; (*legal*) Instanz, *f.*; *v.t.* anführen; **for ~,** zum Beispiel; **in the first ~,** zuerst.

instant, *sb.* Augenblick, *m.*; *a.* sofortig; (*after dates*) dieses Monats; **~ coffee,** löslicher Kaffee; **~aneous(ly),** augenblicklich, Moment-; **~ly,** sogleich, sofort.

instead, (an)statt (*with gen.*).

instep, Spann, Rist, *m.*

instigat|e, anstiften, anreizen; **~ion,** Anstiftung, Anreizung, *f.*; **~or,** Anstifter, *m.*

instil, einflößen.

instinct, Naturtrieb, Instinkt, *m.*; **~ive(ly),** instinktmäßig, unwillkürlich.

institut|e, *sb.* Anstalt, *f.*, Institut, *n.*; *v.t.* stiften, einrichten, einsetzen; **~ion,** Einsetzung; Anstalt, *f.*

instruct, unterrichten, unterweisen; beauftragen; **~ion,** Unterweisung, Vorschrift, *f.*, Auftrag, *m.*; Unterricht, *m.*; **~ional,** Lehr-; **~ive,** lehrreich; **~or,** Lehrer, *m.*

instrument, Instrument, Werkzeug, *n.*; **~al,** mitwirkend, dienlich; **~ board,** Armaturenbrett, *n.*

insubordinat|e, ungehorsam; **~ion,** Ungehorsam, *m.*

insufferab|le, **~ly,** unerträglich.

insufficient, unzulänglich.

insul|ar, Insel-; **~ate,** isolieren; **~ation,** Isolierung, *f.*; **~ator,** Isolator, *m.*

insulin, Insulin, *n.*

insult, *sb.* Beleidigung, *f.*; *v.t.* beleidigen, beschimpfen.

insuperable, unüberwindlich.

insur|e, versichern; **~ance,** Versicherung, *f.*

insurgent, Empörer, Aufrührer, *m.*

insurrection, Empörung, *f.*, Aufstand, *m.*

intact, unberührt, unversehrt.

intangible, unfühlbar.

integ|er, ganze Zahl; **~ral,** vollständig; wesentlich; **~rity,** Rechtschaffenheit, *f.*

intellect, Verstand, *m.*; **~ual(ly),** intellektuell, vernünftig, Verstandes-.

intellig|ence, Verstand, *m.*; (*news*) Nachrichten, *f. pl.*; **~ent(ly),** verständig, intelligent; **~entsia,** die Intelligenz; **~ible,** verständlich.

intemper|ance, Unmäßigkeit, Trunksucht, *f.*; **~ate(ly),** unmäßig.

intend, beabsichtigen, bestimmen (für); **~ed,** *sb* Bräutigam, Verlobter, *m.*, Braut, Verlobte, *f.*; *a.* beabsichtigt.

intens|e, **~ely,** heftig, stark, intensiv; **~ify,** verstärken; **~ity,** Stärke, Heftigkeit, *f.*; **~ive(ly),** intensiv, angestrengt.

intent, gespannt (**on** auf); **~ion,** Absicht, *f.*; **~ional,** absichtlich.

inter, beerdigen.

interce|de, vermitteln (**between** zwischen); **~ssion,** Vermittlung, *f.*

intercept, auffangen; (*aircraft*) abfangen; (*radio*) ab-, mithören; **~ion,** Auf-, Ab-fangen, *n.*

interchange, *sb.* Tausch, Wechsel, *m.*; *v.t.* (ab)wechseln; **~able,** (aus)wechselbar.

intercourse, Verkehr, Umgang, *m.*

interest, *sb.* Anteil, *m.*, Interesse, *n.*; (*money*) Zins, *m.*; *v.t.* interessieren, angehen; **~ing,** interessant, anziehend.

interfere, sich einmengen, stören; einschreiten; **~nce,** Einmischung; (*wireless*) Störung, *f.*

interim, Zwischenzeit, *f.*

interior, *sb.* Innere, *n.*; *a.* inner.

interjection, Ausruf, *m.*; (*gram.*) Interjektion, *f.*

interlock, ineinandergreifen.

interloper, Eindringling, *m.*

interlude, Zwischenspiel, *n.*

intermarr|iage, Mischehe, *f.*; ~y, untereinander heiraten.

intermediary, Vermittler, *m.*

intermediate, *a.* dazwischenliegend, Zwischen-.

interment, Beerdigung, *f.*

intermezzo, Intermezzo, *n.*

internal, ~ly, inner(lich); ~ combustion engine, Verbrennungsmotor, *m.*

international, *a.* international, Welt-, Völker-; *sb.* Länderkampf, *m.*

interpose, dazwischenstellen, dazwischentreten; ~ition, Einmischung, *f.*

interpret, übersetzen; erklären; ~ation, Erklärung, *f.*; ~er, Dolmetsch(er), *m.*

interrogate, befragen, verhören; ~ion, Verhör, *n.*

interrogative, *sb.* Fragewort, *n.*; *a.* fragend.

interrupt, unterbrechen; ~ion, Unterbrechung, *f.*

intersect, durchschneiden, kreuzen; ~ion, Durchschneiden, *n.*; Schnittpunkt, *m.*

intersperse, einstreuen.

interval, Zwischenraum, *m.*; Pause, *f.*; Abstand, *m.*

interven|e, dazwischentreten; ~tion, Vermitt(e)lung, Intervention, *f.*

interview, *sb.* Zusammenkunft, *f.*, Interview, *n.*; *v.t.* interviewen.

intestine, Darm, *m.*; ~s, Eingeweide, *n.*

intim|acy, Vertraulichkeit, *f.*; ~ate, *a.*, ~ately, vertraut, intim; *v.t.* andeuten, zu verstehen geben; ~ation, Andeutung, *f.*, Wink, *m.*

intimidat|e, einschüchtern; ~ion, Einschüchterung, *f.*

into, in; in . . . hinein.

intolera|ble, ~bly, unerträglich; ~nce, Unduldsamkeit, *f.*; ~nt, unduldsam.

intonation, Tonfall, *m.*

intoxicat|e, berauschen; ~ion,

Berauschung, *f.*, Rausch, *m.*

intransitive, intransitiv.

intrepid, ~ly, unerschrocken.

intrica|cy, Verwick(e)lung, *f.*; ~te(ly), verwickelt, verworren.

intrigue, *sb.* Intrige, *f.*, Ränke, *pl.*; Liebeshandel, *m.*; *v.i.* Ränke schmieden.

intrinsic, ~ally, wirklich, innerlich.

introduc|e, einführen; (*person*) vorstellen; ~tion, Einführung, Einleitung; Vorstellung, *f.*; ~tory, einleitend.

intru|de, stören, eindringen; ~der, Eindringling, *m.*; ~sion, Eindringen, *n.*; Zudringlichkeit, *f.*; ~sive, zudringlich.

intuit|ion, Intuition, *f.*; ~ive, intuitiv.

inundat|e, überschwemmen; ~ion, Überschwemmung, *f.*

invade, einfallen in, angreifen; ~r, Angreifer, *m.*

invalid[1], *sb.* Kranke(r); *a.* kränklich.

invalid[2], *a.* ungültig, kraftlos; ~ate, ungültig machen.

invaluable, unschätzbar.

invariab|le, ~ly, unveränderlich.

invasion, Einfall, Angriff, *m.*

invective, Schmähung, *f.*; Schimpfwort, *n.*

invent, erfinden; ~ion, Erfindung, *f.*; ~or, Erfinder, *m.*; ~ory, Inventar, *n.*

invers|e, ~ely, umgekehrt; ~ion, Umkehrung, *f.*

invert, umkehren; ~ed commas, Anführungszeichen, *n.pl.*

invest, (*money*) anlegen; (*besiege*) belagern, einschließen; ~ment, Anlage; (*mil.*) Belagerung, *f.*

investigat|e, erforschen, untersuchen; ~ion, Untersuchung, *f.*

inveterate, eingewurzelt, fanatisch.

invigorate, stärken, kräftigen.

invincible, unüberwindlich.

inviol|able, unverletzlich; ~ate, unverletzt, ungebrochen, unentweiht.

invisib|le, unsichtbar; ~ility, Unsichtbarkeit, *f.*

invit|e, einladen; ~ation, Einladung, *f.*

invocation, Anrufung, *f.*

invoice, Faktura, (Waren)rechnung, f.

invoke, anrufen, anflehen.

involuntar|y, ~ily, unwillkürlich, unfreiwillig.

involve, in sich schließen; verwickeln.

invulnerable, unverwundbar.

inward, ~ly, innerlich; ~s, einwärts.

iodine, Jod, n.

I.O.U., Schuldschein, m.

ir|ate, erzürnt, zornig; ~e, Zorn, m.

iridescent, schillernd.

iris, (anat.) Regenbogenhaut; (bot.) Schwertlilie, f.

irk, ärgern; ~some, lästig.

iron, sb. Eisen, n.; (smoothing-iron) Bügel-, Plätt- eisen, n.; a. eisern; v.t. bügeln; ~ curtain, der eiserne Vorhang; ~ lung, eiserne Lunge; ~monger, Eisenwarenhändler, m.; ~ ore, Eisenerz, n.; ~ ration, eiserne Ration; ~works, Eisenhütte, f.

iron|ical, ironisch; ~y, Ironie, f.

irrational, ~ly, unvernünftig; (math.) irrational.

irreconcilab|le, ~ly, unversöhnlich.

irrecoverab|le, ~ly, unersetzlich, unwiederbringlich.

irregular, ~ly, unregelmäßig; ~ity, Unregelmäßigkeit, f.

irrelevant, ~ly, unanwendbar, belanglos, nicht zur Sache gehörig.

irreligious, gottlos, ungläubig.

irreparab|le, ~ly, nicht wieder gutzumachen.

irreproachab|le, ~ly, untadelhaft.

irresistib|le, ~ly, unwiderstehlich.

irresolute, ~ly, unschlüssig.

irrespective, ohne Rücksicht (auf).

irresponsib|le, unverantwortlich; ~ility, Unverantwortlichkeit, f.

irreveren|ce, Unehrerbietigkeit, f.; ~t(ly), unehrerbietig.

irrevocab|le, ~ly, unwiderruflich.

irrigat|e, bewässern; ~ion, Bewässerung, f.

irrit|ability, Reizbarkeit, f.; ~able, reizbar; ~ant, Reizmittel, n.; ~ate, reizen, erregen; ~ation, Erbitterung; (med.) Entzündung, f.

irruption, Einbruch, m.

is, ist.

isinglass, Hausenblase, f.

island, Insel, f.; ~er, Inselbewohner, m.

isolat|e, isolieren, absondern; ~ed, abgesondert, einzeln; ~ion, Isolierung, f.

issue, sb. Ausgang, m., Folge, f.; (notes, tickets, &c.) Ausgabe, f.; (newspaper) Auflage, f.; (offspring) Leibeserben, Nachkommen, m.pl.; v.t. ausgeben, erlassen; v.i. herausfließen; (originate) herrühren; herkommen.

isthmus, Landenge, f.

it, es, das.

italic|ize, kursiv drucken; ~s, Kursivschrift, f.

itch, sb. Jucken, n., Juckreiz, m.; v.i. jucken.

item, Gegenstand, Punkt; (in an account) Posten, m.

itiner|ant, wandernd; ~ary, Reisebeschreibung, f.; Reiseplan, m.

its, sein(e); ~elf, es selbst, sich.

ivory, sb. Elfenbein, n.; a. elfenbeinern.

ivy, Efeu, m.

J

jab, stoßen, stechen.

jabber, sb. Geschwätz, n.; v.i. schwatzen.

jack, (mech.) Winde, f., Wagenheber, m.; (cards) Bube, m.; (flag) Gösch, f.; (bootjack) Stiefelknecht, m.

jackal, Schakal, m.

jackdaw, Dohle, f.

jacket, Jacke, f., Jackett, n.; (of book) Umschlag, m.; (mech.) Mantel, m.

jade, (horse) Schindmähre, f., Gaul, m.; (woman) Weibsbild, n.; (stone) Jade, Beilstein, f.

jagged, zackig.

jaguar, Jaguar, m.

jail, Gefängnis, n.; ~er, Gefängniswärter, m.

jam, sb. Marmelade, f.; (stoppage) Hemmung, Klemmung, f.; v.t. (radio) stören; v.i. sich klemmen, festsitzen; ~ming, (radio) Störung, f.

janitor, Pförtner, m.

January, Januar, *m.*

japan, *sb.* (japanischer) Lack, *m.*; *v.t.* lackieren.

jar, *sb.* Krug, *m.*, Einmacheglas, *n.*; (*sound*) Knarren, *n.*; *v.i.* knarren, mißtönen.

jargon, Kauderwelsch, *n.*; Jargon, *m.*

jasmin, Jasmin, *m.*

jasper, Jaspis, *m.*

jaundice, Gelbsucht, *f.*

jaunt, *sb.* Ausflug, *m.*, Wanderung, *f.*; ∼y, munter, schmuck.

javelin, Wurfspieß, *m.*

jaw, Kinnbacken, Kiefer, *m.*

jay, Häher, *m.*

jazz, Jazz, *m.*

jealous, ∼ly, eifersüchtig; ∼y, Eifersucht, *f.*

jeans, Jeans, *pl.*

jeep, Kübelwagen, Jeep, *m.*

jeer, *sb.* Spott, *m.*; *v.i.* spotten (*at* über).

jelly, (*fruit*) Gelee, *n.*; (*meat*) Gallerte, *f.*; ∼-fish, Qualle, Meduse, *f.*

jemmy, Brecheisen, *n.*

jeopard|ize, gefährden; ∼y, Gefahr, *f.*

jerk, *sb.* Stoß, Ruck, *m.*; *v.t.* stoßen, rucken; ∼y, ∼ily, stoßweise, stoßartig.

jerry-built, unsolid gebaut.

jersey, wollene Jacke.

jest, *sb.* Scherz, Spaß, *m.*; *v.i.* scherzen, spaßen; ∼er, Spaßvogel; Hofnarr, *m.*

Jesuit, Jesuit, *m.*; ∼ical, jesuitisch.

jet, (*stone*) Gagat, *m.*, Jett, *n.*; (*water*) Wasserstrahl, *m.*; (*gaslight*) Gasflamme, *f.*; (*nozzle*) Düse, *f.*; (*aircraft*) Düsenflugzeug, *n.*; ∼-black, pechschwarz; ∼-propelled, mit Strahlantrieb; ∼-propulsion, Strahlantrieb, *m.*

jetsam, Strandgut, *n.*

jettison, über Bord werfen, abwerfen.

jetty, Damm, Landungsplatz, *m.*

Jew, Jude, *m.*; ∼ess, Jüdin, *f.*; ∼ish, jüdisch.

jewel, Juwel, *n.*; ∼ler, Juwelier, *m.*; ∼lery, Juwelen, *pl.*

jib, *sb.* Klüver, *m.*; *v.i.* scheuen, störrisch sein.

jigsaw puzzle, Zusammensetzspiel, *n.*

jilt, *sb.* Kokette, *f.*; *v.t.* sitzen lassen.

jingle, *sb.* Geklingel, *n.*; *v.i.* klingeln, klimpern.

jingo, Chauvinist, Kriegshetzer, *m.*; ∼ism, Hurrapatriotismus, *m.*

jitter, nervös aufgeregt sein.

job, Geschäft, *n.*, Job, *m.*, Arbeit, *f.*; Auftrag, *m.*; ∼ber, Makler, *m.*

jockey, Jockei, *m.*

jocular, ∼ly, spaßhaft, scherzhaft.

jog, *sb.* leichter Stoß, *m.*, Rütteln, *n.*; *v.t.* stoßen, schütteln; *v.i.* ∼ along, dahinschlendern.

join, *v.t.* verbinden, zusammenfügen; *v.i.* sich verbinden, sich anschließen; ∼er, Tischler, *m.*

joint, *sb.* (*anat.*) Gelenk, *n.*; (*meat*) Braten, *m.*; (*mech.*) Fuge, Verbindung, *f.*; *a.* verbunden, gemeinsam; ∼ly, gemeinschaftlich; ∼-stock company, Aktiengesellschaft, *f.*

joist, Querbalken, *m.*

joke, *sb.* Spaß, Scherz, Witz, *m.*; *v.i.* scherzen; ∼r, Witzbold, *m.*; (*cards*) Joker, *m.*

jolly, fröhlich, lustig.

jolt, *sb.* Stoß, *m.*; *v.* stoßen, rütteln.

jostle, drängen, anrempeln.

journal, (*diary*) Tagebuch, *n.*; (*newspaper*) Zeitung, Zeitschrift, *f.*; ∼ese, Zeitungsstil, *m.*; ∼ist, Journalist, Zeitungsschreiber, *m.*

journey, *sb.* Reise, Fahrt, *f.*; *v.i.* reisen; ∼man, Geselle, *m.*

jovial, ∼ly, lustig.

joy, Freude, Fröhlichkeit, *f.*; ∼ful(ly), freudig, fröhlich; ∼less(ly), freudlos; ∼ous(ly), fröhlich; ∼ride, Bummel, *m.*, Schwarzfahrt, *f.*; ∼stick, (Steuer)knüppel, *m.*

jubil|ant, frohlockend; ∼ation, Jubel, *m.*; ∼ee, (*eccles.*) Jubeljahr; Jubiläum, *n.*

Judaism, Judentum, *n.*

judge, *sb.* Richter, *m.*; *v.t.* richten, beurteilen, entscheiden; *v.i.* urteilen; ∼ment, Urteilsspruch,

m., Urteil, *n.*; Urteilskraft, *f.*;
Judgement Day, der Jüngste
Tag.

judicature, Gerichtsbarkeit, *f.*

judic|ial(ly), gerichtlich; ~ious(ly),
vernünftig, klug.

jug, Krug, *m.*

juggle, gaukeln; ~r, Gaukler, *m.*

juic|e, Saft, *m.*; ~y, saftig.

July, Juli, *m.*

jumble, *sb.* Mischmasch, *m.*; Verwirrung, *f.*; *v.t.* vermengen,
verwirren; ~sale, Ramsch-
verkauf, *m.*

jump, *sb.* (Ab)sprung, *m.*; *v.i.*
(ab)springen, hüpfen; *v.t.* überspringen; ~er, Jumper, *m.*,
Schlupfbluse, *f.*; ~y, nervös.

junction, Vereinigung, *f.*; (*railway*)
Knotenpunkt, *m.*; (*roads*) Weg-
kreuzung, *f.*

juncture, Verbindung, *f.*, Zusammentreffen, *n.*; Konjunktur, *f.*

June, Juni, *m.*

jungle, Dschungel, *m.* or *n.*

junior, jünger, Unter-.

juniper, Wacholder, *m.*

junket, geronnene Milch, *f.*;
Schmaus, *m.*

juridical, gerichtlich.

juris|diction, Gerichtsbarkeit, *f.*;
~prudence, Rechtswissen-
schaft, *f.*

jurist, Jurist, Rechtsgelehrte, *m.*

jury, Jury, *f.*; die Geschworenen,
pl.; ~-box, Geschworenenbank,
f.; ~man, Geschworene(r), *m.*;
~mast, Notmast, *m.*

just, *a.* gerecht; *adv.* eben, bloß,
gerade, fast, nur; ~ as, grade
wie; ~ice, Gerechtigkeit, *f.*;
(*person*) Richter, *m.*; ~ifiable,
zu rechtfertigen; ~ification,
Rechtfertigung, *f.*; ~ify, rechtfertigen.

jut, hervorragen.

jute, Jute, *f.*

juvenile, *sb.* Jüngling, *m.*; *a.*
jugendlich, Kinder-.

juxtapos|e, nebeneinanderstellen;
~ition, Nebeneinanderstellung,
f.

K

kaleidoscope, Kaleidoskop, *n.*

kangaroo, Känguruh, *n.*

keel, Kiel, *m.*

keen, ~ly, scharf, schneidend;
eifrig, energisch; ~ness,
Schärfe, *f.*; Eifer, *m.*

keep, *sb.* (*castle*) Hauptturm, *m.*;
(*food*) Unterhalt, *m.*; *v.t.* halten;
(*support*) unterhalten; (*retain*)
behalten; (*preserve*) erhalten;
(*hinder*) hindern (*from* an);
(*one's room, bed*) hüten; (*shop*)
führen; (*holiday, &c.*) feiern;
v.i. (*food, &c.*) sich (er)halten;
frisch bleiben; (*remain*) bleiben;
~ down, unterdrücken; ~ in,
zurückhalten; ~ off, abhalten,
schützen (*vor*); ~ on, fortfahren, dabeibleiben; ~ up,
aufrechterhalten; Schritt
halten; ~er, Aufseher, Förster,
m.; ~ing, Gewahrsam, *m.* Aufsicht, *f.*; ~sake, Andenken, *n.*

keg, Fäßchen, *n.*

kennel, Hundestall, *m.*

kerb-stone, Prellstein, Randstein,
m.

kernel, Kern, *m.*

kestrel, Turmfalke, *m.*

kettle, Kessel, *m.*; ~drum,
Kesselpauke, *f.*

key, Schlüssel, *m.*; (*piano, typewriter, &c.*) Taste, *f.*; (*switch*)
Taster, *m.*; (*mus.*) Tonart, *f.*;
~board, Klaviatur, Tastatur,
f.; ~note, Grundton, *m.*;
~ position, Schlüsselstellung, *f.*

khaki, *sb.* Khaki, *m.*; *a.* khaki-
farben.

kick, *sb.* Tritt, Stoß; (*horse*) Huf-
schlag; (*gun*) Rückstoß *m.*;
v.t. stoßen; *v.i.* (*horse*) ausschlagen.

kid, *sb.* Zicklein; Kind, *n.*; ~ gloves,
Glacéhandschuhe, *m.*, *pl.*

kidnap, entführen, stehlen.

kidney, Niere, *f.*; ~bean, grüne
Bohne.

kill, töten, erschlagen; schlachten.

kiln, Darrofen, Brennofen, *m.*,
Darre, *f.*

kin, *sb.* Verwandte, *pl.*; *a.* ~ to,
verwandt mit.

kind[1], *sb.* Art, Sorte, Gattung, *f.*;

human ~, Menschengeschlecht,
_n.; in_ ~, in Waren; _of that_ ~,
derartig.

kind² _a._, ~**ly**, gütig, freundlich;
~**liness**, Gütigkeit, _f._; ~**ness**,
Güte, Freundlichkeit, _f._

kindle, _v.t._ anzünden; _v.i._ sich
entzünden.

king, König, _m._; ~**dom**, König-
reich, _n._; ~**fisher**, Eisvogel, _m._;
~**ly**, königlich.

kipper, Räucherhering, _m._

kiss, _sb._ Kuß, _m._; _v.t._ küssen.

kit, Ausrüstung, _f._, Sachen, _f.pl._;
~**bag**, Tornister, _m._, Werk-
zeugtasche, _f._

kitchen, Küche, _f._; ~**ette**,
Kleinküche, _f._; ~**garden**,
Gemüsegarten, _m._; ~**maid**,
Küchenmädchen, _n._; ~**range**,
Herd, _m._

kite, _(bird)_ Steingeier; _(for flying)_
Drache(n), _m._

kitten, Kätzchen, _n._

knack, Kniff, Kunstgriff, _m._

knapsack, Tornister, _m._, Ränzel, _n._

knave, Schurke; _(cards)_ Bube,
_m._; ~**ery**, Büberei, _f._; ~**ish**
schurkisch.

knead, kneten.

knee, Knie, _n._; ~**cap**, Knie-
scheibe, _f._

kneel, knie(e)n.

knell, Totenglocke, _f._

knickerbockers, Kniehosen, _f.pl._

knickers, Schlüpfer, _m._

knick-knacks, Nippsachen, _f.pl._

knife, Messer, _n._; ~, _fork, and
spoon,_ Besteck, _n._; ~**edge**,
Messerschneide, _f._; ~**rest**, Mes-
serstütze, _f._; ~**sharpener**, Mes-
serschärfer, _m._

knight, _sb._ Ritter; _(chess)_
Springer, _m._; _v.t._ zum Ritter
schlagen; ~**errant**, fahrender
Ritter; ~**hood**, Ritterwürde, _f._,
Ritterschaft, _f._; ~**ly**, ritterlich.

knit, stricken; ~**ting**, Strickzeug,
_n._; ~**ting-needle**, Stricknadel, _f._

knob, Knopf, _m._

knock, _sb._ Schlag, _m._; _(at a door)_
Klopfen, _n._; _v.t._ schlagen,
klopfen; _v.i. (door)_ klopfen;
~ _about,_ sich umhertreiben;
_v.t. ~ up,_ wachrufen, wecken;
~**er**, Klopfer, _m._; ~**kneed**,

x-beinig; ~**out**, _(boxing)_
Knockout, _m._

knot, _sb. (in string, &c., naut.)_
Knoten; _(in wood)_ Knorren,
_m._; _v.t._ verknüpfen, knoten;
_v.i._ knotig werden; ~**ty**, _(string,
wood)_ knotig, knorrig; _(difficult)_
schwierig, verwickelt.

know, _(be acquainted with)_ kennen;
(be aware of) wissen; _(understand)_ verstehen; ~ _by heart,_
auswendig wissen; ~**all,**
Besserwisser, _m._; ~**ing,** kundig;
schlau; ~**n,** bekannt.

knowledge, Kenntnis, _f._, Wissen,
_n._; Wissenschaft, _f._; _to my_ ~,
soviel ich weiß; _without my_ ~,
ohne mein Wissen.

knuckle, Knöchel, _m._; ~**duster,**
Schlagring, _m._

kodak, _sb._ Kodak, _m._; _v.t._ kodaken.

L

label, _sb._ Etikette, _f._, Zettel, _m._;
(inscription) Aufschrift, _f._; _v.t._
etikettieren.

labial, _sb._ Lippen-, Labial- laut,
_m._; _a._ labial.

laboratory, Laboratorium, _n._

laborious, ~**ly** mühsam, müh-
selig, schwer; arbeitsam, emsig,
fleißig; ~**ness**, Mühseligkeit, _f._;
Emsigkeit, _f._, Fleiß, _m._

labour, _sb._ Arbeit, _f._; _(trouble, &c.)_
Mühe, Anstrengung, _f._; _(child-
birth)_ Geburtswehen, _pl._; _to be
in_ ~, in Kindesnöten sein, in
Geburtswehen liegen; ~**ex-
change,** Arbeitsamt, _n._; ~**party,** Arbeiterpartei, _f._; ~**saving,** Arbeit ersparend, Hand-
arbeit ersetzend; ~, _v.i._ ar-
beiten _(at an with dat.)_; _v.t._
bearbeiten, ausarbeiten, lab-
oured, schwerfällig, steif; _(of
style)_ unbeholfen, mühsam;
~**er,** Arbeiter, _m._; _agri-
cultural_ ~, Landarbeiter, _m._;
day- ~, Tagelöhner, _m._

laburnum, Goldregen, _m._

labyrinth, Labyrinth, _n._

lace, _sb._ _(boots)_ Schuhriemen, _m._;
(stays, &c.) Schnur, _f._; Spitze,
Kante, Borte, _f._; _v.t._ (zu)-
schnüren.

lack, *sb.* Mangel, *m.*: *v.i.* mangeln, fehlen; *he is ~ing in*, es fehlt ihm an; *v.t.* ermangeln, nicht haben.

laconic, lakonisch, wortkarg.

lacquer, *sb.* Lack, *m.*: *v.t.* lackieren.

lad, Knabe, Junge, *m.*

ladder, Leiter; (*in stocking, &c.*) Laufmasche, *f.*: ~proof, (*of stockings, &c.*) maschenfest.

lad|en, beladen, befrachtet; (*fig.*) belastet; ~ing, Ladung, Fracht, *f.*: *bill of lading*, Frachtbrief, *m.*

ladle, *sb.* Schöpflöffel; (*foundry*) Gießlöffel, *m.*: *v.t.* (aus)schöpfen.

lady, Dame, *f.*: *Our (blessed) Lady*, unsere (liebe) Frau, die Jungfrau Maria: ~ *doctor, friend, &c.*, Ärztin, Freundin, &c., *f.*: ~bird, Marienkäfer, *m.*: ~killer, Damenheld, *m.*: ~in-waiting, Hofdame, *f.*: ~like, fein, wohlerzogen; ~ship, *her, your ~ship*, (die) gnädige Frau, (das) gnädige(s) Fräulein; ~'s maid, Kammer -jungfer, *f.*, -mädchen, *n.*

lag, *v.i.*, ~ *behind*, zurückbleiben.

laggard, *sb.* Saumselige(r), Träge(r).

lagoon, Lagune, *f.*

laid, *new-*~, (*of eggs*) frisch gelegt; ~ *up*, (*ill*) bettlägerig; (*of ship*) aufgelegt.

lair, Lager(platz, *m.*), *n.*

laity, Laien, *pl.*

lake, See, *m.*: (*colour*) Lackfarbe, *f.*: ~dwelling, Pfahlbau, *m.*

lamb, Lamm, *n.*: ~kin, Lämmchen, *n.*: ~skin, Lammfell, *n.*, Lammleder, *n.*

lame, ~ly, lahm, hinkend; (*fig.*) mangelhaft, unvollkommen; ~, *v.t.* lähmen; ~ness, Lähmung, Lahmheit, *f.*, Hinken, *n.*: (*fig.*) Unvollkommenheit, *f.*

lament, *sb.* (Weh)klage, *f.*, Jammer, *m.*, Klagelied, *n.*: *v.i.* trauern (*for um*), klagen; *v.t.* beklagen, betrauern, beweinen; ~able, ~ably, beklagenswert kläglich, jämmerlich, elend; ~ation, (Weh)klage, *f.*: ~ed, verstorben, selig.

lamp, Lampe, *f.*: (*street*) Laterne, *f.*: ~light, Lampenlicht, *n.*: ~lighter, Laternenanzünder.

m.: ~ oil, Lampenöl, *n.*: ~shade, Lampenschirm, *m.*

lampoon, *sb.* Schmähschrift, *f.*: *v.t.* schmähen.

lamprey, Lamprete, *f.*, Neunauge, *n.*

lance, *sb.* Lanze, *f.*: *v.t.* (*surg.*) aufstechen; ~corporal, Gefreite(r), *m.*

lancet, Lanzette, *f.*

land¹, *sb.* Land, *n.*: (*agric.*) Grund, Boden, *m.*: *piece of* ~, Grundstück, *n.*: *dry* ~, festes Land: *see how the* ~ *lies*, sehen (merken), wie die Sache liegt; ~agent, Gütermakler, *m.*: ~holder, Grundbesitzer, *m.*: ~lady, (Haus)wirtin, (Gast)wirtin, *f.*: ~locked, vom Lande eingeschlossen; ~lord, Gutsherr, Hausbesitzer, (Gast)wirt, *m.*: ~lubber, Landratte, *f.*: ~mark, Grenz -zeichen, *n.*, -stein, *m.*: (*fig.*) Markstein, *m.*: ~owner, Grund-, Guts- besitzer, *m.*: ~slide, Bergsturz, Erdrutsch; (*fig.*) Zusammenbruch, *m.*: ~tax, Grundsteuer, *f.*: ~ward(s), landwärts; ~wind, Landwind, *m.*

land², *v.* landen; (*goods*) ausladen, löschen; (*angling*) aus dem Wasser, ans Land, ziehen.

landau, Landauer, *m.*

landing, Landen, *n.*, Landung, *f.*: (*stairs*) Treppenabsatz, *m.*: ~stage, Landungs -stelle, -brücke, *f.*

landscape, Landschaft, *f.*: ~gardener, Landschaftsgärtner, *m.*: ~painter, Landschaftsmaler, *m.*

lane, (*country*) schmaler Weg, *m.*: (*town*) Gasse, *f.*

language, Sprache, *f.*: Ausdrucksweise, *f.*, Stil, *m.*: *bad* ~, Fluchen, *n.*, Schimpfreden, *pl.*

languid, ~ly, schlaff, matt.

languish, (*be exhausted*) ermatten, erschlaffen, dahinschwinden; (*pine*) sich sehnen, schmachten (*for nach*): ~ing, schmachtend.

languor, Mattigkeit, Schlaffheit, *f.*: Schmachten, Sehnen, *n.*: ~ous, schmachtend.

lank, dünn, schmächtig; ~y, schlank; lang und dünn.

lantern, Laterne, *f.*; *magic* ~, see magic; ~-slide, Diapositiv, *n.*

lap¹, *sb.* Zipfel, *m.*; *(of sitting person)* Schoß, *m.*; *(racing)* Runde, *f.*; ~-dog, Schoßhund, *m.*

lap², *v.* *(of waves)* bespülen, schlagen gegen; *(of water)* plätschern; ~ *over*, übergreifen; ~ *up*, auflecken.

lapel, (Rock)aufschlag, *m.*

lapse, *sb.* *(of time)* Verlauf, *m.*; *(of rights, &c.)* Verfall, *m.*; *(slip)* Fehler, Fehltritt, *m.*; Versehen, *n.*; *(theol.)* Abfall, *m.*; *v.i.* verlaufen; verfallen; *(theol.)* abfallen.

lapwing, Kiebitz, *m.*

larceny, Diebstahl, *m.*

larch, Lärche, *f.*

lard, Schmalz, *n.*; *v.t.* spicken.

larder, Speisekammer, *f.*

large, ~ly, groß, breit, dick, stark; geräumig, weit; beträchtlich, bedeutend: zahlreich; *at* ~, frei, ungehindert; ausführlich; im allgemeinen; *as* ~ *as life*, in Lebensgröße; *be in a* ~ *way of business*, ein großes (bedeutendes) Geschäft haben; ~ness, Größe, Weite, Stärke, *f.*

lark¹, *(bird)* Lerche, *f.*

lark², *sb.* lustiger (toller) Streich, Schabernack, *m.*; *v.i.* einen tollen Streich verüben.

larkspur, Rittersporn, *m.*

larva, Larve, *f.*

laryngitis, Kehlkopfentzündung, *f.*

larynx, Kehlkopf, *m.*

lascivious, ~ly, wollüstig, üppig; ~ness, Wollust, *f.*

lash, *sb.* Peitschenschnur, *f.*; *(hit)* Schlag, (Peitschen)hieb, *m.*; *(eye-lash)* Wimper, *f.*; *v.* peitschen; *(fig.)* geißeln, bekritteln; ~ *out*, *(of horse, &c.)* hinten ausschlagen, *(fig.)* über die Stränge schlagen; ~ing, Peitschen, Geißeln, *n.*; *lashings of*, große Massen, *f.pl.*

lass(ie), Mädchen, *n.*

lassitude, Müdigkeit, Mattigkeit, *f.*

last¹, *sb.* *(shoemaker's)* Leisten, *m.*

last², *v.i* dauern bestehen.

bleiben, währen; ausreichen; ~ing, dauernd, bleibend; *(durable)* dauerhaft.

last³, *a.* letzt; *(previous)* vorig; *(utmost)* äußerst, höchst; *at* ~, endlich, schließlich; *to the* ~, bis an (zum) Ende; *breathe one's* ~, sterben; ~ *evening, night*, gestern abend, nacht; ~ *judgement*, das jüngste Gericht; ~ *supper*, das Abendmahl; *sb.* Letzte(r, s) Ende, *n.*; ~ly, *adv.* schließlich, endlich, zuletzt.

latch, Klinke, *f.*; ~-key, Hausschlüssel, *m.*

late, spät, verspätet; *(of news, &c.)* letzt; *(dead)* verstorben, selig; *(former)* vorig; *be (come)* ~, zu spät kommen, sich verspäten; *the clock is 20 minutes* ~, die Uhr geht 20 Minuten nach; *the train is 20 minutes* ~, der Zug hat 20 Minuten Verspätung; *keep* ~ *hours*, spät aufbleiben; ~ly, neulich, vor kurzem; ~ness, Zuspätkommen, *n.*; *(train)* Verspätung, *f.*; ~r, später; ~ *on*, späterhin.

latent, verborgen; ~ *heat*, latente (gebundene) Wärme.

lateral, seitlich, Seiten-; ~ly, seitwärts, von der Seite.

lath, Latte, *f.*

lathe, Drehbank, *f.*

lather, *sb.* Seifenschaum, *m.*; *v.t.* einseifen.

Latin, *a.* lateinisch; *sb.* Latein, *n.*; lateinische Sprache, *f.*; *dog-* ~, Küchenlatein, *n.*

latitude, (geographische) Breite, *f.*; *(fig.)* Weite, *f.*, Umfang, *m.*, Ausdehnung, *f.*

latter, letzter, *m.*; diese(r, s); ~-day, aus der letzten Zeit stammend; ~ly, neuerdings, neuerlich, in der letzten Zeit.

lattice, Gitter, Gitterwerk, *n.*; ~-window, Gitterfenster, *n.*

laudanum, Laudanum, *n.*

laugh, *v.i.* lachen *(at* über); ~ *in one's sleeve*, sich ins Fäustchen lachen; ~ *away, off*, sich lachend über etwas hinwegsetzen; *sb.* Lachen, Gelächter, *n.*; ~able, lächerlich; ~ing, lachend; *it is no ~ matter*, es ist nicht zum Lachen; ~ing gas, Lachgas, *n.*: ~ing-stock, Gegenstand (*m.*) des Spottes; ~ter, Gelächter, *n.*: *break out into fits of ~*, in lautes Gelächter ausbrechen.

launch, *sb.* (*boat*) Barkasse, *f.*, Dampf-, Motor- boot, *n.*; (*from stocks*) Stapellauf, *m.*; *v.* (*ship*) vom Stapel lassen; (*fig.*) ~ *out*, hinaussenden, in Gang setzen; sich ergehen (*into* in).

laundress, Wäscherin, *f.*; laundry, Waschanstalt *f.* : Wäsche, *f.*

laureate, *poet* ~, Hofdichter, *m.*

laurel, Lorbeer, *m.*

lava, Lava, *f.*

lavatory, Waschraum, *m.*

lavender, Lavendel, *m.*; Lavendelfarbe, *f.*; ~~water, Lavendelwasser, *n.*

lavish, ~ly, verschwenderisch, freigebig, übermäßig; *v.t.* verschwenden, vergeuden (*upon* auf); ~ness, Verschwendung, Vergeudung, *f.*

law, Gesetz, Recht, *n.*; Rechtswissenschaft, *f.*; *at* ~, gerichtlich; *go to* ~ *with*, verklagen; *take* ~ *into one's own hands*, sich selbst Recht verschaffen; *canon* ~, Kirchenrecht, *n.*; *criminal* ~, Strafrecht, *n.*; ~~case, Zivilklage, *f.*, Rechtsfall, *m.*; ~~court, Gerichtshof, *m.*; ~ *of nations*, Völkerrecht, *n.*; ~~suit, Prozeß, *m.*: ~~ful(ly), gesetzmäßig, rechtmäßig; ~~less, gesetzlos; zügellos, wild; ~lessness, Gesetzlosigkeit, Zügellosigkeit, *f.*

lawn[1], Rasenplatz, *m.*; ~~mower, Rasenmähmaschine, *f.*; ~ tennis, Tennis, *n.*

lawn[2], (*linen*) Batist, *m.*

lawyer, (*person versed in law*) Rechtsgelehrte(r); (*barrister*) Rechtsanwalt, Advokat, *m.*; (*solicitor*) Sachwalter, *m.*

lax, schlaff, locker; (*morals*) locker; ~ative, Abführmittel, *n.*; ~ity, Schlaffheit, Lockerheit, *f.*

lay[1], *a.* weltlich, Laien-; ~ brother, Laienbruder, *m.*; ~man, Laie, *m.*

lay[2], *sb.* Lied, *n.*

lay[3], *v.t.* (*rails, eggs, cable, &c.*) legen; (*bet*) wetten, setzen (*on* auf); (*ghost*) bannen; ~ *claim to*, Anspruch auf . . . erheben; ~ *the cloth, table*, den Tisch decken; ~ *the fire*, das Feuer anlegen; ~ *siege to*, belagern; ~ *wager*, wetten; ~ *waste*, verwüsten; ~ *aside*, beiseitelegen, weglegen; ~ *down*, niederlegen; (*to rest*) zur Ruhe legen; (*arms*) die Waffen strecken; (*the keel of a ship*) ein Schiff auf Stapel legen; (*principle, rule*) einen Grundsatz, eine Regel aufstellen; ~ *in*, (*provisions*) einlegen, aufspeichern; ~ *off*, (*workmen*) zeitweilig entlassen; ~ *on*, anlegen, auflegen; (*colour*) auftragen; ~ *oneself open to*, sich aussetzen; ~ *open*, bloßlegen, aufdecken; ~ *out*, (*grounds, money*) anlegen, auslegen; (*corpse*) aufbahren, ausstellen; ~ *over*, bedecken, überziehen; ~ *up*, (*save*) sammeln, aufspeichern; (*ship*) auflegen, abtakeln; *be laid up*, bettlägerig sein (*with an* and *dat.* or wegen); layout, *sb.* Anlage, *f.*, Plan, *m.*

layer, Lage, Schicht, *f.*; (*plants*) Ableger, Absenker, *m.*; (*hen*) Legehenne, *f.*

lay figure, Gliederpuppe, *f.*; (*fig.*) Strohmann, *m.*

lazy, lazily, faul, träge, lässig; laziness, Faulheit, Lässigkeit, *f.*; lazy-bones, Faulenzer, Faulpelz, *m.*

lead[1], (*mineral*) Blei, *n.*; (*naut.*) Lot, Senkblei, *n.*; (*typ.*) Durchschuß, *m.*; *swing the* ~, sich drücken; ~~pencil, Bleistift, *m.*; ~, *v.t.* mit Blei überziehen, verbleien; ~en, bleiern, aus Blei; (*sky*) bleifarben, düster; (*fig.*) schwerfällig, unbeholfen; (*eye*) glanzlos; ~s, (*flaches*) Bleidach, *n.*

lead[2], *sb.* Führung, Leitung, *f.*; Vorsprung, *m.*; (*cards*) Vorhand; (*electr.*) Leitung, *f.*, Leiter, *m.*; *take the* ~, die Leitung übernehmen; vorausgehen; *v.t.* führen, leiten, den Weg zeigen (weisen); veranlassen, bewegen; (*cards*) ausspielen; ~ *astray*, irreführen, verführen; ~ *up to*, führen zu; *v.i.* (*road, &c.*) führen (nach zu); voraus-, voran- gehen; (*cards*) die Vorhand haben.

leader, Führer, Leiter, *m.*; (*horse*) Vorderpferd, *n.*; (*newspaper article*) Leitartikel, *m.*; ~**ship,** Führerschaft, Leitung, *f.*

leading, *sb.* Leitung, Führung, *f.*; *a.* leitend, führend, tonangebend, Haupt-, Leit-; ~ **article,** Leitartikel, *m.*; ~ **question,** Suggestivfrage, *f.*; ~**strings,** Gängelband, *n.*

leaf, Blatt, *n.*; (*table*) Tischklappe, *f.*; (*door*) Flügel, *m.*; *turn over the leaves of,* (durch)blättern; *turn over a new* ~, sich bessern; ~**let,** Zettel, *m.*; Flugblatt, *n.*, Broschüre, *f.*; ~**mould,** Lauberde, *f.*; ~**y,** belaubt.

league, *sb.* Bund, *m.*, Bündnis, *n.*; (*sport*) Liga, *f.*; **League of Nations,** Völkerbund, *m.*; *v.i.* ~ *together,* sich verbünden.

leak, *v.i.* (*ship, roof, containers, &c.*) lecken, leck sein; (*liquids, gas, &c.*) auslaufen, auströpfeln, durchsickern; ~ *out,* (*information*) bekannt werden; *sb.* Leck, *n.*, Ritze, *f.*; *spring a* ~, leck werden; ~**age,** Lecken, *n.*, Leckage, *f.*; (*electr.*) Ableitung, *f.*; (*gas, &c.*) Verlust, *m.*; (*information*) Durchsickern, *n.*; ~**y,** leck, undicht, durchlässig.

lean¹, *a.* mager; *sb.* das Magere, mageres Fleisch; ~**ness,** Magerkeit, *f.*

lean², *v.* (sich) lehnen (*on, upon, against* an, auf, gegen); (*rely*) sich verlassen, sich stützen (*on* auf); ~**ing,** (*fig.*) Neigung, *f.* (*to* zu).

leap, *v.i.* springen; *v.t.* überspringen; *sb.* Sprung, *m.*; ~**frog,** Bockspringen, *n.*; ~ **year,** Schaltjahr, *n.*

learn, lernen; hören, erfahren; ~**ed,** gelehrt; ~**er,** Anfänger, *m.*; ~**ing,** Lernen, *n.*; Erlernung, *f.*; Gelehrsamkeit, *f.*, Wissen, *n.*

lease, *sb.* Pacht, Verpachtung, Miete, *f.*; *v.t.* (ver)pachten; (ver)mieten; ~**holder,** Pächter, Mieter, *m.*

leash, Koppelleine, *f.*; *v.t.* koppeln.

least, kleinst, geringst, mindest; *at* ~, wenigstens; *not in the* ~, nicht im geringsten, durchaus nicht.

leather, Leder, *n.*; ~**n,** ledern; ~**y,** lederartig, wie Leder, zäh.

leave, *v.t.* lassen, verlassen, zurücklassen; (*bequeath*) hinterlassen, vermachen; *v.i.* fort-, weggehen, abreisen, abfahren; *be left,* übrigbleiben; ~ *about,* umherliegen lassen; ~ *behind,* zurücklassen; ~ *hold of,* loslassen; ~ *off,* aufhören mit, aufgeben; ~ *out,* aus-, weglassen; ausschließen; ~ *over,* übriglassen; ~ *school,* von der Schule abgehen; ~ *word,* sagen lassen; *sb.* Erlaubnis, *f.*; Abschied, *m.*; ~ *of absence,* Urlaub, *m.*; *by your* ~, mit Verlaub; *on* ~, auf Urlaub; *give* ~, beurlauben; *take* ~, ~ *together,* sich verbünden.

leaven, *sb.* Sauerteig, *m.*, Hefe, *f.*; *v.t.* säuern.

leavings, Überbleibsel, *n.pl.*

lecher, Wüstling, Wollüstling, *m.*; ~**ous(ly),** wollüstig, geil; ~**y,** Wollust, Geilheit, *f.*

lectern, Lesepult, *n.*

lecture, *sb.* Vorlesung, *f.*, Vortrag, *m.*, Kolleg, *n.* (*on* über); (*scolding*) Verweis, *m.*; *v.* Vorlesung, Vortrag, halten; einen Verweis geben, abkanzeln; ~**r,** Vortragende(r); (*univ.*) Dozent, *m.*; ~**room,** Hörsaal, Vorlesungssaal, *m.*; ~**ship,** Dozentenstelle, *f.*

ledge, Sims, *m.* or *n.*, Rand, *m.*, Leiste, *f.*

ledger, Hauptbuch, *n.*

lee, Schutz, *m.*, Lee(seite), *f.*; ~**ward,** leewärts; ~**way,** Leeweg, *m.*, Abtrift, *f.*; *make up* ~**way,** das Versäumte nachholen.

leech, Blutegel, *m.*

leek, Lauch, *m.*

leer, *sb.* lüsterner Blick; *v.i.* lüstern blicken (*at* nach).

lees, Bodensatz, *m.*, Hefe, *f.*

left, *a.* link; *adv.* links; *sb.* Linke, *f.*; *on,* to *the* ~, links; ~-handed, linkshändig; (*fig.*) linkisch; ~wards, (nach) links.

leg, Bein, *n.*; (*mutton, fowl, &c.*) Keule, *f.*; (*compasses, &c.*) Schenkel, *m.*; *be on one's last legs*, im Sterben liegen; *pull a person's leg*, jemand zum Besten haben.

legacy, Vermächtnis, *n.*

legal, ~ly, gesetzlich, gesetzmäßig; *institute,* take ~ *proceedings*, gerichtliche Schritte unternehmen; ~ tender, gesetzliches Zahlungsmittel; ~ity, Gesetzlichkeit, Gesetzmäßigkeit, *f.*; ~ize, rechtskräftig machen.

legate, Legat, *m.*; *papal* ~, Nuntius, *m.*; ~ee, Vermächtnisnehmer, Erbe, *m.*; ~ion, Gesandtschaft, *f.*

legend, Legende, Sage, *f.*; ~ary, sagenhaft.

leggings, Gamaschen, *f.pl.*

legible, ~ly, leserlich, lesbar; ~ility, Leserlichkeit, Lesbarkeit, *f.*

legion, Legion, *f.*; (*fig.*) Schar, *f.*; *foreign* ~, Fremdenlegion, *f.*; ~ary, Legionssoldat, *m.*

legislate, Gesetze geben; ~ion, Gesetzgebung, *f.*; ~ive, legislativ, gesetzgebend; ~or, Gesetzgeber, *m.*; ~ure, Legislatur, *f.*, gesetzgebende Körperschaft.

legitima|cy, Rechtmäßigkeit, (*birth*) eheliche Geburt, *f.*; ~te, *a.* rechtmäßig; (*child*) ehelich, legitim; *v.t.* rechtmäßig (gültig) machen; (*child*) ehelich machen, legitimieren.

leisure, Muße, freie Zeit, *f.*; ~ly, gemächlich, langsam, mit Muße.

lemon, Zitrone, *f.*; ~ade, Limonade, *f.*; ~-coloured, zitronengelb; ~ squash, (Zitronen)limonade, *f.*; ~ squeezer, Zitronenpresse *f.*

lemur, Halbaffe, Maki, *m.*

lend, *v.t.* (aus)leihen, (ver)leihen; ~ *a hand,* assistance, Hilfe leisten; ~er, (Geld)verleiher, *m.*; ~ing library, Leihbibliothek, *f.*

length, Länge, *f.*; (*duration*) Dauer, *f.*; *at* ~, ausführlich; endlich, zuletzt; *at full* ~, in voller Länge; (*painting*) in Lebensgröße; *10 ft. in* ~, zehn Fuß lang; (*days*) länger werden; ~en, verlängern; ausgedehnt; weitschweifig, langweilig; ~wise, ~ways, der Länge nach.

lenien|cy, Milde, *f.*; ~t(ly), milde, nachsichtig (*to* gegen).

lens, Linse, *f.*

Lent, Fasten, *pl.*, Fastenzeit, *f.*

lentil, Linse, *f.*

leonine, löwenartig, löwenstark.

leopard, Leopard, Panther, *m.*

lep|er, Aussätzige(r); ~rosy, Aussatz, *m.*, Lepra, *f.*; ~rous, aussätzig.

lese-majesty, Majestätsbeleidigung, *f.*; Hoch-, Landesverrat, *m.*

less, kleiner, geringer, minder, weniger; ~ *and* ~, immer weniger; *more or* ~, mehr oder weniger; ~en, kleiner (geringer) werden (machen), abnehmen, (sich) vermindern, verkleinern.

lessee, Pächter, Mieter, *m.*

lesson, Lektion, *f.*, Übungsstück, *n.*, Aufgabe, *f.*; Lehrstunde, Unterrichtsstunde, *f.*; Lehre, *f.*

lest, damit nicht, um nicht zu.

let[1], *v.t.* lassen; (*allow*) erlauben, gestatten; (*house*) vermieten; (*land*) verpachten; ~ *me be!* Lassen Sie mich in Ruhe!; ~ *down,* (*bridge, curtain, &c.*) herablassen; (*fig.*) enttäuschen, im Stiche lassen; ~ *go, loose, loslassen*; ~ *in, into,* hereinlassen; ~ *know,* wissen lassen, Bescheid geben; ~ *off,* freilassen, entschuldigen; (*gun*) abschießen, abfeuern; ~ *out,* herauslassen, (*secret*) ausplaudern, ausschwatzen.

let[2], *sb.* (*tennis*) Netzball, *m.*

lethal, tödlich.

lethargic, ~**ically, lethargisch,** träge; ~**y, Lethargie, Schlaf-** sucht; (*fig.*) **Stumpfheit,** *f.*

letter, *sb.* (*of alphabet*) **Buchstabe,** *m.*; (*missive*) **Brief,** *m.*, **Schrei-** ben, *n.*; (*typ.*) **Type, Letter,** *f.*; *by* ~, **schriftlich, brieflich;** *registered* ~, **eingeschriebener** **Brief;** *to the* (*very*) ~, **buch-** stäblich; ~**box, Briefkasten,** *m.*; ~**card, Kartenbrief,** *m.*; ~**case, Briefmappe,** *f.*; ~ **of** **credit, Kreditbrief,** *m.*; ~**press,** **Druck, Text,** *m.*; ~**sorter,** **Briefsortierer,** *m.*; ~**s, Wissen-** schaft, **Literatur,** *f.*; *man of* ~**s,** **Literat, Gelehrte(r),** *m.*; ~**s** **patent: see patent;** *v.t.* **mit** **Buchstaben versehen, betiteln;** ~**ing, Aufschrift,** *f.*; **Titel-** druck, *m.*

lettuce, Lattich, Kopfsalat, *m.*

levee, (Morgen)empfang, *m.*

level, *a.* **waagerecht, horizontal;** eben, **glatt, flach, gerade;** *do* *one's* ~ *best,* **sein Möglichstes** tun; *make* ~ *with the ground,* **dem Boden gleichmachen;** *sb.* (*surface*) **waagerechte Fläche;** (*spirit-level*) **Libelle,** *f.*; (*survey-* *ing*) **Nivellierinstrument,** *n.*; (*fig.*) **Niveau,** *n.*, **Höhe,** *f.*, **Standpunkt,** *m.*; *on a* ~ *with,* **auf gleicher Höhe mit;** *auf* **gleichem Fuße;** ~ *crossing,* **Niveauübergang,** *m.*; ~, *v.t.* **gleichmachen, eb(en)en, pla-** nieren; (*gun, accusation, &c.*) **richten (*at* auf, gegen).**

lever, Hebel, *m.*; ~**age, Hebel-** kraft, *f.*

levity, Leichtsinn, *m.*, **Leicht-** fertigkeit, *f.*

levy, *sb.* (*taxes*) **Erhebung,** (*troops*) **Aushebung, Werbung,** *f.*; *v.t.* (*taxes*) **erheben;** (*troops*) ausheben.

lewd, ~**ly, liederlich, unzüchtig;** ~**ness, Liederlichkeit, Unzüch-** tigkeit, *f.*

lexicographer, Lexikograph, *m.*; ~**y, Lexikographie,** *f.*

liability, Verantwortlichkeit, Ver- pflichtung, **Haftbarkeit,** *f.*; ~**lities, Passiva,** *pl.*, **Schulden,** *f.pl.*; ~**le, verpflichtet, ver-**

bunden; **haftbar** (*for* für); **aus-** gesetzt, **unterworfen** (*to* dat.).

liaison, (*mil.*) **Verbindung,** *f.*; (*Liebes*)verhältnis, *n.*

liar, Lügner, *m.*

libel, Verleumdung, Schmäh- schrift, *f.*; ~**lous**(ly)**, schmä-** hend.

liberal, ~**ly,** *a.* **frei,** (*pol.*) **liberal,** freisinnig; |(*generous*) **freigebig;** *sb.* **Liberale(r), Freisinnige(r);** ~**ity, Freisinnigkeit, Vorurteils-** losigkeit; **Freigebigkeit,** *f.*

liberate, befreien; ~**ion, Be-** freiung, *f.*

libertine, Wüstling, *m.*

liberty, Freiheit, *f.*; *be at* ~**, frei** sein; *take liberties with,* **sich** Freiheiten **herausnehmen** (*with* gegen); *set at* ~**, befreien.**

librarian, Bibliothekar, *m.*; ~**y,** **Bibliothek, Bücherei,** *f.*; *cir-* *culating, lending* ~, **Leih-** bibliothek, *f.*

libretto, Libretto, *n.*; ~**ist,** **Librettoschreiber,** *m.*

licence, *sb.* **Erlaubnis, Konzession,** *f.*, **Erlaubnisschein,** *m.*; **Zügel-** losigkeit, **Ausschweifung,** *f.*; *driving-* ~, **Führerschein,** *m.*; *poetic(al)* ~, **dichterische Frei-** heit, *f.*

license, konzessionieren, erlauben; ~**e, Konzessionsinhaber,** *m.*

licentious, ~**ly, zügellos, lieder-** lich; ~**ness, Zügellosigkeit,** **Liederlichkeit,** *f.*

lichen, Flechte, *f.*

lick, lecken; (*beat*) **schlagen,** durchprügeln; ~ *the dust,* **ins** **Gras beißen;** ~ *into shape,* **zurechtmachen, zustutzen.**

lid, Deckel, *m.*, **Klappe,** *f.*; **Augen-** lid, *n.*

lie¹, *sb.* **Lüge,** *f.*; *v.i.* **lügen.**

lie², *v.i.* **liegen, ruhen;** ~ *down,* **sich niederlegen;** ~ *in wait for,* **jemandem auflauern;** ~ *in the* *way,* **im Wege stehen;** ~ *low,* **sich verborgen halten;** ~ *open,* (*blame, &c.*) **ausgesetzt sein.**

lieu, *in* ~ *of,* **anstatt.**

lieutenant, Leutnant, *m.*; ~**-** **colonel, Oberstleutnant,** *m.*; ~**-** **commander, Kapitänleutnant,** *m.*; ~**-general, General-**

leutnant, *m.*; **lieutenancy,**
Leutnants -rang, *m.*, -stelle, *f.*

life, Leben, *n.*; (*existence*) Dasein,
n.; (*wear*) Dauer, *f.*; (*biography*)
Lebensbeschreibung, *f.*; *early*
~, Jugend, *f.*; *for* ~, fürs
ganze Leben, auf Lebenszeit,
lebenslänglich; *from* ~, (*painting*) nach dem Leben; *high* ~,
die vornehme Welt; *in the
prime of* ~, in der Blüte seines
Lebens; *way of* ~, Lebensweise,
f.; ~**belt,** Rettungsgürtel, *m.*;
~**boat,** Rettungsboot, *n.*;
~**buoy,** Rettungsboje, *f.*; ~**-
guards,** Leibgarde, *f.*; ~**insurance,** Lebensversicherung, *f.*;
~**interest,** Leibrente, *f.*; ~
jacket, Schwimmweste, *f.*; ~
like, wie lebend, naturgetreu;
~**long,** lebenslänglich; ~**pre-
server,** Totschläger, *m.*; ~**size,**
lebensgroß; ~**time,** Lebenszeit, -dauer, *f.*

lift[1], *sb.* Fahrstuhl, Aufzug, Lift,
m.; (*aid*) Hilfe, *f.*, Beistand, *m.*;
give a lift to, jemanden mit-
fahren lassen.

lift[2], *v.t.* (er)heben, erhöhen,
stehlen, wegnehmen; *v.i.* sich
heben; (*mist, &c.*) aufsteigen.

light[1], *sb.* Licht, Tageslicht, *n.*;
Helligkeit, *f.*; ~ *and shade,*
Helldunkel, *n.*; *come to* ~, an
den Tag kommen; *give a person
a* ~, jemandem Feuer geben;
~**er,** Feueranzünder, *m.*,
(Taschen)feuerzeug, *n.*; ~**house,**
Leuchtturm, *m.*; ~**ship,** Feuer-
Leucht- schiff, *n.*; *a.* licht,
hell; *v.t.* anzünden, entzünden;
beleuchten, erhellen; *v.i.* hell
sein, werden; sich entzünden.

light[2], *a.*, ~**ly,** (*not heavy*) leicht;
~**en,** *v.t.* leicht(er) machen,
erleichtern; *v.i.* leicht(er) werden; ~**headed,** leichtsinnig,
leichtfertig, unbesonnen;
schwachköpfig; ~**hearted,**
sorglos, heiter; ~**ness,** Leich-
heit; Gewandtheit, *f.*

lighter[2], (*naut.*) Leichter, *m.*

lightning, Blitz, *m.*; ~**conductor,** Blitzableiter, *m.*

like[1], *a.* gleich, ähnlich; *adv.* als,
wie; ~**n,** *v.t.* vergleichen (*to*

mit); ~**ness,** Gleichheit, Ähnlichkeit, *f.*; (*portrait*) Bild, *n.*;
~**wise,** gleichfalls, ebenso.

like[2], *v.t.* gern haben, gefallen,
mögen; (*of food, drink, &c.*)
gern essen, trinken, &c.; *as
you* ~, wie Sie wollen, wie es
Ihnen gefällt; *if you* ~, wenn
nehm; liebenswürdig; ~**ing,**
Neigung (*for* für, *to* zu), *f.*; *not
to my* ~, nicht nach meinem
Geschmack.

likely, wahrscheinlich; ~**lihood.**
Wahrscheinlichkeit, *f.*

lilac, *sb.* spanischer Flieder;
(*colour*) Lila, *n.*; *a.* lila.

lily, Lilie, *f.*; ~ **of the valley,** Mai-
blume, *f.*, Maiglöckchen, *n.*

limb, Glied, *n.*; (*tree*) Ast, *m.*

lime[1], (*min.*) Kalk; (*bird*) Vogelleim, *m.*; ~**kiln,** Kalkofen,
m.; ~**light,** to be in the ~light,
(*fig.*) Mittelpunkt des Interesses
sein; ~**stone,** Kalkstein, *m.*

lime[2], (*tree*) Linde(nbaum, *m.*),
f.

lime[3], (*fruit*) Limette, *f.*; ~**juice,**
Zitronensaft, *m.*

limit, *sb.* Grenze, *f.*; *v.t.* Grenzen,
ein Ziel, setzen; beschränken,
einschränken (*to* auf); *limited
liability,* (*of company*) mit beschränkter Haftung; ~**ation,**
Beschränkung, Einschränkung,
Grenze, *f.*

limp[1], *a.*, ~**ly,** schlaff, schlapp;
~**ness,** Schlaffheit, *f.*

limp[2], *v.i.* hinken, lahm gehen.

limpet, Schüsselschnecke, *f.*

limpid, ~**ly,** klar, durchsichtig,
hell.

line, (*math., mil., shipping, &c.*)
Linie, *f.*; (*cord*) Schnur, *f.*;
(*type*) Zeile, *f.*; (*poetry*) Vers, *m.*;
(*railway*) Bahn, *f.*, Geleise, *n.*;
(*telephone*) Leitung, *f.*; *hard* ~**s,**
hartes Los, Pech, *n.*; ~ *of
business,* Geschäftszweig, *m.*;
v.t. liniieren; (*of dress, &c.*)
füttern.

lineage, Geschlecht, *n.*; Abstammung, *f.*, Stammbaum, *m.*

linen, *sb.* Linnen, *n.*, Leinwand, *f.*;
(*household*) Wäsche, *f.*; *a.*
leinen, Leinwand-.

liner, (*naut.*) Paket-, Passagierdampfer, *m*.; (*aircraft*) Verkehrsflugzeug, *n*.

linger, (*delay*) zögern, säumen; (*lag*) langsam gehen, schlendern; (*in illness*) dahinschmachten.

lingerie, Damenwäsche, *f*.

linguist, Sprach-kenner, -forscher, *m*.; ~ics, Sprachwissenschaft, *f*.

lining, Futter, *n*.; Fütterung, *f*.

link, Glied, (*chain*) Gelenk, *n*.; *v.t.* verketten, verbinden; *v.i.* verkettet sein, sich verbinden; ~age, Verkettung, *f*.

links, Golfplatz, *m*.

linnet, Hänfling, *m*.

linoleum, Linoleum, *n*.

linseed, Leinsamen, *m*.; ~-oil, Leinöl, *n*.

lion, Löwe, *m*.; ~ess, Löwin, *f*.; ~s, (*sights*) Sehenswürdigkeiten, *f.pl.*; ~'s share, Löwenanteil, *m*.

lip, Lippe, *f*.; (*edge*) Rand, *m*.; (*jug, &c.*) Tülle, *f*.; ~stick, Lippenstift, *m*.

liquefy, schmelzen, (sich) auflösen.

liqueur, Likör, *m*.

liquid, *a.* flüssig; *sb.* Flüssigkeit, *f*.

liquor, Flüssigkeit, *f.*; alkoholisches Getränk, *n*.

liquorice, Süßholz, *n*., Lakritze, *f*.

lisp, lispeln.

list, Liste, Rolle, *f*., Verzeichnis, *n*.; *v.t.* ins Verzeichnis eintragen.

listen, horchen (*to* auf), zuhören; ~ in, (mit)hören.

litany, Litanei, *f*.

literal, ~ly, buchstäblich, wörtlich.

literary, literarisch.

literate, gelehrt, gebildet.

literature, Literatur, *f*.

lithe, ~some, geschmeidig; ~ness, Geschmeidigkeit, *f*.

lithograph, Steindruck, *m*.; ~er, Steindrucker, *m*.

litigation, Rechtsstreit, Prozeß, *m*.

litmus, Lackmus, *m*.

litre, Liter, *n*.

litter, (*carriage*) Tragbahre, Sänfte, *f*.; (*for animals*) Streu, *f*.; (*brood*) Brut, *f*.; Junge(n) *pl.*; (*mess*) Unordnung, *f*.; *v.i.* umherliegen; *v.t.* umherwerfen.

little, *a.* klein, gering; *adv.* wenig; ~ by ~, nach und nach; make ~ of, geringachten; ~ness, *f*.

Kleinheit, Wenigkeit, *f*.

liturgy, Liturgie, *f*.; ~ical, liturgisch.

live[1], *v.* leben; (*dwell*) wohnen; (*feed on*) sich nähren (von).

live[2], *a.* lebend, lebendig; (*shell*) scharf; (*electr.*) geladen; (*coal*) glühend; (*radio*) direkt, live; ~liness, Lebhaftigkeit, *f*.; ~ly, lebhaft, munter.

livelihood, Lebensunterhalt, *m*.

liver, Leber, *f*.

livery, Livree, *f*.

livid, leichenfarbig, bleifarben.

living[1], *sb.* Leben, *n*.; Lebensweise, *f*.; (*eccles.*) Pfründe, *f*.

living[2], *a.* lebend, lebendig.

lizard, Eidechse, *f*.

llama, Lama, *n*.

load, *sb.* Last, Ladung, (*fig.*) Bürde; (*machine*) Belastung, *f*.; *v.t.* beladen; (*gun*) laden; ~ing, Verladung. (Schiffs-) ladung, Fracht, *f*.

loadstone, Magneteisenstein, *m*.

loaf[1], Brot, *n*., Laib, *m*.; sugar-~ Zuckerhut, *m*.

loaf[2], *v.i.* müßiggehen, herumlungern, bummeln; ~er, Müßiggänger, Landstreicher, Bummler, *m*.

loam, Lehm, *m*.

loan, *sb.* Anleihe, *f*., Darlehen, *n*.; *v.t.* ausleihen.

loathe, verabscheuen, hassen; ~ing, Ekel, *m*.; ~some, ekelhaft.

lobby, Vorhalle, *f*., Vorzimmer, *n*.

lobe, Lappen, *m*.; ~ of the ear, Ohrläppchen, *n*.

lobster, Hummer, *m*.

local, ~ly, örtlich, Orts-; ~ity, Örtlichkeit, *f*., Ort, *m*.

lock[1], *sb.* (*door, &c.*) Schloß, *n*.; (*canal*) Schleuse, *f*.; *v.t.* (ver)schließen; *v.i.* sich schließen; ~ in, up, einschließen, einsperren; ~ out, (*workmen*) aussperren; ~-jaw, Kinnbackenkrampf, *m*.; ~-out, Aussperrung, *f*.; ~smith, Schlosser, *m*.

lock[2], (*hair*) Locke, *f*.

locker, Kasten, Schrank, *m*.

locket, Medaillon, *n*.

locomotion, Ortsveränderung, *f*.; ~ve, Lokomotive, *f*.

locust, Heuschrecke, *f.*

locution, Ausdrucksweise, Redensart, *f.*

lodg|e, Hütte, *f.,* Häuschen, *n.;* Portierloge, *f.; v.t.* beherbergen, aufnehmen, unterbringen; ~ *a complaint,* Klage führen (*against* gegen); *v.i.* wohnen, logieren ; ~**er,** Mieter(in, *f.*), *m.;* ~**ing,** Wohnung, *f.;* ~**ings,** (gemietetes) Zimmer.

loft, Boden, *m.,* Dachstube, Bodenkammer, *f.*

loft|y, ~**ily,** hoch, erhaben; ~**iness,** Höhe, Erhabenheit, *f.*

log, *sb.* Block, Klotz, *m.;* (*naut.*) Log, *n.;* ~-**book,** Logbuch, Schiffsjournal, *n.;* ~-**cabin,** Blockhaus, *n.*

logarithm, Logarithmus, *m.*

loggerheads, *at* ~, im Streit, uneins.

logic, Logik, *f.;* ~**al(ly),** logisch.

loin, Lendenstück, *n.,* Nierenbraten, *m.;* ~**s,** Lenden, *f.pl.*

loiter, zögern, schlendern; ~**er,** Müßiggänger, Bummler, *m.*

loll, umherlungern.

lone|ly, einsam, verlassen; ~**liness,** Einsamkeit, *f.*

long¹, *a.* lang; (*lengthy*) langwierig; *adv.* lange; ~ *ago,* vor langer Zeit, längst; *a* ~ *time,* lange; *in the* ~ *run,* am Ende; ~-**boat,** Pinasse, *f.;* ~-**distance,** Fern-, Weit-; ~-**headed,** (*fig.*) klug, schlau, weitsichtig; ~-**lived,** langlebig; ~-**playing record,** Langspielplatte, *f.;* ~-**range,** Fern-; ~-**suffering,** langmütig; ~-**wave,** (radio) Langwelle, *f.;* ~-**winded,** langatmig.

long², *v.i.* sich sehnen (*for* nach); ~**ing,** Sehnsucht, *f.,* Verlangen *n.*

longitude, (geographische) Länge, *f.*

look¹, *sb.* Blick, *m.;* ~**s,** Aussehen, *n.,* Miene, *f.*

look², *v.i.* blicken, sehen, schauen; (*appear*) aussehen, scheinen; ~ *about,* umhersehen, sich umsehen; ~ *after,* aufpassen auf (*acc.*), achten auf (*acc.*); ~ *down on,* verächtlich herabblicken auf (*acc.*); ~ *for,* suchen; ~ *forward to,* erwarten, sich freuen auf; ~ *on,* betrachten

(*as* als) ; zusehen ; ~ *out,* hinaussehen ; (*naut.*) auslugen; ~ *out!* Achtung!; ~ *over,* durchsehen; ~ *up,* aufblicken; (*in dictionary, &c.*) nachschlagen; (*person*) besuchen, aufsuchen; ~ *up to,* mit Achtung zu jemandem aufblicken; ~**er-on,** Zuschauer, *m.;* ~**ing, good-~,** schön; ~**ing-glass,** Spiegel, *m.;* ~-**out,** Ausblick, *m.,* Aussicht, *f.;* Wache, *f.;* (*naut.*) Ausguck, *m.; on the* ~, auf der Lauer ; *keep a sharp* ~, gut aufpassen, ein wachsames Auge haben.

loom¹, *sb.* Webstuhl, *m.*

loom², *v.i.* sichtbar werden.

loop, *sb.* Schlinge, Schleife, *f.; to* ~ *the* ~, sich überschlagen; ~-**hole,** (*fig.*) Ausflucht, *f.*

loose, ~**ly,** lose, los, locker; frei; ~**n,** locker machen, (auf)lösen ; ~**ness,** Lockerheit, *f.;* (*fig.*) Liederlichkeit, *f.;* (*of bowels*) Durchfall, *m.*

loot, *sb.* Beute, *f.; v.t.* plündern.

loquacious, schwatzhaft; ~**ness,** Schwatzhaftigkeit, *f.*

lord, *sb.* Herr; (*Eng. title*) Lord; (*theol.*) der Herr, Gott, *m.; the* **Lord's Prayer,** das Vaterunser; **Lord's Supper,** Abendmahl, *n.; v.t.* ~ *it over,* den Herrn spielen, herrschen (über); ~**ly,** vornehm, edel, stolz; ~**liness,** Hoheit, *f.,* Hochmut, Stolz, *m.;* ~**ship,** Herrschaft; (*title*) Herrlichkeit, *f.*

lore, Kunde, Lehre, *f.*

lorry, Lore, *f.;* Last(kraft)wagen, *m.*

lose, verlieren; (*gambling*) verspielen; (*clock, &c.*) nachgehen; ~ *one's way,* sich verirren ; ~ *sight of,* aus den Augen verlieren; ~ *the train,* den Zug versäumen (verpassen).

loss, Verlust, *m.; at a* ~ (*for*), in Verlegenheit (um).

lot, Los, *n.;* (*fig.*) Los, Schicksal, *n.;* (*auction*) Posten, *m.;* (*quantity*) Menge, *f.; v.t.* cast, draw, ~**s,** um etwas losen; *it falls to my lot,* es fällt mir zu.

lotion, Hautwasser, *n.*

lottery, Lotterie, *f.*

loud, ~ly, laut; (colours) grell, auffallend; ~ness, lauter Schall (Ton), Lärm, m.; ~speaker, Lautsprecher, m.

lounge, faulenzen, müßiggehen, schlendern; ~suit, Straßenanzug, m.

lour, finster (düster) blicken.

louse, Laus, f.

lout, Lümmel, Tölpel, m.; ~ish, tölpelhaft; ~ishness, Tölpelhaftigkeit, f.

love, sb. Liebe, f.; (person) Geliebte(r); in ~, verliebt; ~-affair, Liebeshandel, m.; ~-bird, Sperlingspapagei, m.; ~-letter, Liebesbrief, m.; ~-story, Liebesgeschichte, f.; v.t. lieben, liebhaben, Gefallen (Vergnügen) finden (an); ~ly, lieblich, liebenswürdig; wunderschön; ~liness, Lieblichkeit, Liebenswürdigkeit; Schönheit, f.; ~r, Liebhaber(in), Liebende(r).

low, niedrig, gering, elend; (person) gemein; (sound) leise; ~land, Niederung, f. Tiefland, n.; ~liness, Demut, f.; ~ly, niedrig, demütig; ~-necked, (dress) tief ausgeschnitten; ~ness, Niedrigkeit, f.; ~-pressure, Tiefdruck, m.; ~-spirited, niedergeschlagen; ~-tide, Ebbe, f.; ~er, a. niedriger, Unter-; v.t. (let down) niederlassen, hinablassen; (prices) herabsetzen; (degrade) erniedrigen; lower a boat, ein Boot aussetzen.

loyal, ~ly, treu, loyal; ~ist, Regierungs-, Königs- treue(r); ~ty, Treue, f.

lozenge, Pastille, f., Bonbon, m. or n.

lubricant, Schmierstoff, m., Maschinenöl, n.; ~ate, ölen, schmieren; ~ating oil, Schmieröl, n.

lucid, ~ly, klar, durchsichtig, leuchtend; ~ity, Klarheit, Helle, f., Glanz, m.

luck, Glück, n.; Zufall, m.; ~y, ~ily, glücklich; glücklicherweise.

lucrative, einträglich, gewinnbringend.

ludicrous, ~ly, lächerlich, albern.

lug, schleppen, ziehen, zerren.

luggage, Gepäck, n.; left-~ office, Gepäckaufbewahrungstelle, f.

lukewarm, ~ly, lau; ~ness, Lauheit, f.

lull, v.t. einlullen; v.i. (of wind) sich legen; sb. Windstille (fig.) Ruhepause, f.; ~aby, Wiegenlied, n.

lumbago, Hexenschuß, m.

lumber, Gerümpel, n., Plunder, m.; ~ing, schwerfällig; ~-room, Rumpelkammer, f.

luminous, leuchtend, Leucht-; ~ clock, watch, Leuchtuhr, f.

lump, Klumpen, m., Masse, f., Stück, n.; in the ~, in Bausch und Bogen; ~ sum, runde Summe; ~y, ~ily, klumpig, voller Klumpen.

lunacy, Irrsinn, Wahnsinn, m.; ~atic, Wahnsinnige(r); ~atic asylum, Irrenhaus, n., Irrenanstalt, f.

lunar, Mond-.

lunch(eon), zweites Frühstück, Mittagessen, Lunch, n.

lung, Lunge, f.

lupin, Lupine, f.

lurch[1], v.i. wanken, taumeln.

lurch[2], sb.: leave in the ~, im Stich lassen.

lure, v.t. locken, ködern; sb. Lockspeise, f.

lurid, ~ly, finster, geisterhaft, bleich.

lurk, lauern.

luscious, ~ly, sehr süß, übersüß.

lust, sb. Begierde, Wollust, f.; v.i. gelüsten (after nach); ~ful(ly), wollüstig; ~y, ~ily, kräftig, munter.

lustre, Glanz, m.; (chandelier) Kronleuchter, m.; ~ous, glänzend.

lute, Laute, f.

luxurious, ~iously, üppig, reich; (furnishing) luxuriös; ~y, Üppigkeit, f., Luxus, m.

lye, Lauge, f.

lymph, Lymphe, f.

lynx, Luchs, m.

lyre, Leier, f.

lyric, a. lyrisch; sb. lyrisches Gedicht; ~ poetry, Lyrik, f.

M

macadam, Schotter, *m.*

macaroni, Makkaroni, *pl.*

macaroon, Makrone, *f.*

mace, Keule, *f.;* Szepter, *n.;* Amtsstab, *m.*

machination, Ränke, *pl.*

machine, Maschine, *f.;* ~gun, Maschinengewehr, *n.;* ~ry, Maschinerie, *f.,* Maschinen, *f.pl.,* Mechanismus, *m.*

mackerel, Makrele, *f.*

mackintosh, Gummimantel, *m.*

mad, ~ly, toll, wahnsinnig; ~cap, Tollkopf, *m.;* ~man, Wahnsinnige(r); ~ness, Wahnsinn, *m.;* Tollheit, *f.*

madam, Madame, gnädige Frau, *f.,* gnädiges Fräulein.

magazine, Lagerhaus, *n.; (periodical)* Zeitschrift, *f.*

maggot, Made, *f.*

magic, *sb.* Zauberkunst, Zauberei. *f.; a.* zauberhaft; ~ian, Zauberer, *m.;* ~ lantern, Laterna magica, *f.*

magnanim|ity, Großmut, *f.;* ~ous(ly), großmütig.

magnesi|a, Magnesia, *f.;* ~um, Magnesium, *n.*

magnet, Magnet, *m.;* ~ic, magnetisch; ~ism, Magnetismus, *m.;* ~ize, magnetisieren; ~o, Magnetzünder, *m.*

magnific|ence, Größe, Herrlichkeit, Pracht, *f.;* ~ent(ly), prachtvoll, herrlich.

magnify, vergrößern; *(fig.)* verherrlichen; übertreiben; ~ing glass, Vergrößerungsglas, *n.*

magnitude, Größe, *f.*

magnolia, Magnolie, *f.*

magpie, Elster, *f.*

mahogany, Mahagoni, *n.*

maid, Jungfrau, *f.,* Mädchen, *n.; (servant)* Magd, Hausgehilfin, *f.,* Dienstmädchen, *n.;* ~en, *a.* jungfräulich; ~en name, Mädchenname, *m.;* ~en speech. Jungfernrede, *f.;* ~enhair, *(bot.)* Frauenhaar, *n.*

mail, *sb.* Post, *f.; (armour)* Panzer, *m.; v.t.* mit der Post senden, aufgeben.

maim, lähmen, verstümmeln.

main, *a.,* ~ly, hauptsächlich, Haupt-; *adv.* meistens; *sb.* Hauptteil, *m.; (sea)* hohe See, *f.; (water, gas, &c.)* Hauptrohr, *n.;* ~land, Festland, *n.;* ~mast, Großmast, *m.;* ~spring, Uhrfeder; *(fig.)* Triebfeder, *f.*

maint|ain, erhalten, unterhalten, ernähren; behaupten; ~enance, Unterhalt, *m.,* Erhaltung, *f.*

maize, Mais, *m.*

majest|ic, ~ically, majestätisch; ~y, Majestät, *f.*

major, *a.* größer; mündig; *(mus.)* Dur; *sb.* Major, *m.;* ~general, Generalmajor, *m.;* ~ity, Mehrheit; Mündigkeit, *f.*

make, *sb.* Fabrikat, Erzeugnis, *n.;* Fabrikation; Gestalt, *f.; v.t.* machen, erzeugen, verfertigen; herstellen; (veran)lassen; zwingen; *(money)* verdienen, gewinnen; *(amount to)* ausmachen; *v.i.* ~ away with, stehlen; umbringen; ~ believe, vorgeben; ~ for, sich begeben (nach); *(naut. and fig.)* steuern auf; ~ good, wieder gut machen, ersetzen; ~ haste, sich beeilen, eilen; ~ known, bekannt machen; ~ off, sich aus dem Staube machen; ~ out *(accounts, &c.)* aufstellen; *(understand)* verstehen; ~ over, übertragen; ~ up, *(quarrel)* sich versöhnen, ausgleichen; *(concoct)* erfinden; *(complete)* vervollständigen; *(toilet)* (sich) schminken; *(theat.)* sich verkleiden (als); ~ up one's mind, sich entschließen; ~believe, *a.* angeblich; *sb.* Vorwand, *m.;* ~shift, Notbehelf, *m.;* ~up, *(toilet)* Schminke, *f.,* Make-up, *n.;* ~weight, Lückenbüsser, *m.;* ~r, maker, Fabrikant, Verfertiger, *m.;* making, *in the* ~, im Werden: *he has the* ~s *of,* er hat das Zeug zu.

malady, Krankheit, *f.*

malaria, Sumpffieber, *n.,* Malaria, *f.*

malcontent, unzufrieden.

male, *a.* männlich; *sb.* Mann, *m.; (zool.)* Männchen, *n.*

malediction, Fluch, *m.*
malefactor, Übeltäter, *m.*
malevolen|ce, Bosheit, *f.*; ~t(ly), böswillig.
malic|e, Bosheit, *f.*, Groll, *m.*; ~ious(ly), boshaft; ~iousness, Arglist, Tücke, *f.*
malign, verleumden, beschimpfen; ~ant(ly), boshaft, böswillig; (*med.*) bösartig.
malinger, sich krank stellen, simulieren.
malleable, dehn-, hämmer- bar; (*fig.*) geschmeidig.
mallet, Schlegel, *m.*
mallow, Malve, *f.*
malnutrition, Unterernährung, *f.*
malt, sb. Malz, *n.*; *v.t.* malzen.
maltreat, mißhandeln, schlecht behandeln.
mammal, Säugetier, *n.*
mammoth, sb. Mammut, *n.*; *a.* riesig.
man. sb. (*male*) Mann, *m.*; (*human being*) Mensch, *m.*; *v.t.* bemannen, besetzen; ~ful(ly), mannhaft, tapfer; ~hole, Einsteigeloch, *n.*; ~hood, Mannheit; Tapferkeit, *f.*; Mannesalter, *n.*; ~kind, Menschengeschlecht, *n.*; ~like, männlich; ~liness, Männlichkeit, *f.*; ~ly, männlich; ~of-war, Kriegsschiff, *n.*; ~power, Menschenmaterial, *n.*, Arbeitskräfte, *f.pl.*
manacle, sb. Handfessel, *f.*; fesseln.
manage, *v.t.* leiten, führen, verwalten, managen; (*handle*) handhaben; *v.i.* auskommen; ~ment, Leitung, Verwaltung, Direktion; Behandlung, *f.*; ~r, Verwalter, Direktor, Manager, *m.*; stage-~, Regisseur, *m.*
mandarin, Mandarin, *m.*; ~ orange, Mandarine, *f.*
mandat|e, Mandat, *n.*; Vollmacht, *f.*, Auftrag, *m.*; ~ory, Mandats-.
mane, Mähne, *f.*
manganese, Mangan, *n.*
mange, Räude, *f.*
mangel-wurzel, Mangoldwurzel, *f.*
manger, Krippe, *f.*, Futtertrog, *m.*
mangle, sb. Mangel, Wäscherolle, *f.*; *v.t.* mangeln, rollen; (*fig.*) verstümmeln.

mania, Wahnsinn, *m.*, Manie, *f.*; ~, *a.* wahnsinnig.
manifest, *a.* ~ly, offenbar, augenscheinlich; sb. Ladungsverzeichnis, *n.*; *v.t.* offenbaren; ~ation, Bekanntmachung; Offenbarung, *f.*; ~o, Kundgebung, *f.*
manifold, vielfach.
manikin, Männlein, *n.*; (*model*) Gliederpuppe, Schaufensterpuppe, *f.*
manipulate, handhaben; ~ion, Handhabung, *f.*
manner, Art, Lebensart, *f.*; in a ~, gewissermaßen; ~ism, Manieriertheit, *f.*; ~liness, Manierlichkeit, *f.*; ~ly, manierlich, gesittet, artig; ~s, Manieren, Sitten, *f.pl.*
manœuvre, sb. Manöver, *n.*; Kunstgriff, *m.*; *v.t.* manövrieren.
manor, Ritter-, Land- gut, *n.*; ~ial, herrschaftlich, Ritterguts-.
manse, Pfarrhaus, *n.*
mansion, (herrschaftliches) Wohnhaus; großes Mietshaus, *n.*
manslaughter, Totschlag, *m.*
mantelpiece, Kaminsims, *m.* or *n.*
mantle, sb. Mantel, *m.*, Hülle, *f.*; (*gas*) Glühstrumpf, *m.*; *v.t.* bedecken; bemänteln.
manual, *a.* Hand-; sb. Handbuch, *n.*
manufacture, sb. Fabrikation, Herstellung, Erzeugung, *f.*; Fabrikat, *n.*; *v.t.* fabrizieren, herstellen, erzeugen; ~r, Fabrikant, *m.*
manure, sb. Dünger, *m.*; *v.t.* düngen.
manuscript, Handschrift, *f.*, Manuskript, *n.*
many, viele, manche(r, s) (*numerous*) zahlreich; as ~ as, so viel als; ~ times, oft(mals); ~coloured, bunt, vielfarbig; ~sided, vielseitig.
map, sb. (Land)karte, *f.*; *v.t.* aufzeichnen; entwerfen.
maple, Ahorn, *m.*
mar, beschädigen; entstellen, verstümmeln; verderben, zerstören.
marauder, Plünderer, *m.*
marble, sb. Marmor, *m.*; (*toy*)

Murmel, f. or m.; a. marmorn,
Marmor-.

March¹, sb. März, m.

march², sb. Marsch, m.; Mark, f.,
Grenzland, n.; v.i. marschieren;
v.t. in Marsch setzen; dead ~,
Trauermarsch, m.; quick ~,
Geschwindschritt, m.; ~ past,
Vorbeimarsch, m.

mare, Stute, f.; ~'s-nest, (fig.)
Hirngespinst, n.

margarine, Margarine, f.

margin, Rand; Spielraum, m.

marguerite, Margerite, f.

marigold, Ringelblume, f.; marsh
~, Dotterblume, f.

marine, a. See-; sb. Seesoldat, m.;
~r, Seemann, m.

marital, ehelich.

maritime, zur See gehörig, See-.

marjoram, Majoran, m.

mark, sb. (Ab)zeichen, Merkmal,
n., Spur, f.; (coin) Mark, f.;
(aim) Ziel, n.; (school) Note, f.;
(trade) Marke, f.; not feel up to
the ~, sich nicht ganz wohl
fühlen; overshoot the ~, über
das Ziel hinausschießen; v.t.
zeichnen, markieren; (be)merk-
en; Noten geben; ~ed, hervorragend; deutlich, auffallend;
~ ing-ink, Wäschetinte, f.;
~ing-iron, Brand-, Brenn-eisen,
n.; ~sman, (guter) Schütze, m.

market, sb. Markt; Absatz,
Handel, m.; v.t. auf den Markt
bringen; ~able, gangbar, ver-
käuflich; ~-garden, Handels-
gärtnerei, f.

marl, Mergel, m.

marmelade, Orangenmarmelade, f.

marmot, Murmeltier, n.

maroon, kastanienbraun.

marquee, Markise, f., großes Zelt.

marquis, Marquis, m.

marriage, Ehe, Heirat, (wedding)
Hochzeit, f.; ~ portion, Mitgift, f.

married, ehelich, verheiratet;
~ couple, Ehepaar, m.

marrow, Mark, n.; vegetable ~,
Speisekürbis, m.

marry, v.t. heiraten; sich mit
jemandem verheiraten; trauen;
v.i. sich verheiraten.

marsh, Sumpf, m.; ~ gas, Sumpf-

gas, n.; ~-mallow, Eibisch, m.;
~y, sumpfig.

marshal, sb. Marschall, m.; v.t.
ordnen.

marten, Marder, m.

martial, kriegerisch; ~ law,
Kriegsrecht, n.

martin, Hausschwalbe, f.

martyr, sb. Märtyrer, m.; v.t.
martern, quälen; ~dom, Mär-
tyrertum, n.

marvel, sb. Wunder, n.; v.i. sich
wundern, staunen (at über);
~lous(ly), wunderbar.

marzipan, Marzipan, n.

mascara, Wimperntusche, f.

mascot, Maskotte, f.

masculine, a. männlich; sb. (gram.)
Masculinum, n.

mash, Brei, m.; Gemisch, n.;
(brewing) Maische, f.; v.t.
mischen, mengen; zerdrücken;
~ed potatoes, Kartoffel -brei,
m., -püree, m. or f.

mask, sb. Maske, f.; (fig.) Vorwand,
m.; v. vermummen, maskieren.

mason, Maurer; Freimaurer, m.;
~ic, Freimaurer-; ~ry, Mauer-
werk, n.

masquerade, sb. Maskenball, m.,
Maskerade, f.; v.i. sich maskieren, sich verkleiden, sich
verstellen.

mass, sb. Masse, Menge; (eccles.)
Messe, f.; ~ media, Massen-
medien, n.pl.; ~ production,
Massenherstellung, f.; v. (sich)
anhäufen, (sich) ansammeln;
(troops) massieren.

massacre, sb. Metzelei, f.; v.t.
niedermetzeln.

massage, sb. Massage, f.; v.t.
massieren.

masseur, Masseur, m.

massive, schwer, massig, massiv.

mast, Mast, m.

master, sb. Meister, Herr, Ge-
bieter; Schiffer; (school) Lehrer,
m.; v.t. beherrschen; (be)mei-
stern, bewältigen; ~-builder,
Baumeister, m.; ~-ful(ly), meh-
risch; meisterhaft; ~-key,
Hauptschlüssel, m.; ~-ly, meisterhaft; ~-piece, Meisterstück,
n.; ~-y, Herrschaft; Beherrschung, f.

masticate, kauen.

mastiff, Bullenbeißer, *m.*

mat, *sb.* Matte, *f.*; *v.t.* mit Matten bedecken; ineinander verwirren, verfilzen; ~ted (*hair*), wirr, struppig; ~ting, Matten, *f.pl.*

match, *sb.* (*equal*, *like*) Gleiche(r,s) (*marriage*) Partie, Heirat, *f.*; (*sport*) Wettspiel, *n.*; (*to light*) Streichholz, *n.*; *to be a ~ for*, jemandem gewachsen sein; *v.t.* zusammenbringen, zusammenpassen, vergleichen; *v.i.* passen, zusammenpassen; ~box, Streichholzschachtel, *f.*; ~less(ly), unvergleichlich; ~maker, Ehestifter(in, *f.*), *m.*

mate[1], *sb.* Gefährte, Gehilfe; Gatte, *m.*, Gattin, *f.*; (*naut.*) Maat, *m.*; *v.* (sich) paaren.

mate[2], *a.* (*chess*) schachmatt; *v.t.* matt machen.

material, *sb.* Material, *n.*, Stoff, *m.*; raw ~, Rohstoff, *m.*; *a.* materiell, körperlich; (*important*) wesentlich; ~ism, Materialismus, *m.*; ~ize, verkörpern, materialisieren; zu Stande kommen, in Erscheinung treten.

matern|al, mütterlich; ~ity, Mutterschaft, *f.*; ~ity hospital, Entbindungsanstalt, *f.*

mathematic|al, ~ally, mathematisch; ~ian, Mathematiker, *m.*; ~s, Mathematik, *f.*

matins, Frühmesse, *f.*, Frühgottesdienst, *m.*

matricide, Muttermord; Muttermörder, *m.*

matriculat|e, immatrikulieren, sich immatrikulieren lassen; einschreiben; ~ion, Immatrikulation, Einschreibung, *f.*

matrimon|ial, ehelich; ~y, Ehe, *f.*

matron, Matrone; (*hospital*) Oberin; (*institution*) Hausmutter, *f.*; ~ly, matronenhaft.

matter, *sb.* Stoff, *m.*, Materie, *f.*; (*typ.*) Satz, *m.*; (*med.*) Eiter, *m.*; *it's a ~ of*, es handelt sich um; *it doesn't ~*, es macht nichts; *what is the ~?*, was gibt es?; *what is the ~ with him?*, was fehlt ihm?; *as a ~ of course*, selbstverständlich; *~ of fact*, Tatsache, *f.*, wirklich; *as a ~ of*

fact, tatsächlich, eigentlich; *v.i.* daran liegen, etwas ausmachen; (*med.*) eitern; *what does it ~?*, was tut es? ; *no ~*, gleichviel.

mattock, Hacke, *f.*

mattress, Matratze, *f.*

matur|e, *a.*, ~ely, reif; (*bill*) fällig; *v.i.* reifen; (*bill*) fällig werden; ~ity, Reife; (*bill*) Fälligkeit, Verfallzeit, *f.*

maudlin, rührselig, sentimental, weinerlich betrunken.

maul, *v.t.* beschädigen, mißhandeln, verletzen.

Maundy Thursday, Gründonnerstag, *m.*

mauve, *sb.* Malvenfarbe, *f.*; *a.* malvenfarbig, hellviolett.

maw, Magen, *m.*

mawkish, ~ly, widerlich; (*fig.*) rührselig.

maxim, Grundsatz, *m.*, Maxime, *f.*

maximum, *sb.* Höchstmaß, *n.*; *a.* Höchst-.

May[1], *sb.* (*month*) Mai, *m.*; ~blossom, Weißdorn, *m.*; ~fly, Eintagsfliege; Wasserflorfliege, *f.*; ~pole, Maibaum, *m.*

may[2], *aux.v.* dürfen, mögen, können; ~be, vielleicht; *it ~ be so*, das kann (mag) sein.

mayor, Bürgermeister, *m.*

maze, Labyrinth, *n.*, Irrgarten, *m.*; Verwirrung, *f.*

me, (*acc.*) mich, (*dat.*) mir.

meadow, Wiese, *f.*

meagre, ~ly, mager; dürftig.

meal, (*flour*) Mehl, *n.*; (*dinner*, &*c.*) Mahlzeit, *f.*

mean[1], *a.*, ~ly, (*poor*) niedrig, gemein; ärmlich, armselig; (*stingy*) schäbig, filzig; ~ness, Gemeinheit, Niedrigkeit; Filzigkeit, *f.*

mean[2], *a.* (*average*, *middle*) mittler, mittelmäßig, Durchschnitts-, Mittel-; *in the ~time*, ~while, inzwischen, unterdessen; *sb.* Mittel, *n.*, Mitte, *f.*, Durchschnitt, *m.*; ~s, Mittel, *n.pl.*; Vermögen, *n.*; *by all ~*, jedenfalls, auf alle Fälle; *by no ~s*, keineswegs, auf keinen Fall; *by ~s of*, vermittelst, mittels, durch; *by any (some)* ~s, irgendwie; *by fair ~s or foul*, auf gerechte oder ungerechte Weise; *live beyond one's* ~s, über seine Mittel leben; *live within one's* ~s, seinen Verhältnissen entsprechend leben.

mean[3], *v.* (*intend*) beabsichtigen, wollen; (*signify*) bedeuten, heißen; (*destine*) bestimmen, meinen; ~ *well*, gut meinen; *without* ~*ing to*, unbeabsichtigt: *be meant for*, gelten (*dat.*); ~**ing**, Meinung, Bedeutung, *f.*, Sinn, *m.*; *well-*~**ing**, wohlwollend; ~**ingless**, sinnlos.

meander, sich (herum)schlängeln.

measles, Masern, *f.pl.*; *German* ~, Röteln, *pl.*

measure, *sb.* Maß, *n.*; Maßregel, *f.*; (*rule, standard*) Maßstab, *m.*; (*mus.*) Takt, *m.*; *to* ~, nach Maß. *v.t.* (ab-, aus-, zu-)messen; enthalten, fassen; *v.i.* groß sein; ~**ment**, Maß, *n.*, Messung, *f.*; **measurable**, meßbar.

meat, Fleisch, *n.*

mechan|**ic**, ~**ical**, *a.* mechanisch; *sb.* Mechaniker, *m.*; ~**ics**, Mechanik, *f.*; ~**ism**, Mechanismus, *m.*, Getriebe, Triebwerk, *n.*; ~**ization**, Verkraftung, *f.*; ~**ize**, mechanisieren, auf Maschinenbetrieb umstellen.

medal, Medaille, Denkmünze; Auszeichnung, *f.*

meddle, sich (ein)mischen (*with* in).

media|**te**, vermitteln; ~**tion**, Vermittelung, *f.*; ~**tor**, Vermittler(in, *f.*), *m.*

medica|**l**, ärztlich; (*school, &c.*) medizinisch; ~**ment**, Arzneimittel, *n.*

medicin|**e**, Medizin, Arznei; Heilkunde, Medizin, *f.*; ~**al**, medizinisch, Heil-.

medieval, mittelalterlich.

mediocr|**e**, mittelmäßig; ~**ity**, Mittelmäßig, *f.*

medita|**te**, nachdenken (*on* über); ~**tion**, Nachdenken, *n.*

medium, *sb.* Mittel, *n.*; (*spiritualism*) Medium, *n.*; *a.* mittelmäßig, Durchschnitts-, Mittel-.

medlar, Mispel, *f.*

medley, Gemisch, Durcheinander, *n.*

meek, ~**ly**, mild, sanft(mütig);

demütig; ~**ness**, Sanftmut, Milde, Demut, *f.*

meet, *v.t.* treffen, begegnen; (*demands, expenses, &c.*) nachkommen (*dat.*); erfüllen; (*bill*) honorieren, bezahlen; *v.i.* sich treffen, sich versammeln; ~**ing**, Zusammentreffen, *n.*, Versammlung, *f.*

melanchol|**ic**, schwermütig, trübsinnig; ~**y**, Schwermut, *f.*, Trübsinn, *m.*

mellow, *a.* mürbe, reif; mild, abgeklärt, lieblich; *v.i.* mürbe, reif, abgeklärt werden; ~**ness**, Reife, *f.*

melod|**ious**, ~**iously**, wohlklingend; ~**y**, Melodie, Weise, *f.*

melodrama, Melodrama, *n.*

melon, Melone, *f.*

melt, *v.t.* schmelzen, auflösen; *v.i.* schmelzen, zerfließen, sich auflösen, zergehen; ~**ing-point**, Schmelzpunkt, *m.*

member, Glied; Mitglied, *n.*; ~**ship**, Mitgliedschaft; Mitgliederzahl, *f.*

membrane, Membran, *f.*, Häutchen, *n.*

memento, Erinnerung, *f.*, Andenken, *n.*

memoir, Denkschrift, *f.*; ~**s**, Denkwürdigkeiten, Erinnerungen, *f.pl.*

memor|**able**, ~**ably**, denkwürdig; ~**andum**, Note, Anmerkung, *f.*; ~**ial**, Denkschrift; Denkmal, *n.*; ~**ize**, auswendig lernen, sich einprägen; ~**y**, Gedächtnis, Andenken, *n.*, Erinnerung, *f.*

menace, *v.t.* (be)drohen; *sb.* (Be)drohung, *f.*

menagerie, Menagerie, *f.*

mend, *v.t.* ausbessern; *v.i.* sich bessern.

mendac|**ious**, ~**iously**, lügenhaft; ~**ity**, Lügenhaftigkeit, *f.*

menial, *a.* niedrig, gemein; *sb.* Diener, *m.*

meningitis, Hirnhautentzündung, *f.*

menstrual|**e**, menstruieren, unwohl sein; ~**ion**, Menstruation, *f.*, Monatsfluß, *m.*

mental, ~**ly**, geistig, Geistes-;

~ arithmetic, Kopfrechnen, n.; ~ity, Geistesverfassung, f.

mention, sb. Erwähnung, f.; v.t erwähnen; don't ~ it, bitte sehr!, es ist nicht der Rede wert!

menu, Speisekarte, Speisefolge, f.

mercantile, kaufmännisch, Handels-; ~ **marine,** Handelsmarine, f.

mercenary, sb. Söldner, m.; a. gedungen; käuflich; gewinnsüchtig.

merchandise, Waren, f.pl.

merchant, Kaufmann, Händler, m.; ~**man,** (naut.) Handelsschiff, n.

merci|ful, ~**ifully,** barmherzig, gnädig; ~**iless(ly),** unbarmherzig; ~**y,** Barmherzigkeit, Gnade, f.

mercury, Quecksilber, n.

mere, bloß, lauter; ~**ly,** bloß, nur.

merge, v.t. einverleiben (in), verschmelzen (mit); v.i. aufgehen (in); ~**r,** Fusion, f.

meridian, Mittag, Meridian; (climax) Höhepunkt, m.

merit, sb. Verdienst, n., Vorzug, m.; v.t. verdienen; ~**orious(ly),** verdienstlich, lobenswert.

mermaid, Meerweib, n., Wassernixe, f.

merr||iment, Fröhlichkeit, f.; ~**y,** ~**ily,** lustig, fröhlich, munter; ~**y-go-round,** Karussell, n.

mesh, Masche, f., Netz, n.

mess, sb. (muddle) Unordnung, f.; (dish) Gericht, n.; (mil.) Regiments-, Offiziers-messe, f.; (nav.) Back, f.; v.t. verpfuschen, in Unordnung bringen; ~**mate,** Tischgenosse, m.; (nav.) Backsmaat, m.

message, Botschaft, Mitteilung, f.; Auftrag, m.

messenger, Bote, m.

Messiah, Messias, m.

metal, Metall, n.; (road) Schotter, m.; ~**lic,** metallisch; ~**lurgist,** Metallurg, m.; ~**lurgy,** Metallurgie, Hüttenkunde, f.

metaphor, Metapher, f.; ~**ical(ly),** bildlich, metaphorisch.

metaphysic|al, metaphysisch; ~**s,** Metaphysik, f.

meteor, Meteor, n.; ~**ite,** Meteorit, m.; ~**ologist,** Meteorolog(e), m.; ~**ology,** Wetterkunde, f.

meter, Messer, m.; Gasuhr, f.; (electr.) Zähler, m.

method, Methode, f., Verfahren, n.; ~**ical(ly),** methodisch; ~**ist,** Methodist, m.

methylated, denaturiert.

meticulous, ~**ly,** peinlich genau.

metr|e, Meter, n.; (prosody) Versmaß, Metrum, n.; ~**ic,** metrisch.

mew, (cat) miauen.

mica, Glimmer, m.

Michaelmas, Michaelis, n.

microbe, Mikrobe, f.

microscop|e, Mikroskop, n.; ~**ic,** mikroskopisch.

mid, mitten, Mittel-; ~**day,** Mittag, m.; ~**night,** Mitternacht, f.; ~**shipman,** Seekadett, m.; ~**way,** halbwegs; in der Mitte zwischen; ~**wife,** Hebamme, f.; ~**wifery,** Geburtshilfe, f.

middle, sb. Mitte, f.; a. Mittel-; ~ **ages,** Mittelalter, n.; ~ **classes,** Mittelstand, f.; ~**distance,** Mittelgrund, m.; ~**man,** Zwischenhändler, m.

midge, Mücke, f.

midst, Mitte, f.; in the ~ of, mitten in.

mien, Miene, f.

might, Macht, Gewalt, f.; ~**ily,** ~**y,** mächtig.

mignonette, Reseda, f.

migra|te, wandern, f.; ~**tion,** Wanderung, f.; ~**tory,** wandernd, Zug-.

mild, ~**ly,** mild, sanft; ~**ness,** Milde, f.

mildew, Meltau, m.

mile, Meile, f.; ~**age,** Meilenzahl, f.; ~**stone,** Meilenstein, m.

milit|ant, streitend, kriegführend; ~**arism,** Militarismus, m.; ~**ary,** a. militärisch, kriegerisch; sb. Militär, n.; ~**ary service,** Militärdienst, m.; ~**ate,** sprechen gegen.

militia, Landwehr, Heimwehr, f.

milk, sb. Milch, f.; v.t. melken; ~**maid,** Milchmädchen, n.; ~**man,** Milchhändler, m.; ~**sop,** Weichling, m.; Muttersöhnchen, n.; ~**tooth,** Milch-

zahn, *m.*; ~**y,** milchig; **Milky Way,** Milchstraße, *f.*

mill, Mühle; (*cotton, &c.*) Fabrik, Spinnerei, *f.*; *v.t.* (*corn*) mahlen; (*coins*) rändeln; ~**er,** Müller, *m.*; ~**stone,** Mühlstein, *m.*

millennium, Jahrtausend, Millennium, *n.*

millet, Hirse, *f.*

milli|gram, Milligramm, *n.*; ~**metre,** Millimeter, *n.*

milliner, Putzmacherin, Modistin, *f.*; ~**y,** Putzwaren, *f.pl.*

million, Million, *f.*; ~**aire,** Millionär, *m.*

mimic, *a.* mimisch, Schein-; *sb.* Mime, Nachäffer, *m.*; *v.t.* nachäffen; ~**ry,** Nachäffung, (*zool.*)Anähnlichung,Mimikry,*f.*

mince, *sb.* Hackfleisch, *n.*; *v.t.* kleinhacken; *not to* ~ *matters,* kein Blatt vor den Mund nehmen.

mind, *sb.* Geist, Verstand, Sinn, *m.* Gemüt, *n.*; *presence of* ~, Geistesgegenwart, *f.*; *make up one's* ~, sich entschließen; *change one's mind,* seine Meinung (Absicht) ändern; *give* (*tell*) *a person a piece of one's* ~, jemandem seine Meinung sagen; *have a* ~ *to,* Lust haben zu; *v.t.* achten auf, aufpassen; *v.i.* sich (be)kümmern; *I don't* ~, es ist mir gleich; *never* ~, es macht (tut) nichts; ~**ed,** gesinnt, geneigt; ~**ful,** achtsam; eingedenk, bedacht (auf).

mine[1], *pron.* mein; der (die, das) meinige.

mine[2], *sb.* Grube, *f.*; Bergwerk, *n.*; (*mil.*) Mine, *f.*; *v.t.* graben; **Minen legen;** ~**r,** Bergmann, *m.*; ~**sweeper,** Minensuchboot, *n.*

mining, Bergbau, *m.*

mineral, Mineral, *n.*; ~ *water,* Mineralwasser, *n.*; (*artificial*) Sodawasser, *n.*; ~**ogist,** Mineralog(e), *m.*; ~**ogy,** Mineralogie, Steinkunde, *f.*

mingle, *v.t.* mischen, (ver)mengen; *v.i.* sich mischen.

miniature, Miniaturgemälde, *n.*; (*fig.*) im kleinen.

minimum, Minimum, *n.*, Mindest-.

miniskirt, Minirock, *m.*

minist|er, *sb.* Minister; (*envoy*) Gesandte(r); (*religion*) Geistliche(r), *m.*; *v.t.* versorgen; *v.i.* dienen; ~**erial,** ministeriell; ~**ry,** (*pol.*) Ministerium; (*religious*) Amt, *n.*

minnow, Elritze, *f.*

minor, *a.* kleiner, geringer; unmündig; (*mus.*) Moll-; *sb.* Unmündige(r); ~**ity,** Minderheit; Unmündigkeit, *f.*; *in the* ~*ity,* in der Minderzahl.

minster, Münster, *n.*

minstrel, Spielmann, fahrender Sänger, *m.*; **nigger** ~, Negersänger, *m.*

mint[1], (*bot.*) Minze, *f.*; ~**-sauce,** Minztunke, *f.*

mint[2], *sb.* Münze, Münzstätte, *f.*; *v.t.* münzen, prägen; ~**age,** Münzen, *n.*; Prägung, *f.*

minuet, Menuett, *n.*

minute[1], Minute, *f.*; (*of a meeting*) Protokoll, *n.*; ~**-hand,** Minutenzeiger, *m.*

minute[2], ~**ly,** klein, winzig; (*precise*) genau; ~**ness,** Kleinheit; Genauigkeit, *f.*

mirac|le, Wunder, *n.*; ~**ulous(ly),** wunderbar.

mirage, Luftspiegelung, *f.*

mir|e, Schlamm, Kot, *m.*; ~**y,** schlammig, kotig.

mirror, *sb.* Spiegel, *m.*; *v.t.* spiegeln.

mirth, Fröhlichkeit, *f.*; ~**ful(ly),** fröhlich.

misanthrop|e, Menschenfeind, *m.*; ~**y,** Menschenhaß, *m.*

misapp|lication, Mißbrauch, *m.*, falsche Anwendung, *f.*; ~**ly,** mißbrauchen, falsch anwenden.

misapprehen|d, mißverstehen; ~**sion,** Mißverständnis, *n.*

misbehav|e, sich schlecht benehmen; ~**iour,** schlechtes Betragen.

miscalculate, falsch (be)rechnen; sich verrechnen.

miscarr|iage, Fehlgeburt, *f.*; (*fig.*) Mißlingen, *n.*; ~**y,** (*fig.*) mißlingen, fehlschlagen.

miscellan|eous, gemischt; ~**y,** Gemisch, *n.*

mischance, Unfall, *m.*, Mißgeschick, *n.*

mischief, Unheil, Unglück, *n.*;
Mutwille, *m.*; **~maker**, Unheilstifter, *m.*; mischievous,
~ly, boshaft, mutwillig.

misconceive, falsch verstehen;
~ption, Mißverständnis, *n.*

misconduct, *sb.* Fehltritt, *m.*,
schlechtes Betragen; *v.* ~ *one-self*, sich schlecht betragen.

miscount, falsch zählen, sich verzählen.

misdeal, (*cards*) sich vergeben,
falsch austeilen.

misdeed, Missetat, *f.*

misdirect, falsch leiten, den
falschen Weg weisen; (*letters*)
falsch adressieren.

miser, Geizhals, *m.*; **~ly**, geizig.

miserabl|e, **~y**, elend; erbärmlich.

misery, Elend, *n.*, Not, *f.*

misfire, *v.i.* (*gun*) versagen; (*motor*)
fehlzünden; *sb.* Versager, *m.*,
Fehlzündung, *f.*

misfortune, Unglück, *n.*

misgiving, Besorgnis, Befürchtung, *f.*

mishap, Unfall, *m.*

misinterpret, mißdeuten, falsch
auslegen.

misjudge, falsch urteilen, verkennen.

mislay, verlegen.

mislead, verleiten, irreführen.

mismanage, schlecht verwalten;
~ment, schlechte Verwaltung
(Führung) *f.*

misogyn|ist, Weiberfeind, *m.*; **~y**,
Weiberhaß, *m.*

misprint, *v.t.* verdrucken; *sb.*
Druckfehler, *m.*

mispron|ounce, falsch aussprechen;
~unciation, falsche Aussprache.

misrepresent, falsch darstellen;
~ation, Verdrehung, *f.*

miss¹, *sb.* Fräulein, *n.*

miss², *v.t.* (ver)missen, verfehlen;
(*omit*) auslassen; (*not see*) übersehen; (*train*, &c.) versäumen;
sb. Fehlschlagen, *n.*; Fehlschuß,
Fehlwurf, *m.*; **~ing**, abwesend,
fehlend, verloren; (*mil.*) vermißt; (*aircraft*) verloren gegangen.

missile, Wurfgeschoß, *n.*, Wurfwaffe, *f.*

mission, Sendung, *f.*; Auftrag, *m.*,

Botschaft, *f.*; (*religious*) Mission,
f.; **~ary**, Missionär(in, *f.*), *m.*

mist, Nebel, *m.*; **~y**, neblig.

mistake, *sb.* Irrtum, Fehler, *m.*;
in ~, aus Versehen; *make a* ~,
einen Fehler machen; *v.t.* verkennen, verwechseln; falsch
verstehen; **~n**, irrig, falsch.

mister, Herr, *m.*

mistletoe, Mistel, *f.*

mistress, Herrin, Gebieterin;
(*school*) Lehrerin; (*lover*) Geliebte, Mätresse, *f.*

mistrust, *v.t.* mißtrauen; *sb.* Mißtrauen, *n.*; **~ful(ly)**, mißtrauisch.

misunderstand, mißverstehen;
~ing, Mißverständnis, *n.*

misuse, *v.t.* mißbrauchen, mißhandeln; *sb.* Mißbrauch, *m.*

mitiga|te, mildern, lindern;
~tion, Linderung, *f.*

mitre, Bischofsmütze, *f.*

mix, *v.t.* (ver)mischen; *v.i.* sich
mischen; **~ture**, Mischung, *f.*,
Gemisch, *n.*; (*med.*) Mixtur, *f.*

moan, *v.i.* stöhnen, ächzen; *sb.*
Stöhnen, *n.*

moat, Burg-, Schutz- graben, *m.*

mob, *sb.* Pöbel, *m.*; *v.t.* belästigen,
mißhandeln.

mobil|e, beweglich; **~ity**, Beweglichkeit, *f.*; **~ization**, Mobilmachung, *f.*; **~ize**, mobil
machen.

mock, *sb.* Spott, Hohn, *m.*; *a.*
falsch, nachgemacht, Ersatz-,
Schein-; *v.t.* verspotten, verhöhnen; *v.i.* spotten (*at* über);
~ery, Spötterei, *f.*, Hohn, *m.*;
(*fig.*) Täuschung, *f.*, Blendwerk,
n.; **~ing**, spöttisch; **~ing-bird**,
Spottdrossel, *f.*; **~turtle soup**,
Mockturtlesuppe, *f.*; **~up**,
Modell, *n.*

mode, Art und Weise; Mode;
(*mus.*) Tonart, *f.*

model, *sb.* Muster, Modell, Vorbild; Mannequin, *n.*; *v.t.* modellieren, entwerfen.

moderate, **~ly**, mäßig; (*middling*)
mittelmäßig; *v.t.* mäßigen;
~ness, Mäßigkeit, *f.*

modern, modern, neu; (*of languages*) Neu-; **~ize**, modernisieren.

modest, ~ly, bescheiden, sittsam; mäßig; ~y, Bescheidenheit, *f.*

modif|ication, (Ab)änderung; Einschränkung, *f.*; *(gram.)* Umlaut, *m.*; ~y, abändern; einschränken; umlauten.

moist, feucht; ~en, befeuchten, benetzen; ~ure, Feuchtigkeit, *f.*

molar, Backenzahn, *m.*

molasses, Melasse, *f.*, Sirup, *m.*

mole, *(animal)* Maulwurf, *m.*; *(harbour)* Mole, *f.*, Hafendamm, *m.*; *(on skin)* Muttermal, *n.*; ~hill, Maulwurfshaufen, *m.*; ~skin, Maulwurfsfell, *n.*

molecul|e, Molekül, *n.*; ~ar, molekular.

molest, belästigen, beunruhigen; ~ation, Belästigung, *f.*

mollusc, Molluske, *f.*, Weichtier, *n.*

moment, Augenblick, *m.*; Wichtigkeit, *f.*; ~ary, ~arily, kurz, augenblicklich; ~ous, wichtig; ~um, Moment, *n.*

monarch, Monarch, *m.*; ~ical, monarchisch; ~y, Monarchie, *f.*

monast|ery, Kloster, *n.*; ~ic, klösterlich.

Monday, Montag, *m.*

money, Geld, *n.*; ready ~, Bargeld, *n.*; ~-changer, Geldwechsler, *m.*; ~-lender, Geldverleiher, *m.*; ~-order, Postanweisung, *f.*

Mongol, Mongole, *m.*

mongrel, Bastard, Mischling, *m.*

monk, Mönch, *m.*; ~ish, mönchisch.

monkey, Affe; *(pile-driver)* Rammbär, *m.*; ~-puzzle, Araukarie, Andentanne, *f.*

monologue, Selbstgespräch, *n.*, Monolog, *m.*

monoplane, Eindecker, *m.*

monopol|ize, (Waren) aufkaufen; für sich allein in Anspruch nehmen; ~y, Alleinverkauf. *m.*, Monopol, *n.*

monosyllab|le, einsilbiges Wort; ~ic, einsilbig.

monoton|ous, ~ously, eintönig, langweilig; ~y, Eintönigkeit. Langweiligkeit, *f.*

monsoon, Monsun, *m.*

monst|er, Ungeheuer, *n.*, Mißgeburt, *f.*; Riesen-; ~rous

ungeheuer, kolossal.

month, Monat, *m.*; ~ly, monatlich.

monument, Denkmal, *n.*; ~al, monumental.

mood, Laune, Stimmung, *f.*; *(gram.)* Modus, *m.*; ~iness, Verdrießlichkeit, Launenhaftigkeit, *f.*; ~y, ~ily, launenhaft.

moon, Mond, *m.*; full ~, Vollmond, *m.*; half-~, Halbmond, *m.*; new ~, Neumond, *m.*; ~light, ~shine, Mondschein, *m.*, Mondlicht, *n.*; *(fig.)* Unsinn, *m.*

Moor[1], *sb.* Maure, *m.*; ~ish, maurisch.

moor[2], *sb.* Heide, *f.*; ~-hen, Moorhuhn, *n.*

moor[3], *v.t.* *(naut.)* verankern, vertäuen; ~ings, Vertäuungen, *f.pl.*

mop, *sb.* Wisch-, Scheuer lappen, Bodenmop, *m.*; ~ of hair, Haarschopf, *m.*; *v.t.* ab-, aufwischen; ~ up, *(mil.)* säubern.

moral, ~ist, Sittenprediger, *m.*; ~ity, Sittlichkeit, *f.*; ~ize, moralisieren; ~y, sittlich, moralisch; ~s, Sitten, *f.pl.* Moral, *f.*

morass, Morast, Sumpf, *m.*

morbid, ~ly, krankhaft.

more, mehr; ferner, noch (etwas); once ~, noch einmal; one ~, noch eine(r) (eins); no ~, nicht mehr; ~over, überdies, ferner.

morning, Morgen, Vormittag, *m.*; to-morrow ~, morgen früh.

morocco, Marokkoleder, *n.*, Saffian, *m.*

morose, ~ly, mürrisch, verdrießlich.

morphia, Morphium, *n.*

morsel, Bissen, *m.*

mortal, ~ly, *a.* sterblich; tödlich; *sb.* Sterbliche(r), Mensch, *m.*; ~ sin, Todsünde, *f.*; ~ity, Sterblichkeit, *f.*

mortar, Mörtel; *(vessel & mil.)* Mörser, *m.*

mortgage, *sb.* Hypothek, *f.*; *v.t.* verpfänden; ~e, Hypothekengläubiger, *m.*

mortif|ication, Kasteiung; Demütigung, *f.*; *(med.)* Absterben, *n.*; ~y, kasteien, abtöten.

mortuary, Leichenhalle, *f.*

mosaic, Mosaik, *n.* or *f.*

mosque, Moschee, *f.*

mosquito, Moskito, *m.*; ~net, ~-curtain, Moskitonetz, *n.*

moss, Moos, *n.*; ~y, moosig.

most, *a.* meist; *adv.* am meisten; at the ~, höchstens; ~ of all, vor allem; ~ly, meistens, meistenteils.

motel, Motel, *n.*

moth, Motte, *f.*, Nachtfalter, *m.*; ~-eaten, von Motten zerfressen.

mother, *sb.* Mutter, *f.*; *v.t.* bemuttern; ~ country, Vaterland, *n.*; ~hood, Mutterschaft, *f.*; ~-in-law, Schwiegermutter, *f.*; ~ly, mütterlich; ~-of-pearl, Perlmutter, *f.*; ~ tongue, Muttersprache, *f.*

motion, Bewegung, *f.*; (*resolution*) Antrag; (*med.*) Stuhlgang, *m.*; ~less, bewegungslos.

motive, *sb.* Beweggrund, Zweck, *m.*; Motiv, *n.*; ~ power, Triebkraft, *f.*

motley, bunt, scheckig.

motor, *sb.* Motor, *m.*; (*auto*) Auto (mobil), *n.*; *v.i.* Automobil fahren; ~bicycle, Kraftfahrrad, Motorrad, *n.*; ~-boat, Motorboot, *n.*; ~-bus, Autobus, *m.*; ~-car, Auto(mobil), *n.*, Kraftwagen, *m.*; ~ist, Autofahrer, *m.*; ~ize, motorisieren; ~ lorry, Lastauto, *n.*, Last(kraft)wagen, *m.*; ~way, Autobahn, -straße, *f.*

mottled, gesprenkelt.

motto, Wahl-, Sinn- spruch, *m.*, Motto, *n.*

mould, *sb.* (*for metal, &c.*) (Gieß)-form, *f.*; (*earth*) Komposterde, *f.*; (*mildew*) Schimmel, *m.*; (*fig.*) Schablone, Bildung, *f.*; *v.t.* gießen; kneten, formen, bilden; ~ing, (Ge)sims, *n.*, Fries, *m.*; ~y, schimmelig.

moult, *v.i.* sich mausern; *sb.* Mauser, *f.*

mound, Erdhügel, Wall, *m.*

mount, *sb.* Hügel, *m.*; (*horse*) Reitpferd, *n.*; (*setting*) Einfassung, *f.*; *v.i.* steigen; *v.t.* (*horse*) besteigen; (*jewels*) einfassen; (*picture*) aufziehen; ~

guard, auf Wache ziehen; ~ed, beritten.

mountain, Berg, *m.*; ~ ash, Eberesche, *f.*; ~eer, Bergsteiger, *m.*; ~eering, Bergsteigen, *n.*; ~ous, gebirgig; ~ range, Gebirge, *n.*

mountebank, Scharlatan, *m.*

mourn, trauern, (be)klagen; ~ for, betrauern; ~er, Trauernde(r); ~ful(ly), traurig; ~ing, Trauer, Trauerkleidung, *f.*

mouse, Maus, *f.*; ~trap, Mausefalle, *f.*

moustache, Schnurrbart, *m.*

mouth, Mund, *m.*; (*animals*) Maul, *n.*; (*river*) Mündung, *f.*; ~ful, Mundvoll, *m.*; ~piece, Mundstück, *n.*; (*fig.*) Wortführer, *m.*

mov|e, *sb.* Bewegung, *f.*; (*chess*) Zug, *m.*; *v.t.* bewegen, rühren; *v.i.* sich bewegen, sich rühren; (*chess*) ziehen; *v.t.* (*affect*) rühren; ~able, beweglich; ~ement, Bewegung, *f.*; ~ing (*touching*), rührend.

mow, mähen, schneiden; ~er, Mäher, Schnitter, *m.*; ~ing-machine, Mähmaschine, *f.*

Mr., Herr, *m.*; Mrs., Frau, *f.*

much, viel, sehr.

muck, Mist, Dünger; Schmutz, Kot, *m.*

mud, Schlamm, Kot, *m.*; ~dy, schlammig; trübe; ~guard, Kotflügel, *m.*, Schutzblech, *n.*

muddle, *v.t.* verwirren; verpfuschen; *sb.* Verwirrung, Unordnung, *f.*

muffle, *v.t.* dämpfen; einwickeln; ~r, Halstuch, *n.*

mufti, Zivil, *n.*

mug, Krug, Becher, *m.*

mulatto, Mulatte, *m.*

mulberry, Maulbeere, *f.*

mule, Maul -tier, *n.*, -esel, *m.*; ~s, Slingpumps, *m.pl.*; ~teer, Mauleseltreiber, *m.*

mullet, Meeräsche, *f.*

multifarious, mannigfaltig.

multiple, vielfach.

multipl|ication, Vervielfältigung, Vermehrung; Multiplikation, *f.*; *multiplication table*, das Einmaleins; ~y, multiplizieren, vervielfältigen; sich vermehren.

multitude, Menge, Vielheit, *f.*; Pöbel, *m.*

mumble, murmeln.

mummy, Mumie, *f.*

mumps, Ziegenpeter, Mumps, *m.*

munch, kauen.

mundane, weltlich.

municipal, städtisch, Stadt-; ~ity, Stadtrat, *m.* Stadtgemeinde, *f.*

munificen|ce, Freigebigkeit, *f.*; ~t(ly), freigebig.

munition, Munition, *f.*, Kriegsmaterial, *n.*

murder, *sb.* Mord, *m.*; *v.t.* ermorden; ~er, Mörder, *m.*; ~ous, mörderisch.

murky, dunkel; trübe.

murmur, *v.i.* murmeln; *sb.* Gemurmel, *n.*

musc|le, Muskel, *m.* or *f.*; ~ular, stark, muskulös.

muse, *sb.* Muse, *f.*; *v.i.* nachdenken, sinnen (über).

museum, Museum, *n.*

mushroom, Pilz, *m.*

music, Musik, *f.*; ~al(ly), musikalisch; ~hall, Konzertsaal, *m.* Varieté, *n.*; ~ian, Musiker, Tonkünstler, *m.*; ~stand, Notenpult, *n.*; ~stool, Klavierhocker, *m.*

musk, Bisam, Moschus, *m.*

musket, Flinte, *f.*

muslin, Musselin, *m.*

mussel, Muschel, *f.*

Mussulman, Muselmann, *m.*

must, muß, müssen.

mustard, Senf, *m.*

muster, *v.t.* mustern; aufbringen; *sb.* Musterung; Musterrolle, *f.*

must|iness, Dumpfigkeit, *f.*; ~y, dumpf, muffig.

mutation, Veränderung, *f.*; (*gram.*) Umlaut, *m.*

mute, ~ly, stumm.

mutila|te, verstümmeln; ~tion, Verstümmelung, *f.*

mutin|eer, Aufrührer, Meuterer, *m.*; ~ous(ly), aufrührerisch; ~y, *sb.* Aufruhr, *m.*, Meuterei, *f.*; *v.i.* meutern, sich empören.

mutter, murren; murmeln.

mutton, Hammelfleisch, *n.*; leg of ~, Hammelkeule, *f.*; ~chop, Hammelrippchen, *n.*

mutual, ~ly, gegenseitig; (*friend*) gemeinsam.

muzzle, *sb.* Schnauze, *f.*; (*for dog*) Maulkorb, *m.*; (*of gun*) Mündung, *f.*; *v.t.* einen Maulkorb anlegen; (*fig.*) den Mund stopfen.

my, mein(e); ~self, ich selbst, mich, mir.

myrtle, Myrte, *f.*

myster|ious(ly), geheimnisvoll, rätselhaft, *m.*; ~y, Geheimnis, *n.*

mystic, *a.* mystisch; *sb.* Mystiker, Schwärmer, *m.*

myth, Mythe; Erdichtung, *f.*; ~ical, mythisch; sagenhaft; ~ology, Mythologie, Götterlehre, *f.*

N

nadir, Nadir, *m.*

nag, kleiner Klepper, *m.*; *v.i.* nörgeln.

nail, *sb.* Nagel, *m.*; *fight tooth and nail*, mit aller Kraft kämpfen; *v.t.* (ver)nageln, beschlagen.

naive, ~ly, naiv, einfältig.

naked, ~ly, nackt, bloß; ~ness, Nacktheit, Blöße, *f.*

name, *sb.* Name, Ruf, *m.*; *Christian* ~, Vorname, *m.*; *family* ~, Nachname, Familienname, *m.*; *proper* ~, Eigenname, *m.*; *by* ~, mit Namen; *what is your* ~? Wie heißen Sie?; *v.t.* nennen; ~less, namenlos; ~ly, nämlich; ~sake, Namensvetter, *m.*

nap, Schläfchen, *n.*; (*pile*) Noppe, *f.*; *catch* ~ping, auf der Tat ertappen.

nape, Nacken, *m.*, Genick, *n.*

naphtha, Naphtha, *f.*

napkin, Mundtuch, Serviette, *f.*; (*child's*) Windel, *f.*

narcissus, Narzisse, *f.*

narco|sis, Narkose, *f.*; ~tic, Betäubungsmittel, *n.*

narra|te, erzählen; ~tion, Erzählung, *f.*; ~tor, Erzähler, *m.*

narrow, ~ly, eng(e), klein, schmal; *have a* ~ *escape*, mit genauer (knapper) Not entkommen; ~gauge, schmalspurig; **~-minded**, engherzig; **~ness**, Enge; Beschränktheit, *f.*; **~s**, Meerenge, *f.*; *v.* enger machen; enger werden, sich verengen.

nasal, *a.* nasal, Nasen-; *sb.* Nasallaut, *m.*

nast|iness, Schmutz, *m.*; (*fig.*) Unflätigkeit, *f.*; **~y**, (*fig.*) unflätig; schmutzig; (*smell*) übel; (*taste*) schlecht.

nation, Nation, *f.*, Volk, *n.*; **~al**, national; **~al debt**, Staatsschuld, *f.*; **~alism**, Nationalismus, *m.*; **~alist**, Nationalist, *m.*; **~ality**, Staatsangehörigkeit, Nationalität, *f.*; **~alization**, Verstaatlichung, *f.*; **~alize**, verstaatlichen.

native, *a.* natürlich; angeboren; einheimisch; **~ country**, Heimat, *f.*; *sb.* Eingeborene(r).

nativity, die Geburt Christi.

natural, **~ly**, natürlich; **~ history**, Naturgeschichte, *f.*; **~ist**, Naturforscher, *m.*; **~ize**, einbürgern; (*plants*) akklimatisieren; **~ization**, Einbürgerung, *f.*; **~ness**, Natürlichkeit, Ungezwungenheit, *f.*

nature, Natur, *f.*; (*sort*) Eigenschaft, Beschaffenheit, *f.*; **by ~**, von Natur aus; **from ~**, nach der Natur.

naught, (*figure*) Null, *f.*; (*nothing*) Nichts, *n.*

naught|iness, Unartigkeit, Ungezogenheit, *f.*; **~y**, **~ily**, unartig, ungezogen.

nause|a, Ekel, *m.*; **~ate**, verabscheuen, sich ekeln (vor); **~ous**, ekelhaft.

nautical, See-, Schiffs-.

naval, See-, Schiffs-; **~ engagement**, Seegefecht, *n.*

nave, (*wheel*) Nabe, *f.*; (*church*) Schiff, *n.*

navel, Nabel, *m.*

navig|able, schiffbar, lenkbar; **~ate**, steuern, lenken; **~ation**, Schiffahrt, Seemannskunst, *f.*; **~ator**, Seefahrer, *m.*

navvy, Kanal-, Erd- arbeiter, *m.*

navy, (Kriegs)flotte, (Kriegs)marine, *f.*

neap tide, Nippflut, *f.*

near, *a.* nah(e); (*stingy*) geizig; *prep.* nahe (bei), neben, in der Nähe von; *v.* sich nähern; **~ly**, beinahe, fast; **~ness**, Nähe, *f.*; **~-sighted**, kurzsichtig.

neat, **~ly**, nett, sauber, niedlich; zierlich; (*spirits*) rein; **~ness**, Nettigkeit, Zierlichkeit, *f.*

nebulous, neblig, wolkig.

necessar|y, **~ily**, notwendig, nötig; **~ies**, Bedürfnisse, *n.pl.*

necessit|ate, nötigen, nötig machen; **~ous**, (not)dürftig; **~y**, Notwendigkeit, *f.*; (*want*) Not, *f.*; **of ~y**, notwendigerweise.

neck, Hals, *m.*; **~erchief**, Halstuch, *n.*; **~lace**, Halskette, *f.*; **~tie**, Binde, Kravatte, *f.*

necromancy, schwarze Kunst.

nectarine, Nektarine, *f.*

need, *sb.* Not, *f.*, Mangel, *m.*; **in case of ~**, im Notfalle; **there's no ~ to**, es ist nicht nötig zu; *v.t.* nötig haben; bedürfen; **~less**, unnötig; **~y**, bedürftig.

needle, Nadel, *f.*; **~work**, Näharbeit, Handarbeit, *f.*

nega|te, verneinen; **~tion**, Verneinung, *f.*; **~tive**, *a.* verneinend; *sb.* Verneinung, *f.*; (*photo*) Negativ, *m.*

neglect, *v.t.* vernachlässigen; *sb.* Vernachlässigung, *f.*; **~ful**, nachlässig.

negligen|ce, Nachlässigkeit, *f.*; **~t(ly)**, nachlässig.

negotia|te, unterhandeln (mit); (*bills*) begeben; **~tion**, Unterhandlung, *f.*; **~tor**, Unterhändler, *m.*

negr|o, Neger, *m.*; **~ess**, Negerin, *f.*

neigh, wiehern.

neighbour, Nachbar(in, *f.*), *m.*; **~hood**, Nähe, Nachbarschaft, *f.*; **~ly**, nachbarlich.

neither, *pron.* keine(r, s) von beiden; *conj.* weder; **~ ... nor**, weder ... noch.

nephew, Neffe, *m.*

nerv|e, Nerv, *m.*; (*fig.*) Kraft, *f.*, Mut, *m.*; **~ou(sly)**, nervös; nervig, kraftvoll; furchtsam; **~ousness**, Nervosität, *f.*

nest, Nest, *n.*

nestle, sich einnisten, sich anschmiegen.

net¹, *sb.* Netz, *n.*; *(fabric)* Tüll, *m.*; *(snare)* Garn, *n.*; *v.t.* fangen; ~ting, ~work, Netzwerk, *n.*

net², *a.* netto; ~price, Nettopreis, *m.*; ~weight, Nettogewicht, *n.*

nettle, Nessel, *f.*

neuralgia, Nervenschmerzen, *m.pl.*; Neuralgie, *f.*

neuritis, Nervenentzündung, *f.*

neuro|sis, Nervenkrankheit, Neurose, *f.*; ~tic, nervenkrank.

neuter, *sb.* Neutrum, *n.*; *a. (gram.)* sächlich; unparteiisch.

neutral, neutral; ~ity, Neutralität, *f.*; ~ize, neutralisieren; ausgleichen.

neutron, Neutron, *n.*

never, nie(mals); ~ mind, es tut (macht) nichts; ~more, nimmermehr; ~theless, dennoch, nichtsdestoweniger.

new, neu; frisch; unerfahren; ~comer, Neuling, *m.*, Fremde(r); ~laid, frisch; ~ly, neulich; kürzlich; ~ness, Neuheit, *f.*; **New Year**, Neujahr, *n.*; **New Year's Eve**, Silvesterabend, *m.*

news, Nachricht; Neuigkeit, *f.*; ~agent, Zeitungsverkäufer, *m.*; ~headline, Schlagzeile, *f.*; ~paper, Zeitung, *f.*; ~print, Zeitungspapier, *n.*; ~reel, Wochenschau, *f.*

newt, Wassermolch, *m.*

next, *a.* nächst; *(in time)* folgend; *adv.* zunächst, gleich darauf; ~ but one, two, &c., zweitnächste, drittnächste, &c.; ~door, im nächsten Hause; ~ of kin, Nächstverwandte(n); ~ time, das nächste Mal.

nib, Spitze, Feder, *f.*

nibble, nagen *(at* an); *(fishes)* anbeißen.

nice, ~ly, fein, nett; *(accurate)* genau; ~ness, Feinheit, Nettigkeit; Genauigkeit, *f.*; ~ty, Feinheit, Schärfe, Genauigkeit, *f.*

niche, Nische, *f.*

nick, *sb.* Kerbe, *f.*; *v.t.* kerben; *in the ~ of time*, g(e)rade zur rechten Zeit.

nickel, Nickel, *n.*; ~plated, vernickelt; ~ silver, Neusilber, *n.*

nickname, Spitzname, *m.*

nicotine, Nikotin, *n.*

niece, Nichte, *f.*

niggard|ly, karg, knauserig; ~liness, Kargheit, *f.*, Geiz, *m.*

nigger, Neger, *m.*

night, Nacht, *f.*; *by* ~, nachts; *last* ~, gestern abend; *to*~, heute abend; *stay the* ~, übernachten; ~cap, Schlafmütze, *f.*; *(fig., drink)* Nachttrunk, *m.*; ~dress, Damennachthemd, *n.*; ~fall, Einbruch *(m.)* der Nacht; ~jar, Ziegenmelker, *m.*; ~ly, nächtlich; jede Nacht; ~mare, Alp(druck), Nachtmahr, *m.*; ~school, Abendschule, *f.*; ~shade, Nachtschatten, *m.*; *deadly* ~shade, Tollkirsche, *f.*; ~shirt, Herrennachthemd, *n.*; ~time, Nacht-, Abend- zeit, *f.*

nightingale, Nachtigall, *f.*

nihilis|m, Nihilismus, *m.*; ~t, Nihilist, *m.*

nil, nichts.

nimbl|e, ~y, flink, hurtig; ~eness, Flinkheit, *f.*

nine, neun; ~pins, Kegelspiel, *n.*; ~teen, neunzehn; ~teenth, neunzehnte; ~tieth, neunzigste; ~ty, neunzig; **ninth**, neunte; ninthly, neuntens.

nip, *sb.* *(drink)* Schlückchen, *n.*; *v.a.* kneifen, (ab)zwicken; ~ *in the bud*, im Keime ersticken.

nipple, Brustwarze, *f.*

nit, Nisse, *f.*

nitr|ate, Nitrat, *n.*; ~e, Salpeter, *m.*; ~ic acid, Salpetersäure, *f.*; ~ogen, Stickstoff, *m.*; ~ous, salpetrig.

no, *adv.* nein; *a.* kein; ~body, ~ one, niemand.

nobility, Adel, *m.*

nobl|e, ~y, ad(e)lig; *(fig.)* edel; herrlich; ~eman, Ad(e)lige(r), Edelmann, *m.*; ~eness, Adel, *m.*

nocturnal, nächtlich.

nod, *sb.* Wink, *m.*, Kopfnicken, *n.*; *v.i.* nicken; *(doze)* schlummern.

node, Knoten, *m.*

nois|e, Lärm, *m.*; Geräusch, *n.*; ~eless, still, geräuschlos; ~y, ~ily, lärmend, geräuschvoll.

noisome, widerlich, ekelhaft.

nomad, Nomade, *m.*; ~ic, nomadisch.

nominal, ~ly, dem Namen nach; Namen-, Nenn-; ~ value, Nennwert, m.

nominate, ernennen; vorschlagen; ~ation, Ernennung, Aufstellung, f.; ~ative, Nominativ, m.; ~ee, Vorgeschlagene(r).

non-, nicht, Nicht-; only combinations not formed in this way are included below.

non-commissioned officer, Unteroffizier, m.

nonconformist, Dissident, m.

nondescript, unklassifizierbar, unbestimmt.

none, keine(r, s); ~ but, ausschließlich, nur.

nonentity, Nichtsein, f.; (person) nichtige Person, Null, f.

nonsense, Unsinn, m.; ~ical, unsinnig, albern.

non-stop, ohne Unterbrechung, ohne Pause; (train) durchgehend.

nook, Winkel, m., Ecke, f.

noon, Mittag, m.

noose, Schlinge, f.

nor, noch, auch nicht; neither . . . ~ . . ., weder . . . noch . . .

normal, ~ly, normal, regelrecht.

Norman, sb. Normanne, m.; a. normännisch.

north, sb. Norden, m.; a. and adv. nördlich, Nord-; ~-east, Nordost(en), m., nordöstlich; ~erly, ~ern, nördlich; northern lights, Nordlicht, n.; North Pole, Nordpol, m.; North Sea, Nordsee, f.; ~-ward(s), nordwärts, nördlich; ~-west, Nordwest(en), m., nordwestlich.

nose, Nase, f.; blow one's ~, sich schneuzen; lead by the ~, nasführen; turn up one's ~, die Nase rümpfen (at über); ~-dive, Sturzflug, m.; ~-gay, Blumenstrauß, m.

nostril, Nasenloch, n.

not, nicht; ~ yet, noch nicht; ~ long ago, vor kurzer Zeit.

notable, ~y, bemerkenswert, merkwürdig.

notary, Notar, m.

notation, Aufzeichnung, f.

notch, sb. Kerbe, f.

note, sb. Zeichen, Merkmal, n.;

Notiz, Anmerkung, f.; (mus.) Note, f., Ton, m.; (letter) Briefchen, n.; (bill) Zettel, m.; (distinction) Ruhm, m.; Wichtigkeit, f.; ~ of hand, Schuldschein, m.; take ~ of, Kenntnis nehmen von; take ~s, Notizen machen; v.t. notieren, aufzeichnen, niederschreiben; ~book, Notizbuch, n.; ~d, berühmt, bekannt; ~paper, Briefpapier, n.; ~worthy, merkwürdig, beachtenswert.

nothing, nichts; for ~, umsonst; make ~ of it, nicht daraus klug werden; next to ~, fast nichts; come to ~, nichts daraus werden; to say ~ of, geschweige denn.

notice, sb. Bemerkung, Beobachtung; (of dismissal) Kündigung, f.; give ~, kündigen; at the shortest ~, in kürzester Zeit; take ~, bemerken; take no ~, unbeachtet lassen; until further ~, bis auf weiteres; v.t. bemerken, beachten, Acht geben auf; ~able, ~ably, bemerklich, bemerkenswert.

notification, Benachrichtigung, f.; ~y, benachrichtigen, melden.

notion, Begriff, m., Idee, f., Einfall, m.

notoriety, Offenkundigkeit, f.; ~ious(ly), allbekannt, offenkundig; (bad sense) berüchtigt.

notwithstanding, prep. trotz, ungeachtet; conj. obgleich; adv. dennoch, trotzdem.

nought: see naught.

noun, Hauptwort, Substantiv, n.

nourish, ernähren; (fig.) unterhalten, hegen; ~ing, nahrhaft; ~ment, Nahrung, f.

novel, sb. Roman, m.; a. neu; ~ist, Romanschriftsteller, m.; ~ty, (newness) Neuheit; (thing) Neuigkeit, f.

November, November, m.

novice, Neuling, Anfänger, m.; (eccles.) Novize, m. and f.

now, jetzt, nun; just ~, soeben; well ~, nun denn; ~adays, heutzutage; ~ and then, dann und wann, manchmal.

nowhere, nirgends.

O

noxious, schädlich.

nozzle, Tülle, Düse, Schnauze, *f.*; Endrohr, *n.*

nucle|us, Kern, *m.*; ~ar, Kern-; ~ar fission, Kernspaltung, *f.*; ~ar physics, Kernphysik, *f.*

nud|e, nackt, bloß; *the* ~e, das Nackte, Akt, *m.*; ~ity, Nacktheit, *f.*

nudge, *sb.* leichter Stoß; *v.t.* leise anstoßen.

nugget, (Gold)klumpen, *m.*

nuisance, Unfug, Verdruß, *m.*

null, nichtig, ungültig; ~ify, ungültig machen; ~ity, Nichtigkeit, Ungültigkeit, *f.*

numb, starr, erstarrt (*with* vor); ~ness, Erstarrung, *f.*

number, *sb.* (*arith.*) Zahl, *f.*; (*one of a series*) Nummer, *f.*; (*numeral*) Ziffer, *f.*; (*quantity, number of*) Anzahl, Menge, (*gram.*) Numerus, *m.*, Zahl, *f.*; (*periodical*) Lieferung, *f.*; *v.t.* zählen, numerieren; ~less, unzählbar; ~plate, Nummernschild, *n.*

numeral, Zahlwort, *n.*, Ziffer, *f.*

numeration, Zählung, *f.*

numerical, ~ly, numerisch, Zahl(en)-.

numerous, ~ly, zahlreich.

numskull, Dummkopf, *m.*

nun, Nonne, *f.*; ~nery, Nonnenkloster, *n.*

nuptial, hochzeitlich; ~s, Hochzeit, *f.*

nurs|e, *sb.* Krankenpfleger(in, *f.*), *m.*; Kindermädchen, *n.*; *v.t.* warten, pflegen; (*fig.*) hegen; ~ery, Kinderstube, *f.*; (*plants*) Baumschule, *f.*; ~eryman, Handelsgärtner, *m.*; ~ery rhyme, Kinderliedchen, *n.*; ~ing, (Kranken)pflege, *f.*; ~ing home, Klinik, *f.*

nurture, *sb.* Ernährung; Erziehung, *f.*; *v.t.* ernähren, erziehen, aufziehen.

nut, Nuß, *f.*; (*mech.*) Schraubenmutter, *f.*; ~crackers, Nußknacker, *m.*; ~meg, Muskatnuß, *f.*; ~shell, Nußschale, *f.*

nutri|ment, Nahrung, *f.*; ~tion, Ernährung, *f.*; ~tious, ~tive, nährend, nahrhaft.

nymph, Nymphe, *f.*

oak, Eiche, *f.*; ~apple, Gallapfel, *m.*; ~en, eichen.

oakum, Werg, *n.*

oar, Ruder, *n.*; ~sman, Ruderer, *m.*

oasis, Oase, *f.*

oath, Eid, Schwur; (*curse*) Fluch, *m.*; take the ~, den Eid ablegen; on ~, eidlich.

oat|s, Hafer, *m.*; sow one's wild ~s, sich die Hörner ablaufen; ~cake, Haferkuchen, *m.*; ~meal, Hafermehl, *n.*

obdura|cy, Verstocktheit, Halsstarrigkeit, *f.*; ~te, verstockt, halsstarrig.

obedien|ce, Gehorsam, *m.*; ~t(ly), gehorsam, folgsam.

obelisk, Obelisk, *m.*

obey, gehorchen, folgen.

obituary, Todesanzeige, *f.*, Nachruf, *m.*

object[1], *sb.* Gegenstand; Zweck, *m.*; (*gram.*) Objekt, *n.*; ~ive(ly), *a. and adv.* objektiv, sachlich; *sb.* Ziel; Objektiv, *n.*

object[2], *v.i.* Einwendungen, Einspruch erheben (*to* gegen); ~ion, Einwand, *m.*; *to have no* ~ion, nichts dagegen haben; ~ionable, unerwünscht, nicht einwandfrei.

oblig|ation, Verpflichtung, *f.*; ~atory, verpflichtend, verbindlich; Pflicht-; ~e, verpflichten, nötigen; *I am* ~ed *to you for it,* ich bin Ihnen dafür sehr verbunden; ~ing(ly), verbindlich, gefällig.

oblique, schräg, schief.

obliv|ion, Vergessenheit, *f.*; ~ious, vergessend, vergeßlich.

oblong, *sb.* Rechteck, *n.*; *a.* länglich.

obloquy, Schande, Schmähung, Verleumdung, *f.*

obnoxious, ~ly, anstößig.

oboe, Oboe, *f.*

obscen|e, ~ely, unflätig, unzüchtig; ~ity, Unflätigkeit, Zote, *f.*

obscur|e, *a.*, ~ely, dunkel; niedrig; unklar; *v.t.* verdunkeln; verbergen; ~ity, Dunkelheit; Unklarheit, *f.*

obsequies, Leichenbegängnis, *n.*

obsequious, ~ly, unterwürfig, servil.

observ|ance, Beachtung, *f.*; Brauch, *m.*; ~ant(ly), achtsam, aufmerksam; ~ation, Beobachtung; (*remark*) Bemerkung, *f.*; ~atory, Sternwarte, *f.*; ~e, beobachten; bemerken; achten (auf); ~er, Beobachter; (*av.*) Orter, *m.*

obsess|ed, besessen (*with* von); ~ion, Besessenheit, *f.*

obsolete, veraltet.

obstacle, Hindernis, *n.*

obstin|acy, Hartnäckigkeit, Halsstarrigkeit, *f.*; ~ate(ly), hartnäckig, halsstarrig; eigenwillig.

obstruct, hindern, hemmen; verstopfen; ~ion, Hindernis, *n.*; Verstopfung, *f.*; ~ive, hinderlich.

obtain, *v.t.* bekommen, erhalten, erlangen; *v.i.* sich finden, herrschen; ~able, zu erhalten, erhältlich.

obtru|de, *v.t.* aufdrängen; *v.i.* sich aufdrängen; ~sive(ly), aufdringlich.

obviate, vermeiden, zuvorkommen.

obvious, ~ly, augenscheinlich, augenfällig, deutlich, offenbar.

occasion, *sb.* Gelegenheit, *f.*, Anlaß, *m.*; (*need*) Veranlassung, Notwendigkeit, *f.*; *v.t.* veranlassen; ~al, gelegentlich, zufällig; ~ally, zuweilen.

occident, Westen, *m.*; Abendland, *n.*; ~al, westlich; abendländisch.

occult, verborgen, geheim; ~ation, Verfinsterung, *f.*

occup|ancy, Besitznahme, *f.*; ~ant, Inhaber, Besitzergreifer, *m.*; ~ation, Besitzergreifung, Besetzung, *f.*; (*calling*) Beschäftigung, *f.*, Geschäft, *n.*, Beruf, *m.*; ~ier, Inhaber, Mieter, *m.*; ~y, innehaben, besitzen (*mil.*) besetzen; (*office*) bekleiden; ~y oneself with, sich beschäftigen mit.

occur, sich ereignen, vorkommen, geschehen; *it occurs to me*, es fällt mir ein; ~rence, Ereignis,

n., Vorfall, *m.*

ocean, Ozean, *m.*, Weltmeer, *n.*

ochre, Ocker, *m.*

o'clock: see clock.

octagon, Achteck, *n.*; ~al, achteckig.

octave, Oktave, *f.*

October, Oktober, *m.*

ocul|ar, Augen-, augenscheinlich; ~ist, Augenarzt, *m.*

odd, ~ly, (*number*) ungerade; (*single*) einzeln, vereinzelt; (*strange*) sonderbar, seltsam; ~ity, ~ness, Sonderbarkeit, Seltsamkeit, *f.*; ~s, Ungleichheit; Wahrscheinlichkeit, *f.*; (*chances*) (ungleiche) Wette, *f.*; *at ~s*, uneinig.

ode, Ode, *f.*

odious, ~ly, verhaßt.

odo|ur, Geruch, *m.*; *be in bad ~ur*, schlecht angeschrieben sein; ~rous, duftend.

of, *prep.* von; (*out of, made of*), aus; (*among*) unter; (*time*) an, in; ~ course, natürlich; *a pound of tea*, ein Pfund Tee; *a glass of wine*, ein Glas Wein; *the city of London*, die Stadt London.

off, *adv.*, ab- fort, weg; entfernt; *prep.* von; *int.* fort! weg!; ~ *and on*, ab und zu; *to be ~*, weg-, fort-gehen; *badly* (*well*) ~, schlecht (gut) daran; ~ colour, (*fig.*) nicht auf der Höhe; ~ duty, dienstfrei; ~ season, stille Saison; ~side, abseits.

offal, (Fleisch)abfall, *m.*

offence, Beleidigung, *f.*; Verstoß (*against* gegen) *m.*; Übertretung, *f.* (*with pers.*); *give ~*, beleidigen; *take ~ at*, jemandem etwas übelnehmen.

offend, *v.t.* beleidigen, ärgern; *v.i.* sündigen, verstoßen (*against* gegen); *be ~ed at*, sich über etwas ärgern; ~er, Beleidiger; (*law*) Delinquent, Missetäter, *m.*

offensive, *a.*, ~ly, anstößig, beleidigend; *sb.* (*mil.*) Offensive, *f.*

offer, *sb.*, Angebot, Anerbieten, *n.*; ~ *of marriage*, Heiratsantrag, *m.*; *v.t.* anbieten, darbringen; (*bid*) bieten; (*sacrifice*) opfern; *v.i.* sich zeigen, sich erbieten; ~ing, Opfer; Erbieten, *n.*;

~tory, (eccles.) Kollekte, Opfer-gabe, f.

off-hand, unvorbereitet; auf der Stelle; (person) kurz ange-bunden.

office, Amt, n., Dienst, m.; Büro, n.; Foreign Office, Auswärtiges Amt; post ~, Postamt, n.; ~boy, Laufbursche, m.; ~hours, Amts-, Geschäfts- stunden, f.pl.

officer, (mil.) Offizier, m.; (civil) Beamte(r).

official, a., ~ly, amtlich, offiziell; sb. Beamte(r).

officiate, amtieren; (eccles.) den Gottesdienst halten.

officious, ~ly, zudringlich; über-trieben dienstfertig; ~ness, Zudringlichkeit, f.

offprint, Sonderdruck, m.

offshoot, Sprößling, m.; (fig.) Abzweigung, f.

offspring, Nachkommenschaft, f., Nachkömmling, Sproß, m.

often, oft, oftmals.

ogle, liebäugeln.

ogre, Menschenfresser, m.

oh, oh, ach.

oil, sb. Öl, n.; v.t. (ein)ölen; ~cloth, Wachstuch, n.; ~field, Petroleum-, Öl- feld, n.; ~painting, Ölgemälde, n.; ~skin, (naut.) Ölzeug, n.; ~well, Ölbohrung, f.; ~y, ölig, fettig.

ointment, Salbe, f.

old, alt; ~ age, Alter, n.; ~fashioned, altmodisch; ~ish, ältlich; ~world, altertümlich.

olive, Olive, f.; Ölbaum, m.; ~oil, Olivenöl, n.

omelet, Eierkuchen, m., Omelett, n.

omen, Vorzeichen, n., Vorbe-deutung, f.

ominous, ~ly, drohend, unheil-voll.

omission, Unterlassung, Auslas-sung, f.

omit, unterlassen, auslassen.

omnipoten|ce, Allmacht, f.; ~t, allmächtig.

omniscien|ce, Allwissenheit, f.; ~t, allwissend.

on, prep. (on surface of) auf; (on side of) an; (date) an; (occasion) bei, zu; (causal) aus, mit, von;

(pity, mercy, &c.) mit, über; adv. an, auf, darauf; weiter; and so ~, und so weiter; ~ fire, in Flammen; ~ foot, horseback, &c., zu Fuß, Pferde; ~ purpose, absichtlich; ~ Sundays, &c., jeden Sonntag, &c.; ~ the con-trary, im Gegenteil; ~ the way (to), unterwegs, auf dem Wege (nach); keep ~ (doing some-thing), fortfahren zu; live ~, leben von; put (coat, boots, &c.) ~, anziehen; put one's hat ~, den Hut aufsetzen; turn ~, andrehen.

once, einmal; (formerly) vormals, einst; at ~, sofort, sogleich; ~ more, noch einmal.

one, num. eins, ein(e); pron. einer, eine, eins; (indefinite) man, jemand; any~, jemand; every~, jeder, jede, jedes; no ~, niemand; ~ another, einander; ~ day, eines Tages; the only ~, der, die, das Einzige; it is all ~ to me, es ist mir ganz gleich, einerlei; be at ~ with, mit (jemandem) einverstanden sein; ~ness, Einheit, f.; ~'s, sein(e); ~self, sich (selbst); ~sided, einseitig; ~way street, Ein-bahnstraße, f.

onerous, lästig.

onion, Zwiebel, f.

onlooker, Zuschauer, m.

only, a. einzig; adv. allein, nur; ~ yesterday, erst gestern; he has ~ to, er hat nur (zu); not ~ . . . but also, nicht nur . . . sondern auch.

onslaught, Angriff, m.

onus, Last, f.

onward, vorwärts.

ooze, sb. Schlamm, m.; v.i. ab-fließen, sickern.

opaque, undurchsichtig.

open, a., ~ly, offen, auf; (not hidden) offenbar; (frank) auf-richtig; freimütig; in the ~, im Freien; keep ~ house, offenes Haus halten; with an ~ mind, vorurteilsfrei; with ~ mouth, gaffend; v.t. (er)öffnen, aufmachen; v.i. sich öffnen, aufgehen; ~handed, freigebig; ~ing, Öffnung, f.; (beginning)

Anfang, *m.*; (*opportunity*) Gelegenheit, *f.*; ~-minded, vorurteilsfrei; ~ness, Offenherzigkeit, *f.*

opera, Oper, *f.*; ~-glass, Opernglas, *n.*; ~hat, Klapphut, *m.*; ~house, Opernhaus, *n.*; ~tic, opernhaft.

opera|te, wirken, tätig sein; (*surgery*) operieren; ~tion, Wirkung; Operation, *f.*; ~tive, *a.* wirksam; *sb.* Arbeiter, *m.*; ~tor, Wirkende(r); Operateur, *m.*; *wireless* ~tor, Funker, Funktelegraphist, *m.*

opiate, Opiat, *n.*

opinion, Meinung, Ansicht, *f.*; ~ poll, Meinungsumfrage, *f.*

opium, Opium, *n.*

opponent, Gegner, *m.*

opportun|e, ~ely, gelegen, passend, rechtzeitig; ~ity, Gelegenheit, *f.*

oppose, entgegen-setzen, -stellen; widerstehen.

opposi|te, *sb.* Gegenteil, *n.*; *a.* entgegengesetzt; *prep.* gegenüber; ~tion, Widerstand, *m.*; (*pol.*) Opposition, *f.*

oppress, unterdrücken; ~ion, Unterdrückung, *f.*; ~ive(ly), (er)drückend; ~or, Unterdrücker, *m.*

opprobrious, ~ly, schimpflich.

optic, ~al, optisch, Seh-; ~ian, Optiker, *m.*; ~s, Optik, *f.*

optim|ism, Optimismus, *m.*; ~ist, Optimist, *m.*; ~istic(ally), optimistisch.

option, Wahl, *f.*; ~al, freigestellt.

opulen|ce, Reichtum, *m.*; Wohlhabenheit, *f.*; ~t(ly), wohlhabend.

or, oder; ~ *else*, sonst, andernfalls.

orac|le, Orakel, *n.*; ~ular, orakelhaft, geheimnisvoll.

oral, ~ly, mündlich.

orange, *sb.* Orange, *f.*; (*sweet orange*) Apfelsine, *f.*; *a.* orangefarben; ~-blossom, Orangenblüte, *f.*

ora|tion, Rede, *f.*; ~tor, Redner, *m.*; ~torical, rednerisch; ~torio, Oratorium, *n.*; ~tory, Redekunst, *f.*; (*eccles.*) Orato-

rium, *n.*, (Bet)kapelle, *f.*

orbit, (Kreis)lauf, *m.*, Bahn, *f.*

orchard, Obstgarten, *m.*

orchestra, Orchester, *n.*

orchid, Orchidee, *f.*

ordain, bestimmen, verordnen; (*eccles.*) ordinieren.

ordeal, Gottesurteil, *n.*, (*fig.*) (Feuer)probe, *f.*; Schreckenserlebnis, *n.*

order, *sb.* (*arrangement*) Ordnung, Reihenfolge, *f.*; (*rank*) Rang, *m.*; (*decoration*) Orden, *m.*; (*command*) Befehl, *m.*; (*commerc.*) Bestellung, *f.*; *in* ~ *to*, um ~ zu; *in good* ~, in gutem Zustand; *call to* ~, zur Ordnung rufen; *in* ~, zur Sache (gehörig); in Ordnung; der Reihe nach; *out of* ~, nicht zur Sache (gehörig); nicht in Ordnung; *made to* ~, auf Bestellung gemacht; *payable to* ~, an die Order von ~ zahlbar; *until further* ~s, bis auf weiteren Befehl; *a.* befehlen; (*commerc.*) bestellen; (*arrange*) anordnen; ~ly, *a.* regelmäßig; (*conduct*) sittsam; *sb.* (*mil.*) Ordonnanz, *f.*; ~s, (*eccles.*) geistlicher Stand; *take holy* ~s, in den geistlichen Stand treten.

ordinal, Ordnungszahl, *f.*

ordinar|y, ~ily, gewöhnlich, gebräuchlich.

ordination, (Priester)weihe, *f.*

ordnance, Artillerie, *f.*; ~ map, Generalstabskarte, *f.*; ~ survey, Landesvermessung, *f.*

ore, Erz, *n.*

organ, (*anat. and fig.*) Werkzeug, Organ, *n.*; (*mus.*) Orgel, *f.*; ~ic, organisch; ~ism, Organismus, *m.*; ~ist, Orgelspieler, *m.*; ~ization, Organisation, Einrichtung; Vereinigung, *f.*; ~ize, organisieren, einrichten; ~-stop, Orgelregister, *n.*

orgy, Orgie, *f.*; Festgelage, *n.*

orient, Osten, *m.*, Morgenland, *n.*; ~al, *a.* östlich; *sb.* Orientale, *m.*

origin, Ursprung, *m.*, Herkunft, *f.*; ~al(ly), *a. and adv.* ursprünglich, neu; *sb.* Urbild; Original, *n.*; ~ality, Ursprünglichkeit, *f.*

Originalität, *f.*; ~ate, entstehen, entspringen; ~ator, Urheber, *m.*

ornament, *sb.* Putz, *m.*, Verzierung, *f.*; *v.t.* verzieren, ~al, Zier-; ~ation, Ausschmückung, *f.*

ornate, stark verziert.

orphan, Waise, *f.*; ~age, Waisenhaus, *n.*; Waisenstand, *m.*

orthodox, rechtgläubig; ~y, Rechtgläubigkeit, *f.*

orthography, Rechtschreibung, *f.*

oscilla|te, schwingen; ~tion, Schwingung, *f.*

osprey, Fischadler, *m.*

ossif|ication, Verknöcherung, *f.*; ~y, (sich) verknöchern.

ostensib|le, ~ly, scheinbar, angeblich.

ostenta|tion, Prahlerei, *f.*; Gepränge, *n.*; ~tious(ly), prahlerisch.

ostler, Stallknecht, *m.*

ostrich, Strauß, *m.*

other, ander; *every* ~ *day,* alle zwei Tage; *the* ~ *day,* vor einigen Tagen; *someone or* ~, irgendeiner; ~wise, anders, sonst.

otter, Fischotter, *m.*

Ottoman, Ottomane, *m.*; (*sofa*) Ottomane, *f.*

ought, *aux.v.* sollte(n); ~ *to have.* hätte . . . sollen.

ounce, Unze, *f.*; (*zool.*) Luchs, *m.*

our, unser(e); ~s, (*pron.*) der (die, das) uns(e)rige; ~selves, wir (uns) selbst.

oust, ausstoßen, austreiben.

out, *adv.* aus; draußen; heraus; hinaus; *nicht zu Hause;* (*fire*) ausgelöscht; (*light*) abgedreht; *to be* ~ *of,* nicht mehr haben; *just* ~, soeben erschienen; *speak* ~, frei heraus sprechen; *throw* ~, verwerfen; herauswerfen; ~ *of,* aus, ohne, außer; ~ *of breath,* außer Atem; ~ *of cash,* ohne Geld; ~ *of date,* veraltet; ~ *of doors,* draußen; ~ *of place,* verlegt; unpassend; ~ *of print,* vergriffen; ~ *of sight,* außer Sicht; ~ *of sorts,* unpäßlich; ~ *of stock,* ausverkauft; ~ *of tune,*

verstimmt; ~ *of work,* arbeitslos.

outbreak, Ausbruch, *m.*

outbuilding, Nebengebäude, *n.*

outburst, Ausbruch, *m.*

outcast, *a.* verstoßen; *sb.* Verstoßene(r).

outcome, Ergebnis, *n.*, Folge, *f.*

outcry, Ausruf, Schrei, *m.*

outdo, übertreffen.

outdoor, im Freien; Außen-.

outer, äußer, Außen-; ~ *cover,* (*tire*) Mantel. *m.*; ~most, äußerst.

outfit, Ausstattung, Ausrüstung, *f.*

outgrow, entwachsen.

outhouse, Nebengebäude, *n.*

outing, Ausflug, *m.*

outlast, überdauern.

outlaw, Geächtete(r); *v.t.* in die Acht erklären.

outlay, Ausgabe, *f.*

outlet, Ausgang, *m.* (*commerc.*) Absatzgebiet, *n.*

outline, *sb.* Umriß, *m.*, Skizze, *f.*; Entwurf. *m.*; *v.t.* entwerfen, skizzieren.

outlive, überleben.

outlook, Aussicht, *f.*, Ausblick, *m.*

outlying, fernliegend; auswärtig.

outnumber, an Zahl übertreffen.

outpost, Vorposten, *m.*

output, Ausstoß, Ertrag, *m.*, Produktion, Leistung, *f.*

outrage, *sb.* Schimpf, *m.*, Gewalttätigkeit, *f.*; *v.t.* beschimpfen; jemandem Gewalt antun; ~ous(ly), schimpflich; unerhört.

outright, gänzlich, völlig; (*laugh*) laut.

outset, Anfang, Beginn, *m.*

outside, *sb.* Außenseite, *f.*; *adv.* außen; außerhalb; draußen; *prep.* ausserhalb; *at the very* ~, höchstens; ~ *left,* right, (*football*) Linksaußen, Rechtsaußen, *m.*; ~r, Außenseiter, *m.*

outskirts, Umgebung, *f.*

outspoken, freimütig.

outstanding, (*debt*) ausstehend; (*fig.*) hervorragend.

outvote, überstimmen.

outward, ~ly, äußerlich; nach auswärts; ~s, auswärts.

outwit, überlisten.

oval, *sb.* Oval, *n.*; *a.* oval, eirund.

oven, (Back)ofen, *m.*

over, *prep.* über; *adv.* hinüber, herüber; (*ended*) vorbei; (*excessive*) zu, übermäßig; (*remaining*) übrig; (*entirely*) ganz; all ~, über und über; ganz vorbei; it's all ~ with him, es ist alles aus mit ihm; ~ *and above*, darüber hinaus; ~ *again*, noch einmal; carry ~ (*book-keeping*), übertragen; get ~ (*recover*), überstehen; give ~, aufhören; aufgeben; hand ~, übergeben; remain ~, übrigbleiben.

overall. Arbeitsmantel. *m.*; ~s, Überhosen. *f.pl.*, Arbeitsanzug, *m.*

overawe, in Furcht setzen (*or* halten).

overbearing, gebieterisch.

overboard, über Bord.

overcast, bewölkt.

overcoat, Überzieher, Mantel, *m.*

overcome, überwinden.

overcrowded, überfüllt.

overdo, übertreiben; sich überarbeiten; zu lange (stark) kochen (braten); ~ne, (*fig.*) übertrieben; (*exhausted*) erschöpft.

overdraft, Debetsaldo, *m.*

overdue, überfällig.

overflow, *sb.* Überfluß, Überlauf, *m.*; *v.i.* überfließen.

overgrown, überwachsen.

overhaul, *v.t.* (*overtake*) überholen; gründlich prüfen; *sb.* gründliche Reparatur.

overhead, oben, Ober-; ~ expenses, Generalunkosten, *pl.*; ~ railway, Hochbahn, *f.*

overhear, zufällig hören.

overheat, überheizen; ~ed, überhitzt.

overjoyed, entzückt (*at* über).

overlap, übergreifen.

overload, überladen.

overlook, sehen ... über; beaufsichtigen; (*ignore*) hingehen lassen; (*neglect*) vernachlässigen; übersehen; ~er, Aufseher, *m.*

overpower, überwältigen.

overrate, überschätzen.

override, (*fig.*) überschreiten, umstoßen.

overrule, verwerfen, zurückweisen.

overrun, überlaufen; überwältigen, verheeren.

overseer, Aufseher, *m.*

overshoot, ~ the mark, über das Ziel hinausschießen.

oversight, by an ~, aus Versehen.

oversleep, sich verschlafen.

overstrain, sich überanstrengen.

overtake, einholen, überholen.

overtax, (*fig.*) überbürden.

overthrow, *sb.* Umsturz, *m.*; *v.t.* umstürzen; absetzen.

overtime, Überstunden, *f.pl.*; Mehrarbeit, *f.*

overture, (*mus.*) Ouvertüre, *f.*; (*fig.*) Vorschlag, *m.*

overturn, umwerfen, umstürzen.

overweight, Übergewicht, *n.*

overwhelm, *v.t.* überwältigen; überhäufen.

overwork, *v.t.* überfordern; *v.i.* sich überarbeiten.

ow|e, jemandem schuldig sein; (*fig.*) verdanken; ~ing, schuldig; ~ing to, dank (*with dat.*), zufolge (*with gen.*)

owl, Eule, *f.*

own, *v.t.* (*possess*) besitzen, haben; (*admit*) bekennen, gestehen; *a.* eigen; that is not my ~, das gehört mir nicht; hold one's ~, sich behaupten; ~er, Eigentümer, *m.*; ~ership, Eigentum(srecht), *n.*

ox, Ochs(e), *m.*, Rind, *n.*

oxid|e, Oxyd, *n.*; ~ize, oxydieren.

oxygen, Sauerstoff, *m.*; ~ apparatus, Sauerstoffapparat, *m.*, Sauerstoffgerät, *n.*

oyster, Auster, *f.*; ~-catcher (*zool.*), Austernfischer, *m.*

ozone, Ozon, *n.*

P

pace, *sb.* Schritt, Gang, *m.*; *v.t.* abschreiten; *v.i.* schreiten.

pacific, *a.* friedlich, friedliebend; *sb.* (*with cap.*) Stiller Ozean; ~ation, Befriedung, Beruhigung, *f.*

pacif|ism, Pazifismus, *m.*; ~ist, Pazifist, *m.*; ~y, beruhigen, befrieden.

pack, *sb.* Bündel, *n.*, Ballen, *m.*; (*cards*) Spiel, *n.*; (*hounds*) Meute, *f.*; (*wolves*) Rudel, *n.*;

v.t. (ein)packen; vollstopfen; *v.i.* einpacken; ~age, ~et, Paket, *n.*; ~et-boat, Postdampfer, *m.*; ~horse, Saumpferd, *n.*; ~ice, Packeis, *n.*; ~ing, Verpackung, *f.*; Packmaterial, *n.*

pact, Vertrag, *m.*

pad, *sb.* Polster, Kissen, *n.*; (*of writing*) Schreibblock, *m.*; (*of animal's foot*) Fußballen, *m.*; *v.t.* polstern, wattieren; ~ding, Polsterung, Wattierung, *f.*, Füllmaterial, *n.*

paddle, *sb.* Paddel, *f.* or *n.*; *v.t.* paddeln; plantschen; ~boat, Raddampfer, *m.*; ~box, Radkasten, *m.*

paddock, Gehege, *n.*

padlock, *sb.* Vorlegeschloß, *n.*; *v.t.* mit einem Vorlegeschloß verschließen

padre, Feldgeistliche(r).

pagan, *sb.* Heide, *m.*; *a.* heidnisch; ~ism, Heidentum, *n.*

page, Seite, *f.*; (*boy*) Page, *m.*

pageant, Festzug; Prunk, *m.*

pail, Eimer, *m.*

pain, *sb.* Schmerz, *m.*; Pein, *f.*; *v.t. and i.* schmerzen; ~ful(ly), schmerzhaft; ~less(ly), schmerzlos; ~s, Mühe, *f.*; ~staking, arbeitsam, sorgfältig.

paint, *sb.* Farbe; (*for face*) Schminke, *f.*; *v.t.* malen; (*house*, *&c.*) anstreichen; (*face*) schminken; ~brush, Malerpinsel, *m.*; ~er, (*artist*) Maler; (*house*) Anstreicher, *m.*; (*naut.*) Fangleine, *f.*; ~ing, Malerei, *f.*, Gemälde, *n.*

pair, *sb.* Paar, *n.*; *v.i.* sich paaren.

pal, Kamerad, *m.*

palace, Palast, *m.*; Schloß, *n.*

palat|e, Gaumen, *m.*; ~able, schmackhaft; ~al, Gaumenlaut, *m.*

palatial, palastartig, herrlich.

pale, ~ly, *a.* blaß, bleich; *v.i.* blaß werden; ~ness, Blässe, *f.*

palette, Palette, *f.*

paling, Pfahlzaun, *m.*

pall, *sb.* Bahrtuch; Pallium, *n.*; *v.i.* langweilig werden.

pallet, Strohsack, *m.*

palliat|e, lindern; beschönigen; ~ive, Linderungsmittel, *n.*

pallid, blaß, bleich.

palm, *sb.* (*tree*) Palme; (*of hand*) Handfläche, *f.*; *v.t.* ~ off, (*jemandem etwas*) aufschwindeln; ~ist, Handwahrsager (in, *f.*), *m.*; ~istry, Handwahrsagerei, *f.*; **Palm Sunday**, Palmsonntag, *m.*

palpable, fühlbar, handgreiflich.

palpitat|e, klopfen, pochen; ~ion, Herzklopfen, *n.*

paltry, armselig, erbärmlich.

pamper, verzärteln.

pamphlet, Broschüre, Flugschrift, *f.*

pan, Pfanne, *f.*; ~cake, *sb.* Pfann-, Eier- kuchen, *m.*; *v.i.* (*aircraft*) absacken.

panacea, Allheilmittel, *n.*

pandemonium, Höllenlärm, *m.*

pander, ~to, Vorschub leisten (*with dat.*); (*jemandem*) willfahren.

pane, Fensterscheibe, *f.*

panegyric, Lobrede, *f.*

panel, Füllung, *f.*; Fach, Feld, *n.*; Kassenarztliste, *f.*; ~ling, Täfelung, *f.*

pang, Stich, *m.*; Angst, Qual, *f.*

panic, Panik, *f.*; ~stricken, von Schrecken ergriffen.

panorama, Panorama, *n.*, Rundblick, *m.*

pansy, (*bot.*) Stiefmütterchen, *n.*

pant, keuchen, schnauben; (*nach Luft*) schnappen.

panther, Panther, *m.*

pantomime, Pantomime, *f.*

pantry, Speisekammer, *f.*

pants, Unterhose, *f.*

pap, Kinderbrei, *m.*; (*teat*) Brustwarze, *f.*

papa, Papa, *m.*

pap|acy, Papsttum, *n.*; ~al, päpstlich.

paper, *sb.* Papier, *n.*; (*wall-paper*) Tapete, *f.*; (*leaflet*) Zettel, *m.*; (*newspaper*) Zeitung, *f.*; (*examination paper*) Examensfragen, *f.pl.*; (*dissertation*) Abhandlung, *f.*; *a.* papieren; *v.t.* tapezieren; ~back, Paperback, *n.*; ~bag, Tüte, *f.*; ~fastener, Heftklammer, *f.*; ~hanger, Tapezier(er), *m.*; ~ money, Papiergeld, *n.*; ~-weight, Briefbeschwerer, *m.*

papier mâché, Papiermaché, *n.*

Papist, Papist, *m.*

par, Pari, *n.*; Parikurs, *m.*; at ~, pari.

parable, Parabel, *f.*, Gleichnis, *n.*

para|chute, *sb.* Fallschirm, *m.*; *v.i.* abspringen; ~-schirmjäger, *m.pl.* Luftlandetruppen, *f.pl.*

parade, *sb.* Parade, *f.*; Prunk, *m.*; *v.t.* prunken mit; *v.i.* (in Parade) aufziehen.

Paradise, Paradies, *n.*

paradox, Paradoxon, *n.*

paraffin, (*oil*) Petroleum; (*chem.*) Paraffin, *n.*

paragon, Muster, Vorbild, *n.*

paragraph, Paragraph, Absatz, *m.*

parallel, *sb.* Parallele, Parallellinie; Ähnlichkeit, *f.*; (*of latitude*) Breitenkreis, *m.*; *a.* parallel; entsprechend; *v.t.* vergleichen; gleichsetzen; ~bars, Barren, *m.*; ~ogram, Parallelogramm, *n.*

paraly|se, lähmen; ~sis, Lähmung, *f.*; ~tic, gelähmt.

paramount, oberst, höchst.

parapet, Brustwehr, *f.* Geländer, *n.*

paraphernalia, Zubehör, *n.*, Ausrüstung, *f.*

paraphrase, *sb.* Umschreibung, *f.*; *v.t.* umschreiben.

parasit|e, Schmarotzer, *m.*; ~ic, schmarotzerhaft.

parasol, Sonnenschirm, *m.*

paratrooper, Fallschirmjäger, *m.*

parcel, *sb.* Paket; Stück, *n.*; *v.t.* (ein)teilen; ~post, Paketpost, *f.*

parch, dörren, austrocknen.

parchment, Pergament, *n.*

pardon, *sb.* Verzeihung; Begnadigung, *f.*; *I beg your* ~, (ich bitte um) Verzeihung; wie beliebt?; *v.t.* verzeihen; begnadigen.

pare, schälen; schneiden.

parent, Vater, *m.*, Mutter, *f.*; ~s, Eltern, *pl.*; ~age, Herkunft, Abstammung, *f.*

parenthesis, Parenthese, *f.*

parish, Kirchspiel, *n.*, Pfarre, *f.*; ~ioner, Gemeindemitglied, *n.*

parity, Gleichheit, *f.*

park, *sb.* Park, *m.*; *v.t.* parken; ~ing-place, Parkplatz, *m.*

parlance, Redeweise, *f.*

parley, *sb.* Unterhandlung, *f.*; *v.i.* unterhandeln.

parliament, Parlament, *n.*; ~ary, Parlaments-.

parlour, Empfangszimmer, *n.*; ~-maid, Stubenmädchen, *n.*

parochial, Gemeinde-, Pfarr-.

parody, *sb.* Parodie, *f.*; *v.t.* parodieren.

parole, Parole, Losung, *f.*, Losungswort, *n.*; on ~, auf Ehrenwort.

paroxysm, Paroxysmus, heftiger Anfall, *m.*

parricide, Vatermord; Vatermörder, *m.*

parrot, *sb.* Papagei, *m.*; *v.t.* nachplappern.

parse, analysieren.

parsimon|ious, sparsam, knauserig; ~y, Sparsamkeit, Knauserei, *f.*

parsley, Petersilie, *f.*

parsnip, Pastinake, *f.*

parson, Pfarrer, *m.*; ~age, Pfarrhaus, *n.*

part, *sb.* (An)teil, *m.*; (*district*) Gegend, *f.*; Stadtteil, *m.*; (*theatr.*) Rolle, *f.*; *for my* ~, meinerseits; *for the most* ~, größtenteils; *take in good* ~, gut aufnehmen; *v.t.* teilen, trennen; (*hair*) scheiteln; *v.i.* scheiden, sich trennen, abreisen; ~ *with*, loswerden; aufgeben; ~-song, mehrstimmiges Lied; ~time, Kurz-, Neben-.

partake, teilnehmen (*of* an); (Mahl, etc.) genießen.

partial, ~ly teilweise; parteiisch, eingenommen für; ~ity, Parteilichkeit; Vorliebe, *f.*

particip|ant, Teilnehmer, *m.*; ~ate, teilnehmen (*in* an); ~ation, Teilnahme, *f.*

participle, Partizip(ium), *n.*

particle, Teilchen, *n.*; (*gram.*) Partikel, *f.*

particular, *a.* ~ly, besonder; einzeln; umständlich; wählerisch, genau; *in* ~, im besonderen; *sb.* Einzelheit, *f.*,

Umstand, *m.*; ~ize, ausführlich angeben.

parting, Scheiden, *n.*, Trennung, *f.*; (*hair*) Scheitel, *m.*

partisan, Anhänger, Partisan, *m.*

partition, *sb.* Teilung, *f.*; Scheidewand, *f.*; Fach, *n.*, Verschlag, *m.*; *v.t.* (ab)teilen.

partly, teils, zum Teil.

partner, *sb.* (*trade*) Teilhaber, *m.*; (*cards*) Partner, Mitspieler, *m.*; (*dancing*) Tänzer(in, *f.*), *m.*; *v.t.* (mit jemandem) tanzen, spielen; ~ship, Teilhaberschaft, Assoziation, *f.*

partridge, Rebhuhn, *n.*

party, (*political*, *law*, &c.) Partei; (*pleasure*) Gesellschaft; Partie, Party; (*person*) Person, *f.*; ~line, Parteilinie, *f.*

parvenu, Emporkömmling, Parvenü, *m.*

pass, *sb.* (*way*) (Eng)paß, *m.*; (*safe conduct*, *ticket*, &c.) Reisepaß, *m.*, Freikarte, *f.*; (*fig.*) Zustand, *m.*, Lage, *f.*; (*football*) Zuspielen, *n.*; *v.t.* passieren; (*accounts*, &c.) genehmigen; (*examination*) bestehen; (*football*) weitergeben; (*overtake*) überholen; (*resolution*) annehmen; *v.i.* gehen, vorübergehen; *come to* ~, geschehen, sich ereignen; ~ *away*, vergehen; (*die*) entschlafen; ~ *by*, vorübergehen; ~ *for*, gelten für; ~ *over*, übersehen; ~ *round*, herumreichen; ~ *through*, durchgehen; ~able, passierbar; mittelmäßig; ~book, Kontobuch, *n.*; ~ing, vorübergehend; *in* ~ing, im Vorübergehen, beiläufig; ~key, Hauptschlüssel, *m.*; ~port, Paß, *m.*; ~word, Losungswort, Paßwort, *n.*

passage, (Durch)gang, Korridor, *m.*; (*sea*) Überfahrt, *f.*; (*in book*) Stelle, *f.*; (*of time*) (Ver)lauf, *m.*

passenger, Reisende(r), Passagier, Fahrgast, *m.*

passer-by, Vorübergehende(r).

passion, Leidenschaft, *f.*; Zorn, *m.*; (*of Christ*) Passion, *f.*, Leiden (*n.*) Christi; ~ate(ly), leidenschaftlich; ~flower, Passionsblume, *f.*; ~week, Kar-

woche, *f.*

passive, *sb.* (*gram.*) Passiv, *n.*; *a.*, ~ly, leidend, passiv; ~ resistance, passiver Widerstand.

Passover, Passah, *n.*

past, *sb.* Vergangenheit, *f.*; *a.* vergangen; *prep.* an . . . vorbei; über . . . hinaus; *half* ~ *seven*, halb acht; *quarter* ~ *seven*, Viertel nach sieben, Viertel (auf) acht.

paste, *sb.* Kleister; Teig, *m.*; *v.t.* kleistern, kleben; ~board, Karton, *m.*, Pappe, *f.*

pasteurize, pasteurisieren.

pastime, Zeitvertreib, *m.*

pastor, Pfarrer, *m.*; ~al, ländlich; pastoral.

pastry, Konditorwaren, *f.pl.*, Gebäck, *n.*; ~cook, Konditor, *m.*

pasture, Weide, *f.*

pat, *sb.* leichter Schlag, Klaps, *m.*; (*of butter*, &c.) Klacks, *m.*; *a.* treffend; *v.t.* patschen, klopfen, streicheln.

patch, *sb.* Flicken, *m.*; *v.t.* flicken, ausbessern.

patent, *sb.* Patent, *n.*; (*of nobility*) Adelsbrief, *m.*; *a.* patentiert; offen, bekannt; *v.t.* patentieren; ~ee, Patentinhaber, *m.*; ~ fastener, Druckknopf, *m.*; ~ leather, Lackleder, *m.*; ~ medicine, Markenmedizin, *f.*

patern|al, väterlich; ~ity, Vaterschaft, *f.*

path, Pfad, Weg, *m.*; ~finder, Pfadfinder; (*air*) Zielbeleuchter, *m.*

pathetic, ~ally, pathetisch, rührend, ergreifend.

patholog|ical, pathologisch; ~y, Pathologie, Krankheitslehre, *f.*

pathos, Pathos, *n.*

patien|ce, Geduld, *f.*; ~t, *sb.* Patient(in, *f.*), *m.*; Kranke(r); *a.*, ~tly, geduldig.

patrimony, Erbteil, Erbgut, *n.*

patriot, Patriot, Vaterlandsfreund, *m.*; ~ic(ally), patriotisch; ~ism, Vaterlandsliebe, *f.*

patrol, *sb.* Patrouille, *f.*, Streifzug, *m.*; Spähtrupp, *m.*; *v.i.* patrouillieren; ~ vessel, Vorpostenboot, *n.*

patron, Gönner, Schutzherr, *m.*; ~age, Gönnerschaft, *f.*, Schutz, *m.*; ~ize, beschützen, unterstützen.

pattern, Muster, *n.*

paucity, geringe Zahl, *f.*

paunch, Wanst, *m.*

pauper, Arme(r); ~ism, Armut, *f.*; ~ize, arm machen.

pause, *sb.* Pause, *f.*, Ruhepunkt, *m.*; *v.i.* pausieren, sich bedenken.

pav|e, pflastern; ~ement, Pflaster, *n.*, Bürgersteig, *m.*; ~ing-stone, Pflasterstein, *m.*

pavilion, Zelt, *n.*, Pavillon, *m.*

paw, *sb.* Pfote, Tatze, *f.*; *v.t.* scharren.

pawn, *sb.* Pfand, *n.*; (*chess*) Bauer, *m.*; *v.t.* verpfänden; ~broker, Pfandleiher, *m.*; ~shop, Leihhaus, *n.*; ~ticket, Pfandschein, *m.*

pay, *sb.* Lohn, (*mil.*) Löhnung, *f.*; *v.t.* (be)zahlen; *v.i.* sich rentieren; ~ attention, achtgeben (to *auf*); ~ off, abbezahlen; entlassen, abmustern; ~ out, (*rope*) ausstecken; ~able, zahlbar, fällig; ~ee, Empfänger, *m.*; ~master, Zahlmeister, *m.*; ~ment, Bezahlung, Belohnung, *f.*; ~ pause, Lohnstopp, *m.*

pea, Erbse, *f.*; *sweet* ~, Edelwicke, *f.*; ~nut, Erdnuß, *f.*; ~shooter, Blasrohr, *n.*; ~soup, Erbsensuppe, *f.*

peace, Friede(n), *m.*, Ruhe, *f.*; ~able, ~ably, ~ful(ly), friedlich.

peach, Pfirsich, *m.*

pea|cock, Pfau, *m.*; ~hen, Pfauhenne, *f.*

peak, Gipfel, *m.*, Spitze, *f.*; (*of cap*) Schirm, *m.*; ~hour, Hauptverkehrszeit, *f.*; ~load, Spitzenlast, *f.*

peal, *sb.* (*bells*) Geläute, *n.*; (*thunder*) Gekrach, *n.*, Donnerschlag, *m.*; *v.i.* (*bells*) läuten; (*thunder*) rollen; (*trumpets*) schmettern.

pear, Birne, *f.*; ~tree, Birnbaum, *m.*

pearl, Perle, *f.*

peasant, Bauer, *m.*; ~ry, Bauern, *m.pl.*

peat, Torf, *m.*

pebble, Kiesel, *m.*

peck, picken, hacken.

peculiar, ~ly, eigentümlich; besonder(s); ~ity, Eigentümlichkeit, *f.*

pecuniary, Geld-.

pedagogue, Erzieher, Pädagog(e), *m.*

pedal, *sb.* Pedal, *n.*, Fußhebel, *m.*; *v.i.* radfahren; treten.

pedant, Pedant, *m.*; ~ic, pedantisch; ~ry, Pedanterie, *f.*

peddle, hausieren.

pedestal, Fußgestell, Postament, *n.*

pedestrian, Fußgänger, *m.*

pedigree, Stammbaum, *m.*

pedlar, Hausierer, *m.*

peel, Schale, Rinde, *f.*; *v.t.* schälen; *v.i.* sich schälen.

peep, *sb.* kurzer verstohlener Blick; *v.i.* gucken.

peer[1], Pair, *m.*, Adlige(r), Ebenbürtige(r); ~age, Adel, *m.*; ~less, unvergleichbar.

peer[2], *v.i.* gucken, spähen.

peevish, ~ly, verdrießlich.

peg, *sb.* Pflock; Kleiderhaken, *m.*; *v.t.* ~down, niederhalten; ~out, (ein Stück Land) abstecken.

pelican, Pelikan, *m.*

pellet, Kügelchen, *n.*

pellicle, Häutchen, *n.*

pell-mell, durcheinander, ganz verworren.

pelvis, Becken, *n.*

pen, *sb.* (Schreib)feder, *f.*; (*for sheep*) Hürde, *f.*; (*for submarines, &c.*) Bunker, *m.*; *v.t.* niederschreiben; einpferchen; ~friend, Brieffreund, *m.*; ~knife, Taschenmesser, *n.*; ~nib, Federspitze, *f.*

penal, Straf-; ~ servitude, Zuchthausstrafe, *f.*; ~ize, bestrafen, belasten; ~ty, Strafe, Buße, *f.*; (*football*) Strafstoß, *m.*

penance, Buße, *f.*

pencil, *sb.* (Blei)stift, *m.*; *v.t.* zeichnen; ~sharpener, Bleistiftspitzer, *m.*

pend|ant, *sb.* Gehänge, *n.*; Kronleuchter, *m.*; Wimpel, *m.*; ~ent, *a.* hängend, schwebend; ~ing, *a.* schwebend; *prep.* während.

pendulum, Pendel, *m.* or *n.*

penetrat|e, durchdringen; ~ion,

Durchdringung, *f.*; Scharfsinn, *m.*

penguin, Pinguin, *m.*

peninsula, Halbinsel, *f.*

peniten|ce, Reue, Buße, *f.*; ~t, *sb.* Büßer; *a.*, ~tly, bußfertig; ~tiary, Korrektionsanstalt, *f.*

penmanship, Schreibkunst, *f.*

pennant, pennon, Wimpel, *m.*

penniless, bedürftig, ohne Geld.

penny, Penny, *m.*

pension, *sb.* Pension, *f.*; *old-age* ~, Altersversorgung, *f.*; *v.t.* pensionieren; ~able, pensionsberechtigt; ~er, Pensionär, *m.*, Pensionierte(r).

pensive, ~ly, nachdenklich, tiefsinnig; ~ness, Nachdenklichkeit, *f.*, Tiefsinn, *m.*

Pentecost, Pfingsten, *n.* or *pl.*

penur|ious, dürftig, karg; ~y, Armut, Not, *f.*

peony, Päonie, Pfingstrose, *f.*

people, *sb.* Leute, *pl.*, Volk, *n.*; *v.t.* bevölkern.

pepper, *sb.* Pfeffer, *m.*; *v.t.* pfeffern; ~mint, Pfefferminze, *f.*

per, durch; *as* ~, laut; ~ cent, Prozent, *n.*

perambulat|e, durchwandern; ~or, Kinderwagen, *m.*

perceive, wahrnehmen; bemerken.

percentage, Prozentsatz, *m.*

percept|ible, wahrnehmbar; ~ion, Wahrnehmung, Empfindung, *f.*

perch, *sb.* (*pole*) Stange, *f.*; (*fish*) Barsch, *m.*; *v.i.* sich niederlassen, sitzen (auf).

perchance, vielleicht, von ungefähr.

percolat|e, durchsickern; ~or, Filtrierapparat, Filter, *m.*

percussion, Schlag, *m.*; Perkussion, Erschütterung, *f.*; ~ cap, Zündhütchen, *n.*; ~ instrument, Schlaginstrument, *n.*

perdition, Verderben, *n.*

peremptor|y, ~ily, gebieterisch, dogmatisch; unbedingt.

perennial, ausdauernd;(*bot.*) perennierend.

perfect, *sb.* Perfekt(um), *n.*; *a.* vollkommen, vollendet; *v.t.* vervollkommnen, vollenden; ~ion, Vollkommenheit, Vollendung, *f.*

perfid|ious, treulos; ~y, Treulosigkeit, *f.*

perforat|e, perforieren, durchbohren; ~ion, Durchbohrung, Durchlochung, *f.*; Loch, *n.*; ~or, Locher, *m.*

perform, *v.t.* vollziehen, ausführen, erfüllen; aufführen, vortragen; *v.i.* spielen, wirken; ~ance, Leistung; Vorstellung, Aufführung, *f.*; ~er, Schauspieler(in, *f.*), *m.*

perfume, *sb.* Wohlgeruch, *m.*, Parfüm, *n.*; *v.t.* parfümieren; ~ry, Parfümerien, *f.pl.*

perfunctory, oberflächlich.

perhaps, vielleicht.

peril, Gefahr, *f.*, ~ous(ly), gefährlich.

perimeter, Umkreis, *m.*

period, Periode, *f.*; Zeitraum, *m.*; (*full stop*) Punkt, *m.*; ~ical, *sb.* Zeitschrift, *f.*; *a.*, ~ically, periodisch.

periphrasis, Umschreibung, *f.*

periscope, Sehrohr, *n.*

perish, umkommen, verderben, zu Grunde gehen; ~able, leicht verderblich.

periwinkle, (*bot.*) Immergrün, *n.*

perjur|e, falsch schwören; ~er, Meineidiger(r); ~y, Meineid, *m.*

permanen|ce, Fortdauer, *f.*; ~t(ly), dauernd, Dauer-, beständig; ~t wave, Dauerwelle, *f.*; ~t way, Bahnkörper, *m.*

permeate, durchdringen.

permiss|ible, zulässig; ~ion, Erlaubnis, *f.*

permit, *sb.* Erlaubnis-, Passierschein, *m.*; *v.t.* erlauben.

pernicious, ~ly, schädlich, verderblich.

peroxide, Hyperoxyd, *n.*

perpendicular, *sb.* senkrechte Linie, *f.*; Lot, *n.*; *a.*, ~ly, senkrecht.

perpetrat|e, verüben; ~ion, Verübung, *f.*

perpet|ual, ~ually, immerwährend, ewig; ~uate, verewigen, (für immer) fortsetzen; ~uity, Ewigkeit, *f.*

perplex, verwirren, bestürzt machen; ~ity, Verwirrung, Bestürzung, *f.*

perquisites, Nebeneinkünfte, Sporteln, *pl.*

persecut|e, verfolgen; ~ion, Verfolgung, *f.*

persever|e, beharren, aushalten; ~ance, Beharrlichkeit, Ausdauer, *f.*; ~ing, beharrlich.

Persian, *sb.* (*person*) Perser, *m.*; (*lang.*) Persisch, *n.*; *a.* persisch.

persist, beharren, bleiben (*in, bei*); ~ence, Beharrlichkeit, *f.*; ~ent(ly), beharrlich.

person, Person, *f.*; *in* ~, persönlich; ~al(ly), persönlich; ~ality, Persönlichkeit, *f.*

personat|e, vorstellen, darstellen; ~ion, Darstellung, *f.*

personif|ication, Personifikation, Verkörperung, *f.*; ~y, personifizieren, verkörpern.

personnel, Personal, *n.*

perspective, Perspektive; Fernsicht, *f.*

perspicac|ious, scharfsichtig; ~ity, Scharfblick, *m.*

perspir|e, schwitzen; ~ation, Schweiß, *m.*

persua|de, überzeugen; überreden; ~sion, Überzeugung; Überredung, *f.*; ~sive, überzeugend.

pert, ~ly, keck, vorwitzig; ~ness, Keckheit, *f.*

pertinac|ious, halsstarrig, eigensinnig; beharrlich; ~ity, Beharrlichkeit, *f.*

pertinent, treffend, passend.

perturb, beunruhigen, verwirren.

perus|al, Durchsicht, *f.*, Durchlesen, *n.*; ~e, durchlesen.

pervade, durchdringen.

pervers|e, ~ely, verdorben; verstockt, eigensinnig; ~ion, Verdrehung, Perversion, *f.*; ~ity, Verdorbenheit; Verkehrtheit, *f.*; Eigensinn, *m.*

pervert, *sb.* Abtrünnige(r); perverse(r) Mensch; *v.t.* verführen.

pessim|ism, Pessimismus, *m.*; ~ist, Pessimist, *m.*

pest, Pest, Seuche, Plage, *f.*

pester, plagen, belästigen.

pestilence, Pest, Seuche, *f.*

pet, *sb.* Liebling, *m.*, Lieblingstier, *n.*; *a.* Lieblings-; *v.t.* verzärteln, verhätscheln; ~ name, Kosename, *m.*

petal, Blumenblatt, *n.*

peter, ~ out, verpuffen.

petition, *sb.* Bittschrift, *f.*; Gesuch, *n.*; *v.t.* petitionieren, bitten; ~er, Bittsteller, *m.*

petrel, Sturmvogel, *m.*

petrif|action, Versteinerung, *f.*; ~y, versteinern.

petrol, Benzin, *n.*; ~ pump, Tankstelle, *f.*

petroleum, Petroleum, Erdöl, *n.*

petticoat, Unterrock, *m.*

pett|iness, Geringfügigkeit; Kleinlichkeit, *f.*; ~y, gering; kleinlich; ~y officer, Unteroffizier, *m.*

petulan|ce, Launenhaftigkeit, Verdrießlichkeit, *f.* ~t; übellaunig, verdrießlich.

pew, Kirchenstuhl, *m.*

pewit, Kiebitz, *m.*

pewter, Schüsselzinn, *n.*

phantom, Phantom, Gespenst, *n.*

Pharisee, Pharisäer, *m.*

phase, Phase, *f.*

pheasant, Fasan, *m.*

phenomen|al, phänomenal; ~on, Phänomen, *n.*, Erscheinung, *f.*

phial, Fläschchen, *n.*

philanthrop|ic, menschenfreundlich; ~ist, Menschenfreund, *m.*; ~y, Menschenliebe, *f.*

philatel|ist, Briefmarkensammler, *m.*; ~y, Philatelie, *f.*

Philistine, Philister, *m.*

philolog|ical, philologisch; ~ist, Philolog, Sprachforscher, *m.*; ~y, Philologie, Sprachwissenschaft, *f.*

philosoph|er, Philosoph, *m.*; ~ical(ly), philosophisch; ~y, Philosophie, *f.*

phonetics, Phonetik, *f.*

phosphate, Phosphat, *n.*

phosphor|escent, phosphoreszierend; ~us, Phosphor, *m.*

photograph, *sb.* Photographie, *f.*, Lichtbild, *n.*; *v.t.* photographieren, aufnehmen; ~er, Photograph, *m.*; ~y, Photographie, *f.*

photostat, *sb.* Photokopie, *f.*; *v.t.* photokopieren.

phrase, Phrase, Redensart, *f.*; ~ology, Ausdrucksweise, *f.*

phthisis, Schwindsucht, *f.*

physic|al, physikalisch; körperlich; ~al training, Leibeserziehung, f.; ~ian, Arzt, m.; ~ist, Physiker, m.; ~s, Physik, f.

physiology, Physiologie, f.

pian|ist, Klavierspieler, m.; ~o, Klavier, n.

pick, sb. (implement) (Spitz)hacke; (choice) Auswahl, f.; v.t. (choose) auswählen; (fruit) lesen; (teeth) stochern; ~ a quarrel, Streit anfangen (with mit); ~ out, auswählen; aushacken; ~ up, aufheben, aufnehmen; ~axe, Spitzhaue, f.; ~ed, auserlesen; Elite-; ~pocket, Taschendieb, m.; ~-up (gramophone, &c.), Schalldose, f., Tonabnehmer, m.

picket, sb. Feldwache, f.; Streikposten, m.; v.t. durch Streikposten absperren.

pickle, Pökel, m., Eingepökelte(s), n.; v.t. einpökeln; (in Essig) einmachen; ~s, Pickels, pl.

picnic, Picknick, n.

picture, Bild; Gemälde, n.; ~ postcard, Ansichtskarte, f.; ~s, Kino, n.; ~sque, malerisch.

pie, Pastete, Torte, f.

piebald, scheckig.

piece, sb. Stück, n.; v.t. (zusammen)flicken; ~meal, stückweise; ~work, Stückarbeit, f.

pier, Mole, f., Pier, m.; (of bridge) Pfeiler, m.

pierce, durchdringen, durchbohren.

piety, Frömmigkeit, f.

pig, Schwein, n.; ~-iron, Roheisen, n.; ~sty, Schweinestall, m.; ~tail, Zopf, m.

pigeon, Taube, f.

pigment, Farbstoff, m.

pigmy: see pygmy.

pike, (weapon) Pike, f.; (fork) (Heu)gabel, f.; (fish) Hecht, m.

pile, sb. (heap) Haufen, m.; (stake) Pfahl, m.; (of fabric) Noppe, f., Flor, m. (atomic) Meiler, m.; v.t. aufhäufen; ~ arms, die Gewehre zusammensetzen; ~driver, Ramme, f.; ~d arms, Gewehrpyramide, f.; ~s, Hämorrhoiden, pl.

pilfer, stehlen, mausen; ~ing,

Diebstahl, m., Mauserei, f.

pilgrim, Pilger, m.; ~age, Pilgerfahrt, Wallfahrt, f.

pill, Pille, f.; ~box (mil.), Betonunterstand, Bunker, m.

pillage, sb. Plünderung, f.; v.t. plündern.

pillar, Pfeiler, m.; ~box, Straßenbriefkasten, m.

pillion, Soziussitz, m.

pillory, sb. Pranger, m.; v.t. an den Pranger stellen.

pillow, Kopfkissen, n.; ~case, Kissenüberzug, m.

pilot, sb. (naut.) Lotse; (air) Pilot, Führer, m.; v.t. steuern; lotsen; ~ engine, Vorläufer, m.; ~ scheme, Versuchsprogramm, n.

pimple, Pickel, m.; Pustel, f.

pin, sb. Stecknadel, f.; (mech.) Stift, Pflock, m.; v.t. anstecken; annadeln; festhalten; ~ down, festlegen; ~cushion, Nadelkissen, n.; ~point, v.t. genau treffen; ~prick, Nadelstich, m.; ~up girl, Pin-up Girl, n.

pinafore, Kinderschürze, f.

pince-nez, Kneifer, Klemmer, m.

pincers, Kneifzange, f.

pinch, sb. Kniff, m.; (snuff, &c.) Prise, f.; v.t. kneifen, zwicken; drücken; (steal) klemmen.

pine[1], die Kiefer, f.

pine[2], v.i. schmachten (for nach); ~ away, verschmachten.

pineapple, Ananas, f.

ping-pong, Pingpong, n.

pinion, sb. Fittich, m.; v.t. fesseln.

pink, sb. (colour) Rosa, n.; Fleischfarbe, f.; (flower) Nelke, f.; a. rosa(farbig).

pinnace, Pinasse, f.

pinnacle, Zinne, f.; Gipfel, m.

pint, Pinte, f.; halbes Liter.

pioneer, Pionier, Bahnbrecher, m.

pious, ~ly, fromm.

pip, (fruit) Kern; (on shoulderstrap) Stern, m.

pipe, sb. Rohr, n., Röhre, f.; (tobacco and mus.) Pfeife, f.; v.i. pfeifen; ~clay, Pfeifenton, m.; ~dream, Wunschtraum, m.; ~line, Ölleitung, Rohrleitung, f.; ~r, Pfeifer, m.

piquant, ~ly, beißend; pikant.

pique, sb. Groll, m.; v.t. reizen.

pira|cy, Seeräuberei, f.; unbefugter Nachdruck; **~te,** Seeräuber; Nachdrucker, m.

pistol, Pistole, f.

piston, Kolben, m.

pit, sb. Grube, f.; (theatr.) Parterre, n.; v.t. mit Narben überziehen; gegeneinander hetzen; **~head,** (mine) Schachteingang, m.

pitch, sb. (substance) Pech, n.; (mus.) Tonhöhe, f.; (degree) Grad, m.; (slope) Abhang, m., Neigung, f.; (throw) Wurf, m.; (sport) Spielplatz, m.; v.t. (throw) werfen; (tent) aufschlagen; v.i. (ship) stampfen; (birds, &c.) sich niederlassen; **~blende,** Pechblende, f.; **~dark,** stockfinster; **~ed battle,** regelrechte Schlacht; **~fork,** Heugabel, f.; **~ing** (ship) Stampfen, n.; **~pine,** Pechkiefer, f.

pitcher, Krug, m.

piteous, **~ly,** kläglich, erbärmlich.

pitfall, Fallgrube, f.

pith, Mark, n., Kern, m.; **~y,** markig, kräftig.

piti|able, erbärmlich; **~ful(ly),** mitleidig; kläglich; **~less(ly),** unbarmherzig, mitleidslos.

pittance, kleine Portion, f.; Bißchen, n.; Bettellohn, m.

pity, sb. Mitleid, n.; it's a **~,** es ist schade; v.t. bemitleiden, bedauern.

pivot, sb. Zapfen, Drehpunkt, m.; v.i. sich drehen (um).

placard, sb. Plakat, n.; v.t. anschlagen.

place, sb. Platz, Raum, m., Stelle, f., Ort, m.; (office) Amt, n., Stelle, f.; v.t. stellen, legen, setzen; **~name,** Ortsname, m.

placid, gelassen, ruhig; **~ity,** Gelassenheit, f.

plagiar|ism, Plagiat, n.; **~ist,** Plagiator, m.

plague, Pest, Seuche, f.; (fig.) Plage, f.; v.t. plagen.

plaice, Scholle, f.

plain, sb. Fläche; Ebene, f.; a., **~ly,** (level) eben, flach; (simple) einfach; (clear) deutlich, klar;

(appearance) nicht hübsch; **~clothes,** Zivil, n.; **~dealing,** ehrliches Handeln; **~ness,** Klarheit; Offenheit, Aufrichtigkeit; Einfachheit; Häßlichkeit, f.; **~spoken,** freimütig.

plaintiff, Kläger, m.

plaintive, **~ly** klagend.

plait, sb. Falte, f.; (hair) Flechte, f., Zopf, m.; v.t. flechten.

plan, sb. Plan; Grundriß, m.; v.t. entwerfen, aufzeichnen; planen.

plane, sb. Fläche, f.; (tool) Hobel, m.; (aviation) Flugzeug, n.; Tragfläche, f.; v.t. hobeln; **~tree,** Platane, f.

planet, Planet, Wandelstern, m.

plank, Planke, Bohle, f.

plant, sb. Pflanze, f.; (industry) Maschinen, f.pl., Anlage, f.; v.t. pflanzen, bebauen; **~er,** Pflanzer, m.

plantain, (weed) Wegerich; (banana) Pisang, m.

plantation, Pflanzung, f.; Gehölz, n.

plaster, sb. Verputz, Mörtel, m.; (med.) Pflaster, m.; **~of Paris,** Gips, m.; v.t. verputzen; begipsen; **~er,** Gipsarbeiter, m.

plastic, sb. Kunststoff, Preßstoff, m.; a. plastisch.

plate, sb. (for food) Teller, m.; Silbergeschirr, n.; (metal, photog., &c.) Platte, f.; (engraving) Kupferstich, m.; v.t. überziehen; versilbern, vernickeln; armour—~d, ramiert, Panzergepanzert; gold—~d, vergoldet; silver—~d, versilbert; **~glass,** Spiegelglas, n.; **~layer,** Schienenleger, Streckenarbeiter, m.

plateau, Hochebene, f.

platform, (railway) Bahnsteig, m.; (raised floor) Tribüne, f.; (politics) politisches Programm.

platinum, Platin, n.

platitude, Gemeinplatz, m.

platoon, Trupp, m.

plausib|le, **~ly,** scheinbar gut, annehmbar; **~ility,** das täuschend Einnehmende.

play, sb. Spiel, n.; (theatr.) Schauspiel, n.; (scope) Spielraum, m.; v. spielen; **~back,** Rückspielen, n.; **~bill,** Theaterzettel, m.;

~er, Spieler; Schauspieler, *m.*;
~ful(ly), scherzhaft, spiele-
risch; ~ground, Spielplatz,
m.; ~mate, Spielgefährte, *m.*;
~thing, Spielzeug, *n.*

plea, *sb.* Einwand, *m.*, Einrede, *f.*;
(*law*) Prozess, Rechtsgrund, *m.*

plead, plädieren; sich entschuldigen (mit); ~ *guilty*, sich
schuldig bekennen.

pleasant, ~ly, angenehm; ~ness,
Annehmlichkeit, *f.*; ~ry,
Scherz, *m.*

please|e, gefallen; befriedigen; *if
you* ~*e*, bitte; ~ing, angenehm,
gefällig.

pleasur|e, Vergnügen; Belieben,
n.; ~able, angenehm, ergötzlich.

pleat, *sb.* Falte, *f.*, Plissee, *n.*; *v.t.*
plissieren, falten.

pledge, *sb.* Pfand, *n.*; Bürgschaft,
f.; *v.t.* verpfänden; verpflichten;
zutrinken.

plenipotentiary, Bevollmächtig-
te(r).

plenteous, ~ly, reichlich, voll.

plentiful, ~ly, reichlich, ergiebig.

plenty, *sb.* Fülle, *f.*, Überfluß, *m.*;
~ *of*, genug, reichlich.

pleurisy, Brustfellentzündung, *f.*

pliant, biegsam, (*fig.*) nachgiebig.

pliers, (Draht)zange, *f.*

plight, *sb.* Zustand, *m.*; *v.t.* verpfänden.

plinth, Plinthe, Säulenplatte, *f.*

plod, sich fortschleppen; büffeln,
ochsen; ~der, Büffler, *m.*

plot, *sb.* Anschlag, Putsch, *m.*,
Verschwörung, *f.*; (*of drama*)
Handlung, *f.*; (*land*) Stück
(Land), Grundstück, *n.*; (*grass*)
Rasenplatz, *m.*; *v.i.* sich ver-
schwören; *v.t.* aussinnen;
(*course*) abstecken, bestimmen;
~ter, Verschwörer, Anstifter, *m.*

plough, *sb.* Pflug, *m.*; *v.t.* pflügen;
~man, Ackersmann, *m.*;
~share, Pflugschar, *f.*

plover, Regenpfeifer, *m.*

pluck, *sb.* (*courage*) Mut, *m.*; *v.t.*
pflücken; (*fowl*) rupfen; ~ *up
courage*, Mut fassen; ~y, ~ily,
mutig.

plug, *sb.* Pflock, Stöpsel; (*electr.*)
Stecker, *m.*; *sparking-* ~ Zünd-

kerze, *f.*; *v.t.* zustopfen; ~ *in*,
anschließen, hineinstecken.

plum, Pflaume, *f.*; ~-**pudding**,
Plumpudding, *m.*; ~-**tree**,
Pflaumenbaum, *m.*

plumage, Gefieder, *n.*

plumb, *a.* senkrecht; *v.t.* sondieren;
~er, Klempner, Installateur,
m.; ~-**line**, Lot, *n.*, Lotleine, *f.*

plume, (Schmuck)feder, *f.*

plump, fleischig, feist, rundlich.

plunder, *sb.* Beute, *f.*; Raub, *m.*;
v.t. plündern.

plunge, *sb.* Tauchen, *n.*; Sturz, *m.*;
v.i. untertauchen; sich stürzen;
(*of horse*) ausschlagen; *v.t.* ~ *in*,
hineinstoßen; ~r, Tauch-
kolben, *m.*

plural, Mehrzahl, *f.*

plus, plus; und; mehr; ~ *fours*,
weite Kniehosen, *f.pl.*

plush, Plüsch, *m.*

ply, *sb.* Falte, *f.*; *v.t.* bedrängen;
zusetzen; *v.i.* ~ *between*,
zwischen . . . verkehren;
~**wood**, Sperrholz, *n.*

pneumatic, Luft-, pneumatisch;
~ *tire*, Luftreifen, *m.*

pneumonia, Lungenentzündung, *f.*

poach, *v.i. and t.* wildern; unbefugt betreten; ~ed *eggs*,
verlorene Eier, *n.pl.*; ~er,
Wilddieb, *m.*; ~ing, Wild-
dieberei, *f.*

pocket, *sb.* Tasche, *f.*; *a.* Klein-,
Taschen-; *v.t.* einstecken; ~ *of
resistance*, Widerstandsnest, *n.*;
~ *battleship*, Panzerschiff, *n.*,
Schlachtkreuzer, *m.*; ~-**book**,
Brieftasche, *f.*; ~-**handkerchief**, Taschentuch, *n.*;
~-**money**, Taschengeld, *n.*; ~-
size, Taschenformat, *n.*

pod, Hülse, Schale, Schote, *f.*

poem, Gedicht, *n.*

poet, Dichter, *m.*; ~-**aster**, Dichter-
ling, *m.*; ~**ess**, Dichterin, *f.*;
~**ic(al)**, poetisch; ~**ics**, Poetik,
f.; ~**ry**, Dichtkunst, Dichtung,
Poesie, *f.*

poignan|**cy**, Schärfe, *f.*; ~**t**,
scharf, schmerzhaft.

point, *sb.* (*dot, boxing, rations, &c.*)
Punkt, *m.*; (*sharp*) ~ Spitze, *f.*;
(*of land*) Landspitze, *f.*; (*compass*) Strich, *m.*; (*electr.*) Steck-

kontakt, *m.*: (*of joke*) Pointe, *f.*;
Kern, *m.*; (*object*) Zweck, *m.*;
decimal ~, Dezimalstelle, *f.*;
turning-~, Wendepunkt, *m.*; *to
the* ~, treffend; *come to the* ~,
zur Sache kommen; *on the* ~ *of*,
im Begriffe; ~ *of view*, Gesichtspunkt, *m.*; *v.t.* (*aim*) zielen (*at*
auf); (*pencil*) zuspitzen; ~ *at*,
mit dem Finger zeigen; ~
blank, *sb.* Kernschuß(weite, *f.*),
m.; *a.* direkt: offen; ~duty,
Postendienst. *m.*; ~ed, zuge-
spitzt, spitzig; (*remark*) treffend,
durchschlagend; ~er, Zeiger,
m.; (*dog*) Pointer, Vorstehhund,
m.; ~less, inhaltslos, witzlos;
sinnlos; ~s, (*railway*) Weiche,
f.; (*rations*) Punkte, *m.pl.*

poise, *sb.* Gleichgewicht, *n.*, Haltung, *f.*; *v.t.* im Gleichgewicht
halten, balancieren.

poison, *sb.* Gift, *n.*; *v.t.* vergiften;
~er, Giftmischer, *m.*; ~ gas,
Giftgas, Kampfgas, *n.*; ~ous,
giftig.

poke, stoßen; (*fire*) schüren; ~ *fun
at*, sich über (jemanden) lustig
machen; ~r, Schüreisen; (*game*)
Poker, *n.*

polar, polar, Pol-; ~ bear, Eisbär,
m.; ~ circle, Polarkreis, *m.*;
~ized, polarisiert.

pole, (*North, South, electr.*) Pol, *m.*;
(*wooden*) Stange, *f.*, Pfahl, *m.*;
~axe, Streitaxt, *f.*; ~cat, Iltis,
m.; ~jump, Stabhochsprung,
m.; ~star, Polarstern, *m.*

polemic(al), Streit-; ~s, Polemik, *f.*

police, Polizei, *f.*; ~man, Polizist,
Schutzmann, *m.*; ~ station,
Polizei- amt, *n.*, -wache, *f.*;
~woman, Polizistin, *f.*

policy, Politik, *f.*; (*insurance*)
Police, *f.*

polish, *sb.* Politur, *f.*, Glanz,
Schliff, *m.*; *v.t.* polieren; (*glass*)
schleifen; ~ed, poliert; elegant.

polite, ~ly, höflich; ~ness, Höflichkeit, *f.*

politic, weltklug; schlau; ~al(ly),
politisch; ~al economy, Volks-
wirtschaft, *f.*; ~ian, Politiker,
m.; ~s, Politik, *f.*

poll, *sb.* Wahl, Abstimmung, *f.*;
v.i. (ab)stimmen; ~ing-booth,

Wahlzelle, *f.*; ~ster, Meinungs-
forscher, *m.*; ~tax, Kopf-
steuer, *f.*

pollen, Blütenstaub, *m.*

pollut|e, verunreinigen; ~ion,
Verunreinigung, *f.*

polo, Polo(spiel), *n.*; ~neck,
Rollkragen, *m.*

polygamy, Vielweiberei, *f.*

polyglot, vielsprachig.

polygon, Vieleck, *n.*

pomade, Pomade, *f.*

pomegranate, Granatapfel, *m.*

Pomeranian, (*dog*) Spitz, *m.*

pommel, Degenknauf; Sattelknopf,
m.

pomp, Pracht, *f.*; ~osity, Prah-
lerei, Wichtigtuerei, *f.*;
~ous(ly), pompös; prahlerisch.

pond, Teich, *m.*

ponder, erwägen; ~ous, schwer.

pontiff, Hohepriester; Papst, *m.*;
~ical, päpstlich; feierlich.

pontoon, Ponton, *m.*; ~-bridge,
Pontonbrücke, *f.*

pony, Pony, *n.*

poodle, Pudel, *m.*

pooh! pah!; ~-pooh, spöttisch
verwerfen.

pool, *sb.* Pfuhl, Teich, *m.*; (*gaming*)
Einsatz, *m.*; (*com.*) Ring, *m.*,
Kartell, *n.*; *v.t.* zusammenlegen;
~s, (*football*) Pools, *m.pl.*

poor, arm, dürftig; schlecht;
the ~, die Armen; ~ly, ärmlich;
(*unwell*) unpäßlich; ~ness,
Armut, Niedrigkeit, *f.*

pop, *sb.* Knall, Puff, *m.*; *v.i.*
knallen; ~-gun, Knallbüchse, *f.*

Pop|e, Papst, *m.*; ~ery, Papismus,
m.; ~ish, papistisch.

poplar, Pappel, *f.*

poplin, Popeline, *f.*

poppy, Mohn, *m.*

populace, Pöbel, *m.*, Menge, *f.*

popular, ~ly, volkstümlich; beliebt; ~ity, Volkstümlichkeit,
Beliebtheit, *f.*; ~ize, populari-
sieren, verbreiten.

populat|e, bevölkern; ~ion, Be-
völkerung, *f.*

populous, volkreich.

porcelain, Porzellan, *n.*

porch, Vorhalle, *f.*, Vorhof, *n.*

porcupine, Stachelschwein, *n.*

pore, *sb.* Pore, *f.*; *v.i.*, ~ *over*,

über ... hocken, in ... vertieft sein.

pork, Schweinefleisch, *n.*

pornography, Pornographie, *f.*

porous, porös.

porpoise, Tümmler, *m.*

porridge, (Hafer)brei, *m.*

port, Hafen, *m.*; Hafenstadt, *f.*; (*wine*) Portwein, *m.*; (*of ship*) Backbord, *n.*

portable, tragbar, Taschen-, Reise-.

portal, Portal, *n.*

portcullis, Fallgatter, *n.*

porten|d, vorbedeuten; ~t, Vorbedeutung, *f.*; ~tous, verhängnisvoll.

porter, Träger, Dienstmann, *m.*; Pförtner, Portier, *m.*

portfolio, Mappe, *f.*

portico, Säulengang, *m.*

portion, *sb.* (An)teil, *m.*; Portion, *f.*; *v.t.* austeilen.

port|liness, stattliche Erscheinung; ~ly, stattlich; wohlbeleibt.

portmanteau, Reisetasche, *f.*, Reisekoffer, *m.*

portrait, Porträt, Bildnis, *n.*

portray, schildern; abmalen.

Portuguese, *sb.* (*lang.*) Portugiesisch, *n.*; (*person*) Portugiese, *m.*; *a.* portugiesisch.

pose, *sb.* Pose, Stellung, *f.*; *v.i.* sich ausgeben (für), posieren.

position, Stellung, Lage, *f.*; Stand, *m.*

positive, *sb.* (*gram.*) Positiv, *m.*; (*photog.*) Positiv, *n.*; *a.* ~ly, bestimmt, ausdrücklich, positiv.

possess, besitzen; ~ed, (*mad*) besessen; ~ion, Besitz, *m.*; Besitzung, *f.*; ~ive, Besitz-; possessiv; ~or, Besitzer, *m.*

possib|ility, Möglichkeit, *f.*; ~le, ~ly, möglich.

post¹, *sb.* (*wooden*) Pfosten, *m.*; (*for letters*, &c.) Post, *f.*; (*employment*) Stelle, *f.*; *v.t.* (*bill*) anschlagen; (*letter*) auf die Post geben, einstecken; (*book-keeping*) eintragen; (*person*) stellen, postieren; ernennen, mit Kommando beauftragen; ~age, Porto, *n.*; ~age stamp, Briefmarke, *f.*; ~al, Post-; ~al order, Postanweisung, *f.*; ~card, Postkarte, *f.*; ~er,

Plakat, *n.* Anschlagzettel, *m.*; ~haste, in großer Eile; ~man, Briefträger, *m.*; ~mark, Poststempel, *m.*; ~master, Postdirektor, Postmeister, *m.*; ~office, Postamt, *n.*; ~paid, frankiert.

post², *prep.* nach; ~date, nachdatieren; ~mortem, Leichenschau, Autopsie, *f.*; ~script, Nachschrift, *f.*; ~war, Nachkriegs-.

posterior, später, nachherig.

posterity, Nachwelt; Nachkommenschaft, *f.*

posthumous; ~ly, nachgeboren; (*of books*, &c.) hinterlassen.

postpone, verschieben, aufschieben; ~ment, Aufschub, *m.*

posture, Stellung, Lage, *f.*

pot, *sb.* Topf, Krug, *m.*; *v.t.* einmachen; (*shoot*) umlegen; ~ted meat, Fleischkonserven, *f.pl.*

potash, Kali, *n.*

potassium, Kalium, *n.*

potato, Kartoffel, *f.*

poten|cy, Kraft, *f.*; ~t, ~tly, stark, mächtig; ~tate, Machthaber, *m.*; ~tial, *sb.* Potential, *n.*; *a.* and *adv.*; ~tial(ly), möglich, potentiell.

potion, (Arznei)trank, *m.*

potter, *sb.* Töpfer, *m.*; *v.i.*, ~ about, faulenzen, herumbasteln; ~y, Töpferware, *f.*

pouch, Tasche, *f.*, Beutel, *m.*

poult|erer, Geflügelhändler, *m.*; ~ry, Geflügel, *n.*

poultice, (Brei) Umschlag, *m.*; *v.t.* (jemandem) einen Umschlag anlegen.

pounce, herfallen (*on* über).

pound, *sb.* Pfund, *n.*; *v.t.* (zer)stoßen.

pour, *v.t.* gießen; *v.i.* strömen, rinnen.

pout, schmollen.

poverty, Armut, *f.*; Mangel, *m.*

powder, *sb.* Pulver, *n.*; (*cosmetic*) Puder, *m.*; *v.t.* pudern; ~y, pulverig, staubig.

power, Macht, Kraft, Fähigkeit, *f.*; (*electr.*) Strom, *m.*; (*math.*) Potenz, *f.*; ~ful(ly), kräftig, mächtig; ~less(ly), kraftlos, machtlos; ~loom, mechanischer Webstuhl, *m.*; ~point, Steckdose, *f.*; ~station, Kraftwerk, *n.*

practicab|le, ~ly, praktisch, tunlich, ausführbar; ~ility, Tunlichkeit, Ausführbarkeit, *f.*

practical, ~ly, praktisch, tatsächlich.

practice, *sb.* (Aus)übung, *f.*; Training, *n.*; (*usage*) Brauch, *m.*, Gewohnheit, *f.*; (*doctor's, &c.*) Praxis, *f.*

practise, (aus)üben, trainieren; anwenden; (*med.*) praktizieren.

practitioner, praktischer Arzt.

prairie, Prärie, *f.*

praise, *sb.* Lob, *n.*; *v.t.* loben, preisen; ~worthy, lobenswert.

pram, Kinderwagen, *m.*

prance, sich bäumen.

prank, Possen, Streich, *m.*

prate, schwatzen.

prawn, Garnele, *f.*

pray, beten; ~er, Gebet, *n.*: *the Lord's* ~er; das Vaterunser.

preach, predigen; ~er, Prediger, *m.*

preamble, Einleitung, Vorrede, *f.*

precarious, ~ly, unsicher, ungewiß.

precaution, Vorsicht, *f.*; ~ary, Vorsichts-.

preced|e, vorangehen; ~ence, Vorrang, *m.*; ~ent, Präzedenzfall, *m.*, Beispiel, *n.*

precious, ~ly, kostbar; ~ness, Kostbarkeit, *f.*

precipice, Abgrund, *m.*

precipitate, *sb.* (*chem.*) Niederschlag, *m.*; Präzipitat, *n.*; *a.*, ~ly, voreilig, hastig; *v.t.* beschleunigen; (*chem.*) fällen.

precipitous, steil, abschüssig.

precis|e, ~ely, genau, bestimmt; pünktlich; ~ion, Präzision, Genauigkeit, *f.*

preclude, ausschließen.

precoc|ious, frühreif; altklug; ~ity, Frühreife, *f.*

precursor, Vorläufer, *m.*

predatory, räuberisch.

predecessor, Vorgänger, *m.*

predestination, Prädestination, Vorherbestimmung, *f.*

predicament, Verlegenheit, *f.*

predicate, Prädikat, *n.*

predict, vorhersagen; ~ion, Vor-

hersage, Weissagung, *f.*; ~or, Richtungshörer, *m.*

predomin|ance, Oberhand, *f.*; Übergewicht, *n.*; ~ant(ly), überwiegend, vorherrschend; ~ate, vorherrschen.

pre-eminen|ce, Vorrang, *m.*; ~t, hervorragend.

prefab, Fertighaus, *n.*

preface, *sb.* Vorrede, *f.* *v.t.* einleiten.

prefect, (*school*) Ordner, *m.*

prefer, vorziehen; (*food, drink*) lieber essen, trinken; befördern; ~able, ~ably, vorzugsweise; ~ence, Vorzug, *f.*; Vorzugszoll, *m.*; ~ence share, Prioritätsaktie, *f.*

prefix, *sb.* Vorsilbe, *f.*; *v.t.* vorsetzen.

pregnan|cy, Schwangerschaft, *f.*; ~t, schwanger; (*fig.*) fruchtbar, inhaltsvoll.

prejudic|e, *sb.* Vorurteil, *n.*; Nachteil, *m.*; *v.t.* schwächen; ~ial, schädlich.

prelate, Prälat, *m.*

preliminary, *sb.* Vorverhandlung; Einleitung, *f.*; *a.* vorherig, Vor-.

prelude, Vorspiel, *n.*

premature, ~ly, vorzeitig, vorschnell.

premeditate, vorher bedenken; ~d, vorbedacht.

premier, Premierminister, *m.*

premis|es, Haus, Grundstück, *n.*, Räumlichkeiten, *f.pl.*; ~ses, (*logic*) Prämissen, *f.pl.*

premium, Prämie, *f.*; Lehrgeld, *n.*: *at a* ~, über pari.

premonition, Warnung, *f.*

prepar|e, vorbereiten, verfertigen; ~ation, Vorbereitung, *f.*; Präparat, *n.*; ~atory, vorbereitend, Vorbereitungs-.

prepay, vorausbezahlen; frankieren.

preponder|ance, Übergewicht, *n.*; ~ant, überwiegend; ~ate, überwiegen.

preposition, Präposition, *f.*

prepossessing, einnehmend.

preposterous, lächerlich, unsinnig.

prerogative, Vorrecht, *n.*

Presbyterian, *sb.* Presbyterianer, *m.*; *a.* presbyterianisch.

prescri|be, vorschreiben, verordnen; **~ption**, Vorschrift, *f.*; (*med.*) Rezept, *n.*

presence, Gegenwart, *f.*

present, *sb.* (*time*) Gegenwart, *f.*; (*gram.*) Präsens, *n.*; (*gift*) Geschenk, *n.*; *at* **~**, jetzt; *for the* **~**, vorläufig; *a.* gegenwärtig; *to be* **~**, zugegen sein; *v.t.* (*person, arms, bill*) präsentieren; (*gift*) schenken; (*petition*) einreichen; **~able**, geeignet, annehmbar; **~ation**, Überreichung, *f.*; **~ly**, gleich, bald.

presentiment, Vorgefühl, *n.*, Ahnung, *f.*

preserv|e, *sb.* (*game*) Gehege, *n.*; (*food*) Eingemachte(s), *n.*, Konserve, *f.*; *v.t.* bewahren, behüten; einmachen; **~ation**, Erhaltung, Bewahrung, *f.*; **~ative**, Schutzmittel; Konservierungsmittel, *n.*; **~er**, Retter, Bewahrer, *m.*

preside, den Vorsitz haben (führen), präsidieren; **~nt**, Vorsitzende(r), Präsident, *m.*

press, *sb.* Presse, *f.*; (*for linen*) Schrank, *m.*; (*throng*) Gedränge, *n.*; *in the* **~**, im Druck; *v.t.* pressen, drängen; *v.i.* dringen; drücken (on *auf*); **~agency** Nachrichtenbüro, *n.*; **~button**, **~stud**, Druckknopf, *m.*; **~ing**, dringend; **~man**, Journalist, *m.*

pressur|e, Druck, *m.*; **~e-gauge**, Druckmesser, *m.*; **~ized**, mit Druckausgleich.

prestige, Prestige, *n.*, Geltung, *f.*

presum|e, voraussetzen; sich anmaßen; **~ably**, vermutlich; **~ption**, Mutmaßung; Anmaßung, *f.*; **~ptuous**, anmaßend.

pretence, Vorwand, Schein, *m.*

pretend, vorgeben; beanspruchen; **~er**, Thronbewerber, Prätendent, *m.*

preten|sion, Anspruch, *m.*; Anmaßung, *f.*; **~tious**, anspruchsvoll.

pretext, Vorwand, *m.*

prett|y, **~ily**, hübsch, niedlich; **~iness**, Niedlichkeit, *f.*

prevail, vorherrschen, die Oberhand gewinnen.

prevalent, vorherrschend, geltend.

prevaricat|e, Ausflüchte suchen; **~ion**, Ausflucht, *f.*

prevent, zuvorkommen, verhindern; **~ion**, Verhinderung, *f.*; **~ive**, vorbeugend; Schutz-.

preview, Vorschau, *f.*

previous, **~ly**, früher, vorhergehend.

pre-war, Vorkriegs-.

prey, *sb.* Raub, *m.*; *v.i.* rauben, plündern.

price, Preis, *m.*; **~less**, unschätzbar.

prick, *sb.* Stich, *m.*; *v.t.* stechen; **~le**, Stachel, *m.*; **~ly**, stachlig.

pride, *sb.* Stolz, *m.*; *v.refl.* stolz sein (*auf*).

priest, Priester, *m.*; **~ly**, priesterlich.

prig, eingebildeter Fant, *m.*; **~gish(ly)**, dünkelhaft, eingebildet.

prim, steif, geziert, spröde; **~ness**, Ziererei, *f.*

primar|y, ursprünglich, Anfangs-; **~ily**, anfänglich.

primate, Primas, *m.*

prim|e, *sb.* Blüte, Vollendung, *f.*, Kern, *m.*, Beste, *n.*; *a.* erst-(klassig); ursprünglich; Haupt-; *v.t.* unterrichten, instruieren; (*grenade, &c.*) scharf machen; **Prime Minister**, Premierminister, *m.*; **~er**, Elementarbuch, *n.*, Fibel, *f.*; **~eval**, Ur-.

primitive, einfach, primitiv.

primrose, Primel, *f.*

prince, Prinz, Fürst, *m.*; **~ly**, prinzlich, fürstlich; **~ss**, Prinzessin, Fürstin, *f.*

principal, *sb.* Prinzipal, Direktor, *m.*; (*sum*) Kapital, *n.*; *a.*, **~ly**, hauptsächlich, Haupt-.

principality, Fürstentum, *n.*

principle, Prinzip, *n.*, Grundsatz, *m.*

print, *sb.* Druck, Abdruck, *m.*; (*photo*) Kopie, *f.*; Form, Spur, *f.*; *out of* **~**, vergriffen; *v.t.* drucken; (*photo*) kopieren, abziehen; **~ed matter**, Drucksache, *f.*; **~er**, Buchdrucker, *m.*; **~ing**, Buchdruckerkunst, *f.*; **~ing-ink**, Druckerschwärze, *f.*; **~ing-press**, Druckpresse, *f.*

prior, *sb.* Prior, *m.*; *a.* früher; **~ity**, Priorität, *f.*

prism, Prisma, *n.*; ~atic, prismatisch.

prison, Gefängnis, *n.*; ~er, Gefangene(r).

privacy, Zurückgezogenheit, Heimlichkeit, *f.*

private, *sb.* Soldat, Gemeine(r), *m.*; *a.*, ~ly, privat, geheim; persönlich.

privation, Entbehrung, *f.*

privet, Liguster, *m.*

privilege, *sb.* Vorrecht. *n.*; *v.t.* bevorrechten.

privy, *sb.* Abort, *m.*; *a.* geheim; Privy Council, Staatsrat, *m.*

prize, *sb.* Preis, *m.*; (*ship*) Prise, *f.*; *v.t.* schätzen; ~-fight, Wettkampf, *m.*; ~-fighter, Preisboxer, *m.*

probab|ility, Wahrscheinlichkeit, *f.*; ~le, ~ly, wahrscheinlich.

probe, *sb.* Sonde, *f.*; *v.t.* sondieren, abtasten.

problem, Problem, *n.*; Aufgabe, *f.*; ~atic, zweifelhaft, problematisch.

procedure, Verfahren, *n.*

proceed, hervorgehen, herrühren; fortfahren; ~ *against*, vorgehen gegen; ~ings, Verhandlungen, *f.pl.*; ~s, Ertrag, Gewinn, *m.*

process, *sb.* Verfahren, *n.*; Vorgang, *m.*; *v.t.* (auf)bereiten; präparieren; ~ion, Umzug, *m.*, Prozession, *f.*

procla|im, proklamieren, ausrufen, bekanntmachen; ~mation, Proklamation, Bekanntmachung, *f.*

procrastinat|e, verschieben, zögern; ~ion, Aufschub, *m.* Verzögerung, *f.*

procreat|e, (er)zeugen; ~ion, Zeugung, *f.*

procur|e, besorgen, verschaffen; kuppeln; ~able, erhältlich.

prod, stacheln.

prodigal, *sb.* Verschwender, *m.*; *a.* verschwenderisch; *the* ~ *son*, der verlorene Sohn; ~ity, Verschwendung, *f.*

prodig|y, Wunder(ding), etwas Übernatürliches, *n.*; ~ious, ungeheuer, kolossal.

produc|e, *sb.* Ertrag, *m.*, Erzeugnis, *n.*; *v.t.* (er)zeugen, hervorbringen; (*theatr.*) inszenieren

~er, Erzeuger, *m.*; (*theatr.*) Regisseur, *m.*; ~t, Erzeugnis, Produkt, *n.*; ~tion, Produktion, *f.*; Erzeugnis, *n.*; (*theatr.*) Regie, *f.*; ~tive, fruchtbar.

profan|e, *a.* profan, weltlich; *v.t.* entheiligen, entweihen; ~ation, Entweihung, *f.*; ~ity, Ruchlosigkeit; Gotteslästerung, *f.*

profess, bekennen; behaupten; ausüben; ~ed, erklärt; ~ion, Bekenntnis, *n.*; Beruf, Stand, *m.*; ~ional, *sb.* (*sport*) Berufsspieler, *m.*; *a.* Berufs-, Fach-, berufsmäßig; ~or, Professor, *m.*; ~orship, Professur, *f.*

proffer, anbieten.

proficien|cy, Tüchtigkeit, *f.*; ~t, tüchtig, geschickt.

profile, Seitenansicht, *f.*, Seitenbild, *n.*

profit, *sb.* Gewinn, *m.*; *v.i.* gewinnen (*by* durch); ~able, ~ably, einträglich, nützlich; ~eer, *sb.* Schieber, *m.*; *v.i.* Schiebergeschäfte machen, wuchern.

profliga|cy, Liederlichkeit, *f.*; ~te, ruchlos, liederlich.

profound, ~ly, gründlich, tief.

profus|e, ~ely, übervoll, übermäßig; ~ion, Überfluß, *m.*, Fülle, *f.*

progeny, Nachkommenschaft, *f.*; (*animals*) Junge(n), *n.pl.*

prognosticate, vorhersagen.

programme, Programm, *n.*, Spielplan; (*radio*) Sendung, *f.*

progress, *sb.* Fortschritt, *m.*; *v.i.* Fortschritte machen; ~ive, fortschrittlich; fortschreitend.

prohibit, verbieten; ~ion, Verbot, *n.*; ~ive, verbietend.

project, *sb.* Entwurf, Plan, *m.*; *v.t.* werfen; entwerfen, planen; *v.i.* vorspringen, vorragen; ~ile, Projektil, Geschoß, *n.*; ~ion, Entwurf; Vorsprung, *m.*; ~or, Projektionsapparat; Scheinwerfer, *m.*

proletari|an, proletarisch, Arbeiter-; ~ate, Proletariat, *n.*

prolific, ~ally, fruchtbar.

prolix, weitschweifig; ~ity, Weitschweifigkeit, *f.*

prologue, Prolog, *m.*; Einleitung, *f.*

prolong, verlängern; ~ation, Verlängerung, f.

promenade, sb. Promenade, f.; Spaziergang, m.; v.i. spazieren gehen.

prominen|ce, Hervorragen, n.; ~t(ly), hervorragend.

promiscuous, ~ly, vermischt; unterschiedslos.

promis|e, sb. Versprechen, n.; v.t. versprechen; ~ing, vielversprechend.

promontory, Vorgebirge, n.

promot|e, befördern; gründen; ~er, Beförderer; Gründer, m.; ~ion, Beförderung, f.

prompt, a., ~ly, pünktlich, bereit, schnell; v.t. veranlassen (theatr.) soufflieren; ~er, Souffleur, m.; ~ness, Pünktlichkeit, f.

promulgat|e, verkünden, bekanntmachen; ~ion, Bekanntmachung, f.

prone, geneigt; hingestreckt.

prong, Zinke, f.

pronoun, Pronomen, Fürwort, n.

pronounce, aussprechen; erklären; ~ment, Äußerung, f.

pronunciation, Aussprache, f.

proof, sb. Beweis, m.; (test) Probe, f.; (author's) Korrekturbogen, m.; a.; standhaft, undurchdringlich gegen.

prop, sb. Stütze, f.; v.t. stützen.

propaganda, Propaganda, f.

propagat|e, (sich) fortpflanzen; ausbreiten; ~ion, Fortpflanzung, f.

propel, fortbewegen; ~ler, (Schiffs-, Luft-) schraube, f.; Propeller, m.

propensity, Neigung, f.

proper, eigen; geeignet; richtig; schicklich; ~ly eigentlich; richtig; ~ty, Eigentum, Vermögen, n.; (quality) Eigenschaft, f.

prophe|cy, Prophezeiung, Weissagung, f.; ~sy, prophezeien, weissagen; ~t, Prophet, m.; ~tic, prophetisch.

propitiat|e, versöhnen; ~ion, Versöhnung, f.

propitious, ~ly, günstig.

proportion, Verhältnis, n.; Anteil, m.; ~al(ly), gleichmäßig; in Verhältnis stehend.

propos|al, Vorschlag. (Heirats)-

antrag, m.; ~e, vorschlagen; anhalten um; ~ition, Vorschlag, m; (math.) Satz, m.; (logic) Aussage. f.

propound, vorschlagen.

propriet|ary, patentiert, gesetzlich geschützt ~or, Eigentümer. Inhaber. m.; ~ress, Eigentümerin, Inhaberin, f.

propriety, Schicklichkeit, f.

propulsion, Antrieb, m.

prosaic, (fig.) prosaisch, trocken.

prose, Prosa, f.

prosecut|e, an-, ver-klagen; (study, &c.), nachgehen; ~ion, Anklage; Verfolgung, f.; ~or, (An)kläger, m.

prosody, Prosodie, f.

prospect, Ansicht, Aussicht, f.; ~ive, zukünftig, voraussichtlich; ~us, Prospekt, m.

prosper, gedeihen; gelingen; ~ity, Wohlstand, m.; ~ous(ly), glücklich, günstig.

prostitut|e, sb. Hure, Dirne, f.; v.t. schänden; ~ion, Prostitution, f.

prostrat|e, a. hingestreckt; v.t. niederwerfen; ~ion, Niederwerfung; Erschlaffung, f.

protect, schützen, bewahren; ~ion, Schutz, m.; Schutzzollsystem, n.; ~ive, Schutzsicherungs-; ~or, Beschützer, m.; ~orate, Protektorat, n.

protest, sb. Einspruch, Protest, m.; v.t. and i. protestieren, beteuern; ~ant, sb. Protestant, m.; a. protestantisch; ~antism, Protestantismus, m.; ~ation, Beteuerung, f.

protocol, Protokoll, n.

protoplasm, Protoplasma, n.

prototype, Urbild, n.

protract, in die Länge ziehen; ~or, Gradbogen, m.

protrude, hervorstoßen, ausstrecken; hervortreten.

protuber|ance, Vorsprung, m.; Beule, f.; ~ant, hervorstehend.

proud, ~ly, stolz.

prove, v.t. beweisen; prüfen; v.i. sich erweisen.

proverb, Sprichwort, n.; ~ial(ly), sprichwörtlich.

provide, v.t. versehen (with mit); versorgen; v.i. sich vorsehen;

~d. vorausgesetzt (daß) ; ~nce, Vorsehung; Vorsicht, *f.*; ~nt, sorgsam; ~ntial, der Vorsehung (*genitive*).

provinc|e, Provinz, *f.*, Bezirk, *m.* Gebiet, *n.*; ~**ial**, provinziell, Provinz-, kleinstädtisch.

provision, *sb.* Versorgung; Beschaffung, *f.*; (*stores*) Vorrat, *m.*, Lager, *n.*; (*condition*) Bedingung, *f.*; *v.t.* verproviantieren; ~**al**(**ly**), vorläufig; Behelfs-; ~**s**, Proviant, *m.*, Lebensmittel, *n.pl.*

proviso, Vorbehalt, *m.*

provo|cation, Herausforderung, Reizung, *f.*; ~**cative**, aufreizend; ~**ke**, reizen, herausfordern, hervorrufen; ~**king**, ärgerlich.

prow, Bug, Vorderteil, *m.*

prowess, Tapferkeit, *f.*

prowl, herumschleichen.

proxim|ate, naheliegend, nächst; ~**ity**, Nähe, Nachbarschaft, *f.*

proxy, Stellvertreter, *m.*; Vollmacht, *f.*; *by* ~, in Vertretung.

prude, Spröde, *f.*; ~**ry**, Sprödigkeit, *f.*

pruden|ce, Vorsicht, Klugheit, *f.*; ~**t**(**ly**), vorsichtig, klug.

prune[1], *sb.* Backpflaume, *f.*

prun|e[2], *v.t.* beschneiden; ~**ing-hook**, Gartenmesser, *n.*

prurien|ce, Gelüst, *n.*, Lüsternheit, *f.*; ~**t**, wollüstig, lüstern.

Prussian, *sb.* Preuße, *m.*; *a.* preußisch; ~ **blue**, Berliner Blau, *n.*

Prussic acid, Blausäure, *f.*

pry, spähen, die Nase stecken (in); ~**ing**, neugierig.

psalm, Psalm, *m.*; ~**ist**, Psalmendichter, *m.*

pseudo, Pseudo-, Schein-; ~**nym**, Deckname, *m.*

psychiatr|ist, Psychiatrist, *m.*; ~**y**, Psychiatrie, *f.*

psycho-analy|sis, Psychoanalyse, *f.*; ~**st**, Psychoanalytiker, *m.*; ~**se**, psychoanalytisch behandeln.

psycholog|ical, psychologisch; ~**y**, Psychologie, *f.*

psychopath, Psychopath, *m.*

ptarmigan, Schneehuhn, *n.*

pub, Kneipe, *f.*

puberty, Pubertät, Mannbarkeit, *f.*

public, *sb.* Publikum, *n.*; Öffentlichkeit, *f.*; *in* ~, öffentlich; *a.* ~**ly**, öffentlich, Staats-; ~**an**, Gastwirt, *m.*; ~**ation**, Veröffentlichung; Herausgabe, *f.*; ~ **house**, Wirtshaus, *n.*; ~**ist**, Publizist, *m.*; ~**ity**, Publizität, Reklame, *f.*; ~ **opinion**, öffentliche Meinung, *f.*; ~ **spirit**, Gemeinsinn, *m.*

publish, herausgeben; bekanntmachen; ~**er**, Herausgeber, Verleger, *m.*

puce, purpurbraun.

pudding, Pudding, *m.*

puddle, Pfütze, *f.*

pueril|e, kindisch; ~**ity**, Kinderei, *f.*

puerperal fever, Kindbettfieber, *n.*

puff, *sb.* Hauch; Windstoß, *m.*; (*for powder*) Puderquaste, *f.*; *v.i.* blasen, schnauben; *v.t.* aufblasen; anpreisen; ~**adder**, Puffotter, *f.*; ~**ball**, Bofist, *m.*; ~**paste**, Blätterteig, *m.*; ~**y**, aufgeblasen; schwülstig.

pug, Mops, *m.*

pugilist, Boxer, Faustkämpfer, *m.*

pugnac|ious, kampfsüchtig; ~**ity**, Kampflust, *f.*

pull, *sb.* Zug, *m.*; *v.t.* ziehen; (*pluck*) pflücken; (*oars*) rudern, **pullen**; ~ **through**, durchkommen; ~**over**, Pullover, *m.*

pullet, Hühnchen, *n.*

pulley, Rolle, *f.*, Flaschenzug, *m.*

pulmonary, Lungen-.

pulp, *sb.* Brei, *m.*, (*Frucht*)fleisch, *n.*; *v.t.* zu Brei verwandeln.

pulpit, Kanzel, *f.*

puls|e, Puls, *m.*; Hülsenfrüchte, *f.pl.*; ~**ation**, Pulsschlag, *m.*

pulveriz|e, pulverisieren; ~**ation**, Pulverisierung, *f.*

puma, Puma, *m.*

pumice, Bimsstein, *m.*

pump, *sb.* Pumpe, *f.*; *v.t.* pumpen.

pumpkin, Kürbis, *m.*

pun, *sb.* Wortspiel, *n.*; *v.i.* witzeln.

punch[1], *sb.* (*blow*) Stoß, *m.*; (*instrument*) Punze, *f.*, Locheisen, *n.*; (*drink*) Punsch, *m.*; *v.t.* lochen; schlagen.

Punch[2], Hanswurst, *m.*; ~ *and Judy show*, Kasperletheater, *n.*

punctilious, äußerst genau.

punctual, ~ly, pünktlich; ~ity, Pünktlichkeit, f.

punctuat|e, interpunktieren; ~ion, Interpunktion, f.

puncture, sb. Loch, n., Panne, f.; v.t. durchstechen; v.i. ein Loch bekommen.

pungen|cy, Schärfe, f.; ~t(ly), scharf, beißend.

punish, strafen; ~ment, Strafe, f.

punitive, Straf-.

punt, flacher Kahn.

puny, schwach, winzig.

pup, junger Hund.

pupil, (of the eye) Pupille, f.; (scholar) Schüler(in, f.), m.

puppet, Drahtpuppe, Marionette, f.; (fig.) Werkzeug, n.

purchase, sb. (Ein)kauf, m.; v.t. kaufen; ~r, Käufer, m.

pure, ~ly, rein.

purg|e, reinigen, säubern; abführen; ~ative, Abführmittel, n.; ~atory, Fegefeuer, n.

puri|fication, Reinigung, f.; ~fy, reinigen; ~st, Sprachreiniger, Purist, m.; ~tan, Puritaner, m.; ~tanical, puritanisch; ~ty, Reinheit; Keuschheit, f.

purloin, stehlen.

purple, sb. Purpur, m.; a. purpurfarben.

purpose, sb. Absicht, f., Zweck, m.; on ~, absichtlich; to the ~, zweckentsprechend; v.t. beabsichtigen, im Sinne haben.

purr, schnurren.

purse, (Geld)beutel, m., Portemonnaie, n.; ~r, Zahlmeister, m.

pursu|e, verfolgen; ~er, Verfolger, m.; ~it, Verfolgung, Jagd, f.

purulent, eitrig.

purvey, verproviantieren, liefern; ~or, Lieferant, m.

pus, Eiter, m.

push, sb. Stoß, Schub, m.; v.t. stoßen, schieben; treiben; ~ on, sich beeilen; ~bike, Tretzweirad, n.; ~button, Druckknopf, m.; ~ful, ~ing, aufdringlich, streberhaft.

pusillanim|ity, Kleinmut, m.; ~ous, kleinmütig.

pustule, Bläschen, n.

put, v.t. setzen, stellen, legen; stecken; anwenden; verursachen; (question) stellen; ~ by, weglegen; ~ down, unterdrücken; niedersetzen; anschreiben; (jemandem etwas) zuschreiben; ~ forth, hervorbringen; ~ off, aufschieben; hinhalten; ~ on, (clothes) anziehen; (hat) aufsetzen; (collar) umlegen; (person) auferlegen; ~ out, (extinguish) auslöschen (eyes) ausstechen; (tongue) herausstecken; (person) verwirren, belästigen; ~ to, anspannen; ~ together, zusammenstellen; ~ up, aufstellen; einpacken; einkehren (at in); ~ up with, dulden, sich gefallen lassen.

putref|action, Fäulnis, f.; ~y, faul werden.

putrid, faul, verfault.

puttee, Wickelgamasche, f.

putty, Glaserkitt, m.

puzzle, sb. Rätsel, n.; v.t. in Verlegenheit bringen, verwirren.

pygmy, Zwerg, Pygmäe, m.

pyjamas, Schlafanzug, Pyjama, m.

pyramid, Pyramide, f.

pyre, Scheiterhaufen, m.

pyrotechnics, Feuerwerkerei, f.

python, Python, m., Riesenschlange, f.

pyx, Monstranz, f.

Q

quack[1], sb. Quacksalber, Marktschreier, m.

quack[2], v.i. quaken, schnattern.

quadrangle, Viereck, n.; Hof, m.

quadrant, Quadrant, m.

quadratic, quadratisch.

quadrilateral, vierseitig.

quadruped, Vierfüß(l)er, m.

quadruple, vierfach; ~ts, Vierlinge, m.pl.

quaff, zechen, austrinken.

quagmire, Moorboden, Sumpf, m.

quail[1], Wachtel, f.

quail[2], v.i., verzagen.

quaint, ~ly, wunderlich, seltsam; ~ness, Wunderlichkeit, Seltsamkeit, f.

quake, zittern, beben; ~r, Quäker, m.

qualif|ication, Befähigung, Taug-
lichkeit; Einschränkung, *f.*;
~y, befähigen, berechtigen;
einschränken.

quality, Qualität, Eigenschaft,
Beschaffenheit, *f.*

qualm, Übelkeit, *f.*; (*of conscience*)
Gewissensbisse, *m.pl.*

quandary, Verlegenheit, *f.*

quantity, Quantität, Größe, Menge,
f.

quarantine, Quarantäne, *f.*

quarrel, *sb.* Zank, Streit, *m.*; *v.i.*
(sich) zanken, streiten; ~some,
zänkisch.

quarry, *sb.* Steinbruch, *m.*; (*fig.*)
Fundgrube, *f.*; (*hunting*) ver-
folgtes Wild, *n.*, Beute, *f.*; *v.i.*
Steine brechen.

quarter, *sb.* Viertel, *n.*; Wohnung,
f., Quartier, *n.*; Vierteljahr, *n.*;
(*herald.*) Feld, *n.*; (*mercy*) Gnade,
f., Pardon, *m.*; *from all* ~s,
von allen Seiten; ~ *of an hour*,
Viertelstunde, *f.*; *v.t.* beherbergen, einquartieren; ~day,
Quartalstag, *m.*; ~deck,
Achterdeck, *n.*; ~ly, viertel-
jährlich; ~master, Quartier-
meister, *m.*; ~s, Wohnung, *f.*;
(*mil.*) Quartier, *n.*; *confinement
to* ~s, Stubenarrest, *m.*; *come
to close* ~s, handgemein werden;
in high ~s, in hohen Kreisen.

quartet(te), Quartett, *n.*

quarto, Quarto, Quart(format), *n.*

quartz, Quarz, *m.*

quash, unterdrücken, für ungültig erklären.

quaver, *sb.* Triller, *m.*; (*note*)
Achtelnote, *f.*; *v.i.* zittern;
trillern.

quay, Kai, *m.*

queen, Königin, *f.*; ~bee,
Bienenkönigin, *f.*, Weisel, *m.*

queer, ~ly, wunderlich, seltsam;
verdächtig; unwohl.

quell, unterdrücken; dämpfen.

quench, löschen, stillen; (*metal*)
abschrecken.

querulous, ~ly, nörgelig, quen-
gelig.

query, *sb.* Frage, *f.*; *v.t.* in Frage
stellen, bezweifeln.

quest, Suchen, *n.*; *in* ~ *of*, auf
der Suche nach.

question, *sb.* Frage; Streitfrage, *f.*;
in ~, fraglich, vorliegend; *v.t.*
(aus)fragen; bezweifeln; ~able,
fraglich, zweifelhaft; ~er,
Fragesteller, *m.*; ~mark,
Fragezeichen, *n.*; ~naire,
Fragebogen, *m.*

queue, *sb.* (*of persons*) Schlange, *f.*;
v.i. Schlange stehen, anstehen.

quibble, *sb.* Ausflucht, Zweideutigkeit, *f.*; *v.i.* ausweichen,
Ausflüchte machen.

quick, ~ly, schnell, geschwind;
scharfsinnig; lebhaft; *to be* ~,
sich beeilen; ~en, beschleunigen,
beleben; sich regen; ~firing,
Schnellfeuer-; ~lime, ungelösch-
ter Kalk; ~ march, Schnell-
schritt, *m.*; ~ness, Schnelligkeit,
Geschwindigkeit, *f.*; Scharfsinn,
m.; ~sand, Flugsand, *m.*; ~sil-
ver, Quecksilber, *n.*; ~step
(*dance*) Quickstep, *m.*

quiet, *sb.* Ruhe, *f.*; *a.*, ~ly, ruhig, gelassen; *be* ~, schweigen Sie!; ~
ism, Quietismus, *m.*; ~ist, Quiet-
ist, *m.*; ~ness, Ruhe, Stille, *f.*

quill, Feder, *f.*; (*pen*) Federkiel,
m.

quilt, Steppdecke, *f.*

quince, Quitte, *f.*

quinine, Chinin, *n.*

quintessence, Quintessenz, *f.*

quintet(te), Quintett, *n.*

quire, Buch (*n.*) Papier.

quit, *a.* quitt, los; *v.t.* verlassen,
aufgeben; ~s, quitt.

quite, ganz, völlig.

quiver, *sb.* Köcher, *m.*; *v.i.* zittern.

quiz, *sb.* Quiz, *n.*; *v.t.* quizzen.

quoit, Wurfring, *m.*

quota, Quote, *f.*

quot|e, anführen, zitieren; (*prices*)
angeben, notieren; ~ation, Zitat,
n., Anführung, *f.*; Preisangabe,
f.; ~ation marks, Anführungszeichen, Gänsefüßchen, *n.pl.*

quotient, Quotient, *m.*

R

rabbi, Rabbiner, *m.*

rabbit, Kaninchen, *n.*

rabble, Pöbel, *m.*

rabi|d, rasend, toll; ~es, Hunds-,
Toll- wut, *f.*

race, *sb.* (*breed*) Rasse, *f.*; (*sport*)

Wettlauf, *m.*, Wettrennen, *n.*; (*tide*) Strömung, *f.*; *v.i.* rennen; um die Wette laufen, fahren; **~course**, Rennbahn, *f.*; **~horse**, Rennpferd, *n.*

rack, *sb.* (*torture*) Folter, *f.*; (*for articles*) Gestell, Gepäcknetz, *n.*; (*mech.*) Zahnstange, *f.*; *v.t.* recken, foltern; **~ one's brains**, sich den Kopf zerbrechen.

racket, Schläger, *m.*, Rakett, *n.*; Lärm, *m.*; **~eer**, Schieber, Gewinnler, *m.*

racoon, Waschbär, *m.*

racy, rassig; geistreich; pikant.

radar, Funkmeßgerät, Radar, *n.*

radian|ce, Glanz, *m.*; **~t**, strahlend.

radiat|e, (aus)strahlen; **~ion**, Ausstrahlung, *f.*; **~or**, (*motor*) Kühler; (*central-heating*) Heizkörper, *m.*

radical, *sb.* Radikale(r), *m.*; Wurzel, *f.*; *a.* radikal, gründlich.

radio, Radio, *n.*; **~active**, radioaktiv; **~ location**, Funkmessung; **~ play**, Hörspiel, *n.*; **~ set**, Radioapparat, *m.*, Funkgerät, *n.*; **~ telephony**, Funkgerät, *n.*; **~ telephony**, Sprechfunk, *m.*

radish, Radieschen, *n.*, Rettich, *m.*

radium, Radium, *n.*

radius, Radius, Halbmesser; Umkreis, *m.*

raffle, *sb.* Auslosung, Lotterie, *f.*; *v.t.* verlosen.

raft, Floß, *n.*

rag, Lumpen, Fetzen, *m.*; **~amuffin**, Lumpenkerl, *m.*; **~ged**, zerlumpt.

rage, *sb.* Wut; Mode, *f.*; *v.i.* wüten, rasen.

raid, *sb.* Überfall, Angriff, *m.*; *v.t.* einen Überfall, Angriff, machen; **~er**, Angreifer; Plünderer, *m.*

rail¹, *sb.* Riegel, *m.*, Querholz, *n.*; Eisenbahn; Schiene, *f.*; **~ing**, Geländer, *n.*; **~road**, **~way**, Eisenbahn, *f.*; **~way-guard**, Schaffner, *m.*; **~way-station**, Bahnhof, *m.*

rail², *v.i.* schimpfen, schmähen, scherzen; **~lery**, Spötterei, *f.*

raiment, Kleidung, *f.*

rain, *sb.* Regen, *m.*; *v.i.* regnen;

~bow, Regenbogen, *m.*; **~coat**, Regenmantel, *m.*; **~gauge**, Regenmesser, *m.*; **~proof**, wasserdicht; **~y**, regnerisch, Regen-.

raise, aufheben, erheben; errichten; erhöhen; aufziehen; (*troops*) ausheben; (*breed*) züchten, ziehen; (*ghost*) heraufbeschwören; (*money*) auftreiben; (*taxes*) erheben.

raisin, Rosine, *f.*

rak|e, *sb.* (*implement*) Rechen; (*person*) Wüstling, *m.*; *v.t.* harken; (*with fire*) bestreichen; **~ish**, liederlich.

rally, *sb.* Massenversammlung, Kundgebung, *f.*; (*tennis*) Ballwechsel, *m.*; *v.* (sich) wieder sammeln; sich erholen.

ram, *sb.* (*zool.*) Widder; (*naut.*) Rammbug; Rammstoß, (*mech.*) Rammblock, Stoßheber, *m.*; *v.t.* (ein)rammen.

rambl|e, *sb.* Ausflug, *m.*; *v.i.* herumstreifen; abschweifen; **~er**, Umherstreicher, *m.*; Kletterose, *f.*; **~ing**, umherschweifend; zusammenhanglos; (*of buildings*) unregelmäßig.

ramif|ication, Verzweigung, *f.*; **~y**, (sich) verzweigen.

ramp, Rampe *f.*; Schwindel, *m.*; **~ant**, wuchernd; zügellos; (*heraldry*) aufrecht stehend.

rampart, Wall, *m.*

ramrod, Ladestock, *m.*

ramshackle, wack(e)lig, baufällig.

rancid, ranzig.

ranc|orous, feindselig, erbittert; **~our**, Groll, *m.*, Erbitterung, *f.*

random, *at* **~**, aufs Geratewohl.

range, *sb.* Bereich, Aktionsradius, *m.*; Reichweite, Schußweite, *f.*; (*mountains*) Kette, *f.*; (*kitchen*) Küchenherd, *m.*; (*rifle, artillery*) Schießplatz, *m.*; *v.t.* ordnen; *v.i.* herumstreifen; sich erstrecken; **~finder**, Entfernungsmesser, *m.*; **~r**, Förster, *m.*

rank¹, *sb.* Rang, Dienstgrad, *m.*; Reihe, *f.*; *person of* **~** Standesperson, *f.*; **~** *and file*, Reih und Glied; gemeine Soldaten; *v.i.* gleichstehen (*with* mit); *v.t.* ordnen.

rank², *a.* üppig; übermäßig; äußerst; ranzig.

rankle, (*fig.*) nagen.

ransack, plündern; durchstöbern.

ransom, *sb.* Lösegeld, *n.*; *v.t.* loskaufen.

rant, prahlen, brüllen, übertrieben deklamieren; ~ing, großsprecherisch, prahlend; ~er, Schreihals, Kanzelpauker, *m.*

rap, *sb.* Schlag, *m.*, Klopfen, *n.*; *v.t.* klopfen.

rapac|ious, raubgierig; ~ity, Raubgier, *f.*

rape, *sb.* Notzucht, *f.*; Raub, *m.*; *v.t.* notzüchtigen, vergewaltigen; rauben.

rapid, ~ly, schnell; reißend; ~ity, Schnelligkeit, *f.*; ~s, Strudel, *m.*, Stromschnellen, *f.pl.*

rapier, Stoßdegen, *m.*

rapt, hingerissen; ~ure, Entzücken, *n.*; ~urous, verzückt; leidenschaftlich.

rare, selten; (*precious*) kostbar; (*air*) dünn; ~fy, verdünnen; ~ly, selten; ~ness, rarity, Seltenheit; Kostbarkeit; Dünnheit, *f.*

rascal, Schurke, *m.*; ~ity, Schurkerei, *f.*

rash¹, *sb.* (Haut)ausschlag, *m.*

rash², ~ly, unbesonnen; übereilt; ~ness, Unbesonnenheit, *f.*

rasher, (Speck-, Schinken-) scheibe, *f.*

rasp, *sb.* Raspel, *f.*; *v.t.* and *i.* raspeln.

raspberry, Himbeere, *f.*

rat, Ratte, *f.*

ratchet, Sperrhaken, *m.*

rate, *sb.* (*price*) Rate, *f.*, Preis, *m.*; (*tax*) Abgabe, Steuer, *f.*; (*ratio*) Verhältnis, *n.*; (*speed*) Geschwindigkeit, *f.*; *at any* ~, auf jeden Fall; ~ *of exchange*, Wechselkurs, *m.*; ~ *of interest*, Zinsfuß, *m.*; *v.t.* schätzen; ausschelten; ~able, steuerpflichtig; ~payer, Steuerzahler, *m.*

rather, eher, lieber; ziemlich.

ratif|y, bestätigen; ~ication, Bestätigung, *f.*

rating, Schätzung; Klasse, *f.*; (*naut.*) Matrose; (*taxes*) Steuersatz, *m.*

ratio, Verhältnis, *n.*

ration, *sb.* Ration, *f.*; *v.t.* rationieren; ~book, ~card, Lebensmittelkarte, *f.*

rational, ~ly, vernünftig; ~ism, Rationalismus, *m.*; ~ist, Rationalist, *m.*; ~ization, Rationalisierung, *f.*; *v.t.* ~ize, rationalisieren.

rattle, *sb.* Knarre; Klapper, *f.*; Klirren, *n.*; *v.t.* rasseln (mit); *v.i.* klirren, rasseln (mit); ~snake, Klapperschlange, *f.*

ravage, plündern, verwüsten, verheeren; ~s, Verwüstung, Verheerung, *f.*

rav|e, rasen; faseln (*at* über); schwärmen; ~ing, *sb.* Raserei, *f.*; *a.* rasend.

raven, Rabe, *m.*

ravenous, heißhungrig, gierig.

ravine, Schlucht, Klamm, *f.*

ravish, schänden, notzüchtigen; ~er, Schänder, *m.*; ~ing, bezaubernd, entzückend.

raw, (*unprepared*) roh; (*spirits*) unvermischt; (*weather*) rauh; (*recruits*) unerfahren; ~ material, Rohstoff, *m.*; ~ness, Roheit; Rauheit, *f.*

ray, Strahl, *m.*; (*fish*) Roche(n), *m.*; ~ treatment, Bestrahlung, *f.*

rayon, Kunstseide, *f.*

raze, niederreißen, schleifen; ~ *to the ground*, dem Boden gleichmachen.

razor, Rasiermesser, *n.*; ~blade, Rasierklinge, *f.*

reach, *sb.* Bereich, *m.*; Strecke, *f.*; Hörweite, Schußweite, *f.*; *v.* (er)reichen, sich erstrecken.

react, reagieren, rückwirken; ~ion, Reaktion, Rückwirkung, *f.*; ~or, (*physics*) Reaktor, *m.*

read, lesen; ~able, lesbar; ~er, Leser, *m.*; Lesebuch, *n.*

readi|ly, gern, bereitwillig; ~ness, Bereitwilligkeit; Bereitschaft, *f.*

reading, Lesen, *n.*; Lektüre, *f.*; Lesart, *f.*; ~room, Lesezimmer, *n.*

ready, bereit, fertig; im Begriff; *make* ~, vorbereiten; ~ *cash*, *money*, Bargeld, *n.*; ~made, fertig; ~ *reckoner*, Rechentabellen, *f.pl.*; ~to- *wear*,

Konfektions-.

reagent, Reagens, n.

real, ~ly, wirklich; echt; ~ estate, Grundbesitz, m.; ~istic(ally), realistisch; ~ism, Realismus, m.; ~ist, Realist, m.; ~ity, Wirklichkeit, f.; ~ize, realisieren, verwirklichen; zu Geld machen; sich vorstellen, fassen; ~ization, Realisierung, Verwirklichung; Verwertung, f.

realm, Reich, n.

reap, ernten, schneiden; ~er, Schnitter, m.

rear, sb. (mil.) Nachtrab, m., Nachhut, f.; (background) Hintergrund, m.; a. Hinter-; v.t. heben, errichten; züchten, aufziehen; v.i. sich bäumen; ~admiral, Konteradmiral, m.; ~guard, Nachhut, f.; ~light, Schlußlicht, n.

rearm, v.t. wieder bewaffnen; v.i. aufrüsten; ~ament, Aufrüstung, f.

reason, sb. Vernunft, f.; (motive) Grund, m., Ursache, f.; (right) Recht, n.; lose one's ~, den Verstand verlieren; for that ~, aus diesem Grunde; in ~, billig, vernünftig; v.i. schließen, nachdenken, argumentieren; ~able, ~ably, vernünftig; billig; ~ing, Schlußfolgerung, Beweisführung, f.

reassure, beruhigen, ermutigen.

rebate, Rabatt, Abzug, m.

rebel, sb. Rebell, Empörer, m.; v.i. rebellieren, sich empören; ~lion, Empörung, f.; ~lious, aufrührerisch.

rebound, sb. Rückprall, m.; v.i. zurückprallen.

rebuff, sb. Abweisung, f.; v.t. abweisen.

rebuke, sb. Verweis, m.; v.t. zurechtweisen.

rebut, abschlagen, zurückweisen.

recall, zurückrufen; zurücknehmen; sich erinnern.

recant, widerrufen.

recede, sich zurückziehen.

receipt, sb. Empfang, m.; Quittung, f.; v.t. quittieren.

receive, empfangen, annehmen; erhalten; ~r, Empfänger,

Adressat, m.; (telephone, radio) Hörer, Empfänger, m.; (of stolen goods) Hehler, m.

recent, neu; ~ly, neulich, kürzlich.

receptacle, Behälter, m.

recept|ion, Aufnahme, f., Empfang, m.; ~ive, empfänglich.

recess, Nische, Vertiefung; Unterbrechung, f., Ferien, pl.

recipe, Rezept, n.

recipient, Empfänger, m.

reciproc|al, wechselseitig, gegenseitig, Gegen-; ~ate, austauschen; erwidern; ~ating engine, Kolbenmaschine, f.; ~ity, Gegenseitigkeit, f.

recit|e, vortragen, hersagen; ~al, Erzählung, f.; Konzert, n.; ~ation, Hersagen, n., Deklamation, f.

reckless, ~ly, tollkühn, verwegen; leichtsinnig, rücksichtslos; ~ness, Verwegenheit, f.; Leichtsinn, m.; Rücksichtslosigkeit, f.

reckon, rechnen, schätzen; meinen; ~ing, Rechnen, n.; Rechnung, f.

reclaim, reklamieren.

recline, sich lehnen.

recluse, Einsiedler, m.

recogn|ition, (An)erkennung, f.; ~ition signal, Erkennungssignal, n.; ~ize, (an)erkennen.

recoil, sb. Rückprall, Rücklauf, m.; v.i. zurückprallen; zurückschrecken.

recollect, sich erinnern; ~ion, Erinnerung, f.

recommend, empfehlen; ~ation, Empfehlung, f.

recompense, sb. Vergeltung, Belohnung, f.; v.t. entschädigen, belohnen.

reconcil|e, versöhnen; ~iation, Versöhnung, f.

recondition, wieder instandsetzen.

reconn|aisance, Aufklärung, f.; ~oitre, aufklären, auskundschaften.

record, sb. Verzeichnis, Protokoll, n.; (sport) Rekord, m., Höchstleistung, f.; (gramophone) (Schall)platte, f.; v.t. verzeichnen, protokollieren, registrieren; (sound) aufnehmen; ~er, Registrator; Registrierapparat, m.;

(*mus.*) Blockflöte, *f.*; ~-player, Plattenspieler, *m.*; ~s, Archiv, *n.*

recount, erzählen; noch einmal zählen.

recoup, entschädigen, schadlos halten (für).

recover, *v.t.* wiederbekommen; bergen; *v.i.* sich erholen, genesen; ~y, Wiedererlangung; Genesung, *f.*

recreation, Erholung, Erquickung, *f.*; ~ *ground*, Sport-, Spielplatz, *m.*

recrimination, Gegenbeschuldigung, *f.*

recruit, *sb.* Rekrut, *m.*; *v.t.* werben, rekrutieren.

rectang|le, Rechteck, *n.*; ~ular, rechtwinklig.

rectif|y, berichtigen; (*of electric current*) gleichrichten; ~ication, Berichtigung; Gleichrichtung, *f.*

rector, Rektor; Pfarrer, *m.*; ~y, Pfarrhaus, *n.*

recuperate, sich erholen.

recur, wieder vorkommen; sich wiederholen; ~rence, Wiederkehr, *f.*; ~rent, *(-ring)*, wiederkehrend.

red, *sb.* Rot, *n.*; *a.* rot; **Red Cross**, Rotes Kreuz; ~ *currant*, Johannisbeere, *f.*; ~den, röten; rot machen; ~dish, rötlich; ~haired, rothaarig; ~handed, auf frischer Tat; ~hot, rotglühend; ~ lead, Mennige, *f.*; ~letter day, Festtag, Glückstag, *m.*; ~ness, Röte, *f.*; ~skin, Rothaut, *f.*; ~ tape Bürokratismus, *m.*

redeem, loskaufen, auslösen; (*theol.*) erlösen; (*promise*) erfüllen; (*bonds*) amortisieren; tilgen; ~able, kündbar, tilgbar; ~er, Erlöser, Heiland, *m.*

redemption, Befreiung; Erlösung; Tilgung, *f.*

redouble, verdoppeln.

redoubt, Schanze, *f.*; ~able, furchtbar.

redound, beitragen.

redress, *sb.* Genugtuung, *f.*; Ersatz, *m.*; *v.t.* verbessern, abhelfen.

reduce, verkleinern, vermindern; (*prices*) herabsetzen; (*math. and*

chem.) reduzieren; (*conquer*) bezwingen; ~tion, Verminderung, Herabsetzung, *f.*, Rabatt, *m.*; (*chem.*) Reduktion, *f.*

redundan|cy, Überfluß, *m.*, Überfülle, *f.*; ~t, überflüssig.

reduplicat|e, verdoppeln; ~ion, Verdoppelung, *f.*

reed, Rohr, Schilf, *n.*; Rohrflöte, *f.*

reef, Riff, *n.*, Klippe, *f.*

reel, *sb.* Haspel, *m.* or *f.*, Rolle, *f.*; Rundtanz, *m.*; *v.i.* taumeln.

refectory, Speisesaal, *m.*

refer, *v.t.* hinweisen; *v.i.* sich beziehen (*to auf*); ~ee, *sb.* Schiedsrichter, *m.*; *v.i.* Schiedsrichter sein; ~ence, Verweisung; Beziehung; Referenz, *f.*; *in* ~*ence to*, bezüglich (*with gen.*); ~*ence book*, Nachschlagebuch, *n.*; ~*ence library*, Handbibliothek, *f.*; ~*ence number*, Geschäftsnummer, *f.*; ~endum, Volksabstimmung, *f.*

refill, *sb.* Ersatzfüllung, *f.*; *v.* (sich) wieder füllen.

refine, reinigen, verfeinern; (*sugar, metals*) raffinieren; ~d, (*person*) gebildet, vornehm; fein, schön; ~ment, Feinheit, *f.*, Schliff, *m.*; ~ry, Raffinerie, *f.*; Raffinierofen, *m.*

refit, ausbessern, reparieren.

reflect, *v.t.* zurückwerfen; *v.i.* nachdenken; ~ed, (*light*) reflektiert; ~ing, widerstrahlend; ~ion, Widerstrahlung, Erwägung, Betrachtung; Blamage, *f.*, Tadel, *m.*; ~ive, nachdenklich; ~or, Reflektor; Rückstrahler, *m.*

reflex, Reflex, *m.*; ~ive, reflexiv.

reform, *sb.* Reform, Umgestaltung, *f.*; *v.t.* verbessern, reformieren; *v.i.* sich bessern; *Reformed Church*, Reformierte Kirche; ~ation, Reformation; Besserung; Umänderung, *f.*; ~atory *school*, Besserungsanstalt, *f.*; ~er, Reformator, *m.*

refract, brechen; ~ion, Strahlenbrechung, *f.*; ~ory, widerspenstig; feuerfest.

refrain, *sb.* Kehrreim, *m.*; *v.i.* sich enthalten (*with gen.*).

refresh, erfrischen; auffrischen; ~ment, Erfrischung, *f.*; ~ment room, Erfrischungsraum, m.

refrigerator, Kühler, Eisschrank, Kühlschrank, m.

refuel, (auf)tanken.

refuge, Zuflucht; (in street) Rettungsinsel, f.; ~e, Flüchtling, Emigrant, m.

refund, zurückzahlen.

refuse[1], v.t. verweigern, abschlagen, ablehnen; ~al, Verweigerung, Ablehnung, f.

refuse[2], sb. Abfall, Ausschuß, m.

refute, widerlegen; ~ation, Widerlegung, f.

regal, königlich.

regale, bewirten.

regalia, Regalien, n.pl.; Krönungsschmuck, m.

regard, sb. Achtung, f., Ansehen, n.; with ~ to, mit Rücksicht auf; kind ~s, herzliche Grüße; v.t. achten; auffassen, betrachten (as als); to be ~ed as, gelten für; ~ing, hinsichtlich; ~less, unbekümmert (of um); unachtsam.

regatta, Regatta, f.

regen[cy], Regentschaft, f.; ~t, Regent, m.

regenerat[e], neu beleben; erneuern; ~ion, Neubildung; Wiedergeburt; Erneuerung; (radio) Rückkopplung, f.

regicide, Königsmord; Königsmörder, m.

régime, Regime, n., Regierung, f.

regimen, Lebensordnung, Diät, f.

regiment, Regiment, n.; ~als, Uniform, f.

region, Gegend, f.

regist[er], sb. Verzeichnis, Register, n.; v.t. registrieren; (letter) einschreiben; eintragen; ausdrücken; feststellen; ~rar, Registrator, m.; ~ration, Registrierung; Einschreibung; Eintragung, f.; ~ry, Registratur, f.

regret, sb. Bedauern, Leid, n.; v.t. bedauern; ~table, bedauerlich.

regular, ~ly, regelmäßig; üblich, gewöhnlich; ~ity, Regelmäßigkeit, f.; ~ize, regeln.

regulat[e], ordnen, regeln; regulieren; ~ion, Verordnung, Vorschrift, f.; ~or, Regulator, m.

rehabilitate, wieder einsetzen, re-

habilitieren.

rehears[e], proben; wiederholen; ~al, Probe; Wiederholung, f.

reign, sb. Regierung; Herrschaft, f.; v.i. regieren, herrschen.

reimburse, entschädigen, erstatten; ~ment, Erstattung, f.

rein, sb. Zügel, m.; v.t. zügeln.

reindeer, Renntier, n.

reinforce, verstärken; ~d concrete, Eisenbeton, m.; ~ment, Verstärkung, f., Nachschub, m.

reinstate, wieder einsetzen; ~ment Wiederherstellung, f.

reinsure, rückversichern.

reissue, sb. neue Ausgabe, f.; v.t. wieder ausgeben.

reiterat[e], wiederholen; ~ion, Wiederholung, f.

reject, verwerfen; ~ion, Verwerfung, f.

rejoice, v.t. erfreuen; v.i. sich freuen.

rejoin, v.t. sich wieder anschließen; v.i. erwidern; ~der, Erwiderung, f.

rejuvenate, verjüngen.

relapse, sb. Rückfall, m.; v.i. wieder verfallen in . . .

relat[e], v.t. erzählen; v.i. sich beziehen (to auf); ~ed, verwandt; ~ion, Erzählung; Beziehung, f.; Verwandte(r); ~ive, sb. Verwandte(r); a. verhältnismäßig, relativ; bezüglich; ~ivity, Relativität, f.

relax, v.t. lockern, schwächen; v.i. erschlaffen, nachlassen; ~ation, Erschlaffung; Entspannung; Erholung, f.

relay, sb. Pferdewechsel, m. (tech.) Relais, n.; (sport) Stafette, f.; v.t. (radio) übertragen; ~race, Stafettenlauf, m.

release, sb. Befreiung; Freigabe, f.; v.t. befreien, entlassen, erlösen, freigeben.

relegate, verweisen; ~ion, Verweisung, f.

relent, nachgeben; ~less(ly), unnachgiebig, unerbittlich.

relevant, erheblich, zur Sache gehörig.

reliab[le], zuverlässig, verläßlich; ~ility, Zuverlässigkeit, f.

reliance, Vertrauen (on in), n.

relic, Reliquie, *f.;* ~**t,** Witwe, *f.*

relief, Hilfe, Erleichterung, Linderung; Unterstützung; Ablösung, *f.,* Entsatz, *m.; (sculpture)* Relief, *n.*

relieve, erleichtern, lindern; unterstützen; ablösen, entsetzen, entlasten.

relig|ion, Religion, *f.;* ~**ious,** religiös, fromm, gottesfürchtig, *adv.* ~**iously,** pünktlich, gewissenhaft.

relinquish, aufgeben.

relish, *sb.* Geschmack, *m.;* Würze, Zukost, *f.;* Wohlgefallen, *n.; v.t.* gern essen, schmecken; Geschmack finden an.

reluctan|ce, Widerwille, *m.;* ~**t(ly),** widerwillig.

rely, sich verlassen *(upon auf).*

remain, bleiben; übrigbleiben; ~**der,** Rest, *m.; (bookseller's)* Restauflage, *f.;* Restbestand, *m.;* ~**s,** Reste, Überbleibsel, *pl.*

remark, *sb.* Bemerkung, *f.; v.t.* bemerken; ~**able,** bemerkenswert.

remedy, *sb.* Heilmittel, *n.; v.t.* heilen.

rememb|er, sich erinnern; ~**rance,** Erinnerung, *f.,* Andenken, *n.*

remind, erinnern, mahnen *(of an);* ~**er,** Mahnung, *f.*

reminiscence, Erinnerung, *f.*

remiss, nachlässig; ~**ion,** Erlassung, Vergebung, *f.*

remit, senden; erlassen; ~**tance,** Rimesse, *f.,* Wechsel, *m.*

remnant, Überbleibsel, *n.,* Rest, *m.*

remodel, umbilden.

remonstrate, Einwendungen machen.

remorse, Gewissensbiß, *m.;* ~**less,** reuelos; grausam.

remote, ~**ly,** entfernt, entlegen; ~**control,** Fernsteuerung, Fernschaltung, *f.;* ~**ness,** Entlegenheit, *f.*

remov|e, *v.t.* entfernen, wegschaffen, wegräumen; absetzen; *v.i.* sich entfernen, fortziehen; ~**able,** entfernbar; ~**al,** Wegschaffung, Entfernung, Versetzung, *f.; (furniture)* Umzug, *m.;* ~**er,** *(furniture)* Spediteur, *m.*

remunerat|e, belohnen, vergüten; ~**ion,** Belohnung, Vergütung,

f.; ~**ive,** lohnend.

Renaissance, Renaissance, Wiedergeburt, *f.*

rend, zerreißen.

render, *(make)* machen; *(do)* leisten; *(thanks)* abstatten; *(accounts)* einreichen; *(song, &c.)* vortragen; *(translate)* übersetzen; *(suet, &c.)* ausschmelzen.

rendezvous. Stelldichein, *n.*

renegade, Renegat, Abtrünnige(r), *m.*

renew, erneuern; ~**al,** Erneuerung, *f.*

rennet, (Käse)lab, *n.*

renounce, entsagen; verleugnen.

renovat|e, renovieren, erneuern; ~**ion,** Renovierung, Erneuerung, *f.*

renown, Ruhm, *m.;* ~**ed,** berühmt.

rent, *sb. (tear)* Riß, *m.; (hire)* Pacht, Miete, *f.,* Mietzins, *m.; v.t.* (ver)mieten, (ver)pachten.

renunciation, Entsagung, *f.*

reorganiz|e, reorganisieren, neugestalten; ~**ation,** Reorganisation, Neugestaltung, *f.*

repair, *sb.* Ausbesserung, Reparatur, *f.; v.t.* ausbessern, reparieren, flicken.

reparation, Reparation, Entschädigung, *f.*

repast, Mahlzeit, *f.*

repatriat|e, repatriieren, in die Heimat zurückschaffen; ~**ion,** Repatriierung, Heimschaffung, *f.*

repay, zurückbezahlen; vergelten; ~**ment,** Zurückzahlung, *f.*

repeal, *sb.* Aufhebung, *f.,* Widerruf, *m.; v.t.* aufheben, widerrufen.

repeat, *sb.* Wiederholung, *f.; v.t.* wiederholen; repetieren; ~**edly,** wiederholt; ~**er,** Repetieruhr, *f.*

repel, zurück-stoßen, -treiben; ~**lent,** abstoßend.

repent, bereuen; ~**ance,** Reue, *f.;* ~**ant,** reuig.

repercussion, Widerhall, *m.*

repertory, Repertoire, *n.*

repetition, Wiederholung, *f.*

repine, sich grämen.

replace, zurückstellen; ersetzen *(by durch).*

replenish, wieder füllen.

replete, angefüllt, voll.

replica, Abbild, n., Replik, f.

reply, sb. Antwort, f.; v.i. antworten (to auf).

report, sb. Bericht, m.; Gerücht, n.; (Schul)zeugnis, n.; (of a gun, &c.) Knall, m.; v.t. berichten, melden, anzeigen; ~er, Berichterstatter, m.

repos|e, sb. Ruhe, f.; v.i. (be)ruhen; ~itory, Niederlage, f., Warenlager, n.

reprehensible, tadelnswert.

represent, darstellen, vorstellen; vertreten; ~ation, Darstellung f. Stellvertretung, f.; ~ative, sb. Vertreter, m.; a. repräsentativ.

repress, unterdrücken; ~ion, Unterdrückung, Verdrängung, f.; ~ive, unterdrückend.

reprieve, sb. (Straf)aufschub, m., Begnadigung, f.; v.t. begnadigen.

reprimand, sb. Verweis, m.; v.t. (jemandem) einen Verweis erteilen.

reprint, Neudruck, m.

reprisal, Vergeltung, f.

reproach, sb. Vorwurf, m.; v.t. Vorwürfe machen; ~ful(ly), vorwurfsvoll.

reprobate, Verworfene(r).

reproduc|e, wiederherstellen; nachbilden, wiedergeben; ~tion, Reproduktion, Nachbildung, Wiedergabe, f.; ~tive, reproduktiv.

repro|of, Verweis, m.; ~ve, tadeln, mißbilligen.

reptile, Reptil, n.

republic, Republik, f.; ~an, a. republikanisch; sb. Republikaner, m.

repudiat|e, verwerfen, mißbilligen; ~ion, Mißbilligung, f.

repugnan|ce, Widerwille, m.; ~t, widerwillig.

repuls|e, sb. Zurückweisung, f.; v.t. zurückweisen; ~ive, abstoßend, widerwärtig.

reput|e, Ruf, m.; ~able, angesehen, ehrbar; ~ation, Ruf, m.; Achtung, f., Ansehen, m.

request, sb. Bitte, Forderung, f.; v.t. bitten, ersuchen; by ~, auf Wunsch; in ~, sehr gesucht.

require, erfordern; (need) be-

dürfen; ~ment, Forderung, f., Bedürfnis, n.

requisit|e, sb. Erfordernis, n.; a. erforderlich; ~ion, sb. Requisition, f.; v.t. requirieren, beschlagnahmen.

requit|e, vergelten; ~al, Vergeltung, f.

rescind, aufheben, abschaffen.

rescue, sb. Rettung, Bergung; Befreiung, f.; v.t. retten, bergen; befreien; ~r, Retter, m.

research, Forschung, f.

resembl|e, ähnlich sein; ~ance, Ähnlichkeit, f.

resent, übel aufnehmen; ~ful, grollend; ~ment, Groll, m.

reserv|e, sb. Vorbehalt, m.; (mil.) Reserve, f.; (manner) Zurückhaltung, f.; ~ation, Vorbehalt, m.; (land) Schutzgebiet, Reservat, n.; v.t. aufbewahren, vorbehalten; ~ed, (person) reserviert, zurückhaltend; (place, &c.) bestellt, reserviert, numeriert; ~oir, Reservoir, n.

resid|e, wohnen; ~ence, Wohnort, Aufenthalt, m.; ~ent, sb. Bewohner; Resident, m.; a. wohnhaft.

residue, Rest; (chem.) Rückstand, m.

resign, v.t. aufgeben, niederlegen; v.i. seine Stelle aufgeben; ~ation, Rücktritt, m.; Entsagung, f.; ~ed, ergeben.

resilien|ce, Schnell-, Spann- kraft, f.; ~t, zurückprallend.

resin, Harz, n.; ~ous, harzig.

resist, widerstehen; ~ance, Widerstand, m.

resolut|e, ~ely, entschlossen; ~ion, Entschlossenheit, f.; Entschluß, Resolution, f.

resolve, sb. Entschluß, m.; v.t. auflösen; beschließen; v.i. sich entschließen.

resonan|ce, Resonanz, f.; Widerhall m.; ~t, widerhallend.

resort, sb. Zuflucht, f.; Bade-, Kur- ort, m.; v.i. ~ to, sich an ... begeben, seine Zuflucht zu ... nehmen.

resound, widerhallen.

resource, Hilfsmittel, n., Zuflucht,

f.; ~s, Geldmittel, *n.pl.*; Fähigkeiten, *f.pl.*; ~ful, findig, fähig.

respect, *sb.* Achtung; Hinsicht, *f.*; *v.t.* achten; ~able, ~ably achtbar, anständig; ~ability, Achtbarkeit, Anständigkeit, *f.*; ~ed, geachtet; ~ful(ly), ehrerbietig, höflich; ~ing, hinsichtlich, betreffend; ~ive, respektiv, besonder, eigen; ~ively, beziehungsweise.

respir|e, atmen; ~ation, Atmen, *n.*; ~ator, Respirator, *m.*, Gasmaske, *f.*

respite, Frist, *f.*, Aufschub, *m.*

resplenden|ce, Glanz, *m.*; ~t, glänzend.

respond, antworten; reagieren (*to auf*); ~ent, Beklagte(r).

respons|e, Antwort, *f.*; ~ibility, Verantwortlichkeit, *f.*; ~ible, ~ibly, verantwortlich; ~ive, empfänglich; entsprechend.

rest, *sb.* Ruhe; *f.*; (*remainder*) Rest, *m.*; (*support*) Stütze, *f.*; *v.t.* legen, stützen (*on auf*); *v.i.* ruhen; bleiben; lehnen (*on an*); ~less, unruhig, schlaflos; ~lessness, Ruhelosigkeit, *f.*

restaurant, Restaurant, *n.*; ~car, Speisewagen, *m.*

restitution, Wiederherstellung, Entschädigung, *f.*

restive, störrisch, widerspenstig.

restor|e, wiederherstellen; zurückgeben; restaurieren; ~ation, Wiederherstellung, *f.*; Ersatz, *m.*; Restauration, *f.*; ~ative, Stärkungs-; Belebungs-mittel, *n.*; ~er, *hair-~er*, Haarwuchsmittel, *n.*

restrain, zurückhalten; verhindern; ~t, Beschränkung, *f.*

restrict, beschränken, begrenzen; ~ed, beschränkt; ~ion, Einschränkung, *f.*; ~ive, einschränkend.

result, *sb.* Folge, *f.*, Ergebnis, *n.*; *v.i.* resultieren, enden (*in in*).

resum|e, wiederaufnehmen; wiederanfangen; ~ption, Wiederaufnahme, *f.*

resurrection, Auferstehung, *f.*; ~ist, Leichenräuber, *m.*

retail, *sb.* Einzelverkauf, Kleinhandel, *m.*; *v.t.* im Kleinhandel

verkaufen; ~er, Kleinhändler, *m.*

retain, (bei)behalten; ~er, Gefolgsmann, Vassal, *m.*; Vorschuss, *m.*

retaliat|e, (wieder) vergelten; ~ion, Vergeltung, *f.*

retard, verzögern, aufhalten.

retention, Zurückhalten, *f.*; ~ive, festhaltend; (*memory*) zuverlässig, gut.

reticen|ce, Verschwiegenheit, *f.*; ~t, verschwiegen.

retina, Netzhaut, *f.*

retinue, Gefolge, *n.*

retire, sich zurückziehen; zu Bett gehen; ~d, zurückgezogen, außer Dienst; ~ment, Rücktritt, *m.*; Ausscheiden, *n.*

retort, *sb.* Erwiderung; (*chem.*) Retorte, *f.*; *v.i.* erwidern.

retouch, (*photog.*) retuschieren.

retrace, zurückverfolgen.

retract, widerrufen; zurückziehen; ~able, zurückziehbar.

retreat, *sb.* Rückzug; Zufluchtsort, *m.*; *v.i.* sich zurückziehen.

retrench, einschränken; ~ment, Einschränkung, *f.*, Abbau, *m.*

retribution, Vergeltung, *f.*

retrieve, wiedererlangen; wiedergutmachen; (*sport*) apportieren; ~r, Apportierhund, *m.*

retrogr|ade, rückgängig; ~ession, Rückgang, *m.*

retrospect, Rückblick, *m.*; ~ive, zurückblickend; rückwirkend.

return, *sb.* Rückkehr; Rückgabe; Rückfahrt, *f.*; (*profit*) Umsatz, Gewinn, *m.*; (*election*) Wahl, *f.*; (*report, &c.*) Bericht, *m.*, Liste, *f.*; *by* ~, umgehend, mit umgehender Post; *in* ~, dafür; *many happy* ~*s of the day*, Geburtstagsglückwünsche, *m.pl.*; *v.i.* zurückkehren, zurückkommen; *v.t.* zurückgeben; vergelten; (*ball*) zurückschlagen; (*elect*) wählen; ~ match, Rückspiel, *n.*; ~-ticket, Rückfahrkarte, *f.*

reuni|on, Wiedervereinigung, Versammlung, *f.*; ~te, wieder vereinigen.

reveal, offenbaren; enthüllen.

reveille, Weckruf, *m.*

revel, schmausen; schwelgen (*in* in); ~ler, Schwelger, Schlemmer, Zecher, *m.*; ~ry, Gelage, *n.*, Schwelgerei, *f.*

revelation, Offenbarung, *f.*

revenge, *sb.* Rache, *f.*; *v.t.* rächen; ~ful, rachgierig.

revenue, Einkommen, *n.*; ~ officer, Zollbeamte(r).

reverberate, widerhallen; ~ion, Widerhall, *m.*

revere, verehren; ~ence, Ehrerbietung, *f.*; ~end, ehrwürdig; ~ent(ly), ehrerbietig.

reverie, Traum, *m.*, Träumerei, *f.*

reverse, *sb.* (*back*) Rückseite, *f.*; (*opposite*) Gegenteil, *n.*; (*change*) Wendung, *f.*, Umschlag, *m.*; (*mil.*) Niederlage, *f.*; (*mach.*) Umsteuerung, *f.*; *v.t.* umkehren, umändern; widerrufen; umsteuern; ~al, Umstoßung, *f.*, Widerruf, *m.*; ~ible, umkehrbar; umsteuerbar; ~ion, Umkehr, *f.*; (*law*) Rückfall, *m.*

revert, *v.t.* (*law*) zurückfallen (*to* an); zurückkommen (*to* auf).

review, *sb.* Übersicht, *f.*; (*mil.*) Revue, Parade, *f.*; (*periodical*) Zeitschrift, Rundschau, *f.*; (*criticism*) Rezension, *f.*; *v.t.* Umschau halten über; (*mil.*) besichtigen; (*book*) rezensieren; ~er, Rezensent, *m.*

revile, schmähen.

revise, *sb.* Revision, *f.*; *v.t.* revidieren, durchsehen; ~al, Durchsicht, Prüfung, *f.*

revive, *v.t.* wiederbeleben, auffrischen; *v.i.* wieder aufleben; ~al, Wiederbelebung, *f.*, Renaissance, *f.*

revocation, Aufhebung, *f.*, Widerruf, *m.*

revoke, widerrufen, aufheben; (*at cards*) nicht bedienen.

revolt, *sb.* Empörung, *f.*; *v.i.* sich empören.

revolution, (*political*) Revolution, *f.*; (*mach.*) Umdrehung, Tour, *f.*; ~ary, revolutionär; ~ize, gänzlich umgestalten.

revolve, (sich) umdrehen; ~er, Revolver, *m.*; ~ing, Drehsich drehend.

revue, Revue, *f.*

revulsion, Umschwung, *m.*

reward, *sb.* Belohnung, *f.*; *v.t.* belohnen.

rhapsody, Rhapsodie, *f.*

Rhenish, rheinisch, Rhein-.

rhetoric, Redekunst, *f.*; ~al, rednerisch, rhetorisch; ~ian, Redekünstler, *m.*

rheumatic, rheumatisch; ~ism, Rheumatismus, *m.*

rhinoceros, Nashorn, *n.*

rhododendron, Rhododendron, *n.*, Alpenrose, *f.*

rhomb, Rhombus, *m.*, Raute, *f.*

rhubarb, Rhabarber, *m.*

rhyme, *sb.* Reim, *m.*; *v.t.* and *i.* reimen.

rhythm, Rhythmus, *m.*; ~ical(ly), rhythmisch.

rib, Rippe, *f.*

ribald, zotig, gemein, liederlich.

ribbon, Band, *n.*; Streifen, *m.*; *in* ~s, in Fetzen.

rice, Reis, *m.*

rich, ~ly, reich; (*food*) nahrhaft, fett; (*land*) fruchtbar; ~es, Reichtum, *m.*; ~ness, Reichtum, *m.*; Reichhaltigkeit, *f.*

rickets, Rachitis, *f.*; ~y, rachitisch; wacklig.

ricochet, *sb.* Prallschuß, Abpraller, *m.*; *v.i.* abprallen.

rid, befreien, reinigen (*of* von); *be* ~ *of*, los sein; *get* ~ *of*, sich losmachen von; entlassen; ~dance, Befreiung; Wegschaffung, *f.*

riddle, *sb.* Rätsel, Sieb, *n.*; *v.t.* sieben; durchlöchern.

ride, *sb.* Ritt, *m.*; Fahrt, *f.*; *v.i.* reiten; fahren; ~r, Reiter, *m.*; Zusatzklausel, *f.*

ridge, Grat, Rücken, *m.*; (*of roof*) First, *m.* or *f.*

ridicule, *sb.* Spott, *m.*; Lächerlichkeit, *f.*; *v.t.* lächerlich machen; ~ous(ly), lächerlich.

rife, herrschend, allgemein.

riffraff, Gesindel, *n.*

rifle, *sb.* Gewehr, *n.*; *v.t.* rauben, plündern; ~man, Jäger, *m.*; ~range, Schießstand, *m.*

rift, Riß, *m.*, Spalte, *f.*

rigging, Takelung, *f.*

right, *sb.* Recht, *n.*; rechte Seite, *f.*; *to the* ~, rechts; *by* ~s, von

Rechts wegen; *a.*, ~ly, *adv.*, (*right hand*) recht; (*straight*) gerade; (*correct*) richtig; *all* ~, schon gut, einverstanden; *to be* ~, recht haben; *set* ~, berichtigen; ~ *v.t.* berichtigen; (*naut.*) aufrichten; ~angled, rechtwinklig; ~eous, gerecht; rechtschaffen; ~eousness, Gerechtigkeit; Rechtschaffenheit, *f.*; ~ful(ly), rechtmäßig.

rigid, ~ly, starr, steif; ~ity, Starrheit, Steifheit, *f.*

rigmarole, Gewäsch, *n.*, Unsinn, *m.*

rig|orous, streng; ~our, Strenge, *f.*

rill, Bächlein, *n.*

rim, Rand; Reifen, *m.*

rime, Reif, *m.*

rind, Rinde, Schale, *f.*

ring, *sb.* Ring; (*sound*) Klang, Schall, *m.*, Geläute, *n.*; (*commerc.*) Kartell, *n.*; *v.* klingeln, läuten; ~up, anrufen; ~leader, Rädelsführer, *m.* ~let, Löckchen, *f.*; ~road, Ringstraße, *f.*; ~worm, Ringelflechte, *f.*

rink, Rollschuhbahn, Eisfläche, *f.*

rinse, spülen.

riot, *sb.* Aufstand, Aufruhr, *m.*; *v.i.* sich auflehnen, Aufruhr stiften; ~er, Aufrührer, *m.*; ~ous(ly), aufrührerisch; ausgelassen.

rip, *sb.* Riß, *m.*; *v.t.* reißen.

ripe, reif, *v.*; ~n, reifen; ~ness, Reife, *f.*

ripple, *sb.* Kräuseln, *n.*; *v.* (sich) kräuseln.

ris|e, *sb.* (*sun*) Aufgang, *m.*; (*hill*) Anhöhe, *f.*; (*prices, &c.*) Steigen, *n.*; *v.i.* (*sun*) aufgehen; (*get up*) aufstehen; (*mount*) aufsteigen; (*rebel*) sich erheben; (*prices, &c.*) steigen; (*arise*) entspringen, herrühren; ~ing, *sb.* (*rebellion*) Aufstand (*of meeting*) Aufbruch, *m.*; (*of dead*) Auferstehung, *f.*; *a.* emporkommend; aufgehend; ansteigend.

risk, *sb.* Gefahr, *f.*; Wagnis, *m.*; *v.t.* wagen; ~y, gewagt, gefährlich.

rissole, Frikandelle, *f.*

rit|e, Gebrauch, Ritus, *m.*; ~ual,

sb. Ritual, *n.*; *a.* rituell.

rival, *sb.* Nebenbuhler; Konkurrent, *m.*; *a.* nebenbuhlerisch, wetteifernd; *v.t.* wetteifern (mit); ~ry, Mitbewerbung Konkurrenz, *f.*

river, Fluß, Strom, *m.*

rivet, *sb.* Niet, *m.* or *n.*; *v.t.* nieten.

rivulet, Bächlein, *n.*

roach, Plötze, *f.*, Rotauge, *n.*

road, Straße, *f.*, Weg, *m.*; (*naut.*) Reede, *f.*; ~block, Straßensperre, *f.*; ~hog, Kilometerfresser, *m.*; ~metal, Beschotterung, *f.*; ~sign, Wegweiser, *m.*; ~ surface, Fahrbahndecke, *f.*; ~way, Straßen-, Fahrdamm, *m.*

roam, umherstreifen.

roan, Rotschimmel, *m.*

roar, *sb.* Gebrüll, *n.*; (*guns*) Donner, *m.*; (*sea*) Brausen, *n.*; *v.i.* brüllen; donnern; toben; ~ *with laughter*, in ein schallendes Gelächter ausbrechen.

roast, *sb.* Braten, *m.*; *v.t.* braten; (*ore, coffee, chestnuts*) rösten; *a.* gebraten, Brat-; ~beef, Rinderbraten, *m.*, Roastbeef, *n.*

rob, (be)rauben; ~ber, Räuber, *m.*; ~bery, Raub, *m.*

robe, *sb.* Robe, *f.*, Staatskleid, *n.*, Talar, *m.*; *v.t.* (an)kleiden.

robin, Rotkehlchen, *n.*

robust, stark, rüstig.

rock, *sb.* Felsen, *m.*, Klippe, *f.*; *v.t.* wiegen, schaukeln; rütteln; ~ery, Steingarten, *m.*; ~ingchair, Schaukelstuhl, *m.*; ~inghorse, Schaukelpferd, *n.*; ~salt, Steinsalz, *n.*; ~y, felsig.

rocket, Rakete, *f.*

rococo, Rokoko, *n.*

rod, Stab, *m.*, Rute, *f.*

rodent, Nagetier, *n.*

roe, (*deer*) Reh, *n.*; (*fish*) Rogen, *m.*

rogu|e, Schurke; Schelm, *m.*; ~ery, Schurkerei, *f.*; ~ish, schelmisch.

roll, *sb.* Rolle; Walze, *f.*; Brötchen, *n.*; (*of drums*) Wirbel, *m.*; *v.t.* rollen; wälzen; einwickeln; *v.i.* sich wälzen (*naut.*) schlingern; ~call, Namensaufruf, *m.*; (*mil.*) Appell, *m.*; ~er, Rolle; Walze, *f.*; ~er-skate, Rollschuh, *m.*;

~er-towel, Rollhandtuch, n.;
~ing, Walzen; Schlingern, n.;
Rollbewegung, f.; ~ing-mill,
Walzwerk, n.; ~ing-pin, Teig-
rolle, f.; ~ing stock, rollendes
Material, n.; ~top desk, Zylin-
derbüro, n.

Roman, sb. Römer, m.; a. römisch;
~ Catholic, Römisch-katho-
lische(r), Katholik(in, f.), m.

roman|ce, Roman, m.; Erdich-
tung; Romantik, f.; (lang.)
Romanisch, n.; ~esque, (arch.)
romanisch; ~tic, romantisch;
~ticism, Romantik, f.

romp, sich balgen.

roof, Dach, n.; (mouth) Gaumen, m.

rook, Saatkrähe, f.; (chess) Turm,
m.; ~ery, Krähenhorst, m.

room, Raum, Platz, m.; Zimmer,
n., Stube, f.; Saal, m.; (cause)
Grund, m.; ~y, geräumig.

roost, Hühnerstange, f.; go to ~,
sich niederlegen, schlafen gehen.

root, sb. Wurzel, f.; take ~,
Wurzel fassen, v.i. (ein)wurzeln;
~ out, ausrotten; ~crops,
Hackfrüchte, f.pl.; ~ed, (fig.)
eingewurzelt.

rope, Seil, Tau, n., Strick, m.;
~dancer, Seiltänzer, m.; ~
ladder, Strickleiter, f.; ~
maker, Seiler, m.; ~walk,
Seilerbahn, f.

rosary, Rosenkranz, m.

rose, sb. Rose; (of watering-can)
Brause, f.; a. rosig, rosenfarbig;
~mary, Rosmarin, f.; ~tte,
Rosette, f.; ~wood, Rosenholz, n.

rosin, Harz, n.

roster, Dienstordnung, f.

rostrum, Tribüne, f.

rosy, rosig.

rot, sb. Fäulnis, f.; (slang) Quatsch,
Unsinn, m.; v.i. faulen, modern.

rotat|e, (sich) drehen; ~ion,
Kreislauf, m., Umdrehung, f.;
(crops) Fruchtwechsel, m.; by
~ion, der Reihe nach; ~ory,
Dreh-, Kreis-.

rotten, faul, verfault; ~ness,
Fäulnis, f.

rotund, rund; ~ity, Rundheit, f.

rouble, Rubel, m.

rouge, Schminke, f.

rough, rauh, holprig, uneben; ~

ungebildet; stürmisch; ~cast,
mit Rohputz; ~ copy, Skizze, f.
Entwurf, m.; ~ly, annähernd,
rund; ~ness, Rauhigkeit;
Roheit, f.; ~rider, Pferde-
bändiger, m.; ~shod, scharf
beschlagen; (fig.) rücksichtslos.

round, sb. (turn) Runde, f., Rund-
gang, m.; (of ladder) Leiter-
sprosse, f.; (firing) Salve, f.; (of
ammunition) Schuß, m.; (bread,
beef, &c.) Schnitte, f.; a. rund;
prep. um; adv. herum, umher;
all the year ~, das ganze Jahr
hindurch; come ~, (recover)
wieder zum Bewußtsein kommen; ~ v.t. rund machen; um-
fahren; ~ off, abrunden;
~about, sb. Karussell, n.;
(traffic) Kreisverkehr, m.; a.
weitschweifig; adv. rundherum;
~ers, Schlagball, m.; ~hand,
Rundschrift, f.; ~head, Rund-
kopf; Puritaner, m.; ~ish,
rundlich; ~ly, direkt, rund-
(weg); ~ness, Rundung, f.;
~up, Zusammentreiben, n.

rouse, aufwecken; erregen.

rout, sb. Flucht, Niederlage, f.; v.t.
in die Flucht schlagen.

route, Route, f., Weg, m.;
~ march, (Reise)marsch, m.

routine, Routine, f.

rove, herumstreifen; ~r, Herum-
streicher; Seeräuber, m.

row[1], sb. Reihe, f.

row[2], sb. Lärm, Aufruhr, m.;
~dy, Rowdy, Raufbold, m.

row[3], v.t. and i. rudern, pullen;
~lock, Ruderklampe, f.

rowan, Eberesche, f.

rowel, Spornrädchen, n.

royal, königlich; (naut.) Ober-
bram-; ~ist, Royalist, m.;
~ty, Königtum, n.; Majestät,
f.; (author's) Tantieme, f.

rub, reiben; frottieren; wischen;
~ out, ausradieren; ~ up, (fig.)
auffrischen.

rubber, Radiergummi; (whist,
&c.) Robber, m.; ~ dinghy,
Schlauchboot, n.

rubbish, Schutt, Abfall; (fig.)
Quatsch, Unsinn, m.

rubble, Schutt, m.

rubric, Rubrik, f.

ruby, Rubin, *m.*

rucksack, Rücksack, *m.*

rudder, (Steuer)ruder, *n.*

ruddy, rötlich; frisch.

rude, ~ly, grob, unhöflich, roh; ~ness, Grobheit, Unhöflichkeit, *f.*

rudiments, Anfangsgründe, *m.pl.*

rue[1], bereuen; ~ful, reuig.

rue[2], (bot.) Raute, *f.*

ruffian, Schurke, *m.*

ruffle, *sb.* Krause, *f.*; *v.t.* kräuseln; stören, beunruhigen.

rug, Decke, *f.*, (Kamin)vorleger, *m.*

rugged, rauh, holp(e)rig.

ruin, *sb.* Ruine, *f.*; Verderben, *n.,* Ruin, *m.; v.t.* ruinieren, verderben; ~ous, baufällig; verderblich.

rule, *sb.* Regel; Regierung, *f.; as a* ~, in der Regel; *v.t.* regieren; (*lines*) liniieren; (*decide*) entscheiden; ~r, Herrscher, *m.*; (*for ruling lines*) Lineal, *n.*

rum, sb. Rum, *m.; a.* (*slang*) sonderbar.

rumble, rollen, rasseln.

rumina|nt, Wiederkäuer, *m.*; ~te, wiederkäuen; (*fig.*) nachdenken.

rummage, durchwühlen.

rumour, Gerücht, *n.*

rump, Hinterteil, *n.*; ~-steak, Rumpsteak, *n.*

run, *sb.* Lauf, Anlauf, *m.*; Fahrt; Reihe, *f.*; Zuspruch, *m.*; *in the long* ~, auf die Dauer, mit der Zeit; *v.i.* laufen; rennen; fahren, strömen, fließen; (*melt*) laufen, schmelzen; (*read*) lauten; (*amount to*) sich belaufen (auf); ~ *aground,* stranden; ~ *away,* weglaufen; (*waste*) auslaufen; ~ *down,* (*watch*) ablaufen; (*fluids*) herabfließen; (*decry*) herabsetzen; (*hunt*) abhetzen; (*knock down*) niederrennen; ~ *off,* davonlaufen; gießen; drucken; ~ *on,* fortschreiten; fortsetzen; ~ *out,* knapp werden, zu Ende gehen; ~ *over,* überfahren; (*read*) durchlaufen; ~ *short,* knapp werden; ~ *up,* hinauflaufen; (*prices*) steigern; (*flag*) hissen; ~ *wild,* verwildern; ~-about, Kleinauto, *n.*; ~away, Flüchtling; Ausreißer; (*horse*) Durchgänger, *m.*; ~ner,

Renner, Läufer; (*bot.*) Ausläufer, *m.*; (*of sledge*) Kufe, *f.*; (*strip of cloth*) Läufer, *m.*; ~way, Lauf-, Roll- bahn, *f.*

rune, Rune, *f.*

rung, (Leiter)sprosse, *f.*

running, *sb.* Laufen, *n.*; Verkehr, *m.*; *in the* ~, laufend; *a.* laufend, Lauf-; fließend; *4 days* ~, 4 Tage nacheinander; ~board, Tritt-, Lauf-brett, *n.*; ~ commentary, laufender Kommentar; ~ costs, Betriebskosten, *pl.*

rupee, Rupie, *f.*

rupture, *sb.* Bruch, *m.*; *v.t.* brechen.

rural, ländlich.

ruse, List, *f.*

rush, *sb.* Ansturm, Andrang, *m.*; (*bot.*) Binse, *f.*; *v.i.* sich stürzen, rennen, eilen; ~ hours, Hauptverkehrs-, Hauptgeschäfts-stunden, *f.pl.*; ~hour traffic, Stoßverkehr, *m.*; ~ order, Eilbestellung, *f.*

rusk, Zwieback, *m.*

Russian, *sb.* Russe, *m.*; (*lang.*) Russisch, *n.*; *a.* russisch.

rust, *sb.* Rost, *m.*; *v.i.* (ver)rosten; ~y, rostig.

rustic, ländlich, bäu(e)risch.

rustle, rauschen; rascheln.

rut, *sb.* (*track*) Spur; (*stag*) Brunst, *f.*; *v.i.* brunsten.

ruthless, ~ly, unbarmherzig.

rye, Roggen, *m.*

S

sabbath, Sabbat, Sonntag, *m.*

sable, Zobel, *m.*

sabotage, *sb.* Sabotage, *f.*; *v.t.* sabotieren.

sabre, Säbel, *m.*

saccharine, Sac(c)harin, *n.*

sack, *sb.* Sack, *m.*; Plünderung; Entlassung, *f.*; *v.t.* plündern; entlassen; ~cloth, Sackleinwand, *f.*

sacrament, Sakrament, *n.*

sacred, heilig; ~ness, Heiligkeit, *f.*

sacrifice, *sb.* Opfer, *n.*; *v.t.* opfern; ~ial, Opfer-.

sacrilege, Kirchenschändung, *f.*; Frevel, *m.*; ~ious, kirchenschänderisch, frevelhaft.

sacrist|an, Küster, *m.*; **~y,** Sakristei, *f.*

sad, ~ly, traurig, betrübt; (of *colours*) dunkel; ~den, betrüben; ~ness, Traurigkeit, *f.*

saddle, *sb.* Sattel, *m.*; *v.t.* satteln; ~r, Sattler, *m.*

sadis|m, Sadismus, *m.*; ~t, Sadist, *m.*; ~tic, sadistisch.

safe, *sb.* Geld-, Speise- schrank, Safe, *m.*; *a.*, ~ly, sicher; ~conduct, sicheres Geleit, *n.*; Geleitschein, *m.*; ~guard, *sb.* Schutz, *m.*; *v.t.* beschützen.

safety, Sicherheit, *f.*; ~catch, Sicherung, *f.*; ~pin, Sicherheitsnadel, *f.*; ~razor, Rasierapparat, *m.*; ~valve, Sicherheitsventil, *n.*

sag, sacken, einfallen.

sagac|ious, scharfsinnig; ~ity, Scharfsinn, *m.*

sage, *sb.* Weise(r); (*herb*) Salbei, *m,* or *f.*; *a.* weise.

sago, Sago, *m.*

sail, *sb.* Segel, *n.*; (of *windmill*) Flügel, *m.*; *set* ~ in See stechen, auslaufen; *under full* ~, alles bei; *v.i.* segeln; auslaufen; ~ing, Segeln, *n.*; Fahrt, *f.*; ~ing-vessel, Segelschiff, *n.*; ~or, Matrose, Seemann, *m.*

saint, Heilige(r); ~liness, Heiligkeit, *f.*; ~ly, heilig, fromm; *All Saints' Day,* Allerheiligen, *n.*

sake, *for the* ~ *of,* um ... willen (*with genitive*); *for God's* ~, um Gottes willen; *for my* ~, um meinetwillen.

salad, Salat, *m.*

salary, Gehalt, *n.*

sale, Verkauf; Absatz, *m.*; *for on* ~, zu verkaufen; ~sman, Verkäufer, *m.*

salient, *sb.* Vorsprung, *m.*; *a.* vorspringend.

saline, salzhaltig.

saliva, Speichel, *m.*

sallow, bleich, gelblich.

sally, *sb.* (mil.) Ausfall (*joke*) witziger Einfall, *m.*; *v.i.* ~ forth, einen Ausfall machen.

salmon, Lachs, *m.*

saloon, Saal, Salon, *m.*; (on *ship*) erste Klasse, *f.*

salt, *sb.* Salz, *n.*; *smelling-*~**s,**

Riechsalz, *n.*; *a.* salzig; *v.t.* salzen; ~cellar, Salzfaß, *n.*; ~petre, Salpeter, *m.*; ~works, Saline, *f.*; Salzbergwerk, *n.*; ~y, salzig.

salubrious, heilsam, gesund.

salutary, heilsam.

salute, *sb.* Gruß, *m.*; (*salvo*) Salut, *m.*; *v.t.* grüßen; salutieren.

salvage, *sb.* Bergung, *f.*; geborgene Sachen, *f.pl.*; *v.t.* bergen.

salvation, Heil, *n.*, Rettung, *f.*; *Salvation Army,* Heilsarmee, *f.*

salve, *sb.* Salbe, *f.*; (fig.) Balsam, *m.*; *v.t.* salben; bergen.

salvo, Salve, *f.*; (of *bombs*) Massenabwurf, *m.*

sal volatile, Riechsalz, *n.*

same, der-, die-, das- selbe; *it's all the* ~ *to me,* es ist mir egal.

sample, *sb.* Probe, *f.*, Muster, *n.*; *v.t.* eine Probe nehmen.

sanator|ium, Sanatorium, *n.*; ~y, heilsam.

sancti|fy, heiligen; ~monious(ly), scheinheilig; ~moniousness, Scheinheiligkeit, *f.*

sanction, *sb.* Genehmigung; Bestätigung; (*politics*) Sanktion, *f.*; *v.t.* gestatten, genehmigen, sanktionieren.

sanctity, Heiligkeit, *f.*; ~uary, Heiligtum, *n.*; Asyl, *n.*

sand, Sand, *m.*; ~bag, Sandsack, *m.*; ~bank, Sandbank, *f.*; ~paper, Sandpapier, *n.*; ~s, Strand, *m.*; ~shoes, Strandschuhe, *m.pl.*; ~stone, Sandstein, *m.*; ~y, sandig.

sandal, Sandale, *f.*

sandwich, belegtes Butterbrot, Sandwich, *n.*

sane, (geistig) gesund; vernünftig.

sanguinary, blutig; blutdürstig.

sanitary, sanitär, Gesundheits-; ~ towel, Monatsbinde, *f.*

sanitation, Kanalisation, *f.*, sanitäre Anlagen, *f.pl.*

sanity, gesunder Verstand, *m.*

sap, Saft, *m.*; (mil.) Laufgraben, *m.*; *v.t.* (mil.) minieren; ~ling, Schößling, *m.*; ~per, Pionier, *m.*

sapphire, Saphir, *m.*

sarcas|m Sarkasmus, *m.*; ~tic(ally), sarkastisch.

sardine, Sardine, *f.*

sash, Schärpe, *f.*; (of window) (verschiebbarer) Fensterrahmen, *m.*

satchel, Schulmappe, *f.*

satellite, Satellit, Trabant, *m.*

sat|iate, (über)sättigen; ~iety, Sättigung, *f.*

satin, Atlas, *m.*

satir|e, Satire, *f.*; ~ical, satirisch; ~ist, Satiriker, *m.*; ~ize, verspotten.

satisf|action, Befriedigung, *f.*; ~actory, befriedigend; ~y, befriedigen.

saturate, sättigen.

Saturday, Samstag, Sonnabend, *m.*

sauce, Sauce, Tunke, *f.*; ~pan, Kochtopf, *m.*

saucer, Untertasse, *f.*

sauc|y, frech; ~iness, Frechheit, *f.*

saunter, schlendern.

sausage, Wurst, *f.*

savage, *sb.* Wilde(r); *a.* wild; ~ry, Wildheit, *f.*

sav|e, *v.t.* (rescue) retten; (keep) (er)sparen; (auf)bewahren; *prep.* außer, ausgenommen; ~ings, Ersparnisse, *f.pl.*; ~ings-bank, Sparkasse, *f.*

Saviour, Heiland; Retter, *m.*

savour, *sb.* Geschmack, Geruch, *m.*; *v.i.* schmecken (of nach); ~y, schmackhaft, pikant.

saw, *sb.* Säge, *f.*; *v.t.* sägen; ~dust, Sägespäne, *m.pl.*; ~mill, Sägemühle, *f.*

Saxon, *sb.* (person) Sachse, *m.*; (language) Sächsisch, *n.*; *a.* sächsisch.

saxophone, Saxophon, *n.*

say, sagen; ~ing, Spruch, *m.*, Sprichwort, *n.*

scab, Schorf, *m.*; ~by, räudig.

scabbard, Scheide, *f.*

scabious, Skabiose, *f.*

scaffold, Schafott, *n.*; ~ing, Gerüst, *n.*

scald, verbrennen, verbrühen.

scale, *sb.* (of fish) Schuppe, *f.*; (of a balance) Waagschale, *f.*; (measure) Skala, *f.*; (music) Tonleiter, *f.*; (degree) Grad, *m.*; pair of ~s, Waage, *f.*; on a large ~, in großem Maßstab; ~ of prices, Preisskala, *f.*; to a ~ of, im Verhältnis von; *v.t.*

erklettern, besteigen; *v.i.* (med.) abblättern.

scalp, *sb.* Kopfhaut, *f.*; *v.t.* skalpieren.

scalpel, Skalpell, *n.*

scaly, schuppig.

scamp, *sb.* Schuft, Taugenichts, *m.*; *v.t.* verpfuschen.

scamper, ~away, davonlaufen.

scan, (verse) skandieren; (scrutinize) prüfen.

scandal, Skandal, *m.*; Schande, *f.*; ~ize Anstoß erregen; ~ous(ly), skandalös; schändlich.

scant|y, ~ily, dürftig, knapp; ~iness, Dürftigkeit, *f.*

scapegoat, Sündenbock, *m.*

scar, *sb.* Narbe, *f.*; *v.t.* ritzen, verwunden; *v.i.* vernarben.

scarc|e, knapp; ~ely, kaum; ~ity, Knappheit, *f.*

scare, schrecken, scheuchen; ~crow, Vogelscheuche, *f.*

scarf, Halstuch, *n.*

scarlet, *sb.* Scharlach, *m.*; *a.* scharlachrot; ~ fever, Scharlachfieber, *n.*

scatter, *v.t.* verbreiten, zerstreuen; *v.i.* sich verstreuen.

scavenge, ausspülen, reinigen; ~r, Straßenreiniger, *m.*

scene, Szene, *f.*, Schauplatz, *m.*; ~ry, (landscape) Landschaft, *f.*; (theatr.) Dekorationen, *f.pl.*; ~-shifter, Kulissenschieber, *m.*

scent, *sb.* Geruch Duft, *m.*; (perfume) Parfüm, *n.*; (animal's) Fährte, Spur, *f.*; *v.t.* wittern; parfümieren; ~ed, wohlriechend.

sceptic, *sb.* Skeptiker, *m.*; ~al(ly), skeptisch; ~ism, Skeptizismus, *m.*

sceptre, Zepter, *n.*

schedule, Liste, *f.* Verzeichnis, *n.*; (Fahr)plan, *m.*; ~d, (fahr)planmäßig.

scheme, *sb.* Schema, *n.*, Entwurf, Plan, *m.*; *v.i.* Pläne machen; Ränke schmieden; ~r, Ränkeschmied, *m.*

schism, Kirchenspaltung, *f.*

scholar, Schüler, *m.*; Gelehrte(r); ~ly, gelehrt; ~ship, Gelehrsamkeit, Wissenschaft, *f.*; Stipendium, *n.*

scholastic, schulmäßig; scholastisch.

school, *sb.* Schule, *f.*; *v.t.* unterrichten, schulen; **~boy**, Schuljunge, *m.*; **~girl**, Schulmädchen, *n.*; **~ing**, Erziehung, Ausbildung, *f.*; **~master**, (Schul)lehrer, *m.*; **~mistress**, Lehrerin, *f.*

schooner, Schooner, *m.*

sciatica, Ischias, *f.*

scien|ce, (Natur)wissenschaft, *f.*; **~tific**, wissenschaftlich; **~tist**, Naturwissenschaftler; Gelehrte(r), *m.*

scintillate, funkeln.

scissors, Schere, *f.*

scoff, spotten (*at* über).

scold, schelten.

scoop, *sb.* Schaufel, Schippe, *f.*; (*newspaper*) Erstbericht, *m.*; *v.t.*, **~ out**, aushöhlen; **~ up**, aufschaufeln.

scooter, Straßenroller, *m.*

scope, Spielraum, *m.*

scorch, *v.t.* sengen; *v.i.* (*motoring slang*) dahinsausen.

score, *sb.* (*bill*) Zeche, *f.*; (*games*) Spielergebnis, *n.*, Punkte, *m.pl.*; (*music*) Partitur, *f.*; Zwanzig, *f.*; *v.t.* markieren; (*games*) ein Tor schießen; (*music*) instrumentieren; **~r**, (*football*) Torschütze; Markör, Anschreiber, *m.*

scorn, *sb.* Hohn, Spott, *m.*, Verachtung, *f.*; *v.t.* verachten, verschmähen; **~ful(ly)**, höhnisch.

scorpion, Skorpion, *m.*

Scot, Schotte, *m.*; Schottin, *f.*; **~ch**, **~tish**, schottisch.

scoundrel, Schurke, *m.*

scour, scheuern, reinigen; durchstreifen.

scourge, *sb.* Geißel, *f.*; *v.t.* geißeln.

scout, *sb.* Kundschafter, *m.*, Patrouille, *f.*; *boy* **~**, Pfadfinder, *m.*; *v.i.* ausspähen; *v.t.* (*the idea*) zurückweisen.

scowl, *sb.* finsteres Gesicht, *n.*; *v.i.* finster aussehen, die Stirn runzeln.

scraggy, mager, abgemagert.

scramble, *sb.* Gedränge, *n.*, Balgerei, *f.*; *v.i.* klettern; sich balgen (*for* um); **~d eggs**, Rührei, *n.pl.*

scrap, *sb.* Stückchen, *n.*, Fetzen,

m.; Altmaterial, *n.*; *v.t.* verschrotten, zum alten Eisen werfen; **~book**, Sammelbuch, *n.*; **~ iron**, Alteisen, *n.*

scrape, *sb.* Klemme, Patsche, *f.*; *v.t.* kratzen, schaben.

scratch, *sb.* Riß, *m.*, Schramme, *f.*; (*races*) Startlinie, *f.*; *come up to* **~**, allen Erwartungen entsprechen; *v.t.* kratzen, ritzen; *v.i.* (*sport*) sich zurückziehen.

scrawl, *sb.* Gekritzel, *n.*; *v.t.* kritzeln.

scream, *sb.* Schrei, *m.*; *v.i.* kreischen, (auf)schreien.

screech, *sb.* gellender Schrei; *v.i.* aufschreien; **~owl**, Nachteule, *f.*

screen, *sb.* (Licht)schirm, *m.*; (*cinema*) Leinwand, *f.*; (*photog.*) Scheibe, *f.*; (*technical*) Raster, *m.*; (*for sifting*) Sieb, *n.*; *v.t.* schützen, beschirmen; (*sport*) abblenden; filmen; durchsieben; (*radio*) abschirmen, isolieren; **~wiper**, Scheibenwischer, *m.*

screw, *sb.* Schraube, *f.*; (*pay*) Gehalt, *n.*, Lohn, *m.*; *v.t.* schrauben; **~driver**, Schraubenzieher, *m.*; **~steamer**, Schraubendampfer, *m.*

scribble, *sb.* Gekritzel, *n.*; *v.i.* kritzeln; **~ing-pad**, Notizblock, *m.*

scribe, Schreiber, *m.*

script, Schrift, Schreibschrift, *f.*; (*films*) Drehbuch, *n.*; **~writer**, Drehbuchautor, *m.*

scriptur|e, die Heilige Schrift; **~al**, biblisch.

scroll, Rolle, *f.*; Schnörkel, *m.*

scrub, *sb.* Gestrüpp, *n.*; *v.t.* scheuern, schrubben; **~by**, schäbig.

scruff, Genick, *n.*

scrup|le, *sb.* Skrupel, *m.*, Bedenken, *n.*; *v.i.* Bedenken tragen; **~ulous(ly)**, gewissenhaft; genau, peinlich.

scrutin|ize, prüfen, forschen; **~y**, genaue Untersuchung, *f.*

scud, *sb.* Sprühregen; Wolkenfetzen, *m.*; *v.i.* laufen; (*naut.*) lenzen.

scuffle, Handgemenge, *n.*

scull, *sb.* kurzes Ruder; *v.i.* rudern, skullen.

scullery, Abwaschküche, *f.*

sculpt|or, Bildhauer, *m.*; ~ure, Bildhauerkunst; Bildhauer- arbeit, Plastik, *f.*

scum, Schaum; *(fig.)* Abschaum, *m.*

scurf, Schorf, *m.*; ~y, schorfig.

scurrilous, gemein, grob scherzend.

scurvy, *sb.* Skorbut, *m.*; *a.* *(fig.)* gemein.

scutcheon, Wappenschild, *n.*

scuttle, *sb.* Kohlenkasten, *m.*; *(naut.)* Luke, *f.*; *v.t.* versenken, anbohren.

scythe, Sense, *f.*

sea, See, *f.*, Meer, *n.*; *(fig.)* ratlos: *heavy* ~s, hoher See- gang; ~board, Seeküste, *f.*; ~breeze, Seewind, *m.*; ~gull, Seemöwe, *f.*; ~level, Meeres- spiegel, *m.*; ~lion, Seelöwe. *m.*; ~man, Matrose, *m.*; *able* ~man, Vollmatrose, *m.*; ~manship, Seemannskunst, *f.*; ~plane, Seeflugzeug, *n.*; ~ power, Seemacht, *f.*; ~rescue service, Seenotdienst, *m.*; ~shore, Seeküste, *f.*; ~sick, seekrank; ~sickness, See- krankheit, *f.*; ~side, Seeküste. *f.*, Strand, *m.*; ~weed, Tang, *m.*, Alge, *f.*; ~worthy, seetüchtig, seeklar.

seal, *sb.* Siegel, *n.*; *(zool.)* Seehund. *m.*, Robbe, *f.*; *v.t.* (ver)siegeln; abdichten; ~ing-wax, Siegel- lack, *m.* or *n.*; ~skin, See- hundsfell, *n.*

seam, *sb.* Saum, *m.*, Naht, *f.*; *(coal)* Flöz, *n.*; *v.t.* zusammen- nähen; ~less, nahtlos; ~stress, Näherin, *f.*; ~y side, *(fig.)* Schattenseite, *f.*

sear, brennen, sengen.

search, *sb.* Suchen, *n.*, Unter- suchung, *f.*; *v.t.* (unter)suchen; durchsuchen; ~ing, forschend; ~light, Scheinwerfer, *m.*; ~warrant, Haussuchungs- befehl, *m.*

season, *sb.* Jahreszeit; Saison, *f.*; *v.t.* *(food)* würzen; *(timber)* trocknen; *(fig.)* abhärten, ge- wöhnen; ~able, zeitgemäß; ~ed, gewürzt; akklimatisiert; ausgetrocknet; reif; ~ing, Würze, *f.*; ~ticket, Dauer-

karte, Abonnementskarte, *f.*

seat, *sb.* Sitz; Stuhl; Sattel. *m.*; *(of trousers)* Gesäß, *n.*; *(estate)* Landsitz, *m.*; *take a* ~, Platz nehmen; *is this* ~ *taken?* ist die- ser Platz besetzt?; *v.t.* setzen, stellen; ~ 50, 50 Sitzplätze haben; ~ *oneself*, sich setzen.

sece|de, sich trennen; ~ssion, Trennung, Sezession, *f.*

seclude, absondern; ~d, ab- geschlossen, einsam.

seclusion, Zurückgezogenheit, *f.*

second, *sb.* Sekunde, *f.*; *(in duel)* Sekundant. *m.*; *a.* zweite(r, s); folgend: *on* ~ *thoughts*, bei nochmaliger Überlegung; *v.t.* unterstützen; beistehen; *(mil.)* (ab)kommandieren; ~ary, untergeordnet, ergänzend; ~ary school, höhere Schule; ~hand, antiquarisch; ge- braucht; ~lieutenant, Leut- nant, *m.*; ~ly, zweitens; ~rate, zweiter Qualität, min- derwertig.

secrecy, Verschwiegenheit, Heim- lichkeit, *f.*

secret, *sb.* Geheimnis, *n.*; *a.*, ~ly geheim, verborgen; ~ive, ver- schwiegen.

secretary, Sekretär, *m.*

secrete, verbergen; absondern; ausscheiden; ~ion, Abson- derung, Ausscheidung, *f.*

sect, Sekte, Konfession, *f.*; ~arian, Sektierer, *m.*

section, Schnitt, Durchschnitt; Abschnitt, *m.*, Abteilung, *f.*; *(railway)* Strecke, *f.*; ~al, Abschnitts-; zusammensetzbar.

sector, Ausschnitt, *f.*; *(mil.)* Ab- schnitt, Bezirk, *m.*

secular, weltlich.

secur|e, *a.*, ~ely, sicher; gewiß; *v.t.* sichern; befestigen, fest- machen; sich verschaffen; ~ity, Sicherheit, *f.* Bürgschaft, *f.*; ~ities, Wertpapiere, *n.pl.*

sedan, Sänfte, *f.*

sedate, ~ly, gesetzt, gelassen.

sedative, Sedativ, *n.*

sedentary, sitzend.

sedge, Schilfgras, *n.*

sediment, Bodensatz, Nieder- schlag, *m.*

sediti|on, Aufruhr, *m.*; ~ous|(ly), aufrührerisch.

seduc|e, verführen; ~er, Verführer, *m.*; ~tion, Verführung, *f.*; ~tive, verführerisch.

see[1], sehen, erblicken; *(see to)* besorgen; *(visit)* besuchen, (bei jemandem) vorsprechen; ~ *home*, nach Hause begleiten; ~ *off*, (jemanden) zur Bahn, &c. bringen; ~ *over*, besichtigen; ~ *through*, durchschauen.

see[2], Bischofssitz, *m.*, Bistum, *n.*

seed, *sb.* Samen, *m.*; Saat, *f.*; *v.i.* Samen tragen; *run to* ~, in Samen schießen; ~sman, Samenhändler, *m.*; ~y, schäbig, miserabel.

seek, suchen, trachten.

seem, scheinen; ~ingly, scheinbar; ~ly, anständig, schicklich.

seer, Seher, Prophet, *m.*

see-saw, (Wipp)schaukel, *f.*

seethe, sieden, kochen.

segment, Abschnitt, *m.*

segregat|e, absondern; ~ion, Absonderung, *f.*

seiz|e, *v.t.* ergreifen; sich bemächtigen *(with gen.)*; in Beschlag nehmen; *v.i.* (*of engine*) festfahren; ~ure, Ergreifung; Beschlagnahme, *f.*; *(stroke)* (Schlag)anfall, *m.*

seldom, selten.

select, *v.t.* auswählen, auslesen; *a.* ausgewählt, auserlesen; ~ion, Auswahl, *f.*; ~ *natural* ~ion, natürliche Zuchtwahl; ~ivity, Abstimmschärfe, Selektivität, *f.*

self, *sb.* Selbst, Ich, *n.*; *pron. and pref.* selbst; *by one* ~, allein; ~confidence, Selbstvertrauen, *n.*; ~conscious, befangen; ~control, Selbstbeherrschung, *f.*; ~defence, Notwehr, *f.*; ~evident, selbstverständlich; ~governing, sich selbst regierend; ~propelled, Selbstfahr-; ~respect, Selbstachtung, *f.*; ~restraint, Selbstbeherrschung, *f.*; ~seeking, selbstsüchtig; ~starter, (Selbst)anlasser, *m.*; ~willed, eigenwillig.

selfish, ~ly, selbstsüchtig; ~ness, Selbstsucht, *f.*

sell, verkaufen; ~er, Verkäufer, *m.*

sellotape, Tesafilm, *m.*

semaphore, Semaphor, *m.* or *n.*

semi, Halb-, halb-; ~breve, ganze Note; ~circle, Halbkreis, *m.*; ~colon, Strichpunkt, *m.*, Semikolon, *n.*; ~detached, halb freistehend; ~final, Vorschlußrunde, *f.*; ~quaver, Sechzehntelnote, *f.*; ~tone, Halbton, *m.*

semolina, Grieß, *m.*

senat|e, Senat, *m.*; ~or, Senator, *m.*

send, schicken, senden; *(goods)* spedieren; ~ *for*, holen lassen; ~ *in*, einschicken nach; ~ *in*, einschicken; einreichen; ~ *off*, absenden, befördern; ~er, Absender, *m.*

senile, altersschwach; ~ity, Altersschwäche, *f.*

senior, Ältere(r), Älteste(r); ~ity, höheres Alter; Dienstalter, *n.*

sensation, Aufsehen, *n.*; *(feeling)* Empfindung, *f.*; Eindruck, *m.*; ~al, sensationell, Aufsehen erregend.

sense, Sinn, *m.*; Bedeutung, Vernunft, *f.*; *common* ~, der gesunde Menschenverstand; *out of one's* ~s, von Sinnen; ~less(ly), sinnlos; bewußtlos.

sensib|le, vernünftig; fühlbar; ~ility, Empfindlichkeit, *f.*

sensitive, empfindlich *(to* für*)*; *(of instruments)* fein; ~ness, Empfindlichkeit, *f.*

sensual, sinnlich; wollüstig; ~ity, Sinnlichkeit, *f.*

sentence, *sb. (gram.)* Satz, *m.*; *(legal)* Urteil, *n.*, Richterspruch, *m.*; *v.t.* verurteilen.

sententious, sentenzen-, spruchreich.

sentiment, Gefühl, *n.*, Empfindung; Meinung, *f.*; ~al(ly), empfindsam, sentimental; ~ality, Empfindsamkeit, Rührseligkeit, *f.*

sentinel, sentry, Schildwache, *f.*; sentry-box, Schilderhäuschen, *n.*

separat|e, *v.* (sich) trennen; *a.* getrennt; einzeln; ~ely, besonders, einzeln; ~ion, Trennung, Scheidung, *f.*; ~or, Abscheider, *m.*, Zentrifuge, *f.*

sepia, Sepia, *f.*

sep|sis, Sepsis, *f.*; ~tic, septisch.

September, September, *m.*

sepulchre, Grab(mal), *n.*

sequel, Folge, *f.*

sequence, Reihenfolge, Anordnung, *f.*

seraph, Seraph, *m.*

serenade, Ständchen, *n.*

seren|e, ~ely, heiter; gelassen; ~ity, Heiterkeit, Gelassenheit, *f.*

serf, Leibeigene(r).

serge, Serge, *f.*

sergeant, (*mil.*) Sergeant, *m.*; (*police*) (Polizei)sergeant, *m.*; ~major, Feldwebel, (*cavalry, artillery*) Wachtmeister, *m.*

seri|al, *sb.* fortlaufende Erzählung, *f.*; *a.* Reihen-, Serien-, periodisch; ~es, Reihe, Folge, *f.*

serious, ~ly, ernsthaft; fromm; wichtig; ~ly *wounded,* schwer verwundet.

sermon, Predigt, *f.*

serpent, Schlange, *f.*; ~ine, schlangenförmig.

serrated, gezackt.

serried, dicht zusammengedrängt.

serum, Serum, *n.*

servant, Bediente(r), *f.* or *m.*; Dienstmädchen, *n.*

serve, dienen, (*tennis*) aufschlagen; (*food*) auftragen, auftischen; (*suffice*) genügen; *it* ~*s him right,* es geschieht ihm recht; ~ *time,* Strafe verbüßen.

service, *sb.* Dienst; Gottesdienst, *m.*; (*tennis*) Aufschlag, *m.*; Bedienung, *f.*; Tischgerät, Service, *n.*; *of* ~, von Nutzen; *be in* ~, dienen; *v.t.* (*machines*) warten; ~able, brauchbar.

serviette, Mundtuch, *n.*

servil|e, knechtisch, unterwürfig; ~ility, Unterwürfigkeit, *f.*; ~itude, Sklaverei, *f.*

session, Sitzung, *f.*; (*school, &c.*) Jahr, *n.*

set¹, *sb.* Satz, *m.*; Gerät, *n.*; Service, *n.*; Clique, *f.*

set², *v.t.* setzen; pflanzen; (*trap*) (eine Falle) stellen; (*adjust*) stellen; (*mount*) einfassen; (*limb*) richten; *v.i.* sich setzen; (*sun, &c.*) untergehen; (*become solid*) gerinnen, ansetzen; ~ *about,* anfangen; ~ *apart, aside,* abson-

dern, beiseitelegen; ~ *down,* niedersetzen; aufschreiben; ~ *forth,* darstellen; abreisen; ~ *free,* befreien; ~ *going,* in Gang setzen; ~ *off,* hervorheben; abreisen; ~ *on,* hetzen auf . . ., ansetzen; ~ *out,* bestimmen, festsetzen; abgehen, abfahren; ~ *right,* berichtigen; ~ *to,* an . . . gehen; ~ *up,* aufrichten, aufsetzen; (*type*) setzen; sich niederlassen *a.* festgesetzt, bestimmt; starr; versessen auf; ~back, Rückschlag, *m.*; ~square, Winkellineal, *n.*; ~to, Schlägerei, *f.*

sett, Pflasterstein, *m.*

settee, Polster-, Lehn-bank, *f.*

setter, Vorstehhund, *m.*

setting, Einfassung, *f.*; (*Sonnen-*) untergang, *m.*

settle, *sb.* Lehnbank, *f.*; *v.t.* bestimmen, entscheiden; beilegen; (*accounts*) bezahlen, ausgleichen; *v.i.* sich niederlassen, sich ansiedeln; sich setzen, sich senken, sacken; ~ment, Regelung, Verabredung; (*colony*) Ansiedelung, Niederlassung; (*accounts*) Bezahlung, *f.*; ~r, Ansiedler, *m.*

seven, sieben; ~teen, siebzehn; ~teenth, siebzehnte; ~th, siebente; ~ty, siebzig.

sever, trennen; ~ance, Trennung, *f.*

several, verschiedene, mehrere; ~ly, einzeln.

sever|e, ~ely, streng; ~ity, Strenge, *f.*

sew, nähen; ~ing-machine, Nähmaschine, *f.*

sewer, Abzugskanal, *m.*; ~age, Kanalisation, *f.*; Abwässer, *n.pl.*

sex, Geschlecht, *n.*; ~ appeal, Sex-appeal, *m.*; ~ual(ly), geschlechtlich.

sextant, Sextant, *m.*

sexton, Küster, *m.*

shabb|y, ~ily, schäbig, abgetragen; gemein; ~iness, Schäbigkeit, *f.*

shackle, fesseln; ~s, Fesseln, *f.pl.*

shad|e, *sb.* Schatten; (*lamp*) Schirm, *m.*; Nuance, *f.*; *v.t.* beschatten; (*drawing*) schattieren;

~y, schattig; dunkel, verdächtig.

shadow, *sb.* Schatten, *m.*; *v.t.* heimlich folgen, überwachen.

shaft, *(handle)* Schaft, Griff, *m.*; *(pit)* Schacht, *m.*; *(mech.)* Welle, Spindel, *f.*; *(dart)* Pfeil, *m.*

shaggy, zottig.

shake, *sb.* Erschütterung, *f.*, Stoß, *m.*; *(of the hand)* Händedruck, *m.*; *v.t.* schütteln, erschüttern; *v.i.* beben, zittern; ~ *hands*, sich die Hände geben; ~ *one's head*, den Kopf schütteln; ~ *off*, abschütteln.

shale, Schiefer, *m.*

shall, *(future)* werde(n); *(orders, questions)* soll(en).

shallot, Schalotte, *f.*

shallow, seicht, untief; oberflächlich; ~ness, Seichtheit; Oberflächlichkeit, *f.*; ~s, Untiefen, *f.pl.*

sham, *sb.* Täuschung, *f.*, Trug, *m.*; *a.* falsch, Schein-; *v.t.* vortäuschen, heucheln; *v.i.* heucheln.

shambles, Fleischbank, *f.*; *(fig.)* Schlachtfeld, wüstes Durcheinander, *n.*

shame, *sb.* Scham; Schande, *f.*; *v.t.* beschämen; ~faced, beschämt, verschämt; ~ful(ly), schändlich; ~less(ly), schamlos; ~lessness, Unverschämtheit, *f.*

shampoo, *sb.* Shampoo, *n.*; *v.t.* schampunieren.

shamrock, Klee, *m.*

shank, Schenkel; Stiel, *m.*

shape, *sb.* Form, Gestalt, *f.*; Schnitt, *m.*; *v.t.* bilden, gestalten; lenken; ~d, gestaltet, -förmig; ~less, unförmig; ~ly, wohlgebildet.

share, *sb.* Anteil; Beitrag, *m.*; *(commerc.)* Aktie, *f.*; *(plough-share)* (Pflug)schar, *f.*; *v.t.* teilen; ~holder, Aktionär, *m.*

shark, Hai(fisch), *m.*

sharp, *sb.* ~y, scharf; *(point)* spitz; *(pain)* heftig; *(taste)* beißend; *(clever)* scharfsinnig, klug; *(mus.)* erhöht; zu hoch; ~en, schärfen, wetzen, zuspitzen; aufmuntern; ~er, Falsch-

spieler, *m.*; ~ness, Schärfe; Strenge; Herbheit, *f.*; ~shooter, Scharfschütze, *m.*

shatter, zerschmettern.

shav|e, *sb.* Rasieren, *n.*; *a close* ~e, Entkommen (*n.*) mit knapper Not; *v.t.* scheren; *(person)* rasieren; *v.i.* sich rasieren; ~ings, *(wood)* Hobelspäne, *m.pl.*; *(paper)* Papierschnitzel, *m.* or *n.*; ~ing-brush, Rasierpinsel, *m.*; ~ing-soap, Rasierseife, *f.*

shawl, Schal, *m.*

she, sie.

sheaf, Garbe, *f.*

shear, scheren; ~s, Schere, *f.*

sheath, Scheide, *f.*; ~e, in die Scheide stecken.

shed, *sb.* Schuppen, *m.*; *v.t.* abwerfen; *(tears)* vergießen.

sheep, Schaf, *n.*

sheer, schier, lauter; jäh, steil.

sheet, *(bed)* Bettuch, *n.*; *(paper)* Bogen, *m.*; *(metal)* Blech, *n.*; *(Projektions)*leinwand, *f.*; *(of water)* Wasserfläche, *f.*; *(of ice)* Eisdecke, *f.*; *(of fire)* Feuermeer, *n.*; ~anchor, Notanker, *m.*; ~glass, Tafelglas, *n.*; ~iron, Eisenblech, *n.*; ~lightning, Wetterleuchten, *n.*

sheik, Scheich, *m.*

shelf, Brett, *n.*, Sims, *m.* or *n.*

shell, *sb.* *(egg, nut)* Schale; *(pea)* Hülse; *(mollusc)* Muschel; *(explosive)* Granate, *f.*; *v.t.* schälen; beschießen; ~fish, Schaltier, *n.*; ~proof, bombensicher; ~shock, Kriegsneurose, *f.*

shelter, *sb.* Obdach, *n.*, Schutz(raum), *m.*; *v.t.* schützen, beschirmen; *v.i.* Schutz suchen.

shepherd, Schäfer, *m.*

sherry, Sherry, *m.*

shield, *sb.* Schild; Schutz, *m.*; *v.t.* beschützen *(from vor)*.

shift, *sb.* Schicht, *f.*; *v.t.* versetzen, verlagern; *v.i.* umziehen; ~ *for oneself*, für sich selbst sorgen; ~ing, veränderlich; ~less, hilflos; *v.* unzuverlässig.

shilling, Schilling, *m.*

shin, Schienbein, *n.*

shin|e, *sb.* Glanz, *m.*; *v.i.* scheinen, glänzen; ~**y**, glänzend.

shingle, Steingeröll(e), *n.*

shingles, (*med.*) Gürtelrose, *f.*

ship, *sb.* Schiff, *n.*; *v.t.* verschiffen, einschiffen; ~**builder**, Schiffbauer, *m.*; ~**building**, Schiffbau, *m.*; ~**ing**, Schiffe, *n.pl.*; Schiffahrt, *f.*; ~**owner**, Reeder, *m.*; ~**shape**, in guter Ordnung; ~**wreck**, Schiffbruch, *m.*; ~**wrecked**, schiffbrüchig; ~**yard**, Schiffswerft, *f.*

shirk, sich drücken; ~**er**, Drückeberger, *m.*

shirt, Hemd, *n.*

shiver, *sb.* Schauer, *m.*; *v.i.* frösteln, zittern.

shoal, Menge, *f.*; (*fish*) Zug, *m.*; (*shallows*) Untiefe, *f.*

shock, *sb.* Stoß, Anfall, Schlag, *m.*; Ärgernis, *n.*; ~ *troops*, Stoßtruppen, *f.pl.*; *v.t.* anstoßen, erschüttern; Anstoß geben; ~**absorber**, Stoßdämpfer, *m.*; ~**er**, Schauerroman, *m.*; ~**ing(ly)**, anstößig; empörend.

shod, (*horse*) beschlagen.

shoddy, *sb.* Lumpenwolle, *f.*; *a.* Schund-.

shoe, Schuh, *m.*; Hufeisen, *n.*; ~**black**, Stiefelputzer, *m.*; ~**horn**, Schuhanzieher, *m.*; ~**lace**, Schuhriemen, *m.*; ~**maker**, Schuhmacher, *m.*; ~**polish**, Schuhwichse, *f.*

shoot, *sb.* Sprößling, *m.*; Gleitbahn, *f.*; *v.t.* (er)schießen; abfeuern; leeren; *v.i.* (hervor)schießen; ~**ing-box**, Jagdhäuschen, *n.*; ~**ing-gallery**, Schießstand, *m.*; ~**ing star**, Sternschnuppe, *f.*

shop, *sb.* Laden, *m.*, Werkstatt, *f.*; *v.i.* Einkäufe machen; ~**assistant**, Verkäufer(in, *f.*), *m.*; ~**window**, Schaufenster, *n.*; ~**keeper**, Ladeninhaber, *m.*; ~**lifter**, Ladendieb, *m.*

shore, Ufer, Gestade, *n.*; Strand, *m.*

short, kurz; (*insufficient*) knapp; (*abrupt*) brüsk; ~ *of cash*, knapp bei Kasse; ~**age**, Knappheit, *f.*, Mangel, *m.* (of an); ~ *circuit*, *sb.* Kurzschluß, *m.*; ~**circuit**, *v.* kurzschließen;

~**coming**, Mangel, *m.*; ~**en**, abverkürzen; ~**hand**, Kurzschrift, *f.*; ~**handed**, mit zu wenigen Arbeitskräften; ~**lived**, kurzlebig; ~**ly**, bald; ~**ness**, Kürze, *f.*; ~**range**, Nah-; ~**s**, Kniehosen, kurze Hosen, *f.pl.*; ~**sighted**, kurzsichtig; ~**wave**, Kurzwelle, *f.*

shot, Schuß, *m.*; Schrot, *m.* or *n.*; Kugel, *f.*; Schußweite, *f.*; (*person*) Schütze, *m.*

shoulder, Schulter, Achsel, *f.*; *v.t.* auf die Schulter nehmen; (*arms*) schultern; ~**belt**, Wehrgehenk, *n.*; ~**strap**, (*mil.*) Schulterklappe, *f.*; (*women's dress*) Träger, *m.*

shout, *sb.* Schrei, Zuruf, *m.*; *v.i.* schreien, laut rufen, jauchzen.

shove, *sb.* Stoß, *m.*; *v.t.* schieben, stoßen.

shovel, Schaufel, *f.*

show, *sb.* Schau, *f.*; Schauspiel, *n.*; Ausstellung, *f.*; (*display*) Aufwand, *m.*; (*pretence*) Schein, *m.*; *v.t.* zeigen, sehen lassen; beweisen; ~ *in*, hereinführen; ~ *off*, (*set off*) hervorheben; (*boast*) prahlen; ~ *out*, hinausführen; ~ *over*, herumführen; ~ *up* hervorheben; bloßstellen; ~**man**, Schausteller, *m.*; ~**y**, auffällig, prunkend.

shower, *sb.* (Regen)schauer, *m.*; Überfluß, *m.*; *v.t.* überschütten; ~**bath**, Dusche, *f.*; ~**y**, regnerisch.

shrapnel, Schrapnell, *n.*

shred, *sb.* Stückchen, *n.*, Fetzen, *m.*; *v.t.* zerfetzen; klein schneiden.

shrew, zänkisches Weib, *n.*; (*zool.*) Spitzmaus, *f.*

shrewd, ~**ly**, schlau, klug.

shriek, *sb.* Schrei, *m.*; *v.i.* schreien, kreischen.

shrill, gellend, scharf.

shrimp, Krabbe, *f.*

shrine, Schrein, *m.*, Kapelle, *f.*

shrink, (ein)schrumpfen, einlaufen; zurückschaudern (*from* vor).

shrivel, zusammenschrumpfen.

shroud, *sb.* Leichentuch, *n.*; (*naut.*) Want, *f.*; *v.t.* einhüllen.

Shrove Tuesday, Fastnacht, *f.*

shrub, Staude, *f.*, Strauch, *m.*; ~bery, Gesträuch, *n.*

shrug, (die Achseln) zucken.

shudder, *sb.* Schauder, *m.*; *v.i.* schaudern.

shuffle, (*cards*) mischen; (*feet*) scharren.

shun, vermeiden.

shunt, rangieren.

shut, *v.t.* schließen, zumachen; *v.i.* sich schließen; ~ up! halt's Maul!; ~down, Betriebseinstellung, *f.*; ~ter, (Fenster)laden; (*photog.*) Verschluß, *m.*

shuttle, (Weber)schiffchen, *n.*; ~cock, Federball, *m.*; ~ service, Pendelverkehr, *m.*

shy, ~ly, scheu, schüchtern; ~ness, Schüchternheit, *f.*

sick, krank; *to be* ~ *of*, satt haben; *to be* ~, sich erbrechen; *feel* ~, unwohl sein; ~bay, Lazarett, *n.*; ~bed, Krankenbett, *n.*; ~en, *v.t.* krank machen; *v.i.* erkranken; ~ening, ekelhaft; ~leave, Krankenurlaub, *m.*; ~ly, kränklich; ungesund; ~ness, Krankheit, *f.*; (*vomiting*) Erbrechen, *n.*; ~pay, Krankengeld, *n.*

sickle, Sichel, *f.*

side, *sb.* Seite, *f.*; (*slope*) Abhang, *m.*; (*party*) Partei, *f.*; ~ by ~, nebeneinander; *on this* ~, diesseits; *on the other* ~, jenseits; *v.i.* Partei ergreifen; ~arms, Seitengewehr, *n.*; ~board, Büfett, *n.*, Anrichtetisch, *m.*; ~car, Beiwagen, *m.*; ~light, (*fig.*) Streiflicht, *n.*; ~long, seitwärts; ~saddle, Damensattel, *m.*; ~slip, Rutschen, *n.*; ~walk, Bürgersteig, *m.*; ~ways, seitwärts.

siding, Abstellgeleise, *n.*, Weiche, *f.*

sidle, seitwärts gehen.

siege, Belagerung, *f.*

sieve, Sieb, *n.*

sift, sieben; prüfen.

sigh, *sb.* Seufzer, *m.*; *v.i.* seufzen.

sight, *sb.* (*sense*) Gesicht, *n.*, Sehkraft, *f.*; (*spectacle*) Anblick, *m.*; (*on gun*, &c.) Visier, Zielgerät, *n.*; *at* ~, auf den ersten Blick; *vom Blatt*; *by* ~, von Ansehen; *in* ~, in

Sicht; *v.t.* erblicken, sichten; ~s, Sehenswürdigkeiten, *f.pl.*

sign, *sb.* Zeichen; Schild, *n.*; *v.t.* unterschreiben, unterzeichnen; winken; ~post, Wegweiser, *m.*

signal, *sb.* Zeichen; Signal, *n.*; *a.* ausgezeichnet; *v.t.* signalisieren, Signale geben; ~box, Stellwerk, *n.*; ~ler, Signalwärter, *m.*; (*naut.*) Signalgast, *m.*

signature, Unterschrift, *f.*; ~ tune, Kennmusik, *f.*

significan|ce, Bedeutung, *f.*, Sinn, *m.*; ~t(ly), bedeutungsvoll.

signify, bedeuten.

silence, *sb.* Ruhe, *f.*, Stillschweigen, *n.*; *v.t.* zum Schweigen bringen; ~r, Schalldämpfer, (*mot.*) Auspufftopf, *m.*

silent, ~ly, schweigend; schweigsam; (*film*) stumm; *to be* ~, schweigen.

silica, Kieselerde, *f.*

silk, Seide, *f.*; Seidenstoff, *m.*; *a.* seiden; ~growing, Seidenzucht, *f.*; ~worm, Seidenraupe, *f.*; ~y, seiden(artig).

sill, Fensterbrett, *n.*

silly, einfältig, albern; ~iness, Einfalt, Albernheit, *f.*

silt, *sb.* Schlamm, *m.*; *v.i.*, ~ up, verschlammen.

silver, *sb.* Silber, *n.*; *a.* silbern; *v.t.* versilbern; ~ paper, Stanniol, *n.*; ~plated, versilbert; ~smith, Silberschmied, *m.*; ~y, Silber-.

similar, ~ity, Ähnlichkeit *f.*; ~ly, gleichartig, ähnlich.

simile, Vergleich, *m.*

simmer, wallen, brodeln.

simple, einfach; schlicht; einfältig; ~minded, arglos; ~ton, Dummkopf, *m.*

simplicity, Einfachheit, Einfalt, *f.*

simplific|ation, Vereinfachung, *f.*; ~y, vereinfachen.

simulat|e, erheucheln, vortäuschen; ~ion, Vortäuschung, *f.*

simultaneous, ~ly, gleichzeitig.

sin, *sb.* Sünde, *f.*; *v.i.* sündigen; ~ful, sündhaft; ~fulness, Sündhaftigkeit, *f.*

since, *prep.* seit; *adv.* seitdem; *conj.* da; *long* ~, schon lange.

sincer|e, ~ely, aufrichtig; *yours*

~*ely,* Ihr ergebener; ~*ity,* Aufrichtigkeit, *f.*

sinecure, Sinekure, *f.*

sinew, Sehne, *f.*

sing, singen; ~*er,* Sänger(in, *f.*), *m.;* ~*song,* Singsang, *m.*

singe, versengen.

single, *a.* einzeln; (*ticket*) einfach; (*unmarried*) ledig; *v.t.,* ~ *out,* auswählen, absondern; ~*barrelled,* einläufig; ~ *combat,* Zweikampf, *m.;* ~*file,* Gänsemarsch, *m.;* ~*handed,* alleinig, ganz allein; ~*journey,* Hinreise, *f.;* ~ *line,* einspuriges Gleis, *n.;* ~*ness,* Einzigkeit; ~ *room,* Einzelzimmer, *n.;* ~*s,* (*tennis*) Einzelspiel, *n.;* ~*seater,* Einsitzer, *m.*

singly, einzeln, stückweise.

singular, *sb.* Einzahl, *f.;* *a.* einzeln; einzig; (*strange*) seltsam.

sinister, unheilvoll; böse; (*left*) link.

sink, *sb.* Ausguß, *m.;* ~ *of iniquity,* Lasterhöhle, *f.;* *v.i.* sinken; sich senken; fallen, abnehmen; untergehen; *v.t.* versenken; (*shaft*) abteufen; (*money*) anlegen.

sinner, Sünder, *m.*

sip, *sb.* Schlückchen, *n.;* *v.t.* nippen, schlürfen.

siphon, Siphon, *m.*

sir, mein Herr; (*as title of rank*) Sir.

siren, Sirene, *f.*

sirloin, Lendenbraten, *m.*

sister, Schwester, *f.;* ~*in-law,* Schwägerin, *f.;* ~*ly,* schwesterlich.

sit, sitzen; Sitzung halten; (*of hens*) brüten; ~ *down,* sich setzen; ~ *for,* sich photographieren (*or* malen) lassen; (*parliament*) vertreten.

site, Lage, *f.;* Platz, *m.*

sitting, Sitzung, *f.;* ~*room,* Wohnzimmer, *n.*

situate(d), gelegen; ~*ion,* Lage; Stellung, *f.*

six, sechs; ~*teen*(th), sechzehn(te); ~*th,* sechste; ~*thly,* sechstens; ~*tieth,* sechzigste; ~*ty,* sechzig.

size, Größe, *f.;* Umfang, *m.;* Maß, *n.;* (*book*) Format, *n.;* (*glue*) Kleister, *m.*

skat|e, *sb.* Schlittschuh, *m.;* (*fish*) Roche(n), *m.;* *v.i.* Schlittschuh laufen; ~*ing-rink,* Eisbahn, Rollschuhbahn, *f.*

skeleton, Skelett, Gerippe, *n.;* (*attrib.*) Stamm—; ~ *key,* Dietrich, *m.*

sketch, *sb.* Entwurf, *m.,* Skizze, *f.;* *v.t.* entwerfen, skizzieren.

skewer, Speiler, *m.*

ski, *sb.* Ski, Schneeschuh, *m.;* *v.i.* Ski laufen; ~*er,* Skiläufer, *m.;* ~*jump,* Skisprung, *m.;* Sprungschanze, *f.;* ~*lift,* Skilift, *m.;* ~*stick,* Skistock, *m.*

skid, *sb.* Hemmschuh, *m.;* Ausrutschen, *n.;* *v.i.* ausrutschen.

skiff, Kahn, Nachen, *m.*

skil|l, Geschicklichkeit, *f.;* ~*ful*(ly), geschickt; erfahren, kundig, geübt.

skim, abschäumen; (*milk*) abrahmen; streifen; flüchtig durchsehen.

skimp, *v.t.* knapp halten; *v.i.* knausern.

skin, *sb.* Haut, *f.;* (*hide*) Fell, *n.;* (*peel*) Schale, *f.;* *v.t.* häuten, abdecken; ~*flint,* Geizhals, *m.;* ~*ny,* mager; (*fig.*) geizig.

skip, springen, hüpfen; ~*ping-rope,* Springseil, *n.*

skipper, (Schiffs)kapitän, *m.*

skirmish, *sb.* Scharmützel, *n.;* *v.i.* scharmützeln.

skirt, *sb.* (Frauen)rock, *m.;* *v.t. and i.* begrenzen, entlang gehen; ~*ing-board,* Scheuer-, Wandleiste, *f.*

skit, Satire, Spottschrift, *f.*

skittle, Kegel, *m.;* ~*alley,* Kegelbahn, *f.*

skulk, lauern; scheuen.

skull, Schädel, *m.*

skunk, Stinktier, *m.*

sky, Himmel, *m.;* ~*lark,* Feldlerche, *f.;* (*fig.*) Ulk, *m.;* ~*light,* Oberlicht, *n.;* ~*scraper,* Wolkenkratzer, *m.*

slab, (Stein)platte, *f.*

slack, ~*ly,* schlaff, locker; flau; träge; ~*en,* *v.t.* schlaff machen; abspannen; *v.i.* erschlaffen; ~*er,* Drückeberger, *m.*

slag, Schlacke, *f.;* ~*heap,* Halde, *f.*

slake, löschen; stillen.

slam, *sb.* Knall, *m.*; (*cards*) Schlemm, *m.*; *v.t.* (*door*, *&c.*) zuschmeißen.

slander, *sb.* Verleumdung, *f.*; *v.t.* verleumden; ~**er**, Verleumder, *m.*; ~**ous**(**ly**), verleumderisch.

slang, Slang, *m.*, Sonder-, Zunftsprache, *f.*

slant, *a.* schief, schräg; *v.i.* sich (seitwärts) neigen, abfallen.

slap, *sb.* Klaps, *m.*; *v.t.* klapsen; ~**dash**, oberflächlich, nachlässig.

slash, *sb.* Hieb; Schlitz, *m.*; *v.t.* hauen, schlitzen.

slate, Schiefer, *m.*, Schiefertafel, *f.*; ~**r**, Schieferdecker, *m.*

slattern, Schlampe, *f.*; ~**ly**, schlampig.

slaughter, *sb.* Metzelei, *f.*, Schlachten, *n.*; *v.t.* schlachten; niedermetzeln; ~**er**, Schlächter, *m.*; ~**house**, Schlachthaus, *n.*

slav|e, Sklave, *m.*, Sklavin, *f.*; ~**ery**, Sklaverei, *f.*; ~**ish**(**ly**), sklavisch.

slaver, *sb.* Speichel, Geifer, *m.*; *v.i.* geifern.

slay, erschlagen, töten.

sledge, Schlitten, *m.*; ~**hammer**, Schmiedehammer, *m.*

sleek, glatt; weich.

sleep, *sb.* Schlaf, *m.*; *v.i.* schlafen; ~**er**, Schläfer, *m.*; Schlafwagen, *m.*; (*on railway track*) Schwelle, *f.*; ~**iness**, Schläfrigkeit, *f.*; ~**ing partner**, stiller Teilhaber, *m.*; ~**ing-sickness**, Schlafkrankheit, *f.*; ~**ing-suit**, Schlafanzug, *m.*; ~**less**, schlaflos; ~**lessness**, Schlaflosigkeit, *f.*; ~**walker**, Schlafwandler, *m.*; ~**y**, schläfrig.

sleet, *sb.* Graupelregen, *m.*; *v.i.* graupeln.

sleeve, Ärmel, *m.*

sleigh, Schlitten, *m.*

sleight, ~ **of hand**, Taschenspielerei, *f.*

slender, schlank; knapp, gering; ~**ness**, Schlankheit, *f.*

slice, *sb.* Schnitte, Scheibe, *f.*; *v.t.* zerschneiden.

slid|e, *sb.* Gleiten, *n.*; Gleitbahn, *f.*; (*lantern-slide*) Projektionsbild, Dia(positiv); (*microscopic*) Ob-

jektgläschen, *n.*; *v.i.* (aus)gleiten, schlüpfen; (*on ice*) schlittern; *v.t.* schieben; ~**e-rule**, Rechenschieber, *m.*; ~**ing scale**, bewegliche Skala, Gleitskala, *f.*; ~**ing-seat**, Rollsitz, *m.*

slight, *sb.* Nichtachtung, Geringschätzung, *f.*; *a.* gering, unbedeutend, schwach; *v.t.* vernachlässigen; ~**ly**, etwas.

slim, schlank, schmächtig; ~**ness**, Schlankheit, *f.*

slim|e, Schlamm, Schleim, *m.*; ~**y**, schleimig.

sling, *sb.* Schleuder; Schlinge, Binde, *f.*; *v.t.* schleudern, werfen.

slink, schleichen.

slip, *sb.* Ausgleiten, *n.*; (*mistake*) Fehler, Fehltritt, *m.*, Versehen, *n.*; (*paper*) Stückchen, *n.*, Zettel, *m.*; (*covering*) Überzug, *m.*; (*naut.*) Helling, *m.* or *f.*; *give the* ~ *to*, entwischen; *v.i.* (aus)gleiten, rutschen; entschlüpfen; ~**knot**, Schleifknoten, *m.*; ~**shod**, latschig, nachlässig; ~**stream**, Schraubenstrahl, *m.*

slipper, Pantoffel, *m.*

slippery, schlüpfrig.

slit, *sb.* Spalte, *f.*, Schlitz, *m.*; *v.t.* spalten, aufschlitzen.

slobber, geifern.

sloe, Schlehe, *f.*

slogan, Schlagwort, *n.*

sloop, Schaluppe, *f.*, Kanonenboot, *n.*

slop, *sb.* Lache, *f.*; Spülwasser, *n.*; *v.t.* verschütten; *v.i.* ~ *over*, überlaufen; ~**pail**, Spüleimer, *m.*; ~**py**, matschig; unsauber; sentimental.

slop|e, *sb.* Abhang, *m.*; *v.i.* abfallen; ~**ing**, abschüssig.

slot, Schlitz, *m.*; ~**machine**, Automat, *m.*

sloth, Trägheit, *f.*; (*zool.*) Faultier, *n.*; ~**ful**, träge, faul.

slouch, schlotterig gehen; ~ **hat**, Schlapphut, *m.*

sloven|liness, Schlampigkeit, *f.*; ~**ly**, schlampig.

slow, ~**ly**, langsam; träge; *to be* ~, (*of clock*, *&c.*) nachgehen; (*attrib.*) slow-motion . . . *Zeitlupen...*; ~ *train*, Personen-, Bummel- zug, *m.*; ~**ness**,

Langsamkeit, *f.*; ~-worm,
Blindschleiche, *f.*

sludge, Schlamm, *m.*

slug, Wegschnecke, *f.*; *(bullet)*
grober Schrot.

sluggish, ~ly, träge.

sluice, Schleuse, *f.*

slumber, *sb.* Schlummer, *m.*; *v.i.*
schlummern.

slump, *sb.* Preissturz, *m.*; *v.i.*
fallen, stürzen.

slums, Elendsviertel, *m.*

slur, *sb.* Fleck, Vorwurf, *m.*;
(mus.) Bindung, *f.* Binde-
zeichen, *n.*; *v.t.* beflecken; verleumden; leicht hinweggehen
über; undeutlich aussprechen.

slush, Matsch, *m.*

slut, Schlampe, *f.*; ~tish,
schlampig.

sly, schlau; *on the* ~, verstohlener-
weise.

smack, *sb.* Klaps, *m.*; *(of the lips)*
Schmatzen, *n.*; *(naut.)*
Schmack(e), *f.*; *v.t.* klapsen;
(lips) schmatzen.

small, klein, gering, schwach; ~
hours, frühe Morgenstunden,
f.pl.; ~-arms, Handwaffen,
f.pl.; ~-holder, Kleinpächter,
m.; ~-holding, Kleinpachtung,
f.; ~ness, Kleinheit, *f.*; ~-pox,
Pocken, Blattern, *f.pl.*

smart, *a.*, ~ly schmerzhaft;
beißend, scharf; schneidig,
fesch, elegant; *v.i.* schmerzen;
~ness, Schneidigkeit; Lebhaftigkeit, *f.*, Geist, *m.*

smash, *sb.* Zusammenbruch, Fall,
m.; *v.t.* zerschmettern.

smattering, oberflächliche Kenntnis, *f.*

smell, *sb.* Geruch, *m.*; *v.i.* riechen;
~-ing-bottle, Riechfläschchen,
n.; ~-ing-salts, Riechsalz, *n.*

smelt[1], *sb.* *(fish)* Stint, *m.*

smelt[2], *v.t.* schmelzen.

smile, *sb.* Lächeln, *n.*; *v.i.* lächeln.

smirch, beschmieren.

smith, Schmied, *m.*; ~y,
Schmiede, *f.*

smitten, verliebt, vernarrt.

smock, Kittel, *m.*

smok|e, *sb.* Rauch, *m.*; *v.i.*
rauchen; *v.t.* rauchen; räuchern;
~eless, rauchlos; ~er, Raucher

(abteil, n.), *m.*; ~e-screen,
Nebelwand, Einnebelung, *f.*;
~y, rauchend, rauchig.

smooth, *a.*, ~ly, glatt, eben; *v.t.*
ebnen, (ab)glätten; mildern;
~ness, Glätte, *f.*

smother, ersticken; dämpfen.

smoulder, schwelen.

smudge, *sb.* Schmutzfleck, *m.*; *v.t.*
beschmutzen, beschmieren.

smug, selbstgefällig.

smuggl|e, schmuggeln; ~er,
Schmuggler, Schleichhändler,
m.; ~ing, Schleichhandel, *m.*

smut, (Schmutz)fleck, *m.*; ~ty,
schmutzig; unflätig.

snack, Imbiß, *m.*

snail, Schnecke, *f.*

snake, Schlange, *f.*

snap, *sb.* Knall, Knack, *m.*; *v.*
(ab)schnappen; ~ *one's fingers*,
ein Schnippchen schlagen;
~-dragon, *(bot.)* Löwenmaul, *n.*;
~-shot, Schnappschuß, *m.*;
Momentaufnahme, *f.*; ~ *vote*,
Blitzabstimmung, *f.*

snare, *sb.* Schlinge, *f.*; *v.t.* verstricken, umgarnen.

snarl, *sb.* Knurren, *n.*; *v.i.* knurren.

snatch, *sb.* schneller Griff, *m.*;
v.t. haschen, ergreifen; ~s
schnappen, hastig greifen.

sneak, *sb.* Schleicher; *(tell-tale)*
Petzer, *m.*; *v.i.* schleichen;
petzen.

sneer, *sb.* Hohnlächeln, *n.*; Stich-
elei, *f.*; *v.i.* spötteln, hohnlächeln
(at über); ~ing, spöttisch.

sneeze, *sb.* Niesen, *n.*; *v.i.* niesen.

sniff, schnüffeln.

snigger, kichern.

snip, *sb.* Schnitt, *m.*, Schnitzel,
n.; *v.t.* schnipseln.

snipe, Schnepfe, *f.*; ~r, Scharfschütze, *m.*

snivel, schnüffeln.

snob, Snob, *m.*; ~bery, Snobis-
mus, *m.*; ~bish, snobistisch,
vornehm tuend.

snore, *sb.* Schnarchen, *n.*; *v.i.*
schnarchen.

snort, schnauben.

snout, Schnauze, *f.*

snow, *sb.* Schnee, *m.*; *v.i.* schneien;
~-ball, Schneeball, *m.*; ~ed up,
eingeschneit; ~drift, Schnee-

wehe, f.; ~drop, Schneeglöck-
chen, n.; ~flake, Schneeflocke,
f.; ~plough, Schneepflug, m.;
~storm, Schneegestöber, n.;
~white, schneeweiß.

snub, sb. Verweis, m., Zurück-
weisung, f.; v.t. schelten, abweisen.

snuff, sb. Schnupftabak, m.; v.t.
(candle) putzen; auslöschen.

snug, ~ly, behaglich, gemütlich.

so, (al)so; daher.

soak, (ein)weichen; durchnässen;
~ up, aufsaugen.

soap, sb. Seife, f.; v.t. einseifen;
~boiler, Seifensieder, m.;
bubble, Seifenblase, f.; ~suds,
Seifenwasser, n.; ~y, seifig;
(fig.) süßlich.

soar, sich aufschwingen, schweben.

sob, sb. Schluchzen, n.; v.i.
schluchzen.

sober, ~erly, nüchtern; bescheiden, ernst; ~riety, Nüch-
ternheit; Mäßigkeit, f.

sociable, gesellig; ~ility, Gesellig-
keit, f.

social, ~ly, gesellschaftlich;
gesellig; ~ democrat, Sozial-
demokrat, m.; ~ism, Sozialis-
mus, m.; ~ist, Sozialist, m.

society, Gesellschaft, f.; Verein, m.

sock, Socke, f.

socket, (anat.) Höhle, f.; (mech.)
Rohr, n., Büchse, Pfanne, f.

sod, Rasen, m.

soda, Soda, f.; ~water, Soda-,
Mineral- wasser, n.

sodden, durchweicht; durchnäßt.

sodium, Natrium, n.

sofa, Sofa, n.

soft, ~ly weich; leise; mild(e),
zärtlich; einfältig; ~en, v.t.
aufweichen, erweichen, weich,
geschmeidig machen; mildern;
v.i. weich werden; ~ness,
Weichheit; Sanftheit, f.

soggy, sumpfig; (bread) klitschig.

soil, sb. Boden, m.; v.t. beschmutzen.

solace, Trost, m.

solar, Sonnen-.

solder, sb. Lot, n.; v.t. löten.

soldier, Soldat, m.

sole¹, a., ~ly, allein, einzig.

sole², sb. (of foot, shoe) Sohle;

(fish) Seezunge, f.; v.t. besohlen.

solemn, ~ly, feierlich; ~ity,
Feierlichkeit, f.; ~ize, feiern.

solicit, dringend bitten; (jemanden) ansprechen; ~or, (Rechts)-
anwalt, m.; ~ous, besorgt,
ängstlich; ~ude, Besorgnis,
Bekümmernis, f.

solid, sb. (fester) Körper, m.; a..
~ly, fest; massiv; gründlich;
echt; ~arity, Geschlossenheit,
Solidarität, f.; ~ify, sich ver-
dichten; ~ity, Festigkeit, f.

soliloquy, Selbstgespräch, n.

solitary, ~ily, einsam; einzig;
~iness, Einsamkeit, f.

solo, Solo, n.

solstice, Sonnenwende, f.

soluble, lösbar; ~ility, Lösbar-
keit, f.

solution, (Auf)lösung, f.

solve, (auf)lösen; ~able, lösbar.

solvent, sb. Lösungsmittel, n.; a.
zahlungsfähig; ~cy, Zahlungs-
fähigkeit, f.

sombre, düster, dunkel.

some, etwas, (pl.) einige; ~body,
jemand; ~ day, eines Tages;
~how, irgendwie; ~thing,
etwas; ~time, (future) einmal;
(past) einst; ~ time ago, vor
einiger Zeit; ~times, zuweilen;
~what, etwas; ~where, ir-
gendwo.

somersault, Purzelbaum, m.; turn a
~, einen Purzelbaum schlagen.

somnambulism, Nacht-, Schlaf-
wandeln, n.; ~ist, Nachtwandler,
m.

son, Sohn, m.; ~in-law,
Schwiegersohn, m.

sonata, Sonate, f.

song, Gesang, m., Lied, n.; ~ster,
Sänger; Singvogel, m.

sonnet, Sonett, n.

sonorous, tönend, klingend; ~ity,
Tonfülle, f.

soon, bald, (early) früh; as ~ as,
sobald (als); ~er, lieber, eher;
früher; no ~er than, kaum.

soot, Ruß, m.; ~y, rußig.

soothe, besänftigen, beruhigen.

sop, eingetunkter Bissen, m.; (fig.)
Köder, m., Bestechung, f.

sophism, Trugschluß, m.; ~t,
Sophist, m.; ~tical, sophistisch;

~ticated, verfälscht, verdreht, unnatürlich; ~try, Trugweisheit, *f.*

soporific, einschläfernd.

sorcer|er, Zauberer, *m.*; ~ess, Hexe, *f.*; ~y, Zauberei, *f.*

sordid, ~ly, gemein; schmutzig.

sore, *sb.* wunde Stelle, *f.*; *a.* wundschmerzhaft, empfindlich; ärgerlich, erbittert (*at* über); ~ throat, Halsschmerzen, *m.pl.*; ~ly, sehr, tief; ~ness, Schmerzhaftigkeit, Wundheit, *f.*

sorrow, *sb.* Kummer, Gram, *m.*, Sorge, *f.*; *v.i.* sich grämen; ~ful(ly), traurig.

sorry, traurig, erbärmlich, armselig; *I am ~ for him*, er tut mir leid; *I am ~*, Verzeihung!

sort, *sb.* Art, Sorte, *f.*; *what sort of*, was für; *nothing of the ~*, nichts derartiges; *out of ~s*, unwohl, unpäßlich; *v.t.* sortieren, auslesen.

sortie, Ausfall, *m.*

sot, Trunkenbold, *m.*; ~tish, versoffen; trunksüchtig.

soul, Seele, *f.*

sound, *sb.* Laut, Schall, Klang; (*strait*) Sund, *m.*; *a.*, ~ly, gesund, zuverlässig; stark, tüchtig; triftig; *v.i.* schallen, lauten, klingen, widerhallen; *v.t.* (*blow*) ertönen lassen, blasen; (*measure*) sondieren, loten; (*test*) prüfen, untersuchen; ~barrier, Schallmauer, *f.*; ~box, Schalldose, *f.*; ~film, Tonfilm, *m.*; ~ing, Lotung, Sondierung; Prüfung, *f.*; ~ing-board, Schalldeckel; Resonanzboden, *m.*; ~ing-line, Lotleine, *f.*; ~less, lautlos; ~ness, Gesundheit; Wahrhaftigkeit; Güte, *f.*; ~proof, schalldicht; ~reception, Höraufnahme, *f.*; ~signal, Schallzeichen, *n.*; ~track, Tonstreifen, *m.*, -band, *n.*; ~wave, Schallwelle, *f.*

soup, Suppe, Fleischbrühe, *f.*

sour, *a.*, ~ly, sauer, bitter; *v.t.* sauer machen; (*fig.*) verbittern; *v.i.* sauer werden; ~ness, Säure, *f.*

source, Quelle, *f.*; Ursprung, *m.*

south, *sb.* Süden, *m.*; *a.* and *adv.*
südlich; ~east, Südost, *m.*; ~erly, ~ern, südlich; ~wards, südwärts; ~west, Südwest, *m.*; ~wester, Südwestwind; (*hat*) Südwester, *m.*

sovereign, *sb.* Landesherr, Souverän, *m.*; Zwanzigschillingstück, *n.*; *a.* souverän; höchst; ~ty, Oberherrschaft, Souveränität, *f.*

Soviet, Sowjet, *m.*

sow¹, *sb.* Sau, *f.*

sow², *v.i.* säen; ausstreuen; ~er, Sämann, *m.*; ~ing-machine, Sämaschine, *f.*

soya, Soja, *f.*

spa, Kurort, *m.*, Bad, *n.*

space, *sb.* Raum, *m.*; *v.t.* (*typog.*) sperren; ~ travel, Raumfahrt, *f.*; ~ious, geräumig.

spade, Spaten, *m.*; ~s, (*cards*) Pik, *n.*

span, *sb.* Spanne, Spannweite, *f.*; *v.t.* spannen.

spangle, Flitter, *m.*

spaniel, Wachtelhund, *m.*

spanner, Schraubenschlüssel, *m.*

spar, *sb.* Sparren, *m.*; (*naut.*) Spiere, *f.*; (*min.*) Spat, *m.*; *v.i.* boxen.

spare, *v.t.* (er)sparen; schonen; entbehren; vergönnen; *a.* spärlich, mager; verfügbar, Ersatz-; ~ part, Ersatzteil, *m.*; ~ time, freie Zeit, *f.*

spark, *sb.* Funke(n), *m.*; ~ing-plug, Zündkerze, *f.*

sparkle, *sb.* Funkeln, *n.*; *v.i.* funkeln; (*wine, &c.*) moussieren, perlen.

sparrow, Sperling, *m.*; ~hawk, Sperber, *m.*

sparse, ~ly, spärlich, dünn.

spartan, *sb.* Spartaner, *m.*; *a.* spartanisch.

spasm, Krampf, *m.*; ~odic(ally), krampfhaft.

spatter, bespritzen.

spawn, *sb.* Laich, *m.*; *v.i.* laichen.

speak, sprechen, reden; ~er, Sprecher, Redner, *m.*

spear, *sb.* Speer, Spieß, *m.*; *v.t.* spießen; ~head, (*aircraft*) Spitzenreihe, *f.*; (*troops*) Landekopf, *m.*

special, besonder, Sonder-; ~ist, Spezialist, Facharzt; Fachmann, *m.*; ~ity, Spezialität, *f.*; Sonderfach, *n.*; ~ize, spezialisieren; ~ly, besonders.

specie, Metallgeld, *n.*

species Art, Gattung, *f.*

specific, ~ally, spezifisch, eigen; ~ gravity, spezifisches Gewicht.

specif|ication, Spezifikation, Beschreibung, *f.*; ~y, spezifizieren; einzeln angeben.

specimen, Probe, *f.*, Muster, *n.*

specious, bestechend; (äußerlich) ansprechend.

speck, Fleck, *m.*

speckle, flecken, sprenkeln.

spectacle, Schauspiel, *n.*; Anblick, *m.*; ~s, Brille, *f.*

spectator, Zuschauer, *m.*

spectre, Gespenst, *n.*

spectrum, Spektrum, *n.*

specula|te, spekulieren; nachsinnen, grübeln; ~ion, Spekulation; Betrachtung, *f.*; ~ive, spekulativ, forschend; ~or, Spekulant, *m.*

speech, Sprache; Rede, *f.*; ~less, sprachlos.

speed, *sb.* Eile, Fahrt, Geschwindigkeit, *f.*; *v.i.* eilen, sich beeilen; *v.t.* beschleunigen; ~limit, (zulässige) Höchstgeschwindigkeit, *f.*; ~ometer, Geschwindigkeitsanzeiger, *m.*; ~up, Beschleunigung, *f.*; ~well, (*bot.*) Ehrenpreis, *m.*; ~y, eilig, schnell.

spell, *sb.* Zauber, *m.*; kurze Zeitspanne, *f.*; *v.* buchstabieren; ~bound, (fest)gebannt; ~ing, Rechtschreibung, *f.*; Buchstabieren, *n.*; ~ing-book, Fibel, *f.*

spend, (*money*) ausgeben; (*time*) verbringen, zubringen; ~thrift, Verschwender, *m.*

spent, erschöpft, matt.

spew, ausspeien.

spher|e, Kugel, *f.*; Bereich, Wirkungskreis, *m.*; ~ical, kugelförmig.

spic|e, *sb.* Gewürz, *n.*, Würze, *f.*; *v.t.* würzen; ~y, würzig, pikant.

spick and span, funkelnagelneu.

spider, Spinne, *f.*

spike, Spitze, Zacke, *f.*; Nagel, *m.*; (*corn*) Ähre, *f.*; ~d, mit Spitzen versehen.

spill¹, *sb.* Fidibus, *m.*

spill², *v.t.* verschütten; (*blood*) vergießen.

spin, *sb.* kurze(r) Ritt, *m.*, Fahrt, *f.*; (*av.*) Trudeln, *n.*; (*physics*) Spin, *m.*; *v.t.* spinnen; herumwirbeln; ~ *a yarn*, eine Geschichte erzählen; *v.i.* sich drehen; ~drier, Trockenschleuder, *f.*; ~ner, Spinner(in, *f.*), *m.*; ~ning, Spinnen, *n.*; ~ning-wheel, Spinnrad, *n.*

spinach, Spinat, *m.*

spindle, Spindel, *f.*

spin|e, Rückgrat, *n.*; Stachel, *m.*; ~al, Rückenmark(s)-.

spinster, Ledige, *f.*

spiral, *sb.* Spirale, Schneckenlinie, *f.*; *a.* spiralförmig; ~ staircase, Wendeltreppe, *f.*

spire, Kirchturm, *m.*, Turmspitze, *f.*

spirit, *sb.* (*mind*) Geist, *m.*; (*ghost*) Geist, *m.* Gespenst, *m.*; (*alcoholic*) Spiritus, Sprit, *m.*; (*motor*) Benzin, *n.*; ~s, geistige Getränke, *n.pl.*; *in high* ~s, munter; *in low* ~s, niedergeschlagen; *v.t.* ~ *away*, fortzaubern; ~ed, geistreich, lebhaft; ~level, Libelle, Nivellierwaage, *f.*

spiritual, ~ly, geistlich; geistig; ~ism, Spiritismus, *m.*; ~ist, Spiritist, *m.*

spit¹, *sb.* Bratspieß, *m.*; (*of land*) Landzunge, *f.*

spit², *v.* spucken, speien.

spite, *sb.* Groll, *m.*; *in* ~ *of*, trotz; *v.t.* ärgern; ~ful(ly), boshaft.

spittle, Speichel, *m.*

spittoon, Spucknapf, *m.*

splash, *sb.* Platschen, Spritzen, *n.*; Kotspritzer, *m.*; *v.t.* bespritzen; *v.i.* platschen, spritzen; ~board, Spritzbrett, *n.*

spleen, Milz; Galle, üble Laune, *f.*

splendid, ~ly, herrlich, prachtvoll.

splendour, Herrlichkeit, Pracht, *f.*

splint, Schiene, *f.*

splinter, *sb.* Splitter, *m.*; Sprengstück, *n.*; *v.t.* and *i.* zersplittern.

split, *sb.* Spalt, Riß, *m.*; Spaltung, *f.*; *v.t.* spalten; teilen; *v.i.* bersten, sich spalten.

spoil, *sb.* Beute, *f.*; *v.t.* plündern; verderben; (*child*) verwöhnen;

verziehen; *v.i.* verderben, unbrauchbar werden.

spoke, Speiche, *f.*

spokesman, Fürsprecher, Wortführer, Gewährsmann, *m.*

spoliation, Plünderung, Beraubung, *f.*

spong|e, *sb.* Schwamm, *m.*; *v.i.* schmarotzen; ~y, schwammig.

sponsor, *sb.* Bürge; Pate, *m.*; *v.t.* bürgen, haften (für).

spontan|eity, Selbstentwicklung, Freiwilligkeit, *f.*; ~eous(ly), selbsttätig, freiwillig, ungezwungen, Selbst-.

spool, Spule, *f.*

spoon, Löffel, *m.*

sporadic, sporadisch.

sport, *sb.* Sport, *m.*; *v.t.* zur Schau tragen; *v.i.* spielen, scherzen; ~ing, sportmäßig, sportlich; ~ive, scherzhaft, mutwillig; ~sman, Sportsmann; Sportler; Jäger, *m.*

spot, *sb.* Fleck, *m.*; (*place*) Stelle, *f.*, Ort, *m.*; on the ~, auf der Stelle; *v.t.* beflecken; entdecken, erkennen; ~less, unbefleckt, rein; ~light, Scheinwerfer(licht, *n.*), *m.*; ~ted, befleckt; gefleckt; ~ted fever, Fleckfieber, *n.*; ~ty, fleckig.

spouse, Gatte, *m.*, Gattin, *f.*

spout, *sb.* Rinne, *f.*; (*of vessel*) Tülle, *f.*; Wasserstrahl, *m.*; *v.i.* deklamieren.

sprain, *sb.* Verrenkung, *f.*; *v.t.* verrenken.

sprat, Sprotte, *f.*

sprawl, sich (aus)spreizen.

spray, *sb.* Zweig, Sproß; Schaum, Gischt, *m.*; (*apparatus*) Zerstäuber, *m.*; *v.t.* zerstäuben; bespritzen; besprühen.

spread, *sb.* Ausdehnung; Verbreitung, *f.*; *v.t.* ausbreiten; entfalten; bestreichen; *v.i.* sich verbreiten, sich erstrecken.

sprig, Reis, *n.*

sprightly, lebhaft.

spring, *sb.* (*steel, &c.*) Feder; Federkraft, *f.*; (*leap*) Sprung, *m.*; (*water*) Quelle, *f.*; (*season*) Frühling, *m.*, Frühjahr, *n.*; *v.i.* springen; (*grow*) (empor)schießen; (*water*) sprudeln;

(*fig.*) entspringen, entstehen; ~ a leak, leck werden; ~balance, Federwaage, *f.*; ~board, Sprungbrett, *n.*; ~tide, Springflut, *f.*; ~y, elastisch, federnd.

sprinkle, (be)sprengen; ausstreuen.

sprint, *sb.* Sprint, *m.*; *v.i.* schnell laufen; ~er, Sprinter, Kurzstreckenläufer, *m.*

sprout, *sb.* Sprößling, *m.*; *v.i.* sprossen; Brussels ~s, Rosenkohl, *m.*

spruce, *sb.* Fichte, *f.*; *a.* nett, sauber.

spur, *sb.* Sporn; (*of mountain*) Ausläufer, *m.*; *v.t.* anspornen.

spurious, unecht, gefälscht.

spurn, wegstoßen, verschmähen.

spurt, *sb.* (*racing*) Spurt; (Wasser)strahl, *m.*; *v.i.* (hervor)spritzen; (*racing*) spurten.

sputter, sprudeln, sprühen.

spy, *sb.* Spion, *m.*; *v.i.* spionieren, spähen.

squabble, *sb.* Streit, Wortwechsel, *m.*; *v.i.* zanken.

squad, Rotte, *f.*, Trupp, *m.*; ~ron, (*nav.*) Geschwader, *n.*; (*mil.*) Schwadron, Gruppe; (*air*) Staffel, *f.*; ~ron leader, Major, *m.*

squalid, ~ly, schmutzig.

squall, Bö, *f.*, Windstoß, *m.*; ~y, böig.

squalor, Schmutz, *m.*, Elend, *n.*

squander, verschwenden.

square, *sb.* Viereck, Quadrat, *n.*; (*in a town*) Platz, *m.*; (*chess, &c.*) Feld, *n.*; *a.* viereckig, quadratisch; (*honest*) redlich, rechtschaffen; *v.t.* (*math.*) quadrieren; (*bribe*) bestechen; *v.i.* sich anpassen (*dat.*), übereinstimmen (*with* mit); ~built, vierschrötig; ~ root, Quadratwurzel, *f.*

squash, *sb.* Brei, *m.*; Gedränge, *n.*; *lemon* ~, Zitronenlimonade, *f.*; *v.t.* zerquetschen.

squat, *v.i.* sich kauern, sich ducken; *a.* untersetzt, gedrungen; ~ter, unberechtigter Ansiedler, Eindringling, *m.*

squaw, Indianerweib, *n.*

squeak, *sb.* Gequiek, *f.*; *v.i.* quieken.

squeal, quieken.

squeamish, wählerisch, empfindlich.

squeeze, *sb.* Druck, *m.; v.t.* drücken, pressen.

squint, *sb.* Schielen, *n.; v.i.* schielen.

squirrel, Eichhörnchen, *n.*

squirt, spritzen.

stab, stechen; erdolchen.

stable¹, *a.* fest, dauerhaft; ~ility, Festigkeit, Stabilität, *f.;* ~ilize, stabilisieren.

stable², *sb.* Stall, *m.*

stack, *sb.* Schober, Haufen, *m.,* Schicht, *f.;* Schornstein, *m.; v.t.* häufen, schichten.

stadium, Stadion, *n*

staff, *sb. (rod and mil.)* Stab, *m.,* Personal, *n.; v.t.* mit Personal versehen.

stag, Hirsch, *m.*

stage, *sb. (theatr.)* Bühne, *f.; (platform)* Gerüst, *n.; (bus, &c.)* Haltestelle, Station, Strecke, *f.; v.t.* auf die Bühne bringen, inszenieren; ~coach, Postkutsche, *f.;* ~fright, Lampenfieber, *n.;* ~manager, Bühnenleiter, *m.*

stagger, *v.i.* wanken, taumeln; *v.t.* verblüffen, stutzig machen; ~ed, *(hours. &c.)* gestaffelt.

stagnant, träge, bewegungslos, stockend; ~te, stillstehen, stocken.

staid, gesetzt, nüchtern.

stain, *sb.* Flecken *m.; v.t.* beflecken; ~ed, befleckt; *(glass)* bemalt, bunt; ~less, *(steel, &c.)* rostfrei.

stair, Stufe, *f.;* ~carpet, Treppenläufer, *m.;* ~case, ~s, Treppe, *f.*

stake, *sb.* Pfahl; *(bet)* Einsatz, *m.; at* ~, auf dem Spiel; *v.t.* einsetzen; *(fig.)* aufs Spiel setzen; ~ *out,* abstecken.

stalactite, Tropfstein, *m.*

stale, abgestanden; altbacken; schal; ~mate, *sb.* Patt, *n.; v.t.* patt machen.

stalk, *sb.* Stengel, Stiel, *m.; v.t.* pirschen, beschleichen.

stall, *m. (Verkaufs)stand, m.; (for cattle)* Stand. *m.; (theatr.)* Sperr-

sitz, *m.,* Parkett, *n.; v.i. (motor)* stehenbleiben; *(aircraft)* sacken.

stalwart, stark, kräftig.

stamen, Staubfaden, *m.*

stamina, Ausdauer, *f.*

stammer, stammeln, stottern; ~er, Stammler, *m.*

stamp, *sb.* Stempel, *m.; (postage)* (Brief)marke, *f.; v.t. (letters, &c.)* frankieren; *(mark)* stempeln, markieren; *(coins)* prägen; ~ *out,* ausstampfen, unterdrücken; *v.i.* stampfen.

stampede, *sb.* wilde Flucht; *v.i.* voller Schrecken fliehen.

stand, *sb.* Stand; Ständer, *m.;* Gestell, *n.;* Stillstand, *m.;* Tribüne, *f.; make a* ~. Widerstand leisten; *come to a* ~*still,* zum Stillstand kommen; *v.i.* stehen, aufrecht stehen, sich aufrecht erhalten; *(last)* dauern, bleiben; *(remain)* bestehen; *v.t.* stellen; *(treat)* traktieren; *(tolerate)* ertragen, ausstehen; ~ *at attention!,* stillgestanden! ~ *at ease!,* rührt euch!; ~ *by, (person)* beistehen *(with dat.), (radio)* in Bereitschaft bleiben (für); *(not interfere)* müßig dabeistehen; ~ *one's ground,* nicht weichen, aushalten; ~ *up,* aufstehen; ~ *up for,* für (jemanden) einstehen; ~ing, *sb.* Rang, *m.,* Stellung, *f.; of long* ~*ing,* von lange her; langjährig; *a.* stehend, bleibend; ~ing-orders, Geschäftsordnung, *f.;* Dauerbefehle, *m.pl.;* ~ing-room, Stehplatz, *m.;* ~offish zurückhaltend, reserviert; ~point, Standpunkt, *m.;* ~still, Stillstand, *m.*

standard, *sb. (flag)* Standarte, *f.; (model)* Muster, *n.,* Maßstab, *m.,* Norm, *f.; (class)* Klasse, *f.; a.* musterhaft; klassisch; Einheits-; ~bearer, Fahnenträger, *m.;* ~ gauge *(railway)* Normalspur, *f.;* ~ization, Normierung, *f.;* ~ize, normieren; ~lamp, Stehlampe, *f.;* ~measure, Eich-, Richt-maß, *n.;* ~time, Normalzeit, *f.*

stanza, Stanze, Strophe, *f.*

staple, Haupterzeugnis, n.; (fibre) Faser, f.; a. Haupt-.

star, sb. Stern; (Film)star, m.; v.i. in der Hauptrolle auftreten, gastieren; ~fish, Seestern, m.; ~ shell, Leuchtgeschoß, n.

starboard, Steuerbord, n.

starch, sb. Stärke, f.; v.t. stärken.

stare, sb. starrer Blick; v.i. starren.

starling, Star, m.

start, sb. Start, Ablauf, Abflug, Anfang; Vorsprung, m.; (fright) Auffahren, Aufschrecken, n.; v.i. anfangen, starten, abfahren, losgehen; (with fright) auf-, zurück- fahren; v.t. (mach.) in Gang setzen, anlassen; gründen, anfangen, beginnen; (game) auftreiben; ~er, (sport) Starter; (motor) Anlasser, m.; ~ing-point, Startplatz, m.; Abfahrtsstelle, f.

startle, erschrecken, überraschen.

starv|e, v.i. verhungern; v.t. aushungern; ~ation, Verhungern, n., Hungertod, m.

state, sb. (condition) Zustand; (country) Staat, m.; v.t. erwähnen, erklären, angeben; feststellen, festsetzen; ~ment, Angabe, Aussage, f., Bericht, m.; ~room, Luxuszimmer, n.; (on ship) Luxuskabine, f.; ~sman, Staatsmann, m.; ~smanship, Staatskunst, f.

state|liness, Stattlichkeit, f.; ~ly, stattlich.

static, sb. (radio) Luftstörung, f.; a. statisch; ~s, Statik, f.

station, sb. (rank) Stand; (railway) Bahnhof; (position) Posten, m.; (naut.) Station, f., Standort, m.; v.t. stellen; ~ary, fest(stehend); ~er, Schreibwarenhändler, m.; ~ery, Schreibwaren, f.pl.; ~master, Bahnhofsvorsteher, m.

statistic|al, statistisch; ~ian, Statistiker, m.; ~s, Statistik, f.

statue, Bildsäule, f.

stature, Leibesgröße, f., Wuchs, m.

status, Lage, f., Stand, m.

statut|e, Statut, Gesetz, n.; ~ory, gesetzlich, festgesetzt.

staunch¹, a. treu, standhaft.

staunch², v.t. stillen.

stave, sb. (barrel) (Faß)daube; (ladder) Sprosse; (prosody) Strophe, f., Vers, m.; v.t. ~ in, ein Loch einschlagen; ~ off, abwehren.

stay, sb. (support) Stütze, f.; (stopping) Aufenthalt, m.; (naut.) Stag, n.; v.i. sich aufhalten, wohnen, bleiben; v.t. aufhalten, hindern; ~ up, bleiben; ~s, Korsett, n.

stead, in his ~, an seiner Stelle; ~fast, standhaft; ~fastness, Standhaftigkeit, f.

stead|y, a., ~ily, fest, standhaft; beständig; v.t. festhalten; ruhig machen; ~iness, Beständigkeit, f.

steak, (Fleisch)schnitte, f., Beefsteak, n.

steal, stehlen; ~ away, wegschleichen; ~th, Heimlichkeit, f.; ~thy, ~thily, verstohlen, heimlich.

steam, sb. Dampf, m.; v.i. dampfen; (naut.) fahren; v.t. dämpfen; ~-engine, Dampfmaschine, f.; ~er, Dampfer, m.

steel, Stahl, m.

steep¹, a., ~ly, jäh, steil; ~ness, Steilheit, f.

steep², v.t. einweichen, tränken.

steeple, Kirchturm, m.; ~chase, Hindernisrennen, n.

steer¹, sb. (junger) Ochs(e), m.

steer², v.t. and i. steuern; (motor, &c.) lenken; ~age, Zwischendeck, n.; ~ing-wheel (naut.), Steuerrad; (motor) Lenkrad, n.; ~sman, Steuermann, m.

stellar, Sternen-.

stem, sb. Stiel, Stengel, m.; v.t. aufhalten; dämmen.

stench, Gestank, m.

stencil, Schablone, f., Klischee, n.

stenograph|er, Stenograph, m.; ~y, Stenographie, f.

step, sb. Schritt, m.; (stair) Stufe, f.; (ladder) Sprosse, f.; (carriage, &c.) Tritt, m.; (footstep) Fußstapfe, f.; v.i. schreiten, treten, einhergehen; ~ping-stone, Schrittstein, m.; (fig.) Stufe, f., Mittel, n.

step(brother,&c.),Stief(bruder,&c.).

stereotyped, (fig.) schablonenhaft.

steril|e, unfruchtbar; steril; ~ity,

Unfruchtbarkeit, *f.*; ~ize, sterilisieren.

sterling, *sb.* Sterling, *m.*; *a.* echt; zuverlässig.

stern[1], *sb.* Heck, *n.*

stern[2], *a.* ~ly, streng, ernst; ~ness, Strenge, Härte, *f.*

stethoscope, Stethoskop, *n.*

stevedore, Stauer, *m.*

stew, *sb.* Schmorfleisch, Ragout, *n.*; *v.t.* schmoren.

steward, Verwalter; (*on ship, in club, &c.*) Steward, *m.*; ~ess, Aufwärterin, Stewardeß, *f.*

stick[1], *sb.* Stock, *m.*, Stange, *f.*; (*aeronaut.*) Steuerknüppel, *m.*; (*of bombs*) Reihenabwurf, *m.*

stick[2], *v.t.* (ein)stecken; (*glue*) (an)kleben; (*bear*) ertragen; *v.i.* halten, steckenbleiben, stocken; bleiben bei; ~iness, Klebrigkeit, *f.*; ~y, klebrig.

stiff, ~ly, steif; dick; schwierig; ~en, *v.t.* steifen, verstärken; *v.i.* steif werden, erstarren; ~ness, Steifheit, Dicke, *f.*

stifle, ersticken.

stigma, Brandmal, *n.*, Narbe, *f.*; Schandfleck, *m.*; ~tize, brandmarken.

stile, Zauntritt, *m.*

still[1], *sb.* Destillierapparat, Brennkolben, *m.*

still[2], *a.* still, ruhig; *v.t.* stillen, beruhigen; *adv.* (immer) noch; doch, trotzdem; ~born, totgeboren; ~ life, Stilleben, *n.*; ~ness, Stille, *f.*

stilted, gespreizt, hochtrabend.

stilts, Stelzen, *f.pl.*

stimul|ant, ~us, Reizmittel, *n.*; ~ate, anreizen; ~ation, Reizung, *f.*

sting, *sb.* Stachel; Biß, Stich, *m.*; *v.t.* and *i.* stechen; (*nettle*) brennen; ~nettle, Brennessel, *f.*

sting|iness, Geiz, *m.*; ~y, geizig.

stink, *sb.* Gestank, *m.*; *v.i.* stinken.

stint, knapp halten.

stipend, Gehalt, *n.*, Besoldung, *f.*

stipulat|e, bedingen, festsetzen; ~ion, Bedingung, *f.*

stir, *sb.* Regung, *f.*, Aufruhr, *m.*; *v.t.* (um)rühren, bewegen; ~up, erregen; *v.i.* sich rühren, sich regen; ~ring, aufregend.

stirrup, Steigbügel, *m.*; ~pump, Handspritze, *f.*

stitch, *sb.* Stich, *m.*; (*knitting*) Masche, *f.*; *v.t.* and *i.* nähen, sticken; (*books*) heften.

stoat, Wiesel, Hermelin, *n.*

stock, *sb.* (*store*) Vorrat, *m.*, Lager, *n.*; (*cattle*) Vieh, *n.*, Viehstand, *m.*; (*shares*) Aktien, *f.pl.*; (*family*) Geschlecht, *n.*; (*neck-tie*) Halsbinde, *f.*; (*of gun*) Kolben, *m.*; (*flower*) Levkoje, *f.*; (*soup*) Brühe, *f.*; (*handle*) Griff, Schaft, *m.*; *rolling* ~, Betriebsmaterial, *n.*; *in* ~, vorrätig; *out of* ~, ausverkauft; *v.t.* versehen (*with* mit); *auf Lager haben*; ~ade, Einzäunung, Einpfählung, *f.*; Konzentrationslager, *n.*; ~broker, Börsenmakler, *m.*; ~exchange, Börse, *f.*; ~holder, Aktionär, *m.*; ~raising, Viehzucht, *f.*; ~size, Normalgröße, *f.*; ~taking, Inventur, *f.*

stocking, Strumpf, *m.*

stocky, untersetzt.

stodgy, unverdaulich, dick.

stoic, Stoiker, *m.*; ~al(ly), stoisch.

stoke, heizen; ~hold, Heizraum, *m.*; ~r, Heizer, *m.*

stole, Stola, *f.*

stolid, schwerfällig, phlegmatisch.

stomach, *sb.* Magen, *m.*; *v.t.* sich gefallen lassen, ertragen; ~ache, Magenschmerzen, *m.pl.*

stone, *sb.* Stein, *m.*; *a.* steinern, Stein-; *v.t.* steinigen; (*fruit*) auskernen; ~blind, stockblind; ~cutter, ~mason, Steinmetz, *m.*; ~fruit, Steinobst, *n.*; ~quarry, Steinbruch, *m.*

stony, steinig; (*fig.*) steinern.

stool, Schemel, *m.*; (*med.*) Stuhlgang, *m.*

stoop, *v.i.* sich bücken; (*fig.*) sich herablassen.

stop, *sb.* Stillstand; Aufenthalt, Halt, *m.*; Ende, *n.*, Abschluß, *m.*; (*punctuation*) Punkt, *m.*; (*phonetics*) Verschlußlaut, *m.*; *v.t.* aufhalten, hemmen; hemmen, stoppen; verhindern; (*hole, gap, &c.*) stopfen; (*payment*) einstellen; (*teeth*) plombieren, füllen; *v.i.* anhalten; aufhören; stehenbleiben; wohnen (*at in*), sich aufhalten; **~cock**, Absperrhahn, *m.*; **~gap**, Lückenbüßer, *m.*; **~press**, neueste Nachrichten, *f.pl.*; **~watch**, Stoppuhr, *f.*

stoppage, Hemmung, Verstopfung; Einstellung; Stockung, *f.*
stopper, Stöpsel, *m.*
stopping, Anhalten, *n.*; (*of teeth*) Plombieren, *n.*, Plombe, *f.*
storage, Lagerung, *f.*; Lagergeld, *n.*; *in cold* **~**, im Kühlraum.
store, *sb.* Vorrat, *m.*, Lager, *n.*; (*shop*) Kauf-, Waren-haus, *n.*; *keep in* **~**, vorrätig halten; *have in* **~**, bereit haben (*for* für); *v.t.* lagern, aufspeichern; **~s**, Vorräte, *m.pl.*, Proviant, *m.*
stork, Storch, *m.*
storm, *sb.* Sturm, *m.*; *v.t.* (*mil.*) stürmen; **~y**, stürmisch.
story, (*narrative*) Geschichte, *f.*; *short* **~**, Novelle, *f.*; (*floor*) Stock, *m.*
stout, **~ly**, stark, wohlbeleibt; kräftig; **~ness**, Stärke, *f.*
stove, Ofen, *m.*
stow, stauen; packen; (*bombs on aircraft*) aufhängen; **~away** blinder Passagier.
straddle, sich rittlings setzen; (*target*) eingabeln, decken.
straggle, irren, abschweifen; (*plants*) wuchern; **~r**, (*mil.*) Nachzügler, *m.*
straight, gerade; **~** *away*, sofort; **~** *on*, geradeaus; **~en**, gerade machen; **~forward**, aufrichtig, redlich; einfach; **~ness**, Geradheit, *f.*
strain, *sb.* Anstrengung, *f.*; (*sprain*) Verrenkung, *f.*; (*tech.*) Spannung, *f.*, Druck, *m.*; (*song*) Weise, Melodie, *f.*; (*race*) Geschlecht, *n.*, Art, *f.*; *v.t.* spannen; anstrengen; (*liquid*) durchseihen; *v.i.* sich anstrengen; sich verrenken; **~er**, Filter, *m.*, Sieb, *n.*
strait, (*Meer*)enge, Straße, *f.*; *in great* **~s**, in großer Verlegenheit; *a.* eng; **~** *waistcoat*, Zwangsjacke, *f.*
strand, *sb.* (*shore*) Strand, *m.*; (*rope, wire*) Ducht, Litze, *f.*; (*hair*) Strähne, *f.*; *v.t.* stranden; **~ed**, gestrandet.

strange, **~ly**, fremd; seltsam, sonderbar; **~ness**, Fremdheit; Sonderbarkeit, *f.*; **~r**, Fremde(r).
strangle, erdrosseln; **~ulation**, Erdrosselung, *f.*
strap, *sb.* (Halte)riemen; (*mil.*) Achselstreifen; (*dress*) Träger, *m.*; *v.t.* anschnüren; **~hanger**, Stehplatzinhaber, *m.*; **~hanging**, Stehenmüssen, *n.*; **~ping**, *sb.* Tracht (*f.*) Prügel; *a.* stämmig.
stratagem, (Kriegs)list, *f.*
strategic, strategisch; **~y**, Strategie, *f.*
stratum, Lage, Schicht, *f.*
straw, Stroh, *n.*; **~berry**, Erdbeere, *f.*
stray, *a.* verirrt, verlaufen; *v.i.* sich verlaufen, abirren.
streak, *sb.* Strich, Streifen, *m.*; *v.t.* streifen.
stream, *sb.* Strom, Bach, *m.*; *v.i.* strömen, fließen; wehen, flattern; **~er**, Wimpel, *m.*; **~lined**, stromlinienförmig; schnittig.
street, Straße, Gasse, *f.*; **~arab**, Straßenjunge, *m.*
strength, Stärke, Kraft, Festigkeit, *f.*; **~en**, *v.t.* stärken, befestigen; *v.i.* stark werden.
strenuous, **~ly**, energisch, angestrengt.
stress, *sb.* (Nach)druck, *m.*, Betonung, *f.*; (*tech.*) Spannung, *f.*, Druck, *m.*; *v.t.* betonen.
stretch, *sb.* Strecke, *f.*, Bereich, *m.*; *v.t.* (aus)strecken; ausdehnen; *v.i.* sich (er)strecken, sich ausdehnen; **~er**, Tragbahre, *f.*; **~er-bearer**, Krankenträger, *m.*
strew, (aus)streuen; bedecken.
stricken, betroffen (*with* von).
strict, **~ly**, streng; pünktlich, genau; **~ness**, Strenge; Genauigkeit, *f.*
stride, (weiter) Schritt, *m.*; *v.i.* schreiten.
strident, schneidend, kreischend.
strife, Streit, *m.*
strike, *sb.* Streik, *m.*; *v.t.* schlagen; (*colours, sail*) streichen; (*bargain*) abschließen; (*match*) anzünden; *v.i.* (*stop work*) streiken; (*clock*) schlagen; **~** *on*, stoßen (an), laufen (auf); **~** *out*,

ausstreichen; um sich schlagen; ~ up, (band) aufspielen; (song) anstimmen; ~r, Streikende(r); **striking,** merkwürdig, auffallend.

string, sb. Schnur, f., Bindfaden, m.; (mus. instrument) Saite, f. (series) Reihe, f.; v.t. aufreihen, aufziehen; ~ orchestra, Streichorchester, n.; ~y, faserig.

stringen|t, streng, ~cy, Strenge, f.

strip, sb. Streifen, m.; v.t. abstreifen, abziehen, abschälen; entkleiden; berauben; ~ling, Jüngling, m.; ~tease, Entkleidungsakt, m.; ~-teaser, Nacktänzerin, f.

stripe, Streifen, m.; ~d, gestreift.

strive, streben.

stroke, sb. (blow, clock, med.) Schlag; (mech.) Hub, Takt, (pen) Strich; (swimming) Stoß, m.; four-~, (motor) Viertakt-; v.t. streichen; streicheln.

stroll, sb. Spaziergang, m.; v.i. schlendern.

strong, ~ly, stark, kräftig; ~-box, ~ room Stahlkammer, f.; ~hold, Festung, f.; ~ point, Stützpunkt, m.

strop, sb. Streichriemen, m.; v.t. streichen, abziehen.

structur|e, Bau, m., Gebäude, n.; ~al, Bau-.

struggle, sb. Kampf, m.; v.i. kämpfen, ringen, sich sträuben.

strum, klimpern.

strut, sb. (building) Strebe, f.; Stolzieren, n.; v.i. stolzieren, sich brüsten.

strychnine, Strychnin, n.

stub, Stumpf, m.

stubble, Stoppel, f.

stubborn, ~ly, hartnäckig, unbeugsam; ~ness, Hartnäckigkeit, f.

stucco, Stuck, m.

stud, (collar) Kragenknopf, m.; (horses) Gestüt, n., Rennstall, m.

stud|ent, Student, m.; ~io, Atelier, n.; (radio) Senderaum, m.; ~ious(ly), fleißig; ~y, sb. Studium; Studierzimmer, n.; Studie, f.; v.t. and i. studieren.

stuff, sb. Stoff, m., Zeug, n.; v.t. (aus)stopfen; (cookery) füllen;

~ing, Füllung, f., Füllsel, n.; ~y, schwül, dumpf.

stumbl|e, stolpern, straucheln; ~ing-block, Stein (m.) des Anstoßes.

stump, (tree, limb) Stumpf; (cabbage) Strunk; (cigarette, limb) Stummel; (cricket) Stab, m.; ~y, kurz und dick.

stun, betäuben; ~ning, (slang) famos.

stunt, Kraft-, Kunst- stück, n.; Schlager, m.

stunted, verkümmert.

stupef|y, betäuben; ~action, Betäubung, f.

stupendous, erstaunlich.

stupid, ~ly, dumm; ~ity, Dummheit, f.

stupor, Betäubung, Erstarrung, f.

sturd|iness, Derbheit, Festigkeit, f.; ~ily, ~y, stark, derb.

sturgeon, Stör, m.

stutter, stottern.

sty, Schweinestall, m.; (on eye) Gerstenkorn, n.

styl|e, sb. Stil; Titel; (pen) Griffel, m.; v.t. betiteln; ~ish, elegant, modisch.

sub-, Unter-.

sub-committee, Unterausschuß, m.

subconscious, unterbewußt; ~ness, Unterbewußtsein, n.

subdivi|de, weiter teilen; ~sion, Unterabteilung, f.

subdue, unterwerfen.

sub-editor, Hilfsredakteur, m.

subject, sb. (citizen) Untertan; (matter) Gegenstand, m.; (gram.) Subjekt, n.; a. unterworfen; (liable) geneigt (to zu); abhängig (von); v.t. unterwerfen, aussetzen; ~ion, Unterwerfung, f.

subjunctive, Konjunktiv, m.

sublet, weiter vermieten.

sub-lieutenant, Leutnant (m.) zur See.

sublim|e, erhaben; ~ity, Erhabenheit, f.

submarine, sb. Unterseeboot, U-boot, n.; a. unterseeisch.

submer|ge, v.t. überschwemmen; (of submarine) tauchen; ~sion, Untertauchen, n.; Überschwemmung, f.

submiss|ion, Ergebung; Unter-
würfigkeit f.; ~ive(ly), unterwürfig.

submit, v.t. unterwerfen; unter-
breiten; v.i. sich fügen, sich
unterwerfen.

subordinat|e, sb. Untergeord-
nete(r); a. untergeordnet; ~e
clause, Nebensatz, m.; v.t. unter-
ordnen; ~ion, Unterordnung, f.

subscri|be, unterschreiben; abon-
nieren (to auf); ~ber, Unter-
zeichner, Abonnent, m.;
~ption, Abonnement, n.; Beitrag, m.

subsequent, nachfolgend; ~ly,
nachher.

subservien|t, unterwürfig; ~ce,
Unterwürfigkeit, f.

subsid|e, sinken; abnehmen;
~ence, Einfallen, Einsinken,
n.; Abnahme, f.

subsidiary, Neben-, Hilfs-.

subsid|ize, mit Geld unterstützen;
~y, Beisteuer, Subvention, f.

subsistence, Dasein, n.; (money)
Vorschuß, Unterhalt, m.

subsoil, Untergrund, m.

substan|ce, Stoff, m., Substanz, f.;
Wesen, n.; Vermögen, n.;
~tial(ly), wesentlich; kräftig,
stark.

substantiate, dartun, beweisen.

substantive, Hauptwort, Substantiv, n.

substitut|e, sb. Stellvertreter; Er-
satz, m.; v.t. einsetzen, substi-
tuieren; ~ion, Ersetzung, f.

substratum, Unterlage, f., Sub-
strat, n.

subtenant, Untermieter, m.

subterfuge, Ausflucht, f., Vorwand,
m.

subterranean, unterirdisch.

subtle, schlau, spitzfindig; ~ty,
Schlauheit, f., Spitzfindigkeit, f., Scharfsinn, m.

subtract, abziehen; ~ion, Abziehen, n., Abzug, m.

suburb, Vorstadt, f.; ~an, vor-
städtisch.

subver|t, umstürzen; ~sive, um-
stürzend, umstürzlerisch.

subway, Unterführung, f., Tunnel,
m.

succeed, gelingen, glücken.

success, Erfolg, m.; ~ful(ly),

erfolgreich.

success|ion, Folge; Thronfolge, f.;
~ive, aufeinanderfolgend;
~ively, der Reihe nach; ~or,
Nachfolger, m.

succulen|t, saftig; ~ce, Saftig-
keit, f.

succumb, unterliegen.

such, solche(r, s); so ein; ~ as,
diejenigen, welche; zum Beispiel; ~like, dergleichen.

suck, saugen; ~er, (bot.) Wurzel-
sproß, m.; ~le, säugen; ~ling,
Säugling, m.

suction, Saugen, n.; ~ pump,
Saugpumpe, f.

sudden, ~ly, plötzlich; ~ness,
Plötzlichkeit, f.

suds, Seifenwasser, n.

sue, verklagen.

suède, schwedisches Leder, Wildleder, n.

suet, Nierenfett, n., Talg, m.

suffer, leiden (from an); (punishment) erleiden; (let) erlauben,
gestatten; ~ance, Duldung,
Zulassung, f.; ~ing, Leiden, n.

suffic|e, genügen; ~ient(ly), ge-
nügend, hinlänglich.

suffix, Suffix, n.

suffocat|e, ersticken; ~ion, Er-
stickung, f.

suffrage, Stimmrecht, n.; ~tte,
Frauenstimmrechtlerin, f.

sugar, sb. Zucker, m.; v.t. zuckern;
~-basin, Zuckerschale, f.; ~-
beet, Zuckerrübe, f.; ~-cane,
Zuckerrohr, n.; ~-loaf, Zuckerhut, m.; ~-refinery, Zucker-
raffinerie, f.; ~y, zuck(e)rig.

suggest, eingeben, vorschlagen;
~ion, Vorschlag, Wink, m.;
~ive(ly), andeutend, anregend;
zweideutig, pikant.

suicid|e, Selbstmord; Selbst-
mörder, m.; ~al, selbstmörde-
risch.

suit, sb. (clothes) Anzug, m.; (cards)
Farbe, f.; (law) Prozeß, m.;
(wooing) Werbung, f.; v.t.
passen, gut stehen; ~able,
~ably, passend, angemessen;
schicklich; ~case, Handkoffer,
m.; ~or, Freier, m.

suite, Gefolge, n.; (of furniture)
(Zimmer)einrichtung, f.; (of

rooms) Zimmerflucht, *f.*

sulk, schmollen; ~**ily,** ~**y,** schmollend.

sullen, ~**ly,** mürrisch.

sulph|ate, schwefelsaures Salz; ~**ide,** Sulfid, *n.;* ~**ur,** Schwefel, *m.;* ~*uric acid,* Schwefelsäure, *f.*

sultan, Sultan, *m.;* ~**a,** *(fruit)* Sultanine, *f.*

sultr|iness, Schwüle. *f.;* ~**y,** schwül.

sum, *sb.* Summe; Rechenaufgabe, *f.;* Inbegriff, *m.;* ~ *total,* Summa, *f.; v.t.* ~ *up,* zusammenfassen.

summar|y, *sb.* Auszug, *m.,* Übersicht, *f.; a.,* ~**ily,** summarisch; ~**ize,** zusammenfassen.

summer, Sommer, *m.;* ~**house,** Gartenhaus, *n.*

summit, Gipfel, *m.*

summon, vorladen; auffordern; ~**s,** Vorladung; Aufforderung, *f.*

sumptuous, ~**ly,** prächtig.

sun, Sonne, *f.;* ~**beam,** Sonnenstrahl, *m.;* ~**blind,** Jalousie, Markise, *f.;* ~**burnt,** sonnverbrannt; ~**day,** Sonntag, *m.;* ~**dial,** Sonnenuhr, *f.;* ~**flower,** Sonnenblume, *f.;* ~**light,** Sonnenlicht, *n.;* ~**ny,** sonnig; ~**rise,** Sonnenaufgang, *m.;* ~**set,** Sonnenuntergang, *m.;* ~**shade,** Sonnenschirm, *m.;* ~**shine,** Sonnenschein, *m.;* ~**stroke,** Hitzschlag, Sonnenstich, *m.*

sundry, verschiedene, gemischte.

sup, schlürfen, nippen.

superannuat|e, pensionieren; ~**ion,** Pension; Pensionierung, *f.*

superb, ~**ly,** prächtig, herrlich.

supercharge, Zusatzladung, *f.*

supercilious, ~**ly,** hochmütig, arrogant, anmaßend.

superficial, ~**ly,** oberflächlich; ~**ity,** Oberflächlichkeit, *f.*

superflu|ity, Überfluß, *m.;* ~**ous,** überflüssig.

superhuman, übermenschlich.

superintend, verwalten, die Aufsicht führen; ~**ent,** Aufseher, *m.*

superior, *sb.* Vorgesetzte(r); *a.* höher; überlegen; ~**ity,** Überlegenheit, *f.*

superlative, *sb.* Superlativ, *m.; a.,* ~**ly,** höchst.

superman, Übermensch, *m.*

supermarket, Supermarkt, *m.*

supernatural, ~**ly,** übernatürlich.

supernumerary, *sb.* Überzählige(r); *(theatr.)* Figurant, Statist, *m.; a.* überzählig.

supersede, verdrängen, ersetzen.

superstit|ion, Aberglaube, *f.;* ~**ious(ly),** abergläubisch.

superstructure, Oberbau, *m.*

supertax, Steuerzuschlag, *m.*

supervene, dazwischenkommen.

supervis|e, beaufsichtigen; ~**ion,** Aufsicht, *f.;* ~**or,** Aufseher, *m.*

supper, Abendessen, *n.; The Lord's Supper,* das (heilige) Abendmahl.

supplant, verdrängen.

supple, geschmeidig, biegsam.

supplement, *sb.* Ergänzung, *f.,* Nachtrag, Anhang, *m.; v.t.* ergänzen; ~**ary,** ergänzend, nachträglich.

supplicant, Bittsteller, *m.;* ~**ate,** anflehen.

supply, *sb.* Vorrat; Proviant, *m.;* Versorgung, *f.;* ~ *and demand,* Angebot und Nachfrage; *v.t.* versorgen, liefern; ergänzen; ~**column,** Nachschubkolonne, *f.*

support, *sb.* Stütze; Unterstützung, *f.; v.t.* unterstützen, unterhalten; beistehen; ~**er,** Gönner, Anhänger, *m.*

suppos|e, voraussetzen, vermuten; ~**ition,** Voraussetzung, Vermutung, *f.*

suppress, unterdrücken; verheimlichen; ~**ion,** Unterdrückung; Verheimlichung, *f.*

suppurate, eitern.

suprem|e, ~**ely,** höchst, oberst; ~**acy,** Obergewalt, *f.*

surcharge, Überteuerung, *f.;* Zuschlag, *m.*

sure, ~**ly,** sicher, gewiß; *to be* ~, allerdings, freilich; *to make* ~, sich vergewissern; ~**ness,** Sicherheit, *f.;* ~**ty,** Bürge, *m.;* Bürgschaft, *f.*

surf, Brandung, *f.*

surface, *sb.* Oberfläche, *f.; v.i.* auftauchen; ~**craft,** Überwasserfahrzeug, *n.*

surfeit, Überdruß, *m.;* Übermaß, *n.*

surge, *sb.* Brandung, *f.; v.i.* wogen.

surg|eon, Chirurg, *m.*; ~ery, Chirurgie, *f.*; Sprechzimmer, *n.*; ~ical, chirurgisch.

surl|y, grob, mürrisch; ~iness, mürrisches Wesen.

surmise, *sb.* Vermutung, *f.*; *v.i.* vermuten.

surmount, überwinden.

surname, Zuname, *m.*

surpass, übertreffen.

surplice, Chorhemd, *n.*

surplus, *sb.* Überschuß, *m.*; *a.* überschüssig.

surpris|e, *sb.* Überraschung, *f.*; *v.t.* überraschen; ~ing(ly), erstaunlich.

surrender, *sb.* Übergabe; Abtretung, *f.*; *v.t.* übergeben; abtreten; *v.i.* sich ergeben.

surreptitious, ~ly, heimlich, verstohlen.

surround, umgeben; einschließen; ~ing, umgebend; ~ings, Umgebung, *f.*

survey, *sb.* Überblick, *m.*; Vermessung, Schätzung; (Landes-)aufnahme, *f.*; *v.t.* überblicken; (*land*) vermessen; ~or, Landmesser, *m.*

surviv|e, *v.t.* überleben; *v.i.* fortleben; noch leben; ~al, Überleben, *n.*; ~or, Überlebende(r); Hinterbliebene(r).

susceptib|le, empfänglich; ~ility, Empfänglichkeit, *f.*

suspect, *sb.* Verdächtige(r); *v.t.* in Verdacht haben; vermuten.

suspend, (*hang up*) aufhängen; (*stop*) einstellen, aussetzen; ~er, Strumpfhalter, *m.*

suspense, Ungewißheit, Spannung, *f.*

suspension, *sb.* Aufhebung, *f.*; Aufschub; (*sport*) Ausschluß, *m.*; ~bridge, Schwebe-, Hängebrücke, *f.*

suspic|ion, Verdacht, Argwohn, *m.*; ~ious(ly), verdächtig; argwöhnisch.

sustain, erhalten, aufrechthalten; (*losses*) erleiden.

sustenance, (Lebens)unterhalt, *m.*

swab, *sb.* Schwabber; (*med.*) Abstrich, *m.*; *v.t.* abschwabbern.

swagger, *v.i.* stolzieren, prahlen.

swallow¹, *sb.* Schwalbe, *f.*

swallow², *v.t.* verschlingen, verschlucken.

swamp, *sb.* Sumpf, *m.*; *v.t.* überschwemmen, vollschlagen; ~y, sumpfig.

swan, Schwan, *m.*

swank, *sb.* Großtuerei, *f.*; *v.i.* großtun, prahlen.

sward, Rasen, *m.*

swarm, *sb.* Schwarm, *m.*, Gewimmel, *n.*; *v.i.* wimmeln; (*bees*) schwärmen.

swarthy, schwärzlich, dunkel.

swastika, Hakenkreuz, *n.*

sway, *v.t.* schwenken; lenken; *v.i.* schwanken.

swear, (*oath*) schwören; (*curse*) fluchen.

sweat, *sb.* Schweiß, *m.*; *v.i.* schwitzen; ~er, Sweater, *m.*

sweep, *sb.* Schornsteinfeger; Straßenkehrer; (*reach*) Bereich, *m.*; (*aircraft*) Streife, *f.*; *v.t.* kehren; fegen; (*mines*) räumen, suchen; (*with artillery*) bestreichen; *v.i.* dahinfahren, streifen; ~ing, weitgreifend; ~ing-gear, (*mines*) Such-Räum-gerät, *n.*; ~ings, Kehricht, *m.*; ~stake, Lotterie, *f.*

sweet, *sb.* Bonbon, *m.*; Nachspeise, *f.*; *a.*, ~ly, süß; lieblich; ~bread, Kalbsmilch, *f.*; ~en, süßen, zuckern; ~heart, Liebchen, *n.*; ~meats, Zuckerwerk, *n.*; ~ness, Süßigkeit; Lieblichkeit, *f.*; ~pea, Gartenwicke, *f.*; ~william, Bartnelke, *f.*

swell, *sb.* (*person*) Stutzer, *m.*; (*of sea*) Dünung, *f.*; *a.* elegant; *v.i.* schwellen; zunehmen; *v.t.* aufblasen; ~ing, Geschwulst, *f.*

swelter, vor Hitze ersticken.

swerve, abweichen.

swift, *sb.* Turmschwalbe, *f.*; *a.*, ~ly, schnell, geschwind; ~ness, Schnelligkeit, *f.*

swill, spülen.

swim, schwimmen; ~mer, Schwimmer, *m.*; ~mingly, leicht, nach Wunsch.

swindle, *sb.* Schwindel, *m.*; *v.t.* beschwindeln; ~r, Schwindler, *m.*

swine, Schwein, *n.*

swing, *sb.* Schwung, *m.*; Schaukel,

f.; *in full* ~, in vollem Gange;
v.t. schwingen; *v.i.* schwanken;
baumeln; ~-bridge, Dreh-
brücke, *f.*

swipe, heftig schlagen.

swirl, *sb.* Strudel, *m.*; *v.i.* wirbeln.

switch, *sb.* Gerte, *f.*; (*mech.*)
Schalter, *m.*; (*railway*) Weiche,
f.; *v.t.* umschalten; ~ *on, off*,
an-, ab- drehen, an-, ab-
schalten; ~-back, auf und ab;
~-board, Schaltbrett, *n.*; ~-box,
Schaltkasten, *m.*

swivel, Drehring, *m.*

swoon, *sb.* Ohnmacht, *f.*; *v.i.* in
Ohnmacht fallen.

swoop, *sb.* Stoß; (*aircraft*) Sturz,
m.; *v.i.* herabstoßen.

swop, tauschen.

sword, Schwert, *n.*

sycamore, Sykomore; Platane,
Ahornabart. *f.*

sycophant, Schmeichler, *m.*

syllable, Silbe, *f.*

syllabus, Auszug; Lehrplan;
Prospekt, *m.*

syllogism, (Vernunft)schluß, *m.*

symbol, Symbol, *n.*; ~ic(al),
symbolisch; ~ism, Symbolis-
mus, *m.*; Symbolik, *f.*; ~ize,
symbolisieren; sinnbildlich darstellen.

symmetr|ical(ly), ebenmäßig, sym-
metrisch; ~y, Ebenmaß, *n.*

sympath|etic(ally), mitfühlend;
~ize, Mitleid fühlen für; ~y,
Mitgefühl, Mitleid, *n.*

symphony, Sinfonie, *f.*

symptom, Anzeichen, *n.*; ~atic,
bezeichnend.

synagogue, Synagoge, *f.*

synchronize, *v.t.* synchronisieren;
v.i. gleichzeitig sein, zusammen-
fallen (*with* mit).

syncop|e, Synkope, *f.*; ~ate, syn-
kopieren; ~ation, Synkopie-
rung, *f.*

syndicate, Syndikat, *n.*, Konzern,
m.

synod,   Kirchenversammlung,
Synode, *f.*

synonym, Synonym, *n.*; ~ous,
sinnverwandt.

synopsis, Abriß, *m.*

syntax, Syntax, Satzlehre, *f.*

synthesis, Synthese, *f.*

synthetic, synthetisch, Kunst-.

syphilis, Syphilis, *f.*

syphon = siphon.

syringa, Flieder, *m.*

syringe, *sb.* Spritze, *f.*; *v.t.* einspritzen.

syrup, Sirup, *m.*

system, System, *n.*; ~atic(ally),
systematisch,   planmäßig;
~atize, systematisch ordnen,
in ein System bringen.

T

tab, Schuhriemen, *m.*, Lasche, *f.*
Fähnchen, Anhängeschildchen,
n.

table, *sb.* Tisch, *m.*; Tabelle, *f.*;
v.t. auf den Tisch legen; ~-cloth,
Tischtuch, *n.*; ~-spoon, Eß-
löffel, *m.*; ~ tennis, Tisch-
tennis, *n.*

tablet, (*chocolate, inscription, &c.*)
Tafel, *f.*; (*med.*) Täfelchen, *n.*;
(*soap*) Stück, *n.*

taboo, *sb.* Tabu, *n.*; *a.* verboten.

tabul|ar, tabellarisch; ~ate, in
Tabellen bringen, tabellarisch.

tacit, ~ly, stillschweigend.

taciturn,   schweigsam; ~ity,
Schweigsamkeit, *f.*

tack, *sb.* Stift, *m.*, Zwecke, *f.*;
(*naut., course*) Gang, *m.*; *v.t.*
anheften; *v.i.* (*naut.*) lavieren.

tackle, *sb.* Gerät; (*naut.*) Takel-
werk, *n.*, Talje, *f.*; *v.t.* in
Angriff nehmen, anpacken.

tact, Takt, *m.*, Feingefühl, *n.*;
~ful(ly), taktvoll; ~less(ly),
taktlos.

tactic|s, Kriegskunst, Taktik, *f.*;
~al, taktisch.

tadpole, Kaulquappe, *f.*

taffeta, Taft, *m.*

taffrail, Heckreling, *f.*

tag, Stift; Zettel, *m.*, Anhängsel, *n.*

tail, Schwanz; (*of coat*) Rockschoß, *m.*; (*of coin*) Kehrseite,
f.; *turn* ~, sich davonmachen.

tailor, Schneider, *m.*; ~-made,
Maß-, nach Maß.

taint, *sb.* Flecken, *m.*; Ansteckung,
f.; *v.t.* verderben, anstecken.

take, *v.t.* (an-, ein-, mit-, weg-)
nehmen;   ergreifen; (*illness*)
bekommen; (*require*) erfordern;
(*walk,   &c.*) machen; (*oath*)

leisten; (pleasure in, &c.) finden (an); (likeness) aufnehmen; v.i. wirken, Beifall finden, anschlagen; ~ after, arten nach; ~ care of, in Verwahrung nehmen; ~ cold, sich erkälten; ~ down, niederschreiben; ~ fire, Feuer fangen; ~ in, aufnehmen; betrügen; ~ one's leave, sich empfehlen; ~ off, abnehmen, abziehen; nachäffen; (aircraft) starten; ~-off, sb. Karikatur, f.; (aircraft) Start, Abflug, m.; ~ on, einstellen, aufnehmen; ~ over, übernehmen; ~ part in, teilnehmen an; ~ place, stattfinden; ~ to, sich angewöhnen; sich ergeben; liebgewinnen; ~ up, (hin)aufnehmen.

taking, sb. Nehmen, n.; Einnahme, f.; a. einnehmend; ~s, Einnahme, f.

talc, Talk, m.

tale, Erzählung, f., Märchen, n.; ~bearer, Zuträger, m.

talent, Talent, n., Begabung, f.; ~ed, talentvoll, begabt.

talk, sb. Gespräch, n., Plauderei, f.; Gerücht, n.; v.i. reden, sprechen; ~ative, viel, geschwätzig; ~ie, Sprechfilm, m.

tall, lang, hoch, groß; ~ hat, Zylinderhut, m.

tallow, Talg, m.

tally, passen, stimmen.

talon, Kralle, Klaue, f.

tambourine, Tamburin, n.

tame, a., ~ly, zahm; langweilig, schal; v.t. zähmen, bändigen; ~ness, Zahmheit, f.; ~r, Bändiger, m.

tamper, ~ with, sich einmengen in; fälschen.

tan, sb. Lohe; braune (Haut)farbe, f.; v.t. (leather) gerben; (skin, &c.) bräunen.

tandem, Tandem, n.

tang, (See)tang, m.; Beigeschmack, m.

tangent, Tangente, f.

tangerine, Mandarine, f.

tangible, greifbar.

tangle, Verwicklung, f.; Gewirr, n.; v.t. verwickeln.

tank, Wasserbehälter, m., Zisterne,

f.; (mil.) Tank, Panzerwagen, m.; ~er, (naut.) Tanker, m., Tankschiff, n.

tankard, Krug, m.

tanner, Lohgerber, m.; ~y, Gerberei, f.

tantalize, quälen.

tantamount, gleichbedeutend (to mit).

tap, sb. Klaps, gelinder Schlag; (water, &c.) Hahn, m.; on ~, vom Faß; v.t. (barrel) anzapfen; (tree) anbohren; (telephone, &c.) abfangen, mithören; v.i. klopfen; ~-room, Schenkstube, f.

tape, Zwirnband, n.; Papierstreifen, m.; red ~, Bureaukratismus, m.; ~-recorder, Tonbandgerät, n.; ~-measure, Bandmaß, n.; ~-worm, Bandwurm, m.

taper, Wachsstock, m.; v.i. spitz zulaufen; ~ off, sich verjüngen.

tapestry, Tapisserie, f.

tapioca, Tapioka, f.

tapir, Tapir, m.

tar, sb. Teer, m.; v.t. teeren; ~mac, Steinschotter (m.) mit Teer; (av.) Rollbahn, f.

tardiness, Zögerung, Trägheit, f.; ~ily, ~ly, zögernd, träge; spät.

tare, (bot.) Wicke; (commerc.) Tara, f.

target, Schießscheibe, f.; (in bombing, &c.) Ziel, n.; ~ practice, Scheiben-, Zielschießen, n.

tariff, Tarif, Zoll, m.; Preisliste, f.; ~ protection, Zollschutz, m.

tarnish, v.t. beschmutzen; v.i. den Glanz verlieren.

tarpaulin, Persenning, f., Teertuch, n.

tarry, zögern.

tart, sb. Torte, f.; a. herb, sauer; ~ness, Herbe, Säure, f.

tartar, Weinstein, m.; ~ic, Weinstein-.

task, sb. Aufgabe, f.; Geschäft, n.; take to ~, zur Rede stellen; v.t. in Anspruch nehmen; ~-force, Sondereinheit, f.; ~master, Aufseher, m.

tassel, Troddel, Quaste, f.

taste, sb. Geschmack, m.; v.t. kosten, probieren; v.i. schmecken (of nach); ~ful(ly), tasty, geschmackvoll; ~less(ly), geschmacklos.

tatter, Lumpen, m.; in ~s, zerlumpt.

tattoo, sb. (mil.) Zapfenstreich, m.; Tatauieren, n.; Tatauierung, f.; v.t. tatauieren.

taunt, sb. Hohn, Spott, m.; v.t. verhöhnen.

taut, straff, steif.

tavern, Schenke, f.

tawdry, flitterhaft.

tawny, lohfarbig, gelbbraun.

tax, sb. Steuer, Abgabe, f.; v.t. besteuern; beschuldigen (with mit); ~able, steuerpflichtig; ~ation, Besteuerung, f.; ~collector, Steuereinnehmer, m.; ~payer, Steuerzahler, m.

taxi, sb. Taxi, n., Taxe, f.; v.i. (aircraft) rollen; ~meter, Taxameter, m.

tea, Tee, m.; ~party, Teegesellschaft, f.; ~pot, Teetopf, m.; ~set, Teeservice, n.; ~spoon, Teelöffel, m.; ~urn, Teemaschine, f.

teach, lehren, unterrichten; ~able, gelehrig; ~er, Lehrer(in, f.), m.; ~ing, Lehre, f., Unterricht, m.

teak, Tiekholz, n.

team, Mannschaft, f.; Gespann, n.; ~work, Zusammen -spiel, n., -arbeit, f.

tear¹, Träne, f.

tear², sb. Riß, m.; v.t. (ab-, aus-, zer-)reißen.

tease, plagen, necken; (wool, &c.) krempeln.

teat, Brustwarze, Zitze, f.; rubber ~, Gummilutscher, m.

technical, ~ly, technisch; Fach~ity, technische Eigenart, Eigentümlichkeit, f.; Fachausdruck, m.

techni|que, Technik, f.; ~ology, Technologie, Gewerbekunde, f.

teddy bear, Teddybär, m.

tedi|ous, langweilig, lästig; ~um, Langweiligkeit, f.

teem, wimmeln (with von).

teenager, Teenager, m.

teetotaller, Abstinenzler, m.

telecamera, Fernsehkamera, f.

telegram, Telegramm, n.,

Depesche, f.

telegraph, sb. Telegraph, m.; v.t. telegraphieren; ~ic, telegraphisch; ~ist, Telegraphist, m.; ~pole, Telegraphenstange, f.; ~y, Telegraphie, f.

telephone, sb. Telephon, n., Fernsprecher, m.; v.t. and i. telephonieren; ~booth, -box, Fernsprechzelle, f.; ~exchange, Fernsprechzentrale, f.; ~line, Fernsprechleitung, f.; ~number, Rufnummer, f. ~wire, Telephondraht, m.

telephoto, Fernbild, n.

teleprinter, Fernschreiber, m.

telescop|e, sb. Fernrohr, n.; v.t. and i. (sich) ineinanderschieben; ~ic, teleskopisch.

television, Fernsehen, n., Fernsehrundfunk, m.; ~set, Fernseher, m.

tell, v.t. and i. sagen, erzählen, mitteilen; zählen; erkennen, unterscheiden; Eindruck machen, wirken; befehlen; ~ off, schelten; abkommandieren; ~er, Erzähler; Kassierer; Stimmzähler, m.; ~ing, wirkungsvoll; ~tale, schwatzhaft; verräterisch.

telly, see television.

temerity, (Toll)kühnheit, f.

temper, sb. Gemütsstimmung; schlechte Laune; (steel) Härte, f.; keep one's ~, ruhig bleiben; lose one's ~, ärgerlich werden; v.t. (steel) härten; (fig.) mildern, mäßigen.

temperament, Temperament, n.; ~al, temperamentvoll.

tempera|nce, Mäßigkeit, Enthaltsamkeit, f.; ~te, mäßig; (climate) mild.

temperature, Temperatur, f.

tempest, Sturm, m.; ~uous, stürmisch.

temple, Tempel, m.; (of head) Schläfe, f.

temporal, ~ly, zeitlich; weltlich.

temporar|y, ~ily, vorübergehend, vorläufig.

tempt, versuchen, verleiten; ~ation, Versuchung, f.; ~er, Verführer, Versucher, m.; ~ing, verführerisch.

ten, zehn.

tenable, haltbar.

tenac|ious, zäh, festhaltend; treu; ~ity, Zähigkeit, Festigkeit, f.

tenan|cy, Pacht-, Miet- besitz, m.; ~t, sb. Pächter, Mieter, m.; v.t. bewohnen.

tend, v.t. warten, pflegen, bedienen; v.i. neigen; dienen (to zu); ~ency, Neigung, Tendenz, f.; ~entious, tendenziös; ~er[1], sb. (railway and naut.) Tender, m.; (commerc.) Angebot, n., Offerte, f.; v.t. anbieten.

tender[2], a., ~ly, weich, zart, mürbe; zärtlich; empfindlich; ~ness, Zartheit; Zärtlichkeit, f.

tendon, Sehne, f.

tendril, Ranke, f.

tenement, Mietswohnung, f.

tenet, Grundsatz, m., Lehre, f.

tenfold, zehnfach.

tennis, Tennis(spiel) n.; ~-court, Tennisplatz, m.; ~-racket, Tennisschläger, m.

tenor, Tenor(stimme, f.), m.

tense, sb. Tempus, f., Zeitform, f.; a. gespannt.

tensile, dehnbar; ~ strength, Zugfestigkeit, f.

tension, Spannung, f.

tent, Zelt, n.

tentacle, Fühler, m.

tentative, versuchend, Versuchs-; ~ly, versuchsweise.

tenth, sb. Zehntel, n.; a. zehnte(r, s); ~ly, zehntens.

tenu|ity, Dünne, Zartheit, f.; ~ous, dünn, fein, zart.

tenure, Besitz, m., Innehaben, n.

tepid, lau(warm); ~ity, Lauheit, f.

term, sb. (word) Ausdruck, m.; (period) Periode, Zeit, Frist, f.; (university) Semester, Trimester, n.; (school) Quartal, n.; (law) Sitzungsperiode, f.; v.t. (be-)nennen; ~s, (conditions) Bedingungen, f.pl.; Preis, m.; (relations) Beziehungen, f.pl.

terminal, sb. Endstation, f.; (electr.) Pol, m., Klemme, f.; a. End-.

terminat|e, v.t. beendigen; v.i. enden; ~ion, Ende, n.; Beendigung; (gram.) Endung, f.

terminology, Terminologie, f.

terminus, Endstation, f.

tern, Seeschwalbe, f.

terrace, Terrasse, f.

terra-cotta, Terrakotta, f.

terrain, Terrain, Gelände, n.

terrestrial, irdisch.

terrib|le, ~y, schrecklich, fürchterlich.

terrier, Terrier, m.

terrify, erschrecken.

territor|ial, sb. Landsturmann, m.; a. Landes-; ~ial waters, Hoheitsgewässer, n.pl.; ~y, Gebiet, n.

terror, Schrecken, Terror, m.; ~ize, terrorisieren.

terse, ~ly, kurz und bündig, knapp; ~ness, Bündigkeit, f.

test, sb. Probe, f., Test, m.; v.t. prüfen, untersuchen, testen; ~-case, Präzedenzfall, m.; ~-tube, Reagenzglas, n.

testa|ment, Testament, n.; letzter Wille, m.; ~tor, Erblasser, m.; ~trix, Erblasserin, f.

testicle, Hode, f.

testify, bezeugen.

testimon|ial, Empfehlungsschreiben, Zeugnis; Ehrengeschenk, n.; ~y, Zeugnis, n.; Beweis, m.

test|y, ~ily, reizbar.

tetanus, Starrkrampf, m.

tether, sb. Leine, f.; v.t. anbinden.

text, Text, m.; ~ual, wörtlich; Text-.

textile, gewebt; ~s, Webstoffe, m.pl.

texture, Gewebe, n.; (fig.) Bau, m.

than, als.

thank, danken; ~ful(ly), dankbar; ~less, undankbar; ~s, Dank, m.; ~sgiving, Danksagung, f.

that, pron. jene(r, s); (relative pron.) der, die, das; welche(r, s); conj. daß, damit, weil.

thatch, sb. Dachstroh, n.; v.t. mit Stroh decken.

thaw, v.i. tauen; sb. Tauwetter, n.

the, der, die, das, (pl.) die; ~more, ~ better, je mehr, desto besser.

theatr|e, Theater, n.; ~ical, theatralisch.

thee, dir, dich.

theft, Diebstahl, m.

their, ihr(e); ~s, der (die, das)

ihrige, (pl.) die ihrigen.

them, sie, ihnen; **~selves**, sie (ihnen) selbst; (refl.) sich.

theme, Thema, n., Gegenstand, m.

then, dann, damals; denn, daher, also; now and ~, dann und wann.

thence, von da, von dort; daher.

theolog|ian, Theolog(e), m.; **~ical**, theologisch; **~y**, Theologie, f.

theorem, Lehrsatz, m.

theor|etical(ly), theoretisch; **~ist**, Theoretiker, m.; **~y**, Theorie, Lehre, f.

therapy, Therapie, f., Heilverfahren, n.

there, da, dort, dahin; ~ is, are, es gibt; down ~, dort unten; over ~, da drüben; ~ and back, hin und zurück; **~about(s)**, ungefähr; dort herum; **~after**, danach; **~by**, damit, dadurch; **~fore**, daher, also; **~of**, davon; **~upon**, darauf.

thermal, Wärme-, Thermal-.

thermometer, Thermometer, n.

thermos flask, Thermosflasche, f.

thermostat, Thermostat, m.

these, diese.

thesis, These; Dissertation, f.

they, sie; (impersonal) man.

thick, **~ly**, dick, dicht; (voice) undeutlich; **~en**, v.t. verdicken; v.i. dick (dicht) werden; sich verstärken; **~et**, Dickicht, n.; **~headed**, dumm; **~ness**, Dicke, Dichtheit, f.; **~set**, (person) gedrungen, untersetzt.

thie|f, Dieb, m.; **~ve**, stehlen; **~vish**, diebisch.

thigh, Schenkel, m.

thimble, Fingerhut, m.

thin, **~ly**, dünn, mager; schwach, spärlich; v.t. verdünnen; lichten; **~ness**, Dünne, Magerkeit; Spärlichkeit, f.

thine, dein(er, e, es), der, die, das, deinige.

thing, Ding, n., Sache, f.; Geschöpf, Wesen, n.; **~s**, Kleider, n.pl., Sachen, f.pl.

think, denken, meinen, glauben, halten (für); **~er**, Denker, m.; **~ing**, Denken, n., Ansicht, f.

third, sb. Drittel, n.; a. dritte; **~ly**, drittens.

thirst, sb. Durst, m.; v.i. dursten;

~iness, Durstigkeit, f.; **~y**, **~ily**, durstig.

thirteen, dreizehn; **~th**, dreizehnte.

thirt|y, dreißig; **~ieth**, dreißigste.

this, dies(er, e, es).

thistle, Distel, f.

thither, dorthin, dahin.

thong, Riemen, m.

thorn, Dorn, Stachel, m.; **~y**, dornig, stachelig.

thorough, gründlich, gänzlich; **~bred**, sb. Vollblut, n.; a. Vollblut-, reinrassig; **~fare**, Durchgang, m., Hauptstraße, f.; **~ly**, durchaus, gründlich; **~ness**, Gründlichkeit, f.

those, jene, diejenigen.

thou, du.

though, obgleich, obschon, wenn auch; doch, dennoch; as ~, als ob.

thought, Gedanke, m., Meinung, Absicht, f.; **~ful(ly)**, gedankenvoll; rücksichtsvoll; **~less(ly)**, gedankenlos; leichtfertig.

thousand, sb. Tausend, n.; a. tausend; **~th**, tausendste.

thrash, dreschen; (flog) prügeln; **~ing**, Dreschen, n.; Tracht (f.) Prügel; **~ing-floor**, Dreschtenne, f.

thread, sb. Faden, Zwirn, m.; (of a screw) Gewinde, n.; v.t. einfädeln; **~bare**, fadenscheinig.

threat, Drohung; Gefahr, f.; **~en**, drohen.

three, drei; **~fold**, dreifach.

thresh: see thrash.

threshold, Schwelle, f.

thrice, dreimal.

thrift, Sparsamkeit, f.; **~y**, sparsam, haushälterisch.

thrill, sb. Schauer, m., Sensation, f.; v.t. durchdringen, durchschauern; v.i. schauern; **~er**, Schauer-, Sensations-film, -roman (m.), -drama (n.); **~ing**, spannend, sensationell.

thriv|e, gedeihen; **~ing**, gedeihend, blühend.

throat, Kehle, f., Schlund, m.

throb, pochen, klopfen.

throne, Thron, m.

throng, sb. Gedränge, n.; v.i. (sich) drängen.

throstle, Drossel, *f.*

throttle, *sb. (motor)* Drosselklappe, *f.; open the* ~, Gas geben; *v.t.* erdrosseln.

through, durch; ~-carriage, durchgehender Wagen; ~out, *(prep.)* durch; *(adv.)* durch und durch, durchaus.

throw, *sb.* Wurf, *m.; v.t.* werfen; ~ out, auswerfen; verwerfen; ~ over, up, *(fig.)* aufgeben.

thrush, Drossel, *f.; (med.)* Mundschwamm, *m.*

thrust, *sb.* Stoß, Stich, Schub, *m.; v.t.* stoßen, schieben, pressen.

thud, Dröhnen, *n.;* dumpfer Schlag, *m.*

thumb, *sb.* Daumen, *m.;* ~-print, Daumenabdruck, *m.*

thump, *sb.* Schlag, *m.; v.t.* schlagen.

thunder, *sb.* Donner, *m.; v.i.* donnern; ~bolt, Donnerkeil, *m.;* ~storm, Gewitter, *n.; m.;* ~struck, wie vom Donner gerührt.

Thursday, Donnerstag, *m.*

thus, (al)so.

thwart, vereiteln, hindern.

thy, dein(e); ~self, du (dir, dich) selbst.

thyme, Thymian, *m.*

tiara, Tiara, *f.*

tibia, Schienbein, *n.*

tick, *sb. (sound)* Ticken, *n.; (for beds)* Überzug, Drell. *m.; v.i.* ticken; ~ over, *(motor)* leer laufen.

ticket, Zettel, *m.,* Billett, *n.,* Fahrkarte, *f.,* Fahrschein, *m.* Eintrittskarte, *f.;* ~collector, Bahnsteigschaffner, *m.;* ~office, Fahrkartenschalter, *m.*

tickl|e, kitzeln; ~ish, kitzlig.

tid|e, *sb.* Ebbe und Flut, *f.,* Gezeiten, *f.pl.;* ~al, Flut-.

tid|y, *a.* ~ily, ordentlich, nett; *v.t.* ordentlich machen; ~iness, Ordnung, Nettigkeit, *f.*

tie, *sb.* Band, *n.,* Schnur, *f.;* Halsbinde, *f.,* Schlips, *m.;* (Stimmen)gleichheit, *f.;* unentschiedenes Spiel, *n.; v.t.* binden, knüpfen; *v.i.* gleich sein, unentschieden bleiben.

tier, Reihe, *f.; (theatre)* Rang, *m.*

tiff, Zank, *m.,* Schmollen, *n.*

tig|er, Tiger, *m.;* ~ress, Tigerin, *f.*

tight, ~ly, fest, dicht; straff; knapp; betrunken; ~en, festziehen, enger machen; ~ness, Festigkeit, Spannung; Knappheit, *f.;* ~rope, Drahtseil, *n.;* ~s, Trikothosen, Strumpfhosen, *f.pl.*

tile, Ziegel, *m.,* Kachel, Fliese, *f.*

till[1], *prep.* and *conj.* bis.

till[2], *sb.* (Laden)kasse, *f.*

till[3], *v.t.* bebauen, ackern; ~er[1], Ackersmann, *m.*

tiller[2], Ruderpinne, *f.*

tilt, *v.t.* kippen, neigen, stürzen; *v.i.* umkippen, sich neigen; turnieren; ~ at, stoßen (nach).

timber, Bauholz, *n.*

time, *sb.* Zeit, *f.;* Zeitmaß, *n.,* Takt, *m.;* Mal, *n.,* Zeitpunkt, *m.; at a* ~, zugleich; *at* ~s, zuweilen; *in* ~, mit der Zeit; pünktlich; *in no* ~, im Nu; *what* ~? *v.t.* wieviel Uhr ist es?; *v.t.* abmessen; zur richtigen Zeit tun; ~ bomb, Zeitbombe, *f.;* ~fuse, Zeitzünder, *m.;* ~keeper, Uhr, *f.;* *(sport)* Zeitnehmer, *m.;* ~limit, Zeitgrenze, Frist, *f.;* ~ly, rechtzeitig; ~signal, Zeitzeichen, *n.;* ~table, Fahrplan, Stundenplan, *m.*

timid, ~ly, furchtsam, schüchtern; ~ity, Furchtsamkeit, *f.*

tin, *sb.* Zinn; Weißblech, *n.,* Blechbüchse, *f.; v.t.* verzinnen; einmachen; ~foil, Stanniol, *n.;* ~ned, verzinnt; Büchsen-; ~opener, Büchsenöffner, *m.;* ~plate, Weißblech, *n.*

tincture, *sb. (med.)* Tinktur, Farbe, *f.; (fig.)* Anstrich, *m.; v.t.* färben.

tinder, Zunder, *m.*

tinge, *sb.* Färbung, *f.; (fig.)* Spur, *f.; v.t.* färben.

tingle, prickeln.

tinker, *sb.* Kessel-, Pfannen-flicker, *m.; v.t.* flicken; pfuschen.

tinkle, klingeln.

tint, *sb.* Schattierung, Farbe, *f.; v.t.* färben; schattieren.

tiny, winzig.

tip, *sb.* Spitze, *f.; (of cigarette)* Mundstück, *n.; (gift)* Trinkgeld, *n.*; (*hint*) Tip, *m.*; *v.t.* mit einer Spitze versehen; beschlagen; (*upset*) (um)kippen; (*give*) ein Trinkgeld geben; ~-up seat, Klappsitz, *m.*

tipple, zechen.

tipsy, berauscht, benebelt.

tiptoe, Zehenspitze, *f.*

tip-top, ausgezeichnet, sehr fein.

tire¹, *sb.* Reifen, *m.*

tire², *v.t.* ermüden; *v.i.* müde werden; ~d, müde, erschöpft; ~dness, Müdigkeit, *f.*; ~some, langweilig.

tissue, Gewebe, *n.*; ~-paper, Seidenpapier, *n.*

tit, (*bird*) Meise, *f.*; ~ for tat, wie du mir, so ich dir; ~bit, Leckerbissen, *m.*

tithe, Zehnte, *f.*

titivate, putzen.

title, *sb.* Titel, *m.*; *v.t.* benennen; ~-deed, Eigentumsurkunde, *f.*; ~-page, Titelblatt, *n.*

titmouse, Meise, *f.*

titter, *sb.* Kichern, *n.*; *v.i.* kichern.

tittle-tattle, Geschwätz, *n.*

titular, Titular-.

to, *prep.* nach, an, zu, gegen, vor; (*before infinitive*) zu; ~ and fro, hin und her; *five minutes* ~ *six*, fünf Minuten vor sechs; *two* ~ *one*, zwei gegen eins.

toad, Kröte, *f.*; ~y, *sb.* Schmeichler, Speichellecker, Schmarotzer, *m.*; *v.t.* schmeicheln, schmarotzen.

toast, *sb.* geröstetes Brot, *n.*; Trinkspruch, Toast, *m.*; *v.t.* rösten; (*drink to*) trinken auf; ~ing-fork, Röstgabel, *f.*

tobacco, Tabak, *m.*; ~nist, Tabakhändler, *m.*

toboggan, *sb.* Rodelschlitten, *m.*; *v.i.* rodeln.

tocsin, Sturmglocke, *f.*

to-day, heute.

toddle, watscheln; sich trollen.

toe, Zehe, *f.*

toffee, Zuckerwerk, *n.*, Karamelle, *f.*

together, zusammen.

toil, *sb.* schwere Arbeit, *f.*; *v.i.* sich placken, schwer arbeiten; ~s, Fallstricke, *m.pl.*

toilet, Toilette, *f.*; ~-paper,

Toilettenpapier, *n.*; ~-set, Toilettengarnitur, *f.*

token, Zeichen; Andenken, *n.*

toler|able, leidlich, erträglich; ~ate, dulden; ~ation, Duldung, *f.*

toll, *sb.* (*tax*) Zoll, *m.*; (*of bell*) Läuten, Geläute, *n.*; *v.t.* läuten.

tomato, Tomate, *f.*

tomb, Grab, *n.*

tomboy, Range, *f.*

tom-cat, Kater, *m.*

tome, Band, *m.*

tomfoolery, Narretei, *f.*, Unsinn, *m.*

tommy, (*soldier*) Tommy, *m.*; ~-gun, Maschinenpistole, *f.*

to-morrow, morgen.

ton, Tonne, *f.*; ~nage, Tonnengehalt, *m.*

tone, *sb.* Ton, Klang, *m.*; *v.t.* abtönen; *v.i.* harmonieren.

tongs, Zange, *f.*

tongue, Zunge; Sprache, *f.*; (*of bell*) Klöppel, *m.*

tonic, Stärkungsmittel, *n.*

to-night, heute abend, heute nacht.

tonsil, Mandel, *f.*

tonsure, Tonsur, *f.*

too, auch, ebenfalls; zu.

tool, Werkzeug, Gerät, *n.*

toot, tuten.

tooth, Zahn, *m.*; ~ache, Zahnweh. *n.*; ~-brush, Zahnbürste, *f.*; ~-paste, Zahnpasta, *f.*; ~-pick, Zahnstocher, *m.*; ~-powder, Zahnpulver, *n.*

top, (*mountain*) Gipfel, (*tree*) Wipfel, *m.*, Spitze, *f.*, Oberteil, *m.*, Oberste, *n.*; (*of head*) Scheitel, *m.*; (*toy*) Kreisel, *m.*; (*of mast*) Topp, *m.*, Mars, *m.* or *f.*; *v.t.* übertreffen; ~-boots, Stulpstiefel, *m.pl.*; ~-coat, Überzieher, *m.*; ~-hat, Zylinderhut, *m.*; ~-heavy, oberlastig, kopflastig; ~most, oberst, höchst.

topaz, Topas, *m.*

toper, Säufer, *m.*

topic, Gegenstand, *m.*, Thema, *n.*; ~al, aktuell; örtlich.

topography, Ortsbeschreibung, Topographie, *f.*

topple, umkippen, hinstürzen.

topsy-turvy, kopfüber.

torch, Fackel, *f.*; Taschenlampe, *f.*

torment, *sb.* Qual, *f.*; *v.t.* quälen, peinigen.

tornado, Wirbelsturm, *m.*

torpedo, *sb.* Torpedo, *m.*; *v.t.* torpedieren; ~boat, Torpedoboot, *n.*; ~tube, Torpedorohr, *n.*

torpor, Erstarrung, *f.*

torrent, Gießbach; Strom, *m.*; ~ial, strömend, reißend.

tortoise, Schildkröte, *f.*

tortuous, gewunden.

torture, *sb.* Folter, Marter, *f.*; *v.t.* foltern; ~r, Folterer, *m.*

Tory, Tory, *m.*

toss, *sb.* Wurf, *m.*; *v.t.* (auf)werfen.

total, *sb.* (Gesamt)summe, *f.*; *a.* ganz; total; *v.t.* sich belaufen auf; ~izator, Totalisator, *m.*; ~ly, gänzlich.

totter, wanken, wackeln.

touch, *sb.* Berührung, *f.*; (*sense*) Gefühl, *n.*; (*trace*) Anstrich, leichter Anfall, *m.* Spur, *f.*; (*mus.*) Anschlag, *m.*; *v.t.* berühren; (*concern*) betreffen; *v.i.* sich berühren; ~ down, (*aircraft*) landen; ~-and-go, gewagt; ~ing, rührend; ~stone, Prüfstein, *m.*; ~y, empfindlich.

tough, zäh(e); ~en, zäh(e) machen.

tour, *sb.* (Rund)reise, *f.*, Ausflug, *m.*; *v.t.* bereisen; *v.i.* reisen; ~ist, Tourist, *m.*; ~ist agency, Reisebüro, *n.*

tournament, Turnier, *n.*

tout, *sb.* Anreißer, *m.*; *v.i.* Kunden locken.

tow, Werg; Schlepptau, *n.*; *v.t.* schleppen, bugsieren.

towards, gegen, bis an, auf . . . zu.

towel, Handtuch, *n.*

tower, *sb.* Turm, *m.*; *v.i.* hoch ragen.

town, Stadt, *f.*; ~-clerk, Stadtsyndikus, *m.*; ~-council(lor), Stadtrat, *m.*; ~ hall, Rathaus, *n.*; ~planning, Stadtplanung, *f.*; ~sman, Bürger, *m.*

toy, *sb.* Spielzeug, *n.*; *v.i.* tändeln.

trac|e, *sb.* Spur, *f.*; (*harness*) Zugriemen, Strang, *m*; *v.t.* nachspüren; ausfinden, entdecken; (*draw*) entwerfen, durchpausen; ~er, (*mil.*) Leuchtspur(munition), *f.*; ~ing, Durchpausen, *n.*,

Aufriß, *m.*

track, *sb.* Spur(weite), *f.*; Geleise, *n.*; Pfad, *m.*, Bahn, *f.*; *v.t. der* Spur folgen, verfolgen; ~less, unbetreten; ~suit, Trainingsanzug, *m.*

tract, Strecke, Gegend, *f.*; (*printed*) Traktat, *m.*; ~able, folgsam; ~ion, Ziehen, *n.*, Zugkraft, *f.*; ~or, Traktor, Maschinenpflug, *m.*, Zugmaschine, *f.*

trade, *sb.* Handel, *m.* Gewerbe, Fach, *n.*; *v.i.* handeln, Handel treiben; ~ on, ausbeuten; ~mark, Schutzmarke, *f.*; ~r, Kaufmann, *m.*; ~speople, Handelsleute, *pl.*; ~union, Gewerkschaft, *f.*; ~unionism, Gewerkschaftswesen, *n.*; ~unionist, Gewerkschaftler, *m.*; ~wind, Passatwind, *m.*

tradition, Überlieferung, Tradition, *f.*; ~al(ly), überliefert, traditionell.

traffic, *sb.* Verkehr, Betrieb, *m.*; *v.i.* handeln; ~ light, Verkehrsampel, *f.*; ~ sign, Verkehrszeichen, *n.*

trag|edy, Tragödie, *f.*, Trauerspiel, *n.*; ~ic(ally) tragisch.

trail, *sb.* Spur, *f.*; Schweif, *m.*; (*aircraft*) Kondensfahne, *f.*; *v.t.* schleppen; *v.i.* sich (langsam) hinziehen; ~er, Anhängerwagen, Wohnwagen, *m.*; (*of programme*) Vorschau, *f.*; ~ing edge, Hinterkante, *f.*

train, *sb.* (*railway*) Zug, *m.*; (*dress*) Schleppe, *f.*; (*retinue*) Gefolge, *n.*; (*powder*) Zündschnur, *f.*; *v.t.* lehren, trainieren; (*trees, guns*) richten; *v.i.* trainieren; ~er, Trainer, *m.*; ~ing, Ausbildung, *f.*; (*sport*) Training, *n.*; ~ing college, Seminar, *n.*; ~ing-ship, Schulschiff, *n.*

trait, Zug, *m.*

traitor, Verräter, *m.*

trajectory, Geschoß-, Flug-bahn, *f.*

tram, Straßenbahn, *f.*

trammel, hemmen, verhindern; ~s, (*fig.*)Bande, *n.pl.*, Zwang, *m.*

tramp, *sb.* schwerer Schritt, Tritt; Landstreicher, *m.*; (*naut.*) Frachtschiff, *n.*; *v.i.* trampeln, treten; ~le, (zer)trampeln.

trance, Trance, Bewußtlosigkeit, *f.*

tranquil, ~ly, gelassen, ruhig; ~lity, Ruhe, *f.*; ~lize, beruhigen; ~lizer, Beruhigungsmittel, *n.*

transact, unterhandeln; verrichten; ~ion, Unterhandlung, *f.*, Geschäft, *n.*; Verrichtung, *f.*

transatlantic, transatlantisch.

transcend, übersteigen; ~ental, transzendental, außerordentlich.

transcri|be, abschreiben; (*mus.*) transkribieren; ~ption, Abschrift; Transkription, *f.*

transept, Querschiff, *n.*

transfer, *sb.* Übertragung; Versetzung, *f.*; Umdruck, *m.*; Abziehbild, *n.*; *v.t.* versetzen, verlegen; ~able, übertragbar.

transfix, durchstechen.

transform, verwandeln, umgestalten; ~ation, Verwandlung, *f.*; ~er, Umformer, *m.*

transfus|e, (*blood*) übertragen; ~ion, (Blut)übertragung, Transfusion, *f.*

transgress, übertreten, verletzen; ~ion, Übertretung, Verletzung, *f.*; ~or, Übertreter, *m.*

transient, vorübergehend, vergänglich.

transistor, Transistor, *m.*

transit, Durchgang, Transit, *m.*; ~ion, Übergang, *m.*; ~ional, Übergangs-.

transitive, transitiv.

transitor|iness, Vergänglichkeit, *f.*; ~y, vergänglich.

translat|e, übersetzen; versetzen; ~ion, Übersetzung; Versetzung, *f.*; ~or, Übersetzer, *m.*

transmission, Übersendung; (*radio*) Sendung; (*mach.*) Transmission; (*physiol.*) Fortpflanzung, *f.*

transmit, übersenden, übertragen; (*radio*) senden, absetzen; ~ter, Übermittler; Sender, *m.*; ~ting station, Sendestelle, *f.*

transparen|cy, Durchsichtigkeit, *f.*; ~t, durchsichtig.

transpire, bekannt werden, durchsickern.

transplant, verpflanzen.

transport, *sb.* Transport, *m.*, Ver-

sendung, Spedition, *f.*; (*joy*) Entzückung, *f.*, (*rage*) Anfall, *m.*; Transporter, *m.*; Transportschiff, *n.*; *v.t.* befördern, transportieren; deportieren; entzücken; ~ation, Deportation, *f.*

transpos|e, umstellen; ~ition, Umstellung, *f.*

transverse, quer, schräg.

trap, *sb.* Falle, *f.*; leichter Wagen, *m.*; *v.t.* fangen, ertappen; ~-door, Falltür, *f.*; ~per, Trapper, *m.*

trash, Abfall, Schund, *m.*; ~y, wertlos, kitschig.

travel, *sb.* Reise, *f.*; *v.i.* reisen; ~ler, Reisende(r); ~ling, *a.* Reise-; (*crane*, &c.) Lauf-.

traverse, durchkreuzen, durchwandern.

travesty, Travestie, *f.*

trawl, mit Schleppnetz fischen; ~er, Trawler, Fischdampfer, *m.*

tray, Servierbrett, Tablett, *n.*

treacher|ous, verräterisch, treulos; ~y, Verrat, *m.*

treacle, Sirup, *m.*

tread, *sb.* Tritt, *m.*; (*of tire*) Lauffläche, *f.*; *v.t.* betreten; *v.i.* treten; ~le, Tretbrett, *n.*; ~mill, Tretmühle, *f.*

treason, Verrat, *m.*; ~able, verräterisch.

treasur|e, *sb.* Schatz, *m.*; *v.t.* schätzen; ~er, Schatzmeister, *m.*; ~y, Finanzministerium, *n.*

treat, *sb.* Vergnügen, *n.*, Schmaus, *m.*; *v.t.* behandeln; bewirten, freihalten; *v.i.* unterhandeln (mit); ~ise, Abhandlung, *f.*; ~ment, Behandlung, *f.*; ~y, Vertrag, *m.*

treble, *sb.* Sopran, *m.*; *a.* dreifach; *v.t.* verdreifachen.

tree, Baum, *m.*

trefoil, Klee, *m.*

trek, *sb.* Wanderung, *f.*; *v.i.* (aus)wandern.

trellis, Gitter, Spalier, *n.*

tremble, zittern.

tremendous, fürchterlich; ungeheuer groß.

trem|or, Beben, Zittern, *n.*; ~ulous, zitternd.

trench, *sb.* (Schützen)graben, *m.*;

v.i. Gräben ziehen; *v.t.* (*agric.*) rigolen; ~ant, schneidend.

trend, *sb.* Richtung, Neigung, *f.*; *v.i.* sich neigen.

trespass, *sb.* Übertretung, *f.*; unbefugtes Betreten; *v.i.* sich vergehen; (Land) unbefugt betreten; ~er, unbefugter Eindringling, Rechtsverletzer, *m.*

trestle, Gestell, *n.*

trial, Versuch, *m.*, Probe, Prüfung, *f.*; (*law*) Verfahren, Verhör, *n.*

triang|le, Dreieck, *n.*; ~ular, dreieckig.

trib|e, Stamm, *m.*; ~al, Stammes-.

tribulation, Trübsal, *f.*, Leiden, *n.*

tribunal, Tribunal, *n.*, Gerichtshof, *m.*

tribune, Tribüne, *f.*

tribut|ary, Nebenfluß, *m.*; *a.* tributpflichtig; ~e, Tribut, *m.*; (*fig.*) Achtung(sbezeigung), *f.*

trick, *sb.* Kunststück, *n.*, Trick, *m.*; Hinterlist, *f.*; (*cards*) Stich, *m.*; *v.t.* betrügen, anführen; ~ery Betrügerei, *f.*; ~y, verschmitzt; heikel(ig).

trickle, tröpfeln.

tricolour, Trikolore, *f.*

tricycle, Dreirad, *n.*

trident, Dreizack, *m.*

triennial, dreijährlich.

trifl|e, *sb.* Kleinigkeit, *f.*; (*cookery*) Auflauf, *m.*; *v.i.* tändeln; ~ing, geringfügig.

trigger, Drücker, Abzug, *m.*

trigonometry, Trigonometrie, *f.*

trill, *sb.* Triller, *m.*; *v.t.* and *i.* trillern.

trim, ~ly, niedlich, in Ordnung; *v.t.* einrichten, putzen, stutzen; (*naut.*) trimmen; ~ming, Besatz, *m.*, Verzierung, *f.*

Trinity, Dreieinigkeit, *f.*

trinket, Geschmeide, *n.*, Schmucksache, *f.* (von geringem Wert), Tand, *m.*

trip, *sb.* Ausflug, *m.*, Seereise, *f.*; Fehltritt, *m.*; *v.t.* ein Bein stellen; straucheln machen; *v.i.* trippeln; straucheln; (*fig.*) einen Fehltritt begehen; ~per, Ausflügler, *m.*

tripe, Kaldaunen, *f.*

triple, dreifach; ~t, (*child*) Drilling, *m.*

tripod, Dreifuß, *m.*

trite, abgedroschen, platt.

triumph, *sb.* Triumph, Sieg, *m.*; *v.i.* siegen; ~al, Sieges-; ~ant, siegreich.

trivial, geringfügig, unbedeutend; ~ity Unbedeutendheit, Trivialität, *f.*

troll(e)y, Förderkarren; Teewagen, *m.*

trombone, Posaune, *f.*

troop, *sb.* Schar, *f.*, Trupp, *m.*; *v.i.* sich scharen; ~er, Reiter, Kavalerist, *m.*; ~s, Truppen, *f.pl.*

trophy, Siegeszeichen, *n.*, Trophäe, *f.*

tropic, Wendekreis, *m.*; ~al, tropisch; ~s, Tropen, *f.pl.*

trot, *sb.* Trab, *f.*; *v.i.* traben.

trouble, *sb.* Sorge, *f.*, Kummer, *m.*, Mühe, *f.*; *v.t.* betrüben, beunruhigen; stören; *v.i.* sich kümmern, sich bemühen; ~some, lästig, beschwerlich.

trough, Trog, *m.*, Mulde, *f.*

trounce, durchprügeln.

troupe, Truppe, *f.*

trousers, Hosen, *f.pl.*

trout, Forelle, *f.*

trowel, Kelle, *f.*

troy weight, Troygewicht, *n.*

truant, Schulschwänzer, *m.*

truce, Waffenstillstand, *m.*

truck, Handkarren; Güterwagen, Waggon, *m.*; Lore, *f.*

truculent, roh, wild.

trudge, sich fortschleppen.

tru|e, wahr; echt; treu; genau; ~ism, Gemeinplatz, *m.*; ~ly, wahrhaftig; aufrichtig; *yours* ~ly, Ihr ergebener.

trump, *sb.* (*cards*) Trumpf, *m.*; *v.t.* übertrumpfen; ~ up, erdichten.

trumpet, Trompete, *f.*; ~er, Trompeter, *m.*

truncate, verstümmeln; abkürzen.

truncheon, Knüttel, *m.*

trundle, rollen.

trunk, (*tree*) Stamm, *m.*; (*elephant*) Rüssel; (*body*) Rumpf; (*box*) Koffer, *m.*; ~call, Fernanruf, *m.*; ~ exchange, Fernamt, *n.*; ~line, (*railway*) Hauptlinie; (*telephone*) Fernleitung, *f.*; ~road, Haupt(land)straße, *f.*

trunnion, Zapfen, *m.*

truss, *sb.* (*of hay*) Bündel; (*for rupture*) Bruchband, *n.*; *v.t.* aufbinden.

trust, *sb.* Vertrauen, *n.*; Trust, *m.*, Kartell, *n.*; Obhut, *f.*; *v.t.* (ver)trauen, sich verlassen (auf); Glauben schenken; *v.i.* hoffen; ~ee, Kurator, Verwalter, Fiduziar, *m.*; ~ee securities, mündelsichere Werte, *m.pl.*; ~ful, vertrauensvoll; ~worthy, vertrauenswürdig; ~y, getreu, zuverlässig.

truth, Wahrheit, *f.*; ~ful(ly), wahrhaft.

try, *sb.* Versuch, *m.*; *v.t.* versuchen; probieren, prüfen; (*law*) verhören; ~ing, peinlich, schwierig.

tub, Faß, *n.*, Kübel, *m.*

tub|e, Rohr, *n.*, Röhre, *f.*; Luftschlauch, *m.*; Untergrundbahn, *f.*; ~ular, röhrenförmig.

tuber, Knolle, *f.*; ~culosis, Tuberkulose, *f.*; ~culous, tuberkulös.

tuck, *sb.* Falte, *f.*; Leckereien, *f.pl.*; *v.t.* einschlagen, einwickeln.

Tuesday, Dienstag, *m.*

tuft, Büschel, *m.* or *n.*

tug, *sb.* Schlepper, *m.*; *v.t.* and *i.* ziehen, schleppen.

tuition, Unterricht, *m.*

tulip, Tulpe, *f.*

tumble, *sb.* Sturz, Fall, *m.*; *v.i.* stürzen, fallen; ~down, baufällig; ~r, Trinkglas, *n.*; (*mech.*) Zuhaltung, *f.*

tumour, Geschwulst, *f.*

tumult, Tumult, Aufruhr, Lärm, *m.*; ~uous(ly), lärmend, aufrührerisch.

tun, Faß, *n.*

tune, *sb.* Melodie, Weise; Tonhöhe, *f.*; *sing in, out of,* ~, richtig, falsch, singen; *out of* ~, (*piano*) verstimmt; *v.t.* stimmen; ~ *in,* (*radio*) einstellen, abstimmen; ~ful(ly), melodisch; tuning-fork, Stimmgabel, *f.*

tunic, Tunika, *f.*; (*mil.*) Soldatenrock, *m.*

tunnel, *sb.* Tunnel, *m.*, Unterführung, *f.*; *v.t.* einen Tunnel (durch)stechen.

tunny, Thunfisch, *m.*

turban, Turban, *m.*

turbid, trübe.

turbine, Turbine, *f.*

turbot, Steinbutt, *m.*

turbulen|ce, Aufruhr, *m.*, Verwirrung, *f.*; ~t(ly), stürmisch, aufrührerisch.

tureen, Terrine, *f.*

turf, *sb.* Torf; Rasen, *m.*; *v.t.* mit Rasen bedecken.

turgid, geschwollen; (*fig.*) schwülstig.

Turk, Türke, *m.*, Türkin, *f.*; ~ish, türkisch; ~ish bath, Schwitzbad, *n.*

turkey, Truthahn, *m.*, Truthenne, *f.*

turmoil, Aufruhr, *m.*

turn, *sb.* Wendung, Drehung, Kurve, *f.*; Wendepunkt, Wechsel, *m.*; Reihe, *f.*; Dienst, *m.*; *by* ~s, abwechselnd; *it is my* ~, die Reihe ist an mir; *done to a* ~, gerade recht gebraten (gekocht); *v.t.* drehen, wenden, lenken; umändern; drechseln; *v.i.* sich wenden, sich drehen; (*weather, &c.*) umschlagen; biegen, eine Kurve machen; ~ *back,* zurückkehren; ~ *down,* abschlagen; ~ *in,* einkehren; zu Bett gehen; ~ *off,* absperren; ~ *on,* andrehen; ~ *out* (*person*) hinaustreiben; ausfallen, sich erweisen; ~ *over,* übertragen, anweisen; durchblättern; ~ *to,* sich wenden an; ~ *up,* um-, aufschlagen; zum Vorschein kommen; ~coat, Überläufer, *m.*; ~ing, Wendung; Querstraße, *f.*; *take the second* ~ *ing on the right,* biegen Sie in die zweite Querstraße rechts ein; ~ing-lathe, Drehbank, *f.*; ~ing-point, Wendepunkt, *m.*; ~out, Ausstaffierung, *f.*; Putz, *m.*; Versammlung, *f.*; ~over, Umsatz, *m.*; ~stile, Drehkreuz, *n.*; ~table, Drehscheibe, *f.*

turnip, (weiße) Rübe, *f.*

turpentine, Terpentin, *m.* or *n.*

turquoise, Türkis, *m.*

turret, Türmchen, *n.*; (*nav.* and *mil.*) (Geschütz)turm, *m.*

turtle, (See)schildkröte, *f.*; ~dove, Turteltaube, *f.*

tusk, Fang-, Stoß- zahn, *m.*

tussle, Streit, *m.*; Rauferei, *f.*

tut, pfui!, st!

tutelage, Vormundschaft, *f.*

tutor, (Privat)lehrer, *m.*

twaddle, Quatsch, *m.*

twang, scharfer Klang, *m.*; Näseln, *n.*

tweak, kneifen.

tweezers, Haar-, Feder- zange, *f.*, Pinzette, *f.*

twelfth, zwölfte; ~ly, zwölftens; ~-night, Dreikönigsabend, *m.*

twelve, zwölf.

twent|y, zwanzig; ~ieth, zwanzigste.

twice, zweimal.

twig, Zweig, *m.*

twilight, Zwielicht, *n.*, Dämmerung, *f.*

twill, *sb.* Köper, *m.*; *v.t.* köpern.

twin, Zwilling, *m.*; *a.* Zwillings-, Doppel-.

twine, Zwirn, *m.*, Schnur, *f.*; *v.t.* drehen; *v.i.* sich verschlingen.

twinge, Stich, *m.*; *v.t.* zwicken.

twinkle, funkeln.

twirl, *sb.* Wirbeln, *n.*, Umdrehung, *f.*; Schnörkel, *m.*; *v.t.* wirbeln.

twist, *sb.* Drehung, Windung, *f.*; Geflecht, Maschinengarn, *n.*; Verrenkung, *f.*; *v.t.* (ver)drehen; flechten; verrenken; verzerren; ~ed, gewunden.

twit, tadeln, bekritteln, sticheln.

twitch, *sb.* Zucken, *n.*, Zuckung, *f.*; *v.t.* zupfen; *v.i.* zucken.

twitter, *sb.* Zwitschern, *n.*; *v.i.* zwitschern.

two, zwei; ~-edged, zweischneidig; ~fold, zweifach; ~-piece, zweiteilig; ~-seater, Zweisitzer, *m.*; ~-stroke, Zweitakt-; ~-way, Doppel-.

type, *sb.* (*example, sort*) Typ(us), *m.*; (*model*) Vorbild, Muster, *n.*; (*letters*) Letter, Schrift, *f.*, Buchstabe, *m.*; *v.t. and i.* maschineschreiben, tippen; ~-face, Schriftbild, *f.*; ~founder, Schriftgießer, *m.*; ~script, Maschinenschrift, *f.*; ~writer, Schreibmaschine, *f.*; ~written, maschinegeschrieben.

typh|oid, Typhus, *m.*; ~us, Fleckfieber, *n.*

typhoon, Taifun, *m.*

typi|cal, typisch, charakteristisch; ~fy, als Vorbild (Beispiel) geben, dienen.

typist, Maschinenschreiber(in, *f.*), *m.*; Tippfräulein, *n.*

typograph|ical, typographisch, drucktechnisch; ~y, Buchdruckerkunst, *f.*

tyran|nical, tyrannisch; ~nize, tyrannisieren; ~ny, Tyrannei, *f.*; ~t, Tyrann, *m.*

tyre: see tire.[1]

tyro, Anfänger, Neuling, *m.*

U

U-boat, U-boot, *n.*

ubiquitous, allgegenwärtig.

udder, Euter, *n.*

ugl|iness, Häßlichkeit, *f.*; ~y, häßlich.

uhlan, Ulan, *m.*

ulcer, Geschwür, *n.*; ~ate, schwären; ~ous, geschwürig.

ulterior, jenseitig; weiter; versteckt.

ultimat|e, letzt; ~ely, schließlich; ~um, Ultimatum, *n.*

ultra, ultra-, übermäßig.

umbel, Dolde, *f.*

umbrella, Regenschirm; (*aircraft*) Fliegerschirm, *m.*

umpire, *sb.* Schiedsrichter, *m.* *v.t.* entscheiden; *v.i.* (bei einem Spiel) Schiedsrichter sein.

un-, *the prefix* un- *is added to nouns, adjectives, and adverbs in German, as in English, with the meaning 'not, free from, the reverse of'; only words for which the German equivalent is formed differently from this or for which there is no positive are listed here.*

unadvisable, nicht ratsam.

unaided, ohne Hilfe, allein.

unambitious, nicht ehrgeizig.

unanim|ity, Einstimmigkeit, Einmütigkeit, *f.*; ~ous(ly), einig, einmütig, einstimmig.

unassisted, allein.

unavailing, fruchtlos, vergeblich.

unbalanced, (*mind*) unausgeglichen.

unbar, aufriegeln.

unbiased, vorurteilsfrei, unbefangen.

unbind, losbinden.

unblushing, schamlos.

unbolt, aufriegeln.

unbuckle, aufschnallen.

unbutton, aufknöpfen.

unchain, entfesseln.

uncharitable, lieblos.

uncle, Onkel, Oheim, *m.*

uncoil, abwickeln.

unconcern, Gleichgültigkeit, *f.*; ~ed, gleichgültig.

uncork, entkorken.

uncouple, loskoppeln.

uncouth, roh, ungeschlacht.

uncover, aufdecken, entblößen.

unct|ion, Salbung, *f.*; *extreme* ~ion, letzte Ölung, *f.*; ~uous, salbungsvoll.

undated, ohne Datum.

under, *prep.* unter; *adv.* unten; ~ *age*, unmündig; ~ *way*, in Fahrt; unterwegs; *keep* ~, unterdrücken.

underbid, unterbieten.

under-carriage, Fahr -gestell, -werk, *n.*

undercharge, zu wenig berechnen.

underclothes, Wäsche, *f.*

undercurrent, Unterströmung, *f.*

undercut, *sb.* Filet, *n.*; *v.t.* (*prices*) unterbieten.

underdone, nicht gar.

underestimate, unterschätzen.

underfed, unterernährt.

undergo, erdulden; sich unterziehen.

undergraduate, Student, *m.*

underground, *sb.* Untergrundbahn, *f.*; *a.* unterirdisch; geheim.

undergrowth, Gestrüpp, Gesträuch, *n.*

underhand, heimlich, unter der Hand.

underlie, zu Grunde liegen.

underline, unterstreichen.

underling, Untergeordnete(r).

undermine, untergraben.

underneath, *prep.* unter; *adv.* unten.

underpaid, schlecht bezahlt.

underrate, unterschätzen.

undersell, unterbieten, verschleudern.

underside, untere Seite, *f.*

undersigned, *a.* unterschrieben; *sb.* Unterzeichnete(r).

undersized, unter Normalgröße.

understaffed, unterbesetzt, mit zu wenig Personal versehen.

understand, verstehen, begreifen; erfahren; hören; ~able, verständlich, begreiflich; ~ing, *sb.* Verstand, *m.*, Einsicht, *f.*; Voraussetzung, *f.*; *a.* einsichtsvoll.

understudy, *sb.* Ersatz(schauspieler), *m.*; *v.t.* (als Ersatz) einstudieren.

undertake, unternehmen; ~r, Leichenbestatter, *m.*

undertone, Flüsterton, *m.*; (*fig.*) Unterton, *m.*

undervalue, unterschätzen.

underwear, Leibwäsche, *f.*

underwood, Unterholz, *n.*

underwrite, (*commerc.*) versichern; ~r, Versicherer, *m.*

undisciplined, zuchtlos.

undo, aufmachen; zerstören; *come* ~ne, sich auflösen, aufgehen; *leave* ~ne, ungeschehen lassen, vernachlässigen.

undress, entkleiden; sich ausziehen; ~ed, nicht angekleidet.

undulat|e, wallen; ~ion, Wallen, *n.*, wellenförmige Bewegung, *f.*

unearned, unverdient.

unearth, ausgraben.

uneatable, nicht eßbar.

unemploy|ed, arbeitslos; ~ment, Arbeitslosigkeit, *f.*

uneventful, ereignislos.

unexampled, beispiellos.

unfasten, losmachen.

unfeeling, gefühllos.

unfit, *a.* ungeeignet, untauglich; *v.t.* unfähig machen.

unfix, losmachen; ~ed, lose; unentschieden.

unfledged, nicht flügge.

unfold, (sich) entfalten; darlegen.

unforgettable, unvergeßlich.

unfounded, grundlos, unbegründet.

unfrequented, wenig besucht.

unfrock, (jemandem) das Priesteramt nehmen.

unfurl, entfalten.

ungainly, plump, ungeschickt.

ungodly, gottlos.

ungraceful(ly), nicht anmutig.

ungrudging(ly), gern, willig.

unguent, Salbe, f.

unharness, abschirren.

unhinge, aus den Angeln heben; ~d, (of mind) zerrüttet.

unhook, loshaken.

unicorn, Einhorn, n.

uniform, sb. Uniform, f.; a., ~ly, ein-, gleich- förmig, gleichmäßig; ~ity, Gleichförmigkeit, f.

unify, vereinigen.

unilateral, einseitig.

union, Vereinigung, f., Verein, m.; (trades-union) Gewerkschaft, f.; ~ Jack, britische (National)-flagge, f.

unique, einzigartig.

unison, Einklang, m.

unit, Einheit, f.; Verband, m.; ~e, (sich) vereinigen; ~y, Einheit; Eintracht, f.

universal, ~ly, allgemein, Welt-; ~ity, Allgemeinheit, f.

universe, Weltall, Universum, n.

university, Universität, Hochschule, f.

unjustifiable, nicht zu rechtfertigen.

unkempt, ungekämmt, verwahrlost.

unlace, aufschnüren.

unlatch, aufklinken.

unless, wenn nicht, es sei denn daß.

unlined, nicht gefüttert; ohne Linien.

unload, aus-, ab- laden.

unlock, aufschließen.

unloose, lösen, losmachen.

unmarried, ledig, unverheiratet.

unmask, entlarven, bloßstellen.

unnerve, entnerven.

unobtainable, nicht erhältlich.

unoffending, harmlos.

unofficial, nicht amtlich.

unopposed, ohne Widerstand.

unorthodox, nicht orthodox.

unpack, auspacken, aufmachen.

unpin, ab-, los- heften.

unprejudiced, vorurteilsfrei.

unprincipled, ohne Grundsätze, gewissenlos.

unravel, entwirren, aufwickeln.

unreal, nicht wirklich, wesenlos.

unrepentant, reuelos.

unreserved, ~ly, vorbehaltlos;

rückhaltlos.

unroll, abrollen.

unruffled, ruhig, sanft.

unruly, unbändig, widerspenstig.

unscrew, losschrauben.

unscrupulous, skrupellos, bedenkenlos.

unseal, entsiegeln.

unselfish, selbstlos, uneigennützig; ~ness, Selbstlosigkeit, f.

unsettle, umstoßen; beunruhigen; ~d, (weather) veränderlich.

unsightly, häßlich.

unsound, verdorben; unhaltbar; nicht echt.

unstable, nicht fest; unbeständig.

unsuccessful, ~ly, erfolglos.

unthrifty, verschwenderisch.

untie, aufbinden, lösen.

until, bis (an, zu); not ~, erst (wenn).

unveil, entschleiern; enthüllen.

unwieldy, schwerfällig.

unwrap, auswickeln.

up, adv. aufwärts, hinauf; oben; prep. auf; ~ and down, auf und nieder; ~ to, bis (auf); (equal to) gewachsen (with dat.); well ~ in, bewandert in.

upbraid, tadeln.

upheaval, Erhebung, f.

uphill, bergauf; schwierig.

uphold, aufrecht(er)halten.

upholster, beziehen, polstern; ~er Tapezierer, m.

upkeep, Aufrecht-, Instand-haltung, f.

upon, auf; bei.

upper, ober, Ober-; ~ case, (type) Groß-; ~ class, Oberklasse, f.; ~ hand, Oberhand, f.; ~most, höchst, oberst.

uppish, übermütig; anmaßend.

upright, sb. Ständer, Pfosten, m.; a. and adv. aufrecht; aufrichtig.

uproar, Aufruhr, m.; ~ious(ly), lärmend.

uproot, entwurzeln.

upset, umstürzen, umwerfen; (fig.) bestürzen.

upshot, Ausgang, m., Ergebnis, n.

upside, Oberseite, f.; ~ down, umgekehrt, drunter und drüber.

upstairs, oben.

upstart, Emporkömmling, m.

up-to-date, modern.

upward(s), aufwärts; mehr als.

uranium, Uran, *n.*

urban, städtisch; ~e, gebildet, vornehm; ~ity, Vornehmheit, *f.*

urchin, Schelm; Straßenjunge, *m.*

urge, *sb.* Trieb, *m.*; *v.t.* treiben, drängen; dringend bitten; ~ncy, Wichtigkeit, Dringlichkeit, *f.*; ~nt(ly), dringend.

urin|e, Urin, Harn, *m.*; ~al, Pissoir, *n.*

urn, Urne; Teemaschine, *f.*

us, uns.

usage, Gebrauch, *m.*; Gewohnheit, *f.*

use, *sb.* (Ge)brauch, *m.*, Verwendung, *f.*; Nutzen, *m.*; *it is no* ~, es ist nutzlos; *what is the* ~ *of it?*, was nützt es?; *make* ~ *of*, benützen; *v.t.* gebrauchen, benützen; (*consume*) verbrauchen; (*treat*) behandeln; ~d to, gewöhnt an; *I* ~d *to go*, ich pflegte zu gehen, ich ging früher; ~ful(ly), nützlich; ~fulness, Nützlichkeit, *f.*; ~less(ly), nutzlos, unbrauchbar; ~lessness, Nutzlosigkeit, Unbrauchbarkeit, *f.*

usher, *sb.* Gerichtsdiener; Zeremonienmeister, *m.*; *v.t.* ~ in, einführen; ~ette, Platzanweiserin, *f.*

usual, ~ly, üblich, gewöhnlich.

usurer, Wucherer, *m.*

usurp, sich anmaßen; ~ation, Anmaßung, (widerrechtliche) Besitzergreifung, *f.*; ~er, Usurpator, Thronräuber, *m.*

usury, Wucher, *m.*

utensil, Werkzeug, Gerät, *n.*; ~s, Utensilien, *n.pl.*, Geschirr, *n.*

uterus, Gebärmutter, *f.*

utilitarian, Utilitarier, *m.*; *a.* Nützlichkeits-.

utility, *sb.* Nützlichkeit, *f.*

utilize, nutzbar machen; ~ation, Nutzbarmachung, *f.*

utmost, äußerst; *to the* ~, aufs Äußerste.

Utopia, Utopien, *n.*, Utopie, *f.*; ~n, utopisch.

utter, *a.* äußerst, völlig; *v.t.* äußern, aussprechen; (*coins*) in Umlauf setzen; ~ance, Äußerung, *f.*; ~ly, durchaus.

uvula, Zäpfchen, *n.*

uxorious, der Ehefrau zu sehr ergeben.

V

vacan|cy, Leere; freie Stelle, *f.*; ~t, leer; (*situation*) frei; (*mind*) gedankenlos; (*look*) ausdruckslos.

vacat|e, räumen; niederlegen; ~ion, Ferien, *pl.*, Urlaub, *m.*

vaccin|ate, impfen; ~ation, Impfung, *f.*; ~e, Lymphe *f.*, Impfstoff, *m.*

vacillat|e, wanken, schwanken; ~ion, Wanken, Schwanken, *n.*

vacuum, Vakuum, *n.*, leerer Raum, *m.*; ~ cleaner, Staubsauger, *m.*; ~ flask, Thermosflasche, *f.*

vagabond, Vagabund, Landstreicher, *m.*

vagary, Laune, Grille, *f.*

vagrant, Landstreicher, *m.*

vague, ~ly, vag, unbestimmt; ~ness, Vagheit, Unbestimmtheit, *f.*

vain, ~ly, (*proud*) eitel, dünkelhaft; (*fruitless*) vergeblich; *in* ~, vergebens; ~glorious, ruhmredig.

valerian, Baldrian, *m.*

valet, Kammerdiener, Lakai, *m.*

valiant, ~ly, tapfer.

valid, gültig; ~ity, Gültigkeit, *f.*

valise, Reisetasche, *f.*

valley, Tal, *n.*

valo|rous, tapfer; ~ur, Tapferkeit, *f.*

valuable, wertvoll, kostbar; ~s, Wertsachen, *f.pl.*

valuation, Schätzung, *f.*

value, *sb.* Wert, *m.*; *v.t.* schätzen; ~less, wertlos.

valve, Ventil, *n.*; (*radio*) Röhre, *f.*

van, (Möbel-, Pack-)wagen, *m.*; (*mil.*) Vorhut, *f.*

vane, Wetterfahne, *f.*

vanguard, Vorhut, *f.*

vanilla, Vanille, *f.*

vanish, verschwinden.

vanity, Eitelkeit, *f.*

vanquish, besiegen.

vantage, Vorteil, *m.*

vapid, schal, geistlos.

vapo|rize, verdampfen; ~ur, Dampf, Dunst, *m.*

variable, veränderlich.

variance, Uneinigkeit, Mißhelligkeit, *f.*

variation, Abweichung; Veränderung; (*mus.*) Variation, *f.*

varicose, Krampfader-.

varied, mannigfaltig.

variegated, bunt, scheckig.

variety, Mannigfaltigkeit; Abwechslung; Spielart, *f.*; (*theatr.*) Varieté, *n.*

various, verschieden, mannigfaltig.

varnish, *sb.* Firnis, *m.*; *v.t.* firnissen, lackieren; (*fig.*) beschönigen.

vary, (sich) verändern, abweichen.

vase, Vase, *f.*

vaseline, Vaselin, *n.*

vassal, Lehnsmann, Vasall, *m.*

vast, sehr groß, ungeheuer; ~ness, ungeheure Größe.

vat, Faß, *n.*, Kufe, *f.*

vault, *sb.* Gewölbe, *n.*; Stahlkammer, *f.*; Gruft, *f.*; Sprung, *m.*; *v.i.* springen.

vaunt, prahlen, sich rühmen.

veal, Kalbfleisch, *n.*

veer, sich drehen; (*naut.*) abfieren.

vegetable, *sb.* Gemüse, *n.*; *a.* Pflanzen-.

vegetation, Vegetation, *f.*; Pflanzenleben, *n.*

vehemen|ce, Heftigkeit, *f.*; ~t(ly), heftig.

vehic|le, Fahrzeug, Fuhrwerk, *n.*; Vermittler, Träger, *m.*; Ausdrucksmittel, *n.*; ~ular, Fahr-.

veil, *sb.* Schleier, *m.*; *v.t.* verschleiern, verdecken.

vein, Ader; Anlage; Laune, Stimmung, *f.*

velocity, Schnelligkeit, Geschwindigkeit, *f.*

velvet, Samt, *m.*; ~een, Baumwollsamt, *m.*

venal, feil.

vendor, Verkäufer, *m.*

veneer, *sb.* Furnier, *n.*; *v.t.* furnieren.

venerable, ehrwürdig.

venerat|e, verehren; ~ion, Verehrung, *f.*

venereal, Geschlechts-.

Venetian blind, Jalousie, *f.*

vengeance, Rache, *f.*

venison, Wildbret, *n.*

venom, Gift, *n.*; ~ous, giftig; boshaft.

vent, *sb.* Öffnung, *f.*, (Luft)loch, *n.*; *give* ~ *to,* freien Lauf lassen; *v.t.* (her)auslassen.

ventilat|e, lüften; (*debate*) erörtern; ~ion, Ventilation, Lüftung, *f.*; ~or, Ventilator, Lüfter, *m.*

ventriloquis|m, Bauchredekunst, *f.*; ~t, Bauchredner, *m.*

venture, *sb.* Wagnis, Unternehmen, *n.*; *at a* ~, aufs Geratewohl; *v.* wagen; ~some, verwegen, kühn.

venue, Zuständigkeit, *f.*; Ort, *m.*

veraci|ous, aufrichtig, wahrhaftig; ~ty, Wahrhaftigkeit, *f.*

veranda, Veranda, *f.*

verb, Zeitwort, Verbum, *n.*; ~al, mündlich; wörtlich; ~ally, wörtlich; ~iage, Wortschwall, *m.*; ~ose, wortreich, weitschweifig; ~osity, Weitschweifigkeit, *f.*

verdant, grün(end).

verdict, Urteil, *n.*, Spruch, *m.*

verdigris, Grünspan, *m.*

verdure, Grün, *n.*

verge, *sb.* Rand, *m.*; *v.i.* ~ *on,* sich nähern (*dat.*), grenzen (an).

verger, Küster, *m.*

verif|ication, Bestätigung, *f.*; ~y, bestätigen, beweisen.

vermilion, Zinnoberrot, *n.*

vermin, Ungeziefer, *n.*

vernacular, *sb.* Landessprache, *f.*; *a.* Landes-, einheimisch.

veronal, Veronal, *n.*

veronica, Ehrenpreis, *n.*

versatil|e, gewandt, vielseitig; ~ity, Gewandtheit, Vielseitigkeit, *f.*

verse, Vers, *m.*; Strophe; Dichtung, *f.*; ~d, bewandert (*in* in).

versif|ication, Versbau, *m.*; ~y, in Verse setzen; dichten.

version, Version, Lesart; (*translation*) Übersetzung; (*account*) Darstellung, *f.*

versus, gegen.

vertebra, Rückenwirbel, *m.*; ~te, Wirbeltier, *n.*

vertical, senk-, lot- recht.

vertigo, Schwindel, *m.*

very, *a.* gerade, genau; *adv.* sehr; *the ~ best*, der allerbeste; *the ~ same*, genau derselbe.

Very light, Leuchtsignal, *n.*

vespers, Abendgottesdienst, *m.*

vessel, Gefäß, *n.*; (*ship*) Fahrzeug, *n.*

vest, *sb.* (*waistcoat*) Weste, *f.*; (*undervest*) Leibchen, *n.*; *v.t.* bekleiden, belehnen, verleihen; ~ed, (*interests, rights*) feststehend, altbegründet.

vestibule, Vorhalle, *f.*

vestige, Spur, *f.*

vestment Gewand, *n.*

vestry, Sakristei, *f.*

vetch, Wicke, *f.*

veteran, Veteran, alter Soldat, *m.*

veterinary, Tierarzt, Veterinär, *m.*

veto, *sb.* Veto, *n.*; *v.t.* verbieten, Einspruch erheben (gegen).

vex, plagen, ärgern; ~ation, Ärgernis, *n.*, Verdruß, *m.*; ~atious, ärgerlich; lästig.

VHF, UKW, *f.*

via, über.

viaduct, Viadukt, *m.*

vibrat|e, schwingen, zittern; ~ion, Schwingung, *f.*

vicar, Pfarrer, *m.*; ~age, Pfarrhaus, *n.*; ~ious, stellvertretend.

vice[1], Laster, *n.*

vice[2], (*tool*) Schraubstock, *m.*

vice-, Vize-, Unter-; ~admiral, Vizeadmiral, *m.*; ~roy, Vizekönig, *m.*

vice versa, umgekehrt.

vicinity, Nähe, Nachbarschaft, *f.*

vicious, ~ly, lasterhaft; böse; (*animal*) bösartig; ~ circle, Zirkelschluß, *m.*

vicissitude, Wechsel, Umschlag, *m.*

victim, Opfer, *n.*; ~ize, zum Opfer machen.

victor, Sieger, *m.*; ~ious(ly), siegreich; ~y, Sieg, *m.*

victual, mit Lebensmitteln versorgen; ~ler, Lebensmittellieferant, *m.*; ~s, Lebensmittel, *n.pl.*

vie, wetteifern.

view, *sb.* Aussicht, *f.*; Anblick, *m.*; (*opinion*) Ansicht, Meinung, *f.*; *v.t.* besehen, besichtigen; ~finder, Sucher, *m.*; ~point, Gesichtspunkt, *m.*

vigil, Nachtwache, *f.*; ~ance,

Wachsamkeit, *f.*; ~ant, wachsam.

vigo|rous(ly), kräftig, rüstig; ~ur, Stärke, Kraft, *f.*

vile, ~ly, schlecht, gemein, abscheulich, niederträchtig; ~ness, Gemeinheit, Abscheulichkeit, *f.*

villa, Villa, *f.*

village, Dorf, *n.*; ~r, Dorfbewohner, *m.*

villain, Schurke, *m.*; ~ous, niederträchtig.

vindicat|e, rechtfertigen; ~ion, Rechtfertigung, *f.*

vindictive, rachsüchtig; ~ness, Rachsucht, *f.*

vine, Weinstock, *m.*, Weinrebe, *f.*; ~grower, Weinbauer, *m.*; ~growing, Weinbau, *m.*; ~leaf, Weinblatt, *n.*; ~ry, Rebenhaus, *n.*; ~yard, Wein-garten, -berg, *m.*

vinegar, Essig, *m.*

vint|age, Weinlese, *f.*; (Wein)jahrgang, *m.*; ~ner, Weinhändler, *m.*

viola, Bratsche; (*bot.*) Viole. *f.*

violate, verletzen; schänden; übertreten; ~ion, Verletzung; Schändung; Übertretung, *f.*

violen|ce, Gewalt(tätigkeit): Heftigkeit, *f.*; ~t(ly), gewaltsam; heftig.

violet, *sb.* (*bot.*) Veilchen; (*colour*) Violett, *n.*; *a.* violett.

violin, Violine, Geige, *f.*; ~ist, Violin-, Geigen- spieler, *m.*

viper, Viper, Otter, *f.*

virgin, *sb.* Jungfrau, *f.*; *a.* jungfräulich; ~ity, Jungfräulichkeit, *f.*

viril|e, männlich; ~ity, Männlichkeit; Mannheit, *f.*

virtual, ~ly, eigentlich, so gut wie.

virtu|e, Tugend; Kraft, *f.*; ~ous(ly), tugendhaft.

virulen|ce, Heftigkeit; Bosheit, *f.*; ~t(ly), giftig; bösartig.

virus, Gift, *n.*

visa, Visum, *n.*

visage, Gesicht, *n.*

viscera, Eingeweide, *n.pl.*

visc|id, klebrig; ~ose, Viskose, Zellwolle, *f.*; ~osity, Klebrigkeit, *f.*; Flüssigkeitsgrad, *m.*

viscount, Vicomte, *m.*; ~ess, Vicomtesse, *f.*

visib|le, ~ly, sichtbar; ~ility, Sicht(barkeit), *f.*

vision, Sehen, *n.*; Gesicht, *n.*; Erscheinung, *f.*; ~ary, *sb.* Phantast, Schwärmer, *m.*; *a.* träumerisch, unwirklich, phantastisch, schwärmerisch.

visit, *sb.* Besuch, *m.*; *v.t.* besuchen; ~ation, Heimsuchung, *f.*; ~or, Besucher, Gast, *m.*

vista, Aussicht, *f.*

visual, Seh-, Gesichts-; ~ize, (sich) vorstellen, (sich) vergegenwärtigen.

vital, Lebens-; wesentlich, unentbehrlich; ~ity, Lebenskraft, *f.*

vitamin, Vitamin, *n.*

vitiate, verderben.

vitr|eous, glasig, gläsern; ~ify, verglasen.

vitriol, Vitriol, *m. or n.*

vituperat|e, verunglimpfen; ~ion, Verunglimpfung, *f.*

viva, mündliche Prüfung.

vivaci|ous, lebhaft; ~ty, Lebhaftigkeit, *f.*

vivid, ~ly lebendig, lebhaft; ~ness, Lebendigkeit, Lebhaftigkeit, *f.*

vivify, beleben.

vivisection, Vivisektion, *f.*

vixen, Füchsin, *f.*

viz, nämlich.

vocabulary, Wortschatz, *m.*; Wortverzeichnis, *n.*

vocal, Vokal-, Stimm-; ~ chord, Stimmband, *n.*; ~ist, Sänger(in, *f.*), *m.*

vocation, Beruf, *m.*; ~al, Berufs-, beruflich.

vociferous, laut, schreiend.

vogue, Mode, *f.*

voice, *sb.* Stimme, *f.*; *v.t.* äußern; ~d, stimmhaft; ~less, stimmlos.

void, *sb.* Leere, *f.*; *a.* leer; *null and* ~, ungültig; *v.t.* (aus)leeren.

volatile, flüchtig; flatterhaft; *sal* ~, Riechsalz, *n.*

volcan|o, Vulkan, *m.*; ~ic, vulkanisch.

volition, Wollen, *n.*

volley, (*mil.*) Salve, *f.*; (*tennis, &c.*) Flugschlag, *m.*; (*oaths, &c.*) Hagel, *m.*

volt, Volt, *n.*; ~age, Spannung, *f.*

volte-face, Frontwechsel, *m.*

volub|le, ~ly, zungenfertig; ~ility, Zungenfertigkeit, *f.*

volum|e, Umfang, *m.*; (*book*) Band, *m.*; (*sound*) Lautstärke, *f.*; ~inous, umfangreich, dick.

voluntar|y, ~ily, freiwillig.

volunteer, *sb.* Freiwillige(r); *v.t.* freiwillig dienen; (sich) anbieten.

voluptu|ary, Wollüstling, *m.*; ~ous(ly), wollüstig.

vomit, *v.t.* auswerfen, ausbrechen; *v.i.* sich erbrechen.

voraci|ous, gierig, gefräßig; ~ty, Gefräßigkeit, *f.*

vortex, Wirbel, *m.*

votary, Geweihte(r); Anhänger, *m.*

vot|e, *sb.* Stimme, *f.*; *v.t. and i.*, stimmen (für), wählen; ~er, Wähler, *m.*; ~ing, Abstimmung, *f.*; ~ing paper, Stimmzettel, *m.*

vouch, (sich) verbürgen; Gewähr leisten; ~er, Beleg, Schein, *m.*; ~safe, gewähren, verstatten, geruhen.

vow, *sb.* Gelübde, *n.*; *v.t. and i.* geloben.

vowel, Vokal, Selbstlaut, *m.*

voyage, *sb.* Reise, *f.*

vulcan|ite, Hartgummi, *m.*; ~ize, vulkanisieren.

vulgar, ~ly, gemein, niedrig; (*fraction*) gewöhnlich; ~ity, Gemeinheit, *f.*

vulnerab|le, verwundbar; ~ility, Verwundbarkeit, *f.*

vulture, Geier, *m.*

W

wad, Bund, Bündel, *n.*; Bausch, Pfropfen, *m.*; ~ding, Watte, Wattierung, *f.*

waddle, watscheln, wackeln.

wade, (durch)waten.

wafer, Waffel; (*host*) Hostie, *f.*

waft, *sb.* Hauch, *m.*; *v.t.* tragen, zuwehen; *v.i.* schweben.

wag, *sb.* Schalk, Spaßvogel, *m.*; *v.t.* schütteln, wedeln; *v.i.* wackeln, wedeln.

wage, *sb.* Lohn, *m.*; *v.t.*, ~ *war*, Krieg führen; ~-earner, Lohnempfänger, *m.*; ~-freeze, Lohnstopp, *m.*

wager, *sb.* Wette, *f.*; *v.t. and i.* wetten.

waggle, wackeln, wanken.

wagon, Waggon, Last-, Güterwagen, *m.*

wagtail, Bachstelze, *f.*

waif, verlassenes Kind.

wail, *sb.* Klage, *f.*; *v.i.* wehklagen; wimmern.

wainscot, Tafelwerk, Getäfel, *n.*

waist, Taille, *f.*; ~band, Leibgurt, *m.*; ~coat, Weste, *f.*

wait, *sb.* Lauer, *f.*; *v.i.* warten; (*at table*) bei Tisch aufwarten; ~er, Kellner, *m.*; ~ing-room, Wartesaal, *m.*; ~ress, Kellnerin, *f.*

waive, verzichten (auf).

wake, *sb.* Kielwasser, *n.*

wake(n), *v.t.* aufwecken; *v.i.* aufwachen, erwachen.

walk, *sb.* Gang, Schritt; Spaziergang; Pfad, Weg, *m.*; *v.i.* (zu Fuß) gehen, spazierengehen; ~er, Fußgänger, *m.*; ~ing-stick, Spazierstock, *m.*; ~over, leichter Sieg.

wall, *sb.* Mauer, Wand, *f.*; *v.t.* um- ein- mauern; ~flower, Goldlack, *m.*

wallet, Brief-, Akten- tasche, *f.*

wallow, sich wälzen.

walnut, Walnuß, *f.*

walrus, Walroß, *n.*

waltz, *sb.* Walzer, *m.*; *v.i.* Walzer tanzen, walzen.

wan, blaß, bleich.

wand, Stab, *m.*

wander, wandern; irre reden; ~er, Wanderer, Herumstreifer, *m.*

wane, abnehmen.

wangle, schieben.

want, *sb.* Mangel (*of* an), *m.*; (*requirement*) Bedürfnis, *n.*; (*poverty*) Not, *f.*; *v.t.* (*wish*) wünschen, wollen; (*need*) nötig haben; *v.i.* fehlen, mangeln (*in* an); ~ed, (*in adverts*) gesucht.

wanton, *sb.* Lüstling, *m.*, üppige Person, *f.*; *a.* üppig, lüstern; mutwillig; ~ness, Üppigkeit, *f.*; Mutwille, *m.*

war, *sb.* Krieg, *m.*; *v.i.* Krieg führen; ~fare, Kriegführung, *f.*; ~head, Sprengkopf, *m.*; ~loan, Kriegsanleihe, *f.*; ~

lord, Kriegsherr, *m.*; **War Office**, Kriegsministerium, *n.*; ~ship, Kriegsschiff, *n.*

warble, trillern, schlagen; ~r, Singvogel, *m.*

ward, *sb.* Wache; Vormundschaft, *f.*; (*person*) Mündel, *m.* or *n.*; (*hospital*) (Kranken)saal, *m.*; *v.t.* ~ off, abwehren; ~en, Aufseher; Vorsteher, *m.*; ~er, Wächter, Wärter, *m.*; ~robe, Kleiderschrank, *m.*; ~room, (Offiziers)messe, *f.*

ware, Ware, *f.*; ~house, Warenlager, Magazin, *n.*

warily, vorsichtig, behutsam; ~ness, Vorsicht, Behutsamkeit, *f.*

warm, *a.* warm; herzlich; *v.t.* erwärmen; *v.i.* warm werden; ~th, Wärme, *f.*

warn, warnen (*against* vor); ermahnen; ~ing, Warnung, *f.*

warp, *sb.* (*weaving*) Kette, *f.*; *v.i.* (*wood*) sich werfen.

warrant, *sb.* Vollmacht; Bürgschaft, *f.*; Haftbefehl; (Lager-) schein, *m.*; *v.t.* garantieren; rechtfertigen; ~ officer, Deckoffizier, Feldwebelleutnant, *m.*

warren, (Kaninchen)gehege, *n.*

warrior, Krieger, *m.*

wart, Warze, *f.*

wary, behutsam, vorsichtig.

wash, *sb.* Wäsche, *f.*; (*cosmetic*) Haarwasser, *n.*; Tünche, *f.*; *v.t.* (sich) waschen; (ab)spülen; ~basin, Waschbecken, *n.*; ~er, (Dichtungs)scheibe, *f.*; ~woman, Wäscherin, *f.*; ~hand stand, Waschtisch, *m.*; ~house, Waschküche, *f.*; ~ing, Waschen, *n.*; Wäsche, *f.*; ~leather, Putzleder, *n.*; ~out, Fehlschlag, *m.*

wasp, Wespe, *f.*

waste, *sb.* Verschwendung, *f.*; Verlust, *m.*; Abfall; Verschleiß, *m.*; Putzwolle, Einöde, *f.*; *v.t.* verschwenden; verwüsten; zerstören; *v.i.* abnehmen; ~ful(ly), verschwenderisch; ~fulness, Verschwendung, *f.*; ~heap, Schutthaufen, *m.*; ~paper, Papierabfälle, *m.pl.*; ~paper basket, Papierkorb, *m.*; ~pipe, Abzugsrohr, *n.*;

products, Abfallprodukte, *n.pl.*

watch, *sb.* Wache, Wacht, *f.*; Posten, *m.*; Taschenuhr, *f.*; *be on the* ~, auf der Hut sein; *v.t.* beobachten; *(guard)* bewachen; *v.i.* wachen; ~**dog**, Kettenhund, *m.*; ~**er**, Wächter; Beobachter, Zuschauer, *m.*; ~**ful(ly)**, wachsam; ~**fulness**, Wachsamkeit, *f.*; ~**glass**, Uhrglas *n.*; ~**maker**, Uhrmacher, *m.*; ~**man**, Nachtwächter, *m.*; ~**word**, Losung, Parole, *f.*

water, *sb.* Wasser, *n.*; *v.t.* wässern, begießen, besprengen; verdünnen; ~**closet**, Wasserklosett, *n.*; ~**colour**, Aquarell, *n.*; Wasserfarbe, *f.*; ~**course**, Fluß, Wasserlauf, *m.*; ~**cress**, Brunnenkresse, *f.*; ~**fall**, Wasserfall, *m.*; ~**glass**, Wasserglas, *n.*; ~**ing**, Begießen, *n.*; Bewässerung, *f.*; ~**ing-can**, Gießkanne, *f.*; ~**ing-place**, Badeort, *m.*; Schwemme, *f.*; ~**lily**, Wasserlilie, *f.*; ~**logged**, voll Wasser; sumpfig; ~**mark**, Wasserzeichen, *n.*; ~ **power**, Wasserkraft, *f.*; ~**proof**, *sb.* Regenmantel. *m.*; *a.* wasserdicht; ~**shed**, Wasserscheide, *f.*; ~**spout**, Abtraufe, Speiröhre; Wasserhose, *f.*; ~**tight**, wasserdicht; ~**works**, Wasserwerk, *n.*; ~**y**, wässerig.

watt, Watt, *n.*

wattle, Hürde, *f.*; *(cock's)* Bart, Kehllappen. *m.*

wave, *sb.* Welle, Woge *f.*; Winken; Wehen, *n.*; *v.t.* schwenken; winken; *(hair)* wellen, ondulieren; *v.i.* wehen; wallen; ~**band**, Wellenband, *n.*; ~**length**, Wellenlänge, *f.*; ~**y**, wavy, Wellen-; wellig; wogend.

waver, schwanken; ~**ing**, unschlüssig; wankelmütig.

wax, *sb.* Wachs, *n.*; *(sealing-wax)* Siegellack, *m.* or *n.*; *v.t.* wachsen; *v.i.* wachsen; werden; ~**work**, Wachsfigur, *f.*

way, *sb.* Weg, *m.*; Richtung; Bahn, *f.*; *(means)* Mittel, *n.*; *(Art und)* Weise, *f.*; *the* ~ *out*, der Ausgang; *lose one's* ~, sich verirren; *get one's own* ~,

---

seinen Willen durchsetzen; *in every* ~, in jeder Beziehung; *the right* ~, richtig; *the wrong* ~, verkehrt; *by the* ~, beiläufig; *be in the* ~ *of*, (jemandem) im Wege stehen; *in no* ~, keineswegs; *give* ~, nachgeben, weichen; *lead the* ~, vorangehen; *make* ~ *for*, Platz machen für; *under* ~, unterwegs; ~**farer**, Reisende(r); ~**lay**, auflauern, nachstellen; ~**side**, am Wege stehend; ~**ward**, eigensinnig; launenhaft.

W.C., Abtritt, *m.*, Klosett, *n.*

we, wir.

weak, ~**ly**, schwach; dünn; ~**en**, *v.t.* schwächen; *v.i.* schwächer werden; abflauen; ~**ling**, Schwächling, *m.*; ~**minded**, schwachsinnig; ~**ness**, Schwäche, Schwachheit, *f.*

weal, Reichtum; Wohlstand, *m.*

wealth, Reichtum; Wohlstand, *m.*; ~**y**, wohlhabend, reich.

wean, entwöhnen.

weapon, Waffe, *f.*

wear, *v.t.* Kleidung, *f.*; ~ *and tear*, Abnutzung, *f.*; *v.t.* tragen; abnutzen, verbrauchen; *v.i.* sich tragen; ~ *off*, abnehmen.

wear|iness, Müdigkeit; Langeweile, *f.*; ~**isome**, ermüdend, beschwerlich; ~**y**, *a.* müde; ermüdend; *v.t.* ermüden.

weasel, Wiesel, *n.*

weather, *sb.* Wetter, *n.*, Witterung, *f.*; *v.t.* *(storm)* aushalten; *(cape)* umsegeln; *(fig.)* überstehen; ~**beaten**, abgehärtet; ~**cock**, Wetterhahn, *m.*; ~**forecast**, Wettervorhersage, *f.*; ~**glass**, Barometer, *n.*

weave, weben, flechten; ~**r**, Weber, *m.*

web, Gewebe, *n.*; Membran, Schwimmhaut, *f.*; ~**footed**, mit Schwimmhäuten.

wed, heiraten; ~**ding**, Hochzeit, *f.*; ~**ding-ring**, Trauring, *m.*; ~**lock**, Ehestand, *m.*

wedge, *sb.* Keil, *m.*; *v.t.* verkeilen.

Wednesday, Mittwoch, *m.*

weed, *sb.* Unkraut, *n.*; *v.t.* jäten; ausrotten.

week, Woche, *f.*; *to-morrow* ~, morgen über acht Tage; *yesterday* ~, gestern vor acht Tagen;

~-day, Wochentag, *m.*; ~-end, Wochenende, *n.*; ~ly, *sb.* Wochenblatt, *n.*; *a. and adv.* wöchentlich.

weep, weinen; ~ *for,* beweinen; ~ing willow, Trauerweide, *f.*

weevil, Kornwurm, *m.*

weft, Einschuß, *m.*

weigh, *v.t.* wiegen, wägen; *(anchor)* lichten; schätzen; *v.i.* wiegen; ~ing-machine, Waage, *f.*

weight, *sb.* Gewicht, *n.*; Wucht, *f.*; *v.t.* beschweren; ~iness, Schwere, Gewichtigkeit, *f.* ~y, schwer, gewichtig.

weir, Wehr, *n.*

weird, unheimlich.

welcome, *sb.* Willkomm(en, *n.*), *m.*; Aufnahme, *f.*; *a.* willkommen; *v.t.* bewillkommnen.

weld, schweißen.

welfare, Wohlfahrt, *f.*; ~ work, Fürsorge, Wohlfahrtspflege, *f.*

well[1], *sb.* Quelle, *f.*, Brunnen, *m.*; *(staircase)* Treppenhaus, *n.*; *v.i.* quellen.

well[2], *a.* gut, gesund; *adv.* gut, wohl; leicht; gern; *as ~ as,* sowohl ... wie (als auch); *be ~ up in,* in ... bewandert sein; *all being ~,* wenn alles gut geht; ~-being, Wohlsein, *n.*; ~-bred, wohlerzogen; ~-meaning, wohlmeinend; ~-off, wohlhabend; ~-wisher, Freund, Gönner, *m.*

Welsh, walisisch; ~ rabbit, geröstete Käseschnitte, *f.*

welt, Rand, Rahmen, *m.*

welter, sich wälzen; ~-weight, Weltergewicht, *n.*

west, Westen, *m.*; *a.* westlich; ~erly, ~ern, westlich; ~ward, westwärts; ~wind, Westwind, *m.*

wet, *a.* naß, feucht; ~ *paint!,* frisch gestrichen!; *v.t.* nässen; anfeuchten; ~-nurse, Amme, *f.*

whack, *sb.* Hieb, *m.*; *v.t.* tüchtig schlagen, prügeln.

whal|e, Walfisch, *m.*; ~ebone, Fischbein, *n.*; ~e-oil, Tran, *m.*; ~er, Walfischfänger, *m.*; ~ing, Walfischfang, *m.*

wharf, Schiffslandeplatz, Kai, *m.*

what, was, was für ein, welche(r, s); ~ *for?,* warum?; ~ *is this for?,* wozu dient das?; ~ *is the*

matter?, was ist los?; ~ *sort of,* was für ein; ~ever, was auch; none ~ever, gar kein(e); ~not, Etagere, *f.*

wheat, Weizen, *m.*

wheedle, schmeicheln, beschwatzen.

wheel, *sb.* (Fahr-, Spinn-, Steuer-) rad, *n.*; *(potter's)* Töpferscheibe; *(mil.)* Schwenkung, *f.*; *v.t.* herumfahren, schieben; *v.i.* *(mil.)* schwenken; ~barrow, Schub-, Schieb- karren, *m.*; ~base, Radstand, *m.*; ~wright, Stellmacher, Wagenbauer, *m.*

wheeze, keuchen, röcheln.

whelp, Junge, *n.*

when, *(interrog.)* wann; *(conj.)* als, wenn; ~ce, woher; ~ever, so oft als, (allemal) wenn.

where, wo, wohin; ~abouts, Verbleib, Aufenthalt, *m.*; ~as, da nun, weil; ~at, wobei, woran; ~by, wodurch, ~fore, weshalb; ~in, worin; ~of, wovon; ~upon, worauf; ~ver, wo immer; ~withal, *sb.* Nötige, *n.*; Mittel, *n.pl.*

whet, wetzen; *(appetite)* reizen; ~stone, Wetzstein, *m.*

whether, ob.

whey, Molken, *f.pl.*

which, welche(r, s), der, die, das.

whiff, Hauch, Zug, *m.*

while, *sb.* Weile, *f.*; *conj.* während, indem; *v.t.*, ~away, verbringen, vertreiben.

whilst = while, *conj.*

whim, Grille, *f.*, Einfall, *m.*; ~sical(ly), grillenhaft, launisch.

whimper, winseln, wimmern.

whine, *sb.* Wimmern, *n.*; *v.i.* wimmern,

whip, *sb.* Peitsche, *f.*; *v.t.* peitschen; *(cream)* schlagen; ~-hand, Oberhand, *f.*; ~ped cream, Schlagsahne, *f.*; ~ping, Tracht (*f.*) Prügel.

whirl, *sb.* Wirbel, Strudel, *m.*; *v.t.* wirbeln; ~pool, Strudel, *m.*; ~wind, Wirbelwind, *m.*

whisk, *sb.* Wisch, Staubwedel; (*for eggs, &c.*) Schläger, Quirl, *m.*; *v.t.* (ab)wischen; *(eggs)* schlagen; ~ *away,* schnell abtun.

whiskers, (Backen)bart, *m.*

whisky, Whisky, *m.*

whisper, *sb.* Geflüster. *n.*; *v.i.* flüstern.

whist, Whist(spiel), *n.*

whistle, *sb.* Pfeife, *f.*; Pfiff, *m.*; *v.t.* and *i.*, pfeifen.

white, *sb.* Weiß, *n.*; ~ of egg, Eiweiß, *n.*; *a.* weiß; ~hot, weißglühend; ~ lead, Bleiweiß, *n.*; ~n, weißen; ~ness, Weiße Blässe, *f.*; ~smith, Klempner, *m.*; ~thorn, Weißdorn, *m.*; ~wash, *sb.* Tünche, *f.*; *v.t.* (weiß-)tünchen.

whither, wohin.

whiting, Merlan, *m.*

whitlow, Nagelgeschwür, *n.*

Whitsun|day, Pfingstsonntag, *m.*; ~tide, Pfingsten, *pl.*

whittle, schneiden, schnitzeln.

whiz, sausen, zischen.

who, (*interrog.*) wer; (*relative*) welche(r, s); der, die, das; ~ever, wer auch immer.

whole, *sb.* Ganze, *n.*; *on the* ~, im ganzen; *a.* ganz; wohl, gesund; ~meal, Vollkorn-; ~sale, *sb.* Großhandel, *m.*; *a.* Groß-, im großen; Massen-; ~some, heilsam.

wholly, gänzlich, völlig.

whoop, *sb.* Schrei; Schlachtruf, *m.*; *v.i.* schreien; ~ing-cough, Keuchhusten, *m.*

whore, Hure, *f.*

whorl, (*bot.*) Quirl, *m.*; (*shells*) Gewinde, *n.*

whose, (*interrog.*) wessen; (*relative*) dessen, deren.

why, warum.

wick, Docht, *m.*

wicked, ~ly, böse, gottlos; ~ness, Bosheit, Gottlosigkeit, *f.*

wicker, ~ basket, Weidenkorb, *m.*; ~work, Flechtwerk, *n.*

wide, ~ly, breit, weit; *far and* ~, weit und breit; ~n, erweitern; ~ness, Breite, *f.*

widow, Witwe, *f.*; ~ed, verwitwet; ~er, Witwer, *m.*; ~hood, Witwenstand, *m.*

width, Weite, Breite, *f.*

wield, handhaben, führen.

wife, Frau, *f.*; Weib, *n.*

wig, Perücke, *f.*

wigwam, Wigwam, *m.*

wild, ~ly, wild; roh; grausam; ~erness, Wildnis, *f.*; ~fire, Lauffeuer, *n.*; ~ness, Wildheit, *f.*

wiles, Ränke, *pl.*

wilful, ~ly, eigensinnig; vorsätzlich; ~ness, Eigensinn, *m.*

will, *sb.* Wille; Wunsch; Befehl, *m.*; Testament, *n.*; *v.t.* wollen; ~ing(ly), bereitwillig, gern; ~ingness, Bereitwilligkeit, *f.*

will-o'-the-wisp, Irrlicht, *n.*

willow, Weide, *f.*

wily, schlau, verschmitzt.

win, gewinnen; siegen.

wince, zurückschrecken.

winch, Winde, Haspel, *f.*

wind¹, *sb.* Wind; Atem, *m.*; *v.t.* außer Atem setzen; ~fall, Fallobst, *n.*; Glücksfall, *m.*; ~instrument, Blasinstrument, *n.*; ~mill, Windmühle, *f.*; ~pipe, Luftröhre, *f.*; ~y, windig.

wind², *v.t.* winden, wickeln, aufspulen; ~ up, (*watch*) aufziehen; (*haul up*) aufwinden; (*business*) liquidieren; *v.i.* (*road*) sich schlängeln; (*plants*) ranken; ~ing, Windung, Wick(e)lung, *f.*; ~ing-sheet, Leichentuch, *n.*; ~ing-stairs, Wendeltreppe, *f.*; ~lass, Winde, Haspel, *f.*

window, Fenster, *n.*; ~dressing, (*fig.*) Aufmachung, Reklame, *f.*

wine, Wein, *m.*; ~grower, Winzer, *m.*; ~growing, Weinbau, *m.*; ~press, Kelter, *f.*

wing, Flügel, *m.*; (*aircraft*) Tragfläche, *f.* ~ed, geflügelt.

wink, *sb.* Blinzeln, *n.*; *v.i.* blinzeln.

winn|er, Sieger, *m.*; ~ings, Gewinn, *m.*

winnow, worfeln; scheiden.

wint|er, *sb.* Winter, *m.*; *v.i.* überwintern; ~ry, winterlich.

wipe, (weg)wischen; ~ out, (*fig.*) ausrotten.

wire, *sb.* Draht, *m.*; Telegramm, *n.*; *v.t.* drahten; ~less, *sb.* Radio, *n.*, Funktelegraphie, *f.*; *a.* drahtlos; Funk-; ~less operator, Funker, *m.*; ~less set, Radio-, Funk-gerät, *n.*; ~less station, Radio-, Funk-station, *f.*; ~netting, Maschendraht, *m.*; ~pulling, Intrige, Mache, *f.*; ~**worm**, Drahtwurm, *m.*

wis|e, weise; ~**dom**, Weisheit, *f.*; ~**eacre**, Weisheitsprediger, Gelehrttuende(r), *m.*

wish, *sb.* Wunsch, *m.*; *v.t. and i.* wünschen; begehren.

wisp, Wisch, *m.*

wit, Witz, Geist; (*person*) Witzbold, *m.*

witch, Hexe, *f.*; ~**craft**, Hexerei, *f.*

with, mit; (*by means of*) mit, durch; (*among, in company of*) bei.

withdraw, *v.t.* zurück -nehmen, -ziehen; (*money*) abheben; *v.i.* sich zurückziehen; ~**al**, Zurückziehung, *f.*

wither, verwelken.

withhold, zurückhalten, vorenthalten.

within, *adv.* drinnen; *prep.* binnen; innerhalb.

without, *adv.* draußen; *prep.* (*outside*) außerhalb, vor; (*not having*) ohne.

withstand, widerstehen.

witness, *sb.* Zeuge, *m.*; Zeugnis, *n.*; *v.t.* (*see*) sehen, zugegen sein; (*signature*) beglaubigen, bezeugen.

witt|icism, Witz, *m.*; ~**iness**, Witzigkeit, *f.*; ~**ingly**, wissentlich; ~**y**, ~**ily**, witzig.

wizard, Zauberer, *m.*

wizened, eingeschrumpft, vertrocknet.

woad, Waid, *m.*

woe, Weh, *n.*; ~**ful(ly)**, erbärmlich, elend.

wolf, Wolf, *m.*; ~**ish**, wölfisch.

woman, Frau, *f.*, Weib, *n.*; ~**ish**, weibisch; ~**ly**, weiblich.

womb, Mutterleib, *m.*; Schoß, *m.*

wonder, *sb.* Wunder, *n.*; Verwunderung, *f.*; *v.i.* sich wundern, sich fragen; ~**ful(ly)**, wunderbar.

wont, Gewohnheit, *f.*; ~**ed**, gewohnt, gewöhnlich.

woo, freien, werben um; ~**er**, Freier, Bewerber, *m.*

wood, Holz, *n.*; Wald, *m.*; ~**bine**, Geißblatt, *n.*; ~**cock**, Waldschnepfe, *f.*; ~**cut**, Holzschnitt, *m.*; ~**cutter**, Holzhauer, *m.*; ~**ed**, waldig, bewaldet; ~**en**, hölzern; (*fig.*) steif, unbeholfen; ~**land**, Waldland, *n.*; ~**louse**,

Assel, *f.*; ~**man**, Holzhauer; Förster, *m.*; ~**pecker**, Specht, *m.*; ~**pigeon**, Ringeltaube, *f.*; ~**pulp**, Holzbrei, *m.*; ~**work**, Holzwerk, *n.*, Täfelung, *f.*

wool, Wolle, *f.*; ~**gathering**, zerstreut; ~**len**, wollen; ~**lens**, Wollwaren, *f.pl.*; ~**ly**, wollig.

word, *sb.* Wort, *n.*; Nachricht, *f.*; *v.t.* ausdrücken; abfassen; ~**iness**, Weitschweifigkeit, *f.*; ~**y**, weitschweifig.

work, *sb.* Arbeit, *f.*; Werk, *n.*; Geschäft, *n.*; Beschäftigung, *f.*; *v.t.* bearbeiten; behandeln; verrichten; leiten, in Betrieb haben; (*needlework*) sticken; *v.i.* arbeiten, wirken, gehen; ~**er**, Arbeiter, *m.*; ~**house**, Armenhaus, *n.*; ~**ing**, Arbeit, *f.*; Betrieb, *m.*; ~**ing-day**, Arbeitstag, *m.*; ~**ing-model**, Versuchsmodell, *n.*; ~**man**, Arbeiter, *m.*; ~**manlike**, geschickt; fachmännisch; ~**manship**, Werk, *n.*, Kunst, *f.*, Stil, *m.*; ~**shop**, Werkstatt, *f.*

world, Welt, Erde, *f.*; ~**liness**, Weltlichkeit, *f.*; ~**ling**, Weltling, *m.*; ~**ly**, weltlich; ~**wide**, weitverbreitet.

worm, *sb.* Wurm, *m.*; (*of screw*) Gewinde, *n.*, Schnecke, *f.*; *v.i.* wühlen; sich einschleichen; ~**eaten**, wurmstichig; ~**wood**, Wermut, *m.*

worry, *sb.* Sorge, Plage, *f.*; *v.t.* plagen, quälen; (*of dog*) zerren, totbeißen.

worse, schlechter, schlimmer.

worship, *sb.* Anbetung, Verehrung, *f.*; Gottesdienst, *m.*; *v.t.* anbeten, verehren; ~**per**, Anbeter, Verehrer, *m.*

worst, *a.* schlechtest, schlimmst; *adv.* am schlechtesten, am schlimmsten; *get the ~ of it*, den kürzeren ziehen; *v.t.* besiegen.

worsted, Kammgarn, *n.*

wort, Kraut, *n.*; (*beer*) Würze, *f.*

worth, *sb.* Wert, *m.*; *a.* wert, würdig; *while* der Mühe wert; ~**iness**, Würdigkeit, *f.*; ~**less**, wertlos; ~**y**, ~**ily**, würdig, verdienstvoll.

would-be, vorgeblich, Schein-.

wound, *sb.* Wunde, *f.*; *v.t.* verwunden.

wrangle, zanken, streiten.

wrap, *sb.* Überwurf, *m.*; *v.t.* (ein)wickeln, einschlagen; ~per, Überzug; Umschlag, *m.*, Kreuzband; Packtuch, *n.*

wrath, Zorn, *m.*; ~ful(ly), zornig.

wreath, *sb.* Kranz, *m.*; ~e, *v.t.* flechten; bekränzen; *v.i.* sich ringeln.

wreck, *sb.* Schiffbruch, *m.*; Wrack, *n.*; (*fig.*) Ruine, *f.*; *v.t.* zertrümmern; *v.i.* scheitern; ~age, Wrack, *n.*, (Schiffs)trümmer, *pl.*; ~er, Strandräuber, *m.*

wren, Zaunkönig, *m.*

wrench, *sb.* Verrenkung, *f.*; Ruck, *m.*; *v.t.* verrenken; entreißen.

wrestle, ringen; ~r, Ringkämpfer, *m.*

wretch, *sb.* Schuft, *m.*; ~ed, elend, erbärmlich; ~edness, Elend, *n.*, Erbärmlichkeit, *f.*

wriggle, sich winden, sich schlängeln.

wring, wringen, pressen; herauszwingen; (*hands*) ringen; ~er, Wringmaschine, *f.*

wrinkle, *sb.* Runzel, *f.*; Falte, *f.*; (*hint*) Kniff, *m.*; *v.t.* runzeln; *v.i.* sich runzeln.

wrist, Handgelenk, *n.*; ~let watch, Armbanduhr, *f.*

writ, Gerichtsbefehl, *m.*; Wahlausschreiben, *n.*

write, schreiben; ~r, Schreiber, *m.*; (*author*) Schriftsteller, Verfasser, *m.*

writhe, sich winden.

writing, Schreiben, *n.*, Schrift. *f.*; *in* ~, schriftlich; ~-case, Schreibmappe, *f.*; ~-desk, Schreibtisch, *m.*; ~-paper, Schreibpapier, *n.*

wrong, *sb.* Unrecht, *n.*; *a.*, ~ly, unrecht, verkehrt, falsch; *v.t.* (jemandem) Unrecht zufügen (tun); ~ful(ly), ungerecht; ~headed, verkehrt.

wrought, geschmiedet, gearbeitet; ~ iron, Schmiedeeisen, *n.*

wry, krumm, schief.

X

X-rays, Röntgen-, X- strahlen, *m.pl.*

Y

yacht, Jacht, *f.*; ~ing, Segelsport, *m.*; ~sman, Jachtfahrer, Segler, *m.*

yard, Hofraum, *m.*; (*naut.*) Rahe, *f.*

yarn, Garn, *n.*; (*fig.*) Erzählung, Geschichte, *f.*

yawn, *sb.* Gähnen, *n.*; *v.i.* gähnen.

year, Jahr, *n.*; ~ly, jährlich.

yearn, sich sehnen (*for* nach); ~ing, Sehnen, *n.*, Sehnsucht, *f.*

yeast, Hefe, *f.*; ~y, hefig.

yell, *sb.* gellendes Geschrei; *v.i.* gellen.

yellow, *sb.* Gelb, *n.*; *a.* gelb; ~ fever, gelbes Fieber; ~hammer, Goldammer, *f.*; ~ish, gelblich; ~ press, Hetzpresse, *f.*

yelp, kläffen.

yes, ja.

yesterday, gestern; *day before* ~, vorgestern.

yet, *conj.* doch, dennoch; *adv.* noch, sogar; *as* ~, bisher; *not* ~, noch nicht.

yew, Eibe, *f.*

yield, *sb.* Ertrag, *m.*; *v.t.* (*produce*) erzeugen, hervorbringen; einbringen; (*give up*) aufgeben; *v.i.* sich ergeben, nachgeben; ~ing, nachgiebig.

yodel, jodeln.

yoke, *sb.* Joch, *n.*; *v.t.* an-, unterjochen; zusammenkoppeln.

yokel, Bauerntölpel, *m.*

yolk, (Ei)dotter, *m.*

yonder, *a.* jene(r, s); *adv.* da, dort.

yore, *of* ~, vormals.

you, Sie, du, ihr; (*indefinite*) man.

young, *sb.* Junge, *n.*; *a.* jung; ~ish, jugendlich; ~ster, Junge, Jüngling, *m.*

your, Ihr, dein; ~s, der (die, das) Ihrige (deinige); ~self, Sie, du, selbst.

youth, Jüngling, *m.*; Jugend, *f.*; ~ful(ly), jugendlich; ~ hostel, Jugendherberge, *f.*

Yule, Weihnachten, *n.* or *f.pl.*

Z

zeal, Eifer, *m.*; ~ot, Eiferer, Zelot, *m.*; ~ous(ly), eifrig.

zebra, Zebra, *n.*

zenith, Zenit, *m. or n.*, Scheitelpunkt, *m.*

zephyr, Zephir, *m.*

zeppelin, Zeppelin, *m.*

zero, Null(punkt, *m.*), *f.*

zest, Behagen, Wohlgefallen, *n.*, Lust, *f.*

zigzag, *sb.* Zickzack, *m.*; *v.i.* zickzack laufen (fahren).

zinc, Zink, *n.*

zip(-fastener), Reißverschluß, *m.*

zodiac, Tierkreis, *m.*

zone, Zone, *f.*; Gürtel, *m.*

zoo, Zoo, *m.*; ~logical, zoologisch; ~logist, Zoologe, *m.*; ~logy, Zoologie, Tierkunde, *f.*

zoom, hoch -reißen, -schnellen.

APPENDIX
LIST OF NAMES

Abyssinia, Abessinien, *n.*; **~n,** *sb.* Abessinier, *m.*; *a.* abessinisch.
Adige, Etsch, *f.*
Adolphus, Adolf.
Adriatic, das Adriatische Meer.
Aegean, das Ägäische Meer.
Africa, Afrika, *n.*; **~n,** *sb.* Afrikaner, *m.*; *a.* afrikanisch.
Aix-la-Chapelle, Aachen, *n.*
Albania, Albanien, *n.*; **~n,** Albaner, *m.*; *a.* albanisch.
Alexandria, Alexandrien, *n.*
Algeria, Algerien, *n.*
Alps, die Alpen, *f.pl.*
Alsa|ce, Elsaß, *n.*; **~tian,** *sb.* Elsässer, *m.*; *a.* elsässisch.
America, Amerika, *n.*; **~n,** *sb.* Amerikaner, *m.*; *a.* amerikanisch.
Andes, Anden, *pl.*
Andrew, Andreas.
Ann(e), Anna.
Antarctic, Antarktis, *f.*, das südliche Eismeer.
Anthony, Anton.
Antilles, Antillen, *pl.*
Antwerp, Antwerpen, *n.*
Apennines, the, Apenninen, *pl.*
Arab, Araber, *m.*; **~ia,** Arabien, *n.*; **~ian,** arabisch.
Arctic, Arktis, *f.*; das nördliche Eismeer.
Argentin|a, Argentinien, *n.*; **~e,** argentinisch.
Armenia, Armenien, *n.*; **~n,** *sb.* Armenier, *m.*; *a.* armenisch.
Asia, Asien, *n.*; **~tic,** asiatisch; **~ Minor**, Kleinasien, *n.*
Athens, Athen, *n.*; **~ian,** *sb.* Athener, *m.*; *a.* athenisch.
Atlantic, der atlantische Ozean, Atlantik, *m.*
Augustus, August.
Australia, Australien, *n.*; **~n,** *sb.* Australier, *m.*; *a.* australisch.
Austria, Österreich, *n.*; **~n,** *sb.* Österreicher, *m.*; *a.* österreichisch.
Azores, Azoren, *pl.*

Baltic, Ostsee, *f.*
Barbadoes, die Barbados Inselgruppe.
Basle, Basel, *n.*
Bavaria, Bay(e)rn, *n.*; **~n,** *sb.* Bayer, *m.*; *a.* bay(e)risch.
Belg|ium, Belgien, *n.*; **~ian,** *sb.* Belgier, *m.*; *a.* belgisch.
Bengal, Bengalen, *n.*
Biscay, die Biskaya.
Black Forest, der Schwarzwald.
Black Sea, das Schwarze Meer.
Bohemia, Böhmen, *n.*; **~n,** böhmisch.
Brazil, Brasilien, *n.*
Britain, Great, Großbritannien, *n.*
British, britisch.
Brittany, Bretagne, *f.*
Bruges, Brügge, *n.*
Brunswick, Braunschweig, *n.*
Brussels, Brüssel, *n.*
Bulgaria, Bulgarien, *n.*; **~n,** *sb.* Bulgare, *m.*; *a.* bulgarisch.
Burgundy, Burgund, *n.*
Burm|a, Birma, *n.*; **~ese,** *sb.* Birmaner, *m.*; *a.* birmanisch.
Byzantium, Byzanz, *n.*

California, Kalifornien, *n.*
Cameroon, Kamerun, *n.*
Canad|a, Kanada, *n.*; **~ian,** *sb.* Kanadier, *m.*; *a.* kanadisch.
Canaries, die Kanarischen Inseln.
Cape Colony, Kapkolonie, *f.*
Cape of Good Hope, das Kap der Guten Hoffnung.
Cape Horn, Kap Hoorn, *n.*
Cape Town, Kapstadt, *f.*
Carinthia, Kärnten, *n.*
Carpathians, Karpathen, *pl.*
Caspian, das Kaspische Meer.
Castile, Kastilien, *n.*
Caucasus, Kaukasus, *m.*
Cecily, Cäcilie.
Charles, Karl.
Chile, Chile, *n.*
Chin|a, China, *n.*; **~ese,** *sb.* Chinese, *m.*; *a.* chinesisch.

Christ, Christus; ~ian, sb. Christ,
m.; a. christlich.
Christopher, Christoph.
Cologne, Köln, n.
Constance, Lake, der Bodensee.
Copenhagen, Kopenhagen, n.
Corsica, Korsika, n.
Cracow, Krakau, n.
Crete, Kreta, n.
Crimea, Krim, f.
Cyprus, Zypern, n.
Czech, sb. Tscheche, m.; a.
tschechisch; ~oslovakia,
Tschechoslovakei, f.

Dan|e, Däne, m.; ~ish, dänisch.
Danube, Donau, f.
Dead Sea, das Tote Meer.
Denmark, Dänemark, n.
Dorothy, Dorothea.
Dunkirk, Dünkirchen, n.
Dutch, holländisch; ~man, Hol-
länder, m.

East Indies, Ostindien, n.
Edinburgh, Edinburg, n.
Edward, Eduard.
Egypt, Ägypten, n.; ~ian, sb.
Ägypter, m.; a. ägyptisch.
Elizabeth, Elisabeth.
Elsie, Ilse.
Emily, Emilie.
England, England, n.
English, englisch; ~ Channel,
der Ärmelkanal; ~man, Eng-
länder, m.; ~woman, Eng-
länderin, f.
Eric, Erich.
Ernest, Ernst.
Esthonia, Estland, n.; ~n, sb.
Estländer, m.; a. estnisch.
Eugene, Eugen.
Europe, Europa, n.; ~an, sb.
Europäer, m.; a. europäisch.

Faroes, Färöer, pl.
Fin|n, Finne, Finnländer, m.;
~land, Finnland, n.; ~nish,
finnisch.
Flanders, Flandern, n.
Flemish, flämisch.
Florence, Florenz, n.
Flushing, Vlissingen, n.
France, Frankreich, n.
Frances, Franziska.
Francis, Franz.

Franconia, Franken, n.
Frankfort, Frankfurt, n.
Fred, Fritz; ~erick, Friedrich.
French, französisch; ~man,
Franzose, m.; ~woman,
Französin, f.
Frisian, sb. Friese, m.; a. friesisch.

Gael, Gäle, m.; ~ic, gälisch.
Galilee, Galiläa, n.
Gaul, Gallien, n.
Geneva, Genf, n.
Genoa, Genua, n.
Geoffrey, Gottfried.
George, Georg.
German, sb. Deutsche(r); a.
deutsch; ~y, Deutschland, n.
Ghent, Gent, n.
Gree|ce, Griechenland, n.; ~k,
sb. Grieche, m.; a. griechisch.
Greenland, Grönland, n.
Grisons, Graubünden, n.

Hague, the, der Haag.
Hanover, Hannover, n.
Hebrew, sb. Hebräer, m.; a.
hebräisch.
Hebrides, Hebriden, pl.
Helen, Helene.
Henry, Heinrich.
Herod, Herodes.
Hesse, Hessen, n.
Hilda, Hildegard.
Hindoo, Hindu, m.
Horace, Horaz.
Hungar|y, Ungarn, n.; ~ian, sb.
Ungar, m.; a. ungarisch.

Iceland, Island, n.; ~ic, isländisch.
India, Indien, n.; ~n, sb. Inder,
m.; a. indisch; Red ~n,
Indianer, m.
Ireland, Irland, n.
Irish, irisch; ~man, Irländer,
Ire, m.
Isaac, Isaak.
Isaiah, Jesaias.
Ital|y, Italien, n.; ~ian, sb.
Italiener, m.; a. italienisch.

Jacob, James, Jakob.
Japan, Japan, n.; ~ese, sb.
Japaner, m.; a. japanisch.
Jeremiah, Jeremias.
Jew, Jude, m.; ~ess, Jüdin, f.;
~ish, jüdisch.